Christopher Columbus
and the
Age of Exploration

Christopher Columbus and the Age of Exploration

An Encyclopedia

SILVIO A. BEDINI, Editor
Emeritus, The Smithsonian Institution

Editorial Board

DAVID BUISSERET
The Newberry Library

HELEN NADER
Indiana University

WILCOMB E. WASHBURN
The Smithsonian Institution

PAULINE MOFFIT WATTS
Sarah Lawrence College

DA CAPO PRESS • NEW YORK

Library of Congress Cataloging-in-Publication Data

Christopher Columbus encyclopedia.
  Christopher Columbus and the age of exploration: an encyclopedia / Silvio A.
Bedini, editor; editorial board, David Buisseret . . . [et al.].—1st Da Capo Press ed.
    p.   cm.
  Originally published in 2 v.: The Christopher Columbus encyclopedia. New
York: Simon & Schuster, c1992.
  Includes bibliographical references and index.
  ISBN 0-306-80871-4 (alk. paper)
  1. Columbus, Christopher—Encyclopedias. 2. America—Discovery and explora-
tion—Encyclopedias. I. Bedini, Silvio A. II. Buisseret, David. III. Title.
[E111.C556 1998]
970.01′5—dc21   98-19964
                                                                                CIP

First Da Capo Press edition 1998

This Da Capo Press paperback edition of *Christopher Columbus and the Age of
Exploration: An Encyclopedia* is an unabridged republication of the edition first
published in two separate volumes under the title *The Christropher Columbus
Encyclopedia* in New York in 1992. It is reprinted by arrangement with
Macmillan General Reference/Scribner, an Imprint of Simon & Schuster, Inc.

Published by Da Capo Press, Inc.
A Subsidiary of Plenum Publishing Corporation
233 Spring Street, New York, N.Y. 10013

*Acknowledgments of sources, copyrights, and
permissions to use previously printed materials
are made throughout the work.*

Editorial and Production Staff

Publisher
Charles E. Smith

Editorial Director
Paul Bernabeo

Manuscript Editors
Mary Edwardsen   Stephen Wagley   Cecile Watters

Illustration Editor
David Sassian

Proofreader
Dorothy Bauhoff Kachouh

Executive Assistant
Glady Villegas Delgado

Assistant Project Editors
Debra H. Alpern   Robert M. Salkin

Compositor
The Clarinda Company
Clarinda, Iowa

Illustration Researcher
PAR / NYC Inc.
New York

Illustrator
A Good Thing Inc.
New York

Cartographer
Carta
Jerusalem

Indexer
AEIOU Inc.
Pleasantville, New York

Manufacturing Manager
Margaret Rizzi

Preface

By the end of the fifteenth century, the European states of Portugal and Spain were ready technologically and politically to explore and colonize thousands of miles from their own shores. Although Christopher Columbus was not the first European to arrive in the part of the world soon to be named after Amerigo Vespucci, another European explorer who followed Columbus westward, it was Columbus's first voyage across the Atlantic Ocean that initiated sustained European exploration, colonization, and conquest of what to Europeans was a new world.

The editors of this encyclopedia have planned a series of articles that provides a panoramic view of the age of European exploration from the late fifteenth century to the middle of the seventeenth century, including entries that examine the cultural and political motivations for European exploration as well as the maritime technologies that made this exploration possible. The core of the work includes articles treating Columbus's life and writings in detail. Related entries explore the Columbian legacy in literature, plastic and pictorial arts, and popular culture. The editors have also solicited articles that describe modern research techniques and the ongoing recovery of source materials for this period of history.

In addition to covering Columbus's life, the encyclopedia treats numerous other men and women who participated in the momentous events of his age. Included are the innovators of science and technology, the European leaders who sponsored overseas expansion, and the colonizers who left one world to gain another. Several other entries describe the indigenous ecologies and cultures of the New World encountered by Europeans in the century following Columbus's voyages. The exploitation of the natural resources of the Americas is addressed as is the impact of invasion, conquest, enslavement, and disease upon their human inhabitants.

The aim of this collection of articles, contributed by an international team of scholars, is to illuminate events that promoted the emergence of the modern West. In employing the word *discovery* to refer to Columbus's landfall in the Caribbean on October 12, 1492, our contributors do not deny the prior existence of the so-called discovered.

Nor do we, in referring to the lands previously unknown to Europeans as "the New World," suggest that this world and its peoples did not exist before. We do recognize, however, that what follows from that meeting of cultures, remembered today as the Columbian encounter, is indeed something new in history—a blending of peoples and cultures that constitutes the Americas as we know them today. The name *America* is itself of European origin, and use of the term *Indian* is a European misnomer. Where possible, the following articles are explicit about which Amerindians are under discussion, but ultimately it did not seem practical to abandon conventionally acceptable meanings of the terms *Indian* and *America*.

This encyclopedia does not attempt to trace the entire story of the colonization of the New World. Rather, it focuses on European and American subjects that figure prominently in the European expansionism of the sixteenth century and early seventeenth century. Every plan must set time limits, and ours is the year 1620. Hence, emphasis rests on the Caribbean region and European impact there, but articles are also included that discuss peoples, cultures, and events farther to the north and south, including England's search for the Northwest Passage and the histories of the Incas of Peru and the Tupinambás of Brazil. Pre-Columbian voyages are also covered, for example, in an overview of exploration before 1492, and, more particularly, in entries on Leif Ericsson, Vinland, and Portugal's exploration of Africa.

Thanks are due the more than one hundred scholars who have provided the accumulated learning collected herein. Each of them has played an important part and each is acknowledged within the work for the contribution of particular entries. Special thanks can be paid to Rebecca Catz for unfailing assistance concerning translation and bibliography related to Portuguese topics. Advice was frequently sought and generously given by the project's advisers: Professor Kathleen Deagan of the University of Florida, concerning archaeology; Admiral William Lemos (U.S. Navy, retired), concerning navigation; Vice President Paolo Emilio Taviani, Senate of the Republic of Italy, concerning the European background of the Columbian age; and Commander David W. Waters, honorary member of the Royal Institute of Navigation, Brighton, concerning scientific instruments. Dr. William C. Sturtevant of the Smithsonian Institution was central to the development of articles concerning native American peoples.

Acknowledgment of sources of illustrative material can be found in captions accompanying illustrations. Because so many of the objects illustrated are several hundred years old, special care has been taken to reproduce them faithfully, by electronic means. Translators are acknowledged at the end of each article that has been rendered into English from a foreign language.

The spelling and use of certain names and terms required editorial solutions specially tailored to this work. It was our policy to avoid overturning well-ingrained, common usage and to forgo provoking consternation among general readers by employing a full complement of unfamiliar diacritics in transliterated names. On the other hand, we were eager to balance this service to familiarity with our concern for scholarship. Thus, we have selected forms of personal and geographic names that approximate authentic forms. Cross-references appear throughout the work, including the index, to guide readers to the information they seek under variant forms of names. In addition, where it would not interfere with ease of reading, alternate forms of names are often included within parentheses immediately following the preferred forms.

The very name *Columbus* presented its own special editorial vexations. The encyclopedia discusses several members of the Columbus family who lived in different parts of the world and who spoke, wrote, and are referred to in original sources in various languages, among them, Italian, Portuguese, and Spanish. Members of the Columbus family whose lives centered in Italy are referred to by the Italian form of their name, *Colombo;* those whose lives centered in Spain or in Spanish America, by the Spanish name, *Colón.* To use the Italian *Cristoforo Colombo* or the Spanish *Cristóbal Colón* to refer to the main subject of our work would have been a serious breach of familiarity; therefore, we use the form common in English, *Christopher Columbus.*

Numerous other Europeans and Amerindians are known popularly by various forms of their names derived from different languages. We usually employ authentic forms; thus, the Spanish monarchs who sponsored Columbus's enterprise are known herein by the Spanish forms of their names: Isabel and Fernando; the Aztec emperor of Mexico is known herein as Motecuhzoma, a form of his name reflecting its Nahuatl origins. For these names as well as for numerous others—both personal and geographic—cross-references, parenthetical remarks, and the index will guide the reader to appropriate entries.

The Editors

Directory of Contributors

A

D. K. Abbass
Newport, Rhode Island
Domesticated Animals; Metal

Ann U. Abrams
Atlanta, Georgia
Iconography, *article on* American Painting

Maureen Ahern
Ohio State University
Cabeza de Vaca, Alvar Núñez; Coronado, Francisco Vázquez de

Luís de Albuquerque
Comissão Nacional para as Comemorações dos Descobrimentos Portugueses, Lisbon, Portugal
Dias, Bartolomeu; Indies, The; Lunar Phenomena; Solar Phenomena; Southern Cross; Tristão, Nuno; Vizinho, José; Zacuto, Abraham

Angel Alcalá
Brooklyn College of the City University of New York
Inquisition; Jews, *articles on* Jews in Spain, Conversos, Expulsion from Spain; Torquemada, Tomás de

Ricardo E. Alegría
Centro de Estudios Avanzados de Puerto Rico y El Caribe, San Juan
Indian America, *article on* Taínos

Glenn J. Ames
University of Toledo
Henry the Navigator

José Juan Arrom
North Haven, Connecticut
Pané, Ramón

B

Selma Huxley Barkham
Chichester, England
Exploration and Discovery, *article on* Basque Exploration and Discovery

Frederic J. Baumgartner
Virginia Polytechnic Institute and State University
Charles VIII; France; Louis XI; Louis XII

Silvio A. Bedini
Emeritus, The Smithsonian Institution
America, Naming of; Coat of Arms; Compass, *article on* Declination of the Compass; Humboldt, Alexander von; Museums and Archives, *article on* Collections of Columbus Memorabilia; Signature; Timetelling; Waldseemüller, Martin

Stephen P. Bensch
Swarthmore College
Barcelona

Jerry H. Bentley
University of Hawaii
Fernández de Córdoba, Gonzalo

Frances E. Berdan
California State University, San Bernadino
Malinche

Gordon Bleuler
Dallas, Texas
Iconography, *article on* Philately

Arie Boomert
Alkmaar, The Netherlands
Indian America, *article on* Arawaks and Caribs

Kathleen Bragdon
Colonial Williamsburg Foundation, Williamsburg, Virginia
Indian America, *article on* Indians of New England, Roanoke, Virginia, and the St. Lawrence Valley

Sylvia M. Broadbent
University of California, Riverside
Indian America, *article on* Chibchas

Gene A. Brucker
University of California at Berkeley
Florence; Medici Family

David Buisseret
The Newberry Library, Chicago
Bahamas; Cartography; Colonization, *overview article*; Cuba; Española, La; Jamaica; Puerto Rico; West Indies

Amy Turner Bushnell
University of California, Irvine
Women in the Americas

Joseph P. Byrne
West Georgia College
Cadamosto; Carpini, Giovanni da Pian del; Conti, Niccolò de'; Trade, *article on* Mediterranean Trade; Vivaldi, Ugolino, and Vadino Vivaldi

C

Ilaria Luzzana Caraci
Istituto de Scienze Geografiche, Università de Genova
Vespucci, Amerigo

REBECCA CATZ
University of California, Berkeley
Almeida, Francisco de; Cabral, Pedro
Álvares; China; Cipangu; Columbus,
Christopher, *article on* Columbus in
Portugal; Gama, Vasco da; Madeira;
Pinto, Fernão Mendes; Portugal

S. L. CLINE
*California State University, San
Bernadino*
Cuauhtemoc

D

KATHLEEN DEAGAN
University of Florida
Archaeology, *article on* Land
Archaeology; Settlements, *articles on*
La Navidad, La Isabela

SUSAN M. DEEDS
Northern Arizona University
Indian America, *article on* Indians of
Northern Mexico, Baja, California, and
Southwestern North America

ANGEL DELGADO-GOMEZ
University of Notre Dame
Alvarado, Pedro de; Cortés,
Hernando; Díaz del Castillo, Bernal;
Fernández de Córdoba, Francisco

O. A. W. DILKE
Emeritus, University of Leeds
Marinus of Tyre; Pius II; Ptolemy;
Ruysch, Johan; Strabo; Toscanelli,
Paolo dal Pozzo

JAMES P. DOOLIN
Dallas, Texas
Iconography, *article on* Philately

SIMONE DREYFUS-GAMELON
*École des Hautes Études en Sciences
Sociales, Paris*
Indian America, *article on* Island Caribs

FRANCIS A. DUTRA
University of California, Santa Barbara
Cunha, Tristão da; Elcano, Juan
Sebastián de; Pacheco Pereira, Duarte

E

THERESA EARENFIGHT
Fordham University
Afonso V; Catherine of Aragón;
Charles V; Enrique IV; Isabel; Isidore
of Seville; João II; Juan; Juan II; Juana
de Castilla; Juana I; Manuel I;
Margaret of Austria; María; Maximilian
I; Santángel, Luis de

JUDITH LAIKIN ELKIN
University of Michigan
Jews, *article on* Jews in the New World

DAVID ELTIS
Queen's University, Kingston, Canada
Slavery

HELEN S. ETTLINGER
Central Michigan University
Art and Architecture

F

DONALD L. FIXICO
Western Michigan University
Quincentenary, *article on* American
Indian Perspectives

DONALD W. FORSYTH
Brigham Young University
Indian America, *article on* Tupinambás

G. S. P. FREEMAN-GRENVILLE
York, England
Africa

JOHN BLOCK FRIEDMAN
University of Illinois
Geography, Imaginary

PETER T. FURST
University of Pennsylvania
Flora, *articles on* Psychotropic Flora,
Tobacco

G

FRANCISCO GAGO JOVER
University of Wisconsin
Valladolid

MICHAEL V. GANNON
University of Florida
Exploration and Discovery, *article on*
European Exploration and Discovery
after 1492; Oviedo, Gonzalo Fernández
de

MARGERY ANN GANZ
Spelman College
Verrazano, Giovanni da

STEPHEN D. GLAZIER
Kearney State College
Religion, *article on* Amerindian
Traditions

JOAN B. GOLDSMITH
Northwestern University
England; Henry VII; Henry VIII

BARRY GOUGH
*Wilfrid Laurier University, Waterloo,
Canada*
Canada

EDWARD GRANT
Indiana University
Science, *article on* Science in the Late
Fifteenth Century

CLIVE GRIFFIN
Oxford University
Printing

BARBARA GROSECLOSE
The Ohio State University
Monuments and Memorials

JACQUELINE GUIRAL-HADJIIOSSIF
Université de Nancy II
Valencia

H

J. B. HARLEY
University of Wisconsin at Milwaukee
Cosa, Juan de la

EINAR HAUGEN
Harvard University
Icelandic Sagas

JOHN HÉBERT
Library of Congress
Celebrations

MARY W. HELMS
University of North Carolina at Greensboro
Indian America, *article on* Indians of the Spanish Main and Central America

DAVID HENIGE
University of Wisconsin-Madison
Writings, *article on* Journal

PAUL E. HOFFMAN
Louisiana State University
Ayllón, Lucas Vázquez de (1480–1520); Ayllón, Lucas Vázquez de (1514–1565); Colón, Diego (Columbus's son); Colonization, *article on* Spanish Colonization; Díaz de Solís, Juan; Encomienda; Jiménez de Quesada, Gonzalo; Martínez de Irala, Domingo; Mendoza, Antonio de; Montejo, Francisco de; Orellana, Francisco de; Toledo y Rojas, María de

CHARLES HUDSON
University of Georgia
Indian America, *article on* Indians of La Florida; Soto, Hernando de

I

HELGE INGSTAD
Oslo, Norway
Ericsson, Leif; Vinland

J

CORNELIUS J. JAENEN
University of Ottawa
Cartier, Jacques; Colonization, *article on* French Colonization

WILLIAM R. JONES
University of New Hampshire
Polo, Marco

K

ROBERT W. KARROW, JR.
The Newberry Library, Chicago
Gemma Frisius; Mercator, Gerardus; Ortelius, Abraham

CHRISTOPHER J. KAUFFMAN
Catholic University of America
Columbianism; Columbian Societies

WILLIAM F. KEEGAN
Florida Museum of Natural History, Gainesville
Pacification, Conquest, and Genocide

BENJAMIN KEEN
Santa Fe, New Mexico
Benzoni, Girolamo; Black Legend; Bry, Théodor de; Las Casas, Bartolomé de

HARRY KELSEY
Huntington Library, San Marino, California
Cabrillo, Juan Rodriguez; Narváez, Pánfilo de

MARGARET L. KING
Brooklyn College
Venetian Republic

FRED F. KRAVATH
United States Navy, Retired
Circumference; Distance, Measurement of

L

ASELA R. LAGUNA
Rutgers University
Literature, *article on* Columbus in Hispanic Literature

URSULA LAMB
Tucson, Arizona
Casa de la Contratación; Lawsuits; Ovando, Nicolás de; Santa Fe Capitulations

COLLEEN LEARY
Atmospheric Science Group, Texas Tech University
Azores; Canary Islands; Cape of Good Hope; Cape Verde Islands; Weather and Wind

WILLIAM LEMOS
United States Navy, Retired
Arana, Diego de; Arana, Pedro de; Arms, Armor, and Armament; Equipment, Clothing, and Rations; Méndez, Diego; Niña; Niño, Juan; Niño, Peralonso; Ojeda, Alonso de; Pinta; Pinzón, Francisco Martín; Pinzón, Martín Alonso; Pinzón, Vicente Yáñez; Quintero de Algruta, Juan; Santa María; Shipbuilding; Ships and Crews; Torres, Antonio de; Voyages of Columbus

RUDI PAUL LINDNER
University of Michigan
Ottoman Empire

PEGGY K. LISS
Washington, D.C.
Isabel and Fernando

PATRICK LOUGHNEY
Library of Congress
Iconography, *article on* Film

EUGENE LYON
Flagler College
Menéndez de Avilés, Pedro

M

FRANCIS MADDISON
Oxford University
Armillary Sphere; Astrolabe; Compass, *article on* Marine Compass; Cross-staff; Kamal; Lead and Line; Lodestone; Navigation, *article on* Instruments of Navigation; Quadrant; Timeglass

WILLIAM S. MALTBY
University of Missouri, St. Louis
Guzmán, Enrique de; Philip II;

JOHN A. MARINO
University of California, San Diego
Naples; Social and Economic
Institutions

TERENCE MARTIN
Indiana University
Literature, *article on* Columbus in
American Literature

DARIO G. MARTINI
Edizione Culturali Internationali, Genoa
Literature, *article on* Columbus in
European Literature

LINDA MARTZ
Bethesda, Maryland
Jiménez de Cisneros, Francisco;
Toledo

SCOTT McPARTLAND
*Marymount Manhattan College, New
York*
Science, *article on* Science and
Technology in the Age of Discovery

MICHAEL C. MEYER
University of Arizona
Medicine and Health

NELSON H. MINNICH
The Catholic University of America
Alexander VI; Innocent VIII; Papacy;
Rome

FRANK MOYA PONS
University of Florida
Bobadilla, Francisco de; Settlements,
article on Santo Domingo; Trade,
article on Caribbean Trade

JOHN V. MURRA
*Institute of Andean Research, New
York*
Indian America, *article on* Incas and
Their Neighbors

N

HELEN NADER
Indiana University
Bernáldez, Andrés; Book of Privileges;
Burial Places of Columbus; Columbus,
Christopher, *articles on* Adolescence
and Youth, Early Maritime Experience,
Columbus in Spain, The Final Years,
Illness, and Death; Deza, Diego de;
Fonseca, Antonio de; Fonseca, Juan
Rodriguez de; Granada; Medina
Sidonia, Duke of; Medinaceli, Duke
of; Mendoza, Pedro González de;
Palos de la Frontera; Rábida, La;
Spain; Writings, *overview article*,
article on Last Will and Testament

H. B. NICHOLSON
University of California, Los Angeles
Indian America, *article on* Aztecs and
Their Neighbors; Motecuhzoma II

ANITA WAINGORT NOVINSKY
Universidade de São Paulo
Lisbon

O

JOSEPH F. O'CALLAGHAN
Fordham University
Alfonso X; Boabdil; Herrera y
Tordesillas, Antonio de; Line of
Demarcation; Madrid; Political
Institutions; Reconquista; Treaty of
Alcáçovas; Treaty of Tordesillas

SANDRA L. ORELLANA
*California State University, Dominguez
Hills*
Indian America, *article on* Mayas

P

PAUL PADILLA
University of California, Los Angeles
Alfraganus

DEBORAH PEARSALL
University of Missouri, Columbia
Flora, *overview article*

EUGENIO PÉREZ MONTÁS
*Museo de las Casas Reales, Santo
Domingo*
Settlements, *article on* Concepción de
la Vega

MARY E. PERRY
University of California, Los Angeles
Seville

CARLA RAHN PHILLIPS
University of Minnesota, Minneapolis
Atlantic Rivalry; Iconography, *article on*
Early European Portraits; Myth of
Columbus

WILLIAM D. PHILLIPS
University of Minnesota, Minneapolis
Córdoba; Europe and the Wider World
in 1492

ALFREDO PINHEIRO MARQUES
Universidade de Coimbra
Behaim, Martin; Cão, Diogo;
Colonization, *article on* Portuguese
Colonization of Brazil; Martellus,
Henricus; Pizzigano Chart

CHARLES W. POLZER
University of Arizona
Museums and Archives, *article on*
Overview of Documentary Sources

FOSTER PROVOST
Duquesne University
Bibliography

Q

DAVID B. QUINN
*Emeritus, University of Liverpool
Liverpool, England*
Brendan; Cabot, John; Cabot,
Sebastian; Colonization, *article on*
English Colonization

R

ISABELLE RAYNAUD-NGUYEN
Agrégrée de l'Université, Sèvres
Mappamundi; Nautical Charts;
Portolanos; Sailing Directions

ELIZABETH J. REITZ
University of Georgia
Fauna

PHILIP RICHARDSON
*The Woods Hole Oceanographic
Institution*
Tides and Currents

M. W. RICHEY
*Formerly Director, Royal Institute of
Navigation, Brighton*
Altura Sailing; Astronomy and
Astrology; Columbus the Navigator;
Dead Reckoning; Latitude; Longitude;
Navigation, *article on* Art, Practice, and
Theory; Piloting

JOHN M. RIDDLE
North Carolina State University
Spices

TEOFILO RUIZ
Brooklyn College
Chanca, Diego Alvarez; Fonseca,
Alfonso de; Talavera, Hernando de

RUSSELL RULAU
Iola, Wisconsin
Iconography, *article on* Numismatics

S

NICHOLAS SANCHEZ-ALBORNOZ
New York University
Quincentenary, *article on* Hispanic
Perspectives

JOHN F. SCHWALLER
Florida Atlantic University
Ávila, Pedro Arias de; Balboa, Vasco
Núñez de; Missionary Movement

JEANETTE SHERBONDY
Washington College
Atahualpa; Cuzco; Huascar; Huayna
Capac; Pizarro, Francisco; Pizarro,
Gonzalo; Pizarro, Hernando; Pizarro,
Juan

J. DONALD SILVA
University of New Hampshire
Funchal; Porto Santo

ROGER C. SMITH
*Bureau of Archaeological Research,
Tallahassee, Florida*
Archaeology, *article on* Underwater
Archaeology

WILLIAM C. STURTEVANT
The Smithsonian Institution
Cannibalism; Indian America, *article
on* First Visual Impressions in Europe

T

PAOLO EMILIO TAVIANI
Senate of the Republic of Italy
Arana, Beatriz Enríquez de; Bobadilla,
Beatriz de; Colombo, Domenico;
Colombo, Giovanni; Colombo,
Giovanni Antonio; Colón, Diego
(Columbus's brother); Colón,
Fernando; Columbus, Christopher,
article on Birth and Origins; Cuneo,
Michele da; Fieschi, Bartolomeo;
Fontanarossa, Susanna; Gallo,
Antonio; Genoa; Geraldini,
Alessandro; Perestrelo y Moniz, Felipa;
Pinelli, Francesco

DAVID W. TILTON
University of Wisconsin at Milwaukee
Cosa, Juan de la

AURELIO TIÓ
*Academia Puertorriqueña de la Historia,
San Juan*
Grijalba, Juan de; Ponce de León, Juan

DEBORAH TRUHAN
New York University
Quincentenary, *article on* Hispanic
Perspectives

U

DOUGLAS B. UBELAKER
The Smithsonian Institution
Disease and Demography; Syphilis

V

CONSUELO VARELA
*Escuela de Estudios
Hispano-Americanos, Seville*
Writings, *article on* Letters

DAVID VASSBERG
Pan American University
Agriculture

W

ERIKA WAGNER
*Instituto Venezolano de
Investigaciones Científicas, Caracas*
Settlements, *article on* Nueva Cádiz

MARILYN ROBINSON WALDMAN
The Ohio State University
Muslims in Spain

HELEN WALLIS
The British Museum
Globes; Northwest Passage

WILCOMB E. WASHBURN
The Smithsonian Institution
Exploration and Discovery, *article on*
Exploration and Discovery before 1492;
Landfall Controversy; Vinland Map

PAULINE MOFFITT WATTS
Sarah Lawrence College
Ailly, Pierre d'; Antichrist; Bacon,
Roger; Grand Khan; Prester John;
Religion, *article on* European
Traditions; Spirituality of Columbus;
Terrestrial Paradise; Writings, *article on*
Book of Prophecies

DELNO C. WEST
Northern Arizona University
Library of Columbus; Writings, *article
on* Marginalia

GEORGE D. WINIUS
University of Leiden
Magellan, Ferdinand; Mineral
Resources

SYLVIA WYNTER
Stanford University
Anghiera, Pietro Martire d';
Quincentenary, *article on* Caribbean
Perspectives; Settlements, *article on*
Sevilla la Nueva

Z

CHRISTIAN ZACHER
The Ohio State University
Mandeville, John; Travel Literature

Alphabetical List of Entries

Abbreviations and Symbols Used in This Work

A.D. *anno Domini,* in the year of (our) Lord
A.H. *anno Hegirae,* in the year of the Hijrah
Ala. Alabama
A.M. *ante meridiem,* before noon
Ariz. Arizona
Ark. Arkansas
b. born
B.C. before Christ
B.C.E. before the common era
c. *circa,* about, approximately
Calif. California
C.E. of the common era
cf. *confer,* compare
chap. chapter (pl., chaps.)
cm centimeters
Colo. Colorado
Conn. Connecticut
d. died
D.C. District of Columbia
Del. Delaware
diss. dissertation
ed. editor (pl., **eds.**); edition; edited by
e.g. *exempli gratia,* for example

Eng. England
enl. enlarged
esp. especially
et al. *et alii,* and others
etc. *et cetera,* and so forth
exp. expanded
f. and following (pl., **ff.**)
fl. *floruit,* flourished
Fla. Florida
frag. fragment
ft. feet
Ga. Georgia
ibid. *ibidem,* in the same place (as the one immediately preceding)
i.e. *id est,* that is
Ill. Illinois
Ind. Indiana
Kans. Kansas
km kilometers
Ky. Kentucky
La. Louisiana
m meters
M.A. Master of Arts
Mass. Massachusetts
mi. miles
Mich. Michigan
Minn. Minnesota
Miss. Mississippi
Mo. Missouri

Mont. Montana
n. note
N.C. North Carolina
n.d. no date
N.Dak. North Dakota
Neb. Nebraska
Nev. Nevada
N.H. New Hampshire
N.J. New Jersey
N.Mex. New Mexico
no. number (pl., **nos.**)
n.p. no place
n.s. new series
N.Y. New York
Okla. Oklahoma
Oreg. Oregon
p. page (pl., **pp.**)
Pa. Pennsylvania
pl. plural, plate (pl., **pls.**)
P.M. *post meridiem,* after noon
Port. Portuguese
pt. part (pl., **pts.**)
r. reigned; ruled
rev. revised
R.I. Rhode Island
sc. *scilicet,* namely
S.C. South Carolina
S.Dak. South Dakota
sec. section (pl., **secs.**)

ser. series
sing. singular
sq. square
supp. supplement; supplementary
Tenn. Tennessee
Tex. Texas
trans. translator, translators; translated by; translation
U.S. United States
USNR. United States Naval Reserve
U.S.S.R. Union of Soviet Socialist Republics
v. verse (pl., **vv.**)
Va. Virginia
var. variant; variation
vol. volume (pl., **vols.**)
Vt. Vermont
Wash. Washington
Wis. Wisconsin
W.Va. West Virginia
Wyo. Wyoming
? uncertain; possibly; perhaps
° degrees

A Note on Monetary Systems

Various monetary systems were in use in the Columbian era. The maravedi was a unit of account only, used to record salaries and payments. The Spanish and Genoese maravedi were roughly equal in value and related to different forms of currency as follows:

375 maravedis to 1 gold ducat,
435 maravedis to 1 gold castellano (or peso d'oro),
870 maravedis to 1 gold excelente.

Volume 1
A–K

AENEAS SILVIUS. See *Pius II.*

AFONSO V (1432–1481), king of Portugal (1438–1481). Known as Afonso the African, Afonso V used his military campaigns against the Turks in northwestern Africa to further the exploration of land and sea routes to the spices and gold of the Indies. By 1471 the Portuguese controlled territory in Africa from the Strait of Gibraltar to Tangier. The Portuguese navigators who charted the African coastline enabled Bartolomeu Dias to sail around the Cape of Good Hope.

Son of Duarte I and nephew of Prince Henry the Navigator, Afonso inherited his kingdom at the age of six, but his mother, Leonor, served as regent until Afonso reached his majority in 1446. He married Isabel of Coimbra who bore him two children, Juana and João, later King João II. After Isabel's death Afonso became the suitor and military supporter of Juana de Castilla (la Beltraneja), the alleged daughter and heiress of King Enrique of Castile. Afonso's commitment to Juana resulted in a succession crisis and prolonged war with Castile, which ended in 1479 with the Treaty of Alcáçovas. By the terms of this treaty Afonso renounced his claim to the Castilian throne, but more important for the future discoveries in the New World, Afonso also renounced Portuguese claims to the Canary Islands in return for Castilian recognition of Portuguese territorial rights in Africa. It was the Treaty of Alcáçovas that King João II invoked to support his claim to the lands discovered by Columbus in 1492. During the final years of his reign, Afonso delegated most of the work of overseas expansion to his son, João.

BIBLIOGRAPHY

Albuquerque, Luís. *Introdução a história dos descobrimentos.* Coimbra, 1962.

CHRONICLE OF KING AFONSO V. By Rui de Pina, fifteenth century. The chronicle recounts the life of the Portuguese monarch, the signer of the Treaty of Alcáçovas, an early attempt to address the conflicting claims arising from the voyages of discovery. The illumination in the left-hand column depicts the manuscript of the chronicle being presented to Afonso's nephew, Manuel I.

ARQUIVO NACIONAL DA TORRE DO TOMBO, LISBON

Boxer, C. R. *The Portuguese Seaborne Empire, 1415–1825.* New York, 1969.

Oliveira Marquês, A. H. de. *History of Portugal.* 2 vols. New York, 1972.

Peres, Damião. *História dos descobrimentos portugueses.* Porto, 1943.

Perez Embid, Florentino. *Descubrimientos del Atlántico y la rivalidad castelano-portugesa hasta el tratado de Tordesillas.* Madrid, 1948.

THERESA EARENFIGHT

AFRICA. Columbus's Atlantic voyages had African predecessors. Before 1312, Abu Bakari II, king of Mali, had sent two hundred canoes westward, with orders not to return until they reached the ocean's limits. Only one returned. He then sent two thousand more, but not a single one was seen again. Even though it failed, this initiative was unparalleled among neighboring African states in the Guinea region and on the southern Saharan border.

Trade in gold, salt, and slaves was the basis of an economy linked to the Mediterranean by four trunk routes. From the gold-bearing region and the Niger Bend, two routes converged at Sijilmasa to reach Morocco; two independent routes linked the southeastern Saharan states with Tunis and Tripoli. These and other North African ports linked with Europe. In all western Africa, constitutional monarchies had evolved, some into veritable empires, as economic complexity demanded more organized societies. The easternmost trade route joined the system to Cairo, which, under Mamluk rule since 1250, was the most advanced city of its time. No merchant city in Europe could compare with it in luxury or learning, wealth or splendor. It possessed great palaces, mosques and *madrassa*s (collegiate teaching mosques), hospitals, libraries, khans (hotels) for merchant caravansaries, and dervish monasteries. The whole Islamic world flocked to the university mosque of al-Azhar.

The Mamluk slave dynasty originated from a corps of

THE AFRICAN CONTINENT. Detail from Diego Ribeiro's *mappamundi*, 1529.

professional soldiers instituted by Saladin. They were recruited in their youth chiefly from southern Russia, and their primary loyalty was to the regiment that trained them. This ruling stratum was separate from the Egyptians, who, as agriculturalists, pursued a rural life wholly remote from Cairo and the great seaport of Alexandria. These were cosmopolitan cities, with commercial tentacles that stretched throughout the Mediterranean to western Africa, from Arabia and Syria as far as China, and down the eastern African coast to Kilwa and Mozambique. Chinese porcelain tableware was common among the well-to-do, and in the early fifteenth century a Chinese fleet had voyaged as far as Aden and eastern Africa. The commercial elite included Jews (whose records survive), Armenians, Greeks, and native Coptic Christians. As long as these minorities paid their taxes, they suffered little molestation.

To the south lay small Nubian kingdoms, which to now had been Christian but were giving way to Islam. They were in economic decline. Having burned their forests and made a desert, they could no longer smelt their gold and iron or grow crops. Yet farther south, Ethiopia was beleaguered in its mountains by a ring of small Somali states that controlled the trade routes in the plains. The only Christian state in Africa, Ethiopia had a highly sophisticated polity. It had long enjoyed links with Jerusalem and, through Rome, with Europe. Much of this society was to be destroyed by the Somali Ahmed Grañ's attacks from 1533 to 1535.

Along the eastern coast was a series of city-states, mostly trading centers, like Mogadishu and Pate. Kilwa, however, had a veritable seaborne empire which controlled the coast from the Rufiji to Sofala. Kilwa was a carrying trade entrepôt for the gold of Zimbabwe, which it exported to India. The Kilwa sultans had no internal territorial ambitions; more important were trade connections with Malacca and China.

We know nothing of the peoples who may have lived between the coast and the Great Lakes. Northwest of Lake Victoria a group of kingdoms emerged in Kitara in the twelfth century that had no known contact with the coast. This was the origin of present-day Uganda. In western Africa they had a counterpart south of the Rio Zaire, where highly sophisticated kingdoms emerged before the fifteenth century, albeit with no connection with the outer world. By contrast, in Zimbabwe an empire of Monomotapa had grown up round a local mining industry dependent on Arab and Swahili commercial contacts. All these states were Bantu, from stock that long before had emigrated from the Cameroon Mountains. Family groups were still expanding south of the Limpopo River, pushing the Khoi-San into the Kalahari Desert. These Bantu developed no tribal organizations before the nineteenth century.

Outsiders could have had no overall view of Africa in 1500; European knowledge of Africa was fragmentary. Only one European state had any access to information—Portugal, the poorest of all in wealth and manpower. Labor in Portugal was so short that by 1375 slaves were being imported from Morocco to till the fields. In 1415 Portugal seized Ceuta to serve as a trading base in Africa, and in the same year the half-English prince Henry the Navigator set up a school of navigation at Sagres on the mainland opposite Ceuta.

By the time of Henry's death in 1460, Portuguese trade along the western African coast had been established as far as Sierra Leone. By 1474 Fernão Gomes had advanced trade as far as Cape St. Catherine, south of the Bight of Benin; and by 1486 Diogo Cão had reached Walvis Bay. In 1488 Bartolomeu Dias sailed as far as the Cape of Storms (Cape of Good Hope); although forced to turn back by his seamen, he had nevertheless gained useful knowledge and experience. In the same year Pero da Covilhã was sent to gather intelligence in India and Africa. His story remains veiled in secrecy. From Cairo he traveled down India to Calicut and then back through Aden, along the eastern African coast as far as Sofala. After he returned to Cairo, his report was taken back to Lisbon by the rabbi of Beja while he continued on to Ethiopia. He had performed a journey that was unique for his time. In Ethiopia he was detained at the emperor's court until his death after 1526.

In 1497, therefore, Vasco da Gama set out on a well-reconnoitered route. He reached Natal by Christmas and then sailed up the coast, visiting Mombasa and Malindi. Crossing the Indian Ocean to Calicut he had as guide Ahmed ibn Majid al-Najdi, the foremost pilot of the age. Within a few years the Portuguese had taken Goa; their string of trading posts encircled Africa and reached Macao, off present-day Hong Kong. They now dominated the Indian Ocean commercially and had wrested the spice trade from the Arabs, Egypt, and Venice.

The Portuguese ascendancy had momentous consequences. It inflicted a deathblow on the Mamluk economy, which had depended on the eastern trade. The Mamluks even appealed to the pope to stop the Portuguese. But worse was to come for the Mamluks. In 1516 the Ottoman Turks seized Syria and in 1517 all Egypt. In 1518 Barbarossa (Khayr ad-Din) took the northern African coast as far as Morocco: the whole southern shore of the Mediterranean was now in Ottoman hands. Cairo was reduced to a provincial backwater, although it maintained its status as a center of Islamic learning. Shortly the northern African ports would shelter nests of pirates. Only Morocco, with gold from the south, was able to fend off the Ottomans with arms provided by Elizabeth I of England. In eastern Africa the Portuguese ruined the port towns by maintaining a strict trade monopoly. On the western coast, despite papal prohibitions, Portugal developed a series of slaving ports, chiefly on the coast of present-day Ghana. In the seventeenth century the Dutch, and then the English, followed them. At first the slaves, captured inland by coastal African rulers, were destined chiefly for Brazil and the Spanish colonies. Only in the seventeenth century did the slave trade have much importance north of the Gulf of Mexico, reaching its heyday in the eighteenth century.

The voyages of discovery brought Africa no benefits. The Turks and the Portuguese radically altered the pattern of economic life on the coasts. Cairo was ruined. On the east coast, there would be no stone building for two centuries; on the west, Portugal exploited the Angolan mines; farther north, what eventually numbered forty-two slaving forts drained the continent of manpower. Nevertheless, aside from the periphery that was affected by the Ottomans, Portugal, and, later, other European powers, African states continued to develop along their own lines. The Ottomans never interfered with the trans-Saharan trade. In western Africa, states and empires continued to develop. In the east, Ethiopia went through a long period of disunity and feebleness, threatened by the Somali. Among the Bantu in central Africa, states were developing into empires, to be checked only in the nineteenth century.

BIBLIOGRAPHY

Axelson, E. *South-East Africa, 1488–1530*. London, 1940.

Cambridge History of Africa. 8 vols. Edited by R. Oliver. Cambridge, 1975–.

Freeman-Grenville, G. S. P. *The New Atlas of African History*. New York, 1991.

Lane-Poole, Stanley. *A History of Egypt in the Middle Ages*. London, 1901.

The Oxford History of South Africa. Edited by Monica Wilson and Leonard Thompson. 2 vols. Oxford, 1969, 1971.

G. S. P. Freeman-Grenville

AGRICULTURE. Until the European voyages of discovery in the late 1400s and early 1500s, the Atlantic and Pacific oceans provided a barrier that effectively isolated the Americas from Europe, Asia, and Africa. Because of this isolation, the agricultural systems of the Old World and the New developed independently, along quite different lines.

Old World Agriculture

European agriculture in the fifteenth century was based on a complementary relationship between plant cultivation (mainly of wheat, barley, and rye) and animal husbandry (cattle, horses, poultry, pigs, goats, and sheep). The system was heavily indebted to the ancient Greeks and Romans. Mediterranean Europe continued for the most part the ancient Roman crop-and-fallow system, in which half the arable land was planted each year, while the other half was left idle, to store up moisture and to regain fertility. After harvest, the grain stubble was burned, and animal manure, a fertilizer, was spread among the ashes. In southern Europe, fruits and vegetables—grapes, olives, citrus, figs—were grown in addition to grain. Whereas most European agriculture relied upon natural rainfall, there was some irrigation in the Mediterranean area, mainly on intensively cultivated fruit and vegetable plots along rivers. In some places, intercropping (planting field crops between vines or fruit trees) was practiced, but crops were normally grown separately. Southern Europeans still used the Roman scratch-plow, which did not invert the soil, but merely made a shallow cut in the ground. Plows were almost invariably pulled by oxen.

In northern Europe, fields were worked primarily with horses pulling wheeled moldboard plows. Crops were more heavily fertilized with animal manure than in southern Europe, and through much of the north were planted according to a compulsory three-course rotational schedule (fall grain, spring grain, and fallow or legumes). Northern agriculture was in general more intensive than that of the south: fodder crops were often planted on what would otherwise have been fallow land, thus allowing for the expansion of animal husbandry, and increased attention was paid to selective livestock breeding and to the care of animals within a relatively confined space of pasture and barn. In Mediterranean Europe, by contrast, animals were usually herded over more extensive territory and received comparatively little care.

Agricultural tools throughout fifteenth century Europe remained much the same as in ancient times. Wood was still the basic material for the spade, hoe, pitchfork, rake, harrow, sickle, scythe, and plow. But many of these were tipped with iron for greater durability. An important medieval innovation was the heavy moldboard plow, which permitted the cultivation of tight, well-watered northern European soils that had been impenetrable to the Roman scratch-plow. At the same time, horseshoeing became widespread, and there were numerous improvements in harnessing. In northern Europe, the horse, a faster and more versatile draft animal, increasingly took the place of the ox, which was not displaced until the sixteenth century in southern Europe.

The landowning structure of fifteenth-century Europe was highly complex. The monarchs held ultimate claim to the ownership of all the lands in their kingdoms, but over the centuries they granted enormous territories to nobles, the church, military orders, municipalities, and private citizens. Furthermore, throughout Europe there were ancient communitarian traditions that gave rural villagers free access to certain lands. For example, it was normal to have the right of free use of common pastures. These might be owned by the municipality, by the Crown, or even, in some circumstances, by private parties.

There were infinite variations in the landholding structure. The lands of some agricultural villages were wholly owned by the local bishop, a noble, or a monastery. In such cases, the villagers tended to be tenants or share-croppers. At the other extreme were villages where all arable land was owned by the villagers themselves. The norm was probably somewhere in between, with the average European peasant/farmer using some land of his own, some rented land, and some common land.

In Spain the livestock sector had become extraordinarily important as a consequence of the Reconquista, the eighth-century Christian reconquest of Muslim territory. During the Reconquista, which ended in 1492, the insecurity of the frontier made animal husbandry preferable in economic terms to crop cultivation. As Christian Spaniards expanded into Extremadura (western Spain), they invented cattle ranching, a means of exploiting the semi-arid expanses of the newly won territory with a limited labor force.

New World Agriculture

Agriculture in the Americas probably began somewhat later than in the Old World, and the crops were quite different. By the time of Columbus, agriculture was practiced nearly everywhere in the hemisphere except the frigid far north. There were thousands of different Indian communities, with greatly divergent cultures and economies, but, in general, pre-Columbian Indian peoples depended principally upon agriculture for their food. Hunting, fishing, and food gathering were of secondary importance.

Maize (Indian corn) was the most widely cultivated crop in pre-Columbian America. It was almost invariably grown in conjunction with beans, squashes, and other food plants, combinations that provided a diet with a good balance of proteins and carbohydrates. Maize growers were thus able to expand into geographic areas where it was difficult to obtain animal protein through hunting or fishing.

Maize was the predominant staple of the Indian communities of the eastern part of the present-day United States. Almost all other foods were mixed with corn gruel or baked in little corn cakes. The villages of the Algonquians and Iroquois were surrounded by cultivated fields, which were tended almost exclusively by women and children. Corn and squashes were planted alongside bean plants, which added nitrogen to the soil. But the beans never put into the soil as much nitrogen as corn and other

crops removed. Consequently, fields gradually declined in fertility and were abandoned for new fields cleared from adjacent forest. When the new fields became inconveniently far from the village, the community simply moved the village to a new site, usually only a few miles away. Thus most North American Indians practiced a semipermanent agriculture, remaining in one place only until diminished fertility forced a move.

The Indians of the arid Great Basin and Southwest learned to cultivate crops even under extremely unfavorable natural conditions. The Hopi, for example, developed drought-resistant varieties of maize and irrigated their fields with the silt-enriched floodwaters of desert rainstorms.

In tropical America, manioc, or cassava, became the major food crop. Manioc, a plant native to South America, produces a starchy root that can be made into gruel or bread. The domestication of manioc was of enormous importance to tropical communities, because the plant yields more food per acre than any other crop. Furthermore, manioc tolerates a wide range of soil types, altitudes, and levels of precipitation. Its cultivation is limited to tropical areas, however, as it does not tolerate cold.

One of the most important food plants developed in pre-Columbian America was the potato (now called inaccurately the "Irish" potato), first cultivated in the highlands of South America. The tubers of the potato plant also produced high yields under varied conditions. Though the potato did not grow well in the tropics, the sweet potato (another American root crop) thrived in both temperate and tropical zones. Other crops included the peanut, tomato, papaya, pineapple, avocado, chile pepper, cotton, and cocoa (or cacao). The Mayas and Aztecs valued cocoa highly as a beverage and even used cocoa beans as a medium of exchange.

It took a complex sociopolitical structure to construct, equitably administer, and maintain irrigation systems. The civilizations of Peru and Mexico produced such systems, and a less-complex irrigation was practiced in many other areas. Extensive terracing was used in various parts of the Americas, most notably in the Andean highlands, to permit the cultivation and irrigation of mountain slopes.

In swampy or marshy areas, pre-Columbian agriculturalists developed the technique of farming raised fields (also called ridged, riverbank, and drained fields). These were prepared by digging ditches for drainage and by using the displaced earth (perhaps mixed with upland soil) to raise the level of the area to be planted. The resulting raised fields were above the water level but moist enough to promote growth. This method was labor intensive but also highly productive if more than one crop was grown each year.

Communities in different parts of the Americas developed various techniques to maintain soil fertility. Manuring was done with fish heads (or even whole fish) and with human, bird, bat, and other animal droppings. And green manure (vegetable matter) and fertile silt were sometimes added to fields. Another method of forestalling soil depletion was mixed-cropping: throughout the Americas, maize was almost invariably planted together with nitrogen-producing beans, and the Incas rotated their staple potatoes with beans.

Perhaps the most primitive method of conserving soil fertility is to cultivate periodically, rather than steadily, with a long fallow period between plantings. Clearings for fields cultivated in this system were typically made in the forest. Hence the system is often called "forest fallow," although it was not always practiced in forests but also in areas with scrub brush, reeds, or other low-set vegetation. The large trees were felled, the branches and trunks burned, and crops were planted directly in the ashes. Forest fallow was widely practiced in the pre-Columbian Americas and also in parts of the Old World where climatic and soil conditions were not conducive to permanent agriculture. After several years of planting, fields with unacceptably declining yields were abandoned for periods as long as thirty years or more, depending upon rainfall and other local conditions. This allowed the forest or other spontaneous vegetation to regrow. Meanwhile, cultivation would be shifted to new fields cleared in other areas, until they in turn were abandoned. After the long fallow, the soil would have recovered much of its original fertility and could be cultivated anew, after clearing and burning again.

This long-fallow system of shifting agriculture (also called swidden, *milpa*, *conuco*, or slash-and-burn) offered several advantages: it was an efficient way to prepare large plots for cultivation with a minimum of human labor; the fire loosened the soil and killed weed seeds; and the ashes temporarily enriched the soil. The system continued to be practiced in late twentieth-century American tropical forests, and it was widely blamed for soil erosion and permanent deforestation.

Whereas the pre-Columbian Indians were eminently successful cultivators of plants, they had a poor record as domesticators of animals. Pre-1492 American agriculture had no draft animals, which meant that all cultivation had to be done with hand tools. This limited the scale and organizational level of agriculture. The only domesticated grazing animals were the llama and alpaca of the Andean mountains. These animals provided fiber, manure, and meat, but they were raised only in the central Andes. The dog was domesticated throughout the hemisphere and sometimes was eaten (apparently mainly on ceremonial occasions). Other animals raised for meat included the turkey (despite its name, native to America) and the guinea pig. But domesticated animals provided only a tiny proportion of the diet of pre-Columbian Indians—far less than that of Europeans of the time.

The landholding system of the pre-Columbian Indians was overwhelmingly communitarian, although the Aztec and Inca ruling classes held private hereditary estates. Lands used by the common people were typically controlled by clan and kinship units that allotted arable land to each family. Land was communally owned, and individuals could merely use it. Under this communitarian system, land could neither be sold nor inherited; hence it could not be accumulated as wealth.

The basic agricultural tool throughout pre-Columbian America was the digging stick, or planting stick. In its crudest form, it was no more than a pointed stick. But some had stone tips, or were weighted, to help in breaking clods. Some Indian agriculturalists also used spades and hoes. There were no plows because there was a lack of draft animals to pull them.

Changes in Agriculture after 1492

Within half a century of the voyage of Columbus, Spain had conquered the Aztec, Maya, and Inca civilizations and established an enormous colonial empire spanning North, Central, and South America. The Spanish conquest did not completely destroy the pre-Columbian agrarian system. Instead, it introduced Old World plants, animals, tools, and methods that coexisted with the Indian system. Eventually, each system borrowed elements from the other, irrevocably changing the agriculture of both the Old and New World.

The Spanish—and the other Europeans who followed them—attempted to recreate in America the Old World agricultural system with which they were familiar. The Spanish introduced cattle, horses, donkeys, pigs, goats, sheep, and chickens to their colonies. These Old World animals adapted with astonishing speed to New World conditions. By the mid-1500s, European livestock were abundant, and meat was cheap. Many animals escaped domestication, forming feral herds that thrived on virgin grasslands and in the forests; their numbers quickly multiplied in the virtual absence of natural enemies. These untended herds, and the animals of Spanish ranchers, brought conflict between cultivated agriculture and animal husbandry for the first time in the history of the hemisphere. Spanish colonial authorities introduced the traditional Spanish concept of common pasture rights on woodlands, grasslands, and grain fields after harvest (where the stubble could be foraged). The result was that poorly supervised herds roamed the countryside, often straying into Indian crops and damaging them. The Indians began to erect fences—a new feature on the landscape—to protect their fields. This helped develop the concept of private land ownership among peoples whose previous experience had been almost wholly communitarian.

The Indians immediately recognized the superiority of European iron and steel axes, knives, hoes, and other tools, and it was not long before stone was virtually eliminated as a material for toolmaking. In the Spanish colonies, some Indian villages adopted Old World plows and oxen, while others clung to their pre-conquest planting sticks. By the 1700s, oxen and plows had become fairly common in Spanish-ruled Indian communities.

Cattle and horses, however, were not easily absorbed into pre-Columbian culture and long remained linked primarily to European immigrant agriculture. But if the Indians found it difficult to integrate cattle and horses into their agricultural system, they found that they could readily adjust to the use of smaller animals. Pigs and chickens were relatively inexpensive to acquire and maintain, and Indian families were able to fit them into the niche formerly occupied by pre-Hispanic dogs, turkeys, and guinea pigs. Other small animals, notably goats and sheep, blended easily with the Indian agricultural system, because they required little care and could live off the vegetation on hillside slopes not suited for cultivation.

The importation of ox, horse, and donkey revolutionized transport and travel and encouraged long-distance trade, thus providing new market opportunities for agriculture. Moreover, the tractional power of these animals encouraged an unprecedented expansion of cultivation. The ox (and the horse and mule favored by northern Europeans) could pull a plow through soils that had been too heavy, or too matted with roots, to be penetrated by the Indian planting stick. Livestock as a source of food also became important, as the result of the establishment of ranching on the vast plains of the New World. This began in the Spanish colonies in the sixteenth century and gradually spread into other areas. The result was a massive increase in the amount of animal protein available for human consumption. European colonists and their descendants were the primary beneficiaries, but eventually many Indian communities also turned to Old World animals as a substantial component of their social and economic life.

Desiring familiar foods, European immigrants in America brought with them the full complement of Old World crops. Nevertheless, out of necessity and experimentation, immigrants and their descendants gradually learned to eat maize, manioc, potatoes, and other native American foods. In addition to staple Old World crops, Europeans introduced sugarcane, originally from Asia. Europe seemed to have an insatiable appetite for sugar, even at high prices, and spectacular profits could be made from

its cultivation. But sugar production required a considerable capital investment, expensive machinery, and a large and continuously supervised work force. Sugarcane came to be grown primarily on large plantations worked by imported African slaves, after the native American population could no longer provide an adequate labor supply. European capitalists also imported African slaves to grow cotton (a native American crop) for the world market. Thus a zone of plantations was established, mainly along the coast, from the Chesapeake Bay to Rio de Janeiro, that depended on a work force of slaves imported from Africa. The institution of slavery, which had practically died out in Europe by 1492, was given new vigor in the New World colonies of the Spanish, Portuguese, French, English, and Dutch.

European colonists also introduced rice and bananas, which thrived in warm and humid American lowlands, often in soils not well suited for other crops. There were numerous other Old World crops that could be cultivated on lands not suitable for indigenous crops. Wheat, barley, and European broadbeans, for example, could be grown on mountain slopes at higher altitudes than maize.

Some Old World plants were readily accepted by the Indians. This was the case with many fruits, which were simply added to the Indian food list. Other crops could not easily be integrated into the Indian system. Old World grains, for example, were not normally grown by Indians. And it proved difficult for Indians to engage in large-scale livestock ranching or cash-crop production, because these activities had technological and social requirements that were alien to the indigenous cultures.

The Indian communities of the sixteenth to eighteenth centuries suffered catastrophic population losses to epidemics of Old World diseases to which native Americans had no inborn resistance. This enabled Europeans to encroach on supposedly inviolable Indian lands. The European colonial governments gradually legalized these land seizures, and this led to an increasingly Europeanized and privatized landowning structure.

The post-1492 exchange of plants, animals, tools, and methods of production between Old World and New brought vast alterations to the agricultural patterns of both hemispheres. Farmers now had a greatly increased number of food crops from which to choose. This made it easier to match crops to local soil and weather conditions. They discovered that the immigrant plants often would produce in soils that had been considered unsuitable for agriculture. The greater variety of crops brought not only a greater diversity of foods but also a more dependable food supply, because where one species was damaged by disease, pests, or unfavorable weather, another species often thrived. The increase in food production benefited all humankind, and made possible the massive increase in world population in the nineteenth and twentieth centuries.

The New World was changed far more than the Old. The pre-Columbian Indians had already modified the ecological balance of the Americas with their slash-and-burn agriculture, their irrigation and terracing, and various other practices. But the introduction of Old World agriculture drastically—and perhaps irrevocably—altered the ecology of vast areas of the Western Hemisphere. Cultivation with European plows and overgrazing by European animals brought an acceleration of deforestation and soil erosion. As a consequence of the Europeanization of American agriculture, countless species of native plants and animals were destroyed or reduced in numbers. Their place was taken by a far smaller number of specialized (often Old World) crops and herds and flocks of Old World animals.

Since 1492 the agriculture of the world has become not only more specialized and market-oriented but also more homogeneous. Such changes must be seen in the context of a general trend toward specialized production and the development of an ever more uniform global culture.

[See also *Domesticated Animals; Fauna; Flora; Metal.*]

BIBLIOGRAPHY

Chevalier, François. *Land and Society in Colonial Mexico: The Great Hacienda.* Translated by Alvin Eustis and edited by Lesley Byrd Simpson. Berkeley, 1970.

Crosby, Alfred W., Jr. *The Columbian Exchange: Biological and Cultural Consequences of 1492.* Westport, Conn., 1972.

Donkin, R. A. *Agricultural Terracing in the Aboriginal New World.* Tucson, Ariz., 1979.

Driver, Harold E. *Indians of North America.* Chicago, 1961.

Fussell, G. E. *The Classical Tradition in West European Farming.* Newton Abbot, United Kingdom, 1972.

García de Cortázar, José Angel. *La sociedad rural en la España medieval.* Madrid, 1988.

Hopkins, Joseph W. *Irrigation and the Cuicatec Ecosystem: A Study of Agriculture and Civilization in North Central Oaxaca.* Ann Arbor, Mich., 1984.

Pohl, Mary, ed. *Prehistoric Lowland Maya Environment and Subsistence Economy.* Papers of the Peabody Museum of Archaeology and Ethnology, Harvard University, vol. 77. Cambridge, Mass., 1985.

Sanoja, Mario. *Los hombres de la yuca y el maíz: Un ensayo sobre el origen y desarrollo de los sistemas agrarios en el Nuevo Mundo.* Caracas, 1981.

Slicher van Bath, B. H. *The Agrarian History of Western Europe, A.D. 500–1850.* Translated by Olive Ordish. London, 1963.

Sturtevant, William C., ed. *Handbook of North American Indians.* (20 volumes planned; vols. 4, 5, 6, 8, 9, 10, 11, and 15 published). Washington, D.C., 1978–.

Vassberg, David E. *Land and Society in Golden Age Castile.* Cambridge, 1984.

DAVID E. VASSBERG

AILLY, PIERRE D' (1350–1420), late medieval theologian and conciliarist. Born in Compiègne, d'Ailly was educated at the University of Paris, where he received his doctorate in theology in 1381. Subsequently a prominent administrative figure at Paris, he was named rector of the College of Navarre in 1384 and chancellor of the university in 1389. He was made bishop of Cambrai in 1397 and a cardinal in 1412 by Pope John XXIII. These ecclesiastical offices involved him in the complex conflicts among secular forces, adherents of conciliarism, and competing claimants to the papal throne that marked the Great Schism of the late fourteenth century. He played an active role in both the Council of Pisa (1409) and the Council of Constance (1413–1418).

D'Ailly wrote in both Latin and French. The commentaries, sermons, letters, and treatises that survive reflect the concerns of the academic and political worlds in which he moved. His commentaries on Lombard's *Sentences* and on Aristotle, and the opuscula (minor works) on cosmography and geography derive from his studies at Paris. Other letters and treatises such as *De materia concilii generalis* (1403) were occasioned by his participation in the Councils of Pisa and Constance and related negotiations. A third body of works were predominantly doctrinal or devotional in nature. These include commentaries on selected psalms and the *Song of Songs*, and meditations such as *Speculum considerationis, Compendium contemplationis,* and *De quatuor gradibus spiritualis.*

In the second decade of the fifteenth century, d'Ailly composed a cluster of interrelated works on cosmography, history, and astrology, which proved to be of particular significance in the genesis of Christopher Columbus's "Enterprise of the Indies" later in that same century. These include *Imago mundi* (1410) and *Tractatus de legibus et sectis contra supersticiosos astronomos, Tractatus de concordia astronomice veritatis cum theologia, Tractatus de concordia astronomice veritatis et narrationis hystorice,* and *Elucidarium astronomice concordie cum theologia et hystorica veritate,* all probably composed around 1414. Derived from d'Ailly's reading of a variety of late antique and medieval texts, they explore the interrelationships among Divine Providence, celestial configurations, and significant historical events.

Columbus read and annotated an incunabulum of these works. Published by John of Westphalia between 1480 and 1483, it survives in the Biblioteca Colombina in Seville. Columbus's marginalia indicate that *Imago mundi* was an important source for his plan to reach the Far East by sailing west across the Atlantic Ocean. The opuscula mentioned above supplied him with a larger prophetic and providential framework within which to establish the significance of the discoveries resulting from the "Enterprise of the Indies." These works of d'Ailly thus played an

PAGE FROM D'AILLY'S *IMAGO MUNDI*. Columbus's own copy, showing his notations on length of days at various latitudes.

important role in Columbus's conceptualizing of the voyage that led to the discovery of the Americas and in his understanding of its historical implications.

[See also *Writings*, article on *Marginalia*.]

BIBLIOGRAPHY

Buron, Edmond. *Imago mundi de Pierre d'Ailly.* 3 vols. Paris, 1930. (Includes Columbus's marginal annotations.)

Watts, Pauline Moffitt. "Prophecy and Discovery: On the Spiritual Origins of Christopher Columbus's 'Enterprise of the Indies.'" *American Historical Review* 90 (1985): 73–102.

PAULINE MOFFITT WATTS

ALCÁÇOVAS, TREATY OF. See *Treaty of Alcáçovas.*

ALEXANDER VI (c. 1431–1503), pope (1492–1503). Born Rodrigo de Borja y Borja at Játiva near Valencia in Aragón,

the future pope was the son of local nobility. His father was Jofré de Borja y Doms and his mother was Isabel de Borja y Martí, the sister of Alonso, then bishop of Valencia.

As a youth Borja entered the clerical state and received benefices from his uncle Alonso, whom he followed to Italy, where he studied canon law at Bologna and received a doctorate in 1456. After Alonso was elected pope (as Calixtus III, r. 1455–1458), Borja was appointed administrator of the dioceses of Gerona (1457) and Valencia (1458), and a cardinal (1456) and vice-chancellor of the church (1457), a major post he continued to hold until his own election as pope. Even after the death of his uncle, Borja continued to accumulate lucrative church offices often in Spain.

Borja at first looked to the royal house of his native Aragón to further his own and his family's ambitions (he fathered illegitimately at least four sons and three daughters). In 1472–1473 he returned to the kingdom as papal legate. Although he failed in his primary task of securing Aragonese assistance for a crusade against the Turks, Borja succeeded in putting the heir to the throne, Fernando, forever in his debt.

Entrusted by Sixtus IV to grant or withhold at his discretion a papal dispensation from the impediment of consanguinity, Borja regularized Fernando's earlier (1469) marriage to his cousin Isabel of Castile and worked to secure the support of other Spanish prelates for this marriage, which led eventually to the political union of their kingdoms. As king, Fernando reciprocated the favor by asking Borja to crown his sister Juana as queen of Naples (1477) and to be godfather to his son. The king's kindnesses also extended to the cardinal's children: Cesare and Jofré were legitimized so they could receive Spanish benefices, Pedro Luis was granted the title of duke of Gandia (1485) and betrothed to the king's cousin María Enriquez, Juan succeeded to his brother's title and fiancée, and Lucrezia was initially betrothed successively to two Spanish noblemen. The cordial relations between the king and cardinal were briefly disrupted when Borja secured appointment to the metropolitan see of Seville (1484), which Fernando had wanted for his bastard son Alfonso. But amity was restored in 1486 when the prelate helped the Spanish ruler protect his cousins in Naples by patching up the differences between Ferrante I of Naples (r. 1458–1494) and Innocent VIII. When Fernando and Isabel completed the conquest of Granada in 1492, Borja provided lavish congratulatory celebrations in Rome.

During his thirty-six-year career as a cardinal, Borja earned a mixed reputation in Rome. His enemies saw him as greedy, ambitious, proud, unscrupulous, and lascivious. His friends pointed to his energy and knowledge of canon law, his skills as a diplomat, speaker, and administrator, and his orthodoxy and conventional piety. At the conclave of 1484, Borja was almost elected pope, but for the opposition of his archrival, Cardinal Giuliano della Rovere. With the help of Cardinal Ascanio Sforza, however, Borja triumphed in the conclave of 1492.

As Pope Alexander VI, he continued to further the careers and dynastic ambitions of the Borja family, but now its base shifted primarily to Italy. He often secured for his children there feudal titles and favorable matches. Thus, four of them were married into the nobility of Rome, the ducal family of Ferrara, and the royal house of Naples. His notorious son, Cesare, however, after a career as cardinal (1493–1498), was laicized and then appointed duke of Valence in France by Louis XII and married (1499) to Charlotte d'Albret, the sister of the king of Navarre. With his father's assistance, he nonetheless tried to carve out for himself a dukedom in the Romagna region of the Papal States.

In his foreign policy Alexander proved timorous and uncertain, and was often influenced by Cesare. He initially joined the League of San Marco, allying himself with Venice and Milan against Florence and Naples and their Orsini supporters in Rome. But within months he had reconciled with Ferrante I of Naples for fear of Charles VIII (r. 1484–1498) of France who, urged on by Cardinal Giuliano della Rovere, threatened to descend on Italy to make good his claim to the throne of Naples and to depose the pope for simony. Alexander tried in vain to protect Ferrante's successor, Alfonso II (r. 1494–1495), by forming a broader alliance that would have included Spain and the empire. When the victorious army of Charles VIII stopped at Rome in 1494–1495 on its way to Naples, the pope negotiated terms of peace with the French, but then joined the anti-French league once Charles's position in Naples proved untenable. As a reward to the Spanish rulers for their assistance in expelling the French, Alexander in 1494 reconfirmed their official title of "The Catholic Monarchs." The pope favored the restoration of Alfonso II's son and heir, Ferrandino II (r. 1495–1496), as king of Naples.

In a reversal of his earlier foreign policy, Alexander followed the lead of Cesare in allying with the new French king, Louis XII (r. 1498–1515), who conquered Milan and so helped Cesare to subdue the regions of Romagna and the Marches that in 1501 the pope conferred on this son the title of duke of Romagna. Although Alexander had previously favored the Neapolitan House of Aragona (indeed, two of his children had married into that royal family), he nonetheless agreed to the Treaty of Granada (1500) that called for its deposition and that assigned Sicily to Fernando II of Aragón and Naples to Louis XII of France; he sent his sons Cesare and Jofré to help drive Federico (r. 1496–1501) from the Neapolitan throne. When the French opposed Cesare's growing power in the Papal States, Alexander drew closer to Fernando but never formally acquiesced in his conquest of the Neapolitan mainland in 1503.

Alexander did not provide effective leadership in the area of church reform, although he did support the reform efforts of others. He promoted various forms of Marian devotion, including the building and restoration of churches in honor of Mary. He also took stern measures against heretics and was particularly severe with those who feigned conversion from Judaism. But a serious reform of the Roman Curia ranked low among his priorities, for he devoted his primary energies to politics and nepotism, which led to his appointing unqualified men as cardinals and bishops. The murder of the pope's son Juan in June of 1497 led to a period of repentance during which Alexander planned a sweeping reform of the Curia. But the draft reform bull that resulted from months of careful labor was never signed, and Alexander returned to his customary concerns with family and politics.

Among the pope's primary critics was the Dominican preacher of Florence, Girolamo Savonarola (1452–1498), who attacked the Roman Curia and the pope himself as sources of corruption and helped ally Florence with France in 1494. When Alexander forbade him to preach publicly, the friar obeyed for several months but then resumed his preaching in 1496, denouncing Rome as the new Babylon. The letter Savonarola sent in March 1497 to Charles VIII urging the convocation of a council to depose Alexander VI for simony was intercepted and reported to Rome. The pope excommunicated Savonarola in May of that year, but the friar disregarded this penalty, functioning as a priest at Christmas and preaching in February 1498. When the pope in retaliation imposed an interdict on Florence, city officials sided with him and prohibited Savonarola's preaching. Finally rioting broke out after an ordeal by fire was canceled because of conditions imposed by Savonarola and his followers. The friar was arrested and interrogated, and a confession of fabricated revelations was extracted under torture, a confession he later retracted. The judges sent by the pope from Rome condemned him of heresy and schism and handed him over for execution to civil authorities on May 23, 1498.

Alexander VI's long-standing cordial relations with the rulers of Spain were invaluable to the monarchs in securing full control of the American lands found by Columbus. Because the bulls of Nicholas V (1455), Calixtus III (1456), and Sixtus IV (1481) had given Portugal exclusive possession of all lands from Cape Bojador in West Africa south to India, the Portuguese complained that Columbus's discoveries were in the region of the Indies. The Spanish monarchs thereupon sought papal confirmation of their new territorial claims. In an initial bull, *Inter caetera divinae* dated May 3, 1493, Alexander VI granted the Catholic monarchs sovereignty over the lands discovered by Columbus, provided they were not already owned by a Christian prince. Columbus suggested that in addition to the latitudinal Line of Demarcation earlier approved by the popes, a new longitudinal line be drawn one hundred leagues west of the Azores to separate the Spanish and Portuguese lands. This proposal was adopted in a new version of *Inter caetera divinae* promulgated after the arrival in Rome of a new Spanish delegation in June and backdated to May 4. The revised bull also required that, for any Christian prince other than Fernando and Isabel to retain sovereignty over lands west of that line, he would have to be in possession of them prior to Christmas of 1493.

Also backdated to May 3 was the bull *Eximiae devotionis sinceritas,* which granted to the Spanish monarchs in their new lands the same rights and privileges enjoyed by the Portuguese ruler in his African possessions. Lest any doubts arise regarding Spanish sovereignty over newly discovered lands that might lie in the region of the Indies earlier assigned to the Portuguese, Alexander VI issued on September 26, 1493, the bull *Dudum siquidem,* which allowed the Spanish to take possession of and hold in perpetuity even lands south and east of India and the Orient. Portuguese alarm over this papal grant encouraged King João II to negotiate with Fernando and Isabel the Treaty of Tordesillas of June 7, 1494, which guaranteed their monopolies in accord with a new Line of Demarcation drawn 370 leagues to the west of the Azores and Cape Verde Islands. Julius II confirmed this treaty in 1506.

Alexander VI also made provisions for the propagation of Catholicism in the new lands. The bull *Inter caetera divinae* of May 3, 1493, charged the Catholic monarchs to see that the natives in these lands were instructed in the Catholic faith. To facilitate this task, Alexander VI a month later granted special powers to Bernardo Buil, a member of the recently confirmed Minim order and the person chosen by the Spanish rulers to direct the work of evangelization. To help finance this missionary undertaking, Alexander granted to the Spanish monarchs in 1501 the right to levy and receive from the new lands' inhabitants ecclesiastical tithes to be used to build churches, maintain the clergy, and support worship services. In that same year the work of evangelization had so far progressed that negotiations were begun on establishing a hierarchy in the New World.

The pope also encouraged the Spanish rulers to continue the crusade against the Moors. In 1494 he granted to them in perpetuity the *tercias reales* (the royal portion of one-third of church tithes) to help finance this military undertaking. In addition, beginning in 1494 and renewed annually for several years, Alexander VI allowed the Catholic monarchs to levy a one-tenth tax on all ecclesiastics, both secular and religious, to support a crusade in North Africa. To eliminate any dissension between the

ALEXANDER VI. Detail from Pinturicchio's fresco of the Resurrection in the Borgia (Borja) apartments of the Vatican.

Christian princes of Iberia, the pope in 1494 assigned to the Portuguese as their military area the Kingdom of Fès in Morocco and to the Spanish, Tlemcen and Oran in Algeria. But not until 1505 did the Spanish launch their first serious campaign on the Barbary coast and then with money supplied for the most part by Archbishop Francisco Jiménez de Cisneros of Toledo.

In February of 1502 Columbus drafted a letter to Alexander VI. He recalled that he had wished on the return from his first voyage of discovery in 1493 to visit the pope to tell him in person the great news. But, he said, he had been prevented from doing so because his Spanish rulers quickly sent him back to claim all the lands while the dispute over their ownership between Spain and Portugal was being settled. Columbus protested that after these nine years his desire to visit Alexander VI had not diminished; he wanted to relate to him the significance of his discoveries, which he identified with the Orient and the "Terrestrial Paradise" described by saints and theologians and which he thought lay on the Venezuelan mainland. The purpose of his voyages had been twofold: the propagation of the faith and the recovery of

Jerusalem. To further the missionary work, he asked the pope to provide him with suitable monks and friars. To advance the cause of a crusade, he promised that once he had entered the House of God and visited the Terrestrial Paradise he would contribute 100,000 infantrymen and 1,000 horsemen in two equal installments in the seventh and twelfth years thereafter to conquer the Holy Land. The quantities of gold he had already supplied to the Catholic monarchs, he said, clearly indicated that he could keep his pledge. Although he had been granted perpetual government of these lands, he had been opposed by the forces of Satan who feared he would succeed in his holy enterprise. The mariner apparently was seeking papal assistance in his struggle to regain his governorship and rights to revenues from the new lands. Alexander VI is not known to have received this letter, responded to it, or championed Columbus's cause.

The pope's death on August 18, 1503, was sudden. His son's former secretary and now cardinal, Adriano Castellesi, was accused of having poisoned him and Cesare, who became very ill. The great ambitions Alexander VI had for his family were frustrated. The new head of the House of Borja, the sickly Cesare, was taken prisoner and his control of Romagna crumbled. He fled to Naples, was shipped to Spain, and finally escaped to Navarre where he died in battle in 1507. After the month-long reign of the Sienese reformer Pius III (1503), Alexander's archrival, Giuliano della Rovere, was elected as Pope Julius II (r. 1503–1513).

BIBLIOGRAPHY

Burchard, Johannes. *At the Court of the Borgia.* Edited and translated by Geoffrey Parker. London, 1963.

Cummins, J. S. "Christopher Columbus: Crusader, Visionary, and Servus Dei." In *Medieval Hispanic Studies Presented to Rita Hamilton,* edited by Alan D. Deyermond. London, 1976.

De Roo, Peter. *Material for a History of Pope Alexander VI, His Relatives, and His Times.* 5 vols. New York, 1924.

Mallett, Michael E. *The Borgias: The Rise and Fall of a Renaissance Dynasty.* London, 1969.

Pastor, Ludwig von. *The History of the Popes from the Close of the Middle Ages.* Vols. 5–6. Translated by Frederick Ignatius Antrobus. St. Louis, 1923.

Picotti, Giovanni Battista. "Alessandro VI, papa." In vol. 2 of *Dizionario biografico degli italiani.* Rome, 1960.

Schüller-Piroli, Susanne. *Die Borgia Päpste Kalixt III. und Alexander VI.* Munich, 1980.

NELSON H. MINNICH

ALFONSO V (1396–1458), king of Aragón (1416–1458). Alfonso the Magnanimous was a shrewd ruler and skilled diplomat whose ambitions for territorial expansion resulted in the acquisition of Naples in 1435. The Aragonese presence in Naples set the stage for the prolonged military involvement in Italy of Fernando and Isabel with France, the papacy, and the Holy Roman Empire.

Son of King Fernando I of Antequera and Leonor of Albuquerque, Alfonso represented the Aragonese branch of the Trastámara family. His marriage to his cousin María, the sister of King Juan II of Castile, strengthened the familial and political connections with Castile. This intertwining of the Spanish royal families culminated in the union of the two kingdoms during the reign of Isabel of Castile and Alfonso's nephew Fernando. But close family ties did not prevent armed hostilities. When Alfonso's brothers Juan (later Juan II of Aragón) and Enrique, the infantes of Aragón, interfered in Castilian affairs in 1420, Alfonso became involved also.

Alfonso, a patron of music, literature, the arts, and education, spent the last twenty years of his reign living at his court in Naples in the manner of a Renaissance prince. He was absent from the peninsular realms of the Crown of Aragón during a period of social and economic turmoil, especially in Catalonia. Because Alfonso had no legitimate heir, he bequeathed the Kingdom of Naples to his illegitimate son Ferrante. His brother Juan inherited the realms of the Crown of Aragón.

BIBLIOGRAPHY

Ametller y Viñas, José. *Alfonso V de Aragón en Italia y la crisis religiosa del siglo XV.* 3 vols. Gerona, 1903–1928.

Driscoll, Eileen R. *Alfonso of Aragon as a Patron of Art.* New York, 1964.

Pontieri, Ernesto. *Alfonso il Magnanimo, re di Napoli (1435–1458).* Naples, 1975.

Ryder, Alan. *The Kingdom of Naples under Alfonso the Magnanimous: The Making of a Modern State.* Oxford, 1976.

THERESA EARENFIGHT

ALFONSO X (1221–1284), king of Castile and León, known as Alfonso the Wise. Alfonso's law code, the *Siete partidas* (Seven divisions), was introduced in the sixteenth century into the New World, where it had a profound impact on the legal development of all the Spanish-speaking regions. The son of Fernando III and Beatrice of Swabia, Alfonso X was born in Toledo and succeeded to the throne in 1252. After attending to the colonization of Seville and the recently reconquered territory in Andalusia, he tried to assert his supremacy over his Christian neighbors, especially Portugal and Navarre, but without success. Elected in 1257 as Holy Roman Emperor in opposition to Richard of Cornwall, he incurred great expenses over nearly twenty years in a vain effort to win recognition.

Of greater importance was his plan to invade Morocco so as to deprive the Muslims of easy access to the Iberian peninsula. In preparation he developed a naval base at Cádiz and the nearby Puerto de Santa María, and his fleet plundered Salé on the Atlantic coast of Morocco in 1260. After conquering Niebla to the west of Seville in 1262, he demanded the surrender of Gibraltar and Tarifa. Muhammad I, king of Granada, refused and stirred up rebellion in 1264 among the Muslims subject to Castilian rule in Andalusia and Murcia. While undertaking to contain the revolt in Andalusia, Alfonso X appealed to Jaime I of Aragón, who subdued Murcia early in 1266. Jerez, the last rebel stronghold in Andalusia, capitulated in October, and the king of Granada resumed the payment of a yearly tribute to Castile in 1267. Following the rebellion, Alfonso X expelled the Muslims from the recaptured towns and brought in Christian settlers.

Although tranquillity was restored, Alfonso X soon encountered strong opposition because of his innovations in law and taxation. Intent on achieving greater juridical uniformity, he drew upon Roman law in preparing a code of law for use in the royal court, namely, the *Espéculo de las leyes* (Mirror of the laws), known in its later redaction as the *Siete partidas*. The nobles accused him of denying them the right to be judged by their peers in accordance with their customs. The townsmen, while complaining about the *Fuero real*, a new code of municipal law, were also distressed by the frequent imposition of extraordinary taxes.

When the nobles confronted the king during the Cortes of Burgos in 1272, he modified his plan for a uniform body of law by confirming their customs and those of the towns. Despite that, many nobles went into exile in Granada but were persuaded to return to royal service in 1273. With his realm at peace, Alfonso X journeyed to Beaucaire in southern France where in 1275 he vainly tried to convince Pope Gregory X to recognize him as Holy Roman Emperor.

During his absence, Abu Yusuf, the ruler of the Benimerines of Morocco, invaded Castile. Intent on repelling them, the son and heir of Alfonso X, Fernando de la Cerda, hastened to the frontier, but died suddenly at Villarreal in 1275. Soon after, the invaders routed Castilian forces in Andalusia. At that point, Alfonso X's second son, Sancho, reorganized the defense. A truce was concluded, but the Benimerines invaded again in 1277. Avoiding a battlefield encounter, Alfonso X blockaded Algeciras in 1278 but had to give it up early the next year. In spite of the Moroccan threat, Castile emerged from this crisis without loss of territory.

Meanwhile, the death of his oldest son presented Alfonso X with a serious problem. Fernando de la Cerda's oldest child, Alfonso, could claim recognition as heir to the throne, but Sancho, as Alfonso X's second son, appealed to the older custom that gave preference to a king's surviving sons. After much debate, the king in the Cortes of Burgos in 1276 acknowledged Sancho. Fearing for the safety of her two sons, Fernando de la Cerda's widow, Blanche, took them in 1278 to Aragón, where Peter III kept them in protective custody.

Philip III of France, the uncle of the two boys, pressured Alfonso X to partition his realm for the benefit of Alfonso de la Cerda. Angered by the possibility of losing any portion of the kingdom, Sancho broke with his father during the Cortes of Seville in 1281. The estates of the realm, gathered at Valladolid in April 1282, transferred royal power to Sancho, leaving Alfonso X only the title of king. Abandoned by his family and his subjects, the king turned to Abu Yusuf of Morocco, who invaded Castile again. After an abortive attempt at reconciliation, Alfonso X in his last will disinherited Sancho. The king died at Seville on April 4, 1284, and was buried in the cathedral.

Despite his unhappy end, Alfonso X was one of the greatest medieval kings of Castile, and his impact on the development of Spanish law and institutions was lasting. In collaboration with a team of scholars he published in the vernacular a series of legal, historical, literary, and scientific works without parallel in thirteenth-century Europe. The *Siete partidas*, known in its initial version as the *Espéculo de las leyes*, was an extraordinary achievement. Given its systematic and comprehensive character, the *Partidas* shaped the law in all the peninsular realms and also in the Spanish colonies overseas. The *Fuero real* was an adaptation of the *Espéculo* for the use of municipalities. Alfonso X's collaborators also composed the *Estoria de Espanna*, a history of Spain from the earliest times, and the *General estoria*, or world history. The *Cantigas de Santa María*, a collection of more than four hundred poems written in Galician in praise of the Virgin Mary, was set to music and accompanied by beautiful illuminations. Avidly interested in astronomy and astrology, the king gathered in the *Libro del saber de astronomía* the translations of several Arabic treatises as well as original works on the construction of astronomical instruments. These were used in the compilation of the Alfonsine Tables, based on astronomical observations charting the position of the planets and stars from 1262 to 1272 at Toledo. The Alfonsine Tables were widely known throughout late medieval Europe and were supplanted only in the later sixteenth century. The king's last notable work, the *Setenario*, was a book of theological and moral counsel intended for his successors. By using Castilian for all these works (save the *Cantigas*), he gave great impetus to the development of the language as a proper vehicle for the expression of serious ideas.

BIBLIOGRAPHY

Ballesteros, Antonio. *Alfonso X.* Barcelona and Madrid, 1963. Reprint, Barcelona, 1984.

Keller, John Esten. *Alfonso X, El Sabio.* New York, 1967.

O'Callaghan, Joseph F. "Image and Reality: The King Creates His Kingdom." In *Emperor of Culture: Alfonso X the Learned of Castile and His Thirteenth Century Renaissance.* Edited by Robert I. Burns. Philadelphia, 1990.

Procter, Evelyn. *Alfonso X: Patron of Literature and Learning.* Oxford, 1951.

JOSEPH F. O'CALLAGHAN

ALFRAGANUS (c. 800–861), Arab astronomer and engineer. The name Alfraganus is the Latin corruption of al-Farghani, a ninth-century astronomer-astrologer employed by the Caliph al-Ma'mun (d. 833) and his successors. Al-Farghani was born in Farghana in Transoxania—hence, his name—and died in Egypt after supervising the construction of the Great Nilometer (a canal that connected al-Ja'fariyya, a new city built near the capital city of Samarra, with the Tigris) for the caliph al-Mutawakkil. Very little is known about his life, but his works have survived both in their original Arabic and in Latin translations.

Al-Farghani was responsible for spreading the astronomical knowledge found in Ptolemy's *Almagest,* the single most important work on astronomy in the ancient and medieval worlds. His greatest and most influential work is "Elements of Astronomy," a summary of the nonmathematical portions of the *Almagest.* It is based entirely on Ptolemaic methods and was intended to be an introductory text on astronomy. The popularity of the work can be attributed to both its clarity and its brevity; since it was only thirty chapters in length it was much simpler to use than the *Almagest.* In addition to al-Farghani, al-Battani also wrote a compendium of the *Almagest.* The works of both these individuals were to have a profound impact upon European astronomy until the time of Copernicus.

Like so much of Islamic science and philosophy, the great body of eastern astronomy entered the West through Spain. John of Spain, also known as John of Seville (Johannes Hispalensis), published his translation of al-Farghani's "Elements" in 1135 and Gerard of Cremona completed his translation of the work in Toledo in 1175. Until Regiomontanus's works in the latter half of the fifteenth century, European knowledge of astronomy was derived primarily from the Latin translations of al-Farghani's "Elements." Dante relied on Gerard of Cremona's translation for the knowledge of the stars he displays in his *Vita nuova* and in the *Convivio.* Al-Farghani also wrote two treatises on the astrolabe as well as a commentary on the astronomical tables of al-Khwarizmi; however, the latter work has not survived.

It is known that Columbus, too, referred to at least one of al-Farghani's calculations in planning his voyage of discovery. Columbus the man presents a fascinating dichotomy to the historian. He was a man entrenched in the Old World. Almost everything he said, did, or wrote reflected his Old World mentality. Yet he was also a determined and self-taught man who sought out new horizons. Attesting to this dichotomy are four of his books, which still exist in the Biblioteca Colombina in Seville: Marco Polo's *Description of the World* (1485 edition), Cardinal Pierre d'Ailly's *Imago mundi* (1480 to 1483), Aeneus Sylvius's *Historia rerum ubique gestarum* (1477), and Pliny's *Natural History* (1489). These books were heavily glossed by Columbus; the *Imago mundi* alone contains several hundred marginal annotations.

Columbus, in planning his journey, underestimated the circumference of the earth while at the same time overestimating the size of the Asiatic continent he wished to reach. He rejected Ptolemy's assertion that the distance between Asia and Europe was 180 degrees of longitude. Referring to the works of d'Ailly, Marinus of Tyre, and Marco Polo, he calculated the distance at sixty degrees. Columbus then needed to translate longitude into linear distance. In the *Imago mundi* he found an estimate attributed to al-Farghani of $56\frac{2}{3}$ miles. But he erroneously assumed these to be Italian miles of 1,480 meters each, which translates into forty nautical miles (twenty nautical miles short of the correct distance). Columbus's calculations thus reduced the actual size of the world by one-quarter. These miscalculations, however, served to encourage him in his belief that the distance between Spain and Japan was a relatively short one.

BIBLIOGRAPHY

Al-Farghani. *Alfragano (Al-Fragani) Il 'Libro dell'aggregazione delle stelle.'* Edited by Romeo Campani. Città de Castello, 1910.

Al-Farghani. *Alfragani differentie in quibusdam collectis scientie astrorum.* Edited by Francis J. Carmondy. Berkeley and Los Angeles, 1943.

Carmondy, Francis J. *Arabic Astronomical and Astrological Sciences in Latin Translation: A Critical Bibliography.* Berkeley and Los Angeles, 1956.

Perry, J. H. *The Discovery of the Sea.* Berkeley and Los Angeles, 1974.

Vernet, Juan. *La cultura hispanoárabe en Oriente y Occidente.* Barcelona, 1978.

PAUL PADILLA

ALMEIDA, FRANCISCO DE (c. 1450–1510), first viceroy of Portuguese India. Almeida, born in Lisbon, was a member of a distinguished family who belonged to the highest nobility in the land. His father was Lopo de

Almeida, first count of Abrantes, and his mother, Brites da Silva, served as lady-in-waiting to two successive queens.

He began his military career at the Battle of Toro (1476) in which Afonso V (r. 1438–1481) was routed by a Spanish army under Fernando of Aragón. At the beginning of the reign of João II (r. 1481–1495) he obtained permission to serve in the war of Granada then being fought by Fernando and Isabel of Spain against the Moors, a war in which Columbus is believed to have taken part. The successful conclusion of the campaign against Granada enabled the Catholic monarchs to turn their attention to Columbus and to grant him the ships he needed for his westward voyage.

Almeida may also have been present at court when Columbus visited João II on his return from the first voyage of discovery in 1493. The king was particularly disturbed by the sight of the Amerindians who accompanied Columbus, for they resembled what he had been told the Indians of Asia looked like, and he believed that Columbus had stumbled on land that fell within the sphere of influence granted him by the pope in 1481. As a result, the king decided to send an armada to search for and take possession of the land discovered by Columbus, and he appointed Almeida as admiral. The fleet never sailed because the Spaniards, having heard about it from their spies, convinced João to allow the matter to be settled by negotiation, which eventually led to the Treaty of Tordesillas (1494).

By 1505, after the return of the first four fleets from India, the Portuguese were convinced that it was impossible to wrest the trade monopoly from the Muslims as long as their ships were forced to return to Europe after discharging their cargo. Consequently, King Manuel I (r. 1495–1521) decided to station warships in Indian waters permanently. To initiate this plan he chose Francisco de Almeida as governor-general of Portuguese India, with a provision permitting him to assume the title of viceroy after he had discharged certain duties. On March 24, 1505, Almeida departed for India in command of a fleet of twenty-two ships, taking his only son Lourenço with him. On his way up the east coast of Africa he captured the city of Kilwa, where he built a fort; in Mombasa, he destroyed the city where the Portuguese had been ill treated; and in Malindi, he showered gifts on the sultan who had treated them well.

On September 12, 1505, he reached India and set about building fortresses in the coastal cities where the Portuguese had been well received. He successfully fought the king of Honowar, who challenged him at sea, and wreaked vengeance on the Muslims who had set the Portuguese fort of Cochin afire. He formed an alliance with the rajah of Cochin and on March 15, 1506, he captured Panane, a well-frequented port about fourteen leagues south of Calicut. He sent his son Lourenço to the Maldives and Ceylon to take prizes from the richly laden Muslim vessels that were bypassing the Malabar coast of India. From Ceylon, Lourenço returned triumphantly with a treaty of friendship and tribute in the form of cinnamon.

Early in 1507 the fleet of the sultan of Egypt started for India to expel the Portuguese interlopers from the Indian Ocean. In January 1508 the combined Egyptian and Indian fleets defeated a Portuguese squadron off Chaul in a battle in which the viceroy's son was killed. In the meantime, Afonso de Albuquerque arrived from Hormuz with orders to succeed Almeida as governor of India. Almeida refused to relinquish the command since he was bent on avenging the death of his son. The simultaneous arrival of the annual fleets of 1507 and 1508 swelled his ranks, and on December 12, Almeida set sail for the island of Diu in search of the enemy. Over a hundred Indian vessels had joined the Egyptian fleet when Almeida met them at Diu on February 3, 1509, with only nineteen ships. Nevertheless, he achieved a resounding victory that proved to be one of the decisive battles of Asiatic history. For the next hundred years the dominance of the Indian Ocean remained in Portuguese hands.

Almeida returned to Cochin where Albuquerque, who had waited patiently, now pressed him to hand over his command. Again he refused. Finally, they agreed to leave the matter up to Marshal Fernando Coutinho, who was expected in India momentarily, charged by the king with full powers to act independently. The marshal decided in favor of Albuquerque, thanked Almeida for all he had done, and sent him on his way. On November 19, 1509, Almeida reluctantly sailed for home. After rounding the Cape of Good Hope, he entered the Saldanha Bay where, at the head of 150 men, he went ashore to take on water. There he was slain by the natives, along with fifty of his troops.

His four years in office were notable for a well-run administration and for the many victories he achieved over the Muslims. The only battle he lost was the one in which his son was killed. Though he built fortresses at Kilwa, Angediva, and Cannanore, he is known to have written King Manuel that "as long as you are powerful on the sea, you will have India for Yourself, otherwise, your fortresses on land will avail you little."

BIBLIOGRAPHY

Barros, João de, and Diogo do Couto. *Da Ásia de João de Barros e de Diogo de Couto*. 24 vols. Lisbon, 1778–1788.

Castanheda, Fernão Lopes de. *História do descobrimento e conquista da Índia pelos portugueses*. Edited by M. Lopes de Almeida. 2 vols. Porto, 1979.

Correia, Gaspar. *Lendas da India*. Edited by M. Lopes de Almeida. 4 vols. Porto, 1975.

Prestage, Edgar. *The Portuguese Pioneers*. London, 1933.

REBECCA CATZ

ALTURA SAILING. Altura (height) navigation was introduced at sea by the Portuguese in the latter part of the fifteenth century, probably about 1460. It preceded latitude navigation, which came into practice after the mathematical commission appointed by King João II of Portugal had worked out the procedures and calculated the necessary tables. It is not clear how altura navigation developed, but, at least in its earliest form, sometimes known as the altitude-distance method, it is as likely to have been developed by the pilots as the astronomers. The problem with existing methods arose with the largely north-south voyages from Portugal down the west coast of Africa to Guinea; the return voyage involved a wide sweep westward into the Atlantic to cross the northeast trades and regain the variable and westerly winds in the latitude of the Azores. Some method of checking on a daily basis the north-south component of the position obtained by dead reckoning was highly desirable. The ultimate objective was to attain the parallel on which the destination lay and then steer east or west to it.

The altitude-distance method involved taking an altitude of the meridian passage of the sun or a star and comparing it with a similar observation a day or so later to get the linear distance traveled in a north-south direction. In principle, any star at meridian passage would do, but the seaman was told to use the North Star when the Guards of the Lesser Bear were in the same position in relation to the North Star and, in the case of the sun, to take the second observation not more than a day or two after the first, during which time the declination will not have changed too much. By assuming a figure for the measure of the earth's meridian, the difference between the two readings could be multiplied by this value to give linear distance traveled north or south. One degree of altitude was originally taken to equal 16⅔ leagues, or 4 miles; this was later changed to 17½ leagues.

The medieval seaman was accustomed to using the position of the Guard Stars in relation to the North Star as a form of clock; this involved memorizing their position for every fortnight of the year. To help they imagined a human figure in the sky with the North Star at his breast, the head above, feet below, and arms to right and left. Diagonal lines between the limbs completed the eightfold division of the circle, each of which represented three hours. The same kind of figure was now adopted to help the pilot correct the altitude of the North Star for its counterclockwise movement, which then described a path about the true pole with a radius of about 3½ degrees. The seaman was told initially to observe the North Star on departure when the position of the Guards indicated that it was on the meridian, but later instructions gave the height at Lisbon for all eight positions, from which the heights observed later could be subtracted to get the distance traveled north or south.

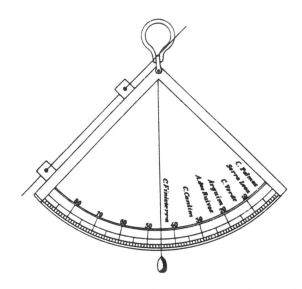

SEAMAN'S QUADRANT. This example is marked with the altitude of various capes. The first marking on the right, for example, is for Cape Palmas, in present-day Liberia.

The first observations were made with the seaman's quadrant, and in 1462 Diogo Gomes records that he marked on the instrument the altitude of the Arctic pole, by which he means the North Star, which by comparison with the altitude of the star at Lisbon gave the distance traveled better (and perhaps more reliably) than the chart. The precise meaning of the note is disputable, but it does reveal that the practice developed among Portuguese pilots of marking the instrument itself with the location at which the plumb line cut the scale when the body observed through the sights was on the meridian. It soon became clear that observations of the sun would be more convenient than observations by night, and, so as to extend the period between observations beyond the one or two days in which the change in declination would adversely affect measurements, tables were prepared giving the meridian solar altitude for each day of the year at Lisbon, Madeira, and other important seaports. Subtracting the altitude observed from, say, the Lisbon figure would give the distance required from Lisbon. In due course the mariner's astrolabe replaced the seaman's quadrant for solar observation; its earliest recorded use was on the Atlantic coast of Africa in 1481.

The mnemonic of the human figure of the sky was revised, initially to avoid ambiguity; the statement, "the Guards are in the right arm," for example, might refer to the right arm of the imaginary figure or of the observer. Later, the cardinal and intercardinal points of the compass were substituted for the eight positions of the Guards, the head becoming north, left shoulder northwest, left arm west, and so on. A yet later system dispensed with the human figure and simply showed the relative positions of the two Guards for each of eight positions of the North Star in its movement about the pole of the sky, two of which (when the Guards lay east-west) indicated the Star's meridian passage. Columbus, in his account of the third voyage, stuck to the old nomenclature and spoke several times of the North Star being elevated five degrees, or, "the Guards in the head." He was attempting to run down the latitude of Sierra Leone, which was given in the manuals at the time as eight degrees north, and it has been suggested that his quadrant must have been marked after the altura fashion, since the correction to the North Star's altitude for that position of the Guards is given as three degrees and if the plumb line on the quadrant fell at five degrees (eight minus three degrees) he would have been on the right parallel. The use of "wheels of the Pole Star," giving the altitude of the North Star for each of the rhumbs indicating the position of the Guards, became the standard method of altura sailing. Such wheels could of course be drawn up for any frequently used seaport or point of departure, but only Lisbon is referred to in the surviving documents.

[See also *Astronomy and Astrology; Dead Reckoning; Navigation.*]

BIBLIOGRAPHY

Albuquerque, Luís de. *Astronomical Navigation.* Lisbon, 1988.
Taylor, E. G. R. *The Haven Finding Art: A History of Navigation from Odysseus to Captain Cook.* London, 1956.
Waters, David W. *Reflections upon Some Navigational and Hydrographic Problems of the 16th Century Related to the Voyage of Bartolomeu Dias, 1487–1488.* Lisbon, 1988.

M. W. RICHEY

ALVARADO, PEDRO DE (1486–1541), Spanish explorer born in Badajoz, Extremadura, in the same province and just one year after Hernando Cortés. Alvarado's parents belonged to the impoverished hidalgo class. In 1510, he and his four brothers sailed to the New World and settled in Santo Domingo. The next year Alvarado took part in the conquest of Cuba. For the next eight years he had a plantation and an encomienda of Indians, but he seems to have shown little interest in them.

In 1518, he participated in the sea expedition to the Gulf of Mexico as captain of one of the ships. A year later, the expedition led by Cortés to conquer Mexico began; Alvarado served as second in command. He was left in charge when Cortés left Tenochtitlán to challenge the expedition of Pánfilo de Narváez. During the celebration of a religious festival, he feared that a rebellion was about to develop and he ordered the merciless slaughter of about four hundred Mexica nobles, an action that caused

a general uprising against the Spaniards and for which Alvarado was universally condemned. He was one of the few survivors among the rear guard during the Spanish flight from the city on June 30, an event known as the Noche Triste (Sad Night). He later led one of the three units that successfully besieged Tenochtitlán, ending the conquest of Mexico in 1521.

The second part of Alvarado's restless life as a conquistador is characterized by increasingly independent actions. On behalf of Cortés he led expeditions to subdue new territories south of Mexico City. In 1523, he conquered Guatemala and the Soconusco region, subduing the Cakchiquel, Quiche, and Tzutuhil Indians and founding the city of Santiago de los Caballeros the next year. As newly appointed captain general of Guatemala, he spent the next two years in a fierce struggle to secure control of an extensive area stretching to present-day El Salvador. In 1527 he returned to Spain to report his exploits in the court of Charles V and to contradict his enemies' accounts. His stay was successful, resulting in a knighthood and appointment as governor of Guatemala. He married Francisca de la Cueva, a woman of high nobility, who died upon arrival in New Spain in 1528.

In Guatemala he soon grew tired of office, and upon news of fabulous riches in Peru, he assembled a major fleet with five hundred men who left Guatemala City at the end of 1533. To avoid interfering with Francisco Pizarro, Alvarado went to Quito in a daring and treacherous crossing of the jungle and the Andes. The suffering proved fruitless because Diego de Almagro had secured control of the area for Pizarro, and Alvarado returned to Guatemala empty-handed after selling his armada to Pizarro for 100,000 pesos. Alvarado then resumed his duties as governor briefly but met with official opposition.

In 1536 he went back to Spain. Still under royal favor, he was confirmed as governor and married his deceased wife's sister, Beatriz. After a few years as governor, he formed yet another expedition of twelve ships to explore the Spice Islands in the Pacific, but convinced by Antonio de Mendoza, viceroy of Mexico, to join forces, he redirected his efforts to find the elusive Seven Cities of Cibola. He was about to embark by sea when he was called by New Galicia's governor, Cristóbal de Oñate, to help crush an Indian uprising. Near Nochistlán he was run over by a horse and died on June 24, 1541.

BIBLIOGRAPHY

Altolaguirre y Duvale, Antonio. *Don Pedro de Alvarado: Conquistador de Guatemala y Honduras.* Madrid, 1905.
Díaz del Castillo, Bernal. *The Discovery and Conquest of Mexico, 1517–1521.* Edited by Genaro García. Translated by A. P. Maudslay. New York, 1956.
Kelly, John Eoghan. *Pedro de Alvarado, Conquistador.* Princeton, 1932.

López Rayón, José. *Proceso de residencia contra Pedro de Alvarado*. Mexico City, 1847.

Taylor, Mark. *Impetuous Alvarado*. Dallas, 1936.

ANGEL DELGADO-GOMEZ

AMERICA, NAMING OF. News of the westward voyages and discoveries of new lands made by Christopher Columbus was slow to circulate in Europe. In the beginning only his account of the first voyage was widely distributed on the continent. His letter of February 15, 1493, describing the voyage and announcing the discovery, was written to Luis de Santángel of Aragón, and a duplicate sent to the royal treasurer Gabriel Sánchez. These letters were written in Catalán dialect and translated into Latin and German for readers throughout Europe.

Despite these many editions, the news of the discovery received little attention in Germany. Columbus's letter spoke only of islands found in the Indies, an unmapped region vaguely defined in terms that did not arouse general interest. Although *The Ship of Fools*, published by Sebastien Brandt in 1494, told of regions to the north—a country of islands he called the Pilappelande and the islands of gold discovered by the Portuguese and the Spaniards—Columbus's name was not mentioned. In contrast, Amerigo Vespucci's widely publicized letters, which appeared a short time later, had great news value and excited imagination with titillating accounts of the natives he had observed.

Upon returning from his voyage of 1501–1502, Vespucci wrote to his former employer in Florence, Lorenzo Pier Francesco de' Medici, describing his voyages. He reported that on his most recent journey he had sailed hundreds of miles along the eastern coastline of a land not yet named, from the fifth to the fifty-second parallel, in search of a passage to India. It was apparent that it was a large land mass, not an Asian island, and he described the region as a "new world" distinct from the known continents. His concept, fundamental and original with him, was that these lands were not part of Asia but a separate continent. The letter was translated from the original Italian into French and was reprinted the following year in Venice under the title *Mundus novus* (The new world). The work quickly spread to other countries and was published in at least fourteen editions between 1503 and 1505.

In September 1504, upon his return from his third voyage, Vespucci wrote another letter, to Piero Soderini, a former schoolmate and at that time chief magistrate of Florence. Vespucci expanded on his earlier account to de' Medici and vividly described the native peoples. This letter, *Quattour navigationes* (The four voyages), was published in Florence and was translated into Latin by the Dominican Giocondo of Verona in Paris and published by the Parisian printer Jean Lambert. It was reprinted immediately in France and Italy, and at least seven editions appeared in Germany. The popularity of the letters was due both to Vespucci's insistence that the newly discovered lands were a new continent, a concept that fired the imagination, and to his vivid description of cannibalism and the sex lives of the inhabitants. These letters were so widely read that as a consequence Vespucci emerged as a major figure in sixteenth-century exploration and discovery, and for more than a generation his claims overshadowed the achievements of Columbus.

It was at about the time that the Vespucci letters appeared that the hitherto dormant science of geography began to experience a renaissance, inspired by the recovery and translation of the Greek manuscript and printed editions of Claudius Ptolemy's geographical atlas. Among the first working in the field was a little group of humanists in the remote town of Saint-Dié in the Vosges Mountains of northeastern France. The current patron of Saint-Dié, Duke René II (1451–1508), did much to promote interest in geography, seeking out well-educated and talented young men to fill his court's administrative positions and diplomatic posts.

One recipient of René's support was Gauthier Lud, who had served as the duke's chaplain and later as director-general of the duchy's mining industry. He was appointed a canon at Saint-Dié and chief official of the community and of the abbey associated with the church. In 1494 he acquired a printing press, which he installed in his home for printing ordinances of the monastic order and which later was used to print books and maps.

Lud, who shared his patron's serious interests in astronomy and cosmography, had published a work on a form of stereographic projection of the terrestrial globe. To promote these interests at Saint-Dié, Lud in 1507 formed a small intellectual circle called the Gymnase Vosgien in imitation of German literary societies. He decided that their first project would be the production of a new translation and updated version of the *Geography*, Ptolemy's world atlas. In addition to Lud, the group consisted at first of his nephew, Nicolas Lud, and Jean Basin de Sandaucourt, vicar of the church of Notre-Dame de Saint-Dié and a distinguished Latinist and poet. The next members to be enlisted were Mathias Ringmann (1482–1511), who could translate Greek and Latin manuscripts, and Martin Waldseemüller (1474–1519), an accomplished draftsman skilled in designing and printing and possessed of an extensive knowledge of geography.

Born in the nearby Vosges Mountains, Ringmann had attended the University of Heidelberg and went on to study mathematics and cosmography in Paris. Although he proved to be a talented poet, Ringmann's preference was the field of geography, and in 1505 he translated Vespucci's letter to de' Medici. Of the many editions of the Vespucci letter that appeared at this time, Ringmann's version was of the greatest interest. He changed the letter's title from *Mundus novus* to *De ora antarctica per regem Portugalliae pridem inventa* (About the Antarctic coast [shore] long ago discovered through the king of Portugal). In comparing Vespucci's account to the works of Ptolemy, he discovered that the lands Vespucci described related to a new world not mentioned by Ptolemy, a world apparently lying under the Antarctic pole. He brought a copy of his publication with him when he arrived at Saint-Dié.

Work there had already begun on the projected atlas when the duke received from de' Medici a copy of the Vespucci letter describing his four voyages as well as several marine charts depicting the newly discovered lands. Excited by the Florentine merchant's accounts, Lud and his associates discontinued work on the atlas to produce a world map and a related treatise to publicize the discoveries. As part of the project, Waldseemüller in 1506 first produced a set of twelve gores, or triangular sections, for a terrestrial globe in which the new continent was named "America." These were engraved on wood, probably to save money, and are believed to be the first to have been printed from woodblocks; previously gores for globes were painted by hand.

Although the date of its production is not certain, Waldseemüller also designed a sea chart that included the name "America" for the new lands. A single copy has survived; it is possible that it was not intended for distribution and that no additional copy was made. The chart was later included in the atlas produced at Saint-Dié, but with the name "America" deleted.

Next Waldseemüller set to work on the preparation of a tract on cosmography to serve as an introduction to the map as well as to the atlas. It was entitled *Cosmographie introductio cum quibusdam geometriae ac astronomiae principiis ad eam rem necessariis. In super quattuor America Vespucci navigationes* (An introduction to cosmography with several elements of geometry and astronomy required for this science, and the four voyages of Amerigo Vespucci). Working together with Ringmann, Waldseemüller began writing the tract in the summer of 1506 and completed it the following winter. Printers were brought from Strasbourg and Basel to help print the first edition, which was issued on April 25, 1507. Four editions were printed at Saint-Dié in that year.

The *Cosmography* consists of two parts. The first contains an explanation of the world map and provides the basic principles of geometry and astronomy to assist readers in understanding the work. The second section contains Vespucci's letter translated into Latin by Basin de

WALDSEEMÜLLER'S *COSMOGRAPHIAE INTRODUCTIO*. A page from the document that first uses the name *America*. Saint-Dié, 1507.

Sandaucourt and one of Ringmann's poems. It is probable that copies were sold with the map. In this work Waldseemüller explains, "So it comes about that while we (having recently set up a printing office in the town of Saint-Dié in the Vosges) were collating Ptolemy's books from a Greek manuscript, and supplementing them from the description of Amerigo's four voyages, we have prepared a representation of the whole world in the form of a globe and in that of a map."

The *Cosmography*, the sections for a globe produced in 1506, and the world map all identified the newly discovered lands by the name "America," here used for the first time. In this volume Waldseemüller explains the reason for the selection of the name:

Now, really these [three] parts [Europe, Africa, and Asia] were more widely traveled, and another fourth part was discovered by Americus Vesputius (as will be seen in the following pages), for which reason I do not see why anyone would rightly forbid calling it (after the discoverer Americus, a man of wisdom and ingenuity) "Amerige," that is, land of Americus, or "America," since both "Europa" and "Asia" are names derived from women. Its location and the customs of its people will be easily discerned from the four voyages of Americus which follow.

The world map is entitled *Universalis cosmographia secunda Ptholemei traditionem et Americi Vespuccii aliorum que lustrationes* (A drawing of the whole earth following the tradition of Ptolemy and the travels of Amerigo Vespucci and others). The earth is depicted in a cordiform (heart-shaped) image and marked in degrees of latitude and longitude. The two parts of the recently discovered American continents are shown separated by a strait with the western coast depicted for the first time but without delineation. In a planisphere at the head of the map, however, the two are joined by land. The delineation of the Atlantic coast of South America appears to have been based on the world portolano (a medieval navigation manual) of the Portuguese cartographer Nicolo Caneiro, and the western coast is shown for the first time. The North American continent extends from the eleventh to the fifty-third degree and is labeled *Terra ulteri incognita*. The South American continent is shown to extend from the ninth degree of latitude to beyond Cape St. Vincent. Its northeastern coast is labeled *tota ista provincia inventa est per mandatum regis Castelle* (all of this province was discovered by mandate of the king of Castile). The name "America" appears approximately in midsection.

The map includes planispheres that depict the Old World and the New as well as a portrait, probably symbolizing Ptolemy, which would indicate that his work provided the source for the Old World cartography. A portrait labeled "Vespucci" next to the New World suggests that he provided the information for that part of the map. Waldseemüller also indicates in the legend that the map was based upon Ptolemy's maps, probably from the Ulm edition of 1482, and upon the published accounts of Vespucci.

The world map was designed as a large wall chart and consisted of twelve sheets, each measuring 450 mm × 500 mm (17.7 × 19.7 inches). The sides of each sheet were made to be trimmed off so that the edges of the map proper could be brought together, although the match proved to be sometimes one or two centimeters off. When assembled, the map would be 1200 mm (47.2 inches) high and 2400 mm (94.5 inches) wide. It is printed in black ink from woodcuts. Some of the place names and descriptions were cut in the woodblock itself, while others were set in printer's type and inserted into openings cut in the wood. Occasional touches of hand-applied color occur, such as red dots for cities and red and yellow coloration in the armorial crests. In the surviving copy a grid of red lines has been drawn by hand in pen and ink over the printing to mark off degrees and a number of handwritten corrections are to be found. The four corners of the map contain long introductory texts within woodcut frames. Neither the mapmaker's name nor the place or date of production appears on the map. The identity of the printer is not known, but Johann Grüninger of Strasbourg is considered to have been the most likely. (Although a number of Strasbourg printers worked for the Gymnase at Saint-Dié, Grüninger had the longest association with the group, and in fact Ringmann had been employed by him as proofreader immediately before joining the group.)

The world map appears to have been widely distributed, for other cartographers quickly copied it and adopted the use of the name "America." Among the earliest copies made from it were maps produced in 1509 by Johann Grüninger, a map dated 1512 by Jan Stobniczy, Johannes Schöner's terrestrial globe of 1515, Peter Apian's map and *Cosmographicus* of 1520, the world map of Gerhard Mercator, and maps produced by Henricus Glareanus, Johannes Honter, Louis d'Albi Boulenger, Erhard Reysch, and others.

If one studies the surviving example of the map, it is clear that it was not part of the first edition, but printed at a later time, probably in about 1516, because it shows ample evidence that the woodblocks from which it was printed were damaged and well worn in many instances. Furthermore, the watermark of the paper on which it is printed coincides with that used for the *Carta marina* designed by Waldseemüller and dated 1516.

After completing the sections for a globe, the *Cosmography*, the sea chart, and the world map, the members of the Gymnase Vosgien resumed work on the new edition of Ptolemy's atlas, to be entitled *Claudii Ptholemei viri Alexandrini mathematicae disciplinae philosophi doctissimi geographiae opus novissima traductione e Graecorum archetypis castigatissime pressum; caereris ante lucubratorum multo praestantis* (The geographical work of Claudius Ptolemy, the man of Alexandria, a most erudite philosopher of mathematical learning, closely reprinted by reproduction of the Greek originals). In order to resolve disparities in place names and textual content the scholars turned to other manuscript and printed copies of Ptolemy's atlas. Ringmann translated place names and texts from Greek to Latin and Waldseemüller designed the maps. Then several factors interfered with the progress of the work. Ringmann died of tuberculosis in the autumn of 1511 and Gauthier Lud experienced increasing financial difficulties. Finally work on the atlas had to be abandoned. The maps, texts, and related materials were acquired by two Strasbourg lawyers who arranged to have the atlas completed and published by the Strasbourg printer Johann Schott. It is probable that Waldseemüller moved to Strasbourg for a time to work with Schott to complete the remaining maps. The atlas appeared in 1513 and was immediately popular. Two more editions were published within the next decade.

During the following years, Waldseemüller and his colleagues accumulated much additional information about the Spanish and Portuguese voyages of discovery. They revised some of their earlier misconceptions, realizing, for example, that the lands discovered by Columbus and those reported by Vespucci were the same.

In 1516 Waldseemüller completed the design of a nautical chart in the form of a large wall map entitled *Carta marina navigatoria Portugallen* (A Portuguese navigator's sea chart); it included the *Tabula terre nove* (Map of the new lands) from the 1507 world map which had also been incorporated into the atlas. The *Carta marina* contained information derived from the voyages of Columbus as well as from Vespucci's letters. The name "America" was deleted, as was the strait between the two American mainlands. The phrase "Brasilia terra sive papagalli" (Brazil, land of parrots) was added to the northeastern coast of South America, and a more complete nomenclature was provided. Cuba continued to be identified as part of Asia, however, and owing to the interruption caused by the borders, the map gave the erroneous impression that the newly discovered lands were a continuation of the east coast of Asia.

Although celebrated in its own time as a magnificent scholarly production containing the latest information about the known world and reportedly published in an edition of one thousand, for several centuries no copies of either the world map or the *Carta marina* were known to have survived. In the course of time Waldseemüller's cartographic work was superseded, and his use of the name "America" was forgotten. It did not come to notice again until 1828 when the American author Washington Irving noted in his *Life and Voyages of Columbus* that the explanation for naming the continent "America" was to be found in the *Cosmography*. Irving's work attracted little attention until 1838 when the German geographer Alexander von Humboldt commented on Irving's report in his *Examen critique de l'histoire de la géographie du nouveau continent aux XVe et XVIe siècles* (Critical examination of the history of the geography of the New Continent in the fifteenth and sixteenth centuries). This led to a search for the missing map in libraries and archives throughout Europe but without success. One explanation for the lack of surviving copies may be its size: the sheets of the world map were usually pasted onto a board or a wall; as the map became worn or damaged it was discarded.

It was not until 1901 that a copy of the world map was found. While Josef Fischer, a professor of geography, was conducting research on the Norse settlements in North America, he discovered a copy in the library of Castle Wolfegg in Wolfegg (in present-day Baden-Württemberg). Its twelve sheets had been bound into a volume together with the twelve sheets of Waldseemüller's *Carta marina*, a star chart by Albrecht Dürer, and two incomplete sets of gores, one for a terrestrial globe and another for a celestial globe. Those for the terrestrial globe had been used to reinforce the binding. The volume is bound in sixteenth-century tooled pigskin bearing the bookplate of the geographer Johannes Schöner, who presumably had them brought together and bound.

Fischer identified the world map from contemporary copies and references, and in cooperation with the German historian Franz von Weiser, he produced a work containing a facsimile of both the world map and the *Carta marina* accompanied by a historical essay published at Innsbruck and London in 1903. In 1983 the unique copy of the map left Castle Wolfegg on a temporary loan and was placed on public display in the National Museum of American History of the Smithsonian Institution in Washington, D.C.

[See also *Cartography* and biographies of Humboldt, Ptolemy, Santángel, Vespucci, and Waldseemüller.]

BIBLIOGRAPHY

Avezac-Macaya, Armand d'. *Martin Hylacomylus Waldseemüller: Ses ouvrages et ses collaborateurs.* Paris, 1867. Reprint, Amsterdam, 1980.

Fischer, Josef, and Franz von Weiser. *The Oldest Map with the Name America of the Year 1507 and the Carta Marina of the Year 1516 by M. Waldseemüller (Ilacomilus).* Innsbruck and London, 1903.

Harris, Elizabeth. "The Waldseemüller World Map: An Appraisal." *Imago Mundi* 37 (1985):30–53.

Humboldt, Alexander von. *Examen critique de l'histoire de la géographie du nouveau continent aux XVe et XVIe siècles.* Paris, 1836–1838. Vol. 4, pp. 101–111.

Laubenberger, Franz. "The Naming of America." *Sixteenth Century Journal* 13, no. 4 (1982).

Morison, Samuel Eliot. *The European Discovery of America: The Southern Voyages, 1492–1616.* New York, 1974.

Schwartz, Seymour I., and Ralph E. Ehrenberg. *The Mapping of America.* New York, 1980.

Skelton, R. A. "Bibliographical Note." In facsimile edition of *Claudius Ptolemaeus. Geographia Strassburg 1513.* Amsterdam, 1966.

SILVIO A. BEDINI

ANGHIERA, PIETRO MARTIRE D'

ANGHIERA, PIETRO MARTIRE D' (c. 1457–1526), humanist, author of earliest description of the New World. Pietro Martire (Peter Martyr) d'Anghiera's career began at the ducal court of Milan; from there he went to Rome to serve as the secretary to the governor, Francesco de Negri. A member of the humanist circle centered on the Roman Academy, d'Anghiera became friends with powerful patrons such as Cardinal Ascanio Sforza and the count of Tendilla, the Spanish ambassador to the papal court. When in 1487 the count of Tendilla persuaded d'Anghiera to relocate to the Spanish court, d'Anghiera

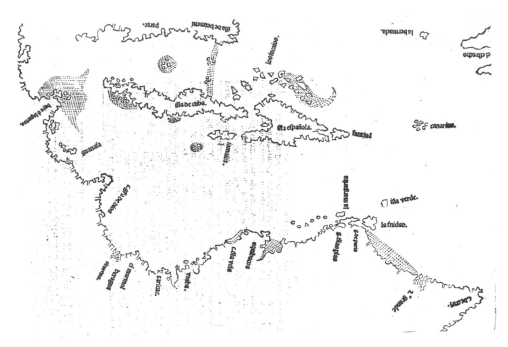

MAP OF THE WEST INDIES. From d'Anghiera's *Decades*, 1511.

promised Sforza that he would write to him regularly about events in Spain. D'Anghiera arrived in Spain in 1488. Ordained as a priest, he was appointed chaplain and humanist at the royal court, where he was well-positioned to observe the events that unfolded in the wake of Columbus's triumphant return from his first voyage. As a member of the Council of the Indies, to which he was appointed in 1518, d'Anghiera was able to supplement first-hand oral accounts from the returning explorers (including Columbus himself), conquistadores, and Indian slave-raiders with the stream of reports, petitions, and official documents related to the events he describes.

D'Anghiera's two major works consisted of letters written to patrons and friends. The *Opus epistolarum* contains eighty-three letters, the first dated 1488 and the last 1525. The *De rebus oceanis et Orbe Novo decades* consists of eight sections, or decades, containing letters written over thirty-two years (1493–1525) and addressed to six patrons, including Sforza.

Both works deal with the New World. D'Anghiera first gives news (in a letter written on September 13, 1493, included in the *Opus*) of the "new discovery" and of Columbus's return "safe and sound" with reports of the "marvelous things" including "gold" as "proof of the existence of mines" that he had found. The historiography of Columbus's *Indias occidentales* begins, however, with *De Orbe Novo*, in which d'Anghiera advances the new thesis of a homogeneous earth, which contradicted, and

ultimately replaced, the premises of classical geography. The *De Orbe Novo* popularized what J. H. Elliot calls the "myth of America" by transposing to the New World Greco-Roman ideas about a golden age and the noble savage in a state of nature. As the anthropologist Jacob Pandian notes, the factual differences of New World cultures and peoples would be seen as signs of human otherness to the "true" rational self and culture of the Europeans. New World peoples would be represented either as noble savages and temporal others who lived "without enforcement of laws" in the peaceful "goulden worlde of which Owlde writers speake so much" (from Richard Eden's translation) or as cannibals who were "savage and monstrous" (Decade 3, book 2).

These interpretations, as Richard Waswo shows in the related case of Edmund Spenser's *Faerie Queene*, would serve to shape perceptions, and therefore to legitimate the social domination of the incoming European settlers over the indigenous peoples of d'Anghiera's New World.

In 1520, d'Anghiera was appointed court historiographer in recognition of his *De Orbe Novo*. In 1524 the king named him to the abbacy of the island of Santiago (Jamaica). This abbacy had been established in 1515 in Sevilla la Nueva, the first town founded, in 1509, by Columbus's son, Diego Colón (then newly appointed viceroy of the Indies), on the site on which Columbus and his crew had been shipwrecked for a little over a year on his return from his fourth and last voyage. D'Anghiera used the tithes from his abbacy to build the first stone church in Sevilla la Nueva and managed to coax matching funds from the emperor, Charles V.

D'Anghiera never set foot in Jamaica or in any part of the New World of which he wrote. However, where his descriptive set pieces were written in terms of the preestablished themes of classical literature, they were interspersed with first-person reports taken fresh from the mouths of the returning participants and through the prism of their cultural perceptions. It is this that gives to *De Orbe Novo* its unique and irreplaceable quality, the quality of a report from the front, as seen by one of the sides in the major confrontation that took place between two worlds that had remained oblivious of each other's existence until, as d'Anghiera begins, "a certain Christopher Columbus, a Genoese, proposed to the Catholic King and Queen, Ferdinand and Isabella, to discover the islands which touch the Indies."

BIBLIOGRAPHY

Anghiera, Pietro Martire d'. *De Orbe Novo: The Eight Decades of Peter Martyr D'Anghera.* Translated by Francis A. MacNutt. New York, 1912. Reprint, 1970.

Anghiera, Pietro Martire d'. *Decades del nuevo mundo.* 2 vols. Edited by Edmundo O'Gorman. Mexico, 1964.

Elliot, J. H. *The Old World and the New, 1492 to 1650.* Cambridge, 1970.

Gerbi, Antonelli. *La natura delle Indie Nove: Da Cristoforo Colombo a Gonzalo Fernandez de Oviedo.* Milan and Naples, 1975.

O'Gorman, Edmundo. *La idea del descubrimiento de America. Historia de esa interpretación y critica de sus fundamentos.* Mexico City, 1951.

Pagden, Anthony. *The Fall of Natural Man: The American Indian and The Origins of Comparative Ethnology.* Cambridge, 1982.

Pandian, Jacob. *Anthropology and the Western Tradition: Towards an Authentic Anthropology.* Prospect Heights, Ill., 1985.

Van Sertima, I. *They Came before Columbus.* New York, 1976.

Waswo, Richard. "The History That Literature Makes." *New Literary History* 19 (1988): 541–565.

Wynter, Sylvia. *New Seville: Major Facts, Major Questions.* Kingston, Jamaica, 1984.

SYLVIA WYNTER

ANIMALS. See *Domesticated Animals; Fauna.*

ANTICHRIST. According to Christian doctrine and legend, Antichrist is a malevolent leader of evil forces who will appear on the eve of the end of time to contest Christ and the church in a final cataclysmic combat. Antichrist is mentioned but four times in scripture. These all occur in the Johannine letters: *1 John* 2:18, 2:22, and 4:3; and *2 John* 7. Other passages drawn from the Old and New Testaments, the Apocrypha, and late antique Jewish and Byzantine apocalyptic and prophetic literature have traditionally been considered to refer to Antichrist as well.

Throughout the medieval period, Antichrist figured prominently in the interweavings of prophecy and political ideology characteristic of a body of authoritative providential histories and related exegetical literature. In such writings, Antichrist and his forces frequently were identified with individuals and groups who threatened social and religious stability from within and without Europe. A number of these works, notably Joachim of Fiore's *Liber concordie Novi et Veteris Testamenti* and *Expositio in Apocalypsim,* and Roger Bacon's *Opus maius* (all written in the thirteenth century), influenced Europeans active in the early phases of the exploration and conquest of the Americas.

Christopher Columbus appears to have been acquainted with the figure of Antichrist and his eschatological role primarily through a cluster of works written in 1414 by the prominent late-medieval theologian Pierre d'Ailly (1350–1420). In these works, d'Ailly drew heavily upon sections of Bacon's *Opus maius,* itself a digest of earlier apocalyptic materials, especially the seventh-century Byzantine apocalypse of Pseudo-Methodius.

Columbus's annotations to d'Ailly's works, the materials he gathered for an unfinished work to be called "The Book of Prophecies," and several letters he wrote to Fernando and Isabel indicate that he anticipated the imminent advent of the Antichrist and the end of time. Although he sought to place his achievements and those of his regents within a historical context that was penultimate, Columbus does not appear to have identified Antichrist with any particular contemporary.

References to Antichrist also appear in a number of works composed by mendicant missionaries active in the evangelization of the indigenous peoples of Mexico subsequent to Hernando Cortés's conquest of the Aztec empire in 1521. Franciscan chroniclers in particular, heirs to the Joachimite tradition of apocalyptic conversion, believed that they were effecting the final Christianizing of the infidel that would presage the end of time. In perhaps the most well known of such chronicles, Gerónimo de Mendieta's *Historia eclesiástica indiana* (completed in 1596), Antichrist is identified with the Protestant leader Martin Luther. The many conversions of Indian souls in the New World, Mendieta argues, will offset the contemporaneous losses to this Antichrist in the Old World.

BIBLIOGRAPHY

Alexander, Paul. *The Byzantine Apocalyptic Tradition.* Berkeley, 1985.

Bossuet, Wilhelm. *The Antichrist Legend.* London, 1896.

Emmerson, Richard Kenneth. *Antichrist in the Middle Ages: A Study of Medieval Apocalypticism, Art, and Literature.* Seattle, 1981.

Phelan, John Leddy. *The Millennial Kingdom of the Franciscans in the New World.* 2d ed. Berkeley, 1970.

Reeves, Marjorie. *The Influence of Prophecy in the Later Middle Ages: A Study in Joachimism.* Oxford, 1969.

Watts, Pauline Moffitt. "Prophecy and Discovery: On the Spiritual Origins of Christopher Columbus's 'Enterprise of the Indies.' " *American Historical Review* 90 (1985): 73–102.

PAULINE MOFFITT WATTS

ARANA, BEATRIZ DE (c. 1465–1522), mistress of Christopher Columbus; mother of his son Fernando Colón. Beatriz Enríquez de Arana was born to Pedro de Torquemada and Ana Núñez de Arana in Santa María de Trassiera. After the death of Pedro de Torquemada, his widow moved to Córdoba, where she died in 1471, leaving two children: Beatriz and Pedro. Their grandmother, Eleonora Núñez, and the maternal aunt, Mayor Enríquez de Arana, took charge of the guardianship of the two orphans.

Beatriz de Arana learned to read and write, a rare achievement in a period in which most wives and daughters of noblemen did not know how to sign their own names. After the death of their grandmother, the minors continued their education in the house of their aunt until her death sometime after May 12, 1478. Thereafter, the guardianship and trusteeship of the minors fell to Rodrigo Enríquez de Arana, a cousin of Ana Núñez, who was the closest relative of the orphans.

How did Beatriz come to meet Columbus? During the first thirty months of his sojourn in Castile (1485–1487), Christopher Columbus chose Córdoba for his residence. The monarchs of Spain were living there in 1485 when Columbus arrived in Castile. It is probable that Columbus did not accompany the sovereigns to Galicia, but joined them some months later in Salamanca, where he was to participate in the council examining his project. Columbus returned to Córdoba when the court did, in the first days of March 1487. Here he resided until March 1488, when he moved to Murcia, where he would again be received by the Catholic monarchs.

During this time Córdoba was a lively place. Because of its strategic position, the monarchs were transforming it into the most important center of Andalusia. There were many Italian merchants present in Córdoba then, prominent among them the Genoese storekeepers Luciano and Leonardo Esbarroya. It was in Esbarroya's shop that Christopher Columbus met Diego de Arana and his father, Rodrigo Enríquez de Arana.

Diego, a cousin of Beatriz, brought the Genoese into his home, and it is probable that it was he who introduced Beatriz to Columbus. By the end of October 1487, their relationship was intimate. In July 1488, in Córdoba, Beatriz gave birth to a son whom Columbus recognized as his and to whom he gave the name Fernando in honor of the Spanish king.

There is no doubt that Fernando eventually became recognized as Columbus's legitimate son. He acquired all the honors of his father and participated in the inheritance. In a public act undersigned by the Admiral in Seville on October 31, 1497, Diego and Fernando were defined as "his legitimate sons," and the title of "don" conferred not only on Diego but also on Fernando. (J. Manzano Manzano gives us a detailed and well-documented analysis of the manner in which the legitimation process must have taken place.)

But at the moment of his birth Fernando was illegitimate—his father was widowed; his mother, unmarried. Bartolomé de las Casas attests that Diego was the legitimate son of the Admiral, and Fernando "his natural son." And Gonzalo Fernández de Oviedo calls don Diego the legitimate and older son, and adds, "and the other son of his, don Fernando."

Columbus never married Beatriz. When he returned from the first voyage, he was given the greatest of honors and elevated to the highest position in Spain. Because of his discovery, he became one of the most illustrious persons at the Spanish court and had to submit, like all the great persons of the time, to customary legal restrictions on matters of marriage and extramarital relations. The Alphonsine laws forbade extramarital relations of concubinage for "illustrious people" (king, princes, dukes, counts, marquis) with plebeian women, if they themselves were or their forefathers had been of inferior social condition.

This is why Columbus, in other ways so scrupulous and pious, did not regularize his relationship with Beatriz but ordered his son and heir, Diego Colón, "to take care of Beatriz Enriquez, mother of don Fernando; let my son provide the necessary means so that she may live honestly, on account of my good name. And let this be done for the relief of my conscience, because it weighs much on my soul. It is not right/lawful to record here the reason."

With these words Columbus reveals his undischarged debt to Beatriz and entrusts to his heir the reparation of his error. Just as revealing are Columbus's words, also directed to Diego in 1502, before the beginning of the fourth and last voyage to the Indies: "I recommend to you for my sake, Beatriz Enríquez, as I would your own mother."

After the discovery, however, Columbus was not very generous toward the woman to whom he owed so much. Fortunately, the revenue from real estate inherited from her own mother and from other close relatives, together with the above-mentioned pension, gave Beatriz a livelihood.

After the death of the Admiral, Beatriz complained to her son Fernando about the lack of punctuality Diego showed in paying the annual pension assigned to her by Columbus. At least, this seems to be the significance of her last known public act. On May 11, 1521, she gave a power of attorney to the Genoese Francesco Cassana, residing in Seville, so that he could collect from the Genoese Juan Francesco de Grimaldo, a Spanish banker, all the maravedis he would be willing to give to her on account of her son Fernando Colón.

Beatriz Enríquez de Arana apparently died not too long after. On September 8, 1532, Diego Colón, who was making his will on the island of Santo Domingo, wrote that the heirs of Beatriz were to be paid all the pensions left unpaid in the preceding three or four years. At her death, all the real estate she possessed in Santa María de Trassierra, consisting of a house with a workshop and a wine press, two orchards, and three vineyard plots, went to her son Fernando. The latter, on August 17, 1525, gave this property as a gift to his cousin Pedro de Arana, one of the sons of Beatriz's only brother.

These events reveal that the behavior of the Admiral and his heir, Diego, was marked sometimes by negligence and forgetfulness, and sometimes by scruples and sincere intentions, if not actual deeds, to remedy a wrongful situation.

BIBLIOGRAPHY

Ballesteros Beretta, Antonio. *Cristóbal Colón y el descubrimiento de América*. Vol. 1. Barcelona and Buenos Aires, 1945.

De la Torre, J. *Beatriz Enriquez de Harana y Cristóbal Colón*. Madrid, 1933.

Manzano Manzano, Juan. *Cristóbal Colón: Siete años decisivos de su vida, 1485–1492*. Madrid, 1964.

Taviani, Paolo Emilio. *Christopher Columbus: The Grand Design*. London, 1985.

PAOLO EMILIO TAVIANI
Translated from Italian by Rodica Diaconescu-Blumenfeld

ARANA, DIEGO DE

ARANA, DIEGO DE (fl. 1490s), marshal of the fleet on Columbus's first voyage. A native of Córdoba, Diego de Arana was a cousin of Beatriz Enríquez de Arana, Columbus's mistress and mother of the Admiral's second son, Fernando. As marshal of Columbus's flagship, *Santa María*, in 1492, Arana was recognized as chief marshal of the fleet with overall authority over the marshals of the other ships in the fleet (each ship had a marshal responsible for maintaining order, resolving disputes among the crew, and punishing offenders).

During the build-up of mutinous feelings among some members of the crews of all three ships in the tense days before the landfall at Guanahani (San Salvador), Arana seems to have earned Columbus's trust. While exploring the north coast of the large island which he named La Española (Hispaniola), Columbus sent Arana ashore with an interpreter to present a gift to the local cacique (chieftain) and to inquire about gold. A few days later, when *Santa María* ran aground and broke up on a reef, Columbus decided to build a fort, which he named La Navidad, to be garrisoned by crew members from *Santa María* and *Niña*. He designated Arana as commander of the settlement. When the ships of the second voyage returned to La Navidad, Columbus learned that Arana's two lieutenants had formed a gang of malcontents that left the fort to maraud for gold and women. An important cacique, Caonabó, had the marauders killed and attacked the fort. Although aided by a friendly cacique, Guacanagarí, Arana and the ten men with him were killed.

BIBLIOGRAPHY

Gould, Alicia B. *Nueva lista documentada de los tripulantes de Colón en 1492*. Madrid, 1984.

Morison, Samuel Eliot. *Admiral of the Ocean Sea: A Life of Christopher Columbus*. 2 vols. Boston, 1942.

WILLIAM LEMOS

ARANA, PEDRO DE

ARANA, PEDRO DE (fl. 1490s), captain of one of the ships of Columbus's third voyage. A native of Córdoba, Pedro de Arana was a cousin of Diego de Arana, commander of the garrison left at La Navidad when Columbus returned to Spain at the end of the first voyage. More significantly, perhaps, Pedro was the brother of Beatriz Enríquez de Arana, Columbus's mistress and mother of Fernando, the Admiral's second son. This kinship quite likely was a factor in his appointment by Columbus as captain of one of the eight ships of the third voyage.

There is no extant record of the name of the ship captained by Arana. It is known, however, that it was one of three caravels, *Garza*, *La Gorda*, or *La Rábida*, loaded with supplies, artisans, farmers, laborers, and *ballesteros* (crossbowmen) for the new colony, Isabela Nueva (now Santo Domingo), established in 1496 by Columbus's brother, Bartolomé Colón, on the south coast of La Española (Hispaniola). Having departed from Sanlúcar de Barrameda on May 30, 1498, as a part of the third voyage fleet, these three caravels were detached at the Canary Islands and instructed by Columbus to proceed independently to Isabela Nueva.

Unfortunately, the pilots of the three caravels lacked Columbus's skill in dead-reckoning navigation and made their landfall at Jaraguá at the western end of La Española, where Francisco Roldán and his rebels were in control. Not knowing about Roldán's rebellion, the captains of the caravels allowed their men to go ashore, where many of them were induced to desert. The captains, remaining loyal to Columbus, finally managed, despite strong headwinds and adverse current, to make their way to Isabela Nueva in their undermanned ships. There the historical record of Pedro de Arana ends.

BIBLIOGRAPHY

Gould, Alicia B. *Nueva lista documentada de los tripulantes de Colón en 1492.* Madrid, 1984.

Morison, Samuel Eliot. *Admiral of the Ocean Sea: A Life of Christopher Columbus.* 2 vols. Boston, 1942.

WILLIAM LEMOS

ARAWAKS AND CARIBS. See *Indian America,* article on *Arawaks and Caribs.*

ARCHAEOLOGY. [This entry includes two articles that introduce the techniques and results of archaeological research concerning European presence in the New World during the early years of contact and European settlement:

Land Archaeology

Underwater Archaeology

See also *Bahamas; Cuba; Cuzco; Española, La; Jamaica; Landfall Controversy; Puerto Rico; Settlements; Vinland; West Indies.* For discussion of related research, see *Disease and Demography.*]

Land Archaeology

Archaeology on sites believed to have been visited or occupied by Christopher Columbus has been carried out intermittently since the nineteenth century. The goals of this research have included the search for and verification of sites at which Columbus is known to have been, the study of the earliest settlements he founded, the recovery of relics related to his ventures, and the investigation of the immediate impacts of his arrival on the people of the Americas.

Most of the New World sites identified with Columbus, and nearly all of those outside La Española (Hispaniola), are Caribbean Indian settlements believed to have been visited by him. One of the most difficult methodological problems in the archaeology of these sites lies in recognizing a European presence (as opposed to the mere presence of European objects) in the archaeological record. European artifacts of the Columbian era in association with contact-era Amerindian remains is provoca-

tive, but could be accounted for by the very active and widespread trade networks among the native peoples of the Caribbean. European items (particularly iron, glass, and glazed ceramics, which were unknown in the Americas prior to European contact) were highly exotic and therefore widely prized by the American Indians, as is amply verified in documents of the era. Such items are likely to have been curated and traded, and they were probably hoarded by the economic elite of native Caribbean society. They are not likely to have been lost or discarded, the most common ways (along with burials) in which articles enter the archaeological record. The most successful identifications of sites occupied by Columbus, therefore, have been those that reveal and date nonartifactual European features and that closely correlate archaeological, documentary, and geomorphological evidence.

A related problem in identifying the presence of Columbus is the fact that it is not possible (except in the extraordinary cases of dated coins) to distinguish artifacts of 1492 from artifacts of 1500. This presents the obvious difficulty of isolating materials left by Columbus from materials left by the many travelers and explorers who followed him during the fifteenth century.

Most of the archaeological efforts related to the presence of Columbus have relied on a relatively limited group of artifacts that can be confidently dated to the closing decades of the fifteenth century. This dating has been based both on the contemporary accounts of Columbus and his companions and on the excavations of sites, such as La Isabela, that are known to have existed only during the Columbian era.

Trade items known to have accompanied all of the voyages include glass beads of blue, green, and yellow; combs, scissors, and mirrors; hawkbells; iron fishhooks; coins; glass bottles; and "tinklers" (brass or copper shapes with a perforation for sewing on clothes). Articles from archaeological sites have included the pottery types of Melado ware (a honey-colored glazed ware) and green bacín; the majolica types of Isabela polychrome, Columbia plain, Caparra blue, and Yayal blue on white; perforated brass crescents, circles, and triangles; tiny doughnut-shaped glass beads in yellow and green; brass finger rings set with a single, colored glass stone; horseshoes; small iron buckles; and Venetian style glassware, both plain and latticinio.

With the advances in transatlantic commerce and the radiation outward from La Española, the material world of Columbus was greatly changed after 1500. This transition has been archaeologically traced at a number of sites throughout the Caribbean.

Much of the archaeology in support of the Columbian quincentenary has been concerned with the issue of the original Bahamas landfall site of October 1492. With regard to this controversial issue, archaeology has been engaged in a supplemental role: to search for contact-period Indian sites in locations hypothesized to have been that of the landfall. Although possible sites have been located, few contain evidence of European presence, and none can definitively be said to have been the landfall site, owing to the methodological problems noted above.

The Long Bay site on San Salvador Island, excavated by Charles Hoffman of Northern Arizona University, has yielded a variety of late fifteenth-century Spanish and Italian artifacts, including glass beads, metal buckle fragments, Castilian coins of the late fifteenth century, and fragments of Spanish pottery. These occur in association with Taino Indian remains and are the kinds of objects (if not the actual objects) brought to the Americas on Columbus's voyages of exploration.

Another approach to the landfall issue has been taken by William Keegan and Steven Mitchell, who have attempted to correlate Columbus's physical descriptions of the Bahamas with geomorphological reconstructions of the islands' coastlines as they may have been in 1492. They are able in turn to correlate these results with archaeological sites.

Columbus visited and named a large number of the Caribbean islands and portions of the South and Central American coastlines during his four voyages. He and the chroniclers accompanying him often described Indian towns and chiefs they visited. Most of these encounters, however, were of a few days duration at most, and there was no long-term European occupation during the Columbian era except for La Española. Relatively little archaeological material related directly to Columbus can thus be identified elsewhere in the Caribbean, although considerable speculation about the specific locations visited has been offered by archaeologists working throughout the islands.

Cuba was briefly explored during the first and second voyages (1492 and 1494), and large Indian towns were described and visited. Cuban and North American archaeologists have identified several Indian sites containing early Spanish materials in the Banes region of northeastern Cuba, known to have been visited by Columbus on his first voyage. These sites contain glass beads; iron buckles and knife fragments; horseshoes and harness hardware; bits of chain, scissors, nails, and coins; and pieces of Spanish pottery. One of these sites, at Yayal, has been extensively excavated over the years and, as Lourdes Dominguez has shown, was apparently occupied well into the sixteenth century by the Cuban Indians.

Jamaica was first visited and described by Columbus in 1494, and he was later shipwrecked and stranded there for more than a year, during his fourth voyage. The site of the shipwreck and camp is believed to be at Saint Ann's Bay, and archaeological work in search of it has been undertaken. Columbus also visited the island's south coast, where he described a very large Indian town on a high hill that appears to correspond to the White Marl site at which John Goggin found fifteenth-century Spanish pottery.

Columbus also met difficulty during his fourth voyage in what is now Panama (then known as Veragua), near the Belen River. Storms forced the fleet into the Belen harbor in January and then silted the river mouth to the extent that Columbus could not leave until the end of April. He built a small settlement and named it Santa María de Belén. From there he and his men traded and fought with the resident Indian population. When storms finally opened the harbor, Indian hostility forced Columbus to abandon the small settlement. He was also obliged to abandon one of his vessels, Gallega, in the Belen River, owing to the considerable worm damage suffered during the stay in the river.

In the Lesser Antilles there are few sites at which European artifacts of the Columbian era have been identified, although Columbus is known to have visited a number of these islands. Neither have fifteenth-century European sites been conclusively identified in Trinidad or at the adjacent Peninsula and Gulf of Paria at the mouth of the Orinoco River (Venezuela). Both of these areas were explored by Columbus during his third voyage.

It was also during the third voyage that the "pearl coast" of northern Venezuela and its associated islands was first recorded by Columbus. This area was later to become a major focus of settlement, because of the economic interest in pearls. Much of the pearl industry was centered on Margarita and Cubagua islands, where the important site of Nueva Cádiz was located and excavated. Although Nueva Cádiz (1515–1545) was not occupied during the Columbian era, the excavation of the site by José Cruxent, Alfred Boulton, and John Goggin during the 1950s yielded a large collection of early sixteenth-century Spanish and Indian materials. These illustrate a transplanted Spanish lifestyle, supported by the exploitive, Indian-slave-based pearl fishing industry.

The earliest and only planned European settlements of the Columbian era were in La Española, primarily in that part which is today the Dominican Republic. The earliest nonintentional settlement, the fortress of La Navidad, was also located in La Española; it was established in 1492 near present-day Cap Haïtien, Haiti.

On Christmas Eve of 1492, Santa María was grounded and could not be repaired. With the assistance of the Indian chief Guacanagarí, the ship was dismantled and unloaded and a small fortress was constructed in or near Guacanagarí's town. Columbus left thirty-nine men there for nine months, during which they all died.

Excavations at Nueva Cádiz, Cubagua Islands, 1960.   Unidad de Fotografia Científica, I.V.I.C.

The site of Guacanagarí's town, and possibly of La Navidad, was located by William Hodges in 1976. It has been subsequently excavated by Kathleen Deagan, working with Hodges, and excavations have verified its date and the presence of European animal and artifact remains from the Columbian era. No structural features definitely attributable to European origin have yet been verified.

Columbus returned to La Navidad on his second voyage in 1492 with seventeen ships and nearly two thousand men (no women). He brought all the resources believed necessary to establish a formal colony, including craftsmen and artisans, animals, and plants. When they found La Navidad burned and all of the men dead, they decided to abandon that area and sail eastward along the north coast of La Española. They established the first Spanish town in the Americas at La Isabela, about seventy kilometers east of La Navidad.

La Isabela had several stone and packed-earth buildings, including a church, fortress, storehouse, and the house alleged to have been occupied by Columbus. It had a limestone quarry and kilns (recently discovered and excavated by José Cruxent) for making tiles, bricks, and possibly simple pottery. The 1,700 inhabitants lived in some two hundred thatch and wood huts.

The site of La Isabela has been known to scholars since its abandonment in 1498. Several of the stone structures have been located, excavated, and identified, as have been the quarry and kiln. The town has been investigated archaeologically a number of times since 1892.

La Isabela was plagued from its start by disease, discord among the settlers, mutinies, Indian attacks, and crop failures. By 1498 it had been largely abandoned, and other Columbus-related settlements took precedence.

Within months of founding La Isabela, Columbus established the small fortress of Santo Tomás, located about three miles from the present town of Janico. Santo Tomás was intended to guard the route between La Isabela and the allegedly gold-rich interior of the island. It was made of wood and packed earth, and had a moat on one side. The site has been located and recorded by Elpidio Ortega, and traces of the moat can still be seen. No excavations have been reported at the site.

In 1495 another fort was established in the interior (referred to as the "Cibao"). This was Concepción de la Vega, which is today, like La Isabela, a Dominican Republic national park. It was intended as a fortified center from which to trade gold, and it soon became a thriving, large town built largely of brick and tile. The site still contains substantial architectural remains, including those from the cathedral, the fort, the monastery, the water and irrigation systems, and other structures. Archaeological work has been underway intermittently since the 1950s, concentrating for the most part on the major architectural elements of the fort and monastery.

A very large and rich assemblage of artifacts reflects a very European material world. These include Spanish and Italian pottery, ornate Venetian glassware, gilded book and chest clasps, and a wide range of ornaments, tools, and domestic household items. This material has not been analyzed or published as of the time of this writing; however, much of it may be seen at the Museo de las Casas Reales in Santo Domingo. The town was destroyed by an earthquake and abandoned in 1562.

The year after the establishment of Concepción de la Vega (1496), Santo Domingo was founded on the south coast of the Dominican Republic by Bartolomé Colón, acting as governor during his brother's absence. The original settlement was on the east bank of the Ozama River, and this site was located in 1986 and has been tested by archaeologists Elpidio Ortega and Marcio Veloz-Maggiolo. Shortly after 1500 the settlement was moved across the river, to its present location. Extensive archaeological work by various agencies of the Dominican government has taken place in Santo Domingo over the years, and

EARLY SIXTEENTH-CENTURY SPANISH ARTIFACTS FROM CARIBBEAN SITES. *Clockwise, from top left:* glass lid finial, from Nueva Cádiz; twisted turquoise glass bead, from Nueva Cádiz; Spanish lustreware pottery, from Concepción de la Vega; gilded belt tip, from Concepción de la Vega; copper alloy scabbard tip, from Concepción de la Vega; gilded, enameled book hardware, from Puerto Real, La Española; *(center)* chain-mail links, from Nueva Cádiz.   FLORIDA STATE MUSEUM, GAINESVILLE

many of the remains are to be found at the Museo de las Casas Reales. Although dense urban occupation has caused considerable damage to the earliest archaeological record of the city, the projects that have been undertaken have permitted the restoration of structures dating to that era, including the cathedral and the house owned by the Columbus family.

By 1500 the settlements established by Columbus were in serious difficulty. Not enough gold had been found to consider the venture an economic success, and there was resentment among the Spanish settlers over the poor living conditions, leading to uprisings and mutinies. The Indian tribute system had also collapsed by that time, owing in great part to the reduction of the Indian populations through disease. Thus in 1500 to Santo Domingo came Francisco de Bobadilla to end the Colón family governorship of the island and to send Columbus back to Spain in disgrace.

The period of Columbus's occupation of La Española (1493–1500) was a time of devastating social and demographic upheaval for the native peoples of the Caribbean. The rapid decline in population among the Caribbean Indians as a consequence of their vulnerability to European diseases is well-documented through ethnohistorical sources. Much of what we know of this period from the native perspective comes from archaeological excavations.

Archaeologists such as Manuel Garcia-Arevalo have located and excavated a number of Taino Indian sites with remains dating to the Columbian era. The earliest such sites are burials, such as the La Caleta site near Santo Domingo, in which European articles (pottery, beads, metal ornaments) were incorporated into traditional Taino burial ritual. Slightly later sites also show evidence of European influence on native craft traditions. Indian-made pottery of that period occasionally makes use of European vessel forms and functions, and aboriginal-style tools are sometimes fabricated from metal.

Columbus also introduced the institutions of Indian slavery and tribute to La Española, although neither survived his tenure as governor because of the virtual disappearance of the Indians. Archaeological work at sites of Indian slavery (such as Concepción de la Vega, Puerto Real in Haiti, Nueva Cádiz, Venezuela, and Santo Domingo), however, show that under these conditions Indian pottery became greatly simplified and lost much of its contact-period form and decorative variation. At Concepción de la Vega, in fact, excavation has revealed a remarkable Indian-made pottery combining traits of European form and South American and Hispaniolan Indian decoration. This suggests to archaeologists that there was a conscious effort very early to direct Indian crafts into directions more appealing to European tastes.

The remains of Columbus's settlements and their legacies can be seen today throughout the Dominican Republic. Archaeology has not only located many of these sites but also helped reveal the nature of life in these very earliest Columbian colonies. It is through these material remains that we get a glimpse of the beginning and the end of the medieval presence in the Americas.

BIBLIOGRAPHY

Brill, Robert. "Laboratory Studies of Some European Artifacts Excavated on San Salvador Island." In *Proceedings of the First San Salvador Conference: Columbus and His World*. Edited by D. Gerace. San Salvador, Bahamas, 1986.

Cruxent, José. "The Origins of La Isabela." In *Columbian Consequences*. Edited by D. H. Thomas. Washington, D.C., 1990.

Deagan, Kathleen. "The Archaeology of the Spanish Contact Period in the Caribbean." *Journal of World Prehistory* 2 (1988).

Dominguez, Lourdes. *Arqueología colonial cubana: Dos estudios*. Havana, 1984.

Garcia-Arevalo, Manuel. "La arqueología Indo-Hispano en Santo Domingo." In *Unidades y variedades: Ensayos en homnenaje al José M. Cruxent*. Caracas, 1978.

Goggin, John. *Spanish Majolica in the New World*. Yale University Publications in Anthropology, no. 2. New Haven, 1968.

Hoffman, Charles. "Archaeological Investigations at the Long Bay Site, San Salvador, Bahamas." In *Proceedings of the First San Salvador Conference: Columbus and His World*. Edited by D. Gerace. San Salvador, Bahamas, 1986.

Mitchell, Steven, and William Keegan. "Reconstruction of the Coastlines of the Bahamas Islands in 1492." *American Archaeology* 6 (1987).

Montas, Eugenio Perez. *Republica Dominicana: Monumentos historicos y arqueológicos*. Instituto Panamericano de Geografia y Historia, no. 380. Mexico City, 1984.

Ortega, Elpidio. *Arqueología colonial en Santo Domingo*. Santo Domingo, 1982.

Ortega, Elpidio. *La Isabela y la arqueología en la ruta de Colón*. San Pedro Macoris, Dominican Republic, 1988.

Sauer, Carl O. *The Early Spanish Main*. Berkeley, 1966.

Willis, Raymond. "The Archeology of 16th-Century Nueva Cádiz." Master's thesis, University of Florida, 1976.

KATHLEEN DEAGAN

Underwater Archaeology

Underwater archaeology is simply archaeology conducted under water. Theoretical concepts are identical to those of terrestrial archaeology, although methodology has been adapted to an aqueous environment. A relatively new branch of the discipline that has grown steadily since the inception of self-contained underwater breathing apparatus (scuba), underwater archaeology has developed techniques to deal with excavating and recording under water, and with the recovery and conservation of waterlogged materials. More specialized forms include marine archaeology, which is conducted in salt water, but which often is confused with maritime archaeology, the study of the remains of seagoing enterprises, whether shipwrecks or harbor works. Another form, nautical archaeology, studies watercraft and their evolution and functions over time.

The origins of underwater archaeology are associated with discoveries by Mediterranean fishermen and sponge divers of significant artifacts like bronze statues. These objects were brought to the attention of archaeologists, who came to realize that shipwrecks preserved an abundance of materials not normally found in terrestrial sites, except perhaps tombs and graves. Attempts to retrieve portions of shipwrecked cargoes followed, with archaeologists directing divers impeded by heavy equipment. With the advent of aqualung diving after World War II, pioneers of undersea exploration tried their hand at shipwreck excavation, followed by traditional archaeologists. In the Americas, scuba divers began to follow the leads of fishermen and explore shipwrecks, especially in the waters of Florida, Bermuda, and the Caribbean. The Smithsonian Institution's program to investigate submerged sites gave birth to underwater archaeology in the Western Hemisphere. As in the Mediterranean, emphasis initially was placed on the recovery of cargoes and armament from shipwreck sites, many of them located through historical research in European archives. Underwater archaeologists became conversant in commercial and military history to help them interpret their finds. They also became proficient in naval architecture, as the remains of ancient wooden ships were increasingly encountered.

Yet, while the sites of classical Greek, Roman, and Egyptian ships came under scrutiny, remains of vessels associated with early European expansion in the Americas still awaited investigation. Thus, the architecture of ships built thousands of years ago became familiar to students of the evolution of seafaring, but components of the ship types that carried Vasco da Gama, Christopher Columbus, and Ferdinand Magellan into distant waters remained a mystery. Of the vast number of underwater sites in the New World, only a handful have begun to shed light on the nautical technology that allowed medieval mariners to sail into the Renaissance, joining two independent worlds for the first time.

The 1554 Fleet. Discovery by beachcombers in 1964 of Spanish coins along a section of Padre Island, Texas, prompted treasure hunters to search for a source offshore. Dates and denominations of the coins led to archival documents connected with the loss of three Spanish merchantmen in 1554. Salvage of one of the wrecks began in 1967, yielding many artifacts that were removed from Texas before the operation was halted by a court order. Legislation established the Texas Antiquities

Committee, and the salvaged materials were returned to the state, where a facility for their conservation was constructed in 1971.

During the next six years, the Antiquities Committee conducted research on the 1554 fleet. Translated documents helped piece together the tragedy of *Santa María de Yciar*, *Espíritu Santo*, and *San Estéban*. Excavated remains of the latter vessel and its cargo were conserved for public display. Publication of the inventory of restored artifacts and the archival documentation provided the most comprehensive study to date of colonial Spanish shipwrecks.

Red Bay Wreck. In the frigid waters of Labrador, investigations of a Basque whaling station at Red Bay led to the discovery of the well-preserved remains of a vessel thought to be *San Juan*, which had lost its moorings in 1565 while preparing to return to Spain loaded with casks of whale oil. Underwater archaeologists from Parks Canada, under the direction of Robert Grenier, began in 1978 to probe the remains of the galleon, unearthing navigational equipment and portions of the vessel's running rigging. The ship's hull lay in ten meters of water, flattened by centuries of winter ice but well preserved by the cold water. Disassembly of its components revealed a ship built for work rather than warfare. Timbers were mapped, pried loose, brought to the surface for recording, and then returned to the seabed. A rubber cast of the central portion of the ship was poured under water to obtain a mirror image of the structure, and a one-tenth scale model was constructed for a three-dimensional perspective of the hull.

The Red Bay wreck represents a well-preserved example of sixteenth-century shipwrightery; reconstruction of the ship's architecture on paper suggests that it was a three-masted vessel of 250 to 300 tons, built and fitted out in the Basque region of Spain. Remains of two other vessels and a small whaling boat were also revealed in the harbor, providing additional examples for the study of early Iberian shipbuilding.

Molasses Reef Wreck. Perhaps the oldest European shipwreck to be found in the Western Hemisphere was discovered by hunters in the 1970s at the crossroads of the Windward Passage and the Old Bahama Channel. The site was situated on a remote reef at the edge of the Caicos Bank, north of Hispaniola, where the ocean floor abruptly rises to within a few feet of the water's surface. Visible wreckage of the ship consisted of a small mound of ballast stones, an anchor, and numerous pieces of artillery. The divers recognized the antiquity of the wrought-iron ordnance and took several pieces as souvenirs. Treasure seekers eventually arrived at Molasses Reef, claiming in 1980 to have found the wreck of Columbus's *Pinta*, hoping to raise funds to work the site. Their unsuccessful attempts to mount an expedition prompted the government of the Turks and Caicos Islands to invite the Institute

of Nautical Archaeology (INA) at Texas A&M University to give the wreck site the scientific attention it deserved.

Three seasons of mapping and excavation began in 1982 under the direction of Donald H. Keith, resulting in the recovery of data and artifacts. The small vessel had been heavily armed with a wide variety of weapons, from two large wrought-iron cannons, called *bombardettas*, to a battery of fifteen smaller swivel guns, or *versos*, mounted on the ship's railings. Unlike later artillery cast in a mold, each piece had been forged by hand, by welding long iron staves together to form the barrel, which was then reinforced by sleeves and rings. Ammunition consisted of cast- and wrought-iron solid shot, solid lead shot, and lead wrapped around an iron cube. The ship's crew apparently cast ammunition at sea because two-part shot molds were discovered on the wreck site. In addition, fragmentary examples of smaller arms were found: two harquebuts, which were an early form of matchlock musket, and the remains of two crossbows. Part of the ship's defensive system, these weapons would also have been carried ashore.

Disassembly of the ballast pile was accompanied by careful recording of stone sizes and stowage patterns in the hold of the ship; petrographic study of samples suggested the ship probably had taken on ballast at some point in Lisbon, England, and the Azores. Fragmentary shards of ceramic vessels collected from the ballast pile represented storage containers for the ship's provisions, basins for washing, pots for waste, and tablewares for the crew. Despite the wreck's exposed situation in the shallow fore-reef zone, fragile portions of tiny glass medicinal vials were unearthed; they may have belonged to a pharmaceutical chest carried on board.

Beneath the ballast stones, remnants of the ship's wooden hull had survived despite shipworms, storms, and centuries under the sea. A section of the bottom of the vessel had been preserved sufficiently to discern at least twenty-two frames and six hull planks. Although these wooden remnants were insufficient to obtain the exact dimensions and shape of the hull, frame spacing and fastening patterns provided clues to the size and method of construction of the ship.

The encrusted artifacts and waterlogged wood were shipped to INA's laboratory where mechanical excavation of conglomerates revealed a cross section of the ship's fittings and tools. Encrustations that once contained iron were injected with molding compounds to create casts of the original objects. Researchers spent thousands of hours to conserve the recovered components so they could be returned to the Turks and Caicos Islands to be displayed in a museum. Comparative analysis of the wreck's ordnance and ceramic and glass types with known examples from Europe and other early Spanish terrestrial sites in the Americas dates the Molasses Reef wreck to the

MOLASSES REEF WRECK. Lifting a wrought-iron cannon (*bombardetta*) from the seabed.

INSTITUTE OF NAUTICAL ARCHAEOLOGY, COLLEGE STATION, TEXAS

first decades of the sixteenth century, although its identity still remains a mystery. Several slaving voyages to the islands occurred during these years, but many more probably went unrecorded. Fragments of sand-tempered native pottery and a pair of iron leg manacles recovered from the wreck site suggest the possibility that the vessel may have been involved in the slave trade.

Highborn Cay Wreck. A similar shipwreck of the same era was discovered by skin divers in 1965, some four hundred miles to the northwest, in the lee of tiny Highborn Cay, an island in the Exuma chain on the edge of the Great Bahama Bank. The site consisted of a small ballast mound with several pieces of encrusted artillery and an anchor. The discoverers obtained a salvage license, and in 1966, all visible iron materials were raised from the site. To learn more about the wreck site and to contrast its components with those at Molasses Reef, an INA research team in 1983 contacted members of the original salvage team for comparative data. From photographs and drawings they learned that the site had contained two *bombardettas* with four associated breech chambers, similar to those found on Molasses Reef. In addition, at least thirteen smaller swivel guns of two types had been found with numerous powder chambers and iron breech wedges. At least one breech block had been loaded; both powder and wooden plug were still in place. Examples of

lead-wrapped iron dice had also been found throughout the site.

As with the Molasses Reef site, a large anchor had been found in association with the two *bombardettas* atop the ballast mound. This pattern of distribution suggested that all three heavy iron objects had been stowed in the holds when the vessels sank. Rather than coincidence, it would appear that small seagoing vessels during this period normally carried heavier ordnance and anchors below decks to lower the center of gravity while underway. Two additional anchors were found some 100 to 150 meters (110 to 165 yards) from the bow portion of the wreck site, suggesting that the Highborn Cay vessel had been at anchor when it sank.

Because of the site's similarity to the wreck at Molasses Reef and the fact that the majority of the ballast had been left undisturbed by previous salvage efforts, the INA team decided in 1986 to reinvestigate the Highborn Cay wreck and examine the ship's surviving structure. The hypothetical location of the vessel's mainmast step assembly and associated structure was deduced from previous survey data compared with the original salvor's site plan. A transverse trench across the ballast pile revealed beneath the coral and stone mantle a large mast step mortice, carved into the keelson. Between bracing timbers were found limber boards designed for easy removal to clear debris from the bilge. Additional boards, called filler planks, protected the bilge area from trash and ballast, which could clog the pump. Two concave cavities had been cut into the keelson to accept cylindrical pump shafts. What may have been the pump box survived only in splinters.

Test excavations of the Highborn Cay vessel provided the kind of constructional details missing from the Molasses Reef wreck. For the first time, dimensions of each of the principal timbers and the manner in which they were joined allowed a detailed image of a discovery-period sailing vessel to be assembled. Together, the remains of both ships and their wreckage represented a major archaeological breakthrough in knowledge of how early sixteenth-century vessels had been built, provisioned, and armed.

Bahía Mujeres Wreck. Another shipwreck undergoing investigation represents the second wave of seafaring conquistadores as their routes shifted from the islands to the Mexican mainland. Entombed by coral in the shallow waters of Bahía Mujeres off the eastern coast of Yucatán, the site was discovered by local divers, who removed examples of wrought-iron ordnance and anchors in the 1950s. Initially and erroneously believed to be the remains of *La Nicolasa*, a ship used by the conquistador Francisco de Montejo in an abortive attempt to establish a colony on Yucatán's shores in 1527, the wreck site and its artifacts are being studied cooperatively by INA and Mexico's National Institute of Anthropology and History (INAH). Surviving ordnance salvaged from the Bahía Mujeres wreck is similar to that of the other sites, but also includes a *verso* of a different type than those found on the Molasses Reef and Highborn Cay wrecks. The number of artillery pieces and the size and weight of the anchor suggest that this vessel may have been smaller than the other two.

With the help of one of the original divers, the wreck site was relocated in 1984 after some twenty-three years. A low mound of ballast stones, almost covered with coral formations, marked the resting place of the ship's hull—the earliest to be discovered in Latin America. A scatter of stones trailed toward the north, where another anchor had been found in the 1960s. Ongoing investigations of the Bahía Mujeres wreck, together with information gleaned from the sites described above, constitute a steadily growing corpus of data on early sixteenth-century ships of a distinctly Atlantic type.

The Search for the Ships of Columbus

The search for remains of Columbus's ships began on the north coast of Jamaica, where the Admiral's fourth voyage to the Indies ended. Beached in a shallow bay in 1504, the sinking caravels *Capitana* and *Santiago* became a survival outpost for more than a year until the marooned mariners were rescued. The last two ships commanded by

Columbus were forgotten until 1935, when amateur archaeologist William Goodwin began to probe a secluded inlet called Don Christopher's Cove near St. Ann's Bay. After three seasons and more than 150 test holes, Goodwin gave up his search, having found only one small ceramic shard for his efforts.

Meanwhile Samuel Eliot Morison was preparing an expedition to retrace the Columbus voyages. When he sailed into St. Ann's Bay in 1940, Morison set out with the help of a local amateur, Charles Cotter, to reconstruct the surroundings of Columbus's unintentional exile. Both scholars rejected Don Christopher's Cove as a possible location for the beached ships because of the inlet's narrow shape and shallow depths. They determined that its name had been derived not from the famous Admiral but from Cristóbal Yssasi, the last Spanish governor of Jamaica, who used the cove to hide from invading seventeenth-century English troops. Morison and Cotter concurred that Columbus's ships probably were abandoned in the western section of St. Ann's Bay, where the island's first European settlement, Sevilla la Nueva, later was established. Morison published this hypothesis in *Admiral of the Ocean Sea* (1942), which contained a map of the proposed resting place of the caravels.

In 1966, while conducting excavations at the sunken city of Port Royal on the south coast of Jamaica, Robert Marx briefly visited St. Ann's Bay. Probing the muddy bottom, he encountered fragments of wood, stone, ceramics, and obsidian. Two years later, Marx returned with an engineer, Harold Edgerton, who produced sonar images of several buried targets in the area that Morison had proposed. Core sampling yielded additional materials, including glass, charcoal, flint, an iron tack, and a black bean. Examined by different laboratories, the samples were judged to be of varying dates and ambiguous origins. Yet the sonar targets raised hopes that both Columbus vessels had been found.

At Marx's urging, the Jamaican government sought international support to begin test excavations, and in 1969, the French diver Frederick Dumas was invited to investigate the site. Several days of dredging turned up ballast stones, artifacts, and glass fragments under the sloping mudbank near a colonial English wharf. Owing to the type and variety of artifacts, and because an old chart depicted two anchors at the location he had tested, Dumas concluded the site probably was an anchorage midden associated with the wharf. Recovery of eighteenth-century wine bottle bases and clay pipe fragments reinforced this hypothesis. The government was told that Columbus's caravels probably were buried elsewhere, and the mystery remained unsolved.

In 1981, INA researchers decided to resume the search for the lost caravels. They reasoned that, if known vessels of discovery could be found and studied, many questions could be answered about the nautical technology that brought Europeans to the Americas and the maritime lifestyles that accompanied them. They also hypothesized that, since the caravels had been beached in the shelter of a bay rather than wrecked on an offshore reef, their remains might be relatively well preserved. Furthermore, because the vessels had been used to house Columbus and his men for more than a year before being abandoned, they might contain archaeological evidence such as food remains and other domestic debris that might help interpret one of the earliest sustained relationships between Europeans and native Americans.

To gather data on geomorphological changes in the bay since the time of Columbus, a series of preliminary cores were undertaken at several locations in St. Ann's Bay. These suggested that portions of the shoreline had variously eroded or accreted over time owing to marine and alluvial action. Other areas had been altered by colonial and modern construction. In conjunction with the government of Jamaica, a cooperative effort to pursue the abandoned caravels began in 1982, combining traditional disciplines of archaeology and history with modern advances in electronics and marine geology. A team of archaeologists and students from the United States and Jamaica, under the direction of Roger C. Smith, assembled at the historic English plantation of Seville, once the site of Sevilla la Nueva and now a national park.

They began a systematic magnetometry survey along the present-day beach and in the shallow waters of the bay to obtain magnetic readings that might represent buried cultural material. A subbottom sonar device also was employed to penetrate marine sediments. Offshore of the old wharf where Marx and Dumas had worked, a cluster of five sonar images was discovered. Test excavations confirmed the site as an anchorage midden with two discrete layers of cultural debris deposited during periods of intense plantation activity in the eighteenth century. Nearby, readings from the instruments led to the discovery of a mid-eighteenth-century English trading vessel preserved under two meters of mud and silt. By the end of the second season, the shoreline and waters of the bay had been surveyed and tested. Additional underwater middens and several other colonial shipwreck sites were encountered, including a salt trader and a merchantman loaded with iron sugar mill apparatus, but none of these sites dated from the sixteenth century. No evidence for early Spanish maritime activities had been found.

The project team decided to return to the area around the old stone wharf where Morison believed the caravels had been beached. The location of the wharf had been well chosen by plantation planners, since a natural deep channel through the bay ran up to the shore at this point, providing ideal access for shipping. The researchers wondered whether the English wharf could have been built on top of an older Spanish structure, which, in turn, might have been constructed from the ballast piles of the abandoned caravels. Electronic sensing and probing of the ruins had proved difficult, since the stones interfered with instrument readings, and subsurface debris hampered coring. Reluctant to dismantle a portion of the historic ruin and undermine its stability, the team devised an alternate strategy for test excavation. A four-foot diameter aluminum culvert pipe was inserted alongside the wharf to form a caisson, within which excavations could be carried out without disturbing the surrounding sediments. As each section was emptied, it sank into the water-saturated soil, and another section was added.

In this manner, more than a ton of river and ballast rock intermixed with hundreds of artifacts was extracted by hand during two seasons of difficult underwater work in tight quarters with no visibility. English trade ceramics, fancy glass stemware, rum and wine bottles, beef, pork, and turtle bones, sailor's buttons and culinary implements, slave-produced pottery, and roof tile and brick fragments all attested to the variety of commerce conducted across the plantation's wharf over three centuries. Oyster shells of a nontropical variety reflected the North American colonial connection; Pacific money cowries found their way via Africa to the West Indian sugar plantations along with the slaves they helped purchase. As late-seventeenth-century materials began to emerge, the stratigraphy became less discrete and the sediments more sterile. Excavation continued as far as the caisson would allow, and then a long core was driven to a total depth of ten meters. No sixteenth-century materials were encountered; no evidence for a Spanish wharf or ship was found. After four seasons, the team discontinued its explorations, and research shifted to the study of early shipwrecks found elsewhere in the Caribbean.

The earliest recorded European shipwreck in the Americas was that of Columbus's *Santa María*, which occurred in 1492 on the north coast of Hispaniola. The remains of this famous vessel became the target of a search that began in 1949, as the pilot Don Lungwitz spotted a dark oval blur inside the barrier reef of Cap Haïtien, Haiti. The blur seemed to rise almost to the surface of the water, but unlike other coral mounds scattered throughout the reefline, this one lay at a right angle to the surf zone and was oval-shaped like a ship.

Ten years before, Morison had sailed into Cap Haïtien Harbor carefully studying the contour of the coastline to retrace the fatal course of *Santa María*. Concluding that the site of La Navidad, partially built from the flagship's timbers, was situated near the present-day fishing village of Limonade Bord-de-Mer, he hypothesized that the vessel had wrecked on one of three small shoals between the shore and the barrier reef. The underwater archaeological methods by which to test his theory had yet to evolve, however.

Some 150 years earlier, the eighteenth-century French historian Moreau de Saint-Méry had recorded the discovery of one of *Santa María*'s anchors in the muddy bottom of Grand Rivière, a mile from its mouth and two miles from Limonade Bord-de-Mer. Over the centuries, the mouth of the river had gradually accreted out into the sea. Saint-Méry conjectured that the anchor was the same one that Diego Alvarez Chanca, the physician of Columbus's second voyage, reported seeing near the burned ruins of La Navidad. This anchor is now on display at the National Museum in Port-au-Prince. In 1955, the underwater explorers Edwin and Marion Link briefly visited Cap Haïtien to search for *Santa María*. Diving far to the west of Morison's hypothesized location, they recovered an early anchor from a reef in the harbor entrance. Although the ring, part of the shank, and the palms were missing, it resembled the anchor found by Saint-Méry. Examined by Mendel Peterson of the Smithsonian Institution, both the Saint-Méry and the Link anchors were conjectured to have come from the same ship, possibly *Santa María*.

In 1967, another explorer, Fred Dickson, came to the north coast of Haiti. Knowledgeable about the Morison and Link expeditions, Dickson met Lungwitz, who offered to fly him over the reefs of Cap Haïtien. Intrigued by what he saw, Dickson organized an expedition and later that year, exploratory excavations began on a mysterious coral mound. Under twelve feet of coral and ballast rock, ship-related materials such as wood, copper and iron fastenings, lead sheathing, and ceramics were recovered. An organization called the Santa María Foundation was formed to raise funds for further investigations.

Dickson decided that more extensive survey of the immediate area was needed, but it was not until 1970 that a magnetometer was employed on the coral mound, revealing a major anomaly at one end. Test excavations produced more wood, ballast, fasteners, and ceramics, but also glass fragments, grapeshot, and two large, square iron bars of a type carried as ballast on warships. The archaeologist Carl Clausen concluded that the artifacts were consistent with an eighteenth- or nineteenth-century shipwreck. Despite frustration and lack of money, Dickson persisted in his efforts to investigate the axis of the mysterious coral mound. While continuing his search for *Santa María* in 1972, he tragically died following a diving accident.

The vagueness of the historical narrative describing the loss of *Santa María,* and dramatic changes that have occurred to the shoreline since that event took place, present serious obstacles to the eventual discovery of its grave. Surviving elements of the ship may no longer be recognizable owing to the offshore environment in which it was lost and the extensive salvage carried out by its crew with the aid of natives. Of the other recorded ship losses sustained by Columbus, the remains of the caravel called *Gallega* have a greater potential to be located and identified.

Left behind in a river on the isthmus of Panama during the first of several disasters that befell the Admiral's fourth voyage, *Gallega* became the object of a search begun in 1987 by a team of archaeologists led by Donald H. Keith. To conclusively identify the remote river that Columbus had named Belén in 1503, an aerial reconnaissance of all rivers along the northern isthmus was conducted. Only the one currently named Río Belén matched the historical descriptions; it too had been visited and identified by Morison in 1940. In conjunction with the Panamanian Institute of Culture, an expedition was organized to map the river mouth. The resulting data indicated that the river's course remained relatively unchanged. Subbottom penetrating sonar and magnetometry, deployed in the shallow riverbed from a small boat, produced several promising anomalies. Continued survey and careful testing of targets may produce evidence of buried ship's wreckage. Río Belén's remote location offers the preserving elements of fresh water and alluvial sediments that may well have protected the remains of a Columbus ship for nearly five hundred years. The discovery of *Gallega* would be a landmark in underwater archaeology.

BIBLIOGRAPHY

Arnold, J. Barto, III, and Robert S. Weddle. *The Nautical Archaeology of Padre Island: The Spanish Shipwrecks of 1554.* New York, 1978.

Frye, John. *The Search for the Santa María.* New York, 1973.

Grenier, Robert. "Excavating a 400-Year-Old Basque Galleon." *National Geographic* 168, no. 1 (1985): 58–68.

Hajovsky, Rick. "Phase II of the Search for Gallega." In *Underwater Archaeology.* Edited by J. Barto Arnold, III. Proceedings from the Society for Historical Archaeology Conference, Baltimore, Md., 1989.

Keith, D. H., and J. J. Simmons. "An Analysis of Hull Remains, Ballast and Artifact Distribution of a 16th-Century Shipwreck: Toward a Better Understanding of Wrecking and Reconstruction." *Journal of Field Archaeology* 12, no. 4 (1985): 411–424.

Keith, D. H., et al. "The Molasses Reef Wreck, Turks and Caicos Islands, B.W.I.: A Preliminary Report." *International Journal of Nautical Archaeology* 13, no. 1 (1984): 45–63.

Myers, Mark D. "An Archaeological Reconnaissance of Río Belén, Panamá." In *Underwater Archaeology.* Edited by James P. Delgado. Proceedings of the Society for Historical Archaeology Conference, Reno, Nev., 1988.

Oertling, Thomas. "The Highborn Cay Wreck: The 1986 Field Season." *International Journal of Nautical Archaeology* 18, no. 3 (1989): 244–253.

Oertling, Thomas. "The Molasses Reef Wreck Hull Analysis: Final

Report." *International Journal of Nautical Archaeology* 18, no. 3 (1989): 229–243.

Smith, Roger C., and D. H. Keith. "The Archaeology of Ships of Discovery." *Archaeology* 39, no. 2 (1986): 30–35.

Smith, Roger C., et al. "The Highborn Cay Wreck: Further Exploration of a 16th-Century Bahaman Shipwreck." *International Journal of Nautical Archaeology* 14, no. 1 (1985): 63–72.

Tuck, James, and Robert Grenier. "A 16th-Century Basque Whaling Station in Labrador." *Scientific American* 245, no. 5 (1981): 180–188.

ROGER C. SMITH

ARCHITECTURE. For discussion of European architecture in Columbus's day, see *Art and Architecture*.

ARIAS DE ÁVILA, PEDRO. See *Ávila, Pedro Arias de*.

ARMILLARY SPHERE. An armillary (from Latin, *armilla*, ring) sphere is an instrument in which the celestial sphere is represented and delineated by rings representing the polar circles, the tropics, the celestial equator, and the ecliptic circle (the apparent path of the sun through a band of constellations [the zodiac] in the course of the year). It derives from a large, fixed, observational instrument, the *astrolabos* or *astrolabon organon* (which is not to be confused with an astrolabe) used by Ptolemy of Alexandria (fl. A.D. 127–148) and employed as an observational instrument in Islamic astronomy. Although the *Libros de saber de astrología* (Burgos, c. 1276) of Alfonso X, known as Alfonso the Wise, describe an observational armillary sphere, the influence of the *Libros*, written not in Latin but in a vernacular (Castilian), appears to have been slight, and the armillary sphere in medieval Europe was primarily an instrument for demonstrational or didactic use.

A small sphere, placed at the center of the sphere, represented the earth and made the sphere a model of the Ptolemaic geocentric system. Star pointers, as on an astrolabe, attached to the constituent rings, demonstrated the apparent rotation of the stars about the celestial pole. Small medieval armillary spheres were attached at the base to vertical handles, but if the sphere were placed in a ring representing the terrestrial horizon, with its polar axis inclined at an angle corresponding to the latitude of a particular place, rotation of the sphere could demonstrate the rising, meridian transits, and setting of stars and of the sun, and could become, like an astrolabe, an analogue computer for solving simple problems in spherical trigonometry. A pair of curved dividers, as used with globes, aided measurement on the sphere. Such dividers were used by João de Castro in 1538 on a *poma* (Portuguese,

ARMILLARY SPHERE. Circa 1425, representing Ptolemaic cosmography. MUSEUM OF THE HISTORY OF SCIENCE, OXFORD

apple), apparently a form of solid or armillary sphere used in navigation, possibly hung from an adjustable suspension ring.

During the latter half of the sixteenth century, the Arsenius instrument workshop at Louvain made armillary spheres with sights (enabling them to be used for observations) and astronomical rings, an observational simplification of the armillary sphere invented by Rainer Gemma Frisius (1508–1535) of the University of Louvain. The astronomical ring was developed by the English mathematician William Oughtred (1575–1660) into the universal equinoctial ring dial, a sundial that became one of the few useful nautical instruments. The large fixed observational armillary sphere was revived in the late sixteenth century by the Danish astronomer Tycho Brahe (1546–1601).

The armillary sphere has often been used as a symbol of astronomy and was given as a heraldic device by King João II of Portugal (1455–1495) to his cousin, Prince Manuel, later, King Manuel I (1469–1521). It thus appears on a gold coin minted for Portuguese India during the reign of Manuel I and is familiar as a motif of Manueline architecture in Coimbra and Lisbon.

[See also *Astrolabe.*]

BIBLIOGRAPHY

Alfonso X. *Libros de saber de astrología.* Edited by Manuel Rico y Sinobas. 4 vols. Madrid, 1863–1866.

Maddison, Francis. *Medieval Scientific Instruments and the Development of Navigational Instruments in the XVth and XVIth Centuries.* Agrupamento de estudos de cartografia antiga, vol. 30. Coimbra, 1969.

Nolte, Friedrich. *Die Armillarsphäre.* Abhandlungen zur Geschichte der Naturwissenschaften und der Medezin, vol. 2. Erlangen, 1922.

Turner, Anthony. *Early Scientific Instruments: Europe 1400–1800.* London, 1987.

FRANCIS MADDISON

ARMS, ARMOR, AND ARMAMENT. Within the vast body of literature devoted to Columbus and his voyages of discovery, there is little information about the armament of his ships or of the arms carried or the armor worn by the seamen and colonists. Historians either ignore the subject completely or suggest, as J. H. Parry has in *The Age of Reconnaissance,* that the explorers sailed in ships meant for the coastal trade. What arms they carried were mostly personal weapons.

Samuel Eliot Morison suggests the same in *The Great Explorers,* indicating that the ships carried a stand of swords, cutlasses, and pikes for use against attackers who might try to fight their way aboard. It is clear, however, from entries extracted by Bartolomé de Las Casas from the lost logs of Columbus's first and third voyages, and in accounts of the second and fourth voyages by Michele da Cuneo and the Admiral's son Fernando, respectively, that all Columbus's ships carried cannons as well as personal weapons of various types. Both Columbus and Cuneo refer to the cannons as lombards. Unfortunately, neither specifies the number per ship nor their size. During the first voyage it was recorded in the log that a lombard was fired as a signal that land had been sighted. Later, after *Santa María* ran aground on a reef off the north coast of La Española, all salvageable equipment, including her armament, was carried ashore. A fort was built for the protection of those members of the crew of *Santa María* who were left behind as the first colony of Europeans in these islands. Lombards were appropriately mounted in the fort, and Columbus ordered a demonstration firing in

the presence of local Indians to impress them with the Spaniards' capacity to protect themselves.

Soon after Columbus's triumphant return from his first voyage, a papal bull, issued in May 1493, granted Spain control of the lands discovered by the Admiral. Despite this, the Spanish sovereigns wanted to make certain that an armed presence was put in place there as soon as possible to guard against any incursion by Portugal. Accordingly, they ordered a large fleet of seventeen vessels to be manned and outfitted with food, arms, munitions, supplies, equipment, and tools for up to twelve hundred crewmen, artisans, farmers, miners, and workmen to establish a self-sustaining colony on La Española.

Setting sail from Cádiz on September 25, 1493, Columbus took a more southerly course than he had followed on the first voyage in order to explore an island chain southeast of La Española that had been described to him on that voyage by his Indian guides. He chose the name Dominica for the first island sighted because of the Sabbath landfall. It was in this island chain that the Spaniards had their first recorded fight with New World peoples, the fierce, hostile, and cannibalistic Caribs. One Spaniard was killed by a poisoned arrow that pierced his buckler. That he was not the first Spaniard to have been killed by native inhabitants, however, was revealed when the fleet, on November 27, reached La Navidad, where the crew of the wrecked *Santa María* had been left on the first voyage. There the entire garrison had been killed.

In March 1494, after establishing the planned colony, which he named La Isabela, at a site on the north coast of La Española to the east of La Navidad and closer to the gold-rich mountains of Cibao, Columbus decided that he must take personal charge of the mining efforts. He assembled the necessary artificers, workmen, miners, munitions, and tools. Because of past incidents of violence on the part of Indians of the Cibao region loyal to the powerful cacique (chieftain) Caonabó, reputed destroyer of the La Navidad garrison, Columbus took with him a substantial and well-armed force composed of a cavalry troop with swords and lances, men-at-arms with crossbows, and hidalgos armed with swords and arquebuses to protect the work force and deter the Indians from any further violence. Washington Irving relates that

On the 12th of March, Columbus set out at the head of about four hundred men well armed and equipped, with shining helmets and corslets; with arquebuses, lances, swords, and crossbows, and followed by a multitude of the neighboring Indians. They sallied from the city in martial array, with banners flying, and sound of drum and trumpet. When the Indians beheld this shining band of warriors, glittering in steel, emerging from the mountains with prancing steeds and flaunting banners, and heard, for the first time, their rocks and forests echoing to the din of drum and trumpet, they might well have taken such a wonderful pageant for a supernatural vision. In this way Columbus disposed of his forces whenever he approached a populous village, placing the cavalry in front, for the horses inspired a mingled terror and admiration among the natives.

Arriving in the foothills of the Cibao mountains, Columbus chose a level field within a bend of a clear stream as the site for a fort and a center for mining operations. Leaving over fifty men under the command of Pedro Margarit, as well as a few horses, which were greatly feared by the inhabitants, Columbus returned to La Isabela. The day after he arrived there, a messenger came from Margarit reporting that the friendly Indians had fled and that the dangerous cacique Caonabó was making preparations to attack. In response, Columbus sent seventy armed men with provisions and ammunition to help Margarit defend the fort and the mining operation.

With the crops planted at La Isabela already beginning to ripen, Columbus decided that it was time to resume his efforts to explore the mainland of "Asia." On April 24, he set sail once again to the west with the three smallest caravels, which he had specifically selected for the mission of exploration, *Niña, San Juan,* and *Cardera.* When he reached the eastern point of Cuba, which he believed to be the eastern extremity of the Asian mainland, Columbus decided, with the concurrence of his pilots, officers, and gentlemen volunteers, that they should explore the south coast rather than the north, 150 miles of which he had already explored on his first voyage.

Hearing reports of gold from the Indians, Columbus headed south to Jamaica, where his three caravels were surrounded by about sixty canoes loaded with apparently hostile Indians. Columbus ordered several blank shots fired from the cannons and the Indians fled ashore. Columbus had portable swivel guns mounted in the bow of each ship's boat and armed the boat crews with crossbows and shields and went ashore. They were met by a hail of stones and responded with arrows from the crossbows and shots from the swivel guns, killing a number of Indians. The following day the well-armed Spaniards again went ashore and were greeted by entirely friendly natives who offered them food and water. Comparable incidents also occurred during both the third and fourth voyages.

Recent findings by nautical archaeologists give a richer picture of the weapons and munitions used during the four voyages than the historical record does. Two shipwrecks of the discovery era have been found in the Caribbean and have yielded excellent evidence of the armament of ships of the period and of the arms carried by their crews and early colonizers. These shipwrecks were surveyed and excavated in the 1980s by a team headed by Donald Keith of the Institute of Nautical Archaeology (INA) at College Station, Texas. One wreck is located on Molasses Reef near the Turks and Caicos Islands and the other just off the northwest shore of Highborn Cay in the northern Bahamas. The size and shape of the reasonably intact mounds of stone ballast at both sites indicates that the ships had been of the approximate tonnage of *Niña* or *Pinta,* a common size for caravels of that period and hence specifically indicative of the arms and armament of the principal type of vessel used by Columbus.

At the Molasses Reef shipwreck site the INA team recovered two authenticated fifteenth-century, wrought-iron, breech-loading cannons (*bombardettas*), with fifteen separate breech chambers; fourteen smaller breech-loading swivel guns, or *versos,* a variety of falconet, with forty separate breech chambers; two lightweight, muzzle-loading swivel guns, or *harquebuts;* two wrought-iron, muzzle-loading shoulder arms, or *arquebuses;* and a large number of various types and sizes of shot for all the weapons. Portions of two crossbows were also found.

Ordnance found at the Highborn Cay wreck included two wrought-iron, breech-loading *bombardettas* with compatible breech chambers and at least thirteen smaller wrought-iron breech-loading swivel guns with eighteen breech chambers and the iron wedges used to lock the chambers in the breech assemblies. Most of the swivel guns were small *versos* of less than 2 meters in length, but two were the larger *versos dobles* and measured 2.7 meters in length. Shot found was of the iron-cored, lead-wrapped variety.

Ten of the fourteen swivel guns excavated from the Molasses Reef wreck appear to have been lashed together in pairs of similar types. The remaining four were found with loaded and plugged breech chambers wedged into the breech assemblies ready to be fired. Had this wreck been the only one found, one might have assumed that the ten lashed pairs were being carried as cargo and that the four loaded swivel guns almost certainly had been mounted on the vessel as her own armament and constituted her total complement of swivel guns. But a comparable number of swivel guns were found at the Highborn Cay wreck, located at a considerable distance from and apparently unrelated to the Molasses Reef wreck. Thus it appears that a discovery-era caravel normally carried a substantial number of swivel guns in addition to a pair of *bombardettas.* The answer may be found in the various accounts of swivel guns being mounted in the ship's boats when explorers went ashore in the presence of natives who might not be friendly. It is also possible that spare swivel guns, the smaller ones of which weighed only about eighty pounds, may have been used to arm the several forts that were built during the period. As for personal weapons such as swords, cutlasses, halberds,

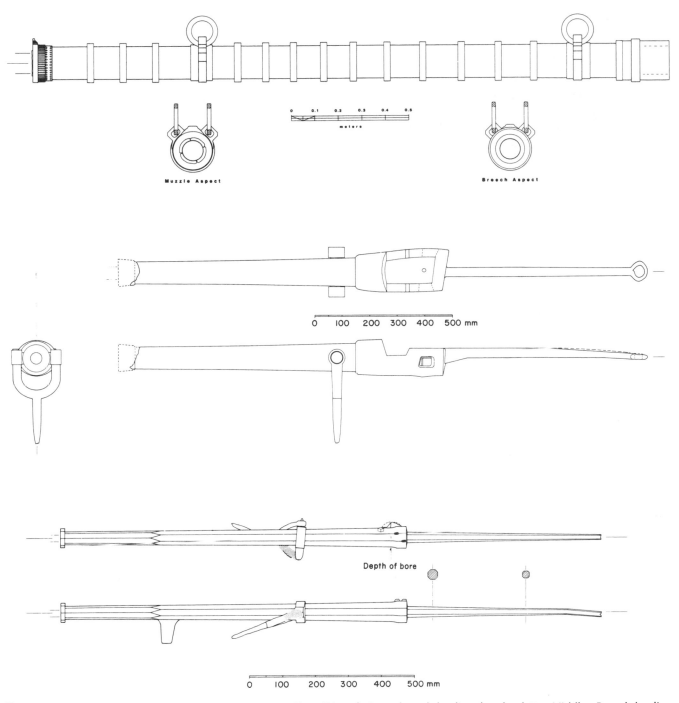

Muzzle Aspect

Breech Aspect

0   0.1   0.2   0.3   0.4   0.5
meters

0   100   200   300   400   500 mm

0   100   200   300   400   500 mm

Depth of bore

Tʜʀᴇᴇ ʀᴇᴘʀᴇsᴇɴᴛᴀᴛɪᴠᴇ ɢᴜɴs ꜰʀᴏᴍ ᴅɪsᴄᴏᴠᴇʀʏ-ᴇʀᴀ sʜɪᴘᴡʀᴇᴄᴋs. *Top*: Wrought-iron, breech-loading *bombardetta*. *Middle*: Breech-loading swivel gun, or *verso*. *Bottom*: Muzzle-loading, lightweight swivel gun, or harquebut.

Iɴsᴛɪᴛᴜᴛᴇ ᴏꜰ Nᴀᴜᴛɪᴄᴀʟ Aʀᴄʜᴀᴇᴏʟᴏɢʏ, Cᴏʟʟᴇɢᴇ Sᴛᴀᴛɪᴏɴ, Tᴇxᴀs

javelins, lances, and knives, none was found at either of the wreck sites. But these are items that survivors of the wrecks would have taken with them.

The heaviest cannons were identified by J. J. Simmons, INA ordnance analyst, as *bombardettas* in the catalog of the Museo del Ejercito (Army Museum) in Madrid. This term is the diminutive of "bombard," the name more commonly found in the historical record of heavier armament. Guns of this type have also been called lombards by some historians. The two *bombardettas* from

WROUGHT-IRON CANNONS FROM THE MOLASSES REEF WRECK. Being raised from conservation tanks.

INSTITUTE OF NAUTICAL ARCHAEOLOGY, COLLEGE STATION, TEXAS

the Molasses Reef wreck measured 8.7 feet in length with bore diameters of about 3.5 inches. The inner surface of the bore of each tube was made up of several iron staves reinforced by alternate abutting sleeves and hoops with their inner surfaces pressed against the inner lining of the staves. The tops of the muzzle hoop and the rear lifting ring hoop have squared-off raised surfaces to serve as gun sights. The separate breech chambers were constructed in the same manner as the gun tubes except that the butt ends were plugged and the forward ends were tapered to fit tightly into the breech end of the gun tube. Breech chambers of two lengths were found. The shorter more numerous chambers measured approximately twenty-four inches in length and the longer ones, presumably loaded with a greater amount of gunpowder for use against more distant targets, measured about thirty inches. No wooden carriages on which the *bombardettas* would have been mounted were found. Such carriages were recovered in excellent condition from the 1545 wreck of HMS *Mary Rose,* which carried a few wrought-iron bombards in addition to numerous more modern cast-bronze and cast-iron cannons.

The most common armament of discovery-period ships was the swivel gun. The types found at the Molasses Reef and Highborn Cay wrecks were called versos, characterized by some as a variety of falconet. Three types of versos were found at the Molasses Reef wreck: *versos lisos, versos normales,* and *versos dobles.* As the names indicate, the *versos normales* were the most common and the most numerous, with smaller numbers of the lighter *lisos* and the heavier *dobles.* The overall length of the most common verso was about 6 feet with a bore diameter of about 1.75 inches. Except for differences in size and weight, all were similar in shape and were made up of

tapering barrels, Y-shaped swivels by which they were mounted in a socket on the ship's rail, integral breech assemblies designed to hold the separate breech chambers, and a permanently attached tiller by which the gun could be swiveled from side to side and up and down. The separate breech chambers were shaped to fit tightly into the breech end of the gun barrel and had an iron handle welded near the butt end at an offset angle from the vertical so as to be clear of the touchhole by which the explosive charge in the chamber was fired with a red-hot iron poker. Each chamber had a horizontal lip fashioned into its sealed butt end slightly below its midpoint. When a retaining wedge was driven through carefully positioned slots in the breech assembly to force the chamber tightly into the gun's breech, the wedge also lay atop that protruding horizontal lip and prevented the chamber from jumping out of the breech assembly when the gun was fired.

Two types of portable wrought-iron, muzzle-loading guns were also found at the Molasses Reef site. One of these types was represented by two small wrought-iron, muzzle-loading swivel guns identified by Simmons as harquebuts. These were similar in form to the versos except that being muzzle-loading guns, they had no breech assembly. One of their distinguishing characteristics was a tang welded to the bottom of the barrel between the muzzle and the swivel. The gun, weighing only about thirty-three pounds, could either be hooked over any convenient rail aboard ship or a ship's boat with the tang acting as a recoil preventer or semipermanently mounted in a swivel socket as was done with the versos. Even more portable were two wrought-iron, muzzle-loading shoulder arms. This type of firearm, identified as an arquebus, had a barrel about 3 feet in length with a bore diameter of about 0.55 inches.

Most of the shot found at the Molasses Reef site were solid cast iron, but small numbers of wrought-iron, hollow cast-iron, iron-cored lead, and solid lead shot also were found. All the solid lead shot were for the harquebuts and arquebuses. Of the remaining shot, some were for the *bombardettas* and some for each of the three types of versos.

Except for the portions of muzzle-loading arquebuses and of crossbows found in the Molasses Reef wreck, no armor or personal arms were found at either site. Since it appears that the crews survived and made it to shore, it is reasonable to assume that they took with them whatever arms and armor they had for self-protection. On the first voyage, the sole purpose of which was exploration, it is probable that such arms as swords were available only to the ships' officers. Every crewman, of course, would have carried his own seaman's knife. It is not likely that any armor was carried on board. The nature of the subsequent

ASSORTMENT OF SHOT AND BRONZE SHOT MOLD. After restoration. From the Molasses Reef wreck.

voyages, however, was such that, particularly on the second and third voyages, which involved the establishment of colonies and subjugation of Indians, personal arms and armor would have been used extensively.

The various types of personal arms carried by caballeros and men-at-arms were mentioned above. As for armor, unfortunately Columbus historians have not addressed the subject except in passing references such as "this shining band of warriors, glittering in steel," in Washington Irving's description of the force led by Columbus into the interior of La Española during the second voyage. On the other hand, historians interested in the subject of armor have provided information about the types of armor used in Spain during the period. One can assume that such information is relevant to early forays in the New World.

It is important to note that much of the armor available in Spain during the Age of Discovery was not made there. Wealthy hidalgos, who could afford the finest equipment, purchased armor in either Germany or Italy. King Fernando, for example, had at least one fashionable suit of armor from Milan. In fact, armor made in Milan was especially popular in Spain at the end of the fifteenth century. Milanese armorers were more than willing to tailor their suits of armor to the particular tastes of their wealthy Spanish clients. The Milanese style could be distinguished by the squared-off shape of the movable sections fastened around the bottom of the solid steel breastplates of that period. For those who could not afford the most elegant styles, or preferred simpler attire, Spanish-made armor of good quality was available in the cities of Zaragoza and Calatayud. They were particularly well known for their fine helmets and a lighter version of

armor that was more popular in Spain than in other parts of Europe.

During the war against the Moors, the Spanish were forced to rely on light cavalry, or *jinetes*, for swift raids and counterraids by both sides. Spanish light cavalrymen learned to ride fast horses in the Moorish style with stirrups high and close to the saddle and their knees high against their horses' flanks, wielding a light lance overarm. Such tactics demanded that less and lighter armor be worn. Swords also became more slender and lighter. The city of Toledo, long famous for the quality of its sword, became a major producer of this new rapierlike weapon.

[See also *Archaeology*, especially the article on *Underwater Archaeology; Equipment, Clothing, and Rations*.]

BIBLIOGRAPHY

Frieder, Braden K. "Arms and Armor in the National Museum of the Viceroyalty, Tepotzotlán, Mexico." Unpublished thesis, University of New Mexico. Albuquerque, N.Mex., 1988.

Irving, Washington. *The Life and Voyages of Christopher Columbus and His Companions.* 3 vols. New York, 1849.

Morison, Samuel Eliot. *The Great Explorers.* New York, 1986.

Parry, J. H. *The Age of Reconnaissance.* London, 1963. Reprint, Berkeley, 1981.

Simmons, J. J., 3d. "Wrought-iron Ordnance: Revealing Discoveries from the New World." *International Journal of Nautical Archaeology* 17 (1987): 25–35.

WILLIAM LEMOS

ART AND ARCHITECTURE. The Age of Exploration coincided with one of the great moments of transformation in art. While Portuguese and Spanish ships were expanding the horizons of the European world, a new style, which became known as "Renaissance," was born in Italy. Innovations in optics and perspective enabled artists to construct a three-dimensional space on a flat surface, which, in turn, led to new developments in navigation and cartography. The invention of engraving allowed artists to create visual images from the written descriptions of the explorers that fired the imagination of a largely illiterate public. Subsequently, still-life painting developed in response to a desire to have a permanent record of perishable flowers and fruits from far-away places, and patrons of the arts such as the Medici began to collect Indian artifacts as both objects of curiosity and admiration.

European art and architecture in the fifteenth century can be divided into two main styles: late Gothic, dominant north of the Alps from the Iberian Peninsula to the Holy Roman Empire; and Renaissance, which originated in Italy beginning around 1400. The latter style, based on the revival and reinterpretation of classical forms deriving from ancient Rome, began to permeate northern sensibilities in a significant way only after the king of France, Francis I, returned from his invasion of Italy in 1517. He brought with him Leonardo da Vinci and a determination to decorate his palace at Fontainebleau in the new style. The Renaissance style gradually spread across Europe and was espoused by Francis's great rival, Emperor Charles V, followed by his son, Philip II of Spain.

The Gothic style had shaped European art and architecture for several centuries. Originally associated in the twelfth century with the French royal house, the style had taken on, by the fifteenth century, local characteristics and become much more florid than the understated elegance of its first manifestations. In France it was called the "style flamboyant," in England, "perpendicular," in Germany, "Spätgotik," and in Spain, "plateresque," but all used the Gothic pointed arch and stressed verticality and light. Many of the cathedrals took decades, if not centuries, to build, and the gradual evolution of the regional styles can be easily seen in them. Some of the finest examples of late Gothic churches of the fifteenth century are the Stephansdom in Vienna, Sankt Lorenz in Nuremberg, Saint-Maclou in Rouen, King's College Chapel in Cambridge, and Seville cathedral.

Late Gothic was not confined to ecclesiastical buildings. Town halls, marketplaces, and private palaces were also built in this manner. The trading town of Bruges in Flanders, one of the wealthiest cities in Europe in the fifteenth century, is virtually a monument to this showy style, which suited the nouveau-riche burghers. Nor was Gothic limited to architecture. Painting, manuscript illumination, lettering, and sculpture were all affected by the fashion for increasing decoration and embellishment. The movement was international; there was a lively exchange of ideas and works of art throughout Europe. The Netherlandish artist Hugo van der Goes was commissioned in 1474 by Tommaso Portinari, the agent for the Medici bank in Bruges, to paint a large triptych (three-part altarpiece). This work, shipped to Florence, created a sensation with its use of oil paint and its contrast to the new Renaissance style. It influenced later fifteenth-century Florentine artists, most notably Domenico Ghirlandaio, in whose workshop Michelangelo served as an apprentice. The central panel has a high vanishing point resulting in a steep angle for the foreground, animated drapery, clear colors and light, and a heavy emphasis on linearity. For all the "realism" with which the shepherds are portrayed, the overall impression is one of brittleness and stylization, characteristic features of the style that had become known as "international Gothic" because of its widespread popularity.

Sculpture had always formed an integral part of church decorations, and there are innumerable figures on late Gothic structures. In addition, by the fifteenth century, complex and enormous wooden altarpieces could be found from the Iberian Peninsula to the eastern Holy Roman Empire. No surface was left smooth or empty. Three-dimensional figures painted and gilded to make them seem more lifelike are surrounded by architectural and botanical forms. Agitated lines abound, from the cascading hair of the Virgin to often graphically explicit Crucifixion scenes. These were especially popular in Germany. One of the outstanding surviving examples is the Sankt Wolfgang altarpiece (1471–1478) by Michael Pacher in the Pilgrimage Church of Abersee.

With the marriage of Fernando and Isabel in 1469, Spanish art received new impetus. The Catholic monarchs undertook large building programs to imprint their sover-

THE PORTINARI ALTARPIECE. Triptych by Hugo van der Goes, 1474.   ALINARI/ART RESOURCE

eignty and Christianity on the newly united kingdoms. But centuries of Moorish culture had left a mark on the arts, particularly as many craftsmen were still Muslim. Spanish Christian art of the fifteenth and sixteenth centuries was an amalgam of late Gothic excess, Flemish-German expressiveness, and Moorish techniques. This latter can be seen most obviously in architectural and decorative forms such as the horseshoe arch and mudejar, the repetitive ornamentation of flat surfaces. A particularly fine example is the cloister of San Juan de Los Reyes in Toledo, built by Fernando and Isabel to celebrate their victory at the Battle of Toro in 1476.

Although in Moorish art and architecture the effect was rhythmical and balanced, the mix with Gothic could result in an overload of often incompatible images and forms. This can be clearly seen by comparing the *mocárabe,* or stalactite plaster work, of the late fifteenth-century Patio de los Leones at the Alhambra, palace of the last Moorish rulers in Spain, with the post-1492 portal of the Colegio di San Gregorio, Valladolid, built by Queen Isabel's confessor. The gentle nonrepresentational organic patterning has given way to a heavily symbolic but disconnected decorative scheme that includes the royal arms held by rampant lions in a pomegranate tree as a memorial to the reconquest of Granada ("pomegranate" in Spanish), putti playing among its branches, and warriors, pages, and wildmen occupying niches encumbered with Gothic trimmings. The name given to this style, plateresque, is derived from the Spanish *platero,* or art of the silversmith, because of its characteristic excessive and precious ornamentality.

This style was not limited to architecture. The enormous carved *retablos,* or altarpieces, of the late fifteenth century exceed even the German taste for crowded surfaces and quantity of decoration. The great *retablo* of Seville cathedral (fifty-nine feet high) has forty-five figurative scenes in addition to all its extra decoration, and the *retablo mayor* of Toledo (1498–1504) is a complete cycle of the Life and Passion of Christ with countless three-dimensional figures separated by elaborate Gothic canopies. Also in Toledo is one of the most extravagant processional *custodias* (tabernacles) ever made: ten feet high and weighing 350 pounds, it is an enormous Gothic steeple of gilded silver and jewels surmounted by a cross made from the first gold brought back by Columbus. Some of this gold was also to find its way to the Spanish pope in Rome, Alexander VI, who used it to gild the ceiling of the early Christian basilica of Santa Maria Maggiore.

Gothic had its proponents in Italy, too. In Venice it blended elegantly with the Byzantine influences on the facades of the palazzi, and in Milan, it was the style for the new cathedral (begun about 1386). In painting and sculpture, the international Gothic remained popular in Italy throughout the fifteenth century. At the same time, Italian

MILAN CATHEDRAL. Construction begun circa 1386.

Renaissance art began to develop with the work and theories of three Florentine artists, the architect Filippo Brunelleschi (1377–1446), the sculptor Donatello (1386?–1466), and the painter Masaccio (1401–1428). The new style involved revived interest in classical proportions and design, increasing realism in portraiture, and closer imitation of the natural world through perspective and foreshortening.

The early Renaissance style gradually transformed to High Renaissance in the second half of the fifteenth century with such masters as the painters Andrea Mantegna (1431–1506) in northern Italy, Giovanni Bellini (c. 1430–1516) in Venice, and the Florentine sculptors-painters Andrea del Verrocchio (c. 1435–1488) and Antonio Pollaiuolo (c. 1431–1498). Of these, Mantegna was the truest to the antique revival. Much of his art contains direct quotations from ancient models and his portrayals of classical monuments are almost literal. At the same time, his work was highly innovative, with dramatic foreshortenings and daring spatial effects, as in, most notably, his oculus in the Camera degli Sposi (1474) in the ducal palace at Mantua, where he was court painter. He was also one of the first to work in the new medium of engraving, and his impact there was considerable.

Giovanni Bellini, Mantegna's brother-in-law, was the chief painter to the state of Venice until his death, despite the growing reputation of the young Titian. His paintings

MONUMENT TO BARTOLOMMEO COLLEONI. By Andrea del Verrocchio, 1483–1488.   ALINARI/ART RESOURCE

impart a monumental stillness and dignity, highly refined perspectival spaces, and a bold, clear light, all apparent in one of his greatest masterpieces, *Saint Francis in Ecstasy* (1485).

Verrocchio, Donatello's heir, worked in many media, including marble, silver, and terra-cotta. His final work was his greatest, the bronze equestrian monument (1483–1488) to the mercenary Bartolomeo Colleoni for the city of Venice. Rather than emulating the calmness of the antique Marcus Aurelius in Rome or even Donatello's own Gattamelata monument of forty years earlier, Verrocchio has made his subject a defiant and bold figure. Standing upright in the stirrups, scowling ferociously at his adversaries, Colleoni is every inch the soldier leading his troops into battle.

Although monuments of a different kind, Pollaiuolo's bronze tombs of Pope Innocent VIII (1492–1498) and Pope Sixtus IV (completed 1493) also show increasing realism in the features. They were deemed of such quality that they were the only tombs saved when the old Saint Peter's was torn down in the sixteenth century. Both were revolutionary. Innocent was given a wall tomb with the enthroned live pope represented over his effigy in death. This double portrait was to become a favorite motif of the Renaissance

and the baroque periods. The tomb of Sixtus, an even more radical departure, is a floor tomb designed to fill the entire chapel with the recumbent pope lying atop a bronze bed surrounded by images of the Liberal Arts and Virtues. The references to Christianity have been allegorized to incorporate non-Christian ideas. But the ultimate power of the monument lies in the beautifully crafted death mask of the powerful, intelligent, and crafty man who built the Sistine Chapel and reestablished the Vatican Library after twenty years of neglect.

It was Sixtus IV who brought the Renaissance to Rome, where it reached its height in the early sixteenth century under the papacy of his nephew, Julius II, patron of Raphael (1483–1520), Donato Bramante (1444?–1514), Andrea Sansovino (c. 1467/71–1529), and Michelangelo (1475–1564). Sixtus founded a museum of antiquities and brought the finest artists of his day—mostly Florentines—to Rome in 1481 to decorate his new chapel with a fresco cycle of the lives of Moses and Jesus intended as a political declaration of the primacy of the pope in the ruling hierarchy of this world. The work was shared by Pietro Perugino (1445/50–1523), Sandro Botticelli (c. 1445–1510), Domenico Ghirlandaio, Cosimo Rosselli (1439–1507), and Luca Signorelli (1445/50–1523), all leading artists of the day. Perhaps the most daring of all artists in Rome during the last quarter of the fifteenth century was Melozzo da Forli (1438–1494) whose extreme foreshortening and skillful perspective make his figures seem to start out of their background and appear three-dimensional. Unfortunately, most of his work has been lost.

But even in the forward-looking world of Italian Renaissance art, the international Gothic continued. Beautiful clear colors, elegant lines, and gilded highlights are all hallmarks of Bernardino Pinturicchio (c. 1454–1513) whose greatest works were fresco cycles for various popes. Among the most famous are the wall paintings (1492–c. 1495) for the papal apartments of Alexander VI. These combine the old style with the new: among the deep tones and gold stucco work are subtle evocations of antiquity and obscure pre-Christian iconography. The pope's daughter, Lucrezia, is depicted as Saint Catherine of Alexandria, a pun on her father's papal name, and Alexander himself kneels at the foot of the cross, his Renaissance profile offset by an extravagant international-Gothic cope heavily encrusted with gold.

While Rome was enjoying its first taste of the Renaissance, there were continuing innovations in northern Italy. In Milan, Bramante, who would become architect of the new Saint Peter's in Rome in 1506, was beginning his experiments with the monumental forms that were to translate so successfully to Rome. Here for the first time was an architect using not only the vocabulary but the scale of ancient architecture. His choir of Santa Maria

TOMB OF SIXTUS IV. By Antonio Pollauiolo, completed 1493. One of two tombs preserved when Saint Peter's was rebuilt in the sixteenth century.

ALINARI/ART RESOURCE

delle Grazie, begun in 1493 as a memorial to the Sforza, the ruling family of Milan, stresses the great size of the space it encloses and overpowers the observer used to the more intimate spaces of Brunelleschi. When the Sforza fell in 1499, Bramante left Milan for Rome, where he found employment first from Cardinal Ascanio Sforza and then from the cardinal's archrival, the newly elected Pope Julius II. After Sforza's death Julius interred his longtime enemy in the choir of Santa Maria del Popolo, in a grand tomb by Andrea Sansovino (1505) under a monumental coffered apse attributed to Bramante.

Florentine art was also changing. By the mid-1480s, Botticelli had executed *The Birth of Venus*, the first full-length painted female nude since antiquity, and Leonardo da Vinci (1452–1519) had established his reputation. Trained in Verrocchio's workshop, Leonardo, by his early work in the 1470s, so impressed the master that Verrocchio swore he would never touch a brush again. His fascination with the natural world led Leonardo to develop the technique of sfumato, which gives a misty quality to his paintings, making it appear as if the objects exist in a real atmosphere. This is in sharp contrast to the clear light of both international Gothic and contemporary Renaissance painting. He also heightened the use of chiaroscuro, a balance between light and shadow in paintings, giving figures greater dimensionality and feeling of being in space. His portrait *Mona Lisa* (1503) is an outstanding example of both techniques. Perhaps his most famous work is *The Last Supper* for the refectory of Santa Maria

delle Grazie in Milan (1495–1498), which began deteriorating almost immediately owing to Leonardo's unfortunate propensity for experimentation with paints. Here for the first time the psychological reaction of the Apostles to Christ's announcement of impending betrayal is shown. Subsequently, movement was to be used in art to display emotion and drama. But Leonardo was also a Renaissance Man in the truest sense. He dissected human bodies to study and draw them. His anatomical drawings are not only exquisite works of art but are also highly accurate. His fascination with technology and war led him to work first for Lodovico il Moro, duke of Milan, and then, after his fall in 1499, for Cesare Borgia, son of Pope Alexander VI, in 1502–1503. Again, his sketches for war machines are sometimes fantastic, but others foreshadow much of modern warfare, such as the tank and the helicopter. He returned to Florence in 1503, where he befriended the young Raphael and competed with Michelangelo. In 1513, he went to Rome and in 1517 accompanied Francis I to France, where he died two years later.

Michelangelo was almost twenty-five years younger than Leonardo. The son of a Florentine magistrate, Michelangelo had to overcome parental opposition to get artistic training. Originally apprenticed to the painter Ghirlandaio, Michelangelo soon found sculpture a more consuming passion. He was befriended by the sculptor Bertoldo di Giovanni, who was the keeper of the Medici sculpture garden and probably an illegitimate Medici. When Lorenzo the Magnificent died in 1492, Michelangelo

PIETÀ. By Michelangelo Buonarroti, completed 1498.

began what was to become a lifelong emotional tug-of-war between Florence and Rome. In 1498 he completed the *Pietà* in Rome. Its great beauty and extraordinary balance of design established his reputation; also impressive was his carving of two figures out of one block of marble (which was inspired by ancient writers praising artistic achievements). Upon his return to Florence he received a commission for the *David* (1501–1504), which created a sensation when it was finished. It was deemed too beautiful to be placed in the site originally planned, high up on the cathedral, and a committee decided to put it next to the entrance of the Palazzo della Signoria as a symbol of the Republic of Florence. Immediately thereafter Michelangelo and Leonardo were engaged in an artistic competition to decorate the Council Hall, but neither of their works was ever finished, and both are known today only from copies. Nonetheless, the abandoned cartoons for Leonardo's *Battle of Anghiari* and Michelangelo's *Battle of Cascina* were so famous that for centuries many artists came to study them.

In 1506 Leonardo left Florence to return to Milan and shortly thereafter Michelangelo received a summons from Pope Julius II in Rome to carve his tomb. From this stay, two of the greatest monuments of the Roman High Renaissance emerged: the statue of *Moses*, part of the never-realized Julius tomb, and the ceiling of the Sistine Chapel (1508–1512). This extraordinary work of art, restored in the 1980s to its original glorious colors, had an immediate and powerful impact. The bold brushstrokes, dramatic colors, difficult poses, and total glorification of the nude ushered in a new era in art. After the death of Julius in 1513, Michelangelo spent the rest of his life working for popes, usually against his will. For Clement VII he created the Medici Chapel in Florence (begun 1524) and for Paul III, *The Last Judgment* (1536–1541). He served as chief architect of Saint Peter's from 1546 until his death in 1564, designing the great cupola and reinforcing the piers to carry the weight. During his own lifetime he was known as "il divino Michelangelo." No other artist has had so serious or continuing an influence on Western art.

During the first decades of the sixteenth century, Italian art became better known north of the Alps, thanks to the travels of such artists as the German Albrecht Dürer (1471–1528), who first visited Venice in 1494. He was a great admirer of Giovanni Bellini and was accused in 1507 of selling pirated copies of Italian engravings in Venice. He must have seen works by Giorgione (c. 1477–1511), whose innovative atmospheric landscape paintings and mysterious subjects made him, with Leonardo, one of the inventors of the High Renaissance style. Just as Raphael followed Leonardo, so Titian (1488/90–1576) succeeded Giorgione.

But it was not such peaceful exchanges that spread Italian taste to foreign lands. As France, Spain, and the Holy Roman Empire became increasingly entangled in Italian wars, their rulers also became aware of the new art that recalled the glory of the ancient Roman Empire. Unfortunately, their artists did not always understand the delicate balance between the structures and their proportions, and there are unhappy examples of a mixture of classical and Gothic motifs. By the end of the sixteenth century this combination had successfully melded into a new international style known as the baroque, which Spanish missionaries carried to the New World.

BIBLIOGRAPHY

Beck, James. *Italian Renaissance Painting*. New York, 1981.

Hartt, Frederick. *History of Italian Renaissance Art: Painting, Sculpture, Architecture*. 3d ed. New York, 1988.

Heydenreich, Ludwig H., and Wolfgang Lotz. *Architecture in Italy, 1400 to 1600*. Translated by Mary Hottiger. Harmondsworth, England, 1974.

Pope-Hennessy, John. *Italian Renaissance Sculpture*. 2d ed. London, 1971.

Snyder, James. *Northern Renaissance Art*. New York, 1985.

Sordo, Enrique. *Moorish Spain: Cordoba, Seville, Granada*. Translated by Ian Michael. New York, 1963.

Swaan, Wim. *The Late Middle Ages: Art and Architecture from 1350 to the Advent of the Renaissance*. Ithaca, 1977.

HELEN S. ETTLINGER

ASIA. For discussion of European knowledge of Asia in the Age of Exploration and how this information compares with the modern view of Asia's history, see *China*. For discussion of Japan, see *Cipangu*.

ASTROLABE. The word *astrolabe* (from Greek, *astrolabos* or *astrolabon organon*) usually refers to the planispheric astrolabe, an instrument deriving from the *planisphaerium* described by Ptolemy of Alexandria (fl. A.D. 127–148). It was used primarily for observation not to determine accurately the position of a celestial body but by day or by night for timetelling, for astrological purposes, for surveying, and for teaching astronomy. The essential circles and star-positions of the celestial sphere, as modeled on an armillary sphere are reduced to a flat surface by the geometrical procedure of stereographic projection, which retains angular measurements undistorted from the center.

The usual form of a planispheric astrolabe consists of a thick (c. ⅛- to ½-inch) main-plate (Latin, *mater*) with a deep recess on one side, leaving only a narrow raised limb, and provided with a suspension-ring attached to the rim. In the recess are a number of separate flat plates (Latin, *tympana*, sing. *tympanum*), prevented from turning by a lug fitting into a notch. Over the plates is a plate (Latin, *rete*) of the same diameter, that can be rotated; the rete is cut away to define circles and pointers. There is a rotatable rule (usually semidiametrical) over this plate; over the flat back of the main plate, there is a rotatable sighting rule (alidade) equipped with a pair of pinhole sight-vanes. The whole is held together by a thick pin, passed through coincident central holes in the main plate, the separate plates, and the cutaway plate, and held secure by a wedge pushed into a longitudinal slot in the pin.

The limb of the front of the main plate is engraved either with a scale of 360 degrees (Islamic astrolabes) or with a scale of twenty-four equal hours in two sequences of one to twelve (European astrolabes). Around the circumference of the back of this plate is a scale of degrees disposed into four quadrants so as to permit altitude measurements and various other scales or graphs (for example, a sine/cosine grid, a shadow "square" [for elementary surveying that avoids the need to know trigonometrical methods] as well as astrological tables [terms, limits, and faces of the planets] on Islamic instruments. Also inscribed are a horary diagram for unequal hours [constituting, with a scale engraved on the alidade, a form of sundial] and a zodiac/calendar scale [correlating the date with the sun's position in the ecliptic; e.g., ten degrees Aries might correspond to March 21] on European instruments). The separate plates are engraved on each side with a stereographic projection from the south celestial pole onto the plane of the equator of the horizon, celestial pole, zenith, circles of altitude between the horizon and the zenith (almucantars), and, below the horizon line, lines of unequal hours. The cutaway plate is a similar projection of the ecliptic circle, of part of the equatorial circle, and of the Capricorn circle (which, in this projection, forms the boundary of the separate plates and the cutaway plate), with pointers attached to the tracery, the tips of which indicate the relative positions of a selection of the brighter stars, the names of which are engraved adjacent to the appropriate pointers. The cutaway plate, or rete, is thus a star-map, similar to a modern plastic planisphere except that it is an external view of the celestial sphere (as seen when looking at a celestial globe), not the sky as seen from the earth. Rotating the rete over the plate immediately below it simulates the apparent rotation of the stars and of the sun about the celestial pole (represented by the center of the central hole) and in relation to the horizon engraved on the plate: an analogue computer, in modern terms.

For use in a particular latitude, the astrolabe was assembled with the plate most appropriate to the latitude on top of the pile of plates in the recess in the main plate, immediately underneath the rete. As an example of use, to tell the time at night, the astrolabe was held by its suspension ring and allowed to hang vertically; the alidade was used to sight one of the stars for which a pointer was provided on the rete, and its altitude above the horizon was noted from the scale of degrees on the limb (after this, it was no longer necessary to suspend the astrolabe). The rete was then turned until the tip of the pointer, representing the star observed, lay on the altitude circle engraved on the plate beneath, corresponding to the observed angular elevation. The star pointer was positioned on the circle either east or west of the meridian line (on an astrolabe of the type described, north is at the bottom, south at the top) according to whether the star, when observed, was east or west of the meridian. The rule over the rete was then turned until it crossed the position of the sun in the ecliptic (that is, the solar declination on the day in question, e.g., twenty-three degrees Leo, ascertainable from astronomical tables or, on a European astrolabe, from the zodiac/calendar on the back). The position of the rule on the hour-scale on the limb then gave the time in equal hours. (On Islamic astrolabes, the

PLANISPHERIC ASTROLABE. Front (*left*) and back (*right*) of a brass astrolabe attributed to Jean Fusoris, circa 1430.

MUSEUM OF THE HISTORY OF SCIENCE, OXFORD

time in unequal [planetary] hours or, sometimes, Babylonian or Italian hours, was found from hour lines engraved on the plate below the horizon line.)

The complexity of design and construction of an astrolabe made it expensive; many of the data it provided were irrelevant to navigation; the use of a solid disk in a wind or on the moving deck of a ship was not conducive to accurate observation. There is no evidence that planispheric astrolabes were ever regularly used at sea, despite the claim of the instrument maker Johann Krabbe of Munden, who described his version of a conventional planispheric astrolabe as especially suited to the needs of seamen in *Neuwes Astrolabium* (1608). Universal (that is, usable in any latitude) variants of the astrolabe described above, not requiring separate plates, and based on stereographic or orthographic projections of the celestial sphere on the colures (great circles) of the solstices, were no more useful to the mariner; the same is true of the rare spherical and linear astrolabes.

Mariner's or Sea Astrolabes. During the latter part of the fifteenth century, an altitude-measuring instrument,

called an astrolabe and intended for employment at sea, came into use. In 1487–1488, Bartolomeu Dias had "astrolabes" on his voyage to the Cape of Good Hope; in 1497 at the bay of St. Helena (southern Africa), Vasco da Gama used, on land (because of the difficulties of making the necessary observations at sea), a large (c. 24-inch diameter) wooden astrolabe, suspended from a tripod. In 1519, Magellan took with him one wooden and six metal astrolabes on his circumnavigation of the earth. The exact form of these sea astrolabes is uncertain. It is not until Alessandro Zorzi's letter of 1517 that an illustration of a mariner's astrolabe of characteristic form is found, and this precedes by eight years the earliest of two drawings on charts by the cartographer Diego Ribeiro of what he called "astrolabio maritimo," but which appears to be a solid disk based on the design of the back of a conventional astrolabe, though the sight vanes on the alidade are placed in the close position characteristic of the mariner's astrolabe.

Vasco da Gama's large wooden instrument was probably nearer in form to the wheel design of the characteristic mariner's astrolabe and was perhaps derived rather from a circular wooden observational instrument, with an alidade, used by medieval astronomers. The characteristic mariner's astrolabe consists of a heavy cast body in the form of a four-spoked wheel, sometimes slightly wedge-shaped in side-view, heavier in the lower part, where part of each of the two void quadrants is symmetrically filled in. There is a suspension ring, similar to that on a conventional astrolabe, and an alidade, with two sight vanes, pierced by pinhole sights, set much farther inward along the arms of the alidade than on a conventional astrolabe. Clearly, the position near the center of the sight vanes would have made it very difficult to use a mariner's observation for stellar observations; it was intended to measure solar altitude (or zenith distances) that, with the aid of appropriate solar-declination tables, permitted the determination of the latitude at the place of observation. The method of making the observation was to hold the astrolabe by the suspension-ring, directing it sideways toward the sun, and to rotate the alidade until the sunlight passing through the pinhole in the foresight fell as a spot of light exactly on the matching pinhole on the backsight; the pointed end of the alidade on the scale on the limb then indicated the sun's elevation. Scales of ninety degrees were graduated on the limb in the upper two quadrants, either (from the horizontal) to measure altitude or, on the later sixteenth-century Portuguese instruments (from the vertical) to measure zenith distance.

Some sixty-five mariner's astrolabes have been recorded (compared with about 1,500 planispheric astrolabes), many found in wrecks. The earliest is Portuguese and dates from 1540; the series continues into the eighteenth century, by which time the mariner's astrolabe was mostly superseded, in northern Europe, at least, by the cross-staff or by the backstaff. Deficiencies of the quadrant (high wind resistance in relation to size, a swinging plumb bob, difficulties in holding it if making a solar observation by the technique described above) doubtless encouraged the development of the mariner's astrolabe, the design of which sought to overcome a seaman's practical difficulties in making an astronomical observation. Columbus's journal of his first voyage (entry for February 3, 1493) mentions that he was unable to use an "astrolabio" because of the rough seas, but what type of astrolabe this was remains unknown. Astronomical observations made with an instrument that are mentioned were made with a quadrant.

[See also *Cross-staff; Quadrant.*]

BIBLIOGRAPHY

North, J. D. "The Astrolabe." *Scientific American*, no. 230 (Jan. 1974), pp. 96–106. Reprint in J. D. North, *Stars, Minds and Fate:*
Essays in Ancient and Medieval Cosmology, pp. 211–220. London and Ronceverte, W.Va., 1989.

Stimson, Alan. *The Mariner's Astrolabe: A Survey of Known, Surviving Sea Astrolabes.* HES Studies in the History of Cartography and Scientific Instruments, vol. 4. Utrecht, 1988.

Turner, Anthony. *Early Scientific Instruments: Europe 1400–1800.* London, 1987.

Turner, Anthony. *The Time Museum: Catalogue of the Collection.* Vol. 1 of *Time Measuring Instruments.* Part 1, *Astrolabes. Astrolabe Related Instruments.* Rockford, Ill., 1985.

FRANCIS MADDISON

ASTROLOGY. See *Astronomy and Astrology.*

ASTRONOMY AND ASTROLOGY. Astronomy and mathematics had little direct effect on navigation until the end of the thirteenth century. However, Greek science (and in particular Ptolemaic ideas of geography), which was transmitted to the Christian West by the Arabs, was to have a profound effect on the world of learning and on cosmographical concepts in the years leading up to the Age of Discovery.

Mathematical scholarship began to flourish in Italy soon after Leonardo of Pisa's (Fibonacci) introduction to the West, in 1202, of the Hindu (Arabic) system of numerals, which replaced the awkward Roman figures that made calculations so complicated. In the Norman kingdom of Sicily, which included southern Italy, Greek texts were being translated from Arabic into Latin with the help of Arab and Jewish scholars, while in Toledo in 1252 King Alfonso X of Castile and León assembled fifty Jewish and Christian scholars to translate scientific texts, including Ptolemy, from Arabic into Castilian.

The compilation, entitled *Libros del saber de astronomia,* included all known works on astronomy and related subjects, and its twenty-four theses summarized contemporary knowledge and gave instructions for making a variety of astronomical instruments, such as the astronomer's astrolabe, the quadrant, the armillary sphere, and so on. Most of the original texts were in Arabic and most of the translators, who rendered the texts into Castilian, were Jewish. Included were the Alphonsine Tables, based on the longitude of Toledo; translated into Latin, they were later circulated widely among astronomers. The astrolabe, an instrument of great antiquity, was introduced into Europe by the Arabs during the tenth century and was used for both astronomical and astrological purposes. It displayed the positions of the stars at night for different times and latitudes and could be used for timekeeping as well as for finding the precise direction of Mecca (which the builders of mosques were required to know). It could also be used to determine the altitudes, azimuths, and amplitudes of stars and, in the armillary type described by Ptolemy in the *Almagest,* enabled the celestial latitude and longitude of a body to be read without having to convert the altitude and azimuth into ecliptic coordinates.

In the Middle Ages the distinction between astronomy and astrology was a fine one. A person's horoscope, for instance, which governed his future, could only be cast if the exact position of the heavenly bodies could be determined as they rose; the position of the heavenly bodies in relation to the zodiac must be established for an exact hour. The astrolabe was in use in Portugal before 1090, and early tables, such as the collection known as the Portuguese Almanacs of Madrid, record a wide variety of astrological, astronomical, and geographical data, including meridian heights of the sun on a given parallel, the coordinates of stars and of geographical locations, dominical letters, and other data for determining movable feasts, eclipses, and the position of the moon in the zodiac, duration of days and nights in each month, and so on. The manuscript, compiled in Coimbra during the reign of King Dinis of Portugal (1261–1325), was derived from the Latin translation of an Arabic almanac calculated for the radix year 1307. King Dinis, the grandson of Alfonso X, is said to have received from his grandfather a copy of the *Libros del saber de astronomia,* which was finished in 1256. The almanacs, for all their astrological leanings, show a level of scientific learning among the astronomers working in Portugal that bodes well for the development of a navigational science.

A small work that was to assume great importance in the history of early nautical astronomy was *De sphaera mundi,* written in the early thirteenth century by the Englishman Johannes de Sacrobosco, or John of Holywood, probably as an introduction to a more advanced course on astronomy and cosmology. It became a standard text during the Age of Discovery and in a translation into Portuguese formed an integral part of the navigation manuals produced at the end of the fifteenth century. It is based largely on the work of the great Arab astronomer Alfraganus (al-Farghani, d. 861) and presents the Ptolemaic system as put forward in the *Almagest.* The treatise gives proofs of the sphericity of the earth, defines astronomical and terrestrial terms such as the ecliptic, equator, small and great circles, meridians, astronomical coordinates, and the twelve signs of the zodiac, and explains various astronomical phenomena, such as eclipses. It was Alfraganus whose calculation of the degree of the meridian—56⅔ miles—so misled Columbus, who failed to take into account the difference between the Arabic and the Italian mile.

The degree of the meridian is the angle subtended at the earth's center between two places on the same meridian, and the linear distance between them will depend on the figure adopted for the circumference of the earth. Early miles—Roman, Mediterranean, and Arabic—were defined in terms of other units unconnected with the size of the earth. Eratosthenes had measured the size of the earth in the third century B.C. and rounded off his findings to 252,000 stadia, so that each degree would have 700 stadia, which is 70 nautical miles. Ptolemy's *Almagest,* on the other hand, which was again in circulation in the fifteenth century, calculated the degree as 62 Roman miles. For the navigator none of this was of importance until, during the Age of Discovery, latitude on the charts became associated with distance. In what seems to be the earliest instruction to the seaman on the observation of altitude, repeated in an archaic addendum printed in the 1563 edition of Valentim Fernandes's *Reportorio dos tempos* (1518), the observer is told that for each degree marked on the scale of his quadrant he must "count 16 leagues and two thirds, which is 2 miles, reckoning 3 miles to a league." This would give a degree of only 50 miles, and later instructions to Portuguese navigators were to count 17½ leagues of 4 miles to the degree, yielding a degree of 70 miles. In *The Haven Finding Art,* E. G. R. Taylor suggests that Portuguese astronomers accepted Eratosthenes' degree of 700 stades, while Spaniards and Catalans chose Ptolemy's 500 stades, both reckoning 10 stades to the mile but each using the local league. To the seaman, however, the earth's size was of little conceptual import, for in the early days of astronomical navigation the navigator thought of his observations not in terms of latitude but rather in terms of the linear distance sailed between observations of the same body.

The first observations were of the North Star made in one of eight positions of the star's counterclockwise path around the pole as defined by the relative positions of the two Guard Stars, whether in terms of the altitude at Lisbon or as a correction to that altitude, and displayed either in terms of an imaginary human figure in the sky or in one of numerous "wheel" diagrams. The navigator was told in the manuals that, disregarding fractions of a degree less precise than those that could be observed at sea, the altitude of the North Star at Lisbon varied between thirty-six and forty-two degrees (giving a latitude of thirty-nine degrees).

There are numerous early Jewish and Islamic works translated into Latin that show how to determine latitude from the meridian altitude of the sun when the declination is known. The earliest, dating back to the ninth century, was by the astrologer Messahalla, but the rules apply only to an observer north of Cancer. The *Libros del saber de astronomia* contained a number of works derived from

Messahalla, including a set of rules that could be adapted for use south of the equator. The Portuguese astrologers who introduced latitude navigation in the Southern Hemisphere, where the North Star became invisible, would thus have had access to sources indicating, if only by analogy, the rules for the determination of latitude from the noonday altitude of the sun in positions with either northerly or southerly declination. Whether the rules set forth by the mathematical commission appointed by King João II of Portugal and set down in the earliest surviving navigation manual were in fact derived from Messahalla is not certain. The Regiment (or Rule) of the Sun in its various forms dealt with the problem of applying the declination to the altitude of the sun to obtain latitude in either hemisphere, when the sun was north or south of the observer and north or south of the equator. The relative positions of the sun and the observer were judged from the direction of shadows. Authorship of the Regiment is generally attributed to José Vizinho, the Jewish astrologer and physician to João II, who was sent on a voyage to Guinea in 1485 to test its efficacy in practice. Columbus refers to his observations.

To use the regiment of the altitude of the pole at noon, as Pedro Nunes was to term the Regiment of the Sun, the navigator needed to know the sun's declination, its angular distance north or south of the celestial equator. Medieval astrologers were accustomed to measuring the sun's position in the sky in terms of one of the twelve signs of the zodiac, each governing thirty degrees of the ecliptic. It was simple to calculate the solar declination from its position on the ecliptic, provided the precise angle between the ecliptic and the equinoctial was known, but astronomers differed on this measure, and so solar declination tables differed. The sun, furthermore, takes a little over a day to get through each degree of the zodiac, and four calendar years pass before the figures repeat themselves (even then a correction factor had to be applied to compensate for the difference between the length of the mean year in the Julian calendar and the duration of the sun's annual course). Tables of the sun's position were thus generally quadrennial, and a correction was made after the four-year period to allow for the sun having advanced 42 minutes and 56 seconds during that time. The most important ephemerides from the point of view of navigation were the tables in Abraham Zacuto's *Almanach perpetuum*. These were calculated from the year 1473 and gave the positions of the sun at noon for the quadrennial period 1473 to 1476 and the declination in degrees and minutes at any point on the ecliptic defined in whole degrees. A correction for use after the four-year period was included with the declination tables. The inclination of the ecliptic was taken to be 22°33'. In his *Tratado em defensam da carta marear*, Nu-

nes found Zacuto's value excessive and based his own tables on an obliquity of 23°30'. Vizinho had been a pupil of Zacuto at Salamanca and translated the introductory parts of the *Almanach perpetuum* into Latin and Spanish; he was no doubt also responsible for adapting the tables for inclusion in the *Regimento do astrolabio e do quadrante*. The sun's declination could of course be calculated by astronomers graphically or with the help of scientific instruments, such as the astrolabe, but few of these methods were suitable for use at sea.

[See also *Distance; Navigation; Science.*]

BIBLIOGRAPHY

Albuquerque, Luís de. *Astronomical Navigation*. Lisbon, 1988.

Cortesão, Armando. *History of Portuguese Cartography*. 2 vols. Coimbra, 1969.

Taylor, E. G. R. *The Haven Finding Art: A History of Navigation from Odysseus to Captain Cook*. London, 1956.

M. W. Richey

ATAHUALPA (d. 1533), Inca emperor. Atahualpa (Spanish, Francisco Atahualpa Inca) was born in Cuzco, the son of Huayna Capac and an Inca princess (Tupa Palla by one account, Tocto Coca by another, and Palla Coca by still another), and the elder brother of Huascar.

He was described as wise, cheerful, and very intelligent, of good appearance and manner, somewhat thickset. He had a large face, handsome and fierce, and his eyes were reddened with blood. He spoke gravely with the authority of a great ruler.

Huayna Capac's death left an ambiguous situation because the son he designated as his successor on his deathbed died in the same epidemic that killed him. Since the Incas had no rule of primogeniture, but settled authority on the one most able and fit to rule, struggles for succession were normal after the death of every Inca ruler. Huascar initially won with the support of the court and administration in Cuzco. Atahualpa had been left in charge of the Inca army at Quito and he probably acted as provincial governor on behalf of Huascar, for whom he was building new palaces at Tumipampa. However, Huascar suspected that Atahualpa was planning treason and sent a militia army to invade Quito; it was defeated by the Inca army, which was loyal to Atahualpa. Atahualpa entered Tumipampa triumphantly and took for himself the Inca crown, the *llautu* (a red woven headband with a fringe that covered the forehead), and title of Sapa Inca (supreme Inca).

The Inca army pursued Huascar's troops to Huanacopampa, west of Cuzco, where it defeated them and took Huascar prisoner. Atahualpa's army entered Cuzco triumphantly with much local support because Huascar had alienated many of his earlier supporters, notably the lineage Hatun ayllu. Atahualpa killed members of Huascar's family and the rival lineage, Capac ayllu. (The story of a northern-southern split of the Inca empire was a fabrication of Garcilaso de la Vega that appealed to the European mentality.)

Atahualpa, celebrating his victory, began to move south slowly with his retinue when he heard of the arrival of Francisco Pizarro's third expedition. He stopped at the hot spring baths near Cajamarca with about 80,000 troops to receive the Spaniards with intentions of capturing them. However, he seriously miscalculated the effect of the Spaniards' weapons and armor and was overconfident and drunk on November 16, 1533, when Pizarro ambushed him in the main square of Cajamarca after the priest Valverde attempted to deliver a sort of *requerimiento* (formal summons to surrender and accept the church and Spanish rule on pain of suffering war and enslavement). About seven thousand of Atahualpa's retinue were killed and his troops surrendered the next morning. Atahualpa was imprisoned but offered the Spaniards a ransom, in return for his life, of a room filled once with gold and twice with silver. He was tried for treason based on rumors that his army was preparing an attack. He was prepared for burning at the stake in the main square, but was garrotted instead when he accepted Christianity and was baptized Francisco.

BIBLIOGRAPHY

Hemming, John. *The Conquest of the Incas.* San Diego, 1970.
Rostworowski de Díez Canseco, María. "Succession, Coöption to Kingship, and Royal Incest among the Inca." *Southwestern Journal of Anthropology* 16 (1960): 417–427.
Rostworowski de Díez Canseco, María. *Historia del Tahuantinsuyu.* Lima, 1988.

JEANETTE SHERBONDY

ATLANTIC RIVALRY. As soon as European explorers ventured out into the Atlantic in search of new lands and commodities to trade, the ocean became part of international rivalries, an extension of the land-based rivalries among contending European states. What might be called the Battle of the Atlantic began several centuries before Columbus's voyages and continued for several centuries thereafter.

One of the earliest European ventures far into the Atlantic reputedly occurred in the sixth century, when an Irish monk named Brendan led a band of followers in search of a pristine land where they could worship God free from the distractions of life at home. It is not clear how far they ventured or even if the voyage occurred at all, but the legend of this monk, who later became Saint

Brendan, continued to inspire European Christians in Columbus's time and beyond. At the start of the eleventh century Viking explorers began sailing westward across the north Atlantic from their Scandinavian homelands to the Shetland and Orkney Islands, and then to Iceland, Greenland, and to what would later be called North America. Neither the voyages of Saint Brendan nor the voyages of Leif Ericsson and his compatriots seem to have inspired rivals, however. They occurred before long-distance trade had developed fully enough to generate much profit, and before the population had risen enough to make the acquisition of new lands very attractive to the countries that rimmed the Atlantic.

Both European trade and population expanded considerably in the centuries after Leif Ericsson sailed, and governments rose that could tap the resources of their people and use them to pursue national goals. Among those goals were new sources of food and trade goods to enhance their countries' wealth. The scope and volume of trade in late medieval Europe had two main poles of development: the northern Atlantic and Baltic coastlines and the Mediterranean. Commercial cities in those two areas became the prime movers of late medieval trade and its main beneficiaries, although inland cities that controlled vital trade goods also played a role. In southern Europe, Portugal was ideally located to participate in both poles of medieval trade. Portugal and its late medieval monarchs identified their interests much more with the Atlantic than with the Mediterranean, however, seeking out supplies of grain and fish along the coasts of northern and western Africa as the population grew. Another powerful African lure was gold, which arrived in the ports of the Mediterranean overland from sources south of the Sahara desert. The trans-Saharan trade was controlled by Muslim merchants, but the Portuguese were quick to see the possibilities of a sea-borne approach to the sources of African gold. Castile, Portugal's neighbor and rival in the Iberian Peninsula, saw the same possibilities in African fishing and trade. Their rivalry would intensify during the fifteenth century.

Partly in pursuit of trade and partly as a continuation of its rivalry with the Islamic world of the Mediterranean, Portugal reached across the Strait of Gibraltar to conquer Ceuta in Morocco in 1415. This conquest gave the Portuguese a trading port in North Africa and a Mediterranean foothold as well. From this foothold, Portuguese merchants exported grain, textiles, and the products of the trans-Saharan caravan trade, primarily gold and slaves. From Ceuta the Portuguese explored westward and southward along the African coast, expanding their trading network and searching for a sea route around Africa toward Asia. Although local African rulers were powerful on land, they had little interest in the sea. Except for

Castile, Portugal had no serious rivals on Africa's Atlantic coast during the fifteenth century.

The situation was similar farther out to sea, although various European powers had been interested in exploring the Atlantic west of southern Europe for several centuries. The first documented voyage after Saint Brendan involved an expedition in 1291 led by two brothers from Genoa, Ugolino and Vadino Vivaldi. At that time attempts to establish overland trade with Asia were being thwarted by the breakup of Mongol authority. Moreover, the last Christian enclave in the Middle East, left from the days of the Crusades, had fallen under Muslim control again. Any future trade would depend on the changeable attitudes of whoever controlled the trade routes. In search of the markets of Asia, the Vivaldi brothers sailed southward from Europe as far as the latitude of the Canary Islands, but they were not heard about thereafter, except in legend.

The Canaries had been known to classical antiquity as the Fortunate Isles, but they and the other Atlantic islands did not engage the serious interest of southern Europeans until the fourteenth century. Sometime before 1340 a Genoese named Lancellotto Malocello explored the Canaries and gave his name to the island of Lanzarote in that chain. In 1341 the king of Portugal launched an expedition composed of Portuguese, Castilians, Florentines, and Genoese to conquer the Canaries, but it evidently failed. Also in the 1340s Clement VI, the pope in Avignon, authorized a nobleman named Luis de la Cerda, who held titles in both Spain and France, to conquer and rule various islands in the Atlantic. While he readied his expedition in France with help from Aragón, both Portugal and Castile argued that they had prior claims. Clearly, the Atlantic islands were becoming valuable prizes. De la Cerda's expedition and his claim came to nothing, however. He died, and Europe was overtaken by the Black Death in 1348. From the 1340s on, the Canaries were visited by several small expeditions, one of them a missionary effort sponsored by the king of Aragón to Christianize the islanders. Mariners from Andalusia also visited the islands regularly at the end of the fourteenth century. In 1402 the Crown of Castile began the definitive conquest of the Canaries, granting patents to captains who would claim the lands for Castile. These captains recovered their investment, first by capturing and selling slaves and later by establishing sugar plantations.

Like the Canaries, the Madeira islands attracted the interest of several rival groups of Europeans from the late thirteenth or early fourteenth century. As mariners ventured out farther into the Atlantic, the winds and currents ensured that they would eventually reach the Madeiras. By the late fourteenth and early fifteenth centuries both Portuguese and Castilian ships stopped there for wood and for the red dye called "dragon's blood," a resin from the so-called dragon tree. The Madeiras were uninhabited, and no serious attempts were made to colonize them until Castile sent a large force to the islands in 1417. In response King João I of Portugal sponsored an expedition of about one hundred people to colonize the islands for Portugal. Grain, sugar, and other agricultural products made the islands of Madeira and Porto Santo profitable colonies from about 1450 on.

The northernmost of the Atlantic islands, the Azores, were discovered in 1427 by Portugal, which probably began to colonize them in 1432. Eventually they produced profitable exports of grain and dyestuffs, but sugar had little success. The Cape Verde Islands, close to the African coast off Senegal, were probably reached by the Portuguese in 1455 and quickly developed into a center for the growing slave trade. The islands were soon producing cotton and cotton cloth, the latter a key item in bartering for slaves on the mainland. Local seashells were also prized, and a certain variety was used as money on the mainland. In all, the Portuguese were able to turn handsome profits from their island colonies, which attracted rivals.

Through the fifteenth century regular voyaging to the Atlantic islands and tentative exploration continued. During the years that Columbus was in Portugal, he became familiar with Portuguese outposts on the African coast and the Atlantic islands and the sea lanes that served them. Undoubtedly this experience contributed to the formulation of his grand design of sailing west to reach Asia. In the meantime, the Portuguese were concentrating their efforts on exploration southward, trying to round Africa to establish a sea route to the Far East. Castilian mariners continued to challenge the Portuguese in these pursuits. Their rivalry in the Atlantic was one of the issues involved in Portugal's intervention in the Castilian civil war of 1475–79. As part of the settlement between Portugal and Castile, the Treaty of Alcáçovas-Toledo set out spheres of influence in the Atlantic for the two Iberian powers. By the terms of the treaty, Castile recognized Portugal's title to the Azores, the Madeiras, and the Cape Verdes in return for Portuguese recognition of Castile's title to the Canaries.

More important, Castile accepted a Portuguese monopoly on new discoveries in the Atlantic from the Canaries southward and toward the African coast. In 1481 the pope granted Portugal a "bull," or charter, ratifying this monopoly. The bull, called *Aeterni Regis,* was followed by four other papal grants in the wake of Columbus's first voyage. In the first two, Pope Alexander VI, fortunately for Spanish pretentions a member of the Borja (Borgia) family of Valencia, granted Castile all lands discovered or to be discovered in the area Columbus had explored. The third bull, called *Inter caetera,* drew a north-south line one hundred leagues west of the Azores and the Cape Verdes. The Portuguese sphere of influence would lie east of the line, the Castilian sphere west of the line.

To that point, Portugal could accept that its interests as well as Castile's were served by papal intervention. The fourth bull, *Dudum siquidem,* changed that perception. Because it extended Castilian control to all lands west, south, and east of India, the main focus of Portuguese efforts, João II of Portugal protested. When the pope refused to change his mind, João approached Isabel and Fernando directly and persuaded them to negotiate. The rival claims of both parties were settled in 1494 with the Treaty of Tordesillas. It redrew Pope Alexander VI's dividing line at 370 leagues west of the Azores and the Cape Verdes, ratifying Portugal's title to its outposts in Africa and its eastern route to India (plus Brazil, as it happened). The recognition was particularly important because Bartolomeu Dias had rounded the cape of southern Africa in 1487–1488, clearing the way for a Portuguese sea route to India. Castile gained an undisputed claim to what would become its empire in the western hemisphere.

Other countries in Europe, especially England and France, were also interested in Atlantic exploration, especially after Columbus's 1492 voyage proved that lands lay close enough to the west to be feasibly explored and exploited. The English sponsored several voyages across the north Atlantic before 1500, the most famous being that of John Cabot (Giovanni Caboto, a Genoese) in 1497. Cabot claimed lands in present-day Labrador and Newfoundland for England. In 1499 the Portuguese Gaspar Côrte-Real followed the same route and claimed parts of Newfoundland for Portugal. In the 1502 map known as the Cantino planisphere, commissioned by a Portuguese nobleman, the lands claimed by Côrte-Real were depicted on the Portuguese side of the demarcation line established by the Treaty of Tordesillas, presumably to avoid conflict with Castile. John Cabot's claims for England were not shown at all. By then Portugal had found another prize in the Atlantic: Brazil. The Portuguese had discovered that the best way to round the landmass of Africa lay in sailing southwestward from Iberia into the Atlantic on the prevailing winds and currents, until intersecting the winds and currents that flowed southeastward. On one of those voyages in 1500, Pedro Álvares Cabral encountered the bulge of Brazil jutting out into the Atlantic, clearly on the Portuguese side of the demarcation line. By 1500, even before Europeans realized that the lands they had found were not in Asia, various countries had staked out claims to own and exploit them and were in the process of having those claims recognized by their European rivals.

In the wakes of Columbus, Cabot, Côrte-Real, and Cabral, dozens of other European mariners obtained charters of exploration for the Atlantic. Undoubtedly many of them believed those lands were a part of Asia, if somewhat removed from the fabled temples and markets of Cipangu and Cathay. Only with the circumnavigation of the globe begun by the Portuguese Ferdinand Magellan in 1519, sailing for Castile, did the true scope and nature of the world's oceans begin to be known. When the remnant of Magellan's small fleet arrived back in Spain in 1521 (minus Magellan, who had been killed in the Philippines), it became clear that a vast expanse of ocean lay between the southern extreme of the new lands and the real Asia known to Europeans since the Middle Ages. The Atlantic Ocean was the route to a New World, rather than the route from one shore of the Old World to the other.

Through most of the sixteenth century the claims that had been warily staked out by 1500 held rivalry in the Atlantic to a minimum. Castile conquered two large empires in the central and southern portions of the Western Hemisphere and created a huge bureaucratic and commercial empire in their place. Early on, pirates from rival European countries hoped to steal Castile's profits from conquest, plunder, taxation, and trade by lying in wait in the eastern Atlantic to ambush inbound voyages. A system of armed convoys organized around 1522 generally thwarted these attempts, and Castile had no serious rivals in its empire or in the sea lanes that served it for most of the sixteenth century. Portugal maintained its claim to Brazil and extracted several items of commercial value from it but did little to colonize the vast interior during the sixteenth century, concentrating instead on its trading posts in Africa and India.

In areas north of the region being developed by Castile, France took the early lead in exploration during the sixteenth century. The Florentine Giovanni Verrazano sailed for Francis I of France in 1524–1528 in search of a passage through North America to the Pacific Ocean and Cathay. Although Verrazano hoped the French would colonize the lands and Christianize the natives of North America, the markets of Asia remained the goal of Francis I and his court. Jacques Cartier's voyages in 1534–1542 continued the fruitless search. Ironically, in the early sixteenth century European rivalry in the Atlantic centered on a battle for the Pacific. The Spanish made similar attempts to find a passage through North America, for the same reasons and with the same results. They made no attempt to colonize or hold the area they explored, although Spanish fishermen and whalers regularly visited the coasts of Newfoundland and Labrador and frequently spent the winter there.

In the late sixteenth century English mariners began to take a greater interest in exploration, and under Elizabeth I a series of expeditions interloped on the monopoly claimed by Spain in the Western Hemisphere while continuing the search for a northwest passage. As relations between England and Spain deteriorated in the 1560s, a new battle for the Atlantic ensued. At stake were control of the lands across the Atlantic and the profits Spain reaped from trade, although the Northwest Passage to Asia remained a central goal of English exploration for centuries to come. Francis Drake, Martin Frobisher, Humphrey Gilbert, and others all made the attempt. Walter Raleigh tried to establish a permanent English colony in 1585–1586 in what was called Virginia, part of the land claimed but not effectively settled by Spain, but the attempt failed. Nonetheless, English and Dutch incursions into the Caribbean intensified in the late sixteenth century, provoking a strong Spanish response.

When pressed, Spain could muster the resources to defend its colonies and its trade monopoly in the Western Hemisphere. Portugal could do likewise, ousting the Dutch from northwest Brazil after a hard-fought struggle in the 1640s. Still, neither Spain nor Portugal could satisfy all the needs of their vast American empires without products from the rest of Europe. The English, French, and Dutch realized that the best hope of profit lay in diplomatic agreements with Spain and Portugal and in founding permanent colonies of their own. By a series of treaties in the seventeenth century, the rest of Europe recognized the titles of Spain and Portugal to their American empires. In exchange, they were able to trade freely with the Spanish and Portuguese empires, either legally through the established monopolies, or clandestinely through a widespread contraband trade that was openly acknowledged by all concerned. By about 1650 rivalry in the Atlantic had established spheres of influence that closely resembled the situation in 1500, with no one power in control of trade and the sea lanes, and the lands in control of whoever could hold them effectively.

[See also *Exploration and Discovery; Trade.*]

BIBLIOGRAPHY

Andrews, Kenneth. *The Spanish Caribbean: Trade and Plunder 1530–1630.* New Haven, 1978.

Davies, K. G. *The North Atlantic World in the Seventeenth Century.* Minneapolis, 1974.

Diffie, Bailey W., and George D. Winius. *Foundations of the Portuguese Empire, 1415–1580.* Minneapolis, 1977.

Fernández-Armesto, Felipe. *Before Columbus: Exploration and Colonization from the Mediterranean to the Atlantic, 1229–1492.* Philadelphia, 1987.

McAlister, Lyle N. *The Growth of the Iberian Empires to about 1650–1700.* Minneapolis, 1974.

Morison, Samuel Eliot. *The European Discovery of America: The Northern Voyages A. D. 500–1600.* New York, 1971.

Morison, Samuel Eliot. *The European Discovery of America: The Southern Voyages A. D. 1492–1616.* New York, 1974.

Parry, J. H. *The Age of Reconnaissance: Discovery, Exploration and Settlement 1450–1650.* New York, 1969.

CARLA RAHN PHILLIPS

ÁVILA, PEDRO ARIAS DE (1440?–1530), Spanish soldier and colonial governor. Disturbing rumors coming out of Tierra Firme (in present-day Panama) in 1513 concerning the conduct of Vasco Núñez de Balboa's government there caused the Spanish king to appoint a courtier, Pedro Arias de Ávila, known as Pedrárias Dávila, governor of the colony and to authorize him to investigate Balboa's actions. Pedrárias, a native of Segovia and a minor member of the Spanish nobility, was a veteran of Spanish campaigns in North Africa. Close to the bishop of Burgos, he was an important royal adviser.

Pedrárias took with him nearly fifteen hundred people, including retainers, settlers, and adventurers. This expedition served as a testing ground for later conquests. Important among the members of the expedition were Hernando de Soto, Bernal Díaz del Castillo, and Gonzalo Fernández de Oviedo. Díaz, in his famous history of the conquest of Mexico, indicates that many members of the expedition who failed to gain wealth moved on to other, later adventures.

The government of Pedrárias in Tierra Firme was marked by cruelty and division. From the outset, the small colony was split between followers of Balboa and those of the new governor, both of whom claimed royal authority over the region. The presence of gold and the growing strategic importance of the place heightened the stakes in the conflict. Balboa opted to move to the Pacific coast, away from Pedrárias's sphere of activities. But he kept in close contact with affairs at court in Spain, sending many letters home denouncing his rival's excesses. Balboa hoped that the reform movement in Spain would eventually call Pedrárias back, allowing Balboa to regain his monopoly in power. But Pedrárias intercepted some of these communications and charged Balboa with treason. When word reached the colony that a royal investigator had been sent out to proceed against Pedrárias, he contrived the arrest of Balboa, who after a brief trial was executed.

In 1519, Pedrárias formally founded the territory of Panama, having moved northward from the original settlement of Santa María la Antigua de Darién. This new territory encompassed all of the original jurisdiction acquired by Balboa, as well as the Pacific coast granted to the latter under his title as adelantado. Although Pedrárias is noted for his ruthlessness, and especially for the execution of Balboa, he is credited with expanding the Spaniards' geographical knowledge of Central America. He organized many expeditions north and south of Panama, laying the groundwork for later conquests of

Nicaragua and eventually of Peru. The important conquistadores Gil González Dávila and Francisco Pizarro served under Pedrárias's direction. His expeditions were basically searches for slaves, gold, and precious stones. Through his exploitation of the region he was able to maintain himself and finance further explorations.

He died while serving as governor of the province of Nicaragua. His career had put his stamp on the southern sector of Central America, much of which he had controlled and explored himself. Service under him became one of the features linking the conquests of Mexico and Peru.

BIBLIOGRAPHY

Alvarez Rubiano, Pablo. *Pedrarias Dávila: Contribución al estudio de la figura del "Gran Justador."* Madrid, 1944.

Sauer, Carl Ortwin. *The Early Spanish Main.* Berkeley, 1966.

JOHN F. SCHWALLER

AYLLÓN, LUCAS VÁZQUEZ DE (1480?–1526), judge of the audiencia of Santo Domingo and colonizer of North America. Ayllón was born in Toledo, Spain, to a family whose ancestors had been leaders of the Mozarabic community (Christians who had remained in Toledo under Muslim rule). Educated in the law, he served as alcalde mayor, or superior judge, of the mining district of La Española from 1504 to 1509. While in Spain from 1509 to 1513, he obtained his licenciate and was appointed one of the judges of the audiencia of Santo Domingo when it was created in 1511 (he served in that office until his death). In 1523 he became a member of the Military Order of Santiago.

On June 24, 1521, a pilot sailing under his sponsorship made the first recorded landing on the coast of South Carolina, at the Santee River. Granted a contract to explore and settle this "new discovery," which he falsely claimed was at the latitude of Andalusia, Spain, Ayllón sent Pedro de Quejo to explore from Cumberland Island, Georgia, to the Delaware Bay in 1525. On or about September 29, 1526, Ayllón founded a Spanish colony, San Miguel de Gualdape, in the territory of the Guale Indians, in the vicinity of Sapelo Sound, Georgia, after initially landing at the Santee River–Winyah Bay area. His death at San Miguel resulted in the abandonment of the site by early November 1526.

Ayllón gained a reputation as a learned if partial judge and as an exploiter of his office for personal gain. In addition to holding properties in Spain and La Española, he engaged in the trade in Indian slaves. As a judge of the audiencia, he was a key figure in royal efforts to vitiate the powers that Diego Colón, Columbus's son and heir, won in his lawsuit over Columbus's privileges. Among other

things, he carried the audiencia's complaints and charges against Colón to Spain in 1521.

Ayllón's colonial activities were part of the wave of continental explorations and settlements that began in 1514. By that date, Columbus's belief that he had found Asian islands and the Malay Peninsula had been discredited, and the early Spanish exploiters of the New World had nearly exhausted the Indian groups and gold mines he had discovered. Also, the limitation in 1511 of Diego Colón's claims of government and a right to a percentage of revenues cleared the way for the king and his officials to encourage exploration and exploitation of areas not found during the Columbian voyages.

Ayllón's claim of the discovery of a new Andalusia survived in the writings of Pietro Martire d'Anghiera (Peter Martyr) and influenced later French and English colonial ventures at Port Royal Sound and Roanoke Island, respectively. Quejo's information about the North American coast was the basis for official Spanish maps until the 1560s.

BIBLIOGRAPHY

Hoffman, Paul E. *A New Andalucia and a Way to the Orient: The American Southeast in the Sixteenth Century.* Baton Rouge, La., 1990.

Malagón Barcelo, Javier. "Un oidor conquistador." *Eme-Eme, Estudios Dominicanos,* no. 25 (July-August 1976): 3–18.

PAUL E. HOFFMAN

AYLLÓN, LUCAS VÁZQUEZ DE (1514?–1565?), contractor for colonization of North America from 1562 to 1564. Born Juan Vázquez de Ayllón at Santo Domingo, this eldest son of Licenciado Lucas Vázquez de Ayllón (1480?–1526) took his father's name after coming of age. While married to Isabel de Pasamonte, niece of his father's political ally Miguel de Pasamonte, he went to Spain in 1547 but did not press his rights, as his father's heir, to colonize North America. In 1561, however, the rediscovery of Chesapeake Bay revealed an area of more promise than those his father had explored and tried to settle. Ayllón then pressed his claim.

Ayllón the Younger was awarded a contract on February 28, 1562, to establish a small agricultural colony, probably at Chesapeake Bay. Problems of raising money and worries about the French colony at Port Royal Sound delayed his sailing until September 1563. His expedition broke up at Santo Domingo, and he fled to Santa Marta (Colombia) to escape debts. Persuaded to engage in conquest there, he was killed by Indians during a slave-and gold-seeking raid.

Ayllón the Younger's colonial venture was the last of the unsuccessful Spanish attempts to colonize North America.

The collapse of Jean Ribault's Charlesfort colony meant that his failure did not have immediate consequences for Spain's claims to the continent, although his venture did delay Spanish occupation three more years, until 1565. By then Philip II was willing once again to put royal money behind a Spanish colony, as he had with Tristan de Luna from 1559 to 1561.

BIBLIOGRAPHY

Hoffman, Paul E. *A New Andalucia and a Way to the Orient: The American Southeast in the Sixteenth Century.* Baton Rouge, La., 1990.

PAUL E. HOFFMAN

AZORES. The Azores Islands, located between latitudes 36°50'N and 39°44'N and between longitudes 25°W and 31°16'W, are about 1,450 kilometers (900 miles) west of Portugal. Between 1440 and 1470 the previously uninhabited islands were colonized by Portugal. The archipelago has nine principal islands: the western islands of Flores and Corvo, the central islands of Fayal, Pico, São Jorge, Graciosa, and Terceira, and the eastern islands of São Miguel and Santa Maria.

Because of their position nearly halfway across the Atlantic Ocean toward Newfoundland, the Azores have a mild maritime climate with plentiful rainfall, particularly from winter storms. The islands lie along the southern boundary of the prevailing westerlies, where winds can be variable but are predominantly from the west. Ocean currents in the vicinity of the Azores flow from west to east, in the region where the warm Gulf Stream broadens as it flows across the North Atlantic Ocean to form the North Atlantic Current. These winds and currents made the Azores an unfavorable place to start westward voyages of discovery.

The Azores were strategically located for sailing on northward and eastward voyages. In spite of the extra distance, it took less time for ships traveling from the west coast of Africa to return to Portugal via the Azores than to fight the northerly winds and the southward Canary Current closer to the African coast. The islands provided much-needed supplies as well as safe harbors. Columbus stopped at the island of Santa Maria after experiencing a strong winter storm on his return from the first trip to the New World.

BIBLIOGRAPHY

Duncan, T. Bentley. *Atlantic Islands: Madeira, the Azores and the Cape Verdes in Seventeenth-Century Commerce and Navigation.* Chicago, 1972.

McAlister, Lyle N. *Spain and Portugal in the New World, 1492–1700.* Minneapolis, 1984.

Morison, Samuel Eliot. *Admiral of the Ocean Sea: A Life of Christopher Columbus.* 2 vols. Boston, 1942.

Rudloff, Willy. *World-Climates.* Stuttgart, 1981.

COLLEEN A. LEARY

AZTECS. See *Indian America*, article on *Aztecs and Their Neighbors*.

B

BACON, ROGER (between 1210 and 1215–1292), philosopher and scientist. Little is known of Bacon's life save for some sparse information that Bacon himself provides in his work. He studied at Oxford University and the University of Paris, where he likely developed his lifelong interest in natural philosophy and optics. He entered the Franciscan order sometime between 1251 and 1257. All three of his major works—*Opus maius, Opus minus,* and *Opus tertium*—were completed by 1267, apparently in response to Pope Clement IV's formal request of June 22, 1266.

Opus maius is the most comprehensive and historically significant of Bacon's works, a kind of encyclopedia or compendium of the knowledge of his day. Following the introductory section, "Causes of Error," the book is arranged in six sections devoted to philosophy, foreign languages, mathematics, optical science, experimental science, and moral philosophy. The work appears to have two principal purposes: to underline the role that knowledge plays in the salvation of the Christian and to demonstrate the power of knowledge as a tool in the rational (as distinct from forcible) conversion of the non-Christian.

Around 150 years after Bacon completed *Opus maius,* the influential late medieval thinker Pierre d'Ailly (1350–1420) copied substantial sections of it into a number of short interrelated works that he composed between 1410 and 1414. Christopher Columbus read and annotated an early edition of these works printed by John of Westphalia between 1480 and 1483. The section of *Opus maius* given to mathematics appears to have been a particularly important source for d'Ailly's and hence Columbus's conceptions of geography and history.

D'Ailly's discussion of the size and shape of the earth and the disposition of the land and sea draws upon important ancient and early medieval sources. In *Opus maius* Bacon had suggested (as had Aristotle before him) that it should be possible to sail from Spain to the Indies. D'Ailly copied this passage into the eighth chapter of one of his works, *Imago mundi.* This chapter, "De quantitate terrae inhabitabilis" (On the extent of the inhabitable earth), was heavily annotated by Columbus. His manifest interest in the contents of *Imago mundi* has led scholars generally to agree that it was a major source for Columbus's "Enterprise of the Indies"—his conviction that the Far East could be reached by sailing west across the Atlantic.

In other parts of the section on mathematics, Bacon outlined an apocalyptic vision of history, paying particular attention to astrological and prophetic materials that he believed provided the basis for marking events that would presage the imminent end of time and the fulfillment of the providential plan. D'Ailly also incorporated these passages into other works contained in the collection used by Columbus. Columbus annotated these works and

ROGER BACON. From a French medal, 1818.

copied a number of passages for inclusion in a work he never completed, his Book of Prophecies.

In the prefatory letter to Fernando and Isabel that accompanies the Book of Prophecies, Columbus indicates that he intended to place his achievements and those of his monarchs within a framework of apocalyptic history traceable back to late antiquity through the works of Bacon and d'Ailly. Columbus was probably not aware that in reading d'Ailly he was frequently reading Bacon. But his indirect use of *Opus maius* gives its thirteenth-century author, Roger Bacon, a significant role in the genesis of the "Enterprise of the Indies."

[See also *Writings*, article on *Book of Prophecies*.]

BIBLIOGRAPHY

Bacon, Roger. *The Opus Maius of Roger Bacon*. Translated by Robert Belle Burke. Philadelphia, 1928.

Watts, Pauline Moffitt. "Prophecy and Discovery: On the Spiritual Origins of Christopher Columbus's 'Enterprise of the Indies.'" *American Historical Review* 90 (1985): 73–102.

PAULINE MOFFITT WATTS

BAHAMAS. The Bahama Islands stretch in a chain about 1,300 kilometers (800 miles) long from near the Florida coast to a point near the north coast of Hispaniola (La Española). There are about seven hundred islands, of which thirty are inhabited. The sea between them is mostly shallow, whence their Spanish name, Bajamar, or "shallow water." In the fifteenth century the Bahamas were inhabited by the Lucayans, a branch of the Arawak family of peoples. We know little about their way of life but must suppose that it resembled that of their better-studied cousins on the Greater Antilles.

After Columbus had crossed the Atlantic in October 1492 he made landfall at the Lucayan island of Guanahani, which has been traditionally identified with the island of San Salvador. Here he found the land "very green and fertile" and the Lucayans friendly, though he soon passed through the chain and into the seas around the Greater Antilles, where he thought there was more possibility of finding gold.

After this initial reconnaissance the islands were largely neglected, except for frequent slaving raids by the Spaniards during the 1490s and 1500s. It has been estimated that forty thousand Lucayans were captured and sent to work in the mines of La Española between 1492 and 1508, with the result that the islands were quite depopulated. Nor were Europeans quick to resettle them, for despite their strategic position covering the routes back to Europe from the Spanish Main, they were not as attractive as the Greater Antilles in terms of agriculture, and indeed they were easily eroded once Europeans did establish intensive agriculture there in the eighteenth century.

[See also *Indian America*, article on *Arawaks and Caribs*. See *Landfall Controversy* for discussion of the Bahamas as the scene of Columbus's first landing in the New World.]

BIBLIOGRAPHY

Craton, Michael. *A History of the Bahamas*. Waterloo, Ont., 1986.

DAVID BUISSERET

BALBOA, VASCO NÚÑEZ DE (c. 1475–1519), Spanish explorer and colonial governor. Although not a conqueror of great empires, Vasco Núñez de Balboa ranks as one of a handful of the most important participants in the discovery and conquest of the Americas. His major accomplishment was the first European sighting of the Pacific Ocean, but his career was paradigmatic of that of many conquerors and early settlers of the Americas.

Balboa came from the Extremaduran town of Jerez de los Caballeros, although some authors claim that he came from the larger nearby city of Badajoz. The exact date of his arrival in the Indies is unknown, but certainly by 1500 he was in the New World. He sailed with Rodrigo de Bastidas and Juan de la Cosa on their expedition to the Gulf of Urabá and the coast of Panama. Following that, he settled in Salvatierra de la Sábana on the island of La Española, where the conqueror of Cuba, Diego Velázquez, also resided.

Following Bastidas's explorations of the Panama coast, the region was hotly contested by two other explorers, Diego de Nicuesa and Alonso de Ojeda. By a royal concession of 1508, Tierra Firme was divided into two parcels, the easterly, called Urabá, under the leadership of Ojeda, and the westerly, Veragua, under Nicuesa. Ojeda had made several expeditions to the northern coast of South America, and by 1505 he had been given the right to explore and settle the Gulf of Urabá. The region had already been visited, not only by Bastidas but also by Cosa on his own, and by others. Cosa had joined with Ojeda, and they had established a town at San Sebastian. Subsequently, Cosa died from a poisoned arrow, and Ojeda fled back to La Española. Nicuesa had little better luck in his concession. Martín Fernández de Enciso was sent from La Española to relieve the settlement which was besieged by Indians. Balboa went with him, having, according to traditional sources, stowed away in a barrel. It was he who suggested that the survivors be resettled on the western side of the Gulf of Urabá where the Indians did not use poisoned arrows. The settlement, Santa María la Antigua del Darién, became one of the more successful of the early attempts at colonization.

Soon after arriving at Darién, Balboa was elected as a justice of the town and ultimately gained near-total control of the settlement. Nicuesa and his followers were brought to Darién, where they were tried for failure to comply with royal authority: Nicuesa had rather foolishly claimed that he had ultimate authority over Darién by virtue of his royal grants. The members of the Fernández de Enciso expedition found Nicuesa guilty, but his death sentence was commuted, pending his appeal before the governor in La Española. The ship made available to Nicuesa and his men for the return to La Española leaked badly, however, and it never reached its destination. Balboa and his supporters then ousted Fernández de Enciso and forced him to return to La Española, thereby making Balboa's control complete.

As the leader of the group, Balboa demonstrated many of the characteristics common among the later Spanish conquistadores. Although he manifested fierce opposition to idolatry and native practices, he was also able to establish an accord with indigenous groups. He maintained peace with the Indians and stipulated regular tribute from them, thereby protecting the Spanish settlers from reprisals while extracting from the Indians a modicum of food and labor.

After making several explorations of the immediate hinterland and collecting information from local inhabitants, Balboa became convinced of a source of gold overland to the west from Darién. In early 1513 he outlined his plans in a letter to the king. This news stirred such excitement that a relief expedition was put together under the leadership of the courtier Pedro Arias de Ávila (Pedrárias), who was also to serve as a judicial investigator into Balboa's rule, especially concerning the trial of Nicuesa and banishment of Fernández de Enciso.

Balboa set off on his expedition to the west around September 1, 1513. About September 27, he caught sight of the Pacific. A few days later, he strode into the surf with sword and banner and claimed the whole sea for the king of Spain. The expedition continued along the Pacific coast, finding important pearl fisheries. By New Year's Day, they were back where they had begun. He had discovered the Pacific Ocean and come across villages that crafted objects in gold, but he had not found the actual source of the gold.

Pedrárias arrived at Darién in June 1514, and thereafter conditions in the settlement worsened. Accompanying him were many Spaniards such as Hernando de Soto and Bernal Díaz del Castillo who would play important roles in further adventures. Pedrárias ruled the region with an iron hand, dispatching numerous punitive raids against what were largely peaceful Indians. Scores of Spaniards, especially among the newcomers, died as a result of Indian resistance and from tropical diseases. The tension between the two captains mounted. Balboa attempted to absent himself from Darién, choosing to occupy the western coast of Panama and begin efforts to exploit his concession as adelantado of that region. He maintained correspondence with the Spanish Crown, continually denouncing the excesses of Pedrárias and hoping that reform efforts on the peninsula might oust his rival. Nevertheless, as a royal investigator was being sent to the colony, Pedrárias arrested Balboa on charges of treason and after a brief trial had him executed.

Balboa was typical of the explorers of his time. He was coolly pragmatic in his dealing with the Indians. He was cruel at times, but overall he recognized the importance of keeping the native peoples as allies rather than making them enemies. He never failed at any of his enterprises. His settlement of Darién and his discovery for the Spanish of the Pacific opened a new chapter in the history of exploration of the continent.

BIBLIOGRAPHY

Romoli, Kathleen. *Balboa of Darien: Discoverer of the Pacific.* Garden City, N.Y., 1953.

Sauer, Carl Ortwin. *The Early Spanish Main.* Berkeley, 1966.

Vigneras, Louis-André. *The Discovery of South America and the Andalusian Voyages.* Chicago, 1976.

JOHN F. SCHWALLER

BARCELONA. The "head and hearth" (*cap i casal*) of Catalonia, Barcelona was the major commercial, naval, and administrative center of the Crown of Aragón during the late Middle Ages. Centrally located on the Catalan coast, it possessed easy communications with the Pyrenean hinterland and a Mediterranean-wide trade network. In 1358, a decade after the Black Death, the city contained roughly thirty-five thousand inhabitants, a size it maintained for a century. Long the hub of royal administration and the depository of extensive royal archives, Barcelona also became the permanent seat of the Generalitat, the standing committee of the Catalan Cortes.

Mediterranean trade laid the foundation for Barcelona's prosperity. Its merchants first redistributed goods produced elsewhere. Fine clothes from northern France and Flanders obtained in southern French ports, Sicilian grain and cotton, North African gold, wax, and slaves, Sardinian coral, Levantine spices and alum, and local leather, pelts, and wine made up the bulk of trade. After 1300 an important textile industry developed. Low-cost cloth, Catalan saffron, glassware, and silverwork increased exports. Together with smaller Catalan ports, Barcelona vied with Genoa for economic domination of the western Mediterranean.

Although subject to royal officials, Barcelona developed independent institutions. King Jaime I established a municipal assembly in 1249, which soon evolved into the Council of a Hundred with an executive body of five magistrates. In 1359 the city gained control over all municipal taxes. To finance public debts, a municipal bank was set up in 1401. Merchants, too, carved out their own jurisdiction. The first Iberian Consulate of the Sea, a maritime guild whose court settled business disputes, was functioning by 1283. The rules established there form the core of the *Llibre del consolat de mar*, the first systematic compilation of maritime commercial law. The construction of a spacious Gothic mercantile exchange, vastly expanded royal shipyards, and an impressive town council hall provided elegant testimony to the city's fourteenth-century prosperity. An ambitious breakwater was begun in 1439; its completion took more than twenty years.

Despite challenges and temporary setbacks, Barcelona retained its preeminence in the Crown of Aragón until the disastrous civil wars of 1462–1472. The municipal leadership had split into two factions, the Busca and the Biga, which were sharply divided over trade protectionism and monetary devaluation. The resulting internal instability and bitter warfare dealt the city a devastating blow. Its population fell to twenty thousand, and its commerce foundered. Fernando of Aragón aided Barcelona by granting it trading and industrial privileges and by reforming the strident town council in 1493 and 1498. A modest recovery ensued, but the damage had been done. Sixteenth-century Barcelona became rigidly stratified and its economy stagnant, profiting only marginally and indirectly from Spain's Atlantic empire.

On April 20, 1493, Fernando and Isabel ceremoniously received Columbus at Barcelona where he arrived with news of his first voyage. Since the city had long ceased to be the preferred residence for Aragonese monarchs, the site of the reception was coincidental but perfectly appropriate. The great Atlantic explorer had come to render homage in the city that centuries earlier had pioneered Iberian Mediterranean expansion.

BIBLIOGRAPHY

Amelang, James S. *Honored Citizens of Barcelona: Patrician Culture and Class Relations, 1490–1714.* Princeton, 1986.

Batlle Gallart, Carmen. *La crisis social y económica de Barcelona a mediados del siglo XV.* 2 vols. Barcelona, 1973.

Capmany y de Monpalau, A. de. *Memorias históricas sobre la antigua ciudad de Barcelona.* 3 vols. 2d ed. Edited by E. Giralt and C. Batlle. Barcelona, 1961–1963.

Carrère, Claude. *Barcelone: Centre économique, 1380–1462.* 2 vols. Paris, 1967.

STEPHEN P. BENSCH

BEHAIM, MARTIN (c. 1436–1507), German geographer. The problems raised by the Martin Behaim globe, the oldest extant globe, dating from around 1492, are similar to those related to the Henricus Martellus map. In both cases we are dealing with what can be regarded as "Portuguese-German" cartography of the end of the fifteenth and the beginning of the sixteenth century—that is, with cartographic objects made by Germans, but based on Portuguese prototypes and geographic knowledge.

The contributions of Martin Behaim (or Martinho of Bohemia, as he was called in Portugal) were probably much overrated in the historiography of the nineteenth century by Alexander von Humboldt and other authors (particularly Germans). Clearly, Behaim's role must have been negligible in the development of the scientific foundation for the Portuguese discoveries, particularly as regards celestial navigation. The reality of the part he played has long since been established in such studies as those of the English author Ernest Ravenstein and the Portuguese writers Joaquim Bensaude, Fontura da Costa, Luciano Pereira da Silva, and more recently, Luís de Albuquerque. Even today, however, some subscribe to the old myths, citing the German influence on Iberian navigational science and the fantastic voyages that Behaim made with the Portuguese to the Cape of Good Hope before Bartolomeu Dias, to America before Columbus, and as far as the Straits of Magellan.

Behaim, who came from Nürnberg, lived in Portugal as a commercial correspondent charged with financial responsibilities, like many other Germans and Italians (Columbus and Amerigo Vespucci are examples). His knowledge of cosmography and mathematics was certainly limited, and his knowledge of nautical and geographical science would have come from the Portuguese. Contrary to what has been suggested by João de Barros, it has been clearly shown that the development of celestial navigation in Portugal was independent of any influence from Behaim, who would have been transmitting the ideas of the German cosmographer Regiomontanus. Portuguese nautical science had its origin in the astronomy of Iberians such as Abraham Zacuto and Joseph Vizinho, not in that of Regiomontanus. The tables of the sun's declination used later in Portuguese celestial navigation, for example, came from the *Almanach perpetuum* of Zacuto, not from the *Ephemerides* or *Tabulae directionem* of Regiomontanus. And certainly there never was an institutionalized board of mathematicians at the service of the Portuguese king João II. There likely were some cosmographers and astrologers from whom the king regularly sought counsel, but they were predominantly Jewish astronomer-astrologers.

In 1492, while on a visit to his native city, Behaim constructed or first presented his famous globe. On it, Africa appears with a great extension to the south and east, in an image similar to that on the Martellus map. Did this extension correspond to the concepts actually prevalent in Portugal or rather reflect a distortion resulting from incorrect information? This is not an easy question to answer, with regard to either Behaim's globe or the Martellus map.

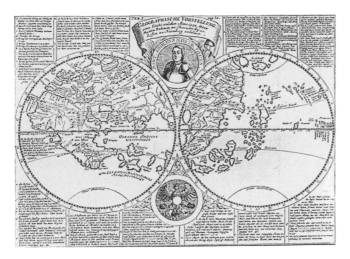

BEHAIM'S GEOGRAPHY OF THE WORLD. Based on his globe of 1492.

ELSEVIER PUBLISHING PROJECTS, AMSTERDAM

BIBLIOGRAPHY

Chillany, Friedrich Wilhelm. *Geschichte des Seefahrers Ritter Martin Behaim, nach der ältesten vorhandenen Urkunden.* Nürnberg, 1853.

Dodge, Robert. "Martin Behaim and His Globe at Nurembergh." In *Memorials of Columbus.* Maryland Historical Society. Baltimore, 1851.

"Martin Behaim and the Astrolabe." *Geographical Journal* 2, no. 2 (1893): 175.

Morris, John Gottlieb. *Martin Behaim, The German Astronomer and Cosmographer.* Maryland Historical Society. Baltimore, 1955.

Ravenstein, Ernest George. *Martin Behaim: His Life and His Globe.* London, 1908.

Ravenstein, Ernest George. "The Voyages of Diogo Cão and Bartholomew Dias, 1482–88." *Geographical Journal* 16, no. 6 (1900): 638–649.

ALFREDO PINHEIRO MARQUES
Translated from Portuguese by Rebecca Catz

There are differences between the two cartographical representations. Behaim places the extreme southern tip of Africa farther north, and he shows Dias's discoveries less clearly. Some interesting information about the Portuguese voyages along the African coast is found only on Behaim's globe, especially regarding those under the command of Diogo Cão—the placement of the first stone pillar erected by the navigator on his second voyage, for example. Behaim undoubtedly had access to Portuguese knowledge concerning the explorations south of the Gulf of Guinea. But this in no way implies that Behaim participated personally in those voyages and explorations—as he would have us believe from a passage he was certainly responsible for in the *Liber chronicarum* of Hartmann Schedel, published in Nürnberg in 1493, when Behaim was in the city. Behaim is even presented here as one of the commanders, together with Diogo Cão, of those voyages, an assertion that certainly does not correspond to reality.

Behaim was married to the daughter of a donatary-captain (grant holder) of the Portuguese islands of the Azores, and though neither a navigator nor a discoverer, he must have been familiar with the Portuguese nautical world. We owe to him the collection and transcription in Latin of an oral report made by a navigator called Diogo Gomes, who in midcentury, in the days of Henry the Navigator, had done some exploring along the African coast. This report, though enigmatic, provides priceless information about the period, for other sources are scarce. Behaim's globe, like the map of Martellus, is valuable for its documentation of the European vision of the world at the end of the Middle Ages, on the eve of the voyage of Christopher Columbus.

BENZONI, GIROLAMO (b. 1519), Italian traveler and chronicler. Born in Milan of humble parents who had been further impoverished by the wars of the time. Benzoni, aged twenty-two, left his native city to travel in France, Germany, and Spain, and in 1541 sailed from Seville for the Indies in search of fortune. During his fourteen years in America—including the West Indies, Tierra Firme (modern Venezuela and Colombia), Peru, and Central America— he probably practiced his trade as silversmith and took part in many expeditions. Having acquired a few thousand ducats, and weary of travel, he determined to return home to write a book telling of "the strange and rare things" he had seen in the New World.

Benzoni's celebrated *La historia del mondo nuovo* (History of the New World) was published in Venice in 1565, with a dedication to Pope Pius IV, and reprinted in 1572 with the addition of the author's own artless line drawings. Numerous editions of the *History* were issued in the sixteenth and seventeenth centuries. The book secured wide diffusion through its inclusion in the *Grands voyages* (Great voyages), a series of handsomely made, profusely illustrated travel accounts published by the Walloon engraver Théodor de Bry and his sons Jean Théodor and Jean Israel in Frankfurt between 1590 and 1634. In this series de Bry included two editions of Benzoni's book: first Urbain Chauveton's Latin translation, issued in three parts between 1594 and 1596, and then Nicolas Hoeniger's German version in 1597. The reasons for the book's popularity are easily explained: its simple, almost naive style; its moving descriptions of Spanish cruelty to the Indians; the numerous anecdotal details; and the general effect of candor and compassion. The impact on European minds of Benzoni's heart-rending descriptions of Spanish cruelty to the Indians was greatly enhanced by de Bry's illustrations, copperplate engravings that vested the Indian figures with classic beauty and grace. The large interest in Protestant countries in works that documented the unworthy character of Spanish Catholic colonization in America certainly contributed to the popularity of Benzoni's book. Benzoni's *History* and Las Casas's *Brevíssima relación de la destruición de las Indias* (Very brief account of the destruction of the Indies) are commonly regarded as the cornerstones of the so-called Black Legend of Spanish inhumanity to the Indians.

Beginning with Benzoni's contemporary, the French chronicler André Thevet, who claimed that Benzoni had never set foot in America, the *History* came under harsh attack from critics who charged Benzoni with a strong anti-Spanish prejudice and with padding out his own scanty historical account with wholesale borrowings without acknowledgment from such chroniclers as Peter Martyr, Gonzalo Fernández de Oviedo, and Francisco López de Gómara. The historical criticism of the nineteenth century dealt severely with Benzoni. As late as 1945 the Mexican historian Carlos Pereyra was inclined to believe that Benzoni's book was a "historical fiction" used by Spain's enemies to strengthen their case.

Most modern studies, however, have tended at least partly to rehabilitate Benzoni and his work. The notion that the *History* was a literary fiction was long ago refuted by the Chilean historian José Toribio Medina, who discovered a colonial document describing Benzoni as a Milanese silversmith living in Honduras who had been pronounced a Lutheran heretic reconciled by the Mexican Inquisition in 1555. Granted the offenses of padding and plagiarism—very common among writers of the time—the book nevertheless contains a substantial body of eyewitness testimony on Spanish dealings with the Indians in the Caribbean area. The claim that Benzoni displayed a violent hostility toward Spain and the Spaniards also appears excessive. Benzoni warmly praised the Dominicans in the Indies for their efforts in behalf of the Indians, and Emperor Charles V for promulgating the famous New Laws in favor of the native peoples. Benzoni even complimented Viceroy Antonio de Mendoza for his prudence in not attempting to enforce the New Laws against the overwhelming opposition of the Spanish colonists. The Argentine historian Rómulo Carbia, a passionate defender of Spain's work in America, compared Benzoni's balanced view of the Spanish Conquest favorably with that of Las Casas. Another champion of Spain's colonial record, the Peruvian Raúl Porras Barrenechea, concluded that Benzoni's book contains valuable data on Peruvian ethnology and the history of the conquest of Peru. After a searching examination of Benzoni's travels in Venezuela, the Venezuelan scholar

Leon Croizat found that as a reporter of what he had himself seen and done, Benzoni was worthy of faith and that there was no reason to doubt that the great majority of the events he relates actually happened.

In the first book of the *History*, Benzoni gave a detailed account of Columbus and his voyages, based almost entirely on such familiar sources as the chronicles of Oviedo and Gómara. However, he defended the Italian nationality of Columbus against the "inventions" of some Spanish historians who could not abide that "an Italian had conquered such great honor and glory, not only among the Spanish nation but among all the nations of the world." For his edition of the Latin translation of Benzoni's book, de Bry prepared a series of plates dealing with Columbus and the Discovery: they include a celebration of Columbus—a triumph with mythological figures; and, among others, scenes depicting the famous anecdote of the egg, Columbus's departure on his first voyage, and his return from the third voyage in chains. They are among the earliest and finest pictorial representations of events related with the Discovery and Columbus's life.

BIBLIOGRAPHY

Benzoni, Girolamo. *History of the New World.* Translated by W. H. Smyth. London, 1857.
Benzoni, Girolamo. *La Historia del mondo nuevo.* With an introduction by Leon Croizat. Caracas, 1967.

BENJAMIN KEEN

BERNÁLDEZ, ANDRÉS (d. 1513?), chronicler, also known as Andrés Bernal. Andrés Bernáldez was born in the town of Fuentes (modern Fuentes de León) and during the reign of Fernando and Isabel served as parish priest of the village of Los Palacios, about twenty-five kilometers (fifteen miles) south of the city of Seville. He wrote an important chronicle of the reign, in which he gives detailed information about Christopher Columbus and his voyages. Columbus and Juan Rodríguez de Fonseca were his house guests in 1496 after the second voyage to America, and the admiral left some of his papers with Bernáldez at that time. The chronicler made excellent use of these documents, particularly the *First Letter from America* and accounts by passengers, such as Diego Alvarez Chanca's letter describing the second voyage.

Bernáldez closely observed natural phenomena in his own environment. His descriptions of earthquakes, locust invasions, droughts, flooding, and epidemics make his chronicle the most vivid narrative of Spain during the reign of Fernando and Isabel. His account of the epidemic (probably typhus) that swept through southern Spain in 1507 reveals the devastation of disease before the age of antibiotics. Bernáldez and his sacristan both became ill and each was bled twice. The priest survived, but his parishioners were not so lucky; in that year Bernáldez buried one-third (160 out of 500) of the children and adults in his village, including all four of the boys who served as his acolytes.

The chronicler's identity has sometimes been disputed, in part because of confusion about his last name. In the baptismal registers from 1488 to 1513 (which disappeared sometime before 1870), Andrés signed his last name both as Bernáldez and Bernal, while the only document from Seville in which he is mentioned calls him Andrés Bernal.

BIBLIOGRAPHY

Gil, Juan. "Noticia de Andrés Bernal, cura de Los Palacios." In *Temas Colombinos*. Seville, 1986.

Carriazo, Juan de Mata, and Manuel Gómez-Moreno. Introduction to *Memorias del reinado de los Reyes Católicos*, by Andrés Bernáldez. Madrid, 1962.

HELEN NADER

BIBLIOGRAPHY. The modern scholarly study of the life and writings of Christopher Columbus has four phases. The first is the discovery of the relevant written documents of an initial "discovery period" embracing Columbus's lifetime and its historical context. These have been found largely in the archives of Genoa and Spain. Except for nonwritten records like archaeological findings, portraits, and so forth, such documents provide all the available evidence. Most of the primary documents now available had been discovered by the turn of the twentieth century, although a few more have turned up since then.

The publication of these documents, frequently in large compendia, constitutes the second phase. Written records of the discovery period have appeared in various collections such as those of G. B. Spotorno, *Codice diplomatico Colombo-Americano ossia raccolta di documenti originali e inediti* (Genoa, 1823); M. F. de Navarrete, *Colección de los viajes y descubrimientos que hicieron por mar los Españoles desde fines del siglo XV . . .* (Madrid, 1825); J. F. Pacheco, et al., *Colección de documentos inéditos relativos al descubrimiento, conquista y colonización de las posesiones españolas en América y Oceania*, series 1, 42 vols. (Madrid, 1864–84), series 2, 25 vols. (Madrid, 1885–1932); and M. del Rosario Falcó y Osorio (the duchess of Berwick), *Autógrafos de Cristóbal Colón y papeles de América* (Madrid, 1892). Single documents have appeared in many and scattered publications: see Foster Provost, *Columbus: A Guide to Scholarship on His Life and Writings* (Providence, R.I., 1991), chapters 1 and 2.

The third phase of Columbus study began in the late nineteenth century. It consists of the preparation, on reliable principles, of critical editions of the primary documents. Such editions attempt to record the exact words intended by the author, with all slips of the pen corrected and all errors of transmission emended as accurately as the available evidence and the disciplines of philology and textual criticism permit. To accompany this corrected and emended, or "critical," text the editor prepares full textual notes recording all of the data on which the corrections and emendations are based, and explaining each of the editor's decisions wherever the critical text departs from the "copy text" on which the edition is based.

The copy text, as currently understood, is the manuscript that most closely represents the author's full and final intention or, if the manuscript is not extant, the earliest printed edition of it. The alternative readings that the editor must consider usually come from other manuscripts or printed editions of the same work, especially those that the author can be shown to have influenced personally. The ideal critical edition will provide the user with all the pertinent readings and make clear the reasons for every correction and every emendation of the copy text.

The primary documents include the writings from Columbus's own hand and the documents recording the context within which these were made. The first and only fully critical edition of the known writings of Columbus is Cesare de Lollis's *I scritti di Cristoforo Colombo*, in the Italian government's monumental *Raccolta di documenti e studi pubblicati dalla R. Commissione colombiana pel quarto centenario dalla scoperta dell'America*, part 1, 3 vols. in 4 tomes (Rome, 1892–1894). In the United States, the difficulty of finding and using the unwieldy and rapidly deteriorating copies of this basic edition has seriously hampered Columbus scholarship.

Since 1894, not only has the canon of Columbus's writings expanded through the discovery of previously unknown documents, but the principles of critical editing have been refined. Consequently a full re-editing has become necessary, and it is not certain that such a project is yet under way. Still, much preparatory work has been done. In recent years, Consuelo Varela's *Cristóbal Colón: Textos y documentos completos, relaciones de viajes, cartas y memoriales* (Madrid, 1982; 2d ed., rev., 1984; 3d ed., rev., 1986) has drawn together almost all the available texts (except for many of the marginal annotations in the books of Columbus's personal library and parts of the Book of Prophecies). This paperbound edition, inexpensive and highly useful, prepared by a careful and knowledgeable textual scholar, unfortunately lacks the textual notes essential to a fully critical edition and so does not answer the scholar's needs fully.

The critical editing of essential primary documents not by Columbus himself also began in the late nineteenth century and continues today. The Italian government's *Nuova raccolta colombiana* (Rome, 1988–), besides including many of the de Lollis texts from the 1892–1894 critical edition, will contain newly transcribed and edited texts of other documents, both those by Columbus that have turned up since 1894 and a large selection of the primary documents not written by Columbus.

Unfortunately, this new collection does not offer a new critical edition of Columbus's writings. A further monumental project, one sponsored by the University of California at Los Angeles, the *Repertorium Columbianum*, initiated by the late Fredi Chiappelli and continuing under Geoffrey Symcox, will present the documents (with facing-page English translations) of the Spanish explorations of the entire discovery period from 1492 to 1519, including Columbus's writings. A considerable philological effort is going into these texts and translations; it remains to be seen whether they will constitute a body of critical texts based on modern principles of copy-text and textual emendation.

In the absence of fully authenticated critical texts, the student of Columbus must have recourse to whatever texts are available. In English translation we have Cecil Jane's *Select Documents Illustrating the Four Voyages of Columbus*, 2 vols. (London, 1930–1933), including a generous selection of the most important documents, and S. E. Morison's *Journals and Other Documents on the Life and Voyages of Christopher Columbus* (New York, 1963), which to some extent supplements Jane's *Select Documents*. Morison continues the emphasis on the voyages but adds important documents from the remainder of Columbus's life. (For further information on texts in various languages, and on studies of these texts as texts, see Provost, *Columbus: A Guide*, chapters 1–3.)

The fourth phase of Columbus study attempts to establish the details of Columbus's life on the basis of the documents and relevant information from allied disciplines such as archaeology. Research has focused on such questions as where and when Columbus was born, what his family and religious backgrounds were, and when, how, and in what order he conceived his "Enterprise of the Indies." Many of these issues have been resolved with much certainty, but since the second, third, and fourth phases of the scholarship depend on the thoroughness with which the tasks of the previous phases have been carried out, historical scholarship on Columbus is still in flux and will remain so until the last relevant surviving document has been discovered, critically edited, judiciously analyzed, and examined in light of the findings of allied disciplines.

Biographical Studies

Even though the textual basis is not uniformly sound, the fourth phase has been intensively developed. Beginning with biographies, we note four basic sources among the hundreds of fifteenth-century accounts of Columbus (all the others being briefer and more fragmentary). First, the initial "decade" of Peter Martyr's *De Orbe Novo* (1511), is available in a new critical edition with copious scholarly apparatus in the *Nuova raccolta*, vol. 6, *La scoperta del Nuovo Mondo negli scritti di Pietro Martire d'Anghiera*, edited by E. Lunardi, E. Magioncalda, and R. Mazzacane (Rome, 1988). There is an English translation by F. A. MacNutt, *De Orbo Novo, the Eight Decades of Peter Martyr d'Anghera* (New York, 1912). The second essential early life is by Columbus's son Fernando, a work usually called the *Historie*, after the title of the unique surviving text, the 1571 Ulloa Italian translation of the much earlier original. There is no critical edition; the best edition is probably that by Rinaldo Caddeo, *Le historie della vita e dei fatti di Cristoforo Colombo* (Milan, 1930). This work has been translated into English by Benjamin Keen as *The Life of the Admiral Christopher Columbus by His Son Ferdinand* (New Brunswick, N.J., 1959).

The third early source of extensive information on Columbus's life is the account of his career in the first volume (1535) of G. F. de Oviedo's *Historia general y natural de las Indias*, edited by J. Amador de los Rios (Madrid, 1851); the material on Columbus will be published in a new edition as volume 10 of the *Nuova raccolta* under the title *Le scoperte di Cristoforo Colombo nei testi de Fernández de Oviedo*, edited by Francesco Giunta.

The last, and best, of the comprehensive early sources is Bartolomé de las Casas's *Historia de las Indias*, which remained in manuscript until finally published in Madrid in 1875–1876. The work is available in a modern transcription by A. Millares Carlo, with an introduction by Lewis Hanke (Mexico City and Buenos Aires, 1951; 2d ed., revised, 1972).

At least one study of each of these biographical sources should be cited. For Peter Martyr, the *Nuova raccolta* volume containing his text is comprehensive. For Fernando Colón's *Historie*, see A. Rumeu de Armas's *Hernando Colón, historiador del descubrimiento de América* (Madrid, 1973), which contains an enormously detailed analysis. For Oviedo, the best modern study is by A. Gerbi, *La natura delle Indie nove* (Milan and Naples, 1975), available in an English translation by Jeremy Moyle, *Nature in the New World* (Pittsburgh, 1986). For Las Casas, the most comprehensive reference is the forthcoming volume 9 of the *Nuova raccolta*, titled *La scoperte di Cristoforo Colombo nei testi di Bartolomeo de Las Casas*, edited by Francesca Cantù.

Modern study of Columbus's life began with William Robertson's *The History of America* (London, 1777), which contains a scholarly, straightforward account that served as the basis of the many popular biographies appearing at the end of the eighteenth century. J. B. Muñoz's *Historia del nuevo-mundo* (Madrid, 1793) and Washington Irving's *A History of the Life and Voyages of Christopher Columbus* (New York, 1828) are based on intense study of documents in the Spanish archives, although Irving's study sprinkles much sentimentality among the genuine scholarship.

The truly classic account among early- and mid-nineteenth-century biographies is that by A. F. von Humboldt in his *Examen critique de l'histoire de la géographie du nouveau continent et des progrès de l'astronomie nautique aux quinzième et seizième siècles,* 5 vols. (Paris, 1836–1839). Henry Harrisse's *Christophe Colomb* (Paris, 1884) is a model scholarly biography except that it is tinged with Harrisse's distrust of Las Casas's account, a prejudice that he later abandoned but that colored historians' views of both Las Casas's *Historia* and Fernando's associated *Historie* until at least 1950, when both works began to be credited as being full of genuine historical information about Columbus.

The new documents that became available in the last quarter of the nineteenth century, beginning with the first volume of Pacheco's *Colección* (Madrid, 1864), made possible a rush of excellent biographies at the time of the fourth centennial. As with several earlier biographies, some are only a part of larger historical studies. Noteworthy among these is John Fiske's *The Discovery of America* (Boston and New York, 1892), a detailed attempt to set Columbus's life and voyages in the context both of European history and of what was then known about aboriginal America at the time of discovery. Equally impressive in its encyclopedic vigor, though somewhat lacking in scholarly method, is J. B. Thacher's *Christopher Columbus: His Life, His Work, His Remains* (New York and London, 1903).

The 1940s brought two salient biographies: S. E. Morison's *Admiral of the Ocean Sea: A Life of Christopher Columbus,* 2 volumes (Boston, 1942) and A. Ballesteros Beretta's *Cristóbal Colón y el descubrimiento de América* (Barcelona and Buenos Aires, 1945). As a narrative, Morison's book is probably the best work on Columbus in English, and the notes in its scholarly two-volume version are thorough beyond the call of duty. Unfortunately, the success of the one-volume version—a condensed popular version stripped of its scholarly apparatus—drove the scholarly version out of print.

Ballesteros's book is a workmanlike account of what could be known of the discoverer's life in the 1940s, cautious and comprehensive. Unfortunately the annotation is limited to the listing, at the end of each chapter, of the items consulted. This approach makes the book as far inferior to Morison's in its annotation as it is superior in its thorough, judicious treatment of the scholarly issues.

The biographies since Ballesteros are generally deriva-tive, with the notable exception of Jacques Heers's *Christophe Colomb* (Paris, 1981), which opens new vistas in Columbus biography with its vigorous attention to fifteenth-century history, especially regarding Genoese activity in Spain, Portugal, and the Atlantic islands.

Concerning Columbus's birthplace and nationality, an overwhelmingly detailed case for his Genoese origin appeared in 1931 in a work so cogent that since that time no responsible scholar has proposed a birthplace outside Liguria: *Christopher Columbus: Documents and Proofs of His Genoese Origin* (Genoa, 1931). P. E. Taviani places this case in the context of the various claims for other birthplaces in *La Genovesità di Colombo* (Genoa, 1987).

Gaetano Ferro reviews Columbus's Portuguese years, 1476 to 1485, in the context of the Portuguese discoveries of the fifteenth century in *Le navigazione lusitane nell' Atlantico e Cristoforo Colombo in Portogallo* (Milan, 1984). A. M. Freitas and R. Maney, in *The Wife of Columbus* (New York, 1893), treat the marriage of Columbus to Felipa Moniz Perestrelo (mother of Columbus's first son and heir, Diego Colón) and her antecedents, Portuguese and Italian.

The Spanish years, 1485 to 1492, constitute the decisive period in Columbus's search for a sponsor. Many of the central issues of this biographical period are developed by Henry Vignaud in *Études critiques sur la vie de Colomb avant ses découvertes* (Paris, 1905). Vignaud, though frequently criticized because of his lifelong contention that Columbus did not expect to reach the Orient on his enterprise of discovery, nonetheless drew together—and commented learnedly on—more documentary evidence about Columbus than anyone else except possibly the indefatigable scholars Henry Harrisse and Alicia Bache Gould. Follow-up studies on major issues include Angel Ortega's *La Rábida: Historia documental crítica* (Seville, 1925–1926); A. Palomeque Torres's "Ambiente político y científico que rodeó al futuro Almirante de Indias d. Cristóbal Colón en la España de los Reyes Católicos," *Studi Colombiani* 2 (Genoa, 1952): 303–355; J. Manzano Manzano's *Cristóbal Colón: Siete años decisivos de su vida, 1485–1492* (Madrid, 1964); and A. Rumeu de Armas's *La Rábida y el descubrimiento de América: Colón, Marchena, y fray Juan Pérez* (Madrid, 1968).

A succinct account of Columbus's voyages, with excellent notes, can be found in S. E. Morison's *The European Discovery of America: The Southern Voyages, A.D. 1492–1616* (New York, 1974). The same material is treated in detail in Morison's *Admiral of the Ocean Sea* (Boston, 1942) and P. E. Taviani's *I viaggi di Colombo: La grande scoperta* (Novara, Italy, 1984).

Among the many questions associated with the first voyage, the dominant one has been the identity of the island in the Bahamas at which the 1492 landfall occurred.

Possibilities include Watlings Island, Grand Turk, and a good many others. The subject is treated vigorously in J. Parker's and L. De Vorsey's *In the Wake of Columbus: Islands and Controversy* (Detroit, 1985; also in *Terrae Incognitae* 15 [1985]). The volume begins with Parker's essay "The Columbus Landfall Problem: A Historical Perspective." A recent attempt to assign the landfall to Samana Cay by J. Judge, "Where Columbus Found the New World," *National Geographic* 170 (Oct. 1986): 566–599, is roundly refuted by various essays in *Columbus and His World,* edited by D. Gerace (Ft. Lauderdale, Fla., 1987).

The most notable single body of twentieth-century research focuses on the first voyage: Alicia Bache Gould's monumental *Nueva lista documentada de los tripulantes de Colón en 1492,* edited by J. de la Peña y Camara (Madrid, 1984), which contains a wealth of information about not only Columbus and his 1492 crew but also a host of related matters.

For the remaining voyages, see Provost, *Columbus: A Guide,* items 331–367. Columbus's life in Spain while not on a voyage (1493–1504) is best studied in the biographies. On his death and the disposition of his body, see C. Fernández Duro, "Noticias de la muerte de d. Cristóbal Colón y del lugar de enterramiento en Valladolid," *Boletín de la Real Academia de la Historia* (Madrid) 24 (1894): 44–46, and A. Álvarez Pedroso, "Los restos mortales del descubridor de América don Cristóbal Colón," *Studi Colombiani* 3 (Genoa, 1952): 15–23.

Other Studies

Other limited studies, addressing single aspects of Columbus's career, can be grouped under the term "Columbiana." The largest body of such works concerns his cosmology and cosmography. There is no book devoted to a survey of this extensive material.

Further examples of Columbiana can be noted briefly. The development of Columbus's project to reach the Indies is treated in three useful books: Vignaud's *Histoire critique de la grande entreprise de Christophe Colomb* (Paris, 1911); P. E. Taviani's *Cristoforo Colombo: La genesi della grande scoperta* (Novara, Italy, 1974); and E. Jos's *El Plan y la génesis del descubrimiento colombino* (Valladolid, 1980).

J. Pérez de Tudela makes a full study of the initial Spanish colonization of La Española during Columbus's lifetime in the following articles: "La negociación colombina de las Indias," "Castilla ante los comienzos de la colonización de las Indias," "La quiebra de la factoria y el nuevo poblamiento de la Española," and "Política de población y política de contratación de las Indias (1502–1505)," in *Revista de Indias* (Madrid) 14 (1954): 289–357 and 15 (1955): 11–88, 197–252, and 371–420, respectively.

A major attempt to delineate Columbus's psychology appears in J. Gil's *Mitos y utopias del descubrimiento,* vol. 1, *Colón y su tiempo* (Madrid, 1988); with its study of new documents, this is one of the most important new studies of Columbus's life in Spain after the first voyage. Treatments of Columbus's language are reviewed in O. Chiareno's "Recenti studi sulla lingua scritta di Colombo," in *Atti I convegno internazionale de studi americanistici* (Genoa, 1976), pp. 107–117.

Columbus's brother Bartolomé Colón and his sons Diego and Fernando are treated in, respectively, A. Albonico's "Bartolomeo Colombo, adelantado mayor de las Indias," *La presenza italiana in Andalusia nel basso medioevo* (Bologna, 1986); L. Arranz Márquez's *Don Diego Colón: Almirante, virrey y gobernador de las Indias* (Madrid, 1982); and A. Rumeu de Armas's *Hernando Colón: Historiador del descubrimiento de América* (Madrid, 1973). The long litigation between Columbus's descendants and the Spanish Crown over the admiral's rights and privileges are treated in Otto Schoenrich's *The Legacy of Columbus* (Glendale, Calif., 1949–1950).

Two medical matters have drawn much interest: the possible transmission of syphilis to Europe by Columbus's crew and the disease *shigella flexneri* (Reiter's syndrome), the cause of Columbus's arthritic condition and eye trouble. A recent summary of what is known appears in P. A. Gemignani's *La scoperta di Colombo e la medicina* (Genoa, 1988).

Columbus's spirituality and millennialism are treated in two recent studies: A. Milhou's *Colón y su mentalidad mesiánica en el ambiente franciscanista español* (Valladolid, 1983) and Pauline Moffitt Watt's "Prophecy and Discovery: On the Spiritual Origins of Christopher Columbus's 'Enterprise of the Indies,' " *American Historical Review* 90 (1985): 73–102. On the abortive nineteenth-century movement to canonize Columbus, see G. Odoardi's "Il processo di beatificazione di Cristoforo Colombo," *Studi Colombiani* 3 (Genoa, 1952): 261–272. On his supposed Jewishness, see Vignaud's "Columbus a Spaniard and a Jew?" *American Historical Review* 18 (1913): 505–512.

On Columbus's navigation, see S. E. Morison's "Columbus as a Navigator," *Studi Colombiani* 2 (Genoa, 1952): 39–48. On portraits of the admiral, see W. E. Curtis's *Christopher Columbus: His Portraits and His Monuments* (Chicago, 1893). On Columbus's ships, see J. M. Martínez-Hidalgo's "Las naves de los cuatro viajes de Colón al nuevo mundo," in *Temi Colombiani (Scritti in Onore del Prof. Paolo Emilio Taviani,* Genoa, 1986), pp. 201–229.

A final topic, of very active interest, concerns Columbus's marginal notes in the books from his personal library. These notes, or "postils," a prime source of biographical information, have traditionally been assigned to the years 1485 to 1492, while Columbus's project was still forming, but recent indications that some notes may have been made later have led scholars to rethink the subject. Two important treatments introduce the new speculations: I. Luzzana Caraci's "La postilla colombiana B 858 e il suo significato cronologico," *Atti del II convegno internazionale di studi colombiani, 1975* (Genoa, 1977), pp. 197–223, and the introductory essay in J. Gil's edition of *El libro de Marco Polo: Ejemplar anotado por Cristóbal Colón y que se conserva en la biblioteca capitular y colombina de Sevilla* (Madrid, 1986).

FOSTER PROVOST

BIBLIOTECA COLOMBINA. See *Library of Columbus.*

BLACK LEGEND. The term "Black Legend" was apparently coined by the Spanish writer Julián Juderías y Loyot; his book of that title, *La leyenda negra* (Barcelona, 1914), charged that foreigners had created a false, distorted image of the Spanish character, wrongly attributing to the Spanish people inherent qualities of intolerance and cruelty, and ignoring the major Spanish contributions to European civilization. He conceded that Spain had once been fanatical and intolerant, but this was at a time when all European peoples shared those traits.

Some three decades later the Argentine historian Rómulo D. Carbia published his influential *Historia de la leyenda negra hispano-americana* (Buenos Aires, 1943), a violent attack on the Black Legend that gave the phrase an even wider diffusion and focused attention on the supposed defamatory treatment of Spain's record in America. Carbia assigned particular responsibility for the creation of the anti-Hispanic Black Legend to Bartolomé de las Casas. According to Carbia, Las Casas laid the solid foundation of the Black Legend with false or exaggerated charges of Spanish cruelty to the Indians, especially in his *Brevíssima relación de la destruición de las Indias* (Very brief account of the destruction of the Indies, Seville, 1552). The charges spread far and wide by the publication of translations of his tracts in French, Dutch, German, English, Italian, and other languages, often with the addition of hair-raising engravings originally published by Jean Théodor and Jean Israel de Bry. Las Casas, according to Carbia, thereby became the instrument of Spain's commercial and political rivals, especially the Protestant powers of England and Holland, who coveted Spain's imperial possessions and sought excuses to seize them for themselves. Carbia's intemperate attacks on Las Casas provided a precedent for a lengthy diatribe by the Spanish scholar Ramón Menéndez Pidal, *El Padre Las Casas, su*

ENGRAVING FROM LAS CASAS'S *VERY BRIEF ACCOUNT*. Illustrations such as this were used by publishers Jean Théodor de Bry and Jean Israel de Bry (sons of Théodor de Bry) in their editions of this work. LIBRARY OF CONGRESS

doble personalidad (Madrid, 1963). Like Carbia, Menéndez Pidal questioned Las Casas's sanity, calling him a "delirious paranoiac."

When considering the origin and evolution of the idea of a defamatory Black Legend of Spanish cruelty and intolerance, two points need to be made. First, the substance of the idea existed centuries before Juderías coined his celebrated phrase. Its rise in Spain coincided with the beginning of Spain's decline as a great power in the second half of the sixteenth century, a decline that accelerated during the Decadencia (decadence) of the seventeenth century. Sensitivity to domestic and foreign criticism and the sense of grievance reflected in the notion of a Black Legend were absent in the heyday of Spanish power; this explains the remarkable tolerance of Emperor Charles V in permitting the publication of Las Casas's fiery tracts in Seville in 1552–1553. But Spanish sensitivity to domestic and foreign criticism of Spain's colonial record grew as the country's power in the Old and New Worlds declined. In the seventeenth century Las Casas's *Very Brief Account* was banned in Spain, and official and unofficial chroniclers harshly scolded him for his services to Spain's enemies.

Second, the notion of the existence of a defamatory, anti-Hispanic Black Legend traditionally drew its principal support in both Spain and Latin America from conservative and reactionary circles. In Spain the struggle against the Black Legend reached its climax in the twentieth century. Facing a growing threat from the forces of liberalism and radicalism, Spanish conservatives and reactionaries developed a historical defense of the traditional order that denounced both the reformist eighteenth-century Bourbon king Charles III and Las Casas as the instruments of a corrupting, debilitating liberalism. Under the dictatorship of Generalissimo Francisco Franco, the need to refute the Black Legend concerning Spain's work in America became the keystone of all teaching of the subject. Meanwhile, conservative circles in Latin America, alarmed by the growth of radical Indianism and a variety of social revolutionary movements, identified themselves more closely with a Hispanic colonial past, which they viewed through nostalgic eyes. These background conditions help explain the twentieth-century upsurge of a historical revisionism predicated on a Black Legend that falsified Spain's past and particularly its work in America.

In recent decades the major premises of the idea of a Black Legend have been questioned as a result of advances in knowledge and understanding of the Spanish colonial process. One major development has been the rehabilitation of Las Casas as a source of historical information. The reliability of his estimates of Indian pre-Conquest populations and their decline following the Conquest, for example, once regarded as the patent exaggerations of a pro-Indian enthusiast, has gained credence as a result of the important work of the so-called Berkeley school of demographic history, whose studies, based on the use of a wide array of documentary sources and sophisticated statistical methods, sometimes offer estimates larger than those of Las Casas. Evidence has also accumulated that the facts cited by Las Casas were in great part drawn from official reports submitted to the Spanish monarchs and the Council of the Indies. Meanwhile the role of Las Casas in creating the Black Legend has been reduced by evidence that Black Legend writers drew their information not only from Las Casas and the Italian traveler Girolamo Benzoni but from such unimpeachably pro-Spanish chroniclers as Francisco López de Gómara and Gonzalo Fernández de Oviedo.

The change in scholarly attitude toward the Black Legend in recent decades is suggested by remarks by the late Charles Gibson in the somber conclusion to his monumental *The Aztecs under Spanish Rule* (Stanford, 1964). Surveying the "deterioration of a native empire and civilization," Gibson went out of his way to resurrect the Black Legend that the revisionists had seemingly buried. "The Black Legend," he wrote, "provides a gross but essentially accurate interpretation of the relations between Spaniards and Indians."

Christopher Columbus's dealings with the Caribbean Indians formed the first chapter in the history of Spanish-Indian relations and provided much material for the Black Legend. Las Casas, who greatly admired Columbus, believing that God had chosen him for his providential task of opening up the New World for the conversion of the Indians, nevertheless harshly criticized the Admiral for his unjust, violent treatment of the natives. Columbus's attitude toward the Indians varied according to the occasion; he sometimes described them as "noble savages," guileless and generous with all they possessed, but when they crossed him they became "filthy dogs." No such ambiguity, however, marked Columbus's conduct with the natives. From his first contact with them, he never recognized their freedom of choice or right of self-determination, kidnapping Indian men and women to serve him as guides or interpreters. Later, on the island of La Española (Hispaniola), he loaded the Indians with intolerable tribute burdens, distributed many as slaves to appease rebellious colonists, and created a situation that Samuel Eliot Morison aptly described as "Hell on Hispaniola." Fearing that Spain's rulers would tire of supporting an unprofitable enterprise of discovery and exploration, Columbus increasingly stressed the importance of the Indian slave trade as a means of making the colonial enterprise self-supporting and a source of royal revenue. In the words of Las Casas, the Indian slave trade became "the Admiral's principal business"; he shipped several thousand Indian slaves to Spain and offered to the Spanish monarchs to send thousands more. Although Queen Isabel rebuked him for enslaving her new vassals and ordered them returned to their homes, few lived to see the islands again. When Columbus landed on La Española, the island held a dense population (Las Casas estimated three to four million, and some modern estimates are even higher) organized in chiefdoms of varying size and supported by a highly productive agriculture. By 1516, thanks to the sinister Indian slave trade and labor policies initiated by Columbus, only some twelve thousand remained.

Columbus's Indian policies reflected his background as a sea captain and trader who was familiar with the slave trade as it operated with relation to Portugal's African possessions and the prevailing European view that slavery was licit under certain conditions. A combination of modern man and medieval mystic, Columbus inflicted these miseries on the Indians not from vulgar greed for gold but from a desire to promote the universal triumph of Christianity, repeatedly urging his royal masters to use the revenue from the Indies to wrest the Holy Land from Muslim hands.

[See also *Encomienda; Exploitation of Indians; Quincentenary;* and biographies of Benzoni, Las Casas, and Oviedo.]

BIBLIOGRAPHY

Gibson, Charles, ed. *The Black Legend: Anti-Spanish Attitudes in the Old World and the New.* New York, 1971.

Keen, Benjamin. "The Black Legend Revisited: Assumptions and Realities." *Hispanic American Historical Review* 49 (November 1969): 703–719.

BENJAMIN KEEN

BOABDIL (d. 1527), sultan of Granada (Arabic, Abu Abd Allah, known as Boabdil by Christians). Boabdil, titled Muhammad XII (r. 1482–1492), was the last sultan of Granada. When Fernando and Isabel began the conquest of Granada in 1481, he revolted against his father, Sultan Abu-l-Hasan Ali (1464–1485), forcing him to flee to Málaga. Though now divided in their allegiance between father and son, the people of Granada determined to resist the Christians. When the Castilians captured Boabdil at Lucena in April 1483, he regained his freedom by pledging homage to Fernando and Isabel, and his father recovered possession of Granada.

In 1485 Boabdil's uncle, al-Zagal, seized control of the government, deposing Abu-l-Hasan Ali who died later in the year. Boabdil initially collaborated with his uncle, but renewed his vassalage to Fernando and Isabel in 1487. When the Castilians occupied the southwestern region, al-Zagal submitted and retired to Morocco, leaving Boabdil as the undisputed sultan of Granada. As Fernando and Isabel tightened the siege of the city, he secretly negotiated with them and capitulated on November 25, 1491. The Castilians took possession of the Alhambra of Granada on January 1–2, 1492, and Fernando and Isabel made their triumphal entry on January 6. The Moors were allowed to retain their property, to worship freely, and to live according to their own law. That situation was altered in 1502 when, following an uprising by the Moors, Fernando and Isabel ordered the Muslims to convert to Christianity or to leave the realm. Most chose to submit, but the problem of assimilating these moriscos, as they were called, was ultimately solved only by their expulsion in 1609–1614. Boabdil, the last of the Nasrid dynasty and the last Moorish sultan in Spain, was assigned a lordship under Castilian sovereignty in Las Alpujarras but chose to withdraw to Morocco in 1493, where he died about forty years later.

BIBLIOGRAPHY

Arié, Rachel. *L'Espagne musulmane au temps des Nasrides (1232–1492)*. Paris, 1973.

Mariéjol, Jean H. *The Spain of Ferdinand and Isabella*. Translated by Benjamin Keen. New Brunswick, N.J., 1961.

JOSEPH F. O'CALLAGHAN

BOBADILLA, BEATRIZ DE (c. 1462–1501), acting captain of Gomera. On his first voyage, Columbus's last port of call in the Old World was San Sebastián, Gomera. During his brief stay on this island, September 3–6, 1492, Columbus was entertained by and reportedly fell in love with the beautiful ruler of Gomera, Beatriz de Bobadilla.

The figure of Beatriz de Bobadilla reveals something of Canarian society in the fifteenth century. Born in Castile of noble lineage, the seventeen-year-old Beatriz came to the Spanish court as a maid of honor to Queen Isabel. An illicit affair between King Fernando and the young maid of honor soon developed. During this time, Hernán de Peraza, governor of Gomera, came to court to explain the death of Juan Rejón, commander of a fleet that had been sent from Castile to conquer La Palma and Tenerife. Rejón had been killed by one of Peraza's vassals when he disembarked on Gomera. Isabel ordered Peraza to be brought before her. Many people, including the powerful duke of Medina Sidonia, interceded for Hernán. The queen was lenient, pardoning him on condition that he help in the conquest of the Grand Canary with some companies of Gomerans. But she imposed on him another, "less onerous penance"—that he marry the beautiful Beatriz de Bobadilla. The queen, writes Joseph Viera y Clavijo, the eighteenth-century historian of the Canaries, "seeing that the King was very fond of the girl, decided to make Hernán Peraza happy by giving him her hand. By this honorable stratagem she rid herself of a rival and secured the loyalty of the Counts of Gomera." Viera y Clavijo does not say whether, on account of the king, Beatriz was no longer a virgin. But only that would explain why marrying her would be punishment.

Immediately after the marriage the newlyweds embarked for Gomera, where their first son, Guillén, was born. The marriage did not last long. Beatriz came to Gomera as a bride in February 1482. In November 1488 her husband was killed by the Guanches, who could not endure his tyrannical government and extraordinary cruelty.

The widowed Beatriz called on the Spaniards of the Grand Canary for aid and abandoned herself to vicious vendettas. Knights, Castilians, and Guanches frequented the castle, which still dominates the beach of San Sebastián. The chroniclers of the time do not furnish details of the many adventures of this femme fatale. They do, however, say that in passing through Gomera in the summer of 1498, Alonso Fernández de Lugo, the conqueror of Tenerife (1496) and the future adelantado of the Canaries (1501), found the famous widow still young and available. People began to gossip indiscreetly about the conduct of the two. Very vocal among the gossips was Francisco Ruiz de Castañeda. Beatriz summoned him at midnight and arrested him. Confessing his imprudence and repenting did not save his life: he was hanged from a beam of the tower, and for a whole day the body hung from a palm tree in the plaza before the castle.

The hanging created a scandal in the islands. The hasty marriage of the adelantado Fernández de Lugo and Beatriz could not stop it, so the newlyweds moved to Tenerife, now controlled by the Spanish Crown, putting Fernán Muñoz in charge of Gomera. That led to new complications. The lord of Lanzarote coveted Gomera for himself, contending that it no longer belonged to Beatriz because her second marriage alienated the inheritance from her first husband, and sought Muñoz's support. When rumors of these plots reached Beatriz she did not hesitate. She and thirty men got in a launch at Los Cristianos one night and crossed from Tenerife to Gomera. At San Sebastián she had Muñoz hanged in the plaza between the tower and the beach and returned to Tenerife.

"Worthy of horror is such cruelty in a sex by nature soft and sensitive," comments Viera y Clavijo. The hanging of Muñoz was the last straw. The widows of Castañeda and Muñoz appealed to the court in Castile, and the monarchs summoned Beatriz to give an explanation. Secure in the protection of her noble relatives, not to mention that of the king, she went to court confidently. But at Medina del Campo a few days after her arrival she was found dead, apparently poisoned, in her bed. Such was the woman for whom Columbus was "touched by love" during his stay on Gomera in 1492.

BIBLIOGRAPHY

Taviani, Paolo Emilio. *I viaggi di Colombo.* Vol. 2. 2d ed. Novara, 1990. Spanish ed., Barcelona, 1989.

Viera y Clavijo, Joseph. *Noticias de la historia general de las Islas Canarias.* Vol. 2. 6th ed. Santa Cruz de Tenerife, 1967.

PAOLO EMILIO TAVIANI

BOBADILLA, FRANCISCO DE   (d. 1502), royal commissioner. A member of the military order of Calatrava, Bobadilla was appointed *juez pesquisidor* of La Española on May 21, 1499. The Crown instructed Bobadilla to go to the island to inquire about Columbus's rule and the rebellion led by Francisco Roldán. Bobadilla arrived in Santo Domingo at the end of July 1500 and immediately demanded from Diego Colón, the Admiral's brother, the delivery of the fortress. Once Bobadilla realized how unpopular Columbus and his brothers were, he ordered their incarceration. Columbus resisted, but Bobadilla managed to outmaneuver him and deported him and his brothers to Spain in shackles in October 1500. As a result, Bobadilla became the de facto governor of the island until his replacement arrived on July 1502.

Bobadilla won the support of Roldán's followers, but he had to adopt further measures to maintain their allegiance. Thus, he freed those imprisoned by Columbus, lowered the tax on gold collected from one-third to

COLUMBUS AND BARTOLOMÉ COLÓN ARRESTED BY BOBADILLA. Engraving from Théodor de Bry's *Americae*. Frankfurt, 1594.

one-tenth, and ratified the system of repartimientos initiated by Columbus two years before. Having observed the lack of beasts of burden, Bobadilla allotted to Roldán's followers the horses he had found on the royal properties, which he mistakenly believed belonged to Columbus. These horses were given as indemnity to those who considered themselves to have suffered losses owing to Columbus's actions and had requested payment in this manner.

Bobadilla proceeded with the repartimientos of land and Indians as a major incentive to the Spaniards. Since there were only 360 Spaniards on the island, Bobadilla ordered them "to join together in couples, forming a partnership and sharing their profits." This measure was designed to protect them from Indian attacks and to give Bobadilla wider acceptance among the Spaniards. The chronicler Bartolomé de las Casas asserts that "because of those favors, endeavors, and advice, they adored him."

By these measures, Bobadilla was adapting himself to the difficult circumstances he encountered. His mission was to carry out the Crown's plan, which was to limit the extensive powers given to Columbus in the Santa Fe Capitulations. The Crown wished, and Bobadilla thus interpreted it, to exclude Columbus as an active partner and administrator from the venture of the Indies. Columbus's rights to the profits from expeditions financed by the Crown would be respected, but the Admiral's political interference in the government of the Indies would be ended.

Bobadilla's rule on La Española was provisional. Once Columbus was removed from La Española, the Spanish monarchs began planning for its colonization according to their own interests and designs. To this end, they appointed Nicolás de Ovando as governor in September 1501. Ovando arrived at Santo Domingo in July 1502 and immediately ordered the departure of Roldán and the main rebel leaders to Spain in the same ships that were to return Bobadilla home. But the ships were struck by a hurricane and sunk off the southeastern coast of La Española. Both Bobadilla and Roldán lost their lives.

BIBLIOGRAPHY

Incháustegui, J. Marino. *Francisco de Bobadilla*. Madrid, 1964.

Las Casas, Bartolomé de. *Historia de las Indias*. 3 vols. Mexico City, 1957.

Moya Pons, Frank. *Después de Colón: Trabajo, sociedad y política en la economía del oro*. Madrid, 1986.

FRANK MOYA PONS

BOOK OF PRIVILEGES. This work is a collection of Castilian royal documents issued to Christopher Columbus between 1492 and 1502. From the moment that King Fernando and Queen Isabel agreed to sponsor Columbus's voyage west to Asia, they began issuing contracts, decrees, privileges, and orders to implement the project. The royal secretarial staff drafted these documents; the royal legal counsel checked the language for accuracy and legality; the queen or both monarchs signed the documents; and finally the chancery clerks recorded them in their registers.

Some documents became outdated once a specific voyage had been carried out. Columbus got into the habit of archiving these by leaving them with a priest in Seville. He left some royal orders and pay vouchers relevant to the first and second voyages, for example, with the chronicler Andrés Bernáldez in 1496, after returning from his second voyage. From the third voyage until the end of his life, he sent outdated documents for safekeeping to the monastery of Las Cuevas in Seville.

Columbus needed to carry other documents with him at all times, and he soon found he needed several copies. In order to govern his growing jurisdictions and responsibilities, he delegated his authority to more and more lieutenants, some in Spain and others in the Americas. All of these deputies needed copies of the official documents in order to carry out their responsibilities. He assembled the texts over a period of ten years and had them copied in varying circumstances.

Shortly before his third voyage in 1498, Columbus commissioned notaries in the city of Seville to make copies of about thirty-five royal documents. These are of two types: warrants and commissions from 1492 through 1494 appointing him admiral and governor of the Indies,

and contracts, pay orders, and instructions dated 1497 preparatory to the third voyage. Columbus carried one copy, known later as the Veragua Codex, completed in March 1498, with him on the third voyage. (The fate of the other 1498 copies is unknown.)

In the city of Santo Domingo on the island of La Española, the Admiral commissioned notarized copies of several royal documents that he had brought with him but had not included in the Veragua Codex. His purpose may have been to leave one copy in the town of Santo Domingo with his lieutenant governor, his brother Bartolomé, while the Admiral himself continued explorations.

But the colonists had become dissatisfied with Columbus's administration, and a royal investigative judge arrested Columbus and his two brothers. Columbus was charged with irregularities in his administration of justice on La Española. Back in Spain, he was exonerated, but the monarchs stripped him of his offices as viceroy and governor-general of the Indies while authorizing other captains to make exploratory voyages. Columbus's years of residence in Spain and his career in the service of the Castilian monarchy could not counter the inherent ambiguities of his position as a foreigner ruling over Castilian citizens.

Columbus turned his energies to recovering his lost authority and status by appealing to the binding legality of the royal documents. In 1502, he updated the collection, adding about twenty-five items. The new additions include a royal mandate ordering restitution of his property, legal opinions as to Columbus's rights to a share of the royal revenues from the Indies and his rights and privileges as Admiral, and Columbus's letters and arguments about his privileges. The Seville notaries finished copying this full set of documents on March 22, 1502.

Columbus regarded the Book of Privileges as the most important document he could leave to posterity. He himself selected the royal documents to be included in the collection, commissioned several notarized copies of the collection, and sent copies to the people he trusted most. Columbus sent two parchment copies of this set, bound and cased, to the San Giorgio Bank and the city government of Genoa. These were confiscated by Napoleon during his invasion of Italy. One remains in Paris in the Bibliothèque Nationale (Paris Codex), while the other has been returned to Genoa and is on display in the Archivio di Stato (Genoa Codex). The Genoa and Paris codices have different covering letters and supplementary materials because, although Columbus sent them to the same person in Genoa, he entrusted them to separate carriers who departed from Seville about a month apart.

Columbus deposited a third copy for safekeeping in the monastery of Las Cuevas in Seville. This is probably the copy in the Library of Congress (Washington Codex), the

FIRST PAGE. Columbus's Book of Privileges. From an 1893 facsimile edition published in London.   LIBRARY OF CONGRESS

only artifact in the United States that Columbus ever held in his hands.

All the original documents (not extant) and codices deposited at Las Cuevas, as well as the 1498 Veragua Codex (now in the Biblioteca Nacional in Madrid), Columbus bequeathed to his son Diego Colón. Most of these remained safe but unused in their Italian and Spanish depositories. The Veragua Codex, however, belonged to Diego and became a living document, the focus of nearly three centuries of litigation between the Castilian monarchy and Columbus's descendants, the dukes of Veragua.

Controversy emerged as early as 1512 in the first two lawsuits. Diego Colón entered copies of portions of the Veragua Codex as evidence in the lawsuit he brought against the monarchy to claim the revenues and offices granted to his father in 1492. The courts ruled in Diego's favor in 1511, restoring the title of viceroy and granting the full revenues and powers of the 1492 contract. The

monarchy initiated a countersuit (settled in its favor in 1512), arguing that Columbus's grant extended only to those places he discovered himself. This argument was based on a strict reading of the 1492 contract and may be the source of two fragmentary collections now in the United States. (One is in the John Carter Brown Library in Providence, Rhode Island, and the other in the Huntington Library in San Marino, California.)

As the claims and counterclaims followed one another with conflicting interpretations of portions of the Book of Privileges, the courts admitted evidence from an ever-widening range of eyewitnesses and experts to define ever-smaller segments of the text. These lawsuits, the Pleitos Colombinos, are of particular interest to scholars because they contain depositions by participants in all eight authorized voyages of discovery of North, Central, and South America between 1499 and 1503. The eyewitness descriptions of flora, fauna, people, topography, equipment, and navigation are an invaluable source of information for natural scientists, geographers, cartographers, and ethnographers.

We must keep in mind, however, that these accounts are self-interested, the witnesses attempting to claim discoveries in order to preserve for themselves a share of the revenues and positions granted in their royal authorizations. They were well aware that their own royal concessions were modeled on the monarchs' 1492 agreements with Columbus and that their rewards would depend on the court's interpretation of the Veragua Codex.

The Book of Privileges is the legal foundation upon which Spanish settlement in America rested. The royal documents instructed Columbus to colonize the Americas and authorized him to establish a system of governance. The monarchs assumed that Columbus would establish towns that would assure an orderly and productive replica of the Castilian homeland and attract the native Indians to the Christian faith. At the time, these objectives were not seen to be inherently contradictory or inappropriate for the Americas.

Almost immediately, however, tensions and conflicts erupted out of the volatile mixture of the monarchs' intentions expressed in the Book of Privileges, Columbus's personal objectives, and the self-interests of native Indians and Spanish colonists. From 1498 on, most parties to the conflicts tried to justify and explain their own actions: Columbus in his letters, memoranda, and Book of Prophesies; Bartolomé de las Casas on behalf of the Indians; Oviedo from the perspective of the Spanish colonists and officials; Andrés Bernáldez and Fernando Colón in defense of the Admiral.

The royal documents granting the discoverer governing powers and a share of the treasure in the Americas shaped the success and failure of Columbus's career in Spain and defined the profit he and his successors would receive from the Americas. During Columbus's lifetime and for 250 years after his death, the wording, intentions, and precedents of the documents in the Book of Privileges were the subjects of litigation brought by the Spanish monarchs, the Columbus family and its descendants, and Columbus's pilots, navigators, rivals, and imitators.

The Book of Privileges contains documents ranging chronologically from a grant issued in 1405 by King Juan II appointing Alfonso Enríquez as admiral of Castile to notarial certificates of the authenticity and accuracy of the copies Columbus commissioned in 1502. The most widely known documents in the collection are the Capitulations of Santa Fe and Granada (the agreements of April 17 and 30, 1492) between Columbus and King Fernando and Queen Isabel. The Washington Codex alone contains the famous papal Bull of Demarcation of 1493, dividing the still-unknown Ocean Sea into Spanish and Portuguese spheres of exploration and settlement.

There are serious historical problems in understanding the Book of Privileges. The first is the same one that the Spanish law courts took years to untangle—the meaning, intent, and precedents of the Spanish original. The documents span one of the most turbulent and innovative periods in the history of the Castilian monarchy, and the secretaries who composed and dictated them were innovating—inventing, borrowing, and adapting terminology and concepts to fit bewilderingly rapid changes in the structure and needs of the royal government. Some of the titles and offices that Fernando and Isabel granted to Columbus in 1492, for example, were their own creations: they created the first Castilian hereditary title of duke in 1475 and appointed the first governor-general in 1484 and the first captain-general in 1492.

The second problem is also historical. Columbus assembled the documents haphazardly, and the notaries copied them exactly as he handed them over. Only after we rearrange them in chronological order can we begin to see the monarchs' changes in vocabulary, their realization that Columbus's discovery was not Asia but a new world, and their hardening attitudes toward Columbus. In 1492, Fernando, Isabel, and Columbus all assumed they were negotiating terms for a relatively familiar world, Asia, made up of large cities and centralized empires and monarchies. The monarchs authorized Columbus to negotiate with the rulers he would encounter and named him their viceroy and governor-general of lands he would discover en route that were not under the jurisdiction of other rulers. The jolting realization that this was not Asia and that all of what Columbus had found might be theirs begins to appear in the 1497 documents and becomes clear in those added to the 1502 codices. The documents

in the Book of Privileges reveal Fernando and Isabel's burst of enthusiastic gratitude after the first voyage and then gradual loss of confidence in the Admiral's governing abilities.

In appearance, the Book of Privileges was only the origin of Columbus's relationship with Fernando and Isabel, but today, in reality, we can see that it shaped the encounter by defining the New World's relationships with the Castilian government. The legal interpretations of the Book of Privileges during the lawsuits were transformed by practical realities of the encounter between Spanish colonists and native cultures. Yet the Book of Privileges set the agenda for debate and provided the format for future Spanish settlements in the Americas.

[See also Lawsuits; Santa Fe Capitulations.]

BIBLIOGRAPHY

Christopher Columbus's Book of Privileges. Translated by Helen Nader and transcribed by Luciano Formisano. Berkeley and Los Angeles, forthcoming.

Davenport, Frances. "Texts of Columbus's Privileges." American Historical Review 14 (1909): 764–776.

Meisnest, Frederick W. "The Lost Book of Privileges of Columbus Located and Identified." Huntington Library Quarterly 12 (1949): 401–407.

Muro Orejón, Antonio. "Cristóbal Colón: El original de la capitulación de 1492 y sus copias contemporáneas." Anuario de Estudios Americanos 7 (1950): 505–515.

Pérez-Bustamante, Ciriaco, ed. Libro de los privilegios del almirante don Cristóbal Colón (1498). Madrid, 1951.

Rumeu de Armas, Antonio. Nueva luz sobre las capitulaciones de Santa Fe de 1492 concertadas entre los Reyes Católicos y Cristóbal Colón. Madrid, 1985.

HELEN NADER

BOOK OF PROPHECIES. For discussion of Columbus's collection of prophecies concerning his plan to find a sea route to Asia, see Writings, article on Book of Prophecies.

BRENDAN (c. 520–577 or 578), Roman Catholic saint, Irish voyager. Apart from his founding Clonfert Abbey in 561, little is known definitely of Brendan's life. He is credited with making voyages to the north and west, during one of which he visited the Scottish island of Iona. His major voyage, in a skin boat with a crew of fourteen monks, became the subject of a long and adventurous story, full of miraculous discoveries and culminating in the Land of the Blessed. This voyage appears briefly in Brendan's Life (c. 800) and is developed in detail in his Navigatio (before c. 900). Varied interpretations have been given these narratives, raising a series of questions. Did

SAINT BRENDAN ON THE BACK OF A GREAT FISH. From Caspar Plautius's *Navigatio in Novum Mundum*.

LIBRARY OF CONGRESS, RARE BOOK DIVISION

Brendan find the Canary Islands? Though this discovery seems improbable, St. Brendan's Isle appears in the Atlantic in this latitude on many marine charts in the fourteenth and fifteenth centuries. Did Brendan sail north to Iceland? The narratives appear influenced by Irish monks who lived in solitude in Iceland from perhaps A.D. 750 onward and traveled to unknown areas to do penance or find solitude for meditation.

Brendan's voyage has long given rise to the claim that he discovered North America, but this claim is grounded in concerns of religious faith, not scientific knowledge. Tim Severin, in two seasons in 1976 and 1977, sailed a skin boat from Ireland to Iceland and on to Newfoundland. His venture proved that these boats could make such long voyages but, obviously, not that Brendan made the voyage. Though thought-provoking to both scholar and student, the *Navigatio* is probably best considered a work of literature rather than a historical account.

BIBLIOGRAPHY

Ireland, John De Courcy, and David C. Sheehy, eds. *Atlantic Visions*. Dublin, 1989.
Severin, Tim. *The Brendan Voyage*. New York, 1978. *The Voyage of St. Brendan*. Translated by John J. O'Meara. Dublin, 1976.

DAVID B. QUINN

BRY, THÉODOR DE (1528–1598), Walloon engraver and publisher. Born in Liège, then under Spanish domination, de Bry, accused of sympathy with the Reformation, left Flanders in 1570 to escape the Spanish Fury and found refuge in Strasbourg, a haven for refugees from persecution and a major center of the Protestant publishing industry and book trade. A distinguished engraver, at first

de Bry worked on order for the German courts and nobility. He finally settled in Frankfurt, in the domain of the Calvinist Frederick III of the Palatinate, and there established a publishing house that specialized in handsomely made, profusely illustrated books. De Bry achieved mastery in the use of copperplate engraving, a technique of reproduction known since the fifteenth century but until recently rejected by publishers because it required twice as much work as wood-engraving, since text and illustration had to be printed separately. Copperplate engraving, however, was infinitely superior to woodengraving in its precision of line and clarity, and it permitted the reproduction of plates over longer print runs.

In the 1580s de Bry made several business trips to England and there met Richard Hakluyt, an ardent promoter of English overseas expansion and author of a great collection of English travels, *The Principall Navigations, Voiages and Discoveries of the English Nation* (1589). Hakluyt encouraged de Bry to pursue a plan he had developed for a new travel collection in four languages. The principal result, as concerned America, was the series known as *Grands voyages* (Great voyages), published by de Bry and his successors in thirteen parts between 1590 and 1634 and comprising some thirty volumes of both large and small folio size. These volumes, published simultaneously in several languages, reached a wide public in the Protestant world and beyond, a public made not only of members of the aristocracy but also of the rising class of merchants and artisans who were fascinated by the voyages of exploration and colonization and the opportunities for enrichment that they offered.

Not unexpectedly, *Grands voyages* reveals an unmistakable anti-Spanish bias, reflected above all in the selection and editing of texts. In this series de Bry published two editions (1594–1597) of Girolamo Benzoni's *History of the New World* (1565), a major source of the so-called Black Legend of Spanish inhumanity to the Indians. To illustrate Benzoni's account of Columbus's career, de Bry attached a series of plates depicting such scenes from the Discoverer's life as the anecdote of the egg, his first departure from Spain, and his return to Spain in chains—probably the earliest attempt at a more or less detailed pictorial record of the Columbian story.

Curiously enough, de Bry omitted from his collection another major source of the Black Legend, Bartolomé de las Casas's *Brevíssima relación de la destruición de las Indias* (Very brief account of the destruction of the Indies, 1552). In 1598–1599, however, following their father's death, his sons Jean Théodor and Jean Israel de Bry published Latin and German editions of Las Casas's tract, accompanied by seventeen illustrations drawn by Iodocus a Winghe. Their beauty of line and the graceful postures struck by the almost nude Indian figures heightened the horror of the scenes of massacre and torture that they depicted. In 1599 the plates were published as a separate; a simply worded legend underneath each plate summarized the event with which it dealt. Repeatedly copied and recopied, these famous illustrations carried to every corner of Europe the message of Spanish cruelty.

Interestingly enough, however, the preface to the 1598 edition of Las Casas's tract is far from being implacably anti-Spanish in spirit. Although the brothers Jean Théodor and Jean Israel de Bry used almost the same words as Las Casas when they declared that the Spaniards in the Indies had committed such cruelties that they could more fittingly be called tigers and lions than men, they disavowed any intent to defame the whole Spanish nation. Indeed, they affirmed that "if we enjoyed the freedom and license that the Spaniards enjoyed in America, with no superior magistrate to hold them in check, we would doubtless be equal to the Spaniards in savagery, cruelty, and inhumanity." Their sole aim, proclaimed these devout

Calvinists, was to make men understand the terrible fruits of that root of all evil, the love of money, and to eradicate that passion from their hearts.

Whatever the political, religious, or practical motives of Théodor de Bry and his successors in publishing a large body of illustrated works dealing with America, their work largely contributed to the development of that image of the American Indian as a Noble Savage living in a Golden Age, free from private property, greed, and kings, which the fantasy of humanists like François Rabelais and Thomas More set in the New World discovered by Columbus. The de Brys did not ignore the brutal aspects of Indian civilization. Théodor de Bry's edition of Hans Staden's narrative of his life as a captive among the Tupinambás of coastal Brazil, for example, was illustrated with skillfully elaborated versions of Staden's own small and crude woodcuts luridly depicting cannibal feasts and the surrounding ritual. More commonly, however, as in the drawings of John White depicting the Indians of Virginia or those of Jacques Le Moyne depicting the Indians of La Florida—drawings brought by Théodor de Bry from London to Frankfurt and engraved on copper, with changes in composition that enhanced their attractiveness—de Bry or his engravers not only endowed the Indians with the classic beauty and poses of Greek gods and goddesses but showed them living peaceful lives of antique simplicity before the coming of the Europeans destroyed their Eden. *Great Voyages,* widely diffused throughout Europe, provided models and sources that profoundly influenced the European artistic vision of the Indian for two centuries.

BIBLIOGRAPHY

Bucher, Benedette. *Icon and Conquest: A Structural Analysis of the Illustrations of de Bry's Great Voyages.* Translated by B. M. Gulati. Chicago, 1981.

BENJAMIN KEEN

AMERICAE, PART 4. Title page of 1594 edition.

BURIAL PLACES OF COLUMBUS. Christopher Columbus was buried in Spain. Between the burial in 1506 and the present century, however, his physical remains were moved around quite a bit. The moves were the products of three impulses in the Columbus family and in Spanish society. First, the burials of wealthy and prominent people customarily took place in two stages: a temporary burial of the full body immediately after death and a permanent burial of the bones several years later. Second, Columbus's son Diego wanted all the family admirals to be buried on the island of La Española, and Diego's son Luis honored that wish. Third, the Spanish monarchy revered Columbus's memory; when it could no longer retain La Española centuries after the Admiral's death, the monarchy moved to keep his remains in Spanish territory.

In medieval and Renaissance Europe, it was customary for the body of a wealthy or prominent person to be interred soon after death and to remain buried for several months or years until only bones were left. Often, this preliminary burial was in a local monastery, where the monks would pray for the soul while it shed the flesh. Meanwhile, the heirs could settle the estate and commission an appropriate burial monument. When the stone monument or slab was ready, the remains were disinterred, placed in a casket, and transferred to the permanent burial site. In the Middle Ages, the permanent monuments were often in the form of statues of the dead persons lying atop their tombs. Because only bones were placed under the monument, it did not need to be life-size. If family chapels became crowded, families could save space by placing the casket of bones in a vault under the floor or a niche in the wall, commissioning smaller monuments, such as an engraved stone or metal slab, to mark the spot. This was the norm in the age of Christopher Columbus.

The fate of Columbus's remains is more complicated than the norm, however, in part because his heirs wanted him to be buried on the island of La Española in the town of Concepción. After Columbus died on May 21, 1506, the funeral ceremonies were celebrated in the parish church of Santa María la Antigua in Valladolid. Immediately afterward, he was buried in the church belonging to the Franciscan monastery in the same town. In 1509, his remains were disinterred and transferred to the Carthusian monastery of Las Cuevas in Seville, where they were buried in the Chapel of Santa Ana (later called Christ Chapel), which had been constructed by order of the prior Diego Luxán.

The next move was to America. Columbus's son, Admiral Diego Colón, made his last will and testament on September 8, 1523. He ordered his heirs to construct a convent of Poor Clare nuns in the town of Concepción, on the island of La Española, for the purpose of providing a permanent burial place in the convent chapel for his and his father's remains. He also ordered that the remains of his mother Felipa Perestrelo y Moniz should be transferred to this family chapel, as well as the body of his uncle Bartolomé Colón, whose remains had also been transferred to the monastery of Las Cuevas. Diego died in 1526 and was buried in Las Cuevas.

About 1541, the transfer from Las Cuevas to La Española was carried out by Diego's son, Luis Colón, the third admiral. The move required several steps. In 1537, Emperor Charles V granted Admiral Luis Colón the space around the main altar—the chancel—in the cathedral of

Santo Domingo for use as the family burial chapel. In 1540 the emperor issued a final decree to the bishop, dean, and chapter of the cathedral to carry out his order. The remains of the great Admiral and his son Diego were buried on the gospel side of the chancel, under the floor in front of the main altar. Soon afterward, Luis was convicted of bigamy by the royal council and sentenced to heavy fines and ten years of military service at Oran in North Africa. He died there in 1572 at the age of fifty, and his remains were later moved to the cathedral of Santo Domingo. Thus, within a century after Columbus's death, he and his male descendants were all buried in La Española in fulfillment of Diego's testamentary instructions. The Columbus dynasty in the Caribbean considered the chancel of the cathedral of Santo Domingo to be their family burial place.

The family funerary chapel was not in Concepción, as Diego had instructed in his last will and testament, because that inland settlement had never flourished. In contrast, the city of Santo Domingo, which the Admiral's brother Bartolomé had established on the south coast in 1496, thrived and became the headquarters of the Caribbean judicial district (Audiencia de Santo Domingo) and archdiocese. Even after 1537, when Luis Colón gave up the family's administrative offices in the Americas in exchange for a perpetual annuity and the noble title of duke of Veragua, Christopher Columbus occupied a place of honor in the seat of Spanish power in the Americas, the empire that he had explored and claimed for Spain.

For this very reason, the Columbus burial site was identified with Spanish rule and subject to the same vicissitudes as the Spanish Empire. In 1655, the plaque over the vault was plastered over or removed when it was feared that an English fleet under Admiral William Penn (father of William Penn, the colonizer) would capture and sack the city. By the end of the next century, Spain and the remains of Christopher Columbus were both expelled from the island of La Española. In all the earlier years of pirate attacks against Spanish ports in the Caribbean, other nations had never succeeded in actually seizing and occupying Spanish territory. But Spain's participation in wars on the European continent during the seventeenth and eighteenth centuries finally drained the monarchy's military and economic resources, and Spain began to give away pieces of its American empire in order to withdraw from the European conflict. Spain ceded part of the island of La Española—the western third now comprising the Republic of Haiti—to France in the Treaty of Ryswick in 1697. A century later, during the wars of the French Revolution, Spain ceded all the rest of the island to France in the Treaty of Basel (July 22, 1795).

Administrators based in Santo Domingo now prepared to transfer Spanish headquarters to the city of Havana. The duke of Veragua at that time did not want his ancestor's remains to fall into the hands of the French and asked the cathedral chapter to permit the remains to be moved to Havana. The commander of the Spanish fleet in the Caribbean, Gabriel de Aristizábal, took charge of disinterring the remains of Christopher Columbus and transferring them to Havana.

Excavations on the gospel side of the main altar revealed a small stone vault. Inside were some lead plates about a foot long, with bones and ashes. On December 20, 1795, Aristizábal, a committee of officials, and representatives of the duke of Veragua carefully collected these fragments and placed them in a lead casket with iron locks. The casket was carried on board the brigantine *Descubridor*, transferred to the ship *San Lorenzo*, and transported to Havana. With reverent ceremony, the casket was taken to the cathedral, where it was placed in a niche on the gospel side of the altar.

Aristizábal and the duke of Veragua were satisfied that Christopher Columbus's remains had been moved to the most honorable place in the cathedral of the headquarters city of the Spanish Caribbean. The Spanish monarchy also prided itself on having treated with respect and care the remains of the founder of the Spanish Empire.

But less than a century later, the identity of the remains in Havana cathedral were thrown into question. The confusion began in 1877, and the main character in the conflict was an Italian bishop, Roque Cocchia, serving as papal vicar to the archdiocese of Santo Domingo. At that time the chancel of Santo Domingo cathedral was being repaired, and the bishop took advantage of that situation to carry out excavations. The actual digs were supervised by a priest of the cathedral, Francisco Javier Bellini. He excavated along the wall of the gospel side of the main altar, and on September 10, 1877, he found a previously unopened vault, containing a lead casket measuring forty-two by twenty-one centimeters. Inside were bones, dust, and a small lead bullet. The casket was found to have several inscriptions on it. The letters cut into the inside lid are abbreviations of the words "Illustrious and famous gentleman Sir Christopher Columbus." Other letters on the sides, front, and top are variously interpreted as initials and "Discoverer of America First Admiral" or "Dignity of Admiralty First Admiral." This lead casket was removed from the cathedral while repairs and excavations continued.

On the other side of the chancel, the epistle side, the investigators found another lead casket with an inscription that indicated it had contained the remains of Christopher Columbus's grandson, Luis Colón. The inscription on this casket correctly identified Luis as admiral but incorrectly listed his noble titles as marquis of Veragua and duke of Jamaica.

Tomb of Columbus in the Cathedral of Santo Domingo
Dominican Tourist Information Center

When repairs in the building were finished and the first casket was brought back to the cathedral in 1878, the dignitaries found a previously unnoticed small silver plate lying inside the casket. The abbreviations inscribed on this plate are interpreted to read "Last of the remains of the first admiral, Sir Christopher Columbus, discoverer." All these inscriptions, on both caskets, are problematic on several grounds. Most troubling, the abbreviations are not standard for the sixteenth century, the titles contain errors, and the workmanship is far below the standard of sixteenth-century Spanish metalworkers.

The Italian bishop nevertheless concluded that what the Spaniards had taken to Havana in 1795 were the remains of the second admiral, Christopher's son Diego Colón. He issued a pastoral letter announcing this and claiming that Christopher Columbus was still buried in the cathedral of Santo Domingo.

The indignant response from Spain came almost immediately. The government was worried, and not just about national pride. In 1795, the Spanish Empire had entered on the most convulsive period in its history. First, all the nations of Europe and America became involved in the conflicts of the French Revolution and Napoleonic Wars, and part of their strategy was to attack and seize parts of the Spanish Empire. Furthermore, the North American colonies that had rebelled against England and won independence in 1776 set an example for the Spanish colonies, which began to rebel and proclaim independence in the 1820s. By 1830, the Spanish Empire in the Americas had been reduced to just a few Caribbean islands, including Cuba and Puerto Rico. By the last quarter of the nineteenth century, many Spaniards believed that the monarchy would not be able to suppress the revolts boiling up on the islands and would surely lose the last of the Spanish Empire. If they had to withdraw from Cuba, they would once again have to make a decision about the remains in Havana cathedral.

In 1879, the Spanish Royal Academy of History submitted to the monarchy a reassuring report. The report published the relevant documents from the Spanish archives, with a historical study of them by one of the academy members, Manuel Colmeiro. It was Colmeiro who established the historical facts of Columbus's five burial places and the dates and circumstances of the Atlantic crossings. Of course, he did not have access to the inscribed lead caskets excavated by the Italian clergymen, nor could he check up on just how much Aristizábal had excavated. The Spanish government was reassured that Christopher Columbus still lay in Spanish territory.

Naturally, this situation did not continue. When Cuba and Puerto Rico rebelled late in the century, the United States decided to help them along, and at the conclusion of the Spanish-American War in 1898, Cuba became an independent country and Havana its capital. Humiliated by its utter defeat in the Caribbean and Philippines, the Spanish monarchy salvaged what dignity it could. Before finally abandoning the island of Cuba, the Spanish government decided to transfer what it still believed to be the remains of Christopher Columbus to Spain. In late 1898, the lead casket was removed from Havana cathedral, transported aboard the ship *Count of Venadito* to Cádiz, and there transferred to the royal yacht *Giralda*. The yacht carried the casket up the Guadalquivir River, flag at half-mast and flying Christopher Columbus's coat of arms, and arrived in Seville on January 19, 1899. The lead casket was placed that same day in the cathedral of Seville. As far as the Spanish government was concerned, Christopher Columbus is still buried in Seville cathedral, behind or under a marble monument sculpted by the Spanish artist Arturo Mélida.

TOMB OF COLUMBUS IN THE CATHEDRAL OF SEVILLE.
NATIONAL TOURIST OFFICE OF SPAIN, NEW YORK

The government of the Dominican Republic believes equally firmly that Christopher Columbus and his grandson Luis are buried in the cathedral of Santo Domingo, and that it is the second admiral, Diego Colón, who is buried in the cathedral of Seville. In order to honor the Admiral and accommodate the many tourists expected to visit the island in 1992, the Dominican government is building a monument to Christopher Columbus. This will be shaped like a lighthouse and will stand on the east coast of the island. The Columbus remains will be transferred to this monument as their "final" resting place. Meanwhile, Santo Domingo cathedral is once again under repair and reconstruction, and the Columbus caskets have been moved to a temporary burial site.

Despite the dignity and veneration with which Christopher Columbus's remains have actually been treated by his family and the Spanish and Dominican governments over the centuries, a great many conflicting claims and counterclaims swirl around the burial places of the Admiral and his descendants. Ironically, the motive for these claims is the very great reverence and admiration that people felt for Christopher Columbus in previous centuries; everyone wanted to claim the honor of being the guardians of the great man's burial place.

There are few prospects of ever resolving this dispute on a scholarly basis. The Spanish historian Antonio Ballesteros Beretta subscribed to Colmeiro's conclusions that Christopher Columbus's remains had been removed to Havana in 1795. Furthermore, Ballesteros published drawings of the artifacts uncovered in 1877, including the inscriptions. The American historian Samuel Eliot Morison subscribed to the Dominican argument, largely on the basis of research published by Rudolf Cronau in 1891. Morison was not troubled by the probability of forgery in the inscriptions and believed that Aristizábal had simply failed to dig far enough, that had he dug closer to the wall he would have found the "real" Christopher Columbus casket in 1795. Instead, Morison believed, the naval commander carried off to Havana the remains of the discoverer's son, Diego Colón, the second admiral, leaving Christopher Columbus buried in Santo Domingo. Ballesteros and Morison, the two giants of their day in Columbus scholarship, could not agree.

After that, a flurry of new research on this problem addressed several important issues, such as the events and decisions surrounding the transfer of the remains of the third admiral, Luis Colón, from North Africa to La Española, and the extent of earthquake and hurricane damage, repair, and relocation within the cathedral of Santo Domingo before 1877. No one has accounted for that small lead bullet.

Scholarly evidence and original documents made no impression on the participants in this paper war, however, nor did they prevent the wildest charges from the most improbable sources. National pride was at stake, and for a century the disputes aroused incredible displays of patriotic competition and ethnic anger. These patriotic and ethnic claims have subsided only in the 1980s. Now that Christopher Columbus is being blamed for starting all the evils of American society, few countries or nationalities want to be associated with him even after death. Meanwhile, we can choose: Christopher Columbus has found refuge in Spain in death, as he did in life, or he rests in his beloved La Española, scene of his grandest dreams and glories.

BIBLIOGRAPHY

Ballesteros Beretta, Antonio. *Cristóbal Colón y el descubrimiento de América*. Vol. 2. Barcelona and Buenos Aires, 1945.

Colmeiro, Manuel. *Los restos de Colón: Informe de la Real Academia de la Historia al gobierno de S. M. El supuesto hallazgo de los verdaderos restos de Cristóbal Colón en la iglesia de Santo Domingo*. Madrid, 1879.

Dozier, Thomas. "The Controversy on Whereabouts of Columbus' Body." *Smithsonian* 5, no. 7 (October 1974): 92–99. Reprinted in *Editor's Choice: Smithsonian: The Best of Twenty Years from Smithsonian Magazine*. Washington, D.C., 1990.

Morison, Samuel Eliot. *Admiral of the Ocean Sea: A Life of Christopher Columbus*. Vol. 2. Boston, 1942.

HELEN NADER

C

CABEZA DE VACA, ALVAR NÚÑEZ (1490?–1556?), Spanish explorer. Cabeza de Vaca made two extraordinary journeys into the interior of the North and South American continents: the first from Florida to Mexico from 1527 to 1536 and the second to Paraguay from 1540 to 1545. He was the first European to walk across the mainland of North America. His *relación*, or account, of that crossing and the years he spent among the indigenous peoples of the gulf coast and southwestern part of the continent is the most gripping narrative of first contact in American letters.

Cabeza de Vaca was born to a distinguished military family in Jerez de la Frontera, Spain. He served in the army of Fernando the Catholic at the Battle of Ravenna in 1512 and later as a steward in the service of the duke of Medina Sidonia. On June 17, 1527, Cabeza de Vaca sailed from Sanlúcar de Barrameda as treasurer or representative of the Crown and provost marshal in the expedition to Florida organized by Pánfilo de Narváez. After the expedition landed near the Bay of Tampa on April 12, 1528, Narváez decided to march overland while his ships explored by sea. As the Spanish struggled through the swamps, they perished in attacks by hostile tribes or died of starvation on the beaches of the Gulf coast where the barges they had constructed from the hides of their horses had been wrecked in storms. Of that fleet of three caravels and some 350 men, only Cabeza de Vaca, Alonso del Castillo Maldonado, Andrés Dorantes, and his black servant Estebanico managed to survive as traders and slaves among the indigenous groups they encountered in what is present-day southern Texas.

Sometime around 1533 the four were reunited at a vast prickly pear harvesting area located near the lower Guadalupe and Nueces rivers. Their successful practice of indigenous healing procedures among the numerous tribes they met earned them reverence as "Children of the Sun." Throngs of friendly Indians accompanied them as they traveled westward toward the Sonora Valley through territories occupied by Piman and Opatan groups and then southward on the middle Yaqui River through Cahitan territory. Although the precise route the party traveled has long been a topic of intense debate, it is agreed that they covered more than 18,000 kilometers (11,000 miles) on foot across the North American continent.

At the climactic moment in the account, when the survivors meet Spanish soldiers somewhere north of Culiacán in May of 1536, Cabeza de Vaca's narrating perspective of "us" includes his Indian friends, and the references to the Spaniards are couched in terms of "they," or separate and other beings. His account of North American tribes, their languages and customs, and the plants, animals, and geography of their native regions includes the first description of a Caribbean hurricane, the buffalo, and the great walled cities in the northern interior. First reported orally to the viceroy in Mexico City in 1536 and later compiled as a joint report written by the three Spanish survivors, it spurred the Crown to send Fray Marcos de Niza and the expedition of Francisco Vásquez de Coronado northward in search of the Seven Cities of Cibola in 1539 and 1540.

Cabeza de Vaca returned to Spain in 1537, where he began writing his own *La relación*, published in Zamora in 1542. It represents a vision of the indigenous peoples and geography of North America through the eyes of a Spaniard living among those societies. To survive, he acculturated to them and defended them against the Spanish abuses he witnessed on the northern frontiers of New Spain.

In 1540 Charles V named him governor and captain

general for Río de la Plata, charged with rescuing the possible survivors of the Pedro de Mendoza expedition to Paraguay. In October 1541 he and his party set out from the island of Santa Catalina off the Brazilian coast, marching more than 1,700 kilometers (1,050 miles) through the jungles of Paraguay to reach Asunción in 1542. On the way the group discovered the falls of Iguazú, and one of his party, Hernando de Ribera, reported news of El Dorado and the Amazons.

Cabeza de Vaca's tenure as governor, however, was short-lived and filled with conflict: his generous attitude toward the Indians caused resentment among his enemies. In 1544 he was taken prisoner by mutinous colonists led by his second in command, Domingo Martínez de Irala, and was sent back to Spain in chains in 1545. His account of that bitter experience was set down in *Los comentarios,* written under his supervision by his secretary, Pedro Hernández, and published together with the edited version of *La relación* in Valladolid in 1555.

BIBLIOGRAPHY

Adorno, Rolena. "The Negotiation of Fear in Cabeza de Vaca's 'Naufragios.' " *Representations* 33 (1991).

Bishop, M. *The Odyssey of Cabeza de Vaca.* New York and London, 1933.

Cabeza de Vaca, Alvar Núñez. *Cabeza de Vaca's Adventures in the Unknown Interior of America.* Translated by Cyclone Covey. New York, 1961. Albuquerque, N. Mex., 1988.

Cabeza de Vaca, Alvar Núñez. *The Narrative of Alvar Núñez Cabeza de Vaca.* Translated by Fanny Bandolier. Edited by John Francis Bannon. With Oviedo's version of the lost joint report translated by Gerald Theisen. Barre, Mass., 1972.

Cabeza de Vaca, Alvar Núñez. *La Relación o Naufragios de Alvar Núñez Cabeza de Vaca.* Edited by Martin A. Favata and Jose B. Fernandez. Potomac, Md., 1986.

Chipman, Donald E. "In Search of Cabeza de Vaca's Route across Texas: An Historiographical Survey." *Southwest Historical Quarterly* 91 (1987).

Molloy, Sylvia. "Alteridad y reconocimiento de los *Naufragios* de Alvar Núñez Cabeza de Vaca." *Nueva Revista de Filología Hispánica* 35 (1987).

MAUREEN AHERN

CABOT, JOHN (c. 1455–1498 or 1499), explorer and navigator. Cabot was born in Genoa, the son of Giulio Caboto and an unknown mother. His family moved to Venice in 1461, living on Chioggia, and Cabot was naturalized as a Venetian in 1476. He claimed to have traveled as a merchant and seaman to the eastern Mediterranean, engaging in the spice trade as he made his way possibly to Mecca. He probably moved to Spain about 1490 with his wife Mattea and their elder sons. He may well have worked as a chart maker, but if he is the same person as Juan Caboto de Montecalunya, he is found planning harbor works at Valencia in 1491–1493. He is described in 1498 as "another Genoese like Columbus, who had been in Seville and at Lisbon seeking to obtain persons to aid this discovery" after his successful voyage of 1497. This description raises the probability that Cabot had early contacts with Columbus, either as a rival or, for a time, as collaborator. He was in Valencia when Columbus passed through in 1493 on his way to report to the Catholic monarchs at Barcelona and so would have heard of Columbus's success. It is likely that this report inspired Cabot to attempt an Atlantic crossing in more northerly latitudes where the distance would be shorter.

The date of his arrival in Bristol, England, is unknown, but it is likely to have been either 1493 or 1494. From about 1491, Bristol was annually sending out exploring expeditions of two to four ships. Bristol could not possibly have afforded to send these expeditions unless profitable cargoes were being brought back. Hence, the conclusion might well be made that the men of Bristol were already fishing off Newfoundland from some time before Cabot's voyage. Cabot had to have time to convince local merchants that he was serious; it may have been in 1495 that he made his first, unsuccessful voyage to the west. This voyage failed, probably because of inclement weather. Cabot's contacts in Bristol were sufficient, however, to get him recommended to Henry VII, who on March 5, 1496, granted, by patent, permission to Cabot and his three sons, Ludovico, Sebastian, and Sancio, to discover and annex lands across the ocean for the Crown. The patent also authorized Cabot and, in succession, his sons to rule these lands in the king's name.

The first expedition under the patent took place between May and August 1497. Cabot's ship left Bristol with a crew of twenty on May 20 and reached "the land first seen" (*terra prima vista*) according to his son Sebastian, on June 24, at forty-five degrees (approximately at Cape Breton). Cabot then sailed up the east coast of Newfoundland, leaving Cape Bauld about July 18. He landed once and found only superficial signs of human occupancy, bringing home "a stick half a yard long pierced at both ends, carved and painted with brazil." (Brazil, a red dye of Asian origin, was clearly iron oxide.) The estimated distance from Bristol to America as eighteen hundred miles was not unreasonable, and the definition of the south-north distance traveled as between the latitudes of the mouth of the Garonne and Dursey Head in Ireland (forty-six to fifty-one degrees) was accurate within a hundred miles. But Cabot's claim to have traversed the coast for four hundred leagues (twelve hundred miles) is absurd; he may have traveled four hundred miles. He made a speedy crossing to Bristol on August 6 and then traveled to London, having agreed to make a world map

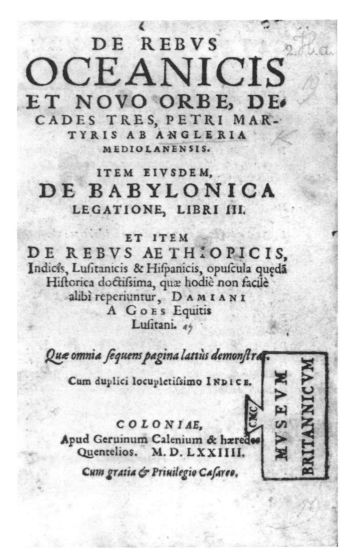

FIRST ACCOUNT OF JOHN CABOT'S VOYAGE TO LABRADOR. Title page of *De rebus oceanicis et novo orbe decades tres...*, by Pietro Martire d'Anghiera (Peter Martyr). Cologne, 1574.

and a globe for Henry VII to illustrate the location of his supposed discoveries in the land of the Great Khan. Henry responded rapidly, giving him a present of ten pounds and a smaller sum to follow (possibly in return for the cartographical evidence). This reward was followed by the generous life grant of twenty pounds a year from the Bristol customs. Cabot's discovery was clearly of an immense island or a continent, presumed by Cabot to be Asiatic.

The king equipped a ship in the Thames for another voyage, and London merchants loaded it with English woolen cloth and other English products, hoping to gain silks and spices in return. The four small Bristol ships that joined it added "slight and gross merchandises, as coarse cloth caps, laces, points and other trifles," showing a skepticism about the luxury trade and suggesting earlier contact with the primitive Newfoundland Boethuks, to whom such items would be attractive. The fleet set out in 1498, provisioned for a year. It met with unknown disasters, including a major storm. One ship, in distress, put in at Ireland. Of the rest of the fleet we know nothing definitive. One vessel may have returned; several persons who were thought to have gone on the expedition were later found alive. Cabot conceivably reached Bristol, though Polydor Vergil wrote in 1512, "he is believed to have found the new lands nowhere but on the very bottom of the ocean." If Cabot survived it was not for long. His pension terminated on September 29, 1509, as did the lease of his house. Sebastian and his mother evidently remained in Bristol; all mention of his brothers is absent.

Cabot's historical importance stems from his being the first clearly recorded discoverer of the North American continent, as was Columbus of South America in the year following the 1497 voyage. In addition, Cabot confirmed the existence of a great fishing ground off Newfoundland. The exploring and fishing expeditions of 1501–1504 followed from this confirmation and his territorial discoveries. A sketch of Cabot's alleged discoveries was sent to Columbus by John Day, a Bristol merchant, who promised later to send a map, presumably a world map. A Spanish ambassador also sent a sketch to his masters in 1498, following his attempt to convince Henry VII that Cabot had infringed the Spanish monopoly under the papal grant and the Treaty of Tordesillas. The long extent of "the sea discovrd by the English" on Juan de la Cosa's map of 1500 certainly impinged on territory that Spain could claim, but this extension could well have been the result of a stretched-out version of an unscaled drawing.

John Day had informed Columbus about John Cabot's voyage very shortly after Cabot's return. Toward the end of 1497 Day wrote to Columbus stating, "It is certain that the cape of the said land was found and discovered in the past by the men of Bristol who discovered Brazil, as your Lordship knows" ("Se presume cierto averse fallado e descubierto en otros tienpos el cabo de la dicha tierra por los de Bristol como dello teine noticia Vuestra Senoria"). This statement implies that both Cabot and Columbus knew of an earlier transatlantic discovery made from Bristol. Brazil was associated with the Island of the Seven Cities (which comprised places that Day designated as being Cabot's discoveries). The words *en otros tienpos* (in the past) have been variously interpreted. Alwyn Ruddock considered this report to be a revised old tale of some distant or supposed discovery. Samuel Eliot Morison classified the report as "Bristol gossip." I regard it as a reference to either a 1481 expedition, reported as being sent "to search for and find the Isle of Brasil," or a voyage made after 1490, conceivably as late as 1494, a date favored by early writers on Cabot.

BIBLIOGRAPHY

Morison, Samuel Eliot. *The European Discovery of America: The Northern Voyages.* New York, 1971.

Quinn, David B. *England and the Discovery of North America.* New York, 1974.

Quinn, David B., Alison M. Quinn, and Susan Hillier, eds. *New American World.* 5 vols. New York, 1979.

Ruddock, Alwyn A. "John Day of Bristol and the English Voyages across the Atlantic." *Geographical Journal* 122 (1966).

Vigneras, Louis-André. "New Light on the 1497 Cabot Voyage to America." *Hispanic-American Historical Review* 36 (1956).

Williamson, James Alexander. *The Cabot Voyages and Bristol Discovery under Henry VII.* Cambridge, 1962.

DAVID B. QUINN

CABOT, SEBASTIAN (c. 1476?–1557), explorer and cartographer. Born in Chioggia, Venice, Sebastian Cabot was the second son of Mattea and Giovanni Caboto (John Cabot). He probably accompanied his family to Spain about 1490, lived in Valencia for most of the years 1491–1493, and then migrated with his family to Bristol, England, in 1493 or 1494. As a young man he appears to have been taught, probably by his father, the art of making charts and possibly globes. At the age of about fifteen, he accompanied his father on his successful 1497 voyage, the first-known large-scale exploration of eastern North America (antedating by a year Columbus's discovery of an American landmass). If Sebastian Cabot was on the 1498 voyage, he was one of the fortunate few who survived it.

From 1501 onward, several syndicates sponsored explorations and cod-fishing expeditions. Sebastian was a leader of at least one such voyage, which in 1504 ranged from New England possibly up the coast of Labrador. For this he was to receive a royal pension for life for his work "in and aboute the fyndynge of the newe found landes." With two ships that, he reported to Pietro Martire d'Anghiera (Peter Martyr), he "equipped at his own cost in Britain" and with three hundred men, he set out in 1508 on a voyage to sail north around the recently discovered landmass to Asia. Cabot later insisted that the ships were provided and equipped by Henry VII. Neither this claim nor that regarding the size of his company appears to be true. It is even suspected that he found finance in the Netherlands. Certainly he was back in England by May 7, 1509, applying for arrears of his pension for part of the period 1506–1509. This pension was subsequently rescinded. He continued to live in Bristol, but he accompa-

nied an English force to France in 1511, where he made a map of Gascony and Guienne. Very shortly after his return, he visited Burgos where he met representatives of King Fernando of Aragón and agreed to transfer to the Spanish service. On September 13, 1512, Fernando wrote to Cabot that his service was sought because of his knowledge of "the navigation to the Indies and the Island of the Bacalaos (Newfoundland)." Cabot then moved to Spain and was in the service of the Spanish Crown until 1548. Henry VIII is not known to have objected.

Cabot had sailed in 1508 from an unknown port; he reached the Labrador coast in July and continued northward. His course thereafter has been a topic of considerable controversy. The Spanish writer Francisco López de Gómera, in 1552, put Cabot's northing as fifty-eight degrees. Cabot himself claimed that he reached some sixty-seven degrees (well up the coast of Baffin Island and north of the Arctic Circle). Given the uncertainty of latitude estimation at this time, he may have entered Hudson Strait at approximately sixty degrees, for he reported encountering numerous icebergs, which is characteristic of that channel in July. He wintered along the eastern shore, probably investigating possible entries into the interior, and finally sailed from North America be-

SEBASTIAN CABOT.   MASSACHUSETTS HISTORICAL SOCIETY

tween twenty-five and thirty-five degrees north, arriving in England shortly before May 7, 1509. Whatever the details of the voyage, it was a notable one and inspired many attempts to find a passage to the Pacific. Cabot's Spanish masters, however, did not attempt to follow him into icy latitudes, choosing rather to send Ferdinand Magellan south to make the circumnavigation, which was completed by Juan Sebastián de Elcano in 1522. Cabot did not give up his plans for a northern voyage. He secretly went to England in 1521 and ingratiated himself with the powerful Cardinal Thomas Wolsey, but failed to convince London merchants to support him. Back in Spain he opened equally fruitless negotiations with Venice.

Cabot taught pilotage and prepared charts on the expanding Spanish empire at the Casa de la Contratación in Seville, where he became head of the pilot office as pilot major in 1518, an office he retained, with one short interval, for thirty years. Holy Roman Emperor Charles V thought highly of Cabot, and, in 1526, he commissioned him to lead an expedition to examine the Río de la Plata, discovered some years before, to determine if there was a passage to the Pacific in a temperate latitude. Cabot did his best to explore the great complex of rivers that combine to create the estuary, but he found neither a trans-American route nor gold. Dissension among his crew forced him to return in 1530, after which he engaged in no further expeditions.

In 1548, he returned to England and spent some years planning a northern route for English trade to the Pacific. In 1553, a northeast passage route was attempted, though this linked trade with northern Russia, not China. Sebastian Cabot remained nominal governor of this Muscovy Company until his death. The world map of 1544 with which he was associated contained notes on early English voyages and was revised by him in 1549. When he died, his considerable achievements had been to build on the discoveries made by his father and on the exploration of eastern Spanish South America in the wake of Columbus, Juan Díaz de Solís, and Magellan.

BIBLIOGRAPHY

Almagià, Roberto. *Comemorazione di Sebastiano Caboto nel IV centenario della morte.* Venice, 1958.

Biggar, Henry P. *Precursors of Jacques Cartier.* Ottawa, 1911.

Morison, Samuel Eliot. *The European Discovery of America: The Northern Voyages.* New York, 1971.

Quinn, David B. *England and the Discovery of North America.* New York, 1974.

Quinn, David B., Alison M. Quinn, and Susan Hillier, eds. *New American World.* 5 vols. New York, 1979.

Toribio, Medina. *El veneciono Sebastián Caboto ene el servicio de España.* Santiago, 1908.

Williamson, James Alexander. *The Cabot Voyages and Bristol Discovery under Henry VII.* Cambridge, 1962.

DAVID B. QUINN

CABRAL, PEDRO ÁLVARES (1467 or 1468–1520), Portuguese discoverer of Brazil. One of more than ten children, Cabral was born in Belmonte, in east central Portugal, the second son of Isabel de Gouveia and Fernão Cabral, lord of the manor of Azurara, civil governor of Belmonte and nobleman of the household of King Afonso V (r. 1438–1481). Like most of the sons of the nobility, at the age of fourteen he entered the court of King João II (r. 1481–1495) where he completed his education. Sometime later, King Manuel I (r. 1495–1521) appointed him to his privy council and offered him the habit of the Order of Christ. As a result of his marriage to Isabel de Castro, he enlarged his holdings considerably and allied himself with one of the most illustrious and powerful families of the day. He was also related by marriage to Afonso de Albuquerque, his mother-in-law's brother.

After the return of Vasco da Gama from his momentous voyage in 1499, King Manuel I decided to send a large armada to India that would impress the Asians with his power and prestige and start the spices flowing from the East. He chose Pedro Álvares Cabral as commander of a fleet of thirteen ships carrying the most experienced pilots and mariners of the day. On March 8, 1500, the day appointed for departure, the king and his court accompanied the mariners to the beach at Restelo, where mass was celebrated by Diogo Ortiz, then bishop of Ceuta, who had been a member of King João II's scientific council when it refused Columbus's request for ships.

Owing to the weather, the fleet did not sail until the following day. On March 14, five days after their departure, they reached the Canary Islands, and on the twenty-second, they touched at but did not stop at Cape Verde. It was there they noticed that Luis Peres's ship was missing, but there had been no adverse weather to account for it. They searched for two days but never found it. The remaining twelve ships of the fleet continued on their way, sailing far to the west. The advantages of following a more southerly route from the Cape Verde Islands, making use of the northeast trade winds, had been apparent during the voyage of Columbus, which is why this course seems to have been chosen. The instructions given to Cabral are supposed to have been dictated by Vasco da Gama, who described a curve after passing the Cape Verdes, the course Bartolomeu Dias had followed, only this time the curve was larger.

On Tuesday of Easter week, April 21, 1500, they saw signs of land, and on the twenty-third they anchored next to the mouth of a river. Since it was not a safe anchorage, on Saturday the twenty-fifth they moved the ships to a safer port, which Cabral named Porto Seguro. They established friendly relations with the natives who brought them a generous supply of food and fearlessly boarded the ships. Cabral decided to linger a while. On Easter Day, they heard mass ashore, which was celebrated in a tent with great solemnity while the natives looked on, enjoying the spectacle. On the first of May, a commemorative pillar was erected on top of a hill near the beach, and on the third of May they departed.

They dispatched Gaspar de Lemos in the supply ship with letters to the king, among them the famous letter of Pero Vaz de Caminha, the ship's scribe. It is a beautifully written letter giving a valuable and detailed description of the ten days they spent in Brazil. The letter is dated May 1, 1500, and is written from "Porto Seguro in your island of Vera Cruz," which proves that Caminha believed Brazil to be a great island. As early as 1501, however, the Portuguese no longer believed that it formed part of Asia.

With the departure of Lemos's caravel, the fleet was reduced to eleven ships. On May 23, as they were approaching the Cape of Good Hope, they were struck by a sudden storm that capsized four of the vessels, with the loss of all hands. One of the ships to go down was that of Bartolomeu Dias, who thus found a grave in the very waters of the cape he had discovered twelve years before. A fifth ship, that of Dias's brother Diogo, carried astray by the storm, took a wide detour into the Indian Ocean and touched the island of Madagascar. His ship, traveling on, approached the mouth of the Red Sea from where it returned around Africa alone without stopping except at Cape Verde. There, in 1501, it met up with Amerigo Vespucci, who was on board the first fleet sent by King Manuel I to explore Brazil.

The remaining six ships proceeded on their way without Diogo's ship. After running through a storm for twenty days, under bare poles and separated from one another, they met again on June 10 off the coast of Sofala. Continuing their journey along the east coast of Africa, they reached Mozambique on July 20, Kilwa on July 26, and Malindi on August 2, where Cabral strengthened the good relations that had been established with the king by Vasco da Gama. From there they departed in the direction of Calicut on August 2, with two Gujerati pilots, dropping anchor on the island of Angediva on August 23, 1500; finally, on September 11, they arrived in Calicut.

There Cabral delivered to the Hindu ruler of Calicut, or the *samuri*, as he was called, a letter from King Manuel, along with the presents he had brought, which, unlike those of Vasco da Gama before him, were deemed satisfactory. The *samuri* granted Cabral the trading rights he sought, and André Gouveia was appointed factor of Calicut. But the Muslim merchants of the city, who had

FLEET OF PEDRO ÁLVARES CABRAL. Detail, from Lizuarte de Abreu's *O sucesso dos visoreis*, mid-sixteenth century. The illustration notes the name of the captain of each vessel and its fate. A storm near the Cape of Good Hope claimed four vessels, one of them (lower right) with Bartolomeu Dias, the cape's discoverer, aboard. THE PIERPONT MORGAN LIBRARY, NEW YORK; M.525, F.7; M.525, F.16v–17.

enjoyed a centuries-old monopoly of the Indian trade, placed a series of obstacles in their way, leading to hostilities that ended with the assassination of Aires Correia and his companions on December 17. According to the chronicler Lopes de Castanheda, Cabral ordered his captains to seize ten Muslim ships that were in port. The cargo was confiscated and the ships set afire with all hands on board. On the following day, Cabral, after bringing his ships as close to shore as possible, ordered the artillery trained on the city, killing and destroying everything and everyone in sight. Even the *samuri* was forced to flee when a cannon ball exploded near him.

A day later, since there was nothing left to destroy, Cabral sailed for Cochin where he had heard that the rajah was friendly to the Portuguese. In Cochin, where he arrived on December 24, he signed a treaty with the rajah and took on pepper. From there he went on to Cannanore, also on the Malabar coast, to load cinnamon. In Cranganore he came across a community of Jacobite Christians. Wisely ignoring a hostile fleet of the *samuri*, which had followed him all the way, he turned homeward, departing from Cannanore on January 31, 1501. He crossed the Indian Ocean and landed in Mozambique, from where he sent Sancho de Tovar to explore the Bay of Sofala, with orders to sail home once he had done so. On his way home, Cabral ran into many storms as far as the Cape of Good Hope, where one of the ships became separated from the fleet and was not seen again on the rest of the voyage. In spite of the dangers he encountered, he eventually rounded the cape on May 21, 1501. He anchored in Cape Verde and finally entered Lisbon harbor on June 23, 1501. Sancho de Tovar arrived later.

King Manuel received Cabral solemnly and conferred various honors on him. He offered Cabral the command of another India-bound fleet of twenty ships, five of which were to form a special squadron under the command of Vicente Sodré. At the last minute, however, for some unknown reason (the chroniclers offer varying explanations), the king changed his mind and offered the command instead to Vasco da Gama who eventually departed on what was to be his second voyage to India. Cabral retired to Santarém and was never again called on to serve the king.

Cabral's voyage was not regarded as a success at the time, but in light of the results, it stands out as one of the greatest of the Portuguese voyages. His achievements consisted of establishing friendly relations with two minor kingdoms—Cochin and Cannanore—on the Malabar coast of India; establishing a factory at the former place, the first permanent factory in India; finding an early Christian settlement at Cranganore; visiting Sofala; and ascertaining a practical sea route to the cape. Though he exercised extreme cruelty toward the Muslims of Calicut, he showed a humanitarian and sympathetic attitude in his treatment of the Amerindians of Brazil, and—unlike Columbus—there is no suggestion that they might have been used as slaves. In the discovery of Brazil, Cabral added to his native land a country that exceeded in area, wealth, and opportunity Portugal itself. It is true that the Portuguese would have discovered America in the course of their voyages to India, probably within a decade, had Columbus not crossed the Atlantic, but this does not lessen the importance of the voyage of Cabral as the first chapter of European history in Brazil.

Just as there are those who question the fact that Columbus discovered America on October 12, 1492, so too there are those who question the fact that Cabral discovered Brazil on April 22, 1500. Was Cabral indeed the first European to discover Brazil, they ask, and if so, was it accidental or intentional? Bailey W. Diffie, one of the doubters, asserts that after Columbus returned to Spain, many other men set out on exploring expeditions, and some of them reached Brazil before Cabral landed in 1500, notably Amerigo Vespucci, Vicente Yáñez Pinzón, and Diogo de Lepe. Many Portuguese historians have held that Cabral had secret instructions from the king to explore en route to India. If such secret instructions ever existed in any form, oral or written, no witnesses have been produced or written documents discovered. These and other questions regarding the voyage of Cabral still remain to be answered.

BIBLIOGRAPHY

Castanheda, Fernão Lopes de. *História do descobrimento e conquista da Índia pelos portugueses*. Edited by M. Lopes de Almeida. 2 vols. Porto, 1979.

Diffie, Bailey W. *Who Was the First to Discover Brazil?* Buffalo, N.Y., 1975.

Greenlee, William Brooks, ed. and trans. *The Voyage of Pedro Álvares Cabral to Brazil and India*. Hakluyt Society Publications, 2d ser., vol. 81. London, 1938.

Peres, Damião. *Pedro Alvares Cabral e o descobrimento do Brasil*. 4th ed. Porto, 1975.

Prestage, Edgar. *The Portuguese Pioneers*. London, 1933.

REBECCA CATZ

CABRILLO, JUAN RODRÍGUEZ

CABRILLO, JUAN RODRÍGUEZ (1498?–1543), soldier and explorer. Often said to be Portuguese, Juan Rodríguez Cabrillo is considered by most historians to be Spanish. Probably born in Seville, he was in the New World by 1510. A tough, self-sufficient boy, he became a merchant-adventurer and served with Pánfilo de Narváez in the conquest of Cuba. Rodríguez could read, write, keep accounts, and trade goods for a profit, but he could also ride a horse, use a crossbow, and handle a sailing ship.

In 1520 Rodríguez went to the mainland with Narváez, joined the army of Hernando Cortés, and served in the second siege of the Aztec capital, Tenochtitlán. Situated in the middle of a lake, Tenochtitlán was vulnerable to attack by ship. Consequently Cortés sent troops to the mountains to cut timber for vessels to be used in retaking the city. Rodríguez commanded a detachment to gather pine resin to mix with tallow and make pitch for waterproofing the ships. Lacking animal fat for tallow, the men used human fat, according to one story, from Indians killed in battle. True or not, the story reflects the reputation of Rodríguez as a tough conquistador.

In 1521 Rodríguez marched through Oaxaca with the soldiers of Francisco de Orozco and then went to Guatemala with the army of Pedro de Alvarado. Fighting and marching almost constantly for the next few years, the army occupied the provinces of Vera Paz, San Salvador, and Nicaragua, finally settling in the new city of Santiago de Guatemala. With a grant of land, plus Indian laborers to work it, Rodríguez became one of the richest men in the country. By 1532 he controlled gold mines, had ships on the Pacific coast of Guatemala, and engaged in trade with the Spanish soldiers involved in the conquest of the Inca Empire.

Though he had children by an Indian woman, Rodríguez returned to Spain about the fall of 1532 to marry the daughter of a prominent family of Seville, Beatríz Sánchez de Ortega, with whom he had two sons. During the 1530s he acquired the name Cabrillo, probably as a nickname, though the meaning is unclear.

Cabrillo built a fleet for Alvarado to use in a daring plan to cross the Pacific and trade with China and the Spice Islands, the lands Columbus had tried to reach in 1492. He joined the fleet with his own ship, *San Salvador*, serving as second in command. When Alvarado died in a misadventure, Cabrillo took the *San Salvador*, a smaller vessel, and a launch and sailed north in 1542. Confident that North America was either joined to Asia or separated from it by a narrow strait, the men expected to reach China by following the coastline north and west. Instead, they found themselves confined by winds and currents to the west coast of North America, unable to sail much beyond forty degrees north latitude. The expedition spent the fall exploring the coastline of present-day California. Winter camp was established on Catalina Island, where the commander was injured in a fall while trying to extricate his men from a fight with the suddenly hostile inhabitants. He died on January 3, 1543, and was buried on the island. His fleet made a second attempt to sail north and probably reached the Oregon coast before returning to New Spain.

Cabrillo's original reports and maps have been lost, but Andrés de Urdaneta interviewed the survivors of his fleet, made a summary of the journal, and sent the coastal map to Europe, where the results appeared in a world map drawn by Andreas Homem in 1559. Urdaneta used Cabrillo's report and map in 1565 when he made the first successful trip across the Pacific to the Spice Islands and back, thus completing the project started by Columbus.

BIBLIOGRAPHY

Kelsey, Harry. *Juan Rodríguez Cabrillo.* San Marino, Calif., 1986.
Mitchell, Mairin. *Friar Andrés de Urdaneta, O.S.A. (1508–1568): Pioneer of Pacific Navigation from West to East.* London, 1964.
Wagner, Henry R. *Spanish Voyages to the Northwest Coast of America.* San Francisco, 1929.

HARRY KELSEY

CADAMOSTO, ALVISE (1432–1488), Venetian navigator, explorer, and merchant. Cadamosto (or Ca'da Mosto), who is credited with discovery of the Cape Verde Islands, was a young trading partner in the Venetian company of Andrea Barbarigo when in August 1454 he entered the service of Prince Henry the Navigator. Henry was preparing a trading expedition to explore the Atlantic coast of Africa, for the Portuguese were very interested in the region as a source of spices, slaves, ivory, gum arabic, and gold. Cadamosto departed as a trading partner in March 1455, and after landing in the Madeiras and Canaries he followed the African coast south to the Senegal River. Along with several Genoese vessels he proceeded up the Gambia River, but returned to Portugal after the crews became restless in the face of hostile natives.

In April 1456, Cadamosto set out from Lagos with the Genoese Antoniotto Usodimare and headed south a second time. Rounding Cape Blanco, they were caught in a wind shift that sent them out to sea, apparently resulting in the discovery of the Cape Verde Islands. Cadamosto explored Boa Vista and São Tiago; then, returning to the coast, he headed south and reached the Bissagos Islands. Although Cadamosto is generally credited with the discovery of the Cape Verde Islands, some, including the historian of Genoa Jacques Heers, claim that Antonio di Noli discovered them in 1460.

Cadamosto wrote an account of his voyages that was first printed at Vicenza in 1507 in the collection *Paesi nuovamenti ritrovati et Novo Mondo da Alberica Vesputio Fiorentino intitolato.* His acute and often vivid observations of the African lands, people, and trading customs are among the earliest European accounts. The cartographer Fra Mauro of Venice used either a portolan map made by Cadamosto, now lost, or his verbal descriptions in constructing his famous world map of 1460.

BIBLIOGRAPHY

Caddeo, Rinaldo. *Le navigazioni atlantiche di Alvise da Ca'da Mosto, Antoniotto Usodimare e Niccololoso da Recco.* Milan, 1928.
"The Voyages of Cadamosto." *Hakluyt Society,* 2d ser., 80 (1937).

JOSEPH P. BYRNE

CANADA. The vision of Columbus and the encounter of the New and Old Worlds evidenced by his four voyages had pronounced influence on the evolution of Canada in the years 1497 to 1550. The Columbian age of Canada's development was one characterized by English, Portuguese, and French attempts to find a Northwest Passage to the rich and profitable lands of the east, including Cipangu (Japan), Cathay, and the Moluccas. Private and government interests in both England and France sought to follow up on Columbus's discoveries and to carve out spheres of influence in the New World once they came to realize that America was not Asia and that, in any event,

America offered resources, labor, foods, and places to settle. Equally important, the English and French entered into arrangements for the first time with the native peoples of Canada. From the natives they learned techniques of survival and travel in a land characterized by long, cold winters. The Europeans introduced diseases unknown to the natives of Canada. Some of the natives they kidnapped. They settled in lands previously occupied by native peoples. Not the least of the features of this cross-cultural encounter was the European desire, chiefly on the part of the French, to expand Christian mission activities. The French were the first to plant the cross on Canadian soil and to commence proselytizing.

On May 2, 1497, John Cabot (Giovanni Caboto), a Genoese navigator who had emigrated to England, sailed in *Mathew* from Bristol on an expedition sponsored by King Henry VII. Following the example of Columbus he sailed due west, but in more northerly latitudes. Cabot made a North American landfall on June 24, possibly at Cape Breton, Nova Scotia. He made an extensive coastal exploration and sailed along the eastern coast of Newfoundland before departing for Bristol. He reported large shoals of fish, and his observation further induced many European fishermen to undertake cod fishery off Newfoundland and Labrador. Bristol merchants had already been sending ships across the North Atlantic to search for the legendary island of Brasil, and some of them may have reached the area now known as Canada before Cabot.

Cabot's discovery is shown on the world map of Juan de la Cosa (1500), now in the Museo Naval, Madrid. Though far from accurate or complete as to details, it indicates English discoveries by showing English flags marking a certain portion of North America; moreover, it verbally attributes discovery to the English. Cabot's 1497 discovery of a New-Founde-Land led Bristol to equip five vessels in 1498 to return to the landfall of the previous year and to coast southward in search of Cipangu, which was thought to lie near at hand. John Cabot and the five ships were never heard of and were presumably lost at sea.

English exploration of Canada was then taken up by Sebastian Cabot, who had sailed with his father on the 1497 voyage. His 1508–1509 expedition, which is clouded in uncertainty, brought him fame if not notoriety. By his claim, he entered a strait, which opened between latitudes sixty-one and sixty-four degrees north, in search of a Northwest Passage and continued westward for about ten degrees of longitude. Cabot claimed that he then turned south into a large sea, which he believed to be the Pacific Ocean. Possibly he had entered the body of water later called Hudson Bay. For many years thereafter, the English concentrated on finding a Northeast Passage above Siberia, a search carried out by the Muscovy Company, of which Sebastian Cabot became the nominal governor. However, in 1575 Sir Martin Frobisher was granted an English license for an expedition to discover a Northwest Passage above Canada. He returned from the Canadian north with some pyrites, thinking they might be gold, and in 1577 he went for a second time, this time to west Greenland for ore. From a third voyage he brought back pyrites, which were truly fool's gold. Meanwhile, in 1578, Sir Humphrey Gilbert had published *A New Passage to Cathaia,* and eventually, when Frobisher's schemes came to nothing, Gilbert was given a license for colonial discovery. In 1583 he sailed to settle Newfoundland and claimed it for England, but died on his return voyage.

Meanwhile the Portuguese had undertaken voyages to seek a Northwest Passage. In 1500 Gaspar Côrte-Real sailed from Lisbon in two ships sponsored by King Manuel I to find the passage and possibly establish Portuguese sovereignty over land discovered by John Cabot in 1497. Côrte-Real sighted a coast that he took for Asia, but it was probably Greenland or possibly Newfoundland. In the following year, he sailed in three ships from Lisbon on a similar expedition and made a landfall probably on the Labrador coast. Two of the ships returned to Portugal with about fifty captive Inuit. Gaspar Côrte-Real was lost at sea, and in 1502 his brother Miguel sailed to Newfoundland to find the lost mariner and reached Newfoundland, but he, too, was never heard of again. In 1520 João Alvares Fagundes visited the vicinity of Newfoundland, Nova Scotia, and St. Pierre and Miquelon, and was given rights of colonization by Manuel. Fagundes may later have tried to settle in this area, but the details are altogether unclear. Portuguese fishermen increased their fishing off Newfoundland in consequence of these voyages.

In 1504 fishing vessels from Brittany began to visit the Grand Banks, and in 1506 Jean Denys, from Honfleur, made the first Norman fishing voyages to Newfoundland. French fishing activities then ensued from Rouen. In 1524, Giovanni da Verrazano sailed from Madeira on an expedition sponsored by Francis I of France. Landing near Cape Fear, North Carolina, he sailed northward until he reached about latitude fifty degrees north off Newfoundland. Ten years later, in 1534, Jacques Cartier, a Breton mariner, who had already sailed "to Brazil and the New Land," was entrusted by Francis I to sail to Newfoundland, where gold and other riches were said to exist. He located the south shore and islands of the Gulf of St. Lawrence. At Gaspé on July 24 he erected a cross, contrary to the wishes of the local chief, Donnacona. Shortly afterwards he captured the chief's two sons and left for the north, assuring Donnacona that they would be returned. On his return to France, Cartier convinced the French court that he had discovered an inland sea. His reported alliance with the local Indians and his optimistic perspectives concerning the possibilities of the passage in those latitudes led to his being allowed to return to the St. Lawrence. In 1535 he undertook his second voyage. With the help of two native guides, he entered the St. Lawrence River. He reached Stadacona, near present-day Québec City, and then the Indian village of Hochelaga, a palisaded town of fifty houses lying below a mountain that Cartier named Mount Royal. From its heights Cartier could see the great cataract known as the Lachine Rapids, which he believed to be the sea route to China; this was to become the highway of French penetration of the continental interior. In 1541 Cartier undertook his third voyage to Canada, with a colonization party under the leadership of Jean-François de La Rocque de Roberval. At Cap Rouge, near Stadacona, Cartier built a fort and nearby Roberval founded his colony, called Charlesbourg Royal. The heavy winter took its toll on the settlers: scurvy, famine, and rebellion were the results, and the colony survived only with native assistance to combat scurvy. Cartier and Roberval did not

remain in Canada. The iron pyrites they found were not gold and the mica was not diamonds. They realized too that no easy passage to China existed.

French interest in Canada lay dormant for half a century and French attempts at settlement were not resumed until Samuel de Champlain, a geographer and cartographer, established a colony in the Bay of Fundy in 1604, moving it to Québec in 1608 to plant the first permanent French settlement in the area now known as Canada. Between Cartier and Champlain the French undertook several fishing and fur-trading expeditions, depending on the Indians for help in fur trading. Champlain's 1612 map offers the first reasonably accurate representation of Canada.

In terms of international law Spain protested to France and also to Rome about Cartier's voyages, claiming that

MAP OF QUÉBEC. Showing Jacques Cartier, Indians, and European settlers. From the Vallard Atlas, 1547.

the lands west of the Line of Demarcation belonged to Spain. Francis I replied that "to pass by and to discover by eye is no title of possession." Pope Paul III did not object to France's claim, perhaps because he needed French support against Spain's dominant power, and because Cartier's third expedition was sent under a commission to extend the Christian faith in lands not already inhabited by any Christian prince. In this way France penetrated lands that Spain thought reserved for itself.

[See also *Northwest Passage.*]

BIBLIOGRAPHY

Cooke, Alan, and Clive Holland. *The Exploration of Northern Canada 500 to 1920: A Chronology.* Toronto, 1978.

The Dictionary of Canadian Biography. Vol. 1. Toronto, 1966.

Hoffman, Bernard G. *Cabot to Cartier: Sources for a Historical Ethnography of Northeastern North America.* Toronto, 1961.

Morison, Samuel Eliot. *The European Discovery of America: The Northern Voyages, A.D. 500–1600.* New York, 1971.

Oleson, Tryggvi J. *Early Voyages and Northern Approaches, 1000–1632.* Toronto, 1963.

Williamson, James A., ed. *The Cabot Voyages and Bristol Discovery under Henry VII.* Cambridge, 1962.

BARRY M. GOUGH

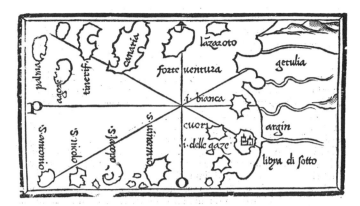

MAP OF THE CANARY ISLANDS. From Benedetto Bordone's *Isolario.* Venice, 1528. NATIONAL MARITIME MUSEUM, GREENWICH

CANARY ISLANDS. The Canary Islands are located between latitudes 27°30′N and 29°30′N and between longitudes 13°20′W and 18°10′W. This places them between 145 and 485 kilometers (90 and 300 miles) west of the southernmost extension of the Moroccan coast, about 485 kilometers (300 miles) south of the Portuguese Madeira Islands, and about 1,695 kilometers (1,050 miles) northeast of the Cape Verde Islands. The Canaries were known to European sailors before 1300, but their conquest and colonization by Spain were not accomplished until the period 1477 to 1497. The seven larger islands that make up the archipelago are Tenerife, Gran Canaria, Fuerteventura, Lanzarote, La Palma, Gomera, and Hierro (Ferro). The smaller named islands are Alegranza, Graciosa, Lobos, Roque del Este, Roque del Oeste, and Montaña Clara. The western islands of Hierro, Gomera, La Palma, and Tenerife have the most rainfall and the most varied topography. The eastern islands of Lanzarote and Fuerteventura have low relief and are quite arid; their climate is a westward extension of the Sahara Desert.

The strategic importance of the Canary Islands for the early explorers lay in their location about six to ten days' sail from Spain. The Canaries provided a convenient stopping point to make repairs and provision ships for westward voyages to the New World. The waters between Spain and the Canary Islands are frequently rough, but the southward Canary Current speeded the passage from Spain. Throughout the year, the Canary Islands lie in the northeast trade winds.

Columbus stopped at the Canary Islands on each of his four westward voyages. On his first voyage, he repaired the rudder of *Pinta* and rerigged *Niña* to a square rig for efficient westward travel.

BIBLIOGRAPHY

Hastenrath, Stefan, and Peter J. Lamb. *Climatic Atlas of the Tropical Atlantic and Eastern Pacific Oceans.* Madison, Wis., 1977.

McAlister, Lyle N. *Spain and Portugal in the New World, 1492–1700.* Minneapolis, 1984.

Morison, Samuel Eliot. *Admiral of the Ocean Sea: A Life of Christopher Columbus.* 2 vols. Boston, 1942.

COLLEEN A. LEARY

CANNIBALISM. Cannibals were reported by Columbus during his first two voyages. He claimed that the Taíno Indians spoke of *canibales, caribales, caniba, canima, cariba, caribe, cariby,* and *carib.* These words, their European derivatives (French, *Caraïbe;* English, *cannibal* and *Caribbean* as well as Shakespeare's *Caliban;* among others) and the tribal or language names *Kalina, Calinago,* and *Galibí* are based on related Indian words that evidently implied ferocity and perhaps enmity. Columbus understood that the Indians of the Greater Antilles applied this name to their enemies in the Lesser Antilles, whom they accused of being eaters of human flesh. The accusation confirmed a common European preconception about savages and barbarians. Spanish law very soon, in 1503, adopted the principle that cannibalism of itself justified war against its practitioners and, moreover, that cannibals were the only Indians who could be enslaved. In light of these functions, as well as the common human tendency to accuse strangers and enemies of atrocities, accounts of cannibalism require careful evaluation.

It is doubtful that any human society has ever engaged in customary cannibalism for purely dietary or subsistence reasons. But it is, on the other hand, certain that many societies, including some in Europe in the sixteenth and even the eighteenth centuries, have engaged in customary cannibalism within narrowly defined limits as to victims, body parts and amounts eaten, and occasions or motives.

The customary cannibalism in the Americas that is best understood, because of the quality and number of qualified observers, is that of the Tupinambás of coastal Brazil during the sixteenth century. Each Tupinambá province or territorial group of villages was engaged in continual warfare with its neighbors, most of whom shared the same language and customs. The purpose of warfare was the capture of prisoners, all of whom were eventually sacrificed and eaten. The treatment of captured enemies was governed by heavily theatrical ritual, which was also certainly full of religious significance, though only hints of the latter are preserved in the documentary sources. There were two principal occasions for the ceremonies: when the captive first arrived at the captors' village, and when he was finally killed and eaten. The two occasions were separated by a period of months and often years. The length of his captivity was the only element of his fate that was not known to the captive, and surely it was psychologically important that this should be so, enabling the captive to play out his role properly until the end came. Only at the beginning and end of the captivity was the victim displayed, taunted, and forcefully reminded of his future. The women undertook particularly important parts in these ceremonies, and the contrasting ritual duties of the sexes is so prominent that it is likely that the treatment of the occasional female captives was also quite different, although the sources say little about these captives except that they too were eaten.

On his arrival at the captor's village, the captive was made to clean the grave of the person whose death his own was now to avenge. He announced to the women met on the path, "I, your future food, have arrived." The men and the women chose the parts of his body each would eat, and often thereafter taunted him with reminders. After his initial reception, the captive was incorporated almost completely into the daily life of the village. He was in effect adopted, replacing the one whose grave he had cleaned. The hammock, weapons, and other property of the deceased were given him, and as wife he was assigned the widow, or else a sister or daughter of his captor or a woman the latter requested for him. Such a marriage was considered prestigious and was not refused. Although it is said that this wife was to keep him from escaping, there was little need for such a guardian. His

own people would not have accepted him should he have returned. Considering him cowardly and believing that his escape implied that they were not strong enough to avenge him, they would probably have killed him. If the captive's wife bore him any children, these too were considered enemies in this patrilineal society, and they were killed and eaten before their father was.

The final ceremonies lasted from three to five days. They included a symbolic recapture and a mock battle in which the captive's movements were constrained by ropes while he shot blunt arrows and threw rocks, potsherds, and hard fruits. At the execution, the victim, the executioner, and even the sacrificial club were heavily decorated. The victim and the executioner engaged in a formalized dialogue emphasizing revenge and threats of revenge. The executioner finally killed him with a blow to the nape of the neck, despite the prisoner's dodging and resisting while he was held by a cord around his waist. The body was then butchered, and the women cooked it, grilling the flesh on a barbecue frame and boiling the entrails. The entire body was eaten, with the possible exception of the brain. Everyone present, guests and villagers, from the oldest to the youngest, had to eat some of the captive. Nursing babies were fed by smearing the victim's blood on their mothers' nipples. If there was insufficient meat to feed everyone, a broth was made so all had at least a taste. There were a few restrictions: the genitalia could be eaten only by someone of the opposite sex, and the executioner had to disgorge what he ate.

The key to understanding Tupinambá cannibalism is their need for vengeance, as they often explained to European inquirers. As Michel de Montaigne wrote in his essay "Of Cannibals" (1580), after interviewing French observers and some Tupinambás brought to Normandy, "it is not, as some think, for nourishment, as it was among the ancient Scythians; it is to carry out the most extreme revenge." The dead had to be avenged, whether they had died in combat or otherwise. The sacrifice was thus a funerary rite, required to appease the spirits of the dead. Ingesting the enemy may also have been a way of regaining and reincorporating the substance and qualities of one's relatives whom the captive had previously eaten. The religious nature of the custom is also shown by the severe restrictions placed on the executioner. He changed his name; he was isolated as though he were ill or in mourning; and he underwent a long period of rigorous fasting. Upon completion of his task, he gained prestige and authority.

Whether or not the Island Caribs accused of cannibalism by their Taíno enemies were in fact eaters of human flesh is a topic of debate. Very likely they practiced endocannibalism, that is, the ingestion of parts of deceased relatives as part of funerary rites. Many South

EUROPEAN DEPICTION OF CANNIBALISM IN THE AMERICAS. The sensational appeal of such images can be supposed from the number produced and their graphic intensity. This engraving is from Caspar Plautius's *Navigatio in Novum Mundum*. Many similar images were published by Théodor de Bry.   LIBRARY OF CONGRESS, RARE BOOK DIVISION

American peoples are documented as ingesting the ground-up bones or ashes of cremated relatives, and some, such as the Guayakí of Paraguay, ate the roasted and boiled flesh of their deceased relatives in order to prevent the souls of the dead from entering their surviving relatives and causing illness and death. The material evidence of funerary endocannibalism and other non-European funerary practices may well have been misinterpreted by Columbus and others as evidence for exocannibalism, the eating of enemies and the hunting of humans in order to eat them. But there does seem to be good evidence for Island Caribs, mainland Caribs, and perhaps Arawaks and others in Venezuela and the Guianas practicing ritualized cannibalism with selected body parts of war captives in a manner and with motives not greatly dissimilar to those of the Tupinambás.

Customary cannibalism is also documented as a minor part of the elaborate sacrificial complex of the Aztecs. The victims were war captives or slaves who were ritually constituted as gods. When they were sacrificed, their bodies were sacred objects and their arms and legs were often eaten. The gods' flesh was thereby consumed as a sort of communion.

Among North American Indians, there is good evidence for the practice of cannibalism as a part of the ritual of the torture of war captives by the Iroquois and Hurons in what is now New York and Ontario in the seventeenth century and before. Here the principal motive seems to have been the incorporation of some of the good qualities of the enemy. It is probable that only particular parts of the body were ingested, rather than essentially the whole body as in Tupinambá practice.

BIBLIOGRAPHY

Abler, Thomas S. "Iroquois Cannibalism: Fact not Fiction." *Ethnohistory* 27, no. 4 (1980): 309–316.

Forsyth, Donald W. "The Beginnings of Brazilian Anthropology: Jesuits and Tupinamba Cannibalism." *Journal of Anthropological Research* 39, no. 2 (1983): 147–178.

Friederici, Georg. "Caribe." In *Amerikanistisches Wörterbuch*. University of Hamburg; Abhandlungen aus dem Gebiet der Auslandskunde, vol. 53. Series B: Völkerkunde, Kulturgeschichte und Sprachen, vol. 29. Hamburg, 1947.

Henríquez Ureña, Pedro. "Caribe." In *Para la historia de los indigenismos*. Biblioteca de dialectología Hispanoamericano, supp. 3. Buenos Aires, 1938.

Métraux, Alfred. "L'anthropophagie rituelle des Tupinamba." In *Religions et magies indiennes d'Amérique du Sud*, pp. 45–78. Paris, 1967.

Sahlins, Marshall. "Culture as Protein and Profit." *New York Review of Books* 25, no. 18 (November 23, 1978).

Sahlins, Marshall. "Cannibalism: An Exchange." *New York Review of Books* 26, no. 4 (March 22, 1979).

Whitehead, Neil L. "Carib Cannibalism, the Historical Evidence." *Journal de la Société des Américanistes* 70 (1984): 69–88.

WILLIAM C. STURTEVANT

CÃO, DIOGO (fl. 1480–1486), Portuguese navigator. From 1480 on, the *mare clausum* (closed sea) policy in the Gulf of Guinea was reinforced by Prince João of Portugal with coast guard squadrons. Diogo Cão appears for the first time in the historical record as a naval captain in one of these missions. These squadrons had orders to execute summarily any intruders found south of the parallel of the Canary Islands as far as a place called Mina, where gold was being extracted.

In 1481, the "perfect prince" ascended the throne as João II and immediately issued orders to Diogo de Azambuja to construct a castle in Mina, in order to exercise control over the gold trade. The castle of São Jorge da Mina (St. George of Elmina), which was finished in about 1482, became the principal source of the precious metal in the fifteenth century, thereby giving Portugal supremacy in this profitable trade. As part of the same strategy, João II ordered the first voyage of geographical exploration commanded by Diogo Cão (1482–1484) to sail beyond the then known limits of the African coast, south of the Gulf of Guinea, below the equator.

Sailing in caravels, Diogo Cão ventured along the coast and reached the Rio Zaire and, farther south, a place called Cape Lobo, located on the coast of Angola. Although this was the farthest point he reached on his first voyage, he thought he had discovered the southern tip of Africa and reached the waters of the Indian Ocean. On the way he made contact with the Kingdom of the Kongo; he established friendly relations with the Kongo people and brought back to Portugal some of the local inhabitants. As a sign that he had passed through these lands, he left some impressive inscriptions engraved on the rocks of Ielala, on the banks of the Rio Zaire, and set up stone pillars at the mouth of the river and at Cape Lobo.

In the meantime, while the first voyage of Diogo Cão was under way, a Portuguese adventurer, João Afonso de Aveiro, was sent overland to explore the interior of Africa, starting from the coasts of Benin and present-day Nigeria. He returned in 1485 with the news that "Ogané" was near. This was an African potentate whom the Portuguese identified possibly with the legendary Prester John of the Indies.

The combined results of the explorations of Diogo Cão and João Afonso de Aveiro may have led the Portuguese to believe that they were about to reach India. In the same year, the Portuguese ambassador Vasco Fernandes de Lucena, in a speech given before the pope in Rome, stated that Portuguese ships had sailed beyond the Promonto-rium Prassum of Ptolemaic geography and discovered the southern tip of Africa.

This must certainly have been one of the reasons the Portuguese king at that time rejected Columbus's proposal to sail west to India. The Portuguese knew that the estimate of the size of the globe on which Columbus based his figures (in accordance with Ptolemy and other written sources) was wrong, and they were above all interested in an African route to the Indies.

During the years 1485–1486, by order of the king, Diogo Cão undertook his second voyage of exploration. Still sailing in caravels, he passed beyond the limit of his first voyage, returned the Kongo people to their homeland, and reached a point on the African coast called Serra Parda. Here he realized he had been mistaken, and that the coastline continued farther south—India was not yet near. Nevertheless, he placed a stone pillar at a point on the coast called Cabo do Padrão (Cape Cross, in present-day Namibia). It is not known whether he died there (as

MONUMENT (*PADRÃO*) OF CAPE CROSS. Placed by Diogo Cão at latitude 21 degrees, 47 minutes south, on the Namibian coast. Such stone monuments were carried on board by Portuguese navigators and were erected to indicate Portuguese claims of dominion. MUSEUM FÜR DEUTSCHE GESCHICHTE, BERLIN

some authors say, basing their judgment on a doubtful reading of a legend on the map of Henricus Martellus) or returned to Portugal. In any case, there is no further reference to him. If he did return to Portugal, it is probable that the king did not forgive him for the high expectations raised by the first voyage but dashed by the second.

In the meantime, in 1488, João II sent Columbus (who was in Spain at the time) an enigmatic letter, assuring him of a safe return to Portugal where his services would be appreciated. This may have reflected the king's disappointment over the results of Diogo Cão's voyages and a subsequent decision to consider the alternate route proposed by Columbus. Or it could have been a diversionary maneuver—to show interest in the western route and thus induce his Castilian rivals to support Columbus's project, leaving the southern route free for the Portuguese to explore at their own pace.

In any case, the Portuguese expedition headed by Bartolomeu Dias departed in 1487. It followed immediately upon Diogo Cão's voyages and finally succeeded in going beyond the southern tip of Africa. When in December 1488 Dias returned to Portugal with the news of his discovery, either Columbus or his brother Bartolomé was probably present when the results of the voyage were announced to the king. With this news, the Portuguese Crown may well have lost any continuing interest in Columbus's plan, for it was then that Columbus last departed for Castile, where he finally found royal support for his westward project.

The voyages of Diogo Cão were consequently of great importance. They brought Portuguese explorations to a new phase and resulted in João II's decision to pursue an African route to India. They also instigated the manufacture of cartographic charts, some of which have survived to this day. The oldest extant signed Portuguese map is the chart of Peter Reinel (c. 1485). It is a direct representation of the explorations of Diogo Cão. Other important cartographic charts reflecting his voyages were prepared in those years, namely the map of Henricus Martellus (c. 1490) and the globe of Martin Behaim (c. 1492), the latter containing specific information about Cão's explorations, including the location of the first stone pillar set up by the navigator on his second voyage.

BIBLIOGRAPHY

Barros, João de, and Diogo do Couto. *Da Asia de João de Barros e de Diogo do Couto.* 24 vols. Lisbon, 1778–1788.

Campos, Viraiato. *Viagem de Diogo Cão e de Bartolomeu Dias.* Lisbon, 1966.

Cordeiro, Luciano. "Descobertas e descobridores: Diogo Cão." *Boletim da Sociedade de Geografia de Lisboa* (1892).

Cordeiro, Luciano. *Diogo Cão.* Lisbon, 1971.

Lewis, Thomas. "The Old Kingdom of Kongo." *Geographical Journal* 31 (1908): 589–615.

Pina, Rui de. *Chronica d'elrey D. João II.* Edited by M. Lopes de Almeida. Porto, 1977.

Prestage, Edgar. *The Portuguese Pioneers.* Pp. 206–211. London, 1933.

Ravenstein, E. G. "The Voyage of Diogo Cão and Bartolomeu Dias, 1482–88." *Geographical Journal* 16 (1890): 625–655.

ALFREDO PINHEIRO MARQUES
Translated from Portuguese by Rebecca Catz

CAPE OF GOOD HOPE.

CAPE OF GOOD HOPE. The Cape of Good Hope, located on the southwest coast of Africa at 34°21'S, 18°29'E near Cape Town in the Republic of South Africa, was first rounded by Bartolomeu Dias in 1488. This voyage was the culmination of over one hundred years of voyages of exploration by Portuguese sailors south along the west coast of Africa. It confirmed hopes that India could be reached by sailing around Africa. Vasco da Gama rounded the Cape of Good Hope in 1497 on the first sea voyage to India from Europe.

Rounding the Cape of Good Hope on a sailing ship was a practical as well as a symbolic victory. A ship sailing southward and eastward had to fight not only adverse head winds but currents as well. The cool Benguela Current flows northward along the west coast of southern Africa, and the warm Agulhas Current flows westward around the southern coast of Africa. Storms with gale force winds in the prevailing westerlies off the Cape of Good Hope can generate waves of twenty feet or higher. In fact, Dias originally named the cape Cabo Tormentoso (Cape of Storms). When no storms are present, the coastal region can experience frequent heavy fog.

Columbus was in Lisbon when Dias returned from the first rounding of the Cape of Good Hope. The success of Dias ended King João II's interest in Columbus's plan to sail westward and resulted in Columbus's return to Spain.

BIBLIOGRAPHY

Bowditch, Nathaniel. *American Practical Navigator.* Washington, D.C., 1966.

Morison, Samuel Eliot. *Admiral of the Ocean Sea: A Life of Christopher Columbus.* 2 vols. Boston, 1942.

Rudloff, Willy. *World-Climates.* Stuttgart, 1981.

COLLEEN A. LEARY

CAPE VERDE ISLANDS.

CAPE VERDE ISLANDS. The Cape Verde Islands, known officially as the República de Cabo Verde, are located between latitudes 14°48'N and 17°13'N and longitudes 22°41'W and 25°22'W, about 640 kilometers (400 miles) west of the bulge of the African coast at northern

Senegal. Between 1455 and 1462, the first Europeans to discover the Cape Verdes claimed the uninhabited islands for Portugal. The first settlers arrived in 1462, and the Cape Verde Islands remained part of Portugal until the republic was founded in 1975.

Located about 1,700 kilometers (1,050 miles) southwest of the Canary Islands, the Cape Verdes provided a safe anchorage for ships traveling to the New World, as well as to and around Africa. The islands lie near the equatorward edge of the northeasterly trade winds, in a region where the ocean current flows southwestward. In spite of their name, the Cape Verdes have a dry desertlike climate similar to that of western Africa.

The ten principal islands of the archipelago are oriented in a rough V shape with the point facing toward Africa. The islands are, in order of decreasing size, São Tiago, Santo Antão, Boa Vista, Fogo, São Nicolão, Maio, São Vicente, Sal, Brava, and Santa Luzia. Although the average elevation of the islands is only 800 meters (2,600 feet) above sea level, the islands are actually the tops of undersea mountains. Fogo has an active volcano, and the adjacent island, Brava, experienced tremors and exhibited signs of volcanic activity in the recent past.

On his third voyage of discovery to the New World, Columbus traveled from the Canary Islands to the Cape Verde Islands before crossing the Atlantic to land on the coast of South America.

BIBLIOGRAPHY

Duncan, T. Bentley. *Atlantic Islands: Madeira, the Azores and the Cape Verdes in Seventeenth-Century Commerce and Navigation.* Chicago, 1972.

Morison, Samuel Eliot. *Admiral of the Ocean Sea: A Life of Christopher Columbus.* 2 vols. Boston, 1942.

COLLEEN A. LEARY

CAPITULATIONS OF SANTA FE. See *Santa Fe Capitulations.*

CARIBS. See *Indian America,* articles on *Island Caribs* and *Arawaks and Caribs.*

CARLOS I. For discussion of the Spanish king Carlos I, see *Charles V.*

CARPINI, GIOVANNI DA PIAN DEL (c. 1180–1252), Franciscan friar and papal envoy to the Mongol khan. Carpini was among the first Westerners to visit the Mongol leader in his home territory. A contemporary of

Saint Francis of Assisi and a native of Umbria, Carpini had become a Franciscan by about 1220. For twenty-five years he served in Franciscan provincial offices in Germany, Spain, and perhaps Barbary. Pope Innocent IV chose Carpini, then about sixty years old, to lead the first of several official missions to the khan, whose fierce armies had invaded Christian eastern Europe, resulting in widespread fear and destruction. Carpini and two other friars were to observe the nature of the Mongol territories, reach the Grand Khan, and register protests against his invasions; they also hoped to gain his aid against Islam.

After leaving Lyons in April 1245, the friars reached Kiev early in 1246 and Karakorum in Mongolia, near the khan's camp, on July 22, 1246. They witnessed the enthronement of a new khan on August 24 and were presented to him formally. In November the khan drafted an imperious reply in Mongol, Arabic, and Latin and sent the Westerners on their way. Their winter journey was filled with hardship, but they reached Kiev in June 1247 and Lyons, where the pope was waiting, seventeen months later. For his services, the pontiff rewarded Carpini with an archbishopric in Dalmatia.

Carpini's formal report, contained in his treatise *Historia Mongolorum,* or *Liber Tartarorum,* contains observations on the territories they traveled through, and the customs, religions, history, and character of the East. He comments on the policies and tactics of the Mongol leadership and suggests ways to oppose them. His work is a solid report, largely devoid of fantasy, on lands that had been closed to Europeans for centuries.

Western leaders regarded the Mongol empire not only as a threat but also as a field for evangelization, a possible trading partner, and a powerful counterweight to Islam. Carpini's perceptive observations were widely circulated; they were abstracted in Vincent of Beauvais's popular *Speculum historiale* (c. 1260; printed in 1473) and alluded to in Roger Bacon's *Opus maius* (c. 1266). The complete work was not published, however, until the nineteenth century.

BIBLIOGRAPHY

Dawson, Christopher, ed. *The Mission to Asia.* Toronto, 1986.

Guzman, G. G. "The Encyclopaedist Vincent of Beauvais and His Mongol Extracts from John of Piano Carpino and Simon of Saint-Quentin." *Speculum* 49 (1974).

Phillips, J. R. S. *The Medieval Expansion of Europe.* Oxford and New York, 1988.

Rachewiltz, I. de. *Papal Envoys to the Great Khans.* London, 1971.

Spuler, Bertold. *History of the Mongols, Based on Eastern and Western Accounts of the 13th and 14th Centuries.* Translated by Helen and Stuart Drummond. Berkeley, 1972.

JOSEPH P. BYRNE

CARTIER, JACQUES (1491–1557), French navigator and explorer. Little is known of Cartier's youth and early career. He was born in Saint-Malo (Brittany) where he rose to the position of master pilot, in part because of his marriage to Catherine Des Granges, daughter of the high constable of the city, in 1520. When King Francis I in 1532 expressed an interest in furthering the exploration of North America begun by Giovanni da Verrazano, the bishop of Saint-Malo, Jean Le Veneur, recommended Cartier, who, he said, had already visited Brazil and the Newfoundland fishery. Of Cartier's navigational skills there is no doubt, having begun his career as a *mousse* (ship's boy) when only thirteen, rising soon to the rank of novice and then sailor. The recommendation was confirmed the following year when Le Veneur obtained from Rome an interpretation of the papal bull of 1493 allowing France to move into territories not already occupied by Spain or Portugal.

Cartier was familiar with the New World that he would be commissioned to explore. There can be little doubt he had contacts with Breton and Norman fishermen who had been coming to Newfoundland waters since at least the late fifteenth century. His accounts also included accurate observations on Brazil. In 1534 he sailed directly to Cape Bonavista and the Strait of Belle Isle as if to a familiar rendezvous.

The royal commission granted him in 1534 ordered him "to discover certain islands and lands where it is said that a great quantity of gold, and other precious things, are to be found." The French Crown obviously hoped to gain access to American treasure and a sea route to the Orient while leaving the costs of initial investigation to private maritime interests. The first expedition, consisting of two sixty-ton ships and a sixty-one-member crew, left Saint-Malo on April 20, 1534, and crossed the Atlantic in twenty days, a remarkably short transatlantic voyage. Cartier's account of his entry into the Gulf of St. Lawrence makes clear that the northern bays and islands were known, frequented, and assigned Breton and Norman names. He even met a fishing vessel returning to La Rochelle. Cartier had taken the route of western European fishermen and marine hunters who in turn probably followed the route beyond Icelandic fishing grounds first navigated by the Vikings. Since the north shore of the gulf, apart from offering havens to vessels in case of storms and supplies of fresh water, seemed uninhabitable, Cartier called it "the land God gave to Cain" (it was popularly believed that Cain was condemned to wander everlastingly in the desolate regions of the earth until the end of the world).

Cartier then headed southward along the west coast of Newfoundland, then westward to the Magdalen Islands and the mainland coastline, searching for a passageway to the Orient. At Chaleur Bay he met some Micmacs with whom he engaged in some brisk trading. Farther north, at Gaspé, he encountered a summer fishing encampment of friendly Laurentian Iroquois with whom he bartered goods sailors normally stocked for such encounters—beads, mirrors, red caps, needles, knives—in return for well-worn beaver cloaks. It was obvious that the natives who came brandishing furs on the end of staves to attract European attention were not novices to such exchanges. His accounts mention at least eleven crosses erected on headlands to serve as navigational aids, but the ten-meter cross erected at Penouille Point, Québec, bearing the arms of the king, appears to have been intended as a formal *prise de possession*. The Iroquoian headman Donnacona so interpreted the ceremony of the erection of the cross and gestured that he wanted it removed as the territory belonged to his people. The chief's sons, Domagaya and Taignoagny, were forcibly taken aboard Cartier's vessel, which headed northward to Anticosti Island but missed the entrance to the St. Lawrence River. These young men subsequently served as interpreters and guides to their permanent base at Stadacona on the St. Lawrence River. By mid-August Cartier thought it advisable to return to France, but he was convinced that a second expedition would enable him to penetrate far to the west to discover fabulous riches.

He was back in Saint-Malo on September 5 and within two months his optimism was shared by Francis I, who granted him a second commission, a promotion, and a subsidy of three thousand livres for the undertaking. The second expedition set out with 110 men and three vessels—*Grande Hermine* commanded by Cartier himself, *Petite Hermine* commanded by a brother-in-law, and *Emérillon* by a compatriot. On board were Domagaya and Taignoagny, who had learned some French during their almost nine-month sojourn in France. This crossing took fifty days, and it was mid-August when the Iroquois captives guided Cartier along "the route toward Canada." He noted passing the "very deep and rapid" Saguenay River and the Ile d'Orléans "where the territory of Canada begins." Donnacona, happy to see his sons again, received the French hospitably. Cartier anchored his ships below the village of Stadacona. He was determined to go farther upstream, though his hosts tried to dissuade him by gifts and then by a display of sorcery. But Cartier would not be deterred from his search for the western passage. With thirty men on long boats he reached the Island of Montréal. Here he was received at the fortified village of Hochelaga, which was surrounded by cornfields near a mountain which he named Mont-Royal. From its summit he could see the widening of the Ottawa River where it joined the St. Lawrence. He was told it led to a "freshwater sea" and to the kingdom of Saguenay where all manner of exotic goods could be had.

When Cartier returned to his base camp he found his men building a fort to defend themselves against increasingly hostile Stadaconans. A harsh winter set in by mid-November bringing scurvy in its wake, which killed twenty-five of Cartier's men. Fortunately Cartier was able to learn the Iroquoian remedy of making an infusion from the bark and needles of the *annedda*, probably white cedar. When spring came, Cartier captured Donnacona and his sons and sailed off to France with seven additional captives. He reached France on July 16, 1536, after an absence of fourteen months.

In October 1540 Cartier was named captain general of a third expedition, but in January 1541 the commission was annulled in favor of a Protestant nobleman, Jean-François de La Rocque de Roberval, who was named commander of a colonization venture with the commoner Cartier as his subaltern. Roberval authorized Cartier to proceed ahead of him with a first contingent of settlers, which he did on May 23, 1541. None of the Iroquois captives survived to return to Canada. Although initially well received at Stadacona, Cartier thought it wise to establish his fortified base upstream at Rivière du Cap-Rouge, which he called Charlesbourg-Royal. In September Cartier made a second trip to the island of Montréal and visited the Lachine Rapids in anticipation of venturing into the upper country the following year. He never realized this objective because relations at Stadacona deteriorated. Charlesbourg-Royal was under constant attack from the natives, who were now decimated by an epidemic, probably of French origin. No fewer than thirty-five Frenchmen had been killed by June 1542, and it was decided to abandon the settlement.

Cartier met the inbound Roberval contingent at St. John's, Newfoundland, but with his vessels loaded with precious metals and having no desire to face the Laurentian Iroquois again, he slipped away under cover of darkness for France. His gold proved to be iron pyrites and his diamonds only quartz. Though he was not punished for having abandoned the Roberval colony, he was never entrusted with another major undertaking. He lived in bourgeois comfort on his country estate at Limoilou during the next fifteen years, until his death at the age of sixty-six during an outbreak of the plague. His widow survived him by eighteen years and as they had no children his papers and charts went to his nephews.

The accounts of Cartier's voyages were published piecemeal: the account of the first voyage was first published in Italian by Ramusio in 1565; the account of the second was published anonymously in French in 1545; and the account of the third was published in a fragmentary English version by Hakluyt in 1600. The Franciscan André Thévet obtained much information about the continent and its native peoples directly from Cartier;

Sebastian Cabot also visited him at Saint-Malo; Rabelais made use of information about Canada in the writing of *Pantagruel*.

Cartier's enduring contribution is the inauguration of the St. Lawrence approach to French exploitation and colonization in North America. The geographical information he provided was soon reproduced on contemporary maps. He also extended the territories of the fishermen, whalers, walrus hunters, and eventually the fur traders.

BIBLIOGRAPHY

Biggar, H. P. *A Collection of Documents Relating to Jacques Cartier and the Sieur de Roberval*. Ottawa, 1930.

Braudel, Fernand, ed. *Le monde de Jacques Cartier*. Montréal, 1984.

Hoffman, Bernard G. *Cabot to Cartier: Sources for a Historical Ethnography of Northeastern North America, 1497–1550*. Toronto, 1961.

Trudel, Marcel. *Les vaines tentatives, 1524–1603*. Vol. 1 of *Histoire de la Nouvelle-France*. Montréal, 1963.

Cornelius J. Jaenen

CARTOGRAPHY. Maps were a nearly indispensable part of the process by which the Europeans settled what they called the New World. Not only were they necessary for navigators, who used them to negotiate the new seas, with their many islands and reef-protected shores, but they also became an important part of the process by which, back in the Old World, kings and queens and statesmen decided where next to send their ships, sailors, and colonists.

Nor were the newcomers the only ones to use maps, for throughout most of what became known as America the indigenous peoples had cartographic skills. In the north they drew maps on such materials as deerskins and walrus tusks, and they made sketches in sand to give cartographic information to the Europeans. Similar mapping traditions existed throughout Central and South America. They were most developed in the Aztec kingdom of Mexico, where maps were drawn showing not only space, but also time, in the form of accompanying genealogical tables. The only area from which no maps have survived seems to be the Caribbean. It may be, though, that some of the region's numerous surviving rock carvings will one day be shown to be maps, and it is highly likely that the Caribbean Amerindians, like those on the rest of the continent, sketched rough maps in the sand.

The Cartographic Tradition in Europe

By the middle of the fifteenth century, three quite separate cartographic traditions had developed in Europe, and these were beginning to influence one another. First, there was the tradition of the medieval *mappamundi* (pl., *mappaemundi*), which went back at least to the eighth century. These became quite numerous from the twelfth century onward. Then, there were the portolan charts, highly accurate delineations of the Mediterranean coastline that emerged about 1300. Finally, there were the maps based on the geographical ideas of Ptolemy (Claudius Ptolemaeus), who lived about A.D. 200 and whose writings began to win new popularity in the early fifteenth century.

When Columbus began to study maps he was able to rely on these three traditions, each of which added something to his vision of the world. Curiously, he probably embarked in 1492 without having seen a globe, since the earliest European example seems to date from that very year, when an "Earth-apple" (as the Germans called it) was constructed in Nuremberg by Martin Behaim. Thereafter, many such globes were built, and they became an ornament of princely courts and libraries.

Mappaemundi. The *mappaemundi* varied greatly in style and detail, but they were nearly always roughly circular and oriented toward the east. The simplest fifteenth-century types are versions of a map that goes back to the eighth century. In these simple versions, the Ocean Sea, or "Mare Oceanum," surrounds the three continents, Asia, Europe, and Africa. Beneath the names of the continents are the names of the sons of Noah whose descendants peopled them: Sem for Asia, Jafeth for Europe, and Cham for Africa. A T-shaped body of water separates the continents, labelled "Great Sea" or "Mediterranean." In other maps of this kind, the stem of the T alone is the Mediterranean, while the left-hand branch is the Black Sea, and the right-hand branch the Red Sea. Obviously a map of this kind is highly schematic and is simply a way of keeping a general outline in one's head. Some historians of cartography compare these maps to modern maps of subway systems, which similarly try to give a general image of the system without pretending to offer accuracy in every part.

One such map is marked with the four cardinal points, "Oriens," "Occidens," "Meridies," and "Septentrio," and may be interpreted either as a flat disk or as a hemisphere. Most commentators agree that people of some learning in the Middle Ages considered the earth round, so these "T–O" maps, as they are called, should probably be envisaged as showing a hemisphere, which they would have called the *oikoumene*, or known world, as opposed to the unknown world, which presumably lay on the other side of it.

Some *mappaemundi* were much more elaborate. The map by Giovanni Leardo of Venice, drawn in 1452, shows the known world surrounded by the Ocean Sea. Jerusalem is in the center, with the Mediterranean Sea stretching away to the west (left) of it. The coastline of the countries

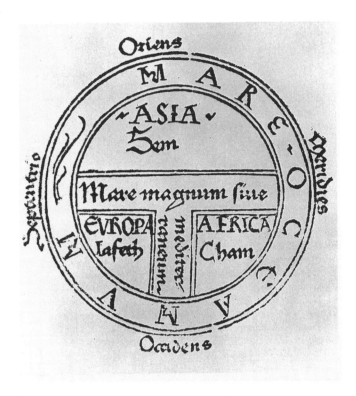

T-O MAP. Fifteenth-century printed version. From *Etymologiarum sive originum libri xx* by Isidore of Seville. Augsburg, 1472.

bordering the Mediterranean is well delineated, as are the Black Sea and Red Sea. Outside the Mediterranean, to the west, the cartographer's knowledge becomes very sketchy; he has some idea of the West African coast but very little of the British Isles and none of Scandinavia. In the east, beyond the Red Sea, Arabia is well shown, but knowledge fades well before India is reached.

This remains a geography very strongly influenced by Christian traditions. The four Evangelists occupy the four corners of the Leardo parchment, with the lion for Mark, the bull for Luke, the angel for Matthew, and the eagle for John. In the extreme east of the map is the terrestrial paradise, named, in red capitals, the Paradixo Teresto. We can also identify Noah's Ark resting on Mount Ararat, the site of Mount Sinai, and the River Jordan. There are also elements that represent ideas from the classical world: to the north is a desert so cold that none could cross it ("Dixerte dexabitado per fredo"), and to the south another desert, this so hot as to defy entry ("Dixerto dexabitado per caldo"). This work by Leardo not only is a summary of the *mappamundi* tradition but also introduces elements from the other two strands of medieval cartographic tradition, the portolan charts and Ptolemaic geography.

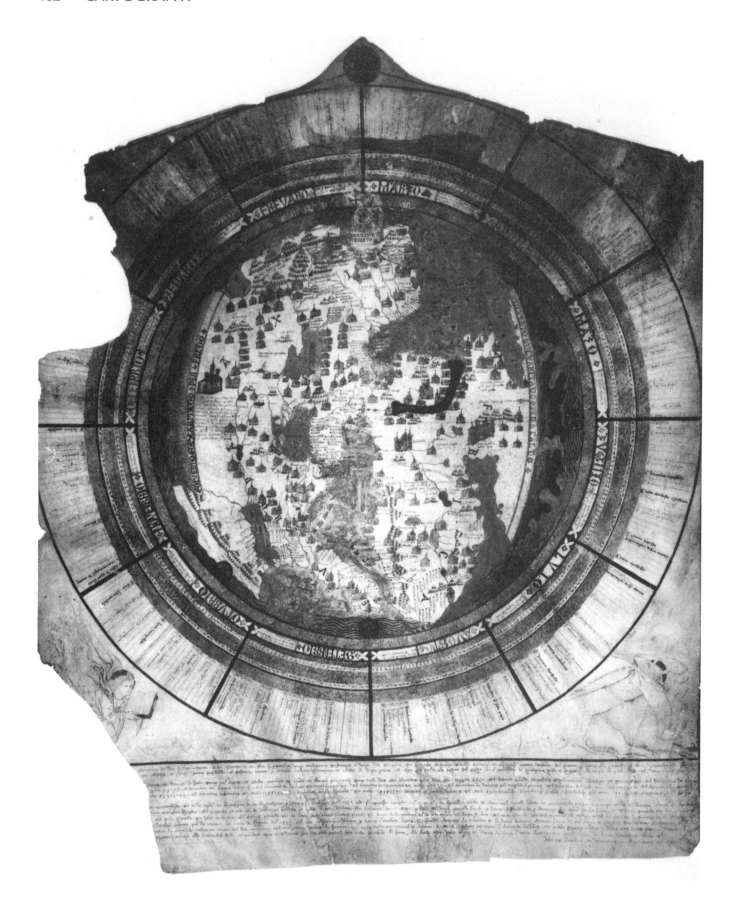

Portolan charts. The portolan chart is a cartographic type that, unlike most, seems to have appeared quite suddenly in almost perfect form. The first such chart known is called the Carte Pisane, because it seems to have originated at Pisa. It dates from about 1300. Its delineation of the Mediterranean Sea is a vast improvement on anything earlier that is known. Scholars have debated a good deal on how such perfection of outline was achieved so suddenly, and the best opinion seems to be that these charts resulted from a combination of established sailing directions (or portolanos) and use of the marine compass, which was beginning to appear in the Mediterranean. Putting these two elements together, the argument goes, allowed the chartmakers to achieve at once something like a perfect outline of the coasts with which they were most familiar.

In the 1456 portolan chart by Petrus Roselli not only the Mediterranean is shown with accuracy, but also the Atlantic coasts of France and Spain as well as the Black Sea. It also includes some Atlantic islands and a summary delineation of the British Isles, but the cartographer's knowledge comes to an abrupt end at the North Sea and at the western coast of Africa. There is very little internal detail—these are, after all, marine charts—and the place-names are written at right angles to the coast. Many islands are shown with a deep, opaque color. Flags fly over territories to indicate their sovereigns, and here and there important cities are shown in profile. These maps

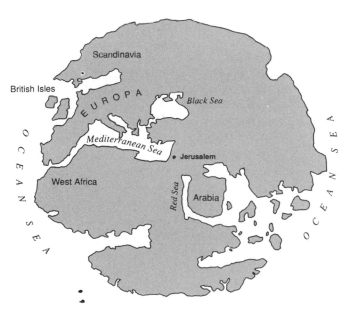

GIOVANNI LEARDO'S WORLD MAP (*facing page*). From a manuscript of 1452. On the schematic representation (*above*), north is at top. On the original (*facing page*), north is at left. The schematic maps accompanying originals in this article are by Tom Willcockson of the Newberry Library, Chicago.

often have scale bars and are covered with a latticework of lines. Originally they were designed to be rolled up on a wooden spindle, which would have been fixed to the right-hand edge of the piece of vellum.

Ptolemaic Maps. The geographical and cartographic knowledge of the ancient world was summarized in the works of Ptolemy, who lived at Alexandria. Ptolemy seems to have been the compiler of a work known as *Geography*, which is essentially a very large listing of the geographical coordinates (latitude and longitude) of many places in the world known to Greece and Rome; it also gives instructions as to how these listings can be used to make maps.

The very idea that any place on the earth's surface could be represented by two sets of figures gives Ptolemy his extraordinary importance. Maps do not have to be constructed in this way—neither the *mappamundi* nor the portolan chart was—but if the coordinates are known, then it is possible to set about recording the shape of the round earth on flat paper in accordance not merely with pragmatic observations but with some kind of mathematical theory. Of course, there is an almost infinite number of possible "projections," but the significance of Ptolemy's system is that his coordinates make it possible to apply the same basic information to any one of these projections.

After the fall of the Roman Empire the ideas of Ptolemy fell into obscurity. Some of his ideas were taken up by Muslim cartographers, for there was a thriving cartography within the empire of Islam. From the twelfth century onward, however, the people of western Europe, and especially of Italy, proved more and more open to ancient learning, which they set about to recover in all its aspects. Roman law was among the first disciplines to be rediscovered; then followed the poetry of Virgil, the physics of Aristotle, the medicine of Galen, and so forth. The geography of Ptolemy was another branch of antique learning recovered during the Renaissance; the process began early in the fifteenth century, when manuscripts of his geography began to circulate among the learned.

One of these Ptolemaic manuscripts, composed about 1460, shows a segment of the world floating, as it were, in space, while angelic heads blow winds upon it. Around the top and bottom edges are the figures of longitude, running from zero at the left to 180 degrees at the extreme right; this is thus meant to represent half the world in longitude. Figures of latitude climb up and down the right-hand edge of the map, beginning at the sharp bend that marks the equator.

Ptolemy's outline of the Mediterranean is markedly less perfect than on the portolan charts. But he shows Europe rather convincingly; indeed, it is hard to imagine how a person living in Alexandria in the second century could have had so accurate a knowledge of the British Isles. Asia Minor and Arabia are also well delineated, as we should

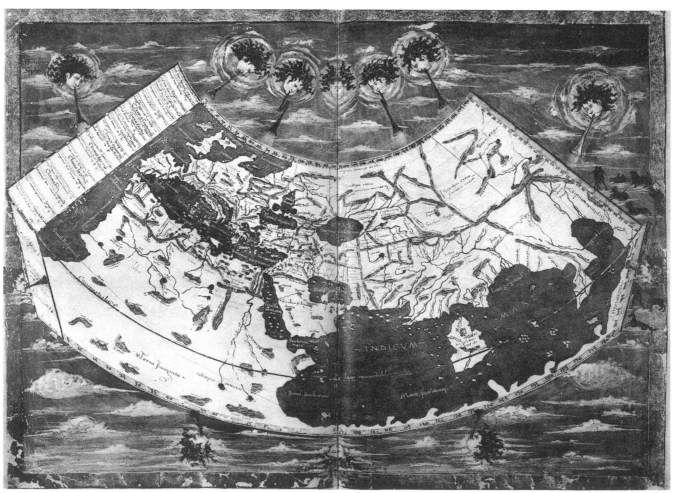

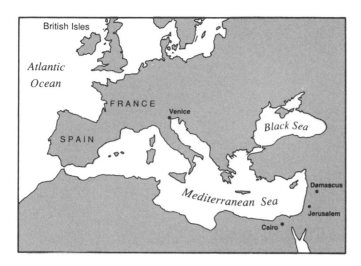

PORTOLAN CHART (*facing page, top*). By Petrus Roselli, 1456. Delineation of the coastline approaches the accuracy of modern maps, as shown in the schematic representation (*above*) of the original. THE NEWBERRY LIBRARY, CHICAGO

expect, and so is the north coast of Africa. However, the southern half of the hemisphere is, as Ptolemy notes, "Terra Incognita," unknown land, and his knowledge of the lands bordering the Indian Ocean is very defective. In particular, he showed a very large island, called Taprobana, in the Indian Ocean; this perhaps represents some distorted notion of the island of Sumatra.

The Ptolemaic vision of the world was very important in the formation of Columbus's own. Note that for Ptolemy the distance between the western tip of Spain and the eastern edge of Asia was something like 200 degrees, leaving 160 degrees for the land "round the back." Columbus in fact carried this error further, but Ptolemy's estimate was already hopelessly optimistic, since in fact

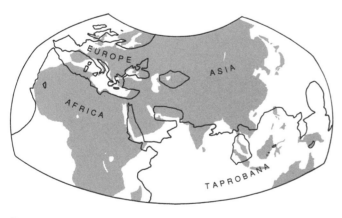

PTOLEMAIC WORLD MAP (*facing page, bottom*). From a manuscript of circa 1460. The shading on the schematic map (*above*) shows the true outlines of landmasses. NEW YORK PUBLIC LIBRARY

the distance from eastern Asia to the western seaboard of Europe is not 160 degrees but about 220 degrees. If the mariners of the late fifteenth century had realized the immense distances involved, they surely would never have set sail—but then they did not know, either, that a New World lay between western Europe and eastern Asia.

After having circulated in manuscript during much of the fifteenth century, Ptolemy's geography was eventually printed and soon ran through many editions. The first edition with maps was printed at Bologna in 1477, and by the middle of the sixteenth century more than twenty other editions in various languages had emerged. It was no doubt this work, more than any other, that made educated Europeans familiar with the idea of having a book—an "atlas," as it would be called—within which was a collection of maps that would give the reader some idea of the outline of the world.

Use of Maps in Early European Exploration

During the reign of Henry the Navigator, the Portuguese were pushing their explorations ever southward down the West African coast. They drew maps as they went, using the techniques of the portolan chart. These techniques were also beginning to be applied in the early fifteenth century to the charting of the Atlantic Ocean. A chart drawn in 1424 by the Venetian Zuane Pizzigano on a single sheet of vellum has the usual latticework of lines radiating from a set of wind-roses. The coasts of western Europe and northern Africa are shown in typical portolan chart style, with an accurate delineation and the names of the towns at right angles to the coast.

The Mediterranean islands are shown with a rich, opaque color, in the usual way, and so are the islands of the eastern Atlantic, the Azores (shown too close to the European coast), Madeiras, Canaries, and two large islands in midocean, Antilia and Satanazes. These last are of course imaginary in the sense that they do not exist where they are shown. But some historians believe that they represent an interpretation of reports by sailors who had in fact crossed the Atlantic; certainly such ideas were in the air for decades before the epic voyage of Columbus.

Early Maps of the New World. The earliest surviving European map to show the New World is the one by Juan de la Cosa, now preserved at the Museo Naval in Madrid. This map strikingly demonstrates the way in which cartographic techniques developed in the Old World were used to map the New, for the Mediterranean region is drawn exactly in the portolan chart style, which is then applied also to the area of the Caribbean and South America that had been explored.

The same stylistic transmission can be seen on the second great manuscript world map surviving from this earliest period, the Cantino planisphere. This large and

PIZZIGANO CHART. Nautical chart of the Atlantic Ocean by Zuane Pizzigano, 1424.

THE JAMES FORD BELL LIBRARY, UNIVERSITY OF MINNESOTA

beautiful map was obtained at Lisbon in 1502 by Alberto Cantino, diplomatic agent of the duke of Ferrara; it was sent back to the ducal library in Modena, where it remains. The Cantino map was almost certainly a copy from the Portuguese *padrão real,* the master map that was kept at Lisbon by the royal chartmakers and constantly updated. The information contained therein was not to be divulged under pain of death.

This is the first map to show the Line of Demarcation fixed by the Treaty of Tordesillas, which was signed by Spain and Portugal in 1494. Spain was to have the territory to the west of the line, and Portugal that to the east. The Portuguese land is marked, as on a portolan chart, with flags flying over what is now Brazil and Newfoundland, which the Portuguese probably claimed because of its rich fisheries. To the west of the line are isolated patches of land, floating in the Western Ocean or "Oceanus Occidentalis." The West Indies are the "Antilles of the King of Castille," but the area to the west of them is left blank. The map reflects growing Portuguese knowledge of the East, for Taprobana has disappeared, the Indian subcontinent has taken on something like its correct form, and the Malaysian peninsula is beginning to emerge.

In the early sixteenth century, the Spaniards and Portuguese did not have printing presses capable of reproducing large and complicated maps. Such maps were printed in Italy and especially Germany. One such map, printed in Rome in 1507 but showing the latest cartographic knowledge from Spain and Portugal, was engraved by Johan Ruysch, with the aim of showing "the known world, drawn from recent discoveries." This type of projection makes it possible to show the whole northern part of the globe; the degrees of longitude run

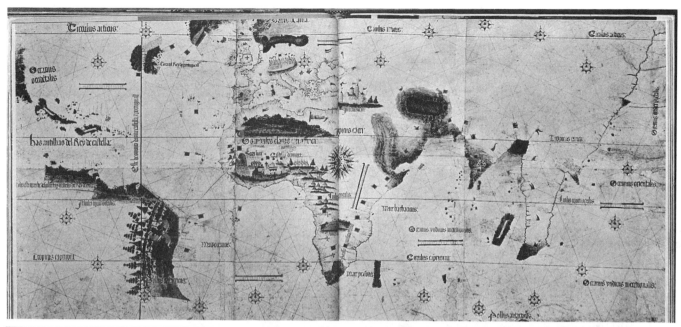

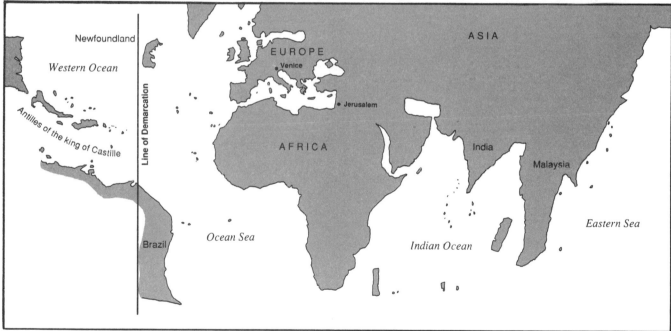

THE CANTINO MAP. Portuguese manuscript world map of 1502.

BIBLIOTECA ESTENSE, MODENA, ITALY

around the semicircle, with two sets from 0 to 180 degrees; the degrees of latitude end at 38 degrees in the Southern Hemisphere.

Ruysch has a fair notion of the shape of the northeastern part of South America, though he has to cover the west coast with a scroll. He also knows the West Indian islands east of Cuba. But he draws in the eastern end of Asia a little way north of Cuba, having absolutely no idea of the existence of North America. Indeed, he writes that "what the Spaniards call Hispaniola is really Japan." At this time

the New World is South America, described here as the "Terra sancte crucis, sive Mundus Novus" (the land of the holy cross, or New World).

All this would change in 1513, when Vasco Núñez de Balboa became the first European to sight the Pacific Ocean, and still more after 1522, when the fleet of Ferdinand Magellan had completed its circumnavigation of the globe. By then the vastness of the ocean one day to be known as the Pacific had become evident. It was plotted particularly well on the charts produced at the

Casa de la Contratación in Seville. Here pilots and cosmographers interrogated ships' masters as they came in from their voyages, plotting accurate information about sites and their latitude and longitude onto the master map, or *padrón real*.

This master map was the Spanish equivalent of the one kept by the Portuguese. The most famous map to emerge from the Casa was no doubt the one drawn by Diogo Ribeiro in 1529, but the previous decades had seen similar efforts, of which about a dozen survive. These are scattered about the archives of Europe, for the only ones that remain are those sent as gifts to foreign princes; seemingly, none survived in Spain itself.

The Salviati world map was probably a gift from the Emperor Charles V (in part of whose huge empire Seville lay) to Cardinal Giovanni Salviati. The Old World is still shown in portolan-chart style, as is the New World. Now

the northeast coast of North America is quite accurately known, ending at the "Tierra de Labrador," and so is the eastern coast of South America, right down to the Strait of Magellan. Very little of the west coast is known, apart from the part bounding Mesoamerica; here two labels distinguish between "Tierra Firme" and the "Mar del Sur," or Pacific. The extent of this great ocean has now been realistically conceived; although there are no figures of latitude and longitude, there are marks at ten-degree intervals along the equator, and similar marks at ten-degree intervals along the lines of latitude.

The Salviati map and the other products of the Casa represent the culmination of the first phase of European world cartography; from this time onward the general extent of the world was known; it was now simply a matter of filling in the various areas with more or less accuracy. The world of the *mappamundi* had exploded outward to

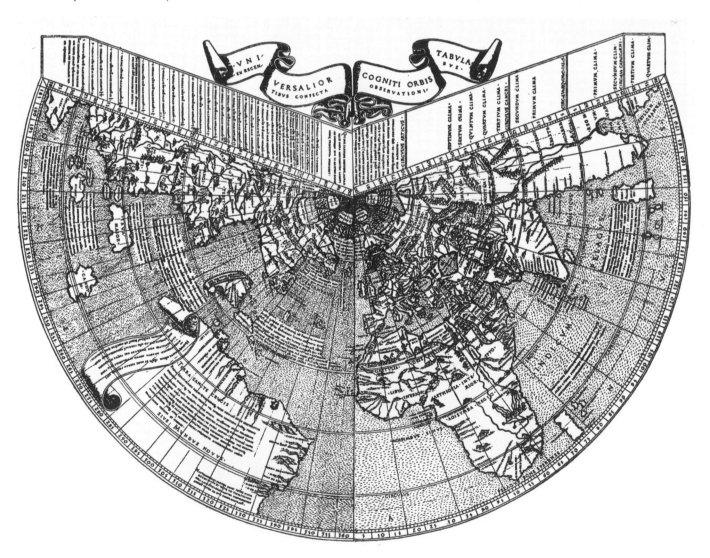

WORLD MAP OF JOHAN RUYSCH. *Universalior cogniti orbis tabula.* Rome, 1507.

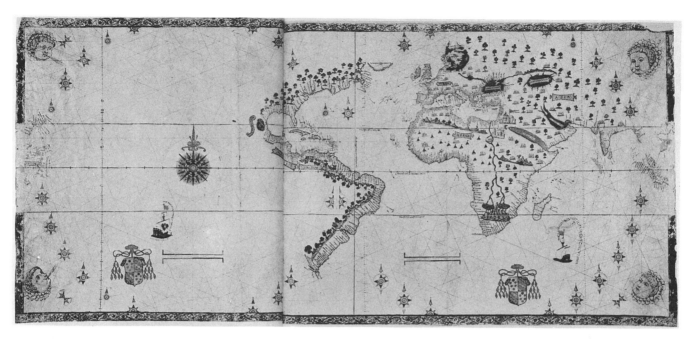

THE SALVIATI MAP. Spanish manuscript world map, circa 1526.

THE VALLEY OF TEPETLAOZTOC, MEXICO. Manuscript map of 1583.

THE HACIENDA OF SANTA INES, MEXICO. Manuscript map of 1569.

give a radically new image of the globe. But this image was constructed using medieval methods. For a long time the style and technique of the portolan chart would still pervade these maps, and they would continue to be constructed according to projections known to Ptolemy, using his system of coordinates. This would not change until after the middle of the sixteenth century, with the adoption of Mercator's projection.

Detailed Land Maps of the New World. When the Europeans came to map the internal regions of the Americas, they often called upon the cartographic expertise of the indigenous peoples. Sometimes this knowledge was transmitted verbally or in transient images like drawings in the sand. At other times the native peoples made drawings on hides or tusks. In Central America, the Aztecs in particular had a rich tradition of portraying places and events in pictorial form. When, for instance,

the Aztec ruler Motecuhzoma II (Moctezuma) heard that strangers (the Spaniards) had been seen landing on his coast, he sent artists to make drawings of these people and the localities through which they were passing. An Aztec map dating from 1583 shows the valley of Tepetlaoztoc, through which a road, marked with footprints, runs. There is a river (though lacking the usual fish symbols) at the top and right, a forest, and low hills jutting into the plain. The inverted shields bear place-names, and the area at the bottom of the image perhaps represents fields, with boundaries between them. Many such maps survive at the Archivo de la Nación in Mexico City, testimony to a lively and widespread cartographic tradition.

When the Spaniards occupied much of the New World, they had maps drawn of the areas under their control; these were often sent back to Spain, to help in the planning of imperial policy. These maps are often an interesting conflation of the European and Amerindian styles, plainly showing elements from each culture. One such map, drawn in 1569 in the course of a dispute over water-rights, delineates the hacienda of Santa Ines, to the north of Mexico City in the Valley of Mexico. Here the Jesuits eventually had a great plantation, the proceeds from which supported their Colegio de Tepotzotlán. We see a church (on the right) and four chapels, outlined on the original in red. The Indians live in the blockish houses scattered more or less at random; care is taken to show the sheep-pens (*corrales*). All these buildings are in a more or less European style. In the fields, however, are New World plants, and on the roads footsteps are shown, in the Aztec style. Such a map obviously cannot give a precise indication of acreage, but it does give a good idea of the layout of the hacienda.

Maps were very important in establishing the power of the European peoples, whether they showed the Saint Lawrence Valley or the Valley of Mexico or the coast of Virginia. Some of the early English maps, indeed, speak very tellingly to this idea of the map as an emblem of power, for they show large English ships approaching a virtually empty continent in which a few small Indian figures can be detected. The reality, of course, was that the invaders approached a vast continent that in places was heavily peopled. True, the European technology, of which the map was an important part, was in some ways superior to that of the Amerindians, but their most potent weapons were those they carried unknowingly: the germs of various diseases until then unknown in the New World.

Eventually, maps would also come to be used to sustain the rights of the Indians, infrequently during the seventeenth century and more often in the modern era. They were a powerful tool for visualizing and, so to speak, "capturing" the vast extent of land that had opened up to peoples used to much narrower horizons. From the beginning, cartography played a central role in the encounter between these different worlds.

[See also *Nautical Charts; Sailing Directions*.]

BIBLIOGRAPHY

Bagrow, L., and R. A. Skelton. *History of Cartography*. Cambridge, 1964.

Cortesão, Armando, and Avelino Teixeira da Mota. *Portugaliae monumenta cartographica*. 6 vols. Lisbon, 1960. New edition, Lisbon, 1987.

Cumming, W. P., R. A. Skelton, and D. B. Quinn. *The Discovery of North America*. London, 1971.

Hale, John K. *The Age of Exploration*. New York, 1966.

Harley, J. B., and David Woodward. *Cartography in Prehistoric, Ancient and Medieval Europe and the Mediterranean*. Vol. 1 of *The History of Cartography*. Chicago, 1987.

Mollat du Jourdin, Michel de La Roncière, and Monique de La Roncière. *Sea Charts of the Early Explorers*. London, 1984.

Morison, Samuel Eliot. *The European Discovery of America: The Southern Voyages, A.D. 1492–1616*. New York, 1974.

Nebenzahl, Kenneth. *Atlas of Columbus and the Great Discoveries*. Chicago, 1990.

Organization of American States and the Instituto Panamericano de Geografía e História. *Precedentes cartográficos del descubrimiento de América*. Mexico City, 1989.

Parry, J. H. *The Age of Reconnaissance*. Berkeley, 1981.

Putnam, R. *Early Sea Charts*. New York, 1983.

Sauer, Carl Ortwin. *The Early Spanish Main*. Berkeley, 1966.

DAVID BUISSERET

CASA DE LA CONTRATACIÓN. The Casa, or House of Trade, was set up by a decree of Queen Juana, dated February 14, 1503. The officials named were a treasurer, a contador (notary), and a factor (i.e., business manager). The establishment of this body signified the change from exploration and discovery to royal commercial enterprise in the Indies. A clearinghouse for the trade, the Casa was also a center for the development of an *artes y oficios de navegar*, or an institute for licensing, controlling, and teaching all aspects of navigation. A pilot major was appointed in 1508, and the Casa was charged with maintaining a *padron real* (mastery map) to instruct pilots in the art of navigation.

Starting to function on January 20, 1503, in the *ataranza* (arsenal) of Seville, the officials of the Casa were to put the relationship of the colonists to the metropolis on a par with the regulation of commerce in other parts of Castile. They collected data on the demand and supplies of the markets and supervised the fleets operating between Seville and the Indies. The assembly and licensing of ships and cargoes resulted in a roster of manifests that were controlled at both terminals of the Indies trade *(carrera de Indias)*. Two early problems of the system involved the casas set up in the Indies, which soon became mere customs houses, and the rivalry between the harbors of Seville and Cádiz. After 1504, incoming tribute, treasure, goods, and people had to be cleared through the Casa in Seville, even if they had arrived in Cádiz.

The special needs of the mercantile and the nautical groups engaged in the Indies trade led to the development of a special branch of the judiciary at the Casa in 1539. The relation of the judges to the local system and the course of appeal of cases before them were gradually defined.

Rounding out the mature institution was a variety of activities: the examination and licensing of pilots and nautical instruments (astrolabes, jacob staffs, compasses, almanacs), the supervision of construction of ships for the trade, instruction in gunnery, and keeping of chronicles.

BIBLIOGRAPHY

Haring, Clarence Henry. *Trade and Navigation between Spain and the Indies in the Time of the Habsburgs.* Cambridge, Mass., 1918.

Haring, Clarence Henry. "Trade and Navigation between Spain and the Indies: A Re-View, 1918–1958." *Hispanic American Historical Review* 40 (1960): 53–62.

Lamb, Ursula. "Science by Litigation: A Cosmographic Feud." *Terrae Incognitae* 1 (1969): 40–57.

Veitia Linaje, José de. *Norte de la contratación de las Indias Occidentales.* Seville, 1672; new ed., Buenos Aires, 1945.

URSULA LAMB

CASAS, BARTOLOMÉ DE LAS. See *Las Casas, Bartolomé de.*

CATHERINE OF ARAGÓN (1485–1536), princess of Castile; queen of England. Born Catalina, the youngest child of Isabel and Fernando, Catherine was married to Arthur, prince of Wales, in 1501. The alliance was the centerpiece of Anglo-Castilian diplomacy, but it was threatened when Arthur died only months after the wedding. Catherine's subsequent marriage in 1509 to Arthur's brother, King Henry VIII, ended in the infamous divorce proceedings that led to the English Reformation.

Catherine spent most of her early childhood as witness to the momentous events of late-fifteenth-century Castile: the conquest of Granada, the Inquisition, the expulsion of Jews and Muslims, and Columbus's reception in Barcelona following his return from the New World. Like her mother, Catherine was deeply pious. She spoke fluent Latin and was schooled in classical literature as well as theology.

Her marriage to Henry appears to have been happy, but unfortunately for Catherine their sons were stillborn or died shortly after birth. Only their daughter, Mary, born in 1516, survived to adulthood. By 1525 there was no hope for a male heir. Desperate to secure the succession, Henry questioned the validity of his marriage to Catherine, basing his argument on the canon law prohibition against marrying the widow of one's brother. Catherine fought the divorce action and marshaled powerful allies, among them her nephew, Emperor Charles V, and Pope Clement VII. The pope ruled in Catherine's favor, but by then Henry had severed ties with Rome and declared himself head of the Church of England. Henry married his mistress, Anne Boleyn, shortly before Catherine's death in 1536.

BIBLIOGRAPHY

Claremont, Francesca. *Catherine of Aragon.* London, 1939.
Mattingly, Garrett. *Catherine of Aragon.* New York, 1941.

THERESA EARENFIGHT

CELEBRATIONS. Although the momentous arrival of Christopher Columbus in the Western Hemisphere was recognized in the first two hundred years after his exploit, there is no evidence of any large public celebrations during that time. It was not until the three-hundredth commemoration that public recognition of the event occurred in the United States. In 1792 celebrations were held in New York City, Boston, Baltimore, Providence, and Richmond to commemorate the voyage. In Boston, Jeremy Belknap presented "A Discourse Intended to Commemorate the Discovery of America by Christopher Columbus" to the Historical Society of Massachusetts on October 23, 1792. During the dinner the memory of Columbus was toasted and Belknap's ode was sung by a choir. Also that year the New York Tammany Society unveiled an obelisk dedicated to Columbus and provided entertainment in celebration of the event.

On the four-hundredth anniversary, in 1892–1893, the celebratory activities increased markedly in contrast to the earlier centennials. Interest stirred in a number of cities to commemorate the Columbian legacy in a broad manner. Columbus had become the embodiment of the United States and inspired strong nationalistic fervor. The *Youth's Companion* magazine introduced the Pledge of Allegiance specifically to mark the four-hundredth anniversary.

Following months of spirited competition among a number of cities, including Chicago, Washington, New York, and St. Louis, Chicago was named as the site of the first major public event in honor of Columbus. The World's Columbian Exposition opened amid great excitement on May 1, 1893. Located on 664 acres on the shore of Lake Michigan, the fair featured forty buildings for main exhibitions, forty-two structures for state exhibitions, and eighty buildings and walkways to accommodate foreign nations, colonies, districts, and corporations. The fair cost over $30 million and attracted 24 million visitors, the largest crowds for any single event in the history of the world to that point. Four times as much money was spent on the Columbian Exposition in 1893 than on the 1876 Centennial Exposition in Philadelphia, which commemorated the independence of the United States.

The fair exhibited statues of Columbus, facsimiles of his letters, a reproduction of the monastery of La Rábida, and full-sized replicas of *Niña, Pinta,* and *Santa María.* The Chicago fair was opened officially by President Grover Cleveland accompanied by Thomas Palmer, president of the U.S. National Commission, and Harlow Higinbotham of the Exposition Company. Among the dignitaries who attended the opening ceremony were the vice president of the United States Adlai Stevenson, the secretaries of state, treasury, navy, interior, and agriculture, various world's fair directors and officers, the governor of Illinois, the duke and duchess of Veragua, and other Spanish notables. The World's Columbian Exposition was consid-

Two views of the World's Columbian Exposition, Chicago, 1893. *Top:* The lagoon and the Palace of Mechanic Arts. *Bottom:* The main basin looking toward the Administration Building, with a statue of Liberty, or Columbia, representing the Republic, in the foreground.

ered the greatest international fair of its time. It was seen as expressing the continuity of the progress of American civilization and opening a new period in humankind's effort to master the environment.

Earlier, in 1892, Columbus-related activities were celebrated in New York City. In October there were five days of parades, floats, fireworks, speeches, marches, naval pageants, statue unveilings, and opera performances. The highlight occurred on October 12, 1892, with the opening of the Columbus memorial corner of Central Park, called Columbus Circle. The federal government, through a congressional joint resolution and a declaration by President Benjamin Harrison, called upon citizens to observe Columbus Day at home, at work, and in school. Congress proposed October 23 as the day of observance, but October 12 remained the popular celebration date. Coins and stamps were issued in honor of the anniversary in the United States and other countries. And in Spain that year, a special event, the Columbian Historical Exhibition, was held in Madrid.

In addition to these world-class spectaculars, a number of complementary activities related to the centennial have occurred over the past century. In many respects, though not as spectacular as a world's fair, some of these events have had an international impact related to Columbus. In the United States the annual Columbus Day celebration has received the strong support of Italians and Hispanics as well as the Knights of Columbus since 1892. Angelo Noce of Denver, Colorado, lobbied for the first official noncentennial Columbus Day in 1905, and its annual observance became state law in 1907. By 1910 Columbus Day had become an official holiday in fifteen states, and in 1938 it became a national holiday, following a proclamation in April 1934 by President Franklin D. Roosevelt. In Latin America, the recognition of the landfall date took a different meaning as the observance of El Dia de la Raza (Day of the Spanish Race) emerged following the 1892 commemoration. By 1938 El Dia de la Raza was celebrated in twenty-two countries in South, Central, and Caribbean America.

For the quincentenary in 1992, Spain plays host to Expo '92, the Universal Exposition, from April 20 to October 12, in Seville. The theme of the exposition, "The Age of Discovery," refers to human discoveries through the ages in every field of activity. The site of the fair, the island La Cartuja in the Guadalquivir River, is the location of the fifteenth-century monastery where Columbus was first buried. Spanish planners hope that Expo '92 will project the modern image of today's Spain, contribute to international unity, and provide an opportunity to improve the environment around the fair area in Seville.

In Genoa, Italy, a specialized exhibition to be held in the summer of 1992 will be devoted to maritime explorations and the technical means and instruments of navigation from Columbus's age to the present day.

A variety of other activities are also planned as the five-hundredth anniversary of Columbus's first voyage to America approaches. By 1990 thirty-two nations and over thirty states and entities of the United States had formed official quincentenary commissions. The National Christopher Columbus Quincentenary Jubilee Commission (United States) was established by law in 1984, and many other countries, including Spain, Mexico, Portugal, Italy, the Dominican Republic, Colombia, and Argentina, also established commissions, some of them functioning several years before that of the United States.

Interpretations of Columbus as representative of one nation's skill or another's genius and the portrayals of him as the agent of capitalist ingenuity and persistence are being challenged by international conferences addressing issues related to the impact of the Columbian voyage on America, Europe, and elsewhere. Planned for the period around October 12, 1992, are conferences on history, law, medicine, music, literature, geography, space exploration, cartography, pre-Columbian studies, library science, and social studies related to the Columbian legacy. Although the directions of these conferences have expanded thematically, they continue to use the opportunity provided by the quincentenary as the occasion for meeting. Out of these activities a new and richer understanding of the consequences of the Columbian voyage and those that followed is emerging.

Throughout the Atlantic world, a wide array of programs has been planned to commemorate, to understand, to debate, and to study the enduring relationship between America and Europe that was set into motion by Columbus's voyage of 1492. Among them are An Ongoing Voyage of the Library of Congress, The Seeds of Change of the Natural History Museum of the Smithsonian Institution, and The Encounter of Two Worlds of the Organization of American States. Unlike the celebrations of 1892, these initiatives seek to establish a broader view of the consequences of the Columbian landfall, although they retain some elements of the nationalistic fervor of a hundred years ago.

[See also *Columbianism; Iconography*, articles on *Numismatics* and *Philately; Quincentenary*.]

BIBLIOGRAPHY

Badger, Reid. *The Great American Fair: The World's Columbian Exposition and American Culture.* Chicago, 1979.

Quinto Centenario del Descubrimiento de America Commission: 500 Years, 500 Programs. Madrid, 1985.

Sale, Kirkpatrick. *The Conquest of Paradise: Christopher Columbus and the Columbian Legacy.* New York, 1990.

JOHN R. HÉBERT

CHANCA, DIEGO ALVAREZ (c. 1463–c. 1515), royal physician; accompanied Columbus on his second voyage to America. Little is known about Diego Alvarez Chanca's early years. He was born in Seville around 1463, but we have no information about his schooling or his training as a physician prior to 1492. His knowledge of Latin, his references to classical literary motifs in his account of Columbus's second voyage, and his medical texts reveal, however, an erudite and solid grounding in the classical and humanistic culture of the late medieval world. Documentary evidence from July 1492 reveals that he held the prestigious post of royal physician, accompanying Fernando and Isabel during the final siege of Granada. As a sign of royal trust, Chanca was named physician to the Infanta Juana, the eventual heir to the throne of Castile and mother of Charles V. On July 7, 1492, Isabel ordered her accounts to pay Chanca 68,750 maravedis in compensation for his services; he retained his position as royal physician until at least 1501. There is some evidence that he may have held this position from a much earlier period and that he may have also served in the retinue of the Infanta Isabel at the Portuguese court between 1481 and 1483.

The Catholic monarchs by a royal letter of May 23, 1493, requested that Chanca accompany Columbus on his second voyage to the New World and ordered the royal accounts to pay him a salary and *ración* (allowance) while in the Indies. The 1493 expedition was not the adventurous sailing into the unknown of Columbus's first voyage. Instead, seventeen ships and more than one thousand men revealed the commitment of the Castilian Crown to the enterprise of the Ocean Sea. Chanca's nomination as physician to the fleet also reflected the interest of the monarchs in the scientific and medical aspects of the voyage.

The best sources for this second voyage are Chanca's letter to the city council of Seville and sections of Andrés Bernáldez's *History of the Catholic Monarchs*. Chanca's letter took the form of a report to the city council of his native city. A copy of the manuscript, now at the Real Academia de la Historia in Madrid, was published by Martín Fernández de Navarrete in his *Colección de los viages y descubrimientos*. Chanca's letter relates Columbus's uneventful second crossing and the discovery and exploration of the Lesser Antilles. Although his account never gained the celebrity bestowed upon some of the contemporary histories of the first age of discovery, such as those of Las Casas, Pietro Martire d'Anghiera (Peter Martyr), and others, it deserves recognition.

His letter, albeit written in a confused and often grammatically incorrect Castilian, is the first "scientific" description of the New World, revealing the awe of Europeans at the sights of these new lands. His was the first attempt at depicting the natural beauty of the Caribbean islands and the diversity and uniqueness of their flora and fauna. Chanca's letter was also the first of what eventually would become a long list of "ethnographic" descriptions of the inhabitants of the New World. His letter contains lyrical descriptions of peaceful and beautiful Indians without clothing, weapons, or visible political organization. His image of a "natural man," when used by more eloquent writers, would become one of the central themes of European thought and a source of utopian ideals in early modern Europe. But Chanca also described, in horrified tones, the warlike and aggressive Caribs and their proclivity toward anthropophagy. His gruesome stories of the Castilians' discovery of dismembered bodies and of emasculated children being fattened for the Caribs' feasts also became part of the European imagination. Scholars currently debate what the Spaniards really did find in the Caribbean and whether their reports transposed the image of the other from classical and medieval literary sources (such as those of Pliny, John Mandeville, and others) or reflected reality. Chanca knew his classics well, but his letter also breathes a feeling of authenticity and of somber adherence to observed reality: the meek and friendly Indians on the one hand and the fierce Caribs on the other.

Chanca's voyage ended at La Española where his services were required to treat the myriad tropical diseases affecting the new colonists. In this sense, he was the first European doctor to come face to face with a host of new illnesses. How he dealt with them is not known. There is no evidence in his later writings that he reflected at all on the medical conditions or problems he faced in the New World. Moreover, he remained in the Americas only for a short period before returning to Seville in 1495.

Married twice without issue, Chanca enjoyed a successful career as a noted scholar on medical matters. In 1499 he published his *Tractatus de fascinatione* and seven years later a treatise, written in the vernacular and printed by Jacob Kronberg, on the afflictions to the sides of the body caused by pestilence, *Tratado nuevo . . . en que se declara de que manera se ha de curar el mal de costado pestilencial*. His last known work, *Commentum novum in parabolis divi Arnaldi de villa nova*, a commentary on the enigmatic medieval physician and philosopher Arnau de Vilanova, was also printed in Seville by Kronberg in 1514. There is an extant will of Chanca from 1510; he probably died around 1515.

BIBLIOGRAPHY

Cecil, Jane, ed. *The Four Voyages of Columbus*. Reprint. New York, 1988.

Morison, Samuel Eliot. *Admiral of the Ocean Sea: A Life of Christopher Columbus*. 2 vols. Boston, 1942.

Paniagua, Juán Antonio. *El doctor Chanca y su obra médica.* Madrid, 1977.

TEOFILO F. RUIZ

CHARLES V (1500–1558), Holy Roman emperor (1519–1556); Carlos I, king of Spain (1516–1556). Charles ruled a vast and far-flung empire that encompassed both the Old World and the New. He dominated European politics through a combination of military prowess, diplomacy, administrative acumen, and overseas exploration. His was a turbulent age: it witnessed the divorce of Henry VIII of England from Charles's aunt Catherine of Aragón, the growth of the Protestant Reformation, the abduction of Pope Clement VII, the conquest and colonization of the New World, and the circumnavigation of the globe by Ferdinand Magellan's fleet in 1522.

Charles was born in Ghent in 1500, the year of Pedro Álvares Cabral's discovery of Brazil. Son of Juana I (Juana la Loca) and Philip the Handsome, archduke of Austria, Charles was the first king to rule a united Spain, which included Castile, Aragón, Naples, Sicily, Mallorca, and territories in the New World. He inherited the Burgundian Netherlands from his father, and upon his election as Holy Roman Emperor (1519) he acquired the hereditary Habsburg estates in Germany and Austria.

He remained in Flanders when his parents went to Castile to claim the Spanish Crown and was raised by his aunt Margaret, regent of the Netherlands. He was educated as a Renaissance prince in the opulent Burgundian court. His tutors included Guillaume de Croy and Adrian of Utrecht, the future Pope Adrian VI.

To solidify the Castilian inheritance Charles married Isabel, infanta of Portugal, daughter of Manuel I and Isabel of Castile, in 1526. Their son Philip II (1527–1598) would inherit the Spanish and Burgundian realms, but the German territories and the title of emperor were granted to Charles's brother Ferdinand.

SHIELD OF CHARLES V. Depicting an allegory of the discovery of the New World.

The demands of his extensive realms required Charles to rule his territories, both in the New World and in Europe, through lieutenants. He spent more time in Spain than elsewhere in his realms, especially in the early years of his reign. He ruthlessly quelled civil unrest in Castile (1521), Navarre (1521), and Valencia (1519–1523). With order restored, Charles appointed Spanish nobles and prelates to serve as his lieutenants and ruled Castile as an absolute monarch.

As king of Spain, Charles supervised the settlement of colonies, established systems of government, and enacted legislation to abolish slavery in the Americas. Early in his reign Hernando Cortés claimed Mexico (1522) and California (1536) for Castile, and Francisco Pizarro explored Peru (1521), territories that brought considerable prestige and wealth to Spain. Charles's treasury was the envy of Europe, but the influx of gold and silver fueled inflation and contributed to a serious economic crisis.

Charles was extraordinarily successful in his military exploits. The Spanish army formed the backbone of the imperial army, which sacked Rome in 1527 and defeated the French at Pavia (1525), the Turks at the Danube (1546), and the German Protestants at Mühlenberg (1547).

In 1554 Charles began to cede territories to Philip, and by the time of his death in 1558, he had abdicated all of his

CHARLES V. The style of dress depicted on this coin makes reference to the rulers of the Roman empire of the ancient world. Minted in Milan. AMERICAN NUMISMATIC SOCIETY

realms. He went into retirement on the estates of the Convent of San Jeronimo de Yuste and was buried in a tomb prepared by his son Philip at San Lorenzo in the Escorial.

BIBLIOGRAPHY

Fernández Álvarez, Manuel. *Charles V: Elected Emperor and Hereditary Ruler.* Translated by J. A. Lalaguna. London, 1975.

Fernández Álvarez, Manuel. *La España del Emperador Carlos V.* Vol. 18 of *Historia de España.* Edited by Ramón Menéndez Pidal. Madrid, 1966.

Rassow, Peter. *Karl V: Der letze Kaiser des Mittelalters.* Göttingen, 1957.

Terlinden, Charles de. *Charles Quint, empereur des deux mondes.* Brussels, 1965.

Tyler, Royall. *The Emperor Charles the Fifth.* London, 1956.

THERESA EARENFIGHT

CHARLES VIII (1470–1498), king of France. The only son of Louis XI, Charles succeeded him at age thirteen in 1483. Because of his youth his older sister Anne of Beaujeu governed for him. Much of the nobility, led by Louis of Orléans and Francis of Brittany, rebelled. In July 1488 Louis was defeated and imprisoned for three years. Francis died shortly after the defeat, leaving his duchy to his daughter Anne, who was persuaded to marry Charles, ending Brittany's autonomy.

By 1491 Charles had begun to govern for himself and set about planning the first French invasion of Italy to make good the Valois claim to Naples, ruled by Ferrante of Aragón. He won the temporary neutrality of Fernando of Aragón by returning Roussillon and Cerdagne in the Pyrenees to him. (In his preoccupation with Naples, Charles passed up the opportunity to fund Columbus's first voyage, when Columbus's brother Bartolomé came to France seeking royal support.) With an army of thirty thousand men and the most powerful artillery train yet seen, Charles invaded Italy in September 1494. Brushing aside limited Italian resistance, Charles marched to Naples and proclaimed himself king. But Fernando of Aragón joined with the major Italian states in an anti-French league. In July 1495 Charles, returning to France, was confronted by an allied force as he crossed the Appenines. The ensuing Battle of Fornova was enough of a French victory to allow him to complete his return to France.

Shortly after, Charles's only child died, which made Louis of Orléans his heir. Three years later, on April 10, 1498, Charles struck his head on a doorway in the Château of Blois on his way to watch a tennis game. Within ten hours he had died, passing the throne to his second cousin Louis XII.

CHARLES VIII OF FRANCE. From Aliprando Capriolo's *Ritratti de cento capitani illustri.* Rome, 1596.

BIBLIOGRAPHY

Bridge, John. *A History of France from the Death of Louis XI.* 5 vols. New York, 1929.

Febvre, Lucien. *Life in Renaissance France.* Translated by Marian Rothstein. Cambridge, Mass., 1977.

Labande-Mailfert, Yvonne. *Charles VIII et son milieu.* Paris, 1975.

FREDERIC J. BAUMGARTNER

CHIBCHAS. See *Indian America*, article on *Chibchas*.

CHINA. Apart from a handful of medieval travelers who left accounts of their wanderings in the East, little was known about China in the West until early in the fourteenth century when Marco Polo's book appeared. During the Renaissance, it was the chief Western source of information on the East, and its influence on Columbus and the European Age of Discovery has never been fully assessed. [See also *Polo, Marco.*]

When Columbus and his contemporaries spoke of China, they were referring to Marco Polo's Cathay, which they did not connect with China; it was not until nearly a century after Columbus discovered America that the mysterious Cathay was located. Later, Europe learned that from 907 to 1125, North China had been ruled by the non-Chinese Liao dynasty, an ethnic group known to the Chinese as Ch'itan or Khitan, and to their Central Asian neighbors as Khitai, from which the word *Cathay* was derived. Since the Arabs who traded at Canton had never used the term *Cathay*, European geographers were confused by the existence of what they took to be two entities, China and Cathay. As for the name China, it is commonly accepted that the word was derived from the Ch'in or Ts'in dynasty that flourished in the third century B.C. and became widely known in India, Persia, and other Asian countries. Confirmation that China and Cathay were one came in 1607 when the Portuguese Jesuit, Bento Goes, reached Cathay by the northern overland route and sent word to Matteo Ricci (1552–1610), who had reached Peking (Beijing) by way of Canton and Macao.

The Cathay described by Marco Polo was the Mongol China of Kublai (or Khubilai) Khan. The Mongol Yüan dynasty ruled over all of China from 1279 to 1368. Mongol rule extended over Korea, but attempts to invade Japan in 1274 and 1281 ended in failure. However, Mongol troops under Batu Khan, a grandson of Genghis (Chingis) Khan, got as far west as Hungary, turning back to Karakorum, the Mongol capital, only because of the death of the Grand Khan Ögödai in 1241.

Of all the medieval accounts of European contacts with the Mongol dynasty, the most famous and the most influential was that of Marco Polo. The effect of his account on Columbus is well known, for in his great enterprise, Columbus let it be known that he was seeking, not a new continent, but a shorter route to the Cathay of Marco Polo.

Kublai Khan died in 1294 at the age of eighty. His nine successors were not outstanding rulers, and the dynasty fell in 1367 after many years of rebellions and internal warfare, to be succeeded by the Ming dynasty (1368–1644), which began reluctantly to open China to the West. The Ming was the last imperial dynasty whose ruling family was of Chinese origin. The major problems facing the early Ming rulers were consolidation of control in China, acceptance of Ming suzerainty by such tributary states as Korea and Vietnam, and the military security of the northern border. The first Ming emperor (r. 1368–1398) was interested in the political aspects of the tribute system, but wanted to restrict trade to a very low level, a policy that struck at the economic livelihood of both Chinese and foreign traders and led to smuggling and piracy.

The second emperor was not a military man, and he proved no match for his uncle, the prince of Yen, who rebelled and seized the throne, reigning as Yung-lo (1402–1424). A successful soldier, he transferred the capital from Nanking to the former Mongol capital in the north, which he renamed Peking. Not long after the beginning of his reign he decided to expand China's contacts. In 1405 he sent Cheng Ho (c. 1371–c. 1433), eunuch commander of the Ming fleet, on a series of expeditions by which China's ships ultimately reached the east coast of Africa and Arabia. The most famous navigator in Chinese history, Cheng sailed the greatest distance of any ship captain up to his time. Yung-lo sent Cheng on a first expedition to southeast Asia, Ceylon, and India, with a fleet of sixty-two ships and nearly twenty-eight thousand men. Later expeditions visited several ports on the Persian Gulf. Cheng's fifth and sixth expeditions (1417–1419 and 1421–1422) explored the Arab and African coasts, and much of Chinese geographical knowledge, prior to the arrival of the Jesuits in the late sixteenth century, was based on Cheng's reports. The Chinese now had some general knowledge of the shape of Africa and heard details about countries of the Mediterranean.

Cheng's expeditions, while endorsed by the emperor, were strongly criticized by a segment of the scholar bureaucracy, who based their opposition on the Confucian concept that China produced all that was necessary for its needs and that foreign expeditions introduced exotic luxuries, which were unnecessary if not harmful.

After Yung-lo's death in 1424, further voyages were banned by his successor, Hung-hsi (d. 1425), who was determined to reverse those of his father's policies that did not conform to Confucian ideas; he put a sudden stop to the expeditions, and issued a decree—that was often ignored—forbidding his nationals from leaving the country. His son, Hsüan-te (r. 1425–1435) permitted Cheng to lead one last expedition (1431–1433) before he retired as military commander of Nanking. However, the Confucian opposition was finally victorious, and even plans for Cheng's ships were later destroyed.

Silk was the major Chinese export to the West in the sixteenth century, despite the fact that trade along the Silk Road was severely limited by the reclusive nature of the Ming. But it was not the only trade route to the West. There were Arab ships trading at Canton and other Chinese ports that continued to call until the Portuguese seized Malacca in 1511, giving them a dominant position in the sea trade of Southeast Asia.

The population of the country is estimated to have been 53,280,000 about the year 1500. In the Yangtze Valley, commerce and industry developed most quickly. Grain transportation to the frontiers came to an end in early Ming time. The rich inland merchants, whose cities bordered on the provinces of Anhui and Chekiang and who had first specialized in the silver trade, spread their activities all over China in the Ming period. They often monopolized the salt, silver, rice, cotton, silk, or tea businesses. In the sixteenth century they had well-established contacts with smugglers on the Fukien coast and brought foreign goods into the interior. Their home was also close to the main centers of porcelain production in Kiangsi, which was exported overseas and to the urban centers. With the development of printing, the paper industry was greatly stimulated, and with the application of block printing to textiles, another new field of commercial activity was opened. There was a growing specialization and division of labor, so that cloth was no longer produced from the raw cotton to the finished product by one worker, but spinning, weaving, and dyeing were done by different specialists, often in diffcrent cities.

The growth of the small gentry, which had its stronghold in the provincial towns and cities, as well as the rise of the merchant class and the liberation of the artisans, are reflected in the new literature of the Ming period. While the Mongols had developed the theater, the novel may be regarded as the typical Ming creation. Together with the development of drama (or, rather, opera) went the modernization of music. Woodcut and block printing developed largely as a cheap substitute for real paintings.

The most widely spoken version of Chinese was—and is—Mandarin, the language spoken by the upper classes and based on the Peking dialect. There were many other dialects, some of which were mutually incomprehensible. More nonstandard dialects existed in the south than in other parts of the country, due to the physical difficulties of communication in mountainous areas. Cantonese and related dialects were spoken in Kwantung province. The written language was never a transcription of the spoken language, and with the passage of time the separation between the two increased.

Ten years after Yung-lo sent Cheng on his Asian expeditions, Prince Henry the Navigator (1394–1460), the third son of King João I of Portugal, took part in the campaign in which Portugal captured the North African port of Ceuta from the Moors. This was the beginning of the period of European expansion that was eventually to see Portuguese ships sail into the Pearl River estuary of Canton. The expedition to Ceuta aroused Henry's interest in Africa and exploration. From 1419 onward he dispatched a series of expeditions down the western coast of Africa, each reaching a bit farther into the unknown. The relentless step-by-step exploration of the West African coast proceeded although commercial rewards were meager.

Prince Henry's death caused only a brief hiatus in the exploration of the West African coast. In 1469 King Afonso V, Prince Henry's nephew, made an agreement with a wealthy Lisbon merchant, Diogo Gomes, who committed himself to discover at least one hundred leagues (about 485 kilometers [300 miles]) of the African coast each year for the next five years. The Gomes contract produced an impressive annual series of African discoveries southward across the equator. When Gomes's contract expired, the king gave the trading rights to his own son, who became King João II in 1481. This was the king who rejected Columbus's appeal in 1484 for support for his projected voyage across the western ocean to what he thought would be Cathay. Nevertheless, one of the voyages João sponsored was that of Bartolomeu Dias who, in 1488, rounded the Cape of Good Hope. Christopher Columbus, who was in Lisbon making another effort to persuade João II to subsidize his projected seaborne expedition, witnessed Dias's return.

Ten years after Dias's rounding of the Cape, Vasco da Gama dropped anchor in Calicut, on the west coast of India. In 1508, King Manuel I, who had succeeded João II in 1495, instructed the commander of one of the subsequent fleets he sent to India to find out all he could about China, which was not yet identified with Marco Polo's Cathay. Between 1513 and 1515, the first contacts with China were made by individual merchant-adventurers who sailed from Malacca for the South China coast in native junks. In 1517, a Portuguese squadron commanded by Fernão Peres de Andrade, the first European ships to appear in Chinese waters, anchored in the Pearl River of Canton. With Peres de Andrade was Tomé Pires, the first European ambassador to China. After some hesitation on the part of the Chinese, Pires was allowed to proceed to Peking and Peres de Andrade established peaceful and profitable relations with the local officials of Canton. But the good impression made by the Portuguese was ruined by Simão Peres de Andrade, brother of Fernão, who visited the Pearl River estuary with a squadron of four ships in 1519 and whose piratical behavior caused a rupture in official Sino-Portuguese relations that lasted for thirty years. However, during the third and fourth decades of the sixteenth century, the Portuguese carried on a clandestine trade with local smugglers in various isolated places in the coastal provinces of China.

About the year 1550, with the development of their trade with Japan—with whom the Chinese were forbidden to trade—it became increasingly urgent for the Portuguese to establish a firm base on the South China coast within easy reach of Canton, where the silk fairs were held. This was secured in 1554 by Leonel de Sousa who, after prolonged negotiations, concluded an agreement with Wang Ho, the acting commander of the coast guard fleet, whereby the Portuguese were allowed to trade in Kwangtung on the same terms as the Siamese. The arrangement was an oral one, and it also seems that the Portuguese were admitted as Siamese, or as foreigners belonging to some other of the Chinese tributary states. This agreement made between Sousa and the provincial authorities at Canton was not reported to the court at Peking, which was not aware of the establishment of the Portuguese at Macao until long afterwards.

Between 1580 and 1615 the lucrative Macao-Japan trade was carried on chiefly by the annual carrack that voyaged from Goa to Macao to the island of Kyushu. Since the Ming court prohibited all direct trade between China and Japan, the Portuguese had the distinct advantage of serving as intermediaries.

The year 1600 may be said to mark a turning point in the history of the Far East. First and most important, it is the date of the decisive battle of Sekigahara (the tenth of October), which gave Tokugawa Ieyasu the mastery of Japan and went far to settle the fate of that country for the next 250 years. Second, it saw the appearance of the first Dutch ship in Japanese waters, whose pilot was the Englishman Will Adams. Third, in December 1600, Queen Elizabeth of England granted a charter to the merchant adventurers who formed the John Company, as the subsequently famous East India Company came to be called. The voluntary dissolution of the English factory at Hirado (Japan) in the year 1624, and the consequent withdrawal of Richard Cocks and his countrymen from Japan, left the Macaonese with only one European competitor in this market, the Dutch. It was the Dutch who were eventually responsible for the dismemberment of the Portuguese empire in the East—with the exception of Macao.

BIBLIOGRAPHY

Boxer, Charles R. *Fidalgos in the Far East.* The Hague, 1948.
Boxer, Charles R. *The Great Ship from Amacon.* Lisbon, 1963.
Boxer, Charles R. *South China in the Sixteenth Century.* London, 1953.
Eberhard, Wolfram. *History of China.* Rev. ed. Berkeley and Los Angeles, 1977.
Prestage, Edgar. *The Portuguese Pioneers.* London, 1933.

REBECCA CATZ

CIPANGU (JAPAN). Europe first heard about Japan from Marco Polo, whose book, *The Description of the World* (Italian title, *Il Milione*) enjoyed widespread popularity in the fourteenth century. Polo had never been to Japan but he described it from hearsay as an island rich in pearls, precious stones, and palaces covered with gold. Of course, he was mistaken, but his book captured the imagination of Columbus, who set out across the Atlantic in an effort to find Cathay and Cipangu—as Polo called Japan—which, he said, was located some fifteen hundred miles east of the Asian continent.

Sometime in the year 1470, a contemporary and compa-

triot of Columbus, the astronomer Paolo dal Pozzo Toscanelli, suggested to King Afonso V of Portugal (r. 1438–1481) that Cathay, Cipangu, and the Spice Islands could be reached more quickly by sailing due west from Portugal than by attempting to find a sea route to Asia around Africa, as the Portuguese were then trying to do. Toscanelli illustrated his proposal with a map on which the island of Cipangu was marked. This map, like his proposal, was obviously based on his reading of Marco Polo. Though Afonso rejected the proposal, there is no doubt that it was later adopted and elaborated by Columbus, who eventually persuaded Fernando and Isabel to sponsor his plan for reaching the east by sailing west.

The name *Japan* entered European history in this form for the first time in the *Suma oriental* of Tomé Pires, which was written between the years 1512 and 1515. It is generally agreed that it is derived through the Malay *Japun* or *Japang* from the Chinese *Jih-pen-kuo* in one or another of its coastal dialect forms, meaning literally "origin of the sun." But Pires's report, which mentions the name *Japan* only briefly, was not published in full for more than four centuries, and the Portuguese chroniclers who used his manuscript did not appreciate the significance of his reference to Japan, still less in connection with Polo's Cipangu.

Columbus failed in his attempt to reach Japan, and a century and a half was to elapse before the first Europeans arrived in that island nation. They were a group of three Portuguese who were caught in a typhoon and blown to Japan aboard a Chinese junk. The merchant adventurer Fernão Mendes Pinto laid claim to being one of them. Although his claim is much disputed, it is certain that he was one of the earliest Portuguese travelers to that country, which he visited four times between 1544 and 1556. As such he had plenty of opportunity to know the real discoverers, whose version of the actual contact in 1542 or 1543 he may have adopted as his own and incorporated into his pseudo-autobiography, *Peregrination* (1614).

The earliest European accounts of Japan that conflict with Pinto's are those of Garcia de Escalante and Jorge Álvares, both of which date from about 1548. Escalante's account is pure hearsay, based on what he was told by a Galician sailor named Pero Diez, who said he had been there in 1544. Although Escalante's account contains some errors, it is of interest as the oldest known report on Japan by a European who had actually visited that country.

The report of the Portuguese captain Jorge Álvares is of greater interest because he was a much better educated and more observant man than the Galician sailor. It is also noteworthy for being the last European report written by a layman for fifty years, since after the arrival of Francis Xavier in 1549, Japan was seen only through the eyes of Christian missionaries until the coming of the Dutch. On his return voyage from Japan in December of 1547, Álvares was accompanied by a Japanese fugitive named Yajiro, whom he presented to Francis Xavier in Malacca.

The most important Japanese account of the European contact is to be found in the *Teppo-Ki* (History of the introduction of firearms into Japan). It was first printed in 1649 but was written during the Keicho period (1596–1614). The author places the arrival of the Portuguese in Tanegashima on the Japanese date corresponding to September 23, 1543, and offers a remarkably accurate description of the Europeans as seen through the eyes of a native.

But all accounts agree that the Portuguese owed their cordial reception in Japan primarily to the novelty of their firearms. The civil strife then endemic in Japan supplied a ready market for their guns and for many years all firearms of this type were known as "Tanegashima," which was the name of the island where the Portuguese first landed and where the firearms were first manufactured.

Not long after Jorge Álvares had presented Yajiro to Francis Xavier, Yajiro, a servant of his, and another compatriot were converted to the Catholic faith. In Goa, where Xavier had enrolled them at the Jesuit College of Saint Paul, they made rapid progress in studying Portuguese. In April 1549 Xavier, accompanied by the three Japanese, two Spanish Jesuits, and two servants, left Goa for Malacca on the first stage of a voyage to Japan. At Malacca they transferred to a Chinese pirate junk, and on August 15, 1549, dropped anchor in Yajiro's home port of Kagoshima, where Xavier stepped ashore for the first time on the south coast of the Japanese island of Kyushu.

The land where Xavier began to preach—with the full permission of the lord of Satsuma—was a land of strife and turmoil. Satsuma itself was not involved in the civil wars, but chaotic feudal anarchy prevailed throughout most of Kyushu and on two of the other main islands, Honshu and Shikoku. Ever since the collapse of the imperial authority and later of the Minamoto shogunate (1200), the provincial war lords had been fighting among themselves in a bewildering series of ever-changing combinations. These endemic civil wars had ceased only for brief spans under the strongest of the Ashikaga shoguns, as when the whole nation combined to repel the Mongol invasions of 1276 to 1281. At the time of the Portuguese contact, Japan was in the middle of the Sengoku-jidai (country at war) period (c. 1460–1600), during which the transition from a patrician to a feudal social and economic order, begun under the Kamakura shogunate (1185–1338), was completed. The emperor at Kyoto still had much of his former moral prestige, but none of his former temporal power.

The condition of the emperor's deputy, the shogun, was not much better. The powerful military dictatorship established in 1192 by Minamoto Yoritomo, after his defeat of the rival Taira clan, had by now shrunk to an empty shell. The Ashikaga shogun, whom the Jesuits usually referred to by his popular title, *kubosama*, exercised only a tenuous authority throughout the *gokinai*, or five home provinces around Kyoto, and none at all elsewhere. However, in one respect the shogunate was better off than the imperial house, since the Ashikagas still possessed considerable landed property from which they derived a fairly substantial income, though they spent it freely on their lavish patronage of the arts. They had delegated many of their administrative duties to provincial constables (*shugo*), who had either become practically autonomous or had delegated their authority to others. The warring daimyo (feudal barons) whether owing a nominal allegiance to the shogun or not, were thus virtually independent of both him and the emperor, ruling their own fiefs as they saw fit.

Another important factor in the political and cultural life of the country was the Buddhist priesthood. Commerce and war lured many of the monks from leading an austerely devout and holy life, but the Buddhist clergy kept the torch of culture alight during this time, in a manner similar to that of the Christian clergy in Europe after the disappearance of the Roman Empire. The fortunes of the Shinto tradition throughout the sixteenth century were completely overshadowed by Buddhism. Nevertheless, the ancient cult was preserved in relatively pristine purity at the great national shrines of Ise and Idzumo. It was some time before the Jesuits grasped the difference between Shinto and Buddhism.

By 1569, the civil wars had reached a point at which there were fewer than half a dozen principal contestants for political supremacy, of whom the most centrally placed was Oda Nobunaga, who in that year had occupied Kyoto on behalf of his puppet, Yoshiaki, the nominal Ashikaga shogun. Nobunaga continued his campaigns to consolidate and extend his dominion and by 1582 he was a master of more than half the provinces of Japan. His career of conquest was cut short by the rebellion of Akechi Mitsuhide, who treacherously attacked and killed him at Kyoto on June 21, 1582.

The discovery of Japan opened a new and most welcome market to the Portuguese, for despite the ravages of civil war, there was a keen demand for foreign goods, and particularly for the Chinese silk yarn, which the daimyo and samurai preferred to the native product.

Because Japanese pirates (*wako*) terrorized the maritime provinces of China and Korea in the fifteenth and sixteenth centuries, the Ming emperor had closed his coasts to them and forbade all intercourse with the Japanese. The Portuguese profited from this situation, since they became not only the carriers but the intermediaries in Japan's trade with China. An agreement made by Leonel de Sousa with the Chinese of Kwangtung in 1554, followed by the acquisition of Macao three years later, virtually placed Portuguese-Chinese relations on an official basis. Within a few years, the Portuguese ships had visited all the harbors on the coast of Kyushu, and not long afterwards the traders were followed by Jesuit priests from the missions at Macao and Goa.

Desire for foreign trade was the primary impulse that accounts for the early success of Christianity in Japan. Some of the daimyo in Kyushu, having noticed the deference the Portuguese traders paid to the priests, favored the Jesuits in hopes of attracting merchant ships to harbors in their own fiefs. After a while, the Jesuits were acting as interpreters and intermediaries, and at times, as brokers, for a fee. The Portuguese annual black ship (kurofune) came to Nagasaki, which had been ceded to them by the local baron, for the first time in 1571. The Jesuits retained the virtual overlordship of Nagasaki until Toyotomi Hideyoshi brought them under the direct control of the central government in 1578 as part of his successful campaign to unify the country.

The rivalry between the various Roman Catholic orders in Japan—Portuguese Jesuits and Spanish Franciscans—was one of the prime causes of the ruin of their missions, and as time went by many things, among them the close connection between politics and religion exemplified by the Portuguese and Spanish in their respective colonial empires, confirmed Hideyoshi's view that Christianity was a political threat. In 1587 he issued an anti-Christian edict, which was not enforced in the Christian fiefs of Kyushu, where the Jesuits were allowed to propagate their faith openly. This proved that Christianity in Japan depended on the annual ship from Macao, and the presence of the Jesuits was thought to be essential to the smooth conduct of the Macao trade at Nagasaki. Hideyoshi's tolerance of Christian propaganda was in direct proportion to the profits he hoped to gain from the Iberian traders. In 1597, Christianity was proscribed and persecution began, but Hideyoshi did not enforce his edict of 1587 because he was occupied with other matters; he died in 1598.

Hideyoshi's successor, Ieyasu, at first displayed a similar tolerance and for similar reasons, hoping to encourage the growth of Japan's merchant marine, while maintaining the country's foreign trade. He offered to open the ports of eastern Japan to Spanish ships, while making it clear that he would not enforce the edicts against Christianity. A Dutch ship arrived in Bungo in 1600; the pilot major of the squadron, an Englishman named Will Adams became a favorite of Ieyasu, advising him on matters of trade and navigation and informing him of the attitude of the Protestant countries of Europe toward the Church of Rome. Ieyasu began to think it preferable and possible to have foreign trade without foreign priests.

In August 1602 the Dutch founded a trading post at Hirado. Although the English tried and failed to establish themselves in Japan, there is no doubt that the presence of the Dutch and English had a decisive influence on the course of Japan's foreign relations at a critical moment in her history.

By 1612 Ieyasu thought that he had little reason to fear the loss of foreign trade, because the Dutch and English were eager to visit his ports, and although there was still no authorized traffic with China, Japanese junks had brought Chinese products from entrepôts in Cochin China and elsewhere. In 1612 and 1613 some Christians were banished, some sanctuaries were destroyed, and fifty Christians were executed. Persecution became more intense in some districts in 1614 and, after Hidetada succeeded Ieyasu in 1616, it became widespread throughout the country, especially after 1617. Hidetada feared that stability and order in his realm would be upset by the presence and the infighting of the Portuguese, the Spanish, the Dutch, and the English. Toward 1622 the shogun Hidetada, suspecting the complicity of the Roman Catholic Church in Spanish plots to invade Japan, began to treat the priests more harshly. In 1624, the cruel and capricious Iemitsu, who succeeded his father, Hidetada, on his retirement in 1623, ordered the deportation of all Spaniards, priests and laymen, and decreed that no Japanese Christian should travel overseas. In 1637, rebellion broke out among the Christians of the island of Amakusa and the Shimabara peninsula, which attracted Christians from neighboring districts. Early in 1638 several thousand of them took possession of a dilapidated feudal castle in Shimabara, where they held out for more than two months. Nearly all were put to the sword and with this massacre, Christianity was virtually exterminated in Japan.

Dread of such uprisings gave the last impulse to the exclusionist sentiment that had been gradually gaining strength in Japan. The English and the Dutch did not come within the scope of the policy of exclusion (the English trading station had been closed in 1623), but after 1640 there were no foreigners in Japan except certain authorized Chinese and a handful of Dutch, who were confined in a small settlement at Nagasaki, to which a few trading ships, strictly limited and closely watched, came annually. Japan had otherwise shut its gates to all foreigners and lapsed into an isolation that lasted for over two hundred years, until July 8, 1853, when an American naval officer, Commodore Matthew C. Perry, forced them open at gunpoint.

BIBLIOGRAPHY

Boxer, Charles Ralph. *The Christian Century in Japan, 1549–1650.* 2d ed. Berkeley and Los Angeles, 1967.

Boxer, Charles Ralph. *Fidalgos in the Far East, 1550–1770.* The Hague, 1948.

Boxer, Charles Ralph. *The Great Ship from Amacon: Annals of Macao and the Old Japan Trade, 1555–1640.* 2d ed. Lisbon, 1963.

Dahlgren, Erik Wilhelm. "A Contribution to the History of the Discovery of Japan." *Transactions and Proceedings of the Japan Society* (London) 2 (1912–1913): 239–260.

Sansom, G. B. *Japan, a Short Cultural History.* Rev. ed. New York, 1943.

Schurhammer, Georg. "O descobrimento do Japão pelos portugueses no ano de 1543." *Anais da Academia Portuguesa da História.* 2d ser., 1 (1946): 9–172.

Schurhammer, Georg. *Francis Xavier: His Life, His Times.* Translated by M. Joseph Costelloe. 4 vols. Rome, 1973–1982.

REBECCA CATZ

CIRCUMFERENCE. Christopher Columbus's views as to the size and shape of the earth came through both study and practical experience. His geographic and geodetic views were formed primarily during the period 1472 to 1484, when he gained his initial experience as a seaman and navigator. But we know, too, that throughout his life, whenever the opportunity arose, he drew, modified, and sold sea charts. (His younger brother Bartolomé had preceded him as a cartographer.) Columbus's convictions as to the earth's dimensions, the distribution of its lands and seas, and the relationship of the earth to the heavenly bodies (collectively and loosely termed "cosmography" in his day) developed through his study of four works: three cosmographical treatises, *Tractatus de sphaera* by Sacrobosco (d. 1256; also known as John of Holywood) and *Tractatus de imagine mundi (Imago mundi)* and *Cosmographiae tractatus duo* by Pierre d'Ailly (d. 1420), and a sensationalist travelogue, *The Book of Ser Marco Polo* (c. 1299).

From Sacrobosco and d'Ailly, Columbus learned that the size of a spherical earth had been estimated, and in some cases measured, by various philosophers, astronomers, and geographers, from Aristotle (384–322 B.C.) to Alfraganus (al-Farghani), a ninth-century Arab astronomer. He also learned that the estimates of the earth's circumference, including those based on attempted measurements, varied widely, although the methods employed were basically similar. The objective in each case was to determine the length, on the surface of the earth along a meridian, of a degree of latitude. Three hundred sixty such degrees would give the circumference of a great circle of the earth's surface. The trace on the earth's surface of a plane intersecting the earth and passing through its center is a great circle; the equator is a great circle, and the meridians, stretching between the North Pole and South Pole, are each one-half of a great circle.

Through the works of Sacrobosco and d'Ailly, Columbus was indirectly introduced to the great geographical, astronomical, philosophical, and natural history writings of Strabo (c. 63 B.C.–after A.D. 23), Pliny (A.D. 23–79), Ptolemy (fl. middle of second century A.D.), Macrobius (Theodosius; fl. A.D. 395–423), Isidore of Seville (fl. c. 560–636), Alfraganus, al-Biruni (973–1048), and Roger Bacon (between 1210 and 1215–1292). Their ideas were covered in sufficient detail to reveal three interesting geographic propositions: one relating to the size of the earth, the second to the length of the Eurasian continent, and the third to the width of the sea that separated Spain and Portugal from the Orient. (There was no knowledge, no inkling, of the existence of the American continents lying between Europe and Asia.)

Columbus learned of Aristotle's arguments for a spherical earth and his estimate of its size: 400,000 stades for the circumference, or 1,111.11 stades for the length of a degree. He learned that Archimedes (d. 212 B.C.), or possibly Dicaearchus of Messana (d. 285 B.C.), had made a measurement (of sorts) of the earth's circumference in which the result obtained was 300,000 stades. He was impressed by the "double-measurement" of the length of a degree carried out between Alexandria and Syene (present-day Aswan), Egypt, by Eratosthenes (c. 276–c. 194 B.C.). Columbus drew some strength from the fact that Eratosthenes' result, 250,000 stades for the earth's circumference, arbitrarily enlarged to 252,000 (so that the length of a degree would be 700 stades), was accorded different equivalent lengths in Roman miles (R.M.) by Strabo, Pliny, and Isidore of Seville, who set Eratosthenes' degree at 87.5 R.M., and by Macrobius and Sacrobosco, who set the degree at 70 R.M. Columbus was pleased to learn that Posidonius (135–51 B.C.), a Greek astronomer and geographer, had made a measurement of a degree between Rhodes and Alexandria and had obtained a degree smaller than that of Eratosthenes. Cleomedes, Posidonius's pupil, reported the result as 666⅔ stades, which, using a stade length of 148.15 to 148.8 meters, or 10 stades to the Roman mile, yields a 66⅔ R.M. degree and a figure for the earth's circumference of 24,000 R.M. Strabo, however, reported that Posidonius's degree measured 500 stades and the earth's circumference 180,000 stades. Using his equivalency of 8 stades per R.M., the degree and the earth's circumference were reduced still further, to 62.5 R.M. and 22,500 R.M., respectively.

There is nothing to indicate that either Marinus of Tyre, a first-century geographer, or Ptolemy ever attempted to measure a degree of latitude. Rather, it appears that both accepted Strabo's interpretation of Posidonius. Columbus was not particularly interested in their views of the size of the earth, because he had come across a reference to Alfraganus's 56⅔-mile degree in both Sacrobosco and d'Ailly. In his *Chronologica et astronomica elementa,* Alfraganus described the measurement of a degree of

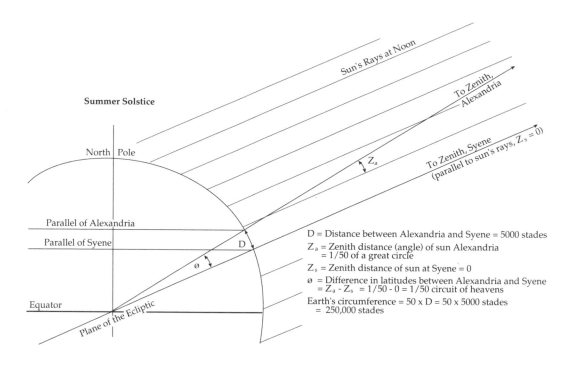

Summer Solstice

D = Distance between Alexandria and Syene = 5000 stades
Z_a = Zenith distance (angle) of sun Alexandria
  = 1/50 of a great circle
Z_s = Zenith distance of sun at Syene = 0
ø = Difference in latitudes between Alexandria and Syene
  = $Z_a - Z_s$ = 1/50 - 0 = 1/50 circuit of heavens
Earth's circumference = 50 x D = 50 x 5000 stades
  = 250,000 stades

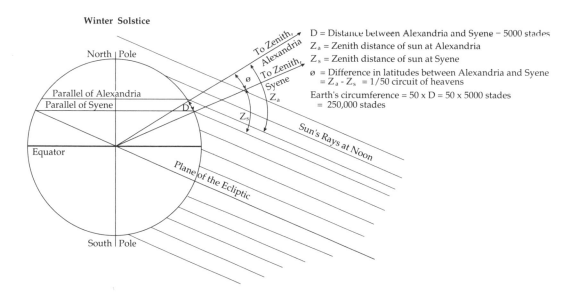

Winter Solstice

D = Distance between Alexandria and Syene – 5000 stades
Z_a = Zenith distance of sun at Alexandria
Z_s = Zenith distance of sun at Syene
ø = Difference in latitudes between Alexandria and Syene
  = $Z_a - Z_s$ = 1/50 circuit of heavens
Earth's circumference = 50 x D = 50 x 5000 stades
  = 250,000 stades

ERATOSTHENES' DETERMINATION OF THE CIRCUMFERENCE OF THE EARTH AT SUMMER AND WINTER SOLSTICES. Eratosthenes chose Syene for its proximity to the Tropic of Cancer: at noon on the summer solstice the sun is directly overhead (*top*). This makes its zenith distance zero. One need only measure the zenith distance at Alexandria, therefore, to obtain the difference in latitudes between the two sites, 1/50 the circuit of the heavens (7°12'). Hence the earth's circumference must be fifty times the distance between the two sites, measured (paced) to be 5,000 stades (circumference = 50 × 5,000 = 250,000 stades). Eratosthenes determined the zenith distance of the sun at Alexandria by means of a skiothern, a hemispherical bowl with a radius equal to the height of a vertical gnomon set in its center. The interior of the bowl was so inscribed with concentric rings around the gnomon that the gnomon's shadow gave a direct measurement of the sun's zenith distance. When Eratosthenes repeated the measurement at noon on the winter solstice (*bottom*), he used skiotherns at both points.

AFTER FRED. F. KRAVATH, CHRISTOPHER COLUMBUS, COSMOGRAPHER, RANCHO CORDOVA, CALIF., 1987, P. 80.

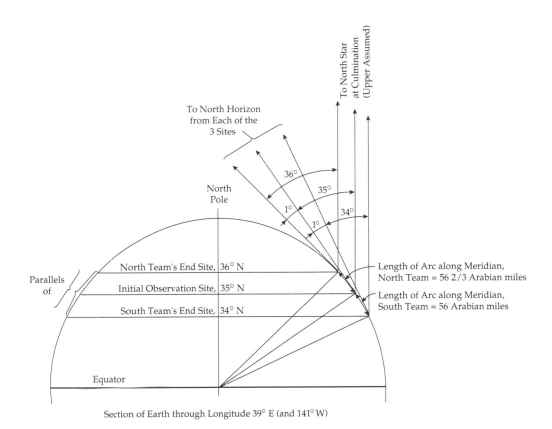

Section of Earth through Longitude 39° E (and 141° W)

PROBABLE METHOD USED BY AL-MA'MUN TO MEASURE THE LENGTH OF ONE DEGREE OF LATITUDE (CIRCA A.D. 830). First, the altitude of the North Star (at its upper culmination) was determined at an initial site at approximately 39° E and 35° N in the desert of Sinjar (Syria). Then, two teams proceeded along the meridian of the initial site, one to the north and one to the south, until they obtained readings of altitude for the North Star one degree greater (for the north team) and one degree less (for the south team) than the altitudes taken at the initial site. One of the teams measured 56⅔ Arabian miles for the surface distance corresponding to one degree of arc; the other measured 56 Arabian miles. The former was selected as the more valid measurement of the length of one degree of latitude. In this illustration, end observation site parallels have been drawn with exaggerated differences in latitude from the initial observation site.   AFTER FRED F. KRAVATH, *CHRISTOPHER COLUMBUS, COSMOGRAPHER*, RANCHO CORDOVA, CALIF., 1987, P. 121.

latitude by the astronomers of the caliph al-Ma'mun in the Syrian desert near Sinjar in A.D. 830. Not only was the result, 56⅔ miles, the smallest numerically of any of the measurements Columbus encountered in the works of Sacrobosco and d'Ailly, but Alfraganus stated that Ptolemy had made his degree too large, in the ratio of 66⅔ to 56⅔. The Arabs' result was stated in Arabian miles. Columbus assumed the Arabian and Roman miles to be identical and adopted the standard of 56⅔ R.M. for the length of a degree of latitude, 20,400 R.M. for the earth's circumference. He claimed to have verified this standard by a measurement at sea, en route from Spain to Guinea, sometime in the period 1482–1484.

In reading Sacrobosco and d'Ailly, Columbus came across a statement from Ptolemy's *Geographic Syntaxis* (Atlas of the world) to the effect that Marinus had given

the habitable world a length of 225 degrees of longitude, stretching from the Fortunate (Canary) Islands, the zero meridian, to Sera, the capital of the Seres and the most easterly inland city of which he had knowledge. Ptolemy arbitrarily reduced this length to 180 degrees. The implication in both cases was that there was an unknown additional stretch of land between Sera and the Atlantic Ocean. Eleven hundred years after Marinus, essential confirmation of his estimate came from Marco Polo, whose book provided details as to the entire continent of Asia and indicated further that 1,500 miles east of the China coast lay the fabulously wealthy island of Cipangu (Japan).

For each of these early geographers, longitudinal distances were determined from the descriptions of travelers' reports, troop movements, caravan operations over reasonably well-known routes, and, where feasible, data

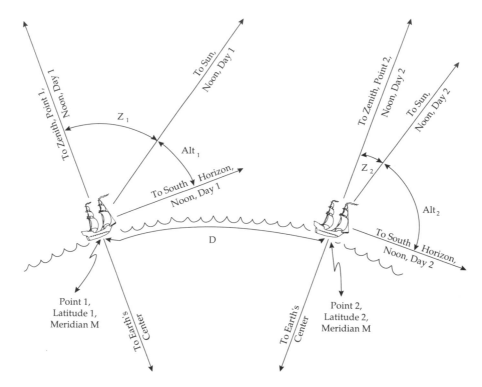

Alt$_1$ & Alt$_2$ = altitudes of the sun at noon on Days 1 & 2

Z$_1$ & Z$_2$ = zenith distances (angles) of the sun at noon
on Days 1 & 2 (zenith distance = 90° - Alt)

Latitude 1 - Latitude 2
$$= (Z_1 + declination_1) - (Z_2 + declination_2)$$
$$= (Alt_2 - declination_2) - (Alt_1 - declination_1)$$

D = surface distance between Points 1 & 2 on Meridian M
= distance traveled due south between noon on Days 1 & 2

Length of 1 Degree of Latitude
$$= \frac{D}{(Alt_2 - declination_2) - (Alt_1 - declination_1)}$$
= 56 2/3 Roman miles, according to Columbus
= 75 Roman miles (111,111 meters), actually

A RATIONALIZATION OF COLUMBUS'S "MEASUREMENT" OF THE LENGTH OF ONE DEGREE OF LATITUDE AT SEA. The length of one degree of latitude is equal to the distance traveled divided by the change in latitude. To use the sun's noontime altitude to determine latitude, one must correct for declination (the sun's zenith distance or angle at the equator). Declination changes day to day. With this change, the end points of the measurement may have been as many as nine degrees of latitude apart, or 675 Roman miles (1,000 kilometers), a four- to eight-day sail in Columbus's time. Whether Columbus even considered declination in his measurement is moot considering the extremely difficult task of taking the sun's altitude aboard a moving ship.

AFTER FRED F. KRAVATH, *CHRISTOPHER COLUMBUS, COSMOGRAPHER*, RANCHO CORDOVA, CALIF., 1987, P. 182.

from the logs of ships engaged in trade. Such data were highly unreliable, for rarely were itinerary reports anything more than a series of estimates of course direction and speed of travel, and they were invariably inflated and inaccurate. In Marinus's use of such reports, and in the interpretations by Columbus and several contemporary geographers of Marco Polo's book, the east-west length of the Eurasian continent was greatly overestimated.

Columbus used Marinus and Marco Polo together to estimate the east-west length of the Eurasian continent, plus offshore islands, somewhere between 280 and 300 degrees. The westward sea voyage from the Canary Islands to Cipangu was allotted 60 to 80 degrees (depending upon the reporting historian). Since this voyage would likely be made at latitudes between 28° N and 36° N, there was involved a sea journey of from 3,000 to 4,000 R.M. at 28° N and possibly as little as 2,750 to 3,670 R.M. at 36° N. Further, the voyage could be broken up by a stop at the island of Antilia (a fictitious place shown on many fourteenth and fifteenth-century portolan charts).

Columbus had heard of correspondence between the Italian astronomer and physician Paolo dal Pozzo Toscanelli (1397–1482) and the Portuguese monarch Afonso V pertaining to the feasibility of a voyage westward from Lisbon to the Indies. It was said that Toscanelli had attached a map to his response. Columbus wrote Toscanelli, giving his own views as to how such a voyage could be made. In return, sometime before his death Toscanelli wrote Columbus, expressing warm approval of his enterprise and attaching a copy of the map he had sent the Portuguese monarch.

Certain of the more prominent biographers of Christopher Columbus, unaware of the extent of Marco Polo's influence over geographers from the time of Columbus to as late as the middle of the sixteenth century, have ridiculed the Great Navigator's enormous extension of the Eurasian continent. The work of the German geographer Henricus Martellus, for example, shows a Eurasian continent with an estimated length of 255 to 265 degrees of longitude. A globe produced by Martin Behaim, a Nürnberg cosmographer and cartographer, in 1492 shows features similar to the Martellus map and a cosmography similar to that of Columbus. J. C. Dopplemayer reproduced Behaim's globe in map form with two hemispheres in 1730.

One of the more interesting maps showing an elongated Eurasian continent is Martin Waldseemüller's world map of 1507, which was responsible for the New World being named after the Florentine Amerigo Vespucci. Despite the necessity of finding room on his map for an American continent and the Greater and several of the Lesser Antilles, Waldseemüller allots a full 270 degrees of longitude for Eurasia, including the Canary Islands (zero meridian), Japan, and the other islands east of China and Southeast Asia.

[See also Cartography; Compass, article on Declination of the Compass; Distance, Measurement of.]

BIBLIOGRAPHY

Bunbury, E. H. A History of Ancient Geography. 2d ed. 2 vols. London, 1883. New edition, New York, 1959.

Dreyer, J. L. E. History of Planetary Systems from Thales to Kepler. Cambridge, 1906. Revised by W. H. Stahl and reissued as History of Astronomy from Thales to Kepler. New York, 1953.

Kimble, George H. T. Geography in the Middle Ages. London, 1938.

Kravath, Fred F. Christopher Columbus, Cosmographer. Rancho Cordova, Calif., 1987.

Morison, Samuel Eliot. Admiral of the Ocean Sea: A Life of Christopher Columbus. 2 vols. Boston, 1942.

Nordenskjold, A. E. Facsimile Atlas to the Early History of Cartography with Reproductions of the Most Important Maps Printed in the XV and XVI Centuries. Stockholm, 1889. Reprint, New York, 1973.

Skelton, R. A. "The Cartography of the First Voyage." Appendix to The Journal of Christopher Columbus, translated by Cecil Jane. New York, 1960.

Skelton, R. A. Explorers' Maps. New York, 1958.

Vignaud, Henry. Toscanelli and Columbus: The Letter and Chart of Toscanelli. First English edition, 1902. Reprint, New York, 1971.

FRED F. KRAVATH

CISNEROS, FRANCISCO JIMÉNEZ DE. See *Jiménez de Cisneros, Francisco.*

CLOTHING. See *Equipment, Clothing, and Rations.*

COAT OF ARMS. As a newly created nobleman, Columbus required the grant of a coat of arms to provide a visible indication of his rank. It is not known when Columbus first conceived of acquiring nobility status, with a title and a coat of arms, as a reward for his achievement—but probably not before 1491. His wish for this status and its accoutrements undoubtedly was based in several factors, including his resentment for having wasted six and a half frustrating years in Spain awaiting royal approval, the summary treatment he had received, and a desire to perpetuate in his family the glory of his achievements.

The coat of arms assigned to him contained the royal arms of the castle and the lion, quartered with his proper bearings, which were a group of islands surrounded by waves. These were specified in a letter patent issued by the Catholic sovereigns on May 20, 1493, confirming his right and that of his descendants to bear arms and declaring:

> You may place above your arms a castle and a lion that we grant you for arms, viz., the gold castle on a green field in the upper quarter of the shield of your arms on the dexter hand and in the other upper quarter on the sinister hand a purple lion rampant with green tongue on a white field, and in the other quarter below on the dexter hand some gold islands in waves of the sea, and in the other quarter below on the sinister hand your own arms which you are accustomed to bear.

It was a singular honor for the sovereigns to allow Columbus to augment his arms with the gold castle of

COLUMBUS'S COAT OF ARMS. A facsimile from a modern edition of Columbus's Book of Privileges, published in London, 1893.

the said ocean sea in the said region of the Indies . . . we do by these presents confirm to you and to your children, descendants and successors, one after the other, now and forever, the said office of Admiral of the Ocean Sea, Viceroy and Governor of the said islands and mainland that you have found and discovered, and of the other islands and mainland that shall by you or your industry be found and discovered henceforward in the same region of the Indies.

No exact description of the coat of arms as quoted in the granting documents has survived, although they are represented in the document of the sovereigns dated June 20, 1493, granting them to Columbus. Undoubtedly each of the vessels that set forth on Columbus's second voyage featured the Admiral's arms emblazoned on their banners and waistcloths.

By the time Columbus had compiled his Book of Privileges in 1502 for the benefit of his descendants, he had made some important alterations in the blazon. He made the chief identical with the royal arms by placing the gold castle on a red field and bringing the lion rampant in accord with the lion of León. Because by this time he had discovered Tierra Firma, he changed the lower dexter quarter so that it now featured an emerging continent as well as a cluster of islands. He added a new sinister quarter to represent the office of the Admiral of the Ocean Sea. This consisted of a group of five golden anchors arranged horizontally on a blue field. The family arms, blazoned as a blue bend on a gold field with a red chief, were now situated in the base between the third and fourth quarters in an arched point.

According to Continental usage, Columbus was within his rights to make the alterations, which had no particular significance. In that period England was the only country having a heralds' college; in all other countries people frequently altered and augmented their escutcheons, few adhering strictly to their original blazon.

If Columbus had pretended to a noble origin, an origin proposed but with no basis in fact by his son Fernando Colón, he would in all likelihood have selected pretentious symbols, like a flock of doves, appropriate to such a claim. A dove, for which the word in Italian is *colombo*, is generally featured in all known arms of patrician families bearing the Columbus name, including the Colombo families of Italy and the Colóns of Castile and Aragón.

The colors of Columbus's arms, consisting of a blue bend on a gold field with red chief, which he afterward quartered with the arms of Castile, probably were derived from the arms of the local guild of clothiers in Genoa, of which his father was a member and occasionally its representative. It is even probable that Columbus's father, a political activist, may have himself used this coat of arms. In European communities during the fifteenth century, members of a trade guild often bore arms, as indeed did

Castile and the purple lion of León, but inasmuch as a difference of the fields was specified, these were not, strictly speaking, the royal arms. No provisions were made, however, for a crest, a motto, or a blazon in the original document assigning the arms to Columbus, which is now among the manuscripts of the duke of Veragua in the Archivo General de Indias in Seville.

These rights and privileges had been conferred conditionally upon Columbus at Granada on April 30, 1492, prior to his departure on his first voyage. After the conditions had been fulfilled with the successful discovery of new lands on the first voyage, it became necessary that the title and arms be officially expressed and formalized. Accordingly, confirmation was issued on May 28, 1493, which repeated the text of the Granada document given above and then went on:

> And now, forasmuch as it has pleased Our Lord that you discover many of the said islands, and as we hope with His aid that you will find and discover other islands and mainland in

other ordinary citizens, for any freeman had a right to assume simple arms. Many of the surviving arms in Continental countries originally were borne by middle-class families. It is to be noted that none of the ingenious promoters of the "real Columbus," whether of Portuguese, Jewish, Catalan, French, or Polish origin, has been able to show that his contender had a coat of arms bearing a blue bend on a gold field under a red chief.

To the family arms as enhanced by Columbus was later added a motto, rendered by Fernando as:

> A Castilla y á León
> Nuevo Mundo dió Colón

> (To Castile and León
> Columbus has given a New World)

In the first edition of his *Historia general de las Indias,* Gonzalo Fernández de Oviedo compounded confusion about the coat of arms with an illustration in which the Columbus arms are further enhanced by the addition of a crest representing a globe surmounted by a red cross and featuring a white ribband containing the motto, which encircled the shield. It is possible that the crest and motto had been added by Columbus's son, Diego Colón, the second admiral.

Much effort has been expended over the years by heraldic experts and others on studies of the "family arms" of the 1502 shield to resolve some of the numerous legends that nineteenth-century writers created around the figure of Columbus. These efforts have not met with much success.

BIBLIOGRAPHY

Colón, Fernando. *Historia del S. D. Fernando Colombo, nella quale s'ha particulare e vera relatione dell'Ammiraglio D. Cristoforo Colombo, suo padre, nuovamente di lingua Spanuola tradotte nell'Italiana dal S. Alfonso Ulloa.* Reprint, Venice, 1571.

Morison, Samuel Eliot. *Admiral of the Ocean Sea: A Life of Christopher Columbus.* 2 vols. Boston, 1942.

Navarette, Martín Fernández de. *Collección de los viajes y descubrimientos que hicieron por mar los Españoles.* Vol. 2. Madrid, 1825–1837.

Oviedo, Gonzalo Fernández de. *Historia general de las Indias.* Vol. 1. Seville, 1535. Reprint, Salamanca, 1851.

Stevens, Benjamin F. *Christopher Columbus: His Own Book of Privileges.* London, 1893.

SILVIO A. BEDINI

COINS. See *Iconography,* article on *Numismatics.*

COLOMBO. Members of the Columbus family whose lives centered in Italy can be found under *Colombo.* For those whose lives centered in Spain or in Spanish America, see *Colón. See Columbus, Christopher,* for several articles detailing the life and achievements of Christopher Columbus.

COLOMBO, DOMENICO (1418–1495/1499), father of Christopher Columbus.

Domenico Colombo, the son of Giovanni Colombo from Mocónesi, was born in Quinto. At the age of eleven, he became an apprentice to Guglielmo de Brabante, a Brabant weaver in Quinto. Ten years later, in 1439, he was a master craftsman.

From 1439 to 1447, Domenico Colombo practiced his trade in Genoa. He was one of many Genoese who became involved in the political rivalry between the Adorno and Fregoso parties in Genoa. He took the side of the Fregosos, acquiring moderate political influence. He was undoubtedly a loyal party member, for in 1447 the new doge Giano appointed him warden of the Olivella gate, a position that customarily lasted thirteen months. Pietro Fregoso had been named captain general of the city on February 3, 1447, the day before Domenico Colombo's appointment, and it is probable that he suggested the appointment to the doge. When Pietro Fregoso became doge, the custody of the Olivella gate was again entrusted to Domenico (October 1, 1450). Domenico Colombo apparently lived comfortably during this period, for he invested money in the purchase of land in Quarto.

Domenico married Susanna Fontanarossa around 1445. Cristoforo Colombo (Christopher Columbus), their eldest son, was born in 1451. From 1452 to 1455, Domenico Colombo resided in Genoa, probably in a house in Vico Olivella. In 1455 he went to live in a house in Vico Diritto. The same building contained both his dwelling and his shop. In February 1470 he was no longer in Genoa, having moved to Savona, where he practiced the trades of weaver and tavern keeper.

Six months later he was back in Genoa with his son Christopher to appear in court, as attested to by the earliest document (September 22, 1470) naming Christopher Columbus. On that day, Domenico was arrested, only to be released a few hours later by a criminal judge who declared that he did not find him *culpabilem.* The reasons for the arrest and for the trip to Genoa were the same: a legal question of a debt that Domenico and his son Christopher owed to a Girolamo del Porto. According to a document dated September 28, 1470, the judge imposed a fine of thirty-five lira on Domenico. In order to raise that sum he sold to a Caprile family some lands "in Ginestreto, potestacie Bisannis," which had been his wife's dowry.

In a document of the Savona weavers' guild dated March 12, 1473, the name Domenico Colombo appears again. On September 24 of the same year, he sold his house on dell'Olivella Street in Genoa. At the beginning of 1477, when he bought land with a house in Légino, near Savona, he sold his house in Vico Diritto, in the Sant'Andrea district. On August 17, 1481, he leased his house in Légino in order to return to Genoa.

In a document dated January 27, 1483, he is cited as a former weaver (*olim textor pannorum*). He was around sixty-five years old, and his wife was probably dead. Of his sons, none had remained by his side. Giovanni Pellegrino, his second son, apparently died young. Christopher and Bartolomé were in Lisbon. Giacomo was also far from home. His daughter Bianchinetta was about to be married to Giacomo Bavarello, son of a cheese maker, who would take his father-in-law's place at the house in Vico Diritto, outside Porta Sant'Andrea. On November 17, 1491, Domenico was in Savona, where he received a sum of money from a debtor, and in 1494, on September 30, he acted as a witness for a notarized document affirming that his sons were "*quondam Dominici.*"

All in all, he is named in seventy-seven notarial acts, attesting to his long and apparently eventful life.

BIBLIOGRAPHY

"Albero genealogico della famiglia Colombo." In part 2, vol. 1 of *Raccolta di documenti e studi pubblicati dalla R. Commissione Colombiana pel quarto centenario dalla scoperta dell'America.* Rome, 1896.

Genoa, City of. *Christopher Columbus: Documents and Proofs of His Genoese Origin.* English-German edition. Bergamo, 1932.

Taviani, Paolo Emilio. *Cristoforo Colombo: Genius of the Sea.* Rome, 1990.

PAOLO EMILIO TAVIANI

COLOMBO, GIOVANNI   (d. around 1442), grandfather of Christopher Columbus. Giovanni Colombo, the son of Antonio Colombo, was born in Mocónesi, a village in the interior of Liguria. Mocónesi had long been the destination of mule teams carrying grain from Piacenza. Here, and in neighboring villages, mills would grind the grain, using the waters of the Lavagna River. The sacks of flour would then be sent, again by means of mules, to Genoa, or more exactly, Quinto. This road from Piacenza to Quinto thus came to be called "the bread road." This was the well-worn route Giovanni Colombo followed as he traveled from Mocónesi to Quinto.

A document preserved in the State Archives of Genoa, dated February 21, 1429, states that Giovanni Colombo of Mocónesi, a resident of Quinto, gave as apprentice his son Domenico, eleven years old, to Guglielmo di Brabante, a Brabant textile weaver. Giovanni Colombo, like his ancestors of Mocónesi, was a peasant, and he wanted his son to become a good artisan. From two documents

preserved in the Columbian Hall of the State Archives of Genoa, Giovanni Colombo appears to have died between September 1440 and January 1444.

BIBLIOGRAPHY

"Albero genealogico della famiglia Colombo." In part 2, vol. 1 of *Raccolta di documenti e studi pubblicati dalla R. Commissione Colombiana pel quarto centenario dalla scoperta dell'America.* Rome, 1896.

Genoa, City of. *Christopher Columbus: Documents and Proofs of His Genoese Origin.* English-German edition. Bergamo, 1932.

Taviani, Paolo Emilio. *Cristoforo Colombo: Genius of the Sea.* Rome, 1990.

PAOLO EMILIO TAVIANI
Translated from Italian by Rodica Diaconescu-Blumenfeld

COLOMBO, GIOVANNI ANTONIO   (c. 1475–c. 1540), cousin of Christopher Columbus and participant in voyages of discovery. During his third voyage Columbus named three captains: Pedro de Arana, brother of Beatriz de Arana, who bore Columbus's son Fernando; Alonso Sánchez de Carvajal, a dignitary of the city of Baeza; and Giovanni Antonio Colombo of Genoa. Thus another relative, another Genoese, makes his appearance, one who did not Hispanicize his surname to Colón, preserving the Italian name Colombo. He had participated earlier in the Columbian enterprise; at the end of 1497 and the beginning of 1498 he was the Admiral's majordomo. Later he was one of the faithful supporters of Columbus during the Roldán rebellion on La Isabela in 1498. Columbus mentions him and his brother Andrea twice in an autograph document for the sale of some gold in Spain sometime between July 1502 and March 1504 and in a letter of January 4, 1505.

When the Admiral died, Giovanni Antonio remained in the service of Columbus's son Diego, who, in his will of February 19, 1515, left him one hundred gold pesos. His brother Andrea, nicknamed "André Ginovés" (Andrew the Genoese), took part in Columbus's fourth voyage as a groom aboard *Santiago* and was in charge of obtaining some provisions on La Española. As procurator to Diego in San Salvador, he testified in an action brought by Diego in 1515 against the treasury. Bartolomé de las Casas says that Giovanni Antonio was "a man of great ability, prudent and authoritative, with whom I held frequent conversations." Las Casas was certain that the brothers, Giovanni Antonio and Andrea, belonged to the Admiral's family. They were probably second or third cousins.

Giovanni Antonio may have been the Johannes de Columbo of Quinto mentioned in a notary's document of October 11, 1496, reproduced in the *Raccolta Colombiana.* The text (from Latin) reads as follows:

Giovanni Columbus of Quinto, Matteo Columbus, and Amighetto Columbus, brothers of the late Antonio, knowing that Giovanni must go to Spain to visit Christopher Columbus, Admiral to the King of Spain, and that whatever expenses are to be borne by the said Giovanni in order to find the said Christopher should be borne by all three of the brothers named above, each of them is paying a third . . . and so they are agreed.

It is not clear whether this is the same Giovanni Antonio or another. Nevertheless, one cannot help but think that when news of the surprising fortune of Domenico's eldest son spread among the Columbuses of Liguria, not a few of them sought him out in quest of some benefit. The Admiral accepted them all—brothers, nephews, and cousins of Liguria and in-laws of Córdoba—placing them in positions of responsibility and command, showing trust for relatives and suspicion of strangers.

BIBLIOGRAPHY

Ballesteros Beretta, Antonio. *Cristóbal Colón y el descubrimiento de América.* Vol. 2. Barcelona and Buenos Aires, 1945.

Columbus, Ferdinand. *The Life of the Admiral Christopher Columbus by His Son, Ferdinand.* Translated by Benjamin Keen. New Brunswick, N.J., 1959.

PAOLO EMILIO TAVIANI

COLÓN, BARTOLOMÉ (1461–1514 or 1515), brother of Christopher Columbus. Bartolomé Colón, the third son of Domenico Colombo, was born in Genoa and, like his brother Christopher, lived there and in Savona.

The Genoese chronicler Antonio Gallo writes that Bartolomé was probably already in Lisbon when Columbus arrived there. Gallo, a neighbor, was a friend of the Colombo family and, at the time he wrote his book, chancellor of the San Giorgio Bank, with which the Admiral had many dealings. Agostino Giustiniani, who cites Gallo in his *Annali della Repubblica di Genova* (1537), adds that Christopher "dedicated himself to the art of navigation and arrived in Lisbon, Portugal, where he learned cosmography . . . [from] a brother who made maritime maps." Although Gallo and Giustiniani were well informed on the subject of Columbus's Ligurian period, neither was familiar with his Portuguese years.

When Christopher Columbus arrived in Portugal in 1476, he was twenty-five years old, and Bartolomé was only fifteen. Thus the latter could not yet have been an expert in cosmography, nor is it clear how he could have gotten to Lisbon. It is more probable that Bartolomé was not yet in Portugal in 1476, but that Christopher himself called him there around 1480.

Bartolomé de las Casas says that Bartolomé was no less an expert in cosmography than was his brother. He adds

that Bartolomé used to compile and draw maps and design nautical instruments. Las Casas also attests that Bartolomé was a better calligrapher than the Admiral. This comparison has led to numerous arguments regarding the attribution to the brothers of various annotations found in the books of the Biblioteca Colombina, Seville.

Above all, however, Bartolomé was a sailor. Before 1492, he sailed to England and probably to Guinea. After the great discovery, he sailed to the New World, becoming an "adelantado de mar," or governor of a region across the sea. And it was Bartolomé who saved the caravel *Bermuda* from shipwreck against a treacherous reef in a terrible storm during the fourth voyage.

From 1480 until the Admiral's death, Bartolomé was close to his older brother. When he was not with him in person, he was helping and promoting his brother's projects. That said, it should be understood that no contribution may be attributed to him for Columbus's project of sailing westward in order to reach the East. Bartolomé was only nineteen when he joined his brother in 1480. Christopher Columbus had already arrived at this notion by himself, with the aid only of the sea and his creative intuition regarding its currents, its winds, and its mysteries.

Although Bartolomé had nothing to do with the genesis of the great design, he was nevertheless present and of immense help during the difficult years that brought the design to fruition. He was a devoted, diligent, and intelligent collaborator. His collaboration was particularly important in times of grave difficulty.

In the winter of 1487–1488, for example, when Columbus had all but abandoned hope of receiving funds from Castile for his proposed voyage, he sent Bartolomé to England to solicit the support of King Henry VII. Bartolomé, however, was captured by pirates before he arrived and endured a long period of captivity before being set free. He arrived finally in England, but was not successful. So he went on to France to enlist the aid of Charles VIII. Here the news reached him that his brother in the meantime had received the help of the Spanish monarchs and had made the great discovery on the other side of the Atlantic.

Bartolomé returned immediately to Seville and, taking with him his nephews Diego and Fernando, went to the court. He then took command of a supply fleet with which he sailed for La Española, where he arrived on June 24, 1493. From this time on he was united with his brother and embarked on enterprises as explorer, colonizer, administrator, and warrior.

As administrator of La Española in Columbus's absence, Bartolomé governed the unruly settlers justly but severely and was feared by them. When the brothers, after the third voyage, were returned to Spain in chains by Fran-

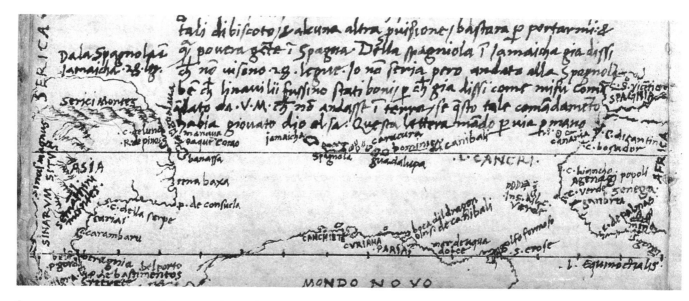

SKETCH MAP OF THE COASTS OF CENTRAL AND SOUTH AMERICA. Drawn by Alessandro Zorzi, based on a map by Bartolomé Colón.

BIBLIOTECA NAZIONALE CENTRALE, FLORENCE

cisco de Bobadilla, Bartolomé helped the Admiral reclaim his rights. Bartolomé went to Rome in 1506, the year of Columbus's death, to solicit from Pope Julius II a recommendation to King Fernando to entrust to him an expedition of discovery. He obtained it three years later and returned to the Indies in 1509 with his nephew Diego. There he held office in the government of Santo Domingo.

Bartolomé died, probably toward the end of 1514 or in the first days of January 1515, in the city of Concepción and was buried in Santo Domingo. He left his estate to Diego.

Two episodes in the eventful life of Bartolomé Colón deserve particular note: the founding of the city of Santo Domingo and the battle he fought during his year at Santa Gloria in Jamaica at the end of the fourth voyage of discovery. The founding of Santo Domingo took place in 1496. Columbus had departed for Europe, leaving to Bartolomé the establishment of a new capital. Bartolomé explored the southern coast of La Española, where he found an excellent natural harbor at the mouth of the Ozama River in an exceptionally fertile region. He named the new colony Santo Domingo in memory of his father, Domenico. In order to confer more solemnity upon his choice of name, Bartolomé led the settlers to the chosen site on a Sunday (*domenica*, in Italian), which that year coincided with the day dedicated by the church to Saint Dominic. Santo Domingo flourished from the beginning. Philip II called it the "escala, puerto y clave de todas las Indias" (stopover, port, and key of all the Indies).

Santa Gloria was a northern beach in Jamaica where Christopher Columbus and his crew were marooned from June 26, 1503, to June 29, 1504. Among the stormy events of that year was the revolt of the Porras brothers, who in 1504 succeeded in convincing the crew to revolt against Columbus. On May 19 they marched on Santa Gloria, where Columbus had entrusted the defense to Bartolomé. Once the armed groups were in position, Francisco de Porras ran to the attack. The boldest of his men surrounded Bartolomé, but with one stroke Bartolomé killed an adversary and then swiftly felled the other five. Francisco de Porras advanced and struck Bartolomé with his sword so violently that he broke Bartolomé's shield and wounded him in the hand. But Porras's sword had penetrated to the hilt, and he could not retrieve it. At this point, Bartolomé could have killed him, but instead he knocked him down, disarmed him, and took him prisoner. Thus, Las Casas recounts, Bartolomé set the rebels to flight. This episode demonstrates that Bartolomé Colón was not only a good cosmographer, as he is usually remembered, but a courageous and able soldier.

BIBLIOGRAPHY

Ballesteros Beretta, Antonio. *Cristóbal Colón y el descubrimiento de América*. Vol. 1. Barcelona and Buenos Aires, 1945.

Columbus, Ferdinand. *The Life of the Admiral Christopher Columbus by His Son, Ferdinand*. Translated by Benjamin Keen. New Brunswick, N.J., 1959.

Las Casas, Bartolomé de. *Historie de las Indias*. Vol. 2. Mexico City, 1951.

Morison, Samuel Eliot. *Admiral of the Ocean Sea: A Life of Christopher Columbus*. 2 vols. Boston, 1942.

Oviedo, Gonzalo Fernández de. *Historia general y natural de las Indias.* 5 vols. Madrid, 1959.

Rubio, V. *Datos para las historia de los origenes de la ciudad de Santo Domingo.* Santo Domingo, 1978.

Taviani, Paolo Emilio. *Christopher Columbus: The Grand Design.* London, 1985.

Taviani, Paolo Emilio. *I viaggi di Colombo.* 2d ed. Vol. 2. Novara, 1990. Spanish ed., Barcelona, 1989.

PAOLO EMILIO TAVIANI
Translated from Italian by Rodica Diaconescu-Blumenfeld

COLÓN, DIEGO (c. 1462–1515), brother of Christopher Columbus. Giacomo Colombo (Spanish, Diego Colón), the second brother of Christopher Columbus, was the son of Domenico Colombo and Susanna Fontanarossa. His name first appears in a document dated September 10, 1485, in which he agrees to become the apprentice of a weaver, Luchino Cadermatori, of Savona, Italy. The will of Susanna Fontanarossa, dated July 21, 1489, lists Giacomo among her heirs.

After Christopher Columbus's return from the first voyage, Giacomo Colombo moved to Spain, where he was called Diego Colón. He became a Spanish subject in 1504; his naturalization documents refer to ecclesiastical honors and benefits, which indicate that he was a cleric. According to Bartolomé de las Casas, Diego Colón was seeking to become a bishop in La Española at this time. Further evidence that he was a cleric is a draft of Columbus's will, dated February 22, 1498, which settles the modest annual income of 100,000 maravedis on him because he was a member of the clergy.

BIBLIOGRAPHY

"Albero genealogico della famiglia Colombo." In part 2, vol. 1 of *Raccolta di documenti e studi pubblicati dalla R. Commissione Colombiana pel quarto centenario dalla scoperta dell'America.* Rome, 1896.

Genoa, City of. *Christopher Columbus: Documents and Proofs of His Genoese Origin.* English-German edition. Bergamo, 1932.

Taviani, Paolo Emilio. *Christopher Columbus: The Grand Design.* London, 1985.

Taviani, Paolo Emilio. *I viaggi di Colombo.* 2d ed. Vol. 2. Novara, 1990. Spanish ed., Barcelona, 1989.

PAOLO EMILIO TAVIANI
Translated from Italian by Rodica Diaconescu-Blumenfeld

COLÓN, DIEGO (c. 1480–1526), Christopher Columbus's son and second Admiral of the Indies. Christopher Columbus's son by his marriage of 1479 to Felipa Perestrelo y Moniz, Diego Colón was born either on Porto Santo in the Madeira Islands or in Lisbon. His mother having died by the time he was four years old, Diego accompanied his father from Lisbon to Spain in the summer of 1485. During the next seven years, he lived at the Franciscan house of La Rábida, or possibly in Moguer with Violante (or Brigulaga, according to Diego's will of 1509) Moniz, his mother's sister, and her husband, Miguel Moliarte.

On May 8, 1492, Diego was appointed a page in the household of Juan, King Fernando and Queen Isabel's only son, but did not go to court until 1494. During the next dozen years, Diego served in a variety of positions in the royal court. He was a page from 1494 to 1497 in Juan's household, and from 1498 to 1503 in Isabel's. On November 15, 1503, he was appointed a *contino* (member of the household guard), a capacity in which he served until Isabel's death the following year. He remained at court until July 1507, but was with his father when he died on May 20, 1506.

Philip I acknowledged Diego as heir to his father's titles and heritable privileges on June 2, 1506, but failed to clarify the geographic area where they applied or the extent of Diego's powers as viceroy, admiral, and governor-general.

In July 1507, Diego obtained permission to take his household to meet Fernando the Catholic, who was returning from Italy to Castile to assume control over its government following the sudden death of Philip I and Queen Juana's mental and emotional retreat from reality (she is known to history as Juana, la Loca [the mad]). By late August, Diego had joined Fernando in Valencia. He followed the court to Burgos where, in October and November 1507, he had an affair with Constanza Rosa, who was said to have borne him a child the following year. Early in 1508 he had a second affair, with Isabel Samba, who bore him a son, Cristóbal Colón, in October 1508.

During the next eighteen months, Colón established himself as his father's successor. Now of age, he sued the Crown to obtain the offices and privileges he believed had been granted to his father; this and subsequent lawsuits are known as the Pleitos Colombinos. Promised that if he would marry he would be named governor-general of the Indies, in the summer of 1508 he married María de Toledo y Rojas, daughter of Fernando de Toledo, brother of the second duke of Alba, thus allying the highest-ranking noble of the Indies with the highest-ranking noble in Castile. They eventually had seven children: Felipa, María, Juana, Isabel, Luís (third admiral of the Indies), Cristóbal, and Diego.

Although his claims had not been satisfied, Colón went to Santo Domingo with his wife to take up his office, arriving on July 10, 1509. Their court and palace gave new life to the capital.

Granted only limited powers by the Crown and subject

DIEGO AND FERNANDO COLÓN. Depicted with their father, Christopher Columbus, and Fernando's mother, Beatriz Enríquez de Harana. Engraving.

to the watchful eye of Miguel de Pasamonte, the royal treasurer—and after 1512 subject to the audiencia judges—Colón managed to use his first period of personal rule at Santo Domingo (1509–1514) to build an extensive base of political support not only on La Española but on Puerto Rico, Cuba, and Jamaica as each was occupied. His judicial and other appointees, often men who had served his father or who were longtime residents of the Antilles, were only a few of those who looked to him for protection and reward. Equally important were the locally resident encomenderos. Granted the right to distribute Indians, Colón seems to have worked out an unofficial arrangement whereby vacant encomiendas were not reported to Spain, but quietly granted (or redistributed) by him to local residents. On a few occasions he even evaded Fernando's orders to grant Indians to absentee courtiers, which, along with his role in the naming of alcaldes (municipal judges) and regidores (municipal councilors) in the municipalities of La Española, eventually came to Fernando's attention and were important reasons for Colón's recall to Spain in 1514.

His political achievement seems to have been only partially matched by financial gain. La Española was in a period of economic and demographic decline. Both the mines and the Indians who were compelled to work them had begun to give out well before Colón arrived. The decline continued in spite of ongoing resettlement of the remaining Indians, the importation of Indian slaves from other parts of the Caribbean, and Fernando's repeated orders to find more gold. Unable to make a living on La Española, Spaniards left for the new colonies or returned to Spain. Nor did the new colonies generate much royal income, of which Colón was entitled to a tenth. Only a little gold was found on Puerto Rico; gold was found on Cuba late in 1514, but proved to be limited as well. Colón did bestow Indians, mines, and farms and ranches on himself, but the extent of his incomes from these sources—as from the tenth of royal income—is not known aside from what can be inferred from some sizable bequests in his will of 1523. And set against these revenues were the heavy expenses of maintaining a court and of patronage on a scale befitting so great a noble.

Although in many respects a victory for Colón, the decision of 1511 in the Pleitos Colombinos proved to be the opening round in the undermining of Colón's quasi-seignorial power in the Caribbean colonies. The court restricted Colón's powers to the Greater Antilles and the eastern part of Venezuela and allowed the Crown to appoint appeals and residencia judges to review the actions of Colón's judicial appointees. Fernando immediately did so, creating the audiencia of Santo Domingo on August 5, 1511, and then appointing residencia judges. In the fall of 1513, Fernando appointed judges to carry out a new distribution of the remaining encomienda Indians, thereby removing Colón's most important tool of patronage. Colón was recalled for discussions in the fall of 1514. He sailed for Spain, which he had visited in 1511 and 1513, in April 1515.

Colón's stay in Spain lasted four and a half years because of Fernando's death and Charles V's succession to the throne in 1516 and because of his own efforts to acquire additional privileges once he had the new king's favor. Ever the courtier, Colón managed to charm the young king and, by late 1518, his restoration to his offices and privileges in the Indies seemed well advanced, only to be further delayed when he demanded observance of other privileges he believed had been granted by the Santa Fe Capitulations. He was also delayed because his enemy, Cardinal Juan Rodríguez de Fonseca, was again the virtual minister of colonial affairs. In the end, by a decree of May 17, 1520, the second lawsuit was settled, largely in Colón's favor. Still unsatisfied, he instituted an appeal that made even more sweeping claims than he had made in the previous suits.

Once Charles left Spain, Colón hastened to Santo

Domingo, sailing from Seville in the fall of 1520. He arrived at his capital on November 12, to find a vastly changed situation from the one he had left. His revenues continued to fall with the economic fortunes of the Antilles and each tax reduction the Crown granted to the islands in hopes of stimulating a reversal of their economic decline. To compensate, Colón arbitrarily, and without clear legal authority, raised taxes and fees. He also invested in a sugar plantation with forty black slaves (making it one of the larger of the nineteen plantations then in existence) and in slaving enterprises on the Venezuelan coast. The latter brought him into conflict with Bartolomé de las Casas and the Dominican reformers, who were attempting to demonstrate there that missions and Spanish farmers could peacefully convert the local Indians into good Spanish Christians. These powerful enemies quickly joined the audiencia's judges in denouncing Colón's actions. And since this was happening during the period of the Comunero Rebellion in Spain—which directly challenged royal power—Colón soon received a royal reprimand and an order to return to Spain, dated March 1523, not long after Charles landed in Spain to reassert his authority. Diego's "Indian summer of political feudalism," as Troy Floyd has so aptly called these three years, was at an end. In September 1523 he set out again for Spain on what proved to be his final journey.

Colón's experience in Spain was similar to his previous visit, but without obtaining what he wanted. After joining the court at Vitoria in late January 1524, he continued to follow it for the next two years and to explain away the charges against him. During this time, Charles treated him with great respect, but Colón's claims never received definitive handling. Twenty years later, Hernando Cortés would receive similar treatment.

When Charles left Toledo for Seville and the celebration of his marriage to Isabel of Portugal, Colón was too ill to travel with the court. Improving somewhat, on February 21, 1526, he left Toledo in a litter, but was forced by his illness to halt at Montalbín, six leagues from Toledo. There he lodged in Alonso Tellez Pacheco's house, where he died on February 23, 1526. Some years later his bones and those of his father were taken to Santo Domingo and buried in the cathedral.

In his will, Colón acknowledged debts totaling 1.6 million maravedis (about 4,253 ducats) in Spain and more than 3,000 pesos de oro (3,600 ducats) in La Española. He claimed that at least 14,350 ducats were due to him (10,000 of which were loaned to Charles V in 1520), as well as the eighth and tenth of the royal revenues from the colonies, none of which had been paid since his father's time. In addition, he had extensive properties on La Española.

Las Casas, who knew Colón well, described him as being tall, large framed, and well proportioned like his father. He had a long face and a dignified bearing and knew how to please as well as how to try to get his way through quiet negotiation and political action. His faults—a tendency to authoritarianism and grasping—seem to have been those of nobles of his rank.

[See also *Lawsuits; Santa Fe Capitulations.*]

BIBLIOGRAPHY

Floyd, Troy S. *The Columbus Dynasty in the Caribbean, 1492–1526.* Albuquerque, N. Mex., 1973.

Nieto y Cortadellas, Rafael. *Los descendientes de Cristóbal Colón: Obra genealógica.* Havana, 1952.

Schoenrich, Otto. *The Legacy of Christopher Columbus.* 2 vols. Glendale, Calif., 1949.

Thacher, John Boyd. *Christopher Columbus, His Life, His Work, His Remains.* 3 vols. 1903–1904. Reprint, New York, 1967.

Winsor, Justin. *Christopher Columbus and How He Received and Imparted the Spirit of Discovery.* Boston, 1891.

PAUL E. HOFFMAN

COLÓN, FERNANDO (1488–1539), historian and bibliophile; son of Christopher Columbus. Fernando Colón was born in Córdoba on August 15, 1488, the son of the Admiral and Beatriz Enriquez de Arana, Columbus's companion during many difficult years of his life.

In 1494 Fernando was received with his older brother, Diego, among the pages of the Infante Juan. After the death of the prince in 1497, Fernando and his brother entered the service of Queen Isabel. He was educated at her court and remained there until May 9, 1502, when with his father and his uncle Bartolomé, he embarked from Cádiz in the small fleet that undertook the fourth voyage of Columbus.

The presence of the fourteen-year-old boy on this voyage was not a mere formality. Fernando and his uncle played an important role in the explorations of the mountain ranges of Veragua (northwestern Panama) beyond Santa María de Belén, a colony that had been founded by Columbus but had failed to prosper because of floods and Indian attacks. In the course of these explorations, in 1503, the Europeans discovered cocaine. Fernando himself wrote about this discovery: "The colonial chief and his dignitaries never neglected to put in their mouths a dry herb and to chew it, and sometimes they would use a certain powder, which they carried with the herb mentioned. Which [custom] seems a very ugly thing."

After returning to Spain, the young Fernando remained with his infirm father. Contrary to legend, Christopher Columbus was not poor. In fact, he was fairly rich, but he had by now become politically marginal. When he died in Valladolid, on May 20, 1506, Fernando was closest at his side among the relatives, friends, and servants who had gathered to catch his last words of faith.

After Christopher Columbus's death, Fernando became actively involved in defending the rights to the titles and revenues that had been granted to Columbus and his descendants in the Santa Fe Capitulations, an agreement signed on the eve of his first voyage, and which the monarchs of Spain no longer acknowledged. These rights were argued in the Pleitos Colombinos, a series of lawsuits with varied outcomes, which started in 1508 and did not end until 1536. To defend his brother in these trials, Fernando elaborated a number of petitions in which he maintained that the Crown should keep all promises made to Columbus, since Columbus had kept his promise—he had presented the monarchs with lands and riches. This intransigent position turned out to be, perhaps, more damaging than useful to his family, even though it was consistent with the position his father had taken all his life.

In July 1509, Fernando made his second and last voyage to America, accompanying his brother, Diego, who had been named governor of the Indies. But two months later, in September, Fernando returned to Spain in order to follow closely the developments of the Pleitos.

In 1512–1513, again on behalf of Diego, he made his first trip to Italy, visiting Rome and his father's native city, Genoa. He had begun by now to accumulate a library, and in the course of this trip and subsequent ones, he purchased books in each city he visited.

With Carlos I's (Charles V) accession to the throne, a new phase began in Fernando's life. Accompanying the king, who went to take possession of the lands he had inherited from the House of Austria and from the Imperial Crown, Fernando Colón undertook a long journey in 1520–1522 to Brussels, Ghent, Louvain, and Worms. Then he went again to Genoa, Milan, Venice, and other Italian cities. From Italy he traveled to Switzerland, Germany, the Netherlands, and London.

In the meantime, his reputation as a cosmographer was growing. In 1524, he was called to join a group of experts that constituted the Committee of Badajoz, which was instituted for the purpose of resolving the problem of delimiting the antimeridian (180 degrees from the Line of Demarcation). In March of 1526 he was entrusted with the task of putting together another group of experts in order to create a general nautical map, which was to serve as a model for maps used by ships going to the New World.

That same year, Diego died, and his wife, María de Toledo, as guardian of her son, Luis, took over the complicated legal and patrimonial affairs of the family. From that time on, Fernando increasingly limited his participation in the business of the Pleitos, which allowed him to devote greater attention to his library.

Containing now more than fifteen thousand volumes, the library had become one of the richest of its time. A part of it, called the Biblioteca Colombina, still exists. He began to build in Seville an edifice to house it and devoted his last years to book collecting. He died in Seville on July 12, 1539.

Fernando Colón wrote several works that have remained, for the most part, in manuscript form. Among them were a politico-historical treatise entitled Colón de concordia, which is lost, and Descripción y cosmographia de España, which remained unfinished. The most famous text attributed to him is Le historie della vita e dei fatti dell'Ammiraglio Don Cristoforo Colombo, a biography of his father. Precisely because it was attributed to Fernando, this biography was long considered the most authoritative source on Columbus, notwithstanding many obvious incongruities and inexactitudes.

The Historie has survived only through an Italian translation by Alfonso de Ulloa, which was published in Venice in 1571, more than thirty years after the death of its presumed author. Doubts about its authenticity, raised since the beginning of the nineteenth century, seem confirmed by recent scholarship. The Historie is apparently a posthumous compilation, based on a writing of Fernando's, but substantially changed by the insertion of false or imprecise statements made with the purpose of exalting the figure of Columbus and bringing glory to his descendants.

Although such reservations diminish the value of the Historie, it remains a fundamental text in Columbian historiography, especially with regard to the narrative of the four voyages, the fourth of which is derived directly from a text whose authenticity is not in doubt.

[See also Lawsuits; Library of Columbus; Santa Fe Capitulations.]

BIBLIOGRAPHY

Belgrano, L. T., and Marcello Staglieno. "Documenti relativi a Christoforo Colombo e alla sua famiglia." In part 2, vol. 1 of Raccolta di documenti e studi pubblicati dalla R. Commissione Colombiana pel quarto centenario dalla scoperta dell'America. Rome, 1896.

Colombo, Fernando. Le historie della vita e dei fatti dell'Ammiraglio Don Cristoforo Colombo. Vol. 8 of Nuova Raccolta Colombiana, edited by Paolo Emilio Taviani and Francesca Cantù. Rome, 1991.

Columbus, Ferdinand. The Life of the Admiral Christopher Columbus by His Son, Ferdinand. Translated by Benjamin Keen. New Brunswick, N.J., 1959.

Harrisse, Henry. Fernand Columb: Sa vie, ses oeuvres. Paris, 1873.

Luzzana Caraci, Ilaria. Colombo vero e falso: La costruzione delle historie fernandine. Genoa, 1989.

Marín Martínez, T. Memoria de las obras y libros de don Hernando Colón. Madrid, 1970.

Rumeu de Armas, Antonio. *Hernando Colón: Historiador del descubrimiento de América*. Madrid, 1973.

Taviani, Paolo Emilio. *Christopher Columbus: The Grand Design*. London, 1985.

PAOLO EMILIO TAVIANI
Translated from Italian by Rodica Diaconescu-Blumenfeld

COLÓN, LUÍS

COLÓN, LUÍS (1521–1572), Christopher Columbus's grandson and third Admiral of the Indies. The eldest son of Diego Colón and María de Toledo y Rojas, Luís Colón y Toledo was born in Santo Domingo and apparently resided there for several years after his mother returned to Spain in 1529 to pursue the privileges she claimed on behalf of her son as his father's heir. Nominally viceroy and governor-general, Luís is not known to have actually exercised any power prior to 1540, even though some royal orders were addressed to him. His mother, as his legal tutor, exercised the powers of his offices.

The final lawsuit in the Pleitos Colombinos was decided by the sentences of June 28, 1536, and the decrees of September 8, 1536, and March 24, 1537. Under terms of these agreements, Colón renounced his claim to 10 percent of royal revenues from the Americas, the title of viceroy, and his right to appoint officials in the colonies. In return, he received a perpetual annuity of ten thousand ducats drawn on the revenues of La Española, fiefs embracing Jamaica and a square of land twenty-five leagues on a side in Veragua (Panama), the titles of duke of Veragua and marquis de la Vega, the title of Admiral of the Indies with all its privileges, and a few minor benefits connected with the island of La Española and his properties there. By separate decrees, his two unmarried sisters, María and Juana (another was a nun), were given lifetime pensions. The fourth sister, Isabel, already seems to have been married to a Castilian nobleman. His youngest brother, Diego, was given an income-producing membership in the Order of Santiago. His other brother, Cristóbal, apparently received nothing. His mother received a grant of four thousand ducats to help repay the costs of litigation and a lifetime income of one thousand ducats a year (she later gave this to her daughter María).

Subsequently, Luís sued to clarify which ports owed dues to him as admiral (1537–1541) and what powers he had in them (1554). His final lawsuit resulted in a new settlement in 1556 under which he gave up his fief in Veragua but retained the title of duke of Veragua, lost all revenues and power associated with the title of admiral (which became honorary), became duke de la Vega, and had his annuity increased to seventeen thousand ducats, seven thousand of which were payable during his lifetime from the customs receipts at Seville. The balance was to be paid from the treasury at Santo Domingo; later, the source of this money was changed to the treasuries of Panama. Settlement of his claims for back payments was made in the form of slave licenses. He received other slave licenses and twenty thousand head of cattle from the royal herds on La Española as royal grants, marks of the king's favor.

These settlements indicate not only that the Crown was determined to recover complete control over the empire, but also to protect Luís Colón's (and his mother's) basic interests: prestige and money. A third interest—love and marriage—became evident during his years as captain general of La Española and during a subsequent period in Spain.

Colón was appointed captain general in 1540, while he was probably in Spain. Returning to Santo Domingo, he soon fathered an illegitimate daughter, Juana Colón de Toledo. In 1542 he and María de Orozco exchanged marriage vows but because of his mother's opposition Orozco was forced to continue on her way to Honduras as part of Pedro de Alvarado's party. Although a legal marriage, according to Spanish common law, the union never received ecclesiastical blessing or consummation. Four years later Luís married María de Mosquera in an elaborate church ceremonial, even though María de Orozco was still alive. Mosquera was the daughter of Juan de Mosquera, a wealthy resident and member of the city council of Santo Domingo. Their honeymoon was spent on the Isthmus of Panama as Colón unsuccessfully attempted to settle his land grant in Veragua. Luís and María de Mosquera had two daughters: María (ca. 1548–1605), who became a nun, and Felipa (1549–1577). The marriage was not a happy one.

When the news of the Pizarro rebellion in Peru reached Panama in 1547, Luís Colón immediately prepared a force to go to the aid of the royal officials in Peru. However, he prudently asked Pedro de la Gasca (the chief royal official in Peru) if he needed help and requested royal permission to leave his post as governor of La Española. The permission was denied. Seven years later he was rewarded with a grant-in-aid of fifteen thousand pesos de oro because of the expenses he had incurred.

Colón returned to Spain in 1551 to seek papal annulment of his marriage to María de Mosquera on the grounds that he had been married to María de Orozco all along. While waiting for action on his petition, he contracted an engagement with Ana de Castro Osorio, daughter of the countess of Lemos. He also pursued his claims and lived extravagantly. In 1555 he obtained a preliminary annulment of his marriages (made final in 1558) and not long afterwards married Ana. Their only child died at birth. Hearing of this marriage, María de Mosquera returned to Spain and filed bigamy charges against Luís. He was arrested in January 1559. He was confined for the next five years in the castles of Arévalo, La Mota (Medina del Campo), Simancas, and Villaverde and at Madrid while his case and appeal were heard. While in Madrid in 1564, he contracted another verbal (but not ecclesiastical) marriage with Luisa de Carvajal; they repeated their marriage contract, also without church sanction, on May 26, 1565, the day that she gave birth to a son, Cristóbal Colón y Carvajal. Luís Colón's sentence to ten years of exile at Oran, North Africa, for bigamy, originally issued in 1563, was upheld by decrees of November 1565 and August 1566. He died in Oran on February 3, 1572. His remains were later taken to the monastery of Las Cuevas, at Seville, and then to Santo Domingo, to lie with his father and grandfather in the cathedral.

According to John Boyd Thacher's account, Luís Colón's will provided that his son Cristóbal would inherit his titles and revenues should his daughter Felipa fail to marry her cousin, Diego Colón y Pravia, the son of his younger brother, Cristóbal Colón y Toledo. (Other accounts suggest that the marriage was a way of compromising competing claims to the succession.) When Felipa did marry Diego, on May 15, 1573, another clause in the will bestowed some money on Cristóbal but Diego refused to pay it. In the end Cristóbal's half sister, the nun María Colón y Mosquera, gave him an annuity of four hundred ducats. Felipa died without heirs in 1577; her husband died two months later, without having remarried. Cristóbal died in 1601, without an heir. The succession then passed through several of Luís Colón's cousins to other families.

BIBLIOGRAPHY

Enciclopedia universal ilustrada. Vol. 14, p. 246. Madrid, 1907?–1930.

Nieto y Cortadellas, Rafael. *Los descendientes de Cristóbal Colón: Obra genealógica.* Havana, 1952.

Schoenrich, Otto. *The Legacy of Christopher Columbus.* Vol. 1, pp. 251–307. Glendale, Calif., 1949.

Thacher, John Boyd. *Christopher Columbus, His Life, His Work, His Remains.* 3 vols. 1903–1904. Reprint, New York, 1967.

Winsor, Justin. *Christopher Columbus and How He Received and Imparted The Spirit of Discovery.* Boston, 1891.

Paul E. Hoffman

COLÓN. Members of the Columbus family whose lives centered in Spain or in Spanish America can be found under *Colón.* For those whose lives centered in Italy, see *Colombo. See Columbus, Christopher,* for several articles detailing the life and achievements of Christopher Columbus.

COLONIZATION. [This entry surveys European overseas colonization of the New World, focusing on the sixteenth century. It includes the following five articles:

An Overview
Spanish Colonization
Portuguese Colonization of Brazil
French Colonization
English Colonization

See also *Exploration and Discovery.*]

An Overview

The idea of founding colonies was not a new one in the fifteenth century. The Greeks had established colonies on the shores of the Mediterranean Sea, and the Romans had extended theirs as far north as Hadrian's Wall in Britain. During the Middle Ages, the series of Crusades to the Holy Land had resulted in the establishment for a while of a European military colony there. Moreover, these various ventures had raised issues met in the fifteenth century and after, such as debates about how to treat subjugated peoples, problems arising from novel patterns of trade, and examples of syncretism, in which the mixing of two ideologies and techniques produced something new. However, the colonizing activity that began in the late fifteenth century soon reached a scale that dwarfed anything that had gone before, and eventually changed the lives of everybody living in European countries and in their colonies.

Fundamental differences in the societies and economies of the countries of western Europe ensured that their colonies would be very different. Spain and Portugal were relatively poor countries, in which the peasants often eked out a precarious existence. The lot of many Spanish peasants became even more difficult during the sixteenth century, with the loss of huge areas of arable land to sheep-farming; there was consequently considerable pressure toward emigration in many parts of the peninsula. In France and England the economic pressures were not so severe. There were, it is true, periodic famines, but nothing to compare with, say, the Great Famine of the 1840s in Ireland, which drove so many Irish people across the Atlantic. In France and England, though, there was religious dissent of a type not found in Spain or Portugal, which played a considerable part in encouraging emigration from those countries.

The extensive transfer of people across the Atlantic was not technically possible before the fifteenth century, when the European peoples, particularly the Portuguese and Spaniards, had developed ships capable of sailing for long periods out of sight of land. These ships could make headway even against contrary winds, could carry supplies to last for many months, and could be defended. Moreover, European sailors could navigate using the sun and stars and use maps to describe the lands to which they went so that others could follow.

The early reception of the Europeans by the American peoples varied widely. Columbus was fortunate in that his first landfall came among a singularly friendly group of "Indians." Other American peoples were often hostile, and the Europeans were able to establish themselves only by taking advantage of existing rivalries; in this way the Spaniards humbled the Aztecs, and the French managed to hold out against the Iroquois. In physical terms, the Americans were often apparently superior to the Europeans; the French in particular were struck by the strength and stature of the peoples they met in northern Florida. However, this outward appearance was deceptive, for the Americans were in fact highly vulnerable to the diseases carried by the Europeans, whereas the Europeans, exposed over the centuries to the great variety of diseases prevalent in the Eurasian landmass, were protected against a wider range of pathogens.

The pace of settlement varied widely. In Central and South America, the Spaniards conquered vast empires in a few decades; in the north, the English and French slowly built up their numbers in the face of Indian hostility. The Spanish conquest was not merely territorial, but also genetic, for, like the Portuguese, they had no qualms about marrying, or at any rate breeding with, native American women. Consequently, in areas that they conquered, a large mixed-blood population soon developed.

This mixing of blood was paralleled by other kinds of "creolization," whether in music, cooking, legal systems, architecture, or any other field of human activity. Astonishingly soon after the Spaniards arrived in Central America, for example, a liturgy developed that was new in music—a mixture of Aztec and Spanish styles. In the same way, the French began adapting their patterns of land settlement to the requirements of Canada, developing a system of "long-lots" without parallel in the Old World, but which still marks the areas of French settlement in North America. The process of "creolization" was much slower in the English colonies, whose inhabitants kept their distance from the Indians and tried as far as possible to duplicate the conditions of life in the old country. But even they were in the end overcome by the new necessities, and in New England as elsewhere new forms of material culture came into existence.

The European governments did their best to retain some sort of control over the colonies, establishing bodies like the English Council of Trade and Plantations or the Spanish Council of the Indies to oversee their affairs. These councils, and the crowns that they represented, were often concerned to regulate what came to be seen as the exploitation of the Americans. However, in every case the interests of the colonists prevailed over the humanitarian sentiments expressed in the European courts; the brute pressures involved in taming a vast continent and its peoples were too much for royal legislation to contend

with. The Spanish Crown was probably the most successful in imposing some degree of control over its burgeoning colonies, often in collaboration with the church. One way in which this was done was to regulate the foundation and growth of towns, which came to be planned in accordance with the Laws of the Indies; this contrasted sharply with the incoherent development of the towns in the areas of English influence.

This was, indeed, a major difference between the colonizing activities of the Spaniards and those of the northern European peoples. As part of Mediterranean civilization, the Spanish culture was primarily urban, and Spanish colonies tended to be organized around the foundation of cities, from Santo Domingo to Lima. The English colonies, on the other hand, were primarily agricultural ventures, allowing cities to form more or less haphazardly where economic activity gave rise to them. In Canada, too, the French colonies remained rural, so that Québec and Montréal were for a long time the only sizeable towns in the St. Lawrence Valley.

The French towns remained small, and dominated to a remarkable degree by the buildings of church and state: the churches, hospitals, and schools run by the church, and the fortifications, magazines, and storehouses erected by the state. The contrast with the more commercially oriented English cities eventually became very striking. They were primarily colonies directed by merchants and planters; the Anglican church played a muted role in the English colonies. It could boast nothing like the Jesuits who labored far out in the wilderness among the Hurons or the Franciscans who founded the distant missions of Mexico.

In fact, until late in the seventeenth century the scale of the Spanish colonizing effort dwarfed that of the other Europeans, even including the Portuguese. The Spaniards had been first in the field, and the combination of royal encouragement and economic necessity had given them an irresistible impetus. Moreover, they had no doubts about what they were doing; from the start, cities like Santo Domingo or Mexico City replicated the institutional framework of Iberian towns, with churches, palaces, and even, sometimes, universities. The stupendous effort needed to sustain this colonizing activity cost Spain dearly, as its own institutions slowly collapsed under the imperial burden, until it was unable even to maintain its position in Europe. But for two centuries Spain led the colonial process, leaving an indelible mark throughout the Americas.

BIBLIOGRAPHY

Bitterli, Urs. *Cultures in Conflict: Encounters between European and Non-European Cultures, 1492–1800.* Stanford, 1989.

Parry, J. H. *The Establishment of the European Hegemony, 1415–1715.* New York, 1966.

Phillips, J. R. S. *The Medieval Expansion of Europe.* Oxford and New York, 1988.

DAVID BUISSERET

Spanish Colonization

Spanish colonization of the Americas went through four phases during the sixteenth century. The initial phase, 1492 to about 1519, involved the Antilles with secondary activity, mostly looting, on the Isthmus of Panama and the northern coast of South America. Attempts to fit Columbus's "another world" (Amerigo Vespucci more accurately called it a "new world") to what was known of Asian geography dictated a primary emphasis on explorations along the Atlantic face of South America, with secondary emphasis on colonization of the Antilles and exploration of the Caribbean Basin from the Antillian centers of colonization. Hernando Cortés's founding of Veracruz and Pedro Arias de Ávila's (Pedrárias) building of Panama City in 1519 marked the beginning of a second, thirty-year phase during which the Spaniards conquered and occupied most of the rest of the areas that are today Spanish America. Explorations north and west of the Antilles and the Magellan-Elcano circumnavigation of the world indicated by 1525 that the Americas were a true New World that stood at a great distance from Asia. Accordingly, Spaniards concentrated on the exploration and colonization of the Americas while still trying to reach Asia by crossing the Pacific Ocean. The third phase embraced the decades of the 1550s and 1560s and was marked by the settlement of such peripheral areas as Florida, western and central Venezuela, and northwestern Argentina. The final phase began about 1570 and ran into the next century. Settlement advanced very slowly in peripheral areas, except for a few leaps such as the settlement of New Mexico.

During the first three phases, the administrative, judicial, ecclesiastical, and economic institutions of the Spanish colonies developed forms that did not significantly change until the late seventeenth century. This institutional history followed a slightly different periodization than did conquest and colonization, with 1524 marking the completion of the initial phase of institution building. By 1573, Spanish colonial institutions and policies had become established in laws that lasted until the reforms of the eighteenth century.

Settlement

Formal settlement on La Española began not with La Navidad, which was an accident, but with La Isabela, founded in 1493 as a typical Spanish city. Discovery of gold placers in the interior of La Española and a subsistence crisis caused the dispersal of the Spanish across the island.

By 1505, when Santo Domingo was moved to its present location, the island was being organized into municipal districts. By that date, too, the Crown had approved the first contract for settlement of another island, Puerto Rico, and slavers and men who bartered with Indians for pearls and gold were operating in the other Antilles, the Bahamas, and along parts of the Venezuelan, Colombian, and Panamanian coasts. In general, Spanish settlements in this period appeared wherever gold was found, although secondary economic activities, such as ranching, expanded colonization beyond the immediate area of the gold mines.

Occupation of the rest of the Antilles and the first Spanish settlements on the mainland occurred between 1509 and 1515. In the former year, Juan de Esquivel began the settlement of Jamaica, and Puerto Rico was invaded by Juan Ponce de León, who completed his conquest with the founding of San Juan in 1511. That same year, Diego Velázquez de León began the conquest of Cuba. After defeating the Indians, he founded Santiago de Cuba in 1514 and Havana the following year. Santa María la Antigua del Darién (Panama), the first Spanish settlement on the mainland, was founded in 1509. For most of the next decade it served as a base from which Spaniards, led by Vasco Núñez de Balboa, explored and raided on the Isthmus of Panama, along the way (1513) discovering the Pacific Ocean and conducting preliminary explorations of the Gulf of Panama. As in the Antilles, the search for gold mines drove this expansion.

At the highest levels of the Spanish government, these years saw much interest in deciphering the geographic mystery that the new discoveries presented while colonizing and exploiting the gold-bearing Antillian and Panamanian discoveries. Variously interpreted as a large island off the coast of Asia (c. 1498–1520) or as a peninsula of Asia (post-1503), South America and its northward extension into Central America continued to be seen in Spain as an obstacle to be gotten around on the way to the spices of the Indian Ocean. In the New World, Spaniards were concerned mostly with exploiting native peoples and resources in an effort to re-create familiar ways of life and acquire wealth that might improve their status in the Indies, as they called Columbus's discoveries, or at home, should they return there after their stay in the colonies.

The settlement of the Antilles was largely the work of men (there were few women) drawn from Andalusia and its seaports, although persons from nearby areas of Spain also took part. The scant available information suggests that by 1519 the society of La Española had many of the hierarchical characteristics of Spanish society, but with the notable differences that Indians had taken the place of the commoners required to pay tribute (no Spaniard in the New World paid the head tax [*pecho*] commoners paid in

Spain) and that social distance among Spaniards seems to have been reduced compared to norms at home. This was the embryo of the society of castes (*castas*) that emerged fully in the mainland colonies. There, social status became a function of racial ancestry.

Hernando Cortés's founding of Veracruz and Pedrárias's building of Panama City in 1519 marked the beginning of the second, thirty-year phase of colonization during which the Spaniards conquered and occupied most of the rest of the areas that are today Spanish America. This continental colonization embraced Mexico (1519–1526) and Central America (1523–1542); outposts along the northern coast of South America at Cumaná (1520), Santa Marta (1525), Coro (1528), and Cartagena (1533); the conquest and settlement of Peru (1532–1535), Ecuador (1533–1537), central Colombia (called New Granada, 1538–1541), and Chile (1541–1550); the short-lived occupation of Buenos Aires (1535–1541); and the permanent occupation of Asunción, Paraguay (1536). Ponce de León's attempt to settle on the west coast of Florida in 1521 and Lucas Vázquez de Ayllón's colony on the east coast of North America (in Georgia) in 1526 were failed attempts to establish a presence in North America.

Many areas, such as central Guatemala, eastern Central America, and parts of modern Colombia and (western) Venezuela, were not brought under Spanish control during these years. Even larger areas in northern Mexico, southeastern and southwestern United States, the western edges of the Amazon Basin, and northern Argentina were explored without any effort being made to settle Spaniards permanently among native inhabitants. In general, the Spanish military style of conquest failed (outside of the Antilles and Panama) wherever the Spaniards encountered Indians living in chiefdoms rather than more highly organized polities. Where the Spanish had outposts in such areas (e.g., coastal Venezuela and Colombia) they were content to loot native cultures for food, gold, and slaves rather than to try to dominate the hinterland. Only later, when Old World diseases, feral cattle, and the destructive effects of raiding on native societies had reduced their abilities to resist did Spanish settlers move into such areas.

In the more densely inhabited highland areas of the Americas, Spanish conquest was followed by the development of a mixed monetary and subsistence economy in which mining was the leading sector. Columbus's efforts to introduce the domesticated plants and animals of Europe into La Española were repeated in each new colony, often with more success (with plants) than had been the case in the Antilles. Cattle, which had overrun the Antilles, multiplied prodigiously on virgin grasslands on the continents, sometimes destroying that environment in drier areas. Vast numbers made beef a cheap staple food and their hides the major bulk export of

colonies all around the Caribbean. Although the consumption of European foods retained a high status value, combinations of American and European foods rapidly developed—the origins of the distinctive national cuisines of today. Alongside native weavers and potters, the Spanish built their own textile factories and pottery works. By the 1570s, a monetarized Hispanic economy existed in all but the more remote areas of the empire. Government officials and merchants used tribute demands, the market, and such devices as the *repartimiento de bienes* (forced sale to Indians of goods needed for "civilized" living) to further expand that economy.

The initial years of this phase produced a final answer to the question of the extent of the discoveries and their relationship to Asia. Explorations to the northwest of Cuba in 1508 (Díaz de Solís and Peralonso Niño) and from 1517 to 1519 (Juan de Grijalba, Francisco Fernández de Córdoba, Alonso Alvarez de Pineda) revealed the continent that rings the Gulf of Mexico. Other explorations by Ponce de León (1513), Esteban Gómez (1523), and Pedro de Quejo (1525) completed the map of the Atlantic face of North America as far as Newfoundland. The Magellan-Elcano voyage of 1519–1523 showed that the Columbian discoveries were separated from Asia by the vastness of the Pacific Ocean. In sum, the Indies truly were a New World, as Amerigo Vespucci had said. Although some Spaniards (e.g., Hernando Cortés) continued to pursue sailing routes to Asia, most turned to exploring and colonizing the vast expanses of the Americas and conquering their various native peoples.

In general, the conquests and settlements of 1519 to 1533 were the work of persons who had survived the difficult early years in the Antilles, although large numbers of persons drawn from Spain came out in 1514 (with Pedrárias) and after 1521 when first Mexico and then Peru offered prospects of quick improvements in economic and social standing. After 1526, royal policy required the organizers of expeditions to supply their manpower needs from Spain, not the rapidly depopulating Antilles, but this policy was not at first effective. By the time of Hernando de Soto's expedition to Florida (1538–1543), however, most new ventures were staffed with persons from Spain.

Limited data indicate that most of the men who participated in these continental conquests were semiskilled youths who were in their early twenties at the time of immigration. They came from landowning peasant backgrounds or were craftsmen and professionals such as notaries. Except for a group sent in 1498, few were criminals nor were many of them veterans of the Italian wars, although some veterans accompanied Pedrárias in 1514. More than 45 percent of the first settlers came from the Spanish provinces of Andalusia and Extremadura. A corridor stretching from León in the north through

Badajoz in the west to Seville in the south supplied about 85 percent of all documented persons. Probably more African slaves (drawn from southern Spain, not directly from Africa) than Spanish women and children came to the colonies prior to the founding of the cities that governed the mainland colonies. One result of the lack of Spanish women was the birth of a large first generation of mestizo children, the fruits of Spanish cohabitation with Indian women. The African slave trade began to grow in the late 1510s as La Española shifted to sugar cultivation. Africans added yet another "caste" to the emerging Latin American society.

By 1548 and the end of the Peruvian civil wars—sparked by personal rivalries and the question of who would control the Indians and under what terms—and of the great epidemic of 1546–1548 in Mexico, the rapid expansion of Spanish conquest and settlement had spent itself. But expansion of the area of settlement continued in response to economic, religious, and military needs. Two periods may be distinguished, the 1550s and 1560s, and the last thirty years of the century.

The expansion of Spanish settlement during the 1550s and 1560s took place in Venezuela, northern Mexico, Florida, and Chile. In western Venezuela the founding of the Spanish towns of Pamplona (1549), Ibagué (1551), Barquisimeto (1552), Trujillo (1556), and Mérida (1558) built a line of settlements based on mining and agriculture in the southwestward curving valleys of the Cordillera de Mérida. To the east, the founding of Valencia in 1555 marked a first step toward settlement of central Venezuela's lush mountain valleys. That progression was completed with the founding of Caracas (1568) and the extension of Spanish agriculture throughout the central highlands. Only the lack of a good port retarded the economic and demographic growth of central Venezuela.

In Mexico, the discovery of the silver deposits at Zacatecas (1548) and elsewhere in the northern interior basin produced a period of frontier expansion into the progressively drier (as one goes north) region of semino-madic peoples whom the sedentary agricultural Indians of Mexico called Chichimecs (sons of dogs). By 1570 Spanish mining centers employing wage laborers and slaves (rather than coerced Indians) reached to within a few hundred miles of the present U.S.-Mexican border. Ranches (haciendas) developed along the roads to the mines to supply them with draft animals, meat, tallow (for illumination), and hides and to provide security for travelers against nomadic raiders. Missions, too, began to be founded in this area after 1560 as the mendicant orders sought to save souls and the government sought a way to end the rapidly escalating costs of defending Spanish interests against the nomads.

In North America the Spaniards finally—in the face of French attempts to occupy ports near the mouth of the Bahama Channel (Port Royal, 1562; the St. Johns River, 1564)—founded a permanent town, St. Augustine (1565), and another, Santa Elena (on Parris Island in Port Royal Sound), that lasted from 1566 to 1586. These settlements never developed into the self-sustaining agricultural communities that their founders envisioned. Instead, they became garrisons dependent on Mexico and Cuba for their sustenance. They were valued primarily for their strategic locations near the Bahama Channel. Hegemony over the inland Indian polities, established in 1566, collapsed in the early 1570s. Spanish control along the coast between their towns increased during the 1580s and 1590s as the Franciscans built missions in coastal Georgia. These survived the abandonment of Santa Elena and the Indian revolt of 1597 and anchored weak Spanish control of the area until the 1670s.

The final area of expansion in the 1550s and 1560s was in Chile. Along its southern frontier, a bitter war with the Araucanian Indians that began in 1553 had come to a temporary end in 1557. The troops thus freed were used in 1562 to found the cities of Mendoza and San Juan east of the Andes in present-day Argentina. Thereafter, Spanish settlement slowly filled in the territories surrounding their initial towns.

The persons who carried out this third phase of colonial expansion have not been studied, but were probably similar in age and occupations, if not in regional origins, to the persons who carried out exploration, conquest, and colonization during the pre-1548 period. Elsewhere in the Spanish empire, immigrants came from a wider cross section of Spanish provinces, especially in Old Castile, and were more likely to be servants of officials or minor nobles going out to serve in the colonies or to try to remake their fortunes there.

After the expansive activities of the 1550s and 1560s, the pace of new settlement slowed. The occupations of New Mexico in the 1590s and of Buenos Aires in 1580 stand out in an era when the Crown was generally unwilling to provide either permission or resources for new frontier settlements. Private interests, moreover, found it more profitable to exploit the existing colonial economy rather than to seek resources speculatively in areas offering mostly agricultural possibilities and usually at a great remove from access to world and even regional markets.

Institutional Development

Spanish colonization of the New World began under mixed signals so far as governmental and economic institutions were concerned. In his contract with the Catholic monarchs, Columbus secured the titles of viceroy (vice-king), admiral, and governor, indicating that he expected eventually to rule a large free population with an extensive maritime commerce, rather like the Kingdom of

Catalonia. Yet the expedition of 1493 was organized as a royal monopoly company, although not everyone in the colony was an employee. To compound the confusion, La Isabela, in La Española, was organized as a standard Spanish municipality, although its officers were also key employees of the royal company.

This mixture of institutional forms quickly broke down because of the Columbus brothers' inability to govern, the desires of the unemployed Spaniards to exploit the natives and the gold mines, and the determination of King Fernando and Bishop Juan Rodríguez de Fonseca, Fernando's unofficial minister of colonial affairs, to void the terms of Columbus's contract so that licensed private interests could take over the expense and risk of colonization and, to a lesser degree, exploration. In 1499, Francisco de Bobadilla was sent to investigate conditions on La Española, and licenses were issued for voyages in which Columbus had no part. Bobadilla's *visita,* or ad hoc investigation, was the first of a long series by which the Crown attempted to restrain independent-minded officials and to check abuses. In this case, it quickly turned into a residencia, a formal inquiry into an official's conduct in office made at the time that he left office. This device, too, was a means through which the Crown tried to maintain control over its officials during the centuries that followed.

Nicolás de Ovando, who began to serve as royal governor of La Española in 1502, carried out a complete reorganization of the government of the colony so that it conformed to an idealized peninsular province. Fifteen municipalities were organized, each with a council and its local justices (alcaldes ordinarios) and minor officials such as notaries. Judicial appeals and certain felony cases were placed under two superior judges (alcaldes mayores). Treasury officials, present since 1493, became more concerned with collecting taxes on commerce and mining, both now freed from the earlier monopoly, than with administering the royal mines and property. In Spain, the House of Trade (Casa de la Contratación) was created in 1503 to administer navigation acts that opened the discoveries to all Spaniards. Finally, the Crown sent out additional secular as well as regular clergy and pressed the papacy for the creation of two bishoprics and rights of patronage (patronato) to those sees. A bull of 1508 granted royal control over the church in the colonies. In short, by 1509, when Ovando was removed from office and colonization was beginning to move to other islands, Spanish society on La Española had been given the political, economic, and religious institutions of those areas of the peninsular kingdoms under direct royal rule. In addition, the Crown had control over the Catholic church to an extent that it did not have in most of Spain.

Ovando's other great work was to settle the question of the place of the native Americans in the new colonial society. Drawing on the experience of his military order in Andalusia and orders from the Crown, he systematically conquered the native polities of the island and distributed them (by caciques or chiefs) as encomiendas to be administered by selected Spaniards. Under this system, the Indians were required to work for the Spaniards, in part to earn money to pay their tribute (head tax) but mostly because they were a subject people and because their labor was essential to the colonies. Spaniards were required to care for their charges' spiritual and physical welfare in accordance with decrees that the Crown issued at frequent intervals. Ovando's method of incorporating the native Americans remained standard Spanish practice down to the end of the continental conquests.

Ovando's government was followed by a brief period, 1509–1523, during which the Crown prevented the reestablishment of the seigneural power of the Columbus family, which had won a lawsuit over the terms of Columbus's contract. The institutional means used were treasury officials and their taxing authority and the audiencia, an appeals court instituted in 1511 to oversee the work of the judges whom Diego Colón, Columbus's son and successor, was allowed to appoint (judicial authority was, with control of economic resources, the basis of most seigneural power in Europe). In addition, since all royal orders had the force of law and were thus subject to judicial interpretation, the audiencia had ample grounds for interfering with Colón's administration of the Antillian colonies. An uncommon institution in Spain (there were only two in the sixteenth century), the audiencia here became, as it later remained elsewhere in the empire, the keystone in the arch of royal control over viceroys (Colón's title) and all lesser officials. Hernando Cortés and Hernando Pizarro discovered in turn the power of these two royal institutions to prevent the development of quasi-seigneural power in the colonies. Audiencias were subsequently created in Mexico City (1528), Panama (1538), Lima (1542), Guatemala (1542), New Galicia (northwestern Mexico, 1548), and Bogotá (1549). The office of viceroy, which was ended when Colón returned to Spain (1523), was revived for the government of Mexico (1535) and Peru (1544) with powers similar to those it had in Catalonia.

The final step in creating the political-administrative-judicial system of the empire was the founding of the Council of the Indies in 1524, patterned on the Council of Aragón (1494). Its founding was a recognition that, given their numbers, the Spanish colonies, and in particular the populous "kingdom" of New Spain, had outgrown administration by one man or by other royal councils as their secondary business. The Council of the Indies advised the Crown on appointments and policy matters and served as the court of appeal from the audiencias in capital offense cases and in civil suits involving large sums. In the beginning it supervised the final auditing of the accounts of treasury officials in the Indies, but this function was delegated to special accounting tribunals in the New World in the early seventeenth century.

In the years between 1524 and 1573, the institutions established prior to 1524 were transferred to each new Spanish colony in turn, but with certain modifications to fit changing circumstances. Whether acting under royal authority or independently of it (as at Veracruz in 1519), the first formal act of the Spanish in a new territory was the creation of municipalities to divide and govern the land. Treasury officials usually accompanied each new, royally licensed expedition. Conquest and periods of personal rule by expedition leaders (who had varying titles) regularly gave way to rule by royally appointed alcaldes mayores, governors, viceroys (for Mexico and Peru), and audiencias. Encomiendas were distributed, often without regard to the intricate sociopolitical systems of native societies. Mendicant (regular) clergy and secular priests accompanied new expeditions, ministering to the Spanish and trying to convert native Americans. The establishment of bishoprics followed. Increasingly, the secular and religious institutions of each new colony were fully elaborated and staffed when the first soldier began the conquest. Of the institutions and practices established prior to 1524, three underwent significant modification by 1574: the operational structure of the Roman Catholic church, trade practices, and, most important, the systems for using Indian labor.

In Europe, the secular or parish clergy of the Catholic church dominated church operations, with the mendicant orders performing mostly acts of charity and prayer. In the early Spanish colonies, however, the shortage of established churches and "livings" meant a shortage of secular priests. The mendicants, especially the Franciscans and Dominicans, and after 1560 the Jesuits (who were not mendicants), filled the void. Using authority granted to them in 1521–1522 to administer the sacraments in areas where there was no secular priesthood, they became the principal, often the only church presence in most Indian communities and many Spanish ones as well. In time, however, the growth of the number and power of the secular clergy produced demands that the friars relinquish parishes in nonfrontier areas to the seculars. A decree of 1574 settled this quarrel in favor of the seculars. Thereafter the mendicants could administer parishes only on the frontiers of the empire and only until the secular clergy were ready to take over the new parishes.

Like the operations of the Catholic church, so the trading system underwent change in this era. European wars and their attendant raids on Spanish shipping caused the abandonment of the original "sail when ready" system of commerce with the Indies. Group sailings, even in

SKETCH OF THE SPANISH PORT NOMBRE DE DIOS. On the Caribbean coast of present-day Panama. A port used by the Spaniards to transship gold from Peru. This sketch is from *Histoire Naturelle des Indes*, often called the Drake Manuscript, and could be from the hand of Sir Francis Drake himself, who raided Spanish shipping here.   THE PIERPONT MORGAN LIBRARY, NEW YORK; M.3900, F.97

peacetime (1521), and then convoying that reached to the Canary and Azores islands (1520s onward) and then into and back from the Caribbean (1543–1545, 1552–1559) restricted competition among merchants and led to a system of fairs at Nombre de Dios (Panama) and Veracruz and to the establishment of the merchant guild (*consulado*) of Seville (1543). Thus granted corporate advantages during the wars of Charles V, the *consulado* merchants obtained their continuation during the official European peace after 1559. Resumption of the convoys (1561) and the legal exclusion from the Indies trades of non-Spanish but naturalized merchants during the 1560s were among the means they used to solidify their monopoly in a form that became infamous throughout Europe.

The third institution to be modified during the years

before 1573 was the encomienda. Prior to 1530, the Crown pursued a policy of issuing increasingly more detailed regulations concerning the treatment of the Indians, many of them responses to the Dominicans' complaints of continuing abuses. Then, in 1530, the Crown put all Indians not already in private encomiendas under the supervision of royally appointed corregidores de indios and began to claim encomiendas upon the deaths of their owners. The New Laws of 1542 carried this process to its logical conclusion by ending Indian slavery, all unpaid Indian service to individuals (but not to the church or the community), and all encomiendas upon the deaths of their holders. All Indian labor would thenceforth be obtained by request from a corregidor de indios under a system of fixed-term labor drafts generally referred to under its Peruvian name, the mita.

Because these laws challenged the labor basis of the Spanish colonies and provoked threats (carried out in Peru) of Spanish rebellion if enforced, the Crown had to give up trying to end the encomienda immediately. It was able, however, to insist that the encomienda was a sinecure administered by royal officials rather than the encomenderos themselves. Continuing depopulation and the development of a pool of wage laborers eventually made the encomienda and the mita less important as sources of wealth and labor except in the mines of Bolivia.

Parallel with the emergence of the so-called tamed encomienda was the development in the continental colonies of separate republics of Indians and Spaniards. The origins of this development lay in the initial residential and cultural separation of the two communities (although members of each group could be found in the other's towns), Indian unwillingness to give up their cultures, royal laws restricting Spanish residence in the native communities in order to protect them from abusive, direct exploitation, and the desire of many of the early mendicant missionaries to keep the Indians separate from the vices of European society. Additionally, there were several notorious "failures" to convert Indians into "Spaniards" during naive experiments in Mexico in the 1530s. The process was completed by the pragmatic recognition that the Indians required special legal "privileges" if they were to receive justice from the unfamiliar political and juridical world the conquest had forced upon them. For example, they were granted unlimited, free access to the audiencias' judicial processes. Special courts, the juzgados de Indios, were also created. At the same time, the governments of many Indian communities were forced into the mold of Spanish municipal government, and the role of chief (or headman) was transformed from its preconquest norms into ones that fit the demands of the Spanish republic, especially for labor through the mita. Indian towns that lost large parts of their populations to disease were occasionally "congregated" into new towns organized along Spanish lines and controlled by friars and royal officials. This also helped to segregate Indians into their own so-called republics.

Finally, out of the struggle for justice that swirled around the problem of Indian labor, there emerged a new royal policy on future additions to the empire. As early as the 1560s, but definitively in the laws of colonization of 1573, Spanish activity in new areas was limited to the exercise of their rights under the law of nations (jus gentium) to create their own settlements in areas not used by the Indians, to peaceful trade, and to missionary activity. In general these strictures seem to have been obeyed.

In addition to the three major institutional developments from the 1524 to 1574 era, others produced the forms and customs that remained common until the reforms of the eighteenth century. Examples are the repartimiento de bienes system for distributing goods to the Indians, procedures for annual audits of treasury accounts, the regular use of the residencia, and the development of elaborate processes of consultation in decision making.

The issuance of the laws for new colonization in 1573 and the decree of 1574 laying down the jurisdictional rules for the regular and secular clergy marked the end not only of the second phase of institutional development in the Spanish colonies but also of the major institutional innovations that accompanied Spanish colonization in the Americas. Institutionally, as territorially, the Spanish empire had attained the essential form it would hold for the next two centuries.

[See also Cuba; Encomienda; Española, La; Jamaica; Puerto Rico; Settlements; West Indies.]

BIBLIOGRAPHY

Burkholder, Mark A., and Lyman L. Johnson. Colonial Latin America. New York, 1990.

Crosby, Alfred W. The Columbian Exchange: Biological and Cultural Consequences of 1492. Westport, Conn., 1972.

Floyd, Troy. The Columbus Dynasty in the Caribbean, 1492–1526. Albuquerque, 1973.

Hanke, Lewis. The Spanish Struggle for Justice in the Conquest of America. Philadelphia, 1949.

McAlister, Lyle N. Spain and Portugal in the New World, 1492–1700. Minneapolis, 1984.

Parry, J. H. The Discovery of South America. New York, 1979.

Sauer, Carl O. The Early Spanish Main. Berkeley, 1966.

Simpson, Lesley B. The Encomienda in New Spain: The Beginnings of Spanish Mexico. Rev. ed. Berkeley, 1966.

Super, John C. Food, Conquest and Colonization in Sixteenth Century Spanish America. Albuquerque, 1988.

PAUL E. HOFFMAN

Portuguese Colonization of Brazil

For Brazil, the relationship between history and geography is of the utmost importance: the country's size and tropical environment to a great extent determined its history. The discovery and claim of the land of Brazil by Pedro Álvares Cabral in 1500, part of the Portuguese explorations of the fifteenth and sixteenth centuries, took place against the background of the international diplomatic problems entailed by the division of the newly discovered lands. The importance of the Treaty of Tordesillas (1494), in which Portugal and Castile divided the planet between them, was only beginning to be realized. Determining a strict demarcation of the line was very difficult. No agreement as to the Line of Demarcation had ever been reached *in loco,* creating diplomatic and economic problems regarding spheres of influence from the New World to the Moluccas. In South America, these persisted until the eighteenth century. This was the context within which Brazil was formed. It was constantly expanded and defended by the Portuguese, in moves later recognized by the Spaniards, far beyond the limits of the Line of Demarcation. Thus, a country-continent was created, a giant occupying nearly half the space of South America.

Some historians have hypothesized that there were precursors to Cabral. Among Portuguese explorers, Duarte Pacheco Pereira and Bartolomeu Dias (1498) have been mentioned, and among the Spanish, Alonso de Ojeda (who took Amerigo Vespucci with him), Vicente Yáñez Pinzón, and Diego de Lepe, who navigated along the northern coast of South America in 1499, some months before Cabral, Gonçalo Coelho, and Amerigo Vespucci touched at Porto Seguro. The fact remains, however, that it was with Cabral that the effective exploration and development of Brazil began. Spanish explorations of the northern coast, even if they took place (which is debatable) had no significant impact.

During the early years of the century, after Cabral took official possession of Brazil in 1500, the exploration of the coastline was undertaken. The exploratory voyages were related to the trade in brazilwood, the first material wealth from the new land traded commercially. Coelho and Vespucci participated in this process in important ways. The commerce of the new land had been leased to the merchant Fernão de Loronha.

The French and the Spanish also began to appear along the coast at this time. The former traded sporadically in brazilwood (the first Frenchman to touch the coast of Brazil must have been the trader Goneville, in 1504). The latter hoped to procure a passage to the "Southern Sea"; this was the motivation for the Spanish expedition commanded by Juan Díaz de Solís, who arrived in Río de la Plata (the Plate River) in 1516 (note that the Plate estuary

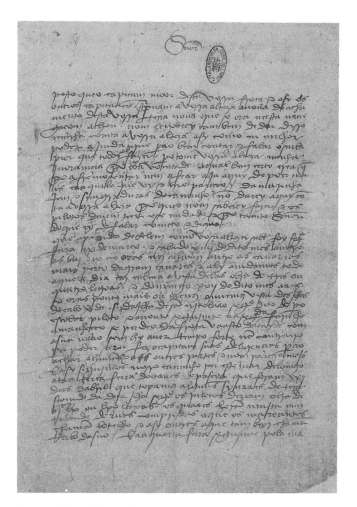

LETTER TO KING MANUEL I GIVING NOTICE OF THE DISCOVERY OF BRAZIL. Dated May 1, 1500, this letter is one of three surviving documents relating to the India-bound voyage of Pedro Álvares Cabral that landed on the Brazilian coast.

ARQUIVO NACIONAL DA TORRE DO TOMBO, LISBON

had already been visited by Portuguese ships), and that commanded by Ferdinand Magellan in 1520.

With the expeditions and coastal armadas under the command of Christopher Jacques in 1516–1519 and 1526–1528, and with the establishment of a permanent trading post in 1516, further steps were taken by Portugal to keep other Europeans at a distance. The repression of the French and the exploration of the southern and northern territorial boundaries took on fresh energy with the expedition of Martim Afonso de Sousa in 1530–1533. The initial steps toward a systematic colonization were undertaken: the founding of São Vincente and the first town in the interior (the future São Paulo), the establishment of an embryonic administrative organization, the settling of colonists, and the first expeditions into the backlands. The Portuguese were also preoccupied with the idea of expanding their zone of influence in the direction of the

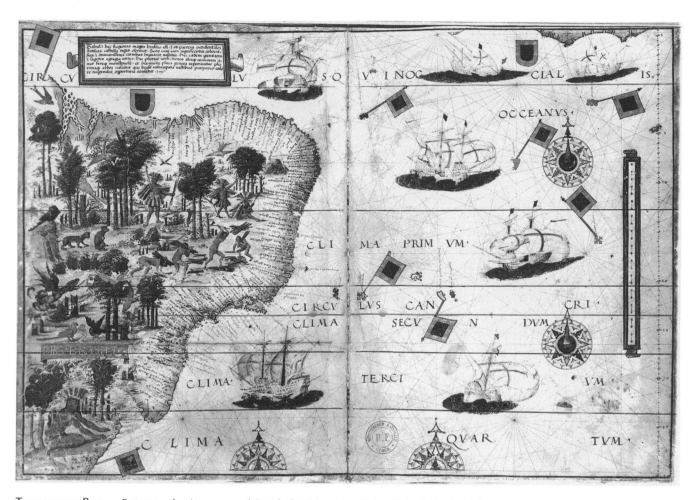

THE COAST OF BRAZIL. Between the Amazon and Río de la Plata. From Pedro Reinel's Miller Atlas.

Río de la Plata estuary (Pero Lopes de Sousa reached the region in 1531), and up the north coast to the Amazon region. The exploration was carried out as far as the mouth of the Amazon.

Soon after the expedition of the Sousa brothers, the Portuguese Crown ordered the division of the territory into hereditary captaincies. Although this regime failed in most of the regions, it allowed for the maintenance—and in some cases, the reinforcement—of the Portuguese presence, especially in the regions of Pernambuco in the northeast and São Paulo in the south. The foundation was thereby laid for the transformation of these areas into two great centers of Portuguese Brazil. On the northern coast, however, the failure of colonization efforts was overwhelming. At the end of the century these territories were not effectively controlled by the Portuguese. Not until the period of the union between the Crowns of Portugal and Castile during the seventeenth century were the territories secured and the Indians and foreign intruders driven out.

The administrative and economic characteristics of these hereditary captaincies in the sixteenth century are still debated: were they remnants of a feudal economy or nascent capitalist enterprises? Old words can hide new realities. Consequently, it is useful to distinguish institutions and ideologies, however archaic and medieval they might be, from economic structures that were developing in the direction of a modern market—a monoculture of exportation and colonial commerce in capitalist terms.

Between the two geographic poles of development in sixteenth-century Brazil—the Pernambuco and São Vincente regions—were extensive coastal territories. Here the captaincies failed and foreigners continued to trade sporadically with the natives.

This situation changed during the second half of the century, owing to the introduction of a central government by the Portuguese Crown and that government's establishment of a new administrative center in Bahia. From this new center, which was eventually transformed into an administrative, military, and religious capital, the successors of the first governor, Tomé de Sousa (1549), oversaw the consolidation of control of the entire eastern coast, the establishment of Portuguese population centers, and the expulsion of foreigners. Tomé de Sousa, in cooperation with the natives, created a true administrative, economic, and military apparatus in the new city. His successor, Mem de Sá, soon attacked and expelled the French of Villegaignon, who were trying to install themselves in Guanabara Bay. Once victorious, the Portuguese founded the city of Rio de Janeiro. The Jesuits began to arrive in the middle of the century, instituting an almost exclusively missionary program and establishing ascendancy over the Indians.

The sixteenth century, then, was a period of occupation and defense of the coast; the next two centuries were devoted to an expansion into the interior. By the end of the sixteenth century the Portuguese presence in Brazil had been consolidated along the eastern coast, where there were two principal centers: the northeastern region of Pernambuco and Bahia and the southeastern region of São Vincente and São Paulo.

The Brazilian northeast, that "most ancient of all the Brazils," began in the last three decades of the century to build its prosperity as a "sugar civilization." New Brazils would be joined to it, born of a multifaceted, decentralized, and continuous geographic expansion. But this region would remain as the historic "cradle" of Brazil.

The economic and social structures of the northeast were based on sugar as the dominant product, with brazilwood, cotton, tobacco, and rum of lesser importance. Thus arose a culture of estates and a laboring class whose continuance was assured by an influx of slaves (already being imported from Africa in the last decades of the sixteenth century). The sociologist Gilberto Freyre characterized this system as a patriarchal society and an economy of "mansions and shanties." But a mestizo class and a generalized acculturation of the three basic components of Brazilian society began to emerge. The Portuguese element was omnipresent, but an African culture predominated on the coast and an Indian culture in the interior.

The indigenous population was of major importance in the sixteenth century; only later, with the arrival of massive numbers of Africans, was it superseded. There were numerous tribes in the Brazilian territory, especially those of the two great linguistic families of the Tupi and Tapuiya. Their social organization and material culture corresponded in a general way to that of hunter-gatherers everywhere. Among the Tupi, however, there was an incipient agriculture. Cannibalism was practiced.

The native peoples moved into the new societies created by the Europeans and even became integrated with them, though the process involved a kind of devolution of the once powerful native peoples into dependents and slaves even as their demographic destruction was

taking place. But their heritage persisted, especially in regions where miscegenation and mutual acculturation were common.

To northeastern Brazil was joined, in the late sixteenth and early seventeenth centuries, all of Brazil of the northern coast. This expansion occurred because of military conquest by the Portuguese-Spanish Crown from 1584 to 1616, during which foreign intruders were expelled and enemy tribes repressed. In 1614 the French were ousted from the Maranhão, where they had tried to establish themselves as "Equinoctial France," and in 1616 Francisco Caldeira de Castelo Branco arrived at the mouth of the Grão Pará River and founded the fortress that became the city of Belém. From this city the Portuguese during the next two centuries defended, explored, and finally occupied all the immense regions not only of the Pará but also of the Río Negro as far as Peru. Thus was born northern Brazil, which in the second half of the eighteenth century would achieve prosperity.

In the meantime the growing colony suffered attacks by the Dutch in the "sugar wars" of the first half of the seventeenth century. Taking advantage of the weakness of the Portuguese in the final period of the Iberian union, they attacked the heart of the northeast and in 1630 conquered Pernambuco. The Dutch remained there for nearly twenty-five years and were expelled by the Portuguese-Brazilian forces only after the independence of Portugal had been regained. The regaining of Portuguese independence from Spain was, in part, motivated by the difficulties in which Brazil found itself during the period of its alliance with Spain because it was attacked by the enemies of the Spanish monarchy. Brazil was already the "crown jewel" of the overseas Portuguese empire. Since India had in great part been lost, Portuguese interests now centered on the South Atlantic with its Euro-Afro-American trade.

But while the colony was experiencing these difficulties in the northeast, it was developing a notable vitality in its remote territories farther south. A great expansion took place in the center and the south, stimulated by the São Vincente and São Paulo population centers. From the city of São Paulo the great movement of the Paulist (as those from São Paulo are known) *bandeiras* arose—expeditions of backlanders into the interior in search of Indian slaves and mineral wealth. By promoting the capture of Indians and the destruction of the Spanish Jesuits who were trying to advance to the east, energizing the search for alluvial gold and the advance to the south, penetrating into the interior, and surpassing the limits defined by the Treaty of Tordesillas, the Paulist expansion created central and east central Brazil.

It was the Paulist *bandeirantes* who, in the final years of the seventeenth century, found gold in the region of

Minas Gerais. From this time, the region was linked to the northeastern sugar bowl by the colonization (encouraged also by a flourishing cattle industry) along the São Francisco River, which came to be called the "river of national unity." Thus finally were joined two economic activities—sugar and gold mining—creating a unified Brazil from the northeast to the southeast. Beginning with the gold economy and the settlement of Minas Gerais, the prosperity of this interior colony was developed. A great demographic density was created, and local agriculture continued the development initiated by the gold rush.

The gold rush extended to the far west, to the lowlands of Mato Grosso, Goiás, and the borders shared with Brazil's Hispanic neighbors. The "Monsoons" were regular voyages by river that gave continuity to the movement of the *bandeirantes* and expanded the fluvial highways of the Mato Grosso in the direction of the Amazon. Thus were set the limits of Brazilian territory along its western boundaries.

As for the actual occupation of the Amazon region, the Portuguese always had the advantage over their Hispanic neighbors (though the Spaniards had made the earliest explorations). From the city of Belém in the Pará region, after 1616 the *entradas* (raids) of the *tropas de resgate* (liberation troops) began. The Portuguese controlled the Amazon basin for some two centuries, exploiting it for its vegetable products such as cocoa. In 1669 São José do Rio Negro, precursor of Manaus, was founded.

The advance to the south continued at the instigation of the Portuguese Crown, which created after 1680 the colony of Sacramento, an isolated fortress on the Río de la Plata, directly in front of the Spanish city of Buenos Aires. This Portuguese entrepôt eventually depended for its livelihood on trade and contraband with its adversary on the other side of the river, appropriating part of the flow of silver exported from there. This solitary outpost—at times a thorn in the side of the Spanish, at times a go-between in diplomatic affairs—allowed the Portuguese-Brazilian rear guard to advance, thereby colonizing the entire south over the next hundred years. The Portuguese-Brazilians took possession of the regions of Santa Catarina, Paraná, and Rio Grande do Sul, where by the beginning of the eighteenth century had developed that great source of wealth: cattle.

Thus the Paulist expansion was probably primarily responsible for the creation of the central and west-central parts of Brazil and for the early reclamation of the south. The official expansion instigated by the Portuguese Crown led to the rise of the northeast, the southeast, and the north and the defense and settlement of the south. But the distinction between the two formative influences should not be too closely drawn. As historian Jaime Cortesão has pointed out, both factors were at work in each region. For example, António Raposo Tavares was without doubt one of the most important of the Paulist *bandeirantes*, but his connection with the Portuguese Crown was obvious. Raposo Tavares undertook the *bandeira* of 1649, covering a great territory, from the Río de la Plata to the Amazon, across the upper Paraguay River, and from the Guaporé to the Madeira rivers. This circuit defined a unity that would later be consolidated as the Brazilian national territory. In contrast to other European colonies in America, Brazil, when it became an independent state, was already fully formed.

[See also *Portugal*.]

BIBLIOGRAPHY

Boxer, Charles Ralph. *The Dutch in Brazil, 1624–1654*. Oxford, 1957.

Boxer, Charles Ralph. *The Golden Age of Brazil, 1695–1750: Growing Pains of a Colonial Society*. Berkeley, 1962. Reprints, 1969, 1975, 1984.

Boxer, Charles Ralph. *Salvador de Sá and the Struggle for Brazil and Angola, 1602–1686*. London, 1952. Reprint, Westport, Conn., 1975.

Marchant, Alexander. *From Barter to Slavery: The Economic Relations of Portuguese and Indians in the Settlement of Brazil, 1500–1580*. Baltimore, 1942.

Morse, Richard McGee. *The Bandeirantes: The Historical Role of the Brazilian Pathfinder*. New York, 1965.

Sanceau, Elaine. *Captains of Brazil*. Porto, 1965.

Schwartz, Stuart B. *Sovereignty and Society in Colonial Brazil: The Judges of the High Court of Bahia, 1586–1750*. Berkeley and Los Angeles, 1974.

Tomlinson, Regina Johnson. *The Struggle for Brazil: Portugal and "The French Interloper," 1500–1550*. New York, 1970.

ALFREDO PINHEIRO MARQUES
Translated from Portuguese by Rebecca Catz

French Colonization

Breton, Norman, and Basque fishermen from France were active off the Atlantic coast of northeastern North America as early as the closing decades of the fifteenth century. After European Atlantic fishermen were closed out of Icelandic fishing grounds in 1478, they looked for other sources of "sea silver" to meet the demand in Europe, where the religious calendar indicated over 150 days of abstinence from meat and dairy products in a year. The first official record of annual cod-fishing expeditions from French ports is dated 1504. By 1510 Breton and Norman fishermen kept the market at Rouen supplied with "Terreneufve" cod. In 1520, Jean and Raoul Parmentier combined their fishing with loading furs in Cape Breton. There followed a marked increase in the size of the fishing fleets, especially after 1540 as the fishermen selected a favorite beach for landing and later for drying fish. Although some men wintered in Cape Breton, there was as yet no true colonization. By 1578 an eye-witness report confirmed that the French were the most numerous in spite of the Wars of Religion at home.

In addition to cod, fishermen became interested in the walrus of morse, the "beast of the great teeth." The French began hunting them sometime after 1510 for their "white gold," or ivory, their fat oils, which were used as sealant on ships, and their tough hides, which were used for shields and armor as well as for ropes and rigging. The islands of the Gulf of St. Lawrence provided the most profitable rookeries for exploitation. Jacques Cartier's nephews had an interest in the Magdalen Islands establishments and by the end of the century the French had succeeded in driving out the Portuguese and the English, with the help of Micmac warriors, from the gulf. Exploitation of the walrus rookeries led to the first French colonization venture on the coastal islands. In 1598, a Breton nobleman, Marquis Troilus de la Roche, was granted letters patent to found a colony on Sable Island and was authorized to recruit hardened criminals "chosen by the best judges in France." Sable Island, however, failed to attract immigrants and the colony was eventually abandoned.

The slow development of the fur trade out of the cod fishery led to more permanent colonization. When the explorer Jacques Cartier visited Chaleur Bay in 1534, he was approached by Micmacs who "set up a great clamor and made frequent signs to us to come to shore, holding up to us some furs on sticks." His crew frightened the Micmacs off, but, when they returned the following day, bartering ensued at a brisk pace. Obviously, this was not the first trading encounter for the Micmacs, nor were the French caught without appropriate goods to exchange. The lasting consequence of Cartier's second voyage in 1535 was the discovery of the St. Lawrence River entrance to the continent, although he did not realize at the time that the river led to the Great Lakes basin in the heart of North America. France decided to pursue exploration in this region and to found a colony to establish its sovereignty. In 1541 Cartier was commissioned to undertake a third voyage, as part of a colonization scheme to be headed by a nobleman from southern France, Jean-François de La Rocque de Roberval, to "enter deeper into these lands, to converse with the peoples found there and live among them, if need be." Cartier arrived near the Laurentian Iroquois village of Stadacona (Québec) with a first contingent of settlers and established a base camp that he called Charlesbourg-Royal (Cap Rouge), then proceeded to explore upstream as far as the Iroquoian villages of Hochelaga and Tutonaguy (Montréal Island). A combination of a particularly harsh winter, shortage of

food, scurvy, and increasing native hostilities as an epidemic swept the Laurentian Iroquois villages, together with the discovery of what were believed to be gold and diamonds, convinced Cartier and the colonists to return to France in June 1542. Putting in at the natural harbor of St. John's (Newfoundland), he met the Roberval contingent with its settlers, cattle, and equipment. Cartier slipped away under cover of darkness, leaving Roberval and the second contingent to face the rigors of a Canadian winter and native hostility before it too abandoned the settlement scheme.

Settlements were not seriously attempted again until 1603, when Henry IV granted Pierre de Monts, a distinguished Calvinist soldier and administrator, a trade monopoly in North America with the obligation to establish sixty colonists a year and promote Catholic missionary work among the native peoples. De Monts organized an association of merchants from several cities and named the Dutchman Cornelis de Bellois as chief shareholder to finance a joint Catholic-Protestant expedition to explore and colonize Acadie. (Most of the sixteenth-century French overseas ventures had involved Protestants and there was even a proposal to solve the religious problem in France by sending all the Protestants to the colonies.) Three vessels carrying artisans, soldiers, vagabonds, two Catholic priests, and a Huguenot pastor sailed into the Bay of Fundy, where a first settlement called Sainte-Croix was laid out on Dochet Island. The following year it was decided to move the settlement across the Bay of Fundy to the Annapolis valley at Port Royal. In 1611 the marquise de Guercheville bought out the merchant association's interest in Port Royal and sent out Jesuit missionaries to work

MAP OF NEW FRANCE. With representations of Indians. From Ramusio's *Navigatoni e viaggi*. Venice, 1556.

among the Micmacs. The colony in Acadie survived but was subject to raids by interlopers in the fur trade monopoly, to corsairs, and to attacks from the English colonies established along the Atlantic littoral.

Since de Mont's trade monopoly extended to the St. Lawrence valley, in 1608 he named Samuel de Champlain, an experienced geographer, his lieutenant charged with establishing a beachhead at "the point of Québec" where a century earlier the Laurentian Iroquois village of Stadacona had stood. The French were aware that the northern Algonquian bands and the Hurons were at war with the Five Nations Iroquois to the south; Champlain therefore fortified his "habitation" at Québec in 1608. In July 1609, Champlain and a party of Frenchmen joined a raiding party into Iroquois country; the ensuing encounter resulted in a century of Iroquois hostility that at times threatened the very survival of the French colony. The French had little choice but to join with their fur-trading partners in this intertribal war. Exploration of the "upper country" of Canada progressed well, but there were few colonists who came out from France. Champlain sent out young men to live among the Hurons and Algonquians to learn their languages and ways and in return received a few native children to be given a French education. In 1615 missionaries of the Recollet order, a branch of the Franciscans, arrived to undertake missionary work; they soon chose the sedentary agricultural Huron tribes along Georgian Bay as their main center of activity. The Hurons lived at the northern limits of corn culture, were noted traders with neighboring tribes, had established themselves as middlemen in the French trade, and were strategically located in the Great Lakes basin, which gave access by waterways to the Mississippi valley, the Far West, Hudson's Bay, and the St. Lawrence entrance from the Atlantic. However, they were still engaged in sporadic but interminable warfare with the Five Nations Iroquois to the south.

In 1627 Cardinal Richelieu intervened to set the colony on a firm financial foundation. A monopoly company known as the Company of New France (popularly the Hundred Associates) was charged with the administration of Canada, its settlement, and its social organization in return for a fifteen-year monopoly of commerce and perpetual control of the fur exports. The company undertook to bring out four thousand settlers within fifteen years, but a three-year occupation of Québec by the English, constant harassment by Iroquois war parties, and the general unattractiveness of the region to persons not involved in the fur trade rendered the company's mandate unrealizable. In 1645 the company ceded its fur-trade monopoly to a small group of local merchants, known as the Community of Habitants, in return for assuming the administrative costs of the struggling colony.

The charter of the Company of New France had stipulated that no foreigners or Protestants were to be permitted to settle permanently in the Laurentian outpost. What measure of success there was in this period was achieved largely by religious organizations. The Jesuits joined the Recollets as missionaries in 1625 and by 1634 were the sole evangelizers in Canada. They had their headquarters at Québec but sent out missionaries in pairs to the nomadic Algonquian bands and to some Iroquois villages and established a large mission among the Hurons with a regional headquarters in 1639 at Sainte-Marie-des-Hurons (Midland, Ontario). Shortly before his death, Champlain had established a second settlement at Trois-Rivières. In 1642, a lay religious millenarian group known as the Société de Notre-Dame, an off-shoot of extensive revivalistic activity in France associated with the Catholic Reformation, founded Ville-Marie (Montréal) on the island of Montréal. This third settlement was ideally located in good agricultural land, at the confluence of trading and communications routes, and at a strategic point for dealing with native peoples.

In 1639 two women's religious communities arrived to inaugurate important hospitals, schools, and houses of charity. The colony could even boast of a Jesuit college, founded in 1635. These extraordinary advances in the social and cultural fields masked a slow progress in settlement and in the development of an agricultural base.

The inability of private entrepreneurs to attract a significant number of immigrants and of the French fur traders to provide a base for commercial and artisanal development convinced King Louis XIV to extend his personal rule to the colony under the system known as royal government. Canada, from its earliest stage of development, required centralized public direction and initiative and state intervention in the economy to ensure its survival and progress. Tasks first undertaken by private entrepreneurs, merchant associations, and religious zealots were now taken up by the bureaucratic, military, and ecclesiastical establishments within the French state. Each created its own dominant elite and clientele and each assumed responsibility for a sector of public affairs under the Crown. Settlement proceeded along lines of the native strategy of territorial occupation—for example, penetrating the waterways of the continent or establishing settlements at strategic points of communication, trade, and defense. As early as 1665, the French government decided that the strategy of extending French sovereignty over a vast hinterland also required restriction of French settlement to the narrow ribbon of the St. Lawrence valley and recognition of native independence and self government in all regions beyond the riverine colony. In native ancestral lands the French might with permission establish mission stations, trading posts, and military garrisons, following the native tradition of sharing resources and offering hospitality.

Under the system of royal government introduced by stages in 1663, New France came under the jurisdiction of the Ministry of Marine and Colonies in Versailles. The colonial administration consisted of a governor-general at Québec, who was the king's representative with responsibility for military matters and relations with native peoples; an intendant who was responsible for justice, commerce, and public order; a bishop, who as the chief ecclesiastical official supervised the church's mandate in education, social welfare, hospitalization, and missionary work; and an appointed sovereign council at Québec, made up of local notables who sat as a court of appeal and acted as a chancery registering all royal edicts and colonial legislation to give them colonial application. In the eighteenth century, under the Regency and during the reign of Louis XV, the sovereign council was enlarged and its legislative role greatly restricted; it retained its judicial role and was renamed superior council. While the governor held the most prominent position in the power structure, it was the intendant who wielded the greatest influence over daily affairs through control of financial affairs, the justice system, and correspondence with Versailles, as well as the presidency of the Superior Council. The bishops found their role increasingly relegated to purely spiritual matters, especially in the eighteenth century, in keeping with the Gallican maxim that "the church is in the state" and so was subject to the temporal power.

The colony reflected the social distinctions and ranking that prevailed in France itself, although in the early decades of settlement the pioneer environment imposed some social leveling and stimulated a spirit of independence. There was less upward social mobility in the eighteenth century as the class structure became more entrenched. Nevertheless, when faced with unwilling immigration, pioneer hardships, and external threats from the English colonies, the administration adopted a sense of social responsibility to all classes—an attitude that has been called paternalism. Royal instructions in 1663 said that "the general spirit of government ought to lean in the direction of gentleness, it being dangerous to employ severity against transplanted peoples, far removed from their prince. . . ." Religion was important in inculcating a kind of social conscience, a sense of just price and reasonable labor, and respect for authority. Though there were no parliamentary institutions, there were periodic consultative assemblies called by the governor and intendant dealing with matters of general concern such as brandy trafficking, price controls, statute labor, and parish boundaries. The general rule remained, however, that "each should speak for himself, and none for all."

Government could consult but mass petitioning would not be tolerated.

The Custom of Paris became the customary Canadian legal code regulating property rights, inheritance, contracts, and marriage and family relations. Its inheritance rules, for example, provided for all the children "male and female, living and not in holy orders" and protected the right of women to property. The royal courts were located in the three principal towns and provided rapid and relatively cheap justice to those living nearby. Fees were fixed and there was little litigation about seigniorial dues, which were fixed in the contracts, or about tithing, whose rate was set by the state officials. Criminal law was harsh and the punishments barbaric, as in Europe, but only crimes against God and the king were brutally punished. Proceedings were adversarial and inquisitorial, with judicial torture provided for in extreme cases; the accused had to prove his innocence to the judges. Capital punishment was meted out publicly, as were lesser punishments that used such instruments as the stocks, the pillory, and the wooden horse, or amende honorable (judicial penance) in nightshirt and candle at the door of the parish church.

The population of New France was largely rural, and it was not until the end of the French regime that villages emerged as markets and service centers. Outside the three towns—Québec, Montréal, and Trois-Rivières—the people were for the most part settled on seigneuries. In theory all the land belonged to the Crown, which made grants of estates to the privileged orders, the clergy, and the nobility. At the beginning of royal government, the religious owned about 11 percent of cultivated lands, but by the end of the French regime almost one-quarter of the land was in their hands. Initially it appeared that the lay seigneuries would be restricted to the nobility but this never became the rule. There was little speculation in land because land was readily available and required time and labor to become productive as an investment. The traditional French seigniorial system underwent a few changes in Canada. The estates were surveyed as trapezoidal parallelograms running back from the St. Lawrence River in such a way that each censitaire (landholder) had access to the river as the transportation axis and the source of water, fish, and marine animals. Each farm cut across the grain of the land affording a variety of soils and vegetation—wet fodder lands, heavy soils for cereals, upland meadows for grazing, and wood lots for fuel and lumber at the upper reaches of the property. The habitants, as the peasants preferred to be called, enjoyed privacy on their individual farms of about 150 meters frontage, yet were not too distant from neighbors. Besides retarding the emergence of villages, this pattern of settlement also shielded the rural population from the constant supervision of the seigneur or parish priest. As the seigneuries became populated and all arable land was brought into production, seigneurs began to exact all the customary dues and to exercise their traditional privileges and honors.

The population generally practiced its religion out of conformity and social convention and loved the ritual and ceremonial aspects, but was not excessively zealous. The state found it necessary to legislate observance of Sunday rest and attendance at mass, the closing of taverns during divine office, the payment of tithes, the maintenance of church property, and even respectful behavior in church. The church did succeed in exercising effective censorship, in controlling education, and in offering adequate hospitalization and welfare services in the major centers. It did not stamp out popular superstitions, eliminate the brandy traffic, or convert the majority of the native peoples. Recruitment of the parish clergy never kept pace with population growth, so that at the end of the French regime there were about 240 seigneuries but only 114 parishes served by a mere 169 priests, including seminary, missionary, and chaplaincy personnel. Instead of a priest-ridden colony, there was a crisis of religious vocations.

Though population growth outstripped religious vocations, immigration never reached the levels experienced in other European colonies. At the introduction of royal government in 1663 there were less than four thousand colonists. By 1700 there were still only about 15,000 colonists in spite of state-supported schemes to settle soldiers, brides, artisans, and professionals. Over more than a century an estimated 11,000 French remained permanently in the colony and founded families.

Québec remained the chief port, administrative center, and fortified capital of the colony. From here a threefold colonial strategy had been elaborated during the final years of the reign of Louis XIV. First, peace was concluded with the Iroquois Confederacy in 1701 and its neutrality in international wars was guaranteed. Second, a settlement was permitted at Detroit in the upper country and a plan evolved for settlements in the Illinois country, a colony at the mouth of the Mississippi river, and a chain of forts linking these distant places to the Laurentian colony. By 1713 it was clear that Canada should be held not for its economic value but for geopolitical reasons, as a strategic outpost capable of containing the English colonies along their Atlantic seaboard and forcing Britain to maintain overseas garrisons and a navy. Third, the native peoples had to be supplied with the goods they desired and conciliated to French sovereignty in order to retain their support against the British.

During the Seven Years' War large contingents of French regulars, *troupes de terre* from the Ministry of War, under their own commanders arrived to assume the brunt of the fighting against British land and naval invaders, resulting in the adoption of European formation fighting supported by artillery when the British attacked using traditional siege tactics. Since the seventeenth century engagements against the Iroquois, the Canadian militia had adopted the guerilla tactics of the native auxiliary forces in raids on English settlements and in thwarting invading forces. The colonial strategy championed by the Governor Vaudreuil was jettisoned, causing him to complain, "Now war is established here on the European basis . . . . It is no longer a matter of making a raid, but of conquering or being conquered. What a revolution! What a change!" The colonial militia and the native auxiliaries became marginal to the conflict and New France fell finally to British forces with the capitulation of Montréal in September 1760. Military occupation and martial law were imposed until the definitive treaty of peace, the Treaty of Paris, was signed in 1763 bringing the French regime to an end.

BIBLIOGRAPHY

Eccles, W. J. *Canada under Louis XIV, 1663–1701.* Toronto, 1964.

Jaenen, Cornelius J. *The French Relationship with the Native Peoples of New France.* Ottawa, 1984.

Miquelon, Dale. *New France, 1701–1744: A Supplement to Europe.* Toronto, 1968.

Stanley, George F. G. *New France: The Last Phase, 1744–1760.* Toronto, 1968.

Trudel, Marcel. *The Beginnings of New France, 1504–1663.* Toronto, 1973.

CORNELIUS J. JAENEN

English Colonization

There was little coherence in the initiatives of the English Crown in regard to North America in the sixteenth century aside from the fact that all derived directly from it. John Cabot in 1496 was given wide-ranging powers to rule the non-Christian lands that he might annex to the English Crown, much as Columbus was given in Spain, but nothing came of this or subsequent patents in the years following. After 1505, no English activity was formally authorized until 1553, when what later became the Muscovy Company was given a monopoly on trade with the northeast and northwest, including that part of North America north of about fifty degrees. This authorization was superseded in 1577 by the patent creating the Company of Cathay, which was authorized to exploit the (nonexistent) gold reserves of Baffin Island and to control English access to the supposed Northwest Passage. These powers collapsed with the company in 1578. The patents of 1553 and 1577 created companies that were operated by their subscribers and a governor and council. From 1578 onward, patents relating to North America were normally granted to individuals or small syndicates; these patents granted very wide powers to the recipients if they succeeded in their objectives.

Early English Colonies and Explorations of North America

A new interest in North America followed the collapse of the Company of Cathay. On June 15, 1578, Sir Humphrey Gilbert was given a patent that authorized him to annex and colonize all lands that were not yet occupied by a Christian power (though only eastern North America was intended). Gilbert interpreted his authority widely and drew up plans by which vast feudal estates were to be conferred on associates and subscribers under a code of laws drawn up by Gilbert himself. His ideas often outran his practical capacity, however. He ultimately conceded some rights to form a consultative council by the larger proprietors, although this council remained under his control. In August 1583, he formally annexed Newfoundland to the Crown and assumed control of its inshore fishery. This annexation, however, came to nothing, as Gilbert was drowned at sea on a return voyage.

Roanoke Island. Gilbert's patent (excluding Newfoundland) was regranted to his half brother, Walter Raleigh, on March 25, 1584, but Queen Elizabeth would not let Raleigh take part in the subsequent voyages in person. His reconnaissance vessels of 1584 located a possible site for a colony on Roanoke Island, and in July 1585, Governor Ralph Lane and 108 colonists maintained the first English colony until mid-June 1586. Among its discoveries was the deep-water harbor of Chesapeake Bay. The colony produced little economic return and was brought back to England in July 1586.

Raleigh lost interest in direct participation in the colony for a time and surrendered his rights over the Chesapeake Bay area to a syndicate. John White and his twelve assistants were given authority to settle a colony of families on lands that were not fully occupied by Indians. By chance, the expedition landed on Roanoke Island and was forced to make its way overland to the Elizabeth River in present-day Virginia. White returned to England for supplies, leaving a party on Roanoke Island to guide him to the colony when he came back. The Spanish war, however, delayed his return. Indeed, in 1588, Raleigh planned a new venture on the shores of Chesapeake Bay as an advance base against the Spanish fleet, but his ships were countermanded to help fight the Armada that year. In 1590, White made a brief call at Roanoke Island only to find the island deserted. The lost colonists remained out of contact with England, though they were assumed to be still alive, at least until 1603. Raleigh authorized minor searches around 1600–1602 and some exploration of New

England in 1602–1603, but his patent lapsed in the latter year. These colonists were finally killed about 1606 by Powhatan, the Algonquian ruler of southern Virginia.

Jamestown. A new period of English colonization started in 1606. Thus far, no known English colonies had been established in North America. The Virginia Company Charter of April 10, 1606, created a commercial company drawn mainly from London merchants, with a parallel company based at Plymouth. Both enterprises were to be controlled by a royal council, as was the Consejo de Indias in Spain. The Plymouth Company settled a small colony on the Kennebec (Sagadahoc) River in 1607, but it was underfinanced and its members unfamiliar with the fur trade. In the autumn of 1608, it was abandoned.

Attention then focused on the Chesapeake Bay area. Christopher Newport conveyed a group of about one hundred colonists, all servants of the company, to the James River in 1607. The first settlement was on Jamestown Island, which offered the advantage that ships could moor close to its shore. The site's superficial attractions soon faded, however, because the environment was extremely unhealthy. The company had nominated Edward Maria Wingfield as the first governor and named his councillors. While a fort, church, and houses were being built, Newport proceeded to explore the James River valley until he was stopped at the river's fall line in the vicinity of modern Richmond, beyond which navigation was not possible. (Only brief reconnaissance beyond the falls was attempted.) Newport was able to bring home only a few samples of indigenous products.

Among the remaining 104 persons in the colony, division and illness (more than half the original settlers died from drinking brackish water or from typhoid or other diseases) led to the deposition of Wingfield in September. Powhatan, who ruled most of the Indian tribes in the area from Weromacomoco on the York River, welcomed the Jamestown settlement as a source of copper and iron, and of knives, tools, and other European goods. Capt. John Smith, however, was captured by Indians in December 1607 and was formally adopted as a leader under Powhatan, who henceforth regarded Jamestown as a subordinate unit in his domain.

When Newport returned in January 1608 with fifty additional colonists, he was shocked at the condition of the settlement. Smith was released in time to meet him, but the village was burned down a few days later. Newport had brought insignia from King James in order to make Powhatan a vassal of the English Crown, which he did in February. (Neither Smith in December 1607 nor Powhatan in 1608 understood the implications of the ceremonies in which they were involved.) Newport was once again dissatisfied with what had been produced in the colony, especially as reports in 1607 of a possible gold deposit had

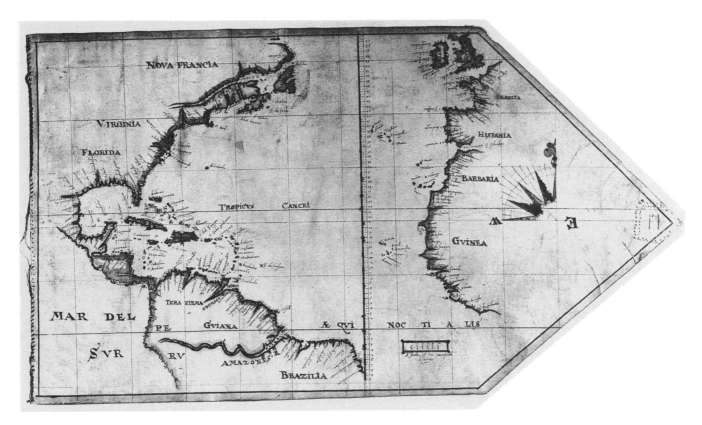

THE VIRGINIA COMPANY CHART. Circa 1607–1609. Manuscript map on vellum.   NEW YORK PUBLIC LIBRARY

been shown to be false. In June, Smith set out on his exploration of the Chesapeake basin and its rivers. He found that the fall line everywhere obstructed further navigation. The Potomac River was especially disappointing, as the obstructions above the site of present-day Washington were formidable barriers to further penetration. His pioneer work in mapping the area and locating Indian settlements, however, has proved invaluable to modern scholars.

Newport made a third visit, with yet another group of colonists. Smith had been made governor and had set the colonists to clearing land, growing crops, and lading processed timber. The colony's death rate had slowed, but it still remained high. Crops that were grown in comparable latitudes in Europe (37 to 38 degrees), such as olives and sugar cane, could not thrive in the misunderstood continental climate of North America.

A complete reorganization of the company was then undertaken. It was relaunched under a second charter of May 25, 1609, which expanded the membership to over six hundred subscribers, abandoned the Royal Council, and entrusted the company's council with some royal authority. The Royal Council, as its last act, appointed Sir Thomas Gates as governor, naming his council and providing him

with extensive instructions. Of the eight ships sent out from England, six reached Virginia. The flagship carrying Gates, his council, and his instructions went aground on Bermuda. Gates and Sir George Somers organized their men to maintain themselves and salvage enough from the ship to equip two pinnaces, which, with a cargo of wild pigs and pork, reached Jamestown in May 1610. There they found disaster had almost destroyed the colony. The addition of some five hundred settlers was impossible for Smith to assimilate. His credentials as governor were challenged amid severe dissension. He did succeed in getting the bulk of the newcomers to create a major new settlement, Henrico, near the falls, but he himself had to leave for England, owing to injuries incurred in an accident.

Under George Percy and Francis West, the colony had deteriorated. Powhatan, in effect, had declared war on these intruders who had overthrown the arrangements he considered he had made with the Jamestown colony. Supplies of corn from most of the Indian villages ceased, and, in return, vicious and brutal raids were made on a number of those villages. In the winter, the colonists had died in great numbers. When Gates and Somers appeared, only some sixty remained alive. They could give

Nova Britannia.

OFFERING MOST

Excellent fruites by Planting in
VIRGINIA.

Exciting all fuch as be well affected
to further the fame.

LONDON
Printed for SAMVEL MACHAM, and are to befold at
his Shop in Pauls Church-yard, at the
Signe of the Bul-head.
1 6 0 9.

ENGLISH PROMOTIONAL TRACT ADVERTISING OPPORTUNITIES IN VIRGINIA.
Printed in London, 1609. The text promises "a most comfortable
subsistence" to those who would make the voyage and settle in
the New World.   NEW YORK PUBLIC LIBRARY, RARE BOOK DIVISION

allowing his daughter Pocahontas to become a Christian
and to marry the colonist John Rolfe.

In 1616, earlier promises that land would be distributed
to subscribers and settlers of seven years' seniority came
due, but it was 1618 before final arrangements were made.
Sir George Yeardley was authorized to begin the process
of distribution and to initiate grants of extensive blocks of
land to individuals or syndicates for "particular plantations." He arrived on April 19, 1619, and a period of hectic
colony building began (the Indians now appearing too
weak to resist). Among other innovations was permission
to create a general assembly. Yeardley incorporated a
number of towns, and from them and "particular plantations" a body was elected, which formed, with the
governor and council, a legislative body that modified the
strict legal code of 1610 and dealt with local matters. This
was an important precedent for local self-government,
though it did not become a continuing part of Virginia
government until 1639.

Under the direction of the treasurer of the company, Sir
Edwin Sandys, some five thousand colonists had been
sent out by 1624; the colony expanded over most of the
James-York peninsula. The death rate remained high, but
the production of glass, soapash, and, above all, the new
tobacco, together with plans for a major ironworks, gave
hope of a varied and prosperous community. The process,
however, was abruptly checked by an Indian uprising.
Opechancanough had succeeded Powhatan in 1618, and
his forces were strong enough on March 22, 1622, to
sweep through the colony, destroying many new settlements (though not taking Jamestown) and killing some 150
colonists.

This uprising led to a retraction of the colony to a
relatively small area; many colonists died of starvation and
epidemics, even though extensive help came from England. The company went bankrupt, and the king was
obliged to step in, declaring the Virginia Company dissolved in 1624. The new king, Charles I, promptly reestablished Virginia as a royal colony in 1625, with a governor
and council appointed by him and under government
control. This act may be said to have created the basis for
a continuing expansion of royal authority over increasing
areas of eastern North America.

The Pilgrims at Plymouth Harbor. In 1620, the Pilgrims
landed at Cape Cod and soon moved to Plymouth Harbor
where they established the first autonomous colony that
owed nothing to royal authority. Nonconforming Congregationalists had been driven into the Netherlands in 1607,
but they had retained English contacts. In 1619–1620, they
obtained backing from London merchants and other
Congregationalists in England who were being persecuted. They had a grant for a "particular plantation" from
the Virginia Company when they sailed from Plymouth on

them first aid, but they could not restore the colony. They
were in the process of evacuating the colonists when Lord
De La Warr, a new governor, intercepted them. From June
1610, the colony, which remained at war with Powhatan
until 1614, was governed by a strict body of laws. In effect,
Sir Thomas Dale governed the small colony like a military
garrison between 1612 and 1616, gradually weakening
Indian power and slowly leading the colony toward
self-sufficiency. During this period, John Rolfe experi-
mented with Trinidad tobacco (*Nicotiana tabacum*) as a
possible export crop. A final reorganization of the company took place in 1612. The charter of March 12, 1612,
extended membership and authorized participation in
quarterly courts to which the treasurer and council were
elected. In 1614, Powhatan made peace with the colonists,

September 26, 1620, for the northern fringe of the company's territory. But they put ashore on the first land they came to, Provincetown Harbor, on November 31, and drew up the famous Mayflower Compact, forming a civil society of their own. Their move to Plymouth Harbor was completed on December 16. More than half of the Pilgrims died that winter, but under the guidance of William Bradford they proceeded with remarkable skill and endurance to establish a settlement that was to be a singular and lasting one on the site of a former Indian village. They remained for a long time a unique religious and political grouping with no formal recognition of royal authority.

Bermuda. Because Bermuda had seemed so attractive to Gates and Somers, the Virginia Company set up a subsidiary body to colonize it in 1611. A master carpenter and builder, Richard More, was chosen as governor. With a party of colonists, he landed at St. George's Harbor on July 11, 1612. For three years he concentrated on building fortifications to protect from a possible Spanish attack.

Colonists flooded into Bermuda, especially when it obtained a separate charter in 1614. Early conditions were chaotic, but the island was surveyed and divided into parishes, most of which were allocated to major investors. It took some time to establish that tobacco was the easiest and most profitable crop, but under the governors Daniel Tucker and Nathaniel Butler the colony gradually found a balanced existence, though it never became the paradise for growing subtropical fruits and other products that Somers had envisaged in 1610.

Newfoundland. From 1583 to 1608 only occasional plans were made for the colonization of Newfoundland. In the latter year John Guy of Bristol explored its eastern shores, where a fishery, operating between May and September, had become a major industry. As a result of cooperation between London and Bristol capitalists, a patent was obtained on May 2, 1610, for a company to colonize Newfoundland. A treasurer and council were to govern the company and to appoint a governor for any colony it should establish.

John Guy accepted the post of first governor, and an expedition of thirty-nine men landed at Conception Bay in August 1611, creating the colony of Cupids Cove. Their remit was to explore and engage in fur trading as well as cod fishing and drying. Guy, who directed the planting of root crops, the construction of a warehouse large enough for building boats in the winter, and the exploration of territories while the snow was still on the ground, was an able commander. Additional settlers, including women, came out in 1612, and the first two years yielded good fishing returns and some furs, which were sent back to England. Before returning to Bristol to report progress in 1611, however, Guy unwisely imposed regulations on the inshore fishermen, who had a long-standing stake in the

summer fishery. These regulations led to a campaign against the colony that was ultimately fatal to its expansion, without which it could not pay its way. In 1612, the pirate Peter Easton disrupted the fishery, though he did not attack the colony. Plans for a second settlement were abandoned, and in 1613 colonists began to drift homeward. Guy and the treasurer John Slany quarreled, and after Guy's departure in 1613 the colony declined to a handful of people.

By 1616 the colony was bankrupt and kept going only by selling concessions to other interested parties, five in all, covering most of southeastern Newfoundland. Several parties never took up their grants, but others made interesting, though ultimately unsuccessful, experiments in the 1620s. The company survived until 1631, but as early as 1621, the fishing interests began a campaign against colonization. This campaign hampered and, in the end, virtually destroyed opportunities for colonization until much later.

Quest for the Northwest Passage. The search for a Northwest Passage, in which the English were leaders, affected the exploration of the whole of northern North American waters. Under a patent granted in February 1584, John Davis explored and defined the shorelines of Greenland, Baffin Island, and northern Labrador (1585–1587), paving the way for later explorations but finding no passages that were not blocked with ice. In 1600, the East India Company was constituted and given, among many other things, rights over any northern passages. It financed an expedition in 1602 under George Waymouth, which appears to have entered Hudson Strait but which was unable—as a result of both ice and crew problems—to establish any hopeful prospect of finding a passage.

An unofficial syndicate of London merchants in 1610 financed the voyage of Henry Hudson during which he discovered Hudson Bay. While Hudson wintered in James Bay, he was cast off in a shallop by a mutinous crew, a few of whom survived to tell the tale. In 1612, Thomas Button explored the main outline of Hudson Bay and brought back indications that a passage might be found. An explosion of interest ensued, and a patent was granted to the powerful North-West Passage Company on July 26, 1612. A resulting 1613 voyage was a fiasco. In 1615, Robert Bylot and William Baffin extended the range of exploration north of the bay, but they too failed to find a passage. In 1616, a final attempt was made by the English north of Davis's exploration of 1587, which brought the expedition into new high latitudes before being checked by ice. Though valued for its explorations, the company collapsed and exploration by the English ceased for some fifteen years. The various ventures had revealed much of northern North America, but from the perspective of imperial expansion, they were a waste of money that might otherwise have been used to establish effective colonies farther south.

The English Record of the Early Years

It can scarcely be argued that by the end of 1620 England had anything that resembled an empire in North America. A single colony, Virginia, had showed promise, only to be shortly checked by indigenous resistance. Many experiments in planning and governing colonies had been made, but almost all were unsuccessful. Nevertheless, with the creation of its general assembly in 1619, the Virginia Company by the next year was showing indications of a process that was to differentiate English colonization from that of other powers. The Pilgrim venture, not yet defined by the end of 1620, revealed that collective initiatives impelled by noneconomic forces could be promising. Direct royal authority remained the source of all other colonial activity, mediated through chartered companies or powers entrusted to individuals, without any supervisory body. (The experimental Royal Council of 1606–1609 was not repeated.)

Religion, theoretically, played a part in most ventures. There was extensive writing about converting native peoples. One goal of these writings was to remove the perception by Roman Catholics that the Church of England was merely a narrow sectarian heresy with no influence outside England. In practice, however, little was done, except to provide colonists with clergy. In Virginia, church building, compulsory church attendance, and an unbroken supply of clergy to carry on the work of maintaining Anglicanism were permanent features. In the years 1620–1622 a serious attempt was made to raise money to found a missionary college for Indians, but the 1622 uprising put an end to this effort.

Although a fishery might flourish in the summer, misunderstandings about climate and the failure to ensure the self-support of the colonies at an early stage led to the repeated failure to find a staple crop with which to provide profits for those who supplied the capital for the colonies. (From 1618 onward, tobacco at last provided such a staple.) The self-supporting efforts of the lost colonists and the Pilgrims composed a distinct strand in colonization, but they had produced no substantive results by the end of 1620. There was, indeed, no effective English imperial achievement of any consequence down to this date, only a series of experiments that provided guidelines for later ventures on what not to do.

BIBLIOGRAPHY

Andrews, Charles McLean. *The Colonial Period of American History.* 4 vols. New Haven, 1934.
Andrews, Kenneth R., Nicholas P. Canny, and E. H. Hair, eds. *The Western Enterprise.* Detroit, 1978.
Axtell, James. *After Columbus.* New York, 1988.
Barbour, Phillip, ed. *The Complete Works of Captain John Smith.* 3 vols. Chapel Hill, 1987.
Madden, Frederick, and David Fieldhouse, eds. *The Empire of the Britaignes, 1175–1688.* Westport, 1985.
Quinn, David B. *England and the Discovery of America.* New York, 1974.
Rose, J. Holland, Alfred Percival Newton, and Edward A. Bern-ansi, eds. *The Cambridge History of the British Empire.* 8 vols. Cambridge, 1929.
Williamson, James Alexander. *A Short History of the British Empire.* 2 vols. London, 1930.

DAVID B. QUINN

COLUMBIAN EXCHANGE. For discussion of the transfer of plants, animals, and technologies between the Old World and the New World that resulted from the encounter of European and American cultures, see *Agriculture; Disease and Demography; Domesticated Animals; Fauna; Flora; Metal; Syphilis.*

COLUMBIANISM. As the people of the thirteen colonies that became the United States were shifting from colonial to national identity, they harked back to the origins of the New World and adopted "Columbia," the feminine adjectival form of "Columbus," a name that became the poetic identity for the new nation. Infused into the romantic nationalism of the early Republic, Columbia first entered the American ethos in literary discourse.

Two anonymous poets first referred to Columbia, but such references were prior to the political movements of the 1770s. Mrs. Mercy Warren, wife of Gen. James Warren and sister of James Otis, Jr., colonial patriots in the War for Independence, was the first to place Columbia in the context of the American Revolution. Published in the *Boston Gazette* of February 13, 1775, her poem identifies Columbia as a land "where Liberty, a happy Goddess reigned / where no proud Despot rules with lawless sway / Nor orphans spoils became the Minion's prey."

Albert J. Hoyt, the scholar who traced this poem, was responding to George H. Moore's claim that Phillis Wheatley, a freed slave, coined the literary form "Columbia." Hoyt's discovery was first published in 1886, but because little is known of his research, Phillis Wheatley is still identified as the name's original source. Though she may not have minted the name, her poetry popularized the term, thereby infusing the coinage into the general parlance.

Wheatley, the first known African American poet, was born in Africa and was the slave of a Boston businessman who granted her manumission in 1773. With a background in Latin and a command of contemporary English and

American literature, Wheatley manifested an awareness of the latinized name for Great Britain, "Britannia," in a poem in 1773. After she received her freedom Wheatley visited England where she published her first book of poetry. Benjamin Franklin and other notables visited her, and Voltaire expressed his approval of her poetry.

Wheatley's "Columbia" was included in her poem "His Excellency General Washington": "Fixed are the eyes of Natives on the scales, / for in their hope Columbia's arm prevails." Washington was so gratified by the poem he invited Wheatley to his headquarters in Cambridge, Massachusetts. The poem became widely known when Thomas Paine published it in his *Pennsylvania Gazette*. In a 1776 poem Wheatley placed Columbia on an Olympus of mythicized figures representing European nationalities: Britannia, Gallia, Germania, Scotia, and Hibernia.

The direct link between Columbus and Columbia is found in a 1778 poem by Joel Barlow. Apparently familiar with the Wheatley poem, Barlow recited his "The Prospect of Peace" as a commencement piece at Yale College. A year later he stated, "The discovery of America made an important revolution in the history of mankind. It served the purpose of displaying knowledge, liberty and religion."

Barlow's 1787 epic poem of nine books, *The Vision of Columbus*, identified Columbia as the land of liberty; he rendered the American Republic as the culmination of a new era inaugurated by Columbus. The poem was replete with biases imbedded in the Black Legend, which portrays Spain in terms of the cruelties of the Inquisition and perceives Columbus as a man who transcended the Catholic superstition of his era. The identification of Columbia with liberty had already achieved some popularity prior to Barlow's poem when New York's Kings College was renamed Columbia in 1784.

Thomas Jefferson, James Madison, and the three commissioners charged with responsibility for the capital informed Pierre L'Enfant, its first architect, that the home of the federal government would be called Washington and would be located in the federal territory of Columbia. Without any evidence concerning the commission's rationale, one may infer that the commissioners' decision intended to give the capital the aura of liberty rather than authority. Perhaps the commissioners' rationale included this idea: Columbia had severed itself from Britannia; hope had guided Columbus to the New World; Columbia symbolized the hope of the new nation.

These early manifestations of Columbianism illustrate Robert Bellah's notion of a civil religion (or, as Martin E. Marty prefers, public religion): creed, code, and cult unite diverse people into a common sense of their American nationality identified with sacred texts—the Declaration of Independence, the Constitution, the Bill of Rights, the Gettysburg Address; with special feast days—Thanksgiv-ing, the Fourth of July; with hymns; with flag-raising rituals; and with the nation's particular place in God's providential design.

The first monument to Columbus reflected the early phase of civil religion. According to oral tradition, the idea for the monument originated at a dinner party in early 1792 hosted by the French consul in Baltimore, Chevalier Charles-François Adrien Le Paulmier d'Annemours. A guest lamented the absence of a monument to Columbus as a suitable site for commemorating the tricentennial of the landing on San Salvador. The chevalier d'Annemours, the story goes, decided then and there to erect such a monument on his property about a mile north of the city boundary. Designed as a simple obelisk, the monument, inscribed "sacred to the Memory of Christopher Columbus," was erected in a grove of cedar and ash trees about one hundred yards from Le Paulmier d'Annemours's home. Though it was nearly fifty feet in height, this first monument was a private tribute remote from the people of the city. To the French absorbed in the independence movement the monument represented loyalty to Columbus and to the land "Columbia," so symbolic of the American ethos of liberty.

The Saint Tammany Society of New York, which changed its name to the Society of Tammany, or the Columbian Order, in 1789, was one of several patriotic fraternal societies of the day. Named after Saint Tammany, a native American convert and martyr for Christianity, the society chose Christopher Columbus as a patron, and it was the first to celebrate Columbus Day, in 1790. Its observation of the tricentennial of Columbus's landing included a parade, patriotic oratory, and a grand banquet. A twelve-foot portable obelisk was erected for the occasion, one that was intended to be displayed each Columbus Day.

Jeremy Belknap's *Ode to Columbus and Columbia* that was sung by a soloist and choir in a Boston celebration of Columbus Day, 1792, resounded with discordant notes on the themes of the Black Legend and anti-Catholicism:

> Black *Superstition's* dismal night
> Extinguished *Reason's* golden ray;
> And *Science,* driven from the light
> Beneath monastic rubbish lay
> The *Crown* and *Mitre,* close allied
> Trampled whole nations to the dust
> Whilst *Freedom,* wandering far and wide
> And pure *Religion,* quite was lost.
> Then, guided by th' Almighty Hand
> *Columbus* spread his daring sail,
> *Ocean* received a new command
> And Zephyrs breathed a gentle gale.
> . . . Sweet Peace and heavenly truth shall shine
> on Fair Columbia's ground
> There Freedom and Religion join
> And Spread their influence all around.

A hundred years later, at the Chicago World's Columbian Exposition, dedicated in October 1892 and opened in the spring of 1893, Columbianism's role in the tradition of civil religion dominated the festive atmosphere. Professor John Knowles Paine of Harvard College wrote the following lyrics to accompany his Columbian march, composed for the dedication of the main exposition building:

All hail and welcome, nations of the earth
Columbia's greeting comes from every state.
Proclaim to all mankind the world's new birth . . .
Let war and enmity forever cease
Let glorious art and commerce banish among
The universal brotherhood of peace
Shall be Columbia's high inspiring song.

The twentieth century, so profoundly affected by two world wars, by economic recessions, and by periods of social conflict, has witnessed the decline of romantic nationalism associated with Columbianism, and devotion to Columbia has lost its hold on the public's poetic self-understanding.

BIBLIOGRAPHY

Belknap, Jeremy. *Intended to Commemorate as Discourse the Discovery of America by Christopher Columbus.* Boston, 1792.

Dickey, J. M. *Christopher Columbus and the Monument Columbia.* Chicago, 1892.

Hoyt, Albert J. "The Name Columbia." *New England Historical and Genealogical Register,* July 1886.

Kilroe, Edwin Patrick. *Saint Tammany and the Origin of Tammany of Columbian Order in the City of New York.* New York, 1913.

Williams, John Alexander. "The First American Hero: Columbus in Columbia, 1775–1792." Typescript, 1986.

CHRISTOPHER J. KAUFFMAN

COLUMBIAN SOCIETIES. In the latter quarter of the nineteenth century many second-generation Catholic immigrants assimilated into American culture through societies that blended patriotism with a religious devotion to the Catholic "origins" of the New World, with particular focus on the great navigator, Christopher Columbus. These Columbian societies include the Knights of Columbus (founded in 1882) and two sororal societies, originally formed in association with the Knights, the Daughters of Isabella (1897) and the Catholic Daughters of the Americas (1903).

A unique blend of faith and fraternalism, the Knights of Columbus is the largest organization of Catholic laity in the world. Over its history it has responded to the myriad needs of local churches and societies in the United States, Canada, Mexico, Cuba, Puerto Rico, and the Philippines.

Michael J. McGivney, the New Haven priest who founded the Knights of Columbus in 1882, implicitly fostered an American Catholic apologetic, one that promoted harmony between religious liberty and Catholicism. Concerned with the strong appeal of the prohibited secret societies among Catholic youth and with the plight of widows and children who had suffered the loss of their breadwinner, he was eager to form a fraternal insurance society imbued with deep loyalties to Catholicism and to the American experience.

The Knights' Columbianism was born on February 6, 1882, when a small group of New Haven laymen chose Columbus as the patron of their fraternal society. One of those present at this meeting invoked the cause of Catholic civil liberty when he asserted that, as Catholic descendants of Columbus, they "were entitled to all rights and privileges due to such a discovery by one of our faith." In short, the founders perceived Columbus as a source of identity for Catholics of all ethnic groups, a cultural symbol infused into their sense of American Catholic peoplehood. Just as the ship *Mayflower* was a sign of Protestant identity, so *Santa María* was a symbol of Catholic legitimacy. The term *knight* conveyed a commitment to struggle against the forces of nativism and anti-Catholicism that periodically erupted into hysteria among groups eager for scapegoats.

Besides establishing a united front in defense of the church, the Knights cultivated patriotic sentiments based on the Catholic component in the American heritage. The initiation ceremonies were dramatic renditions of the heroic faith of Columbus, of the "Catholic baptism" of the American continent, and of the nobility of religious liberty and American democracy. In a sense, the ceremonials provided the candidates for Knighthood with a rite of passage—from Old World ties to loyalty to the Republic. Though the leaders were all second-generation Irish-Americans, they were realists on the ethnic issue. Hence, in Boston they allowed the establishment of the Teutonia Council for German-American Knights and the Ansonia Council for Italian Americans.

Thomas Cummings, one of the most impassioned proponents of Columbianism, wrote of the order's idealism. He predicted that if the Knights "honorably practiced their beliefs," then it would mean "the creation of a new type of Catholic manhood," a new spirit of lay activism in the church:

Under the inspiration of Him whose name we bear, and with the story of Columbus's life, as exemplified in our beautiful ritual, we have the broadest kind of basis for patriotism and true love of country. . . . [B]y drawing close the bonds of brotherhood, we make for the best type of American citizenship. For the best American is he who best exemplifies in his own life, that this is not a Protestant country, nor a Catholic country, nor a Hebrew country, any more than it is an Anglo-Saxon or Latin country, but a country of all races and all creeds, with one great, broad, unmolterable [sic] creed of fair play and equal rights for all.

For the first ten years the order was primarily a Connecticut organization, but it expanded from New England throughout the nation. By 1905 the Knights were in every state in the Union, five of the nine provinces in Canada, Mexico, and the Philippines, and were poised to enter Cuba and Puerto Rico. The Knights' expansion during this period owed much to the strong sense of Catholic Columbianism it had exhibited during the celebration of the quadricentennial. Catholics in every diocese throughout the nation had manifested their loyalty to the nation and the faith by parades and religious liturgies.

Originally a women's auxiliary of Russell Council of the Knights, the Daughters of Isabella was founded in New Haven in 1897. The Columbian motif was represented in its initiation rites, which featured Isabella's role in sponsoring Columbus's first voyage. The Catholic Daughters of America (CDA) was also originally entitled Daughters of Isabella. Founded in Utica, New York, in 1903 in association with the Knights, it too ritualized Columbianism. As a result of a 1921 court case, however, the Utica society lost its right to the Daughters name and became the CDA.

Each of the three Columbian societies through the years has engaged in extensive work in projects for the Roman Catholic church as well as community and volunteer services for the handicapped, the homeless, and the aged. All three have also provided insurance benefits for their memberships, which by 1990 had reached 96,000 in the Daughters of Isabella, 145,000 in the CDA, and 1.5 million in the Knights of Columbus. Though the vast majority of Catholics have been assimilated into American society, these organizations still foster the Columbian bonds of unity and charity; they still render Columbus and Isabella as models of dedication to religion and culture.

BIBLIOGRAPHY

Kauffman, Christopher J. *Faith and Fraternalism: The History of the Knights of Columbus, 1882–1982.* New York, 1982.

Kerwin, P. K. "Catholic Daughters of America." In *New Catholic Encyclopedia.* Vol. 3. Washington, D.C., 1967.

Maguire, J. F. "Daughters of Isabella." In *New Catholic Encyclopedia.* Vol. 4. Washington, D.C., 1967.

CHRISTOPHER J. KAUFFMAN

COLUMBUS, CHRISTOPHER. [This entry provides a biography of Columbus in six articles:

Birth and Origins
Adolescence and Youth
Early Maritime Experience
Columbus in Portugal
Columbus in Spain
The Final Years, Illness, and Death

For detailed discussion of the events of Columbus's four voyages to the Western Hemisphere, see *Voyages of Columbus.* See also biographies of numerous figures mentioned herein. Biographies of several members of the Columbus family can be found under *Colombo* (for those whose lives centered in Italy) or under *Colón* (for those whose lives centered in Spain or in Spanish America). For discussion of Columbus's literary remains, see *Writings.* For analysis of Columbus's legacy in scholarship, art, and literature, see *Bibliography; Celebrations; Columbianism; Columbian Societies; Iconography; Literature; Monuments and Memorials; Museums and Archives.*]

Birth and Origins

Christopher Columbus (1451–1506) was Genoese by birth and culture. The roots of his genius and his enterprise lie in the flowering of the Italian Renaissance and in the cultural, naval, and cartographic traditions of Genoa. The term *Genoese* must, however, be broadly defined, for a fifteenth-century Genoese could be from Corsica or even Chios.

Columbus's Genoese origins are confirmed by numerous documents. One principal document is a *majorat* (entail) in which Columbus designates the heir to his titles and privileges. In this *majorat,* which played an important part in the two centuries of legal proceedings involving the claimants to the Admiral's estate, Columbus states: "that, having been born in Genoa, I came to serve them [the Spanish monarchs] in Castile, and discovered for them the Indies and the aforesaid islands to the west of terra firma."

A copy of this document, which dates back to the early seventeenth century and had been officially sent from Spain to the Republic of Genoa, is conserved in the State Archives of Genoa. The supposed original is in the Archive General de Indias in Seville.

Cesare de Lollis observes that "the history of this important document is so clear that there is no doubt about its authenticity." Both Rinaldo Caddeo and Antonio Ballesteros Beretta maintain that it is authentic. Henry Harrisse, however, considers it a forgery from a later period. Even if the document is on the whole authentic, the suspicion of interpolation cannot be excluded. This suspicion, however, has no effect on the basic fact of the Genoese birth and cultural background of Columbus. This claim is confirmed by many other documents and by recorded testimony.

There is, for example, an important letter sent by the Admiral to the San Giorgio Bank in Genoa. This letter, the authenticity of which is beyond question, begins, "Although my body may be here, my heart is there constantly." "There" is Genoa. Similarly, there exist two other letters, addressed to Nicoló Oderico, ambassador of the Republic of Genoa to the court of Spain. In these letters, Columbus states that he has assigned 10 percent of his

The Columbus Family

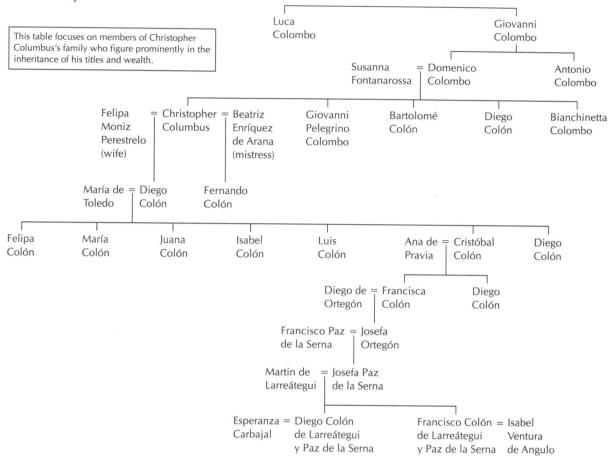

This table focuses on members of Christopher Columbus's family who figure prominently in the inheritance of his titles and wealth.

bequest to the San Giorgio Bank in order to alleviate the taxes on grain, wine, and other foodstuffs for the poor of Genoa.

Even more definitive are the public and notarial acts—original copies of which are conserved in the archives of Genoa and Savona—regarding Columbus himself, his father, his grandfather, and other relatives. There are more than a hundred such documents, clearly indicating that Columbus was from a Ligurian family. His great-grandfather lived in Mocónesi, where his grandfather, Giovanni, was born. His father, Domenico, who was born in Quinto, lived for a long period of time in Genoa and then in Savona. Today, Quinto is part of Genoa's urban complex, but in the fifteenth century it was a village a short way from the city. Christopher Columbus spent his childhood and the first years of his youth in Vico Diritto, under the gate of Sant'Andrea.

According to documents that we are certain are authentic, the date of his birth is usually set between August 25 and October 31, 1451. In a document dated October 31, 1470, Columbus declares himself *major annis decemnovem* (nineteen years old); in another document, dated August 25, 1479, which will be discussed below, he

declares himself *annorum vigintiseptem vel circa* (about twenty-seven). Between August 25 and October 31, 1451, Domenico Colombo, Christopher's father, was the keeper of the Olivella gate and thus lived next to the gate itself. This, therefore, is where Christopher would have been born.

Another doubt remains to be settled: can we be sure that all the documents cited concern the Christopher Columbus who was later to become the Admiral of the Ocean Sea? In a legal document dated September 22, 1470, a judge convicts Domenico Colombo. The conviction concerns a debt owed by Domenico—*together with his son Christopher* (explicitly stated in the document)—to a certain Girolamo del Porto. In the will dictated by Columbus in Valladolid, the dying navigator remembers this old debt, which had evidently not been paid.

Still more important is an act drawn in Genoa on August 25, 1479, by a notary, Girolamo Ventimiglia (series 2a, 1474–1504, n. 266). This act is known as the Assereto Document, after the scholar who found it in the State Archives in Genoa in 1904. Following is the part in which Columbus is cited:

Lodovico Centurione, appearing by law and in the presence of the venerable Office of Merchandise, says and states that which he will or hopes or doubts to have with Paolo Di Negro, son of the late Luca, he himself or his brother Cazano with the aforementioned Paolo, and since he has some witnesses who are informed of the rights of said Lodovico, who must shortly leave this city of Genoa and depart on a long journey, thus requests that said witnesses, in eternal memory of the fact and for as long as the belief in truth does not perish, be received and examined.

First he intends to prove and to attest to the truth of the fact that was and is that other times in the past year, during the time in which the witnesses . . . will say, Paolo Di Negro, commissioned by him Lodovico and by the aforesaid Cazano or one of them to the island of Madeira in order to purchase a certain quantity of sugar, and Lodovico having sent 1,290 ducats therefore, that is to say 1,290 "grossati" or their value to said Paolo, who was supposed to purchase 2,400 and more rubbi of sugar, Christopher Columbus, on the order of said Paolo, was sent to the island of Madeira and here he secured and purchased the aforementioned amount of sugar.

Witnesses in favor of Lodovico Centurione.

In nomine Domini amen. May all who see the present public testimonial document know that, having appeared in the presence of myself, the notary and the undersigned witnesses, summoned and requested for the express purpose, Christopher Columbus, citizen of Genoa, summoned here as a witness, must be received and examined as such.

When asked if he has to depart soon, he answered: yes, tomorrow morning for Lisbon. When asked how old he is, he answered that he was about twenty-seven years of age.

In addition, several notarial acts confirm the identification of the Genoese Christopher Columbus, son of Domenico, with the Admiral of Spain. For example, an act dated October 11, 1496, says: "Giovanni Colombo of Quinto, Matteo Colombo and Amighetto Colombo, brothers of the late Antonio, in full understanding and knowledge that said Giovanni must go to Spain to see M. Christopher Columbus, Admiral of the King of Spain, and that any expenses that said Giovanni must make in order to see said M. Christopher must be paid by all three of the aforementioned brothers, each one to pay a third . . . and to this they hereby agree."

In an act drawn in Savona on April 8, 1500, Sebastiano Cuneo requested that Christopher and Giacomo (called Diego), the sons and heirs of Domenico Colombo, be summoned to court and sentenced to pay the price for two lands located in Légino. This document confirms the brothers' absence from the Republic of Genoa with the words: "dicti conventi sunt absentes ultra Pisas et Niciam" (the summoned parties are absent and beyond Pisa and Nice).

Another notarial act, drawn in Savona on January 26, 1501, is more explicit. A group of Genoese citizens, under oath, "said and say, together and separately and in every more valid manner and guise, that the Christopher, Bartholomew, and Giacomo Colombo, sons and heirs of the aforementioned Domenico, their father, have for a long time been absent from the city and the jurisdiction of Savona, as well as Pisa and Nice in Provence, and that they reside in the area of Spain, as was and is well known."

Finally, there is a very important document from the notary Bartolomeo Oddino, drawn in Savona on March 30, 1515. With this act, Leon Pancaldo, the well-known Savonese who would become one of the pilots for Ferdinand Magellan's voyage, sends his own father-in-law in his place as procurator for Diego Colón, son of the Admiral. The document demonstrates how the ties, in part economic, of the discoverer's family with Savona survived even his death.

These documents, along with some seventy other Genoese and Savonese documents, irrefutably demonstrate that Christopher Columbus, the discoverer of America, was Cristoforo Columbo, son of Domenico.

BIBLIOGRAPHY

Ballesteros Beretta, Antonio. *Cristóbal Colón y el descubrimiento de América*. Vol. 1. Barcelona and Buenos Aires, 1945.

Genoa, City of. *Christopher Columbus: Documents and Proofs of his Genoese Origin*. English-German edition. Bergamo, 1932.

Morison, Samuel Eliot. *Admiral of the Ocean Sea: A Life of Christopher Columbus*. 2 vols. Boston, 1942.

Sammartino, Peter. *Columbus*. Rome, 1988.

Taviani, Paolo Emilio. *Christopher Columbus: The Grand Design*. London, 1985.

Taviani, Paolo Emilio. *Cristoforo Colombo: Genius of the Sea*. Rome, 1990.

Thacher, J. B. *Christopher Columbus: His Life, His Work, His Remains*. New York, 1903.

PAOLO EMILIO TAVIANI

Adolescence and Youth

In 1502, at the height of his fame and power, Admiral Christopher Columbus was in Spain writing with fond sentiment to the directors of the San Giorgio Bank in his native city of Genoa: "Though my body is here, my heart is always with you." His love of Genoa is one part of the abundant evidence that Christopher's youth in Genoa was happy and that he grew up in a loving and prosperous family.

Two aspects of his youth were significant in preparing him for a career: his education and his family life. Ambition and the desire for education had been behind the Colombo family's move from the mountain village of Mocónesi to the city of Genoa. Christopher and his brothers received the type of education that would carry the family even further—to foreign countries.

Italians in the fifteenth century believed that all family

members, including the children, were part of the family work force. The work of boys was to study, and for that purpose, the wool guild of Genoa maintained a school on Pavia Street. It was here that young Christopher learned to read and write and do basic arithmetic. His son Fernando later confused this grammar school with the famous University of Pavia, and so mistakenly introduced the idea that Christopher Columbus had a university education. The curriculum in the grammar school was much more humble. Children entered grammar school between the ages of five and seven. First, they learned to write using chalk on a slate or a stylus on waxed boards. By the time they left the school at age eleven or twelve, they knew how to read and write in Latin and do basic addition and subtraction. Only when they came to write their own letters did they write on paper, mixing the ink, sharpening a quill to form a pen point, folding a sheet of paper to form its own envelope, and sealing it with string and hot wax.

The usual method for teaching Latin was memorization of whole sentences chosen from the Bible and ancient classics to teach grammatical rules and inculcate morality and manners. They were not intended to give students a love of literature or make them proficient in writing beautiful Latin. Rather, the sentences Columbus learned in his grammar school were functional tools for a business career. Italian businessmen needed to be able to read contracts and political documents in Latin because it was the language of church and government records throughout Italy. As an adult, Columbus read the Latin language with ease; he bought Latin books about geography and cosmography as soon as they came off the new printing presses and wrote Latin notes (often containing errors) in their margins commenting on the texts.

After grammar school, some boys learned a profession by serving a six- or seven-year apprenticeship. That is what Columbus's father, Domenico Colombo, had done. Domenico had been apprenticed at the age of eleven to a cloth weaver for six years. In exchange for the boy's labor in his shop, the master taught his apprentice all aspects of the weaver's trade, from purchasing and processing the raw materials, through weaving several patterns, to selling the finished products. By the age of twenty-one, Domenico was a master weaver and he, in turn, brought apprentices into his household.

Domenico taught his sons the weaver's trade at home to prepare them to enter the wool guild, but he had ambitions for his family. The city of Genoa had rigid status divisions, even under the new constitution adopted in 1418, which divided the seats in the city council half and half between nobles and guildsmen, with half the guildsmen merchants and the other half artisans. In Genoa the highest-status occupation was international merchant; the

doges during the fifteenth century came from the merchant guilds. Domenico Colombo made sure that his sons received the appropriate education for the merchant profession.

The next stage of education for a future merchant was the study of mathematics. In the fifteenth century, mathematical computations were undergoing a drastic change in Italian cities. Medieval Europeans did not write down numbers to do computations. Instead they drew an abacus on a table top (or, in England, covered a table with a checkered cloth), performed computations by moving counters on this counting table, and recorded the sums in Roman numerals in their ledgers. Now this old system was being challenged by a system adopted from Arab merchants. The Arabs computed as we do today; they used algorithms, writing out their computations as they went along in Hindu-Arabic numerals. Computation involving large numbers was more rapid and sophisticated, and the change created a great demand for teachers of the new mathematics. Merchants in northern Europe sent their sons to study with Italian teachers, but Christopher had to walk only a few blocks to a local teacher.

In a city like Genoa, international commerce depended on mastery of the sea, so that the mathematical basis of navigation was an essential part of a businessman's education. Computations were performed in Arabic numerals, although sums and dates were still recorded in Roman numerals: most city governments considered the new numerals easier to counterfeit than Roman numerals and so did not accept them as evidence in litigation.

Young Christopher must have learned these lessons well, for he calculated interest income and currency exchange rates with great facility throughout his life. During his voyages he handled navigational computations with confidence and accuracy; his miscalculations of the earth's circumference were due to incorrect geographical assumptions, not computational errors. He followed the custom of using Roman numerals in business documents, but in personal letters he sometimes used Arabic numerals to record large numbers, such as the year.

The next stage of a boy's education for international commerce was accounting. Italian businessmen used double-entry bookkeeping. In this method, each transaction is recorded twice, on one page under a debit heading and on the opposite page under a credit heading. Double entry enabled a businessman to draw up a balance sheet showing his personal worth—an exercise the prudent Italian merchant carried out in private at the end of every month. Drawing up a balance also was used to distribute profits and losses among partners or to close an account no longer active. Near the end of his life, Columbus advised his son Diego: "I order you under penalty of being found disobedient to personally draw up a balance of your household expenses every month and sign it with your name, because otherwise all your employees and money will be lost, and enmities will develop."

Christopher's mathematical and accounting education indicates that his family intended him to follow a career on a larger stage than the ones his father and grandfather had occupied. The family was moving up in the world, from Giovanni's small-town farming career, to Domenico's big-city manufacturing and commerce, and now to Christopher's intended international career of import and export merchant.

Domenico's economic ventures wrought many changes in his family's life and provided a model of entrepreneurship for Christopher. In 1440 Domenico, while still a bachelor practicing his wool-weaving trade in Genoa, leased a house and land, situated in dell'Olivella Street, from the monks of the Benedictine monastery of Santo Stefano. He became involved in city politics and joined the Fregoso party, whose policy was alliance with France against Aragón. Their opponents, the pro-Aragonese Adorno party, gained power on January 4, 1447, when Barnaba Adorno was elected doge, but Barnaba was overthrown at the end of the month in an assault led by Giano da Campo Fregoso. Giano brought eighty-five men by galley to the city at night and attacked the doge's palace, which was defended by six hundred soldiers sent by King Alfonso of Aragón, uncle of the future King Fernando.

The victors appointed their supporters to all the political and military offices of the city. On February 4, 1447, Domenico was appointed warden of the Olivella city gate and tower near his house, and his brother Antonio was appointed warden of the lighthouse (Capo di Faro) at the entrance to the harbor. The usual term of appointment was thirteen months, so that by April 1448, Domenico was no longer warden of the tower, and he and his brother were living in Quinto. During the next two years, the Fregoso party ruled the city. Giano died and was eventually replaced as doge by Pietro Fregoso, who had been captain general of the city since February 3, 1447, and probably was Domenico Colombo's political sponsor. On October 1, 1450, Domenico was again appointed warden of the Olivella tower and gate for another thirteen months. Domenico's anti-Aragonese politics was probably the reason Christopher never talked about his Genoese past after he moved to Spain.

Clearly, Domenico was prospering. He married Susanna Fontanarossa. As dowry, her parents gave her land in the village of Ginestreto. In 1451, Domenico bought farmland in Quarto, the village next to Quinto, for five hundred Genoese lire and leased it to the seller on the same day. The two oldest sons, Christopher and Giovanni Pelegrino, were probably born in the house in Quinto that Domenico and his brother Antonio inherited from their father. From 1452 to 1455 Domenico and his family lived in Genoa, probably in their house on dell'Olivella Street.

With a growing family and prospering business, Domenico and Susanna needed more space and resources. In 1455, the family moved to their permanent home—a substantial house and garden that Domenico leased from the monastery of Santo Stefano, on Diritto di Ponticello Street, near the Soprana city gate. Two younger boys, Bartolomeo and Giacomo, and a daughter, Bianchinetta, were probably born in this house. It is likely that Susanna gave birth to several more children, but this was an age when 25 percent of newborns died before the age of five, and only five of their children survived into adulthood. Diritto Street where Christopher and his brothers and sister grew up was in a new section of the city, called Borgo Santo Stefano, that had been in the countryside before being enclosed by city walls built a century earlier. The new house had everything necessary for a comfortable city home. At the front on the ground floor was the shop, where Domenico and his sons and apprentices

THE COLOMBO FAMILY HOUSE ON DIRITTO DI PONTICELLO. Near the Soprano gate. The plaque attests to Columbus having spent his boyhood and early youth in the house.   ALINARI/ART RESOURCE

manufactured cloth on large looms and sold it. At the back of the ground floor was a kitchen with its well, fireplace, and storage rooms, and upstairs were the bedrooms. Behind the house was an enclosed garden that reached to the old city wall. The neighbors on either side were Giovanni de Paravania and Antonio Bondi and their families.

Satisfying the family's growing food needs was the responsibility of Susanna and her servants and daughters. The staple of the Italian diet was wheat bread. (Pasta was eaten occasionally but did not become daily fare in Italy until late in the nineteenth century.) The Genoese had to import their wheat because most of the local countryside was too steep to plow. Fish was the principal source of complete protein, but, curiously, the waters around Genoa do not have much fish, so the Genoese imported preserved fish: herring from Flanders, salted fish from Provence or eastern Spain, tuna preserved in oil from Andalusia, and caviar from Asia. Susanna made large cash outlays for these imported staples.

Domenico and Susanna could supply most of their other food needs from their own land. Most city people depended on butcher shops, where they bought daily portions of fresh veal and pork, but families like Domenico's that owned farmland could also butcher whole hogs in the countryside to make a year's supply of sausages and hams. All of this preserving of food required enormous amounts of salt, which was one of Genoa's biggest imports and an important part of the import-export trade. Olive oil also served as a preservative, as well as the principal cooking fat; much of it came from the villages around the city, whose terraced hills were planted with perennials, such as the olive trees on the land Domenico owned in Quarto.

Susanna provided the rest of the family's food needs from her garden at the back of the house. Here on the traditional planting day, Easter Sunday, she would plant vegetables to supplement and diversify the family diet. Her principal crops were peas and broad beans to be dried for the winter, lettuce and other salad greens, onions, garlic, carrots, parsley, and basil. Tomatoes and potatoes, indigenous to the Americas, were not yet known in Europe. Susanna's new garlic would have been sprouting by Easter, and her perennials showing their spring renewal, with the fruit trees and rosemary bush in bloom, and the sage plant putting out new leaves.

Using table and garden scraps for feed, Susanna probably raised chickens to supply the family with eggs, an important source of protein. There would not have been enough feed in the city garden to raise a milk animal, so she would buy cheese in the village. Susanna was responsible for the health of the family, and she would have raised herbs in her garden for medicinal purposes.

Christopher learned these remedies and resorted to them for himself and his men in the Americas; for example, he wrote marginal notes about parsley as a diuretic.

Domenico began to branch out and diversify his business activities, adding commerce to manufacturing. He described himself as a cheese merchant during the 1460s, perhaps buying cheeses from farm housewives in the countryside around Quarto and Quinto to sell wholesale to the many cheese shops in the city. Throughout the same decade, he was also buying and selling wool cloth. He must have prospered in this venture, because he bought wool cloth from several men on credit, an indication that he was considered creditworthy. By late 1469, he was diversifying again, now describing himself in business documents as wool weaver and taverner.

From this fact of having become a wine dealer, some authors about a century ago concluded that Domenico was a drunkard. But this accusation reflects an ignorance of the role that wine played in the European diet. Wine and water were the daily beverages, for little else was available. The Asian drinks of coffee and tea had not yet been incorporated into the European diet, and hot chocolate was unknown because its basic ingredient, cocoa, is indigenous to the Americas.

Country people drank the wine that they produced themselves. After the harvest, farm families stored a year's supply of wine for their own use and sold the rest. Each region had its own preferences; in Genoa the favorite grape varieties were muscadet and grenache, which were a specialty of the region. Because of the city's large population, there was a great demand for wine, and in the local countryside grapes were an important commercial crop. Wholesale merchants bought the wine and transported it by pack train from villages in the mountain valleys or brought it by ship from villages along the Riviera, like Savona, one of the most important of these wine-exporting towns.

Prosperous city people owned vineyards in the country as close to the city as possible. Domenico and Susanna had their land in Quarto and Ginestreto. Traditionally, the whole family went out to prune, tie up, and weed the vines in March and April and to help the hired hands harvest the ripe grapes and make the wine in October. City people who owned no land in the country depended on the local wine merchant—the taverner—for their wine. Every day as part of her food purchases, the city housewife took the family's large flask to the taverner, who filled it from the wineskins he decanted from the casks in his cellar.

The family's life in the city lasted throughout Christopher's adolescence. But just when he was old enough to start a career himself, Domenico and Susanna moved to the smaller city of Savona on the Riviera coast east of

Genoa. Scholars have proposed several reasons for this move, although the destruction of much of Genoa's notarial archives in a bombardment of the city by the forces of Louis XIV in 1684 makes any firm conclusion difficult. The move could have been inspired by a political reversal; the city's government was taken over by the dukes of Milan in 1464. In Italian politics, such reversals usually resulted in exile for members of the losing party, and even if Domenico was not important enough to be banished from the city outright, the Fregoso supporters would have lost favorable treatment in official and political affairs.

Another reason for moving might have been Domenico's increasing involvement in the lucrative wine trade. He and Susanna bought a farm with vineyard in Légino, just outside Savona. Their house in Savona, on San Giuliano Street, was also a tavern, so Domenico had acquired the cellars necessary for business as a wine dealer.

Savona may also have represented an improvement in the family's living conditions. Domenico had represented the Genoa wool guild in negotiating an agreement of mutual membership with the wool guild of Savona. This made it possible for Domenico to move his family to the calmer and less crowded Savona and join the guild there without losing his membership in the Genoa guild. Savona may also have been attractive because many of its wool weavers came from the Fontanabuona Valley, where the Colombo family originated. Susanna and Domenico both had several cousins living in Savona.

Family solidarity was as important as political connections in the life of the Italian businessman. Domenico had a close relationship with his older brother, Antonio, who, after a brief venture in Genoese politics, remained in Quinto the rest of his life. In 1460, when Antonio apprenticed his son Giannetto to a tailor for six years, it was Domenico who acted as surety for the contract. Christopher often acted as the dutiful oldest son and conscientious big brother. After he became Admiral of the Ocean Seas, he brought his brothers and cousins from Genoa, Savona, and Quinto to command his ships and fill the offices in his admiralty.

By the time the Colombo family moved to Savona, Christopher was almost twenty years old and ready to launch his business career. Domenico had trained his son well. Every aspect of Domenico's business life had a profound and lasting impression on Christopher: the disciplined training in technical, mathematical, and linguistic skills, the constant striving for economic and social improvement, the restless moves from one place to another, and the constant involvement with family. All through his life he would follow his father's example, daringly taking the initiative in international trade to further the fortunes of the whole family.

BIBLIOGRAPHY

Airaldi, Gabriella, et al. *Cristoforo Colombo nella Genova del suo tempo*. Genoa, 1985.

Belgrano, Luigi Tommaso, and M. Staglieno, eds. "Documenti relativi a Cristoforo Colombo e alla sua famiglia." In part 2, vol. 1 of *Raccolta di documenti e studi pubblicati dalla R. commissione Colombiana pel quarto centenario dalla scoperta dell'America*. Rome, 1892.

Genoa, City of. *Colombo*. Genoa, 1931.

Heers, Jacques. *Gênes au XVᵉ siècle: Activité économique et problèmes sociaux*. Paris, 1961.

Swetz, Frank J. *Capitalism and Arithmetic: The New Math of the 15th Century*. La Salle, Ill., 1987.

Taviani, Paolo Emilio. *Christopher Columbus: The Grand Design*. London, 1985.

HELEN NADER

Early Maritime Experience

By the time Christopher Columbus settled in Spain, he was an experienced and astute import-export merchant who understood the commercial value of a new route to Asia and had developed his navigational skills during years at sea. Like other Genoese seagoing merchants, his early career had developed in the family import-export business, which was both promoted by the city government and threatened by the city's turbulent politics. The city's power to protect Genoese commerce declined during Columbus's youth, with the result that Genoa lost most of its share of Asian commerce in the eastern Mediterranean while Venice increased its share. It is some indication of Columbus's genius that he conceived a daring new solution for this problem out of the common knowledge and everyday experiences of an Italian merchant's life at sea.

The city of Genoa gave birth to Columbus's earliest maritime experience long before he went to sea. Genoa's busy harbor would have attracted any boy. The city's economy was shaped by its strategic location on a strip of coast just where the mountains came down closest to the sea. Since ancient times, the major highway between Italy and France had snaked along this narrow coastal route. Genoa's advantage over its neighbors on this coastal highway was its splendid harbor, which was deep and protected. The city government constantly maintained and improved these natural advantages. Year after year, young Christopher would have seen city work crews building and expanding wharves, docks, sea walls, a customs house, lighthouses, shipyards, and an arsenal. The harbor of Genoa was one of the maritime wonders of Europe, bustling with the coming and going of merchant ships. Columbus and his brothers must have spent hours watching the dock workers load and unload cargoes, observing the repair and refitting of merchant vessels at the arsenal, and tracing the emergent forms of new ships as they were built in the city shipyards.

Antonio Gallo, a friend of the Colombo family and official chronicler of Genoa, wrote that the brothers Christopher and Bartolomeo went to sea when they were barely teenagers. Boys from poor families would have gone at a younger age; in the western Mediterranean, boys who planned to be sailors went to sea as cabin boys or ships' apprentices as early as age ten. But Columbus's family intended him to go to sea as an international merchant, not as a sailor. So when he was ten, he was still in school finishing his study of Latin and mathematics and beginning his study of navigation and accounting.

After completing his formal education, he would have learned international commerce by practicing it. We may suppose that Columbus first went to sea as a merchant's assistant at about the age of thirteen or fourteen. Every merchant needed help on his business trips, someone to pack merchandise for the voyage, find lodging when they landed in a new port, count pieces, weigh loads, accompany him while he invested his profits in local loans or merchandise, record these sums in the ledgers, and transport the new merchandise back to the ship.

After working with an international merchant, Columbus joined his father, Domenico, who transformed the family business from manufacturing wool cloth to exporting it. In the Italian city-states, business was family business and involved every family member. Fathers held absolute control over their children's career, education, and marriage choices. Sons were an important source of skilled labor for the family's business. Traditionally, teenage sons went abroad to learn the export business by practicing it in a friend's employ and then as young adults traveling the known world to buy and sell merchandise for their father's business. They did not return to take up permanent residence at home until they married in their late twenties or thirties.

Because they were away so much, Italian businessmen in the fifteenth century wrote letters almost constantly, producing a volume of correspondence that is unique in Europe. They wrote home to report on business, currency exchange, and political developments that might affect prices and markets. Every prudent businessman kept a travel journal recording his routes, transactions, expenses, and receipts to be posted later to the ledgers in the home office. Wherever he did business he paid notaries to record even the most trivial business contracts and credit operations. Unfortunately, many Genoese legal and notarial records perished in 1684 in a fire that started when the ships of King Louis XIV bombarded the city. French artillery made direct hits on the College of Notaries and city hall, where the historical documents were kept,

as well as inflicting serious damage on the Borgo Santo Stefano, including the house of the Colombo family. None of their private letters or ledgers survived, but a Genoese author interested in the history of the Colombo family had copied many of the legal and notarial documents in 1602. These copies, together with Columbus's own reminiscences, documents from Savona, Quarto, and Quinto, and the documents that survived the 1684 fire, enable us to piece together Columbus's travels for the family business.

Where he sailed is not difficult to discover. Columbus boasted that he had sailed all the seas of the world before he went to the court of Fernando and Isabel. In his journals of his voyages to America he mentioned the Genoese-controlled island of Chios in the Aegean and the Portuguese trading post of São Jorge da Mina on the Guinea coast of West Africa. At various times he claimed that he had commanded a ship during an attack on Tunis carried out by King René of Anjou, that he was shipwrecked in a battle off the coast of Portugal and was taken in by Genoese merchants in Lisbon, and that he sailed as far north as England, Ireland, and Iceland.

Scholars once thought that these claims were exaggerated, that he had only heard about these distant places from other mariners, but most of these stories now are accepted as true to at least some degree. We know that Genoese merchants traveled everywhere it was possible for Europeans to go by sea. Genoese merchants for centuries had sailed from the Black Sea to England and Flanders. They had established trading posts with powers of self-government on the shores of the Black Sea, on islands in the Aegean Sea, outside the walls of Constantinople, and on the island of Corsica. Colonies of Genoese merchants flourished in the port cities of Trebizond, Beirut, Alexandria, Tunis, Naples, Málaga, Seville, Lisbon, Bristol, London, Paris, and Bruges. Columbus's travels fit the model of a young Genoese merchant traveling for his father's import-export business.

His travels for the family business began in 1470 and ended when he moved to Portugal and married in 1479. These were difficult and tumultuous years in Genoa's political and economic history. When Domenico Colombo set up his wool cloth manufacturing shop in the 1440s, economic opportunities seemed vast. Since the Middle Ages, citizens of Genoa had participated in lucrative commerce with Asia. Genoese businessmen traveled overland through the Middle East and Central Asia to buy high-profit spices and aromatics and brought them back to Genoese trading stations on the shores of the Black Sea, and from there through Genoese colonies in Constantinople and the Aegean islands. Other Genoese merchants in Beirut and Alexandria bought spices and aromatics directly from Arab merchants who had transported them overland from the Red Sea and Indian Ocean countries.

But by the time Columbus was a young man, Genoese possibilities in the East were shrinking drastically. The Ottoman Turks were expanding, conquering Genoese colonies and cutting off Genoa's direct access to Asian trade. The list of losses during Columbus's lifetime is sobering. The Ottoman Turks conquered Constantinople and its Genoese merchant colony of Pera in 1453; Focea in Asia Minor, whose loss had grave consequences for Genoese alum merchants, in 1455; the Aegean islands of Enos, Imbros, Samothrace, and Lemnos (whose lordship had belonged to the Genoese Gattilusio family) in 1456; Trebizond, a seaport on the Asian shores of the Black Sea with its flourishing Genoese colony, in 1461; Lesbos, the last Aegean island possessed by the Gattilusio family, in 1462; and Caffa, a Genoese colony on the Crimean Peninsula in the Black Sea, in 1475.

To compensate for these losses, western routes became all-important to Genoese shipping. Genoese merchants increased their trade with Muslim and Christian Spain, and in 1452, they formed a corporation of shareholders, the Granada Company, to do business in Málaga, the principal port of the Muslim Kingdom of Granada. Genoese merchants had been established, with their own stock exchange and chapel, in the Christian city of Seville since 1261, and by the end of the fifteenth century their numbers had swelled to about three hundred merchants, representing three hundred Genoese companies.

Political upheaval in the city of Genoa, however, moved Columbus and many other Genoese merchants away from traditional routes and products. In 1458, the Fregoso doge of Genoa invited France to take control of the city in exchange for helping Genoa attack Naples in order to wrest Sardinia from the Aragonese. The French took over the city, but their policy of imposing taxes and forced loans to finance the Neapolitan expedition sparked a reaction, and Genoa expelled the French in 1461. The Fregoso party's inability to protect Genoese colonies and trading stations in the East discredited their government and threw the city into political turbulence.

Internal strife became so disruptive that the pro-Aragonese Adorno party asked the duke of Milan to impose order. Genoa was a tempting target for the Sforza dukes of Milan, always in need of seaports for their landlocked territory. In 1464, Duke Francesco Sforza took control of Genoa's government, but he died in 1466, leaving his widow to govern for their minor son. When Duke Galeazzo Maria Sforza came of age in 1468, he began to administer Genoa with the same administrative skill and authority he exercised in Milan.

This loss of political autonomy affected the status and safety of Genoese citizens active in pro-French politics. It drove Domenico Colombo and his Fregoso allies out of the city and cut them off from the shipping facilities of Genoa's harbor. In 1470, the Colombo family moved to Savona, an independent port city federated with Genoa. In March Domenico was doing business there, describing himself as a wool weaver and taverner and participating in the Savona wool guild. For the next few years, Domenico and his wife, Susanna, described themselves as residents of Savona, not Genoa.

With Domenico virtually exiled from Genoa, Columbus began traveling as his father's agent. From 1470 through 1476, he appears in notarial documents in Savona acting in concert with his father or in Genoa acting alone. While Domenico in Savona bought and stored merchandise, his son leased cargo space and transported the merchandise to sell in foreign ports.

Because we have no direct documentary evidence of Christopher Columbus's early maritime experience, it has been a matter of much speculation. It is possible, however, to reconstruct these "lost years" by placing other surviving documents in the context of an Italian family business.

In Savona on October 25, Domenico sold the note that he held from Bartolomeo de Castagneli to Antonio Rollero for a load of cloth worth twelve lire. In Genoa, on October 31, 1470, Columbus bought a load of wine from Pietro Bellesio, paying part of the sale price in cash and signing a note for the remainder, a significant sum of more than forty-eight lire. Because Columbus was not old enough to contract debts, his father cosigned for him.

This, the first appearance of Christopher Columbus in a document, has special significance. First, it attests that he and his father were considered creditworthy by the wine vendor. Second, Columbus was the principal merchant in the transaction and owner of the wine, thus protecting the merchandise from confiscation in case his father's property were at risk. Third, Columbus was going to export this Italian wine; he swore that he would be liable for the debt in law courts in several countries including England and France. He was taking a cargo of wine to sell abroad, and he probably laid over in England or Flanders that winter. Later, he displayed a sure knowledge of the leasing arrangements for the North Atlantic; in 1494, during his second voyage to America, he advised Fernando and Isabel that the most profitable and least expensive way to lease the resupply ships for La Española was by tonnage, the same way that merchants leased ships for Flanders.

The merchant's year followed a seasonal pattern, determined by the weather, winds, and current. Traditionally, May 20 to September 24 was considered a safe period for sailing; September 24 to November 22, risky; November 22 to March 20, dangerous; and March 20 to May 20 risky. The harbor would be busy with ships coming and going from the end of February to late November; then traffic slowed during the winter layover. Traffic revived in February when merchants returned from their layovers abroad and rushed to reembark in order to take full advantage of the safe season. August saw another flurry of activity in preparation for a short round-trip voyage, probably to the western Mediterranean islands.

Seafaring merchants had a great deal of paperwork to dispatch just before a voyage; they cleared their accounts, were called by litigants to depose in legal matters, signed powers of attorney, wrote their wills, and signed for goods they had bought on consignment or on credit. Columbus signed nearly all his documents in the months of February and March, before embarking on the long voyages to the eastern Mediterranean or northern Europe, and in August before the last short trip of the sailing season. The short trips would have included trade in the famous triangle of the western Mediterranean: Genoese wool cloth to Sicily, Sicilian wheat to Ibiza or Barcelona, Spanish salt to Genoa.

Columbus was back home by March 20, 1472, when he acted as witness to a neighbor's testamentary deed in Savona, describing himself as a wool dealer in Genoa. He and Domenico began acquiring new merchandise to sell abroad. The most common Genoese export was wool cloth—thousands of bolts of it every year. Domenico in Savona began to purchase wool cloth in wholesale quantities, purchases that can be correlated with his son's voyages. Columbus would take the cloth to sell in Spain, North Africa, or the Middle East, and with the profits buy local products, especially wheat, to sell in Genoa. Domenico used the profits from each voyage to buy more wool cloth for export.

In June 1472 Domenico bought 316 pounds of wool cloth on credit from Giovanni de Signorio for forty lire. Columbus probably sold these in Sicily or another western Mediterranean port just in time to buy the new grain harvested and threshed during the summer. In late summer, he was back in Savona, probably with a cargo of wheat to sell at a good profit.

On August 26, 1472, Columbus and Domenico together bought another 736 pounds of wool cloth from Giovanni de Signorio, for 140 lire payable in six months. Columbus could have made another round trip during these six months and returned with enough profit to enable Domenico to buy 418 pounds of Savona wool cloth on credit from Andrea Drago on February 12, 1473.

On June 4, 1473, Domenico bought seven white wool cloths on consignment from Ludovico Multedo, citizen of Savona, to be paid for within five months, with Domenico keeping the profits or incurring the loss. Two months later, in Domenico's shop in Savona, Columbus and his brother Giovanni Pelegrino agreed to their parents' sale of their house on dell'Olivella Street in Genoa to the Genoese wool weaver Petro de Cella. Giovanni Pelegrino

was now old enough to share with Christopher the burden of owning legal title to their parents' property in Genoa.

The most profitable Genoese imports were spices and aromatics from the eastern Mediterranean. Although Ottoman expansion had deprived the Genoese of their traditional markets and sources, they were still able to participate indirectly in the Levant trade because Genoa held Chios, an island in the middle of the sea lanes through the Aegean Sea. A consortium of Genoese shipowners, who called themselves the Giustiniani family, controlled all trade and shipping on Chios. By the last half of the fifteenth century, Genoese shippers were using very large ships that carried high-value cargo directly from Chios to winter over in England and Flanders, without stopping to trade in Mediterranean ports.

While Chios was an important entrepôt for goods in transit from the Muslim East to the Christian West, its importance to the story of Christopher Columbus revolves around a local product, gum mastic. Gum mastic is the sap of certain kinds of acacia trees that grow mostly in East Africa and Asia. Because the substance is slightly soluble and eventually dissolves when chewed, it was used in early medicine as a carrier that would release drugs slowly. It is also known as gum arabic, because the first sugar traders, the Arabs, got the idea of mixing gum with sugar as a thickening agent in candies and sweets (it is the basis of jujube, marshmallow, and licorice paste). Gum mastic and related resins fetched a very high price per ounce, and since the only place in Europe where that variety of acacia grows is in Chios, the Giustiniani were able to control the price by spacing the harvest of sap from the trees and by limiting the number of fleets that sailed from Genoa to Chios to just one or two every decade.

Columbus was obviously familiar with this lucrative trade; he mistakenly reported finding the Chios variety of acacia trees on more than one Caribbean island. This seems conclusive evidence that Christopher Columbus traveled to Chios as a young man. This trip could have taken place only on Genoese fleets, and that fact places the voyage in 1474 or 1475, the only years during Columbus's youth when Genoese fleets went to Chios. The first of these, Gian Antonio di Negro's fleet, left from Savona for Chios in May 1474. The second, Goffredo de Spinola's fleet, left from Genoa in September 1475. Two of the ships in the 1475 voyage were owned by Paolo di Negro and Nicolò Spinola. Although Columbus's name does not appear on the passenger or crew lists, he probably sailed on the ships of one or both of these men; he named them and their heirs among his creditors in the codicil to his will. While in Chios, the fleet would have learned of another disaster; in the summer of 1475, the Ottoman Turks captured Caffa, the last Genoese trading post on the Black Sea.

Meanwhile, the Colombo family business flourished.

Father and son bought merchandise on a large scale, obtaining credit for sums of money equal to one-half the price of a farm or city house. Domenico's status in Savona continued to rise, and he changed his self-description from wool weaver (*textor pannorum*) to wool dealer (*lanerius*). On April 14, 1474, Domenico acknowledged receipt of 250 lire in full payment for his farm in Ginestreto. Six months later, he bought a farm in Legino, a village in Savona's territory, for a total price of 250 lire. Domenico agreed to pay 50 lire in wool cloths every year on Saint Michael's Day (September 25) as payment for the farm, which included a vineyard, grain fields, an orchard, woods, and a farmhouse. This farm was next to that of the vendor, Corrado da Cuneo, whose son Michele would accompany Columbus on his second voyage to America.

While the family at home was prospering, Columbus was exposed to all the dangers and novelties of the sea, from the vagaries of weather, shifting currents, and high winds to pirate attacks. Piracy was part of warfare and a constant menace to shipping in the western Mediterranean. The richest shipowners hired military professionals to defend their ships from pirates and sailed together in fleets in order to help one another in case of attack. Because Genoa was under French domination and at war with Aragón during most of Columbus's youth, the most dangerous routes for Genoese ships were the Straits of Gibraltar and the western Mediterranean routes from Sardinia to Sicily.

From 1468 to November 1476, when Genoa was under the rule of pro-Aragón Milan, the danger came in Atlantic waters from French pirates. On August 13, 1476, Columbus was involved in a battle off the coast of Portugal. A fleet of five Genoese ships (probably including ships returning from Chios) embarked in Noli and passed through the Straits of Gibraltar headed for England. The Genoese convoy included one galleass belonging to Goffredo Spinola, one whaler belonging to Nicolò Spinola, one galleass belonging to Terano Squarcifico, one galleass commanded by Gian Antonio di Negro, and one "bechalla" (a ship of Flemish construction) commanded by Cristoforo Salvago, which had many Savonese aboard, probably including Christopher Columbus. This fleet was attacked by a French squadron commanded by the vice admiral Guillaume Casenove (Coulon). Only two Genoese ships survived—those of Goffredo Spinola and Gian Antonio di Negro. The others sank, along with four French ships. The bechalla caught fire, everyone jumped overboard, and Columbus saved himself by grabbing a floating oar and swimming. He told his son Fernando a garbled story of swimming about two leagues (seven to eight miles) to the coast and coming ashore not far from Lisbon, where he was taken in by Genoese merchants.

Although Columbus survived, he lost a great deal in this shipwreck. His merchandise in the cargo hold, now at the bottom of the sea, was probably covered by marine insurance. His personal possessions in his sea chest, however, would have been a total loss. Inventories of sailors' chests show that he would have taken on board enough clothing, liquid assets, and personal possessions to last the voyage and a winter in the North.

In 1493, Genoa was suffering an outbreak of bubonic plague, which was believed to be transmitted on merchandise, especially cloth. When ships whose crews had experienced deaths at sea from the illness came into port, the government confiscated the sea chests of the deceased sailors, inventoried their contents, and had them purified as a public health measure. (Health officials sprinkled the goods with vinegar or exposed them to dry air to purify them.) The inventories of two of these chests (on p. 172) suggest what the contents of Columbus's sea chest would have been, although his would have contained more clothing and property than the common sailor's and less military equipment than the soldier's. Also, Columbus would have been carrying account ledgers and probably more paper, ink, and books than either of the two men who died in 1493.

Columbus did not remain in Lisbon long following his shipwreck in 1476. On September 12, a new fleet left Genoa to pick up the remnants of the shipwrecked fleet in Lisbon and go on to England. Financed cooperatively by the Genoese merchant colony in London, the fleet may have continued from London to winter over in Bristol. This voyage would have a lasting effect on Columbus's imagination and ambition. He told his son Fernando that in February 1477 he had been to an island called Thule that was as large as England and lay seventy-three degrees north of the equator. The winter of 1476–1477 was an exceptionally mild one in the North Atlantic, and some scholars speculate that it was Iceland he visited.

While Columbus traveled on this, the most far-reaching of his early maritime experiences, the political situation back home in Genoa once again turned in favor of the Colombo family. The loss of Caffa and Milanese inability to protect Genoese shipping in the western Mediterranean weakened the Sforza position in Genoa. Domenico Colombo dared to reenter the city and conduct some business there on November 5, 1476. A few days later, Duke Galeazzo María Sforza died in Milan at the hands of assassins. Genoa allied again with France. Still, the city had lost much of its attraction for Domenico and Susanna, and in January 1477 they transferred title on their first Genoa house, on dell'Olivella Street, having received payment of the final installment.

By this time, Columbus was twenty-five or twenty-six years old, legally an adult and able to contract debts and marriage without his parents' consent. In 1478, he was back in Lisbon. At that time, he was the agent of a Genoese merchant, Paolo di Negro, who was buying and

Inventories of Two Sailors' Chests (Genoa, September 27, 1493)

Inventory, compiled by order of the Health Office of the Commune of Genoa, of the objects and property retrieved from the chest of the deceased Valarano Frastaria, seaman on the ship of the noble Giovanni Jacopo Spinola. The objects and property listed below were consigned by orders of the Office to Melchione Marenco to be purified with the chest.

A gilded silver ring in a small, light leather purse.

A long sword with scabbard.

A large basket full of dates weighing about 35 lbs.

Three pairs of stockings, two made of black wool and the third of white wool.

A round basket of Morisco palm.

Two vests of turquoise wool with sleeves and another without sleeves.

A man's garment of green wool.

A wool tunic.

Two shirts.

Wool underpants.

A black cap.

Four linen handkerchiefs.

Two small hampers, empty.

A lead bullet.

A pair of scissors.

Iron tongs with wood handles.

A long sheet of parchment, written on and erased.

Inventory, compiled by order of the Health Office of the Commune of Genoa, of the objects and property found in the chest of the deceased Paulino, artilleryman on the ship of the noble Giovanni Jacopo Spinola. The objects and property listed below were consigned by orders of the Office to Melchione Marenco to be purified with the chest.

A Morisco purse containing 7 coins from Ebosa and two handkerchiefs, one larger than the other.

A pair of short swords with hilts and scabbard decorated with silver.

A spherical pearl that must be worth about 40 soldi, wrapped in a sheet of paper and piece of black silk cloth.

A piece of jasper and a piece of rock for touching gold and silver, in a little sack.

An open pin.

A heavy black cap.

A *scarsella* (?) of light colored leather.

A wool *pappafico* (?).

Another black cap, used.

A man's garment of red wool, another of green wool, and a very old one of fustian.

Three pairs of lined stockings of red wool, one of them almost new.

A man's garment in linen.

Two black wool vests.

A man's black wool tunic.

A piece of heavy black wool cloth.

A bundle of various scraps and pieces of wool cloth.

A man's garment of black wool, not finished.

Nine men's shirts.

Six towels, some in good condition, others in bad shape.

A long sack about six palms in length.

One blanket.

Three handkerchiefs.

A small piece of wool cloth.

A hemmed towel about five palms in length.

Two hides.

A pair of long, fine knee boots.

One shirt sleeve.

A piece of white wool cloth.

A red fur hood.

Some scraps of velvet tied up.

A piece of red wool cloth.

Two shoes.

A prayer book written on paper with leather-bound covers.

A printed book with covers.

A pair of linen stockings.

A long sword with scabbard.

A short sword with scabbard.

Two shoes.

One pickax.

One inkwell made of cypress wood.

A small box with a few odds and ends.

A hemp sack containing some squid bones (? *ossa sepiarum*)

A lump of iron weighing about 10 pounds.

A *verrina* (?)

A small basket, about one palm in diameter and pretty, with its cover.

Two bunches of string.

shipping sugar from Madeira to Genoa with the money and instructions of Luigi Centurione in Genoa. With the money that Centurione had forwarded to Paolo, Columbus went to Madeira in June and bought twenty-one tons of sugar ready to be loaded on the ship of Fernando Palencia, then in the harbor.

Many years later, Columbus referred to the Atlantic sugar trade in knowledgeable detail. In the letter to the Spanish monarchs in which he advised them to lease ships for America the same way ships were leased for the Flanders trade, Columbus also offered advice on purchasing sugar from Madeira. In 1494, the Spaniards on La Española were suffering an epidemic, and sugar was one of the most recommended foods for the ill. Columbus wrote:

> For the sustenance of the healthy as well as for the sick, it would be very good to have 50 pipes of sugar syrup from the island of Madeira, because it is the best and most healthful sustenance in the world. It usually does not cost more than 2 ducats without the cask. If Their Highnesses would order a caravel to stop over there on the way back here, it could buy the syrup and also 10 boxes of sugar, which are desperately needed. This is the best time of year, between now [January 30] and the month of April, to find it available and get a good price on it.

Columbus now had enough experience and stature to command a ship. He told his son Fernando that he had once tried to attack an Aragonese ship while commanding a ship in a French attack on Tunis. The details have never been clear, which is not surprising; the story would have been an embarrassing admission that Columbus had fought against King Fernando's father, King Juan II of Aragón. The events must have taken place while the Angevins were at war with the Aragonese from 1472 to 1479. Columbus claimed that King René of Anjou sent him to Tunis to capture the Aragonese galleass *Fernandina.* Near the island of San Pietro off Sardinia they found the ship with three others. His crew wanted to go back to Marseille for reinforcements. Columbus agreed, only to fake the ship's course by night, so that the next morning, when the crew expected to be off Marseille, they found themselves off Cape Carthage in North Africa.

In August 1479, Columbus was in Genoa and ready to embark on another voyage. Either Luigi Centurione had not received the sugar shipment or Paolo's efforts did not satisfy him, because now, more than a year after the fact, he called Columbus to depose about the matter. On August 25, Columbus testified that he had received the money in Lisbon from Paolo di Negro and had used it on Madeira to purchase the sugar for Centurione. Considerable doubt is cast on this statement by the fact that, just before he died, he ordered his son Diego to pay thirty thousand Portuguese reales to the heirs of Luigi Centurione. In 1479, however, his deposition pictured him as a prosperous young man with many possibilities. He described himself as twenty-seven years old and possessing more than a hundred florins in cash, and stated that he was embarking the next morning. It was his last visit to his native city and probably his final voyage in the Mediterranean.

The shift from the Mediterranean to the Atlantic had been gradual. Columbus may well have found Lisbon a more congenial setting for his future than Genoa, with its precarious political and economic situation.

His maritime experience had encompassed both the Mediterranean and the Atlantic, often on the same voyages. For years, he moved back and forth from Genoa to Lisbon, where he was part of the colony of foreign businessmen. He formed lifelong connections with the Genoese merchants in Lisbon; on his deathbed, Columbus ordered his son to pay twenty-five hundred Portuguese reales to "Antonio Vazo, a Genoese merchant who used to live in Lisbon," and the equivalent of a half mark of silver to a Jew who used to live at the entrance to the Jewish quarter in Lisbon, though he did not recall this man's name.

Portuguese merchants, in turn, were also moving back and forth between the Atlantic and the Mediterranean. One example alone indicates the degree to which ships, merchants, and merchandise that we traditionally associate with the Atlantic where equally part of Mediterranean commerce. If Columbus had been in Genoa during the winter layover of 1474–1475, he could have met a Portuguese ship's captain named Bartolomeu Dias, who on January 3, 1475, received a safe-conduct from the city government of Genoa. Dias was the future discoverer of the Cape of Good Hope, carrying on trade in sugar and slaves between the Atlantic and the western Mediterranean. He was also engaged in piracy and the slave trade in the Mediterranean. In 1478, Dias, captain of the ship *Charachone,* again arrived in an Italian port city, Porto Pisano, with a cargo of sugar on the account of a Florentine company, the Cambini. The same ship probably unloaded sardines sent from Lisbon by the merchant-banker Bartolomeu Marchionni. On his return from Porto Pisano, Dias stopped in Genoa to buy slaves and continued from there to Lisbon, indulging along the way in a bit of piracy on behalf of King João II, who was at war with Castile. In Lisbon on June 21, 1478, King João issued an acknowledgment of debt granting Dias one-fifth of the prisoners he had captured at sea in payment of the twelve thousand reals that Dias had spent on the slave he had bought for the king in Genoa.

Columbus married a Portuguese woman, Felipa Moniz y Perestrelo, probably in 1479, and from then on used

Lisbon, already familiar to him, at his home port. Now Columbus was no longer a foreigner. By virtue of his marriage, he acquired Portuguese citizenship and therefore the right to trade in all Portuguese overseas possessions. He probably had not participated in the Africa trade earlier, because the Portuguese monarchy tried to reserve it for Portuguese citizens and ships, just as Genoa reserved trade with Chios for its own citizens and ships. What does seem certain is that, after 1479, Columbus made his living navigating the Atlantic and doing business in Atlantic ports. The most lucrative Portuguese trade formed a triangle: Portuguese slavers loaded slaves from sub-Saharan Africa, sold them to sugar plantations on the Portuguese island of Madeira, and used the profits to buy sugar, which they would sell in Europe.

Columbus, through his Portuguese citizenship, acquired the opportunity to participate in this trade, which placed him in the midst of the Atlantic currents and winds that would eventually carry him to America. Through observation, he made those winds and waters his own. He also gained access to the nautical lore and wisdom of Portuguese mariners and shipbuilders, who were at that time making many subtle and ingenious improvements in ship design, sails, and navigational equipment to cope with Atlantic conditions.

These years in the Mediterranean and the Atlantic were a crucial period in Columbus's life. In the Mediterranean, he became accustomed to the piracy, violent storms, and warfare that were constant dangers for merchant shipping. In Genoa's slave market he learned to see humans from Asia and Africa as commodities. In Genoa's eastern trade with Asia, he learned the financial and military risks associated with trading posts and colonies financed and governed by merchant companies without a government to protect them.

In the Atlantic voyages he traveled farther north and south than the Mediterranean allowed and encountered oceanic conditions that existed nowhere else. In the mid-Atlantic, counterclockwise ocean currents and winds made sailing straight north from sub-Saharan Africa difficult without first going west. Coping with these conditions had driven Portuguese and Spanish merchant ships far out into the Atlantic, and there they had discovered the Madeiras, the Azores, and the Canary and Cape Verde islands. King João II sent a heavily manned and armed fleet to build a fortified trading post, São Jorge da Mina, on the West African coast south of Cape Bojador in 1482.

Columbus traveled these same Atlantic routes and integrated their lessons into a scheme for reestablishing direct trade with Asia by sailing west. He learned the currents and winds for both the outward and homeward passages to Africa. He calculated the latitudes of Atlantic locations as far north (Thule) and south (Mina) as Europeans had ever sailed in order to calculate the circumference

of the earth. His writing is full of Atlantic Ocean vocabulary and Atlantic nautical terms; it is nearly devoid of such terms from the Mediterranean. He knew the flora and fauna of the Atlantic—its birds, seaweed, and marine life. He knew the Portuguese slave trade in Africa and its importance to sugar production on Madeira. He knew the only Portuguese site on the African mainland, São Jorge da Mina, whose survival depended on royal financing and protection.

Columbus's maritime expertise was the product of long experience in the import-export trade of the Atlantic and Mediterranean. He knew that the king of Portugal acted as a partner in the commercial voyages of Portuguese ships, and that, though Portuguese merchants sacrificed a fifth of their profits to the king, they received royal financial and military backing. Everything in Christopher Columbus's early maritime experience had taught him that partnership with the monarchy provided a level of protection unknown in the precarious and high-risk world of the Genoese merchant companies.

BIBLIOGRAPHY

Ballesteros Beretta, Antonio. *Cristóbal Colón y el descubrimiento de América*. 2 vols. Barcelona, 1945.

Borghesi, Vilma. *Il Mediterraneo tra due rivoluzioni nautiche (secoli XIV–XVII)*. Florence, 1976.

Columbus, Ferdinand. *The Life of the Admiral Christopher Columbus*. Translated by Benjamin Keen. New Brunswick, N.J., 1959.

Documenti relativi a Cristoforo Colombo e alla sua famiglia. Compiled and edited by L. T. Belgrano and M. Staglieno. In *Raccolta Colombiana*. Part 2, vol. 1.

Fonseca, Luis A. *O essencial sobre Bartolomeu Dias*. Lisbon, 1987.

Genoa, City of. *Colombo*. Bergamo, 1932.

Grendi, E. "Traffico portuale, naviglio mercantile e consolati genovesi nel Cinquecento." *Revista Storica Italiana* 80 (1968): 593–629.

Heers, Jacques. *Gênes au XVe siècle: Activités economiques et problèmes sociaux*. Paris, 1961.

Heers, Jacques. "Le royaume de Grenade et la politique marchande de Gênes en Occident (XVe siècle)." *Moyen Âge* 63 (1957): 87–121.

Lane, F. C. "The Mediterranean Spice Trade: Evidence of Its Revival in the Sixteenth Century." *American Historical Review* 45 (1940): 581–590.

Martini, Dario G. *Cristoforo Colombo tra ragione e fantasia*. Genoa, 1987.

Morison, Samuel Eliot. *Admiral of the Ocean Sea: A Life of Christopher Columbus*. 2 vols. Boston, 1942.

Phillips, Carla, and William D. Phillips, Jr. *The Worlds of Christopher Columbus*. Cambridge, forthcoming.

Pryor, John H. *Commerce, Shipping, and Naval Warfare in the Medieval Mediterranean*. London, 1987.

Pryor, John H. *Geography, Technology, and War: Studies in the Mediterranean, 649–1571*. Cambridge, 1988.

Salinero, Giulio. *Annotationes Julii Salinerii iureconsulti savonensis ad Cornelium Tacitum.* Genoa, 1602.

HELEN NADER

Columbus in Portugal

Christopher Columbus first arrived in Portugal in May 1476 during a naval battle in which the ship he was serving on was destroyed. Forced to swim for his life, he landed on the beach at Lagos, near Cape St. Vincent, where Prince Henry the Navigator had first set in motion the systematic exploration of the West African coast that was eventually to lead the Portuguese to India.

Columbus's Experience as a Merchant. After recovering from his wounds and the long swim, Columbus went to Lisbon and soon joined a second fleet sent from Genoa to pick up the survivors of the battle of Cape St. Vincent; at the end of December 1476, the Genoese fleet continued the voyage interrupted five months before.

One of the organizers of the second Genoese fleet was Paolo di Negro (or di Negri), who was well known for his trading activities in the route from Lisbon to the Netherlands by way of England. His fleet would have brought Columbus to England about February 1477. He probably arrived at Southampton and he may have gone to London; two prominent Genoese trading families, the Spinola and di Negro, maintained establishments in both cities. It is most probable that Columbus visited Bristol, where he was introduced to English commerce with Iceland. The return route of the Bristol trading vessels was by the west coast of Ireland, their first objective there being the port of Galway. At that time the English merchants had a virtual monopoly of the Iceland fish trade. They brought the fish from Iceland along the western coast of Ireland, making landfall at Galway, and transferring the fish to Portuguese vessels to meet the insatiable Portuguese demand for bacalao, or cod.

The little that is known about Columbus's voyage to Iceland comes on the authority of his son Fernando, quoting from a now lost memorandum from his father:

In the month of February 1477 I sailed one hundred leagues beyond the island of Tile [Iceland]. Its southern part is seventy-three degrees north and not sixty-three degrees as some say. Furthermore, it does not lie on the meridian where Ptolemy says the West begins, but a great deal farther west. To this island, which is as big as England, the English merchants go, especially those from Bristol. And at the time when I was there the sea was not frozen, but there were vast tides, so great that they rose and fell as much as twenty-six fathoms [about fifty feet] in depth.

This passage, which was intended to prove that the Arctic zones were habitable, contains so many improbabilities that some critics refuse to believe that Columbus ever went to Iceland. His report of the height of the tides is wrong; the maximum range at Reykjavík is less than fifteen feet. His statement that the southern coastline of Iceland is at seventy-three degrees is wrong; it is in fact at sixty-three degrees, sixty minutes. There seems little doubt, however, that Columbus did visit Iceland in 1477 because of an annotation in the margin of his personal copy of the *Historia rerum ubique gestarum* (*History of memorable things that have happened in my time*) by Enea Silvio Piccolomini (Pius II): "Men of Cathay, which is toward the Orient, have come hither. We have seen many remarkable things, especially in Galway, in Ireland, a man and a woman of most unusual appearance have come to land in two boats."

The Iceland voyage appears to be the only occasion on which he could have visited Galway. His assumption that the two bodies he saw came from the Orient suggest that he was already obsessed with the idea of Marco Polo's Cathay. The unusual appearance of the two dead bodies strongly suggests that they were Inuit (Eskimos) who were probably caught in an Atlantic storm off Labrador and eventually dashed lifeless against the Irish coast. These elements do fit together with the trade route pioneered by the Bristol men, and the Portuguese vessel to which Columbus transferred would have brought him back in the autumn of 1477 to Portugal, where he was to stay for nearly a decade.

It is not known how much time he spent at sea or in Lisbon, where his younger brother Bartolomé was living. Antonio Gallo (d. 1510), who was the official chronicler of the republic of Genoa from 1477 until his death, says that Bartolomé had settled in Lisbon before Christopher arrived, opened a chart-making business, took his elder brother into partnership, and imparted to him the ideas that led to his voyage to the New World. Andrés Bernáldez of Seville, in whose house Columbus lived when he returned from the second voyage to America, describes him in his contemporary history of the reign of the Catholic monarchs as a "hawker of printed books . . . very skilled in the art of cosmography and the mapping of the world." Samuel Eliot Morison (1942) believed that Columbus was a skilled chart maker, and that the two brothers became partners in providing articles for which the Portuguese maritime expansion created a great demand. Like every sailor in other centuries, he may have worked at several trades, as a mapmaker and bookseller in the winter months and as a merchant seaman at other times. It is possible that he may have had a commercial career as factor or agent for the rich Genoese merchants in Lisbon. Some Columbus scholars, for example, David B. Quinn, believe that for the first twenty-five years of his life Columbus was primarily a trader, part of the widespread network of Genoese traders who had outposts in the Iberian lands, and who were active in the later fifteenth century as far afield as Chios in the east, England and France in the north, and Madeira and Guinea in the west and south. One family, the Spinolas, appears to have been prolific enough to have had members or even trading concerns in most if not all of these places; a Spinola is named in Columbus's will. But most of the Genoese trade at that time was between Genoa and Portugal, England, and Flanders, a new pattern of trade that was established about 1466 due to the loss of most of the Genoese colonies in the eastern Mediterranean, as well as to political strife at home that increased the flow of emigration from Genoa to the west.

Of all the voyages that Columbus may have made during his early Portuguese years, his voyage to Madeira in 1478 and 1479 is fairly well documented. In 1478, Paolo di Negro, a Genoese living in Lisbon who had organized the fleet in 1477, commissioned Columbus to go to Madeira to purchase sugar on behalf of Luigi Centurione, a resident of Genoa. Columbus chartered a Portuguese vessel and sailed from Lisbon for Madeira in July 1478, but without having received 1,290 ducats that Centurione had sent to di Negro. In Madeira, Columbus placed an order for the sugar with Erogio Catalão, expecting any day to receive the money from Lisbon with which to pay for it. But when he received from di Negro only 103 ducats and woolen goods that found no buyers, he was able to load only a small portion of the sugar he had ordered. When Columbus finally reached Genoa, it was only natural that protests were lodged by the ship captain, who wanted payment for the entire amount of the freight even though he had not carried all the merchandise stipulated in the contract, and by Centurione, who wanted to know why Columbus had only delivered a fraction of the merchandise he had ordered and paid for in advance.

Both protests were heard and duly recorded by a notary public, Gerolamo Ventimiglia, who signed the notarial documents in Genoa on August 21, 1479, in the presence of Columbus as both witness and concerned party. In his sworn statement before the notary, Columbus declared that he was a citizen of Genoa, that he was about twenty-seven years old, that he had one hundred florins on his person, and that he intended to depart for Lisbon the following day. (This record, the "Asseretto document," was discovered in 1904 by Hugo Asseretto; it is held in the notarial archives of the government of Genoa.)

Columbus's Marriage to Felipa Perestrelo y Moniz. It was probably in the year 1479 that the twenty-eight-year-old Columbus took a decisive step in his private life and one that was to prove equally important to his future career. He married Felipa Perestrelo y Moniz, the daughter of Isabel Moniz and Bartolomeu Perestrelo, the first governor of the island of Porto Santo in the Madeiras. Practically all that we know of this marriage is derived from the

writings of the principal biographers of Columbus, namely, Fernando Colón, youngest son of the Admiral, and Bartolomé de las Casas, his friend and admirer.

Much has been written about how and why Christopher Columbus, the son of a humble weaver, a part-time seaman and trader, and dealer in books and maps, came to meet, woo, and marry a woman of aristocratic birth on both sides of her family. According to Fernando, they met at the Convento dos Santos in Lisbon where Columbus used to attend mass. The convent belonged to the nuns of the military order of Santiago; its purpose was to provide a home for the wives and daughters of the knights of the order while the knights were at war. For an ambitious young man eager to marry into upper-class society, there could have been no better place to choose for his churchgoing, since only in church was it possible for the men and women of different social strata to meet.

Nothing is known about the appearance of Felipa, but whether she was attractive or not, she was undoubtedly a good catch. As for Columbus himself, Gonzalo Fernández de Oviedo, who first saw him in Barcelona in 1492, fourteen years after Felipa met him, describes him

as a man of fine appearance, well built, taller than most, and with strong limbs. His eyes were lively and his features in good proportion. . . . His hair was very red and his face ruddy and freckled. He spoke well, was tactful in his manner and was extremely talented. He was a good Latinist and a very learned cosmographer, gracious when he wished, but hot tempered if he was crossed.

Fernando explains the attraction that Felipa had for him in the following manner: "Inasmuch as he behaved very honorably, and was a man of such fine presence, and withal so honest, that she held such conversation with him and enjoyed such friendship with him that she became his wife." As far as Columbus was concerned, whether or not he was deeply attracted to Felipa, the advantages of the match were immense. She was to prove the key that opened the way for his acceptance into a world where power and influence could be courted and obtained. Though very little is known about Felipa herself, a great deal is known about her family.

The Moniz and Perestrelo families. On her mother's side, Felipa came from the powerful family of Moniz, which had been in close contact with the Portuguese royal family since the twelfth century, when its founder, Egas Moniz, became governor under Afonso Henriques, the first king of Portugal. One of the gates in the Castle of St. George, an enormous fortress overlooking Lisbon and the Tagus River, still bears the name of Egas Moniz, who defended the gate by himself during a battle against the Moors in 1147, preventing them from penetrating the walls. The grandfather of Felipa, Gil Ayres Moniz, ruled one of the richest seigniories of the Algarve, the last of the lands conquered from the Moors, and accompanied Henry the Navigator when he took part in the conquest of Ceuta in 1415.

On her father's side, the family was no less illustrious and perhaps more powerful. Felipa's father, Bartolomeu, descended from the Italian Pelestrellos or Pallastrellis of Piacenza, one of whom, Filippo or Filippone Palestrelli, moved to Portugal in the year 1385; he established himself first in Porto and later in Lisbon and dedicated himself to commerce. With him when he left Italy was his wife, Catarina Sforza. On January 8, 1399, Filippo obtained a tax exemption from King João I, after proving that he was descended from an aristocratic line (in those days, the nobility did not pay taxes). Filippo had four children—Richarte, Isabel, Branca, and Bartolomeu; the last was the father-in-law of Columbus. The oldest son, Richarte, sometimes called Rafael, took holy orders and rose to become prior of the parish of Santa Marinha of Lisbon. He fathered two children whom he legitimized in 1423. Later, his descendants played outstanding roles in the enterprise of India; one of his grandsons was among the first Portuguese to visit China. Isabel and Branca became the mistresses of the great churchman and powerful political figure, Pedro de Noronha, archbishop of Lisbon, who was related to the reigning families of both Castile and Portugal.

Noronha's mother was the daughter of King Fernando of Portugal (r. 1367–1383) and his father was related to the royal family of Castile. One of his brothers was count of Vila Real; another, Sancho, was count of Odemira; his sister Constanza married Afonso, count of Barcelos, later duke of Braganza, bastard son of King João I. In 1424, when Pedro de Noronha was barely twenty-eight years old, he was elected archbishop of Lisbon. With Isabel Perestrelo he had a son, João. With the younger sister Branca he had three children—Isabel, Diogo, and Pedro. Despite his position as head of the Portuguese church, he had all his offspring officially legitimized in 1444 and saw to it that Isabel married into the royal house of Braganza and his two sons rapidly reached the highest posts in the state and in the church. Branca Perestrelo, the younger sister, was eventually abandoned by Noronha and retired to a convent until her marriage to Eanes de Beja.

Bartolomeu Perestrelo, Captain Donatário of Porto Santo. On the basis of Columbus's two earliest biographies, by his son Fernando and by Las Casas, the view has been traditionally held that Bartolomeu Perestrelo, Columbus's father-in-law, had been given the hereditary captaincy of the island of Porto Santo because of his seamanship and valorous deeds. Both Fernando Colón and Las Casas elaborate a story about papers and instruments and hints about islands to be discovered that

Perestrelo's widow was supposed to have given her son-in-law, Columbus. The part played by Columbus's father-in-law in the discovery of Porto Santo is described by Las Casas in the following manner:

> As days went by, the mother-in-law realized how bent on the things of the sea and of cosmography was Cristóbal Colón . . . so that . . . she told him how her husband, Perestrelo, had also been a person leaning to affairs of the sea, and how, by order of Prince Henry, he had gone in company with two other gentlemen to the island of Porto Santo, recently discovered, and soon after, he alone was entrusted with the task of populating the island; and the Prince [Henry the Navigator] granted him properties in it; and as in those days there was a great boiling over of the practice and exercise of discoveries on the coast of Guinea and on the islands of the Ocean Sea and the said Bartolomeu Perestrelo had the hope of discovering other islands from his, as indeed they were discovered . . . he probably had instruments and papers and pictures on navigation which the mother-in-law gave Colón, from seeing and reading which, he received much pleasure. . . ."

It is plain that Las Casas himself suggests that the existence of "instruments, papers, and pictures" belonging to Perestrelo is a mere conjecture. Salvador de Madariaga, a twentieth-century biographer of Columbus, believes that it was the connection of the Perestrelo family with Archbishop Noronha that supplies the key to the reputation of Bartolomeu Perestrelo as a discoverer and populator.

Perestrelo's name is not included among the discoverers of Porto Santo by the chronicler João de Barros, who entitled a chapter in his *Décadas da Ásia* (1552) "How João Gonçalvez and Tristão Vaz discovered the island of Porto Santo, owing to a tempest which took them there." Barros claims to have gotten his information from the chronicler Gomes Eanes de Zurara, who wrote about a hundred years before him. Referring to João Gonçalvez and Tristão Vaz, Barros writes that the two knights, who were sent on a discovery voyage by Prince Henry the Navigator, accidentally discovered the island of Porto Santo. Henry was extremely pleased to hear about the discovery and even more pleased when the two discoverers told him that they wanted to return to colonize it. Many others who had heard about the discovery also offered to settle there, among them Bartolomeu Perestrelo, who was a "gentleman of the household of Prince João," Prince Henry's brother. Henry then had three ships outfitted, one of which he gave to Bartolomeu Perestrelo and the two others to Gonçalvez and Vaz, the original discoverers. In the two years that they lived on Porto Santo, it was impossible to sow or plant anything because of the overpopulation of the rabbits that Perestrelo had brought there, and so the colonizers began to hate the work and their way of life, and Bartolomeu Perestrelo decided to return to Lisbon.

From Barros we also learn that the knights who discovered the island of Porto Santo, even if much against their will, were definitely Gonçalvez and Vaz; Perestrelo was a hanger-on of Prince João who was attracted by the prospect of profit and was given a ship through favoritism; and his efforts toward populating the island that his widow, in Las Casas's version, says was entrusted to him alone were limited to breeding rabbits.

Nevertheless, his influence at court convinced Prince Henry in 1425 to entrust him with another expedition to populate Porto Santo. His lack of success does not seem to have warranted a long stay, for in 1431 he was given a house in Lisbon, where in 1437 he was registered as a municipal councilor. In 1446, over twenty years after his two unsuccessful attempts and two years after the legitimization of his sisters' children had demonstrated the power of Pedro de Noronha, Perestrelo was granted by Prince Henry the title of capitão donatário (grant-holder) of Porto Santo.

The Perestrelo family, then, enjoyed power and social standing and a well-known permanent connection with the island of Porto Santo, the captaincy of which was hereditary. And since Bartolomeu Perestrelo lacked a talent for seafaring and competence as a colonizer, it is obvious, though it was not to Las Casas, that his supposed "papers and instruments" could not have been the cause or the inspiration of Columbus's design. This fact strengthens the argument that the scheme or "urge" toward discovery was active in Columbus's mind before he ever married Felipa Perestrelo and therefore that he probably married into the Perestrelo family because it was so powerful in Porto Santo, which was an admirable base for exploring the western seas.

The marriage of Bartolomeu Perestrelo with Isabel Moniz—Columbus's mother-in-law—must have taken place in 1449 or 1450. It seems that Isabel was his second or third wife. With his first wife, Perestrelo had had three children; and he had three children with Isabel Moniz: Bartolomeu, Felipa, who married Columbus, and Violante or Briolanja, with whom Columbus maintained good relations long after the death of his wife.

Bartolomeu Perestrelo lived in Porto Santo from 1446 probably until his death in 1457, when Isabel Moniz moved back to Lisbon. She had looked for someone capable of taking charge of the captaincy of Porto Santo and found no one more apt than Pedro Correia da Cunha, who was married to a daughter from her husband's first marriage. He belonged to the highest nobility and was a gentleman of the court of the infante, Prince Henry, who made him donatário of the Azorean island of Graciosa. Isabel Moniz had sold the captaincy of Porto Santo for three hundred thousand reis in 1458, when the young

Bartolomeu Perestrelo was only eight years old. When he was old enough, he served in Africa and, on his return, he reclaimed the captaincy of Porto Santo, which he obtained when the king annulled the previous grant with the obligation on the part of Perestrelo of returning to his relative Pedro Correia the 300,000 reis.

It is interesting that Columbus never mentions the name of his wife in any of his papers that have survived, though he does refer to her twice: once in a letter of 1500, and the second time in his testament of August 25, 1505, when he recommends to his son Diego that he should have mass said for "the souls of my father, my mother, and my wife."

The island of Porto Santo was, and still is, not as prosperous as the island of Madeira, and many of Columbus's biographers believe that not long after his marriage, Columbus moved to Madeira, where he probably engaged in trade and went on a number of voyages. There he probably met with and listened to the tales of mariners who, long before him, had sailed into the Atlantic, and where signs of land to the west were constantly being washed ashore.

Portuguese Knowledge of Western Islands. During the years that he lived in Portugal and its island territories, Columbus amassed considerable evidence of exotic lands to the west. From what Las Casas tells us, he either heard of or saw definite physical clues of transatlantic lands with exotic flora, as well as indefinite rumors of islands. One day he was told by a pilot of the king of Portugal, Martim Vicente, that at about 450 leagues west of Cape St. Vincent, he had picked up from the sea a piece of carved wood that, as far as he could see, was not cut by iron. Since the wind had been fixed in the west for many days, he came to the conclusion that this piece of wood had come from some island or islands lying further west.

Another pilot, Pedro Correia da Cunha, who was married to the sister or half-sister of Columbus's wife, told him that he had picked up a similar piece of driftwood in the harbor of Porto Santo. He also told him that he had seen some very thick reeds or canes that would easily hold three large measures of wine or water. Columbus himself says that he heard the king of Portugal say the same thing and that the king had these reeds shown to him. The king thought, as Columbus says, that they had come from some island, not very far off, or had been brought from India by the strong winds and swift currents, since no such reeds were known to exist in Europe. Columbus thought that these reeds must be the bamboo of India described by Ptolemy. Morison determined that though large pieces of driftwood rarely come ashore on the outer Azores, Central American treetrunks—probably of the light cuipo tree—did wash ashore on the island of São Miguel in a storm in 1869 (the Azores are about 1,100 kilometers [700 miles] northwest of Madeira).

According to Las Casas, Columbus was also informed by

some of the people who lived in the Azores that when strong westerly and northwesterly winds blew, the sea carried pine trees that washed up on the shore, especially on the islands of Graciosa and Faial, although there were no pine trees growing in the Azores. Others told him that on Flores Island, also in the Azores, two corpses had come aground, with very broad faces and features quite unlike those of European men. On another occasion, near Cape Verga on the west coast of Guinea, long, narrow canoes with moveable deckhouses ran aground; they may have been sailing from one West Indian island to another when strong winds or currents drove them off course, their crews died, and their boats drifted to Africa. Antonio Leme, a resident of Madeira, assured Columbus that he once had caught sight of three islands far in the west. Whether this was true or not, it is common for sailors from the Azores and from Gomera and Hierro islands in the Canaries to report that they have seen islands lying toward the west. But Columbus says that in 1484 he knew of a resident of Madeira who went to ask the king for a caravel to discover a certain land that he swore he caught sight of every year and always in the same way, which agreed on this point with what the Azoreans maintained.

The tale of the unknown pilot. Though it appears, then, that Columbus had definite physical clues as well as indefinite rumors of lands in the west, it was also rumored that he had definite information about them. Not long after he returned from his first voyage of discovery in 1493, it was said that he had known all along exactly where he was going and when he would get there because of what he had learned from an unknown pilot who died in his arms.

Almost all the chronicles of the West Indies mention the pilot, about whom nobody seemed to know anything definite. Las Casas relates that he first heard about him in 1500 when he was living in La Española. But it was not until 1535 that the tale of the unknown pilot first appeared in print in the first part of the *General and Natural History of the Indies, Islands and Mainland of the Ocean Sea* by Gonzalo Fernández de Oviedo (1478–1557). According to Oviedo

some say that a caravel that was sailing from Spain to England, charged with merchandise and provisions, such as wine and other things which are usually shipped to that island . . . was subjected to such mighty and violent tempests and foul winds that she was forced to run westward for so many days that she picked up one or more of the islands of these regions and Indies; and [the pilot] went ashore and saw naked people . . . and when the winds moderated which had driven him thither against his will, he took on water and wood to return to his first course. They also say that the better part of the cargo which this vessel carried consisted of provisions and things to eat and wines, whereof they were able to sustain life on so long a voyage.

But since it took four or five months to return, everyone except three or four mariners and the pilot died en route, and all save he arrived in such bad condition that they died shortly after.

Moreover it is said that this pilot was a very intimate friend of Christopher Columbus, and that he understood somewhat of the latitudes, and marked the land which he found, and in great secrecy shared it with Columbus, whom he asked to make a chart and indicate on it the land which he had seen. It is said that Columbus received him in his house as a friend and sought to cure him, as he too landed very weak; but that he died like the rest, and thus Columbus was informed of the land and navigation of those regions, and he alone knew the secret. Some say that this master or pilot was Andalusian, others have him Portuguese, others Basque; some say that Columbus was then living on the island of Madeira and others in the Cape Verde Islands; and that there the aforesaid caravel came to harbor, and in this way Columbus learned of the land. Whether this was so or not, nobody can truly affirm; but so the story ran among the common people. As for me, I hold it to be false."

In his *History of the Indies* (1552), Francisco López de Gómara (1512–1572) attributes the discovery of the Indies to the unknown pilot and describes his voyage in a manner similar to that of Oviedo:

There are also some who say that the caravel reached Portugal, others say Madeira or one of the islands of the Azores; but no one affirms anything. Only that they all agree that that pilot died in Columbus's house, in whose hands he left the log of the caravel and the relation of that whole long voyage, with the mark and latitude of the lands newly seen and found. . . . Columbus lived on the island of Madeira where I think he resided at the time that the said caravel arrived there. Columbus took him into his house and he told him about the voyage he had undertaken and the new lands he had seen, so that he could copy it onto a chart. In the meantime, the pilot died and left him the relation, sketch, and latitude of the new lands and that is how Columbus found out about the Indies [for] he had never thought of such a thing until he came across the pilot who found them by fortunes of the sea.

Las Casas devotes Book 1, chapter 14, of his *History* to the pilot. Las Casas, who was living in La Española at the time the story was current, gives us more or less the same version as Oviedo except that he advances an argument in favor of the unknown pilot's existence by relating the tradition among the Indians of the bearded white man who had visited the islands not long before the arrival of Columbus. However, Las Casas concludes that since there were so many other reasons to inspire Columbus to make the voyage of discovery, the story of the unknown pilot may well be ignored. He adds it is certain that Columbus "was so sure of discovering what he discovered and of finding what he found, that it was as though he had it all locked up in a room under lock and key." But he does not come out for or against the tale of the unknown pilot.

Morison summarizes the different versions of the story of the unknown pilot:

> Some name the unknown pilot as Alonso Sánchez and give his home as Palos, Huelva, Galicia, or Portugal; some say the ill-fated caravel was engaged in commerce between the peninsula and Madeira or the Canaries or the Gold Coast; she is "blown across" in 28 or 29 days by an "east wind of great fury and relentlessness" in 1484; in the different versions she returns to Graciosa, Terceira, Madeira, Porto Santo, or the Canaries, in each of which Columbus performs his well-rewarded act of charity.

For twenty years, writes Ballesteros Beretta in his *Christopher Columbus and the Discovery of America* (1945), he believed in the truth of the tale since it offered a plausible explanation for Columbus's tenacity. "Today," says Ballesteros,

> we no longer believe in the fairy tale. It is a sailor's tale in which Oviedo does not believe and which Las Casas doubts. Some other data, document, or indication, would be needed to incline the balance in favor of the fantastic pilot. Until the present time everything is up in the air and covered with clouds.

Morison suggests that the story appeared credible to people in the sixteenth century because the winds in the Atlantic had not been charted. Perhaps a seaman did die in Columbus's house and people later believed that he had told Columbus his tale. Most probably, the story was concocted by someone in La Española to cast doubt on Columbus's originality.

The westward voyages of the Portuguese. It was inevitable that Columbus should learn from both his own activities at sea as well as his work in his brother's chart- and mapmaking business of the voyages that were taking place almost every year along the African coast and in the Atlantic. These voyages must have been the common talk of the waterfront.

Columbus mentions some of the voyages that contributed to his training in his own notes, as excerpted by Las Casas. He says that in 1452 Diogo de Teive, one of Prince Henry's captains, discovered the two westernmost islands of the Azores, Flores and Corvo. Teive was a well-known Madeiran who, in 1452, was ordered by Prince Henry to build the first sugar mill on that island. Sailing southwesterly from Faial in the Azores, Teive had run into the Sargasso Sea, the sea of weeds that forty years later, Pedro de Velasco, the Spanish pilot who accompanied Teive on the 1452 voyage, told Columbus not to fear. On the second half of that voyage, Teive continued on a northeast course in search of the mythical island of Brazil and reached the latitude of Cape Clear, Ireland. Unequipped for the cold weather he ran into, and quite unprepared for so long a voyage, he turned back to Portugal, where Teive

put it on record that he was convinced that there was land to the northwest. Not only is it certain that Columbus heard about Teive's voyage, but in the year 1492, when Columbus was hiring the crew that was to sail with him to America, Velasco, who was living in Palos at the time, proved to be of invaluable assistance. He came forward and volunteered the information about "the land of the Indies." Moreover, he publicly encouraged the people, urging them to sign on board with Columbus, assuring them that "they would find a very rich land." Las Casas says that the Portuguese pilot Vicente Dias, on a voyage from Guinea to the Azores, thought that he had seen an island, which he later sought in vain.

The general belief that there were lands lying farther west in the Atlantic found support in several official Portuguese documents. They show that under a royal charter of February 19, 1462, João Vogado was granted the nonexistent islands of Lovo and Capraria that often appeared on charts of the period. They were islands derived from the legend of Saint Brendan, the seagoing Irish saint of the sixth century whose saga of ocean voyaging was one of the most popular stories of the Middle Ages. Much as Columbus stumbled on a New World when in search of the Indies, so the captains of Prince Henry, when searching for the mythical Saint Brendan isles, found the Azores. Seven of them had been discovered by 1439, and in 1452, as mentioned above, Teive came upon far-flung Flores and Corvo.

On October 29, 1462, King Afonso V granted to his brother Fernando a nonexistent island that Gonçalo Fernandes claimed to have sighted west-northwest of the Canaries and Madeira, on his return from the fisheries off the African bay known as the "River of Gold," not far from Cape Bojador. The king, on the ground that Fernando had frequently and unsuccessfully sought an island "that appears over against the island of São Tiago" in the Cape Verdes, conferred the island on his sister Brites, wife of the duke of Viseu. The duchess made no profit on that grant, for the Cape Verde Islands were already known and no more islands were to be found in those waters.

A charter of June 21, 1473, granted João Gonçalves da Câmara, for his service in Africa, an island that he hoped to discover. Another royal document, dated January 28, 1474, granted to Fernão Teles any islands he might discover, a grant that was extended to the Island of the Seven Cities (Antilia) or other inhabited islands, by a charter of November 10, 1474, provided they were not in the region of Guinea. It was in this same year that the Florentine cosmographer Paolo dal Pozzo Toscanelli wrote to Fernão Martins, encouraging the Portuguese to seek Asia by sailing westward and not by sailing around Africa. Ten years later, a royal charter of June 30, 1484, granted Fernão Domingos do Arco an island that he intended to discover; this was the year that Columbus laid his "Great Enterprise" before King João II.

These charters show that a growing number of people in Portugal believed in the existence of islands or a mainland to the west, and that some believed they had caught sight of them. These beliefs in turn prove that sailing on the high seas, far from the African coast and even west of the known archipelagoes, had become frequent and that the Portuguese felt no apprehension in doing so. On the other hand, these lands are never identified with Asia in Portuguese documents, nor is there any talk of crossing the Atlantic to seek out the Far East. Thus, there are no signs that anyone wanted to follow Toscanelli's advice until Columbus came along.

In 1474 Fernão Teles had sought Antilia in vain. But the story of its existence would not die, and Columbus's certainty that he could find it en route to the Indies, if properly equipped and suitably rewarded, probably had something to do with the detailed and significant letters patent of donation issued in 1486 by King João to Ferdinand van Olm, or Fernão Dulmo as he was known in Portugal. Dulmo was a Fleming and a gentleman of the royal household who had settled in the Azores. He established himself on the north coast of Terceira and was appointed captain of that part of the island. The terms of Dulmo's grant betray a new and livelier interest on the part of the king in Atlantic discovery. According to a long entry in the registry of the royal chancellery, Dulmo declared that he proposed "to seek and find a great island or coast of a mainland, which is presumed to be the island of the Seven Cities (or Antilia), and all this at his own proper cost and expense." He prays that he may have a royal donation of any such islands or mainland, populated or unpopulated, as he or anyone acting under his orders may "have discovered or found," together with civil and criminal jurisdiction over the same, these rights with their fees and incomes to be hereditary. The king granted his request and on March 3, 1486, issued letters patent accordingly, and further promised that he would confer upon Dulmo if he were successful "such titles of honor as would appear to us to be reasonable"—a reflection of Columbus's ambition to be viceroy and admiral. One clause in particular shows a keener interest in the generation-old search for islands:

> In the event that he cannot conquer the said islands and mainland, We shall send with the said Fernão Dulmo men and fleets of ships with Our power to effect the same, and the said Fernão Dulmo shall always be Captain General of the said fleets, and is acknowledged by Us always for his King as Our subject.

Dulmo evidently found the enterprise too much to accomplish alone. Three months later he brought in João Afonso do Estreito of Madeira as a partner, praying that the king admit him to a share of the enterprise and the profits, on certain conditions. Estreito was required to provide two good caravels fully equipped and provisions for six months, to be ready to sail on March 1, 1487, while Dulmo would engage pilots and mariners for the fleet and pay their wages. Estreito would command one caravel and Dulmo the other, and for forty days after their departure, Dulmo was to be captain general and set the course for both caravels and possess all lands discovered in that space of time, after which Estreito was to be captain general and possess all other lands discovered thereafter and until their return to Portugal. The king confirmed all this, and much more in the way of detail, on July 24 and August 4, 1486, promising that Estreito would enjoy all such privileges, liberties, and franchises in his share of the discoveries as Dulmo had been granted originally. Perhaps for this voyage the king congratulated himself on driving a much better bargain than he could have concluded with Columbus, who demanded so much more.

Whether Dulmo and Estreito ever undertook their expedition is not known. The only further mention of it is one oblique reference in Las Casas, who says that the pilot Pedro de Velasco told Columbus that on the voyage he took with Diogo de Teive in 1452, they saw land to the west of Ireland that they believed was the land that "Hernan Delinos" sought to discover, "as shall presently be told." Hernan Dolinos is most likely a Spanish form of Fernão Dulmo. Unfortunately, Las Casas neglects to tell more, and Dulinos's story has perished. It is not difficult to imagine why Dulmo and Estreito did not succeed if they did sail. The month of March, in which they proposed to sail, is a bad one for sailing westward from the Azores, for it is the month of tempestuous west to northwest winds.

The Dulmo-Estreito expedition was the last effort of the Portuguese, of which we have any record, to discover new lands in the west before the first voyage of Columbus. And there may well be some connection between their failure and the cordiality of King João's letter of March 20, 1488, to Columbus, who by that time was already living in Spain.

There is no doubt that the westward voyages of the Portuguese were made possible by contemporary technical advances. Improvements in shipbuilding, progress in the pilot's art culminating in navigation by the stars, development of chart making leading to the introduction of the scale of latitudes, study of weather and ocean current conditions, and the consequent tracing of the best routes taking into account the winds and currents of each area—all these factors made it possible to create a real system of high-seas navigation in the Atlantic, while the old system of sailing characteristic of coastal navigation, by dead reckoning only, continued to be used in the Mediterranean. Columbus came on the scene precisely when half a century of progress in these spheres was leading to spectacular practical results, at the outset of what has been described as the period of great sea discoveries.

Columbus's Appeals for Royal Support. Not long after the birth of Columbus's first son, Diego, in Porto Santo, his wife died and Columbus returned to Lisbon. It was during this period that Columbus sailed one or more times to the west coast of Africa, which the Portuguese called Guinea, where they were engaged in trade and in building a fortified factory or trading post at São Jorge da Mina. It was on his voyages to West Africa with the Portuguese that he observed that the winds in this area blew predominantly from the northeast, which is ideal for running down a latitude in a westerly direction. He, as well as the Portuguese who had preceded him, had discovered that phenomenon, the northeast trade winds, upon which the economy of Europe was to depend for centuries to come. At any rate, it must have been on these voyages under the Portuguese flag, if not before, that he became a proficient navigator.

No one can say for certain at what moment Columbus conceived the idea of sailing westward across the Atlantic to reach the Indies. But it must have been on his mind during the early years he spent in Lisbon. The best evidence of this is to be found in the correspondence he is known to have had with a Florentine physician, Paolo dal Pozzo Toscanelli. In 1474, Toscanelli corresponded with a canon of Lisbon cathedral, Fernão Martins, who had been trying to convince King Afonso V that there was a quicker way to the Indies than around the southernmost point of Africa. Toscanelli, who took the writings of Marco Polo very seriously, believed that the earth was a great deal smaller than it actually is. Some time later, perhaps in 1481, Columbus wrote to Toscanelli, enclosing a sphere with his letter, in which he expressed a desire to open communications with the East by a direct voyage west across the Atlantic. Toscanelli sent him a chart based on his conception of the earth, largely derived from Marco Polo's account of the Far East, and enclosed with it a copy of the letter he had earlier sent to Fernão Martins. In that letter, Toscanelli had maintained that a course west out of Lisbon would bring the navigator to the Chinese province of Mangi (Man-tzu, a territory south of the Yellow River conquered by the Mongols in 1276) after about 8,000 kilometers (5,000 miles)—though 18,000 kilometers (11,000 miles) would have been nearer the mark—and "passing by the island of Antilia, after only two thousand miles [thirty-two hundred kilometers] he would reach 'Cipangu,'" the Japan that Marco Polo had described, an island rich in all precious metals and stones, which stirred Columbus's imagination.

But the important thing that Columbus obtained from Toscanelli, apart from the prestige of having an eminent scholar approve his enterprise, was the Florentine's approval of Marco Polo. Columbus, however, thought that the ocean was even narrower than Toscanelli supposed. At any rate, by the time that Columbus returned from his voyage to Africa, probably in 1484, he was ready to make an amazing proposition to King João II of Portugal.

Columbus's proposal to João II. João, who succeeded his father Afonso V in 1481, was undoubtedly the right man for Columbus to approach with his project of a great voyage to the west. Known in history as João the Perfect, he was as ambitious for his country overseas as he was determined to ensure Portugal's stability by curbing the power of the nobles at home. Unfortunately, the state of the kingdom of Portugal was such that João was far too preoccupied in the 1480s with potential civil war and disputes with Spain to devote much time to the extension of Portuguese sea exploration. But it is evidence enough of his eagerness to promote such adventures that he agreed in 1484 to consider the plan of the importunate Genoese.

Apparently, Columbus experienced none of the difficulties in obtaining an audience with King João that he was later to encounter in meeting with Isabel and Fernando. He may have used the influence and connections of his powerful in-laws, for he knew that without the backing of the king there could be no hope of his securing the ships and men he needed for the voyage.

Armed with all the information he had been collecting over the years, Columbus appeared at court. He was now thirty-one years old. He proposed to João II an expedition that would sail west into the Atlantic, rather than following the current Portuguese practice of attempting the circumnavigation of Africa. He would thus reach the desired lands and "the kingdom of the Great Khan" by the direct westward route. Actually, there is no direct evidence concerning the exact nature of his proposal. But that he presented his proposal to João of Portugal is confirmed by his son Fernando and by Las Casas, as well as by the Portuguese chroniclers Rui de Pina, García de Resende, and João de Barros who, years later, after Columbus's return from his first voyage, alluded to it.

According to Las Casas's account of that momentous meeting, Columbus held out a promise of rich rewards: "He proposed the project to the King, which was as follows: that going by way of the west toward the south he would discover great lands, islands and terra firma, all very prosperous, rich in gold and silver, pearls, and precious stones, and an infinite number of people."

Columbus's own demands in return for the vast fortune that he was offering King João were in keeping with the grandiosity of his ideas. First he thought that he should be granted nobility, which carried with it the right for him and his descendants to be called "Dom" and to be armed as a knight with golden spurs. He asked that he be granted the title of Grand Admiral of the Ocean Sea with all the same honors, privileges, rights, and dues enjoyed by the grand admiral of Castile. He wanted to be appointed the "perpetual viceroy and governor of all the islands and lands which he might discover or which might be discovered by anyone else under his command." He also demanded "a tenth of all the income accruing to the king from all the gold, silver, pearls, precious stones, metals, spices, and other valuable things, and from every kind of goods bought, exchanged, discovered, or acquired within the region of his admiralty." He concluded by stipulating that in any future expeditions he should have the right to put up one-eighth of the expenses in return for receiving one-eighth of the profit.

These demands were the same as those he presented years later to the Catholic monarchs and are not confirmed in the Portuguese sources. Some critics have even accused Las Casas of merely copying these demands as they appear in the Santa Fe Capitulations made to the Catholic monarchs. But Antonio Ballesteros Beretta, a modern Columbus scholar, believes they are authentic because if Columbus could have made the same demands in Castile, when he was weary and disconsolate after years of waiting, without giving up one of his points, he must have been even firmer in Portugal, where his situation was clearer and he was not worn out or disillusioned. Ballesteros cannot explain why Columbus asked for the same rights as an admiral of Castile, a demand that certainly would have offended the Portuguese.

Columbus's demands and overbearing manner were so outrageous that the king had his doubts about having anything further to do with him. Nevertheless, João showed him special consideration by referring his proposal to a scientific council. The council returned an unfavorable report. However, it appears that the king remained interested in the project and determined to put it to the test himself. It was said that he secretly chartered two caravels and ordered their masters to sail westward from the Azores to find the great Island of the Seven Cities, the legendary Antilia. The caravels returned after being heavily buffeted by head winds and the project was abandoned. The Portuguese who rejected Columbus's project did only what might have been expected of any well-ordered government dealing with an adventurer of vast pretensions but meager attainments.

Charles E. Nowell, in his penetrating article, "The Rejection of Columbus by John of Portugal," examines the possible reasons for the rejection. First, Columbus failed to give the king's advisers a convincing demonstration that a westward route to the Indies existed. Since Columbus lacked the requisite intellectual background to impress the king's learned councilors, he could offer them no respectable calculation regarding the westward distance to Cipangu. Second, João made it his policy to distinguish between national and private enterprise. His treasury financed the explorations down the African coast that year by year were bringing him closer to his goal of rounding Africa. This constituted a national enterprise. The men whom he sent on these expeditions, like Diogo Cão or Bartolomeu Dias, were royal agents, sent to do a particular task; none of these discoverers acquired private rights in the regions they explored. Columbus wanted to be the king's agent, but he also wanted to make his terms in advance, contrary to established policy. His projected voyage fell rather within the category of private initiative, the Portuguese pattern of discovery in the Atlantic and its islands. Without money and financial backing, Columbus proposed to enter a field hitherto dominated by private entrepreneurs, and, even more, he claimed rewards far greater than any other entrepreneurs had thought of demanding. In keeping with João's policy, the private speculator had to finance himself. On successful completion of the type of discovery voyage proposed by Columbus, he would generally have received proprietary rights and some economic privileges, but nothing like the noble title of Dom that Columbus demanded, or the rank of an admiral, or ships supplied by the Crown. Private discovery missions cost the Crown nothing; hence permission for them was easily granted. But for the Crown to outfit an adventurer and then to step into the background in that adventurer's favor was out of the question.

Although Columbus remained on friendly terms with the king, he knew that it was time to look elsewhere for a patron. With his dreams of financial success in ruins, and with his even greater dream of discovering the Indies dismissed by the king's advisers, Columbus left for Spain, clandestinely, it was said, to avoid his creditors. Interestingly enough, Fernando attributes the reason for his father's departure from Portugal to the fact that King João had secretly sent an expedition to where his father had proposed to sail, and as a result, he "formed such a hatred for that city and nation that he resolved to depart for Castile with his little son Diogo . . . ," his wife having died in the meantime. He took ship for Palos, not far from Huelva, where his wife's sister Violante lived, intending, it is believed, to leave the child with her.

Second approach to João II. But Columbus was not finished with Portugal. Near the end of 1487, he contacted King João again. Writing from Seville, he asked João to be allowed to return to Portugal under a safe conduct that would protect him—it is presumed from his creditors, though there is no mention of them in the king's letter. Columbus's letter to the king is lost, but it is obvious from the king's reply that it was the future Admiral who had initiated the correspondence. Writing from Avis on March 20, 1488, João urged him to return to Portugal in an extremely cordial letter.

On the outside the letter is addressed to "Christovam Collon [sic], our special friend in Seville." Inside it reads:

Christoval Colon [sic]: We, Dom Joham, by the grace of God King of Portugal, the Algarves on this side and beyond the sea in Africa, and lord of Guinea, send you warm greetings:

We have seen the letter you wrote us and we thank you very much for the good will and affection expressed therein for our service.

As for your coming here, we not only desire you to come, for the reasons you give, but for other reasons as well, for we will have great need of your ability and fine talent. Therefore, we would be very pleased if you would come. Moreover, all matters concerning you will be taken care of in such a way that you must needs be content.

And if by chance you are in fear of our justice officials owing to some obligation you have incurred, we, by means of this letter, can assure you that during your coming, your stay, and departure, you will not be arrested, detained, accused, summoned, or prosecuted, for any reason whatsoever, under the civil and criminal code. By virtue of this selfsame letter, we hereby command all our justice officials to comply with these orders as set forth herein. Therefore, we beg you and urge you to come soon and not to be reluctant to do so for any reason whatsoever. Moreover, we will be grateful to you for doing so and will regard it as being of great importance to our service.

Written at Avis, on the xx day of March in the year 1488. The King.

Columbus did not know at the time that he wrote to the king that two years before, in 1486, João had sent another expedition down the coast of Africa. This one was led by Bartolomeu Dias, who had been dispatched from Lisbon with three caravels to continue the southward exploration of Africa beyond the limits that had already been reached by Diogo Cão. At the time that Columbus wrote to the king, Dias had been away for many months; he had rounded the Cape of Good Hope and discovered the dream of Henry the Navigator—the sea route to the Indies. Columbus was in Lisbon in December 1488 when Dias returned triumphant. It must have been a moment of intolerable bitterness for him, for the prospect of reaching Asia by way of Africa meant the end of any chance he might have had of arousing the king's interest in his own project for a westward route. Once again, Columbus left Lisbon for Spain, a disappointed man.

Perhaps it was for his own good fortune that he was rejected by the king of Portugal. Had his project been accepted, he probably would have set out in high latitudes from the Azores, as earlier Portuguese explorers before him had done. In that event, he would have been forced to buck the westerlies and we would have heard no more

of him. But sailing for Spain, as he did in 1492, he had no choice but to depart from the Canaries, a Spanish possession, where he picked up the trade winds that blew him, on an almost perfect course, to America.

Unexpected Return to Portugal. Columbus returned to Portugal on an unexpected visit that put his life and the success of the 1492 voyage in jeopardy. In February 1493, on the first homeward-bound voyage from America, Columbus was forced to make two unscheduled stops in Portuguese territory before returning to his home port in Spain.

The island of Santa Maria in the Azores. Overtaken by a storm as he was approaching the Azores, he put in on the island of Santa Maria in the Azores. Another storm, a few days after his departure from the Azores, forced him to land at Lisbon.

The Portuguese chroniclers of the period have described the stopover in Lisbon in great detail, but they have nothing to say about Columbus's brief stop in the Azores during the ten days from February 18 to 28, 1493, which Columbus himself describes in his log. On February 10, Columbus reckoned that his two ships were about on the latitude of Flores in the Azores. Two days later a gale blew up and *Pinta* and *Niña* ran before the wind under bare poles. On the night of February 13, the two ships lost contact with each other. Battered by the storm and drenched by the sea, the crew of *Niña* prayed and three times drew lots to see which of them should make pilgrimages of devotion to Santa María de Guadalupe, to the shrine of Santa María de Loreto, and to Santa Clara de Moguer, not far from their home port of Palos. Finally, all hands vowed to make a pilgrimage, clad only in their shirts, to the nearest church of Our Lady at whatever place they should first make land.

The island of Santa Maria was sighted shortly after sunrise on Friday, February 15, and an unsuccessful

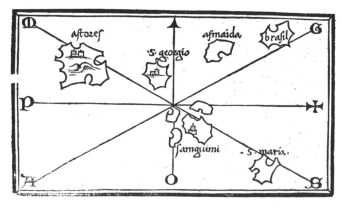

MAP OF THE AZORES. From Benedetto Bordone's *Isolario*. Venice, 1528.

attempt to anchor was made on February 15. It had never been Columbus's intention to call at the Azores and he had carefully avoided all the Portuguese islands, but ship and seamen had taken such a beating that he decided to take a chance in the hope of obtaining wood, water, fresh provisions, and a bit of rest.

After sunrise on Monday, February 18, Columbus anchored on the northern side of the island and sent the boat ashore. The local people told his sailors that they were on the island of Santa Maria in the Azores and showed them where they could find a safer anchorage for the caravel on the other side of a high rocky cape called Punta dos Frades. After sunset on Monday, February 19, three islanders visited the ship. Since the next day was Shrove Tuesday, they brought, according to Columbus's log,

> fowls and fresh bread, and other things that were sent by the captain of the island, who was called Juan de Castañeda [João de Castanheira in Portuguese], saying that he knew me very well, and that as it was night he did not come to call, but at daybreak he would come and bring more refreshments with the three men of the caravel who remained there, whom he did not send back because of the great pleasure that he had with them, hearing about events of the voyage.

Informed that there was a little shrine near the sea dedicated to Our Lady, Columbus decided to fulfill the third vow that had been made at the height of the storm. At daybreak on Tuesday, February 19, he sent half the crew ashore in *Niña*'s one boat, asking the messengers who returned with them to seek out the village priest to say mass, after which the men were to return to the ship while Columbus with the other half of the crew went ashore to hear mass. As the first group was at mass, clad only in their shirts, they were taken prisoner by the villagers, acting under Castanheira's orders.

About eleven in the morning, Columbus, anxiously awaiting the return of his boat from the village that he was unable to see, decided that either the boat had been wrecked on the rocks or the crewmen detained. Weighing anchor, he sailed *Niña* around Punta dos Frades and came upon a troop of well-armed men commanded by Castanheira. They came out to the ship with the obvious intention of arresting Columbus. Columbus attempted to lure Castanheira aboard *Niña* in order to hold him hostage, while Castanheira tried to lure Columbus into the boat in order to take him prisoner along with the men who had been captured at prayer. Columbus said that he was "the Admiral of the Ocean Sea and Viceroy of the Indies which belong to their Highnesses," and that he would return to Castile with half his crew if the others were not released and see to it that the offending Portuguese were suitably punished. Castanheira replied

that "they did not recognize the King and Queen of Castile here, nor their letters, nor were they afraid; rather, they would have us understand that this is Portugal, and they said this in a threatening way." Rash and angry words were exchanged before Columbus returned to anchor in the harbor where he had first arrived, the anchorage that the villagers had warned him about.

On February 20, *Niña*'s cables broke and Columbus made sail for the island of São Miguel, which is usually visible from Santa Maria in fair weather; because of foul weather *Niña* was unable to reach the island by nightfall. Also, it was very difficult to handle the ship because only three of the crew left aboard were seamen; the rest—soldiers, landsmen, and Indians—were not very useful for navigating the ship. At sunrise on February 21, Columbus decided to return to Santa Maria and see whether he could negotiate the release of his crewmen. As *Niña* lay at anchor in the bay east of Punta dos Frades, the *Niña*'s boat appeared, carrying five of the captured seamen, two priests, and a notary public. The priests and the scribe scrutinized the Admiral's credentials, expressed themselves satisfied, and granted him free entry. Castanheira released the rest of *Niña*'s crew, who said that the real reason for their release was Castanheira's failure to capture Columbus; the seamen alone were too unimportant for him, they said.

With its full crew restored, *Niña* left this uneasy anchorage for the last time on February 23, and sailed around Santa Maria to the west, in search of a good place to take on wood and stone ballast. However, since the weather was favorable for going to Castile, Columbus gave up the idea of taking on ballast and ordered the course to the east. Before daylight, *Niña* was well beyond the inhospitable island. A few days later he ran into another, more violent storm that carried *Niña* to the mouth of the Tagus River. On the night of March 2 and 3, the fifth day of the storm, a violent squall split the sails and placed *Niña* in grave danger because, as Columbus knew by dead reckoning and the look of things, he was very near the coast of Portugal. At 7:00 P.M. on March 3, the seamen sighted land dead ahead by the light of a full moon. At daybreak on March 4, Columbus recognized the Rock of Sintra, north of the mouth of the Tagus River. He decided to enter the Tagus because, as he says in his logbook, he could do nothing else. This stopover in Portugal was to cause him some difficulties on his return to Spain where he was unfairly accused of having visited Lisbon for the express purpose of betraying the Catholic monarchs, a charge repeated by a number of modern writers.

The court of João II. Shortly after sunrise, *Niña* entered the Tagus estuary and came to anchor at 9:00 A.M. on Monday, March 4, off the beach of Restelo. Learning that the king was in the country, Columbus requested permission to proceed upstream to Lisbon. He cited his credentials from Fernando and Isabel, and informed King João that he was coming from the Indies and not from Guinea. Having written to King João, Columbus added a postscript to the letter to Fernando and Isabel announcing his discovery that he had composed at sea and dated at Santa Maria on February 15, and sent it off to Spain.

Moored near *Niña* was a great Portuguese warship whose master was Bartolomeu Dias, discoverer of the Cape of Good Hope. Dias came aboard *Niña* and ordered Columbus to return with him and give an account of himself to the captain of the warship, Álvaro Damão. Columbus stood on his dignity as Admiral of the Ocean Sea and replied that he could not come unless by force of arms; he also refused to allow Vicente Yáñez Pinzón, captain of *Niña,* to convey the ship's papers to Damão. Dias then asked to see his papers, which Columbus was only too glad to show him. After Dias made his report to Damão, Damão then came aboard *Niña* himself to pay a visit of courtesy to the new Admiral of the Ocean Sea and offered to do all he commanded.

On Friday, March 8, 1493, Martim de Noronha, a gentleman of the king's court, delivered a letter from King João himself inviting the Admiral to visit him. The king ordered his agents to supply *Niña* with provisions and with whatever stores she needed at his expense. Mules were provided by Noronha, and Columbus, on starting out, probably took with him some of the gold and a few other souvenirs he had found in the Caribbean, as well as some of the captive Indians, to exhibit at court. He found the king at the monastery of Santa Maria das Virtudes (Saint Mary of the Virtues), situated in a pinewood at the foot of the Vale do Paraíso (Paradise Valley), a rich farming region about fifty kilometers (thirty miles) from Lisbon, where the court had gone to escape an outbreak of the plague. The meeting of the king and the Admiral, both men of high courage and inflexible will, must have been dramatic. Columbus was then forty-two years old, King João thirty-eight. Columbus had seen him as a petitioner in 1484 or 1485 and had been rejected; he had been summoned by him to court in 1488 and had again been dismissed.

Columbus gave an account of their meeting in his log for March 9:

> The King ordered that I should be received with great honor by the principal personages of his household, and he himself received me with great honor and showed me much respect, asking me to sit down and talking very freely with me. He told me that he would order everything done which would be of use to your Highnesses [the Catholic monarchs] even more fully than if it were for his own service. He indicated that he was greatly pleased that the voyage had been accomplished successfully, although he understood that in the capitulation between the Sovereigns and himself the conquest belonged to him. I told him that I had not seen the capitulation and did not know anything other than that the Sovereigns had commanded me not to go to La Mina [São Jorge da Mina] nor to any part of Guinea, and that this had been proclaimed in all of the ports of Andalusia before I started on the voyage. The King graciously responded that he was certain that there would be no need for mediators in this matter. He made me the guest of the Prior of Crato, who was the most important person there, and from whom I received many honors and favors.

There are several other accounts of his interview with King João written by three Portuguese chroniclers that give a somewhat different version of what took place at court that day. The first was written by Rui de Pina (1440?–1533?), who not only was present at court when Columbus arrived, but also took part in the diplomatic negotiations between Spain and Portugal over the boundaries of their respective discoveries. In his *Chronicle of King John II,* Pina reports that on March 6, 1493, an Italian by the name of Christovam Colombo dropped anchor in the port of Lisbon, inbound from a voyage of discovery to the islands of Cipangu and Antilia. He had with him a few natives of those lands as well as gold and some other things he had found there. He had been given the title of admiral of those islands. The king summoned him to Vale do Paraíso. Pina claims that João II was both dismayed and chagrined by Columbus's visit, not only because he believed that the discovery fell within his sphere of influence, but also because the Admiral's attitude was arrogant and the account of his discovery greatly exaggerated. Columbus upbraided the king for having refused to accept his enterprise of the Indies when first proposed. Pina reports that the courtiers were so outraged by his behavior that they suggested that he be secretly murdered, which would put an end to his discovery, but the king would not hear of it; on the contrary, he dismissed the Admiral with honor and favor.

Garcia de Resende (c. 1470–1536) also describes the king's interview with Columbus in his chronicle of the reign of King João II (1533). Much of what he wrote was copied from Rui de Pina, except for an addition that extolls the role of the king in directing the negotiations of the Treaty of Tordesillas from afar, and in wisely distributing his bribes in order to obtain the favorable terms he sought for the treaty.

The best description of Columbus's visit to Portugal in 1493 was written by João de Barros (c. 1496–1570). The first volume of his *Decades of Asia,* published in 1552, contains the most detailed account of the visit. Barros repeats much of the same information found in the works of Pina and Garcia de Resende. He describes Christóvão Colom not as an Italian, as do his two predecessors, but as a Genoese (which is important in view of the later polemics over the nationality of Columbus), and claims that the reason King João sent for him was that he knew him personally and he was aware of the fact that King Fernando of Castile had sent Columbus on a voyage of discovery about which he wanted to hear. Columbus came to court, according to Barros, not so much to please the king as to spite him. He adds that the king was quite perturbed when he saw the natives who accompanied Columbus because they fit the description he had been given of the Indians of Asia. He explains that Columbus had "imagined," as he told the king in 1484 or 1485, that he could reach Cipangu by sailing west because of his reading of Marco Polo, what he had heard of the western discoveries made in the days of Prince Henry the Navigator, the discussions he had had with the Portuguese mariners about their past discoveries, and his reliance on the experience of foreign navigators. Barros goes on to speak of King João's thwarted attempt to send an armada in search of Columbus's discovery, the disputes that arose between Spain and Portugal over the location of the discovery, and the dispatching of embassies from one kingdom to the other. After more than a year of procrastination on the part of the Spanish sovereigns who were waiting for Columbus to return from his second voyage with more specific information about the location of his discovery, the Treaty of Tordesillas, which divided the non-Christian world into two zones of influence, was finally signed, on June 7, 1494. In principle, the treaty followed the papal bull issued in 1493 by Pope Alexander VI, which fixed the demarcation line along a circle passing 100 leagues west of the Cape Verde Islands and through the two poles. This division gave the entire New World to Spain, but Africa and India to Portugal. However, at the objection of the Portuguese, the Treaty of Tordesillas, as it was finally signed, shifted the demarcation line to a circle passing 370 leagues west of the Cape Verde Islands, thus giving Portugal a shadowy claim to Brazil.

From these three Portuguese accounts, it is apparent that it must have been with smoldering anger that King João heard a firsthand relation of Columbus's voyage.

A stopover in Madeira. Columbus visited Portuguese territory one last time, again unexpectedly, in Madeira in 1498, on his third voyage to America. Spain was at war with France and it was rumored that a French armada was lying in wait for him and his six ships off Cape St. Vincent. The Admiral sailed south, passing near the African coast, instead of following a direct course for Porto Santo. Eight days later, on June 7, 1498, his fleet arrived in Porto Santo, after having sailed at least 1,050 kilometers (650 miles). When Columbus decided to take on wood, water, and provisions, and to hear mass, the inhabitants confused his fleet with that of the French corsairs and fled inland with their flocks. Finding no one in Porto Santo, Columbus sailed for Madeira that same night, reaching Funchal, no more than sixty kilometers (forty miles) from Porto Santo,

on June 10. Las Casas writes that Columbus "was given a very fine reception and much entertainment, for he was well known there, having been a resident thereof for some time."

That was the last known time that Columbus set foot on Portuguese soil.

BIBLIOGRAPHY

Ballesteros Beretta, Antonio. *Cristóbal Colón y el descubrimiento de América.* Barcelona and Buenos Aires, 1945.

Bradford, Ernle. *Christopher Columbus.* New York, 1973.

Columbus, Ferdinand. *The Life of the Admiral Christopher Columbus by His Son Ferdinand.* Translated by Benjamin Keen. New Brunswick, N.J., 1959.

Fuson, Robert H. *The Log of Christopher Columbus.* Camden, Me., 1987.

Las Casas, Bartolomé de. *Historia de las Indias.* 3 vols. Edited by Agustín Millares Carlo. Mexico and Buenos Aires, 1951.

Madariaga, Salvador de. *Christopher Columbus: Being the Life of the Very Magnificent Lord Don Cristobal Colon.* 3d ed. New York, 1967.

Morison, Samuel Eliot. *Admiral of the Ocean Sea: A Life of Christopher Columbus.* 2 vols. Boston, 1942.

Morison, Samuel Eliot. "Christophe Colomb et le Portugal." *Boletim da Sociedade de Geografia* (July–September 1956): 269–278.

Morison, Samuel Eliot. *Portuguese Voyages to America in the Fifteenth Century.* Cambridge, Mass., 1940.

Mota, Avelino Teixeira da. "Christopher Columbus and the Portuguese." *Journal of the American Portuguese Cultural Society* 2, nos. 1, 2, 3 (Winter, Spring, Summer 1968): 1–22.

Nowell, Charles E. "The Rejection of Columbus by John of Portugal." *University of Michigan Historical Essays* (1937): 25–44.

Quinn, David B. "Columbus and the North." Paper delivered at University of California, Los Angeles, June 6, 1989.

Ruddock, Alwyn A. "Columbus and Iceland: New Light on an Old Problem." *Geographical Journal* 132, part 2 (June 1970): 177–189.

Sale, Kirkpatrick. *The Conquest of Paradise: Christopher Columbus and the Columbian Legacy.* New York, 1990.

Taviani, Paolo Emilio. *Christopher Columbus: The Grand Design.* Translated by William Weaver. Edited by John Gilbert. London, 1985.

Vigneras, L. A. "Columbus in Portugal." Paper presented at the first annual meeting of the Society for the History of Discoveries, Washington, D.C., December 28, 1961.

REBECCA CATZ

Columbus in Spain

Columbus was a Genoese businessman living in exile most of his adult life. His ideas and hopes had been shaped by his Italian background, but circumstances in the eastern Mediterranean dictated that he could not realize these hopes in the city of Genoa. During his early maritime experience, Columbus had witnessed in the Black and Aegean seas the ending of two centuries of Genoese trade with Asia. He kept the hope of Asian trade alive by transferring the Italian dream to Castile, the most dynamic and prosperous monarchy in Europe. In Spain he found employment at the highest levels possible to a foreigner, royal interest in his Asian trade proposal, government officials with the expertise to expedite such a venture, and experienced seamen to carry it to completion. These resources and benefits impelled Columbus to spend more of his adult life in Spain than in any other country—most of the twenty years from late 1485 until his death in 1506.

A Move to Spain. Settling in Spain was not his original intent. Genoese businessmen lived in constant motion, moving by sea from one country to another in order to buy low and sell high. Even after a merchant married and established a permanent household, home for him was a base of operations, not a place of continuous residence. Columbus had many reasons to base himself in Portugal; by the early 1480s he was a family man, with Portuguese wife, children, household, and business based in Lisbon, and he was a Portuguese citizen by virtue of his marriage. Yet he transferred his base of business operations from Portugal to Spain in late 1485. The move was more than the usual business trip. Things were not going well in Portugal for his wife's family, who were friends and followers of the duke of Braganza. In May 1483, King João II had had the duke of Braganza executed for treason, and in August 1484, the king personally executed the duke of Viseu, the queen's brother. Portuguese politics may well have been a factor in Columbus's decision to move to Spain.

His years there were very long for an international merchant, but conditions in Castile were particularly favorable for an experienced trader. King Fernando and Queen Isabel needed supplies and provisions for two great projects. The royal children were growing up, and all five of them married between 1490 and 1500. Their parents wanted to supply luxury gifts, clothing, and furnishings of premium quality for trousseaus and wedding festivities on an unprecedented scale. At the same time, the monarchs were carrying on a war of conquest against the Kingdom of Granada. From 1482 to 1492, Castilian armies commanded by Fernando were conquering one Muslim city after another, and they needed to sell their war booty. For the Genoese, the war required an adjustment because their traditional trade with Muslim Málaga dropped off sharply. Increasingly, the Italians dealt with the monarchy, basing themselves principally in the city of Seville.

Columbus had traded in Spanish ports since he first went to sea in the early 1470s. The most logical place to set himself up in Spain was the city of Cádiz. It was well known to him as the traditional stopover on Genoese voyages from Chios to northern Europe, and there was at hand an advantageous person to work with, a Castilian businessman with influence at the royal court. On the north shore of Cádiz Bay lay the town of Puerto de Santa María, which belonged to the duke of Medinaceli. The duke had developed the shipping business in this port, and in the 1480s he was developing the village of Rota, on the peninsula opposite Cádiz, into another important port. He put Columbus on his staff, presumably employed in his shipping business.

Columbus became much more than just a member of the duke's staff, because he had a startling proposal to make. The idea had developed in response to events he had observed at the Portuguese royal court in Lisbon. In May 1485 he witnessed an important event in the Portuguese search for a way to Asia. A land navigator, José Vizinho, returned from an epic trek across Africa and gave King João a report on the distance across Africa at the equator. (The Portuguese had earlier sought an opinion on this subject from an Italian scientist in Florence, Paolo dal Pozzo Toscanelli.) Vizinho's information led João to the conclusion that the distance and obstacles across Africa were so great that an overland route linking the Atlantic and the Indian oceans was not commercially feasible. The Portuguese turned their efforts once again to finding a sea route south and east around Africa.

Columbus, however, drew a startlingly different conclusion from this same information because, as usual, he underestimated the size of the globe. If Asia extended as far into the ocean as Toscanelli believed, then the Ocean Sea must not be very wide. If Africa turned out to be as long from north to south as it was wide from west to east, the shortest and fastest route to Asia would not be around Africa; it would be directly west across the Ocean Sea. By taking the western route ships could avoid both the long detour around Africa and the trip across the Indian Ocean, going directly to the rich market cities of Cathay. He proposed such a voyage to the duke of Medinaceli. The duke was responsive to the idea and calculated that three or four caravels would be sufficient for a one-year voyage. But then the duke realized that the project was more suitable as a royal enterprise and wrote to his uncle, Cardinal Pedro González de Mendoza, introducing Columbus to the court.

Columbus Enters Royal Service. The year when Columbus left the duke's staff and entered Castilian royal service has been a matter of fierce debate in Columbus scholarship. On January 14, 1493, Columbus wrote in his Diario that he had entered the service of the Spanish monarchs "seven years ago on January 20, this very month." That seems to be a direct statement, but it is problematic. If we count back in the modern way by subtracting 7 from 1493, he would have entered royal service on January 20, 1486, in

Alcalá de Henares, where the monarchs were spending a few days in late January that year. But if Columbus counted both the first and last of the seven years (the method he apparently used in calculating his age in a Genoese document of 1470), then the first service was on January 20, 1487, in the city of Salamanca, where the monarchs were spending the winter. By then, he had been in the duke's service long enough to win the confidence of this important person who could provide him with an introduction to the royal court. The year 1487 is further supported by contemporary documents.

Columbus went to court to propose that the monarchs sponsor an exploratory commercial voyage west to Asia. He must have been very persuasive, because King Fernando and Queen Isabel took him seriously. Spanish monarchs followed a standard procedure with proposals; they appointed a subcommittee of the royal council to make a feasibility study. The chairman of the committee was one of the queen's confessors, Hernando de Talavera, bishop of Ávila. The rest of the committee were royal councillors, experts in subjects important to the success of such a proposal: royal finances, law, and foreign affairs. A Franciscan friar, Antonio de Marchena, who had a reputation as an astronomer, may have been brought in as a scientific expert.

The committee began its deliberations in Salamanca and continued as the royal court resumed its incessant travels around the realms of Fernando and Isabel. On January 30, the monarchs began traveling south on their way to resume the war against Granada. They arrived in the city of Córdoba on March 2, and Isabel established the court there for the duration while Fernando mobilized municipal militias and royal forces for the campaign. Córdoba was the heart of the war effort, the place where supplies and equipment were collected, where administrators planned strategy and dispatched armies to carry it out, and where the royal treasury disbursed payments to suppliers and employees.

In Córdoba, Columbus appeared on the royal payroll, reporting to Bishop Talavera in some activity administered by the queen's comptroller of finances, Alfonso de Quintanilla. On May 5 Columbus received his first payment from the royal treasury—three thousand maravedis—probably for the months of February, March, and April, because royal employees were paid quarterly for services rendered. The payments continued through June 16, 1488, for a total of seventeen thousand maravedis in five payments. This was a small amount of money—about equal to a seaman's annual wages.

Payments from the monarchy provided only part of his income. He was still in business, and in the time-honored Italian tradition, he employed his younger brother, Bartolomé, as his agent in northern Europe. The chronicler

COLUMBUS AT THE COUNCIL OF SALAMANCA. Bronze relief, detail from the Rogers Doors (sculpted by Randolph Rogers, 1858) in the Rotunda of the U.S. Capitol. The doors depict various scenes from the life of Columbus.   ARCHITECT OF THE CAPITOL

Andrés Bernáldez reports that Columbus was selling printed books—a growth industry at that time—in several cities in southern Spain. He probably also sent books to Bartolomé, who was based in Lisbon and trading with France and England.

The nature of Columbus's employment with the Castilian monarchy was never divulged. The journal entries written by the royal accounting clerks give only the vaguest sense of what his service to the monarchy was: "On this day I gave 3,000 maravedis to Christopher Columbus, foreigner, who is here on Her Majesty's secret service." This means not that he was a spy but that the project was still too sensitive to be made public. Several possibilities concerning his activities have been suggested, among them that Columbus had already started some preparations for the momentous voyage west, and that the secrecy was necessary to prevent Portuguese spies from finding out about the project. But this is unlikely because, as Columbus himself complained, the monarchs did not approve the project immediately.

Another suggestion, more credible, is that Columbus was involved in selling war booty for the royal treasury. The monarchs during 1487 and 1488 were following a new strategy, attacking the coast in order to outflank the Muslim capital in Granada and cut it off from trade and assistance from the sea. On May 7, the king set siege to the city of Málaga, which, contrary to the monarchs' expectations, refused to surrender and put up the most stubborn resistance of the entire war. On May 23, Isabel left Córdoba to join Fernando in the royal encampment outside Málaga while the siege dragged on, costing more time and money than the monarchs had anticipated and arousing their determination to deal harshly with the Malagueños once they were defeated. On August 18, the monarchs launched a massive assault against the city and its fortress and then returned to the royal encampment while their troops destroyed the defeated city and enslaved its inhabitants. Ten days after taking this potentially lucrative prize, the queen sent Columbus four thousand maravedis from the royal treasury "so that he could go to the royal encampment at Málaga." The coincidence is probably significant.

In this world of war booty and government contracts, the Genoese were the most famous but by no means the only operators. In Spain Columbus did business with Italians from Florence, Milan, and Naples, and with Castilian, Aragonese, and Portuguese merchants, nobles, and monarchs. Although Columbus was traveling almost constantly, moving merchandise from one city or country to another, his years in Spain are the best-documented period of his life, for wherever Italian businessmen went they left a paper trail. Several hundred Spanish documents by and about Columbus and his business associates, only recently discovered and examined by historians, yield a fairly full picture of Columbus's career during this period. They reveal that Columbus studies published before 1980 were romantic fictions and show that he was, first and foremost, interested in commerce and profit.

If Columbus was involved with the war at all, it may have concerned the transport and sale of enslaved Muslim war captives. He formed a business association with a Florentine merchant in Seville, Juanoto Berardi, who had been engaged in slave trading in Portugal and then moved to Spain about 1485. Berardi would later finance Columbus's huge investment in the momentous 1492 voyage, and the two Italians maintained their association until Berardi's bankruptcy and death in 1495.

A more attractive explanation of Columbus's employment by the Castilian monarchy centers around the queen's primary concern at the time—preparations for the marriage of her eldest daughter, Princess Isabel. A marriage between the Castilian and Portuguese royal families had been anticipated in the Treaty of Alcáçovas that the two monarchies had signed in 1479 ending Portuguese participation in the Castilian succession war. Princess Isabel (born October 7, 1470) was now of marriageable age, and her parents began negotiations for a marriage with the crown prince of Portugal, Afonso. Queen Isabel threw herself into the arrangements with all the force of her personality.

The marriage alliance with Portugal fulfilled Castilian objectives at the highest level, resolving foreign policy issues of overwhelming significance. Negotiations, appropriately, were carried out by high-level diplomats in secrecy. But at another level, the marriage posed an embarrassing dilemma involving Castilian prestige and the queen's personal pride. The Portuguese court prided itself on being the most elegant in Europe. Members of the royal family wore the latest hat fashions from Flanders when having their portraits painted, and they furnished their palaces with luxurious tapestries and tableware.

The Spanish royal family lived in utter simplicity compared to the Portuguese. The Castilian royal court was ambulatory, moving all year except for the coldest winter months. The royal family did not have a residence, except for a couple of hunting lodges and castles, such as the Alcázar in the city walls of Segovia and the fourteenth-century Alcázar Palace that had been built by King Pedro in Seville. In every other place to which they traveled, Fernando and Isabel borrowed someone's house, usually a bishop's palace. When they were on campaign, as they frequently were from 1474 until 1492, they set up camp and lived in tents. If any housewifely impulses stirred in Queen Isabel, she satisfied them with needle and thread; she made and embroidered all King Fernando's shirts.

This level of personal and domestic simplicity would not do for the marriages of her children, and no one could have been more aware of it than the queen; she herself had not had a trousseau because she and Fernando had eloped. Queen Isabel's personal pride was at stake in every aspect of her daughter's wedding, clothing, and future household. Requiring samples of the latest Lisbon fashions and furnishings, she may well have turned to someone like Columbus, who had access to the Portuguese royal court and moved between the two societies at a certain practical level.

In early 1488, he wrote to King João II, asking for permission to return to Portugal under a safe conduct. Columbus and Berardi may also have been offering to sell Muslim slaves to the Portuguese. On March 20, João replied to Columbus's letter, addressing him as "our special friend in Seville," assuring him of royal protection, and urging him to return to Portugal where his services would be appreciated.

Columbus also had powerful personal reasons to return to Portugal; his wife had died during his absence. (Columbus once reminded Queen Isabel that in order to enter her service he had left behind "wife and children whom I never saw again.") But now that he worked for the Castilian queen, he needed guarantees from arrest by the suspicious Portuguese king so that he could settle his wife's estate and pick up his one remaining child in Portugal, Diego.

Although Columbus stayed in Portugal for about two

years, there is no record of his activities in that country either for then or for any other period. Nevertheless, the overall timing and tenor of Spanish documents indicate that he was probably working at least part time on the project that preoccupied Isabel during this period, arrangements for the royal wedding.

On May 12, 1489, Queen Isabel sent a letter to the city council of Seville instructing the city to give free lodging and provisions to Columbus, whom she expected to return to Seville soon. But Columbus did not come, and so he missed the most spectacular Spanish event of the year 1490. The Portuguese envoy arrived in Seville to finalize the marriage contract, and Queen Isabel personally supervised preparations for the wedding festivities, gifts, and bride's trousseau. The bride's table service alone, all of gold and silver, cost 3,277,227 maravedis. Princess Isabel signed the contract in Seville on April 18, 1490, and the festivities were elaborate. The bride's brother, Prince Juan, organized processions, plays and masques, jousts, sports competitions, and banquets. The expenses of costumes, gifts, horse trappings, and food were so great that the monarchs had to borrow money to pay for them.

By the time the contracts were carried to Portugal for Afonso to sign there, the hot summer of southern Spain made travel dangerous. Fernando and Isabel, justifiably as it turned out, could not bring themselves to bid good-bye to their firstborn child until November. The doomed bridegroom and his splendidly costumed entourage met her at the Portuguese border, and the bridal procession moved slowly through an elaborate series of wedding festivities that outshone even the spectacles in Seville. But by July 1491, Prince Afonso was dead, trampled after a fall from his horse during a racing competition. Princess Isabel returned to Castile in widow's garb and was met by her grieving parents in Íllora, just outside Granada.

The Portuguese marriage, in which Castile had invested so much money and hope, had failed, and that failure coincided with Columbus's return to Spain later that year. He was deeply depressed and in desperate financial straits. Despite King João's cordial invitation to him in 1488, the stay in Portugal had left him destitute. He reentered Spain through the port of Huelva, intending to leave his son with his wife's sister Violante (or Briolanja) Moniz and her husband, Miguel Molyart, only to find that the couple had moved. Columbus was now a stranger; no one in the towns of Huelva or nearby Moguer or Palos remembered having seen him before. And his years away apparently affected his ability to speak Castilian; years later, witnesses recalled that he spoke with a heavy foreign accent.

The father and his twelve-year-old son now set out on foot in the direction of Seville. They got as far as the Franciscan monastery of La Rábida and there made friends

La Rábida Monastery.

with the friar Juan Pérez. Columbus's talent for winning the loyalty of expert and well-connected supporters once again served him well; Pérez had trained as a clerk in the queen's treasury office. Pérez sent a letter to the queen, informing her of Columbus's arrival and asking her to permit Pérez to come to court as Columbus's agent and representative.

Receiving a favorable reply two weeks later, Pérez rented a mule from a citizen of the town of Moguer and went to join the court in Santa Fe, where he told the queen that Columbus and his son were ragged, without connections, and without funds. Pérez worked miracles with his old colleagues on the queen's accounting staff. The monarchs sent twenty thousand maravedis in gold coins to Columbus—payment for his two years of service in Portugal.

Proposal for a Western Voyage Revived. Pérez must have also told the monarchs what the Portuguese had learned about Africa. Events in Lisbon had once again stirred Columbus's ambition to find a western route to Asia. He was present at the Portuguese court in December 1488 when Bartolomeu Dias returned from a nearly two-year voyage and announced his discovery of the route around the Cape of Good Hope. Now that Africa had been rounded, the southern route to the Indian Ocean became available to Portuguese shippers. But Columbus drew his own conclusions. Africa extended much farther south than the Portuguese had hoped. They would have direct access to Asian trade, but the new route was not going to be shorter and more profitable than going through the Venetian trading stations in the eastern Mediterranean. The Portuguese king had entered the competition, but he had not won it. The field was still open for the Spaniards.

Now everything seemed in place for Castile to venture forth on a western voyage to Asia. King Fernando had conquered every Muslim city remaining in Spain except the capital itself, Granada. Because this city was completely cut off from supplies and allies, it agreed to capitulate without a fight. Once the Castilian diplomats had established surrender terms with the king of Granada, negotiations between the monarchs and Columbus began in earnest.

Fernando and Isabel were represented in these negotiations by the king's secretary Juan de Coloma, and Friar Juan Pérez acted as agent for Columbus. Coloma and Pérez worked out terms (capitulations) for a business partnership in which the monarchs would venture capital and Columbus would risk his life. Once the negotiators agreed on the terms, Pérez informed Columbus, who left Diego with the friars in La Rábida and traveled to the court on a rented mule. He arrived to see Castilian flags flying over the conquered city's fortresses.

Although he could now enjoy the wonders of one of Europe's largest and most sophisticated consumer societies, Columbus still faced obstacles. The monarchs once again placed the proposal and the new information about Africa before a subcommittee of the royal council. The proposal was the talk of Santa Fe that season; years later a witness named Miguel Toro testified that he had heard many people in the royal encampment discuss the question. The Castilian scientists, lawyers, and mariners were aware that Columbus's assumptions about the size of the globe were incorrect, and they pointed this out again to the subcommittee. The royal council confirmed the judgment of the earlier subcommittee; Columbus was wrong about the distance that a voyage from Spain to Asia would have to cover.

Columbus left the court in discouragement, but at this point King Fernando stepped in and turned the proceedings around. The capture of the city of Granada had changed Castilian perspectives on the possibilities of Asian trade. What the Spaniards found in Granada when they entered the city on January 2, 1492, could only have whetted their appetites for exotic goods. The marketplaces for silk, ceramics, and spices, as well as stunning palaces and mosques, had survived intact because the city had been spared a bombardment. If this was any indication of what Asia's cities held, it was worth the risk of failure. After all, the monarchs themselves would not be in any danger, and Castilian seamen were experienced and competent enough to take care of themselves.

The king, Bishop Talavera, and Bishop Diego de Deza therefore decided to explore the possibilities for financing the voyage as an experiment. Fernando's pensions clerk, Luis de Santángel, found the right argument to persuade the queen. His reasoning was economic: a relatively small investment by the king and queen held the potential for returning great profits. The journey, if it succeeded, could

solve an urgent financial dilemma. The royal treasury faced the continuing expense of further weddings, and within a year the monarchs would need an additional 24,250,000 maravedis, which they had agreed to pay the Muslim king as indemnity for Granada.

Royal officials who had thought there was no money to spare for a risky voyage now began a serious search of the accounts for any overlooked fund. The royal council, in its capacity as supreme court of law, had recently handed down a decision in a case brought by the king of Portugal. João accused seamen from the town of Palos of having violated Portuguese fishing territory off the west coast of Africa. The Castilian royal council found the defendants guilty and sentenced the town council of Palos to provide two caravels for royal service for one year. Queen Isabel thus had two ships available for which she would not have to pay leases.

Still, the voyage would require a cash outlay to charter a third ship and to outfit the ships, buy provisions and equipment, and pay the crews' wages. The monarchs did not have cash on hand, nor did they have any collateral available for a loan. The war had strapped royal finances so seriously that the queen had pawned her jewels to pay for the siege of the city of Baza two years earlier. But Santángel, who was familiar with every intricacy of court finance, pointed out that there was now a peace dividend. The federation (Santa Hermandad) of Castilian cities and towns whose funds had previously been allocated for the war effort had a surplus balance. Santángel advanced 1.4 million maravedis from the Hermandad's treasury to finance the voyage.

For the Spanish monarchs, the venture was purely and simply economic. They were at this point not trying to convert souls or reclaim the Holy Land, as later papal bulls (decrees) made politically necessary; rather, they sought pearls, gold, silver, spices, and other merchandise and resources of any sort. Even Bartolomé de las Casas, himself a fervent missionary to the Indians, reports Santángel's speech to Isabel without the missionary motive that weighed so heavily later. On behalf of the monarchs, Coloma had negotiated a strictly commercial agreement forming a business partnership between the monarchs and Columbus.

Columbus's prime vocation, of course, was international commerce, and his major preoccupation at this point was to secure royal partnership, on the Portuguese model, for a major voyage of commerce to Asia. Columbus, however, wanted more than the usual business partnership. Perhaps inspired by the example of his Portuguese in-laws on Porto Santo, he demanded military and governing authority over any islands or mainland he might discover in the Atlantic, and he wanted these as hereditary offices, not just as lifetime appointments. The granting of hereditary offices, especially to foreigners, went against royal policy, and at first the monarchs refused. On the other hand, Fernando and Isabel wanted to gain legal possession of any islands Columbus might find in the Atlantic. The monarchs intended to settle and develop them as entrepôts and supply stations on the way to Asia. Castile's claims to legal possession would be strongest if Columbus were a royal official, not just the monarchs' business partner.

On April 17, 1492, the monarchs signed the partnership terms known as the Santa Fe Capitulations. The partners agreed that Fernando and Isabel would supply two fully outfitted ships, their crews, and provisions and receive nine-tenths of any revenues. Columbus would provide his management and expertise and receive one-tenth of the revenues. If he wanted to invest money in the enterprise, he could supply up to one-eighth of the cost of outfitting the voyage and receive one-eighth of the profits.

In Granada on April 30, 1492, the monarchs issued a letter patent giving him title to everything he had asked, a document now known as the Capitulations of Granada. They decreed that, once he discovered and took possession of any islands or continent, he would be their hereditary admiral of the Ocean Sea and viceroy and governor of what he discovered, and he and his descendants would be addressed as "sir."

Throughout the negotiations and preparations, the purpose and the destination of the voyage were state secrets. Fernando and Isabel imposed strict security, issuing only sketchy orders to the fleet's outfitters and officers. If the Spanish monarchs had made public their intention of sailing west to Asia, spies would have reported the news immediately to Portugal. Thus the monarchs described the fleet's destination in the vaguest possible terms—"certain parts of the Ocean Sea."

The First Voyage. Columbus and Juan Pérez returned to the monastery on the night of May 22. For the next two months, Columbus worked to equip and man his little fleet in Palos. Fernando and Isabel issued orders implementing their part of the contract, instructing the town council of Palos to provide Columbus with two ships for a year. The town council probably used municipal funds to lease two caravels, *Niña* and *Pinta,* from members of the Pinzón family, who may have been involved in committing the trespass in the first place.

Columbus chartered a third ship, the cargo carrier *Santa María,* which he found in the port of Sanlúcar de Barrameda and leased from its owner, Juan de la Cosa. Columbus apparently did this as his share of financing the voyage, using money from his business partner, Juanoto Berardi. Berardi must have had an enormous amount of cash on hand, or he and Columbus borrowed from investors; Columbus's share of the expedition's total cost

of 4 million maravedis has been estimated at 500,000 maravedis.

Columbus persuaded members of the Pinzón family, a highly regarded shipping dynasty in Palos and Moguer, to serve as captains of two ships, and the Pinzóns then helped persuade other seamen from Palos, Huelva, and Moguer to sign on as crew. The monarchs guaranteed that during their service on the voyage the seamen's private property would not be seized and sold to pay any court-ordered damages and fines. Juan de la Cosa also agreed to go on the voyage, and he may have persuaded *Santa María*'s crew, who were mostly from the Basque lands, to sign on. Columbus himself hired two translators, whom he expected to need in the Indian Ocean where the long-distance shippers and pilots were Arabs.

During the spring and summer, Fernando and Isabel ordered merchants and outfitters to sell supplies and equipment to Columbus at reasonable prices. They instructed government officials not to collect royal taxes on the sales, extending these exemptions to Columbus's purchases for his personal needs. The monarchs issued a total of 1.4 million maravedis to Columbus as reimbursement for the money he spent to buy equipment and provisions.

These preparations for the first voyage were begun at the worst possible time of year for provisioning a fleet. By the time Columbus left Granada on May 12, 1492, the previous year's wheat supplies would have been almost depleted, and the new crop would not be harvested until June and threshed until July. Until the end of the summer, wheat would be scarce for making the ship's biscuit (unsalted twice-baked bread) that would be the staple food during the journey. Columbus had calculated that it would take six weeks to reach Asia. He expected to find islands all along the way but could not count on finding food on them; experience had shown that most Atlantic islands were not inhabited. He had to provision the ships on the assumption that the fleet would not get fresh supplies before reaching its destination. Well aware that Dias had taken almost two years to explore around the tip of Africa and back, Columbus had outfitters and provisioners load enough supplies for a year. The amount of wheat required to prepare ship's biscuit for almost one hundred men for so long must have strained the resources of the countryside around Palos that summer. Fernando and Isabel sent a royal agent, Juan de Peñalosa, to the coast to supervise the collection of supplies and equipment.

Preparations reached a peak of activity in July. Dockworkers loaded carefully packed supplies and merchandise in the holds. Able seamen rigged the sails, tested the lines, and brought their own sea chests on board. Columbus secured a home and revenues for his son

Diego. At his request, the monarchs had appointed Diego a page in the household of Prince Juan, with a yearly allowance for clothing and expenses. But Diego did not go to court yet; he went to live with Columbus's mistress, Beatriz de Arana, for whom Columbus had probably bought a house in Seville.

All was ready in time to take advantage of the safe sailing season at the beginning of August, but the departure had to be postponed for the benefit of the crew. The region around Huelva and Palos celebrated the Feast of the Virgin on August 2, and this was the traditional day to settle accounts, pay annual rents, and sign contracts for the coming year. Columbus paid the crew four months' wages in advance. The crewmen made their final arrangements for their families and property; they gave powers of attorney to their wives, deposed testimony in pending litigation, or became engaged to marry. The fleet left the port of Palos just before dawn on August 3, 1492, put in to the Canary Islands for repairs, fresh water, and additional provisions on August 9, and sailed from the last Spanish port on September 9.

After making landfall in the Bahamas at dawn on October 12, Columbus explored the coasts and named a large number of islands, including Cuba and La Española. He landed and spoke with the islanders in several languages, including Arabic, but without finding a common tongue. Most disappointing of all, he found no cities,

much less luxury consumer goods. Columbus's imagination did not fail him now; he concluded that these must be offshore islands close to the Asian continent. Since he could find no Great Khan or any other ruler with sovereignty over all of any one island, he felt justified in claiming each as Castilian territory. With the act of possession, he became an officer of the Kingdom of Castile—Admiral of the Ocean Sea and viceroy and governor of whatever he claimed for Castile. He would not prove equal to the challenge.

On the island of La Española Columbus had his first opportunity to act as governor of a Spanish territory. The results were not happy. On Christmas Day, *Santa María* ran aground, and there was insufficient space on the remaining ships for all the crews. Columbus salvaged timbers and planking from *Santa María* to construct a palisaded trading post, which he named La Navidad. Here he left behind thirty-eight unfortunate men under the command of the fleet's marshal, Diego de Arana, cousin of Beatriz. He sailed for Spain on January 4, 1493.

Columbus returned to Palos on March 15, 1493, and began a new style of life in Spain as a noble and honored hero. He could not know how brief this moment of glory would be. The monarchs, who were visiting Fernando's Aragonese domains, immediately summoned him to the royal court in Barcelona. According to the Capitulations, as soon as he had encountered and taken possession of an island, he was transformed from plain Christopher Columbus to Sir Christopher Columbus. In the royal letter, the rulers addressed him as Admiral of the Ocean Sea, viceroy and governor of the islands, and "sir."

Leaving most of the crew in Palos to happy reunions with family and friends, weddings, and years of tale-telling, the Admiral went to Seville with his Indian captives, exotic souvenirs, and some of the crew and then traveled by land to the court. Years later, Bartolomé de las Casas recalled what a deep impression this little entourage had made on his boyhood imagination; he had been fascinated by the large balls the Indians carried, which, when thrown to the ground, bounced back up as high as they started. These were the first samples of rubber Europeans had seen. Las Casas did not mention what he learned later—that throughout the Caribbean basin Indians played a deadly game with these rubber balls, a form of basketball in which the captain of the losing team lost his life.

Fernando and Isabel received Columbus with joy when he finally arrived in Barcelona. Now that the enterprise had become a reality and Columbus had fulfilled the terms of the contract by actually discovering and taking possession of islands, the monarchs and the Admiral rushed to formalize their agreements and prepare a return voyage. In a confirmation drawn up in Barcelona in March 1493,

DEPARTURE OF COLUMBUS FROM PALOS. Bronze relief, detail from the Rogers Doors (1858) in the U.S. Capitol.

ARCHITECT OF THE CAPITOL

the royal secretaries made public for the first time the partnership contract and privileges of the Capitulations.

A Return Voyage. The first concern of Columbus and the monarchs was a return voyage to resupply the unfortunate crew left behind at La Navidad. Despite Columbus's assurances that the native people were meek and peaceful, no one could expect good relations to continue when the Europeans' provisions ran low. And indeed the crew had to barter for food by offering European goods of little value to Caribbean islanders; most of the European merchandise was wool cloth. The metal tools and equipment were highly desirable to the island people who had none, but European coins had no value in the local barter economy.

Thus, within a month of Columbus's return to Spain, he was instructed to organize another transatlantic crossing. In addition to relieving La Navidad, the monarchs, in the time-honored tradition of Castilian expansion in the Iberian Peninsula, wanted to lay effective claim to the islands by having Castilian citizens settle and cultivate the land. They appointed Juan Rodríguez de Fonseca as their agent to supply and organize the fleets to America. Columbus and Fonseca traveled from Barcelona to Seville together and, in these early stages, cooperated amicably to prepare a massive second voyage. Fonseca proved to be a superb administrator and soon was supervising all government contracts, fleet outfitting, emigration, and navigational matters concerned with America.

Because of Fonseca's amazing endurance and capabilities, the second voyage assumed a scale unimagined for the first. Over twelve hundred men were on board when the ships departed during September 1493. Hundreds of Spanish farmers and artisans, carrying tools, seeds, seedlings, and livestock, went as settlers to the new Castilian territory, and dozens of Italian and Spanish merchants now clamored to invest in contracts with Columbus. His boyhood friend Michele da Cuneo and his youngest brother Diego came from Italy to embark on the voyage. Five or six baptized islanders whom Columbus had brought to Spain six months earlier returned to the Caribbean with him to act as translators. The monarchs insisted that Columbus take a military force of cavalry, and sent the first Christian priests to America, a team of clergy led by Friar Bernardo Buil, to minister to the spiritual needs of the new colony and convert the natives. Other passengers who would later play distinguished roles in the American venture were the Seville physician Diego Alvarez Chanca; the cartographer Juan de la Cosa; Francisco de las Casas, father of Bartolomé; and Juan Ponce de León and Alonso de Ojeda, businessmen turned explorers.

Seventeen vessels of various types and capacities made the journey, Fonseca and Columbus having chartered them from private owners. Several probably belonged to

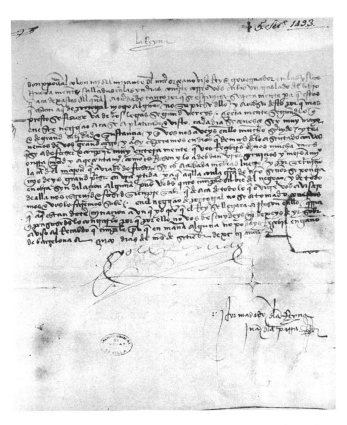

LETTER FROM QUEEN ISABEL TO COLUMBUS. Dated Barcelona, September 5, 1493. Isabel, with this letter, is returning a book Columbus had lent her and asks that he send her a certain navigation chart, if finished. She further requests that he not delay the departure of his voyage.

ARCHIVO GENERAL DE INDIAS, SEVILLE

the duke of Medinaceli, who had wasted not a minute in asking the monarchs to use his town of Puerto de Santa María as the port for future trade with America.

Everything we know about the preparations for the second voyage indicates a close and harmonious understanding between the Spanish monarchs and the Admiral of the Ocean Sea. Columbus and Fonseca together selected the settlers and merchants who were allowed to embark. Columbus himself drafted the specifications for the voyage, which the monarchs issued in Barcelona on May 29. The instructions covered the conduct of the voyage, the order of departure, the organization of the fleet, the course, and the procedure to be followed on arrival.

Isabel, Fernando, and Columbus all had the same hopes for the second voyage: to establish a permanent Castilian town on the island of La Española. The townspeople would supply food and textiles for sale to colonists, merchants, and natives. With this base, the Admiral could create a royal trading post through which all commerce with Asia would be conducted, collect or mine gold, and provide manpower for further exploration. Optimistic, but sadly mistaken hopes prevailed for the future of Spanish trade with Asia.

The monarchy's second concern was to gain public acknowledgment of Castilian sovereignty over the islands and western Ocean Sea. Publicity was essential. For this, Fernando's secretaries made extracts from the journal Columbus had kept of the first voyage and from a letter he had sent from Lisbon. The king published this Castilian extract, known as the *First Letter from America*, in Barcelona and then commissioned a Latin translation for publication in Rome and other cities throughout Europe. This publicity was intended as groundwork for gaining clear legal title to the islands.

Rather than reopen old disputes with Portugal, the monarchs turned to the only international court of appeals

<small>DEPICTION OF ISLANDS DISCOVERED BY COLUMBUS. Woodcut from the Basel edition of the *First Letter from America*, 1493.</small>

<small>NEW YORK PUBLIC LIBRARY, RARE BOOKS DIVISION</small>

in Christendom, the papacy. Pope Alexander VI issued a series of bulls, dividing the Ocean Sea into Spanish and Portuguese spheres of exploration and settlement and rested legal title to islands and continents squarely on conversion of the native people to Christianity. Fernando and Isabel, by seeking legitimation from the church, transformed the nature of European government in America from its purely commercial Spanish and Italian origins to an enterprise infused with religious objectives. The Admiral, who had now arrived in America, did not yet know about the papal conditions imposed on the enterprise, though he would have approved of them heartily. Instead, he had his hands full coping with the natives and settlers of these islands from which he had promised so much.

By the time the Admiral returned to Seville in June 1496, the hard realities of the Caribbean had become apparent. He could not know that these realities would continue to decimate every Spanish expedition and settlement that followed for the next century, but he certainly knew that the signs were ominous for his own reputation and fortune. Despite his first glowing reports to the monarchs in 1493, the experience of the second voyage showed that the Caribbean environment could not support a European society without major compromises. The native peoples, the soil, and the climate were hostile. All the Admiral's expectations from the islands were disappointed: he found no cities, no money economy, no metal tools, manufactures, or ores.

Meanwhile, his new city—La Isabela—and trading post were floundering. The city council of La Isabela, which convened its first meeting on April 24, 1494, was helpless to avert the impending collapse of the colony. The European crops the Castilian farmers planted—wheat, barley, grapes, olives, cotton, fruits, legumes, and vegetables—failed in the tropical climate, and the food and feed supplies brought from Seville suffered an alarming rate of spoilage. Columbus refused to issue provisions from the stock he kept in the fortified royal warehouse, the only stone structure he built in La Isabela. Desperately hungry, Spaniards moved to island villages and "went native."

The demographic consequences for this and future Spanish colonies were appallingly apparent to the royal court in Castile. The modern popular notion that only Indians suffered from the bacterial and viral infections Europeans brought with them, that Europeans were immune to disease, is both biologically and historically incorrect. The monarchs could see that Europeans in the Americas died in large numbers from disease as well as warfare and shipwreck. Of the ninety crew and officers on the first voyage, thirty-nine died in La Navidad during 1493. Of the twelve hundred crew, staff, and passengers on the second voyage, three hundred died of disease in La Isabela during 1494, despite the heroic care of Dr. Chanca. Columbus himself almost died in this epidemic, and he suffered serious aftereffects for the rest of his life. He also reported to the monarchs that every contingent of Spaniards who went into the interior of the island returned with yellow complexions and seriously ill.

The weather was also hostile. A hurricane in 1495 destroyed all the ships in the harbor of La Isabela, including those that Columbus's financial backer Berardi had leased and loaded with merchandise. Columbus was able to return to Spain only by patching together two ships from the wreckage. He rounded up twelve hundred captured native Americans and selected five hundred for sale in Spain.

Columbus's Reputation Fades. Columbus's report to the monarchs when he arrived in Seville in June 1496 confirmed rumors they had already heard from the resupply ships that had crossed the ocean during 1494 and 1495. Fernando and Isabel gave the Admiral a distracted if not cool reception. They were busy with another royal wedding, even more spectacular and fateful than the first; this one—between Prince Juan and Margaret of Burgundy—would link their family to the Habsburg rulers of the Netherlands, Austria, and the Holy Roman Empire. They were also negotiating a second Portuguese marriage for the widowed Princess Isabel, to Prince Manuel, brother of her deceased husband Afonso. In April, the court celebrated the wedding of Juan and Margaret of Burgundy. Columbus played no part in these crucial negotiations and events.

Instead, the royal government kept him waiting in Seville, where he told his story to Andrés Bernáldez and Juan Rodríguez de Fonseca and tried to sell his American captives in the Seville slave market. Las Casas believed that the monarchs' neglect of the Admiral was based on a positive coolness to his slaving activities. Queen Isabel had developed a neat legal distinction between trading in slaves from other countries and enslaving her own subjects, a distinction that would later be adopted by the English colonists of North America. She suspended the sale of American natives and chastised the slavers.

By the time the monarchs summoned Columbus to court in Burgos and held an audience with him in April 1497, relations were decidedly cool. Furthermore, the royal treasury was once again empty. The monarchs approved a third voyage and granted Columbus some personal favors, but their funding and paperwork for the voyage moved at a glacially slow pace. No American-bound ships embarked from Spain that year, and since there were no sailing ships left in the islands, 1497 was the only year after 1492 that ships have not crossed between Spain and the Americas. Furthermore, when the monarchs issued orders for the new crossing, they did so with such a profusion of details as to indicate a lack of confidence in the Admiral's judgment and reliability.

In this threatening atmosphere, Columbus returned to the Andalusian coast to organize and launch his third voyage, which left Spain on May 30, 1498, and explored the coast of Venezuela. There the Spaniards encountered rivers whose force and volume emptying into the sea constituted clear evidence that they drained a very large continent, not just an island. No one knew how far north and south this continent might extend or how wide it was.

The only good news came in La Española, where the Spaniards had found gold nuggets, which they were collecting through placer mining. The news started a gold rush. In 1498, for the first time, Columbus had good reason to believe he would realize a profit on his Asian venture. Nevertheless, when he and his brothers returned to Spain in 1500, they were under arrest and accused of mismanaging their responsibilities as royal governors of the Spanish colonies. They had persisted in refusing to distribute provisions from the royal warehouse; their continued denial of self-government to Spaniards who moved out of La Isabela to establish new towns and grow their own food had inspired a rebellion among the colonists. The royal government no longer trusted the Admiral as administrator of Spanish law and justice.

Fernando and Isabel also reconsidered their Asian policy. The monarchs had come to grips with new realities. Columbus had not arrived at the Spice Islands; he had been wrong about the extent of the Ocean Sea, and apparently a continent stood between them and Asia. In the five years from 1492 through 1497, they had invested millions of maravedis and received no profit. In fact, they had lost ships, men, and cargo on an appalling scale for peacetime voyages. They did not necessarily blame Columbus for these losses, but they did decide to develop a new policy. They would no longer send all their ships to one island under the command of one admiral. Instead, they authorized Fonseca to commission one or two voyages each year, financed by corporations of stockholders and commanded by experienced merchant shippers. Between May 1499 and June 1505, eleven of these "Andalusian voyages" systematically explored the coast and islands of South and Central America.

The monarchs permitted Columbus to make a final voyage in 1502, this time as a private venture without their partnership. They continued to address him as Admiral, but they forbade him to exercise any governing powers on the islands he had brought under their sovereignty. His administrative failures in America had diminished his reputation in Spain, and the disastrous fourth voyage damaged public opinion of his seamanship. The heady days of 1493, when all ahead seemed promising and everyone praised his acumen, had come to earth in just ten years. He spent his last years in a shadowy existence in Spain—a distrusted foreigner of faded glory and tarnished reputation.

[See also *Española, La; Granada; Isabel and Fernando; Rábida, La; Reconquista; Settlements,* articles on *La Navidad* and *La Isabela; Spain; Treaty of Alcáçovas; Voyages of Columbus.*]

BIBLIOGRAPHY

Ayala, Juan de. *A Letter to Ferdinand and Isabella, 1503.* Translated by Charles E. Nowell. Minneapolis, 1965.

Ballesteros Beretta, Antonio. *Cristóbal Colón y el descubrimiento de América.* 2 vols. Barcelona and Buenos Aires, 1945.

Cartas de particulares a Colón y relaciones coetáneas. Edited by Juan Gil and Consuelo Varela. Madrid, 1984.

Casas, Bartolomé de las. *Historia de las Indias.* Edited by André Saint-Lu. Vol. 1. Caracas, 1986.

Columbus, Christopher. *Los cuatro viajes: Testamento.* Edited by Consuelo Varela. Madrid, 1986.

Columbus, Christopher. *Textos y documentos completos: Relaciones de viajes, cartas y memoriales.* Edited by Consuelo Varela. Madrid, 1984.

Columbus, Christopher. *The Diario of Christopher Columbus's First Voyage to America, 1492–1493.* Edited and translated by Oliver Dunn and James E. Kelley, Jr. Norman, Okla., 1989.

Columbus, Ferdinand. *The Life of the Admiral Christopher Columbus by His Son Ferdinand.* Translated and annotated by Benjamin Keen. New Brunswick, N.J., 1959.

Fernández-Armesto, Felipe. *The Canary Islands after the Conquest: The Making of a Colonial Society in the Early Sixteenth Century.* Oxford, 1982.

First Images of America: The Impact of the New World on the Old. Edited by Fredi Chiappelli. Berkeley, 1976.

Floyd, Troy S. *The Columbus Dynasty in the Caribbean, 1492–1526.* Albuquerque, 1973.

Gil, Juan, and Consuelo Varela. *Temas colombinos.* Seville, 1986.

Giménez Fernández, Manuel. *Bartolomé de las Casas.* 2 vols. Seville, 1953, 1960.

Ladero Quesada, Miguel Angel. *Spain in 1492.* Translated by Helen Nader and Roland Pearson. Bloomington, Ind., forthcoming.

Manzano Manzano, Juan. *Cristóbal Colón: Siete años decisivos de su vida, 1485–1492.* Madrid, 1964.

Manzano Manzano, Juan. *Los Pinzones y el descubrimiento de América.* 3 vols. Madrid, 1988.

Morison, Samuel Eliot. *Admiral of the Ocean Sea: A Life of Christopher Columbus.* 2 vols. Boston, 1942.

Phillips, Carla, and William D. Phillips, Jr. *The Worlds of Christopher Columbus.* Cambridge, forthcoming.

Ramos, Demetrio. *Audacia, negocios y política en los viajes españoles de "descubrimiento y rescate."* Valladolid, 1981.

Roberts, David. *Great Exploration Hoaxes.* San Francisco, 1982.

Rumeu de Armas, Antonio. *El "Portugués" Cristóbal Colón en Castilla.* Madrid, 1982.

Rumeu de Armas, Antonio. *Hernando Colón, historiador del descubrimiento de América.* Madrid, 1973.

Rumeu de Armas, Antonio. *Itinerario de los Reyes Católicos, 1474–1516.* Madrid, 1974.

Rumeu de Armas, Antonio. *La Rábida y el descubrimiento de América: Colón, Marchena y Fray Juan Pérez.* Madrid, 1968.

Torre, José de la. *Beatriz Enríquez de Harana y Cristóbal Colón.* Madrid, 1933.

Varela, Consuelo. *Colón y los florentinos.* Madrid, 1988.

HELEN NADER

The Final Years, Illness, and Death

In 1506, Columbus could have looked back on his career and felt satisfied that he had accomplished what he had wanted to achieve when he came to Spain. At age fifty-five he was rich, famous, and honored. But Columbus was not satisfied with these achievements; he wanted more. And when he did not get more, he complained bitterly. Hence, paradoxes once again emerge in the story of Columbus. The Admiral died rich, but he complained about poverty. King Fernando and Queen Isabel showered him with honors and favors, but the letters that Columbus wrote in his final years are full of grievances.

The explanation for these paradoxes lies in several complicated changes that occurred in the final years of Columbus's life. Most of these changes, both administrative and personal, resulted from a growing awareness of the realities of America, realities that Columbus refused to acknowledge. A disparity between the Crown's accommodation and the Admiral's inflexibility surfaced during Columbus's third voyage (1498–1500), leading to disastrous results for the Admiral's prestige and authority.

Colonization of La Española was one of the principal objectives of the third voyage, but Columbus was unable to work harmoniously with the Spanish colonists. This conflict was not inevitable, nor was it strictly the result of hostility between Spaniards and Italians. Columbus remained on good terms with Spanish mariners, especially with the seamen of Palos. He did not expect to control these Spanish mariners; they had sailed the high seas before his 1492 voyage, and they continued to go on independent voyages. Yet Columbus failed to realize that Spanish farmers and artisans were equally independent and experienced. When he sought to control the actions of Spanish colonists, the consequence was revolt.

Spanish settlers in La Española found his government oppressive. The first Spanish city he had established on the island suffered a devastating epidemic and crop failure in 1494; most of the settlers died or returned to Spain. Those who remained on La Española claimed that Columbus's brothers, whom he left in charge while he explored other islands, did not understand the Spanish form of self-government through town councils.

If Columbus had any understanding of the settler's expectations, he had no intention of allowing them to live in the traditional Castilian way. He managed his city of La Isabela as if it were a Genoese trading station, or factory, in the Black Sea. Such a factory was simply a mercantile exchange, where businessmen could collect and store their merchandise and engage in currency exchanges until the fleet returned to Genoa.

The monarchs had agreed to Columbus's form of municipal governance in La Isabela, and, of course, they expected to make a substantial profit on their partnership with the Admiral. But they also assumed that the Spanish farmers of La Isabela would be able to provide enough food for the whole colony.

The settler's European crops failed to mature in the tropical climate, but Columbus remained inflexible. He refused to distribute supplies from the royal storehouse and forbade the colonists to farm elsewhere on the island. The ships that returned to Spain for resupply in 1494 carried may disillusioned settlers. Their disgruntled reports shattered the euphoria that had prevailed in the preparations for the second voyage.

Queen Isabel was very sensitive to the complaints from the returned settlers and understood the relationship between agricultural production and local self-government. In preparation for the third voyage, she gave the Admiral explicit instructions for establishing towns and distributing farm land. Such instructions had not previously been issued for the Americas; they were such an integral part of Castilian life that there had seemed no need to write them down.

Columbus accepted these instructions, but he did not implement them. Consequently, he had great difficulty recruiting farmers and other colonists for the third voyage. A comparison of his projected recruits in 1497 and the fleet's actual musters in 1498 show a serious shortage of colonists in all professions except the military.

When Columbus reached La Española, he found the entire island in turmoil. The Spanish crops had once again failed to mature, and Bartolomé and Diego Colón had

COLUMBUS IN CHAINS. Bronze relief, detail from the Rogers Doors (1858) in the U.S. Capitol. An interpretation of the events surrounding Columbus's arrest on La Española.

ARCHITECT OF THE CAPITOL

Occupations of Recruits for the Third Voyage

PARTIAL LISTING	PROJECTED RECRUITS (1497)	EMBARKED RECRUITS (1498)
Military officers	40	20
Enlisted men	0	57
Able seamen	30	15
Ship's apprentices	30	6
Gold miners	20	1
Unskilled workmen	100	50
Artisans	20	18
Farmers and gardeners	60	28
Women	30	6

refused the colonists' demands for seed and supplies from the royal storehouse. The colonists had gradually left La Isabela and followed the traditional methods of starting new towns. The man whom Columbus had appointed as appellate judge for the island, Francisco Roldán, led nearly one hundred Spaniards to the southwestern peninsula, where they established the town of Jaraguá. They started clearing fields, elected a town council, established a town marketplace, and petitioned Columbus for recognition of their town.

Though the settlers of Jaraguá had acted in accordance with Queen Isabel's instructions to Columbus, the Admiral called their actions rebellion. He refused to grant the Spaniards authority to live autonomously and declared the squatters rebels. In response to the rebels' complaints, the monarchs sent a royal judge, Francisco de Bobadilla, to investigate. By the time Bobadilla arrived in Santo Domingo, disputes between the Columbus brothers and the colonists had reached a stage of open rebellion and repression. Bobadilla sent Columbus and his brothers back to Spain under arrest.

King Fernando and Queen Isabel released Columbus immediately, but they took the complaints of the colonists very seriously and initiated some reforms. They stripped Columbus and his brothers of governing authority over Spanish settlers, appointed Nicolás de Ovando royal governor of La Española, and banished Columbus and his brothers from the island.

Failures in governing the colonists did not alienate the monarchs from their Admiral. They apparently agreed with the colonists' assessment that Columbus was acting out of ignorance because he was a foreigner. Far from rejecting him, the monarchs continued to support him and treat him as a respected business partner. Columbus had come full circle to his original role in the Santa Fe Capitulations, that is, as business partner to the monarchs. Money and commerce again dominated his career, and Genoese merchants in Seville again became his business associates.

His failures at governing had serious but not disastrous consequences for his financial affairs. Leaving a rich inheritance for his son Diego became the obsession of the Admiral's final years. Columbus expended much of his declining energy from 1498 to 1506 making sure that his financial privileges would remain intact and that his son Diego would inherit a rich estate.

Despite the disastrous financial losses the royal monopoly suffered on the first and second voyages, Fernando and Isabel treated Columbus with as much generosity as their treasury would allow. According to the Capitulations, Columbus's revenue from the Americas was to be one-tenth of the net royal income and one-eighth of the profits on voyages he helped to finance. But for the first five years of Spanish presence in the Americas, the monarchy received no income at all. Consequently, neither Columbus nor his financial backers received any profits.

Once the commercial difficulties began to emerge, the monarchs began modifying the original terms of commerce with the Americas. In order to compensate Columbus for his efforts and investments, the monarchs changed the partnership terms. On June 2, 1497, they ordered that Columbus, without having to invest anything at all, would receive one-eighth of the royal gross for the next three years and, thereafter, one-tenth of the royal net income.

By 1500, Columbus's income from America would have been considerable. Settlers from La Isabela had moved to the south shore of the island after they had found gold nuggets in the streams feeding into the Ozama River. By 1496, this gold rush to the south coast created a squatter settlement, Santo Domingo, to which Columbus's brother Bartolomé transferred his headquarters. The amount of wealth that passed through the city of Santo Domingo during the next few years made it the hub of Spanish government and trade in the Caribbean for the next three centuries. The Admiral appointed Alonso Sánchez de Carvajal, a former member of Queen Isabel's staff, as his business agent in Santo Domingo. Carvajal collected 240,000 maravedis as Columbus's share of the royal profits for 1494 through 1498, and 1500. (The account book for 1499 does not survive.) His income increased every year until the end of his life.

Though Columbus was rich, he was having trouble transferring his wealth from his agent in Santo Domingo to his financial backers in Seville, and this embittered Columbus against the royal treasurers in Seville. Small discrepancies between the Admiral's accounts and the treasury's audits turned into serious obstacles. At the time that he organized the third voyage, Columbus's accounts were being handled by his cousin Juan Antonio Colón. Juan Antonio's failure to balance his accounts prompted the royal treasurers to monitor the Admiral's accounts with extraordinary care. For example, while Columbus was still in Burgos in 1497, Pedro de Terreros signed on as his butler for the third voyage and received pay in advance from King Fernando's treasurer. Since he should have waited and received payment in Seville from the fleet treasurer, Bernardo Pinelo, the king's treasurer asked Pinelo for reimbursement and debited his accounts. Though all drafts associated with the voyage required Columbus's signature, Columbus never signed the voucher. Finally, Pinelo stopped all payments to the Admiral, pending the necessary transfer. Thus, even though Carvajal in Santo Domingo credited the correct amount of gold to the Admiral's account, the royal treasurer in Seville would not allow the Admiral or his creditors to withdraw the gold delivered to Seville.

The Admiral became frustrated. The monarchy's three-year grant to Columbus was drawing to a close. He wanted the grant extended or made permanent, but he also wanted to change some of its terms. He did not want to be dependent on the royal treasurers for an accounting of how much gold was being shipped from the Americas, and he wanted his own agents on both sides of the Atlantic free to draw from his accounts.

By September 1500, Carvajal was in Burgos, lobbying the monarchs for Columbus's demands. He stayed at the court until Juan Antonio Colón arrived in February 1501, apparently bringing Columbus's gold with him; during March and April, the two of them commissioned a silversmith to make a seal and a gold chain of forty-seven links for the Admiral. Clearly, the abrupt end of his governorship had not prevented Columbus from receiving gold in large amounts from the Americas.

Carvajal's tireless campaigning at court led to Columbus's regaining of some of his privileges. On December 27, 1501, the monarchs drafted a declaration of new procedures that permitted Columbus to have his own agent on La Española receive his share of the gold. He appointed Carvajal. According to the new regulations, both the Admiral's agent and the monarchy's inspector,

Diego Márques, had to be present when gold was minted and marked in Santo Domingo. Carvajal received the one-tenth of the minted gold for Columbus, as well as the one-eighth of the net profits on his investments. Carvajal remained in Santo Domingo, managing Columbus's business affairs in the islands and collecting the Admiral's share of the wealth of the Americas until 1502.

While in Spain Columbus made another commercial investment in the Americas. Ironically, this involved him in the voyage that transported to Santo Domingo his replacement as governor, Nicolás de Ovando. This investment also brought into the open serious conflicts between Columbus's profit motives and the colonists' consumer needs. The monarchs instructed fleet comptroller Jimeno de Brivicsca to permit Columbus to invest one-eighth of the cost of the voyage. Columbus did not hesitate to make arrangements for a huge investment in merchandise.

The Admiral's associates for the Ovando fleet were four Genoese businessmen in Seville: Francisco de Riberol, Francisco Doria, Francisco Cataño, and Gaspar de Spínola. These merchants had so much faith in the profitability of the Americas that they loaned Columbus more than 188,000 maravedis to pay his expenses in Spain in exchange for the privilege of selling their merchandise in America. Their one-eighth of the commercial cargo consisted of the usual Genoese merchandise—woolen cloth. When the merchandise reached Santo Domingo in 1501, the monarchy's business agent, Fernando de Monroy, refused to accept the goods. He claimed that they were "not things that could be sold here very quickly and were priced higher than their worth." Monroy's response reflects the fact that the royal treasurers in Seville suspected the investors of falsifying their accounts by recording higher prices than they had actually paid for the goods.

The queen needed to take emergency measures to preserve the colony. She broke the Admiral's monopoly and allowed other merchants to engage in commerce in the Indies. In September 1502, she contracted two Spanish merchants, Juan Sánchez de la Tesorería and Alonso Bravo, to send six caravels to the Americas. The terms of the contract made clear that this was a commercial voyage. The two merchants had to deliver only limited supplies to the royal agent in Santo Domingo—no more than 3,600 bushels of wheat and flour, six horses, and 1,200 bushels of barley as feed for the horses. Beyond this, they were free to sell on their own any amounts they wanted of food, clothing, cloth, merchandise, African slaves, and mares. The monarchs again allowed Columbus to invest one-eighth in the voyage, but he and his agents appear not to have done so (though Carvajal and the Admiral later tried to claim one-eighth of the profits).

The Admiral's failure to invest in this very lucrative voyage was not because of lack of funds. His share of the gold was still coming to Seville. While Columbus was in the Caribbean on his fourth voyage (1502–1504), his business agent in Spain, Luis de Soria, invested 130,000 maravedis of Columbus's money in another commercial voyage to Santo Domingo and received one-eighth of the royal profit for the Admiral's accounts. In Santo Domingo in September 1504, after his rescue from Jamaica, Columbus had enough gold waiting for him to pay his crew two years of back pay and living expenses in cash and to pay a quarter of a million maravedis in gold to charter and supply ships for a return voyage to Seville, where he had accumulated fifteen million maravedis in gold in his accounts.

This period of enormous profits for Columbus from the Americas was soon tarnished. During early 1503, Fernando and Isabel held discussions with a colonial delegation from Santo Domingo. The delegates reported that the colonists could not buy the manufactured goods they needed from the royal storehouse. Instead of supplying necessities, such as metal tools, lightweight clothing for the tropical climate, paper, and medicines, the royal storehouse stocked overpriced merchandise that was not useful to the colony. For example, the colonists charged that Columbus had sent thick woolen broadcloth from England, which was suitable for northern European or central Asian climates but not for tropical islands.

For the monarchs, the problem seemed clear: the colonists could not flourish without supplies from Spain, and Columbus and his investors would never send the right supplies. As the colonial delegates pointed out, the royal treasury could not make a profit on undesirable merchandise; the unwanted goods rotted in the storehouse, even though the colonists had money to spend and needed European goods.

The monarchs solved this problem in mid-1503 by opening trade in the Americas to all Spaniards. Beginning in early 1504, any Spanish subject of the crowns of Castile or Aragón could export anything to La Española, except slaves, horses, arms, gold, and silver, and they could import anything from the Americas, except brazilwood.

For Columbus, this action by Fernando and Isabel was a cruel rebuff. Though he was seriously ill and crippled after the fourth voyage, he again took charge of his business affairs as soon as he got back to Spain, and he never stopped complaining about the free trade. In a letter to his son Diego in 1504, he criticized the new policy: "The privilege of the one-eighth is worthless because anyone can send merchandise to sell, without investing in outfitting the fleet and without having an account or partnership with anyone." He urged Diego, who had recently joined the queen's staff, to persuade the monarchs to reverse this policy. When this produced no results, he sent his other son, Fernando, his brother Bartolomé, and the tireless Carvajal to help Diego pressure the monarchs.

Columbus wanted desperately to be at the royal court, which was spending the winter of 1504–1505 in northern Castile, in the town of Medina del Campo. Queen Isabel was terminally ill, and Columbus wanted to see her one more time. He wanted the queen to promise on her deathbed that the monarchy would permit his son Diego to inherit his wealth, offices, and privileges.

The Admiral's gold from America had not made him happy. Columbus was a millionaire by any standard and expected his income to grow in the coming years. Although he complained that free trade had reduced his income by ten million maravedis, he had much to bequeath to his son. It was, however, this very wealth that made him anxious. He could not be sure that Diego would inherit it.

He could have solved this problem by becoming a Castilian citizen. Throughout Europe, only citizens enjoyed the protection of the law; foreigners did not have the right to dispose of their property by testament nor did the usual laws of inheritance apply to their property. The monarchs could simply seize a foreigner's property after his death and leave his heirs with nothing. Other Genoese in Spain, including the Admiral's brother Diego and his business associates Juanoto Berardi and Francisco de Riberol, became naturalized citizens of Castile. But Columbus remained a foreigner, and that left him in a tenuous position.

Columbus had already employed a device to avoid the terrible inheritance consequences of noncitizenship. He asked for and received from the monarchs the privilege of establishing a perpetual trust, and he placed all his offices, privileges, and income in that trust. But the monarchs whittled away at the contents of the trust, and Columbus could not be sure that the process would stop when he died. The possibility that the monarchy might reclaim more of his offices or continue to reduce his privileges haunted Columbus during his final years.

If he had been well, he might have fought and won this battle at court. But he could not travel because he was sick and crippled. His health problems had begun on the second voyage, when he, along with hundreds of other Europeans, fell seriously ill. Most of those who survived recovered fully. Columbus, in contrast, suffered crippling aftereffects for the rest of his life. During the third voyage, just after exploring the delta of the Orinoco River and realizing that he had reached a continent, Columbus became seriously ill. He ran a high fever and was in severe pain. His eyes became so inflamed that they bled, and he became temporarily blind. These symptoms recurred during the fourth voyage with such severity that, during the shipwreck on Jamaica, he could not walk without

assistance, and his vision was so bad that his teenage son Fernando had to act as his secretary, reading and writing for him. By the time he returned to Spain in the fall of 1504, he was dangerously ill.

The cause of Columbus's symptoms is unknown. Retrospective diagnoses are always guesswork, especially after nearly five hundred years. The most common diagnosis is that Columbus suffered from Reiter's syndrome, a genetic disorder. This syndrome produces a cluster of ailments that include crippling arthritis and inflammation of the eyes and the urinary tract. In persons with a genetic predisposition to Reiter's, onset is triggered by a severe illness, such as viral dysentery or the epidemic that occurred on La Española during Columbus's second voyage.

Whatever the disease, Columbus could travel and write only with great pain and difficulty during his final months. Though he spent several restful weeks in Santo Domingo before his last transatlantic crossing in 1504, he was dangerously ill by the time he arrived in Seville. He wrote often to his son Diego, but he explains, he could not write to his friend Diego Méndez "because of my illness, which does not permit me to write except at night, because during the day my hands are too weak."

Columbus wanted to go north to the court, but he could not even ride a horse. Carriages were unknown in Spain, and he could not have stood the roughness of a cart. In desperation, he made arrangements to borrow from Seville Cathedral an enclosed litter that had brought the body of the late cardinal archbishop to Seville. But he was advised against attempting the trip, for, he writes, "my illness is so severe, and the weather is so cold for someone in my condition, that I could end up in a dangerous state in some roadside inn."

Finally, after he had recovered somewhat and the coldest part of the winter had passed, Columbus decided to ride a mule to court. For this, he needed royal permission, because in 1494 Queen Isabel had issued a decree forbidding anyone except clergy and pregnant women to ride mules. (The breeding of mules reduced the production of horses, which were needed by the military.) After the victory of Granada, the monarchy attempted to replenish the supply of horses by depressing the desirability and price of mules. Being forbidden to ride mules was a hardship for everyone; the mule's smooth and surefooted gait made it the preferred means of travel in Castile. Nevertheless, the monarchy's need for war horses took precedence over custom. King Fernando and Queen Isabel set the example by riding horses, and all classes of society, from nobles to farmers, conformed to the royal decree.

Columbus apparently was so crippled that he could not have sat a horse on the steep roads of Castile. The journey

DEATH OF COLUMBUS. Bronze relief, detail from the Rogers Doors (1858) in the U.S. Capitol. In this depiction, the last rites are administered, as friends and attendants surround the ailing Columbus. The humble setting is meant to indicate the circumstances of Columbus's final years.   ARCHITECT OF THE CAPITOL

were Spaniards. A local notary and witnesses were called, and Columbus dictated final instructions for Diego and confirmed the perpetual trust he had established. He died during the night of May 20, 1506.

Columbus performed amazing feats of world importance in Spain. Spain, especially Castile, welcomed and nurtured his talents and rewarded his deeds. With the labor and expertise of Spanish seamen Columbus had made a western voyage and claimed for Castile many islands in the Ocean Sea, just as he had predicted. On Castilian ships he had explored and claimed a continent, which he called a "New World," whose existence no European had ever imagined. Spanish seamen had risked their lives to rescue him and his brother and son from Jamaica.

He never became a citizen of Castile. The Admiral trusted few outside his circle of family and Italian friends. He expressed regret that his son Diego did not have more brothers: "Ten brothers would not be too many for you, because I myself never found in the whole world any better friend than my own brothers." He sent his most precious documents, the Book of Privileges, to Genoa and his gold and jewels to an Italian priest in Seville, Gaspar Gorricio, for safekeeping. And he recommended to the Castilian monarchs that his successor be the Italian navigator Amerigo Vespucci, who had been his original contact with the slave dealer Berardi in Seville.

from Seville to the royal court in Valladolid was over five hundred miles, and it crossed Spain's deepest river valleys and highest mountain ranges. He left Seville in May 1505 and made the journey in agonizing stages. When he reached his sons and brothers in the city of Segovia, where the widowed King Fernando and his court were residing during the summer, he confirmed his perpetual trust—an indication that he felt near death.

By the time he followed the royal court to the town of Valladolid, Columbus could go no further. He never succeeded in regaining his governing privileges from the king, but Fernando did begin discussions for Diego to marry a Castilian woman, which would give him citizenship in Castile. With these negotiations in early stages, Columbus sent his sons and brothers to give the oath of vassalage to the new queen, Juana, and her husband, who were expected soon to arrive on the north coast. When the new monarchs landed at La Coruña on April 26, however, they made no promises.

The Admiral could wait no more. His devoted employees stood watch during his final moments: Bartolomeo Fieschi, Alvaro Pérez, Juan de Espinosa, Andrea and Fernando Vargas, Francisco Manual, and Fernán Martínez. Most of them had been his mates at sea, and all but one

CASKET IN THE CATHEDRAL OF SANTO DOMINGO, DOMINICAN REPUBLIC. Said to contain remains of Columbus. Columbus was first buried in Spain, but his remains were moved several times. His son Diego wanted all the family admirals buried on La Española, and Diego's son Luis honored that wish. When the Spanish monarchy, which revered Columbus's memory, lost control of the island, the Crown acted to keep the remains within Spanish territory. The ultimate destiny of the remains, however, is the subject of much controversy.   PHOTOGRAPH © WALTER R. AGUIAR

BIBLIOGRAPHY

Ballesteros Beretta, Antonio. *Christóbal Colón y el descubrimiento de América.* Vol. 2. Barcelona and Buenos Aires, 1945.

Gil, Juan. "Las cuentas de Colón." In *Temas Colombinas,* edited by Juan Gil and Consuelo Varela. Seville, 1986.

Morison, Samuel Eliot. *Admiral of the Ocean Sea: A Life of Christopher Columbus.* Vol. 2. Boston, 1942.

Weissman, Gerald. *They All Laughed at Christopher Columbus: Tales of Medicine and the Art of Discovery.* New York, 1987.

HELEN NADER

COLUMBUS THE NAVIGATOR. One of the difficulties in assessing Columbus's skill as navigator lies in reconciling the legends about his early life with the few established facts. In his journal of the first voyage to America, in the entry for December 21, 1492, he writes: "I have spent twenty-three years at sea without coming off it for any length of time worth mentioning, and I have seen all the east and west . . . and I have gone to Guinea." This alludes to 1469; yet, in signing a deed in 1472, Columbus describes himself as a "woolworker from Genoa." In 1474 he was in Chios, then a Genoese outpost, trading for the firm of Spinola and Di Negri. In 1477 he was in England, whence he claims to have visited Iceland and one hundred leagues beyond. The following year he was in Lisbon, and from there he sailed to Madeira to buy sugar for the same Genoese firm. He claims to have sailed to Guinea in the same ship as José Vizinho, the astronomer sent by King João II of Portugal to work out the procedures for determining latitude through observation of the sun. On these voyages, Columbus tells us, he would watch the work of the pilots and occasionally attempt to duplicate their observations.

In all this there is no evidence that Columbus sailed as a professional seaman. More probably, he traveled in the capacity of a ship's factor, a post that nevertheless demanded a knowledge of geography and familiarity with the port books. What he knew of navigation he had acquired through the nautical circles he frequented in Lisbon. He had read widely, but his cosmology was gravely at fault. The force of this viewpoint is not so much to detract from the legend of the great navigator as to suggest that his genius and considerable gifts lay elsewhere. As commander of an expedition, he would have conferred frequently with the pilots and masters on matters of navigation, but he would not have been expected to navigate the expedition, nor is there any hard evidence that he was equipped to do so.

The practice in navigation at the end of the fifteenth century was to establish the latitude (or *altura*) of the destination and sail along it east or west until familiar landmarks were sighted. The oldest extant Portuguese manual of navigation, the so-called Munich Regiment for the Astrolabe and Quadrant, was probably first printed in 1494, but it can be dated to before 1485, when the rules for observing the sun for latitude were drawn up. There is evidence in Columbus's journal that he had access to and possibly possessed a hand-copy of an early version of the manual, which contains a list of latitudes of the principal land features on the Atlantic coast, from the equator to Cape Finisterre, including all the reference points mentioned by Columbus and to an accuracy well beyond that achieved by Columbus in his own observations. E. G. R. Taylor has shown that while Columbus had studied the rules and procedures for observing the North Star and sun, he had failed to understand them properly and in particular misapplied the declination of the sun. His method for establishing the measure of the degree, for instance, was to compare the ship's run with successive altitudes of the sun, irrespective of any change in solar declination, a procedure probably suggested by the out-of-date version of the manual he had studied. He had trouble too with the precise conventional nomenclature used to describe the position of the Guard Stars in relation to the North Star, a technique used to find the correction to the North Star's altitude; in his letter describing the third voyage he uses an ambiguous phraseology long since abandoned by the Portuguese. Again, in a passage referring to the Guinea voyage, Columbus records that in the island of Los Idolos, off Sierra Leone, he found himself five minutes of latitude from the equinoctial. In fact the island lies 9° N, and the five minutes recorded was the sun's northerly declination for that day, for the date was March 11, the day of the spring equinox in the Julian calendar. Two weeks later he found the noonday sun directly overhead at Elmina and assumed that the fort thus lay on the equinoctial; in fact its latitude is 5½° N and the sun's declination for that day was 5°37' N. Other of his gross errors in measurement of latitude can be pointed up, as for example on October 30, 1492, off the coast of Cuba, where "in the opinion of the Admiral, he was distant from the equinoctial line forty-two degrees to the north." The sun's declination for the day was 17° N, which subtracted from 42° would have given the more reasonable figure of 25° N.

The good navigator is of course not necessarily the one who obtains the most accurate information, but rather he who makes the best use of the information available to him. Here Columbus may have been on surer ground. For all his adoption of too small a measure for the degree, his convoluted juggling of the day's run, and his occasionally lame explanations of his disagreements with the pilots, he does seem to have been possessed of a sea-sense that enabled him, in uncharted waters and with imprecise methods of navigation, to find his way about the ocean with a degree of caution that ensured success. His navigational achievements were probably due more to his seamanship than to his occasional observations and cosmological small talk.

[See also *Myth of Columbus*.]

BIBLIOGRAPHY

Morison, Samuel Eliot. *The European Discovery of America: The Southern Voyages*. New York, 1974.

Taylor, E. G. R. "The Navigating Manual of Columbus." *Journal of the Institute of Navigation* 5, no. 1 (1952): 42–54.

M. W. Richey

COMPASS. [This entry includes two articles, *Marine Compass*, focusing on the development of the compass's use at sea, and *Declination of the Compass*, focusing on the phenomenon of compass variation, which European navigators experienced the farther they traveled in unknown waters.]

Marine Compass

In Latin the compass is called *pixis*, in German, *Kompas*, in Italian, *bussola*, and in French, *boussole*. An early (mid-thirteenth-century) use of the word *compasso* meant sailing directions, comprising the portolano (strictly speaking, the written guide) and the nautical chart. The development of the magnetic compass as a marine instrument is poorly documented, but is probably no earlier than the first use of a magnetized needle pushed into a straw and floated on water in a bowl. There are serious practical difficulties in the use even of this improvement upon the floated lodestone (i.e., a piece of natural magnetic ore) described by Petrus Peregrinus (Pierre le Pèlerin) de Maricourt in his *Epistola de magnete* (1269). The introduction of a pivot to support the magnetized needle in a dry bowl was essential to the further development of the compass, and the pivot seems, like the magnetic compass itself, to have derived from China. Petrus Peregrinus had already described a pivoted compass needle: two pivots, above and below a vertical arbor carrying the needle. The earliest surviving instrument with a compass-needle pivot is the small astronomical *compendium* (a simple astrolabe and sundial for finding Muslim prayer-times and the direction of Mecca from various places) made in A.H. 767 (A.D. 1366/1367) by the important astronomer, 'Ali b. al-Shatir. There are no other surviving magnetic compasses that can be dated before those incorporated toward the end of the fifteenth century in sundials and a globe, and none of these instruments was intended for nautical use.

Transmission of the magnetic compass from China to Europe would suggest Islamic culture as a vector, and the earliest-cited reference to use of the lodestone in a portable nautical context seems to be in a mid-ninth-century Arabic poem. However, the first known mention of the use of a compass at sea is Alexander Neckam's (1157–1217) reference in his *De utensilibus* to mariners' finding their course when sun or stars were invisible by means of a north-pointing needle, and in his *De naturis rerum*, he describes the needle as being placed on a pivot; both treatises belong to the last quarter of the twelfth century. Neckham's priority has led some historians to seek a northern European origin for the magnetic compass. Between 1204 and 1208, Guyot de Provins wrote in his poem *La Bible* some verses concerning a needle (*aiguille*) that had touched a lodestone (*magnette*, "an ugly and brownish stone") and then been inserted in a straw (*festu*) and placed in water; this needle pointed to the polestar. Before about 1218, Jacques de Vitry, bishop of Acre, had written that the compass was "very necessary" to those navigating on the sea, and by 1225 the navigational use of the compass was apparently a commonplace in Iceland. Petrus Peregrinus, in his *Epistola*, envisaged navigation that was astronomical when he said that his compass would enable the traveler to reach all places, on land or at sea, as long as he knew his longitudes and latitudes. By the second half of the thirteenth century, use of the magnetic compass at sea must have become general in European and North African waters: the *Siete partidas*, a legal encyclopaedia edited between 1256 and 1263 under the supervision of King Alfonso X of Castile, uses a simile that refers to sailors finding their way on a dark night with "the needle which is a mediator between the star [the polestar] and the stone [the lodestone]." Likewise, the Egyptian scientist, Baylak al-Qipjaqi, wrote that the captains of ships on the sea route between Syria and Egypt, when the night was too dark for stellar observation, would take a vessel filled with water and place it inside the ship, protected from the wind; they would then take a needle and insert it in a reed (or the like) such that the latter formed a cross (perhaps to keep the needle central in the vessel), and when this was floated on the surface of the water, magnetize the needle by bringing a large lodestone over the needle, twisting the lodestone to the right (thereby turning the floating needle) and then removing the lodestone rapidly. Baylak says that he saw this procedure with his own eyes during his voyage from Tripoli to Alexandria in A.H. 640 (A.D. 1242/1243).

It might be assumed that the use of a pivot for the compass needle was common by the end of the fourteenth century or at the beginning of the fifteenth. No descriptions, illustrations, or artifacts document the history of the marine compass until the illustration of a compass box and, possibly, compass rose drawn in the margin of a manuscript of *La sfera*, a cosmological poem by Gregorio Dati (1363–1436) or by Leonardo Dati written in the first half of the fifteenth century, but it is not absolutely clear that the "star" in the picture represents a compass rose on a fly rather than just the Stella Maris on the lid of the box. Crude illustrations of mariner's compasses drawn on fifteenth-century charts show a round box and a pivoted fly, similar to those of later marine compasses, of which the earliest good illustration is perhaps in the 1562 portrait of the lord high admiral Edward Fiennes, Lord Clinton and Saye (in the Ashmolean Museum, Oxford University). There is, however, an allegorical drawing by Leonardo da Vinci, dated about 1515 to 1516, in which a wolf, seated in a sailing boat, is looking at a fixed compass that clearly has a fly.

Fiennes's compass is probably not far removed in design from the Genoese and Flemish compasses used by Columbus. It is contained in a round wooden box, slightly less than a handsbreadth in diameter. There is a fly bearing a compass rose (that is, the pivoted magnetized needle, or wire frame, is attached underneath a disk of paper-covered pasteboard on which are drawn the cardinal points separating the eight "winds" of 45 degrees each, subdivided into four "quarters" of 11¼ degrees, instead of having a simple needle pivoted within a fixed scale of divisions). The fly may derive from a cross or disk used to keep a floating needle central in its bowl, and its invention is probably not much later than the introduction of charts drawn with rhumb lines. Conceptually, it is easier to set a ship's course along a rhumb if the compass has a graduated fly, rather than a simple needle that points to a surrounding scale. For example, given that the meridian axis of the compass box is aligned on the longitudinal axis of the ship, sailing on a course a quarter west with a fly requires only the quarter west division on the fly to be kept opposite the meridian axis of the compass, whereas a simple needle has to point on the surrounding scale to the quarter east division. Fiennes's compass shows no sign of any gimbal mounting (Cardan suspension), though the idea of such a mounting was known to medieval technology (e.g., in the Sketchbook of Villard de Honnecourt, c. 1235), and its use for a compass was envisaged by Leonardo da Vinci around 1500. Compasses were kept in a box or cupboard (*gisola*, binnacle/bittacle); the inventory of a ship sold in Genoa early in 1495 includes "four needles for navigating . . . two binnacles." A marine compass, made in Lisbon in 1711 by Josep' da Costa Miranda (Whipple Science Museum, Cambridge), may be further rare evidence for the form of Columbus's compasses, though it may be slightly more elaborate.

MARINE COMPASS. This Portuguese compass, although eighteenth-century, is close to that used by Columbus in that it has no gimbals. Opposite sides of the painted wooden box containing the fly are fitted with sights for taking solar bearings.

WHIPPLE MUSEUM OF THE HISTORY OF SCIENCE, CAMBRIDGE

Some of the problems that Columbus encountered in using his compasses may have arisen because the Genoese compass makers may have placed the magnetic needle under the fly, aligned with true north, whereas the Flemish makers allowed for the declination. It is clear from A. Crichton Mitchell that Columbus did not discover, as has been claimed, the magnetic declination. From the evidence of the German roadmaps (c. 1492 or 1500) of Erhard Etzlaub of Nürnberg and the less certain evidence of portable sundials with compasses, it seems that an easterly declination of about 11¼ degrees had been observed in northwestern Europe before Columbus sailed on his first voyage. Columbus's observations on September 13–14, 1492, suggest that he was close to the agonic line (i.e., line of zero declination), but he deduced no general space variation of declination from these observations.

[See also *Lodestone.*]

BIBLIOGRAPHY

Gouk, Penelope. *The Ivory Sundials of Nuremberg 1500–1700*, pp. 73–74 and 84–88. Cambridge, 1988.

Grant, Edward, ed. *A Source Book in Medieval Science*. Cambridge, Mass., 1974.

Körber, Hans-Günther. *Zur Geschichte der Konstruktion von Sonnenuhren und Kompassen*. Veröffentlichungen des Staatlichen Mathematisch-Physikalischen Salons—Forschungsstelle—Dresden-Zwinger, vol. 3. Berlin, 1965.

Maddison, Francis. *Medieval Scientific Instruments and the Development of Navigational Instruments in the XVth and*

XVIth Centuries. Agrupamento de estudos de cartografia antiga, vol. 30. Coimbra, 1969.

Mitchell, A. Crichton. "Chapters in the History of Terrestrial Magnetism. Chapter I—On the Directive Property of a Magnet in the Earth's Field and the Origin of the Nautical Compass." *Terrestrial Magnetism and Atmospheric Electricity* 37 (1932): 105–146.

Mitchell, A. Crichton. "Chapters in the History of Terrestrial Magnetism. Chapter II—The Discovery of the Magnetic Declination." *Terrestrial Magnetism and Atmospheric Electricity* 42 (1937): 241–280.

Needham, Joseph, Wang Ling, and Kenneth Girdwood Robinson. "Physics." Part 1 of vol. 4 of *Science and Civilisation in China*. Cambridge, 1962.

Radelet de Grave, P., and D. Speiser. "Le *De magnete* de Pierre de Maricourt. Traduction et commentaire." *Revue d'histoire des sciences et de leurs applications* 28, pt. 3 (1975): 193–234.

Taylor, E. G. R. "The South-Pointing Needle." *Imago Mundi* 8 (1951): 1–7.

FRANCIS MADDISON

Declination of the Compass

The declination, or variation, of the compass at any point on the earth's surface is the difference in angular degrees between the direction to magnetic North and geographic North. Although the phenomenon had become apparent from the time that compass steering was generally practiced, it was not until the sixteenth century that its cause became known. Mediterranean pilots usually blamed the needle's variation either on careless shipboard use of the lodestone to magnetize the needle or, more frequently, on faulty workmanship by the compass maker. Later, as pilots began to keep careful logs and compared notes with other pilots, they became aware that declination, or variation, existed and also that declination varied from place to place.

It was not until navigation of the "Western Ocean" was first attempted that the strange behavior of the compass needle from place to place became a matter of serious concern. It was Christopher Columbus who made the earliest record of the phenomenon. In his journal of the first voyage westward he noted that for most of the time the compass rarely pointed true north, although it had done so at a point 2½ degrees east of Corvo in the Azores. The needle's erratic behavior caused considerable consternation among the superstitious crew and almost led to mutiny.

Columbus's entry in his journal for September 13, 1492, noted, "This day at night fall, the needles deviated to the North-West, and on the morrow they deviated slightly in the same direction." Four days later he recorded,

> The pilots took an observation of the north, and found that the needles deviated a good quarter to the north west, and the

mariners were afraid and were dismayed and did not say why. And the Admiral observed it and bade them repeat the observations of the north at dawn, and they found that the needles were correct: the reason was that the star, which they saw, moved, and not the needles. (Dunn and Kelly, eds., *The Diario of Christopher Columbus's First Voyage to America, 1492–1493*)

Although Mediterranean pilots had long been aware of the occasional variation of the compass needle, magnetic variation in the Mediterranean was practically negligible until the mid-seventeenth century, and it was not an important factor in navigation. The phenomenon observed by Spanish seamen obviously was new to them, however; if it had been generally known among European navigators and seamen prior to Columbus's first voyage, there would have been no reason for the fear expressed by the sailors.

In his diary of the second voyage, Columbus noted that he was equipped with both Genoese and Flemish compasses. This was a combination that substantially multiplied the navigator's confusion because in addition to noting the needle's variation in some locations and not in others, he also observed differences in the readings between the two types of compasses. This discrepancy was due to the fact that the Genoese needle pointed to true north while the needle or wire of the Flemish compass was oriented to point east.

A significant passage in Fernando Colón's biography of his father relates to the return voyage on Coumbus's second visit to the Indies:

> This morning the Dutch [Flemish] compasses vary'd as they used to do, a point; and those of Genoa, that used to agree with them, vary'd but a little, but afterwards sailing east vary more, which is a sign we are a 100 leagues, or somewhat more, west of the Azores. . . . and the Dutch needles vary'd a point, those of Genoa cutting the north point; and when we are somewhat farther E.N.E. they will alter again; which was verified on Sunday following being the 22nd day of May; by which and the exactness of his account, he found he was 100 leagues from the islands Azores, which he was somewhat surpriz'd at, and assigned this difference to the several sorts of load-stones the needles are made by; for till they come to that longitude they all vary a point, and there some held it; and those of Genoa exactly cut the north star. (Churchill and Churchill, *Collection of Voyages*, vol. 2.)

With growing awareness of variation, it had become the practice for navigators to set the needle beneath the card slightly askew to compensate for the amount of variation that occurred in a particular region. This shipboard modification became so common that compass makers eventually began to mark the variation in compasses they sold. Compasses produced in Italy—Genoa, Sicily, and Venice—generally had the needles set three-quarters of a point eastward, while the needles of compasses produced in Spain, Portugal, France, and England were set one-half of a point eastward. One point, *una quarta,* was equal to 11¼ degrees. This was only a temporary solution, however, practical for short cruises but not for longer voyages.

Although Columbus was the first to record the compass's variation, he failed to recognize its true cause. The first recorded scientific observation was made by Felipe Guillén of Seville in 1525, and a decade later Francisco Faleiro published a navigational manual containing directions for determining declination by means of an instrument similar to that devised by Guillén. In his *History of the Indies* the Spanish historiographer Gonzalo Fernández de Oviedo dealt at some length with northeasting and northwesting of the compass needle, but he neglected to mention that Columbus had reported it.

Columbus's report of the phenomenon was noted in his journal edited by Bartolomé de las Casas as well as in Fernando Colón's biography of his father, but the report did not become known to subsequent transoceanic voyagers until 1571 when the translation of Fernando's biography into Italian by Alfonso de Ulloa became available. Little note was made of it even then, for the work had limited distribution and it was not translated into other languages until more than a century later. It was, in fact, not until 1789 when Martín Fernández de Navarrete discovered the Las Casas manuscript that Colombus's observations of the phenomenon became known, long after the phenomenon of magnetic variation had become common knowledge.

On voyages undertaken during the years 1538–1541, João de Castro compiled the most complete set of observations of compass variation to that time. Pedro Nuñez, in his *De arte atque ratione navigandi* (1546), promoted the use of the compass's variation as a means of determining longitude. And it was in a preface by Giovanni Maria Negri in a book by Niccola Negri published in 1574 that for the first time magnetic variation of the compass was mentioned in a manner indicating that by then it had become general knowledge among Spanish navigators.

It is believed that compass makers in Flanders and Germany may have had some knowledge of magnetic declination prior to Columbus's voyages, and that variation for those regions were marked on Flemish compasses by their makers. The increasing growth of sea trade resulted in the rapid development of the manufacture of compasses and lodestones in Flanders from the fourteenth century on, and it is possible that by the second half of the fifteenth century, compass makers had begun to correct their compasses for variation observed in northwestern Europe. This was first achieved by mounting the compass card on the needle where it indicated magnetic north instead of where it indicated true or geographic north. The practice was copied by other compass makers in Nürnberg and elsewhere in northern Europe. Such instruments were sold widely throughout the continent by itinerant salesmen.

The earliest confirmed evidence that German compass makers and mapmakers had knowledge of magnetic variation is to be found in the work of Erhard Etzlaub, a Nürnberg physician who drew maps and made compasses. He marked the magnetic variation for Nürnberg first on a horizontal dial drawn upon a 1501 map of Germany, and he also produced and sold rectangular, wooden, folding sundials with the same feature. Magnetic variation also appears in the figure of a sundial drawn as part of the *Carta itineraria Europae,* a map of Europe produced in 1511 by Martin Waldseemüller and Mathias Ringmann. On the basis of these maps, there is no doubt that magnetic variation had become known to German mapmakers and compass makers by the beginning of the sixteenth century, if not before.

BIBLIOGRAPHY

Churchill, A., and J. Churchill. *The History of the Life and Actions of Adm. Christopher Columbus and His Discovery of the West-Indies.* In vol. 2 of *Collection of Voyages.* 3d edition. London, 1744.

Denne, W. *Magnetic Compass Deviation and Correction.* 3d edition. New York, 1979.

Dunn, Oliver, and James E. Kelly, Jr. *The Diario of Christopher Columbus's First Voyage to America, 1492–1493.* Norman, Okla., 1989.

Heathcote, N. H. de Vaudrey. "Christopher Columbus and the Discovery of Magnetic Variation." *Scientific Progress,* no. 105 (July 1932): 82–103.

Mitchell, A. Crichton. "Chapters on the History of Terrestrial Magnetism." In *Terrestrial Magnetism and Atmospheric Electricity* 38 (1932): 105–146; 42 (1937): 241–280; 44 (1939): 77–80.

Waters, David W. *The Art of Navigation in England in Elizabethan and Early Stuart Times.* London, 1958.

SILVIO A. BEDINI

CONCEPCIÓN DE LA VEGA. See *Settlements,* article on *Concepción de la Vega.*

CONQUEST. For general discussion of European expansion in the New World, see *Pacification, Conquest, and Genocide.* For discussion of particular European efforts, see *Colonization; Exploration and Discovery.*

CONTI, NICCOLÒ DE' (c. 1395–1469), Venetian merchant-adventurer. Probably born in Chioggia, Conti set out in 1414 on a trading expedition along the eastern spice trade routes that would last some twenty-five years. Having learned Arabic in Damascus, he followed the caravan routes to Baghdad and thence along the Tigris and Euphrates to Basra. He sailed down the Persian Gulf to Hormuz and then to Kalhat (present-day Qalhat, Oman), where he learned some Persian. Over the ensuing years he explored and traded along the coasts of India, Burma, and Sumatra, the origins and transit points of the spices for which Europeans were so eager. Apparently he worked out of a trading base on the western coast of India, and he may have even reached China. About 1439 Conti returned to Europe via Socotra, the Red Sea, Mount Sinai, and Cairo.

Two contemporary accounts of his travels survive. One of these Conti related in 1448 to the humanist papal secretary Poggio Bracciolini, and the second was recorded by the Spanish merchant Pedro Tafur, whom Conti met while trading in the Mediterranean. The narration to Poggio was a form of penance imposed by Pope Eugenius IV for Conti's having reportedly abjured the Christian faith while in the lands of the "infidel." Poggio included this in his *De varietate fortunae* (On the diversity of fortune), of which some thirty-one manuscript copies, mostly from the fifteenth century, survive from Italy, Germany, France, and England. The first printed Latin edition came out in 1492. This narrative contains a good deal of information about the peoples among whom Conti traveled, although there is speculation that Poggio took some of this, especially in the second half of the narrative, from sources other than Conti. The extent of Conti's exposure to the sources of Egyptian and Syrian transit trade was perhaps unique, and his account certainly was. The bounty of contemporary, pre-Columbian texts of his story attests to both Mediterranean and northern interest in this mysterious world.

BIBLIOGRAPHY

Longhena, M. *Viaggi in Persia: India e Giava di Niccolò de Conti.* Milan, 1929.

Major, R. H., ed. *India in the Fifteenth Century.* London, 1857. Reprint, New York, 1971.

JOSEPH P. BYRNE

CONVERSOS. See *Jews,* article on *Conversos.*

CÓRDOBA. Located on the Guadalquivir River in the southern Spanish region of Andalusia, Córdoba was settled in prehistoric times. During the Roman period it was the capital of Hispania Ulterior and, later, Baetica.

After the Muslim conquest, Córdoba became capital of Umayyad Spain (756–1031). During the Umayyad dynasty, the city attained the general plan it would retain into modern times, and the mosque and other Islamic architectural monuments were constructed. Twelfth-century Córdoba was the home of the distinguished philosophers Averroës (Ibn Rushd) and Maimonides (Moses ben Maimon). In 1236 King Fernando III conquered the city from the Muslims and began its Christian resettlement.

By the late fifteenth century, Córdoba was a prominent Andalusian city with an urban population of some 25,000; another 125,000 people lived in surrounding towns and villages under the city's jurisdiction. It was a royal city whose representatives sat in the Castilian Cortes (parliament). Its municipal government was dominated by local nobles, whose bands controlled the political scene. As the seat of a bishop, it was also a center of ecclesiastical jurisdiction.

Córdoba served as a commercial transshipping point for agricultural and mining products produced in the surrounding territory. The city was located in the center of a large agrarian region whose varied topography supported fields of wheat and barley, olive groves and vineyards, and irrigated plots for fruit and vegetables. Livestock raised on extensive pastures produced meat for local consumption and hides and wool for export. Local entrepreneurs and workers manufactured leather goods (Cordovan leather), soap, and woolen textiles. The wool clipped locally or purchased from neighboring regions was exported or woven into cloth.

Christopher Columbus often visited Córdoba between 1485 and 1492, while seeking Castilian support for his enterprise of the Indies. In Córdoba Columbus also established a romantic liaison with Beatriz de Arana, an orphan living under the care of her cousin, Rodrigo Enríquez de Arana, whose wife, Lucía Núñez, owned looms and employed weavers of linen and woolen cloth. Some writers suggest that Columbus, a weaver's son, could have met Beatriz there or through the Genoese pharmacists Lucián and Leonardo de Esbarroya, whose shop was a popular meeting place. Whatever the circumstances, in June 1488, Beatriz bore a son named Fernando.

BIBLIOGRAPHY

Edwards, John. *Christian Córdoba: The City and Its Region in the Late Middle Ages.* Cambridge, 1982.

La Torre y del Cerro, José de. *Beatriz Enríquez de Harana y Cristóbal Colón.* Madrid, 1933.

WILLIAM D. PHILLIPS, JR.

CÓRDOBA, GONZALO FERNÁNDEZ DE. See *Fernández de Córdoba, Gonzalo.*

CORONADO, FRANCISCO VÁZQUEZ DE (1510–1554), Spanish explorer.

Coronado's expedition in search of the Seven Cities of Cíbola provided the first relatively accurate geographical knowledge of western North America and the indigenous peoples of the greater Southwest.

Coronado was born in Burgos, Spain, and came to New Spain in 1535 in the service of the first viceroy, Antonio de Mendoza. In August 1538 he was named governor of New Galicia, the northernmost Spanish frontier outpost. In 1536 Alvar Núñez Cabeza de Vaca had brought news of large cities in the far north, and in 1539 the viceroy commissioned Coronado commander of the army that was being assembled to explore the Kingdom of Cíbola and its Seven Cities that Fray Marcos de Niza had sighted beyond the Great Sonoran Desert.

On February 22, 1540, Mendoza personally reviewed the army at Compostela in Guadalajara and received the muster call of some 336 Spaniards of whom 225 were mounted horsemen, hundreds of Indian guides and bearers, and more than 1,500 horses, mules, and livestock. On April 22, 1540, Coronado set on ahead from Culiacán toward Cíbola with a small vanguard of eighty horsemen and twenty-five to thirty foot soldiers; the main army with the livestock and baggage train followed later. On May 9, 1540, two ships commanded by Hernando de Alarcón sailed up the northwestern coast of Mexico with supplies for the army. Although he never established direct contact with the main expedition, Alarcón navigated the Colorado River 250 miles to its confluence with the Gila River, established alliances with the Cocopas and other Yuman peoples, and observed that Baja California was not an island.

Coronado's advance guard reached northern Sonora in late May. From there it pushed through southern Arizona, finally reaching the Colorado Plateau and the outskirts of the walled Zuni city of Hawikuh on July 7, 1540. When Coronado led the assault on the adobe terraces, he was knocked senseless by a barrage of heavy stones, narrowly escaping death when two of his captains, García López de Cárdenas and Hernando de Alvarado, threw themselves over his body to protect him. "Everything was the reverse of what Fray Marcos de Niza had said," the commander wrote to Mendoza.

In the final quarter of 1540 Coronado sent his captains on a great circle of inland exploration: Pedro de Tovar to the Hopi villages; Cárdenas west to the brim of the Grand Canyon and the Colorado River; Melchior Díaz southwest to the lower Colorado River and into California. Alvarado swung east on a long reconnaissance mission with two chiefs from Cicuye (Pecos) to Acoma, the Tiguex villages along the Rio Grande valley, north to the pueblos of Santo Domingo, San Felipe, and Cochiti, finally reaching Pecos on the eastern edge of the Pueblo world and the buffalo country.

The main army had reached Hawikuh in late November and moved eastward into the Rio Grande valley in late December 1540, forcing the Tiguex to vacate one of their pueblos and provide food and blankets for the Spanish army. After Indian prisoners were burned alive at Arenal, Coronado led a winter-long siege that ended with two hundred dead Indians, ten or more slain Spaniards, and twelve Tiguex pueblos burned or abandoned.

A third phase of exploration began on April 22, 1541, when Coronado set out with guides from Pecos onto the plains, "so vast that I did not find their limit anywhere I went." The army swung east to Tucumcari, to the Texas Panhandle along the Canadian River, and then southward into the Staked Plains where they explored the Tule and Palo Duro canyons. A Plains Indian guide given them at Pecos, whom they called "the Turk," had told them of a rich province to the north whose rulers used golden vessels. Coronado sent the main army back to Tiguex and with a detachment of thirty horsemen rode north, meeting vast buffalo herds and the nomadic Querechos, probably Apaches, and the Teyas. In July 1541 the horsemen reached Quivira at the bend of the Arkansas River. It turned out to be a series of Wichita Indian villages of grass huts set in fine country for a Spanish settlement, near present-day Lyons, Kansas. After nearly a month of exploration that uncovered no gold, the Turk confessed that he had led the Spaniards astray on the plains on orders of the people of Cicuye who hoped to rid themselves of the invaders. Their return to the Rio Grande valley followed an Indian route that would become in the future the Santa Fe Trail.

Just after Christmas in 1541 Coronado was thrown under the hooves of another horse in a riding accident that nearly killed him. A strong minority of sixty men wanted to stay and hold the country; others wanted to return to Quivira. But the ailing Coronado was determined not to divide his command, and his army began the return march to Mexico City in early April 1542.

The Crown conducted a full inquiry into Coronado's conduct of the Cíbola expedition, from which he was exonerated of charges of incompetence and ill treatment of the natives. He died at age forty-two in 1554. In two short years his explorations had produced the information that transformed the geography of North America from the medieval island imagery of Columbus to that of a new continent.

BIBLIOGRAPHY

Works by Members of the Coronado Expedition

Castañeda de Náçera, Pedro de. *La relación de la jornada de Cíbola.* 1563? MS. 1596, New York Public Library.

The Coronado Expedition. Transcribed, translated, and edited by George Parker Winship. Washington, D.C., 1896. Reprint, Chicago, 1964.

Narratives of the Coronado Expedition, 1540–1541. Edited and translated by George P. Hammond and Agapito Rey. Vol. 2 of Coronado Cuatro Centennial Publications. Albuquerque, 1940.

Works about the Coronado Expedition

Bolton, Herbert Eugene. *Coronado: Knight of Pueblos and Plains.* Albuquerque, 1949. Also published as vol. 1 of Coronado Cuatro Centennial Publications.

Day, Arthur Grove. *Coronado's Quest: The Discovery of the Southwestern States.* Berkeley, 1942.

"In Coronado's Footsteps." *Arizona Highways* 60, no. 4 (1984).

Lecompte, Janet. "Coronado and Conquest." *New Mexico Historical Review* 64 (1989).

Mora, Carmen. "*La relación de la jornada de Cíbola* de Pedro Castañeda Nájera, ¿un texto censurado?" *Insula* 522 (1990).

Sauer, Carl P. *The Road to Cibola.* Berkeley, 1932.

Spanish Explorers in the Southern United States, 1528–1542. Edited by Frederick W. Hodge and Theodore H. Lewis. New York, 1907. Reprint, New York, 1965.

Udall, Stewart L. *To the Inland Empire: Coronado and Our Spanish Legacy.* Photographs by Jerry Jacka. New York, 1987.

Weber, David J. "Coronado and the Myth of Quivira." *Southwest Review* 70 (1985).

MAUREEN AHERN

CORTÉS, HERNANDO (1485–1547), Spanish explorer born in Medellín, a small town in Extremadura in the Spanish southwest. Cortés's parents were both of the hidalgo class, a lower nobility with little income. At the age of fourteen, he was sent to Salamanca where he received some formal education; two years later he returned home tired of studying and without the law degree his parents wanted him to pursue.

In 1504, Cortés sailed for La Española, attracted like many in his class by the expected but as yet unrealized riches of the New World. He was soon appointed notary of the new town of Azúa. He remained there until 1511, when he participated in the conquest of Cuba under Diego Velázquez, who as the first governor of Cuba appointed Cortés his secretary. In the following years, he prospered in his farming and mining activities as an encomendero and in his administrative career as mayor of Santiago de Baracoa, then the capital of the island. He married Catalina Juárez in 1515 and lived an uneventful life as a settler for the next three years, showing no interest in the expeditions of Francisco Hernández de Córdoba (1517) and Juan de Grijalba (1518), which were launched from Cuba to explore the mainland. On news that there were significant riches in Mexico, he maneuvered to obtain from Velázquez the command of the next expedition to explore the Yucatán and northern coast.

Velázquez seems to have had doubts about Cortés's loyalty, owing to rumors that Cortés intended to gain wealth for himself, but in February 1519 a fleet of some twelve ships with five hundred Spaniards, some Caribbean Indians, and sixteen horses left hastily for Yucatán. After some reconnaissance of the coast they disembarked at Tabasco, where Cortés quickly proved Velázquez's fears to be well founded. In a skillful political maneuver, he convinced his troops that news about a fabulous empire nearby demanded a new course of action, namely a military campaign to subdue the territory to the west in the name of the king of Spain, its rightful owner according to the papal donation. With the boldness and determination that would make him famous, he sank his ships to avoid retreat and proceeded to the interior from Veracruz, a city he had just founded in April of 1519.

The long march to Tenochtitlán took five months. His message to the Indians consisted of just one option, that of accepting immediate servitude to the Spanish Crown or being declared rebels and suffer the consequences. This ultimatum was naturally met with opposition, sometimes violent, but Cortés, an inexperienced soldier, proved an effective military leader whose able and disciplined army quickly overcame any resistance. He also was, however, a skillful diplomat, ready to make new alliances founded upon sweet promise and fierce intimidation. He took early notice that many communities such as the Cempoallans were disgruntled subjects of Motecuhzoma II (Moctezuma), the powerful leader of a triple alliance based in Mexico whose vast territories constituted a large empire, and he accordingly offered them political and financial liberation. On the other hand, he found independent republics like Tlaxcala that lived in a state of permanent war with the Mexicans, and to them he offered a solid alliance against the Mexica power. His strategy worked, and the march progressed as the confused Motecuhzoma, who may have thought the Spaniards to be deities, had strong doubts about the proper course of action. He tried to avoid the impending peril by offering rich presents and gold, but the effort was in vain.

On November 8, 1519, Cortés and his men entered Tenochtitlán, the magnificent city on the water, and were received as guests of Motecuhzoma. Soon after Cortés arrested the ruler under a feeble pretext and made him sign a pledge of allegiance to Charles V. Cortés then spent a few months strengthening his control of the city and the Mexican territories, but in May of 1520 a powerful fleet under the command of Pánfilo de Narváez was sent by Governor Velázquez to punish Cortés. In a shrewd commando-style night operation Cortés managed to overcome Narváez near the coast, but in the meantime Tenochtitlán had rebelled because of the unruly behavior of Pedro de Alvarado who had been left in charge. Cortés rushed back to the city, but after a brief pause in the conflict the general rebellion resumed, and he was forced to flee the night of June 30, the so-called Noche Triste (Sad Night) in which he lost half of his troops and most of

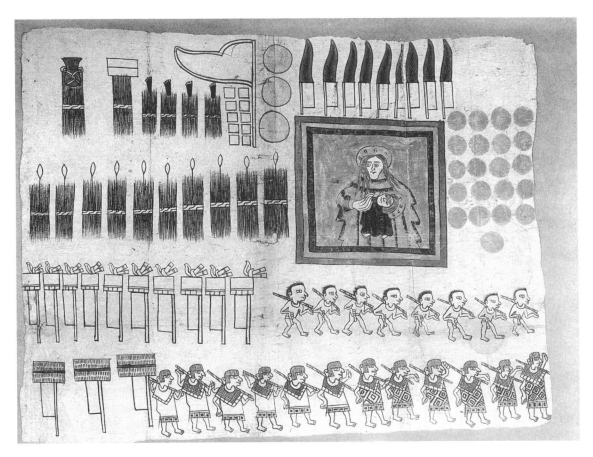

THE HUEJOTZINGO CODEX. Detail from an Aztec manuscript, circa 1531, that is a pictographic record of a lawsuit brought by Aztecs against Spanish colonial authorities to recover costs of Aztec aid to Cortés.

LIBRARY OF CONGRESS, HARKNESS COLLECTION

Motecuhzoma's treasure. After fending off an attack in Otumba, the army retreated to the allied republic of Tlaxcala. Undeterred by the costly setback, Cortés had no thoughts of abandoning his goal. He spent the winter of 1520 preparing the siege of Tenochtitlán, which lasted from late May until August 13, 1521, when Cuauhtemoc, the new lord of the Mexica who had led a heroic resistance, was captured and his people surrendered.

Cortés now controlled a vast territory, larger than Motecuhzoma's, that stretched from Veracruz to the Pacific coast; Cortés named it New Spain. Charles V, acknowledging the importance of this expansion over the objections of Velázquez, appointed Cortés governor and captain general of New Spain. Cortés then tried to combine his military role with a civilian one by expanding his control of the country to the south, founding new cities, and promoting agriculture and mining. He also organized the reconstruction of Tenochtitlán (later called Mexico City), which had been destroyed by the war and decimated by new diseases introduced by Europeans. In October 1524, he led an unsuccessful land expedition to

Honduras, during which he almost died. In his absence, chaos erupted in Mexico City, and upon his return he was stripped of his office and subjected to an official enquiry that lasted for many years.

In 1528 Cortés sailed back to Spain for the first time. He was received with honors, and Emperor Charles knighted him with the title Marquis of the Valley, a nobility status with vast territories and a huge encomienda of Indians. Although he was never to recover his governorship, he was granted permission to explore the Pacific coast, an activity to which he dedicated his best efforts in the 1530s, with mixed results. In January 1540 he left New Spain never to return. His last years in Spain remain clouded in mystery. Little is known apart from his ongoing writing of claims and demands to the Crown. He participated in an unsuccessful sea expedition to Tunisia, but otherwise he seems to have lived a life of quiet retirement with Juana de Zúñiga, his second wife, first in Valladolid and then in Seville, where he died on December 2, 1547.

The legacy of Cortés can hardly be overstated, and unlike other conquistadores, he seems to have had a good grasp of the complex issues surrounding his actions. His ideas are clearly stated in his *Cartas de relación*, the five long dispatches he sent to Charles V between 1519 and 1526. He thought of his enterprise in both political and religious terms, as a universal expansion of Charles's empire as well as a providential crusade for the Christian religion. He was also aware of the abuses committed against the Caribbean Indians, and although he supported the encomienda system, he encouraged humanitarian efforts. By expanding the Spanish possessions into the American continent, Cortés created a new perception of the New World—hitherto perceived by many in Europe as little more than some exotic islands of primitive people—as a land endowed with resources and populated by civilizations akin to those in the Old World. As such, he was able to describe with admiration the urban and artistic accomplishments of the Aztecs, but as a man of his time he understood their future only in terms of political and cultural assimilation to the European mode of life.

Cortés quickly achieved legendary status as one of the best known figures of modern times. In his own day, the spectrum of opinion about him knew the extremes of praise and blame, even in Spain. On the one hand, his official biographer, Francisco López de Gómara, hailed him as a hero whose exploits surpassed those of Caesar, and this was the prevalent view of Europeans of his time; on the other hand, Bartolomé de las Casas, protector of the Indians, accused him of exemplifying the evils of the forceful conquest of the New World. In the West, a generally favorable view of Cortés prevailed until the twentieth century, when frequent criticism of his actions reflected a reassessment of European imperial expansion overseas.

BIBLIOGRAPHY

Cortés, Hernán. *Letters from Mexico.* New York. 1971. Translated and edited by Anthony R. Pagden. Reprint, New Haven, 1986.

Díaz del Castillo, Bernal. *The Discovery and Conquest of Mexico, 1517–1521.* Edited by Genaro García. Translated by A. P. Maudslay. New York, 1956.

Gómara, Francisco López de. *Historia de la conquista de México.* 2 vols. Mexico City, 1943.

Guzmán, Eulalia. *Relaciones de Hernán Cortés a Carlos V sobre la invasión de Anáhuac.* Mexico City, 1958.

León-Portilla, Miguel. *Cortés y la Mar del Sur.* Madrid, 1985.

Madariaga, Salvador de. *Hernán Cortés, Conqueror of Mexico.* London, 1942.

Martínez, José Luis. *Hernán Cortés.* Mexico City, 1990.

Navarro González, Alberto, ed. *Hernán Cortés.* Salamanca, 1986.

Orozco y Berra, Manuel. *Historia antigua y de la conquista de México.* Vol. 4. Mexico City, 1880. Reprint, Mexico City, 1960.

Wagner, Henry R. *The Rise of Fernando Cortés.* Berkeley, 1944.

ANGEL DELGADO-GOMEZ

COSA, JUAN DE LA (d. 1510), master of *Santa María*, cartographer, explorer. Little is known of Juan de la Cosa's early life, but by the end of the fifteenth century he was one of Spain's most respected navigators and cartographers. Controversy surrounds his life and career, including his birthplace. Late-fifteenth-century documents have been variously interpreted to suggest that he was born either at Puerto de Santa María, a city on the bay of Cádiz, or at Puerto de Santoña, a small village on the coast of Cantabria. Several theories attempt to reconcile this discrepancy (Ballesteros Beretta, 1987, and Berreiro-Meiro, 1970) including one, now discredited, that suggests that there were two Juan de la Cosas (Morison, 1942).

As owner and master of Columbus's flagship, *Santa María*, Cosa took part in the famous first voyage, but his ship sank off the coast of La Española on Christmas Eve, 1492. In his log entry for December 25, 1492, Columbus blamed the wreck on the ship's master, accusing him of negligence and cowardice; however, Columbus later helped him receive restitution from the Crown for the loss of his ship, calling this accusation into question. On Columbus's second voyage to America, Cosa is listed as a master chart maker and seaman and upon his return he remained in Spain until 1499, when he made the first of several voyages to Tierra Firme (South America). In mid-May, he signed on as chief pilot for Alonso de Ojeda and explored the north coast from the Boca de la Sierpe (Serpent's Mouth, the southern entrance to the Gulf of Paria) to Cabo de la Vela on the Guajira Peninsula.

Cosa's historic manuscript map—the earliest surviving European map to show part of America—was compiled upon his return to Spain in mid-June 1500. The date of the map has been debated, though recent research using X-ray, reflection-ray, and ultraviolet-ray analysis suggests that the inscribed date of 1500 is accurate. Drawn on parchment, the original map, in the Museo Naval in Madrid, measures 183 by 96 centimeters (72 by 38 inches). It shows both the Old and New Worlds. Recording the voyages of Columbus, Ojeda, Amerigo Vespucci, Martín Alonso Pinzón, and John Cabot, among others, it is given special authority by Cosa's participation in some of the voyages. The map, in the portolano style, shows the equator, both tropics, and a meridian apparently corresponding to the Line of Demarcation established by the Treaty of Tordesillas of 1494. At the west end of the map, occupying unknown lands, is an image of Saint Christopher carrying the Christ Child on his shoulders, said by some to symbolize Columbus carrying Christianity to the shores of the New World. Beneath this image is an inscription: "This map was made by Juan de la Cosa at Puerto de Santa María in the year 1500."

In February 1501, Cosa again sailed to Tierra Firme, as a pilot for Rodrigo de Bastidas. They coasted south from

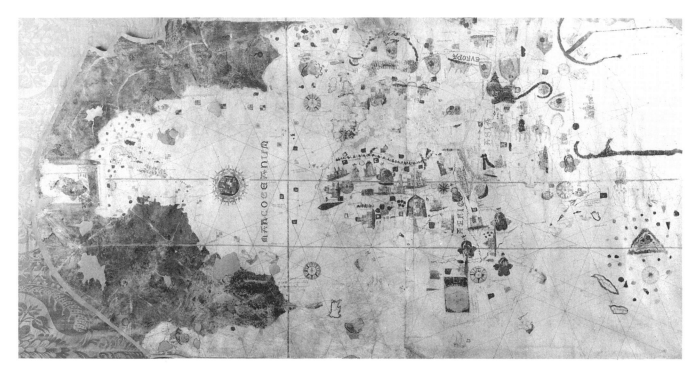

JUAN DE LA COSA'S MANUSCRIPT MAP OF 1500. The earliest surviving world map to show both the Old and New Worlds. The Old World (at right, faintly visible) is represented in white on the original, the New World (at left), in green. The two halves are in different scales, with the American portion greatly enlarged. At center left is a portrait of Saint Christopher, said to be an allusion to Columbus. The dark patches are holes in the original.   MUSEO NAVAL, MADRID

Cabo de la Vela exploring Caramairi and Urabá (the northwest coast of Columbia) and then headed north along the east coast of Panama to near Puerto del Retrete. Here they turned back after trading with the Indians, returning to Spain in September 1502.

Cosa was held in high regard by the Spanish Crown. It was perhaps due to his influence that Isabel changed her opposition to slavery; in 1503 she excluded the natives of Cartagena and Urabá from royal protection. Her decision offered the prospect of riches for Cosa, who had recently been appointed alguacil mayor (chief constable) of Urabá, granting him a share of a potentially lucrative slave trade. Perhaps in return for such favors, he undertook a secret mission to Portugal in 1503 to investigate suspected Portuguese infringements on Spanish territorial claims to Tierra Firme. His mission was discovered and he was imprisoned for a short period of time.

Following his release, Cosa prepared to claim his appointment as alguacil mayor of Urabá, though he did not reach the north coast of South America until late 1504. There he joined the Cristóbal Guerrera expedition, which had left Spain a few months earlier, and carried out a series of brutal raids that even their contemporaries condemned. Referring to Cosa and Guerrera, the sixteenth-century chronicler Gonzalo Fernández de Oviedo

states, "It seems to me this manner of exploring and bartering should be better called laying waste." But the Spaniards were repaid in kind. Death, disease, and combat took a heavy toll, and in March 1506 Cosa returned to Spain with only a handful of men. Oviedo saw a moral in these events: "See, those of you who can read, how few of the many Christians remained . . . so that you understand how much this gold costs."

In 1508, Cosa's status as the most experienced navigator in the West Indies was acknowledged by his participation (along with Vespucci, Pinzón, and Juan Díaz de Solís) in the Junta de Burgos. He contributed not only his geographical knowledge but also his technical skill as a pilot and cartographer. Both the office of pilot major in the Casa de la Contratación and the proposal for the creation of a master map of the Spanish discoveries (the Padrón Real) were initiated at this meeting.

The Junta also decided to impose Spanish authority over Tierra Firme. To this end, an expedition under the direction of Alonso Ojeda, with Cosa as second-in-command, was sent to occupy Urabá in late 1509. Shortly after landing on February 28, 1510, Cosa led a slaving raid inland, taking a village named Turbaco. The Indians counterattacked, killing seventy Spaniards including Cosa, whose body was riddled with poison arrows.

According to Oviedo, this was retribution for his previous transgressions. He left a widow and at least one daughter.

Juan de la Cosa sought wealth and found death in the New World. He was recognized by his contemporaries for his skill but condemned for his cruelty. Las Casas claims that he was the most experienced navigator in the West Indies. Pietro Martire d'Anghiera states that his maps were the most valued of their day. The world map of 1500 survives as one of the foundation documents in the early history of America.

BIBLIOGRAPHY

Anghiera, Pietro Martire d'. *Decadas del nuevo mundo.* Translated by Agustín Millares Carlo. 2 vols. Mexico, 1964.

Ballesteros Beretta, Antonio. *El cantabro Juan de la Cosa y el descubrimiento de America,* 2d ed. Cantabria, 1987.

Barreiro-Meiro, Roberto. *Juan de la Cosa y su doble personalidad.* Madrid, 1970.

Campbell, Tony. "Portolan Charts from the Late Thirteenth Century to 1500." In *The History of Cartography.* Vol. 1: *Cartography in Prehistoric, Ancient, and Medieval Europe and the Mediterranean.* Edited by J. B. Harley and David Woodward. Chicago, 1987.

Cerezo Martínez, Ricardo. "Aportación al estudio de la carta de Juan de la Cosa." In *Géographie du monde au moyen âge et à la Renaissance.* Edited by Monique Pelletier. Paris, 1989.

Morison, Samuel Eliot. *Admiral of the Ocean Sea: A Life of Christopher Columbus.* 2 vols. Boston, 1942.

Puente y Olea, Manuel de la. *Los trabajos geográficos de la Casa de Contratación.* Seville, 1900.

Vigneras, Louis-André. *The Discovery of South America and the Andalusian Voyages.* Chicago, 1976.

Watts, Pauline Moffitt. "Prophecy and Discovery: On the Spiritual Origins of Christopher Columbus's 'Enterprise of the Indies.'" *American Historical Review* 90 (1985): 73–102.

J. B. HARLEY and DAVID W. TILTON

CREW. See *Ships and Crews.*

CROSS-STAFF. An angle-measuring instrument (usable vertically or horizontally), the cross-staff consisted of a bar or rod (the staff), with a sliding transversal bar, the transversary. The cross-staff was also called the sea staff or Jacob's staff (Latin, *baculus Jacobi,* perhaps from the staff of the pilgrim to Santiago de Compostela). In other languages it was called *baculus geometricus* or *radius astronomicus* (Latin), *bâton de Jacob* (French), *balestilha* or *balestinha* (Portuguese), *ballestilla* (Spanish, perhaps from the word for crossbow). These terms were applied to the astronomer's, surveyor's, and seaman's cross-staves, and theoretical distinctions in their application were not

consistently maintained. The transversary was called in Latin *tabula* or *transversarius.*

In nautical use, the cross-staff was similar in principle to the *kamal,* and it has been suggested that the Portuguese navigators' acquaintance with the *kamal* led to their interest in the cross-staff. An observer held the end of the staff to his eye and moved the transversary along the staff until the upper edge of the transversary, viewed from the end of the staff, appeared to cut through the celestial body being observed, and the lower edge appeared to lie on the horizon (or similarly between any two objects, celestial or otherwise, of which the angular separation was to be measured). A scale engraved on the staff enabled the angle (or a function of it) to be read off from the position of the transversary. The problem of the position of the eye in relation to the axis of the staff (parallax error) and consequential inaccuracies in the observations were recognized from the outset and discussed in the literature. Improvements to the cross-staff included the attachment of sight vanes at the ends of the transversary, a lockable

USE OF THE CROSS-STAFF. For determining the altitude of the polestar, when the Guard Stars are in a particular position. Reproduced from Pedro de Medina's *Regimiento de navegación.* Seville, 1563.

NATIONAL MARITIME MUSEUM, GREENWICH

NAUTICAL CROSS-STAFF. Of wood, dating from circa 1596.   RIJKSMUSEUM, AMSTERDAM

sliding sleeve holding the transversary on the staff, changes in the proportions of the staff to the transversary (of which several of different sizes were provided), and changes in the nature of the scales. Because a cross-staff required the user to look directly at the observed object, it could not be conveniently used to make solar observations. João de Lisboa, writing of solar observations with the cross-staff made "from above" so that the sun's disk was covered by the transversary, says that a quarter degree of the measured altitude should be deducted, corresponding to the approximate apparent diameter of the sun. The back staff (or Davis quadrant), devised toward the end of the sixteenth century, obviated this difficulty.

The cross-staff was usually of hardwood, but sometimes of brass with a central wooden core. It was probably invented by the Jewish Provençal philosopher and scientist, Levi ben Gershom (1288–1344), who described it in his *Sefer tekunah*; the part of this treatise describing the cross-staff was translated from Hebrew into Latin by Peter of Alexandria in 1342. Regiomontanus and his patron, Bernhard Walther, knew of Levi's treatise, and Walther used a cross-staff *(radius astronomicus)* for many of his astronomical observations at Nürnberg from 1476 to 1504. Large and elaborate cross-staves were used by astronomers until well into the seventeenth century. The average size of the cross-staff may be judged from the woodcut in Pedro de Medina's *Regimiento de navegación* (1563).

Although the cross-staff was in principle available to Columbus, or any other fifteenth-century navigator, there is no evidence that it was used by seamen before the sixteenth century; the first navigational work to mention it is the *Livro de marinharia* of João de Lisboa, but parts of this work date from the middle of the sixteenth century. It is certain, however, the cross-staff was in use at sea by João Gomes before 1524. The type of cross-staff described by Levi ben Gershom had scale divisions that could not be

read directly in degrees of arc, and seamen would have required a table to convert to degrees the readings obtained. The scale on the seaman's cross-staff, therefore, read directly in degrees. The earliest surviving cross-staves are probably those made at Louvain in 1563 and 1571 by Gualterus Arsenius, nephew of Rainer Gemma Frisius, who had published, at Antwerp and Louvain in 1545, a comprehensive book on the cross-staff; but these brass instruments were presumably not for nautical use. The earliest surviving nautical cross-staff is probably that left at Novaya Zemlya in 1596 or 1597 by the Dutch explorers Jacob van Heemskerck and Willem Barents.

[See also *Kamal.*]

BIBLIOGRAPHY

Albuquerque, Luís de. *Curso de História da náutica.* 2d ed. Coimbra, 1972.

Maddison, Francis. *Medieval Scientific Instruments and the Development of Navigational Instruments in the XVth and XVIth Centuries.* Agrupamento de estudos de cartografia antiga, vol. 30. Coimbra, 1969.

Roche, John J. "The Radius Astronomicus in England." *Annals of Science* 38 (1981): 1–32.

Waters, David W. *The Art of Navigation in Elizabethan and Early Stuart Times.* London, 1958.

FRANCIS MADDISON

CUAUHTEMOC (c. 1495–1525), the last Mexica (or Aztec) king. Cuauhtemoc, whose name means "descending eagle," ascended to the rulership of the Aztec Triple Alliance in 1520. As ruler, Cuauhtemoc tried to defeat the Spaniards who had arrived in Central Mexico in 1519. The Aztec ruler Motecuhzoma II (Moctezuma), unsure how to deal with the invaders, was captured and later killed, and the Spaniards were forced to abandon the Aztec capital of Tenochtitlan (now Mexico City). Cuitlahuac succeeded

Motecuhzoma, ruling for only eighty days; in that time he organized the first active resistance to the Spaniards. After Cuitlahuac's death from smallpox, Cuauhtemoc continued the resistance. From April through August 1521, Tenochtitlan was besieged by the Spaniards. During the siege, Cuauhtemoc called a council to decide whether to continue resistance or sue for peace. His concern was that the people of Tenochtitlan were suffering from the lack of food and water and from disease. Native priests argued for war to the death, advice which Cuauhtemoc followed. War continued until August 13, 1521, when Tenochtitlan fell. Cuauhtemoc sought to escape in a canoe, but the Spaniards captured him, later torturing him to learn where gold was hidden. Though he continued as king, Cuauhtemoc was no longer a sovereign monarch, but an instrument of Spanish rule. In 1525 he was compelled to accompany Hernando Cortés on his expedition to Honduras. En route Cuauhtemoc was allegedly involved in a conspiracy and was executed. In modern Mexico, Cuauhtemoc is a national hero, a symbol of resistance to the Conquest.

BIBLIOGRAPHY

Cortés, Hernando. *Letters from Mexico.* Translated and edited by A. R. Pagden. New York, 1971.
Díaz del Castillo, Bernal. *Historia verdadera de la conquista de México.* Mexico City, 1980.
Sahagún, Bernardino de. *The Conquest of New Spain, 1585 Revision.* Translated by Howard F. Cline. Edited by S. L. Cline. Salt Lake City, 1989.

S. L. CLINE

CUBA. Almost 1,300 kilometers (800 miles) long and over 160 kilometers (100 miles) broad in places, Cuba is by far the largest of the West Indian islands. It is generally hilly, with three well-defined groups of mountains in the east, center, and west. The eastern range, known as the Sierra Maestra, is the largest. Along the coast are river valleys and plains where intensive agriculture is possible. Two of the most fertile of these plains are in the southeast, at Santiago de Cuba and Guantánamo.

"Guantánamo," with its distinctive initial letters *(gua)*, is characteristic of the place-names given by the original inhabitants. The oldest aboriginal groups were the Ciboney and Guanahatabey, who by the fifteenth century were largely confined to the western end of the island. The rest of the island was occupied by the more recently arrived Tainos, a subgroup of the Arawaks, who made up perhaps 90 percent of the population of about 100,000 people.

The Amerindian peoples of the northern West Indies seem to have shared much in terms of culture and

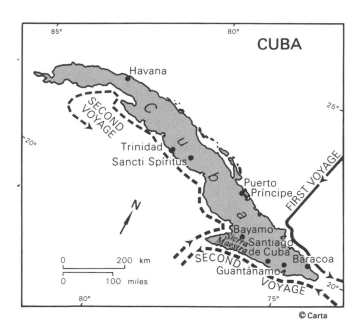

economy. They all relied heavily on fish, which was supplemented by the cassava root, which will grow in very unpromising conditions. They lived in villages under headmen known as caciques and were peaceable, without territorial ambitions. They had animistic religious beliefs and held various sports in high esteem. Some of their artifacts are remarkable: they wove fine hammocks, crafted superb canoes from huge trees, and created distinctive pottery.

Columbus reached Cuba during his first voyage, on October 28, 1492. He named the island Juana, after the daughter of Fernando and Isabel, but the native name of Cuba eventually prevailed. On the first voyage Columbus sailed along the northeast coast of the island before heading eastward. He returned during his second voyage, in the spring of 1494, and this time sailed along the south coast, visiting Taino villages and exchanging goods with the residents.

After the voyages of Columbus there was a considerable interval before the Spaniards came back to Cuba. Further efforts were undertaken from their base in La Española. In 1510 Diego Velásquez was commissioned to settle the island, and in 1511 he established himself at Baracoa. During the next few years seven towns were founded on the island, which was thus taken over by the Spaniards. The Tainos rather quickly died out, partly through conflict with the newcomers, but more through the ravages of European diseases.

Despite its size, Cuba was not an important part of the Spanish empire. In the early sixteenth century the settlement of La Española engaged the Spaniards, and after 1521 and the conquest of Mexico they were wholly preoccupied by the conquest of the mainland. So Cuba became a sort of backwater, a land of cattle ranches and a few sugar plantations whose main importance was as a staging post for the homeward-bound fleets, which would stop over at Havana.

[See also *Indian America*, articles on *Island Caribs* and *Tainos*.]

BIBLIOGRAPHY

Portuondo, Fernando. *Curso de historia de Cuba*. Havana, 1945.
Suchlicki, Jaime. *Historical Dictionary of Cuba*. Metuchen, N.J., 1988.

DAVID BUISSERET

CUNEO, MICHELE DA (c. 1450–c. 1511), gentleman explorer and a friend of Columbus. Born into a noble family of Savona, Michele da Cuneo was the son of Corrado da Cuneo who, in 1474, sold to Domenico Colombo, father of Christopher, a house with two pieces of land in Légino. Michele da Cuneo was an educated man, who spoke not only Genoese and Latin but also Castilian and Tuscan, the latter being the Italian language of the learned. Columbus, on the other hand, being a plebeian, knew only Genoese and Latin at the time of his departure from Genoa.

Cuneo was a participant in Columbus's second voyage. Although the reason for his accompanying Columbus is not known, the fact that he did not stop at La Isabela with the Castilian noblemen who also made the journey gives support to the claim that for him scientific curiosity exceeded the economic and military interests of the expedition.

Cuneo, after his return from the voyage, wrote a letter dated December 15, 1495, which is preserved at the University Library in Bologna. Addressed to another Savonese nobleman, Gerolamo Annari, the letter is the first European document, after Columbus's journal, to give extensive details on the flora and fauna of America. Cuneo was also something of a gossip. It was he who wrote of a flirtation between Columbus and Beatriz de Bobadilla of Gomera, who was as beautiful as she was sensual and cruel.

Cuneo and Columbus seem to have been good friends. The Admiral presented him with an island, southeast of La Española, which to this day bears, in his honor, the name of Saona.

Apart from being a friend, Cuneo was also a great admirer of Columbus. He wrote about the Admiral: "I want you to know well, that in my humble opinion, since Genoa is Genoa, there is no born man as magnanimous and as expert in navigation as the said Admiral." These praises refer not only to Columbus as expert sailor, but

also to the tenacity with which he faced difficult situations and his sparing the members of his crew onerous tasks: "as soon as the storm was gone, he would raise the sails while the others slept."

BIBLIOGRAPHY

Morison, Samuel Eliot. *Admiral of the Ocean Sea: A Life of Christopher Columbus*. 2 vols. Boston, 1942.
Taviani, Paolo Emilio. *I viaggi di Colombo*. 2d ed. Vol. 2. Novara, 1990. Spanish ed., Barcelona, 1989.
Vannini, Marisa de Gerulewicz. "Traducción y notas de novitatibus insularum oceani hersperii repertarum a Don Christoforo Columbo genuensi por Michael de Cuneo." Special issue of *Revista de Historia*. Caracas, 1965.

PAOLO EMILIO TAVIANI
Translated from Italian by Rodica Diaconescu-Blumenfeld

CUNHA, TRISTÃO DA (c. 1460–1539), Portuguese leader of 1506 expedition to India; discoverer of the island of Tristan da Cunha. Tristão da Cunha was the son of Nuno da Cunha, chamberlain of Prince Fernando, nephew and heir of Prince Henry the Navigator and the younger brother of King Afonso V (r. 1438–1481). Cunha himself was chamberlain of Prince Fernando's son, the ill-fated Dom Diogo, duke of Viseu, older brother of the future King Manuel I. After Dom Diogo was stabbed to death by King João II in 1484, Cunha became a member of João's household. When Manuel became king in 1495, Cunha served as councilor and trusted adviser to the monarch, accompanying him to Castile in 1498 so that they could be acclaimed heirs to the Castilian and Aragonese thrones.

In 1505 Cunha was named to be *capitão-mor* (commander) of the seventh armada to India and governor of Portuguese Asia for three years. However, illness prevented him from going to India and Dom Francisco de Almeida took his place. By 1506 Cunha had been restored to health and was named *capitão-mor* of the expedition of fourteen to sixteen ships that left Lisbon in the spring of that year and included the famed Afonso de Albuquerque. His instructions were to establish a fortress on the island of Socotra in the Arabian Sea the better to control non-Portuguese shipping through the Red Sea, and then to continue to India to take on a cargo of spices.

En route, probably in October 1506, Cunha discovered an archipelago of three small uninhabited islands and two islets in the south Atlantic about 1,900 kilometers (1,200 miles) south of the island of Saint Helena, 2,400 kilometers (1,500 miles) west of the Cape of Good Hope, and about 2,900 kilometers (1,800 miles) east of Uruguay (37°6′ S latitude and 12°15′ W longitude). The largest island (with an area of approximately 100 square kilometers [40 square miles] and reaching about 2,080 meters [6,760 feet] above sea level) and the archipelago itself now bears an anglicized version of his name (Tristan da Cunha). The smaller islands (later named Inaccessible and Nightingale) are about 16 kilometers (10 miles) apart. All three islands, because of their precipitous cliffs, were not easily accessible to shipping and Cunha did not land there. Since the region is subject to dangerous squalls, it was avoided by most seafarers during the Age of Discovery.

Arriving in Mozambique too late to catch the favorable wind to India, Cunha explored the island of Madagascar and attacked several East African Muslim strongholds. After leaving the African coast, the forces led by Albuquerque and Cunha captured Socotra after a bitter fight. In August 1507, while Albuquerque remained on the island to supervise the building of a fortress, Cunha sailed to India where he helped lift the Muslim siege of Cannanore. He also aided Viceroy Almeida in the struggle against the ruler of Calicut. In early December 1508, Cunha embarked for Portugal in command of five ships loaded with spices, pearls, and precious stones. After an absence from the Portuguese capital of almost twenty-six months, Cunha arrived in Lisbon on June 1, 1508. Four of the five ships reached Portugal safely, the fifth having been captured by the French corsair Mondragon.

In 1513 Cunha was named to head the Portuguese embassy sent to Rome to pledge King Manuel's obedience to the newly elected pope, Leo X. The embassy included three of Cunha's sons as well as Manuel's delegates to the Fifth Lateran Council. On March 12, 1514, the Portuguese embassy made its triumphal entrance into Rome accompanied by musicians, an elephant from Malabar, India, and its mahout, and a Persian on horseback accompanied by a cheetah on a leash, the latter animal a gift to King Manuel by the ruler of Ormuz. In a letter to António Carneiro, Portugal's secretary of state, Cunha wrote that "all said it was the most honored and richest embassy that ever entered Rome." Cunha later presented the animals to the pope, along with richly decorated vestments and altar cloths.

Little is known of the last two-and-a-half decades of Cunha's life. His oldest son, Nuno da Cunha, served as governor of India from 1529 to 1538 and died on the return voyage to Portugal early in 1539, predeceasing his father, who died sometime before September 6 of the same year.

BIBLIOGRAPHY

Andrade, António Alberto Banha de. *História de um fidalgo quinhentista português: Tristão da Cunha.* Lisbon, 1974.
Brander, Jan. *Tristan da Cunha, 1506–1902.* London, 1940.

Francis A. Dutra

CURRENTS. See *Tides and Currents.*

CUZCO. Cuzco was the capital of the Inca state Tahuantinsuyu until its capture by Spaniards in 1533. It is located in the easternmost range of the Andes of Peru, at fourteen degrees south latitude. It was built in a wide, well-watered valley on the Huatanay River, a tributary of the Vilcanota. At 3,250 meters above sea level, it has a semiarid climate with high daytime and low nighttime temperatures and a short rainy season.

Inca oral tradition states that Manco Capac, the original Inca, founded Cuzco at an undetermined date. By the mid-fifteenth century, when the city had attained considerable size, Pachacuti Inca rebuilt it as an elite administrative and ceremonial center. On the outskirts and scattered throughout the valley were the villages of the common people. The only eyewitness estimate of the population for the Cuzco valley gave 40,000 residences, which may have housed 100,000 to 200,000 inhabitants. Three major languages were spoken: Quechua, Aymara, and Puquina. People of different ethnic groups were required to wear distinctive clothing and hairstyles.

Cuzco impressed the Spanish conquerors as large, rich, clean, and well ordered. It was constructed of stone buildings with gabled thatched roofs along narrow, straight stone-paved streets. The river and streams were lined with stone. Palaces and temples were built as *cancha,* several rooms around an enclosed courtyard. Some included *kallanka,* long halls for ceremonies in inclement weather. The most distinguishing stylistic feature was the trapezoidal aperture for doorways, windows, and niches. Sheets of gold covered the walls of important temples.

The city was divided socially and geographically in two. In the upper half were two large open squares separated by the Huatanay River. Life-sized gold figures of people, maize, llamas, and alpacas were embedded in the fine gravel that paved one of the squares, Haucaypata. Facing it were the temple to Viracocha, the creator deity, three palaces (Cassana, CoraCora, and Amarucancha), and the Acllahuasi, the palace for the *aclla,* the women chosen to weave the enormous quantities of textiles the Incas needed and to brew the corn beer for their festivals. Coricancha, the temple to the sun, where the mummies of the Incas were kept, also had gold figures planted in its garden. Above Cuzco was the fortress-temple, Sacsahuaman.

Inca religion was based on reverence for the earth, sky, and the ancestors. The fertile, cultivated earth was revered in the form of the feminine deity Pachamama; earthquakes as the masculine deity, Pachacamac; and the largest mountains as lords. In the Cuzco area there were many official sacred places that were significant landscape features, such as springs, lakes, hills, and rock outcroppings. Of them, 329 were encoded onto a system of imaginary lines that radiated from Coricancha like spokes of a wheel; their care and worship was the responsibility of the major *ayllus* (lineages) of Inca Cuzco. The thunderbolt (Illapa) and the sun (Inti) were worshiped primarily by men and the moon (Mamaquilla) by women. Most importantly, the Incas revered their ancestors, whose mummies had extensive lands and large retinues dedicated to their care. The Incas also considered themselves children of the sun, thereby incorporating that deity as one of their ancestors.

The surrounding hillsides were terraced and watered by an extensive network of irrigation canals. Maize was grown on the lower slopes and potatoes on the higher, and at the highest elevations were pastures for herds of llamas and alpacas, used for transportation, sacrifices, wool, and meat. Cuzco and the entire Inca state were divided into four quarters connected by four major highways that originated at the two central squares, Haucaypata and Cusipata. The road to the northern province, Chinchaysuyu, reached present-day Ecuador; the road to the western province, Cuntisuyu, went to the southern coast of present-day Peru and into Chile; the road to the southern province, Collasuyu, went to present-day Bolivia; and the road to the eastern province, Antisuyu, went to the slopes of the Andes that descend into the Amazonian lowlands of Peru.

The Spaniards under Francisco Pizarro conquered Cuzco in November 1533 and refounded it as a Spanish city on March 23, 1534. Manco Inca presented himself as an ally to the Spaniards, who crowned him as a puppet Inca in December 1533. However, in 1536 Manco Inca organized a rebellion and burned Cuzco, which was rebuilt with tile roofs. Manco Inca retreated to Vilcabamba, where he set up an Inca government-in-exile until his assassination in 1544.

The colonial city became a major provider of supplies on the route from Lima to the silver mines at Potosi. Francisco, Gonzalo, and Hernando Pizarro and Diego de Almagro fought over their respective shares of the former Inca empire, which resulted in a factional war and the execution of Almagro in 1538. Almagrist forces, however, had Hernando Pizarro imprisoned in Spain (1540) and murdered Francisco (1541, in Lima) and Gonzalo Pizarro (1548). Almagrist and Pizarrist forces continued to struggle against each other and against the increasing power of the Spanish colonial state, as did the Incas from their exile state in Vilcabamba. The last claimant to the Inca throne, Tupac Amaru, a descendant of Manco Inca, led an unsuccessful rebellion against the Spaniards. He was captured and executed in Cuzco in 1572, thus ending Inca resistance to Spanish conquest. The indigenous population was reorganized into parish towns by the Viceroy Francisco de Toledo, marking the beginning of an era of strong control by the Spanish Crown over the viceroyalty of Peru.

BIBLIOGRAPHY

Hemming, John. *The Conquest of the Incas.* New York, 1970.

Hemming, John, and Edward Ranney. *Monuments of the Incas.* Boston, 1982.

Gasparini, Graziano, and Luise Margolies. *Inca Architecture.* Bloomington, Ind., 1980.

Porras Barrenechea, Raúl. *Antología del Cuzco.* Lima, Peru, 1961.

Rowe, John Howland. "What Kind of a Settlement Was Inca Cuzco?" *Ñawpa Pacha* 5 (1967): 59–76.

JEANETTE E. SHERBONDY

D

DA GAMA, VASCO. See *Gama, Vasco da.*

DEAD RECKONING. The dead reckoning position, as opposed to a navigational fix, is determined by advancing the course and distance made good since the last known position. The art of dead reckoning was perfected during the late medieval period in the Mediterranean, where the tideless environment enabled the magnetic compass, the nautical chart, the sandglass, and the *toleta de marteloio* (a form of traverse table) to be used to produce a purely mathematical solution to the problem of position at sea. Conditions on the Atlantic coasts of Europe, where the ebb and flow of the tide so largely dominated passage making, were not so favorable, but during the fifteenth century the traditional skills of pilots schooled in such conditions were combined with Mediterranean practices to produce the method of navigation characteristic of the Age of Discovery. Toward the end of the century, when the long ocean voyages began, a form of astronomical navigation emerged that verified one element of the dead reckoning, but, until the problem of fixing longitude was finally solved some three hundred years later, dead reckoning remained the basis of all navigation.

A vivid, if somewhat colorful, picture of Mediterranean methods is painted by the German monk Felix Faber who went on pilgrimage to the Holy Land in a three-masted galley in 1483. His account is nonetheless instructive for being that of a landsman. The pilot (or "pirate," as Faber mistakenly calls him) is described as a powerful officer who knew the shortest and safest ways across the sea but who would hand over to local officers (local pilots, one must assume) in any area he did not himself know. "Besides the pilot," Faber writes,

there were other learned men, astrologers and watchers of omens who considered the signs of the stars and sky, judged the winds and gave directions to the pilot himself. And they were all expert in judging from the sky whether the weather would be stormy or fair, taking into account besides such signs as the colour of the sea, the movement of dolphins and of fish, the smoke from the fire and the scintillations when the oars were dipped in the water. At night they knew the time by the inspection of the stars.

Faber then goes on to talk of the magnetic compass (calling it a Stella Maris), of which the ship had two, one near the mast and a second on the upper poop deck:

And beside it all night long a lantern burns, and they never take their eyes off it and there is always a man watching the star [i.e., the compass rose]. Nor does the helmsman dare move the tiller in the slightest degree except at the order of the one watching the Stella Maris from which he sees whether the ship ought to go straight on or curve or turn sideways.

The narrator then goes on to describe the nautical chart,

on which is a scale of inches showing length and breadth, and on which thousands of lines are drawn across the sea and on which regions are marked by dots and numbers of miles. Over this chart they hang, and can see where they are even when the stars are hidden.

He ends up with a passage about how the navigation of the vessel is organized, saying that the captain does not interfere in matters of navigation, nor does he know the art, but he orders the ship to go this way or that.

Though the account is impressionistic, it clearly points to the care with which navigation was conducted, both as to the course steered and in the observation of natural phenomena that might reflect on the ship's position. The "thousands of lines" drawn across the sea of course refers to the rhumbs emanating from the wind roses on the chart by means of which the pilot, using two pairs of dividers, "pricked off" his position on the chart and then laid off the new course.

Although Faber makes no mention of it, a sandglass would be turned, probably by the helmsman, every half hour, both to regulate the watchkeeping duties and to keep up the dead reckoning, for out of sight of land the measurement of (intervals of) time, in conjunction with an assessment of speed by the pilot was the only way of calculating distance run. Mediterranean books of sailing directions, such as the late thirteenth-century *Compasso da navigare* gave precise distances to be run on given courses over hundreds of miles, instructions that could be followed only by accurate steering, plotting, and estimation of distance run. Further, the *toleta de marteloio*, the form of traverse table used when the ship was forced off her intended track by headwinds, would have been useless without an accurate assessment of the distance run. The glass, whether half-hour or hour, was reset each noon, when the sun bore due south.

Although there is no documentary evidence of the *toleta de marteloio* being used outside the Mediterranean, it seems highly probable that it was and that it was adapted early in the fifteenth century to make it more suitable for use in an open ocean with currents of unknown velocity. It formed an essential part of Mediterranean dead-reckoning navigation. First referred to by the Catalan mathematician and scholar Ramon Lull (1233–1315), the tables, or in another form, as on Andrea Bianco's atlas of 1436, the diagram, resolved the problem of the "traverse" caused by the necessity in headwinds to tack on either side of the mean line of advance. What was important to the medieval navigator, before there was any indication of latitude and longitude on the chart, was the angle between the course he wanted to make good and the course he actually had to steer. Essentially, the *toleta de marteloio* in two tables told the pilot how far he had sailed away from his desired course, the distance he had made good in the intended direction, and how to get back to the intended track. Chartwork, in the sense of resolving such problems graphically, was of course impossible on the portolan chart. The tables solved the problem geometrically, that is to say, without accounting for any drift or set. They were replaced, when altura navigation was introduced, by the Rule, or Regiment, of Leagues, which used the measured change of altitude (in effect, latitude) in place of the estimated distance sailed. The rule told the seaman how far he had to sail along a given rhumb to alter the altura by one degree, which was taken to equal 16⅔ leagues. David W. Waters in *Reflections upon Some Navigational and Hydrographic Problems of the XVth Century Related to the Voyage of Bartolomeu Dias, 1487–1488* contends that the Rule of Leagues was used long before latitude (as opposed to altura) navigation was practiced and probably dates from the first rather than the last quarter of the fifteenth century. The successive attempts to estimate the length of a degree of the meridian and to fix the value of the league and of the mile are not relevant to the subject of dead reckoning.

[See also *Altura Sailing; Navigation.*]

BIBLIOGRAPHY

Crone, Ernst. *How Did the Navigator Determine the Speed of His Ship and the Distance Run?* Coimbra, 1969.

Lane, F. C. *The Invention of the Compass.* London, 1969.

Waters, David W. "Early Time and Distance Measurements at Sea." *Journal of the Institute of Navigation* 8, no. 2 (1955): 153–173.

Waters, David W. *Reflections upon Some Navigational and Hydrographic Problems of the XVth Century Related to the Voyage of Bartolomeu Dias, 1487–1488.* Lisbon, 1988.

M. W. RICHEY

DEATH OF COLUMBUS. See *Burial Places of Columbus; Columbus, Christopher,* article on *The Final Years, Illness, and Death; Writings,* article on *Last Will and Testament.*

DECLINATION OF THE COMPASS. See *Compass,* article on *Declination of the Compass.*

DE LA COSA, JUAN. See *Cosa, Juan de la.*

DEMARCATION, LINE OF. See *Line of Demarcation.*

DEMOGRAPHY. See *Disease and Demography.*

DEZA, DIEGO DE (1443–1523), friend of Columbus, archbishop of Seville. A Dominican priest, Deza was the tutor of the crown prince, Juan. In the summer of 1486, Queen Isabel appointed him to the commission of experts she asked to evaluate Columbus's ideas. Deza rose quickly in the church hierarchy, becoming successively bishop of Zamora, Salamanca, Jaén, and Palencia and finally archbishop of Seville from 1505 until his death in 1523, while serving as King Fernando's confessor in 1492 and inquisitor general from 1498 to 1507. He gained a reputation for strict censorship among the humanists editing the texts of the Polyglot Bible. But Columbus remembered Deza as a warm supporter of his ideas and, after his disastrous fourth voyage, chose the archbishop as arbiter in his disputes with the king.

Deza's nephew, the Dominican priest Pedro Suárez de Deza, was appointed bishop of Concepción de la Vega on the island of La Española in 1513 and allied himself with Bartolomé de las Casas as a defender of the Indians. In December 1515, nine Indians—six women and three men—who had been captured and survived the voyage to Spain, were sent to Seville, where Diego de Deza was expected to teach them Spanish and convert them to Christianity, so that they could return to convert their own people on La Española. In 1516, Deza founded and endowed the Colegio de Santo Tomás in Valladolid, which became a haven for Las Casas and other Dominicans engaged in the great debate over the nature and status of the Indians.

BIBLIOGRAPHY

Azcona, Tarsicio de. *La elección y reforma del episcopado español en tiempo de los Reyes Católicos.* Madrid, 1960.

Bataillon, Marcel. *Erasmo y España.* 2 vols. Mexico City, 1950.

Gams, Pius Bonifatius. *Die Kirchengeschichte von Spanien.* Vol. 3. Regensburg, 1879.

Giménez Fernández, Manuel. *Delegado de Cisneros para la reformación de las Indias.* Vol. 1 of *Bartolomé de las Casas.* Seville, 1953.

HELEN NADER

DIARIO. For discussion of Columbus's journal of his first voyage, see *Writings,* article on *Journal.*

DIAS, BARTOLOMEU (c. 1450–1500), Portuguese navigator. In voyages made in the years 1487 and 1488, Dias was the first European to go from the Atlantic Ocean to the Indian Ocean. His fleet, which sailed from Lisbon in August 1487, consisted of three ships under the command of Dias himself, his brother Diogo Dias, and the infante João.

The flotilla traveled safely, using the new astronomical procedures applied to navigation in the second half of the fifteenth century. Knowledge of these new procedures are the subject of an annotation made by Christopher Columbus in one of his books. Columbus reports that he attended an interview between Dias and King João II soon after Dias's return. Dias had assessed latitudes by means of an astrolabe, surely taking account of the position of the sun. He states that he traveled to a promontory that he named the Cape of Good Hope and that he had determined with an astrolabe that the cape was forty-five degrees from the equator. This figure is ten degrees farther south than the approximate latitude of the cape, although it may be the latitude of the southernmost point

reached by Dias, since it is known that he went farther south than the southernmost point of Africa.

King João apparently made no public recognition of Dias's voyage, even though it meant the realization of the king's dream of reaching the Indies and its spices by a direct sea route. The discovery of this route had radical repercussions on European geographical concepts, which were derived primarily from Ptolemy's *Geography.* The planispheres reproduced in this work showed the Indian Ocean as an inland sea and the African continent as exceedingly wide to the south, thus giving the impression that the Atlantic was also a landlocked sea. Though maps by less prestigious authors, such as Fra Mauro, presented Africa as circumnavigable, the predominant geographical image was derived from Ptolemaic cartography. For example, Duarte Pacheco Pereira in his *Esmeraldo de situ orbis* (Emerald of the earth), written between 1505 and 1508, states that the seas are landlocked *(medi terrani).*

Bartolomeu Dias's trip, therefore, was a revelation to Europe: it was possible to reach the Indian Ocean from the Atlantic by ship. A map drawn by Henricus Martellus Germanus in 1489 or 1490 spread this novel idea throughout Europe. In 1490 the publication of Ptolemy's *Geography* was suspended until new data about the world could be collected. The book was republished in 1507 with new tables that sought to give a new and realistic configuration of lands and seas.

Little is known about the life of Bartolomeu Dias, except that he navigated the Atlantic in order to determine current and wind conditions. João Barros writes that he experienced many "dangers at sea" during the voyage that made him famous. He was responsible for numerous activities related to navigation in the city of Lisbon and was a member of the fleet of Pedro Álvares Cabral as the commander of a caravel. Caught in a sudden storm on May 23, 1500, he and all his crew were drowned at sea.

BIBLIOGRAPHY

De Lery, Jean. *History of a Voyage to the Land of Brazil Otherwise Called America.* Translated by Janet Whatley. Berkeley, 1990.

Diffey, Bailey W. *Prelude to Empire: Portugal Overseas before Henry the Navigator.* Lincoln, Neb., 1960.

Diffey, Bailey W., and George D. Winius. *Foundations of the Portuguese Empire, 1414–1850.* Edited by Boyd C. Shafer. Minneapolis, 1977.

Morison, Samuel Eliot. *Portuguese Voyages to America in the Fifteenth Century.* New York, 1965.

LUÍS DE ALBUQUERQUE
Translated from Portuguese by Paola Carù

DÍAZ DEL CASTILLO, BERNAL (1495?–1584), Spanish soldier and chronicler born in Medina del Campo, in northern Castille. Díaz sailed for Tierra Firme, Panama, in 1514 to join the recently appointed governor, Pedro Arias de Ávila (called Pedrárias Dávila). He then moved to Cuba and participated as a soldier in three expeditions launched by its governor, Diego Velázquez, to the Mexican coast: the first led by Francisco Fernández de Córdoba (1517), the second by Juan de Grijalba (1518), and the third by Hernando Cortés, which resulted in the long campaign of conquest of Mexico (1519–1521). In 1523 Díaz accompanied Captain Luis Marín in the conquest of Chiapa and a year later he accompanied Cortés in his expedition to Honduras. Upon his return to Mexico City in 1526, he was granted an encomienda of Indians in Chamula and later was appointed regidor of Coatzacoalcos. After a brief trip to Spain in 1540, he settled in Guatemala in 1541, where he married Teresa Becerra in 1544, with whom he had several children. During another trip to Spain in 1550 he was appointed regidor of Guatemala City. He spent the rest of his long life there, active in local politics and as a landholder.

Unlike other famous conquistadores, Díaz never distinguished himself in military deeds. His fame rests solely on his *True History of the Conquest of New Spain,* an account of his participation in the campaign, designed to inform the royal officials of his service to the Crown. Such accounts were often written by conquistadores, but Díaz's is distinguished as a comprehensive history that reacts vigorously against Francisco López de Gómara's *Conquest of Mexico* (1552), which praises Hernando Cortés while making little mention of his soldiers. Díaz was fully aware of his technical inability as a historian, since, unlike Gómara, he did not have the training to write in the appropriately high literary style. But he believed his personal account of the facts more than compensated for his poor rhetoric. Díaz admired Cortés no less than Gómara, but the *True History* provides a wider perspective than Gómara's account. The book also rebuts Bartolomé de las Casas's negative view of the conquest. Like Cortés, Díaz believed he was participating in the advance of Christianity. Endowed with a prodigious memory, Díaz identified the names of all persons and places of the conquest and provided memorable descriptions of Tenochtitlán, powerful portraits of Cortés, Alvarado, Motecuhzoma II, Cuauhtemoc, and others, and enriched his account with innumerable personal anecdotes. His major success lies in his ability to recreate and evaluate his own perceptions and feelings as a conquistador, which he conveys in a sincere and almost conversational style.

BIBLIOGRAPHY

Alvar, Manuel. "Bernal Díaz del Castillo." In vol. 1 of *Historia de la literatura hispanoamericana.* Edited by Luis Iñigo Madrigal. Madrid, 1982.

Cerwin, Herbert. *Bernal Díaz: Historian of the Conquest.* Norman, Okla., 1970.

Díaz del Castillo, Bernal. *The Discovery and Conquest of Mexico, 1517–1521.* Edited by Genaro García. Translated by A. P. Maudslay. New York, 1956.

Díaz del Castillo, Bernal. *Historia verdadera de la conquista de la Nueva España.* Edited by Carmelo Sáenz de Santamaría. Madrid, 1982.

Graham, R. B. Cunninghame. *Bernal Díaz del Castillo.* New York, 1915.

ANGEL DELGADO-GOMEZ

DÍAZ DE SOLÍS, JUAN   (?–1516), pilot and explorer. Born in Lebrija near Seville in the last half of the fifteenth century, Díaz de Solís's career prior to 1508 is obscure. According to one story, before 1495 he was involved with French commerce raiders in an attack on a Portuguese royal caravel, but this account appears improbable in light of Díaz de Solís's claim of service as a pilot in Portugal's Asian trades after 1498. Whatever his previous experience, by 1508 he was known as an experienced and apparently accurate pilot.

Díaz de Solís's fame rests on two voyages he undertook in search of a way to Asia around the New World. In 1508, Fernando V commissioned Díaz de Solís and Vicente Yáñez Pinzón to sail north and west from Honduras, which Columbus had reached in 1503, to see if they could round the "island" of the New World and cross the supposed Great Gulf to India. Although the chronicler Antonio Herrera y Tordesillas raises doubts about whether and where this voyage went, more contemporary sources indicate that it resulted in the discovery of Yucatán and may have sailed as far north in the Gulf of Mexico as twenty-three degrees north. The voyage of 1508–1509 was marked by a disagreement between its leaders. Diego Colón, Columbus's son and heir, later sued, probably because he believed that Díaz de Solís and Pinzón had trespassed the area of his father's discovery.

These legal problems did not prevent Díaz de Solís's selection as chief pilot of the Casa de la Contratación in 1512 and his commission to sail to India for the purpose of determining the Line of Demarcation in the Eastern Hemisphere. However, Portuguese protests and doubts by members of the Casa de la Contratación regarding Díaz de Solís's fitness for command caused the suspension of preparations for this voyage. New preparations in 1513 were also suspended because of an investigation of unknown charges against the chief pilot.

Díaz de Solís's second attempt to round the New World took place in 1515 to 1516. He sailed from Sanlúcar de Barrameda on October 8, 1515. On February 2, 1516, he sailed his ships into the Río de la Plata, which he explored to a point on the Uruguayan shore where he landed to lay claim to the region for Spain. He and most of his party were killed by Charrúa Indian archers. Survivors of the expedition returned to Seville and spread Díaz de Solís's belief that the Río de la Plata was the beginning of a strait through the continent.

BIBLIOGRAPHY

Parry, John H. *The Discovery of South America*. New York, 1979.
Morison, Samuel Eliot. *The European Discovery of America: The Southern Voyages, A.D. 1492–1616*. New York, 1971.

PAUL E. HOFFMAN

DISEASE AND DEMOGRAPHY. When Christopher Columbus ventured into the Americas in 1492, he encountered a large, diverse population that spoke many languages and displayed many different customs. Just how many American Indians were present at that time was unknown to Columbus and Europeans immediately following. Estimates of population size of the Americas have perplexed scholars ever since. Clearly, Europeans brought new diseases to the Americas that ultimately combined with cultural changes to reduce dramatically the size of the population after 1492. The magnitude and timing of this population reduction as well as which diseases were brought by Europeans and which were already in the Americas continue to fuel scholarly debate.

Information on the size of the American Indian population in 1492 can be obtained from many sources, but none offers exact figures. Much information about population size originates from the writings of early European explorers like Christopher Columbus, Capt. John Smith, Samuel de Champlain, and Bénard de La Harpe. Many of these Europeans in early contact with American Indians were concerned about population size and related their estimates. In some cases, these estimates include direct counts, but mostly they consist of impressions and information the explorers had gathered from other Europeans or the Indians themselves. To use this information, scholars must interpret how well the Europeans knew the particular Indian group, whether the information was based on firsthand observation or on hearsay, the political context of the estimate (whether the Europeans had reason to exaggerate or minimize the estimate), and the date of the information.

A special problem in estimating the size of the American Indian population prior to European contact from European accounts is the likelihood that population size may have previously shifted. The first European to estimate population size usually postdated by many years the first European contact with most groups. The researcher hopes that early information on population size includes evidence of past declines or increases, but it is difficult, if not impossible, to be certain. The problem is compounded by the likelihood that European-introduced disease may have spread among American Indian populations even prior to the initial European contact in a given area. Although many American Indian groups were isolated from one another by language and geographical barriers, others were linked through trade networks, economic activity, and various aspects of their culture.

To supplement the information available from ethnohistorical sources, archaeologists have attempted to estimate population size from excavations. This work involves assessing the amount of village refuse (garbage) and the number of people-years needed to produce it. Excavations can reveal the size and number of houses occupied, the size and distribution of villages, and the approximate number of years a village was occupied. To interpret such archaeological data, scholars must estimate how long it would take a person to accumulate refuse and how many persons lived together in one house. Were all houses in a village occupied simultaneously by a large population, or did a smaller population move to new houses several times?

In recent years, scholars have attempted computer simulations and theoretical arguments to focus on population size. For example, by assuming that epidemics of new diseases like smallpox and measles would have caused a particular mortality in the population, scholars can work backward in time to estimate what the population must have been originally to result in a known figure for a later date. Obviously, such approaches make many assumptions about the accuracy of the recent estimate and the impact of epidemics that may not be justified.

Even bones can offer information about population size. For example, in the mid-Atlantic area of the United States, American Indian ossuaries have been found archaeologically that contain a large number of skeletons. Such deposits apparently represent a custom whereby every few years the remains of all who had died during that time were brought together for communal burial. Analysis of skeletons after excavations can reveal the ages at death of individuals, and these ages can be grouped to reconstruct mortality curves, survivorship curves, and even life tables that characterize the populations they represent. Such research tells us that people living in the mid-Atlantic area in the fifteenth century experienced a very high infant mortality rate, so that life expectancy at birth was only about twenty-three years. Although this figure seems very low, it actually is close to that estimated for cities of Europe at that time.

If the number of years represented by a skeletal sample is known, then population size can be estimated directly from the reconstructed life table. This technique can be highly accurate if the number of years represented by the sample is known and if the sample contains all of the deceased from the population.

Given the probable inaccuracy and incompleteness of the information available, and the difficulty in interpreting all the variables involved, it is not surprising that scholarly estimates of American Indian population size in 1492 vary greatly. Estimates of the size of the population of the U.S. region in 1492 range from 294,000 to 5 million. Estimates for North America for the same period range from 900,000 to 7 million and for the Western Hemisphere from 8.4 million to 72 million. For the most part, the variation in these estimates reflects the different methods used and the assumptions made by the scholars involved. But it also reflects differences in the definition of geographic areas and dates in question. For example, some scholars define North America as north of Mexico or north of the Rio Grande; for others, North America is north of "civilized" Mesoamerica. The date focused on varies from A.D. 1200 to the middle of the seventeenth century. All these problems complicate the comparison of estimates.

A 1988 study at the Smithsonian Institution in Washington, D.C., synthesized estimates made of each North American tribe by experts on each tribe. These estimates for North America (north of the urban civilizations of central Mexico) at about 1492 ranged between 1,213,475 and 2,638,900 with the "best estimate" of 1,894,350. These figures suggest a population density (number per 100 square kilometers) between 7 and 15. The area showing greatest density was California (75), followed by the northwestern coast (54) and the Southwest (18). Areas of sparse occupation were the subarctic (2), arctic (3), and Great Basin (4).

Most scholars agree that the size of the population of the Americas in 1492 culminated from a long period of population growth originating with the first migrations of people from Asia. There is some evidence that between A.D. 1000 and 1492 in some areas, population size was already declining or at least oscillating owing to disease and climatological or cultural factors.

Disease in the Americas prior to 1492

Many of the Europeans in early contact with American Indians were impressed with their good health and vitality. Such impressions have led some scholars to suggest that prior to European contact, American Indians were living in a largely disease-free environment that made them especially susceptible to the pathogens introduced from Europe.

American Indian vulnerability to many European diseases is well documented and was a major factor leading to depopulation in the sixteenth through the nineteenth centuries. But rapidly accumulating evidence suggests that morbidity was high in many areas of the New World prior to European contact. This evidence largely originates from analysis of samples of human remains recovered in archaeological contexts.

Techniques of paleodemography, as mentioned above, enable mortality curves, survivorship curves, life tables, and other demographic statistics to be computed from the study of skeletons. But these computations require accurate estimates of age at death for each skeleton in the sample.

For infants and children, age at death can best be estimated by examining the stage of dental formation as revealed in X rays. Observations on the development of the crowns and roots of the teeth provide the most accurate estimates, and observations on the eruption of the teeth, the length and size of the bones, and the appearance and fusion of epiphyses, or small bony caps, on the ends of the bones offer other useful information, although they are less accurate than dental formation data. To estimate age at death in adults, scientists examine the extent of arthritic change, metamorphosis of the pubic symphyseal face (area where two pubic bones come together in the front), fusion of the bones of the skull, and microscopic changes in bones and teeth. These techniques have been developed from the study of skeletons of individuals whose age at death is known.

The sex of the individual can be determined accurately from the appearance of the bones of the pelvis. Sex differences are also marked in the size of most other bones of the skeleton; bones of males are slightly larger than those of females. These differences are not well marked in the bones of children; thus sex is usually estimated in skeletal samples only for adults.

Demographic analyses of samples of human remains dating prior to European contact indicate that mortality rates were increasing through time and were at relatively high levels in most areas of the New World immediately prior to 1492. The studies suggest that in many areas, as American Indians developed agriculture, they shifted their settlement pattern to a more sedentary lifestyle and began living in larger, more densely populated villages. This pattern probably resulted in sanitation problems, polluted water sources, and increased levels of infectious disease. The demographic consequence was a temporal increase in infant and child mortality, which created a decrease in life expectancy at birth.

Paleopathology is the science of interpreting diseases of past populations. Mostly this involves assessing lesions or abnormalities on archaeologically recovered human bones or preserved soft tissue on the bones. Other evidence derives from depictions on artifacts or from the study of coprolites (preserved feces). Unfortunately, few environments allow preservation of soft tissue or coprolites; thus most interpretation must focus on bone. The field is limited further in that relatively few diseases affect bone, and some diseases affect bone in similar ways. In recent years, technological advances and improvements in research design have greatly facilitated the capability to diagnose disease. Current researchers hope to identify immunoglobulins (defense proteins of the body that respond to disease) in ancient bones, which would enable them to detect specific diseases.

Artistic representations of disease have been found on ceramic vessels bearing images of deformed and diseased persons, although these have been limited largely to certain cultures in Peru and Mexico. The best such evidence comes from the Moche culture of northern coastal Peru, which dates from about A.D. 100 to 750. Missing limbs, skin diseases, blindness, cleft palate, clubfoot, and various mutilations have been recognized in the artistic depictions on these vessels.

Studies of preserved coprolites in archaeological contexts document the pre-Columbian New World presence of several parasites that previously were thought to be of Old World origin. These parasites include the hookworm (*Ancylostoma duodenale*), the whipworm (*Trichuris trichura*), the common roundworm (*Ascaris lumbricoides*), the broad fish tapeworm (*Diphyllobothrium spp.*), the pinworm (*Enterobius vermicularis*), the hairworm (*Strongyloides spp.*), the louse (*Pediculus humanus*), and Zoonoses, or diseases originating in nonhuman animals (*Moniliformis clarki*, *Trichinella spiralis*, and *Echinococcus granulosis*).

In 1973, examination of a pre-Columbian Peruvian mummy of the Nasca culture revealed not only bony changes indicative of tuberculosis but also soft tissue containing the acid-fast bacilli, which indicate terminal miliary tuberculosis. Numerous other examples of skeletal changes consistent with those documented for tuberculosis have been found in archaeologically recovered samples, all dating from the pre-Columbian period. The temporal-geographic occurrence of remains with tuberculosis indicates an association with large, dense populations living in the last few centuries prior to European contact.

For many years, scholars have debated the origin of syphilis. After 1492, the disease was a problem in both the Old and New World. To date, pre-1492 examples suggestive of syphilis have been found only in the New World. This suggests that syphilis originated in the Americas and was transported to Europe after 1492. The problem is complicated in that other diseases (yaws, pinta) produce lesions similar to those produced by syphilis and are difficult to distinguish.

Other disease conditions present in the New World prior to 1492 were bacillary and amoebic dysentery, viral influenza and pneumonia, arthritis, dental disease, and various congenital disorders and nutritional deficiencies. Research indicates that most of these health problems were increasing in frequency prior to 1492. Certainly, the increase in frequency of these infectious diseases correlates with increasing population size, density, and sedentism. These problems probably were major factors in the increasing infant mortality rate also apparent in the samples. Changes in agriculture that resulted in a less varied diet with a higher starch component apparently produced nutritional problems in some areas, as well as increases in dental caries. Samples from many areas of the New World show temporal increases in evidence of anemia, reflecting both dietary reliance on low-iron foodstuffs and the effects of dysentery and parasitism. All these problems seem to correlate with high population density and sedentism, since earlier samples from populations with more mobility, less population density, and a more varied diet seem to show less evidence of disease.

Impact of European-Introduced Disease

Columbus's arrival in La Española in 1492 marked the beginning of the end to thousands of years of isolation between the Old World and the New World. This isolation applied not only to human populations but to microbes as well. Movements of peoples throughout Europe, Asia, and Africa had created a large pool of disease microbes maintained by the large human population densities. In contrast, the comparatively smaller population density in the New World and its long isolation from the Old World allowed fewer major diseases. Although, as mentioned above, some evidence suggests that syphilis may have moved from the New World to the Old World, most other major epidemic diseases traveled in the other direction, with devastating results.

The first major epidemic following Columbus's arrival occurred in about 1520. This epidemic was smallpox, a disease that struck American Indian populations repeatedly and ultimately caused the greatest mortality of all introduced diseases. Smallpox was followed by measles, bubonic plague, cholera, typhoid, pleurisy, scarlet fever, diphtheria, mumps, whooping cough, and gonorrhea. Malaria and yellow fever probably were introduced from Africa.

The spread of the diseases and the magnitude of their impact were affected by the density of the American Indian populations, their geographic location, extent of contact with one another, and the extent of their contact with Europeans. In general, the epidemics moved from east to west, loosely following the extent of European–American Indian contact. Clearly, in some areas, disease spread in advance of actual European contact, facilitated by Indian trade networks. The timing of the first major outbreaks of disease in the New World populations was roughly as follows: smallpox, 1520–1524; measles, 1531–1533; influenza, 1559; bubonic plague, 1545–1548; diphtheria, 1601–1602; typhus, 1586; cholera, 1832–1834; scarlet fever, 1637; typhoid, 1528; and malaria, 1830–1833. Many of these diseases struck American Indian groups consecutively and repeatedly, causing great mortality.

Other factors causing population reduction among American Indians were alcoholism, warfare, genocide, cultural disruption, and declines in fertility. Beginning shortly after 1492, Europeans introduced disease and cultural disruption that dramatically reduced the size of the Indian population. In North America, the total dropped to about 1.8 million by 1600, 1.4 million by 1700, 1 million by 1800, 770,000 by 1850, and a low of below 500,000 in the early twentieth century. The rate of reduction ranged from about 95 percent in California to about 53 percent in the arctic, or an overall reduction of about 73 percent. After reaching their lowest number in the early 1900s, populations of native North America began a slow but steady recovery, reaching over 600,000 by 1925, nearly 800,000 by 1950, and over 1 million again by 1970.

Estimates of the contemporary population size of American Indians in the United States are complicated by different definitions of Indian membership. For example, the 1980 U.S. Census estimated that 1,478,523 citizens considered themselves to be American Indians (excluding Eskimos and Aleuts). A total of 1,120,245 of these identified themselves as from particular tribes. The remaining 358,278 listed themselves as "American Indian" or "tribe not reported." Note that these figures represent self-declaration; and the large increase in the total from similar estimates in 1970 probably includes incorporation of formerly non-Indians into the Indian sample and changes in census procedures. In 1970, ethnic categories from rural western areas were determined from observation by census workers. In 1980, such data were collected entirely by self-declaration.

In contrast, in 1980 only 339,475 American Indians were living on U.S. reservations (excluding Alaska). Most of them were concentrated in the Southwest, the Great Plains, and the Northeast. Official government records of tribal enrollment totaled 891,208 in 1981. Including estimates of Indian population size in northern Mexico and Canada, the North American Indian population size in 1980 would have been about 1,921,182, using the U.S. Census data; 1,390,990, using tribal enrollment data; or 872,257, using reservation data. In 1980, the census suggested that just over 232,000 citizens considered themselves to be Cherokee. In contrast, over 55,000 were enrolled in one of the Cherokee groups (North Carolina, Shawnee, or Tahlequah), and just under 5,000 were living on reservations.

However one counts the size of the contemporary population of the United States, it is clear that a remarkable population recovery is underway. By some counts, the number of Indians in North America in recent years may have reached or exceeded their numbers in 1492. As health conditions and medical care continue to improve, the demographic recovery is likely to continue.

[See also Syphilis.]

BIBLIOGRAPHY

Baker, Brenda J., and George J. Armelagos. "The Origin and Antiquity of Syphilis: Paleopathological Diagnosis and Interpretation." Current Anthropology 29 (1988): 703–737.

Cohen, Mark N., and George J. Armelagos, eds. Paleopathology at the Origins of Agriculture. Orlando, Fla., 1984.

Denevan, William M., ed. The Native Population of the Americas. Madison, Wis., 1976.

Dobyns, Henry F. Their Number Became Thinned: Native American Population Dynamics in Eastern North America. Knoxville, Tenn., 1983.

Johansson, S. Ryan. "The Demographic History of the Native Peoples of North America: A Selective Biography." Yearbook of Physical Anthropology 25 (1982): 133–152.

Snow, Dean R., ed. Foundations of Northeast Archaeology. New York, 1981.

Thornton, Russell. American Indian Holocaust and Survival: A Population History since 1492. Norman, Okla., 1987.

Ubelaker, Douglas H. "North American Indian Population Size, A.D. 1500 to 1985." American Journal of Physical Anthropology 77 (1988): 289–294.

DOUGLAS B. UBELAKER

DISTANCE, MEASUREMENT OF.

While Columbus adopted in principle what he believed to be Alfraganus's measure of a degree of latitude, 56⅔ Roman miles (R.M.) to the degree, in practice he employed the seamen's standard of his era, 60 R.M. to the degree, or 1 mile to the minute of latitude.

In fifteenth-century practice, distance was determined by estimating the speed of the ship and recording the length of time the ship remained on the same course at the same estimated speed. Speed was determined by estimating the rapidity with which bubbles in the wake of a ship recede, a frustrating operation, for the wake disappears rapidly. Time that a ship remained on a specific course or at a specific estimated speed was determined from the ampoletta, or "hourglass," which required reversing every half-hour. Rough seas tended to slow the rate at which sand passed from the upper portion of the instrument to the lower. This factor, together with forgetfulness on the part of the ship's boy tending the ampoletta in recording each reversal or tardiness in making the reversal, worked to yield a shorter time on course than actual, which tended to offset the invariably inflated estimates of ship's speed made by the navigator or mate. Finally, *course* was determined from the mariner's compass whose needle pointed to the north magnetic pole. The direction of the ship's travel was shown by the lubber line drawn on the forward edge of the bowl containing the floating or gimballed compass card.

The magnetic compass, however, is subject to variation, that is, the angle between true north and magnetic north. Variation differs from place to place on the surface of the earth and from day to day in any particular locality. In Columbus's day nothing had been published on variation in the Atlantic Ocean. Columbus encountered it and coped with it by usual navigator's practices. At night, he took "readings" of the position of the North Star, Polaris, by the "pilot's blessing method," in which an observer in close proximity to the compass faces the North Star. Raising his arm and pointing to the star, he lowers his arm to the level of the compass, attempting to include in a single plane both star and compass. It is readily apparent if there is a significant angular difference between compass north and North Star. Repeated trials might point to variation and result in course corrections if the navigator became convinced that this was necessary.

The technique by which Portuguese and Spanish seamen navigated was known as *dead reckoning*. Employed was a mariners' chart, essentially blank except for the delineation of known features of coastline, home and other ports, and islands (known, such as Azores, Canaries, and Cape Verde; or mythical, such as Antilia and St. Brendan's). Sometimes the only horizontal line shown would be the Tropic of Cancer, approximately 23 degrees 30 minutes north latitude. There might also be entered a series of vertical lines spaced at anywhere from one to five degrees of longitude. The proposed course to be followed on a sea voyage would be plotted before embarking. Then, as the ship proceeded, with the navigator and pilot attempting to follow the proposed course, estimates of the course actually followed would be entered upon the chart.

Columbus attempted on many occasions to take readings of the altitude of the North Star. (The altitude of the Celestial North Pole gives a direct reading of the latitude of the observer.) Such readings were inaccurate for several reasons: for one, the North Star in Columbus's time (and today as well) was not identical with the Celestial North Pole but described a path with a radius of 3 degrees 27 minutes around the pole; for another, it was extremely difficult to get a reasonably accurate reading of altitude of a not very bright star from the deck of a ship undergoing various and varying degrees of heave, surge,

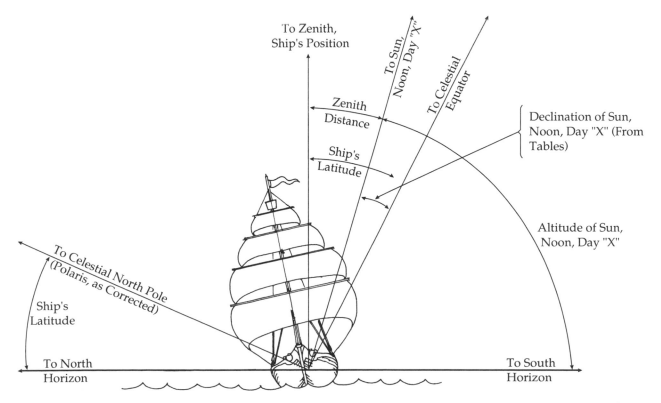

DETERMINING LATITUDE AT SEA. Relationships between ship's position and the heavenly bodies available for determining latitude.

AFTER FRED F. KRAVATH, *CHRISTOPHER COLUMBUS, COSMOGRAPHER*, RANCHO CORDOVA, CALIF., 1987.

sideslip, yaw, roll, and pitch while using a mariner's astrolabe or a marine quadrant hung from a tripod or bracket on the ship. Still, repeated attempts, all recorded, together with the plot of the estimated actual course followed, in which the north-south component of the Roman miles traversed could be converted to degrees of latitude and the east-west component to degrees of longitude, provided a number of checks. Unusually sensitive and resourceful navigators like Columbus appeared rarely to be greatly off course or in a position from which they could not return to their home ports or continue on to other explorations.

The correction for Polaris's circumpolarity was not known prior to Columbus's crossing. Columbus discovered that Polaris was circumpolar through the practice of comparing Polaris's bearing with magnetic north as given by the mariners' compass. Thus, he was at least alerted to the unreliability of a single reading of Polaris's altitude. Taking readings, however, as was the practice, at dusk and dawn (approximately twelve hours apart during the greater part of his first voyage) provided a set of altitudes and azimuthal differences between Polaris and compass magnetic north that could be averaged. Even though Polaris had a circumpolarity of 3.5 degrees, averaging

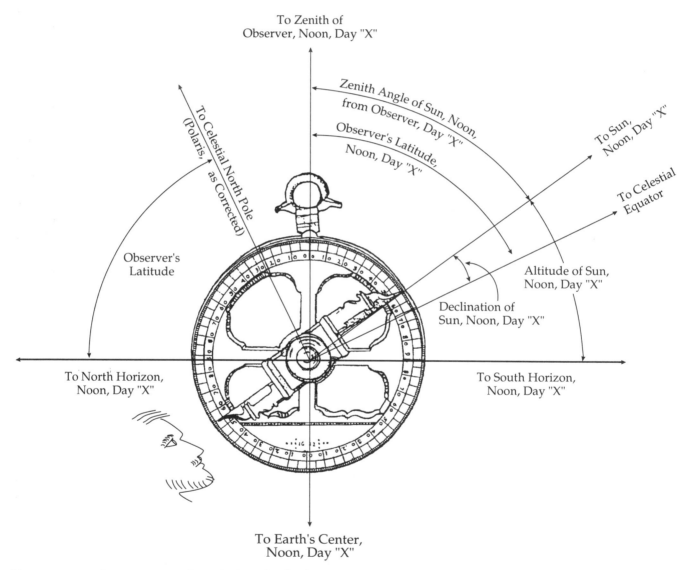

USE OF THE MARINER'S ASTROLABE. To obtain the latitude of a ship by observation of the sun's zenith angle (90 degrees minus altitude) at noon, between March 21 and September 22: If the ship is north of the equator, add the sun's declination (from tables) to the zenith angle of the sun at noon; if the ship is south of the equator, subtract this value. Between September 23 and March 21: If the ship is north of the equator, subtract the sun's declination from the zenith angle of the sun at noon; if the ship is south of the equator, add this value.

AFTER FRED. F. KRAVATH, *CHRISTOPHER COLUMBUS, COSMOGRAPHER*, RANCHO CORDOVA, CALIF., 1987.

reduced error in determining azimuth and altitude to 0.75 degree or less.

Correction for declination was required in order to utilize the sun's altitude at noon to determine latitude. Latitude, at noon, is equal to the zenith distance (or zenith angle) plus declination. Since altitude of any heavenly body is equal to 90 degrees minus the zenith distance, latitude of the observer's position is also given by 90 degrees minus altitude plus declination. While declination of the sun at noon on specific days of the year was not yet available in published charts or ephemerides in Columbus's day, it was not difficult for a navigator to construct his own set of approximate declinations. Declination is simply the zenith distance of the heavenly body (in this case the sun) with reference to the equator. All professional navigators knew that the declination of the sun at noon on the days of the vernal and autumnal equinoxes was zero, on the day of the summer solstice declination was approximately plus 23.5 degrees, and on the day of the winter solstice, minus 23.5 degrees. Ptolemy had indicated how the declination varied from day to day in his *Geographic Syntaxis*. Pilots had various methods of approximating declination. During the spring, for example, one simple method was to add 23 degrees for each of the first 31 days after the vernal equinox, 17 degrees for each of the next 31 days, and 5.5 degrees for each of the last 31 days. These measurements would then be accurate to within 6.5 nautical miles, 8.12 Roman (Italian) miles, or (in 1492) 2.03 Spanish *leguas* (leagues)—a tolerable error.

The Roman Mile and the League. The earliest linear measurement units were anatomical, or body-related. The thumb, fingers, palm, hand, forearm, upper arm, full arm, and foot were favorite appendages for indicating lengths—singly, in multiples, and in combinations. The Roman system was an outgrowth of the ancient Greek system, just as the Greek system was an outgrowth of the

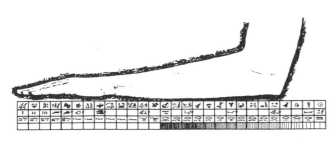

THE CUBIT. The twenty-four-digit small cubit, commonly measured from elbow to fingertips, compared to the twenty-eight-digit royal cubit, represented here by a hieroglyphics-covered royal-cubit rod from approximately 1550 B.C.

FROM MISCELLANEOUS PUBLICATION NUMBER 272, NATIONAL BUREAU OF STANDARDS

earlier Egyptian and Babylonian systems, particularly the former. These systems were similar in many respects but not identical. All units of linear measure were relatable to digit length or breadth. However, the manner of determining the finger size varied, not only between the various civilizations, but within each from time to time and place to place.

Another type of linear measure, which developed hand-in-hand with anatomical units, was botanical in origin. It developed from the requirement for units somewhat smaller or larger than the body-related units available. Since the smallest body unit was the finger, one way of subdividing the finger into smaller units was to relate it to one of several types of seeds. The barley grain was used in Europe and Asia for just such a purpose. Usually, four lengths of a grain of barley, or six widths, was equal to the width of a digit, about 18.5 millimeters or 1/54 meter.

In areas of the world such as Mesopotamia and the Nile delta, where there is considerable marshland, reeds were used. A small reed was made equivalent to four small elles (cubits) or twelve palms; a medium reed was defined as six medium elles (cubits) or twenty-four palms, and a large reed was equated to six large elles (cubits) or thirty palms. By the beginning of the Christian era, the digit, or finger, of approximately 1/54 meter (18.31 to 18.79 millimeters) was in use in Egypt, Assyria, Persia, Syria, Asia Minor, Greece, Italy, and the Roman colonies, including Great Britain. However, while apparently the dominant size, this was not the only digit in use. A somewhat later unit adopted by the Greeks that spread wherever Hellenic influence was strong was the finger (also referred to as the Parthenon or Olympic finger) defined as 1/16 Attic foot of 0.3083 to 0.309 meters or 19.27 to 19.31 millimeters. Even larger fingers than the Olympic came into use, some as large as 22.5 millimeters in breadth.

Itinerary Units of Measurement. All ancient linear systems had itinerary units related, at first, to human performance and later augmented to include the performance of animals such as the horse and camel. Some, for instance, defined the distance that troops could march in four hours without rest, or per day on a continuous basis, allowing for rest. Units such as the Roman mile, schoenus, parasang, and league came into being to express such distances. It was more convenient to say 12 miles than 12,000 paces or 60,000 feet, and it was still more convenient to express a longer distance as, say, six schoeni, or parasangs, than as the equivalent number of miles.

An important itinerary unit in the ancient world was the Greek stade, or stadion. This unit was originally defined as the distance a strong man could run without stopping for breath. Later, it became the standard length of the Olympic track and was equated to 100 fathoms, 500

Relationship between Greek Olympic and Roman Systems of Measure

GREEK OLYMPIC SYSTEM								ROMAN SYSTEM BASED ON ANCIENT GREEK SYSTEM					
Unit	Length in Meters	Finger	Palm	Foot	Cubit	Plethron	Stadion	Unit	Length in Meters	Digit	Foot	Pace	Stadium
Finger[a]	0.01929	1	¼	1/16	1/24			Digit	0.0185185	1	1/16		
Knuckle	0.03858	2						Uncia	0.0247		1/12		
Palm	0.07716	4	1	¼	1/6			Palm	0.074074	4	¼		
Handbreadth	0.11574	6	1½		¼								
Lick "Little span"	0.15432	8											
Handlength	0.1929	10	2½										
Span	0.23148	12											
Foot	0.30864	16	4	1	⅔			Foot (pes)	0.2963	16	1	⅕	
Pygme[b]	0.34722	18											
Pygon[c]	0.3858	20						Palmipes[e]	0.37037	20			
Cubit	0.463	24	6	1½	1			Cubit (ulna)	0.4444	24	1½		
Step[d]	0.7716	40	10	2½				Step	0.74074	40	2½		
Xylon	1.3888	72	18		3			Pace (passus)	1.48148	80	5	1	
Fathom	1.8518	96	24	6	4								
Pole	3.0864	160	40	10	6⅔			Pole	2.96296	160	10	2	
Cable	18.5184	960	240	60	40								
Plethron	30.864	1600	400	100	66⅔	1	⅙	Actus	35.556	1920	120	24	
Stadion	185.184	9600	2400	600	400	6	1	Stadium	185.185	10,000	625	125	1
Ride	740.736	38,400	9600	2400	1600	24	4						
Roman mile	1481.472	76,800	19,200	4800	3200	48	8	Roman mile	1481.48	80,000	5000	1000	8
								Miglio geografico[f]	1851.85	100,000	6250	1250	10

While the table shows only one value for each unit of measurement, a range of values actually existed to comply with the relationships shown. Other ancient cultures also had systems of measure incorporating the same units but assigning different values. The relationships shown between units apply for most systems based on larger feet such as the Babylonian (0.3142 to 0.31161 m) and the Drusian (0.3349 to 0.3415 m).

[a]Contrary to this widely accepted value, W. M. Flinders Petrie believed the Greek finger to be based on the Egyptian digit (0.018295 to 0.01879 m). He set 6 Olympic feet (4 cubits) equal to 100 Egyptian digits.
[b]One pygme = one lick + one handlength.
[c]One pygon = one foot + one palm.
[d]One step = one foot + one cubit.
[e]One palmipes = one palmus + one pes.
[f]Miglio geografico may date from a few centuries after the ancient Roman system proper.
SOURCE: After Fred F. Kravath, *Christopher Columbus, Cosmographer*, Rancho Cordova, Calif., 1987.

remens, or 600 Greek Olympic feet. Alexander the Great and his armies introduced the stade (stadion) into the Middle East and probably India. The Romans, in their zeal for standardization, made their own stadium equal to the Greek Olympic stadion. Strabo (62 B.C.– A.D. 19), the Greek historian and geographer, said eight stadia made the Roman mile, which yields a mile with a length of 1,481.5 meters.

Was the unit of measurement known as the Roman (Italian) mile—and defined as equivalent to 8 stadia, 1,000 paces, 5,000 feet, 80,000 digits, and 1,481.5 meters—the unit employed by Columbus at sea? Martinus Capella (fl.

third century), whose geography became somewhat of a standard in the medieval period, set the Roman mile at 1,000 paces, or 8 stadia; Macrobius (fl. c. 395–423), in describing Eratosthenes's and Ptolemy's differing metrologic conclusions, still set the Roman mile at 5,000 Roman feet or 1,000 paces; and Isidore of Seville (fl. c. 560–636) set the stadium at 625 Roman feet and the Roman mile at 8 stadia. There is, however, some evidence that in at least some areas the Roman mile grew to 1,488 meters (because of changes in the size of the basic foot, pace, and stadium); this measure was referred to as the "miglio Romano," in contrast to the "milliarium" or "mille pas-

Comparison of Various Stades (Stadions, Stadia) Found in the Literature

Historiographic Interpretation	Stade Length in Meters[a]	Stade Composition: Unit (Length in Meters) × Number	Stades per Roman Mile[b]
Herodotus-Gossellin stade[c]	99.75 m	Assyrian cubit (0.494 m) × 200	14.85
Pliny (interpreted by Macrobius) Pliny (interpreted by d'Anville)	148.2 m	Pelasgic foot (0.2963 m) × 500 Schoenus (5928 m) ÷ 40 Assyrian cubit (0.494 m) × 300	10
Pliny (interpreted by Hultsch) Pliny (interpreted by Dreyer/Stahl)	157.5 m	Schoenus (6300 m) ÷ 40 Royal cubit (0.525 m) × 300	9.41
Lehmann-Haupt	165 m	Plinian foot (0.275 m) × 600 Talmudic cubit (0.550 m) × 300	9
Polybius "Palesgic" stade	177.9 m	Pelasgic foot (0.2963 m) × 600	8.33
Strabo-Pliny Olympic stade and Roman stadium	185.2 m	Olympic foot (0.3086 m) × 600 Roman foot (0.2963 m) × 625 Egyptian remen (0.3704 m) × 500	8
Drabkin Philetaerian stade	197.6 m	Assyrian cubit (0.494 m) × 400	7.5
Ptolemaic or Royal Egyptian stade of Hultsch	210 m	Royal cubit (0.525 m) × 400	7
Lehmann-Haupt	296.4 m	Double Assyrian cubit (0.988 m) × 300	5
Babylonian and Assyrian ush (stadion)	355.68 m	Assyrian cubit (0.494 m) × 720	4.166
Klein's "superstadion"	1896 m	?	0.78

[a]One meter = 3.28084 U.S. customary feet.
[b]For this table, 1 Roman mile = 1482 meters.
[c]Based on an Egyptian itinerary measurement between Thebes and the mouth of the Nile River.
Source: After Fred F. Kravath, *Christopher Columbus, Cosmographer*, Rancho Cordova, Calif., 1987.

sus," the ancient Roman mile of 1,481.5 meters. There is also evidence that other Italian miles, such as the Tuscan (Florentine) mile and the "miglio geographico" (equal to 1,851 to 1,853 meters, essentially one minute of latitude, or of longitude at the equator), came into use for land measurements around Columbus's time or before. Closer to the Columbian era, Sacrobosco defined the Roman mile as equal to 10 stadia of 500 Roman feet each, which maintains the 5,000-foot equivalency.

Sometime during the period 1526–1528, some thirty-four to thirty-six years after Columbus's first voyage, Jean Fernel, the celebrated French physician known as "the modern Galen," undertook to measure the length of a degree of latitude on the Paris–Amiens road "where the road ran true north and south." In describing the reason for his undertaking, he indicated that authorities of his era considered Eratosthenes' degree of 700 stades to be equivalent to 87½ Italian (Roman) miles. Johann Müller (1436–1476, known as Regiomontanus), publisher of astronomical ephemerides used by Portuguese, Spanish, and Italian navigators, including Columbus, had reduced Eratosthenes' degree to 640 stadia or 80 Italian miles. Ptolemy's 500-stadia degree was in Fernel's time considered equivalent

to 62½ Italian miles; but Fernel himself accorded the degree only 60 Italian miles (the mariners' degree used by Columbus). Hence, the impetus to "straighten things out." After his measurement, which resulted in a degree length of 68,095¼ paces, Fernel equated this to 68 Italian miles and 95¼ paces (68.09525 Italian miles), or 544 Roman stadia and 95¼ paces (544.762 stadia).

Despite his insistence, for promotional purposes, that a degree measured 56⅔ Italian (Roman) miles, Columbus used the 60-Italian-mile degree that had adherents among not only mariners but also at least a modicum of sixteenth-century cosmographers. This mile was equivalent to 8 stadia, which unit was most likely used in estimating the speed of his ship, or one-quarter league (sometimes used for plotting a ship's course in dead reckoning). The league, however, unlike the Roman (Italian) mile, had an extremely variable value—over the years, from place to place, and even at a given place and time, depending on the context of its use. The literature reveals at least thirty-one values for this unit, from a low of 1.5 Roman miles to a high of over 4.58 Roman miles.

[See also *Circumference; Latitude; Longitude; Navigation*, article on *Instruments of Navigation*.]

BIBLIOGRAPHY

Berriman, A. E. *Historical Metrology.* London, 1953.

Delambre, J. B. J. *Histoire de l'astronomie du moyen âge.* Paris, 1821. Reprint, New York, 1965.

Gillings, Richard J. *Mathematics in the Time of the Pharaohs.* Cambridge, 1972. Reprint, New York, 1982.

Haws, Duncan. *Ships and the Sea.* Göteborg and New York, 1975.

Kravath, Fred F. *Christopher Columbus, Cosmographer.* Rancho Cordova, Calif., 1987.

Landstrom, Bjorn. *Columbus: The Story of Don Cristóbal Colón, Admiral of the Ocean Sea, and His Four Voyages Westward to the Indies.* New York, 1966.

Morison, Samuel Eliot. *Admiral of the Ocean Sea: A Life of Christopher Columbus.* 2 vols. Boston, 1942.

Phillips-Birt, Douglas. *A History of Seamanship.* New York, 1971.

FRED F. KRAVATH

DOMESTICATED ANIMALS. Before Christopher Columbus crossed the Atlantic, the only domesticated animals in the New World were the dog, the turkey, the guinea pig, the alpaca, and the llama. Native Americans had no horses, cattle, sheep, goats, pigs, cats, or chickens. The North American cowboy and the gaucho of the Argentinian pampas developed only after cattle and horses reached the New World from Spain. Even the North American Plains Indians, commonly portrayed as horsemen in the modern popular media, did not have horses until the eighteenth century.

In 1493 Columbus brought twenty-four horses, ten mares, and three female mules to the New World, as well as cattle, sheep and goats, hogs, dogs, and probably cats and chickens. These were the first European domesticated animals to have a significant influence on the New World. The Vikings had brought horses, cattle, and other animals earlier to Greenland, but their animals did not survive the abandonment of that colony; and the English, Dutch, and French colonists did not bring their animals to northeastern North America until more than a hundred years after Columbus.

Every Spanish fleet after 1493 brought more animals. These animals multiplied and spread from the early ranches in the Caribbean to the mainland, reaching as far as New Mexico and Chile by the mid-1500s. As they spread, the animals brought about extensive and permanent ecological changes in the New World.

Routes to the New World. Spanish animals came to the New World by two main sailing routes. The first was via the Canary Islands to La Española. The voyage from Spain to the Canaries might be as short as eight to twelve days. At certain times of the year, the prevailing winds from the Canaries to the outer Antilles could be so steady and favorable that the voyage took as few as twenty days.

Another five days brought ships to La Española. Most of the animals brought to the Spanish colonies came by this route.

By Columbus's time, moving animals by watercraft was common, based on six thousand years of Mediterranean and north European maritime experience. The only difference between this early animal transport and that of the transatlantic passage was in the length of the voyages. As soon as mariners understood the patterns of winds and currents, they easily carried smaller animals to La Española from herds established on the Canaries, and they brought horses from Spain by this route until late in the sixteenth century.

Once in the New World, however, voyages between the islands of the Caribbean and along the mainland coasts could be very difficult. Although unfavorable winds and contrary currents on these routes took their toll of animals, livestock from La Españolan herds spread first to Puerto Rico and then to Jamaica, and from Jamaica to Honduras and to Nicaragua. La Española supplied stock for Cuba, and from Cuba animals were carried to New Spain. From there the animals moved north overland to what is now New Mexico. From La Española animals also moved to the north coast of South America and to Panama. Animals crossed the Isthmus of Panama, sailed down the west coast of South America to Peru, and then marched overland to Chile. This process took less than fifty years.

The second route from Spain and Portugal to the New World went via Cape Verde to the east coast of South America. This passage was very difficult because it crossed the doldrums and the so-called horse latitudes, those bands of windless sea at the intersection of major air patterns, where ships were becalmed for long periods and where dead animals were thrown overboard. On these voyages, the loss of animal life may have been as high as one-third, and perhaps one-half for horses.

Crossing the North Atlantic, the English, French, and Dutch ships met contrary winds and currents. These difficult and stormy voyages are much better known in North America than are the easier voyages of the Spanish ships. Confusion of the North Atlantic route and the route to South America with the favorable Middle Atlantic passage leads to an exaggeration of the difficulty of moving animals to the New World.

Growth of the Herds. The pattern of herd development in each of the Spanish colonies was similar. The conquistadores first brought their horses and dogs for war. They also brought some animals for provisions, but usually relied on foodstuffs provided by native Americans.

Once an area was under Spanish control, the land and its native American inhabitants were divided among the conquistadores. The ownership of a horse and arms was

NORTH AMERICA

GREENLAND

British Isles

1750

1730

1770

1773

1719

1600

1690

1540

1665

1567

1520

1665 from France

1629 from England

1660 from Flanders

1620 from England

ATLANTIC OCEAN

Iberian Peninsula

Canary Islands

AFRICA

La Española (Hispaniola)

1493 from Spain

Jamaica

Puerto Rico

Cape Verde Islands

1514

1519

Isthmus of Panama

1509, from La Española to Puerto Rico and to Jamaica

PACIFIC OCEAN

Peru

SOUTH AMERICA

1530

1540

1560

1535

1580

Chile

1540 from Spain (failed)

INTRODUCTIONS AND DIFFUSION OF OLD WORLD
DOMESTICATED ANIMALS IN THE AMERICAS

sometimes prerequisite to receiving a land grant, and horsemen received a greater portion of treasure than did foot soldiers.

As the Spanish colonial economies developed around herding and ranching, the newly introduced domesticated animals increased dramatically in numbers. Although this increase can be attributed to the lush New World environment and its vacant ecological niches and to the lack of natural predators, the speed of the increase varied depending on the type of animal.

The increase in the herds was most immediate and obvious among pigs, sheep, and goats. Called *ganado menor,* these small animals have short breeding cycles, produce multiple births, and are relatively easy to transport. Mariners commonly left them to breed on uninhabited islands as future provisions for ships and expeditions. The small animals are rarely mentioned in the historical records, except in unusual circumstances.

Sheep spread to many areas of the New World, but they were never as important economically as they were in medieval Spain. Goats were usually found along with sheep and sometimes in great numbers where the land was poor. The pig's short reproductive cycle made it one of the most economically useful of all animals. Eating pork not only provided an important source of meat protein, but it also distinguished the Catholic Spaniard from Jewish and Muslim contemporaries. Hernando Cortés, Hernando de Soto, and Francisco Vázquez de Coronado all took swine on their expeditions, and Francisco Pizarro, known as a swineherd in Spain, had as many as three thousand to five thousand pigs in Peru.

Other small animals brought by the Spaniards included dogs, cats, and chickens. Dogs were greatly effective in war and interbred with indigenous breeds, multiplying so rapidly as to become a nuisance. We know of the presence and value of domestic housecats only from rare descriptions of their sale and their importance in the control of vermin.

Chickens may have spread throughout the New World the most rapidly of all the European animals because they were economically interchangeable with the indigenous turkey. Native Americans traded both fowl widely, and chickens arrived in northern New Spain well in advance of the Spanish explorers. Other small European animals present, but not mentioned directly in the historical sources, were rats, insects, parasites, and disease organisms.

Horses and cattle were called *ganado mayor.* It was very difficult to establish these larger animals in herds because they make a great physical investment in their offspring. Their reproductive cycle is longer than that of the smaller animals and they typically produce single births. The long period of dependency of the young on the mother makes the young more vulnerable to predators. Stock was also depleted when colonists consumed their animals during "starving times" and when native Americans added beef and horsemeat to their diets.

Horses are the best documented of all the animals brought to the New World because of their military and economic importance and because they occupied a special place in medieval and Renaissance European culture. To own and raise horses was a symbol of aristocracy; the words for *knight* in Romance languages—*caballero* in Spanish—are derived from the words for *horse.*

The conquistadores believed in the special effectiveness of their cavalry. Bernal Díaz del Castillo, Alvar Núñez Cabeza de Vaca, Pedro de Castañeda, Garcilaso de la Vega, and Bartolomé de las Casas all describe the formidable advantages of cavalry in war, although the usefulness of cavalry depended on compatible terrain and the ready availability of forage and water. In the early years of the Conquest, the Spanish explorers encouraged native Americans to believe horses to be divine. However, information regarding the limitations and mortality of horses quickly passed along indigenous trade and communication networks, and many native Americans were already familiar with large quadrupeds, such as the bison, the llama, and the alpaca. They quickly took advantage of the limitations of cavalry, practiced guerrilla warfare, avoided open combat, and cut off supplies.

Cattle followed the same paths in the New World as the other animals, although the herds of the pampas grew from cattle brought overland from Peru and Chile, not transported by the difficult transatlantic crossing from Cape Verde. As early as 1538, the cattle herders of New Spain established the *mesta,* modeled after the medieval Spanish sheepherders' association. The New World *mesta* organized cattlemen, held meetings, regulated brands, disposed of strays, and mediated disputes. Cattle from New Spain eventually reached Texas to become the foundation of the North American cowboy tradition.

The relationship between European animals and the environmental changes arising from their introduction is very clear in the example of cattle in New Spain. The discovery of silver on the northern frontier of New Spain increased the demand for leather, hides, and tallow. The resultant tremendous growth of cattle herds led to overgrazing that, along with the seasonal drought and the burning of scrub, created semidesert badlands. This ecological change in turn caused an inevitable decline in herding on the Mexican plateau and helped to create an accompanying economic depression.

Although herding and ranching were the foundation for colonial Spanish economies, the Spanish soldier-colonists considered most agricultural pursuits, except the raising of horses, to be of low social status. They relied instead on native Americans to supply labor for their ranches. As the herds and their attendant demand for labor increased and the native American populations drastically declined, black African slaves were brought to provide the necessary labor. Chroniclers also proclaimed the abundance and fertility of the New World in an effort to encourage farm laborers to emigrate from Spain to the New World.

Extensive ranches based on large land grants and their associated native American labor were absent in North America. The North American natural environment was comparatively hostile, and the native American populations were smaller, less dense, and not so highly organized as many Central and South American groups. The English, French, and Dutch economies were based on fur trading and farming, supported mainly by the colonists' own labor. Although it took longer to establish European animals in North America, they, too, ultimately displaced indigenous species and altered the precontact environment.

BIBLIOGRAPHY

Abbass, D. K. "Horses and Heroes: The Myth of the Importance of the Horse to the Conquest of the Indies." *Terrae Incognitae* 18 (1987): 21–41.

Abbass, D. K. "Herd Development in the New World Spanish Colonies: Conquistadors and Peasants." In *Themes in Rural History,* edited by Richard Herr. Ames, Iowa, 1991.

Crosby, Alfred W. *Ecological Imperialism: The Biological Expansion of Europe 900–1900.* Cambridge, 1986.

Denhardt, Robert Moorman. *The Horse of the Americas.* Norman, Okla., 1975.

Dusenberry, William H. *The Mexican Mesta.* Urbana, Ill., 1963.

Johnson, John J. "The Introduction of the Horse into the Western Hemisphere." *Hispanic American Historical Review* 23 (1943): 487–610.

Marcus, G. J. *The Conquest of the North Atlantic.* New York, 1981.

Patiño, Victor Manuel. *Animales domésticos introducidos.* Vol. 5 of *Plantas cultivadas y animales domésticos en América Equinoccial.* Cali, Colombia, 1970.

Roe, F. G. *The Indian and the Horse.* Norman, Okla., 1955.

Rouse, John E. *The Criollo.* Norman, Okla., 1977.

Varner, John, and Jeannette Varner. *Dogs of the Conquest.* Norman, Okla. 1983.

D. K. ABBASS

DOÑA MARINA. See *Malinche.*

ECONOMIC INSTITUTIONS. See *Social and Economic Institutions.*

ELCANO, JUAN SEBASTIÁN DE (1487?–1526), Basque navigator, member of Ferdinand Magellan's expedition, and first to sail around the world in one voyage. Elcano, the third son of Domingo Sebastián de Elcano and Catalina del Puerto, was born in the Cantabrian port town of Guetaria in the Basque province of Guipúzcoa. Little is known of his early life except that he followed a maritime calling and captained one of the ships that transported troops across the Mediterranean in Cardinal Jiménez de Cisneros's North African campaign in 1509–1510.

In late 1518, in Seville, Elcano joined Ferdinand Magellan's expedition. Magellan, though Portuguese, had received permission from Carlos I to seek an all-Spanish route to the Far East. Initially, Elcano held the post of *contramaestre* but was soon named master of *Concepción*, the third largest ship in the armada. The five-ship fleet sailed from the outport of Sanlúcar de Barrameda on September 20, 1519.

At Port St. Julian in southern Argentina where the fleet was wintering, Elcano, who believed that Magellan was not following a course in conformity with royal instructions, sided with Gaspar de Quesada, captain of *Concepción*, and more than forty other mutineers. Although initially condemned to death, Elcano and most of the others were pardoned and sentenced to hard labor for the remainder of the stay at Port St. Julian.

When the fleet continued its voyage, Elcano was restored to his post of master of *Concepción* and helped negotiate the strait later named after Magellan. On November 28, 1520, Magellan's flagship *Trinidad*, along with *Victoria* and *Concepción*, entered the Pacific Ocean.

After almost a hundred days at sea, they landed at Guam on March 6, 1521. From there, they proceeded to the Philippines where, on April 27, Magellan was killed. Elcano had missed the fateful sortie owing to illness.

Because of a lack of manpower and questions about her seaworthiness, *Concepción* was burned off the island of Bohol in the Philippines, leaving only *Trinidad* and *Victoria* to continue the voyage. Under the leadership of the Portuguese pilot, João Lopes de Carvalho, the expedition drifted from island to island, exploring, plundering, arranging treaties, and repairing the two ships. When Carvalho was deposed in the latter part of September, Elcano, who was now master of *Victoria*, was elected captain of the ship and treasurer of the expedition.

On November 8, 1521, the remnants of the Magellan expedition reached their destination of the Moluccas, landing in Tidore, where the local leader pledged allegiance to Castile. After loading both ships with cloves, the men decided that *Trinidad* should remain behind for repairs. On December 21, 1521, *Victoria*, under the leadership of Elcano and with fifty-nine others aboard, set sail for Spain via the Cape of Good Hope. Aided by Moluccan pilots, Elcano sailed through the maze of islands and, on February 11, 1522, began an epic voyage across the Indian Ocean, using a southwesterly route to avoid detection by Portuguese shipping, since that part of the world was off-limits to non-Portuguese. Fear of the Portuguese prevented Elcano from seeking aid in Mozambique, and the mariner had difficulty rounding the Cape of Good Hope. After five months of sailing in a leaking ship without fresh provisions, Elcano reached the harbor of Rio Grande on Santiago, a Portuguese Cape Verde island, pretending he had been blown off course coming from America. By then only thirty-five men remained aboard. The Portuguese gave them some supplies, but

COAT OF ARMS GRANTED ELCANO BY CARLOS I (CHARLES V). Embellished with cinnamon, cloves, nutmegs, and a globe with the words *Primus circumdedisti me* (You were the first to circumnavigate me). AFTER F. H. H. GUILLEMARD, *THE LIFE OF FERDINAND MAGELLAN* (LONDON, 1890), P. 308.

seized thirteen men. Elcano and his crew quickly set sail for Spain via the Azores.

Fifty-four days later, on September 6, 1522, *Victoria* with Elcano, seventeen Europeans, and three East Indians arrived at Sanlúcar, a little less than three years after the voyage had begun. Elcano was well received by King Carlos I (Emperor Charles V), who, among other rewards, allowed him to use a coat of arms embellished with cinnamon, cloves, nutmegs, and a globe with the words *Primus circumdedisti me* (You were the first to circumnavigate me).

In the spring of 1524, Elcano served on the Castilian side of the mixed Commission of Inquiry that met to determine whether the Moluccas were on the Spanish or Portuguese side of the Line of Demarcation agreed upon in the 1494 Treaty of Tordesillas. (A fellow commissioner was Fernando Colón, son of Christopher Columbus.)

On May 24, 1525, a seven-ship expedition with 450 men under the command of García Jofre de Loaisa, with Elcano as pilot-major of the venture and captain of *Sancti Spiritus,* set sail from La Coruña for the Moluccas, following Magellan's route. Near the Strait of Magellan, Elcano's ship was wrecked and he transferred to Loaisa's flagship, *Santa María de la Victoria.* The lengthy voyage through the strait during winter and a stormy voyage in the Pacific took its toll: the overcrowded flagship separated from the rest of the fleet and sickness decimated the crew. On July 30,

1526, Loaisa died and Elcano succeeded him as captain-general. But Elcano, also ill, died just a few days later, on August 4, and was buried at sea about a month's sail from the Marianas.

Elcano's relative importance has been heatedly debated. Pro-Magellan writers have tended to denigrate the Basque navigator's achievements. One of the seventeen European survivors who reached Spain with Elcano in 1522 was the Italian chronicler Antonio Pigafetta, a great admirer of Magellan. His eyewitness account, the chief historical source for the voyage, fails to mention Elcano by name. On the other hand, some writers have tried to elevate the Spanish-born Elcano at the expense of the Portuguese-born Magellan, arguing that since he died in the Philippines, Magellan was not the first to sail around the world, that honor belonging instead to Elcano.

BIBLIOGRAPHY

Mitchell, Mairin. *Elcano: The First Circumnavigator.* London, 1958.

Morison, Samuel Eliot. *The European Discovery of America: The Southern Voyages A.D. 1492–1616.* New York, 1974.

Navarrete, Eustaquio Fernandez de. *Historia de Juan Sebastián del Cano.* Vitoria, 1872.

Nowell, Charles E., ed. *Magellan's Voyage around the World: Three Contemporary Accounts.* Evanston, Ill., 1962.

FRANCIS A. DUTRA

ENCOMIENDA. Creation of the formal, or legal, institution of the encomienda began during Nicolás de Ovando's rule as governor of La Española (1502–1509). During this period, Ovando systematically subjugated the native American chiefdoms of the island, placing their villages under the "care" of individual Spaniards who were to see that the Indians worked in the Spanish economy and lived "like Christians."

Ovando's model for this legal institution seems to have been the encomiendas that his military order, Alcántara, held in southern Spain. However, Columbus's demand that the Indians pay tribute, in gold, and earlier royal decrees requiring them to work and to receive Christian instruction had prepared the way for Ovando's actions. Another basis for the institution on La Española and in Paraguay was the service obligations of lower status kinsmen to the husbands of Indian women of high status. In both locations, Spaniards who took or were given the daughters of chiefs as their concubines discovered that her kinsmen began to offer food and labor services similar to those they owed the chief. In Paraguay, at least, this kin relationship tempered the exploitive nature of the institution.

The institution was legally formulated in a series of royal orders first drawn into a code in the Laws of Burgos of 1512 to 1514 and then in the New Laws of 1542. The orders and the law codes were responses to protests by Dominicans over the continuing abuse of Indian laborers and the rapid decline in the Indian population, a decline they attributed to the abuses.

Until 1542, Spanish law required the Indians to labor for their Spanish masters for fixed periods (as much as two-thirds of the year) in exchange for instruction in Christianity and Spanish ways of living and for legal and military protection. With the New Laws, the labor obligation was transformed into a tribute obligation, and personal service to the encomendero (master of a particular encomienda) was strictly forbidden. Supervision of the Indians' forced labor (to earn money to pay the tribute) was turned over to corregidores de indios, officials first appointed for New Spain in 1530. Native caciques, or village headmen, were made responsible for supplying the number and kind of laborers demanded by the corregidor. An attempt to abolish the encomienda system altogether provoked an insurrection by Spanish colonists in Peru. Elsewhere in the Spanish empire, the men charged with implementing the New Laws in fact suspended them to prevent insurrection. While continuing to award encomiendas to the descendants of the original conquerors, the Crown gradually brought more and more Indians into the "royal encomienda," or direct vassalage.

By 1600 the encomienda had largely ceased to be an important source of income for private persons. However, the derivative labor system, the mita, continued to be important in Peru as a method of supplying labor to the silver mines, especially at Potosi; elsewhere it was a source of seasonal labor for Spanish agriculture and public works projects. Although legally the encomienda was only a grant of the labor of a given group of Indians, it often provided a basis for the creation of haciendas as encomenderos obtained land and used the encomienda Indians as the labor on these properties.

BIBLIOGRAPHY

Chamberlain, Robert A. "Simpson's *The Encomienda in New Spain* and Other Recent Encomienda Studies." *Hispanic American Historical Review* 34 (1954): 238–250.

Keith, Robert G. "Encomienda, Hacienda, and Corregimiento in Spanish America: A Structural Analysis." *Hispanic American Historical Review* 51 (1971): 431–446.

Lockhart, James. "Encomienda and Hacienda: The Evolution of the Great Estate in the Spanish Indies." *Hispanic American Historical Review* 49 (1969): 411–429.

Simpson, Leslie B. *The Encomienda in New Spain: The Beginning of Spanish Mexico.* Rev. ed. Berkeley, 1966.

PAUL E. HOFFMAN

ENEA SILVIO. See *Pius II.*

ENGLAND. The earliest description of Tudor England was written by Polydore Virgil, an Italian historian who lived and worked at the royal court under the patronage of King Henry VII. Virgil divided the kingdom into four parts, "which all differ among themselves": the area south of the Thames, the Midlands south of the Trent, the six western counties "towards Wales," and the seven northern counties "towards Scotland." The key element in Virgil's description was his recognition of the extreme differences that set each area off from the others. Each sector had its own regional accents, traditions and ancient customs, unique agricultural patterns, communal organization, regional produce, and local industries.

Geographically, England rises slowly from the lowland southeastern shires to the northern highlands on the Scots border. In the southeast and southwest the land is best suited to fruit orchards, vegetables, and cereal crops with only a few cattle and almost no sheep. Until a climatic shift toward colder summers occurred in the fourteenth century, vineyards and a wine industry thrived in Kent. The Midlands and southern half of Yorkshire are composed of flat, well-drained, fertile land. Here, a variety of grain was grown, mostly wheat and oats. This area also contained a large number of cattle and huge flocks of sheep. In the far west and north— the regions that border on Wales and Scotland—the land is rocky and inhospitable. The large, crop-growing fields of the Midlands are replaced with broad expanses of meadow and grazing land that supported immense herds of sheep and the indigenous, long-haired highland cattle. Then as now, the land in the northern shires was distinctive for its emptiness, running on for mile upon endless mile of sheep runs separated by long, low-lying stone dikes and the occasional small stone shepherd's hut or larger stone cluster of monastic buildings.

England's organization of dwelling sites and patterns of landholding varied as much as did its geography. In the late fifteenth and early sixteenth centuries, the rural countryside was composed of innumerable villages, most of which traced their origins back through at least eight hundred to a thousand years of history. The villages in the southern shires of Kent, Sussex, and Hampshire were small, with house sites strung out in a linear pattern along innumerable High Streets. Peasant-farmers in this region owned individual, compact plots of land enclosed by high hedges. In contrast, the individual dwellings in Midland villages clustered haphazardly around a small stone church. Moreover, these villages sat in the center of a vast, unfenced, open-field system in which peasant-farmers owned strips of land. Life here was more communal for men and women in that all shared use of the village green, the central well, and the meadow and forest lands that surrounded the fields. Finally, the far west and north contained only hamlets and truncated, single farmsteads that supported a clan organization of clustered kinship groups, much like the Scots clan system. There was no recognizable village organization, and one parish church serviced a wide area of individual dwellings.

Population growth in this diverse land was slow. On the whole, the population of medieval England had suffered a dramatic decrease from the mid-fourteenth century through the early years of the fifteenth owing primarily to the devastating Black Death of 1348–1350 and the cyclical epidemics of bubonic plague that ravaged the kingdom thereafter. By the middle of the fifteenth century, however, population recovery was underway, and by 1485— when the first Tudor king succeeded to the throne— England as a whole already felt the quickening of the population growth. This increase continued unabated— despite the introduction of a new epidemic disease, the "sweating sickness," which first appeared in the late fifteenth century and was indigenous to the island.

The growing population was self-sufficient to a large extent. Practically all necessities of life—food, clothing, fuel, and housing materials—came from native resources of which the immense natural forests was the most important. Agricultural and industrial production was organized into innumerable small units, and peasant families lived on what they grew or made for themselves and on the sale of any surplus produce at local markets. Without doubt, population growth stimulated the proliferation of local town markets, which in turn contributed greatly to the development of the high level of economic prosperity that characterized life in late Tudor England, specifically during the reign of Elizabeth I.

On a broader economic level, sixteenth-century England was one of the primary producers of many of the raw materials that fueled various industries of continental Europe. Tin and lead mined in Cornwall and the Mendip Hills near Wales fed the smithies of southern Europe; and the cloth workshops of Flanders and northern Italy absorbed massive quantities of both raw wool and, later, finished woolen cloth.

But England had other "business" to accomplish on the continent in addition to the growth of commerce. As a nation-state, it played an increasingly important part in the continual power struggles that characterized diplomatic life at this time. When Henry VII ascended the throne in 1485 England was a virtual nonentity in European politics. But with an eye toward foreign alliances, Henry established his kingdom's presence as an important ally at the negotiating table or on the battlefield. In the early days of Tudor rule, captains of English ships, such as John and Sebastian Cabot, took part in the great voyages of discovery that had begun to chart the existence of whole "new worlds" far distant from the European continent. Later and throughout the Tudor century, English armed support was actively sought by France, Spain, and the Holy Roman Empire as well as the smaller Flemish and Dutch powers. In early Tudor years, England remained tied firmly to Spanish interests through an alliance sealed by the marriage of Catherine of Aragón to Henry VII's son Prince Arthur and after Arthur's death to his brother Henry VIII. This alliance of English and Spanish interests reached a high point in the mid-sixteenth century, when Queen Mary Tudor (1553–1558) married Philip II, king of Spain and Naples. But during the reign of the second Tudor queen, Elizabeth I, the relationship deteriorated quickly and finally ended when Spain sent its famed, albeit doomed, armada to try to destroy the smaller English navy and to land invasion troops on English shores in 1588.

In its social structure, early Tudor England was organized around the concept of a status hierarchy based on possession of land. A continuity that extended from the dawn of the Middle Ages, land was deemed valuable because it carried with it social status, economic wealth, and, most important, political power. Land ownership dictated the rank of each individual on the hierarchical ladder: the larger the amount of land owned by a single family, the higher the social status, the greater the wealth, and the more political power it could wield. Land possession was linked to territorial titles from a duke at the top of the pyramidal structure down through an earl or baron to a knight at the bottom of the land-owning strata. Because political enfranchisement was linked to possession of land—not the mere rental of land as a tenant—early Tudor England really consisted of only two classes: the politically enfranchised, land-based elite and everyone else in the lower reaches of the hierarchy.

Regardless of whether they were nobles or knights, merchants or farmers, all English men and women lived a life dominated by the liturgical rituals of the church. At the beginning of the Tudor century, this church was a single entity—Roman Catholic—led, technically, by the pope in Rome. But by the time the dynasty died out in 1603, the center of the Ecclesia Anglicana—the Church of England—had shifted from Rome to Canterbury in Kent, the supreme leadership over that church was now vested in the Crown, and instead of unity, religion in England varied in the extreme, from Anglican-Protestant to Puritan, including a small but committed group of secret Catholics. The constitutional break with Rome came in the reign of Henry VIII, and the doctrinal shift from a Catholic liturgy to a new Protestant liturgy centered primarily in the reign of Henry's son, Edward VI (1547–1553), and continued on into the reign of Elizabeth (1558–1603).

In political organization as in economic and industrial organization, England looked to locally powerful families to maintain social order and a modicum of peace and stability. Administration of the provinces was carried out through royal appointment of a single lord lieutenant, a single sheriff, and several justices of the peace who were chosen from among the male heads of landed, wealthy families. At the top of the hierarchy sat the Crown on the head of the current king or queen. Early Tudor monarchy was personal monarchy at its best: the monarch had the right to declare the law through arbitrary proclamation or through statute, made in tandem with Parliament. All men and women in *his* kingdom belonged to *him* and his will or whim was directly impressed upon all and sundry. Moreover, in line with continental monarchies, the individual who wore the Tudor Crown was believed to have been divinely chosen by God to reign over the realm. These Tudor monarchs—an extraordinary, glittering group of three men and two women—collectively built the strong base upon which their successors constructed an empire that one day would extend its rule to all corners of the globe.

[See also *Canada; Colonization,* article on *English Colonization.*]

BIBLIOGRAPHY

Bindoff, S. *Tudor England.* Harmondsworth, Eng., 1950.
Lockyer, R. *Henry VII.* New York, 1968.
Palmer, M. *Henry VIII.* London, 1971.

JOAN B. GOLDSMITH

ENRIQUE IV (1425–1474), king of Castile (1454–1474). Enrique's reign was a continuation of the chaos, factionalism, and monarchical weakness characteristic of that of his father, Juan II. Like his father, Enrique disliked the business of ruling and relied excessively on his close advisers Juan Pacheco and Beltrán de la Cueva. The questionable paternity of his daughter Juana provoked a crisis in the succession, which led to the accession of Isabel the Catholic as queen of Castile.

Enrique was born on January 5, 1425; little is known of his childhood. He married Blanca of Navarre in 1440 but the marriage was nullified in 1453 because Enrique was alleged to be impotent. The following year he married Juana of Portugal and a daughter, Juana, was born in 1462. Her paternity was not questioned until later, when it was alleged that Enrique was impotent and Juana was the daughter of Beltrán de la Cueva; hence she is known as "La Beltraneja." The issue of Juana's paternity never was resolved completely. Although Enrique maintained that Juana was indeed his daughter, his inconsistent support of her obscures the truth. Under pressure from his nobles,

ENRIQUE IV. Depicted on a Spanish coin.

Enrique named his brother Alfonso heir in 1464. When Alfonso died in 1468, Isabel was declared heir, but Enrique repudiated her when, against his wishes, she married Fernando of Aragón in 1469.

Enrique's reign ended in failure and disgrace. He was unable to curb the power of a faction of rebellious nobles who dethroned him in a dramatic ceremony in Ávila in 1465, and the chaos of civil war dominated the last years of his reign. His death in 1474 followed a long illness.

BIBLIOGRAPHY

Amézaga, Elias. *Enrique Quarto.* Madrid, 1974.
Ferrara, Orestes. *Un pleito sucesorio: Enrique IV, Isabel de Castilla y la Beltraneja.* Madrid, 1945.
Miller, Townsend. *Henry IV of Castile, 1425–1474.* Philadelphia, 1972.
Phillips, William D., Jr. *Enrique IV and the Crisis of Fifteenth-Century Castile, 1425–1480.* Cambridge, Mass., 1978.
Sitges, J. B. *Enrique IV y la excelente señora, llamada vulgarmente Doña Juana la Beltraneja, 1425–1530.* Madrid, 1912.

THERESA EARENFIGHT

EQUIPMENT, CLOTHING, AND RATIONS. The equipment carried aboard Columbus's ships on his first voyage of discovery was limited to essentials. Life aboard ship in the Age of Discovery was not easy. Seamen had to put up with numerous privations and during foul weather perform hard physical labor for extended periods of time. To do this, they needed an ample supply of nourishing food and a reasonable level of assurance that, however indefinite the length of the voyage might be, they eventually would return safely to their homes. Thus, high on the list of priorities were those items needed to maintain the crew's physical ability to withstand the rigors of an ocean voyage and to temper their mental image of the dangers facing them in sailing off into the unknown.

Maintaining their physical well-being required adequate

means for preparing and serving food, and for providing necessary rest. On ships of this era, neither was easily accomplished. It should be understood that the serving of meals on these ships was for the basic purpose of providing nourishment rather than a pleasurable experience. The cooking stove called a *fogon* was an open square metal box with raised sides and back, lashed down somewhere on deck out of the weather. A layer of sand in the bottom of the box provided insulation for the wood fire. A cooking pot, hanging from an iron rod spanning the box, swung freely as the ship rolled. Food was ladled out of the pot into each crewman's wooden bowl, which he carefully held level against the rolling of the ship. He then ate with his fingers while sitting on a convenient coil of rope, one of the hatches, or on the deck wherever he could find room. He had no fork. If the food needed to be cut, the crewman used his personal knife, which he carried with him at all times for a variety of needs. If there was gravy or a heavy broth, he sopped it up with hardtack, a biscuit that needed some moistening to be edible. The only beverages available were water and wine, which became either unpalatable or unavailable after several weeks at sea.

The ship's watch schedule governed the time that food was served. Watches were of four hours' duration. In Columbus's time, the watch was changed at three, seven, and eleven o'clock day and night. In modern times, watches change at four, eight, and twelve around the clock, except the evening watch, which is commonly split into two watches, four to six and six to eight. This permits the evening meal to be served at the convenient time period of five to seven to one group of watch-standers just before they go on watch and to the other group just after they come off watch. These two-hour periods are called dog watches. They have the added advantage that their use staggers the watch schedule so that the same group of watch-standers does not always have the midwatch, the four-hour period from midnight to four in the morning. There is no indication that dog watches were used in the discovery era.

Although there is no historical comment as to when and how often the crewmen were fed, there are records of the food and drink carried by ships of the period. The basic staples were sea biscuits, or hardtack, salted flour, salt fish (cod, sardines, and anchovies), salt meat (beef and pork), olives, olive oil, vinegar, cheese, dry legumes (peas, chick-peas, black-eyed peas, and lentils), rice, garlic, almonds, raisins, honey, molasses, wine, and water. The olive oil, and perhaps olives, were carried in large earthenware jugs. All other provisions were stored in wooden casks, which occasionally, according to some reports, were of cheap and faulty construction, permitting the preserving brine to leak out of the meat casks and moisture to invade the casks of dry provisions. All were

stored in the hold, the driest section of which was normally reserved for those casks carrying dry provisions. The cooper was responsible for keeping the casks as tight as possible, with allowance made for their condition when loaded aboard.

Getting necessary rest was not easy. Cabins normally were available only to the admiral and the captain. The master and the pilot usually had open bunks in steerage under the raised quarterdeck clear of the massive tiller by which the helmsman steered the ship. Everyone else not on watch had to bed down somewhere out of the way on the main deck or in the hold. Some of the senior ratings had thin mattresses and others had straw mats, all of which were rolled up and stowed when not in use. The spare sails stowed in the hold would have been a favored spot for stretching out, particularly in foul weather.

Maintaining a healthy mental attitude among the crew was especially difficult on Columbus's first voyage largely because of the seamen's innate fear of the unknown. To assuage this fear, Columbus may have made use of a particular item of personal equipment. That was his copy of Toscanelli's chart from which, together with his study of Marco Polo, Ptolemy, and Marinus of Tyre, he had developed his firm belief that he would find Cipangu (Japan) only 750 leagues (2,115 nautical miles) west of Ferro in the Canary Islands. Since the three ships had on some occasions sailed as far as 50 leagues in a day, and could probably average 35 leagues per day, they should make a landfall within fifteen to twenty-two days, or so they probably were told.

Insistence by Columbus on careful use of the three principal navigational instruments available in the late fifteenth century would have been an important element in his efforts to develop his crew's confidence that the location of the ships was known at all times. These instruments were the compass, the half-hour sand glass, and the traverse board.

Compared to the modern compass, that of Columbus's time was very crude. The circular compass card, divided into thirty-two equally spaced compass points, had a magnetized needle fastened to it and a small, hollow, brass cone mounted over a small hole at the midpoint of the card. The complete assembly was suspended on a brass pivot mounted vertically in a wooden bowl by setting the hollow brass cone on the point of the pivot, about which the compass card was free to rotate. A black vertical line called the lubber line was drawn on the forward edge of the bowl. Since the magnetized compass needle always sought the earth's magnetic north pole, the point on the circumference of the compass card in line with the lubber line indicated the heading of the ship, subject to an important proviso: the orientation of the compass had to be fixed in a position such that a radial line from the center of the compass card passing through the lubber line was parallel to the keel of the ship. This was done by mounting the compass in a properly and securely aligned wooden box called the *bitacora*, or binnacle. In addition, to ensure that the compass card remained horizontal so that the compass card could rotate freely about its pivot despite the rolling and pitching of the ship, the compass was suspended within the binnacle by means of a brass gimble system. The binnacle was provided with a hood to protect the compass from the weather and with a small brass or copper oil lamp for illumination at night.

Two such binnacle assemblies were required, one on the main deck just forward of the tiller for the helmsman to steer by and the other on the quarterdeck for the captain or officer of the watch to monitor. There was an open hatch in the quarterdeck through which the officer of the watch called down to the helmsman the course to be steered. Other important items of equipment associated with the compass were the iron compass needles and the all-important lodestones needed to magnetize them. A number of each were carried on every ship.

In the Columbus era, and until the late sixteenth century, four items of shipboard equipment were used in conjunction with each other to indicate the approximate time of day. One was a simple diagram, sometimes referred to as the Polaris clock, for indicating time from the orientation of the axis of the Little Dipper as it appeared to rotate in a counterclockwise direction around the polestar. The second was an instrument called a nocturnal with which it was possible to measure with some precision the orientation of that axis. The third was an almanac that recorded that orientation at midnight for every night of the year, and the fourth was the half-hour sand glass, or *ampolleta*.

The Polaris clock diagram consisted of the figure of a man circumscribed by a circle with the time of day represented by twenty-four hourly points equally spaced around its circumference. The polestar, Polaris, at the end of the handle of the Little Dipper, was located at the man's navel, and a radial line from that point to Kochab, one of the two brighter stars at the Dipper's outer edge, defined the axis of the constellation. Thus, a ship's pilot, estimating the orientation of the axis of the Little Dipper and comparing it with the midnight orientation given in the almanac for that date could make a reasonable approximation of the local time. With the nocturnal, by sighting Polaris through a hole at the center of the instrument and rotating the movable radial arm until it was aligned with Kochab, it was possible to obtain a more accurate orientation of the axis of the Little Dipper and hence a more accurate estimate of the time. Obviously, use of these three items of equipment was limited to nights on which the Little Dipper was visible at least part of the time.

The only means available for keeping track of time on a continuing basis was the *ampolleta*, or half-hour sand glass. A gromet, or ship's boy, was assigned the tedious but essential task of watching the sand glass and turning it over promptly when all the sand had run out of the upper globe. These sand glasses were very fragile and each ship normally carried a dozen or more. Seamen of the period thought of time in terms not of hours but of *ampolletas* and *guardias*, sand glasses and watches, eight sand glasses to a watch. The crewmen of each ship were divided into two groups or watches, usually referred to as the port watch and the starboard watch. Every four hours, or eight *ampolletas*, the men on watch would be relieved of duty by the oncoming watch. At that time, the ship's pilot, sharing with the master the duty of being in charge of either the offgoing or the oncoming watch, would estimate the ship's position from the record of its estimated course and speed as recorded on the traverse board at half-hour intervals during the prior watch.

The traverse board consisted of a wooden compass rose with eight equally spaced holes drilled through the lines radiating from its center to each of the thirty-two compass points. Each hole represented one half hour of the watch. Each time the half-hour sand glass was turned over, the helmsman would call out his average course for the past half hour and a peg would be inserted in a hole for the specified compass course, starting from the center and working out toward the circumference as the watch progressed. Below the compass rose were eight horizontal lines with about ten equally spaced vertical lines superimposed on them. Each horizontal line represented one half hour of the watch and each vertical line one mile per hour of ship's speed and were so marked. The number of vertical lines was arbitrary and varied in accordance with the maximum speed a particular ship was capable of attaining. Holes were drilled at each intersection of the two sets of lines so that pegs could be inserted to record the estimated speed during each half-hour period.

These were the principal items of equipment used in the Columbus era for dead-reckoning navigation. During that period, the connotation of doom suggested by the term *dead reckoning* was not altogether false. Although the term is a contraction of *deduced reckoning* and is the presumed trace of the ship's course on a chart, the accuracy of this form of navigation diminishes markedly in direct proportion to the distance traveled from the known position of the point of departure and in inverse proportion to the skill of the master and pilot in estimating the true course and speed of their ship. The true course of a ship is dependent on several variables, which, in the uncharted waters of the discovery voyages, were of unknown size. For example, magnetic variation of the earth can cause the magnetic compass to be offset by several degrees either to the east or west from true north, and the direction and strength of the current can cause the true geographical course of the ship to differ significantly from its compass heading. The extent of these variables in the vast expanse of the Atlantic Ocean was completely unknown in the Columbus era. The diligence and skill of the helmsman in maintaining the assigned compass heading in variable wind and sea conditions was yet another factor. No instruments were available for determining a ship's speed, and its estimation totally depended on the experience and skill of the watch officer. Similarly dependent was the estimation of leeway, the amount that a ship is pushed sideways. These variables were cumulative, and as time and distance increased from a known location so too did the possibility of significant errors. The later increased use of celestial navigation made it possible to eliminate the cumulative effect of these errors.

The only two instruments available to Columbus for celestial navigation were the astrolabe and the quadrant. Although the cross-staff had been invented prior to 1500, there is no evidence that Columbus or any of his Spanish contemporaries ever used one. The astrolabe consisted of a disk of brass or bronze with degree markings from 0 to 90 etched into its upper semicircle. A small ring attached at the ninety-degree point permitted the astrolabe to be suspended so that a line connecting the zero-degree points would be horizontal. By sighting Polaris through the peepholes of the rotatable arm, the altitude of the polestar could be read from the etched degree markings, providing a reasonable approximation of the latitude of the viewer. The quadrant was a simple quarter-circle of hardwood or bronze with peephole sights attached along one edge, a light plumb line attached to the apex, and a scale of ninety degrees scribed into the arc. By sighting a star through the peepholes, its altitude could be read at the position of the plumb line. Accurate readings were difficult to obtain with these instruments when using them aboard a rolling and pitching ship. Even in calm weather a ship has enough motion so that the suspended instrument sways. Vasco da Gama, when attempting to establish the latitude of an important landmark during his voyage to India in 1497–1499, is said to have disembarked and hung his astrolabe from a tree in order to obtain an accurate reading. Columbus had very little success with either instrument, whereas his prowess as a dead-reckoning navigator has been acclaimed by many.

One item of equipment particularly important to historians was the ship's log book in which the ship's captain kept a record of each day's events. Entries in the log naturally depended on the writing skills of the captain and on his level of interest in events that occurred. In a well-kept log, the record would show the place and time of departure, courses and speeds for every watch, a daily estimate of the ship's position, weather conditions including wind direction and velocity, unusual conditions and sightings, occasional comments about the adequacy of

provisions and the health and morale of the crew, position and time of landfalls, place and time of arrival at destination, and any other happening that might be of historical interest.

Ships of the period normally carried seven anchors: four bower anchors, two of which were kept in readiness to let go on short notice with mooring cables attached, and two stowed either in the forecastle area or in the hold; one large sheet anchor for use in storm conditions, almost always stowed in the hold for reasons of ship stability; and two warping grapnels used for moving the ship around in a harbor. Occasionally a kedge anchor of moderate weight would be carried for use in hauling a grounded ship from a sandbar. The anchors had heavy wooden stocks and, in the case of Spanish anchors, relatively thin shanks and arms. As one would expect, the weights of the various sizes of anchors were related to the size of the ship on which they were carried. A bulky merchant nao such as Santa María carried bower anchors of about a thousand pounds each, whereas those of the smaller and less bulky caravels weighed only half as much.

In addition to the anchor cables fastened to the bower anchors in constant readiness, spare cables of various circumferences and lengths were stowed in the hold. Also stowed there were spare sails; various sizes of hemp rope for repair of rigging; tools and equipment for the carpenter, caulker, and cooper for effecting repairs to the ship; and the many casks of wine, water, salted fish and meat, hardtack, and other provisions. Two important items for the caulker, who was responsible for the watertightness of the ship, were tar and tallow with which the underbody of the hull was coated to protect it against shipworms. Other items required for the safe navigation of ships not only in the Age of Discovery but right up to the development of electronic instruments were the sounding lead and the deep-sea lead and their associated lead lines. The sounding lead, used for measuring depths of water of no more than twenty fathoms, weighed only a few pounds; the deep-sea lead, used for measuring depths of as much as two hundred fathoms, was heavier.

The one cabin on board, occupied by the captain or the admiral, was sparsely furnished. On the larger naos, with a cabin under the raised poop deck at the aft end of the half deck, there was enough room for a table, tableware, one or two chairs, a lamp, a seaman's chest, a built-in bunk with appropriate bed covers, a washstand, and perhaps a separate desk. Functional items of equipment included a shield, pieces of armor, a sword, an astrolabe, a quadrant, and perhaps a compass if the captain or admiral wished to monitor the course without having to go out to the quarterdeck to check the one there. The admiral had a royal standard and flags of Castile and León in readiness for carrying ashore when claiming possession of an island in the name of the Spanish sovereigns. He

FIFTEENTH-CENTURY CLOTHING OF SPANISH SAILORS. *Left:* A sailor caulking a hull. *Right:* Towing boats in Barcelona harbor.

may also have had a copy of Toscanelli's chart, or one of his own, hanging on the bulkhead, as well as an image of the Virgin Mary.

Clothing worn by seamen in the Columbus era could in no sense be described as uniform. Typically, clothing was of wool and loose fitting except for stockings, which, when worn, were of the leotard type. Some form of hat was always worn. Two general types were common: one, a red wool stocking cap from Catalonia and the other, also of red wool, a bonnet from Toledo. Blouses with full sleeves were favored and occasionally had hoods, which were useful in foul weather. Often, a lightweight sleeveless tunic was worn over the blouse.

Regardless of the weather, the Spanish always remained fully clothed, even in the tropics. This may have been the reason they were so astounded by the nakedness of the Indians, comments on which abound in every report. On board ship, when rousing the next watch to come on duty, there was no need to allow time for dressing. None would have undressed when coming off the previous watch.

In colder weather, an overcoat of coarse brown cloth was common. Columbus often wore such a coat, which some authors have referred to as a Franciscan habit, associating his choice of drab clothing with his fondness for that religious order. But whenever Columbus went ashore to claim new lands in the name of the Spanish sovereigns or to impress native caciques (chiefs), he invariably was royally adorned in red.

[See also *Arms, Armor, and Armament; Navigation; Timetelling.*]

BIBLIOGRAPHY

Landstrom, Bjorn. *Columbus.* New York, 1966.
Martinez-Hidalgo, José María. *Columbus' Ships.* Barre, Mass., 1966.

Morison, Samuel Eliot. *Admiral of the Ocean Sea: A Life of Christopher Columbus.* 2 vols. Boston, 1942.

WILLIAM LEMOS

ERICSSON, LEIF (fl. 1000), called the Lucky, Norse explorer and settler in Newfoundland. Leif Ericsson is widely accepted as the European discoverer of America in about A.D. 1000. During the Viking age, from shortly before A.D. 800, there was a special sea route, the western route across the North Atlantic, followed by the Norwegians and, after the discovery of Iceland, also by the Icelanders. The Norsemen sailed from island to island, farther and farther west, settling in the lands they reached. First they came to Shetland, Orkney, the Hebrides and the Faeroes; then Iceland and Greenland were found and settled; and as a final, logical consequence of the western route, none-too-distant America was reached.

Leif's father was Eric the Red, born about A.D. 950, who emigrated with his family from southwestern Norway to Iceland, where he settled and married. Leif Ericsson was born there. As the result of conflict with powerful families, Eric was outlawed and had to flee Iceland. He sailed westward, discovered Greenland, and explored its southwestern coast. He returned to Iceland three years later and in 986 led a large expedition of emigrants to the new land, which he called Greenland. Eric settled at Brattahlid, a favorable area at Ericsfjord and became the leader of the Greenland community, an independent state; this community existed for about five hundred years. When Leif came to Greenland with his family, he must have been a fairly young boy; he grew up in the new country, and became a Greenlander.

Two Icelandic sagas are our most important sources for Leif's discovery of Vinland and other regions in America. These sagas, which are found in thirteenth- and fourteenth-century manuscripts, are *Eiríks saga Rauða* (The saga of Eric the Red) and *Grœnlendingasaga* (The saga of the Greenlanders).

Eiríks saga relates that Leif Ericsson sailed from Greenland to Norway, where the Norwegian king Olafr Tryggvason commissioned him to Christianize Greenland. On his return voyage, Leif lost his way and came to an unknown country where he found vines and fields of wild wheat. That same summer he sailed to Greenland, where he preached Christianity. This version is probably largely unhistorical.

The *Grœnlendingasaga*, which is found in an Icelandic manuscript known as the Flatey Book (*Flateyarbók*, 1387), gives a radically different version. This saga states that Bjarni Herjulfsson lost his way when sailing to the colony in Greenland and sighted a strange coast that he followed to the north and east, finally reaching the eastern colony in Greenland. Leif Ericsson then set out on an expedition with a crew of thirty-five, in order to find the coasts Bjarni had seen, following the latter's route, but in the opposite direction. He came first to a barren, flat land with glaciers, which he called Helluland (Flatstone land, probably Baffin Island), then to a land that he gave the name Markland (Land of forests, presumably Labrador), and finally to a land with much grass, which he called Vinland (Land of meadows; the Old Norse syllable *vin* with a short *i*, meaning "meadow," was misinterpreted by Adam of Bremen to mean "wine" and accepted by the writer of the saga). Here he settled and built large houses.

The location of Leif's Vinland has been the subject of much discussion. The sagas state that Leif found vines and grapes, and therefore it has been fairly generally accepted that Vinland must lie comparatively far south, in parts where wild grapes grow. But after Helge Ingstad's discovery of a Norse settlement at L'Anse aux Meadows (51°35' N) in northern Newfoundland, a number of scholars agree that this site must be identical with Vinland. It is clear that Vinland was a good land with meadows that provided pasture, important to a people contemplating emigration with their livestock. There was a river here, and we know from the saga that it held salmon. Leif explored the land, but half his men always stayed near the houses; although they met no natives, they must have feared them.

Leif returned to Greenland after having spent a year in Vinland. During his return voyage he saved fifteen people wrecked on a reef and became known as Leif the Lucky. Now Leif, after succeeding his father as leader of the Greenland settlement, lived at Brattahlid. His advice must have been of decisive importance for the later expeditions to Vinland led by Thorfinn Karlsefni, by Freydis, Leif's sister, and by his brother Thorvald, who was killed by the natives.

We know little about Leif's person, although the *Grœnlendingasaga* describes him as "big and strong, of striking appearance, shrewd, and in every respect a temperate and fair-dealing man." It seems likely that he became a Christian, although his father, Eric the Red—and probably most of the other Greenlanders—remained pagans. Eric's wife, Thjodhild, however, was baptized, and built a church not far from Brattahlid. The remains of this church have been excavated by Danish archaeologists. It was built of turf and measured only 3.5 by 2 meters (11 by 6.5 feet). One of the 144 skeletons that have been excavated from its churchyard is probably that of Leif Ericsson, the European discoverer of America.

[See also *Icelandic Sagas; Vinland.*]

BIBLIOGRAPHY

Columbus, Ferdinand. *The Life of the Admiral Christopher Columbus.* Translated by Benjamin Keen. New Brunswick, N.J., 1959.

Ingstad, Helge. *Land under the Pole Star.* London and New York, 1966. English translation of *Landet under Leidarstjernen.* Oslo, 1959.

Storm, Gustav. *Studies on the Vineland Voyages.* Extraits des Mémoires de la Société royale des antiquaires du nord 1888. Copenhagen, 1889.

HELGE INGSTAD

ESPAÑOLA, LA. In December 1492 Columbus arrived at the western end of an island that he named "La Isla Española," known later by its Latin name, Hispaniola. Its native name was Ayti, meaning "mountainous land," and this is the name, spelled "Haiti," now applied to the western third of the island. The remaining portion comprises the Dominican Republic. The land is indeed mountainous, with five distinct ranges running from east to west. As on the other large West Indian islands, the central mountainous region is bordered by extensive plains, many of which are fertile.

By the late fifteenth century La Española was inhabited by about 600,000 Taínos, a subgroup of Arawaks, who had replaced earlier peoples. Those on La Española lived much like their neighbors in Cuba, except that they were more exposed to the hostile Caribs, who from their bases in the eastern Caribbean were at this time raiding Taíno settlements on the island. The Caribs, a warlike people, were skilled archers and were capable of ranging great distances in their swift canoes.

Columbus visited the island during his first voyage and was welcomed by the Taínos, whose gold ornaments particularly interested him. After *Santa María* had been wrecked, Columbus established a settlement at La Navidad and then sailed back to Spain, encountering some hostile Indians (perhaps Caribs) during his voyage along the island's northeastern coast. He returned in

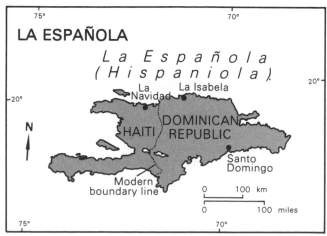

November 1493 to find the La Navidad settlement ruined; he then established a larger Spanish town at La Isabela and set about systematically subjugating the island's inhabitants.

Expeditions penetrated the different regions, and the Taínos were obliged to provide the Spaniards with food and to labor in the newly opened gold mines. As elsewhere, they were also inadvertently brought into contact with European diseases. The result was that by 1508 only about a tenth of the original 600,000 Indians were still alive. The survivors did their best to hold out in the mountains, and Africans were imported as laborers. Meanwhile, the conquest went on; it was consolidated during the governorship of Nicolás de Ovando (1502–1509) with the foundation of fifteen towns.

The site Columbus had chosen at La Isabela proved unsuitable, and so in 1496 the capital was moved to the south coast, where Nueva Isabela was founded on the left bank of the Ozama River. After this town was destroyed by a hurricane, the city of Santo Domingo was established in 1502 on the right bank of the river. Here the Spaniards constructed churches, monasteries, and public buildings, many of which survive to the present day, making Santo Domingo easily the oldest permanent city established by Europeans in the Western Hemisphere.

La Española continued throughout the sixteenth century to produce sugar and gold, and Santo Domingo became the center of an extensive administrative area known as an audiencia. Even after the Spanish conquest of the mainland in the 1520s and 1530s, Santo Domingo continued to enjoy a certain importance as the main Spanish base in the Caribbean; it was not until the late sixteenth century that it began to feel the effects of attacks by French, Dutch, and English pirates.

[See also *Indian America*, articles on *Taínos* and *Island Caribs*; *Settlements*, articles on *La Isabela*, *La Navidad*, and *Santo Domingo*.]

BIBLIOGRAPHY

Moya-Pons, Frank. *Historia colonial de Santo Domingo*. Barcelona, 1974.

DAVID BUISSERET

EUROPE AND THE WIDER WORLD IN 1492.
Educated Europeans in 1492 knew quite a bit about the universe they lived in, even before the voyages of Columbus. The great oceanic expeditions sponsored by Portugal and Spain would expand Europe's incomplete knowledge of Africa and Asia and introduce them to the vast American continents as well. Only a half century later a new view of the cosmos would prove to be equally fundamental. When Copernicus published his notion that the sun and not the earth was the center of the universe, he challenged ancient and medieval wisdom about the heavens quite as much as the voyages of Columbus and his successors challenged accepted knowledge about the earth.

Models of the Universe and the Earth

The astronomical knowledge of medieval Europe, and of the Islamic world as well, relied on the model proposed by the classical astronomer and geographer Ptolemy, a Greco-Egyptian trained in Hellenistic science who had lived in the second century A.D. His seminal work on astronomy had been translated into Latin in the twelfth century, although it generally continued to be known by the title of its Arabic translation, the *Almagest*. Ptolemy proposed a geocentric universe in which the moon, the planets, the stars, and the heavens all revolved around the spherical earth on perfectly formed, transparent crystalline spheres. Ptolemy's model included ten concentric layers around its earthly core: (1) the moon; (2) Mercury; (3) Venus; (4) the sun; (5) Mars; (6) Jupiter; (7) Saturn; (8) the firmament, or starry heaven; (9) the prime mover, or crystalline heaven; and finally (10) the empyrean, or habitation of God. Even if—as we know now—the basic theory was wrong, it held great importance throughout the Middle Ages in both the Christian and Islamic worlds.

Medieval astronomers were careful observers. Even if their basic geocentric model was incorrect, they knew that the moon had no light of its own and depended on reflected light from the sun. They also knew that eclipses of the moon occurred when the earth cast a shadow upon it and that eclipses of the sun occurred when the moon blocked the sun's light from reaching the earth. They had no telescope (the telescope was invented in the seventeenth century), but careful naked-eye observations persuaded them that the planets did not describe perfect circles in their seeming circuit about the earth. Medieval astronomers accounted for these discrepancies by accepting Ptolemy's suggestion that each planet described tiny circles (epicycles) on the surface of its crystalline sphere while the whole sphere revolved. By refining Ptolemy's model to account for observations that seemed to contradict it, medieval astronomers were able to retain a geocentric model of the universe for centuries.

The first frontal assault on that model came from the work of the Polish astronomer Nicolaus Copernicus (1473–1543), whose research and astronomical observations spanned the first decades of the sixteenth century—the very time that Iberian mariners were spanning the terrestrial globe. Copernicus's *De revolutionibus orbium coelestium*, published in 1543, placed the sun at the center of the solar system, but it took over a century and a half before the heliocentric idea would be widely accepted by scholars, and even longer before ordinary people would know about it. Because the English language was set while the geocentric model still held sway, we still speak of the sun rising and setting, although we know that our phrases describe only what our eyes observe, and not what is really happening.

The Spherical Earth. Educated Europeans, who had access to the cosmographical theorists such as Ptolemy, also knew perfectly well that the earth is a sphere. Popular works, too, made that knowledge more widely available among the literate. Around 1220, John Holywood, also known by the Latin version of his name, Sacrobosco, wrote a basic textbook called *De sphaera mundi,* based on his reading of a translation of the *Almagest* and various Muslim and Hellenistic geographers. Holywood's book was widely circulated in the later Middle Ages and went through many printings in the fifteenth and early sixteenth centuries.

Maps depicting the lands of the earth relied on the traditional medieval assumption that only a portion of the earth, well above the equator, was habitable. These maps also reflected the traditional Judeo-Christian idea that God had created the earth, and the Christian notion that spirituality continued to define it. Because Christian geographers believed that the most important event in human history was the death and resurrection of Jesus, they held that Jerusalem must be in the center of the inhabited world. In many medieval maps, the continents were arrayed around Jerusalem, with Asia at the top, Europe in the lower left and Africa in the lower right. Europe and Africa together were about the size of Asia by itself. Such depictions have come to be called T-O maps, because of their general layout, the Mediterranean forming the vertical base of a T with Jerusalem at its head, and the Nile River to the right and the Black Sea and the Don or Dnieper River to the left forming the arms of the T. Surrounding the land mass was an all-encompassing and uncharted ocean, the O of the map. To many scholars, these maps displayed Christian zeal but a profound ignorance of geographical reality. (In fact, similar maps were also produced by Muslim geographers in the Middle Ages.) More recently scholars are coming to suspect that the makers and users of medieval T-O maps knew quite well that they did not depict geographical reality. Instead they portrayed the spiritual reality of the world and its component parts, transcending the physical world.

That physical world was depicted fairly accurately in the late medieval period by another sort of map. The beautiful sailing charts called portolanos, common in Mediterranean countries, combined great aesthetic appeal with accurate depictions of the coasts and compass directions linking major ports. They are generally identified by their compass roses and rhumb lines emanating from the various compass points, so that mariners could use them

to sail from port to port. The so-called Catalan Atlas, attributed to the Majorcan Jew Abraham Cresques and presented to King Charles V of France around 1375, owed much to the portolano tradition. In addition, it contained information about the world beyond Europe and depicted it in a more accurate fashion than the T-O maps. Scholars, mapmakers, merchants, and mariners of late medieval Europe all profited from the advances made in academic geography and by the collection and dissemination of information about Asia and Africa by literate travelers. Full knowledge was still lacking, but sufficiently accurate, though incomplete, information circulated among scholars and informed laymen to inspire them to believe that ocean routes to India might be discovered.

Academic Geography. In 1268 Roger Bacon (c. 1214–1294) published his *Opus maius,* summarizing ancient geographical knowledge and integrating the contributions of Muslim geographers in the Middle Ages. He accepted the view of the world depicted in the T-O maps, specifically that the habitable portion of the world was composed of three parts (Asia, Africa, and Europe) and that the rest of the globe was covered by an encircling ocean. Earlier authorities had asserted that the "torrid zone"— lands located near the equator—would be too hot for habitation, but Bacon suggested that Africa and Asia were habitable south of the equator. Bacon's ideas influenced many other geographers between his time and the era of Iberian exploration.

In the early fifteenth century Pierre d'Ailly (1350–1420), a cardinal of the Roman Church, published a geography called *Imago mundi* that was to have a great influence upon Columbus. D'Ailly relied on geographical treatises by classical writers and Muslim scholars, but he disregarded the accounts of recent travelers such as Marco Polo. Perhaps because he seemed so careful with evidence, d'Ailly's conclusions carried great weight, although he made several fundamental errors. Two of these directly informed Columbus's mistaken conception of the world: that Asia covered much more of the globe from east to west than it actually does *and* that the oceans cover much less of the globe than they actually do.

As a geographical authority, d'Ailly's *Imago mundi* was greatly overshadowed by the translation of two works by Ptolemy. In addition to the *Almagest* on astronomy, Ptolemy also produced an influential geographical treatise, the *Geography,* translated into Latin in the early fifteenth century. As soon as it became available in that common language of European intellectual life, Ptolemy's *Geography* provided educated Europeans with a convenient framework for depicting the globe in a graphic form, particularly for those who already knew and trusted his work on the heavens. Ptolemy's division of the earth into 360 degrees became the basis for subsequent European maps. Ptolemy did, however, make two fundamental mistakes. First, he believed that Africa and Asia were joined by lands connecting their southern tips, making the Indian Ocean a landlocked sea, inaccessible to ships sailing from Europe around Africa. Fortunately for those who were trying to find just such a route, the humanist Enea Silvio Piccolomini, who became Pope Pius II, rejected the idea that the Indian Ocean was an enclosed sea when he published his own work summarizing much of Ptolemy's *Geography*. Columbus and others with dreams of global sea routes read Piccolomini's work and took inspiration from its conclusions. Ptolemy's other error, which did influence Columbus, postulated that the earth was about one-fifth smaller than it is.

The geographical ideas of the late fifteenth century found physical expression in a now-famous globe by Martin Behaim, made in 1492 (the earliest known globe to date), which presented a view of the world that was almost identical to the concept that Columbus had formed. The Americas are totally absent, of course. Cipangu (Japan) is located far distant from the mainland of Asia, and the ocean between Europe and the East is amply strewn with islands. Whether Columbus and Behaim had close contact with one another is unknown, but Behaim's depiction of the world and Columbus's concept of it both grew out of the academic geography available at the end of the fifteenth century. Both men had lived in Lisbon and had gained access to the Portuguese court, where courtiers and experts regularly discussed the latest geographical discoveries.

World Geography

The world depicted in the limited maps and geographies of the fifteenth century bore some relation to the world as it really was in 1492, but the vision was far from complete. Europe had quite limited information about the great civilizations that existed in Asia and Africa. Contacts with the Muslims had taught Europeans something about the interior of Africa, including that gold was obtained there. During the early fifteenth century, Portuguese voyages down the western shore of Africa added more direct practical knowledge as well. Europeans had no knowledge of the civilizations in the Americas, despite the Scandinavian voyages that had reached some part of North America around the year 1000. By the fifteenth century, however, Scandinavians were going no farther west than Greenland, and memory of their earlier voyages had not entered the mainstream of European thought. Implausible as it may seem, European scholars and merchants in the fifteenth century probably knew more about distant Asia than about any other part of the world outside Europe.

Asia. Despite the hostility felt by European Christians for the Islamic world, Muslim merchants served as crucial intermediaries between Europe and the vastness of Asia. Western Europeans had acquired first-hand knowledge of the western fringe of Asia during the Crusades (1095–1291), when religiously motivated armies from western Europe established the Kingdom of Jerusalem and related principalities along the eastern shore of the Mediterranean, thus wresting control of Christian holy places from the Muslims. Even though the crusaders failed to maintain control of the Holy Land and lost their few strongholds eventually, their ventures spawned a long-lasting commercial development. During the Crusades, merchant communities from the Christian Mediterranean seized the economic initiative in the region from the Muslims and maintained it thereafter. The Crusades foreshadowed the worldwide expansion of Europe that began in the fifteenth century and gathered momentum with Columbus.

By the time of Columbus, the spice trade provided one of the most important motivations for European expansion. During the Crusades, Europeans had first developed a taste and demand for exotic spices, which improved the palatability of food in the thousands of years before the development of advanced preservation techniques. The European elite consumed increasing amounts of spices during the late medieval centuries. Most of the spices that entered European markets were grown in the Far East, especially in India and the South Asian islands, and were then brought by Muslim traders across the Indian Ocean to the Persian Gulf and the Red Sea. In eastern-Mediterranean ports, such as Alexandria, the most important emporium, Italian merchants bought spices from Muslims to resell in Europe, where they commanded high prices. The Venetian Republic, in particular, reaped enormous profits from this trade. Even if the buyers of Asian spices and other luxury goods formed only a tiny part of the total European population, their purchasing power helped to keep the entire structure of long-distance trade functioning. Because of the profits to be made from the spice trade, many other Europeans were eager to participate in it, but the Italians and their Muslim trading partners held an effective monopoly by their control of the eastern Mediterranean.

By the fourteenth century, many Europeans knew where spices came from. Indeed, many European missionaries and merchants had traveled to Asia—some as far as China—and had reported on what they had seen. They generally reached Asia by overland caravan routes through central Asia. Those routes were open to travelers during the thirteenth and fourteenth centuries because of what has been called the Pax Mongolica, the period when Mongol rulers held sway from North China to the Black Sea and guaranteed safety along the trade routes.

Mongol ascendancy began when Genghis Khan (1167–1227; born Temüjin, he assumed the title "ruler of the universe") secured the unity of the Mongols and related tribes in 1206. Fierce mounted warriors who relied for mobility on their powerful horses, the Mongols had a powerful bow and good steel arms and armor. From the Chinese, they learned the siege tactics necessary to capture fortified towns. All their military skills were put to good use in the rapid conquests of North China, Persia, and Russia. By the death of Genghis Khan in 1227, Mongol authority stretched from East Asia to eastern Europe.

Reports about the Mongols had filtered through to Europe, where, despite the horrifying and lurid nature of many of the tales, they inspired Western interest in contacting the Mongols, especially on the part of religious leaders. Although such interest may seem puzzling at first, it sprang from a logical source. The Mongols were a distant threat and not yet the enemies of Europe. The Muslims were close by and had been enemies for centuries. Consequently, popes and, later, kings thought that the Mongols might prove useful against the Muslims at a time when the crusader states faced increased Muslim pressure.

A joint Egyptian-Turkish army reconquered Jerusalem from the crusaders in 1244. In the next year, 1245, Pope Innocent IV sent an envoy, Giovanni da Pian del Carpini (c. 1182 or 1200–c. 1252) to the Mongol khan, charged with finding out more about these mysterious people. Carpini went by land from Kiev to the Mongol capital of Karakorum and was present at the coronation of Güyük (or Kuyuk) Khan. Carpini gave the khan the pope's letter calling on him to join an alliance against the Muslims and to recognize papal supremacy. Not surprisingly, the khan declined to recognize papal supremacy and nothing came of the military alliance, but Europe at least learned more about Asia. Carpini's written account of his journey found its way into the world history of Vincent of Beauvais (d. before 1264), court historian to Louis IX of France, who sought to strengthen contacts with the Mongols by sending other western ambassadors: Andrew of Longjumeau in 1248 and Willem van Ruysbroeck and Bartholomew of Cremona in 1253 to 1255. Their accounts, too, have survived. Taken together, the Christian missions to the Mongols prepared the way for the Christian merchants who soon followed.

In the later Middle Ages, many Italian merchants, especially Genoese and Venetians, were willing to try new ventures in the search for economic gain. One of the best known episodes began around the year 1260, when two Venetian merchants, Niccolò and Maffeo Polo, departed from the Crimean peninsula in the Black Sea, where other Italian merchants had been established for some time. Their trading expedition through Mongol lands eventually brought them to China. They returned to Venice in 1269 and left again for China a few years later, this time taking with them Niccolò's son Marco. Marco Polo (c. 1254–1324) remained for eighteen years in China, where he served as a bureaucrat in the court of the Mongol khan, Kublai. He traveled throughout China and returned to Europe after having visited India. At the same time other European merchants and missionaries also traveled to Asia. While Marco Polo resided at the Mongol court, Giovanni da Montecorvino arrived in Peking and later became its first Catholic archbishop, presiding over a large archdiocese but few Christians.

After Marco Polo returned to Venice, he was captured by the Genoese and spent several years as a prisoner of war. In prison he recounted the tale of his travels through Asia to Rustichello of Pisa. Although Rustichello embellished the story in places, and misunderstood some of it, his story of Marco Polo's travels provided one of the best and most accurate accounts of China and the east that Europeans had at their disposal, although many readers thought the tale more fanciful than real. Accounts by other travelers also appeared and spread through Europe, some of them genuine and others woven from legend rather than practical experience. John Mandeville (the name is a pseudonym) wrote a purported travel guide in the fourteenth century that included fabulous races of human beings with monstrous characteristics; some had no heads, others enormous tails, others extra limbs. Mandeville's book was extraordinarily popular, especially in the early days of printing in the late fifteenth century, and undoubtedly fed European enthusiasm for travel to real places, even as it confirmed ancient legends of monstrous humans and fanciful beasts. Based on the information from Marco Polo and others, Francesco Balducci Pegolotti was able to write a commercial guide in 1340 called *La pratica della mercatura* that included information about the spices and other products of Asia. He even provided a generally accurate indication of where those products originated. Both Polo and Pegolotti told their readers that it was possible to buy spices directly from their Asian sources, and Polo, at least, was an important inspiration for Columbus.

The Mongols suffered a series of reverses in the later thirteenth century and their empire broke up in the fourteenth. As long as it lasted, however, the Pax Mongolica opened Central and East Asia to a number of intrepid European missionaries and merchants, whose experiences taught them enough about Asia to spur great interest in long-distance trade and gave them a much greater knowledge of the world and a better idea of the extent of Muslim power. Unfortunately for Europeans who might wish to put the information about Asia and its markets to practical use, political conditions in the Middle East made it impossible.

After the collapse of the Mongol Empire, three new and aggressive Muslim empires gained importance in the Middle East. By the end of the fifteenth century they held sway from the Mediterranean to India. The Ottoman Turks in Anatolia and southeastern Europe had delivered the death blow to the Christian Byzantine Empire in 1453 by capturing Constantinople. Muslims now controlled the key ports and trade routes leading to the markets of Asia, and they severely restricted Christian trading opportunities: the Ottoman authorities permitted western merchants to frequent coastal markets such as Alexandria, but they would not allow them free passage along the routes they controlled. Consequently, some Europeans contemplated a bold alternative that had been discussed for centuries: to bypass the Muslims altogether by finding a sea route to India in order to purchase the spices directly at their sources.

Two adventuresome brothers from Genoa named Vivaldi had made a very early voyage out into the Atlantic to seek the sea route to Asia. In 1291 their small fleet sailed through the strait of Gibraltar with the aim of reaching India. They never returned, and left no traces of their fate except for some equivocal signs on the African coast opposite the Canary Islands. Although we can assume that the Vivaldis failed in their attempt, the hope of finding a sea passage to India remained alive to inspire the Portuguese and the Spaniards as they added new areas of Africa and the Atlantic to European knowledge in the fifteenth century.

With the benefit of hindsight, we know that Europeans would find a very favorable situation to develop their Asian trade once they had rounded Africa. Muslims from the Middle East—mostly Arabs and Persians—had established regular trade in the Indian Ocean. Making use of the annual cycle of monsoon winds, which blow from the northeast from October to March and from the southwest from April to September, they traveled from India in the east to the Red Sea, the Persian Gulf, and East Africa in the west. Although Muslim traders were able to maintain their monopoly in the northern reaches of the Indian Ocean, they did not dominate southeastern Africa or the ocean passage from there to India. Consequently they could not prevent the Portuguese and other Europeans from sailing to India. On Vasco da Gama's first voyage from Portugal to India, he picked up a skilled Muslim pilot in east Africa who guided the Portuguese fleet across the Indian Ocean.

Beyond India, China might have challenged European incursions into its sphere of influence, and could even have rivaled Europe on the unexplored oceans of the globe, but the Chinese chose not to. Chinese maritime technology and military capability easily equaled European achievements, and in the early fifteenth century, the Chinese had sent out seven large naval expeditions under the command of the admiral Cheng Ho. These spectacular Chinese fleets visited many Asian ports and islands, including places on the coast of India and Ceylon. They also reached the entrances to the Persian Gulf and the Red Sea and several places on the East African coast. After the last of these impressive voyages, however, the Ming emperors of China shifted the center of their operations away from the coast and made efforts to isolate China from the rest of the world. And Japan, the golden-roofed Cipangu of Marco Polo's tale, had not developed an important long-distance seafaring tradition. Once European voyagers learned how to sail around Africa, the markets of Asia lay open to them.

Africa. Although the 1291 voyage of the Vivaldi brothers aimed to reach India, their attempt to sail westward and southward from the Mediterranean exemplified the growing southern European interest in Africa and the Atlantic. In the late Middle Ages, Genoese, Catalans, and other Christian merchants of the Mediterranean had established a series of trading posts in the ports of North Africa from Egypt to Morocco. Through agreements with the local Muslim rulers, they were able to maintain residences, offices, and warehouses, usually in segregated districts. There they bought the products of North Africa and, in the eastern Mediterranean, Asian goods as well. In the western Mediterranean, they were especially taken with the goods of West Africa brought across the Sahara Desert by Muslim caravan traders.

Among the West African products available in North African ports was gold. Since the time of the later Roman Empire, western Europe had tried to increase its meager internal supplies of gold. Optimists kept hoping that alchemy would find a way to convert baser elements into the precious metal that served as the standard of wealth. Realists settled for trade to obtain it. The Muslim world was better provided with gold than Europe, largely by tapping into sources south of the Sahara. By the later Middle Ages, the most important gold supplies were in West Africa in three major mining areas: Bambuk, Boure, and Akan. Muslim caravan traders acquired gold in sub-Saharan Africa and took it across the desert to North Africa. In the exotic ports of the southern shore of the Mediterranean, European merchants, especially Italians and Spaniards, acquired it through trade, but often on unfavorable terms. Although the Muslims maintained a monopoly on the Saharan caravan routes, Europeans knew enough about Africa to realize that black Africans had rich kingdoms in the lands to the south of the Sahara, where the Muslims purchased slaves and gold, as well as other goods.

European knowledge of the black African kingdoms of West Africa can be gauged by the Catalan Atlas (c. 1375) mentioned earlier, attributed to Abraham Crescas and presented to King Charles V of France. On the map depicting Africa, the kingdoms of the Sudanic belt of grasslands south of the Sahara are represented by the figure of a black king, seated on a throne and holding a

DETAIL FROM THE CATALAN ATLAS, CIRCA 1375. This detail, an inset placed in northwestern Africa, depicts the king of Mali and an Arab trader on a camel.   BIBLIOTHÈQUE NATIONALE, PARIS

golden orb and scepter. The caption describes him as Musse Melly (Musa Mali), "lord of the Negroes of Guinea," and attributes his power to the abundance of gold found in his country.

By the fifteenth century, one of the primary Portuguese motivations for exploring the African coast was to intersect the gold trade. The city of Ceuta, on the Moroccan coast opposite Gibraltar, was closely linked with the trans-Saharan caravan trade, which was one factor in the Portuguese decision to conquer the city in 1415. Thereafter, the Moroccans diverted most of the trade away from Ceuta, although it remained an important outpost for the Portuguese. Later in the century they sought the gold-producing regions south of the Sahara, undercutting the Muslims' monopoly of the gold trade. Those early profits would help finance continuing Portuguese exploration.

Pseudo-knowledge of Africa coexisted with reality in European minds. Along with the real kings of Africa, a legendary king called Prester John—supposedly a powerful Christian monarch whose lands lay somewhere beyond the area under Muslim control—occupied a prominent position in the expansive dreams of the Portuguese. After completing the reconquest of their territory from the Muslims in the thirteenth century, the Portuguese thought to carry a Christian holy war to the heart of Islam. The curious legend of Prester John encouraged the Portuguese to think that, if only they could find him, he would become an ally in the struggle against Islam. The problem was that no one in Europe knew where to find him. Rumors in the twelfth and thirteenth centuries placed him in Asia; by the fifteenth he was believed to be in Africa. Portuguese captains on voyages down the Atlantic coast of Africa in the early fifteenth century had instructions to collect news or even rumors about Prester John's kingdom. In the late fifteenth century, contemporary with

Columbus, the Portuguese king João II sent an overland expedition into the Middle East to seek Prester John. The Portuguese did eventually find Ethiopia, a kingdom in East Africa whose people had been Christian since the fourth century, converted by the Copts of Egypt. But their ruler was a weak imitation of the legendary Prester John, totally lacking the resources to launch any sort of crusade against Islam. Given the scope of the Portuguese efforts, there is little doubt that the politico-religious goal of attacking the Muslims from the rear held an important place among European motives for expansion. That the results of their efforts did not measure up to expectations is beside the point.

The Portuguese had other reasons for their African and Atlantic ventures. For one, they sought to expand sugarcane production. European knowledge of sugarcane and the methods for growing and processing it had expanded greatly during the Crusades. After the Crusades were over, Europeans spread sugarcane cultivation throughout the Mediterranean areas they controlled. As the Spaniards and Portuguese discovered the islands of the eastern Atlantic, they found new opportunities for the expansion of sugarcane. Spaniards in the Canary Islands, and Portuguese in the Madeiras founded sugar plantations and mills, whose production could be sold very profitably in Europe. Sugarcane production was one of the ways that newly discovered lands might be used, and the profits derived from it helped to sponsor further explorations down the African coast.

A similar pattern applied to the slave labor acquired to work in cane fields and mills. Although cane could be grown in small plots or large, the need to process the cane immediately after harvest meant that large plantations with their own processing plants were the most profitable. Also, although the hard labor in the fields and the mills could be done by anyone, it was most profitably done by some form of coerced labor, whether slave or free. The opportunities for this kind of agricultural production were more plentiful outside Europe than within. For labor on their Atlantic island plantations, Europeans frequently used slaves, especially black slaves from Africa. At first, Portuguese voyages tended to raid native settlements for slaves, but soon they found that it was easier and more profitable to make agreements with local rulers to supply them with slaves in exchange for European trade goods. The slave trade soon produced profits that made continued exploration possible.

Much more ordinary motives for Portuguese expansion into Africa existed as well. Portuguese merchants bought wheat in North Africa, particularly Morocco, to supplement production at home and to trade for other goods in West Africa. In addition, both the Portuguese and the Castilians had well-established fishing fleets that provided for home consumption as well as for exports. They saw the Atlantic waters off Africa as suitable places to extend their fishing grounds. Like sugar plantations and the slave trade, the expanded fishing grounds and grain trade developed as part of a generalized search for profitable opportunities in Africa and elsewhere.

At some point, as the Portuguese explored and traded southward along the African coast, they began seriously to look for a sea route to Asia. As we have seen, the cosmography of the day held that the world's land masses were closely linked to one another, surrounded by vast oceans that covered the rest of the globe. To reach Asia by the most efficient sea route required a voyage around Africa, which was held to be much smaller than in fact it was. Luckily for the Portuguese, the African coastal trade and the products of the Atlantic island economies were profitable enough to finance continuing efforts to find a way around the vast continent.

The search went on decade after decade before Bartolomeu Dias finally reached the southern tip of Africa in 1488, which he appropriately dubbed the Cape of Good Hope. That hope came true when Vasco da Gama took a Portuguese fleet to India in 1497 and returned to tell the tale, revealing in the process extensive geographical knowledge about the southeast coast of Africa, the Indian Ocean, and India itself. The search for India also motivated Columbus and the monarchs of Spain who eventually backed his enterprise, and he began his first voyage in the years between Dias's discovery of the Cape and Da Gama's voyage to India. The difference was that Columbus proposed a westward approach to Asia, which was widely considered more dangerous and less promising among the experienced mariners of the day. A westward voyage would mean a confrontation with the still largely unknown Atlantic.

The Atlantic and the Americas. For centuries rumors and legends told of numerous islands out in the Atlantic. Many of these islands were only legendary: Hy Brasil, St. Brendan's Isle, and Antilia, for example, have never been found. But in the fourteenth and fifteenth centuries, Iberians found four island groups to conquer and settle, pushing back the southern and western frontiers of the known Atlantic. The Portuguese-held Azores, Madeiras, and Cape Verdes and the Castilian-held Canaries encouraged monarchs and mariners to hope that still more previously unknown islands could be found. The discoveries of islands in the eastern part of the south Atlantic had taught Iberian mariners the rudiments of the ocean's wind and water movements. Their later voyages would reveal the full range and extent of the oceanic patterns of winds and currents.

For the North Atlantic, the picture was murkier in 1492. The largest gap in European knowledge of the world was the nearly total ignorance of the American continents. Early in the Middle Ages Irish monks had journeyed out into the unknown North Atlantic, but their daring exploits, undertaken to find a quiet place to contemplate and serve God, had no known consequences. Around the year 1000 Scandinavian explorers traveled from island to island across the far north Atlantic, visiting the Shetlands and Orkneys, Iceland, and Greenland, and finally arriving in North America. But the exploits of Leif Ericsson and others did not usher in an era of general European expansion and global change. Instead, the voyages had no known effect on the wider European world and were very little known outside Scandinavia. Scandinavian settlements in North America were quickly abandoned, and the colony in Greenland existed in greatly reduced circumstances by the fifteenth century.

It is safe to assume that the only people with knowledge of the Americas in 1492 were the Americans themselves. The ancestors of human societies that Spanish explorers encountered in the fifteenth century had discovered America from Asia in prehistoric times. Their great trek across the land bridge between Siberia and Alaska, where the Bering Strait exists now, forms an important chapter in the ancient history of human migration, but it did not have the effect of linking America with the rest of the world. Instead, the descendants of the migrants lost contact with their Asian homeland, and America and its first human inhabitants developed in isolation from the Old World of Europe, Africa, and Asia.

Consequently, the Americas became strikingly different from the Old World in plants, animals, and human populations. By the fifteenth century, millions of people populated the continent from the Arctic Circle south to the tip of South America. They had settled in almost all the regions of the Americas suited for human habitation. Whether on plains, highlands, deserts, forests, jungles, or islands, native Americans had developed societies and economies that took good advantage of the topographies and the ecologies in which they lived. Their social organizations varied from groups of hunter-gatherers to highly developed urban civilizations. The latter had evolved in three areas: the Yucatán peninsula, the central valley of Mexico, and the highlands of the Andes in South America. The Mayas had built an advanced civilization, particularly learned in astronomy, in the Yucatán peninsula and the adjacent areas of Central America. They had reached their peak from about 400 B.C. to A.D. 1000 but had declined thereafter, perhaps because of soil exhaustion, perhaps from some other cause. In the central valley of Mexico, the Aztecs, or Mexica, created a large empire surrounded by tributary groups. Their empire was still flourishing in 1500, although many of the tributary groups chafed under the Aztec yoke. The empire of the Incas extended from what is today Peru north to modern Ecuador and south to Chile. Like the Aztecs, the Incas presided over a collection of tributary groups, and their empire was also flourishing in Columbus's time. As impressive as the great civilizations of the Americas were, their stone-age technology would prove to be no match for that of the Europeans, either on land or sea.

At the beginning of their global exploration in the fifteenth century, Europeans found the oceans of the world open to them, with no competing maritime powers anywhere on the face of the earth. The civilizations of the Americas lacked the technology for deep-ocean sailing. Similarly, the kingdoms of Africa south of the Sahara had no ocean-going vessels. Europe's strongest political enemy in the Old World—the Ottoman Empire—had only a Mediterranean navy. In the early sixteenth century the Ottomans would extend their sway to Egypt and North Africa as far west as Algeria. Their land attacks on Europe would reach as far as the gates of Vienna in 1529, and their Mediterranean navy would cause serious problems for the states of Italy and Spain in the sixteenth century. Nonetheless, the Ottoman Empire was in no position to challenge Portugal or Spain in the Atlantic or the Indian Ocean.

Beyond the Ottoman Empire to the east, the successor states to the Mongols were still gathering strength. In Persia, the Safavid Empire would be founded in 1502 and would continue in power for over two centuries. The Turkish Moguls, entering India from Afghanistan in the early sixteenth century, would carve out an empire that embraced much of northern and central India. Neither of these land-based empires could challenge European dominance of the world's sea lanes. The Portuguese and Castilians of the Iberian peninsula were ideally situated to lead European world exploration. Of all the peoples on earth in the late fifteenth century, they enjoyed the most effective combination of strong motives for overseas expansion and the maritime technology necessary to carry it out. They were encouraged to do so by what they knew and by what they suspected about the rest of the world. And no one else was in a position to challenge them.

The World after Columbus. Columbus was fortunate to have lived at a time when many Europeans were interested in exploring the oceans beyond Europe. Had he failed to obtain funding for his plan to reach Asia by sailing westward, other Europeans would have made the voyage and happened upon the Americas before too long. King João II of Portugal licensed at least one expedition to explore west from the Azores in the 1480s. English mariners probed the North Atlantic to the west in the same decade. Their efforts succeeded when John Cabot, a Genoese mariner, captained an English voyage to Newfoundland in 1497. In 1500 the Portuguese captain Pedro

Álvares Cabral reached Brazil, either by accident or design, as he sailed west and south to catch the winds for a voyage to southern Africa.

Columbus's voyages began the unification of the world, bringing the previously isolated Americas into the networks of trade and communication that already linked Asia, Africa, and Europe. The far-reaching consequences of his voyages, for good and for ill, have undoubtedly earned Columbus a place in world history. Nonetheless, he was not the first human being to discover America, or even the first European to do so. The ancestors of the Indians he encountered in the Caribbean had discovered and settled the land millennia before. Even among Europeans, Scandinavians had preceded Columbus by five hundred years.

Columbus was the first European to reach America since the Vikings, and his voyage occurred at a time when Europe as a whole was poised to exploit that discovery. Columbus had prepared his plans carefully, relying on his wide knowledge of contemporary European ideas—both correct and incorrect—about the world beyond Europe. His first voyage, and the later voyages he and others made during his lifetime, linked the Americas with the rest of the world, but they did not immediately allow Europeans to understand the true size of the earth or the relation of the continents to one another. The first circumnavigation of the globe between 1519 and 1522 did far more than Columbus's voyages to reveal the size and nature of the earth. That expedition, sponsored by Spain, begun under the command of Ferdinand Magellan and completed by his lieutenant Juan Sebastián de Elcano proved that vast oceans lay between the lands visited by Columbus and the kingdoms of Asia visited by Marco Polo.

Even after 1522, extensive exploration and observation would be necessary to map the earth fully and assign it its proper place in the universe. That work would not be complete until the twentieth century. By the mid-sixteenth century, however, some fifty years after Columbus's first voyage, all the global centers of high civilization and the major commercial networks had been connected directly or indirectly by sea. Geographers in Seville and Lisbon had a fairly accurate view of the earth and its parts. Although the details would change and although there were many unknown lands still to be explored, an educated European in 1550 could form a conception of world geography that would not differ in broad outlines from our own, although it would be startlingly different from the European conception of the world in 1492. In 1543 Copernicus allowed his heliocentric model of the universe to be published. Once his theory triumphed, Europeans could begin to explore the true nature of the heavens as well as the earth.

[See also *Cartography; Exploration and Discovery; Geography, Imaginary;* and biographies of figures mentioned herein. For more detailed discussions of particular places, see *Africa; Asia; China; Cipangu; England; Florence; France; Genoa; Naples; Ottoman Empire; Portugal; Rome; Spain; Venetian Republic; Vinland.* For discussion of the indigenous peoples and cultures encountered by Europeans in the Western Hemisphere, see *Indian America.*]

BIBLIOGRAPHY

Bovill, E. W. *The Golden Trade of the Moors.* 2d ed. Oxford, 1970.

Broc, N. *La géographie de la Renaissance, 1420–1620.* Paris, 1980.

Cassidy, Vincent H. *The Sea around Them: The Atlantic Ocean, A. D. 1250.* Baton Rouge, 1968.

Chaudhuri, K. N. *Trade and Civilisation in the Indian Ocean: An Economic History from the Rise of Islam to 1750.* Cambridge, 1985.

Chaunu, Pierre. *European Expansion in the Later Middle Ages.* Translated by Katharine Bertram. Amsterdam, 1979.

Dawson, Christopher, ed. *Mission to Asia: Narratives and Letters of the Franciscan Missionaries in Mongolia and China in the Thirteenth and Fourteenth Centuries.* New York, 1966. Reprint, Toronto, 1986.

Diffie, Bailey W., and George Winius. *Foundations of the Portuguese Empire, 1450–1580.* Minneapolis, 1977.

Fernández-Armesto, Felipe. *Before Columbus: Exploration and Colonization from the Mediterranean to the Atlantic, 1229–1492.* Philadelphia, 1987.

Jones, Gwyn. *The Norse Atlantic Saga.* 2d ed. London, 1983.

Mollat, Michel. *Les explorateurs de XIIIe au XVIe siècle: Premiers regards sur des mondes nouveaux.* Paris, 1984.

Olschki, L. *Marco Polo's Asia.* Berkeley and Los Angeles, 1960.

Parry, J. H. *The Age of Reconnaissance.* New York, 1963, and later editions.

Parry, J. H. *The Discovery of the Sea.* Berkeley and Los Angeles, 1974.

Penrose, B. *Travel and Discovery in the Renaissance, 1420–1620.* Cambridge, Mass., 1967.

Phillips, J. R. S. *The Medieval Expansion of Europe.* Oxford, 1988.

Rogers, Francis M. *The Quest for Eastern Christians: Travel and Rumor in the Age of Discovery.* Minneapolis, 1962.

Scammell, G. V. *The World Encompassed: The First European Maritime Empires c. 800–1650.* Berkeley and Los Angeles, 1981.

Southern, R. W. *Western Views of Islam in the Middle Ages.* Cambridge, Mass., 1962. Reprint, 1980.

Wolf, Eric R. *Europe and the People without History.* Berkeley and Los Angeles, 1982.

WILLIAM D. PHILLIPS, JR.

EXPLORATION AND DISCOVERY.

[This entry includes three articles on overseas exploration:

Exploration and Discovery before 1492
European Exploration and Discovery after 1492
Basque Exploration and Discovery

For further discussion of European overseas interests, see *Atlantic Rivalry; Europe and the Wider World in 1492; Trade;* and entries on particular nations and city states. For discussion of overseas exploration and discovery by other civilizations, see *Africa; China.* See *Colonization* for discussion of the settlement efforts that followed European contact with the New World.]

Exploration and Discovery before 1492

Although the name Columbus is indelibly linked with European discovery of America, the Norsemen without question arrived in the New World five hundred years earlier, and other Europeans may have arrived a thousand years earlier. It does not minimize Columbus's achievement to put it in the context of Europe's knowledge of lands beyond the Atlantic from the time of the Greeks and Romans and perhaps earlier.

Some scholars postulate voyages to the Atlantic islands and even to the American continent by Stone Age or Bronze Age sailors from Europe. A thousand years later Phoenicians and Carthaginians ventured from the Mediterranean Sea to repeat the feats of these shadowy early navigators. Greeks and Romans followed. The Atlantic islands discovered were sometimes exuberantly reported as the site of the Hesperides (producer of golden apples), the Fortunate Islands, the Terrestrial Paradise, or other attractive locales. Although these early navigators are sometimes thought to have made transatlantic discoveries, most scholars limit their findings to islands in the Atlantic.

During the time of Alexander the Great, the Greek Pytheas of Massilia claimed to have visited an island called Thule, probably Iceland, which became known as the "ultimate," or farthest land from Europe; the sea around this land was often thought to be congealed. In medieval times (sixth to eighth centuries A.D.) Irish monks such as Saint Brendan (c. 520–578) set sail in seagoing, leather-skinned, willow-framed coracles, seeking variously the earthly paradise or solitude on deserted islands to which they were sometimes guided by a flight of birds. Because the earthly paradise was assumed to lie in the extreme East, the effort to sail west to reach it indicates a recognition of the sphericity of the earth and a belief that the width of the Atlantic separating Europe from Asia was not great. Reports of the voyages of Irish monks were to litter the maps of the period with mythical islands.

Norse Explorations and Settlements

Beginning in the eighth century A.D., Norsemen moved west from Scandinavia, often finding Irish already established on islands such as Iceland, which the Norse reached in the ninth century. The distance between Iceland and Greenland is much less than the distance between Iceland and the lands from which the settlers from Europe had come. Hence it is not surprising that, before the end of the tenth century, the Norsemen had reached Greenland and, shortly after, Vinland the Good (the North American continent). Some scholars assume the Irish were ahead of the Norse, even in America, but hard archaeological evidence is lacking to support the Irish claim, whereas it exists for the Norse.

That the Norse planted settlements—however briefly—on the mainland of North America has long been accepted, despite the fact that the Icelandic saga evidence upon which that assumption was based for many years was treated cautiously by scholars like Fridtjof Nansen because of its oral, folkloristic, and mythical elements. Indeed, the Massachusetts Historical Society, when asked to report on a nineteenth-century proposal to erect a statue in Boston to Leif Ericsson, responded, "There is the same sort of reason for believing in the existence of Leif Ericsson that there is for believing in the existence of Agamemnon; they are both traditions accepted by later writers, but there is no more reason for regarding as true the details related about his discoveries than there is for accepting as historic truth the narratives contained in the Homeric poems." But with the discovery in 1961 by Helge and Anne Stine Ingstad of some house ruins at L'Anse-aux-Meadows in northern Newfoundland containing European artifacts such as a Norse spindle-whorl dating from around A.D. 1000, the few remaining doubts about Norse pre-Columbian settlement in the New World were largely erased.

The Norse settlements on mainland America were an outgrowth of the activities of Eric the Red of Iceland who established a colony in Greenland in the late tenth century. Eric's son Leif may have been the first European to set foot on American soil, but the story of the accidental discovery and later occupation of a portion of "America" involves not only Eric and Leif but Bjarni Herjulfsson, Leif's brother Thorvald, and Thorfinn Karlsefni Thordarson.

The land west of Greenland that was discovered and temporarily settled (until conflict with the native inhabitants caused the Norsemen to withdraw) consisted of three distinct but apparently connected regions: Helluland, Markland, and Vinland. The first two areas are usually identified as Baffin Island and Labrador, but the last named is subject to great debate because of the assumption that vines grew there.

Questionable claims to pre-Columbian Norse sites have been made for New England, Minnesota, and other parts of Canada. Fourteenth-century voyages into the interior of Canada and the United States have periodically been reported—for example, as recorded on the Kensington Rune Stone found in 1898 near Kensington, Minnesota. This artifact occasioned a bitter debate among scholars and amateurs and was eventually judged to be a modern

fraud, although theories of its authenticity periodically reemerge. The elastic character of ancient "inscriptions" on rocks can be judged from the fact that the puzzling inscriptions on the Dighton Rock near Taunton, Massachusetts, have been read to support both Norse and Portuguese pre-Columbian discoveries.

Another potential Norse site is on Kodlunarn Island (White Man's Island) in Frobisher Bay, where the English explorer Martin Frobisher led three expeditions in 1576, 1577, and 1578. The Arctic explorer Francis Hall in the mid-nineteenth century rediscovered the site and recovered an iron bloom from it, and a Smithsonian Institution expedition in 1981 excavated the site and discovered several additional iron blooms dating from the twelfth and thirteenth centuries. There are many explanations for the unusual dating of these objects that would preclude a Norse presence in the area during those centuries, but the possibility of a Norse presence cannot be ruled out. It is even conceivable that advocates of a pre-Columbian discovery by the legendary Welsh prince Madoc, around A.D. 1170, may, with the discovery of these artifacts, reemerge.

The fact that Vinland is clearly recognized by modern geographers as part of the North American mainland while Greenland and Iceland are identified as islands adjacent to the mainland but not necessarily within the Western Hemisphere, emphasizes the artificial nature of contemporary descriptions of what constitutes "discovery" of the "New World." Our present-day knowledge of the existence of a continent separated from both Europe and Asia by vast oceans impels us to consider any discovery within what we now know to be the mainland of that continent to be a discovery of the whole, while discovery of offshore islands is not given the same importance. Such thinking, indeed, is often used to rob Columbus of the distinction of discovering "America" because he discovered "only" outlying islands on his first two voyages and did not reach the mainland of South America until the third voyage, in 1498. But the explorations and settlements of the Norse on the mainland of North America, though known in Europe, had little impact on those who sought to reach the Asia described by Marco Polo, a land of immense, civilized, wealthy, and powerful populations. Rather, the reports that filtered back to Europe inspired at best curiosity about a cold and uninviting northern frontier similar to the northern reaches of the Scandinavian peninsula, with which the new discoveries were often confused in the telling and conjoined on some maps. [See also *Icelandic Sagas; Vinland; Vinland Map.*]

Classical Exploration

The Atlantic Ocean was the source of idyllic and paradisaical images for some classical writers but was described in forbidding terms by other classical and medieval writers as an impassable, shallow, muddy barrier to navigation. Such reports were derived principally from the story of Atlantis reported by Plato in the middle of the fourth century B.C. Atlantis, a powerful kingdom occupying a gigantic continent larger than Europe or Africa, had sought to conquer Europe but was destroyed in a cataclysmic series of earthquakes and floods, which caused it to disappear beneath the sea, leaving the Atlantic impenetrable because of the shoals of mud and dangerous reefs. In contrast to the tales of fortunate islands or isles of the blessed, other tales of giant sea monsters, huge eels, spouting whales, and the like were sometimes reported by fearful commentators, whose visions were later to adorn the maps of medieval Europe. The Roman poet Horace (first century B.C.) spoke of "godless ships bound madly in contempt o'er channels not allowed" and warned that the gods were appalled by this "violation" of strange seas and sacred waters.

It should be recalled that the Atlantic was thought by most classical and medieval scholars to be merely an arm of a great ocean surrounding the central landmass of Europe, Asia, and Africa. Prior to the efforts of those who sought to reach the East by sailing west, traders, diplomats, and explorers tried to reach the East by sailing east, starting from the eastern Mediterranean or the Red Sea (which were intermittently connected by a canal) and sailing across the Indian Ocean. Classical reports of attempts, some successful and some not, to sail around Africa, either from the east to the west or the west to the east, can also be found in the literature. The earliest known attempt to circumnavigate Africa from east to west was undertaken by Phoenician seamen at the beginning of the sixth century B.C. on the order of the Egyptian king Necho. Reported by Herodotus, the voyage, in the opinion of some modern scholars, did take place and did succeed in its mission.

In the second century B.C., Agatharchides of Cnidus in his *On the Erythraean Sea* (which included the Indian Ocean, Red Sea, and Persian Gulf) discusses the history of the area following Alexander the Great's conquests (336–323 B.C.), which opened up the area to Greek enterprise. Alexander's successors in Egypt, the four Ptolemies, promoted explorations down the African coast and into the surrounding ocean. By the first quarter of the second century B.C. the secret of the monsoon route to India from Africa had been discovered.

The Greek navigator Eudoxus of Cyzicus, in the last two decades of the second century B.C., twice sailed to India from Egypt's Red Sea ports, probably utilizing the hitherto closely held Arab knowledge of the monsoon seasons that facilitated such voyages. Subsequently, he tried to sail directly from the Mediterranean to India by circumnavigating Africa from west to east. He failed in his first attempt and made a second effort, during which he may

have been cut off by Carthaginians, who jealously guarded the Atlantic jumping-off places of the route around Africa, which they, as well as Phoenicians and Persians, had earlier—probably unsuccessfully—attempted to accomplish in a west-east direction.

Medieval Exploration

Voyages into the Atlantic, some with the goal of circumnavigating Africa, continued in the Christian Era. In 1291 the Vivaldi brothers, Ugolino and Vadino, of Genoa sailed into the Atlantic through the Straits of Gibraltar with the intention of reaching India and were never heard from again. The Venetians Niccolò and Antonio Zeno may have discovered land in the western ocean in the fourteenth century. Genoese navigators, in the service of Portugal in the fourteenth and fifteenth centuries, sailed to the Canaries and down the African coast. In the course of such voyages in the great ocean surrounding the land masses of Europe, Asia, and Africa, it is not inconceivable that sailors were blown off course, shipwrecked, or otherwise carried to "American" lands, in the same way that the Portuguese voyager Pedro Álvares Cabral "discovered" Brazil while sailing around Africa to India in 1500.

Periodic reports of Roman coins or other tantalizing evidence of a pre-Columbian presence in the New World, or in the islands lying between the New and Old Worlds, must always be treated with skepticism given the difficulty of establishing historical facts. The same must be said for the evidence of native American myths such as that of the white, bearded god Quetzalcoatl, expected to return from the East, whose assumed arrival in the form of the Spanish conquistador Hernando Cortés caused the Aztec ruler Motecuhzoma II (Moctezuma) effectively to disarm himself and lose his kingdom.

Pre-Columbian discoveries can also be attributed to explorers, navigators, fishermen, merchants, and others from Asia, who may variously have sailed, been blown off course, or been carried by the Japan Current northeast along the Aleutian Islands and down the West Coast of America. It is more difficult to conceive of a trans-Pacific route eastward across the southern Pacific to South America, though Polynesians have been given credit for the achievement by some; a more plausible route runs in the opposite direction, as has been demonstrated theoretically by Thor Heyerdahl. In any event, pre-Columbian contact between Asia and the western coast of North and South America has been hypothesized because of the similarity of pottery types in Japan during the early to middle Jomon period and the Valdivia pottery of Ecuador in the period 3500 to 2000 B.C. The similarity of pottery types on two sides of a vast ocean suggested trans-Pacific contact to Smithsonian anthropologists Betty Meggers, Clifford Evans, and their collaborator Emilio Estrada, though their thesis has been accepted by only a few scholars. But while images of Asian animals, similarities of items of clothing, pottery, and so forth can be used to demonstrate the possibility of transpacific exploration and discovery, the evidence is too insubstantial, and the effects too transient to threaten the importance of the first transatlantic discoveries that did have immediate and substantial consequences.

The Historians' Debate

Two scholarly vices, hypercriticism, on the one hand, and imaginative inferences, on the other, coexist in the historical profession, creating an ever-present tension between those who want to believe what cannot be proved and those who want to prove false what is in fact believable. The historian must steer a strict course between both extremes when dealing with the evidence for pre-Columbian contact between the Old World and the New.

Columbus's achievement has been denigrated by historians unwilling to concede that he had the ability or the luck to achieve his great enterprise. Skeptics have suggested that someone—possibly an anonymous pilot, possibly an Indian floating across the Atlantic, possibly a now-lost map—showed him the way. The presence of large islands such as Antillia in pre-Columbian maps of the Atlantic Ocean has encouraged some scholars to assume that these land masses represent pre-Columbian discoveries. Thus the island of Antillia—reputedly the refuge of seven bishops and their people who left Portugal in the eighth century to escape the Moors—on the 1424 map of Zuane Pizzigano (now in the James Ford Bell Library in Minneapolis) was judged in 1954 by the Portuguese scholar Armando Cortesão to represent the "forefront of America" and to reflect a pre-Columbian Portuguese voyage across the Atlantic.

Similar claims for pre-Columbian discoveries, particularly in the last quarter of the fifteenth century, have been made in behalf of the English (particularly those from Bristol), Danes, Flemings (in the service of Portugal), Basque fishermen from the Bay of Biscay, and Portuguese from the Azores. The documentation of each such claim is complex and clouded, as in the letter written in the winter of 1497–1498 by John Day, an English merchant in Andalusia, to the "Lord Grand Admiral" of Spain (Columbus) speaking of transatlantic discoveries by "men from Bristol in other times," which may or may not refer to pre-Columbian times.

Those who accept the various hypotheses of pre-Columbian discoveries of America frequently imply that Columbus does not deserve to be called the discoverer of America. Important scholars, particularly in an earlier era, frequently subscribed to such views, but they are increasingly rare among scholars of the late twentieth century.

Cortesão, for example, has received little support for his theory about the 1424 map from present-day Portuguese scholars.

More relevant, though not necessarily contradictory of the idea that Columbus discovered America, is the frequently voiced complaint that Columbus did not discover America because it had been discovered before, by its own inhabitants. Of course, it is true that ancestors of present-day Native Americans, who found, perhaps fifteen thousand years ago, a land bridge to the "New World," perhaps while hunting game, were the first men and women to discover the land geographers now categorize as the Western Hemisphere, or North and South America. But the term *discovery*, as used by Europeans, always meant "discovery by Europeans." It was not meant to suggest that the native inhabitants either did not know where they were or had not earlier discovered for themselves the lands now discovered by the Europeans. In each case the term is specific to the discoverers.

BIBLIOGRAPHY

Adam of Bremen. *History of the Archbishops of Hamburg-Bremen.* Translated with an introduction and notes by Francis J. Tschan. New York, 1959.

Agatharchides of Cnidus. *On the Erythraean Sea.* Translated and edited by Stanley M. Burstein. Hakluyt Society, 2d ser., vol. 172. London, 1989.

Cassidy, Vincent H. *The Sea around Them: The Atlantic Ocean, A.D. 1250.* Baton Rouge, La., 1968.

Fitzhugh, William W., and Jacqueline S. Olin. "Archeology of the Frobisher Voyages: Contributions to the Archeology of Kodlunarn Island, Frobisher Bay, N.W.T., Canada. Results of a 1981 Smithsonian Expedition." Report submitted to the Government of the Northwest Territories, Prince of Wales Northern Heritage Center, Yellowknife, N.W.T., Canada. Typescript. June 1990.

Ingstad, Helge. *Westward to Vinland: The Discovery of Pre-Columbian Norse House-sites in North America.* Translated by Erik J. Friis. New York, 1969.

Jones, Gwyn. *The Norse Atlantic Saga: Being the Norse Voyages of Discovery and Settlement to Iceland, Greenland, America.* London, 1964.

Keen, Benjamin. *The Aztec Image in Western Thought.* New Brunswick, N.J., 1971.

Magnusson, Magnus, and Hermann Palsson. *The Vinland Sagas: The Norse Discovery of America: Graenlendinga Saga and Eirik's Saga.* New York, 1966.

Oleson, Tryggvi J. *Early Voyages and Northern Approaches, 1000–1632.* Canadian Centenary Series. London, 1964.

Sauer, Carl O. *Northern Mists.* Berkeley, Calif., 1968.

Thiel, J. H. *Eudoxus of Cyzicus: A Chapter in the History of the Sea-Route to India and the Route round the Cape in Ancient Times.* Groningen, [1966].

Wahlgren, Erik. *The Kensington Stone: A Mystery Solved.* Madison, Wis., 1958.

Winsor, Justin. "Pre-Columbian Explorations." In vol. 1 of *Narrative and Critical History of America*. 8 vols. Boston, 1884–1889.

WILCOMB E. WASHBURN

European Exploration and Discovery after 1492

Following Columbus's first voyage to the Western Hemisphere and before the close of the fifteenth century, numerous non-Columbian expeditions sailed from Spain or England for the New World. Four of those departures are described in the recently discovered Libro de Armadas in the Archivo General de Indias, Seville. A fleet of four caravels commanded by Juan Aguado sortied in 1495 with supplies for Columbus's second settlement, La Isabela, on the northern coast of La Española (Hispaniola). A second supply fleet under Giannotto Berardi sailed in January 1496 but all its vessels foundered in a storm immediately upon leaving Cádiz; the Libro suggests that the business agent and chandler for that expedition, Amerigo Vespucci, sailed in one of Berardi's vessels. The same source records the departure for La Española of the ship *Catalina* and two caravels, *Santa María de Guía* and *Lázaro*, in June 1496, and the dispatch of the royal visitor Francisco de Bobadilla to the same island in 1499.

In the last years of the century three other expeditions departed Spain for the New World. Alonso de Ojeda, with three caravels and Vespucci and the mapmaker Juan de la Cosa among his passengers, left Cádiz in May 1499 with the intention of plundering and slaving in the pearl fisheries between Margarita Island and the Venezuelan mainland; he would return for the same purpose in 1502. La Cosa led two expeditions with similar goals to the region in 1504 and 1508. A second 1499 voyage was commanded by Peralonso Niño, who had commanded Columbus's *Santa María*. Niño left Palos in June in a single caravel and returned the following April with sizable treasure from the Pearl Coast. Other minor voyages to the same region followed in the next decade, such as that of Rodrigo de Bastidas in 1500; one of his passengers was Vasco Núñez de Balboa, who would cross the Isthmus of Panama in 1513 and sight the Pacific Ocean, on which the Portuguese were already sailing from the opposite direction.

The third and last significant non-Columbian Spanish effort of the century was commanded by Vicente Yáñez Pinzón, captain of *Niña* in 1492. From his native Palos in November 1499 Pinzón sailed down the African coast to the Cape Verde Islands and then in twenty days crossed the Atlantic to the shoulder of Brazil. After exploring the Amazon and loading a cargo of logwood (valued as a dyewood) and twenty native slaves, but having lost half his own men, he returned to Palos in September 1500.

Though his Brazilian landfall is not accepted by all historians, no one rejects his two subsequent voyages to the Caribbean, in 1502–1504 and 1508–1509; on the latter he was joint commander with Juan Díaz de Solís.

Another notable voyage in the 1490s was sponsored by Henry VII of England and commanded by the Venetian John Cabot. With one ship and a crew of eighteen, Cabot departed Bristol on May 20, 1497. Taking a high-latitude course in search of a northwest strait to the Indies, he raised the northern peninsula of Newfoundland in thirty-three days, explored the island's eastern capes, islands, and bays, and re-entered Bristol on August 6. In May of the following year he returned to "the newe founde lande" with five ships, four of which, with Cabot, disappeared without a trace. A son, Sebastian, who possibly sailed with his father in 1497, may have sailed to Newfoundland in 1508; it is certain that he reached the Río de la Plata on his own in 1525–1528.

In one of the most important voyages before the end of the decade, the Portuguese navigator Vasco da Gama sailed in a completely different direction, south and east around the Cape of Good Hope to the southwest coast of India, which he reached at Calicut in May 1498. A second Portuguese expedition in 1500 under Pedro Álvares Cabral was the first to exploit the newly opened Asian trade. Da Gama followed him in his second (1502) and third (1524) voyages to consolidate the Portuguese presence, particularly at Goa.

Credit is usually given to the Portuguese Cabral for the discovery of Brazil. Though he probably followed Pinzón by a few months, Cabral, having made an accidental landfall (he was bound around the Cape of Good Hope for India) on April 22, 1500, east of Monte Pascoal, formally opened Brazil to further exploration and commerce. He named the country, which he thought to be an island, Ilha da Vera Cruz. He thereupon proceeded around the Cape of Good Hope and returned to Lisbon, much depleted in ships and men, in summer 1501.

Several Portuguese and Anglo-Azorean expeditions made northern voyages in the period 1500 to 1536, among them the voyage in 1500 of João Fernandes, who conferred the name Lavrador (husbandman) to Greenland (a name later translated to eastern Canada), and others establishing a steady cod fishing industry on the Newfoundland banks.

The southern latitudes absorbed Iberian interest in the same period, and the peninsula's two most visible captains were the Florentine Amerigo Vespucci and the Portuguese Ferdinand Magellan. Having survived the wreck of Berardi's fleet off Cádiz in 1496, Vespucci sailed with Ojeda in 1499 and with the Portuguese Gonçalo Coelho in 1501. (There is no evidence for a western voyage that he claimed to have made in 1497.) The Coelho-

Vespucci fleet out of Lisbon made landfall on Brazil, where the Florentine made copious notation of native lifeways and the local flora and fauna. In 1503 he commanded a vessel in a second Coelho voyage that established a garrison on the Brazilian coast. In two widely circulated letters he described with some inflation his role and experiences in that *Mundus Novus,* leading the Lorraine cartographer Martin Waldseemüller to emblazon "America" across his 1507 depiction of South America. Spain continued to call the new lands Las Indias (the Indies).

In 1515, armed with a charter from King Fernando, the Spanish *piloto mayor* Juan Díaz de Solís sailed for Brazil and rounded Uruguay where he entered and gave a first European name to the Río de la Plata estuary: La Mar Dulce, later called Río de Solís, and still later Río de la Plata. Somewhere on the Uruguayan coast Solís and seven men went ashore where all but one were clubbed to death and eaten by natives. The remaining crewmen, less one ship of their three and one-third of their complements, returned to Seville in 1516.

Magellan, tantalized by tales of the Spice Islands (Moluccas) of Asia, and considering, it appears, that the Pacific was a narrow body of water, thought that those fabled sources of clove, cinnamon, and nutmeg might best be reached by a strait through Spanish America. Accordingly, on September 20, 1519, the five ships of his Armada de Molucca left Sanlúcar de Barrameda.

Sailing down the African coast to elude two fleets sent by a competitive Portuguese monarch to intercept him, Magellan crossed the Atlantic to the shoulder of Brazil, which he reached on November 29. His ships coasted south to Rio de Janeiro, Montevideo, and Patagonia, during which time he put down several mutinies. On November 1, 1520, he sighted the strait that he had sought, and made an unusually direct negotiation of its 334 nautical miles of tricky currents and dead ends. Although he named it Todos los Santos it soon acquired the name Strait of Magellan. On November 27 the fleet, now down to three ships, debouched into the trackless Pacific, which he also named.

Magellan hugged the Chilean coast north as far as Valdivia and then struck westward on a four-month crossing that took him past the Marshall Islands, through the Marianas, and finally to the Philippine archipelago at Leyte Gulf. At Mactan Island north of Mindanao, Magellan intervened militarily in a conflict on the side of the Mactanese against nearby Cebu. Tactical errors forced a Spanish withdrawal and Magellan, covering the retreat, was killed.

Down to two ships and a fraction of their force, the survivors succeeded in reaching the Moluccas on November 8, 1521. One ship, *Trinidad,* loaded with cloves from

Tidore, was captured by Portuguese ships sent around the Cape of Good Hope to deny the spiceries to Spain. The other, *Victoria,* captained by Juan Sebastian de Elcano, rounded the cape and, completing the first circumnavigation of the globe, put in at Seville on September 8, 1522, with enough spices to more than pay the monetary cost of the voyage, though hardly the cost in lives (227).

Meanwhile, Spain launched an ever-widening circle of voyages of discovery from her bases in the Caribbean Sea. Juan Ponce de León, who had sailed with Columbus in 1493, sailed northwest from Puerto Rico through the Bahama chain and on April 2, 1513, sighted the coastline of a large "island" to which he gave the name La Florida. Recent studies indicate that his landfall was probably south of Cape Canaveral. Sometime between 1514 and 1516 the slaver Pedrode Salazar reached the mainland at a higher but unknown latitude. In 1521 Ponce de León returned to what Alonzo Alvarez de Pineda had proved by that date to be a peninsula, but his landing party was repulsed, and he himself was mortally wounded by Calusa natives on the lower Gulf Coast.

Francisco Fernández de Córdoba sailed out of Havana in 1517 and discovered the Yucatán Peninsula of Mexico. His pilot, Antonio Alaminos, was the most experienced navigator of the region, having sailed with Columbus in 1493, Ponce in 1513, and numerous expeditions in between. Juan de Grijalba, with Alaminos aboard, followed to the Mexican coast in 1518. And in the same year Hernando Cortés, with Alaminos, left Baracoa, Cuba, for the lands that he would conquer and name Nueva España (New Spain).

Disaster met the expedition of Lucas Vázquez de Ayllón, which sailed from Santo Domingo in 1526 bound for La Florida with about six hundred settlers. After founding a town named San Miguel de Gualdape at Sapelo Sound, Georgia, on September 29, the colonists were quickly overcome by exhaustion, hunger, cold, and disease. What had been Europe's first settlement in territory that would later be part of the United States was abandoned after less than two months, and some 150 half-famished survivors (not including Ayllón) made their way by ship to various ports in the Antilles.

Pánfilo de Narváez landed at Tampa Bay in 1528 and explored the Florida interior as far as Apalache Bay, where, hungry and under incessant native attack, he and 245 of his men built barges and sailed west along the Gulf shore seeking refuge in Mexico. Most, including Narváez, were drowned in a storm. Four survivors among those who safely made the Texas coast eventually crossed by foot to the Pacific, then reached Mexico City in 1536. Their leader, Álvar Núñez Cabeza de Vaca, five years later walked nearly 950 kilometers (580 miles) across pathless Brazil from Santa Catarina Island to Asunción.

With a force of over six hundred people, some two hundred horses, and a herd of swine, the Extremaduran Hernando de Soto landed at Tampa Bay in 1539 and embarked on an overland reconnaissance that took his men through Florida and into areas comprising nine other present-day southeastern U.S. states, an exploration that covered 4,000 miles in four years. De Soto was the first European to reach the Mississippi River and died on its banks in 1542. About 310 survivors eventually reached Mexico City. A similar long march into the North American interior was led out of Mexico by Francisco Vázquez de Coronado, who penetrated as far as present-day Kansas in 1540–1542.

Sailing from Cádiz, Pedro Menéndez de Avilés founded St. Augustine, Florida, in September 1565. From there he explored the peninsular shoreline and the East Coast as far north as Santa Elena (Parris Island, South Carolina), where he established a second settlement (1566–1587). From Santa Elena in 1566 and again in 1567 Menéndez sent Captain Juan Pardo and 150 men to search the interior for an overland route to the mines of New Spain. Though he understandably failed in his primary mission, Pardo returned from both marches with the first significant information about the American interior since the expedition of De Soto a quarter century before. During the next half-century Spanish pilots out of St. Augustine conducted intensive reconnaissance of the coast northward. Typical were the expeditions of Fernández de Ecija in 1605 and 1609, which hunted details of the English settlement of Jamestown in Virginia.

Numerous navigators explored the coast of the Gulf of Mexico. On the basis of their information the Viceroy of Mexico authorized Tristán de Luna y Arellano to found a settlement at Pensacola Bay. After three difficult years (1559–1562), the colony failed. Spanish seaborne exploration continued, though it was left to a Frenchman sailing downriver in 1682, Robert Cavalier, sieur de La Salle, to discover the mouth and delta of the Mississippi. Despite additional Spanish attempts to pacify and settle the Gulf lands, particularly the expeditions of Luis de Carvajal y de la Cueva in 1580 to 1590, the expanse of shore between the Río Pánuco in Mexico and the Menéndez family claims in Florida remained unsubjugated wilderness at the close of the sixteenth century.

France had since 1504 exploited the cod banks of Newfoundland, but it was only after news of Magellan's strait that it began serious exploration of its own, and in a different region: the thirteen degrees of latitude north of Florida, where it was hoped her navigators could find a northern passage to Cathay. The first seeker to sail under French sponsorship was the Dieppe-based Florentine, Giovanni da Verrazano. With a single naval ship, *La Dauphine*, Verrazano made a landfall near Cape Fear,

North Carolina, in early March 1524, then explored the Outer Banks, at one point fancying that across them he sighted the Pacific Ocean. Proceeding north he closed Barnegat, New Jersey, entered New York Harbor as far as the Narrows, then resumed coasting to Maine and the east coast of Newfoundland. Verrazano returned in July 1524 to Dieppe, where he mounted two more transatlantic expeditions, one in 1527 to cut logwood in Brazil and the second in 1528 to the Lesser Antilles, where Caribs killed him.

Obsessed by the search for a northern passage, France showed casual indifference to the great North American mainland that Verrazano was the first to explore, and subsequent French voyagers hunted instead in the far northern reaches of the present-day Maritime Provinces of Canada. Jacques Cartier made three such voyages. In the first, with two ships, he departed Saint-Malo in April 1534 and reached Newfoundland twenty days later. For three and a half months he explored the south coast of Labrador, the west of Newfoundland, Prince Edward Island, and the Gulf of St. Lawrence with its islands and bays. Cartier made the first contacts with the Hurons. He returned to these waters with three ships in the spring of 1535 and expanded his reconnaissance up the St. Lawrence River as far as the Rock of Québec and Montréal. Despite many hardships, including scurvy, the French survived the following winter in Canada and returned to France fourteen months after setting out.

Having opened up an east-west waterway that conceivably could be the long-sought strait, Cartier made a third and final voyage to establish a colony on its banks in 1541, though this time as subaltern to a nobleman, Jean-François de La Rocque de Roberval. Cartier reached the St. Lawrence ten months before Roberval, passed another severe winter above Québec, then on his way home met Roberval at Newfoundland and refused the latter's order to stay.

One winter proved enough for Roberval, too, and France abandoned interest in the far north for over half a century. In 1562 an expedition under Jean Ribault founded Charlesfort in Carolina, and two years later René de Laudonnière built Fort Caroline on the St. Johns River in Florida. The first was abandoned and the second was destroyed by Pedro Menéndez de Avilés in 1565. Not until 1604 to 1608, when Samuel de Champlain began the permanent settlement of Canada, did France take advantage of its Laurentian discoveries.

Spain, too, was active in the wake of Magellan. The Dominican García Jofre de Loaysa passed through the Strait of Magellan in 1525 but his seven vessels met disaster either at the strait or in the Pacific. Ending a long controversy with Portugal about the position of the Moluccas along the papal Line of Demarcation, Charles V in 1529 yielded the Spice Islands to Portugal in exchange for 350,000 gold ducats. In 1564 the Augustinian Andrés de Urdaneta oversaw a voyage from the west coast of Mexico to Cebu, which became Spain's first colony in the Philippines, not supplanted in importance until the foundation of Manila in 1571. By discovering the westerlies that brought him home to Acapulco by way of a California landfall, Urdaneta made possible the Manila galleon trade that opened in 1573.

Pedro de Mendoza followed Sebastian Cabot to the La Plata basin in 1534, founding Buenos Aires but losing his own life and about 1,850 others. An expedition commissioned by Bishop Gutiérrez de Varga Carvajal just barely negotiated the Strait of Magellan in 1540 to inaugurate trade with Chile and Peru. In 1557–1558 Juan Fernández Ladrillero from Chile proved that the strait could be traversed from west to east.

Cortés, conqueror of Mexico by 1521, began soon afterward to explore the Pacific coast northward. In May 1535 he discovered the lower tip of California. His lieutenant Francisco de Ulloa explored much of the Baja California littoral in 1539 and 1540. The first sighting of Alta California is credited to the expedition of Juan Rodriguez Cabrillo and Bartolomé Ferrelo, also out of Mexico, in 1542. The present state of California would not be seen by Europeans again until thirty-seven years later, by the crew of England's Francis Drake.

Drake's voyage in 1577 to 1580 began as a privateering expedition against Spain and resulted in the second circumnavigation of the earth. On his initial southwest course Drake by-passed the Strait of Magellan, rounded Henderson Island south of Tierra del Fuego, and made a wide sweep north into the Pacific. Only one ship, *Golden Hind,* of the original fleet of six survived. Perhaps seeking a western entrance to the northwest passage, which some called the Strait of Anian, Drake raised the coast of Oregon. He did not tarry long before turning south to northern California, where he found an agreeable bay and anchored from June 17 to July 23, 1579, naming the pleasant countryside Nova Albion (New England). Historians debate at which of three California bays *Golden Hind* anchored: Drake's Estero, San Quentin Cove, or Bolinas Lagoon. On his subsequent westerly passage Drake followed roughly the track of Elcano's *Victoria* fifty-eight years before, reaching Plymouth in September 1580.

The Englishman Thomas Cavendish circumnavigated the earth from 1586 to 1588, as did the Dutch Oliver de Noort from 1598 to 1601 and George Spilbergen from 1614 to 1617. The growing Dutch position among maritime powers was further demonstrated by the chartering of the Dutch East India Company in 1602, the establishment of the New Netherlands colony near Albany, New York, in 1614, and the discovery of Cape Horn by Wilhelm Cornelison Schouten and Jacob Le Maire in 1615–1617.

While Drake was exploring the Pacific, his countryman Martin Frobisher made three fruitless voyages (1576–1578) to the bay that bears his name, north of Labrador. Sir Humphrey Gilbert, financed mainly by his family and friends, and after one false start, explored the Canadian Maritime provinces in 1583, but lost his life off the Azores on the return. In three voyages between 1585 and 1587, the privateer and shipmaster John Davis explored the sounds and capes bordering Davis Strait between Greenland and Baffin Island in a fruitless search for a northwest passage, just missing the opening of one at Lancaster Sound.

In 1584 Humphrey Gilbert's half-brother Walter Raleigh, together with Philip Amadas and Arthur Barlowe, sailed from Plymouth to the temperate North American latitudes first sighted by Verrazano. On his return, having liked what he saw at the Carolina Outer Banks, Raleigh gave the region the name Virginia (the Spanish knew it as Jactán) and organized a fleet under Richard Grenville's command to establish a colony there, which its first governor, Ralph Lane, placed at Roanoke Island, in 1585. From that base Lane explored as far north as Chesapeake Bay. The colony faltered because of poor relations with the Indians, and after one year 103 survivors were withdrawn by Sir Francis Drake. Encouraged by nautical chronicler Richard Hakluyt and others, Raleigh sponsored a second Virginia colony in 1587, which settled at the same Roanoke site under governor John White. Unaccountably, it vanished almost without a trace.

The sixteenth century ended with only one European power, Spain, boasting a permanent toehold north of New Spain, at St. Augustine. In 1609, Santa Fe, New Mexico, was established. England founded Jamestown in Virginia in 1607. In the following year Champlain raised the fleur-de-lis above Québec. The Dutch opened New Netherlands in 1614. And in 1620 the Puritan Pilgrims established the second New England in Massachusetts. By then the stage was set for a three-nation struggle for hegemony over the continent that led to numerous new discoveries, both overland and downriver. In Mexico, the Central American isthmus, and South America the writs of Spain and Portugal ran unimpeded, and discovery there proceeded equally apace.

BIBLIOGRAPHY

Chaves, Alonso de. *Quatri partitu en cosmographia practica, y por otro nombre espejo de navegantes.* 1537. Reprint, Madrid, 1983.

Hakluyt, Richard. *The Principall Navigations, Voiages and Discoveries of the English Nation.* London, 1859.

Hanna, Warren L. *Lost Harbor: The Controversy over Drake's California Anchorage.* Berkeley, 1979.

Herrera y Tordesillas, Antonio de. *Historia general de los hechos de los Castellanos en las islas y tierra firme del mar Océano.* 4 vols. Madrid, 1601–1615.

Hoffman, Paul E. *A New Andalucía and a Way to the Orient.* Baton Rouge, 1990.

La Roncière, Charles de. *Jacques Cartier.* Paris, 1931.

Libro de Armadas. Archivo General de Indias, *Contratación,* legajo 3249.

Manzano Manzano, Juan. *Los Pinzones y el descubrimiento de América.* 3 vols. Madrid, 1988.

Morison, Samuel Eliot. *The European Discovery of America: The Northern Voyages A.D. 500–1600.* New York, 1971.

Morison, Samuel Eliot. *The European Discovery of America: The Southern Voyages A.D. 1492–1616.* New York, 1974.

Paige, Paula Spurlin, trans. *The Voyage of Magellan: The Journal of Antonio Pigafetta.* Englewood Cliffs, N.J., 1969.

Quinn, David B., ed. *North American Discovery, circa 1000–1612.* Columbia, S.C., 1971.

MICHAEL GANNON

Basque Exploration and Discovery

Although Basques were renowned as competent seamen from early medieval times and though a Basque navigator, Juan Sebastián de Elcano, was the first man to return safely with his ship from a voyage around the world (1519–1522), no fifteenth- or sixteenth-century Basque ever claimed to have discovered America, as later legend would claim. If there had been any genuine tradition of a pre-Columbian Basque discovery of either North or South America, the Basque historians Esteban de Garibay and Lope de Isasti (both born in the sixteenth century), would certainly have mentioned the fact. Instead, those writers, as well as other contemporary documents, provide solid evidence for the remarkable trading opportunities offered by the New World and exploited by Basque merchant mariners once "the navigation to Terranova had been discovered" and once the Indies had been conquered. In other words, Basques actively participated in but did not initiate the exploration and exploitation of North America, and Basques showed their genius more as merchants and shipbuilders than as explorers and conquerors. The importation from the New World of vast quantities of dried cod and whale oil and the exportation of iron and other goods to the West Indies, for instance, were two highly successful branches of commerce for Basques throughout most of the sixteenth century, while from about 1505 onward their well-built ships formed the backbone of the West Indies run.

Starting in the 1540s, several Basque navigators took part in exploration along the Pacific Coast of North America northward from Mexico. Probably the most outstanding exploit of any Basque in the Pacific was that of Andrés de Urdaneta who, at the king's bidding, left his monastery in Mexico City to accompany another native of the Basque province of Guipúzcoa, Miguel López de Legazpi, on a voyage undertaken for the conquest of the Philippines. The course from Mexico to the Philippines

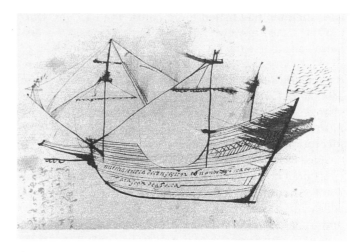

SKETCH OF A BASQUE SHIP. From 1611, found in the files of a notary in Guipúzcoa in northern Spain. PHOTOGRAPH BY MICHAEL BARKHAM

was relatively easy, but Urdaneta, in 1565, was the first pilot to find an efficient return route via the coast of California, so that the Manila galleons could thereafter make a safe easterly passage from the archipelago to Acapulco.

Unlike Urdaneta and Legazpi's expeditions, Basque voyages to northeastern North America (from about 1517) were entirely promoted by private enterprise. These expeditions made a clear contribution to knowledge of North American geography since many place names were bequeathed by Basque fishermen and two small volumes of sailing directions were written by Martin de Hoyarsabal and Pierres Detcheverry "Dorre" (published respectively in Bordeaux and Bayonne, in 1579 and 1677). The final pages of the 1579 volume reflect the detailed knowledge Basques possessed of the Atlantic coasts of Canada, from Cape Breton Island and southeastern Newfoundland, where many of their codfishing stations were located, to the Labrador shore of the Strait of Belle Isle, where before 1550 they had established major whaling stations. Pilots of other nationalities had left short descriptions of eastern Newfoundland, but none at that date was as professional as those of Hoyarsabal, while Detcheverry's description of the island's west coast was only superseded a century later by the surveys of Captain James Cook (1764–1767).

A larger number of Basque place names have survived on the western side of Newfoundland than on any other coast of North America because an almost exclusively Basque seasonal presence was maintained there for nearly two hundred years, while the rest of the Atlantic seaboard was often shared by fishermen of various nationalities. Although well over one thousand Basques went annually to the Strait of Belle Isle whaling stations during the peak years of the whaling industry (about 1565 to 1585), the toponymy of the strait remained basically Breton as Breton codfishermen had fished there before the Basques. During the 1580s, however, Basques were some of the first Europeans to use the Gaspé region and the north shore of the St. Lawrence River for fishing and fur-trading and were particularly successful as traders. References exist to the Montagnais Indians learning Basque during trading exchanges, while later Eskimo traders who often met Basques as far south as Portuchoa (now Port-au-Choix) incorporated Basque words into their trading language.

Since Basque whalers frequently stayed on the Labrador coast until January and occasionally wintered there, many deaths occurred in icebound harbors. The oldest known wills written north of Mexico resulted from these voyages, and as large sums of capital were invested in whaling vessels the voyages also spawned litigation. Early lawsuits, notarial records, and insurance documents testify to the importance of the Basque whaling industry, and archaeological evidence has supported the documentation. It is evident that the frequent impressment of Spanish Basque ships for royal armadas gradually undermined Basque shipbuilding and trading activities toward the end of the sixteenth century. However, a few Spanish and many French Basques continued to participate in transatlantic fishing and trading throughout the seventeenth and on into the eighteenth century.

BIBLIOGRAPHY

Detcheverry Dorre, Pierres. *Liburuhauda jxasoco nabigacionecoa: Martin de Hoyarzabalec egiña Francezes.* Bayonne, 1677. Facsimile edition, San Sebastian, 1985.

Garibay, Esteban de. *Compendio Historial.* 4 vols. Antwerp, 1571.

Huxley, Selma, ed. *Los vascos en el marco Atlantico Norte, Siglos XVI y XVII.* Vol. 3 of *Itsasoa.* San Sebastian, 1987.

Isasti, Lope de. *Compendio historial de la muy noble y muy leal provincia de Guipuzcoa.* Facsimile edition, Bilbao, 1972.

SELMA HUXLEY BARKHAM

EXPULSION FROM SPAIN. For discussion of the Expulsion of the Jews from Spain, see *Jews,* article on *Expulsion from Spain.*

F

FARGHANI, AL-. See *Alfraganus*.

FAUNA. The New World animals encountered by Columbus and those who followed him in the sixteenth century were diverse. The fauna commonly used by pre-Columbian peoples reflected a number of environmental factors. One major influence was whether they lived on an island or a continental mainland. Continental North and South America support a wide range of terrestrial animals, whereas the West Indian islands have very few. On the continents, climate and altitude are important factors. For example, animals living along the coast of Mexico or Peru are quite different from those found in the highlands of those countries. Although coastal peoples throughout North and South America used marine resources extensively, the ones they exploited depended upon whether there were salt marshes, reefs, banks, beaches, rivers, swamps, or other habitats nearby. Finally, the animals of South America are quite distinct from those of North America, with Central America serving as a bridge between them.

Since it is not possible to review the natural history of the entire New World, I will include here only those marine, aquatic, and terrestrial animals whose pre-Columbian use has been verified by archaeological evidence. And the discussion will be further restricted to those regions that were actively colonized by Spaniards during the sixteenth century: the West Indies, Spanish Florida, Mexico and Central America, and parts of South America.

One problem with archaeological evidence is that it is difficult to determine why a specific animal is found at a given site. The majority were probably eaten, but animals were used also for tools, drugs, rituals, jewelry, clothing, and shelter. Some, such as dogs and songbirds, were kept as pets or for protection, and animals used for these purposes might or might not also be eaten. Other animals were attracted to human residences and their refuse inadvertently became part of the archaeological deposit. Sometimes remains are found that appear to have been curios—for example, fossilized shark teeth. It is possible in some cases to determine the role animals played at a specific site, but it is unwise to assume that all animals were eaten, even though most probably were.

West Indies. The Gulf of Mexico and the Caribbean Sea define a subtropical and tropical basin. The islands of the West Indies separate this basin from the Atlantic Ocean while the coasts of North and South America form the continental rim. Although there are some differences between the animals of the Gulf of Mexico and those of the Caribbean, the Gulf Stream current unifies the marine animals of the West Indies and those of the adjacent continental coasts. The islands of the West Indies support terrestrial animals that are derived primarily from Central and South America rather than from North America. The Bahamas, Cuba, Jamaica, Hispaniola (La Española), Puerto Rico, and the Virgin Islands differ in faunal characteristics from the Lesser Antilles, which extend south from the Virgin Islands almost to continental South America. The islands of Grenada, Trinidad, Tobago, Margarita, and the Netherland Antilles are not considered part of the West Indies. The West Indies and the north coast of Venezuela are the only New World locations actually explored by Columbus.

The tropical waters of the Caribbean, as Columbus noted, support many fish, and these played an important role in pre-Columbian economies. Depending upon the site, over 90 percent of the animals were from the sea. Inshore or estuarine fish taken by West Indians included ladyfish, bonefish, porgies, mullets, puffers, and porcupinefish. Banks and reefs form the most common marine habitat in the West Indies and contributed sea basses, jacks, snappers, grunts, angelfish, wrasses, parrotfish, and surgeonfish. Sharks, tarpons, barracudas, mackerels, tunas, and triggerfish were also used. Columbus reported catching mullets and soles and also wrote that West Indians fished with remoras, which attached themselves to turtles and other fish. Remoras, however, are not common in pre-Columbian archaeological sites.

Caribbean waters support other marine animals used by pre-Columbian peoples. These include monk seals and manatees. Columbus thought that the three West Indian sirens (manatee) he saw were not as beautiful as they were usually pictured. He described sea turtles, which were commonly caught, as being like great wooden shields. Archaeological evidence of such invertebrates as mussels, arks, pearl-oysters, tree-oysters, lucines, jewelboxes, coquinas, venuses, limpets, topsnails, nerites, ceriths, conchs, slippersnails, murexes, whelks, and crabs are often found. Columbus wrote that conchs were tasteless.

Freshwater resources were occasionally used by West Indians. Although pond turtles were taken on some islands, freshwater fish have not been reported from West Indian sites. Marine fish that spend at least a portion of their lives in brackish waters or freshwater streams, such as eels, clingfish, needlefish, and sleepers, are sometimes found.

As Columbus noted, terrestrial mammals, although not numerous, were used by West Indians. These included insectivores, rice rats, an extinct family of rodents including *Quemisia*, hutias, and spiny rats. Some of these mammals had become extinct before 1492, but many survived into the sixteenth century only to become extremely rare or extinct during the post-Columbian period.

Other terrestrial and avian animals were used by West Indians. On some islands, iguanas and land crabs were consumed in large numbers. Columbus reported that some iguanas were six feet long and had white meat that tasted like chicken. Although he marveled at the large number of different kinds of birds, some of which sang very sweetly, birds do not appear to have been significant resources for West Indians. Those that have been found in West Indian sites include grebes, shearwaters, tropicbirds, boobies, herons, flamingos, ducks, rails, gulls, pigeons, doves, macaws, and owls. Columbus wrote in his log that some small birds were tamed and kept in houses

NEW WORLD FAUNA. Three drawings by John White of the Virginia colony, circa 1590: iguana, terrapin, flying fish.

and that there were so many parrots they darkened the sun. Among the foods and other presents given to him were parrots.

There is good evidence in the West Indies of animals introduced from South America and of West Indian animals transported to new islands within the Indies. Guinea pigs and a nonnative hutia have been reported on Hispaniola. Although the hutia might have been introduced to Hispaniola from Cuba, the guinea pig originated in South America. Other South American animals brought to the West Indies included opossums and agoutis. Perhaps the best known introduced animals are dogs, which probably came with peoples immigrating into the West Indies from South America. According to Columbus, some of these dogs could not bark and others were the size of mastiffs and pointers. Some hutias, a flightless rail, and a macaw might have been taken within the West Indies to islands where they were not native and hence were at least captive if not domesticated.

Spanish Florida. The coastal plain of what was once Spanish Florida is a low, flat region fringed by barrier islands and estuaries stretching from Texas into Virginia. The terrestrial and aquatic fauna are temperate North American animals, whereas marine animals are a combination of tropical and temperate species. Although occasional explorations were made into the upper coastal plain and beyond, the Spaniards generally stayed within the coastal mainland and islands for most of the three hundred years they occupied this area.

Marine resources might have contributed over 80 percent of the diet of natives living along the coastal fringe. The fish most frequently taken by these peoples were from the estuaries that border the coastal plain. In both the Atlantic Ocean and the Gulf of Mexico, tropical animals gradually decrease as temperate species increase. Tropical marine species may live in waters as far north as North Carolina, but only in the deeper waters of the continental shelf edge where water temperatures are more stable and warmer than closer to shore. Animals from the offshore area were not exploited by North Americans in Spanish Florida until several centuries after contact. Marine fish taken by coastal residents were primarily sharks, rays, sea catfish, sheepsheads, drums, and flounders. Although they were more common and abundant in warm Caribbean waters, sea basses, jacks, snappers, and porcupinefish were also taken. By far the most common fish used along the coast were members of the drum family, including silver perches, seatrouts, spots, croakers, black drums, red drums, and star drums.

Other marine resources were used in Spanish Florida. Porpoises and manatees are found occasionally in coastal sites. Sea turtles, common in the West Indies, also live in the area's warm waters and were taken on a seasonal basis. Diamondback terrapins were frequently used by coastal peoples. Invertebrates from coastal sites include mussels, arks, bittersweets, oysters, coquinas, stout tagelus, marshclams, quahog and venus clams, periwinkles, conchs, whelks, nassas, shrimps, and blue crabs.

Aquatic animals were used by coastal peoples as well as by those living farther inland. Beavers and otters were the primary mammals taken from this environment. Alligators, snapping turtles, pond turtles, musk and mud turtles, and softshell turtles are common freshwater residents, although some of these animals can live in estuarine waters. Freshwater fish found in archaeological sites include gars, bowfins, pikes, suckers, bullhead catfish, sunfish, and perches. Further inland, many species of the large freshwater mussel family Unionidae as well as campelomas, riversnails, rocksnails, and hornsnails are common.

Unlike the West Indies, continental Spanish Florida supported many terrestrial mammals. These include opossums, rabbits, squirrels, coyotes, foxes, bears, raccoons, weasels, minks, skunks, cougars, and bobcats. The white-tailed deer was an important part of the diet of North Americans living inland from the coast.

Other terrestrial and avian resources were also used. These include the terrestrial box turtles and gopher tortoises. The latter were frequently consumed by colonists in Spanish Florida, although apparently not often by native Americans. The gopher tortoise range extends north from peninsular Florida along the coastal plain to the Georgia–South Carolina border, but they are far more common in peninsular Florida than they are farther north. As in the West Indies, birds were not commonly used in Spanish Florida, although herons, ducks, quails, and common turkeys were found there. Inland sites sometimes contain a wider variety of birds, including the now-extinct passenger pigeon.

The only domestic animals in Spanish Florida were dogs, which may occasionally have been used for food as well as other purposes. Although the common turkey was domesticated elsewhere, this was not the case in Spanish Florida.

Mexico and Central America. Both North American and South American animals live in the Mexican–Central American region, with their ranges depending upon latitude, altitude, and rainfall patterns. This area is characterized by primarily temperate zone animals in Mexico and mostly tropical animals south of Mexico. There are significant altitudinal and climatic differences among the eastern coastal plain, the highlands, the deserts, the tropical rain forests, and the western coastal plain, and these are reflected in the animals living in each area. While the eastern coast of Mexico and Central America is inhabited by animals of the warm Gulf of Mexico and the Caribbean, the western coast is also bordered by warm tropical waters. These warm Pacific waters extend the length of Mexico and Central America to just south of the equator in South America.

A wide variety of fish were important in the economies of Mexican and Central American coastal communities, but the percentages are highly variable. The continental edge of the circum-Caribbean basin is frequented by many of the same fish found in the West Indies and Spanish Florida. Depending upon nearby habitats, people may have used sharks, sawfish, stingrays, eaglerays, tarpons, bonefish, sea catfish, toadfish, needlefish, snooks, sea basses, jacks, snappers, tripletails, mojarras, grunts, porgies, drums, wrasses, parrotfish, mullets, barracudas, sleepers, triggerfish, puffers, and porcupinefish. Different but closely related species were taken on the Pacific side of Mexico and Central America.

Other marine resources were available. On the Caribbean side of Mexico and Central America, manatees were used occasionally. Sea turtles are found off both the circum-Caribbean and Pacific beaches. Invertebrates from coastal sites include mussels, arks, oysters, jewelboxes, surfclams, marshclams, pointed-venus, nerites, hornsnails, periwinkles, queen conchs, moonsnails, crown conchs, melampus, blue crabs, and stone crabs.

Freshwater resources found throughout Mexico and Central America include reptiles, fish, and mollusks. Reptiles such as crocodiles, snapping turtles, pond turtles, and musk and mud turtles were often used. The region supports many species of freshwater characins, catfish, and cichlids that do not live farther north or in the West Indies. These are frequently found in sites adjacent to freshwater sources. Some freshwater mollusks, such as applesnails, were also used.

With few exceptions, the mammals of Mexico and Central America were rare or absent in Spanish Florida and none lived in the West Indies. Terrestrial mammals include opossums, armadillos, rabbits, Mexican porcupines, agoutis and pacas, foxes, raccoons, coatis, tapirs, collared and white-lipped peccaries, brocket deer, and white-tailed deer. These animals live on the coastal plain as well as in the highlands.

Other terrestrial animals included iguanas and birds. Iguanas live throughout Mexico and Central America. The use of birds by pre-Columbian residents of this area varied, depending upon cultural preferences for brightly colored feathers. In some locations, remains of boobies, frigatebirds, herons, wood storks, hawks, curassows, quails, wild common turkeys, ocellated turkeys, gallinules, coots, sandpipers, pigeons, parrots, owls, and songbirds are abundant. More often, birds found in archaeological sites are quails, turkeys, pigeons, doves, and parrots.

Two domestic animals were present in Mexico and Central America. One of these was the common turkey. Its range extends south into Mexico from the United States, in portions of which the birds were not domesticated. They were domesticated, however, in the southwestern United States, the highlands of Mexico, and the Yucatán. The common turkey should not be confused with the wild ocellated turkey which is confined to the Yucatán Peninsula and was not domesticated. Dogs were the other domestic animal. They have been found in contexts that indicate they were eaten by some groups and served as hunting companions, sacrifices, and protection for others.

South America. The South American fauna is largely a tropical one, although altitude and rainfall are important in the distribution of these animals. The animals of the Caribbean islands of Grenada, Trinidad, Tobago, and the Netherland Antilles are also South American. Many animals that are native to the continent but not found in the West Indies, such as monkeys, anteaters, and armadillos, are present on these islands and were used by islanders prior to 1492. Although the coastal plain of Venezuela, Colombia, and part of Ecuador is characterized by mangrove swamps, savannas, and tropical forests, the coastal plain from southern Ecuador to northern Chile is a desert virtually devoid of terrestrial animals. Beyond the coastal plain, the highland Andes have temperate and cold climates with distinct animals generally dissimilar to those living along the Pacific or Caribbean coasts. Unfortunately we know little from archaeological evidence of the resources used over much of this area.

Marine fish were very important in the Caribbean and Pacific coastal economies of South America. The coastal fish of Venezuela, the offshore islands, and Colombia east of Panama are Caribbean species similar to those found elsewhere in the circum-Caribbean basin. The fish in the warm waters off Colombia west of Panama are similar to those of Mexico and Central America. Just south of the equator there is a distinct change in Pacific fish. The waters off Peru and Chile are characterized by upwellings of nutrients, which support an abundant temperate and cold water marine life. Coastal sites in Ecuador contain the remains of more warm water animals than do sites farther south. Fish important to coastal populations in Ecuador include sharks, rays, herrings, sea basses, jacks, grunts, drums, mullets, barracudas, mackerels, tunas, and flounders. Fish important to coastal populations in Peru include different species of herrings, anchovies, sea basses, jacks, grunts, drums, mackerels, and tunas.

Other marine resources were also important. Sea turtles have been found in Ecuadorian collections, and whales, sea otters, fur seals, and sea lions were used by coastal peoples farther south. Invertebrates from coastal sites include mussels, scallops, thorny-oysters, surfclams, wedgeclams, venuses, limpets, tegulas, periwinkles, slippersnails, rocksnails, chitons, lobsters, crabs, and sea urchins.

Aquatic resources are almost absent on the western side of the Andes below the equator, owing to limited rainfall and few freshwater sources. On the other hand, pond turtles and freshwater fish such as characins, catfish, and cichlids may be locally abundant in archaeological sites near lakes and streams.

The presence of coastal terrestrial mammals is also influenced by the presence of freshwater. The coast of Ecuador supports opossums, armadillos, rabbits, rice rats, agoutis, spiny rats, foxes, skunks, cougars, tapirs, white-lipped and collared peccaries, brocket deer, and white-tailed deer. In contrast, the Peruvian desert coast supports very few terrestrial mammals. These are primarily rabbits, mice, foxes, cougars, guanacos, and white-tailed deer.

Other terrestrial resources might be locally significant. Iguanas and *Dicrodon* lizards were more commonly used in Ecuador and on the north coast of Peru than farther south. Terrestrial tortoises have been found in two sites on the island of Trinidad. Although birds are not a common feature elsewhere in the New World, along the Pacific coast of South America many birds attracted by the marine upwellings are abundant in coastal sites. These include fulmars, shearwaters, penguins, boobies, pelicans, cormorants, and gulls. In Ecuador, more tropical birds such as tinamou, ducks, curassows, doves, and parrots were used.

A number of diverse habitats extend away from the coastal plain into the Andes. The upper valleys are separated from each other by altiplano grasslands and snow-capped peaks. Although the terrestrial fauna of the Andes is limited, some terrestrial mammals were extensively used. These included opossums, rabbits, guinea pigs, agoutis, viscachas, chinchillas, foxes, spectacled bears, kinkajous, skunks, otters, margays, cougars, guanacos, vicuñas, brocket deer, huemul deer, and white-tailed deer.

Other highland species are found in Andean sites. Iguanas have been identified occasionally. Birds from sites in the Andean highlands include tinamous, herons, ducks, vultures, hawks, pigeons, owls, and parrots, as well as birds more typical of the coast such as boobies, pelicans, cormorants, gulls, and terns. Aquatic fish and invertebrates are not common in the Andes, although some characins, catfish, and freshwater mussels have been identified.

In addition to dogs, several South American animals were domesticated. Chief among them were llamas and alpacas, members of the same family which includes the wild guanaco and vicuña. Although llamas and alpacas were originally domesticated in the Andean highlands,

they soon became common in coastal locations. Guinea pigs were also domesticated in the highlands and are found as domestic animals in sites on the Pacific coast and in the West Indies. Another South American domestic animal, the muscovy duck, has become widespread throughout the world.

[See also *Agriculture; Domesticated Animals; Flora.*]

BIBLIOGRAPHY

Chirichigno, Norma F. *Catálogo de especies marinas de interés económico actual o potencial para América Latina: Parte II, Pacífico Centro y Suroriental.* Rome, 1982.

Emmons, Louise. *Neotropical Rainforest Mammals: A Field Guide.* Chicago, 1990.

Fuson, Robert H., trans. *The Log of Christopher Columbus.* Camden, Maine, 1987.

Hoese, H. Dickson, and Richard H. Moore. *Fishes of the Gulf of Mexico.* College Station, Tex., 1977.

Landstrom, Bjorn. *Columbus.* New York, 1966.

Larson, Lewis H. *Aboriginal Subsistence Technology on the Southeastern Coastal Plain during the Late Prehistoric Period.* Gainesville, Fla., 1980.

Mares, Michael A., and Hugh H. Genoways, eds. *Mammalian Biology in South America.* Special Publication Series Pymatuning Laboratory of Ecology, vol. 6. Pittsburgh, 1982.

Meyer de Schauensee, Rodolphe. *A Guide to the Birds of South America.* Philadelphia, 1970.

Nowak, Ronald M., and John L. Paradiso. *Walker's Mammals of the World.* 4th ed. Baltimore, 1983.

Randall, John E. *Caribbean Reef Fishes.* Jersey City, N.J., 1968.

Wing, Elizabeth S., and Elizabeth J. Reitz. "Prehistoric Fishing Economies of the Caribbean." *Journal of New World Archaeology* 5 (1982): 13–33.

Woods, Charles A., ed. *Biogeography of the West Indies: Past, Present, and Future.* Gainesville, Fla., 1989.

ELIZABETH J. REITZ

FERDINAND. For discussion of Fernando of Aragón, see *Isabel and Fernando.*

FERNÁNDEZ DE CÓRDOBA, FRANCISCO (c. 1475–1526), Spanish explorer of Central America.

The date of Fernández de Córdoba's arrival in the New World is not known, but around 1520 he participated in several campaigns as a lieutenant of Pedro Arias de Ávila (Pedrárias), first governor of Castilla del Oro. Since the discovery of the Pacific Ocean by Balboa, Pedrárias had sought to find a sea passage between the two oceans. In 1524, upon receiving news that Gil González de Ávila was exploring the coast of Honduras, Pedrárias formed an expedition to Nicaragua under the command of Fernández de Córdoba. The goal was to explore the Pacific coast to the north of the Isthmus of Panama and take possession of that territory for Pedrárias, who had a claim to it based on an earlier expedition he had sent in 1516 under Hernando Ponce. Strictly following Pedrárias's instructions, Fernández marched inland and in 1524 he founded the town of Bruselas, near present-day Puntarenas, the first Spanish settlement in Costa Rica. He then discovered Lake Nicaragua, founded the city of Granada on its southwest shore, and began evangelizing the Indians. Continuing eastward, he founded the first city of León ("la Vieja"). Entering Honduras, he founded Segovia on the Yare River but then ran into the expedition of González de Ávila. In the ensuing clash, González skillfully overpowered Fernández.

A third party then intervened in the dispute: Cristóbal de Olid, sent from Mexico by Hernando Cortés (who was claiming the territory as part of New Spain). After landing in Honduras, Olid decided to break with Cortés, proclaiming himself governor. In a clash with González Olid managed to prevail. González was imprisoned together with Francisco de las Casas, who had been sent by sea to punish Olid, but who had been captured upon his arrival in Honduras. The two prisoners came to an agreement, broke free, executed Olid in January 1525, and then left for Mexico to inform Cortés. Fernández took advantage of their absence to proclaim himself governor of Nicaragua with the encouragement of Pedro Moreno, who had arrived from Santo Domingo to support González, but in González's absence decided to change sides. Fernández's own lieutenant, Juan Ponce de León, did not approve this independent move; he was arrested but managed to escape with the help of his fellow lieutenant Francisco de Campañón. Both returned to Panama to inform Pedrárias, who quickly arranged a naval expedition to punish Fernández. In a desperate move, Fernández then tried to get the support of Cortés, who had arrived in Honduras after the departure of González and Francisco de las Casas. Cortés seems to have been close to making an agreement with Fernández for a joint exploration of Nicaragua, but the deteriorating state of affairs in Mexico prompted Cortés's hasty departure from the area in April of 1526. Left alone, Fernández was not able to overcome Pedrárias, who had him executed in León, Nicaragua, in June of 1526.

BIBLIOGRAPHY

Alvarez Rubiano, Pedro. *Pedrárias Dávila*. Madrid, 1944.
Anderson, C. L. G. *Old Panama and Castilla del Oro*. Boston, 1946.
Gámez, José D. *Historia de Nicaragua*. Managua, 1889.

ANGEL DELGADO-GOMEZ

FERNÁNDEZ DE CÓRDOBA, GONZALO (1453–1515), Spanish army commander. Often known as the Great Captain—*el gran capitán*—Córdoba organized the disciplined, professional army that built the Spanish empire during the sixteenth and seventeenth centuries. Córdoba was a tactician and military organizer who quickly identified combinations of troops, tactics, weapons, equipment, and organizational units that would be most effective in the various military situations he faced. He waged brilliant campaigns in both Spain and Italy. In Spain, he directed the last phase (1482–1492) of the Reconquista, the conquest of the Muslim kingdom of Granada, depending upon mobile light cavalry; he ended the conflict with an experienced army of battle-tested veterans. In 1495 he went to Italy to support the Aragonese monarchy of Naples against the invading army of King Charles VIII of France, who also claimed the Neapolitan throne. There he relied on mobile infantry and firearms in two campaigns (1495–1497 and 1501–1504) that effectively expelled French forces from Italy. By 1504 the weak dynasty of Naples had collapsed, and Córdoba incorporated the kingdom into the growing Spanish realm. From 1504 to 1506 he governed Naples as viceroy of the king of Spain. Though he had no direct connections with Christopher Columbus or Spanish expansion overseas, his work contributed to the success of Spanish forces in America, for many of the early conquistadores acquired their military discipline and gained battlefield experience in Córdoba's armies in Spain or Italy.

BIBLIOGRAPHY

Elliott, J. H. *Imperial Spain, 1469–1716*. New York, 1963.
Parker, Geoffrey. *The Military Revolution: Military Innovation and the Rise of the West, 1500–1800*. Cambridge, 1988.

JERRY H. BENTLEY

FERNÁNDEZ DE OVIEDO, GONZALO. See *Oviedo, Gonzalo Fernández de*.

FERNANDO. For discussion of Fernando of Aragón, see *Isabel and Fernando*.

FIESCHI, BARTOLOMEO (c. 1470–c. 1530), captain on Columbus's fourth voyage. Bartolomeo Fieschi was a member of a noble Genoese family that belonged to the Fregoso party, the political party of which Columbus's father, Domenico Colombo, was also a member. The fortunes of Columbus's father were tied to this party; his moving from Genoa to Savona was occasioned by its final eclipse. His successes, especially the lucrative post as warden of the Olivella gate, came about because of the influence of the Fieschi family. It is therefore not surprising to find Bartolomeo Fieschi a companion of Columbus and a participant on the fourth voyage.

In 1503, while Columbus and his crew were marooned on Jamaica, Bartolomeo Fieschi and Diego Méndez made a daring canoe voyage from Jamaica to La Española to secure help. Their trip was later recorded in detail in Fernando Colón's biography of his father. After returning to Spain, Fieschi remained with Columbus, helping him draw up his will on May 19, 1506, at Valladolid, signing it as a witness, and helping on the occasion of his death the next day.

The historian Cesare de Lollis believes that Fieschi went home immediately after the Admiral's death, identifying him with the Bartolomeo Flisco who, according to Agostino Giustiniani, was an instigator of a popular uprising in Genoa in July 1506. The uprising resulted in Fieschi and his family going into exile and Louis XII of France sending troops to intervene. In 1525, having returned to Genoa, Bartolomeo Fieschi was elected captain of a fleet of fifteen Genoese ships that sailed to fight France. In 1527, he was declared *padre del comune* (city father).

BIBLIOGRAPHY

Morison, Samuel Eliot. *Admiral of the Ocean Sea: A Life of Christopher Columbus.* 2 vols. Boston, 1942.

Taviani, Paolo Emilio. *I viaggi di Colombo.* Vol. 2. 2d ed. Novara, 1990. Spanish ed., Barcelona, 1989.

PAOLO EMILIO TAVIANI

FILM. For discussion of Columbus as a figure in film and motion pictures, see *Iconography*, article on *Film*.

FIRST VOYAGE. See *Voyages of Columbus*.

FLORA. [This entry includes three articles on native American flora and on crop exchange between the Old World and the New:

An Overview
Psychotropic Flora
Tobacco

For related discussions, see also *Agriculture; Domesticated Animals; Fauna.*]

An Overview

When Christopher Columbus made landfall in 1492, he set in motion an exchange of plants between the Old and New Worlds, landmasses that had been separated since the breakup of Pangaea (the ancient supercontinent) nearly 200 million years before. Although in the years to follow useful plants would move both ways across the Atlantic and Pacific oceans, changes in the flora of the New World were the most profound. Alfred W. Crosby has pointed out that the long geographic isolation of the New World rendered its inhabitants, human, plant, and animal alike, vulnerable to Old World diseases and ill-adapted for competition. Humans fell victim to smallpox and other contagions; native vegetation succumbed to the pressures of grazing by cattle, pigs, and horses. Soon the New World began to resemble the Old, with European crops, herds, and weeds spreading into all hospitable environments.

What plants did Europeans bring to the New World? Which species did they carry back to Europe and across the Pacific? In both instances, economically useful plants, especially foods, formed the core of the exchange. These transplanted crops had significant impacts on the diet, health, and economic well-being of the inhabitants of both hemispheres. To understand this phenomenon, it is necessary to begin with the plants themselves.

Crops of the New World. The pre-Columbian flora of the New World was tremendously varied; so too were the manipulations of it by humans. The history of crop domestication in the New World is centered largely in the tropical latitudes. Jack Harlan has described two independent areas of domestication in the tropics, one in Mesoamerica (central Mexico and Guatemala) and another, larger area in South America. The major crops native to these regions include:

Grain: maize (corn)
Root crops: manioc (cassava), sweet potato, white potato
Pulses: common bean, lima bean, peanut, jack bean
Vegetables: squash, tomato, quinoa, amaranth
Fruits: avocado, pineapple, papaya, guava, passion fruit
Spices/stimulants: chile pepper, cacao, tobacco, coca
Utility: cotton

Plant domestication in South America probably occurred in many locations, with crops evolving both in the lowland zones (manioc, sweet potato, peanut) and the highland zones (white potato) of the continent. The earliest stages of plant domestication are difficult to document, but by 5000 B.C. fully evolved crops were present in both Mesoamerica and South America. Maize was domesticated in Mesoamerica, but spread early into South America. Species of beans, chile peppers, squashes, and cotton were domesticated independently in both areas. Recent research has also documented a temperate zone area of New World plant domestication, in eastern North America. By the time of contact, however, most of the indigenous crops of this region—small-seeded annuals like chenopod and sumpweed—had been replaced by maize.

Crops of the Old World. Four independent areas of crop domestication existed in the Old World: in the Near East (NE: eastern Mediterranean), Africa (A: tropical Africa), north China (C), and Southeast Asia and the South Pacific (SEA: eastern India, southern China, Southeast Asia, south Pacific). In addition, central Europe (E) was a secondary area where several local crops evolved from weeds growing in fields of introduced grains. The major crops of Old World origin include:

Grains: wheat, barley (NE); sorghum, finger millet, pearl millet (A); rice, broomcorn millet, foxtail millet (C); sugarcane, rice (SEA); oats, rye (E)

Root crops: beet, turnip, carrot, radish, onion (NE); yams (A); taro, yams (SEA)

Pulses: lentil, pea, chick-pea, broad bean (NE); cowpea (A); soybean (C); rice bean, mung bean (SEA)

Vegetables: lettuce, cabbage (NE); cucumber (C); eggplant (SEA)

Fruits: fig, olive, apple, grape, melon (NE); watermelon (A); peach (C); banana, plantain, mango, breadfruit, citrus fruits, plum (SEA)

Spices/stimulants: coffee (A); tea (C); clove, black pepper, nutmeg, turmeric (SEA)

Utility: flax (NE); cotton, gourd (A)

By the fifteenth century, many of these Old World crops had spread far from their areas of origin. Citrus fruits—lemons, limes, and oranges—were domesticated in Southeast Asia but were known in Europe by the thirteenth century; bananas and plantains were introduced into Africa early in the Christian era. Many crops domesticated in the Near East spread millennia earlier into Europe. Einkorn wheat, for example, spread to central and western Europe during the fifth millennium B.C., attaining a wide distribution during the Bronze and early Iron Ages. Olives were known to the Romans; figs to the ancient Greeks. The foods carried by the first Europeans traveling to the New World were thus a mixture of plants from many regions of the Old.

European Crops in the Americas. The history of European crops in the Americas begins with the second voyage of Columbus. As Crosby relates, Columbus, on his return to La Española, brought seeds and cuttings for wheat, chick-peas, melons, onions, radishes, salad greens, grape vines, sugarcane, and fruit trees, including the olive. Here, with the vegetable mainstays of Mediterranean cuisine, the newcomers set about re-creating the gardens and orchards of home.

The Caribbean is not the Mediterranean, however, and not all the new crops prospered. Wheat, barley, olives, and grapes would not grow, for example. Other orchard crops, such as figs, oranges, and lemons, did well, as did melons and some vegetables. Sugarcane, and a slightly later introduction, the banana, did very well in the hot climate of the Caribbean.

The success of the early introductions of European crops to the Caribbean depended on the temperature, rainfall, and day-length requirements of the individual species. Because he made his first landfall in the tropical latitudes of the New World, Columbus missed the region preferred by many of the European staples, especially grains—the temperate zone. But sugarcane, banana, and citrus, among other crops of the Old World tropics, prospered in the new setting.

Six examples will serve to illustrate how and where European crops adapted to the New World and the impact of the vagaries of plant geography on indigenous peoples and colonists alike. Wheat, grapes, and two legumes (peas, broad beans) illustrate the pattern for the temperate zone crops; sugarcane, bananas, and yams, for the tropical crops.

Wheat (*Triticum* spp.) is the most important cereal in the world today, followed closely by rice. It is essentially a temperate zone crop, but can be grown successfully at higher elevations in the tropics. In the mountains, one finds the cooler temperatures needed for wheat's successful growth and development. There are five species of cultivated wheats—common or bread wheat, spelt, durum, emmer, and einkorn. Their domestication and evolution under cultivation occurred initially in the Near East and continued as the species spread throughout the temperate regions of the Old World.

Attempts were made in the sixteenth century to grow wheat in the Caribbean and Spanish Florida, but these largely failed, owing to the combination of high summer temperatures and high humidity in this region. To grow wheat under such conditions requires cultivation during the drier, cooler season, with irrigation to provide the necessary moisture. This was not the cultivation practice in Europe.

As the Spanish exploration of the tropical New World progressed, however, higher elevation lands suitable for growing wheat were soon discovered. One of the first successful introductions of wheat was to the highlands of Mexico in 1529. Wheat was carried soon after into the Andes of South America, where it found a productive niche: the higher elevation zone favored by the potato. Peru became the wheat breadbasket for the Spanish New World, supplying wheat flour to the lower, wetter regions. The English settlers of North America had less trouble establishing this mainstay of diet; it was introduced successfully early in the seventeenth century and spread westward with the settlers.

The case of the domesticated grape *(Vitis vinifera)* is less the story of a crop finding its natural range in a strange land and more a story of adaptation. Grapes prefer regions with Mediterranean climates: hot, dry summers and cool, rainy winters. Grapes were carried on all the early voyages of discovery and were introduced into the eastern United States, Spanish Florida, Mexico, and South America. Mediterranean climates were eventually found in California and the southern Andes, but grapes were successful in other regions as well. This was in large part due to the hybridization of the cultivated grape with native, wild grapes. Such crosses resulted in vigorous offspring, better adapted to the local growing conditions. In eastern North America the concord grape developed; in the Caribbean, crosses with a local species produced grapes that were resistant to disease and tolerant of heat and moisture.

The pea *(Pisum sativum)* and the broad bean *(Vicia faba)* are two temperate latitude pulses introduced into the New World by Europeans. Peas were domesticated in the Near East and introduced early into the northern Mediterranean and Europe. They spread east to India and China and south into central Africa before the age of European exploration. Because peas require a cool, humid climate, they do poorly in the tropics except at higher elevations. Like wheat, however, they can be grown as a winter crop at lower elevations if sufficient moisture is present. Peas are one of the four most important seed legumes today and are an excellent source of vegetable protein.

The broad bean, or field bean, like the pea, is a very old Near Eastern domesticated plant. It was the only edible bean known in Europe before the discovery of the New World and the introduction of the American *Phaseolus* beans. It is a crop that does poorly in hot weather, even in the temperate zone, when it may flower but not produce fruit. It can be grown in the summer at higher elevations in the tropics or as a winter crop at the edges of the tropical zone.

In contrast to temperate zone crops like wheat, grapes, peas, and broad beans, for which only high-elevation terrain proved productive in Spanish and Portuguese America, Old World crops of tropical origin were preadapted to the extensive lowlands of the New World. With the exception of some fruits and spices, however, these African and Asian crops were not at the core of European cuisine. Why, then, did the Spanish and Portuguese introduce crops like sugarcane, bananas, and yams to the New World? The answer is twofold: for profit and to feed the African slaves introduced to replace the dying indigenous populations.

Sugarcane *(Saccharum officinarum)* was domesticated in the islands of Southeast Asia, where its stems, or canes, were chewed for their sweetness. The practice of extracting the juice and boiling it down to make sugar probably originated in India. Sugarcane had spread as far as Persia by the sixth century, where it was adopted by Arab peoples, who carried it to northern Africa and eventually to the northern Mediterranean and Spain. By the time of Columbus's voyages, sugar was a lucrative industry in the Iberian Peninsula and the recently conquered Canary Islands. Demand in Europe was high, but land suitable for cultivation limited.

Sugarcane requires hot weather, plenty of rain and

sunshine, a long frost-free period, and well-drained soil. It is a perennial crop that can be planted on the same land for many years. These characteristics combined to make sugarcane cultivation one of the most powerful forces for vegetation change in the tropical New World. Forests were clear-cut for cane fields that never went out of production; deforestation led to erosion, reduced rainfall, and more vegetation change. Soon after their discovery, the islands of the Caribbean were transformed into vast sugar mills. Sugarcane cultivation was introduced in the early sixteenth century into Mexico, Peru, and Brazil, with similar results.

As native peoples died from disease and hardship, African slaves were brought in to work the cane fields. Feeding these workers required staple crops that would produce abundantly in the lowland tropics. In their explorations of West Africa in the fifteenth century, the Portuguese encountered a variety of such crops, some of which they introduced into the Canary Islands. Among these was the banana, which was taken from the Canary Islands to La Española in 1516.

Bananas *(Musa* spp.) originated in Southeast Asia. They were introduced into Africa perhaps as early as the fifth century A.D. Ripe bananas are sweet and easily digested raw. Unripe fruits are starchy and must be cooked. In this

BANANAS. Sketch of an Old World plant made in the New World, circa 1590, by which time species of bananas had already become well-established in the Caribbean region. From *Histoire naturelle des Indes*, often called the Drake Manuscript; perhaps a sketch from Sir Francis Drake's own hand.

THE PIERPONT MORGAN LIBRARY, NEW YORK; M.3900, F.11v

form they are often called plantains, but there are also true plantains, strains that are starchy even when ripe. Plantains are high in carbohydrates (about 35 percent) and a good source of vitamins and minerals. They have been important staples in many parts of Africa for centuries, supplementing the native and Asian yams and the introduced New World tuber, manioc.

Yams (*Dioscorea* spp.) evolved independently as cultivated plants in the New World, African, and Southeast Asian tropics. Like the banana, the Asian, or greater yam, was introduced into Africa from the East during the first millennium A.D. and spread across the continent. Readily accepted by agriculturalists accustomed to the native yellow or Guinea yam, the greater yam became an important West African food. Yams were used for victualing of slave ships sailing from West Africa and were carried to both the Caribbean and Brazil soon after contact.

The African slaves who worked the sugarcane fields subsisted on a diet high in starches—a combination of New World crops, including the highly productive manioc, and introduced crops familiar to them, such as bananas and yams. As the temperate latitudes and higher elevation tropics began to mirror Europe, the lowland tropics were transformed by the plantation system and the blending of African, Asian, and indigenous crops.

American Crops in the Old World. In the years following the discovery of the New World, food plants from the Americas were carried back to Europe with the other fruits of conquest. First viewed as curiosities, some of these crops came to play major roles as food staples. Crosby suggests that the introduction of new food crops into sixteenth-century Europe resulted in an increase in the quantity and quality of food, which in turn contributed to population growth. Many New World crops found productive niches in the Old World, where they complemented native crops. Maize, for example, is a genetically plastic grain, able to adapt to many different growing conditions. From its hearth in Mesoamerica, it had spread prehistorically throughout the New World, from the Amazon basin to the Great Lakes region of North America. In the Old World, it was suitable for land too wet for wheat and too dry for rice, thriving in both the temperate and tropical latitudes.

Many New World plants had an impact on European, Near Eastern, African, and Asian cuisines and customs. Chili peppers spice up food around the world; chocolate (from cacao) transformed candy; the tomato is indispensable in Italian cooking; smoking tobacco is a common practice around the world. Food staples have had the greatest impact on health and nutrition, however. Maize, bean, manioc, and potato will serve as illustrations.

Maize, or corn *(Zea mays)*, is the most important cereal in the world after wheat and rice. In tropical regions, it is

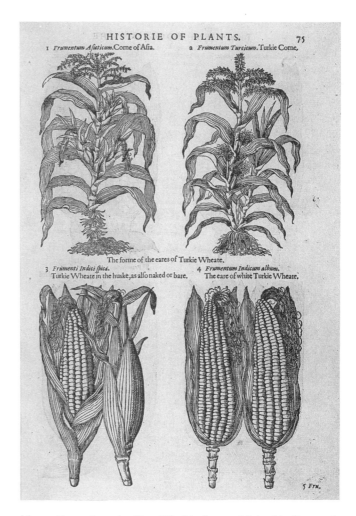

MAIZE. Engraving of a New World plant published in Europe in 1597, by which time maize had been established in temperate regions of the Old World. From J. Gerarde's *The Herball*.

LIBRARY OF CONGRESS

used primarily as a starchy staple for human consumption; in the temperate regions, its primary role is as livestock feed. European settlers throughout the New World survived on maize when their own crops failed.

The first European reference to maize was made by Columbus, who recorded its cultivation on Long Island in the Bahamas. He took seeds back to Spain, where the plant was described and grown as a garden curiosity. Sixteenth-century herbals illustrate two varieties, one similar to the flint corn of eastern North America, the other to Caribbean maize. The potential of maize was quickly recognized, however, and cultivation spread from Spain around the Mediterranean and into North Africa. Both Spanish and Portuguese explorers carried maize with them on their explorations of the tropics; it was introduced into West Africa in the early sixteenth century and was carried by Ferdinand Magellan around the world, becoming established first in the East Indies and the Philippines and then spreading to the Asian mainland. Maize was introduced into India either by sea by the Portuguese or overland from the Near East by Arab peoples.

Maize quickly became a dietary staple in the warm temperate regions of the Old World, where its cultivation rivaled that of the traditional Near Eastern grains. In the tropics—for example, in Africa—maize also replaced traditional grains, which here were sorghum and the millets, and during the height of the slave trade (seventeenth and eighteenth centuries), it became a major cash crop. Maize assumed these roles because it is high yielding and nutritious for the labor required and is compact and easily stored or transported. In Asia, rice remained the preferred grain, but maize found a role, replacing lower-yielding native millets on terrain too dry for rice.

The major New World bean species, the common bean (Phaseolus vulgaris) and the lima bean (Phaseolus lunatus), are among the most important sources of vegetable protein in the world today. Domesticated independently in Mesoamerica and South America, beans were grown throughout the temperate and tropical regions of the New World. The common bean was introduced into Europe in the sixteenth century and carried around the world by Spanish and Portuguese explorers. A genetically plastic crop, the common bean thrived throughout the temperate zones of the Old World and in areas of medium rainfall in the tropics. It was cultivated widely in Europe by the seventeenth century and became an important source of vegetable protein there.

Lima beans were introduced into the Philippines and Asian mainland by Spanish explorers. They were also introduced into Africa, along with the common bean, where they became the major pulse crop in wetter regions. Lima beans tolerate higher rainfall than the common bean. They fulfilled an important dietary function in wet tropical Africa, providing protein to complement the high-starch diet of grains, root crops, and plantains. The native African pulse, the cowpea, is primarily a crop of the drier, savanna habitat. Neither of the New World beans became very important in tropical Asia, where two native Phaseolus species, mung bean and rice bean, were already established.

Two root crops, manioc and potato, round out the picture of the role American crops played in Old World agriculture. The story of manioc is primarily African, the potato European.

Manioc, or cassava (Manioc esculenta), originated in the low-elevation tropics of South America. It was the primary carbohydrate source of the tropical-forest agricultural system. Manioc is a highly productive crop that can tolerate prolonged drought and soils of marginal fertility. It is often grown as the last rotation under shifting cultivation, after soil is too depleted to grow maize. Some strains, referred to as bitter manioc, have high levels of hydrocyanic acid (HCN), which must be destroyed by cooking or fermentation. The toxin serves to protect the plant from animal and insect predation.

These characteristics—high yield, ability to tolerate drought and low soil fertility, and natural pest protection—make manioc an attractive choice in tropical regions with uncertain rainfall and depleted soils. Manioc was introduced into Africa and elsewhere in the tropics by the Portuguese late in the sixteenth century. It had a relatively limited distribution and use from then through the eighteenth century, however, becoming widespread only in the mid-nineteenth century and after. African agriculturalists preferred the yam. Manioc production increased dramatically only after its cultivation was encouraged as protection against famine and locust attacks. It performed well, but with manioc now dominating agriculture in some regions of Africa, protein deficiency and HCN toxicity have become serious problems.

The white potato (Solanum tuberosum) has also been a mixed blessing to Old World agriculture. Overdependence on the potato led to the death of a million people in nineteenth-century Ireland when blight destroyed the crop; nevertheless, today potatoes rank fourth in world food production, behind wheat, rice, and maize.

Originating in the central Andes of South America, in the Lake Titicaca region, the potato spread south into Chile and north into Ecuador and Colombia before European contact. The Andean potato was a crop of short days and cool growing conditions. Its spread to the north was checked by the heat of the Central American lowlands. It was only after contact that potato cultivation spread to Mesoamerica and North America. In the latter case, the potato arrived in the seventeenth century by way of Europe, after strains adapted to long daylight conditions had been developed.

The potato was introduced into Europe twice, first from Colombia to Spain in about 1570 and then to England sometime around 1590 with goods seized from Spanish treasure ships. The potato was illustrated in herbals of the period and by late in the sixteenth century was grown in Spain, Italy, and southern France, where it was suitable as a winter (short-day) crop. By the seventeenth century the potato had been introduced into Ireland, but it was not until the late eighteenth or early nineteenth century that potato cultivation spread throughout Europe, where it became a mainstay of peasant agriculture.

With maize and the potato among the top four food crops of the world, it is clear that the New World has contributed crops vital to the life and health of people around the globe. Plants domesticated by native Americans are grown today both under mechanized production and on small peasant farms, expanding the land that can be cultivated and providing essential components of the human diet. The crops of the New World were among its greatest gifts to the Old.

BIBLIOGRAPHY

Burton, W. G. *The Potato: A Survey of Its History and of Factors Influencing Its Yield, Nutritive Value, Quality, and Storage.* Wageningen, Holland, 1966.

Chadha, Y. R., ed. *Maize in India.* New Delhi, India, 1977.

Crosby, Alfred W. *The Columbian Exchange.* Westport, Conn., 1972.

Crosby, Alfred W. *Ecological Imperialism.* Cambridge, 1986.

Finan, John J. *Maize in the Great Herbals.* Waltham, Mass., 1950.

Harlan, Jack. *Crops and Man.* Madison, Wisc., 1975.

Hawkes, J. G. *The Potato: Evolution, Biodiversity, and Genetic Resources.* Washington, D.C., 1990.

McAlister, Lyle N. *Spain and Portugal in the New World, 1492–1700.* Minneapolis, Minn., 1984.

Purseglove, J. W. *Tropical Crops: Dicotyledons.* New York, 1974.

Purseglove, J. W. *Tropical Crops: Monocotyledons.* 2 vols. London, 1972.

Root and Tuber Crops, Plantains and Bananas in Developing Countries: Challenges and Opportunities. Food and Agriculture Organization of the United Nations (FAO). Plant Production and Protection Paper, no. 87. Rome, 1988.

Simmonds, N. W., ed. *Evolution of Crop Plants.* London, 1976.

Deborah M. Pearsall

Psychotropic Flora

Soon after Columbus and his men set foot on land in what came to be called the West Indies, they were confronted by a phenomenon that, like everything else the native inhabitants believed and practiced, was unfamiliar and shocking to them: to contact their gods the Taínos intoxicated themselves with a potent snuff. Commissioned by Columbus on his second voyage in 1496 to record Taíno ceremonies and "antiquities," Ramón Pané described rites in which the natives inhaled cohoba, an intoxicating herb that was "so strong that those who take it lose consciousness," believing themselves to be in communication with the supernatural, while "sorcerers" customarily inhaled the drug together with their patients so as to learn the cause and proper treatment of the affliction.

Since then, ethnobotanists have identified more than a hundred ritual plant hallucinogens, not counting tobacco, which the Spaniards identified with cohoba. Because the custom soon died out in the West Indies, along with

Ceremonial snuff holder. From the West Indies.

virtually the entire native population, the identification of cohoba as tobacco was accepted until 1916, when an influential American botanist, William A. Safford, insisted that cohoba could not have been tobacco but was the same as *yopo,* the hallucinogenic snuff Indians in Colombia and elsewhere in northern South America derive from the seeds of a leguminous tree, *Anadenanthera peregrina.* Recent research, however, suggests that the Spaniards may well have been right, and that the West Indian cohoba may indeed have been pulverized tobacco of the potent species *Nicotiana rustica.*

The genus *Anadenanthera* also has a highland species, *A. colubrina,* from whose seeds Andean Indians prepared a snuff called *willka. Willka* was used not only in Peru: from bone-dry burials in the Atacama Desert of northern Chile, archaeologists and looters have recovered *willka* powder as well as hundreds of beautifully carved hardwood snuff tablets dating to around A.D. 800.

Snuffs were derived from the *Virola* tree in addition to the two species of *Anadenanthera*. On the Upper Orinoco, some Yamomami Indians and their neighbors prepare a vision-inducing powder from the dried shavings of the inner bark. This is mixed with the powdered leaves of an acanthaceous weed, *Justicia pectoralis,* and the ash of the bark of a leguminous tree, *Elizabetha princeps.* The former, a powerful hallucinogen, is also cultivated and used by itself.

In western Amazonia, Indians brew a powerful hallucinogenic beverage from *Banisteriopsis caapi* and related species, often with the addition of other plants that also contain psychoactive compounds. The drink has many names—Quechua-speakers call it *ayahuasca,* "vine of souls," a name adopted by some non-Quechua peoples east of the Andes. Others call it *caapi, mihi, dapa, pinde,* or *natéma.* The most common admixture is an extract of *Brugmansia,* a tree *Daturas* with showy trumpet-shaped flowers. *Brugmansia* is also used by itself. Shrub *Daturas,* including *D. stramonium,* the so-called jimsonweed of the eastern United States, and *D. inoxia,* the *toloáche* of Mexico and California (from the Aztec *toloátzin*), were employed in divination and curing by Mexican Indians, and in initiations and vision seeking by Indians in California, just as Virginia Indians used *D. stramonium. D. inoxia* is sacred and retains a divinatory use even today among the Pueblo Indians. *Datura* use is not without a certain danger, however. Of all the ritual plant hallucinogens now employed by American Indians, only the solanaceous *Daturas* are so toxic as to pose physiological risk. On the other hand, none is addictive.

Another ritual hallucinogen, of importance in the southern plains at the time of Spanish exploration and, on the archaeological evidence, for more than ten thousand years before, was *Sophora secundiflora.* The red and black seeds were widely employed in the initiation rites of ecstatic-shamanistic medicine societies. Caches of the beans have been found in Texas rock shelters in association with the remains of a long extinct giant bison and projectile points dating between 8400 and 8120 B.C., making *Sophora* the oldest continuously used hallucinogen in the New World. The mescal bean cults died out only in the late nineteenth century A.D.

First mentioned by sixteenth-century Spanish chroniclers among the divine intoxicants of the Aztecs, the little peyote cactus, *Lophophora williamsii,* remains at the core of the indigenous religion of the Huichols of the Sierra Madre Occidental. But it has also achieved a unique role north of Mexico, as a sacrament of a pan-Indian religion, the Native American Church, which has some 250,000 adherents from the Río Grande to the Canadian plains.

Peyote is a veritable factory of alkaloids. More than thirty have been identified, but the one chiefly responsible for the color-saturated visions it induces is mescaline. This is also the principal hallucinogenic alkaloid in San Pedro, *Trichocereus pachanoi,* a tall columnar cactus with a very long history in Andean ritual. First depicted on Peruvian pottery and textiles dating to 1000 B.C., San Pedro continues to play an important role in the curing rituals of Andean folk medicine.

The Spanish colonial authorities tried in vain to stop Mexican Indians from using peyote. But they had no more success with the little cactus than with *ololiuhqui,* as the Aztecs called the revered seeds of the white-flowered morning glory *Turbina corymbosa.* What brought on the extraordinary effects described by the Indians was a matter of controversy until the 1960s, when the Swiss chemist Albert Hofmann identified the hallucinogenic compounds as lysergic acid derivatives, closely related to the synthetic LSD-25 he and an associate had discovered in 1938. *Ololiuhqui* is still used by some Mexican Indians today, as are the seeds of the purple morning glory *Ipomoca violacea.*

Nor were the Spaniards able to stamp out the sacred mushrooms the Aztecs called *teonanácatl,* "divine flesh." At the time of the Conquest, at least half a dozen species seem to have been in ritual use in Mexico, but many more, previously unknown, species have been identified in recent years in Mexico and elsewhere, all of the genus *Psilocybe* and related genera. Several indigenous peoples continue to employ them for divination and curing. In any event, stone sculptures of mushrooms dating to the first millennium B.C. in highland Guatemala and pre-Columbian mushroom effigies of cast gold found in Colombia confirm that veneration of mushrooms was already ancient in the New World when the Spaniards first encountered it nearly five centuries ago and that it was far more widespread than formerly assumed.

BIBLIOGRAPHY

Furst, Peter T. *Hallucinogens and Culture.* San Francisco, 1986.
Schultes, Richard Evans, and Albert Hofmann. *Plants of the Gods.* New York, 1979.

PETER T. FURST

Tobacco

Although the genus *Nicotiana* occurs naturally not only in the Americas but also in parts of Africa, Oceania, and Australia, nowhere but in the New World were any of its more than sixty species cultivated or used for tobacco. Moreover, the largest concentration—almost 60 percent—is in South America. And it is from the South American continent that the genus is believed to have dispersed naturally millions of years before two of Columbus's men, Luis de Torres and Rodrigo de Jerez, became, according to the Admiral's journal entry of November 6, 1492, the first Europeans to see Indians smoke cigars made of the herb called *tabaco* in the Arawakan language.

It was not long before Europeans took up this curious custom and promptly became addicted. "I have known Spaniards in this isle of Hispaniola who were wont to take them," wrote Bartolomé de las Casas of the Indian cigars in his *Apologética historia de las Indias* (c. 1527), "and being reproved for it and told that it was a vicious habit, they replied that it was not in their power to stop taking them." Because Las Casas's work and Columbus's journal were not published until considerably later, the first printed description of tobacco smoking appeared in Gonzalo Fernández de Oviedo's *Historia general y natural de las Indias, islas y tierra-firme del mar océano,* dated 1535. The first books, however, to depict native American tobacco ritual were not European but the Mixtec *Codex Vindobonensis,* or *Codex Vienna,* and a handful of other pre-Hispanic pictorial manuscripts that survived the conquest of Mexico.

Johannes Wilbert, in *Tobacco and Shamanism in South America,* a book on tobacco as a ritual intoxicant of South American shamans and the biochemistry of nicotine intoxication, comments that "man's historic interest in *Nicotiana* has been exclusively because of the nicotine alkaloid it contains." Not all *Nicotianas* synthesize nicotine; some contain it in large amounts, others in small, and some none at all. Hence, writes Wilbert, Indian peoples selected only a dozen or so for tobacco cultivation, of which two, *Nicotiana rustica* and *Nicotiana tabacum,* became widely disseminated throughout the Americas. The former, with a nicotine content as high as 18.76 percent, many times that of Virginia blends, achieved almost the same wide distribution as maize—from the southern limits of agriculture in Chile to Canada. *N. tabacum,* which contains up to half as much nicotine as *N. rustica,* never made it beyond the tropics in pre-Columbian times. Botanically, the *Nicotianas* belong—along with such food plants as the pepper, eggplant, tomato, and potato, and such psychoactive and medicinal species as *Datura,* mandrake, deadly nightshade, and *Atropa belladonna,* and such garden flowers as the petunia—in the family of the Solanaceae (ironically, petunia derives from *petún,* the name the Tupían-speaking Indians of Brazil apply to tobacco).

The designation *Nicotiana rustica* notwithstanding (*rustica* is Latin for "wild"), both it and *N. tabacum* are cultigens, and both are hybrids whose parent species may have been the earliest plants to be cultivated by South American Indians, earlier even than the beginnings of agriculture some eight thousand years ago. *N. rustica* is almost certainly the older as well as the hardier and more potent; its center of origin is thought to be north-central Peru. *N. tabacum* may have begun on the eastern slopes of the Bolivian Andes, from where it diffused into Amazonia, the Guianas, and ultimately the West Indies, possibly, but not certainly, as late as the early sixteenth century. *N. tabacum* also became the basis of the commercial blends, *N. rustica* having been found to be too potent for general consumption. In any event, if, as Columbus's men thought, the potent snuff with which they saw the native people of the West Indies intoxicate themselves in visionary rituals was tobacco, it would have had to be the nicotine-richer *N. rustica,* the species of choice in South American tobacco shamanism as well as the *piciétl* of the Aztecs and the "Indian tobacco" of eastern North America.

South American Indians ingest tobacco in many more ways than inhaling its smoke or taking it in powder form. Wilbert lists the following: snuffing, smoking, drinking, chewing, licking, sucking, sniffing, and eating. Tobacco is made into poultices, pastes, jellies, juice, and enemas. It is absorbed through the mucous membranes, skin, intestines, eyes, nose, and ears. It is given to the gods and spirits as their sacramental, indeed, their only proper food, blown in the shaman's spit or as therapeutic smoke on his patients, pressed on wounds and stings and foodstuffs as a magical as well as practical disinfectant, burned for divination, and used externally against insects and internally against worms and intestinal parasites. It is taken to enhance vitality, reduce pain, induce vomiting for physical and ritual purification, relieve hunger and thirst, conjure the spirits, exorcise demons, and cure disease. Above all, it is smoked or otherwise ingested by shamans in enormous quantities to trigger the ecstatic-visionary trance state that is everywhere the hallmark of shamanism and that other practitioners of the shamanic arts attain with the hallucinogenic flora or by nonchemical means.

As Wilbert notes, the action of nicotine absorbed into the system in such prodigious quantities is deeply implicated in almost every characteristic of South American shamanism, from the experience of initiatory sickness, death, and resurrection, and other ordeals of the shaman's novitiate to various bodily transformations, such as the shaman's special guttural and dark-timbered speaking and singing voice, the experience of "magical heat," distinctive sight and improved night vision, and combative behavior.

Generally speaking, tobacco did not become a recreational drug until it was adopted by Europeans and rapidly diffused throughout the Old World. Ironically, only after it had circled almost the entire globe and arrived among tribal Siberians did it once again attain some of the magico-religious status and the connection with shamanism it had enjoyed and, at least in the case of *N. rustica,* still enjoys, among Native Americans.

BIBLIOGRAPHY

Furst, Jill L. *Codex Vindobonensis Mexicanus I: A Commentary.* Albany, N.Y., 1977.

Las Casas, Bartolomé de. "Apológetica historia de las Indias." In *Nueva Bibliotéca de Autores Españoles,* edited by M. Serrano y Sanz. Madrid, 1909.

Oviedo y Valdés, Gonzalo Fernández de. *Historia general y natural de las Indias, islas y terra-firme del mar océano.* Asuncíon del Paraguay, 1944.

Wilbert, Johannes. "Tobacco and Shamanistic Ecstasy among the Warao Indians of Venezuela." In *Flesh of the Gods: The Ritual Use of Hallucinogens.* Edited by Peter T. Furst. New York, 1972. Revised edition, Prospect Heights, Ill., 1990.

Wilbert, Johannes. *Tobacco and Shamanism in South America.* New Haven, Conn., 1987.

PETER T. FURST

FLORENCE. When Columbus was born in 1451, Florence was one of the premier cities in Italy and, indeed, in Europe. Its urban population of some fifty thousand placed it among the five largest cities in Italy; it governed a territory of forty-five hundred square miles. Florence had a republican government, though its polity was gradually drifting under the control of the Medici family in the later fifteenth century. As one of the five most powerful states on the Italian peninsula, it had been involved in a long series of debilitating wars, which finally ended in 1454 with the Peace of Lodi. Thereafter, the city enjoyed a forty-year period of peace, broken only sporadically by minor conflicts.

Florence's power and reputation were based upon its productive and diverse economy, which for centuries had played an important role in European and Levantine commerce. The city had developed a thriving cloth industry, specializing in the production of fine woolens and silks. Its merchants were active in every major port in the Mediterranean and in European markets from London to Budapest. In the fifteenth century, Florentine galley fleets regularly sailed to England, the Low Countries, and the Levant. The most prosperous segment of the city's economy was banking, which involved particularly the papal finances. The wealth of the Medici and that of other leading families (Strozzi, Pazzi, Bardi, Salviati, Altoviti) came largely from the profits gained from the papal fisc.

In 1300, Pope Boniface VIII had called the Florentines the "fifth element" in the universe, referring to their economic power and their ubiquitous mercantile presence throughout Christendom. Two centuries later, the city was still known for its entrepreneurial activities, but even more for its cultural achievements. In the early 1400s,

Florence was the laboratory for the creation of a new Renaissance culture based upon the revival of classical antiquity. Later in the century, when Lorenzo de' Medici was Florence's leading citizen, the city became (in Eugenio Garin's words) "the cultural capital of the world." It counted among its artists such luminaries as Andrea del Verrocchio, Filippo Lippi, Leonardo da Vinci, and Michelangelo, and among its scholars Marsilio Ficino, Angelo Poliziano, Christoforo Landino, and Paolo del Pozzo Toscanelli. On June 25, 1474, Toscanelli, a distinguished scientist, wrote a letter to a Portuguese cleric, Fernam Martins, in which he suggested the possibility of reaching the Orient by sailing westward. A copy of this document survives in Columbus's handwriting; it was a key piece of evidence used by the Genoese explorer to justify his Atlantic voyage.

After Lorenzo de' Medici's death in 1492, Florence's fortunes declined. The city was occupied in 1494 by the French army of King Charles VIII, and for the next four decades it experienced almost continuous warfare, political upheavals, and economic disruption, culminating in its siege and occupation by imperial forces in 1530. Florence's republican government was replaced by a Medici principate under Duke Cosimo I (r. 1537–1574). In these troubled years, many Florentines chose to pursue their fortunes abroad. Two of the city's most illustrious exiles were Amerigo Vespucci (1454–1512) and Giovanni da Verrazano (1480?–1527?), who participated in early voyages to the Americas.

BIBLIOGRAPHY

Brucker, Gene. *Renaissance Florence.* Berkeley and Los Angeles, 1983.

Butters, Humfrey. *Governors and Government in Early Sixteenth-Century Florence.* Oxford, 1985.

Garin, Eugenio. *Portraits from the Quattrocento.* New York, 1972.

Hale, John R. *Florence and the Medici: The Pattern of Control.* London, 1977.

Weinstein, Donald. *Savonarola and Florence.* Princeton, N.J., 1970.

GENE A. BRUCKER

FLORIDA, LA. For discussion of the Indians of La Florida, see *Indian America,* article on *Indians of La Florida.*

FONSECA, ALFONSO DE (1418–1473), archbishop of Santiago and Toledo. A descendant of a noble and influential Galician family, Alfonso (or Alonso) de Fonseca began his ecclesiastical career as archdeacon of the cathedral of Santiago de Compostela, a see that, by the late fifteenth century, had almost become the private fief of the Fonseca family. Fonseca rose to prominence as chaplain to the Infante Enrique, heir to the Castilian throne, being named bishop of Ávila in 1445 and archbishop of the wealthy see of Seville in 1453. In 1460 his nephew, also named Alfonso de Fonseca, the archbishop of Santiago de Compostela, faced popular unrest and opposition in his diocese. Uncle and nephew exchanged ecclesiastical dignities, supposedly because the elder Fonseca had the energy and connections to deal more successfully with the problems. Once the disturbances were quelled, however, the younger Alfonso refused to vacate the see of Seville, and his uncle had to seek legal recourse from the pope to recover his position in Seville. This he finally did in 1463.

Active in Castilian politics during the reigns of Juan II and of Enrique IV, Fonseca often found himself opposing the royal favorite, the enigmatic Álvaro de Luna, during the turbulent years of the early and mid-fifteenth century. After Enrique IV's ascent to the throne in 1454, Fonseca served him well during the first years of his reign, but the archbishop joined the rebellious magnates in their antiroyal league (the League of Burgos) in 1464. That same year, Fonseca played an important role in the "farce of Ávila," the ritual and theatrical dethroning and humbling of Enrique IV's effigy. Nevertheless, although opposed to the king, Fonseca worked for the reconciliation of the king and his half-brother, the Infante Alfonso, the magnates' candidate. At the death of the latter, the archbishop of Seville returned to Enrique's allegiance. It was in this later role as the king's adviser that Fonseca was instrumental in the drawing up of the Pact of the Toros de Guisando, the agreement that served as the legal basis for Isabel's claim to the Castilian throne upon Enrique IV's death in 1474.

BIBLIOGRAPHY

Fernández, Luis Suárez. Nobleza y monarquía: Puntos de vista sobre la historia castellana del siglo XV. Valladolid, 1975.

Mariéjol, J. H. The Spain of Ferdinand and Isabella. Translated and edited by Benjamin Keen. New Brunswick, N.J., 1961.

MacKay, Angus. "Ritual and Propaganda in Fifteenth-Century Castile." Past and Present 107 (1985): 3–43.

TEOFILO F. RUIZ

FONSECA, ANTONIO DE   (d. 1533), financial adviser to the Spanish Crown. The brothers Antonio de Fonseca and Juan Rodríguez de Fonseca dominated the administrative and accounting affairs of the Indies between the years 1493, when Juan was in charge of provisioning and outfitting Columbus's second voyage, and 1533, when Antonio died. Antonio, the older, was lord of the towns of Coca and Alaejos in the north of Castile. A close ally of

King Fernando, he negotiated the marriage contract between Princess Juana and Philip of Burgundy in 1495 and became chief auditor (contador mayor) of Castile in 1503. As auditor of the Castilian royal revenues from the royal patrimony and the Indies, Antonio influenced the policies of the new king, Juana's son Charles. Together, the Fonseca brothers enjoyed a considerable income from the Americas in the form of monopolies and encomienda revenues. When Charles needed cash to secure election as Holy Roman Emperor, Antonio advanced him large sums (some speculate as much as 16,000 ducats), drawn against future revenues from the Americas. The Fonseca brothers opposed efforts to reform Spanish administration of American Indians, which would have reduced their own income. In May 1520 Charles left the government of Castile under the administration of a royal council that included both Antonio, as captain general of the Kingdom of Castile, and Juan. Antonio's military and political blunders during the Comunero Revolt, the tax rebellion that swept over Castile in 1520–1521, weakened the influence of the Fonseca brothers over American affairs, although Antonio became grand commander (comendador mayor) of the Order of Santiago in 1526.

BIBLIOGRAPHY

Giménez Fernández, Manuel. Bartolomé de las Casas. Vol. 2, Capellán de s.m. Carlos I, poblador de Cumaná (1517–1523). Seville, 1960.

Haliczer, Stephen. The Comuneros of Castile: The Forging of a Revolution, 1475–1521. Madison, Wis., 1981.

Lovett, A. W. Early Habsburg Spain, 1517–1598. Oxford, 1986.

HELEN NADER

FONSECA, JUAN RODRÍGUEZ DE (1451–1523), prelate and adviser to the Spanish court. Fonseca was born in the city of Toro, son of the lord of the towns of Coca and Alaejos and his second wife. His family intended him for a career in the church and was sufficiently close to the monarchy to place him at the seat of power from the beginning of his education as a priest and apprenticeship for a prelacy. They sent him to the royal court, where he became a member of the household of Queen Isabel's confessor, Hernando de Talavera. He received several benefices that gave him a comfortable income and in 1492 formed part of the team that negotiated Aragón's annexation of Rosellón and La Cerdagne from France. Juan accompanied Fernando and Isabel to Barcelona, where he was ordained as a subdeacon on March 2, 1493, and as a priest on April 6.

Fonseca was present when Columbus arrived at the royal court to report on his first voyage to America, and on May 20 the monarchs appointed Fonseca to create a fleet in Seville for Columbus's second voyage. Certainly he succeeded—the fleet counted seventeen ships and twelve hundred men—but Columbus had preferred a smaller fleet that could leave right away. The two men were locked in conflict from then on, because the monarchs entrusted Fonseca with responsibility for supervising the European side of Spain's transatlantic trade.

In April 1495, Fonseca established regulations and procedures for trade with the Americas. These included government contracts with joint stock companies to systematically explore the South American coast (these expeditions are called the Andalusian voyages), restriction of the Americas trade to ports where royal customs officials could inspect the cargoes, posting of royal customs officials to the Americas to inspect the loading and unloading of cargoes there, and issuance of government clearances for individuals to travel to the Americas.

The Americas trade grew so much that on January 1, 1503, the monarchs established a branch of the royal treasury, the House of Trade (Casa de la Contratación), in Seville to house the customs, mint, navigation, licensing, and judicial offices. Fonseca probably recommended the regulations that went into effect on that date, as well as the expanded and revised regulations for the House of Trade that were issued on June 13, 1510, and March 18, 1511. Fonseca shaped policy for all the Americas trade until his death in 1523. The next year, Charles V created a royal council, the Consejo de Indias, to replace the position Fonseca had held.

Although the Americas had been Fonseca's principal responsibility, he had also carried out many diplomatic assignments for the monarchs and advanced his career in the church. He escorted members of the royal family to and from the Netherlands and England in 1499, 1500, and 1501; acted as witness of Queen Isabel's will in 1504 and carried the news of her death to the Netherlands; attended King Fernando on his deathbed in 1516; and welcomed the new king Charles in Aguilar in 1517. In 1518, he organized the fleet for Ferdinand Magellan's expedition to circumnavigate the world, and the next year he organized the fleet that transported the royal court to Germany for Charles's coronation.

BIBLIOGRAPHY

Alcocer y Martínez, Mariano. *Juan Rodríguez de Fonseca*. Valladolid, 1926.

Giménez Fernández, Manuel. *Bartolomé de las Casas*. 2 vols. Seville, 1953–1960.

"Ordinances for the Casa de la Contratación, 1503." In *The Conquerors and the Conquered*. Vol. 1 of *New Iberian World: A Documentary History of the Discovery and Settlement of Latin America to the Early 17th Century*. Edited by John H. Parry and Robert G. Keith. 5 vols. New York, 1984.

HELEN NADER

FONTANAROSSA, SUSANNA (c. 1425–c. 1480), mother of Christopher Columbus. Daughter of Jacobi de Fontanarubea (Giacomo Fontanarossa), Susanna Fontanarossa was born to an affluent Catholic family. The name Susanna was very common in the Catholic families of Liguria, owing, in part, to the fact that in the middle of the fifteenth century a Genoese pope had restored the church of Santa Susanna in the center of Rome.

Her family owned substantial real estate in Quezzi, a little village in the low-lying valley of Bisagno (part of the present-day city of Genoa). In the fifteenth century, it was necessary to go through the Olivella gate, where Christopher Columbus's father was custodian for two terms, in order to travel from the valley of Bisagno to Genoa.

Susanna Fontanarossa brought to her marriage to Domenico Colombo a dowry of a house with land. This property was soon sold; a record of the sale, dated May 25, 1471, is in the State Archives in Genoa. (Columbus's mother is also mentioned in two other documents, dated August 7, 1473, and January 23, 1477, which are found in the State Archives in Savona.)

The marriage between Susanna Fontanarossa and Domenico Colombo was apparently harmonious. The names of five children are known: Christopher (Cristoforo), Giovanni Pelegrino, Bartolomé (Bartolomeo), Diego (Giacomo), and Bianchinetta. It is likely that she bore other children, for, at this time, child mortality exceeded 50 percent. The exact date of her death is unknown, but it is probable that she died around 1480.

BIBLIOGRAPHY

"Albero genealogico della famiglia Colombo." In part 2, vol. 1 of *Raccolta di documenti e studi pubblicati dalla R. Commissione Colombiana pel quarto centenario dalla scoperta dell'America*. Rome, 1896.

Genoa, City of. *Christopher Columbus: Documents and Proofs of His Genoese Origin*. English-German ed. Bergamo, 1932.

Taviani, Paolo Emilio. *Cristoforo Colombo: Genius of the Sea*. Rome, 1990.

PAOLO EMILIO TAVIANI

FOOD. See *Equipment, Clothing, and Rations*.

FOURTH VOYAGE. See *Voyages of Columbus*.

FRANCE. In the Age of Exploration, France was a monarchy ruled by the Valois dynasty. Except for Charles VIII (r. 1483–1498), whose strong-willed sister Anne of Beaujeu governed during his first years, the kings of this era—Charles VII (r. 1422–1461), Louis XI (r. 1461–1483), Louis XII (r. 1498–1515), Francis I (r. 1515–1547), and

Henry II (r. 1547–1559)—came to the throne as adults and provided France with generally strong rule. The kingdom they governed was the most populous and largest in western Europe. It had a population of perhaps as many as 14 million people in 1500, and the number was rapidly increasing. Containing much of the best agricultural land in Europe, France exported considerable grain and, of course, wine. French was the language of most of the people; but in Brittany, Gascony, and the Midi, local dialects were in use, and the rural folk probably understood only a few phrases of French.

France had begun to expand beyond its long-term medieval borders but still was about 20 percent smaller than the modern republic. Provence and Dauphiné had recently been incorporated into the realm, but many regions of modern France—Calais, Flanders, Artois, Lorraine, Alsace, the Franche-Comté, Savoy, Roussillon, and northern Navarre—remained outside of it. All were the objects of much diplomatic and military activity.

Before France could expand its borders farther, the monarchy had to gain greater control over the feudal magnates. Louis XI did much in that respect by crushing the League of the Common Weal in 1465. His skillful intrigue and diplomacy led to the death of Charles the Bold of Burgundy at the hands of the Swiss at the Battle of Nancy in 1477. Louis seized control of the duchy of Burgundy, but he was not able to pressure Charles's heiress, Mary of Burgundy, into marrying his son. Instead she married Maximilian of Habsburg and passed most of Charles's lands, including Flanders and the Franche-Comté, to the House of Austria. When Charles VIII married Anne of Brittany in 1491, the last autonomous principality of medieval France passed under royal control.

The Hundred Years' War had come to an end in 1453, but continued English control of Calais and its claim to the French throne resulted in numerous episodes of war until 1559. Nonetheless, by 1494 Charles VIII was secure enough to lead an army of thirty thousand men and the best artillery train yet seen in the first French invasion of Italy. His goal was to make good a two-hundred-year-old French claim to the Kingdom of Naples. Brushing aside ineffective Italian resistance, Charles marched to Naples and proclaimed himself king. It was a member of the House of Aragón whom Charles ousted, however, and Fernando of Aragón organized an anti-French league against Charles. Although Charles quickly returned to France, the army he left behind to occupy Naples remained there until 1503, when a Spanish force crushed it in the Battle of Cerignola.

The second French invasion, led by Louis XII in 1499, and the third invasion, led by Francis I in 1515, centered on Milan. When Francis claimed the title of duke of Milan

FRANCIS I. Portrait by Jean Clouet.

after his victory at Marignano (1515), he gave Holy Roman Emperor Charles V a pretext for war, since the duchy was nominally an imperial fief. The Valois-Habsburg feud was fought in Flanders, the Franche-Comté, Roussillon, and Navarre, but Milan was still the main prize. The Battle of Pavia in which Francis was captured was fought near there in 1525. His ransom, agreed upon in 1530, required paying 3 million crowns and giving sovereignty over Flanders and Milan to Charles V. Nonetheless, hostilities continued, and the French sought to balance the vast array of Habsburg forces with a tacit alliance with the Ottoman Empire, extending to the use of Toulon as a base for the Turkish fleet in 1542. The war continued into the reigns of Henry II and Philip II, but it ended with the Peace of Cateau-Cambrésis in 1559. France conceded Spanish control of Italy but gained Calais and the three bishoprics of Lorraine.

The French army that fought those wars had undergone vast change in a century's time. In 1439 Charles VII had created fifteen lance companies, each to consist of one hundred armored lancers and five mounted support troops for each lancer, paid for by the king. Recruited from the nobility, the lance companies remained the heart of the French army until 1559, but by then the use of mounted pistoleers was threatening their primacy. Efforts to create a native infantry foundered on the long-ingrained fear among French nobles of putting weapons in the hands of their peasants. France had to depend on foreign mercenaries, mostly Swiss and German. The special strength of the French army was its artillery. A vast number of high-quality bronze guns, which fired iron balls instead of stone, gave the French an extraordinary ability to reduce fortifications until the design of forts began to change after 1500. The French also developed the first mobile gun carriages, permitting the artillery to keep up with the army.

The major French contribution to war at sea was the gunport. French seamen began to raid Iberian transoceanic shipping shortly after 1492. Their success led Charles V to create the flota system with its galleons for transporting treasure and goods from the Americas. The acquisition of Provence in 1480 provided the French with several ports to base a galley fleet for use in the Mediterranean. In the 1500s this fleet made its mark largely in joint operations with the Turkish fleet.

The revenues for the enhanced French military came largely from a property tax, the taille. In 1444 Charles VII gained the power to levy it without permission of the Estates General, and it quickly became permanent, but by 1465 the nobles and the clergy had obtained a permanent exemption. In 1550 the taille provided 80 percent of royal taxation. The clergy irregularly provided a "gift" of 10 percent of its income; this *décime* became annual under Francis I. Although taxes and the traditional revenues from tolls and the royal domain reached 8.3 million livres by 1547, royal expenses always exceeded revenues, and the kings resorted to borrowing. In 1559 royal indebtedness totaled some 43 million livres.

The Estates General was supposed to control taxation, but the inability of its three constituent bodies, the clergy, the nobility, and the commoners, to work together undercut its effectiveness. It met only sporadically until 1506 and then not again until 1561. The existence of provincial estates in most of the realm, which were far more likely to agree to royal demands for revenues, also undermined the Estates General. Far more powerful a factor in French government was the Parlement, the law court. The Parlement had authority to register royal edicts, which could not take effect until it did so, but the king retained the right to go in person to require that edicts be registered. The chief administrative officer of the state, the chancellor, usually was chosen from among the presidents of the Parlement. His appointment was for life, and his purview extended to virtually all the routine matters of government. Issues of special importance were decided by the royal council, over which the king usually presided and which varied in size from one reign to the next.

The theoretically absolute power of the monarchy was also limited by the presence of numerous corporate bodies in the realm such as the nobility, the cities, and the guilds. The most powerful was the church. The French church was imbued with Gallicanism and claimed autonomy for itself from the papacy in such matters as finances and episcopal appointments. The key Gallican document was the Pragmatic Sanction of Bourges of 1439, which ended the payment of funds to Rome and papal appointment of bishops for French sees. The papacy regarded the situation as schismatic and was quick to accept Francis I's offer to negotiate a new arrangement in 1515. The resulting Concordat of Bologna, which remained in effect until 1790, gave the right to nominate bishops to the king with papal approval and permitted the transfer of funds to Rome.

The concordat provided the French monarchs with a powerful incentive to remain Catholic, since there was now little benefit in their becoming Protestant. The kings did little to correct the abuses in the church, where corruption and ignorance among the clergy were commonplace. Early French Protestantism, however, was disorganized and had little success until John Calvin, himself French, began to provide strong leadership and an attractive theology. After 1550 the number of Huguenots, as French Protestants became known, began to increase rapidly, and by 1559 they may have reached 15 percent of the population.

The monarchy's efforts to repress religious dissent, the attraction of many nobles to the new religion, and the weakness of the monarchy after Henry II's accidental death in 1559 all contributed to the Wars of Religion that wracked France until 1598. Until they were concluded, they distracted the French from overseas exploration. French interest in the lands revealed by Iberian expeditions was limited in the years after 1492. Charles VIII had ignored a request from Bartolomé Colón for aid for a voyage across the Atlantic. Having no claim to any newly discovered lands, France was left out of the papal Line of Demarcation of 1493. Francis I would later ask to see "where in Adam's will the world was thus divided." French fishermen worked the waters off Newfoundland before 1500, but little is known of their voyages. Frenchmen also had reached Brazil before 1504. Royal support for exploration began only in 1523 with Giovanni da Verrazano's voyage along the east coast of North America. It was followed by Jacques Cartier's voyages to eastern Canada from 1534 to 1542. Under Henry II, Nicolas de Villegaignon attempted to found a colony in Brazil, but Portuguese attacks and the death of the king doomed it.

Thus in the century after Columbus discovered the New World, France was little involved in the discovery and conquest of the new lands. Only after 1600 did the French follow up on the claim to Canada that Cartier's voyages had created.

[See also *Colonization,* article on *French Colonization.*]

BIBLIOGRAPHY

Baumgartner, Frederic J. *Henry II, King of France.* Durham, N.C., 1988.
Bridge, John. *A History of France from the Death of Louis XI.* 5 vols. New York, 1929.
Febvre, Lucien. *Life in Renaissance France.* Translated by Marian Rothstein. Cambridge, Mass., 1977.
Kendall, Paul. *Louis XI: The Universal Spider.* New York, 1971.
Knecht, R. J. *Francis I.* Cambridge, 1982.
Labande-Mailfert, Yvonne. *Charles VIII et son milieu.* Paris, 1975.
Lavisse, Ernest. *Histoire de France.* Vols. 4–5. Paris, 1900–1911.
Quilliet, Bernard. *Louis XII: Père du peuple.* Paris, 1986.
Vale, Charles. *Charles VII.* Berkeley, Calif., 1977.

FREDERIC J. BAUMGARTNER

FUNCHAL. The capital city of the Madeira Islands, Funchal is a seaport situated on the south coast of Madeira Island, 978 kilometers from Lisbon. It was officially recognized as a town *(vila)* in 1452 by Afonso V, king of Portugal. On November 1, 1450, the duchy of Funchal had been granted by royal charter to João Gonçalves Zarco, whose family ruled as lord proprietors until 1497. The city's population in 1480 is estimated at eight thousand. It was designated a city in 1508 by Manuel I. Funchal is named for *funcho,* or fennel.

Italians dominated the sugar trade in Funchal from 1470 through the 1480s. Among these merchants were Baptista Lomelino, Francisco Galvo, Micer Leão, João Antonio, Bartolomeu Marchioni, Jeronimo Sernigi, Luis Doria, and Christopher Columbus. Columbus visited Funchal at least three times and spent from one to two years (1479–1481) using it for his base of operations while representing Genoese firms in Lisbon.

On his first visit in 1478, Columbus represented Paolo Di Negro, a powerful Jewish financier, for whom Columbus purchased a cargo of sugar to deliver to Genoa. When he arrived in Genoa, the firm hailed him before a notary to explain under oath why the order was not complete. On August 25, 1479, Columbus gave his age as twenty-seven, related that he was sailing to Lisbon the next morning, and testified that he had not been given credit to cover the whole order.

Before his second visit to Funchal, Columbus married Felipa Perestrelo Moniz in 1479 in Lisbon. Their son Diego was born the next year while he was living with his brother-in-law, the governor of Porto Santo, an island to the northeast of Madeira.

During this time, Columbus made friends with Jean de Esmenaut (João Esmeraldo), a Flemish merchant exporter from Picardy who owned extensive lands southwest of Funchal. It is traditionally claimed that Columbus lived at the residence of Esmeraldo when he was in Funchal. Columbus visited Funchal late in 1481 when he joined Diogo d'Azambuja on a voyage to the Gulf of Guinea, and then many times from 1483 to 1484 as master or officer of trading expeditions to São Jorge da Mina. His last visit to Funchal, in 1498, was at the beginning of his third voyage across the Atlantic. The landfall was for the purpose of taking on water and wood, and Columbus remarked, "In the town I was given a fine reception and much entertainment, for I am well known here, having been a resident for some time."

[See also *Madeira.*]

BIBLIOGRAPHY

Carita, Rui. *História da Madeira, 1420–1566.* Funchal, 1989.
César, César Figueira. *Ilha da Madeira.* Funchal, 1982.
Cossart, Noël. *Madeira: The Island Vineyard.* London, 1984.
Farrow, John, and Susan Farrow. *Madeira: Pearl of the Atlantic.* London, 1987.
Silva, J. Donald. *Bibliography on the Madeira Islands.* Durham, N.H., 1987.

J. DONALD SILVA

GALLO, ANTONIO (d. around 1510), Genoese chronicler. Gallo recorded the most reliable information we have about the early years of Columbus's life. A notary public, he lived and worked in the second half of the fifteenth century and the beginning of the sixteenth. From 1491 to 1510, he was chancellor in the office of the San Giorgio Bank. Gallo wrote three Latin commentaries on Genoese history, to which he added a fourth on Columbus's voyages. They were published by the historian Lodovico Antonio Muratori in his *Rerum Italicarum scriptores* (1723–1738). The importance of these commentaries as a source of information on Columbus has been demonstrated by Gianbattista Spotorno in his *Literary History of Liguria* and was confirmed by a little codex found in the State Archives of Genoa. This codex attests to the relationship, based on interests and friendship, between Gallo and the relatives of Columbus. Gallo declares that he saw a letter signed by Columbus, from which he took some of the information he records. His commentary was compiled between 1496 and 1498—that is, after Columbus's second voyage and before his third.

Gallo's testimony is of exceptional value, for it confirms the many notarial documents that have been found in the Archives of Genoa and Savona. He notes, for example, Christopher and Bartolomé were brothers of Ligurian nationality who were born of plebeian parents in Genoa and that their father was a wool weaver who lived in the quarter of Sant' Andrea's Gate.

BIBLIOGRAPHY

Belgrano, L. T. *Relazione sulla casa abitata da Colombo.* Genoa, 1887.

Gallo, Antonio. *De navigatione Columbi per inaccessum ante Oceanum comentariolum.* Manuscript of 1506, published by A. Muratori, in book 23, part 1 of *Rerum Italicarum scriptores,* edited by E. Pandiani. Cittá di Castello, 1910.

Colombo, Fernando. *Le historie della vita e dei fatti dell' Ammiraglio Don Cristoforo Colombo.* Vol. 8 of *Nuova Raccolta Colombiana,* edited by Paolo Emilio Tavaini and Ilaria Caraci. Rome, 1991.

Staglieno, M. *Il borgo di S. Stefano ai tempi di Colombo e le case di Domenico Colombo.* Genoa, 1881.

Taviani, Paolo Emilio. *Christoforo Colombo: Genius of the Sea.* Rome, 1990.

PAOLO EMILIO TAVIANI
Translated from Italian by Rodica Diaconescu-Blumenfeld

GAMA, VASCO DA (1460?–1524), discoverer of the maritime route to India. Da Gama was admiral of the Indian Ocean, the first count of Vidigueira, sixth governor of Portuguese India, and its second viceroy. The date and place of his birth are uncertain, but he may have been born at Sines, a seaport in the south of Portugal, where his father, Estêvão da Gama, became civil governor after 1478. His mother, Isabel Sodré, was a granddaughter on her mother's side of a Sudley, who settled in Portugal.

Nearly ten years after Bartolomeu Dias rounded the Cape of Good Hope (1488), King Manuel I made plans to continue that historic voyage. To that end, he appointed Vasco da Gama commander of a fleet of four ships, which departed from Lisbon on July 8, 1497. Books, maps, and charts were supplied by Diogo Ortiz de Vilhegas, titular bishop of Tangiers and one of the three royal commissioners who had discredited Columbus's plans for a voyage to Cipangu (Japan).

On July 15 the fleet sailed past the Canary Islands. The following night the ships became separated in a fog but came together July 26 at the Cape Verde island of Santiago, where they remained for a week. Leaving the Cape Verdes on August 3, they steered southwestward into an unknown ocean. To escape from the doldrums and currents of the Gulf of Guinea, where Dias's experience had shown that unfavorable weather might be expected, Da Gama conceived the bold idea of shaping a circular course through the Atlantic in order to reach the Cape of Good Hope. In September, the fleet reached its westernmost limit, coming within six hundred miles of South America, and then headed back to the cape. On November 7 the ships dropped anchor at St. Helena, a bay on the west coast of Cape Province. Since leaving the Cape Verdes the fleet had spent ninety-six days in the South Atlantic and had sailed fully forty-five hundred miles. No navigator of whom there is any authentic record had ever completed so long a voyage without sight of land. Columbus himself had covered only twenty-six hundred miles between his departure from the Canary Islands and his first landfall at San Salvador.

Da Gama's fleet remained at St. Helena for eight days to careen the ships, and on Thursday, November 16, the voyage was resumed. Owing to contrary winds, however, they were unable to double the cape until the twenty-second. Three days later they anchored in Mossel Bay, where they remained for thirteen days, breaking up the

VASCO DA GAMA. From *O sucesso dos visoreis*, by Lizuarte de Abreu, mid-sixteenth century. Colored ink drawing.

THE PIERPONT MORGAN LIBRARY, NEW YORK; M.525, F.7; M.525, F.16V–17.

store ship and transferring its contents to the other vessels. On December 8 the fleet set sail but soon encountered a dangerous storm that forced them to run under bare poles. Eight days later they passed the Great Fish River, the farthest point reached by Dias. During the next five days they encountered considerable difficulty because of the Mozambique current, which at times made them run backward. They got past this obstacle and on December 25 reached Natal, whence they followed the coast. On January 11 they stopped at the mouth of the Limpopo River, and on the twenty-fourth they anchored in the estuary of the Kilimane where they saw the first signs of Eastern civilization. For thirty-two days, from January 24 to February 24, they remained there, careening and repairing the ships and nursing the crew through an epidemic of scurvy. They stopped successively at Mozambique on March 22, at Mombasa on April 7, and at Malindi on April 13. Contrary to what had happened to them in Mozambique and Mombasa, where they had to defend themselves against Muslim machinations, they were well treated in Malindi. The sultan there gave them a Gujerati pilot with whom they departed on April 24.

On May 20, less than a month later, they anchored in front of Calicut, India, where Da Gama spent several months in negotiations over trade with the local rajah, or *samuri*, as he was called. At first, the Portuguese were made welcome, but later the *samuri*'s attitude changed, probably owing to the intrigues of the local Muslim merchants who feared the loss of their trade monopoly. Finally, Da Gama decided to return home, convinced that only a stronger expedition than his would have the power to bring negotiations to a successful conclusion.

At the end of August 1498, the fleet turned homeward. This time, the crossing of the Indian Ocean took three months and was beset with almost insuperable difficulties—calms, contrary winds, and violent attacks of scurvy, which decimated the crews. On January 7, 1499, the fleet anchored at Malindi where, for lack of hands, *São Rafael* was burned and the crew distributed between the other two ships. On March 20 the ships, *São Gabriel* and *Berrio*, rounded the cape together, but a month later they were parted by a storm. *Berrio* held on its way and entered Lisbon harbor on July 10, 1499, two years and two days after it had left, while Vasco da Gama proceeded to Cape Verde. From there he dispatched *São Gabriel* to Lisbon, while he took his dying brother Paulo da Gama (in a hired ship) to the Azores, where he expired the following day. Vasco da Gama reached Lisbon on September 8, 1499, and made a triumphal entry into the city nine days later, receiving many honors and rewards from King Manuel I.

There is no doubt that Da Gama's outward voyage was the finest feat of seamanship recorded up to that time, far greater than Columbus's. It took 209 days and covered a distance of over twelve thousand miles, five times that

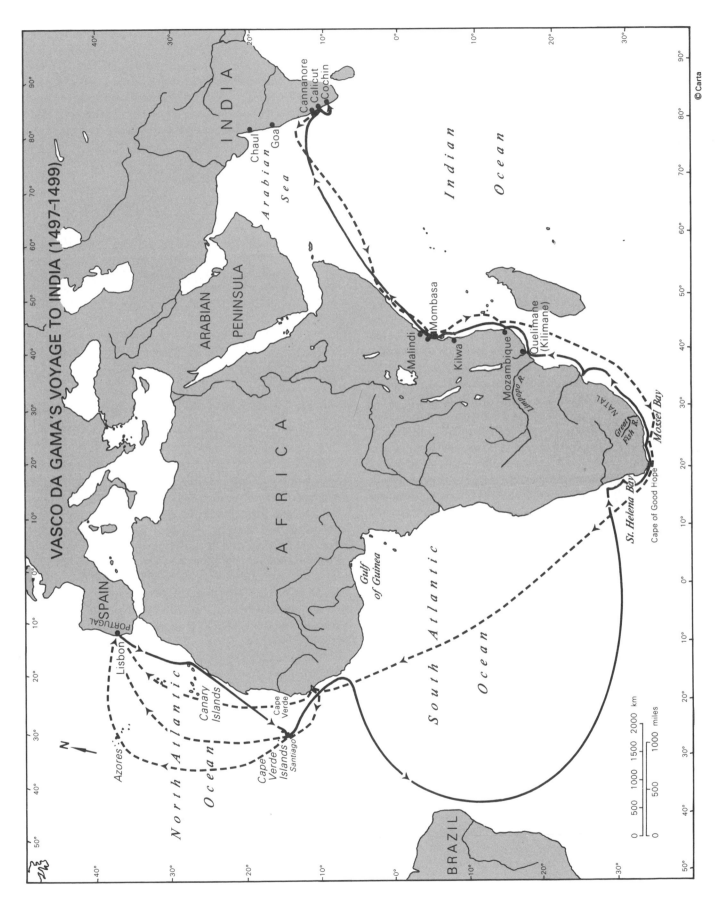

VASCO DA GAMA'S VOYAGE TO INDIA (1497-1499)

INDIA

Cannanore
Calicut
Cochin

Chaul
Goa

Arabian
Sea

ARABIAN
PENINSULA

Indian
Ocean

AFRICA

Malindi
Mombasa
Kilwa
Mozambique
Quelimane
(Kilimane)
Limpopo R.

NATAL
Great
Fish R.
Mossel Bay

Cape of Good Hope
St. Helena Bay

Gulf
of Guinea

South Atlantic
Ocean

SPAIN
PORTUGAL
Lisbon

North Atlantic
Ocean

Azores

Canary
Islands

Cape
Verde

Cape
Verde
Islands
Santiago

BRAZIL

N

500 1000 1500 2000 km

500   1000 miles

© Carta

289

traversed by Columbus. Not only did Columbus have a much shorter distance to travel, but, favored by the wind, he could proceed almost straight from the Canaries to the Caribbean. In scientific knowledge, Da Gama also proved himself the superior, for the accuracy of his charts was in marked contrast to the errors made by Columbus. In the late fifteenth and early sixteenth centuries, the general goal was to reach the spice countries. Thus the results of Columbus's voyages were disappointing, but the news of the arrival of the Portuguese at Calicut stirred the minds of people in every country and filled them with wonder, envy, or alarm. Though his diplomatic mission was a failure, owing to the enmity of the Muslims, he had found India and brought back samples of its products.

Vasco da Gama made two more voyages to India, in 1502 as commander of a fleet of twenty ships, and in 1524 as viceroy of Portuguese India. The highlights of his second voyage included a stop at Kilwa on July 12, 1502, where he forced the East African sultan to become tributary to Portugal, though according to historian Fernão Lopes de Castanheda, the tribute was paid by the hostage himself, who knew he would not be ransomed. On his approach to the coast of India, Da Gama captured a ship underway to Mecca, confiscated the cargo, and set it afire, killing most of the occupants, with the exception of twenty children who were later baptized. He committed many other cruel and barbarous acts against the Muslims and bombarded the unfortunate city of Calicut, all in the name of avenging the ill treatment accorded Pedro Álvares Cabral two years before. In Cochin he signed a treaty of friendship with the rajah and set up a factory, and he did the same in Cannanore. His ships fully laden, on December 28, 1502, Da Gama left for home with a squadron of thirteen ships. After passing Mozambique, he was struck by a storm during which one of the ships became separated from the fleet, but apart from that, the rest of the voyage home was uneventful. He reached Lisbon on September 1, 1503, where he paraded his accomplishments before an admiring crowd, preceded by his page who was carrying a basin full of the gold tribute he had exacted from the sultan of Kilwa as well as the two treaties he had signed with Cochin and Cannanore. In addition to many other honors and emoluments, King Manuel I rewarded him with the titles of admiral of the Indian Seas and count of Vidigueira.

Twenty-one years later, when the affairs of Portuguese India had begun to decline, Vasco da Gama was again called on, this time by King João III (r. 1521–1557), in the hope that he could improve matters. On April 9, 1524, he departed from Lisbon, with an appointment as viceroy of Portuguese India, at the head of a fleet of fourteen ships. After losing two vessels on the way, he anchored at the Indian port of Chaul on September 5, 1524, and reached Goa, then the capital of Portuguese India, at the end of the month, where he arrived with great pomp befitting his station. He tried to do away with corruption, but his harsh policies spread fear and dread among the inhabitants, many of whom fled inland. Three months later, on the night of Christmas, 1524, the viceroy died, more feared than loved. His body was transferred to Portugal in 1538, where he received more honors than had ever been given to anyone of nonroyal blood.

BIBLIOGRAPHY

Castanheda, Fernão Lopes de. *História do descobrimento e conquista da Índia pelos portugueses.* Edited by M. Lopes de Almeida. 2 vols. Porto, 1979.

Cortesão, Armando. *The Mystery of Vasco da Gama.* Coimbra, 1973.

Góis, Damião de. *Chronica do felicíssimo rei Dom Manuel.* 4 vols. Coimbra, 1949–1955.

Jayne, K. G. *Vasco da Gama and His Successors, 1460–1580.* Lisbon, 1910.

Ravenstein, E. G. *A Journal of the First Voyage of Vasco da Gama, 1497–1499.* Hakluyt Society Publications, 1st ser., vol. 99. London, 1898.

Sanceau, Elaine. *Good Hope: The Voyage of Vasco da Gama.* Lisbon, 1967.

REBECCA CATZ

GEMMA FRISIUS (1508–1555), Dutch mathematician, cosmographer, cartographer, and instrument maker. Gemma Frisius was born in Dokkum, Friesland. The name Gemma (Latin for "gem") was evidently an allusion to his intellectual abilities and his small stature. His father's name was Reynier, and the son was sometimes referred to as Gemma Reyneri or Reinerus Gemma. He was slight, frail, and born crippled, a condition of which he was miraculously cured at the age of six. He got his early education in Groningen and enrolled as one of the "poor students" in Lily College of Louvain University in 1526. He took his master's degree in 1528 and at the age of twenty-one was well enough grounded in geography and astronomy to publish an edition of the popular book of cosmography authored by Peter Apian (Peter Bennewitz). Gemma's version enjoyed a long and useful life, going through thirty-three editions in five languages over the course of the next eighty years. In 1530 Gemma published a pair of globes (terrestrial and celestial), although neither has survived.

The booklet that accompanied these globes is extant, however, and includes a prescient paragraph on a method for determining the longitude of places, a serious problem in all oceanic voyaging. Gemma's solution was to carry a timepiece set to local sun time at the point of origin. Comparing the difference between the time shown on the clock and the local sun time at the remote location would yield the longitude. As Gemma explained (in Richard Eden's translation of 1555):

> We see that in these owre dayes certeyne lyttle clockes are verye artificially made the whiche for theyr smaule quantitie are not comberous to be caryed abowt in all vyages. These often tymes moue continually for the space of xxiiii houres: and may with helpe continewe theyr mouynge in maner perpetually. By the helpe therefore of these the longitude may bee founde after this maner. Before wee enter into any vyage, wee muste fyrste foresee that the sayde clocke exactly obserue the houres of the place from whense we departe: And ageyne that in the way it neuer cease. Accomplysshynge therefore xv. or xx. myles of the vyage, if wee desyre to knowe howe much in longitude we are dystant frome the place of owre departure, we must tary untyll the poynt or style of the clocke do exactly come to the poynt of sum houre: and at the same moment by our Astrolabie or globe, owght wee to seeke the houre of the place where we bee.... And so shall the longitude bee founde. And by this arte can I fynde the longitude of regions althowgh I were a thousand myles owt of my attempted course & in an unknowen distance. (*The Decades of the Newe Worlde*, London, 1555, p. 361)

Gemma's technique was correct in principle, but the "lyttle clockes" and watches of the day, although they might run twenty-four hours on a winding, were not sufficiently accurate to yield usable results. The practical solution of the longitude problem had to await the chronometers of John Harrison in the eighteenth century.

In 1533 Gemma published the second of his vital contributions to cosmography, a description of the use of triangulation in surveying. The geometrical bases of triangulation were, of course, well known, but he was the first to print a full description of the technique for mapping purposes, including the measurement of base lines, the means for setting the scale of a map, and the use of resectioning for orienting the instrument (which was very like a modern surveyor's compass). Within a few years after the appearance of Gemma's description, all the provinces of the Netherlands had been mapped using the new technique, and its wide dissemination ushered in a new era in the making of large-scale regional maps.

In 1534 Gemma married and, presumably to better provide for his family, embarked on the study of medicine. He continued to be involved in the production of globes and, together with the young Gerardus Mercator and another engraver, Gemma produced a new pair of globes in 1536–1537. The terrestrial globe shows a wide bay in North America that connects with the South Sea. Labeled "Arctic Straight or Straight of the Three Brothers by which the Portuguese attempted to sail to the Orient & Indies & Moluccas," this may have been a reference to a voyage of Sebastian Cabot and his brothers.

Gemma published an influential world map in 1540. No copy has survived, but we know from contemporary descriptions that it was a nautical chart, with radiating rhumb lines, a wind rose, and scales. The map continued to be sold for at least twenty years. Gemma's most popular work was a handbook of practical arithmetic, which was first published in 1540. With seventy-five editions printed over the next one hundred years, it was the most widely read arithmetic book of its day.

Gemma was awarded the degree of doctor of medicine in 1541, and although he became a highly respected physician, he continued to write and publish in the field of cosmography and navigation. He also established a considerable reputation as a maker, or at least designer, of instruments. No surviving instrument bears his name, but he certainly designed an improved cross-staff, made of brass, which he hoped would make it possible to read angles with sufficient exactness to determine lunar distances for calculating longitude. This method was also theoretically correct but, as with the clocks, required a level of accuracy and precision unobtainable in the sixteenth century. Gemma's version of the cross-staff came into rather general use in England. His last book, published posthumously, dealt with the astrolabe, the standard instrument of navigators until the seventeenth century.

Gemma Frisius died in 1555 in Louvain, aged only forty-six years. His theoretical solution of the longitude problem, his perfection of triangulation as a surveying technique, his work as a cartographer and instrument maker, and his contribution to the spread of mathematical knowledge make him a figure of major importance in the annals of navigation and cosmography in the sixteenth century.

BIBLIOGRAPHY

Bagrow, Leo, and Robert W. Karrow, Jr. *Mapmakers of the Sixteenth Century and Their Maps: The Catalog of Cartographers of Abraham Ortelius, 1570.* Chicago, forthcoming.

Ortroy, Fernand G. van. *Bio-bibliographie de Gemma Frisius.* Académie Royale de Belgique, Classe des lettres et des sciences morales et politiques. Mémoires, 2d ser., vol. 11, fasc. 2. Brussels, 1920. Reprint, Amsterdam, 1966.

Pogo, A. "Gemma Frisius: His Method of Determining Differences of Longitude by Transporting Timepieces (1530) and His Treatise on Triangulation (1533)." *Isis* 22 (1935): 469–505.

Smet, Antoine de. "Gemma Frisius." *National biografisches woordenboek* 6 (1974): 315–331.

Vocht, Henry de. "Gemma Cosmographer." In Part 2 of *History of the Foundation and Rise of the Collegium Trilingue Lovaniense, 1517–1550.* Volumes 10–13 of Humanistica Lovaniensia. Louvain, 1953. Vol. 11, pp. 542–565.

ROBERT W. KARROW, JR.

GENOA.   In the mid-fifteenth century, when Christopher Columbus was born, Genoa was about to become, as Fernand Braudel has put it, a "metropolis of European capitalism." For centuries Genoa, endowed with a perfect harbor and overlooking a deep bay almost in the center of the Mediterranean, had been a maritime capital. It had successfully fought for control of the Tyrrhenian Sea against the Saracens and against Pisa, Provence, and Catalonia. Freedom of movement and control over the sea routes to the Ligurian Sea were indispensable for its men and ships. The Genoese moved about the Mediterranean in search of strongholds from which they could travel farther inland in the quest for goods and markets. Since the early eleventh century, the Genoese had been in Sardinia and Corsica, and then along the coastlines of Tunis and Spain. They were thus established in the West before they made contact with the East, where they arrived only with the First Crusade, whose fleets embarked from their harbor.

In this way a Genoese colonial empire was formed, although it was an economic, not a political empire. Its private citizens sent capital, ships, men, and commercial ventures to various parts of the Mediterranean, going so far as to act against the directives and political alliances of their mother country. Genoese settled in Spain, in North Africa, and in the Aegean and Black seas. Their intricate network of interests extended both west, toward Portugal, England, and Flanders, and east, toward Persia, India, and China.

From this Mediterranean perspective, the West and the East appeared not so much antithetical worlds as potential markets in the vast Genoese commercial circuit, and subject to the Republic's vigilant attention. It was not at all strange, then, that even before he landed in Spain, Columbus had made a voyage to Chios, the island in the archipelago of the Southern Sporades that was one of the pillars of the Genoese colonial empire.

By the fifteenth century, Genoa had an economic regime that could be defined as capitalistic, or, if one prefers, mercantilistic. It had already emerged from the feudal Middle Ages, which knew nothing of free enterprise except what was carried on occasionally or surreptitiously. The young Christopher Columbus grew up in this mercantile world, hearing around him the language of money-making—purchases, sales, interest, percentages, commissions, profits. He left Genoa with this kind of economic background and then, having traveled the British seas, engaged in commerce with the Portuguese and Spanish islands in the Atlantic and off the coast of Africa and lived in Portugal, where he entered into negotiations with the king before leaving for Seville and Córdoba.

In Spain Columbus found a substantial Genoese settlement of Adornos, Dorias, Centuriones, Grimaldis, Pinellis, Spinolas, De Maris, and Di Negros—the best names of the rich class of merchants from that richest of cities, Genoa. The political and economic power the Genoese had accumulated in Seville and Córdoba was nothing short of incredible: they lent money to the court and to the municipal administrators, and they allocated local taxes. There were so many Genoese nationals that in 1473 Genoa dared to solicit the pope to appoint a Genoese bishop in Seville in order to better safeguard the Republic's interests. Some Genoese took advantage of a law granting citizenship after ten years of residence in the kingdom and became citizens of Seville or Córdoba. Others, in exchange for services rendered to the Crown, hoisted their ships' flags with the royal coat of arms. A Genoese company obtained a monopoly over the mercury trade from the sovereigns. Francesco Pinelli was especially successful; he was an adviser and confidant to the Catholic monarchs, the financier for the sovereigns' Granada venture, the director of the Treasury of Santa Hermandad, and a friend of Christopher Columbus and of the Catalonian minister Luis de Santángel, whom he supplied with part of the capital necessary to finance the first voyage of discovery.

But a paradox emerges here. Christopher Columbus, the progressive who looked forward to the Renaissance, could also be a reactionary who looked back to the Middle Ages in economic matters. In Genoa, Portugal, Seville, and Córdoba, Columbus was the typical man of mercantilism, or incipient capitalism. He dealt in percentages,

GENOA. Woodcut, from *Liber chronicarum*, 1493.

commissions, interest, and profits with the king of Spain and his ministers, with his Genoese compatriots, with the Florentines, and with converted Jews. But when in 1499–1500 in Santo Domingo he had to choose a political and social system that could be implemented in the newly discovered lands—and found himself trapped in the struggles between the Indians and the colonists as well as the Castilian conquistadores—he had to resort to establishing the encomienda. The encomienda was an institution inherited from the Castilian Middle Ages. The encomendero—the colonist or landowner—had and would have for centuries in the Spanish Empire of the Americas the same rights over Indian workers that the medieval feudal vassals had had over their serfs. These workers were not marketable slaves—unlike those in the colonies of Portugal, England, and Holland, countries that were already capitalistic and mercantile—but servants bound to the land. Hence, even Columbus's economic practices can be traced to Genoa, just as his ideas in another field—geography—can.

In the fifteenth century Genoa was among the capitals of nautical cartography, along with Venice, Mallorca, and the Arabian schools. When the young Columbus attended the school of the wool weavers' guild, he learned the basics of geography and the nautical arts in a city with great sensitivity toward and knowledge of these subjects. Genoa, then, can be seen as the cultural homeland of the discoverer of the Americas.

BIBLIOGRAPHY

Bradford, Ernle. *Christopher Columbus.* New York, 1971.

Howard, Edmund. *Genoa: History and Art in an Old Seaport.* Genoa, 1971.

Taviani, Paolo Emilio. *Christopher Columbus: The Grand Design.* London, 1985.

Taviani, Paolo Emilio, Piero Sanavio, Adriana Martinelli, and Caterina Porcu Sanna. *Cristoforo Colombo nella Genova del suo tempo.* Turin, 1985.

PAOLO EMILIO TAVIANI

GENOCIDE. See *Pacification, Conquest, and Genocide.* See also *Disease and Demography.*

GEOGRAPHY, IMAGINARY. When Columbus made his first voyage to America in 1492, he met the inhabitants of the West Indies and was surprised to find that contrary to what he had expected, they were physically similar to Europeans. Since he was entering a region of exotic geography, it had seemed likely that he would find there fabulous beings as well. Agreeably surprised, he insisted over and over again on the physical attractiveness of the

inhabitants by the standards of his own world. Later, in a letter to Fernando and Isabel, Columbus reassured them that whatever earlier geographers might have said, there were no "monstrous" men in America, only "savage" men.

Monstrous men and animals were such an important feature of the legendary geography of Columbus's age that they were a commonplace of any exotic travel narrative. Columbus's assumptions about the appearance of the people of the New World were much like those of "Europeans" from antiquity to the late Middle Ages who made real or imaginary voyages to places such as India or Africa. Beyond the boundaries of the European known world were believed to live monstrous races of beings whose oddity, according to some thinkers, was caused by climatic extremes of heat or cold in their habitat. These monstrous beings invariably differed in physical appearance, such as possessing extra body parts, and in social practices from the person describing them, who often gave them names derived from these qualities. Their diet was particularly important in characterizing their otherness. Chroniclers told of races who lived solely on the smell of apples; of troglodytes who dwelt in caves and ate their prey raw; of beings who were physically or socially unusual but not anomalous, such as pygmies, giants, and Amazons; and of others who were truly fabulous, such as the Four-Eyed Maritime Ethiopians or the Blemmyae, men with their faces on their chests.

The exotic geographical inheritance of Columbus contained about fifty distinct races, living always far from Europeans, for distance was a precondition of their existence. They inhabited places like India, Ethiopia, Albania, or Cathay, whose outlines were vague to the medieval mind but whose names evoked mystery. As

BLEMMYAE. Illustration from a manuscript edition of John Mandeville's *Travels*, fifteenth century.

BIBLIOTHÈQUE NATIONALE, PARIS

geographical knowledge grew through the voyages of Columbus and others, the existence of these people was disproved by actual experience and the monstrous races were consigned to less well known regions, such as Lapland.

These fabulous peoples posed a number of theological and cosmographical questions for Europeans. Even their humanity became an issue. Did they have souls? Were they rational? Were they descended from the line of Adam as were all other members of the human family, or did they have a separate lineage? How had they survived the Flood? Could they be converted to Christianity? Was their existence a portent of God's intentions toward humankind? If so, what was their significance in the Christian world scheme?

The monstrous beings whom Columbus expected to find in the New World were races—that is, they would possess inherited physical and cultural characteristics. He

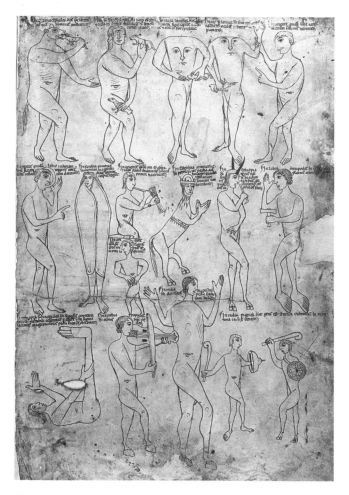

CATALOG OF MONSTROUS TYPES. From a manuscript from the Middle Rhine, late twelfth century.

did not anticipate supernatural or infernal beings, or the polymorphic creatures found in Romanesque and Gothic art, who were chiefly animal in composition, each differing from the next. Nor were they to be simply ordinary humans monstrous because of birth defects, though classical and medieval discussion of them often involved matters more properly associated with embryology.

The term *monster* (Latin, *monstrum*) to Columbus and his age had three different senses. Chiefly, it meant something outside the existing order of nature. Aristotle considered anomalous births as monsters *(terata)* who were defects of nature, which had deviated from the mean; he examined their physiological causes and classified them by type. The Romans discussed these births as portending the will of the gods because they showed *(monstrare)* something to humankind. Both of these senses signified individual unusual beings rather than races. It remained for the Roman encyclopedist Pliny the Elder to see both individual prodigies of the womb and the legendary races of the East as indicating God's power and desire to revitalize humanity's sense of the marvelous. Monsters, individual or as a species, fascinated and terrified the antique and medieval worlds because they challenged human understanding and pointed up the fragility and uncertainty of traditional conceptions of human beings.

The first Western accounts of these beings came from two Greek geographers, Ctesias who lived in the early fifth century B.C. and Megasthenes who lived in the fourth. They described their voyages in India in works of dramatic anthropology, focusing on the way such races were unusual or dissimilar to Greeks. Pliny described thirty distinct races in his *Natural History,* and Latin versions of the legends of Alexander the Great, who was believed to have encountered many hostile monstrous men in his Eastern exploits, were another important source for descriptions of perhaps twenty more. The conqueror was believed to have written a *Letter of Alexander to Aristotle on the Wonders of the East.* A new feature of Pliny's collection was the idea that many of the races lived in Ethiopia, which was confused with India. Indeed, the names of these two regions in medieval travel works and world maps should really be understood as vague literary terms rather than as denoting specific places.

Although there is no early medieval tradition of illustrated editions of Pliny's *Natural History* or of the Alexander cycle, portrayals of the monstrous races were quickly adopted by the compilers of medieval world maps. The two main kinds were the Noachid, or tripartite maps, sometimes called T-O maps, and the Macrobian zone maps. The former showed the world as a flat pie-like shape, with the world disk surrounded by a ring of ocean forming the shape of a letter O. Within the O and dividing it into three parts was a shape resembling the letter T, whose stem was formed by the Mediterranean imagined as a narrow vertical mass (north being generally to the left and east to the top in these maps) and whose cross bar was formed by the rivers Don and Nile. The area within the O was thus divided into three continents believed to have been created by Noah when he gave Europe, Asia, and Africa to his sons Japheth, Shem, and Ham, respectively, after the Flood. The continent of Africa on these maps usually contained at its outermost edge a band of monstrous races.

Macrobian zone maps were more theoretical; they divided the globe into regions of excessive cold or heat with two temperate zones suitable for human habitation between them. Some zone maps added an austral continent, which was the home of such monstrous beings as the sciopod, or shadow-footed man, who reclined with his foot over his head serving as an umbrella. The Antipodes also gave rise to a race of men believed to have their feet turned backward, or to be literally "opposite-footed."

Thus theories about the monstrous races were highly ethnocentric from the beginning. As the Aristotelian ideal of a mean between extremes gave rise to the notion of a mean climate found at the middle of the earth, extreme climates whether hot or cold had of necessity to be "un-ideal," deforming the inhabitants in mind and body. Each European nation thought of itself as a "middle people" superior in appearance, manners, and climate to all other peoples. Indeed, a Frenchman, Guy de Bazoches, observed that because of its climate and geographical situation, "France alone has no monsters, but abounds in wise, strong, and eloquent men." Another Frenchman, Benoît de Sainte-Maure, suggested that where the days are hot and burning there are various races "who have no law, religion or reason, justice or discretion; not knowing the difference between right and wrong, they are more felonious than dogs." Men in these torrid regions, he went on, are large, black, chinless, horned, and hairy right down to the ground with hanging ears, long noses, and huge feet. These features were the result of the extremes of temperature at the world's edges.

Much the same Aristotelian ideal was applied to the Plinean peoples' habitats. Visual depictions of them—for example, the illustrations in the very popular *Travels* of Sir John Mandeville—place them on mountains or crags that deviate from the norm in height. Mountains inspired great fear and distaste in the medieval populace. Antique fondness for landscapes that show the influence of art over nature made mountains unattractive for aesthetic reasons. The Bible associates topographical height with pride and with Satan, and in the Midrash, mountains are the earth's punishment for the sin of Adam. In the ninth-century Latin text *Liber monstrorum*, however, mon-

strous races live not only in the mountains and forests but in swamps, at the bottoms of deep pools, and in the vast wilderness of deserts and other hiding places at the edges of the world. They have deservedly been banished from the centers of civilization, their deviation from the physical appearance and social customs of Europeans responsible for their exile and their danger to humans. For example, races called the unclean peoples of Gog and Magog were believed to live in the Caucasus Mountains, safely walled up by Alexander the Great behind a great gate of brass. They ate their own afterbirths and periodically broke free of their gate to do terrible harm to Europeans. Although a contrary tradition made certain of the races, such as the Indian Bragmanni, or naked wise men who engaged in philosophical dialogue with Alexander, into noble savages and saw them in the light of romantic primitivism, even these lived not in cities and houses but in caves or waste places and had no political organization beyond simple kingship.

In the medieval *mappaemundi*, or world maps, available to Columbus, the monstrous men were always marginalized at the farthest point—usually eastward—from the center of the disk. Thus they were symbolically farthest in creation from Christ and hence from Jerusalem, the center of Christianity, which was usually represented in the exact center of the disk on the T-O maps. This metaphoric positioning eventually came into conflict with geography.

On the eve of the great discoveries, the chief problem of the Christian thinkers who took the geographic lore of Pliny seriously and expected to find monstrous races in the New World was how to fit them into the narrative of events recorded in scripture. If they descended from Adam, how had they survived the Flood and how had they gotten to the New World? Many theologians of Columbus's day wondered if it would be possible to convert them to Christianity. Were they redeemable like others? If they had descended from Adam, Augustine said, they must have souls, and if they had souls, they could be saved by grace. But were they so descended? This seemed questionable. As only hairy men and pygmies are mentioned in the Bible, the Plinean peoples seemed to have no scriptural genealogy and thus were not included in the single-family creation theory of *Genesis*.

Some said the monstrous races were distorted in form and manners and lived in remote places because they descended from children of Adam who disregarded his warning not to eat certain herbs. Others took them to be descendants of either Cain or Noah's rebellious son Ham, whose crimes had earned them exile in the waste places of the earth. A more extreme idea, found in the Midrash, was that the Plinean races' supposed ancestral father, Cain, was not Adam's child at all but the offspring of Eve's copulation with Satan. The curse that Noah laid upon his son Ham was also a genealogical explanation, for many theorized that this curse was blackness and physical deformity, so that black peoples, especially the supposed Ethiopians, and later the Moors and Saracens, were assigned a descent from Ham.

Another line of thought, which stemmed from Roman legal interpretations of monstrous births, also questioned the humanity of the Plinean races and of their actual counterparts in the New World. The legal and religious status of those of anomalous birth was of considerable interest to medieval jurists commenting on Roman law and to their contemporaries the canon lawyers. The former, as might be expected, considered *monstra* with respect to human form, laws of inheritance, and place in society, whereas the latter were concerned with their salvation as rational creatures having souls. The Cynocephali, or dog-headed men, and the pygmies particularly interested medieval thinkers in this way because their physical shape or size and social customs raised questions concerning their human status.

In Roman law, monstrous births, such as hermaphroditic babies, were instantly killed because they suggested a breakdown in cosmic order and portended an imminent danger to the state. Thus the Laws of the Twelve Tables, dating from as early as 450 B.C., stated that a father should immediately put to death a son who was a monster or who had a form different from members of the human race. For the Romans, human form was a prerequisite for human social or legal status. Not only did the *monstrum* reveal the gods' anger and serve as a focal point of danger to all; it lacked a place in society because it was unable to perform within it. The great legal commentators of the Middle Ages like Baldo Ubaldi slightly broadened this narrow definition of humanity: since form gives essence to a thing, that which does not have the form of a man is not a man, but if the creature has something of human form—like the dog-heads—he has civil status. The parish priests' manuals, popular embodiments of canon law, counseled how to baptize a creature with two heads: ought it to be baptized as one being or two? The answer: two heads meant two separate souls and so baptism as two persons.

The Scholastic philosophers of Columbus's immediate intellectual background speculated on the humanity of creatures like the Cynocephali who supposedly lived naked or wore animal skins and on pygmies who departed from the mean in human size. Albertus Magnus, for example, advanced the argument that the pygmy is the most perfect of animals, as he makes use of memory and understands by audible signs. In this he seems to imitate reason without truly possessing it, for he cannot through syllogistic reasoning elicit universals from past experience and apply them to similar cases in matters of art and learning. Pygmies, then, are subhuman because they lack the true reason inseparable from the forms of Aristotelian thought.

All these philosophical speculations as well as the literary conquests of Alexander the Great provided the underpinnings of the pattern of Western conquest and subjugation in the New World. Immodest dress, sexual license, and a lack of written history and laws—traits that had long offended the West in its dealings with the peoples of fabulous geography—were assumed to characterize the New World natives as well.

These qualities in New World monsters were dealt with by the sixteenth-century Aristotelian thinker Juan Ginés de Sepúlveda, who in 1550 engaged in a celebrated argument with Bartolomé de las Casas on the correct methods of propagating Christianity and Spanish capitalism in the New World. Las Casas argued for benign treatment and peaceful conversion to Christianity of the wild men, who were New World forms of the Anthropophagi, Donestre, and Hairy Wild Men of the Alexander legends; Sepúlveda countered that these men—if they were not more beasts than men—were the natural slaves of whom Aristotle spoke in the *Politics* and that their servitude to the conquerors and their conversion should be induced by force, stressing as part of his argument their sinful sexuality and their lack of written history and laws. Sepúlveda had in effect exported the ethnocentrism of the earliest Greek accounts of the fabulous geography of India and Africa to the New World and transformed the Indians of the Americas into Cynocephali, pygmies, and Hairy Wild Men. The myths of the monstrous races, though geographically obsolete by Columbus's day, were too vital to discard, for they provided a ready and familiar way of looking at the inhabitants of the New World.

[See also *Cartography*; *Travel Literature*.]

BIBLIOGRAPHY

Campbell, Mary. *The Witness and the Other World: Exotic European Travel Writing, 400–1600*. Ithaca, N.Y., 1988.

Friedman, John Block. *The Monstrous Races in Medieval Art and Thought*. Cambridge, Mass., 1981.

Kappler, Claude. *Monstres, démons et merveilles à la fin du moyen âge*. Paris, 1980.

Wittkower, Rudolf. "Marvels of the East." *Journal of the Warburg and Courtauld Institutes* 5 (1942): 159–197.

JOHN BLOCK FRIEDMAN

GERALDINI, ALESSANDRO (1455–1525), bishop of Santo Domingo. Columbus, thinking that a region of the coast of Venezuela was an island, named it "Isla de Gracia." This name, which did not survive, was an expression of appreciation to the Umbrian bishop,

Alessandro Geraldini, who had supported Columbus's cause at the court of the Spanish monarchs. The name of Geraldini's mother was Gracia.

She had married Andrea del Segale and then, having become widowed, Pace Busitani. She had two sons: from the first husband, Antonio; from the second, Alessandro. The stepbrothers were adopted by their maternal uncle, Angelo Alessandrini.

Antonio Geraldini, papal nuncio at the court of the Catholic monarchs, long supported Columbus's projects. When he died in 1488, his stepbrother, Alessandro Geraldini, was nominated by Pope Innocent VIII to be his delegate at the Spanish court. After the discovery of the lands across the sea, he was named bishop of Santo Domingo, thereby becoming the first bishop to reside in the New World. When he died in Santo Domingo in 1525, he left behind a work of Columbian bibliography that is considered among the best from the point of view of chronology: *Itinerarium ad regiones sub aequinoctiali plaga constitutas* (1631).

Alessandro Geraldini was especially helpful during the Council of Santa Fe, which was convened in the winter of 1492 to decide on the feasibility of the enterprise proposed by Columbus. The council was composed primarily of prelates rather than geographers and cosmographers. On that occasion, Columbus had many supporters, but Geraldini's arguments were particularly important in surmounting the doubts regarding the cosmography that was at the heart of Columbus's proposal to sail westward to reach the East.

Geraldini recorded his intervention in his *Itinerarium:*

Christopher Columbus, of Italian nationality, had his origins in the city of Genoa, in Liguria; he is an expert in Cosmography, Mathematical Sciences, and in the knowledge of the dimension of the sky and of the earth; above all he is renowned for his great courage. . . . In the process of measuring the sky's circuit, he realized, during his long navigations on the Ocean, that he could reach the lands of the Equinox, that is, the Antipodes. But such an expedition was rejected by King John of Portugal. Columbus decided to go to Spain where King Fernando and Queen Isabel were in those days waging war against the Arabs.

Thereupon, Antonio Geraldini, my brother, papal nuncio and most esteemed person, who had recently come back from the legation to the Sovereign Pontiff Innocent the VIII, offered his very powerful help to Columbus. But once my brother's death had taken place, Columbus had remained without any human succor whatever, and came to such dire circumstances that he went, dejected and entreating, to a monastery of Saint Francis where he might be given the food necessary for life.

Thereupon Fra Giovanni de Marchena, a man esteemed everywhere for his life, religion and sanctity, seeing Columbus, a man remarkable in every aspect, and having had compassion for him, left for Granada in order to see King Fernando and Queen Isabel. These, moved by the authority of such an honorable person, called for Columbus. Nonetheless, many Spanish bishops were judging him guilty of heresy, because Nicholas of Lyra had maintained that there was no land in the Southern Hemisphere, and because Saint Augustine had asserted that there existed no Antipodes. Then I approached Cardinal Mendoza, and had him reflect on the fact that Saint Nicholas of Lyra and Saint Augustine were great for their sanctity and doctrine, yet lacking in cosmographical science; for so much was true, that the Portuguese had already reached the regions below the Southern Hemisphere.

This argument by Alessandro Geraldini, meant to resolve the conflict between science and faith, helped dispel Queen Isabel's concern regarding the heretical implications of Columbus's enterprise.

BIBLIOGRAPHY

Baggio, Sebastiano. *Alessandro Geraldini di Amelia, primo vescovo residente nelle diocesi riunite d'America.* Grotte di Castro, Italy, 1985.

Geraldini, Alessandro. *Cristoforo Colombo ed il primo vescovo di Santo Domingo mons. Allassandro Geraldini d'Amelia.* Amelia, Italy, 1986.

Geraldini, Alessandro. *Itinerarium ad regiones sub aequinotiali plaga constitutas.* Vols. 12 and 14. Rome, 1631.

Masetti, P. "L'amicizia fra Cristoforo Colombo e Alessandro Geraldini." *Columbus '92* (Genoa) 2, no. 7–8 (1986).

Tisnés, R. M. *Alejandro Geraldini, primer obispo residente de Santo Domingo en la Española. Amigo y defensor de Colón.* Santo Domingo, 1987.

PAOLO EMILIO TAVIANI
Translated from Italian by Rodica Diaconescu-Blumenfeld

GERMANUS. See *Martellus, Henricus.*

GLOBES. Arab astronomers and geographers were making celestial globes in the Middle Ages. Though no European medieval globes survive, scholars such as Gebert of Aurillac (c. 945–1003; later Pope Sylvester II) used celestial globes and armillary spheres in teaching the astronomical sciences. The earliest extant European celestial globe is that made by Nicholas of Cusa at Nürnberg in 1444. The revival of Ptolemy's *Geography* (written around A.D. 150), first published with maps in 1477, reinforced the concept of a spherical earth. The cosmographer Nicolaus Germanus (c. 1420–1490), famous for the Ulm edition of Ptolemy's *Cosmographia* (1482), made a pair of terrestrial and celestial globes for the Vatican in 1477. They were presumably lost in the sack of Rome in 1527.

The earliest surviving terrestrial globe is the "Erdapfel" (Earth apple), which Martin Behaim (1459–1507) made at

Nürnberg in 1492 (and which is now preserved in the city's National Museum). The geographical features were drawn on vellum by the miniaturist Georg Holzschuler, and the map was pasted on a sphere about fifty centimeters (twenty inches) in diameter. The globe is famous as the only one now known that dates from before Columbus's discovery of America.

Scholars have puzzled over the fact that the globe appears to reflect the ideas of Columbus, yet there is no evidence that Columbus and Behaim had met. The explanation is found in records indicating that Behaim received payment for "a printed *mappamundi* embracing the whole world," which he used for the globe. This has been identified as the large world map of Henricus Martellus of about 1490 (now in the Beinecke Rare Book Library of Yale University). Columbus apparently consulted this map or a prototype for planning his voyage. Behaim's globe is also notable for its depictions of Portuguese discoveries along the coast of Africa, derived partly from information Behaim obtained in Portugal.

Globes were essential geographical instruments in the age of discovery, for they depict direction, distance, and area more accurately than does the plane chart. Columbus's papers include references to globes as well as to charts, and his brother Bartolomé Colón was skilled in making or painting spheres.

John Cabot's discovery of North America for Henry VII in 1497 was recorded on both a globe (probably the first English one) and a map, as the ambassador of the duke of Milan reported in a letter of December 18, 1497: "This Messer Zoane has the description of the world in a map, and also in a solid sphere, which he had made, and shows where he has been. In going towards the east he passed far beyond the country of the Tanais [i.e., the Don]." On this globe Cabot's discoveries in the region of Newfoundland must have been shown as located on a cape of Asia.

The earliest printed globe gores, or triangular sections, are those made by Martin Waldseemüller, professor of cosmography in Lorraine, dated 1507 and probably published at Strasbourg. The globe is a simplified version of Waldseemüller's large world map of 1507 and is described in an accompanying text, *Cosmographiae introductio* (St. Dié, 1507). On both the map and the globe Waldseemüller names the southern part of the New World "America" in honor of Amerigo Vespucci, who navigated the coasts of South America from 1499 to 1501. By the time Waldseemüller recognized Columbus's priority of discovery, the name of America was firmly established (such is the power of the printed word). The globe, like the map, shows the New World as a separate landmass, divided by a strait.

The Lenox globe in the collections of the American Geographical Society has been described as the oldest extant post-Columbian globe. An engraved copper ball, unsigned and undated, it was probably made about 1510. The New World, shown as South America, is named "Mundus Novus, Terra Sancta Crucis." To the north are islands and open ocean between Europe and Asia; there is no North American continent. The gilded copper globe, 7.3 centimeters in diameter, in the Jagellonian University Library, Cracow, is similar in its geographical features.

The "Globe Vert," or Green Globe, in the Bibliothèque Nationale, Paris, named for the bright green color of its seas, is a painted wooden sphere twenty-four centimeters in diameter, unsigned and undated, probably from about 1515. It bears similarities to Waldseemüller's globe gores and is the earliest cartographic document to give the name of America (which appears four times) on both the northern and southern continents of the New World. A legend names Columbus as the discoverer of the Antilles. To the south of South America an unnamed southern land is similar to that named "Brasilie regio" on Schöner's globe of 1515.

Johann Schöner (1477–1547), mathematician and geographer, was the most influential globe maker of his day. He was the first to undertake globe production on a considerable scale and in association with many astronomical and cosmographical publications. His woodcut globe made in 1515 ranks as the earliest printed and mounted terrestrial globe. Two of these survive, in

ANONYMOUS GLOBE GORES, INGOLSTADT, CIRCA 1518. Facsimile, mounted as a globe.

NORDENSKJÖLD COLLECTION, UNIVERSITY OF HELSINKI

Weimar and in Frankfurt. An accompanying pamphlet dated 1515 reveals Schöner's authorship. The strait that appears between "America" and the southern landmass "Brasilie regio" has prompted the speculation that Ferdinand Magellan was familiar with this globe and that it guided him in 1520 to the discovery of the strait named after him. Globe gores, published about 1518, probably in Ingolstadt, show America in a form similar to that on Schöner's globe—without a southern continent.

Schöner's manuscript globe of 1520 provides another interpretation of the discoveries of the time. The New World comprises five landmasses, from Terra Corterealis in the northeast to Brasilia Inferior as a substantial southern continent in the south. In 1523 Schöner issued another globe, now apparently lost, which he refers to in his treatise *De nuper . . . repertis insulis ac regionibus . . . epistola* (An epistle concerning islands and regions recently discovered). The text seems to suggest that Schöner now gave North America ("Parias," as he called it) an Asiatic connection.

F. C. Wieder identified the lost globe of 1523 with the Stuttgart globe gores, but this is no longer accepted. The gores, which would make a globe thirty-five centimeters in diameter, appear to date from about 1535 and to have been made in Nuremberg. They display the track of Magellan's ship *Victoria* around the world. The artist may have been from the school of Schöner. The Gilt, or De

Bure, globe in the Bibliothèque Nationale is similar to the Stuttgart globe gores and also shows the track of *Victoria*. In both these works America is joined to Asia, whereas most globes of the period are notable in showing the New World as a land or lands independent of Asia. The globe gores by Georg Hartmann, published at Nuremberg in 1535, illustrate a typical conception of America.

Another globe depicting Magellan's voyage and identified for some years mistakenly as Schöner's lost globe of 1523 is that known in the form of globe gores in the New York Public Library. In its mounted form, it is called the Ambassadors' Globe, from its inclusion in Hans Holbein's portrait of ambassadors at England's Hampton Court in 1533. It is notable in displaying the Line of Demarcation between the Spanish and Portuguese spheres as determined by the Treaty of Tordesillas, 1494. The instruments in the picture, including a celestial globe (probably that by Peter Apian first published in 1530), express in graphic form the theme of Henricus Cornelis Agrippa's book on the vanity of the arts and sciences, *De incertitudine et vanitate omnium scientiarum & artium liber*, first published at Antwerp in 1530.

The invention of printing and engraving techniques gave mapmakers and artists as well as instrument makers the opportunity to take up globe making. The artist Albrecht Dürer (1471–1528) proposed in 1525 the globe-biangle (gore) as a means of transferring the sphere to a

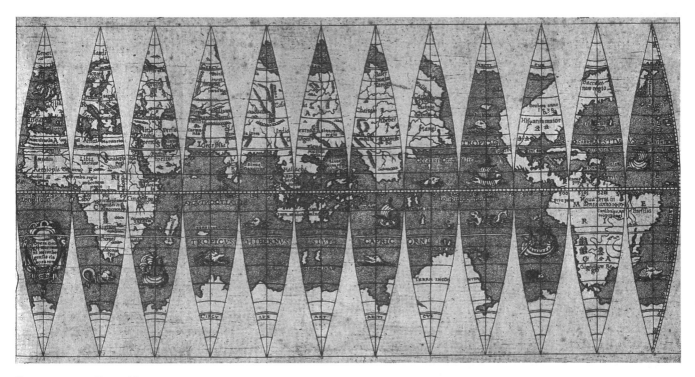

GLOBE GORES BY GEORG HARTMANN. Nürnberg, 1535.

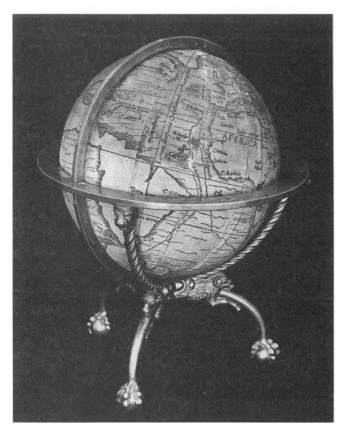

THE AMBASSADORS' GLOBE. Mounted facsimile of globe gores published possibly in Nürnberg, circa 1530.

NORDENSKJÖLD COLLECTION, UNIVERSITY OF HELSINKI

GEMMA FRISIUS. Constructing a celestial globe at his workshop in Louvain.

BIBLIOTHÈQUE ROYALE DE BELGIQUE, BRUSSELS

flat surface. The Swiss professor Henricus Loritus Glareanus in 1527 was the first to explain how to construct globe gores. His *Poetae laureati geographia liber unus* (Basel, 1527, with later editions to 1542) includes a chapter, illustrated by a diagram, that describes the method. The construction is simple but not completely correct mathematically.

As geographical studies advanced in the sixteenth century, globe makers became interested in exploring the relationship between the terrestrial and celestial spheres. They found that the most effective way of conveying the relationship was to make a matching pair of terrestrial and celestial globes, often accompanied by a book on their use. Gemma Frisius, professor of mathematics at the University of Louvain, made the earliest pair now extant, 36.5 centimeters in diameter, the terrestrial dated 1536, the celestial, 1537. They were engraved by Gemma Frisius's celebrated pupil Gerardus Mercator. The globes became well known throughout Europe and were of particular interest in England because the terrestrial showed the northwest passage Sebastian Cabot claimed to

have discovered while in English service many years before.

Mercator's pair of globes, forty-one centimeters in diameter, the terrestrial published in 1541, the celestial in 1551, superseded the globes of Gemma Frisius and were in standard use in the later part of the sixteenth century. The terrestrial globe displays innovative features. Loxodromes, or rhumb lines, are marked from the numerous compass roses as a guide for seamen, and these became a standard feature on globes. The second device was the depiction of stars as seen at various places on land and sea to help the traveler orient himself at night. This did not inspire others to follow suit, however.

In England the first pair of globes was published to great acclaim in 1592. They were made by Emery Molyneux, a Lambeth mathematician and instrument maker, with the help of Cambridge mathematician Edward Wright, engraved by the Dutchman Jodocus Hondius, and produced at the expense of the London merchant-adventurer William Sanderson. Measuring two feet two inches in diameter, they were the largest printed globes yet made.

TERRESTRIAL (LEFT) AND CELESTIAL (RIGHT) GLOBES BY ÉMERY MOLYNEUX. First published in London, 1592. Second edition in 1603.

COURTESY OF THE MASTER AND BENCHERS OF THE MIDDLE TEMPLE, LONDON GRANADA

The terrestrial globe provided a full record of England's explorations and discoveries abroad, and the arms of Elizabeth on the continent of North America were designed to encourage her plan for an English empire there.

Globes featured in pictures and portraits of the sixteenth century as emblems of statecraft. They symbolized the territorial ambitions and spiritual power of the monarch. Henry VIII, for example, had a great hall built at Calais for a banquet to entertain Emperor Charles V on July 12, 1520, after their meeting at the Field of the Cloth of Gold. Eight hundred feet around, the hall contained "the whole sphere" on its roof.

In more mundane affairs geography was taught using globes, and ships on voyages of discovery were equipped with them. At international conferences, such as the Council of Badajoz to settle the territorial disputes between Spain and Portugal, the diplomats had globes as well as maps to consult.

[See also *Cartography.*]

BIBLIOGRAPHY

Babicz, Jozéf. "The Celestial and Terrestrial Globes of the Vatican Library Dating from 1477, and Their Maker Donnus Nicolaus Germanus." *Der Globusfreund* 35–37 (1987): 155–168.

Krogt, Peter van der. *Old Globes in the Netherlands: A Catalogue of Terrestrial and Celestial Globes.* Utrecht, 1984.

Muris, Oswald, and Gert Saarmann. *Der Globus im Wandel der Zeiten.* Berlin, 1961.

Nordenskiöld, A. E. *Facsimile-Atlas to the Early History of Cartography.* Stockholm, 1889. Reprint, New York, 1961.

Ravenstein, E. G. *Martin Behaim: His Life and His Globe.* London, 1908.

Shirley, Rodney W. *The Mapping of the World: Early Printed World Maps, 1472–1700.* London, 1983.

Stevenson, Edward Luther. *Terrestrial and Celestial Globes.* 2 vols. New Haven, 1921.

Wallis, Helen. "Some New Light on Early Maps of North America, 1490–1560." In *Land- und Seekarten im Mittelalter und in der frühen Neuzeit,* edited by Cornelis Koeman. Munich, 1977.

Wieder, F. C. *Monumenta cartographica.* Vol. 1. The Hague, 1925.

HELEN WALLIS

GRANADA. Granada in the time of Christopher Columbus was transformed from the capital city of the last Muslim kingdom in the Iberian Peninsula into a defeated and deeply divided outpost on the periphery of Castile. From 1482 to 1485, Castilian frontal attacks against the city itself failed; the surrounding terrain was too rugged for a rapid Christian advance, and the Christian supply line ran through hostile territory. Finally, Fernando and Isabel isolated the city of Granada from its seaports and surrounding farmland. They besieged and captured the coastal city of Málaga in 1487, enslaving eleven thousand to fifteen thousand of its citizens because the city had resisted so fiercely. The lesson was not lost on the Granadines. As one port after another fell to the Christian armies, citizens of the capital escaped to Africa. After Granada was surrounded, it surrendered without a fight, receiving very favorable terms of capitulation. The defeated Muslim ruler, Boabdil, formally transferred sovereignty to Fernando and Isabel, who entered the city on January 2, 1492.

Under the terms of the capitulation agreement, the Muslims were allowed to retain their religion, laws, and customs. But the taxes they once paid to Muslim rulers they now paid to the Christian monarchs. In religion, too, the old dues *(habices)* that had previously supported Muslim religious and charitable institutions now went to support the Christian cathedral and churches. Only after accomplishing this conquest and transfer did the Catholic monarchs turn their attention to Christopher Columbus's proposal for his voyage of discovery, which they agreed to in a contract signed in the royal encampment of Santa Fe, outside the walls of Granada.

From this point on, Granada began a long decline punctuated by episodes of crisis. The most serious effects were loss of population and a decline in silk manufacturing. In 1499–1500, Fernando and Isabel crushed a Muslim uprising by military force and ordered all Muslims to convert to Christianity or leave the Kingdom of Castile. The archbishop of Toledo, Cardinal Francisco Jiménez de Cisneros, launched a successful military attack on North Africa, which inspired counterattacks on Spanish ports and shipping all along the Granadine coast. A serious food shortage in 1506 and an epidemic (probably typhus) in 1507 devastated the local population and discouraged immigration to the city from other parts of Castile. Silk production dropped, and the traditional trade patterns with North Africa were broken. The population of about 100,000 at the time of the conquest had dropped by half by the end of the sixteenth century, with a corresponding decline in production levels and rate of economic transactions. But silk thread and cloth continued to be the largest exports, and the silk tax was the monarchy's principal income from Granada.

The old Muslim consumer economy, epitomized in the luxuriously decorated Alhambra Palace overlooking the city, was replaced by an administrative service economy. The palace was the captain-general's headquarters for the Kingdom of Granada and housed a large portion of the military personnel and their families. The archbishop of Granada and the cathedral's staff supervised the ecclesiastical administration of eastern Andalusia, and the royal appellate court for southern Castile, the *chancillería,* moved permanently to Granada in 1505. The minutes of the Granada city council, which survive almost intact from 1497 to the present, show that, though the city was amply provisioned with food from the surrounding countryside, the variety and volume of manufactures shrank during the sixteenth century.

BIBLIOGRAPHY

Domínguez Ortiz, Antonio, and Bernard Vincent. *Historia de los moriscos: Vida y tragedia de una minoría.* Madrid, 1984.

Grabar, Oleg. *The Alhambra.* London, 1978.

Ladero Quesada, Miguel Angel. *Granada: Historia de un país islámico (1232–1571).* Madrid, 1969.

Rosenthal, Earl E. *The Palace of Charles V in Granada.* Princeton, 1985.

HELEN NADER

VIEW OF GRANADA. Woodcut from Pedro Medina's *Libro de grandezas de España,* 1548.

LIBRARY OF CONGRESS, RARE BOOK DIVISION

GRAND KHAN. "Khan" was the title given by Turkish and Mongol tribes to the man whom their warriors proclaimed the leader. Although khans were frequently descendants of previous khans, the title was not hereditary or continuous but apparently activated by the exigencies of combat. When on occasion a number of tribes banded together, usually for military purposes, they chose a common leader who bore the title "gurkhan." Throughout the early medieval period, western Europe was buffered from the periodic westward thrusts of these nomadic peoples by the intermediary civilizations of Byzantium and Islam. Accurate knowledge of inner Asia and the Far East was negligible. What information Europeans had was derived from ancient sources and the legends and romances based upon them.

Early in the thirteenth century, however, a Mongol of noble descent named Temüjin (1167–1227) consolidated control of the Mongols, Kairites, and Uighur Turks of outer, eastern, and western Mongolia. In 1206, he took the name Genghis (Chingis) and the title "kah khan," or "the emperor of mankind." In his quest to conquer the world he amassed an army of nomadic horsemen capable of traversing the great steppes of inner Asia with extraordinary speed and efficiency. A series of campaigns in the second and third decades of the thirteenth century gave him control of northern China, Manchuria, and the central Asian Muslim empire of Khwarazm.

Direct contact between the forces of Genghis Khan and central Europeans occurred in the second decade of the thirteenth century when Hungary, Poland, and Silesia were overrun in a Mongol offensive that reached the shores of the Adriatic Sea. These fierce hordes receded rather abruptly before the mobilizing armies of western Europe could engage them, probably in the aftermath of the death of Genghis in 1227. A subsequent Mongol offensive in 1240 resulted in the conquest of Christian Romania.

The sudden, devastating appearances of these horsemen terrified Europeans, who called them "the scourge of God" and "the devil's horsemen." Such apocalyptic apprehensions did not, however, prevent Pope Innocent III from seeking to establish diplomatic relations with Genghis's successor, the Grand Khan Güyük (or Kuyuk). The legate chosen by the pope to journey eastward to meet the Grand Khan was the Franciscan friar Giovanni da Pian del Carpini (1180–1252). After a rapid passage across inner Asia on relay teams of horses, Carpini and a companion were received at the court of Güyük. Upon his return, he wrote an account of his journey of 1245 to 1247 titled *History of the Mongols*. This work marks the beginning of a new phase in European knowledge of the peoples of central Asia and the Mongol empire.

Carpini was followed by another Franciscan, Willem van Ruysbroeck, who in 1253 was sent by the French king Louis IX to locate and proselytize the communities of Nestorian Christians presumed to exist in parts of Asia. The two-year expedition culminated with eight months spent in the court of Güyük's successor, Mangu Khan. Willem provided a detailed account of his experiences in a work known as *The Journey* and also informed other

writers such as Roger Bacon, who made use of the information in parts of his *Opus maius*.

In 1260, two Venetian merchants, Niccolò and Maffeo Polo, seeking to establish new trade networks in Russia and Persia, were stranded by local conflicts in the important Muslim trade center of Bukhara. They were invited by Barak, the Muslim khan of Turkestan who controlled Bukhara, to accompany him on a diplomatic visit to his overlord, the Grand Khan Kublai, whose court was located near present-day Beijing (Peking). The Polo brothers returned to Italy in 1269 as envoys from Kublai Khan to the pope. Upon finding the pope recently deceased and the papacy vacant, the brothers in 1271 elected to return to the court of Kublai Khan, taking with them Niccolò's son Marco, then probably around fifteen years old.

Marco Polo spent almost two decades in China and southeastern Asia. His activities and movements during this period are not altogether clear, though he does appear to have been associated with the court of Kublai Khan. In 1292 he returned to Venice not by the ancient overland routes established by silk and spice traders but by sea from Southeast Asia to the Persian Gulf port of Ormuz and thence by land to the shores of the Mediterranean. Some six years later he was captured and imprisoned by the Genoese in a sea battle with the Venetians. While in prison he dictated his story of his years in the Far East to a fellow inmate, one Rustichello of Pisa. The *Travels* (also known as *Il milione*), originally written in French, enjoyed great popularity from the time it began to circulate and was soon translated into other vernaculars. Many manuscripts and early printed editions survive; the work generated an important pictorial tradition as well.

The title grand khan disappeared in the late fourteenth century with the demise of Mongol power, but western Europeans, unaware of such dynastic shifts, continued to believe that this at once alluring and terrifying leader ruled the Far East. Marco Polo's exotic and opulent description of the court of Kublai Khan, contained in the famous third chapter of the *Travels*, was an important stimulus to the Spanish and Portuguese voyagers of the fifteenth and sixteenth centuries. Prompted by a desire to find a sea route to India and the Far East that would bypass the routes controlled by Muslim traders, Prince Henry the Navigator (1394–1460) masterminded a series of Portuguese expeditions down the west coast of Africa beginning in 1510. These culminated in Vasco da Gama's circumnavigation of the Cape of Good Hope in 1497–1498 and the subsequent establishment of Portuguese maritime trade networks in the seas once traveled by Marco Polo on his return journey from China to Italy some two hundred years earlier.

The Portuguese successes in discovering new sea routes to what Marco Polo called the "marvels of the East" undoubtedly played an important part in Fernando and Isabel's decision to underwrite Columbus's voyages. And Columbus, who read and heavily annotated a copy of Marco Polo's *Travels,* clearly expected to find the riches described therein by sailing west. His own letters and various other sources indicate that he was particularly interested in reaching Cipangu (Japan), described by Marco Polo as being even richer than the territories held by Kublai Khan, who coveted it.

On his first voyage Columbus took a converso named Luis de Torres whom he thought would serve as an interpreter in the interviews he expected to have with the Grand Khan. According to Bartolomé de las Casas, Columbus thought that the Tainos whom he encountered on the island of Cuba spoke of "El Gran Can." He dispatched a diplomatic party headed by Luis de Torres to meet this nonexistent leader in a land he did not yet know existed, poignant proof of the enduring power of the legend of the Grand Khan in the age of European expansion.

[See also the biographies of Carpini and Polo.]

BIBLIOGRAPHY

Chambers, James. *The Devil's Horsemen: The Mongol Invasion of Europe.* New York, 1985.

Dawson, Christopher. *Mission to Asia.* Toronto, 1980.

Polo, Marco. *The Travels.* New York, 1958.

Rossabi, Morris. *Khubilai Khan: His Life and Times.* Berkeley, 1988.

Wittkower, Rudolf. "Marco Polo and the Pictorial Tradition of the Marvels of the East." In *Allegory and the Migration of Symbols.* London, 1977.

Yule, Henry. *Cathay and the Way Thither: Being a Collection of Medieval Notices of China.* Taipei, 1966.

PAULINE MOFFITT WATTS

GRAVE OF COLUMBUS. See *Burial Places.*

GRIJALBA, JUAN DE (1489–1527), Spanish explorer. Juan de Grijalba and his uncle Diego Velázquez, Cuba's first governor, were both from Cuellar in Spain. In Cuba, Velázquez heard about the riches of a land known as Culhua, recently discovered in 1513 and 1516 by Juan Ponce de León, who had been appointed adelantado of Bimini and Florida. Under this title, he had exclusive rights to explore and settle territory extending from the Río de Palmas, forty leagues north of Panuco, up to Newfoundland's Grand Banks.

Lacking such a title to Culhua, Velázquez was allowed to outfit expeditions only for the purpose of barter with the Indians. Ponce de León complained to King Fernando that Velázquez had illegally taken off some three hundred

Indians from the territory he had been granted, so on July 22, 1517, a 1502 decree declaring that all Indians were free men was reconfirmed.

Velázquez then tried to obtain a grant to explore Culhua from the Hieronymite friars who governed La Española, while sending Friar Benito Martín to Spain to seek his appointment as adelantado (a title granted so far only to Bartolomé Colón, Columbus's eldest brother, and Ponce de León).

Although lacking such a grant, Velázquez dispatched in 1517 three ships under Francisco Fernández de Córdoba with pilot Antón de Alaminos, who had served as pilot when Ponce de León explored these coasts. While bartering with the Indians, however, the expedition was attacked, and the captain wounded. It was forced to return to Cuba by way of Florida, landing where Alaminos said he had been with Ponce de León.

Next, in May 1518, Velázquez sent four ships with 160 men to Culhua in an expedition captained by his nephew, the "young and beardless" Juan de Grijalba. He was ordered to barter with the Indians, seek gold, and deliver a full report of the land (called Mayab, but named Yucatán, meaning "don't understand"). He landed at Cozumel Island and then at Asunción and San Juan de Ulúa bays, so named by Ponce de León. They bartered for gold and Indian objects, which Grijalba sent to Velázquez. He then sailed toward Campeche. There the party was attacked by Indians and was forced to return to Cuba; the trip was considered a failure.

Velázquez organized yet another expedition under Grijalba and his secretary, Hernando Cortés, in a three-man private partnership. Because he still lacked a grant, the expedition was supervised by a government overseer and a treasurer. In October 1519 Cortés led ten ships to explore and settle "the islands of San Juan de Ulúa, Ponce, and Yucatán." They were also to barter with the Indians and rescue shipwrecked and captive sailors. Grijalba falsely claimed that Spaniards had not sailed along those shores before, hoping to be recognized as the pioneer explorer. He was demoted by Velázquez and died in Nicaragua.

BIBLIOGRAPHY

Wagner, H. R., trans. *Discovery of New Spain in Fifteen Eighteen by Juan de Grijalva.* 1942. Millwood, N.Y., 1969.

AURELIO TIÓ

GUZMÁN, ENRIQUE DE (d. 1492), second duke of Medina-Sidonia. Enrique de Guzmán inherited the richest of the Castilian duchies in 1478, having been recently legitimized by his father. The estate, which included vast territories around the mouth of the Guadalquivir River, was contested unsuccessfully by the counts of Alba de Liste, who were descended from a legitimate daughter of the first duke.

The second duke spent most of his career in a bitter feud with the marqués of Cádiz, who regarded him as "my enemy incarnate." This struggle, which occasionally degenerated into open warfare, was a major concern of the Catholic monarchs who were able to secure only a temporary truce. Medina-Sidonia nevertheless came to the aid of his enemy in 1482 when the marqués was besieged by the Moors after capturing Al-Hamma. The duke's refusal to accept a share of the booty earned him the respect of other grandees, but the feud was revived in later years. For the remainder of the Granadan war, Medina-Sidonia participated chiefly in local defense, though his son commanded the family's troops in several major campaigns.

Shortly after Columbus arrived at Seville in 1485, he approached the duke in the hope of securing his support. He was encouraged to do so by Antonio de Marchena, who was no doubt aware of Medina-Sidonia's investment in the Canaries campaign. Negotiations were abandoned when the duke returned to his estates after yet another outbreak of his feud with the marqués of Cádiz. Medina-Sidonia died on August 25, 1492, only three days before the passing of his mortal enemy, Cádiz.

BIBLIOGRAPHY

Ladero Quesada, Miguel Angel. *Spain in 1492.* Bloomington, Ind., forthcoming.

Vassberg, David. *Land and Society in Golden Age Castile.* Cambridge, 1984.

WILLIAM S. MALTBY

HENRY. For discussion of the Castilian king Henry IV, see *Enrique IV*.

HENRY THE NAVIGATOR (1394–1460), prince of Portugal. Born in Oporto, Henry was the third surviving son of João I, founder of the Aviz dynasty, and Philippa, daughter of John of Gaunt of England. Prince Henry played a seminal role in the early stages of European overseas expansion. He was a patron of pioneering voyages to Madeira, the Azores, and the west coast of Africa, and his private court at Sagres was responsible for notable advances in cartography, navigational instruments, and ship design. His elusive goal—not realized until Vasco da Gama's epic voyage some four decades after the prince's death—was the maritime passage to Asia, the coveted prize for a spice-starved and Christian Europe eager to outflank the middlemen of the Levant trade while extending the crusade against Islam.

Henry's biographer, Gomes Eanes de Zurara, states that the prince and his brothers, Duarte and Pedro, convinced their father to continue the crusade against Islam in North Africa so they might win their knightly spurs in true combat. The Portuguese Crown was also no doubt eager to win a share of the trade in slaves and gold that had hitherto proved so lucrative for the Moors. An expedition sailed for Ceuta in July 1415. Prince Henry played a prominent role in the capture of this place and was promptly named governor. This position gave him access to ships, and he soon began to sponsor voyages of discovery. Between 1418 and 1420 his squires, João Gonçalves Zarco and Tristão Vaz Teixeira, rediscovered the islands of Porto Santo (destined to play a notable role in the life of Columbus) and Madeira.

After the prince returned to Portugal, he was given the titles of duke of Viseu and lord of Covilhã and was appointed governor of the Algarve. He left Lisbon in 1419 to take up this post in Portugal's southernmost province, selecting the windswept and rocky promontory of Sagres, near Cape St. Vincent, as the site for his court. There he gathered sailors, cartographers, astronomers, and shipbuilders to help in his quest for exploration and discovery.

In 1420 Prince Henry's projects received welcome support when he was named grand master of the Order of Christ, the successor in Portugal to the crusading order of the Templars. Henry used revenues from this order to finance his expeditions. Thereafter, his ships bore the red cross of the order on their sails and had as an ancillary objective the conversion of pagans to Christianity.

In the decades that followed, Prince Henry dispatched scores of ships from the nearby port of Lagos. According to Zurara, Henry had six motives for his grand enterprise: to learn what lay beyond the Canaries and Cape Bojador, to open profitable new trades with Christian peoples, to investigate the extent of Islamic power, to win converts, to make alliances with any Christian rulers who might be found (e.g., Prester John), and to fulfill the predictions of his horoscope, which compelled him to engage in "great and noble conquests" and to seek "the discovery of things which were hidden from other men." During the 1420s the prince's expeditions explored the Azores and Canaries and colonized the Madeira Islands. These activities suggest that Henry may have been considering a western passage to Asia of the type that Columbus would later attempt.

Before King João died in 1433, he exhorted his son not to abandon his quest. The following year Gil Eannes succeeded in doubling Cape Bojador, and by 1436 Henry's

HENRY THE NAVIGATOR. From *Crónica do descobrimento e conquista da Guiné*, by Gomes Eanes de Zurara, 1543.

BIBLIOTHÈQUE NATIONALE, PARIS

caravels had nearly reached Cape Blanco. But renewed warfare in Morocco (including a disastrous 1437 attack on Tangier), King Duarte's death in 1438, and Afonso V's stormy minority with Pedro as regent hindered Henry's work.

Exploration began anew in 1441 when Antão Gonçalves returned with the first slaves and gold from the Guinea coast and Nuno Tristão reached Cape Blanco. A burst of maritime activity characterized the remainder of the 1440s: Nuno Tristão reached the Bay of Bight in 1442, Tristão and Dinis Dias reached the mouth of the Senegal and Cape Verde in 1445, Alvaro Fernandes pushed on to Sierra Leone in 1446, and Prince Henry in 1448 had a fort and warehouse built on Arguin Island to exploit the Guinea trade, perhaps the first European trading post established overseas.

The year 1449 witnessed the culmination of the struggle between Afonso V and Pedro. After trying without success to act as peacemaker in this feud, Henry sided with his young nephew without taking part in the bloody skirmish at Alfarrobeira (May 1449) that ended with Pedro's demise.

The final decade of Henry's life was dominated by the colonization of the Azores and Madeira, the further exploitation of the Guinea trade, a last campaign in Morocco, and the sponsorship of more voyages along the African coast. In 1458 Henry accompanied Afonso V (flush with crusading zeal but little enamored with the work of maritime discovery) in the campaign against Alcacer Ceguer. Earlier, he had dispatched the Venetian Alvise Cadamosto, who between 1455 and 1456 explored Senegal and Gambia, discovered the Cape Verde Islands, and mapped a significant section of the African coast beyond Cape Vert.

When Prince Henry died in 1460 in his town near Cape St. Vincent, he was in the midst of preparations for additional voyages. Although late medieval conventions of propriety had prevented him from personally embarking on exploratory voyages, his patronage of such trips justly ensured his place as the initiator of the great Age of Discovery. Prince Henry's activities made Portugal the leading European power in the quest for overseas conquest and the center of navigational and geographic knowledge of the age. This legacy attracted the young Columbus to Lisbon and exerted a profound influence on his life and theories. The prince's voyages also ensured Portuguese dominance of the African route to the Indies, thus compelling Columbus to search for a western passage.

BIBLIOGRAPHY

Dinis, A. J. Dias, ed. *Monumenta Henricina*. 8 vols. Coimbra, 1960–.

Godinho, V. M. *A economia dos descobrimentos Henriquinos*. Lisbon, 1962.

Major, R. H. *The Life of Prince Henry of Portugal, Surnamed the Navigator*. London, 1868. Reprint, London, 1967.

Prestage, Edgar. *The Portuguese Pioneers*. London, 1933. Reprint, New York, 1966.

Zurara, Gomes Eanes de. *Chronicle of the Discovery and Conquest of Guinea*. Translated and edited by C. R. Beazley and Edgar Prestage. 2 vols. London, 1896–1899.

GLENN J. AMES

HENRY VII (1457–1509), king of England. Henry Tudor succeeded to the English throne in 1485 at a time when the kingdom was racked by the Wars of the Roses—a series of dynastic battles fought between the feuding families of York and Lancaster since mid-century. When the head of the Lancastrian faction, Henry VII, married the Yorkist Princess Elizabeth, he cemented the two factions together, ending more than thirty years of civil war. He then rebuilt the strength and power of the monarchy and amassed a fortune, replenishing the royal treasury.

Henry increased and protected English commercial interests through a series of skillfully negotiated trade

HENRY VII. Bust by Torrigiano.

HENRY VIII (1491–1547), king of England. Henry VIII, probably the best known of English monarchs, has been portrayed as a glittering Goliath who hovered menacingly over those around him—particularly the women. Popular views aside, Henry VIII is best understood as a study in contrasts.

In his early years Henry was noted for his beauty, height and athletic prowess. He exercised daily in the tiltyard or on the tennis court (a game he made popular in England). He enjoyed the hunt and regularly outrode his companions. But by the end of his life, ill health had made it impossible for him to sit a horse and, as his suits of armor illustrate, he had grown obese. When he died there was little trace of the energetic young man who had captured the hearts of his subjects.

Henry VIII was a deeply pious and orthodox Catholic. In 1520 he wrote a treatise defending the Roman Catholic church against Martin Luther's accusations, which prompted the pope to award him the title "Defender of the Faith." Yet he also engineered a constitutional revolution within the English church and, with Parliament, enacted laws that broke with Rome and created an English catholic church with himself as supreme head in place of the pope. Although he allowed little doctrinal change in

treaties and political alliances with continental countries. Because of his awareness of the importance of trade, Henry in 1496 issued a license to John Cabot and later to his son Sebastian to search for "unknown lands beyond the . . . seas." By the end of his reign he had helped write laws that dealt with standardization of weights, measures, and coinage—all of which encouraged the growth of internal and external commerce.

In foreign policy, Henry VII was motivated by his desire to place England on a par with the great continental powers of France, Spain, and the Holy Roman Empire. To this end he allied himself with Spanish interests through the marriage of his eldest son, Arthur, to Catherine of Aragón, princess of Castile and daughter of Fernando and Isabel. After Arthur's early death, Henry refused to return Catherine's dowry and kept the young widow in England, close to the throne through unofficial promises and plans to marry her to his second son and heir, the future Henry VIII. By the time of his death in 1507, Henry's pragmatic political negotiations in combination with England's growing prosperity and slowly centralizing royal power had made the kingdom an important player in the complex game of maintaining the balance of European power.

BIBLIOGRAPHY

Alexander, M. *The First of the Tudors.* Totowa, N.J., 1980.
Lockyer, R. *Henry VII.* New York, 1968.
Storey, R. L. *The Reign of Henry VII.* London, 1968.

JOAN B. GOLDSMITH

HENRY VIII. Portrait by Hans Holbein.

the catholic liturgy, the nationalization of church wealth, dissolution of monastic houses, and publication of an English Bible loosened ties to the old church and opened the way for the Protestant Reformation during the reigns of his children Edward VI and Elizabeth I.

Henry VIII perceived himself as a patriarch, loyal to the institution of marriage. During his marriage to his first wife, Catherine of Aragón, he wrote a work defending the sacrament of marriage in reaction to its exclusion in the new Lutheran faith. Yet by the end of his life, Henry had been married six times, divorced twice, and widowed three times—twice at the hands of the royal executioner. In the words of a contemporary, he was "the greatest Prince in Christendom" and "the uncommonest man who ever lived!"

BIBLIOGRAPHY

Scarisbrick, J. J. *Henry VIII.* Los Angeles, 1968.
Smith, L. B. *The Mask of Royalty.* London, 1971.

JOAN B. GOLDSMITH

HERALDRY. See *Coat of Arms.*

HERNÁNDEZ. See *Fernández.*

HERRERA Y TORDESILLAS, ANTONIO DE (1549–1624), Spanish historian of the Indies. Herrera, who was appointed Chief Chronicler of the Indies and Chronicler of Castile and León by Philip II of Spain, is best known for his *Historia general de los hechos de los castellanos en las Islas y Tierra Firme de el Mar Océano* (General history of the deeds of the Castilians in the Islands and Mainland of the Ocean Sea), first published in 1601. Preceded by his study of the West Indies, *Descripción de las Islas y Tierra Firme de el Mar Océano que llaman Indias occidentales,* the *History* is divided into eight sections or decades, chronicling the discovery, exploration, and colonization of the New World from the era of Columbus until 1554.

Influenced by the Roman historian Tacitus, whose *Annales* he translated, Herrera supplied his history with a multitude of details, always striving to magnify the Spanish enterprise and to minimize anything untoward, harsh, cruel, or unjust. He has been accused of plagiarizing from many authors, including Bartolomé de las Casas, Gonzalo Fernández de Oviedo, and Fernando Colón. In reply to the complaint that he had never visited the Indies, he pointed out that neither Livy nor Tacitus had seen all the lands they wrote about. Despite these criticisms, his description and history of the Indies still provide a useful overview of the establishment of the Spanish overseas empire.

BIBLIOGRAPHY

Herrera y Tordesillas, Antonio de. *Historia general de los hechos de los castellanos en las Islas y Tierra Firme de el Mar Océano.* Edited by Antonio González Barcía. Madrid, 1726–1730. Reprint, 2 vols., Asunción, 1944–1947.
Prescott, William H. *History of the Reign of Ferdinand and Isabella.* 3 vols. Philadelphia, 1872.

JOSEPH F. O'CALLAGHAN

HISPANIOLA. See *Española, La.*

HORSES. See *Domesticated Animals.*

HOURGLASS. See *Timeglass.*

HOUSE OF TRADE. See *Casa de la Contratación.*

HUASCAR (d. 1532), Inca emperor, successor to Huayna Capac and rival of Atahualpa. Huascar was the son of Huayna Capac and Rahua Ocllo, Huayna Capac's sister but not his *coya* (queen). Huayna Capac had left Huascar in charge of the Inca state in Cuzco while he was campaigning in Ecuador, but Huascar was never designated coruler. After the deaths of Huayna Capac and his son and designated successor, Ninan Cuyuchi, there was much dissension among the *orejones* (Inca ruling class). The rivalries between the surviving sons led to the formation of factions. Because of Rahua Ocllo's influence, Huascar obtained court and administrative support in Cuzco and was elected successor to Huayna Capac as emperor of Tahuantinsuyu (the Inca state). However, Huascar did not maintain good relations with his supporters and antagonized the powerful lineages of Cuzco by threatening to confiscate their lands and property and to end their autonomy. He had a reputation for being tactless, violent, cruel, and cowardly. He finally rejected the nobles of Cuzco and surrounded himself with foreigners, especially the Cañaris and the Chachapoyas (northern ethnic groups), who formed his personal bodyguard.

Huascar feared that his brother Atahualpa was organizing a rebellion in the north and sent a militia army to invade Quito. The Inca army supported Atahualpa and repulsed Huascar's troops. Subsequently, Atahualpa took the title of Inca emperor. Huascar's army was definitively defeated at the battle of Huanacopampa, west of Cuzco, and Huascar was captured. Atahualpa's army triumphantly entered Cuzco. Huascar was killed shortly after Atahualpa was captured by Francisco Pizarro at Cajamarca.

BIBLIOGRAPHY

Hemming, John. *The Conquest of the Incas*. San Diego, 1970.
Rostworowski de Díez Canseco, María. "Succession, Coöption to Kingship, and Royal Incest among the Inca." *Southwestern Journal of Anthropology* 16 (1960): 417–427.

JEANETTE SHERBONDY

HUAYNA CAPAC (d. 1525?), Inca emperor. Huayna Capac was born Tito Cusi Hualpa in Tumipampa (Quito) while his father, the Inca Tupac Yupanqui, was conducting the campaign for the northern expansion of Tahuantinsuyu (the Inca state) into what is today southern Colombia. He was quite young when he succeeded to the throne. His mother, the *coya* (queen) Mama Ocllo, begged him to stay close to Cuzco, where for several years he inspected the many ethnic groups near the capital that had already submitted to Inca rule.

He essentially maintained the vast territory his father had conquered, which extended from central Chile to southern Colombia. While he was leading his armies through the southern quarter of Tahuantinsuyu, he heard of rebellions in the north and marched to Quito. The northern ethnic groups formed a strong alliance against the Inca troops, among whom there was much dissension. At one point Huayna Capac's troops even dropped his litter, which angered him for many years. Huayna Capac personally led his army and spent many years in Tumipampa fighting against and finally incorporating the northern ethnic groups into the Inca state.

He heard reports of the arrival of Francisco Pizarro's expedition along the coast of Ecuador in 1526. Shortly thereafter he died in Quito during an epidemic of smallpox and measles that also killed most of his court, the generals of his major military command, and the son he had named as his successor, Ninan Cuyuchi. He was succeeded by his son, Huascar.

BIBLIOGRAPHY

Hemming, John. *The Conquest of the Incas*. San Diego, 1970.
Rostworowski de Díez Canseco, María. *Historia del Tahuantinsuyu*. Lima, 1988.

JEANETTE SHERBONDY

HUMBOLDT, ALEXANDER VON (1769–1859), German naturalist, traveler, and statesman. Friedrich Wilhelm Heinrich Alexander von Humboldt was born in Berlin, the son of a major in the Prussian army who later became a royal chamberlain. Originally destined for a financial career, while at the universities of Frankfurt an der Oder, Berlin, and Göttingen, Humboldt's passion for travel and his early interest in geology and botany redirected him into a lifelong study of the natural sciences. In 1790 he traveled to Holland, England, and France with George Forster. In 1792 he entered the Prussian mining service, and was appointed a mining superintendent in Upper Franconia. Moving to Paris in 1798, he contributed to the first relatively conclusive determination of magnetic inclination. Later that year he journeyed to Spain and thereafter undertook a scientific expedition in company with the French botanist Aimé Bonpland, traveling during the next six years through the Spanish colonies in Venezuela, Cuba, Colombia, Peru, Ecuador, and Mexico, gathering plant specimens, mapping the regions, recording observations of natural phenomena, and studying volcanoes, the origin of tropical storms, and the igneous origin of certain rocks. On his return journey in 1804, he visited the United States, meeting several times with President Thomas Jefferson and cabinet members, to whom he reported on his travels. In 1829 he made a long-postponed scientific expedition to Russian Asia. In his later years he was often employed on diplomatic missions for the Prussian government. He died in Berlin after a prolonged illness at the age of ninety.

Humboldt's travel journals, never completed, were published in thirty-four volumes over a period of twenty-five years. Among his most important works was *Kosmos* (1845–1862), in which he provided a description of the physical universe. In a five-volume work that appeared in 1814–1834 entitled *Examen critique de l'histoire de la géographie du nouveau continent aux XVe et XVIe siècles* (A critical examination of the history of the geography of the new continent in the fifteenth and sixteenth centuries), Humboldt directed attention to a generally overlooked passage in Washington Irving's biography of Columbus in which Irving noted that the name America had been invented in 1507 by Martin Waldseemüller and his associates and first published in *Cosmographiae introductio*, as well as in a set of globes and a world map.

BIBLIOGRAPHY

Dictionary of Scientific Biography. Vol. 6, pp. 549–555. New York, 1972.
Encyclopaedia Britannica. 11th ed. Vol. 13, pp. 873–875.
Humboldt, Alexander von. *Examen critique de l'histoire de le géographie du nouveau continent aux XVe et XVIe siècles*. 5 vols. Paris, 1814–1834.
Irving, Washington. *The Life and Voyages of Christopher Columbus*. New York, 1828.
Nouvelle biographie générale depuis les temps les plus reculés jusqu'à nos jours. Vol. 25, cols. 510–525. Paris, 1861.
Terra, Helmut de. *Humboldt: The Life and Times of Alexander von Humboldt*. 6th ed. New York, 1968.

SILVIO A. BEDINI

I

ICELANDIC SAGAS. The sagas of Iceland are relevant to the story of Columbus in two ways: they recount the explorations by Europeans who preceded him to the New World and there is a hint in the records that Columbus may have visited Iceland. The Icelandic sagas indisputably document the presence of Icelanders and other Norsemen on American shores several centuries prior to Columbus. The term *saga* is an Old Norse word meaning "tale," originally an oral narrative, which began to be committed to writing in the twelfth century by Icelandic scribes. The sagas are of various kinds; they range from sober historical accounts of past events, primarily relating to happenings in which Icelanders were involved, to more fanciful stories that must be identified as romances. The chroniclers of Iceland were keenly aware of their special history as an island colony of Scandinavian (primarily Norwegian) enterprise. After their gradual Christianizing in the tenth and eleventh centuries, they began busily recording past and contemporary events in their history. Preservation of these sagas was at first casual but became systematic in the sixteenth century with the collecting of documents in the royal libraries of Scandinavia, especially in Denmark, which at this time held dominion over Iceland. An Icelandic repository did not come into being until well into the twentieth century.

Information about the Icelandic discovery was actually available before the sagas, in the *History of the Archbishopric of Hamburg* (c. 1070) by the German cleric Adam of Bremen. Adam wrote that the king of Denmark had told him of an island in the North called "Winland," which had the peculiar quality that "vines grow wild there which yield the best of wine" as well as "grain unsown." Around 1130 a Christian historian of Iceland, Ari Thorgilsson, known as "the Learned," wrote his *Íslendingabók* (Book of the Icelanders) in which he mentioned "Vinland" and its native inhabitants, whom he called "skraelingar," apparently a derogatory term referring either to American Indians or Eskimos.

For our purposes the most valuable sources are the Icelandic sagas that were written between 1100 and 1300, some of which deal specifically with the discovery of America. They offer two differing versions, which we distinguish by the manuscript compilations that contain them, called the "Hauk's Book" and the "Flatey Book." These are both from the fourteenth century. A third version, "AM. 537 qto." from the fifteenth century, is largely identical with the Hauk's Book. Scholars have long debated the relative merits of the two versions without coming to any definite conclusion.

The Flatey Book version concentrates on the family of Eric the Red and his son Leif Ericsson, who was the first to explore Vinland. Eric was born in Norway and became the first Norse settler of Greenland, having emigrated as an outlaw from Iceland in 986, but he held back from exploring Vinland. The first person to view Vinland was Bjarni Herjulfsson, who skirted its coast after losing his way from Norway to Greenland. His sighting of the unknown coast encouraged Leif to undertake an expedition that is recounted in some detail in the Flatey Book. Because of his exploration and his success Leif came to be known as "the Lucky." He was also commissioned by the king of Norway, Olafr Tryggvason, to convert the natives to Christianity (including his recalcitrant father). Leif was the first to apply Norse names to the American coast: from north to south, Helluland, "land of rocks"; Markland, "land of forests"; and Vinland, "land of vines" (possibly "of wine"). Just which part of the American coast was designated by these names is still a matter of discussion.

According to the Flatey account, Leif was not the only son of Eric to explore America. His brother Thorvald became a victim of the natives' arrows and lost his life. A third brother, Thorstein, also made the attempt but was driven back by storms. A sister named Freydis followed because "people fell to talking of the journey to Vinland, for this seemed an open road to wealth and honor." Freydis apparently had nothing but wealth in mind, for her expedition resulted in the massacre of many participants.

The Hauk's Book version (also known as Eric the Red's Saga) is more interested in the family of the later explorer Thorfinn Karlsefni, who was the first to make a serious attempt to settle the new land. One suspects that the saga writer's interest was determined by the fact that Thorfinn and his wife, Gudrid, were direct ancestors of Hauk Erlendson, the compiler of Hauk's Book. Thorfinn was an Icelandic trader who came to Greenland and equipped a fleet of three ships with 160 men, many accompanied by their wives. He brought "all sorts of livestock" with him and did not head directly to Vinland, but crossed the Davis Strait and sailed down the coast of Labrador at least as far as Newfoundland. Like Leif he found lands that he named Helluland, Markland, and Vinland.

But he also found and named other areas: a headland named Kjalarnes (Keelness), long, sandy beaches named Furdustrandir (Wonderstrands), Straumfjord (Streamfjord), a mysterious area named Hvitramannaland (White Men's Land), and finally an area named Hop, where he encountered natives with whom he first traded and later fought. This encounter can be seen as the first clash between Indians and Europeans, and it was disastrous for the outnumbered Icelanders; after their third winter they retreated back to Greenland. In the words of historian Gwyn Jones, "They were unwilling to woo and unable to conquer." The Norse settlements in Greenland have left abundant remains in the form of dwellings and churches, which were abandoned only with the extinction of the Norse colonies in the fourteenth century or possibly the early fifteenth.

There can be no doubt that the expeditions to Vinland actually took place in the tenth and eleventh centuries, but the exact location of their "Vinland" is still in doubt, in spite of the assurance of the sagas. Vinland has been sought in modern times from Labrador in the north to Florida in the south. In 1965 a new angle was offered by scholars at Yale University in the form of a purported "Vinland Map." The map got its name by including on a rectangular mappamundi a figure to the west and south of Greenland representing a "Vinlanda Insula" (Island of Vinland). Its appearance in a sumptuous Yale publication was a scholarly sensation.

In the meanwhile an experienced Norwegian explorer, Helge Ingstad, who had been pondering the problem of the Norse colonies in the New World, undertook explorations in northern waters from 1961 to 1968. He first announced his findings in *National Geographic* (November 1964) and published his first book on the subject, *Westward to Vinland,* in 1969. Ingstad was the first to locate Norse remains on an American coast, at a place in northern Newfoundland known as L'Anse aux Meadows. This was an even more startling discovery than the Vinland Map, for it concentrated attention on a more northerly area than had been customary. It had the merit of reflecting more accurately the directions of the sagas in terms of days' sailings. After exploring the American and Canadian east coasts thoroughly, Ingstad came upon sites that had never been excavated and that proved to contain indubitable evidence of Norse settlement around A.D. 1000. He and his archaeologist wife, Anne Stine Ingstad, spent seven summers, assisted by other experts, digging up the remains.

In Ingstad's words: "The results may be briefly summarized as follows: Eight larger or smaller house-sites . . . one of them a smithy, four boat-sheds, three large outdoor pits of which two may have been cooking pits. Various finds have been made at the sites and in the many test trenches." Among the rather sparse finds Ingstad mentions stone tools, nails, fragments of iron, a stone lamp, a whetstone for needles, and a soapstone spindle-whorl. A larger publication edited by Anne Stine Ingstad appeared in 1977, detailing the finds with an abundance of maps and illustrations, plus carbon datings. The Ingstads are convinced that this was the Vinland of the sagas, but questions remain about the fact that the sagas also include expeditions to more southerly climes. Ingstad admits the possibility. Otherwise we have to dismiss the sagas' stories of grapes and self-sown wheat and the active contact with the Skraelings.

The possibility of Columbus's having visited Iceland is based on a passage in his son Fernando Colón's biography of his father. He cites a letter from Columbus stating that in February 1477 he sailed "a hundred leagues beyond the island of Tile" (i.e., Thule, Iceland). But there is no reference to his having stopped in Iceland or spoken with anyone, and in any case it is unlikely that anyone he spoke to would have known about the Icelandic discovery of Vinland. More significant may be the fact that he refers to Bristol, England, as the starting point of this voyage; Bristol had connections with Iceland. On the whole, however, it is hardly important. If Columbus had learned anything, he would have mentioned it in his plans for exploration.

[See also *Vinland; Vinland Map;* and the biography of Ericsson.]

BIBLIOGRAPHY

Haugen, Einar. *Voyages to Vinland: The First American Saga.* New York, 1942.

Ingstad, Anne Stine. *The Discovery of a Norse Settlement in America.* Oslo, 1977.

Ingstad, Helge. *Westward to Vinland.* New York, 1969.

Jones, Gwyn. *The Norse Atlantic Saga.* London, 1964.

Magnusson, Magnus. *Viking Expansion Westwards.* London, 1973.

Skelton, R. A., Thomas E. Marston, and George D. Painter. *The Vinland Map.* New Haven and London, 1965.

EINAR HAUGEN

ICONOGRAPHY.

[This entry includes five articles that explore the Columbian legacy in painting, coins, stamps, and motion pictures:

Early European Portraits
American Painting
Numismatics
Philately
Film

For further discussion of visual representations of Columbus, see *Monuments and Memorials.* See *Literature* for explorations of the Columbian theme in literature.]

Early European Portraits

As far as we know, Columbus was never painted in his lifetime. Yet virtually every book about him contains a portrait, and many general textbooks do as well. The 1893 World's Columbian Exposition in Chicago displayed seventy-one portraits of Columbus, which William Eleroy Curtis discussed in *Christopher Columbus: His Portraits and Monuments.* None could be considered authentic, and few even remotely resembled extant descriptions of his physical characteristics.

The only firm evidence about Columbus's appearance comes from a few brief descriptions written by persons who knew him or at least were his contemporaries. The descriptions have a good deal in common and may have borrowed from one another. They describe a strongly built man of more than average height for the time. All agree that he had a ruddy complexion; he may have had freckles as well. His hair is variously described as bright red or blond when he was a young man and as having turned gray when he was about thirty. His face was oblong, neither full nor thin and distinguished by an aquiline nose and lively eyes. The commentaries in Italian describe their color as *bianchi* (pale or light). One Spanish commentator uses the word *garzos*, which nowadays is usually translated as "light blue," but which seems to have connoted "light gray-green" or "hazel" to Columbus's contemporaries. These distinctive physical characteristics provide a standard by which to evaluate the portraiture of Columbus.

PORTRAIT BY SEBASTIANO DEL PIOMBO (1485–1547). Oil on canvas.
THE METROPOLITAN MUSEUM OF ART, GIFT OF J. PIERPONT MORGAN, 1900.(00.18.2)

Only a few representative portraits will be discussed here, but they served as models for scores of others. Sculpture and other art forms will not be discussed, nor will the large historical scenes and murals that feature events in Columbus's life.

The most representative portraits of Columbus fall within several families or types. The first, and probably the best known, is the Piombo type, based on Sebastiano del Piombo's portrait in the Metropolitan Museum of Art in New York. The man in Piombo's portrait has a fleshy face and nose, large round eyes, dark hair, full lips, and a double chin. He is wearing a black angled hat, a full dark cape, and a vertically pleated shirt. An inscription across the top of the painting gives the date as 1519 and reads, "Haec est effigies liguris miranda Columbi antipodum primus rate qui penetravit in orbem" ("This is the likeness of the Ligurian mariner Columbus, the first in the world who penetrated the antipodes").

There is no doubt that the portrait is by Piombo, who was a younger contemporary of Columbus, and the inscription on the painting would seem to identify it conclusively. Nonetheless, the face does not reflect the written evidence we have about Columbus, and art historians have recently questioned its identification on

ENGRAVING FROM THÉODOR DE BRY'S *GRANDS VOYAGES*. Piombo type.

LIBRARY OF CONGRESS

depictions associated with the Italian Paolo Giovio (1483–1552), archbishop of Nocera in the early sixteenth century. The archbishop's palace on Lake Como displayed a large and important art collection, and his portrait of Columbus, probably commissioned between 1530 and 1540, was copied by many other artists. Unfortunately, the location and identity of the painting owned by Archbishop Giovio are no longer certain, and several paintings have been claimed as the original over the centuries.

Further confusion relates to a book Giovio wrote called *Elogia virorum bellica virtute illustrium* (1549). An edition published in Basel by Petrus Perna in 1575 contained an engraving commonly attributed to Tobias Stimmer that is often claimed to be the oldest firmly dated portrait of Columbus. There is no evidence, however, that Stimmer ever saw the portrait owned by Giovio or indeed that the engraving bears any resemblance to that portrait. The engraving shows a man with a firm expression, short curly hair, and large round eyes, dressed in what appears to be

other grounds. Michael Hirst, in his book about Piombo, says the inscription "is a later addition and there is, therefore, no reason to suppose that it is the likeness of the navigator or that the painting was done in about 1519–20." He concludes that a stylistic analysis of Piombo's development hints that "the picture may one day prove to be of one of the clerics present in the winter of 1529–30 at Bologna."

During the sixteenth century, however, the Piombo type of likeness became accepted as authentic. Théodore de Bry's *Grands voyages*, published in Frankfurt in 1595, included an engraving of the Piombo type, which Bry claimed was based on a copy of a portrait commissioned by King Fernando of Aragón before Columbus's voyage. Portraits of the Piombo type continued to be popular in the succeeding centuries. Constantino Brumidi's two paintings of Columbus in the U.S. Capitol Building, painted in the mid-nineteenth century, clearly used Piombo as a model, and twentieth-century artists have found inspiration in Piombo and his followers as well. Nonetheless, Piombo's painting cannot be taken as an authentic or even plausible representation of Columbus.

Another family of Columbus portraiture stems from two

PORTRAIT BY CONSTANTINO BRUMIDI. Piombo type. Adorns a ceiling in the Senate wing of the U.S. Capitol.

ARCHITECT OF THE CAPITOL

a monk's robe. It does not actively contradict the evidence from contemporary descriptions of Columbus, although no one ever wrote that he had curly hair.

Thus, there are two types of Columbus portraiture associated with Paolo Giovio, although many authors seem unaware of the distinction. One type descended from the painting owned by Giovio or its numerous copies; the other, from the engraving in his *Elogia virorum*.

The painting is best exemplified by the so-called di Orchi portrait, named for Dr. Alessandro di Orchi of Como, who owned the portrait in the late nineteenth century. Many claim this is the original portrait of Giovio's collection, because the Giovio male family line died out in 1849, and this portrait passed to Antonia Giovio, wife of di Orchi. The unknown artist shows the worn face of a man in later middle age, with dull eyes and a firm expression. His garb is semiclerical. The di Orchi portrait has inspired many imitators over the years. Whether or not it depicts Columbus in old age, it seems to represent a real person rather than an idealized hero.

THE SO-CALLED DI ORCHI PORTRAIT. An anonymous work named for Alessandro di Orchi, who owned the portrait in the nineteenth century. Giovio type. The work presently hangs in the Museo Civico, Como.   SCALA/ART RESOURCE

ENGRAVING ATTRIBUTED TO TOBIAS STIMMER. Capriolo subtype. From the 1575 Basel edition of Giovio's *Elogia virorum bellica virtute illustrium*.   PAR/NYC, INC.

In 1552 Cristofano dell'Altissimo was sent to Como by Cosimo de' Medici to copy the Giovio portrait. His copy has hung in the Uffizi palace in Florence ever since, belying the sometime claim that it is the original Giovio portrait. The Florentine/Uffizi portrait is very similar to the di Orchi portrait, but the subject has a thinner face and harsher expression. It seems to have been painted by a less skilled hand than the di Orchi portrait, which reinforces the notion that it is a copy rather than the original owned by Giovio.

The type of Columbus portrait descended from the engraving in Giovio's *Elogia virorum* is best represented by Aliprando Capriolo's engraving in *Ritratti di cento capitani illustri*, first published in Rome in 1596. Capriolo's rendering of the facial features, expression, and garb of Columbus is similar to Stimmer's, although Capriolo depicts Columbus's hair as long and straight rather than short and curly.

Many later portraits clearly descend from the Capriolo engraving, including a painting in the Museo Naval in Madrid. The Spanish government commissioned the portrait in 1838 from Charles Le Grand, who added age lines

FLORENTINE/UFFIZI PORTRAIT. Presumed to be a copy of the original Giovio portrait.

LIBRARY OF CONGRESS

and a more anxious expression to the face but followed the general aspect and garb set out by Capriolo. The artist shows Columbus with a noble head, round light eyes, a very high forehead, a receding hairline, straight blond hair, and a long straight nose with flaring nostrils. Many other artists since have used Capriolo and Le Grand as models.

Another commonly used depiction of Columbus is the Cevasco portrait, named for the donor who gave it to the city of Genoa. The Cevasco portrait fits in no obvious category, although it bears more resemblance to the Capriolo family of portraiture than any other. The artist depicted Columbus with a round, soft face, round, rather dull eyes, a soft cap, and a simple tunic. The portrait has been attributed to Ridolfo Ghirlandaio (1483–1561), although most sources simply say the artist and date are unknown.

The last family of Columbus portraiture to be considered here descended from a portrait by Lorenzo Lotto, signed and dated 1512. The portrait was discovered in Europe in the late nineteenth century and, despite the doubts of some scholars, soon gained a reputation as the most authentic likeness of Columbus. The portrait shows a young man with a very high forehead, a long face, straight fair hair, and fair skin. The reputation of the Lotto portrait relates not only to its close adherence to contemporary descriptions of Columbus but also to its provenience. Lotto painted it for Domenico Malipiero, a Venetian senator and historian, on the recommendation of Angelo Trevisan, secretary to the Venetian ambassador in Granada in 1501. Both Trevisan and his ambassador knew Columbus well, which puts the Lotto portrait closer to its subject than any other painting known. An engraving of the Lotto portrait by T. Johnson in 1892, contained in an article by John C. Van Dyke for *Century* magazine, gave Columbus a suspicious, piercing glance and an aspect rather different from the original.

The Lotto family of Columbus portraiture includes two distinguished paintings. One is *The Virgin of the Navigators* by Alejo Fernández, a Spanish artist active in Seville from 1508 and in Córdoba before that. Fernández could have met or at least seen Columbus before the latter died in 1506, though there is no proof that the two had any contact. *The Virgin of the Navigators,* painted in 1531–1536, hangs in the Reales Alcazares in Seville and depicts several famous explorers at the Virgin's feet. They have been variously identified, but the figure in lavish robes in the left foreground has often been identified as Columbus. Whether or not Fernández ever saw Columbus, it is likely that he used a local model for the painting, because his Columbus greatly resembles King Melchior in the *Epiphany* that Fernández's workshop painted for the cathedral of Seville. In other words, however closely Fernández's portrait may resemble descriptions of Columbus, one cannot argue that it is an authentic likeness.

The other distinguished portrait of the Lotto type was painted by the Spanish artist Joaquin Sorolla y Bastida (1863–1923). Sorolla's *Departure of Columbus from the Port of Palos* was commissioned by the American collector Thomas Fortune Ryan and currently hangs in the Mariner's Museum in Newport News, Virginia. Besides doing research, the artist used a descendant of Columbus, the duke of Veragua, as his model. In Sorolla's masterful full-length portrait, Columbus has sharp features and a penetrating gaze, which reflect his character far better than the mild and noble visages depicted by Lotto and Capriolo.

Dozens of other portrayals of Columbus follow these four families of portraiture—Piombo, di Orchi, Capriolo, and Lotto—either singly or in combination. Others span the range of European physical types and bear little or no relation to contemporary descriptions of Columbus. Depending on the source, Columbus can be depicted as a bearded buccaneer, a corpulent burgher, a brooding intellectual, a dashing cavalier, or a pensive ascetic. He can be clean-shaven or bearded; thin or fat; blond,

ENGRAVING BY ALIPRANDO CAPRIOLO. From his *Ritratti de cento capitani illustri*. Rome, 1596. Capriolo subtype.

ENGRAVING AFTER THE LE GRAND PORTRAIT. This engraving by Henri Lefort (France, 1891) closely follows the 1838 portrait by Charles Le Grand in the Museo Naval, Madrid. Capriolo subtype.

OIL PORTRAIT BY LORENZO LOTTO. Signed and dated 1512.

ENGRAVING BY T. JOHNSON. From *Century Magazine*, 1892. Lotto type.

OIL PORTRAIT BY JOAQUIN SOROLLA Y BASTIDA. Lotto type.   COURTESY OF THE MARINERS' MUSEUM, NEWPORT NEWS, VIRGINIA

ALEJO FERNÁNDEZ, *THE VIRGIN OF THE NAVIGATORS*. Oil, 1531–1536. The figure in lavish robes in the left foreground is often identified as Columbus.   MAS, BARCELONA

brunet, red-headed, totally gray, or nearly bald. Because we have no portraits painted from life, and none even dated in his lifetime, there is no authentic portrait of Columbus. Nonetheless, a comparison of written descriptions with the available portraiture suggests that the best approximations of his appearance are the Lotto or Capriolo type of portrait for the prime years of his life and the di Orchi type for his old age.

BIBLIOGRAPHY

Berenson, Bernard. *Lorenzo Lotto*. London, 1956.
Bianconi, Piero. *All the Paintings of Lorenzo Lotto*. Translated by Paul Colacicchi. New York, 1963.
Curtis, William Eleroy. *Christopher Columbus: His Portraits and Monuments*. Chicago, 1893.
Hirst, Michael. *Sebastiano del Piombo*. Oxford, 1981.
Honour, Hugh. "L'image de Christophe Colomb." *Revue du Louvre* 26 (1976): 255–267.
Peel, Edmund, et al. *The Painter Joaquin Sorolla y Bastida*. London, 1989.
Van Dyke, John C. "The Lotto Portrait of Columbus." *Century* 44 (October 1892): 818–822.
Volpe, Carlo, ed. *L'opera completa di Sebastiano del Piombo*. Milan, 1980.

CARLA RAHN PHILLIPS

American Painting

Depictions of Christopher Columbus in American art are diverse because artists have imagined his likeness so differently. But they are also monotonously similar because painters portray identical incidents. Such events as his meeting with clerical scholars in Salamanca, his departure from Palos, his landing at San Salvador, his triumphal appearance before the Spanish court, and his return in chains after being arrested by Spanish authorities frequently found their way into paintings and prints. During the nineteenth century the landing at San Salvador was by far the most popular Columbus subject, perhaps because it best seemed to embody the metaphor of "discovery" by picturing the first permanent European presence on American shores.

One of the earliest depictions of Columbus by an American artist was Benjamin West's *An Indian Cacique of the Island of Cuba* (Chicago Historical Society), created as an illustration for Bryan Edward's *History of the British West Indies*, published in 1794 shortly after the tercentenary of Columbus's first voyage. Six years later Edward Savage and David Edwin issued a large engraving entitled *The Landing of Columbus* (American Antiquarian Society, Worcester, Mass.), which features a large burly figure of the Admiral in Renaissance attire accompanied by a priest and several soldiers. Three immigrant artists—Michael Corne (private collection), Frederick Kemmelmeyer (National Gallery of Art, Washington, D.C.), and John James Barralet (Library of Congress)—created Landing of Columbus scenes in the early years of the nineteenth century. All three of these artists placed an unprecedented emphasis on the Catholic orientation of the landing party and stressed the importance of American commerce. Around 1825, an anonymous folk artist rendered a most unusual version of the *Landing of Columbus* (New York State Historical Association, Cooperstown), featuring two natives, one playing a flute, the other aiming a bow and arrow at a landing party in the background. Were it not for the inscription attached beneath ("Christopher Columbus

FREDERICK KEMMELMEYER, *FIRST LANDING OF CHRISTOPHER COLUMBUS*. Oil on canvas, 1800–1805.

NATIONAL GALLERY OF ART, WASHINGTON, D.C.

Landing upon the Island of St. Salvador; October 12, 1492"), one would have no way of identifying the subject, especially since the setting looks a great deal like the rocky coast of New England.

After Washington Irving's popular *History of the Life and Voyages of Christopher Columbus* was published in 1828, artists interpreting events from the Admiral's life patterned their compositions after the many descriptive passages in the biography. John Vanderlyn acknowledged that he consulted Irving's text when painting *The Landing of Columbus on San Salvador,* which was installed in the Capitol rotunda in 1847 and has become the most famous Columbus painting in the United States. After he received the commission from Congress in 1836, Vanderlyn (then in his sixties) traveled to the Caribbean to make sketches of the foliage and the terrain before renting a studio in Paris to complete the painting. While the work was in progress, Americans visiting the French capital sent home glowing reports, no doubt realizing that the composition—with the heroic Columbus planting the standard of Fernando and Isabel on the tropical shore—epitomized the discovery as did no other painting that preceded or followed it.

Vanderlyn's work became such a familiar icon of popular culture that copies appeared on U.S. stamps, souvenirs, advertisements, and even the side panel of a turn-of-the-century circus wagon (Circus Museum, Baraboo, Wis.).

Among other unusual American works from the mid-nineteenth century are William James Hubard's *The Dream of Columbus* (Valentine Museum, Richmond), which pictures the Admiral as a youthful dreamer envisioning his future empire, and four versions of *Columbus at Salamanca* by Robert Walter Weir (West Point Museum), William Henry Powell (Kennedy Gallery, New York City), Frank Duveneck (Cincinnati Art Museum), and William Merritt Chase (private collection). Between 1842 and 1855, the German-American artist Emanuel Leutze executed a series of paintings devoted to episodes from Columbus's life, including *The Return of Columbus in Chains to Cadiz* (1842, Masco Corporation, Detroit, on loan to U.S. State Department), *Columbus before the Queen* (1843, Brooklyn Museum), and *The Departure of Columbus from Palos* (1855, Fumi International Collection, Tokyo). All of Leutze's compositions are theatrical spectacles that exaggerate the Admiral's lonely heroism and

dramatize his mistreatment by the Spanish court. *The Departure from Palos,* which depicts the dramatic moment on the deck of *Santa María* just as the large sail was being hoisted, is perhaps the most riveting because Columbus in the center of the composition points westward toward the lands he will "discover." In the early 1880s, William Morris Hunt created an allegorical mural entitled *The Discoverer* for the New York State capitol in Albany, featuring a brooding figure of Columbus accompanied by several goddesses. Shortly after its completion, Hunt's painting began to deteriorate and subsequently had to be covered.

The 1892 quadricentenary inspired many American painters and printmakers to delineate episodes from Columbus's life. Thomas Moran and Albert Bierstadt painted tropical landscapes with tiny representations of Columbus and his crew, Thomas Eakins made a sketch of *Columbus in Prison* (Kennedy Gallery), and James A. McN. Whistler designed a *Discoverer* mural for the Boston Public Library, although the project was never completed. In the early twentieth century, the illustrators Edward

ANONYMOUS, *LANDING OF COLUMBUS*. Watercolor, circa 1825.

NEW YORK STATE HISTORICAL ASSOCIATION, COOPERSTOWN

JOHN VANDERLYN, *THE LANDING OF COLUMBUS ON SAN SALVADOR*. Installed in the Rotunda of the U.S. Capitol in 1847.

ARCHITECT OF THE CAPITOL

ROBERT WALTER WEIR, *COLUMBUS AT SALAMANCA*.   WEST POINT MUSEUM, NEW YORK

EMANUEL LEUTZE, *COLUMBUS BEFORE THE QUEEN*. Oil on canvas, 1843.   THE BROOKLYN MUSEUM, NEW YORK

ROBERT COLESCOTT, *KNOWLEDGE OF THE PAST IS THE KEY TO THE FUTURE: SOME AFTER THOUGHTS ON DISCOVERY*. Acrylic on canvas, 1986.   COURTESY OF THE PHYLISS KIND GALLERY, NEW YORK AND CHICAGO; PHOTOGRAPH BY ADAM REICH

Austin Abbey (Yale University) and N. C. Wyeth (Annapolis Museum) created dramatic landing scenes that featured a fair and youthful Columbus claiming the "New World" for Spain. By the 1930s, films began to replace paintings as the major source for Columbus imagery, while at the same time adherence to modern trends seemed to end the long history of narrative paintings devoted to episodes from Columbus's life. But the subject has not vanished entirely, even though such recent works as Robert Colescott's *Knowledge of the Past Is the Key to the Future: Some After Thoughts on Discovery* (1986, Metropolitan Museum of Art, New York City) and Alexander M. Frankfurter's *Columbus Triptych* (1980s, property of the artist) have responded to ethnic and racial sensitivites and thus attempted to counteract the very myths that once motivated artists in the United States.

BIBLIOGRAPHY

Abrams, Ann Uhry, and Barbara Groseclose, eds. *Christopher Columbus/U.S.A.* Forthcoming.

Brown, Milton W. et al. *American Art: Painting, Sculpture, Architecture, Decorative Arts, Photography.* New York, 1979.

ANN UHRY ABRAMS

Numismatics

Christopher Columbus was not widely depicted in coins or medals until the twentieth century. The 1592, 1692, and 1792 anniversaries of his first voyage passed without numismatic notice, although a medal struck by the Columbian Order (Tammany Society) of New York City in 1789 may have honored Columbus. The first medal to salute him specifically was a French bronze piece issued by Amedée Durand in 1819 as part of a series of medals honoring the world's famous men. The first coin to depict Columbus was an eight-real (dollar) piece issued by Guatemala in 1854.

The four-hundredth anniversary of the first voyage was commemorated by four nations. The United States, Colombia, and El Salvador issued half-dollar coins (approximately 31 millimeters in diameter) in 1892; the American coin was reissued in 1893 and the Salvadoran coin in 1893 and 1894. The United States also issued a silver quarter-dollar in 1893 portraying Queen Isabel. El Salvador placed Columbus's effigy on its 37-millimeter silver pesos issued between 1892 and 1914. The fourth nation, Costa Rica, named its new monetary unit the colón in 1897 and placed

COLUMBIAN SILVER DOLLAR. Minted by the United States in 1892 and 1893, the world's first coin of general circulation to honor Christopher Columbus. Over 2,500,000 pieces were struck at the Philadelphia mint. Size: 31 mm.

SILVER QUARTER DOLLAR. Honoring Queen Isabel, minted by the United States in 1893. Only 24,000 pieces were struck at the Philadelphia mint. Size: 25 mm.

ALL COINS ILLUSTRATED IN THIS ARTICLE ARE FROM THE COLLECTION OF RUSSELL RULAU.

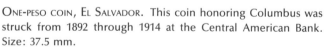

FIFTY-CENTAVO COIN, COLOMBIA. Colombia struck only 4,800 pieces of this 1892 denomination honoring Columbus. Size: 31 mm.

ONE-PESO COIN, EL SALVADOR. This coin honoring Columbus was struck from 1892 through 1914 at the Central American Bank. Size: 37.5 mm.

Columbus's portrait on its gold two-, five-, and ten-colón coins issued from 1897 to 1928.

There were no other Columbus coins until Italy pictured Columbus's three ships (without naming them) on its silver five-hundred-lire coins between 1958 and 1987. Other nations began to honor Columbus on coins intended for collectors in the 1960s. The Bahamas, where Columbus first landed in the New World, very likely on Watlings Island (Guanahani or San Salvador), issued a gold one-hundred-dollar piece in 1967; other Bahamian issues

appeared between 1971 and 1988. Haiti issued Columbus coins between 1967 and 1974, Jamaica between 1972 and 1989, the Turks and Caicos Islands between 1975 and 1986, the Cayman Islands in 1988, the Dominican Republic between 1984 and 1988, the Cook Islands in 1989, Cuba in 1981, Belize 1989, Nicaragua in 1989, Italy in 1990, and El Salvador between 1984 and 1988.

In 1989, Spain issued a set of four gold and eight silver coins to honor Columbus, his discoveries, and the times in which he lived. Each coin was struck to the standards of

TWO-THOUSAND PESETA COIN, SPAIN. This large (40-mm) silver coin was struck in an issue of 235,000 at the Madrid Mint in 1989. Its value approximates the eight-real "Spanish dollar" of the sixteenth century.

TWO-HUNDRED PESETA COIN, SPAIN. An astrolabe such as that used by Columbus is featured on this small (20-mm) 1989 issue, approximately equal to one real in sixteenth-century coinage. This and the two-thousand peseta coin are part of a twelve-coin issue initiating a massive memorial minting saluting the 1992 Quincentennial.

TEN-THOUSAND CORDOBA COIN, NICARAGUA. This 1989 silver coin recalls the discovery of the country by Columbus during his final voyage in 1502. Ten thousand pieces were struck. Size: 38 mm.

the fifteenth century. The U.S. Congress authorized gold five-dollar, silver one-dollar, and nickel-clad fifty-cent coins for the five-hundredth anniversary in 1992.

BIBLIOGRAPHY

Eglit, Nathan N. *Columbiana: The Medallic History of Christopher Columbus and the Columbian Exposition of 1893*. Chicago, 1965.

Forrer, Leonard. *Biographical Dictionary of Medalists*. 9 vols. Reprint, London, 1987.

Hibler, Hal E., and Charles V. Kappen. *So-Called Dollars*. New York, 1963.

Hobson, Burton. *Historic Gold Coins of the World*. London, 1971.

Krause, Chester L., and Clifford Mishler. *Standard Catalog of World Coins*. Iola, Wis., 1990.

Rulau, Russell. *Discovering America: The Coin Collecting Connection*. Iola, Wis., 1989.

RUSSELL RULAU

Philately

From the first issuance of postage stamps in Great Britain in 1840 to the present day, many countries of the world have honored Christopher Columbus with designs on their stamps; over fifteen hundred such stamps have been issued. The first country to so honor Columbus was Chile, which used his portrait on its first postal issue in 1853—a five-centavo denomination in brown-red. In fact, all of Chile's postal issues until 1900 utilized his portrait in the design.

The initial stamp issued by the United States to commemorate Columbus was the fifteen-cent bicolor stamp of the 1869 regular postage series, which showed a classic landing scene of Columbus's discovery of the Americas. This particular denomination has also been found with the center inverted, which is a very scarce and valuable stamp. Its value ranges from $17,500 to $145,000, depending on condition and color, and whether used or unused.

The nineteenth century was a period of considerable movement of people from Europe to the United States and then westward across the continent. In the course of this expansion, more than forty towns named Columbus were established, of which only nineteen have survived with an operating post office into the latter half of the twentieth century.

A major event commemorating Columbus's discovery of the New World was the World's Columbian Exposition held in Chicago, Illinois, from May 1 to October 30, 1893. In that year the U.S. Post Office issued an unusual series of sixteen commemorative stamps in horizontal format, in denominations of 1¢ to $5.00, for a total face value of $16.34. These stamps depicted various scenes pertaining to Columbus and his voyages to the New World. Quantities issued included 1.4 billion of the two-cent denomina-

UNITED STATES, ISSUES INCORPORATING THE "LANDING SCENE." *Above:* Pictorial issue of 1869, fifteen-cent denomination engraved and printed in brown and blue by the National Bank Note Company. *Below:* Columbian commemorative issue of 1893, two-cent violet engraved and printed by the American Bank Note Company. Both issues use an engraving after *Landing of Columbus* (1842–1844), a painting by John Vanderlyn commissioned for the Rotunda of the U.S. Capitol.

tion and 26,000 to 55,000 of the five different dollar values in the series. The designs in this set were engraved and printed by the American Bank Note Company. A complete set of these stamps is considered one of the key series of U.S. philatelic collectibles.

One of the many firsts associated with the Columbian Exposition was the release of a series of beautifully lithographed souvenir postal cards. It consisted of twelve designs printed in full multicolor. These cards, printed on the back of the one-cent, black U. S. Grant postal card, were released as the official world's fair souvenir cards through a concession contract held by Charles W. Goldsmith. Approximately two million of Goldsmith's cards

UNITED STATES, POSTAL ITEMS FROM THE 1893 WORLD'S COLUMBIAN EXPOSITION. *Above:* Columbian Exposition postal stationery; one-cent blue entire postmarked with machine cancellation of the Exposition's postal station. *Middle:* One-cent Ulysses S. Grant postal card with machine cancellation of the Exposition's postal station, dated September 1, 1893. This is the postal card stock on which the multicolor Goldsmith designs (below) were printed. *Below:* Lithographed, multicolor souvenir postal card, showing a portrait of Columbus and a view of the Exposition's Fisheries Building. These souvenir cards were printed by the American Lithographic Company and distributed by Charles Goldsmith.

UNITED STATES, COLUMBIAN COMMEMORATIVE ISSUE OF 1893. Complete set of sixteen denominations, from one cent to five dollars, with various Columbus-related scenes. These are impressions from the original plates. *Top to bottom, left to right:* one cent, a clean-shaven Columbus, as pictured by artist William Powell, is shown in sight of land from the deck of *Santa María*; two cents, only a day later, Columbus lands, in an engraving after John Vanderlyn, but he now has a full beard; three cents, *Santa María*; four cents, *Niña, Pinta,* and *Santa María*; five cents, Columbus asks Isabel to finance his trip; six cents, Columbus is welcomed in Barcelona after his return from the first voyage; eight cents, Columbus restored to favor after meeting with Isabel; ten cents, Columbus presents a group of American Indians to Isabel; fifteen cents, Columbus relates his discoveries (the platform from which he spoke can still be seen at the Cathedral of Barcelona); thirty cents, Columbus at La Rábida (the first time a dog was ever pictured on a stamp); fifty cents, Columbus is recalled to Barcelona by Isabel prior to the first voyage; one dollar, depiction of legendary scene in which Isabel pawns her jewels to finance the first voyage; two dollars, Columbus is returned to Spain in chains; three dollars, Columbus tells the Spanish court of his discoveries after his third voyage; four dollars, portraits of Isabel and Columbus (this is the first time a U.S. stamp featured portraits of royalty or someone who was not a U.S. citizen); five dollars, Columbus and allegorical figures in a design taken from a commemorative half-dollar issued for the 1893 World's Columbian Exposition.

were sold during the fair, and many were mailed to foreign destinations, thus publicizing the Columbian Exposition. Although printed on U.S. government postal stationery, they are considered to be the first illustrated postal cards in the United States.

The Columbian Exposition also maintained and operated a World's Fair Station post office. Mail collected from various points on the fairgrounds was taken to the station for canceling and handling. Special World's Fair Station machine and hand-stamp markings were applied on this mail. Thus, there are a range of U.S. postal markings under this category for the collector of Columbian material.

Other privately printed Columbian four-hundredth anniversary postal cards and stationery as well as illustrated envelopes and letterheads were issued during this period. A special "Puck" postal card (*Puck* magazine) was given away to visitors at the Puck Building on the fairgrounds.

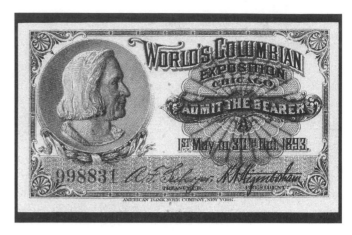

SOUVENIR TICKET, WORLD'S COLUMBIAN EXPOSITION OF 1893. Showing a medallion portrait of Christopher Columbus. From a group of six designs that were engraved and printed by the American Bank Note Company.

OTHER ITEMS OF FOUR-HUNDREDTH ANNIVERSARY VINTAGE. *Top left*: Wells Fargo domestic frank commemorating the anniversary. *Top right*: Unusual use of three Columbian entires that have been overlapped as one cover to make the five-cent foreign mail rate. Mailed from New York to Christiania, Norway. *Bottom*: Trade card published by Ayer's Sarsaparilla.

COLUMBIAN COMMEMORATIVE ISSUE STAMPS ON SELF-PROMOTIONAL BUSINESS ENVELOPES. *Top*: Stewart Fruit Company, Baltimore; postmarked 1894. *Bottom left*: W. F. Snyder of Mifflintown, Pennsylvania, evidently in the furniture-moving business. *Bottom right*: J. F. Collins, dry goods retailer, Smith, North Carolina; postmarked 1894.

TURN-OF-THE-CENTURY ISSUES FROM CENTRAL AND SOUTH AMERICA. The four-hundredth anniversary inspired many postal designs in the Spanish-speaking countries. *Left:* El Salvador, one-centavo postal card with printed frank showing the landing of Columbus; issued 1892. Background design shows ships with a map of the route of one of Columbus's voyages. *Right:* Chile, government postal card. Three-cent denomination with portrait of Columbus; issued 1905.

Another interesting Columbian Exposition collectible is a series of six beautifully engraved and printed souvenir admission tickets, each with a different portrait. These tickets were engraved and printed by the American Bank Note Company. One has a portrait of Christopher Columbus.

In 1893 the U.S. Post Office also issued four envelopes (entires) in denominations of one cent, two cents, five cents, and ten cents. This commemorative postal stationery group has embossed portraits of Columbus and Liberty against a background of the Eastern and Western Hemispheres.

Other countries, including Argentina, Chile, Honduras, El Salvador, Nicaragua, and Venezuela, also issued stamps and postal stationery in observance of the four-hundredth anniversary. Interestingly, Spain was not among them. The first stamp issued by Spain in recognition of Columbus's achievement was included in a series issued for the Seville and Barcelona Exposition in 1929. The one-centavo greenish blue stamp shows the flagship of Columbus, *Santa María,* offshore from the city of Seville.

In 1930, Spain allowed a privately produced postage set

and two airmail sets commemorating Christopher Columbus to be used. Limited quantities of these sets were given to the Spanish postal authorities, who placed them on sale for a short time. They are attractive, large-size stamps with designs relating to Columbus. Several of the series were printed in multicolor.

During recent years a number of countries, primarily in South and Central America but also elsewhere, have issued Columbus stamps that may be considered as early commemoratious of the five-hundredth anniversary. And in 1990, the United States tentatively scheduled several souvenir-type sheetlets bearing "stamp on stamp" designs taken from those included in the 1892 series of U.S. World's Columbian Exposition commemoratives.

It is interesting to compare how the European countries Columbus knew most intimately have commemorated him on their stamps in the nineteenth and twentieth centuries. For example, Portugal has never recognized Columbus on its postage or commemorative issues and has expressed no intent to do so for the quincentenary. Spain recognized Columbus with issues in 1929 and 1930, and it has already started issues for the quincentenary.

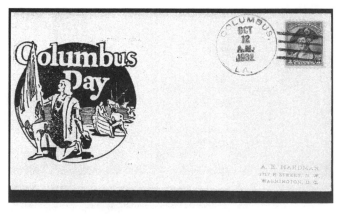

POSTMARKS OF U.S. CITIES NAMED COLUMBUS. *Top left*: North Carolina, 1932; design of envelope shows Columbus at court of Isabel. *Top right*: Kansas, 1894. *Bottom*: Louisiana, 1932.

SPAIN, 1930. Various denominations and designs from the three Columbus sets issued in September 1930.

Though Italy has released many special issues over the past seventy-five years, Columbus has received little recognition. Emphasis has, rather, been placed on the achievements of Marco Polo. There are, however, indications that Italy will recognize Columbus with an issue in 1992.

BIBLIOGRAPHY

Bleuler, Gordon, and Jim Doolin. "Columbian Exposition Revisited." *American Philatelist* 94, no. 8 (1980): 713–726.

Bomar, William J. *Postal Markings of U.S. Expositions.* North Miami, Fla., 1986.

Doolin, Jim. *1893 Columbian Exposition Admission & Concession Tickets.* Dallas, 1981.

Maineri, Ronald J. *Checklist of Christopher Columbus Related Postage Stamps.* 2d ed. San Bernardino, Calif., 1987.

GORDON BLEULER AND JIM DOOLIN

Film

Christopher Columbus has been the subject of a wide variety of motion-picture productions throughout the twentieth century, ranging from one-reel films in the early silent era to scientific expeditionary footage, animated educational short subjects, a television miniseries, and a major feature film in the age of sound.

The importance of motion pictures is often ignored in assessments of the cultural landscape of the twentieth century. Films, in all their variety, have played an important role in perpetuating the iconography of Columbus that was established in Europe and America, through the end of the nineteenth century. Indeed, it is the entire body of those pre-cinema stereotypes and iconographic depictions, which began accumulating during Columbus's lifetime and were nurtured and polished in popular expressions between the sixteenth and nineteenth centuries, that became the grist for motion pictures of all kinds in the twentieth.

Christopher Columbus was of interest to early filmmakers because of his obvious link to the origins of America. But there was another more direct reason why Columbus was regarded by the first film producers as a historical figure of particular interest to contemporary audiences. The age of commercial development of motion pictures began the year after America celebrated the quadricentennial of Columbus's discovery in 1892. During this period of precinematic popular entertainment, an enormous output of amateur and professional plays, novels, songs, poems, and other works was produced on the life of Columbus. (The outpouring of these works actually began prior to 1880 and continued to appear with unusual frequency through the early part of the twentieth century.) In the decade of the 1890s alone, the United States Copyright Office registered over forty dramatic compositions based on the life of Columbus, plus numerous biographies, historical novels and other written and graphic works as well.

By the end of the nineteenth century, filmmakers began turning to fictional and historical subjects for plot and character ideas that could be made into short entertainment films. These early productions, though primitive by modern standards, were nevertheless usually based on scripts or scenarios that were derived from existing source materials that had already demonstrated, to some degree in a nonfilm venue, their popularity with a mass audience. Early film producers looked toward all the precinema, large audience entertainments for successful works that could be adapted to film. No good narrative idea or plot was ignored regardless of its original venue or format: grand opera, the Broadway theater, novels, popular songs and poems, magazines and pulp fiction, and vaudeville or burlesque sketches.

The commercial development of motion pictures, particularly in America, grew therefore directly out of the ideas and subjects that formed the content of popular entertainments as they existed at the end of the nineteenth century. When the makers of film entertainments discovered that all that had gone before them was adaptable to the screen, Columbus was among the prime group of historical figures whose life stories were virtually already prepared for endless adaptations to the motion picture medium.

The first feature-length American motion picture about Columbus was the three-reel production *The Coming of Columbus,* released by the Selig Polyscope Company of Chicago in May 1912. The scenario was written by C. E. Nixon and the starring roles were played by Charles Clary, Thomas Santschi, Bessie Eyton, and Herbert Rawlinson. The film is of special interest because the producer, William N. Selig, filmed many scenes on board replicas of *Niña, Pinta,* and *Santa María* that had been presented to the United States by the queen regent, María Cristina of Spain, for display at the World's Columbian Exposition of 1893. In an effort to achieve authenticity and publicity, Selig also secured the use of the log of the first voyage as a prop in the film.

The earliest extant theatrical motion picture about Columbus known to be in an American film archive is a 1910 French production by the Gaumont Company entitled *Christopher Columbus,* in the collection of the Library of Congress. It was imported and released by George Kleine, a Chicago-based film distributor. The most widely distributed and best-known English-language, sound-era feature film on the life of Columbus is the 1948 J. Arthur Rank production, *Christopher Columbus,* starring Fredric March and Florence Eldridge. Though the Gaumont, Selig,

FROM *THE COMING OF COLUMBUS*, UNITED STATES, 1912. The three-reel Selig Polyscope production. *Top*: Columbus is made an admiral by Isabel and Fernando before taking command of his ships. *Bottom left*: Reproductions of *Niña, Pinta,* and *Santa María*, which were given as gifts by the Spanish government to the World's Columbian Exposition of 1893 and refitted by the Selig company for the film. *Bottom right*: Columbus is received at the court of Isabel and Fernando after the first voyage.

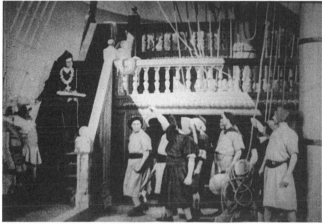

FROM *CHRISTOPHER COLUMBUS*, FRANCE, 1910. The Gaumont Company production. *Above:* Columbus persuades Isabel and Fernando to sponsor his voyage. *Below:* Columbus quiets his rebellious crew.   LIBRARY OF CONGRESS

In addition, motion pictures have been directed to purposes other than theatrical entertainment since the making of narrative films began in the early 1900s. In 1923, for example, the Yale University Press Film Service produced a biographical film entitled *Columbus,* based on

FROM *CHRISTOPHER COLUMBUS*, UNITED STATES, 1948. The J. Arthur Rank production. Two scenes of Columbus at court. *Above:* Columbus (Frederic March) entreats Isabel (Florence Eldridge) and Fernando. *Below:* Columbus's triumphal return after his first voyage.   THE MUSEUM OF MODERN ART, FILM STILLS ARCHIVE

and Rank productions span almost forty years, they depict the identical dramatic events of Columbus's life in the same reverent and conventional manner that characterized mainstream commercial biographical films until the 1960s.

Short-subject productions from the same period created humor by incorporating Columbus's name in their titles. Examples include the 1911 Thanhouser one-reeler *A Columbus Day Conspiracy,* the 1933 Vitaphone short *Double Crossing of Columbus* (starring the vaudeville act Vanessi and the Maxellos), the 1934 Walter Lantz cartoon *Chris Columbus, Jr.* (with animation by Tex Avery), and the 1938 Terrytoon *Chris Columbo.*

As with the majority of important historical figures whose lives have been dramatized in motion pictures, Columbus has also been the target of occasional satires, as in Chico Marx's fine cameo burlesque in the otherwise forgettable *The Story of Mankind* (Warner Bros., 1957).

FROM *CHRISTOPHER COLUMBUS*, UNITED STATES, 1948.   The J. Arthur Rank production. Columbus (standing), before his arrest, is interrogated by Bobadilla.

Irving Berdine Richman's book *The Spanish Conquerors*. This film, along with others in the series Chronicles of America Photoplays, was produced partly as a rebuttal by the academic community to the costume melodramas of commercial producers in New York and Hollywood, who were criticized at the time for their lack of regard for historical facts. The series was also intended to promote the use of film as an educational medium.

One of the more interesting noncommercial applications of motion pictures was made in 1939 by the historian Samuel Eliot Morison, who used the medium to record his expedition retracing the first voyage of Columbus.

Numerous short films and filmstrips about Columbus and other explorers have also been produced for educational markets, especially in the period following World War II. Productions of this type that continue to be circulated by distributors of educational films include *Christopher Columbus* (BBC/Time-Life, 1976), *Christopher Columbus* (Churchill Films, 1982), and *Christopher Columbus—The Voyage of Discovery* (American Films, 1989).

Two notable productions on the life of Columbus have appeared on American television networks. The first is the 1971 CBS Television News broadcast *You Are There: Columbus and Isabella,* which was hosted by Walter Cronkite. The second is the six-hour miniseries *Christopher Columbus* (1985), also broadcast by CBS. Produced by Radiotelevisione Italiana with international financing, the series was widely seen throughout Europe and the Americas.

BIBLIOGRAPHY

Dramatic Compositions Copyrighted in the United States, 1870–1916. 2 vols. Washington, D.C., 1918.

Educational Film and Video Locator. 4th ed. 2 vols. New York, 1990.

Filmography

Christopher Columbus. Gaumont Film Company, France, 1910.

The Coming of Columbus. Selig Polyscope Company, 1912.

Columbus. Yale University Press Film Service, 1923.

Harvard Columbus Expedition, 1939. Samuel Eliot Morison/ Richard S. Colley.

Christopher Columbus. J. Arthur Rank Productions, 1948.

PATRICK LOUGHNEY

IMAGINARY GEOGRAPHY. See *Geography, Imaginary.*

INCAS. See *Indian America,* article on *Incas and Their Neighbors.*

INDIAN AMERICA.

[This entry provides an overview of the peoples and cultures of the Western Hemisphere that figure prominently in the earliest phases of European presence in the Americas. The lead article, *First Visual Impressions in Europe,* surveys the earliest representations of what to Europeans was a new world. It is followed by twelve articles on particular peoples from the Caribbean region, South America, and North America:

Taínos
Island Caribs
Arawaks and Caribs
Tupinambás
Indians of the Spanish Main and Central America
Chibchas
Incas and Their Neighbors
Mayas
Aztecs and Their Neighbors
Indians of Northern Mexico, Baja California, and Southwestern North America
Indians of La Florida
Indians of New England, Roanoke, Virginia, and the St. Lawrence Valley

For further discussion of the Western Hemisphere before Columbus's voyages across the Atlantic and the consequences of encounter, see *Agriculture; Colonization; Disease and Demography; Encomienda; Fauna; Flora; Mineral Resources; Pacification, Conquest, and Genocide; Settlements; Slavery; Syphilis; Trade,* article on *Caribbean Trade; Women in the Americas.*]

First Visual Impressions in Europe

There is no evidence that Columbus or anyone on his voyages made pictures of what they saw in America, nor are any pictures known of the people or the natural and artificial curiosities they took back to Europe. However, the earliest illustrations that claim to show American subjects do appear in editions printed before 1500 of Columbus's letter announcing his discovery. One of

these, issued in two versions in Basel in 1493 and 1494, shows a Mediterranean forty-oared galley approaching "Insula hyspana" (La Española), where there is a waiting crowd of about twelve natives, entirely unclothed as Columbus reported the men to be, but with short hair and at least one man bearded, as were no Indians seen or described by Columbus. No artifacts are shown, and no distinctive flora or fauna. The other woodcut, which was first issued in 1493 with G. Dati's Italian verse translation of Columbus's letter, also shows a crowd of Indians, the men bearded and unclothed, the women wearing leafy girdles, and both with long wavy hair. The women's girdles reflect Columbus's brief verbal description, as do a badly depicted palm tree beside the Indians and two large branched trees behind them. There are also two roofed sheds, which are pure inventions of the (unknown) artist. This scene was repeated without useful variations in three other Italian editions of this poem, published in 1493 and 1495.

Illustrations of Vespucci's Account. The next known published European illustrations of America are woodcuts accompanying various versions and translations of accounts by Amerigo Vespucci. One is a variant of the Dati scene. In the others most of the elements are based on

FRONTISPIECE OF GIULIANO DATI'S *LETTERA.* Published in Florence, 1493. King Fernando of Spain points across the Atlantic to the landing of Columbus. None of the details is based on American reality.

LIBRARY OF CONGRESS, RARE BOOK DIVISION

FROSCHAUER WOODCUT, AUGSBURG, 1505. Tupinambá Indians of Brazil in a hand-colored woodcut. This is the first picture of New World natives to contain some relatively accurate details.

NEW YORK PUBLIC LIBRARY

Vespucci's verbal descriptions of South American Indians, especially their nakedness, or on the artists' conventional preconceptions, and do not directly reflect or depict American reality. Several of them include clearly non-American elements, such as curly hair, full beards, and the wrong kinds of clubs, buildings, and canoes. However, there are one or two exceptions that provide the first true, or approximately true, European images of America.

The best known is a woodcut on a broadside probably printed by Johann Froschauer in Augsburg in 1505; it is accompanied by four lines in German that paraphrase Vespucci's description of the Tupinambá Indians of coastal Brazil. Much of the scene is invented by the anonymous artist, either following his European preconceptions (for example, the full beards on three of the men, the composition of a mother with three children, the stalk probably meant to represent maize but with milletlike seeds), or following Vespucci's overly brief verbal descriptions (the cannibalistic cooking and eating, probably the stone ornaments inset in the men's chests and faces). But several of the feather ornaments worn by the Indians resemble known examples from the Tupinambás or from much later Brazilian Indians in details that cannot be based solely on verbal descriptions. Examples are a rosette-shaped bustle, crowns of upright feathers, short feather capes or collars, perhaps ankle and arm bands, and perhaps the skirts of long feathers. Almost certainly these details are based on actual examples brought from Brazil that were available to the artist in Augsburg (or perhaps Nürnberg). Only two examples of this woodcut survive, in Munich and New York; they are impressions

from the identical block, although the text beneath has slightly varying type settings.

The broadside was evidently once common, for it served as the model for a crude, simplified version used by Jan van Doesborch in Antwerp on two broadsheets printed about 1510 to 1515. It may have influenced another woodcut illustrating Vespucci's *Mundus Novus* printed in Leipzig or Nürnberg in 1505 or 1506; this also survives in only two examples, different impressions from the same woodblock, one of them appearing above a long text in German after Vespucci. The latter print may well be based also on Brazilian objects brought to Germany as souvenirs or trophies that provided ideas about the appearance of feather crowns, skirts and leg bands, and long clubs. Another related woodcut, by Jörg Breu the Elder, was printed in Augsburg in 1515 to depict the inhabitants of Sumatra described in a German translation of the *Itinerario* of Ludovico Varthema. Some of Breu's feather ornaments and the postures are related to those on the 1505 woodcut. But one headdress with a vertical feather resembles a form known from nineteenth-century Brazil

DRAWING BY ALBRECHT DÜRER, 1515. From the *Gebetbuch Maximilians*. The figure wears a Tupinambá feather skirt, a feather collar, a downy feather cap, and holds a feather scepter.

BAYERISCHE STAATSBIBLIOTHEK, MUNICH

the skirts may in fact have been capes, for one is too short to go fully around the model's waist. This misunderstanding may be the origin of the skirt of long feathers that became part of the European visual symbol representing Indians and America in general. Although there is no evidence for eastern Brazilian Indians wearing such skirts in recent times, and they seem impractical for everyday wear, there are a few examples of Tupinambá Indians shown wearing them—in particular in a ritual dance—in illustrations on sixteenth-century maps where other details seem quite accurate reflections of ethnographic reality.

Another very early accurate European illustration of Tupinambá objects is a panel painted in oils for the high altar in the cathedral at Viseu, Portugal. This is attributed to Vasco Fernandes and dated about 1505 (or even 1501); it is an Adoration of the Magi in which the usual African king is replaced by a figure with brown skin (but not otherwise especially Indian in appearance) who wears rich European clothing (Tupinambá nudity being inappropriate in the context), carries a long heavily fletched arrow that is Brazilian in form, and wears a feather crown, feather necklace, belt of short feathers, and a downy feather cap, which are all probably accurate depictions of objects brought from Brazil.

Indians on Early Maps. The first depictions of American topics made from life reflect visits to the coast of Brazil after it was discovered by Cabral in 1500, and not the voyages of Columbus in the Caribbean region. The emphasis on the Tupinambás in European depictions continued throughout the first century after 1492. Some fifteen manuscript French and Portuguese maps drawn between 1525 and 1579 bear colored figures of Indians and Indian activities in America, many of them very skillfully done. Although Indians in northern South America, Mexico, and around the mouth of the St. Lawrence are also shown, only scenes of Tupinambás seem to be based directly on observations. The best, in the amount of detail and the apparent accuracy, are on a map of Brazil by Jean Rotz, 1542 (in his *Boke of idrography* preserved in the British Library). Other excellent depictions are on maps by Nicolas Vallard (1547), Pierre Desceliers (1553), Guillaume Le Testu (1555), and Jacques Vaudeclaye (1579). Less accurate, but not wholly invented, are Tupinambás depicted by Pedro and Jorge Reinel in the Miller Atlas (c. 1525), on maps by Juan Vespucci (1526) and Diogo Ribeiro (1529), on the Harleian world map in the British Library (c. 1544), and on maps by Pierre Desceliers (1546, 1550), Sancho Gutiérrez (1551), Diogo Homem (1558, 1568), and Sebastião Lopes (1565). Less reliable are figures on a woodcut map published by Giovanni Ramusio in 1556 and on a large map by Sebastian Cabot printed probably in 1544. Non-Brazilian Indians are shown in the Miller atlas

TUPINAMBÁ MEN AND WOMEN. Tupinambá feather ornaments, clubs, and bows and arrows in a woodcut by Hans Burgkmair from the *Triumph of Maximilian*, circa 1516-1519. American monkeys, a macaw, and the first clear illustration of maize are included.   LIBRARY OF CONGRESS

but not otherwise documented for the sixteenth century. Other indications of the presence of Tupinambá Indian objects in Augsburg to serve as models are three feather skirts and a long feathered scepter in Breu's woodcut, which resemble examples depicted in a beautiful 1515 drawing by Albrecht Dürer of an unidentified man. The skirts reappear on many figures in a woodcut scene of a triumphal procession done in 1516 to 1519 by Hans Burgkmair.

More Tupinambá Models. Soon after 1519 Burgkmair or another in his circle painted two watercolors of Indians wearing very similar skirts, and also feather capes, crowns, and downy caps, which seem accurately drawn Tupinambá objects, although one crown is worn backward and

ADORATION OF THE MAGI, CIRCA 1501-1505. Oil pànel depicting the Epiphany attributed to Vasco Fernandes. The central figure, taking the place of the traditional African king, evidently wears Tupinambá feather ornaments and carries a Tupinambá arrow.

MUSEU GRAO VASCO, VISEU, PORTUGAL

America, along with surprisingly accurate snowshoes and an impossibly accurate painted tepee), Ramusio (imaginary structures and clothing along the St. Lawrence, plus some canoes that may remotely reflect observations of Indian birchbark canoes), and Fernão Vaz Dourado (1568, dubious Patagonian archers).

Tupinambá Reality. There are two very early depictions of a Tupinambá village filled with figures engaged in various typical activities that were done from life not in America but in France. An elaborate imitation Brazilian village set up in Rouen for the entry of King Henry II in 1550 included among the occupants fifty Brazilian Indians and 250 Frenchmen said to have learned how to act like Indians while living with the Tupinambás in Brazil (as many Normans had, but probably not 250). There are two contemporary illustrations of this scene, a watercolor that shows few details although it does indicate the customary red body paint worn by the otherwise naked Indians (and Frenchmen); and a woodcut that is crowded with details that are quite small and rather poorly executed, but obviously only one or two removes from observed reality.

Much more accurate details of Tupinambá artifacts and activities (although the compositions and scale are distorted) appear in forty-two small crude woodcuts illustrating a book published in 1557 in which Hans Staden tells how he escaped being sacrificed and eaten by Tupinambás during his captivity among them in 1553 and 1554, and ends with a brief but systematic account of Tupinambá customs. The illustrations obviously reflect Staden's own observations; while they cannot be versions of drawings done directly from life, they may reflect his own sketches done later or at least must have been prepared under his critical supervision.

More skillfully done, but hardly more accurate, are seventeen woodcuts published by André Thevet in 1557–1558, 1575, and 1584. These are based on Thevet's own observations during some three months in Brazil in 1555 and 1556, and perhaps on some Tupinambá objects he is known to have brought back to France. Some of Thevet's illustrations are derivatives of works in other sources, and a few obviously have no basis in reality (for example, war between Amazons; a view of Trinidad; some Patagonian giants), while others are quite dubious ("portraits" of Motecuhzoma and Atahualpa; three views of Indians of New France and Newfoundland that are largely imaginary but include snowshoes and houses only several removes from Canadian reality).

Better depictions of Tupinambá Indians than Thevet's were published by Jean de Léry in 1578, in a work based on his own experiences in Brazil in 1557. Léry criticized Thevet's work, largely justifiably, but used one of Thevet's engravings as the basis for an improved version, and in a second edition in 1580 added three new woodcuts copied

(northern South America, fictional), in the Rotz atlas (fictional in most of eastern North America and South America, but with accurate wigwams and possible tailored clothing in Labrador), by Desceliers (1546, imaginary St. Lawrence scene; 1550, fictional North American Indian houses and clothing), Vallard (fictional figures in northern South America and in North America), Gutiérrez (invented figures in North America), Cabot (several figures may be based ultimately on Mexican Indian clothing, although they are misplaced), Le Testu (invented figures in southern South America, Peru, Mexico, and eastern North

from Thevet without improvements. French knowledge of Tupinambás is also reflected in two woodcuts showing a man and woman with quite accurate feather ornaments in a costume book by François Deserps (or Desprez) published in Paris in 1562 and reissued and copied later. A woodcut of a Tupinambá man with accurately depicted feather cape and leg bands was published in 1599 by Ulisse Aldrovandi in a book on ornithology. The watercolor that lies behind this illustration survives in Bologna. It was certainly based on Brazilian objects in Aldrovandi's natural history collection, as was another watercolor and engraving of a woman of Florida (probably a Timucua Indian), which is more difficult to evaluate because no examples of the clothing and ornaments she wears survive. Other engravings published by Aldrovandi show, quite accurately, Mexican Indian artifacts in his collection.

An anonymous Portuguese painting in oils of about 1550 shows the Devil presiding in hell over the vividly depicted torturing of the damned. Curiously, among the strange accoutrements of the Devil are a feather crown, a feather skirt, and perhaps a short feather cape that seem to be influenced by Tupinambá examples, although he also wears an entirely invented tailored feather shirt and perhaps also feathered trousers.

The Allegorical Figure of America. From these and perhaps other, now lost, depictions of Tupinambá Indians was derived the long-standard allegorical figure of America, which then underwent diffusion and stylistic development entirely divorced from American reality. America's career begins with the invention of allegorical personifications of the four continents, which appeared almost simultaneously in Flanders, Italy, and France in the 1570s. America is usually an undraped female figure wearing a feather crown and often a feather skirt, sometimes a feather collar or cape, based on Tupinambá originals (usually at several removes). She often carries a bow and arrows, not especially Brazilian in form, and frequently has a long club shaped like the Tupinambá club used to sacrifice victims in cannibalistic rituals, and she is often shown with a severed human head or another body part alluding to cannibalism. Each of the continents is usually accompanied by a typical animal; for America there is an alligator, a large South American armadillo, or sometimes a parrot. This kind of figure came to represent America for Europeans in many contexts well into the nineteenth century, while in America itself in the seventeenth and eighteenth centuries it usually was understood to be an Indian. What has been termed the Tupinambization of eastern North American Indians resulted when they adopted the crown of upright feathers from the non-Indian stereotype. Finally, in the late nineteenth century the older feather crown influenced the adoption of the

VESPUCCI DISCOVERING AMERICA.   An allegorical ink drawing by Jan van der Sreet, called Stradanus, 1589. A remote descendant of a Tupinambá club leans against the tree at left.

THE METROPOLITAN MUSEUM OF ART, GIFT OF THE ESTATE OF JAMES HAZEN HYDE, 1959. (1974.205)

AMERICA.   Allegorical drawing by Marten de Vos, 1594. The armadillo is American (although far too large), as is the anchor axe. The rest is imaginary.

MUSEUM PLANTIN-MORETUS EN STEDELIJK PRENTENKABINET, ANTWERP

ings by Gonzalo Fernández de Oviedo, some of which were converted into woodcuts illustrating his books on the natural and civil history of America that were published between 1526 and 1547. Most depict artifacts, including a fire drill, tobacco-snuffing tube, and two houses. A few show activities, including canoe paddling and gold mining. Oviedo was not a skilled artist, but he succeeded in producing informative illustrations of the Indian cultures of La Española, Central America, Peru, and Patagonia, as well as many pictures of the flora and fauna of these regions. Other good illustrations of the Indians of the West Indies, the Spanish Main, Central America, and Peru are the sixteen published in 1565 in Girolamo Benzoni's Italian history of the New World, based on his own observations between 1541 and 1556. A few other illustrations of South American topics—Indians and their

DRAWING OF A PINEAPPLE BY FERNANDEZ DE OVIEDO.   From the original manuscript of his natural history, created before 1547.

THE HUNTINGTON LIBRARY, SAN MARINO, CALIFORNIA

Plains Indian war bonnet of sloping eagle feathers to stand for Indians in many contexts.

Accurate Representations. In the earliest period after Columbus, American Indians were occasionally pictured as fantastic figures transferred from other regions imagined by Europeans. These included humanoid figures without heads but with faces on their chests, figures with dog heads, giants, Amazons living without men, and wild men with heavy body hair wearing leaves and carrying large crude clubs.

The first relatively accurate illustrations of the aborigines of the Greater Antilles are among twenty-odd draw-

excellent standing colored figures of Indians in an entirely European style. There are many illustrations of Mexican Indians influenced to varying degrees by the native manuscript-painting tradition. Probably the best known are the hundreds drawn by Mexican Indian artists for the use of the Franciscan missionary and proto-ethnographer Bernardino de Sahagún between 1558 and his death in 1590.

There are very few sixteenth-century depictions of North America. All those done by Jacques Le Moyne de Morgues in Florida in 1562 and 1564–1565 survive only in the many engravings based on them published by Théodor de Bry in 1591, and in excellent manuscript copies done by John White about 1580 of two Le Moyne drawings of a standing Timucua Indian man and woman. White's

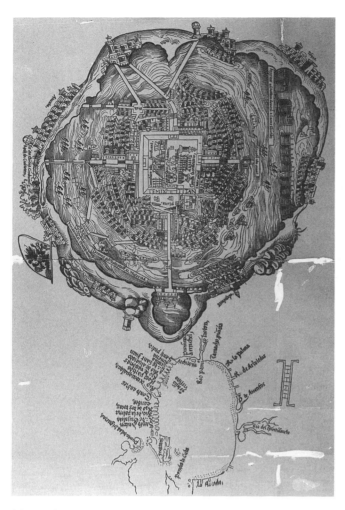

MAP OF TENOCHTITLAN. Woodcut, from the Latin translation of Hernando Cortes's letter to Charles V published in Nürnberg, 1524. The temple precincts are shown clearly, with Motecuhzoma's zoo adjoining one corner.

NEW YORK PUBLIC LIBRARY, RARE BOOK DIVISION

artifacts, plants, animals—are in a manuscript by Galeotto Cey describing his travels between 1539 and 1552, and in a curious manuscript work in French by an unknown shipmate of Francis Drake that must have been compiled soon after 1586.

There are more good sixteenth-century illustrations of Mexico than of any other part of America. They begin with a 1524 woodcut map of Tenochtitlan with some recognizable details. There follow eleven fine, detailed colored drawings of Aztec Indians brought by Cortés to the court of Charles V in 1529, where they were depicted by Christoph Weiditz, a visiting German artist. Another manuscript source is the Codex Tudela (1553), which includes both copies of native Mexican paintings and six

NATIVE MEXICAN PAINTING OF TLALOC. From the Codex Ixtilxóchitl. The Aztec deity was rendered in a very Europeanized style by a native artist working in Texcoco in 1580.

BIBLIOTHÈQUE NATIONALE, PARIS

KING AND QUEEN OF FLORIDA.   Engraving by Théodor de Bry, 1591, after a lost original watercolor by Jacques Le Moyne de Morgues, showing a Timucua couple, circa 1564-1565.

THE SMITHSONIAN INSTITUTION

own depictions, based on his observations near Roanoke, North Carolina, in 1584 to 1587, are among the very best and most important sixteenth-century illustrations of American subjects. Of these, eighteen original watercolors survive, and there are many more quite accurate engraved derivatives of White's drawings published by De Bry in 1590. The subjects include plants and animals as well as Indian figures and scenes. White also painted some Baffinland Eskimos captured by Martin Frobisher in 1576 and 1577, either as a member of Frobisher's expedition or as an observer of the captives in England, where they were drawn by two or three other artists. There is an earlier portrait of Eskimos, a woodcut in several versions done in Antwerp showing a Labrador woman and child exhibited there in 1566.

Depictions of Flora and Fauna. Another genre of illustrations of America are botanical drawings. Three herbals, in addition to those already mentioned, are by Mexican Indian artists. The Badianus manuscript was written in Nahuatl in 1552 by Martín de la Cruz and translated into Latin by Juan Badiano. La Cruz probably is responsible for the 184 small paintings, in a mixed Aztec and European style, of plants and trees of medicinal importance. Other Mexican botanical drawings are among those in the works

of Sahagún. The massive work on plants, animals, and minerals compiled in Mexico between 1571 and 1577 by the Spanish physician Francisco Hernández, which contained hundreds of illustrations, many by named Indian artists, was burned in 1671. Many woodcuts based on the drawings were printed in 1651. A medical work by Nicolas Monardes depicted American plants that he grew in Spain, including the first printed illustration of tobacco. The English translation, *Joyfull Newes Out of the Newe Founde World* (London, 1577) is perhaps better known than the more conservatively titled Spanish original (Seville, 1569).

American plants appeared with Old World Plants in several sixteenth-century herbals. Their origins were sometimes unknown, since the drawings, paintings, and woodcuts were usually based on plants grown in Europe rather than dried specimens or drawings imported from America. Among the works including American plants are those by Otto Brunfels (1530; woodcuts by Hans Weiditz, a pupil of Dürer), Leonhart Fuchs (1542; illustrations by Albrecht Meyer), Pierandreo Mattioli (1544, 1554), Plantin (about 1565–1573; the main artist was Pierre van der Borcht), and John Gerard (1597; with perhaps the first printed illustration of the potato). Early illustrations of several American plants, including maize, pineapple, and prickly pear, appeared in G. B. Ramusio's collection of voyages published in Venice in 1556. Konrad Gesner (Conrad Gessner; 1516–1565) did many drawings of American plants and animals. One of his students, Ulisse Aldrovandi (1522–1605), employed painters, draftsmen, and engravers in Bologna to illustrate his huge collection of natural history specimens. Thirteen large folio volumes were eventually published between 1599 and 1688, illustrated with woodcuts of many American plants, mammals, birds, fishes, reptiles, and minerals, along with Aldrovandi's text descriptions. For early illustrations of American

TURKEYS. A woodcut after a painting by Pierre Gourdelle, from Pierre Belon's *L'Histoire de la nature des oyseaux*, Paris, 1555. Belon thought the bird originated in Asia.

HOUGHTON LIBRARY, HARVARD UNIVERSITY

BISON. The first published picture of the North American bison; a woodcut perhaps based on a sketch from life. From López de Gómara's history of the Indies, 1552.   THE SMITHSONIAN INSTITUTION

mammals and birds (especially the macaw) maps are among the most important sixteenth-century sources, including most of those mentioned above.

[See also *Geography, Imaginary.*]

BIBLIOGRAPHY

Alegría, Ricardo E. *Las primeras representaciones gráficas del Indio Americano, 1493–1523.* San Juan, Puerto Rico, 1978.

Honour, Hugh. *The New Golden Land: European Images of America from the Discoveries to the Present Time.* New York, 1975.

Honour, Hugh. *L'Amérique vue par l'Europe.* Paris, 1976. Corrected version of *The European Vision of America,* 1976.

Hulton, Paul. *America 1585. The Complete Drawings of John White.* Chapel Hill, N. Car., 1984.

Kohl, Karl-Heinz, ed. *Mythen der Neuen Welt: Zur Entdeckungsgeschichte Lateinamerikas.* Berlin, 1982.

Robertson, Donald. *Mexican Manuscript Painting of the Early Colonial Period: The Metropolitan Schools.* New Haven, Conn., 1959.

Sturtevant, William C. "First Visual Images of Native America." In *First Images of America: The Impact of the New World on the Old,* edited by Fredi Chiappelli. Berkeley, 1976.

WILLIAM C. STURTEVANT

Taínos

The Taíno Indians, who lived in the Bahama Islands and the Greater Antilles (Cuba, Jamaica, La Española [Hispaniola], and Puerto Rico), were the first people of the New World to have contact with the Spanish explorers and conquerors. Their culture was the first to be described by European explorers and chroniclers such as Cristopher Columbus, Bartolomé de las Casas, Gonzalo Fernández de Oviedo, and Pietro Martire d'Anghiera.

The Taínos descended from Arawakan Indians, who approximately 2,500 years ago began to migrate from the coasts of South America (Venezuela and Guyana) to the archipelagoes of the Antilles. Evidence of this migratory movement has been discovered in the region of the Orinoco River, on the coasts of Venezuela, on the island of Trinidad, and in the Lesser Antilles. Archaeology reveals that by the sixth century A.D. the culture of these Indians in Puerto Rico had already attained characteristics that differentiated them from their South American predecessors; there is evidence of a cultural expansion by the tenth century in Puerto Rico and La Española, from which they began to emigrate to Jamaica, Cuba, and the Bahamas.

Archaeologists such as Irving Rouse have distinguished the Taínos of Puerto Rico, La Española, and eastern Cuba, who attained a more complex level of cultural and political development, from the Indians of central Cuba, the Bahamas, and Jamaica, who are considered Sub-Taíno. The Sub-Taínos of the Bahamas were called Lucayos.

The term *Taíno* was used by the Indians of La Española to indicate to the Spanish conquerors that they were "good, noble" Indians, as opposed to the Caribs, the warlike Indians of the Lesser Antilles. The word *Taíno* has been used by archaeologists and ethnohistorians since the nineteenth century as the name of the Indians of Arawakan origin who lived in the Greater Antilles at the time of the Discovery.

It is difficult to determine the population of the Greater Antilles at the time of the European discovery. Some chroniclers, such as Las Casas, say that in La Española there were over a million inhabitants and that in Puerto Rico and Jamaica there were more than 600,000 Indians. Modern knowledge of the indigenous economy and historical data on the number of Indians distributed among the colonists suggest that these figures are exaggerated. As early as 1509 the conquerors recount that because in La Española and Puerto Rico there were few Indians, they had to import Indian slaves from the Bahamas, the South American coast, and the Lesser Antilles. New demographic studies are needed to reach a realistic conclusion, which will undoubtedly show a much smaller figure than Las Casas's. In the case of Puerto Rico the population was probably not larger than sixty thousand.

The Taínos were agriculturists who had brought with them from South America to the Antilles the cultivation of the yucca, with which they made their cassava bread, together with corn, sweet potatoes, yautia (malanga), peanuts, and numerous other food plants. They also grew fruit trees such as guava, soursop, sweetsop, yellow mombin, mammee, papaya, and other plants such as pineapple, annatto, red pepper, tobacco, and cotton. High yields of manioc and sweet potatoes were obtained by planting them in rows of low mounds of dirt heaped up in the fields, or *conucos*.

Besides agricultural products, the Taínos complemented their diet with birds and a small rodent similar to a rabbit that they called *jutía*. They also hunted manatees, snakes, large iguanas, and sea turtles. Taínos fished with bone and shell fishhooks, with nets, and with bows and arrows. They also used a plant extract that numbed fish and brought them to the surface. They also ate oysters, clams, and conchs from the coastal reefs, as well as mute dogs that they bred.

Taínos lived in settlements near the coasts of the islands and in the interior valleys near rivers. According to Las Casas some of these villages, which the Taínos called *yucayeque*s, contained hundreds of *bohío*s (communal houses), each of which housed an extended family. The *bohío*s were made of tree trunks, reeds, and straw roofing. Taínos used hanging nets called *hamaca*s as beds.

The Taínos, like other inhabitants of the tropical regions, wore almost no clothes. Men and unmarried women walked about completely naked. Married women used some small aprons woven of cotton called *naguas*. The caciques and the shamans sometimes used cotton mantles and clothing made of feathers of various colors. Taínos frequently painted their bodies totally or partially with drawings of red, white, and black pigments derived from annatto (*Bixa orellana*), genipap, and earth and ochre coloring. Body ornaments of stone, bone, shell, clay, seed, feather, cotton, and straw included counting necklaces made of tubular granite or marble beads, pendants or amulets that often had anthropomorphic and zoomorphic representations, radial crowns with feathers of different colors, and woven-cotton belts and head ornaments. They also worked gold nuggets into thin sheets that they shaped and embossed. The cacique wore a golden disk as a sign of his status in the social hierarchy.

Taíno society was governed by a cacique, or hereditary chief, who was the political and religious authority. The office was matrilineally transmitted; as a result, the cacique's mother and sisters enjoyed high prestige. The caciques in the Greater Antilles acquired great political power and their authority extended over several villages. According to some chroniclers, the cacique Agueybaná was the most important cacique of the island of Boriquén (Puerto Rico) and other caciques were subordinate to him. Las Casas says that in La Española there were five powerful caciques and numerous minor caciques under them. There was also a social class called *nitaíno*s that the Spanish colonists called the nobles; they functioned as subcaciques in the villages, directing the *naboria*s (workers) who attended to agricultural activities, fishing, and hunting.

The caciques were permitted many wives; some marriages were the results of alliances with neighboring caciques. The cacique was privileged in dress, ornaments, and food. He was the owner of the most powerful idols. In some cases, when the cacique died, he could be turned into a demigod and his remains could become part of an idol. The chroniclers tell us that, in some cases, when the cacique died, some of his favorite wives were buried with him.

The Taínos were the heirs of an ancient and complex magicoreligious tradition that had its sources in the Amazon regions of South America. It included a rich mythology about the origins of islands, of plants, of animals, and of human beings. Some aspects of Taíno mythology were collected by Ramón Pané at the beginnings of the conquest of La Española. They believed in a supreme being or creator called Yocahu Maorocón and in a goddess who was associated with fecundity and known by several names, including Apito and Atabei.

The Taínos' principal cult concerned the tutelary spirits

INDIAN AMERICA

N o r t h
A t l a n t i c
O c e a n

Jamestown (founded 1607)
Roanoke Island

St. Lawrence R.

Colorado R.

Red R.

Mississippi R.

Tennessee R.

Alabama

Rio Grande

Sierra Madre Occidental

Sierra Madre Oriental

Gulf of Mexico

Tenochtitlán

Cuba

Jamaica

La Española
(Hispaniola)

Puerto
Rico

Caribbean Sea

SPANISH MAIN

Trinidad

Orinoco R.

Pacific
Ocean

Amazon R.

Cuzco

Paraná R.

Río de
la Plata

South
Atlantic
Ocean

ETHNIC AND LANGUAGE GROUPS

Ais & Tequestas (1)
Algonquians. *See* Beothuks;
  Micmacs; Passamaquoddies;
  Roanoke Island Algonquians;
  Virginia Algonquians.
Apaches (2)
Arawaks (3)
Aztecs (4)
Beothuks (5)
Calcusas (6)
Caribs (7)
Cenus, Dabeibas, & Quimbayas (8)
Chibchas (9)
Chinchas (10)
Conchos (11)
Dabeibas, Cenus & Quimbayas (8)
Guaranis (12)
Hochelegans. *See* Iroquois.
Hokan Language Family. *See*
  Seris; Yumans.
Hopis (13)
Huastecs (14)
Incas (15)
Iroquois (St. Lawrence River
  Region: Hochelagans &
  Stadaconans) (16)
Island Caribs (17)
Karankawans (18)
Lencas (19)
Lucayos (20)
Mayas (21)
Mayos (22)
Micmacs (23)
Mississippian Chiefdoms
  Apalachees, Casquis, Chicazas,
  Cofitachequis, Coosas,
  Guales, Ichisis, Naguatezes,
  Ocutes, Pacahas, Quigualtams,
  Tascaluzas (24)
Mixtecs (25)

Mocozos & Ozitas (26)
Navajos (27)
Ocales & Urriparacoxis (28)
Opatas (29)
Otomís (30)
Ozitas & Mocozos (26)
Passamaquoddies (31)
Payas (32)
Pimas (33)
Piplis (34)
Pueblos (35)
Quimbayas, Cenus, & Dabeibas(8)
Roanoke Island Algonquians (36)
Seris (37)
St. Lawrence Iroquois. *See*
  Iroquois.
Stadaconans. *See* Iroquois.
Taínos (38)
Tarahumaras (39)
Tarascans (40)
Tepehuans (41)
Tequestas & Ais (1)
Timucuans. *See* Ocales;
  Urriparacoxis; Utinas; Yustegas.
Totonacs (42)
Tulas (43)
Tupinambás (44)
Urriparacoxis & Ocales (28)
Utinas (45)
Uto-Aztecan Language Family.
  See Conchos; Hopis; Mayos;
  Opatas; Pimas; Tarahumaras;
  Tepehuans; Yaquis.
Virginia Algonquians (46)
Waraos (47)
Xincas (48)
Yaquis (49)
Yumans (50)
Yustegas (51)
Zapotecs (52)

0   400   800 km
0 200 400 600 miles

© Carta

Taíno ceramic effigy jar of a man. Eleventh to fifteenth century, La Española. Surviving Taíno pottery is mostly unpainted bowls and jars decorated in low relief. Effigy vessels are rare, and this is perhaps the finest known example.

(*cemíes*) of their ancestors. Statuettes were carved from wood, stone, bone, and shell or made of clay and woven cotton. These objects, which were associated with the magicoreligious cult, manifest the high level of Taíno art. The idols and paraphernalia used in the *cohoba* ceremony represent some of the best examples of Taíno art. Other objects of high artistic value were the cacique's *dujos* (ceremonial chairs), low benches, generally with four legs, carved from wood or stone. They were also enriched by incrustations of sheets made of gold and shell. Trigono-lites (three-pointed stones) found in Puerto Rico and the Dominican Republic often represent a humanoid head or the head of an animal at one end and "frog legs" at the other.

The Taínos were relatively peaceful and, according to the chroniclers of the conquest, they fought among themselves only on rare occasions. They resorted to war in order to defend their villages from the frequent attacks carried out by the Island Caribs from the Lesser Antilles.

Their weapons included spear throwers, bows and arrows, and the *macana*, a kind of wide sword made of the hard wood of the corozo palm that was used as a club for hand-to-hand combat. They also used noxious gases produced by throwing pepper into clay pots full of burning coals.

They were good sailors, using boats called *canoa*s that they carved from the trunks of big trees and propelled with paddles. They traveled from island to island to exchange products.

It was among the Taínos that the conquerors saw for the first time a ball made of rubber. It was used in *batey*, a game that had both a ceremonial and a recreational character, occasionally being played to discern the gods' desires. One of the representative objects of the Taínos of Puerto Rico, the stone belt, is associated with the *batey* game. These monolithic arcs, which in the past were called "stone yokes," attest to the high level of Taíno stoneworking technology. Among the best examples of Taíno art were these monolithic belts and *codo*s (elbow stones), which were part of a belt, completed with a wooden arc.

The Spanish conquest and the colonization of the Greater Antilles began in La Española in 1494. The Spaniards soon established the encomienda system in which between fifty and three hundred Indians, under a cacique,

Taíno ceremonial stool.   Thirteenth to fifteenth century, La Española. This example, reportedly preserved in a dry cave, is one of the finest known, and the only one to show gold leaf (in the eyes and mouth and on the shoulders of the figure). Such stools, called *dujo*s, were the property of chiefs, who occupied them on important occasions.

were assigned to work for a colonist, who was obliged to contribute to their conversion to Christianity and to their adjustment to Spanish customs. Such policies were harshly criticized by the Dominican friars, especially Las Casas, because they facilitated abuses against the Indians who, although they were vassals of the Crown by Spanish law, suffered from an exploitation that was equivalent to slavery. The Lucayo Indians (Sub-Taínos) of the Bahamas were forcibly uprooted from their islands to work in La Española, Puerto Rico, and Cuba, since the Spaniards considered their islands *inútiles* (useless) and never colonized them. The conquest and the colonization of Puerto Rico began in 1508, that of Jamaica in 1509, and that of Cuba in 1510. The encomienda system that began in La Española and was responsible for the deaths of thousands of Indians was also introduced into Cuba. The Taínos of La Española, Puerto Rico, Cuba, and Jamaica tried to free themselves from the oppressive yoke of the Spanish conquerors, but their weapons and their knowledge of war could not compete with the conquerors' powerful weapons, horses, and dogs.

In 1512 to 1513, even before the Dominican friars protested to King Fernando, the Laws of the Indies were meant to correct some of the abuses, but they did not abolish the encomiendas, thus permitting the extinction of the indigenous society of the Antilles. Until 1518 there were attempts to establish free Indian villages in the Greater Antilles, but they did not succeed and the indigenous population continued to diminish rapidly. In 1542, Spain granted total freedom to the Indians. For the Taínos of La Española, Cuba, Jamaica, and Puerto Rico, however, it was already too late, since there was only a small number of them left. In Puerto Rico, the bishop in charge of granting freedom to the Taínos reported that he could only find sixty native Indians.

The wars against the conquerors, who robbed them of their land, their freedom, and their magicoreligious beliefs; the European and African diseases against which they had no natural defense; the mistreatment they suffered when they were obliged to work in the mines; the change in diet that was imposed on them by the conquest; and the collective suicide they sometimes committed to free themselves from their sufferings: all these factors contributed to the disappearance of Taíno society in little more than a century after the initial contact. However, because the Spaniards were used to racial miscegenation, they cohabited with the Indians from the beginning of contact, and so there soon arose a mestizo society that retained many cultural characteristics of the Taínos. Its language influenced the Spanish spoken in Cuba, the Dominican Republic, and Puerto Rico, and some Taíno words have entered English and other modern European languages: *hamaca* (hammock), *savana* (savan-

nah), *tabac* (tobacco), *maíz* (maize), *huracán* (hurricane), *cayo* (cay), and cacique. Their physical type, their diet, some of their handicrafts (such as the weaving of baskets and hammocks), the use of the maraca, and other characteristics of their culture still survive among the populations of the Greater Antilles.

BIBLIOGRAPHY

Alegría, Ricardo E. *Ball Courts and Ceremonial Plazas in the West Indies.* New Haven, 1983.
Fewkes, J. Walter. *The Aborigines of Porto Rico and Neighboring Islands.* Washington, D.C., 1907.
Las Casas, Bartolomé de. *History of the Indies.* Translated by Andree M. Collard. New York, 1971.
Loven, Sven. *The Tainan Culture of the West Indies.* Göteborg, 1935.
Morison, Samuel Eliot, ed. *Journals and Other Documents on the Life and Voyages of Christopher Columbus.* New York, 1963.
Pané, Ramón. *Relación acerca de las antiguedades de los Indios.* Edited by José J. Arrom. Mexico City, 1974.
Rouse, Irving. "Prehistory of the West Indies." *Science* 144 (1964): 499–513.
Rouse, Irving. "The Arawak." In vol. 4 of *Handbook of South American Indians.* Washington, D.C., 1948.
Willey, Gordon R. *An Introduction to American Archaeology.* Vol. 2. Englewood Cliffs, N.J., 1966.

RICARDO E. ALEGRÍA

Island Caribs

The word *carib* is unknown in the language of the inhabitants of the Lesser Antilles, who have been called Caribs since the discovery of America. The term, a corrupt form of *cariba, caniba, caribata,* is borrowed from Taíno, a language of western Hispaniola (La Española), where Christopher Columbus landed in November 1492. According to Douglas R. Taylor, the word meant "harmful, hurtful nation" or "quarrelsome people," which the inhabitants of the northwest coast used to designate the peoples of the east. These aggressive and redoubtable neighbors were said to be dogfaced, one-eyed monsters who ate humans. These details were related by Spaniards who evidently did not understand the native language well, and who were guessing, fantasizing, and embellishing, influenced by European literary descriptions of fantastic peoples, especially in the writings of Pliny.

During his first stay on La Española, Columbus had encountered inhabitants of the northeastern peninsula, who with their very long hair, black facial paint, and bows and arrows differed in appearance from the natives he saw around him; he quickly concluded that these were the "Caribs." In November 1493, on the second voyage, Columbus and his companions went ashore on Guadeloupe, where they found human bones in villages deserted by their inhabitants, who had fled into the forest. They were therefore convinced that they had found those "cannibals" of whom they had been told the previous year. From that time the word *carib* was applied to the islanders of all the Lesser Antilles, and subsequently also to the cannibals of the mainland, with whom they were for a long time confused. The mainland peoples are known in anthropological literature as the Karinyas or the "true Caribs." They speak a language of the Cariban family, which bears no relation to the native language of the Island Caribs of the Lesser Antilles.

Contrary to the Spanish interpretations of Taíno tales, it is doubtful that the Caribs of the Lesser Antilles carried out raids on La Española since extremely strong currents flowing from west to east in the Caribbean Sea would have made it impossible for them to return home in their canoes. It is more likely that, besides their traditional annual expeditions to the Orinoco and farther to the east on the South American continent, they made forays onto the island of Borinquén (now Puerto Rico), to the northeast of their territory. Such raids were documented during the sixteenth century, Puerto Rico being by then a Spanish colony. Borinquén and La Española shared the same language and culture; it is possible that the inhabitants of La Española knew of the raids carried out on Borinquén and mentioned them to the Spaniards. However, there is no proof that these raids took place in pre-Columbian times and that they were not attributable, in the sixteenth century, to the presence of Europeans. One must in any case disregard the myth of the Carib raids on La Española and acknowledge that the sociopolitical system of the Lesser Antilles was aligned with the South American continent, and the inhabitants were more closely linked by war and trade with local populations than with the Taíno group of the Greater Antilles, which was close geographically but quite distant socially and culturally.

From St. Christopher in the north to Grenada in the south, all the small islands were inhabited by peoples who spoke a language that belonged to the same Arawakan family as did Taíno, shared the same institutions and rituals, and who visited one another frequently from island to island. They comprised more than just one ethnic population; rather they formed a social and political unit occupying the archipelago that was bounded on the north by the Virgin Islands (uninhabited during the fifteenth century, except St. Croix) and Borinquén, and on the south by the island of Chaleibe (present-day Trinidad). This society was composed of networks of alliances, both matrimonial and political, which united the local groups. These groups were for the most part exogamous and composed of one single extended uxorilocal family, the headman of which was the father of married daughters and lived with his sons-in-law. Thus a man of common

status after marrying would go to live in the village of and under the authority of his wife's father. He would establish his own village when his father-in-law died, and he himself became a father-in-law when his own daughters married. This fluctuating structure, by which the village populations were spatially redistributed with each generation, was based on the ties between the wife's father and the daughter's husbands, not between kin of the same sex. Sisters were quite likely to live separately when their husbands became village chiefs. Hence, it would be inappropriate to speak of matrilocality or, especially, matrilinearity in this cognatic society that did not recognize lineal descent.

Some villages were more important and more populous than others. In these more important villages the headman was recognized as a war chief because of his feats, the number of prisoners he had taken on his expeditions, and, consequently, by the magnitude of the anthropophagic rituals he held in which the prisoners were sacrificed. To acquire this status the prospective war chief had to undergo a lengthy initiation, which included fasting, flagellation, being bitten by ants, and seclusion. Once attained, this status remained tenuous and had to be maintained by frequent expeditions. The war chief, whose status was tenuous, had to be able to forge for himself a clientele with his kindred as its nucleus. The more expeditions he made the more prestige and partisans he gained and the more privileges accrued to him. He was exempt, for example, from the "bride service" obligatory in uxorilocal villages. Warring expeditions were directed not toward the Antilles but toward the South American continent around the mouth and the valley of the Orinoco and the Guyanas where the islanders had both long-term and occasional allies and enemies. The wars were accompanied by trading, as the result of a system of partnership by which the warriors had "friends" in the enemy villages with whom they traded and whom they never took prisoner. Most of their enemies were cannibalistic and went out on expeditions and abducted women. Thus, on the continent, the island peoples participated in a polity structured by war and the exchange of goods, women, and values, in which social and ideological communication was characterized by reciprocal positions and relationships.

The long-time confusion between the islanders and their Karinya or Kalinya allies (the "true" Caribs) of the continent springs from a remarkable social practice that has been misinterpreted. It was said that the men and the women of the islands spoke two different languages—the women's language belonging to the Arawakan family and the men's language belonging to the Cariban family. It was suggested that the abduction of Arawak women by Carib invaders explained this oddity. In reality the maternal language of all of the islanders was Arawakan. In this language their name for themselves was *Kaliponam*. The men, who by their overseas expeditions and trading had close links with continental groups, notably with the Karinyas, made numerous lexical borrowings from their language. Among themselves, at their gatherings at the men's house (in the central plaza of the village), they used this mixed speech, with its Arawakan structure and partially Karinya vocabulary, which one can consider to be a social marker of the hierarchical difference between the sexes. Moreover, on the continent a pidgin was spoken in interethnic relations to permit communication between groups who often spoke unrelated languages. It appears that Karinya was the dominant element, which explains how it influenced the speech of male islanders to the extent that they called themselves Kalinago, from the name of a mythical ancestor who invoked a link with the Karinyas.

Though they were doubtlessly weakened by epidemics and deadly battles with the Europeans, the Kaliponams/ Kalinagos (the so-called Island Caribs) were able to continue their traditional social life and their continental expeditions throughout the sixteenth century. The Spaniards were occupied with conquering Mexico beginning in 1519 and with conquering Peru beginning in 1532. Aside from some attempts at establishing a settlement in Dominica, which was a stopover point for their fleets, they did not seek to colonize the Lesser Antilles, which lacked the richness in minerals they sought and which were staunchly defended by warlike and terrifying natives. The situation changed radically in 1624 when the English and the French simultaneously decided to establish colonies in the Lesser Antilles as strategic bases supporting their colonial undertakings to the north (in Virginia) and to the south (in the Guyanas). The first island to be conquered was St. Christopher, which the English and the French shared, and where, in 1629, they carried out the partial massacre of the island Indians. Those who survived took refuge on the other islands, especially on Guadeloupe. The French settled there in 1635, at the same time that they settled on Martinique. Until 1678, there were incessant attacks throughout the archipelago followed by bloody retaliation between the colonists and the Indians, who defended themselves with the energy born of despair, but who succumbed in great numbers to the bullets, swords, and diseases of the Europeans. In 1678 a treaty was signed by, on one side, the French and English, and on the other side the "Caraibes," which stipulated that the Indians had to abandon all the islands except Dominica and St. Vincent, which were recognized as their property. This treaty was not honored by the colonists, who continued to settle on St. Vincent and to bring African slaves there. Many fugitive slaves from plantations found refuge with the Indians, but the latter disappeared little by little from St. Vincent during the eighteenth century, absorbed by intermarriage with blacks whose population was rapidly increasing. The black Caribs carried out a guerrilla war of harrassment against the colonists until they were defeated and deported en masse in 1797 to the British colony of Honduras (now Belize) where they settled. The Indian population of Dominica dwindled, and the social structure collapsed, deprived of its political framework, which had been dependent on wars, rituals, and long-distance trading.

BIBLIOGRAPHY

Breton, Raymond. *Dictionnaire françois-caraïbe*. Auxerre, 1666.

Dreyfus, Simone. "Historical and Political Anthropological Inter-connections: The Multilinguistic Indigenous Polity of the 'Carib' Islands and Mainland Coast from the 16th to the 18th Century." *Antropológica* 59–62 (1983–1984): 39–55.

Dreyfus, Simone. "Territoire et résidence chez les Caraïbes insulaires au XVIIe siècle." In vol. 2 of *Actes du XLIIe Congrès international des Américanistes*. Paris, 1977.

Taylor, Douglas R. "Carib, Caliban, Cannibal." *International Journal of American Linguistics* 14 (1958): 156–157.

Taylor, Douglas R. "Kinship and Social Structure of the Island Carib." *Southwestern Journal of Anthropology* 2 (1946): 180–212.

Taylor, Douglas R. "The Place of the Island Carib within the Arawakan Family." *International Journal of American Linguistics* 24 (1958): 153–156.

SIMONE DREYFUS
Translated from French by Elizabeth Keller

Arawaks and Caribs

At the time of the European discovery, the islands of Trinidad and Tobago, the coastal zone of Guiana and the lower and middle reaches of the Orinoco River in Venezuela were inhabited by Amerindian groupings of varying ethnicity, linguistic affiliations, subsistence strategies, and levels of sociopolitical integration. Most of these peoples spoke languages belonging to three major linguistic families, Arawakan, Cariban, and Waraoan; the two former language stocks are still widely dispersed on the South American mainland, especially in the Amazon Basin. Waraoan forms an isolated speech community, without known linguistic relations, found today exclusively in the Orinoco Delta and the adjoining portion of Guyana. It may be the survivor of an originally widespread substratum language, which was displaced by Arawakan and Cariban.

Although sixteenth- and seventeenth-century written sources reveal a multitude of Amerindian names, each claiming to refer to a particular ethnic unit, it is likely that the actual situation was much less complicated. Apart from Waraos, two major Amerindian ethnic groups can be distinguished in the Southeast Caribbean: Arawaks and Caribs, along with a variety of smaller groups such as Guaianas, Nepoios, Yaios, Shebaios, Chaimas, and Paragotos.

The Amerindian people referred to in the early documentary sources as the Aruacas or Aroacas represent a grouping that in the period of initial contact inhabited South Trinidad, the lower Orinoco Valley and parts of the Guiana coastal zone. Sixteenth-century maps suggest that the Arawaks originally occupied the lower reaches of the major rivers, especially in the western portion of the latter area. They are mentioned for the first time in 1520 when a Spanish report speaks of a region, situated beyond the Gulf of Paria, "que dize de Aruaca" (that is called Aruaca). Under Spanish pressure the Arawaks disappeared from Trinidad and the Orinoco Valley in the seventeenth and eighteenth centuries and their numbers became greatly reduced. The present Arawaks, who still live in scattered settlements in Guyana, French Guiana, and Suriname, call themselves Lokono (the [own] people); the alternative name, Arawak, is probably derived from the name of a major Lokono settlement on the lower Orinoco, called Aruacay. The Spaniards of the pearl-producing islands of Cubagua and Margarita maintained close trading contacts with Aruacay throughout the sixteenth century. The Lokono language is documented since the 1590s, when Dutch and English sailors collected Arawak word lists in South Trinidad. The ethnographic literature often refers to the Lokono as the "True" or "Mainland" Arawaks, in order to distinguish them from the Taíno or "Island" Arawaks who occupied the Greater Antilles in the period of contact. The two Amerindian groupings are unrelated except for a linguistic bond which can be compared to that between English and German or Dutch.

The supposed "traditional enemies" of the Arawaks were the Cariban-speaking Kalinas. Sixteenth-century documentary and cartographic evidence suggests that the ancestors of the Kalinas, Indians whom the Spaniards called Caribes, occupied the northern third of Trinidad, the reaches of the Guiana rivers upstream from the Arawak, and the middle Orinoco Valley. The name Caribes is derived from Caniba or Canaiba, both Spanish corruptions of *kalinago*, the word (a combination of *kalina*, "the [own] people," and the honorific suffix *-go*) that the male Caribs of the Lesser Antilles used to refer to themselves.

The fierce resistance that the Caribs of the West Indies made against European colonization and slave raiding earned them a negative reputation in the documentary sources, whereas the Arawaks tended to be shown in a favorable light by Spaniards. This obviously resulted from their sixteenth-century trade relationships.

Most Amerindian peoples of the southeast Caribbean were organized sociopolitically as tribes, that is, as egalitarian societies consisting of a series of semi-independent villages, each normally having some three hundred to five hundred inhabitants. The livelihood of most people depended on a form of subsistence that combined swidden (slash-and-burn) cultivation with hunting for small game, fishing, and the unspecialized collecting of edible wild plants, seeds, and shellfish. Only a few peoples, including the Waraos, specialized in nonagricultural subsistence strategies. Political organization was typically tied to kinship and did not extend beyond the village. The village headman was chosen for his abilities as a leader of war and trade expeditions. A few communities of the southeast Caribbean had a more complex type of political organization, with a principal chief and subordi-

NATIVE OF TRINIDAD. Working an elaborate parrot trap, which uses the cries of a captive parrot to lure other birds. From *Histoire naturelle des Indes*, known as the Drake manuscript, which contains sketches and drawings of the Caribbean region made at the behest of Sir Francis Drake.

THE PIERPONT MORGAN LIBRARY, NEW YORK; M.3900, F.83.

nate chiefs. The Lokono town of Aruacay on the lower Orinoco is an example. Sixteenth-century Spanish sources note that Aruacay consisted of some four hundred large round houses, each forming the dwelling of a *parentela*, obviously a kinship group, perhaps a localized clan. Furthermore, Aruacay is described as being ruled by nine chiefs, subordinate to one principal chief, who also functioned as the main shaman. The town probably owed its preeminent position to its strategic geographical position at the apex of the Orinoco Delta, which was conducive especially to maintaining extensive ties of ceremonial exchange and trade with other peoples.

The boundary between exchange and war was ambiguous, however. Although constant warfare characterized the Amerindian societies of the southeast Caribbean in pre-Columbian times, the hostilities between traditionally antagonistic peoples such as the Caribs and Arawaks never interrupted their mutual trade. Major items of Caribbean ceremonial exchange, the famous *kalukulis* (zoomorphic or crescent-shaped breast and nose ornaments made of a gold-copper alloy) found their way from the mainland of South America into the Antilles through peaceful exchange between the Arawaks of the lower Orinoco Valley and Trinidad and the Caribs of the Lesser Antilles. These ties of Arawak-Carib trade show that, among the Amerindian societies of the southeast Caribbean, exchange and war could be considered merely two different expressions of the same reciprocal pattern of social interaction.

BIBLIOGRAPHY

Boomert, Arie. "The Arawak Indians of Trinidad and Coastal Guiana, ca. 1500–1650." *Journal of Caribbean History* 19 (2) (1984): 123–188.

Sued Badillo, Jalil. *Los Caribes: Realidad o fábula.* Río Piedras, P.R., 1978.

Whitehead, Neil L. *Lords of the Tiger Spirit: A History of the Caribs in Colonial Venezuela and Guyana 1498–1820.* Dordrecht and Providence, R.I., 1988.

ARIE BOOMERT

Tupinambás

The name Tupinambá refers to the Indians inhabiting the coast of Brazil from the region of São Paulo to the mouth of the Amazon River. Closely related to the Guaranis of southern Brazil and Uruguay, Tupinambás were divided into a number of tribal groupings that, although culturally similar and speaking mutually intelligible dialects, were often in a state of bitter and perpetual warfare with one another. In fact, the Tupinambás were recent migrants to the coastal regions, having displaced earlier occupants.

The first recorded contact between Tupinambás and Europeans occurred in 1500 when Pedro Álvares Cabral, a Portuguese captain on his way to India, anchored briefly off the Brazilian coast. Subsequent European contacts were generally friendly, often involving the exchange of European manufactures for raw materials from the Brazilian coast. Serious efforts at colonization by the Portuguese began in the 1530s. After 1550 colonization intensified along much of the Brazilian coast, both on the part of the Portuguese and the French. At first the Tupinambás welcomed contact with the Europeans, finding the economic exchanges beneficial. Various Tupinambá groups formed trading and military alliances with the French and Portuguese, incorporating the Europeans in their internecine warfare. Over time, however, Portuguese expansion put greater and greater pressure on the Tupinambás and their way of life.

Tupinambá subsistence was based on a mixed economy of swidden horticulture, hunting, fishing, and gathering. Horticultural work was done primarily by women, while men dedicated themselves to hunting, fishing, and warfare. Villages were moved often, due primarily to the deterioration of local agricultural lands caused by swidden agriculture.

Tribal groupings resided in dispersed, fortified settlements throughout well-demarcated tribal areas. Tribes lacked any sort of overarching, centralized political structure. Each individual community was theoretically independent of the others, although there were long-standing alliances forged by kinship, friendship, common interests, feasting, and mutual aid in warfare. The local community or village consisted of four to seven *malocas*, long houses composed of various extended families and housing between forty and several hundred people. Each *maloca* was presided over by a *morubixaba* (principal), to whom the resident members were related through kinship or close friendship. Each nuclear family occupied its own area within the *maloca*. Village leadership was provided by a chief, usually the *morubixaba* of one of the *malocas*, but some villages had more than one such chief. Leadership was exercised through persuasion and prestige. Village chiefs had no power to compel compliance in day-to-day activities, although their counsel and supernatural power were greatly esteemed. The *morubixabas*, almost invariably older men who had demonstrated great valor and success in warfare, formed a village council that deliberated important matters related to village activities, particularly with respect to warfare and village movement. Also essential in village leadership were the *pajés* (shamans), whose divinations were necessary before any important undertaking.

Law among the Tupinambás was based primarily on the principles of *lex talionis* (law of retaliation) and private justice. Since no police or formal judicial system existed for redress of grievances, the Tupinambás emphasized strongly the principle of retribution and revenge for offenses. If one Tupinambá injured another, the guilty party or a close relative should suffer the same injury, and it was up to the aggrieved person and his or her relatives to press for settlement of disputes. In the case of capital offenses, the kinsmen of the perpetrator were required to themselves kill the guilty party in recompense or face feud and warfare. Thus, feud was always a threat and occasionally broke out among groups that had once been allies and kinsmen. The retributive principle was one of the major causes of warfare among the Tupinambás.

Tupinambá warfare, driven by ideology, demographic pressure, and economic and social factors, was chronic. By means of success in warfare, men gained prestige and political influence in society. One of the primary motivations for warfare was to take vengeance for relatives killed or eaten in religious rituals by their enemies. Consequently, much Tupinambá warfare took on the aspect of continual feud in which the losers always sought to revenge themselves on the winners.

Great importance was placed on the capture of enemies. A captive was taken to the village of the captor, incorporated into his household and, if a male, married to his daughter or other close female relative. Female captives generally became the wives of the captor. Captives were treated in many respects as if they were a member of the household, playing roles similar to those of other members of the local community. However, their fates were quite distinct, since at some time in the future, they would be ceremonially executed in the public square and then roasted and eaten.

The process of revenge warfare was closely integrated into other aspects of Tupinambá culture. Warfare could be static, the contending parties engaging in an endless series of raids and counter raids. Warfare also had a dynamic aspect. At times, tribal groups were able to drive their enemies from their lands, occupying the areas thus vacated. Given the lack of political centralization, this occupation did not lead to larger and larger territorial control by successful tribes. Rather it took the form of groups migrating from less desirable or ecologically overused lands to more productive ones. These migrations, often under the leadership of pajés, took on the guise of messianic movements in search of a legendary earthly paradise; there were also powerful demographic and ecological motivations behind these movements. Tupinambá subsistence practices led to a deteriorating ecological balance, which necessitated shifting cultivation. With population growth, migration and warfare became mechanisms for alleviating such pressures on local tribes.

Much warfare took the form of raids, which involved relatively small forces making incursions into enemy territory, with the intent of seizing prisoners and then fleeing back to friendly territory. Weaponry was simple but effective, consisting of bows and arrows and the tacape (hardwood club). But very large expeditions, involving several thousand warriors, also took place, often involving siege tactics against enemy villages, which, because of the constant threat of attack, were characteristically palisaded and contained other defensive features. This form of larger-scale battles was intensified as a result of European contact and incursion in the form of colonization, slaving, and attempts to subdue the native groups and seize their lands.

Kinship was a central principle of social organization among the Tupinambás. The malocas were composed principally of kinsmen, and the preferential forms of marriage—mother's brother with sister's daughter and cross-cousin—reinforced kin relations based on affinal ties. Kin ties, together with success in warfare, were the primary means by which a man built a following and gained prestige and influence in the community and tribe. Men were not generally allowed to marry until they had captured and ritually killed an enemy in warfare. Even then it might be difficult for young men to marry, as it was customary to marry young, nubile daughters and sisters to older, accomplished males, thus extending or enhancing the father's or brother's ties to important people. As it was common for older males to practice polygyny, a young man often was not able to find an acceptable wife until he had gained some renown. Thus, there was a strong gerontocratic aspect to both kinship and political power. When finally able to marry, a young man was usually required to live in the maloca of his in-laws, and to labor on behalf of his father- or brother(s)-in-law, and to serve under their direction, until such time as he could recompense them by providing a daughter in marriage. Thus daughters were greatly esteemed, as their marriages enabled a man not only to free himself from heavy obligations to his in-laws, but to make important alliances within the community and tribe.

There was considerable inequality in status between males and females. Although status differences existed within each gender, women were generally subordinate either to their fathers or brothers, or to their husbands. The husband's considerable authority and power over his wives was checked to some degree by the wife's male relatives, who might react adversely if she were mistreated. A woman's status was derived primarily by ascription—a daughter or sister of a renowned warrior or principal had high status and tended to marry a male of high status. However, some women, particularly female shamans, could gain prestige and status in their own right. Females cultivated the fields and carried out practically all the domestic chores. Such was the division of labor that a male was virtually unable to function without a spouse or female relative to care for him.

PORTRAITS OF TUPINAMBÁ MAN AND WOMAN, CIRCA 1640, BY ALBERT ECKHOUT. Portuguese colonization rapidly changed Tupinambá life and culture to conform to the needs and values of colonial society. Such changes are reflected in the dress and personal adornment of the two subjects. The man holds a a typical Tupian bow and arrows, with which the native Brazilians were exceptionally proficient. Acculturated or mixed-blood Tupinambás were often employed by Europeans as hunters or auxiliaries in war.

NATIONAL MUSEUM OF DENMARK, DEPARTMENT OF ETHNOGRAPHY

Shamanism was an important religious function. Through auguring, divination, and healing, individuals and groups could discern the outcome of events and restore health. Tupinambás believed in and feared a great number of spirits, including the spirits of the dead, who, if not properly buried and reverenced, could cause injury and death to the living. The souls of the dead who had exemplified the ideals of society, especially bravery in warfare, were believed to journey to a land of happiness, abundance, and joy where a man was reunited with his ancestors, especially his male ancestors. Wicked or cowardly persons could never attain this land.

The effects of European contact on Tupinambá culture were dramatic. At first, rival tribes aided the Europeans in raids against their traditional enemies, but the colonists soon made little distinction among the groups they would raid for slaves. Moreover, epidemic diseases, to which the natives had little resistance, devastated Indian peoples, as did the practice of slavery. As a result of this process, Indians were able to avoid assimilation or death only by fleeing farther and farther into the interior. Thus, as European colonization ensued over several centuries, Tupinambá culture disappeared except in the most remote areas of Brazil.

BIBLIOGRAPHY

Brandão, Ambrósio Fernandes. *Dialogues of the Great Things of Brazil.* Translated and annotated by Frederick H. Hall, William F. Harrison, and Dorothy W. Welker. Albuquerque, N.Mex., 1987

Hemming, John. *Red Gold: The Conquest of the Brazilian Indians.* Cambridge, Mass., 1978.

Metraux, Alfred. "The Tupinamba." In *Handbook of South American Indians.* Vol. 3. Washington, D.C., 1963.

Staden, Hans. *Hans Staden: The True History of His Captivity 1557.* Translated and edited by M. Letts. London, 1928.

DONALD W. FORSYTH

Indians of the Spanish Main and Central America

The term *Spanish Main* was the English phrase applied in part to the mainland territory opposite the islands of the West Indies. It included the south coast of the Caribbean Sea from the Paria Peninsula, opposite Trinidad, and west along the coast of northern South America to and including lower Central America. At the time of first European contact this environmentally diverse coastal region (including northern Venezuela, northern Colombia, Panama, eastern Costa Rica, eastern Nicaragua, and eastern Honduras) was populated by several dozen native societies, most of which were organized into chiefdoms of varying sizes and degrees of political complexity.

The majority of the population in each of these chiefdoms consisted of commoners, who were governed in political and religious matters by a small group of aristocratic elites. In addition, war captives worked as laborers and servants and sometimes were absorbed by marriage or adoption into the general population. Elites and commoners were differentiated in part by the relative honor accorded their respective ancestors and in part by overall lifestyles. Elites displayed rare and valuable ornaments made of gold alloys and precious and semiprecious stones and wore robes and mantles of exceptionally fine woven textiles. They were carried in litters by retainers, lived in large, elaborately decorated houses located in ceremonial centers, and were buried in tombs richly stocked with items reflecting wealth. Commoners, in contrast, lived in the countryside surrounding the elite center in plainer and smaller homes, had fewer and less elaborate ornaments and clothing, and were more simply buried.

Commoners focused their lives on daily subsistence activities and kin group affairs. To raise manioc and other root crops such as maize, peanuts, chili peppers, and various tree crops, including pejibaye palm, they cleared and burned agricultural land and planted it with the aid of pointed sticks; mountain slopes and hillsides were sometimes terraced and irrigated by canals. Commoners

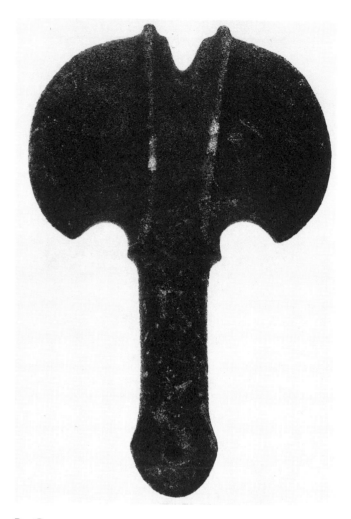

PRE-COLUMBIAN DOUBLE-HEADED STONE AXE. From present-day Costa Rica.   REPRODUCED BY COURTESY OF THE TRUSTEES OF THE BRITISH MUSEUM

hunted abundant land and aquatic animals including deer, peccary, iguanas, ground birds, turtles, water fowl, and manatee and fished in rivers and ocean, providing food for themselves, for the elite, and for ceremonial occasions. They also worked agricultural lands for their lords and built the chiefs' compounds and ceremonial centers, but they paid no taxes or other formal tributes.

Elites focused their attention primarily on foreign affairs, creating complex regional networks of high-level contacts through diplomatic marriages (chiefs were polygynous), warfare, and trade with lords of other polities. Trade involved a wide range of crafted and natural goods, including salt, raw cotton, woven textiles, raw gold, finished gold jewelry, dried fish, emeralds, seashells, and pearls. By such means, ties were established between Panamanian elites and lords of the mountains and lowlands of northern Colombia (e.g., Dabeiba, Quimbaya, Cenu), between chiefs of coastal Colombia and chiefs of interior highland peoples (e.g., Chibchas), between elites of northwest Venezuela (including the Lake Maracaibo area) and those of northeast Colombia and the Venezuelan Andes, and between lords of northeast coastal Venezuela and the grassland (llanos) peoples of the interior.

Spanish contact had a devastating effect on many of the indigenous cultures of the Spanish Main. Expeditionary raids and forays in search of portable wealth (gold, gems) and exportable slaves quickly depleted many of the sizable native populations as people became victims of the raids and of new diseases. Survivors sought refuge in the more inhospitable depths of mountains and forests. The Spaniards then utilized select ports along the Caribbean, most notably Cartagena and Portobelo, as jumping-off points for expeditions farther into the interior and as transshipment points for the crucial trade that eventually linked the South American colonies with Europe.

BIBLIOGRAPHY

Gordon, B. LeRoy. *Human Geography and Ecology in the Sinu Country of Colombia.* Berkeley, 1957.

Helms, Mary W. *Ancient Panama: Chiefs in Search of Power.* Austin, Texas, 1979.

Helms, Mary W. "The Indians of the Caribbean and Circum-Caribbean at the End of the Fifteenth Century." In *Colonial Latin America.* Vol. 1 of *The Cambridge History of Latin America.* Edited by Leslie Bethel. Cambridge, 1984.

Sauer, Carl O. *The Early Spanish Main.* Berkeley, 1969.

MARY W. HELMS

Chibchas

The Chibchas lived in the high valleys of the eastern cordillera of the Andes in what is now central Colombia, an area of year-round cool climate, moderate rainfall, and fertile soils. Estimates of the preconquest population have run as high as one million. The Spanish conquest of the Chibchas began in 1537, when about 170 men led by Gonzalo Jiménez de Quesada arrived via the Magdalena Valley. Two years later, two more expeditions arrived: one, from Venezuela, under Nicolás Féderman, and the other, from Ecuador, led by Sebastián de Belalcázar, each apparently unaware of the other. The three leaders returned to Spain to claim the rewards of conquest, leaving Hernán Pérez de Quesada in charge. So-called "rebellions" that followed probably constituted the main Chibcha resistance; they were put down with considerable bloodshed, especially for the Chibcha nobility. Smallpox epidemics, starting about 1560, also claimed many lives. However, a considerable Chibcha population remained through the colonial period.

Colonial-period sources describe the Chibchas as organized into two kingdoms, which were probably fairly loose confederations of towns headed by caciques (local chieftains), who may have had some hierarchical relationships among themselves, but any hegemony of the Zipa of Bogotá and the Zaque of Tunja (the "kings") was probably recent and weak. The division may reflect some kind of dual organization not understood by the Spaniards. The local communities (towns) were internally divided into a variable number of entities called (in English) parts, each having a hereditary leader (captain); the cacique was captain of his own part. Inheritance of part membership and of leadership positions was strictly matrilineal and remained so for three hundred years after the Spanish conquest. The parts were neither exogamous nor endogamous, but may have been localized.

The food supply was based on agriculture; corn, potatoes, and a variety of other crops were grown in an extensive system of raised-bed fields, traces of which have been discovered in recent years. Deer, guinea pigs, and other animals were hunted, and fishing was important, perhaps to the extent of fish-farming in the ditches between the raised-bed fields. Cotton was grown in the lower-altitude parts, and was spun and woven into fine textiles decorated with painted as well as woven designs. Besides serving as clothing, textiles were important items of trade; their use for such purposes as ceremonial gifts, prizes, and religious offerings suggests that weaving and textiles may have had symbolic values similar to those reported ethnographically for the linguistically related Kogi. Other crafts included pottery, woodworking, and metallurgy, mainly in gold and copper and for ornamental and religious purposes rather than for tools. Gold was obtained by trade, which was an important activity; established marketplaces and specialized traders are reported. Besides textiles, the main trade item was salt, produced abundantly at several localities, especially Zipaquirá, still an important source of this mineral.

Houses and temples were built of wood with thatch roofs, circular in plan; early colonial-period maps sometimes have little drawings of them. Little architectural use of stone has been found, and the perishable building materials have left no monumental ruins. However, the numerous palisaded settlements were impressive enough to remind the first Spaniards of Moorish fortresses in southern Spain; they called the Bogotá region Valle de los Alcázares.

Chibcha religion involved a considerable pantheon of divinities, the chief of whom seem to have been a creator god, Chimingagua; the Sun, Xue; his wife the moon, Chía; and a culture hero, Bochica or Nemquethaba, who traveled through the country teaching the people to spin and weave and live good lives, and then disappeared. Relations with these and other spiritual beings were the responsibility of specialized priests, whose lengthy training started in boyhood, and who led celibate and very ascetic lives. They made offerings of gold objects, emeralds, miniature textiles, and other objects in temples and other places. Temples, large and small, public and private, were numerous; the most important was located at Sogamoso, north of Tunja. Future caciques were secluded in temples for training. An elaborate ceremony at Lake Guatavita for the cacique of that town seems to be the origin of the legend of El Dorado.

BIBLIOGRAPHY

Broadbent, Sylvia M. "The Formation of Peasant Society in Central Colombia." *Ethnohistory* 28 (1981): 259–277.

Broadbent, Sylvia M. "A Prehistoric Field System in Chibcha Territory, Colombia." *Nawpa Pacha* 6 (1968): 135–147.

Broadbent, Sylvia M. "The Site of Chibcha Bogotá." *Nawpa Pacha* 4 (1966): 1–13.

Simón, Pedro. *Noticias historiales de las conquistas de Tierra Firme en las Indias Occidentales.* 1625. 9 vols. Bogotá, 1953.

SYLVIA M. BROADBENT

Incas and Their Neighbors

Tahuantinsuyu (Tawantinsuyu), the Inca state, was no more than a century old in 1532 when, after a short campaign, 155 Europeans overthrew it. Such a swift collapse convinces some observers that it had been a state without coherence, a makeshift ethnic conglomerate. Protracted military campaigns far from familiar geographic conditions had certainly enfeebled it, particularly in the equatorial north. Dynastic squabbles between royal lineages also contributed to the European victory. But considering what had been achieved in the century before the European invasion, the Inca state was a remarkable socioeconomic and technological structure.

In 1532 the Incas ruled over twelve million people, including dozens of ethnic groups speaking at least twenty different languages. Tahuantinsuyu stretched from present-day northern Ecuador to Mendoza in west-central Argentina and the Maule River in central Chile. What impressed the Europeans most and very early were the roads—more than 25,000 kilometers (15,500 miles) linking territories that today are part of five modern republics— and the thousands of warehouses, strung along the roads and in the administrative centers, full of food and textiles. One of the best early sources on the Americas, Gaspar de Espinosa, member of a prosperous slave-trading and banking family, who had financed the invasion of the Andes by Francisco Pizarro and Diego de Almagro, wrote to Charles V in 1533 that these Indians were good candidates to be made to serve the Spaniards in light of their experience as members of the Inca state, and that "these Indians of the provinces of Peru are very skilled at making and opening roads and causeways and fortresses

and other buildings of stone and earth and at opening water canals and at this building it is said that they are far in advance of us."

The Inca state also transferred populations for productive or strategic purposes. In the last few decades before the arrival of the Europeans, when the Inca armies found themselves fighting farther and farther from home, special measures had to be taken to ensure the supply of commodities that the troops expected as their reward. While high-altitude tubers and their conversion to storable, freeze-dried *chuñu* formed the bulk of the food supply, maize and its by-product, beer, were held in much higher esteem and were expected by the troops. Eventually state maize plantations were set up in present-day Bolivia, worked by highlanders sent down on rotation. Because soldiers also expected regular issues of high-status cloth, state manufactures were established using as many as a thousand carders, weavers, and feather ornamentors. The European chroniclers who reported these exotic features of Inca military organization noted that the troops were likely to rebel if they did not receive regular issues of commodities rare in the villages.

Since Inca rule outside the Cuzco region was so recent, many ethnic groups, large and small, were still distinguishable and retained their sense of identity within Tahuantinsuyu. Some of them still recalled a time, less than a century before 1532, when their own lords competed with Cuzco for political hegemony. And since the Incas were not the first overarching polity to emerge in the Andes, the dynastic oral traditions of each ethnic group recalled periods in the past when their own lords had achieved power beyond their immediate valleys and pastures. Some of them also recalled decades of "war of all against all," as described by Guamán Poma de Ayala (Waman Puma), an Andean writer. In 1615, Poma finished a twelve-hundred-page "letter" to the Spanish king Philip III, describing not only Inca glories but also his own ancestors' rule in pre-Cuzco times. This memory of past independence also encouraged many local lords to favor the Europeans against the Incas; they lived to regret it.

Although the Incas were a high-altitude, mountain dynasty, the political structure they eventually cobbled together included many coastal polities. While some of these had resisted Inca rule, others were folded into the Inca state without resistance. Some of these coastal polities were small, others made up of several valleys; all depended on irrigation, since the Peruvian coast is a desert. As these polities expanded in pre-Inca times, so did their irrigation network; in some cases waters from the rainy highlands were diverted at will from one valley to another. Several languages and ethnic groups prevailed on the Andean coast. Their achievements are better understood—even though their descendants no longer speak the mother tongue and frequently have no histori-

EFFIGY VESSEL, STANDING MUSICIAN. From Chimu, fourteenth to fifteenth century. Silver and turquoise.

THE METROPOLITAN MUSEUM OF ART, THE MICHAEL C. ROCKEFELLER MEMORIAL COLLECTION, GIFT OF NELSON A. ROCKEFELLER, 1969. (1978.412.219)

cal awareness of their past—because archaeologists have long preferred to concentrate on the desert coast, and the presence of gold, emeralds, and other treasure in the graves has favored the study of coastal civilizations over Inca civilization.

One coastal society that has received attention from historians, even though its metallic treasure was rare, is the Chincha. Eyewitnesses of the Inca defeat in 1532, at Caxamarca, reported that only one lord other than King Atahualpa was carried in a litter. When asked about the lord's identity, the interpreter explained that he was the "lord of Chincha, master of 100,000 rafts on the sea." While the exact number of these craft need not detain us, the sea-borne traffic is startling both for the number quoted and distances traveled.

The balsa wood used to build the rafts came not from the arid Peruvian coast but from the distant warm waters of the Gulf of Guayaquil, in present-day Ecuador. The sailors maneuvered their craft with the help of sails and a keel. Cabins to protect the goods and the crew were built on the raft; some had crews of as many as twenty sailors. The rafts carried vast amounts of spondylus shells; like the balsa wood, these mollusks did not grow in the cold waters of the Peruvian coast. It is unclear what the southerners, like the Chincha (who used spondylus shells to encourage rainfall and to feed the gods) sent north in exchange. María Rostworowski, a leading Peruvian scholar of Andean history, suggests that in exchange for spondylus, metals—arsenic alloys for bronzes at an earlier stage and the more familiar tin bronzes in Inca times—were shipped north.

The Inca dynasty was aware of the strength of ethnic diversity throughout the realm and the separatist dangers implicit in such differences. The royal road and the army were only some of the methods used to foster coherence. The cult of the sun, identified originally with the Incas in their Cuzco homeland, was extended to the rest of the realm, sometimes incorporating local deities, at other times repressing them. Another tactic was to ignore local ethnic and linguistic differences and loyalties and to impose a decimal system for reorganizing and governing conquered groups. This decimal system reflected the organization of the official Inca historical and accounting records, quipu, made by knotting strings. The conquered peoples were divided into units of ten to ten thousand "households." Surviving records for part of the Huánuco region imply that a "hundred households" unit was composed of five hamlets in close geographic proximity. This method of classifying subjects was ignored by the Europeans, but occasionally the decimal vocabulary does appear in North Andean records, where this method of accounting apparently originated. Finally, there was an attempt to impose Runa Simi, the language of Cuzco, as the common language for the whole realm. Today some ten million people in four republics speak variants of this language (called Quechua), but much of its spread occurred after the colonial period, when the Spaniards continued the Inca campaign against local dialects and languages.

Sun worship was the state religion of the Incas, but the religious beliefs and practices of other pre-Incan peoples continued in some form up to the time of the Spanish conquest. In addition to Inti, the sun god, the Inca pantheon contained his wife Mama-Kilya, the moon goddess; Viracocha, the creator god; and Apu Illapu, the rain giver. Priests presided over the Inca religion and resided at all important shrines and temples. The Incas held monthly religious festivals, performed divination, and practiced sacrifice ranging from daily offerings of burnt corn for the rising sun to human sacrifice at times of defeat, famine, or pestilence.

The Inca version of their history cannot be readily studied because they apparently did not write. The quipu decimal records are said to be limited to matters that could be expressed in quantitative terms. Eyewitnesses of the invasion refer to "maps" kept by the state's record keepers. At an early moment in the invasion these "maps" had permitted the Europeans to learn of ethnic groups, their size, their geographic distribution, and their leaders before they had ever seen them. As late as 1575, the viceroy Francisco de Toledo sent to Philip II in Madrid a collection of four "maps" kept by descendants of Andean authorities, but these have not yet surfaced. Both quipu and the use of ethnic "maps" were abandoned by the Spaniards soon after the invasion, possibly because the office of custodian was a religious office.

Knowledge of Inca history is thus severely limited when compared, for example, with contemporary knowledge of the Maya past. Inca history may be illuminated in two ways, by examining the archaeological record (many Inca cities are still standing along the Qhapaq Ñan, the royal highway), and by searching for additional sixteenth-century administrative and ecclesiastic records, which were compiled by eyewitnesses but remain inaccessible, locked up in convent and private libraries.

[See also *Cuzco.*]

BIBLIOGRAPHY

Hemming, John. *The Conquest of the Incas.* San Diego, 1973.
Hyslop, John. *The Inka Road System.* San Diego, 1984.
Hyslop, John. *Inka Settlement Planning.* Austin, Tex., 1990.
Morris, Craig, and Donald Thompson. *Huánuco Pampa: An Inca City and Its Hinterland.* London, 1985.
Murra, John V. *The Economic Organization of the Inka State.* Greenwich, Conn., 1980.
Murra, John, Nathan Wachtel, and Jacques Revel. *Anthropological History of Andean Polities.* New York, 1986.
Steward, Julia H., ed. *Handbook of South American Indians.* Vol. 2: *The Andean Civilizations.* Washington, D.C., 1946.

JOHN V. MURRA

Mayas

The Maya region stretches from Tabasco and Chiapas in Mexico to the western parts of El Salvador and Honduras. It includes all of Yucatán, Guatemala, and Belize. In the late twentieth century there were about 2.5 million Maya Indians, but there were between six and seven million in 1519. After the Spaniards arrived, the native population declined, dropping 80 to 90 percent in some areas and becoming extinct in others. The Maya region is composed of three main geographical zones: the highlands, the lowlands, and the Pacific coastal plain and piedmont.

The Classic Mayas

During the Classic period (A.D. 250 to 900), the Mayas developed one of the most complex and sophisticated civilizations in the Petén lowlands of Mexico and Guatemala. The elite class of rulers and higher administrators formed the upper level of a diverse society that consisted of lesser bureaucrats, merchants, craftsmen, farmers, and unskilled laborers.

Carved monuments called altars and stelae document the histories of the rulers of many of the important sites such as Tikal, Copan, Yaxchilan, Calakmul, and Quirigua. At one time Maya scholars thought the depictions on these monuments were priests and that the accompanying hieroglyphs mainly dealt with religion and the passage of time. Classic Maya society was perceived to be basically theocratic and peaceful. More recent work and increasing ability to read Maya texts have demonstrated that Maya society was quite militaristic and that the monuments record dynastic histories and conquests as well as astronomical information. Emblem glyphs, or those that identify individual sites, show that some of the larger sites, such as Tikal, dominated smaller nearby centers.

Architecturally, lowland Maya structures are some of the finest produced in ancient Mesoamerica. Vast trade networks spanned the Petén leading to the Gulf of Mexico, the Pacific coast, highland Guatemala and southeast to Copan and Quirigua. Classic Maya civilization was already declining by the late ninth century. By the early tenth century, most of the sites had been abandoned, and the jungle had begun to encroach upon the ruins. The Mayas of the Petén region were not to be rediscovered until the nineteenth century.

Maya Culture at Contact

In 1519 the Mayas were fragmented into many small, autonomous polities that engaged in constant warfare. There were around sixteen of these in northern Yucatán and several in highland Guatemala and Chiapas. Boundaries between adjacent groups were not clear and were often disputed. Other causes of war were desire for tribute, trade routes, land, and slaves. Walled, palisaded, and moated centers were common. In the Guatemala highlands major sites (*tinamit*) were located on mountain slopes and hilltops for defense. The larger Maya sites were residences of the elite and centers of political, ritual, and economic activities. Commoners inhabited smaller villages scattered throughout the countryside.

The Petén (central lowlands) was not densely populated. The most important sites were located on islands in

Lake Petén-Itzá and Yaxhá. The elite lived in these island centers, and the commoners inhabited scattered mainland villages. The Itzás of Tayasal had a political system similar to that of Yucatán and warred against their neighbors. Other Petén groups, such as the Lacandóns, seem to have had a village-level political organization.

Maya sites in highland Chiapas were small. Some were politically aligned with the Chontal Mayas, but others were independent and ruled by local nobles. Centers in the Chiapas Plateau, such as Zinacantán, faced Aztec intervention and encroachment from the nearby Chiapanecs.

Sociopolitical System. Throughout the Maya area the most important groups had a corporate form of lineage organization. The lineages were ranked, and the highest political offices were held by male leaders of the highest-ranking lineages. The lineages were grouped into a larger entity known generally as the *chinamit*. Members were not always related, but the *chinamit* was called by the surname of the highest-ranking male. A territorial and political unit, the *chinamit* was responsible for its members' actions. It was a resource and land-holding group, and the members lived together within a walled area. Highly ranked members married outside the *chinamit* and sometimes out of their center. Commoners married within the *chinamit*. In highland Guatemala principal lineages were associated with multifamily dwellings called big houses. Such dwellings were also constructed in Yucatán, Acalán, and Tayasal and probably characterized most Maya groups.

Socially, the Mayas were divided into two main groups, the nobles who received tribute and the commoners who paid it. The nobles dominated the higher offices, wore fine clothing, and lived in large houses in major centers. Commoners, who were lesser officials, farmers, fishermen, unskilled laborers, foot soldiers, craftsmen, and burden bearers, lived in outlying villages. Warriors, merchants, and skilled artisans formed a middle status group but still paid tribute. There were also serfs who originally seem to have been conquered people who were attached to and inherited with the land. Some became trusted servants, warriors, and guardians of valuable lands and rose in society. Slaves were war captives, criminals, debtors, and those sold into slavery.

Economic System. The Maya economic system consisted of local agricultural and crafts production, commercial agriculture, local and long distance trade—the latter primarily involving luxury products—and tribute. Local agricultural products consisted of such crops as maize, beans, chili, honey, cotton, and salt and fish. These were the staples of daily life along with such craft products as pottery, obsidian and flint tools, and weaving and rush mats. Other crops, such as cacao and cotton, were raised on large plantations.

There were many local and regional markets, the most important ones being held in major centers. People selling the same items were grouped together, and luxury as well as everyday items were sold. Markets in important centers were located near temples, and there were judges to settle disputes. Cacao was the most common medium of exchange, but salt and gold were also used.

There were several long-distance trade networks. Much of the sea trade route that stretched from the Chontal area, around Yucatán, and down to the Sula plain of Honduras was controlled by Chontal traders who had large canoes. One such canoe was sighted by Columbus in 1502, and it was filled with trade goods. The Chontals received such goods as cloth, gold ornaments, copper and obsidian items, cochineal, rabbit furs, and slaves from the Aztecs. Aztec merchants had enclaves in Chontal territory, especially at the port of Xicalango. They took cacao, jaguar skins, carved tortoise shells, feathers, and precious stones back to Mexico. Salt, fish, cotton, slaves, honey, and beeswax came to Acalán from Yucatán. The Chontals had extensive cacao plantations in Potonchan, Chetumal, and Honduras. They had enclaves and ports in Cozumel, Chetumal, Nito, and Naco. Another trade route probably passed overland through the Petén, to Tayasal and on to the Caribbean, and one went from Yucatán south to northern Belize.

In Guatemala the most important trade network involved the highland and Pacific coastal exchange. Maize, lime, timber, salt, obsidian, copper, and fish were highland products which were exchanged for lowland cacao, feathers, shrimp, turtles, iguanas, cotton, and fruit. Quetzal feathers were exported from Verapaz and jade from the Motagua area. Gold was imported from Soconusco and Honduras.

Tribute payers ordinarily paid items grown or made in their local area. They paid prescribed amounts over fixed periods of time, and the tribute does not seem to have been a severe hardship. Labor service to the lords was given and involved such activities as working in the lords' fields or building their houses.

Arts and Architecture. The period immediately preceding the Conquest was one of decay in Maya arts and architecture. Much construction was shoddy, and art forms often imitated past styles. In architecture Maya style was combined with such Mexican elements as twin temples placed on a single substructure, round temples, dance platforms, skull racks, colonnaded multiroomed structures, and ball courts in the shape of a capital *I*. Buildings at major centers were usually made of stone and were arranged around plazas.

Mixteca-Puebla influence appears in murals found at several Maya sites. The walls of the palace of the Quiché Cawek lineage at Utatlán were covered with such frescoes portraying important events in the lives of the lords. The best preserved are at Tulum in a two-story building where Xux Ek, the Venus deity, is portrayed. The style is Mixteca-Puebla, but the content is Maya.

During this period, most pottery was local or regional although some Mixteca-Puebla pieces turn up in Maya sites. Chinautla polychrome, a red-and-black-on-white ware from the Guatemala highlands, was traded as far south as El Salvador. Incense burners are found throughout the Maya area. Most pottery and monumental stone sculpture were undistinguished and poor in quality. At Naco, pottery used by the elite living in the central precinct differed from that used by the common people and suggests the higher class had ties with the lowland regions to the north. Other important arts were woven cotton textiles, feather garments, gold, silver and jade items, and painted hieroglyphic books.

Religion. The Mayas had some deities who had been worshiped for a long time, such as Itzamná (a reptilian diety), the Chacs (or rain gods), Ix Chel (the rainbow deity), and Ek Chuah (the merchant god). Mexican-derived gods, such as Kukulcan, and the gods of impor-

THE QUICHÉ IDOL IK.

FROM LEONHARD SCHULTZE, *LEBEN, GLAUBE UND SPRACHE DER QUICHÉ VON GUATEMALA,* JENA, 1933.

tant lineages were also prominent in the period immediately before the conquest. The Maya religious system was polytheistic, and many local deities and spirits were also worshiped. Shrines and pilgrimage centers, such as that dedicated to Ix Chel on Cozumel, also existed.

The gods were portrayed in sculpture and painted hieroglyphic books (codices). They were also worshiped in the form of effigies made out of wood, clay, or stone. The effigies were believed to speak to their people through chosen interpreters or prophets. Dressed in fine clothing and adorned with precious stones and gold, the effigies were kept in temples or were hidden in caves and were the focus of rituals involving fasting, dancing, drinking, and burning incense. The gods were fed food, drink, and human blood. The hearts of living victims were removed by priests, and the victims' blood was smeared on the idols. Birds and animals were also sacrificed by individuals who hoped to attain health, fortune, or some other desire.

The religious organization was headed by a high priest who was assisted by many subordinate priests. They resided in a multiroomed structure near the temple. Priests were in charge of the hieroglyphic books that contained the 260-day divinatory and the 365-day calendars and other religious texts. The *Popol Vuh,* the sacred book of the Quiché Mayas, contains mythology and legends as well as historical accounts of the Quiché forefathers and their Mexicanized gods that are remnants of a much larger body of sacred material that existed before the Conquest. In Yucatán the cult of the *katuns* (twenty-year periods) involved prophecies based on the idea that whatever happened in the past would happen again in another *katun* of the same name. In highland Guatemala sacred bundle cults, such as that of the Pizom Qáqál mentioned in the *Popol Vuh,* were important.

Post-Contact Maya Culture

The period of fighting in the Maya area lasted around twenty years. Some areas were quickly subdued, and others, such as Yucatán (northern lowlands) and the Petén (central lowlands), took longer to conquer.

The Conquest Period: 1517–1542. It was not until 1542 that Francisco de Montejo, father and son, were able to found a capital in Yucatán at Mérida. The conquest of Yucatán was difficult because there was no supreme native ruler to defeat and the provinces defended themselves with guerrilla warfare. Revolts continued throughout the sixteenth century in Yucatán. The conquest of the eastern Maya area around the Gulf of Honduras was achieved quickly, and the Indians were almost entirely obliterated at Nito and Naco. Chetumal held out until 1544; most of its inhabitants fled after the conquest.

Diego de Mazariegos began the conquest of Chiapas in 1528 and rapidly subdued the population. Pedro de

Alvarado entered Guatemala in 1524 and soon conquered the highland groups. He established a permanent capital at the foot of Agua volcano in 1527. This capital was destroyed in an eruption of 1541, and a new capital was founded at present-day Antigua. In 1524 Alvarado also conquered Cuzcatlán (El Salvador), and Honduras was taken by Cristóbal de Olid. The Itzás of the Petén were the last Maya group to remain independent and were not conquered until 1697.

The conquest of the Mayas was facilitated by the superior arms and military strategies of the Spaniards, by the failure of the Indians to put aside local conflicts and join together to fight the common enemy, and by the willingness of both Mexican and Maya Indians to give aid to the Spaniards.

The first Spanish institution imposed on the Indians by the Crown was the encomienda, a grant of a certain number of Indians to reward a conqueror for his service to Spain. The encomendero had the right to receive tribute and labor service from his encomienda Indians. The conquerors tended to exploit their encomiendas as they wished, and there were few limits on their demands. The turbulent times and the small number of Crown officials in the Maya area made it impossible to curb the excesses of the conquerors, whose goals were to become wealthy as quickly as possible and return home to positions in Spain. Sources of gold, silver, and precious stones were quickly exhausted, and the encomienda was used to deplete the Indians rapidly of their wealth.

The upper level of the native sociopolitical structure was greatly affected by the Conquest. Rulers lost their independence and could no longer conduct war and were reduced to the level of local authorities as regional units were dissolved. Agriculture remained in Indian hands as the Spaniards were not initially interested in farming. The conquerors did, however, take over long-distance trade networks. Some of these, such as the sea route from Yucatán to the Gulf of Honduras, were disrupted, but not all the trade was destroyed.

By the 1540s it was becoming clear that the situation could not continue as before. Severe population decline had occurred as a result of fighting and diseases introduced by the Spaniards, reducing the value of encomiendas. Initial sources of wealth were exhausted, and colonists resented the removal of Indians because their labor was needed in local areas.

Establishment of Spanish Authority: 1542–1600. Beginning in 1542, with the passage of the New Laws, which abolished Indian slavery and prohibited the colonists from interfering in most aspects of native life, the Crown took steps to ensure its control and protect the remaining Indians. A new administrative structure was imposed, and more priests were sent to Christianize and protect the

natives. The New Laws were resisted, but by 1550, control passed to the audiencias, administrative bodies staffed by officials from Spain. The Audiencia de los Confines, established in 1543, included the area from Chiapas to Costa Rica, except Yucatán, which was initially a part of the Audiencia of Mexico.

Two policies in particular established the basic format of Indian life throughout the sixteenth century: congregation (the gathering of scattered native settlements into focal towns) and the implementation of the Indian town-government system. Many hilltop and remote villages were abandoned for more accessible sites. Towns were laid out according to the Spanish town plan with the church, cabildo (town council), and other main buildings being placed around the plaza. Indian houses surrounded the central area.

The Guatemala and Chiapas highlands received more Spanish colonists than tropical areas and Yucatán. Both Yucatán and Chiapas remained areas of Indian agriculture. By 1550 many Spaniards had left Chiapas or had begun to raise cattle and sugar in the Grijalva River valley. As they took more land, Indians were forced to leave home in search of work. This migration, also found in the Guatemala highlands, destroyed the lineage structure in towns, such as Zinacantán and possibly Atitlán, which were severely affected by loss of men. Many died in tropical areas working on cacao plantations. More remote towns, such as Chamula and Sacapulas, retained the pre-Hispanic social organization.

The Spaniards transferred the people of Itzamkanac to coastal Tixchel in 1557 as the interior had few Indians left. This severely weakened the trade system linking the southern and northern lowlands, and few wealthy Acalán merchants survived by the end of the sixteenth century. The Pacific coastal piedmont area became a focus of Spanish exploitation. Indians owned and cultivated cacao, but most of the harvest was drawn off as tribute or in trade. Because of steep population decline, external competition, and the lack of proper attention, the piedmont cacao plantations gradually declined, and the area was eventually impoverished.

By the mid-sixteenth century, most of the Indians resided in remote highland areas of Chiapas and Guatemala and northern Yucatán. The majority of Spanish colonists resided in a few large towns in temperate areas and lived off encomiendas, through trading, or on government salaries.

Another important local institution introduced by priests after 1550 was the cofradía (religious sodality). Cofradías were dedicated to a patron saint, and became the focus of Indian religious life. By this time priests had destroyed most of the Maya effigies and hieroglyphic books and had ended human sacrifice. Some of the aspects of aboriginal religion objectionable to the Spaniards went underground, however, and did not completely disappear in the sixteenth century. The Mayas were allowed to retain much of their religious life, as long as they were outwardly Catholic. They mixed pagan beliefs with Catholicism through *cofradía* rituals. Drinking, dancing, fasting, incense, sacred bundles, and diety worship in the form of a cult of the saints continued.

By the end of the sixteenth century, the Spanish had implemented the colonial system that was to exist for the next two hundred years in the Maya region. Indian culture was not destroyed in all areas, and many aspects of pre-Hispanic life endured. Indians living close to Spanish towns or in the lowlands experienced more disruption and exploitation than those inhabiting remote highland areas. Loss of traditional lands and migration also affected the continuity of Maya social organization. Many of the methods used by the Spaniards to control the Indians were variations of aboriginal practices, but they were often much harsher. Along with the introduction of epidemic diseases, these methods led to the gradual lowering of Indian society to a peasant level and to the destruction of ancient sources of wealth.

BIBLIOGRAPHY

Carmack, Robert M. *The Quiché Mayas of Utatlán: The Evolution of a Highland Guatemala Kingdom.* Norman, Okla., 1981.

Edmonson, Munro. *The Book of Counsel: The Popol Vuh of the Quiché Maya of Guatemala.* Middle American Research Institute, no. 35. New Orleans, 1971.

Hill, Robert M., and John Monaghan. *Continuities in Highland Maya Social Organization: Ethnohistory in Sacapulas, Guatemala.* Philadelphia, 1987.

Lovell, George W. *Conquest and Survival in Colonial Guatemala: A Historical Geography of the Cuchumatán Highlands, 1500–1821.* Kingston, Ont., and Montréal, 1985.

MacLeod, Murdo J. *Spanish Central America: A Socioeconomic History, 1520–1720.* Berkeley and Los Angeles, 1973.

Morley, Sylvanus G., and George W. Brainerd. *The Ancient Maya.* 4th ed. Revised by Robert J. Sharer. Stanford, Calif., 1983.

Orellana, Sandra L. *The Tzutujil Mayas: Continuity and Change, 1250–1630.* Norman, Okla., 1984.

Roys, Ralph L. *The Indian Background of Colonial Yucatán.* Norman, Okla., 1972.

Scholes, France V., and Ralph L. Roys. *The Maya Chontal Indians of Acalán-Tixchel. A Contribution to the History and Ethnography of the Yucatán Peninsula.* Norman, Okla., 1968.

Wasserstrom, Robert. *Class and Society in Central Chiapas.* Berkeley and Los Angeles, 1983.

SANDRA L. ORELLANA

Aztecs and Their Neighbors

Although, strictly speaking, *Aztec* (Nahuatl, *Azteca*, Person of Aztlan, the legendary homeland) designated only the ancestors of the Mexica of the twin cities of Mexico Tenochtitlan and Tlatelolco, it has proved useful as a generic term for the late pre-Hispanic peoples of Central Mexico. Most spoke dialects of a common language, Nahuatl, shared an essentially similar culture, and were organized into a number of city states that were dominated by a coalition of the three most powerful: Mexico Tenochtitlan, Tetzcoco, and Tlacopan (in Spanish these Nahuatl names became, respectively, Tenochtitlán, Texcoco, and Tlacopán)—constituting what is usually referred to as the Triple Alliance or Aztec empire.

Traditional History. Mexico Tenochtitlan achieved the supreme position in the coalition. According to one version of Mexica official history, their ancestors were commanded to leave Aztlan, described as an island in a lake, by their patron deity, Huitzilopochtli, in 1116. After a long migration, which included a period of servitude in Colhuacan, they encountered the sign that signaled the end of their wandering, an eagle perched on a nopal cactus growing from a rock. This occurred on a swampy island in the western portion of the saline lake that covered much of the floor of the Basin of Mexico. There they founded their city, Mexico Tenochtitlan (Place of the Mexica–Next to the Stone Nopal Cactus Fruit) around 1325. A divisive group of Mexica leaders established a short distance to the north another city, Tlatelolco (Place of the Globular Islet), that eventually became a serious rival of its southern sister city.

This lake zone was controlled by the Tepaneca of Azcapotzalco, on the western shore, capital of the city-state that had superseded Colhuacan as the paramount power in Central Mexico. Although still tributary to the Tepaneca, the Mexica of Mexico Tenochtitlan, now also called the Tenochca, were able in 1376 to crown their first official ruler, Acamapichtli, a part-Mexica scion of the Toltec-descended royal dynasty of Colhuacan.

At the outset of the reign of the fourth Tenochca ruler, Itzcoatl (r. 1428–1440), a general revolt of most of the Central Mexican city-states tributary to Azcapotzalco was successful. In the early 1430s a new imperial order, the Triple Alliance, was formally established. Mexico Tenochtitlan was joined by Tetzcoco, which under its part-Mexica ruler, the famed "poet king," Nezahualcoyotl (r. 1431–1472), controlled the eastern Basin of Mexico, and Tlacopan, the junior partner, which had inherited the remnant of Tepanec power. This coalition generated great military strength and under a succession of able and aggressive rulers, particularly the nephew and successor of Itzcoatl, Motecuhzoma I (r. 1440–1469), steadily expanded the territory subject to its control. At the time of the Conquest, the Triple Alliance imperium included most of Central and Southern Mexico, and into its capitals regularly flowed a huge amount of rich tribute from hundreds of communities within this extensive territory. Mexico Tenochtitlan, ruled by Motecuhzoma II (r. 1502–1520), the great-grandson of Motecuhzoma I, had, with its twin city, Tlatelolco (which it had conquered in 1473), grown to a great, canal-laced island metropolis, connected by four main causeways to the mainland, with perhaps as many as a quarter-million inhabitants.

Although Motecuhzoma II continued to extend the boundaries of the empire, focusing particularly on the Mixtec-speaking polities of southwestern Oaxaca, the era of spectacular Triple Alliance military expansion was nearly over. Soon after his accession, the first vague reports of the operations of the Spanish in the Caribbean drifted into his realm (Columbus himself, on his fourth and final voyage, in the summer of 1502, reached the Bay Islands off the north coast of Honduras). According to post-Conquest tales, various signs and portents of impending catastrophe plagued Motecuhzoma's last years. The ruler of Mexico Tenochtitlan's chief imperial partner, Nezahualpilli of Tetzcoco, who had succeeded Nezahualcoyotl in 1472, died in 1516, reputedly prophesying dire events to come. A favorite of Motecuhzoma, Cacama (r. 1516–1520), one of Nezahualpilli's sons by a Mexica wife, was chosen the new lord of Tetzcoco—and Mexico Tenochtitlan's preponderance in power within the Triple Alliance became steadily more manifest.

In 1517, two caravels from Cuba were blown off their course and found themselves off a low, unknown shore, the northeastern corner of Yucatan (Spanish, Yucatán). The next year a small fleet of four ships cruised up the coast of Motecuhzoma's Gulf Coast dominions. His representatives there, after engaging in trade with the strangely attired newcomers, reported this unexpected visitation to their emperor. When they returned to the coast, bearing Motecuhzoma's gifts and official message of greeting, the "houses that floated on the water" had sailed away.

In 1519 a much larger fleet of thirteen ships appeared off the same coast. On Good Friday, April 22, Hernando Cortés stepped onto the sandy shore at the edge of Cemanahuac Tenochca Tlalpan (The Whole Earth, the Land of the Tenochca). A little over a year later the most powerful native ruler in North America, a bewildered prisoner in his father's palace, fell under a hail of stones hurled by his own people. Huitzilopochtli's children rallied for a desperate defense of their empire, but, in spite of their stoic heroism, most of their leaders perished in the flaming ruins of the great city that had grown up on the spot where their ancestors had encountered the eagle on the cactus on the rock. Nezahualpilli's prophecy had been fulfilled.

The Triple Alliance Empire. The imperial territory was divided into a number of tributary provinces, comprising various towns and their dependencies. One of the main towns served as the headquarters for the *calpixqui,* the imperial official and his staff, who supervised the collection of the tribute and forwarded it to the capital(s). Provinces of particular strategic importance were governed by high ranking military officers, who commanded garrisons of imperial troops.

A wide range of products constituted the regular tribute levies, which were most commonly collected every eighty days. Various pictorial and textual sources, particularly the *Matrícula de tributos* and its cognate, Part II of the Codex Mendoza, provide itemized lists of them, province by province. Large quantities of foodstuffs and condiments were exacted, mainly from the more centrally located provinces. The prized cacao, the source of chocolate, was collected from certain lowland provinces. Both male and female clothing of cotton and maguey fiber was a standard item, as were elaborate warrior costumes and shields and jade, rock crystal, amber, and gold ornaments. A greater amount of tribute was demanded of provinces that had militarily resisted the Triple Alliance armies. As long as the provinces paid their tribute on time and did not otherwise create problems for their masters, they were allowed a high degree of internal autonomy.

The empire of the Triple Alliance was an intricate mosaic of numerous peoples speaking many different languages, among which Nahuatl—which also served as a lingua franca throughout most of Mesoamerica—was clearly dominant. Another important language of Central Mexico was the unrelated Otomi and its linguistic congeners (Matlatzinca, Mazahua, Ocuilteca), whose center of gravity was to the west and north. To the southeast, centered particularly in Oaxaca and neighboring territory, other languages were spoken, most of them at least remotely related to the Otomian family, the most important of which were Mixtec and Zapotec. To the east, in the Gulf Coast region, were Huaxtec (only their southernmost communities had been added to the empire), Tepehua, and Totonac. Directly to the west was a large block of Tarascan (Purepecha)-speaking communities, which had been organized into an extensive empire, ruled from Tzintzuntzan. This powerful polity had successfully resisted the westward thrust of the Triple Alliance, inflicting on Axayacatl (r. 1469–1481) the greatest military defeat ever suffered by the imperial army. The southeastern border of the empire touched on the territory of the speakers of the Mayance languages. However, although some Triple Alliance dynastic marital alliances had apparently been entered into with the Quiche- and Cakchiquel-speaking polities of Highland Guatemala, any more serious moves to extend the empire in this direction were forestalled by the Spanish Conquest.

The imperialistic thrusts from the Basin of Mexico had radiated out in a somewhat irregular fashion, often leapfrogging or bypassing still-resisting areas, and, at the time of the Conquest, there were various enclaves of unconquered territory within the extensive area dominated by the Triple Alliance. The most important of these were three populous city-states and their lesser allies just to the east of the Basin of Mexico: Tlaxcallan, Huexotzinco, and Chollollan. Just before the Conquest, Tlaxcallan and Huezotzinco had had a serious falling out, resulting in the former dominating the latter, and Chollollan had entered into an uneasy truce with Mexico Tenochtitlan. Tlaxcallan, however, was still a formidable military power, as became evident when in 1519 it formed a pact of friendship with Cortés, and the Tlaxcaltecas long served as the most potent and faithful native allies of the Spaniards. Other significant enclaves were Yopitzinco, along the Costa Grande of Guerrero, east of Acapulco, and a cluster of Mixtec-speaking polities, headed by Tototepec, in southwestern and coastal Oaxaca.

Subsistence. Aztec subsistence was based primarily on intensive agriculture, with some subsidiary hunting, gathering, and fishing. A variety of crops was cultivated, with maize, beans, and squash preeminent. Cotton and maguey provided most of the fiber for the weaving of clothing. The fermented saccharine exudate of maguey constituted the standard intoxicating beverage, pulque (Nahuatl, *octli*). Cacao, which provided the elite, luxury drink, chocolate, was cultivated in certain favored tropical locations.

The simple digging stick was the basic agricultural tool. Intensive rainfall cultivation was widespread in the semiarid highlands, while the slash-and-burn (swidden) system prevailed in the tropical lowlands. Where feasible, irrigation, flood-water farming, and terracing were employed on a limited scale. Food-storage facilities were well developed, with large, sturdily constructed granaries of both quadrangular pole and adobe vasiform (*cuezcomatl*) types.

Economy. Large agricultural surpluses could be produced both for satisfying tribute obligations and for commercial purposes. Aside from routine domestic household production, particularly the weaving of clothing by the women to satisfy family needs, small-scale "industrial" production featuring numerous specialized crafts played a significant role in the economic system.

In general, commerce, both local and long range, was of great importance. Although most transactions were conducted by barter, cacao beans and standard-sized cotton mantles served as a kind of supplemental currency. The major metropolitan centers held organized markets daily, the lesser communities normally every five days. The two most important Central Mexican markets were in Tlatelolco, where, according to Cortés, sixty thousand persons gathered daily, and Chollollan (Cholula), in the Basin of Puebla, a special holy city and pilgrimage center that also served as a great mercantile emporium. The highly

organized professional merchants (*pochteca/oztomeca*) joined with the merchants of other communities in undertaking great trading caravans that penetrated as far east as Guatemala and even beyond. They were much favored by the Triple Alliance rulers, who employed them as commercial agents and gatherers of useful military intelligence.

Sociopolitical Structure. The fundamental sociopolitical unit was the city-state, a dominant major town (*altepetl*) or group of allied towns that politically controlled a number of smaller dependent satellites. Even if the city-states paid tribute to more powerful polities—as most of them did within the Triple Alliance empire—they typically were permitted to manage most of their internal affairs. The larger communities were subdivided into smaller units (*calpolli, tlaxilacalli*), largely endogamous residential wards that exercised various corporate functions, particularly those involving land tenure.

All family members cooperated closely in subsistence and economic activities. By the age of ten most boys left their families to attend either the ward's military school (*telpochcalli*) or, particularly if they were members of the nobility, temple schools (*calmecac*). Some girls also attended the temple schools, but most were instructed in domestic skills by their mothers in their homes. Girls normally married quite early, boys somewhat later, after a period of military service. Polygyny was standard among the aristocracy, while most commoner marriages, mainly for economic reasons, were monogamous.

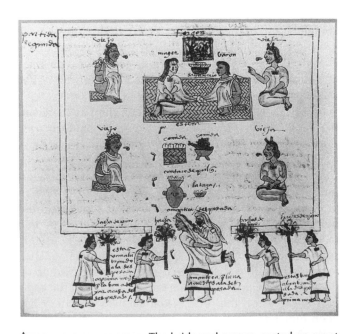

AZTEC MARRIAGE CEREMONY. The bride and groom, seated on a mat, literally "tie the knot," as his shift is tied to her blouse. From the Codex Mendoza, folio 61r.   LIBRARY OF CONGRESS

The society was highly stratified, with two major classes, the nobility *(pipiltin)* and the commoners *(macehualtin)*, with various distinctions of rank within each stratum. Most of the former possessed their own patrimonial lands, which were worked for them by commoners as well as tenants attached to them. All other commoners were required to pay taxes and fulfill additional obligations, including corvée labor on public works and military service. Nobles were usually free from local tax levies but were expected to serve in various leadership roles, particularly in the military sphere. Slaves *(tlacotin)* were owned mainly by the upper class and performed many of the more menial tasks. However, they possessed definite legal rights and were not considered mere chattel property.

Most of the major city-states at the core of the empire were governed by a ruler *(tlatoani,* speaker) who possessed great power as the earthly representative of his community's patron deity but was expected to consult with an advisory council composed of the highest ranking nobles before making important decisions. An extensive bureaucracy administered both local and imperial affairs, particularly the collection of taxes and tribute. Many of the higher officials also performed judicial duties, functioning within a complex, hierarchically organized system of local and imperial courts. They applied a rich body of traditional law based on both formal codes as well as recognized precedents.

Religion. The pervasive role of religion has long been recognized as one of the leading features of pre-Hispanic Mesoamerica. Typically, the Aztec religious and ritual system was extraordinarily rich and complex. From birth to death, the individual was immersed in incessant religious activities. Aside from a considerable amount of household ritual, most religious activities focused on the temple *(teocalli).* In the larger communities, a highly organized professional priesthood *(teopixque)* served in these temples. The priests lived together, practicing sexual abstinence, in monastic-type establishments *(calmecac)* that also served as schools for the sons of the nobility. In addition to the priest who served his community as a whole, there was also the practitioner of both white and black magic *(nahualli)* who mainly served individuals, especially in divination and curative medicine.

The rich theatrical ritualism was largely regulated by the two principal calendric cycles, the (13×20) 260-day cycle *(tonalpohualli)* and the (18×20+5) 365-day cycle *(xihuitl),* geared to the vague tropical year. The former was primarily employed for divination, each day and its numerical coefficient possessing a fortunate, unfortunate, or neutral connotation. The latter regulated the principal public ceremonies that honored the major deities. The typical ceremony involved a preparatory fasting period, offerings (especially food), processions, deity imperson-

ation, dancing, singing, and often human sacrifice with attendant ritual cannibalism.

The most striking feature of Aztec cosmogony was the concept of four great cosmic eras, or "suns," that had preceded the present age and had terminated with different types of cataclysmic destructions. The current era, the fifth and last, was to be terminated with mankind's final destruction by great earthquakes.

Aztec cosmology conceived the earth as a quadrangular land mass surrounded by ocean. From its center four quadrants extended to the cardinal directions. The celestial sphere consisted of thirteen tiers, the highest of which constituted the abode of the supreme creative divinities. Beneath the earth's surface were nine levels, the lowest, Mictlan, being the final resting place of most of deceased humanity.

An extensive pantheon of individualized deities was believed to control the various spheres of the universe. The majority expressed different aspects of certain fundamental themes, three of the most important being celestial creativity, agricultural fertility, and war/sacrifice/sanguinary nourishment of the sun and earth. The major supernaturals included Tezcatlipoca, the omnipotent "supreme god," Huitzilopochtli, the patron "war god" of the Mexica, Tlaloc, the ancient rain/fertility god, Ehecatl Quetzalcoatl, the wind deity, Chicomecoatl, the principal maize goddess, and Teteoinnan, the earth mother.

Writing. An embryonic writing system was employed, both for religious and secular purposes. It was essentially pictographic but contained some phonetic elements, utilizing the principle of the rebus, or "phonetic transfer," in place and name signs. Besides divinatory and ritual manuals, Aztec writings covered a wide range of subjects, including histories, genealogies, maps and plans, and

COLOSSAL STONE JAGUAR. A *cuauhxicalli*, or ritual vessel for human hearts, in the form of a jaguar. Discovered one block north of the Cathedral of Mexico City in 1901.

MUSEO NACIONAL DE ANTROPOLOGÍA, MEXICO CITY

administrative records such as taxation and tribute lists, censuses, and cadastres.

Aztec culture constituted the final synthesis of the ancient civilization of Mesoamerica. Cut off in full flower by the sudden, wholly unexpected Spanish invasion, much still survives of the lifeways of the indigenous peoples of Central Mexico, albeit in considerably modified form. Certainly no satisfactory understanding of modern Mexico can be achieved without full appreciation of the importance within its cultural fabric of the heritage of Mexico Tenochtitlan, today's Mexico City, and the many peoples over which this great New World Venice once ruled.

BIBLIOGRAPHY

Anderson, Arthur J. O., and Charles E. Dibble, eds. and trans. *Florentine Codex: General History of the Things of New Spain, Fray Bernardino de Sahagún.* Monographs of the School of American Research, Santa Fe, N.Mex., No. 14, Parts 1–13. Salt Lake City, 1950–1982.

Barlow, Robert H. "The Extent of the Empire of the Culhua Mexica." In vol. 28 of *Ibero-Americana.* Berkeley, Calif., 1949.

Berdan, Frances E. *The Aztecs of Central Mexico: An Imperial Society.* New York, 1982.

Carrasco, Pedro. "The Social Organization of Ancient Mexico." In vol. 10 of *Handbook of Middle American Indians,* edited by Robert Wauchope. Austin, Tex., 1971.

Clark, James Cooper, ed. and trans. *Codex Mendoza: The Mexican Manuscript Known as the Collection of Mendoza and Preserved in the Bodleian Library, Oxford.* 3 vols. London, 1938.

Davies, Nigel. *The Aztecs: A History.* Reprint, Norman, Okla., 1980.

Davies, Nigel. *The Aztec Empire: The Toltec Resurgence.* Norman, Okla., 1987.

Gillespie, Susan. *The Aztec Kings: The Construction of Rulership in Mexíca History.* Tucson, Ariz., 1989.

Gillmor, Frances. *Flute of the Smoking Mirror: A Portrait of Nezahualcoyotl, Poet-King of the Aztecs.* Reprint, Albuquerque, N.Mex., 1968.

León-Portilla, Miguel. *Aztec Thought and Culture.* Norman, Okla., 1963.

Matos Moctezuma, Eduardo. *The Aztecs.* New York, 1989.

Nicholson, H. B. "Religion in Pre-Hispanic Central Mexico." In vol. 10 of *Handbook of Middle American Indians,* edited by Robert Wauchope. Austin, Tex., 1971.

Nicholson, H. B., with Eloise Quiñones Keber. *Art of Aztec Mexico: Treasures of Tenochtitlan.* Washington, D.C., 1983.

Pasztory, Esther. *Aztec Art.* New York, 1983.

H. B. Nicholson

Indians of Northern Mexico, Baja California, and Southwestern North America

The human landscape encountered by Spanish explorers in northwestern New Spain in the sixteenth century was even more varied than the arid physiographic area

that sheltered it. Ranging across mountains, plateaus, canyons, river valleys, and deserts were Uto-Aztecan speakers (among them, Tepehuan, Tarahumara, Concho, Yaqui, Mayo, Opata, Pima, and Hopi Indians); Pueblo Indians of the Tanoan, Keresan, and Zunian linguistic groups; Apache and Navajo speakers of Athapaskan languages; and Seri and Yuman subgroups of Hokan speakers.

Nor did these peoples exhibit cultural unity. Although the native groups within this vast region had trade and exchange ties in the late prehistoric period (perhaps extending into Mesoamerica) and some of them had hierarchical sociopolitical structures, at least by 1600, the indigenous peoples of northern New Spain were characterized by relatively small, predominantly egalitarian communities that were independent of one another economically and politically. Their economies rested on varying combinations of agriculture (carried out by both men and women), gathering (mainly by women), and hunting (by men). Pueblos lived in compact adobe villages and practiced intensive irrigated and dry-farm agriculture. Roving-band peoples could be hunters and gatherers exclusively (as in Baja California) or, like the Navajos and some Apaches, also engage in limited agriculture. The largest number of northern Indians lived in scattered settlements of noncontiguous dwellings called rancherías where they practiced dry farming and floodplain agriculture, depending upon their location. Some changed ranchería locations within the course of the year and supplemented farming with hunting and the gathering of wild foods. In spite of differences in subsistence, kinship organization, and habitat, many inhabitants of this region (particularly the Uto-Aztecan groups) shared some common features, cultivating maize, beans, and squash; twilling baskets and mats; making pottery; and weaving cotton. Elders of individual communities constituted a type of moral authority in peacetime; tribal war leaders emerged in times of conflict. Shamans, whose power derived from dreams, predicted future events and possessed supernatural powers related to weather and curing. Ceremonial life included ritual dancing and the use of intoxicants. A common cosmological framework included belief in stages of creation, a universal flood, dominant male and female supernatural beings related to heavenly bodies, and opposition between supernatural beings who controlled wet and dry seasons.

Estimates of population at the time of contact range from one to two million. Within a hundred years after contact (a process that itself occupied a century), these numbers diminished by more than 90 percent due primarily to epidemic diseases such as smallpox, measles, and typhus. The demographic decline was the greatest ally of the Spaniards in bringing Indian peoples under their control. Hopis, Navajos, Apaches, and Yumans, living at the margins of Spanish empire, successfully resisted incorporation, but even they underwent profound changes in material culture. The introduction of Spanish livestock nearly everywhere diversified small-scale subsistence. Most groups experienced attempts by Franciscans and Jesuits to reorganize them in mission communities where native subsistence strategies and cosmologies clashed with Spanish coercive practices designed to extract surplus production and inculcate Christianity. Indigenous responses, often initially receptive, eventually took varying forms of accommodation and resistance, resulting in a wide range of acculturation.

BIBLIOGRAPHY

Hall, Thomas. *Social Change in the Southwest, 1350–1880.* Lawrence, Kan., 1989.

Ortiz, Alfonso, ed. *The Southwest.* Vols. 9 and 10 of *Handbook of North American Indians,* edited by William C. Sturtevant. Washington, D.C., 1983.

Spicer, Edward H. *Cycles of Conquest: The Impact of Spain, Mexico and the United States on the Indians of the Southwest, 1533–1960.* Tucson, 1962.

SUSAN M. DEEDS

Indians of La Florida

The Spaniards who explored sixteenth-century La Florida—roughly the southeastern United States—encountered a large number of native societies that differed in language, culture, and social structure. Many, but not all, had been powerfully shaped by an economic and social transformation that began about five hundred years before the Spaniards arrived. Beginning around A.D. 1000, this Mississippian transformation entailed a shift from hunting and gathering wild food to a significant dependence on corn grown in cleared fields. The native people of the Southeast had been cultivating several plants on a small scale for 3,000 years or more, but the food from these cultivated plants was little more than an accessory to the wild food they procured from hunting and collecting. Even in the Mississippian period (A.D. 1000–c. 1550), the cultivation of corn, beans, and squash never completely supplanted hunting and gathering. But the demands of corn dependency shaped the Mississippian way of life in a way that previous cultivation had not.

Only a small percentage of the soils in the Southeast are rich enough to have been cultivated without a heavy investment of labor. These favored soils—especially the alluvial soils along the margins of rivers and ox-bow lakes—became crucially important to the Indians of the Mississippian era and were worth fighting for.

Along with this economic change, there were far-reaching social changes during the Mississippian period. Most notably, many people in the Southeast organized themselves into chiefdoms that were hierarchical in structure. The people of a chiefdom were ranked in terms of their birth-order distance from the chief.

Chiefs and their closest relatives and retainers were supported by "gifts," which were voluntarily given, though they could be informally sanctioned, but the chiefs of larger chiefdoms were supported by tribute extracted by coercion or the threat of coercion. The chiefs of the larger Mississippian societies were set apart in life by special clothing, special ritual treatment, and possession of finery; in death they were set apart by burial in sanctified places accompanied by elaborate grave goods.

Just as the members of chiefdoms were ranked with respect to each other, so too were their communities ranked. The typical Mississippian chiefdom was not more than about twenty miles in diameter, and its population numbered in the thousands or low tens of thousands. The central town of a Mississippian chiefdom, which was not always the largest town in size or population, was normally a site with one or more flat-topped mounds on which there were buildings in which the chief lived, where councils and rituals were held, and where venerable things were kept. But chiefdoms might also include secondary towns with mounds, as well as smaller villages and homesteads with no mounds.

In addition, in a number of places in the interior of the Southeast, chiefs gained ascendancy or influence over other chiefdoms, becoming paramount chiefs. Notably unstable because of internal and external conflict, paramount chiefdoms could be short-lived.

One of the principal concerns of Mississippian chiefdoms was the waging of warfare. Southeastern warriors were most adept at one-on-one combat using bows and arrows and warclubs, but they also organized units of combatants against distant enemies. They were devotees of the swift attack from ambush, and they symbolically identified themselves with the cougar and the peregrine falcon. Warfare between some chiefdoms was so endemic and so long-lasting, the combatants were separated by very large uninhabited wildernesses. The Indians warily entered these wildernesses to hunt, fish, and collect wild foods.

The Indians of the Mississippian Southeast created a variety of technically proficient and aesthetically pleasing art forms. This included wooden and stone temple statuary, repoussé copper, engraved shell, and, most particularly, pottery. In the early Mississippian era a complex of symbols known as the Southeastern ceremonial complex became widespread in Mississippian chiefdoms.

The expeditions of Hernando de Soto (1539–1543), Tristán de Luna (1559–1561), and Juan Pardo (1566–1568) all penetrated the interior of the Southeast and came into contact with the paramount chiefdoms. The most notable of these paramount chiefdoms were Coosa, dominating the ridge and valley area of Tennessee, northwestern Georgia, and northeastern Alabama; Ocute, on the middle Oconee River in Georgia, and with probable influence over people living on the western headwaters of the Savannah River, the Guale on the coast, and perhaps Ichisi below the falls at the Ocmulgee River; Cofitachequi, controlling the Wateree River in South Carolina, and with influence over societies between the mountains and the coast; Tascaluza, whose domain lay along the Alabama River; Apalachee, commanding the area between the Aucilla and Ochlockonee Rivers; Chicaza, dominating the middle course of the Tombigbee River and its western tributaries; Pacaha, commanding both sides of the Mississippi River from perhaps thirty miles above and below present Memphis; Casqui, commanding the upper St. Francis River in Arkansas; Naguatex, commanding the great bend of the Red River in southwestern Arkansas; and Quigualtam, commanding the Mississippi River below the mouth of the Arkansas River down to about the mouth of the Yazoo River.

In addition, the European explorers encountered a number of smaller chiefdoms that may not have been incorporated into paramount chiefdoms. The most important of these were Capachequi and Toa on the Flint River in Georgia; Guatari, on the Yadkin River in North Carolina; Apafalaya, on the Black Warrior in Alabama; Quiguate, on the middle St. Francis River in Arkansas; Coligua, on the upper White River in Arkansas; Cayas, on the upper Arkansas River; Quipana, on the upper Ouachita River; Autiamque, on the middle Arkansas River; Anilco, on the lower Arkansas; Guachoya, on the Mississippi River below the mouth of the Arkansas River; and Aminoya, on the Mississippi River above the mouth of the Arkansas River.

Finally, on the margins of the Southeast there were a number of small chiefdoms and tribal societies that were based on hunter-gatherer economies, or societies that were agricultural but not fully Mississippian. The most notable of these were the buffalo-hunting Tula of northwestern Arkansas; the hunter-gatherer Karankawans of the coast of east Texas, among whom Álvar Núñez Cabeza de Vaca and his companions suffered; the Tequesta and Ais of southern Florida, both small societies of hunter-gatherers; the Calusa of southwestern Florida, a chiefdom with a hunter-gatherer economy; and the Ozita and Mocozo of Tampa Bay, who appear to have relied mainly on hunting and gathering. In addition, there were several who in later times were loosely called Timucuans, the most important of whom were the Urriparacoxi and Ocale, agriculturalists in the Withlacoochee River wetlands; the agricultural Yustega of northern Florida; and the Utina of eastern Florida.

Spain had a continuous presence in the Southeast after 1564. But Spain's sphere of influence never extended much beyond the missions of northern Florida and the Georgia coast. The missionaries were effective within this sphere, converting the Indians to Catholicism and instructing them in the Spanish language and in useful skills. But the diseases that the Spaniards brought from the Old World to the New had a catastrophic impact on the native people. One disease after another struck in the late sixteenth century and throughout the seventeenth century. The native population declined precipitously, the paramount chiefdoms fell apart, and the survivors reorganized themselves into new societies to face the challenge of the eighteenth century.

BIBLIOGRAPHY

Dye, David H., and Cheryl Anne Cox, eds. *Towns and Temples along the Mississippi*. Tuscaloosa, Ala., 1990.
Galloway, Patricia, ed. *The Southeastern Ceremonial Complex: Artifacts and Analysis*. Lincoln, Neb., 1989.
Hudson, Charles. *The Southeastern Indians*. Knoxville, Tenn., 1976.
Milanich, Jerald T., and Susan Milbrath, eds. *First Encounters: Spanish Exploration in the Caribbean and the United States, 1492–1570*. Gainesville, Fla., 1989.
Smith, Bruce D., ed. *The Mississippian Emergence*. Washington, D.C., 1990.
Thomas, David Hurst, ed. *Columbian Consequences: Archaeological and Historical Perspectives on the Spanish Borderland East*. Vol. 2. Washington, D.C., 1990.

CHARLES HUDSON

Indians of New England, Roanoke, Virginia, and the St. Lawrence Valley

At the time of Columbus's explorations, the natives of the northern and mid-Atlantic coast and the St. Lawrence Valley of North America were a large and varied array of communities and cultures. Natives of the St. Lawrence River basin and northern New England were members of two distinct cultural traditions, one the northern Algonquian maritime-hunting cultures such as the Beothuks, Micmacs, and Malecite-Passamaquoddies. The other tradition was Iroquoian and included groups known collectively as the St. Lawrence Iroquoians.

The St. Lawrence Iroquoians practiced a mixed economy, including farming, hunting, and fishing. First encountered by French explorers in 1534, these natives occupied two distinct territories, one centering around the Île d'Orléans, and the other on Montréal Island, and they may have been divided into correspondingly separate political and cultural entities. They are today sometimes known as Stadaconans and Hochelagans, after their principal fortified towns. By 1535, the Stadaconans had established themselves as trading intermediaries between the French and native groups farther inland. Rivalry between them and the equally powerful Iroquoian and Algonquian groups to the west probably led to their defeat and dispersal in the late sixteenth century.

The Algonquian-speaking people of the St. Lawrence basin and northern coastal regions were also hunters, subsisting mainly on game, fish, wild vegetable foods, nuts, and seeds. Their material culture was well-suited to the harsh climatic conditions of their territory; they exhibited superior workmanship in hide clothing, snow shoes, and hunting and fishing gear. Coastal groups, such as the Micmacs of the Gulf of St. Lawrence and Maritime provinces, and the Passamaquoddies of the lower St. John River valley, were sea-mammal hunters, while inland groups hunted moose, caribou, and other game. Religious ritual was shamanistic, with emphasis on divination, healing, and the accumulation of personal spiritual power. The northern Algonquians were organized into bands with leaders chosen for their skill at hunting and diplomacy and sometimes for their shamanistic abilities as well. In the late sixteenth century, some of these leaders were exploiting long-distance coastal trade routes for the benefit of their lineages and bands, and it was these men who first negotiated with Europeans in the early decades of the seventeenth century.

Natives of southern New England and the Atlantic seaboard were also Algonquian speakers, but, unlike their northern relatives, they were more sedentary, with women's agricultural products providing a large portion of their diet. Many were organized into communities led by hereditary leaders, known in some areas as sachems, who were entitled to tribute and empowered to allocate land, conduct diplomacy, and wage war. Their cosmology included a belief in an afterlife and in the efficacy of *manitou* (spirit helpers) in gaining success as providers, warriors, and leaders.

Some of the earliest known illustrations of eastern woodlands people are of the Indians of Roanoke Island, completed by the artist John White in 1585. The Roanoke Indians were Algonquian-speakers, and, like the natives of coastal Virginia, were farming people, ruled by elected or hereditary chiefs. The religious ceremonies of the Virginia and Roanoke Algonquians included an elaborate burial cult and belief in frightening and powerful spirits to whom ritual sacrifices were made.

At the time of the establishment of Jamestown in 1607, the natives of eastern Virginia were united into a confederacy under a paramount chief known as Powhatan, a confederacy perhaps influenced by previous encounters with Europeans, particularly the Spanish, who had established an ill-fated Jesuit mission on the York River in 1576.

The size of the aboriginal population in the Northeast varied with ecological conditions. Northern and inland

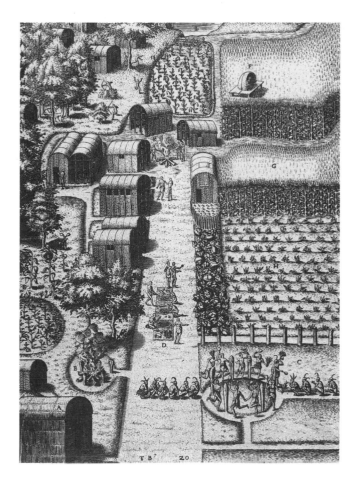

DEPICTION OF AN INDIAN VILLAGE BY JOHN WHITE. The type of village commonly found along the Atlantic seaboard south of New England at the time of first contact with Europeans. This engraving, after a drawing by White, appeared in Thomas Hariot's *A Brief and True Report of the New Found Land of Virginia*. Frankfurt, 1590.

NEW YORK PUBLIC LIBRARY, RARE BOOKS DIVISION

regions may have supported as few as three to ten people per one hundred square kilometers, while the same area supported as many as one hundred people in more temperate and coastal regions. Contact with Europeans after 1492 led to a series of disastrous epidemics throughout the native populations of the Northeast, with losses up to 95 percent in certain regions. These debilitating losses, accompanied by political instability and exacerbated by early trade rivalries, severely affected but did not destroy the majority of native cultures in the region.

BIBLIOGRAPHY

Fitzhugh, William W., ed. *Cultures in Contact: The European Impact on Native Cultural Institutions in Eastern North America A.D. 1000–1800*. Washington, D.C., 1985.

Quinn, David. *North America from Earliest Discovery to First Settlements: The Norse Voyages to 1612*. New York, 1977.

Trigger, Bruce C. *The Northeast*. Volume 15 of *Handbook of North American Indians*, edited by William C. Sturtevant. Washington, D.C., 1978.

KATHLEEN BRAGDON

INDIES, THE. For Europeans of the fourteenth and fifteenth centuries, India was a vast, poorly defined territory of the Orient, subdivided into India Major and Minor (India below and above the Ganges). India was important because it was the source of spices that made the European diet palatable. Pepper and clove, cinnamon, mace, and ginger were shipped from parts of Hindustan to Europe, mainly from Calicut. Most of them were shipped through India from other parts of South Asia. Pepper and cinnamon did come from India, but clove originated in the Moluccas and mace in the Banda Islands. There were other products besides spices: dyes (such as anil), medicinal plants (such as cardamom), precious stones (such as rubies, pearls, and emeralds), silks, musk, lacquer, and many other goods that found a ready market in Europe. Europeans paid premium prices for these products because kings and territorial lords along the trade routes between the centers of production and consumption added surcharges in the form of imposts or duties on transit rights.

In the last centuries of the Middle Ages and until the end of the fifteenth century, the distribution of such merchandise was mainly in the hands of the Muslim traders who transferred it from parts of India, especially from western Hindustan, to Genoese or Venetian ships in ports of the Near East or the Black Sea. European merchants, especially those who came from the small states or cities of the Italian peninsula tried at times to establish direct ties with the producers of spices, though with little success.

The most famous of these merchants was Marco Polo (1254–1324), who went to Asia personally at the end of the thirteenth century in order to take direct charge of his business affairs. He was relatively well acquainted with India, although he was based in China. The importance of Marco Polo for fifteenth-century Europe can be attributed to his sometimes confused description of the areas from which much-sought-after luxury products were imported into Europe. *The Description of the World* (also called *The Book of Marco Polo*) enjoyed a wide readership in the Western world during the fourteenth and fifteenth centuries and was eventually translated into the vernacular languages. It attracted the attention of travelers who, like Christopher Columbus, elaborated plans to make contact with the Orient that the Venetian adventurer described in his work, at times with some exaggeration.

The plan to reach the East Indies directly, thereby eliminating the Muslim intermediaries, took shape only during the second half of the fifteenth century as the result of the Portuguese expansion along the west coast of Africa. In effect, the so-called India plan (meaning direct access to the Indies by sea) was laid only after Prince João (1455–1495; after 1481 King João II) assumed responsibility for the administration of overseas affairs in 1473. The plan became reality only after he encouraged southward voyages along the African coast in the hope of finding, despite the ideas of Ptolemy, a maritime link between the Atlantic and Indian oceans. Between 1481 and 1488 two or three voyages under the command of Diogo Cão (fl. 1480–1486) explored the African coast. In 1488 Bartolomeu Dias (c. 1450–1500) sailed into the waters of the Indian Ocean, off southeast Africa.

King João based his expectation of the success of the India plan on many sources of information on the Indies and the Orient that were known in Europe even in the early fifteenth century, before European expansion began. Marco Polo was the first source of much of the information about the Orient disseminated throughout the Western world. But there were other sources of knowledge available to scholars and merchants as well as to the simple curious reader.

Among written sources were *Liber Tartarorum* of the Franciscan Giovanni da Pian del Carpini (c. 1180–1252), a curious account of the lives and customs of the Tatars mixed with some fabulous reports, and the description of the itinerary of the Franciscan Odoric of Pordenone (c. 1265–1331), whose report contained objective observations but was also permeated with symbols, myths, and marvels.

Oral traditions were as important—if not more important—than written documents and pseudogeographical novels. Oral relations were rooted in antiquity and were widely disseminated. Kings and great lords had occasional recourse to storytellers, though not all of them deserved the confidence placed in them. Because their accounts often gave free rein to the imagination, whenever projects related to India were planned, it was considered indispensable to obtain precise information directly from trustworthy persons.

João II was absolutely sure of being able to reach India by way of the Cape, perhaps as a result of the information obtained from Diogo Cão, who believed that he had almost reached the Indian Ocean on his first voyage. For that reason, in 1487, King João sent two men, Afonso de Paiva and Pero de Covilhã, to the Orient to gather accurate information on Ethiopia and the spice markets (the king suspected that Ethiopia and India were different places). Covilhã accomplished his mission, visiting the Malabar Coast (Calicut), Kanara (Goa), and Hormuz and perhaps following the Muslim maritime commerce along the East

African coast as far as Sofala (on the central coast of Mozambique). Paiva died before he reached Ethiopia, and Covilhã took his place after transmitting to the king his impressions of the world of active commercial exchange with which he had come into contact in the Indian Ocean. That the news sent by Covilhã was a determining factor in the king's plan is proven by the fact that in 1498 Vasco da Gama sailed directly to the port of Calicut and stayed there from the middle of May to the end of August.

Muslim merchants had reached India many years before Da Gama. They carried the message of their religion but did not forcibly convert followers of other religions. Because of their tolerance, they were able to gain markets without arousing opposition. Perhaps for that reason they gained faithful followers and eventually dominated the economy of the Indian hinterland. The Muslims followed all the routes of local commerce from the Red Sea to Malabar, Bengal, Malacca, Kanara, the Banda Islands, and Java. They navigated the Strait of Hormuz to follow routes along the east coast of Africa as far as Sofala. Eventually they came to enjoy enormous influence in all the major commercial entrepôts. Such accomplishments were achieved without difficulty or friction, and without claiming for themselves exclusivity or privileged treatment.

In the first half of the fifteenth century, when, for reasons even today only partly understood, Chinese overseas expansion ended (though their ships still continued for several years to visit Malacca, where the Portuguese encountered them), the Muslims dominated commerce in this active world of trade that included Gujaratis, Malays, Bengalis, and Javanese, among others. Muslim merchants were aware of their ability to dominate trade in India, but, recognizing the greater complexity of Indian culture, they had little difficulty in adapting to it and deriving economic benefits from supplying its products to Western markets.

The Portuguese operated much differently. Although the offensive capability of Da Gama's fleet was obviously insufficient in 1498, the first Portuguese in India employed the artillery mounted on their ships to force open markets and engage in a commerce that would have been impossible for them to win otherwise. In a short time, Portuguese activity brought about a reaction: the Turks appeared in Cambay, descending the coast in the direction of Calicut. They attacked and besieged the bar of Chaul (1508); in the ensuing battle, Lourenço de Almeida, son of the viceroy of India, was killed. The Portuguese realized that their foothold in India was vulnerable, and their sense of vulnerability was confirmed in the sixteenth century. They never succeeded in occupying Aden (on the southwest coast of Arabia) and Turkish galleys ran freely along the coast of Arabia and penetrated the Strait of Hormuz. Afonso de Albuquerque had captured Hormuz and con-

structed a fortress there; other fortresses were built in strategic Arabian ports. But the Portuguese presence in Arabia (which guarded the routes to India) was placed in jeopardy when Ottoman armies descended the Euphrates and captured Basra in 1547. The Turks besieged the Portuguese fortress of Diu (in northwestern India) in 1538 and supported a second attack, by the king of Cambay, in 1546.

In view of this situation, the Portuguese government of India felt compelled to develop a new commercial policy. Instead of allowing freedom of trade, it adopted a permanent control of merchants and merchandise. Navigation was permitted only to holders of a *cartaz* (license to sail, or safe conduct). On the other hand, various products (such as pepper from Malabar, horses from Iran, and cinnamon from Ceylon) were traded on a monopoly basis by the Portuguese.

Portuguese mercantile policy encountered innumerable difficulties. The Portuguese offended a great number of merchants, Muslim and non-Muslim alike, who usually become their declared enemies. In addition, they lacked the military power and population to impose their policy.

Christopher Columbus was in Lisbon in 1485 and he must have followed with great interest the steps taken to implement the India plan. In view of the uncertainty of rounding southern Africa, he conceived an alternative plan based on his readings of Nicole d'Oresme (c. 1325–1382), Pierre d'Ailly, and other writers: to sail westward across the Atlantic to Asia. But Columbus's calculation of the circumference of the earth was incorrect; he assumed that the earth is smaller than it is and therefore that the distance west from Europe to Asia is smaller than it is. And he did not suspect the existence of a vast continental landmass between western Europe and eastern Asia.

King João II had at his disposition better estimates of the dimensions of the earth. He also knew, or thought he knew, that the route via the Cape of Good Hope would be the most convenient. He therefore rejected Columbus's project. Considering his immediate objectives, King João was right; it was impossible to know the importance of Columbus's voyages in the fifteenth or early sixteenth century. The Portuguese wanted to reach the Indies, and, at the time, João II was the great victor in the race to get there. Columbus failed after enduring great hardship and being imprisoned, yet he was convinced that he had visited parts of Asia. Vasco da Gama had actually reached Asia and won for Lisbon the means of trading with the East. At that time no one had as yet the least idea of the importance that America would assume later.

If Columbus never reached India, he did reveal to the world the existence of new continents. So insistent was he that he had reached Asia that the whole group of islands in the Caribbean were designated as the "West Indies" or the "Indies of Castile." His error also prevented the two continental masses from being named after him. They are called the Americas after Amerigo Vespucci, because he, and not his fellow Italian, Columbus, succeeded in demonstrating that the lands they explored were continents and not islands off the coast of Asia.

[See also *Trade*. For discussion of uses of the name Columbus, see *Columbianism*. On the name America, see *America, Naming of*.]

BIBLIOGRAPHY

Albuquerque, Afonso de. *Albuquerque, Caesar of the East.* Translated and edited by T. F. Earle and John Villiers. Warminster, England, 1990.

Cortesão, Armando. *The "Suma Oriental" of Tomé Pires and the "Book of Francisco Rodrigues."* Hakluyt Society Publications, 2d ser., vols. 89 and 90. London, 1944.

Danvers, Frederick Charles. *The Portuguese in India,* 2d ed. 2 vols. New York, 1966.

Lach, Donald F. *Asia in the Making of Europe,* vol. 1, bks. 1 and 2. Chicago, 1965.

Prestage, Edgar. *The Portuguese Pioneers.* London, 1933.

Whiteway, R. S. *The Rise of Portuguese Power in India, 1495–1550,* 2d ed. London, 1967.

LUÍS DE ALBUQUERQUE
Translated from Portuguese by Rebecca Catz

INNOCENT VIII

INNOCENT VIII (1432–1492), pope. Born in Genoa, Giovanni Battista Cibò was educated at Padua and Bologna and during his early career in Naples fathered an illegitimate son and daughter. Entering the clerical state, he was employed by Cardinal Filippo Calandrini and was named bishop of Savona (1466–1472), of Molfetta (1472–1484), and datary (1471–1473), before becoming a cardinal (1473–1484). He owed his rapid promotions to Cardinal Giuliano della Rovere, who at the conclave of 1484 also secured his election as pope.

Amiable and kind, Innocent VIII was also frequently ill, lacking in financial resources, and subject to the influence of Cardinal della Rovere. As a result, he accomplished little as pope. Civil rulers took advantage of his weakness to gain greater control over local churches. Much of his time and energy was consumed in a protracted (1484–1492) military and diplomatic conflict with Ferrante I (1458–1494) of Naples over disputed territories, unpaid tribute, and independent church appointments. Threats of French intervention and of relocating the papacy outside Italy, coupled with the mediating services of Fernando and Isabel of Spain, led finally to the settlements of 1486 and 1492.

Although dissension and death among Christian princes undid his earnest efforts to launch a crusade against the Turks in 1490, his obtaining custody in 1489 of Cem, brother of Sultan Bayezid II (Bajazet), who lived as a

INNOCENT VIII. Papal medal, 1484.   AMERICAN NUMISMATIC SOCIETY

hostage in the Vatican palace and could be used to stir up civil war in the Ottoman Empire, led Bayezid to sue for a truce. He paid tribute to keep his brother as prisoner and presented the relic of the Holy Lance to the pope as a gift.

To encourage the Reconquista efforts of Fernando and Isabel in Spain, Innocent issued in 1486 the bull *Orthodoxae fidei* extending their traditional ecclesiastical patronage rights to bishoprics and major benefices in the conquered lands of Granada, the Canary Islands, and the town of Puerto Real recently founded by the Spanish monarchs near Cádiz. When Granada fell in 1492, the pope is said to have confirmed their traditional title of *los Reyes Católicos* (the Catholic monarchs).

According to a story told in the circles of Martín Alonso Pinzón of Palos, captain of *Pinta*, Pinzón visited Rome during the reign of Innocent VIII and found in the Vatican library an ancient account of a transatlantic voyage to Japan that so impressed him that he tried on his own to organize such a voyage. He is said to have shared this information with Columbus, encouraged him to seek royal authorization and financing, and put together the fleet Columbus eventually used for his first voyage of discovery. There is no evidence that Columbus himself had contact with his fellow Genoese countryman Innocent VIII.

BIBLIOGRAPHY

Brezzi, Paolo. "Innocenzo VIII, papa." In *Enciclopedia Cattolica.* Vol. 7. Vatican City, 1951.

Burchard, Johannes. *The Diary of John Burchard, Bishop of Orta.* Vol. 1. Translated by Arnold H. Mathew. London, 1910.

Morison, Samuel Eliot. *Admiral of the Ocean Sea: A Life of Christopher Columbus.* 2 vols. Boston, 1942.

Paschini, Pio. *Roma nel Rinascimento.* Vol. 12 of *Storia di Roma.* Bologna, 1940.

Pastor, Ludwig von. *The History of the Popes from the Close of the Middle Ages.* Vol. 5. Translated by Frederick Ignatius Antrobus. St. Louis, 1923.

Rodocanachi, Emmanuel P. *Histoire de Rome: Une cour princière au Vatican pendant la Renaissance (1471–1503).* Paris, 1925.

NELSON H. MINNICH

INQUISITION. The Spanish Inquisition was an ecclesiastical tribunal established in 1478 by Isabel and Fernando to determine whether the conversos were practicing Christianity and not their former Jewish rites. This definition, however, requires an explanation of what is meant by the Inquisition's being Spanish, as well as of its origin, structure, procedures, and goals.

The first inquisition was established in 1231 as a juridical tribunal. When Pope Gregory IX (r. 1227–1241) saw the inactivity of the bishops of southern France in pursuing the Cathars, or Albigensian heretics, he appointed members of the newly founded Dominican order as his direct representatives to deal with them. This inquisition was thus a papal, and not a royal, institution, although its activities did contribute to the definitive French domination of the region, which had been hesitating between France and Aragón.

Whereas the French tribunal was never an organ subordinate to the French Crown, the Spanish Inquisition was a department of government. In other nonpolitical aspects, however, it was essentially a continuation of the French, or papal, inquisition, and adopted its provisions and by-laws regarding arrest of defendants, trial procedures, confiscation, secrecy, witnesses, and other procedures. The medieval inquisition was dominant in France especially in Languedoc. In Spain the Inquisition extended only to the Crown of Aragón comprising the three kingdoms of Aragón proper, Catalonia, and Valencia, but never to Castile. It was dormant in the fifteenth century. The *Directorium inquisitorum* written by the Catalan inquisitor Nicolau Eymerich (1376) was the primary procedural guide of the Spanish Inquisition, so much so that some scholars contend that there was only one Inquisition.

In order to deal with the alarming number of conversos who some people believed to be Marranos (Jews who submitted to forced conversion but maintain Jewish practices in secret) several proposals were advanced in the fifteenth century by the constable, Alvaro de Luna, and King Enrique IV, either to extend the Aragonese Inquisition to Castile or to establish a new one with a special orientation. The new Inquisition, however, seems to have been a personal initiative of King Fernando based on reports by anticonverso friars like Alonso de Espina in his *Fortalitium fidei* (1460) and on the alarm raised by Pedro González de Mendoza, archbishop of Seville, who discovered important groups of secret Judaizers in that city and in Andalusia. It took the shrewdness of the king and the greed of Pope Sixtus IV to agree on the terms of the bull *Exigit sincerae devotionis* (November 1, 1478), which authorized the monarchs to appoint inquisitors. Nothing was done for several months until the accidental discovery of a plot of Jews and conversos in Seville set in motion the machinery that resulted in the first *auto de fe* ("act of faith," a term used for the formal announcement of the Inquisition's judgment and the execution of its sentence) held in that city on February 6, 1481.

Many of the suspect conversos fled the city and even Spain; some protested in writing (most interesting is a famous letter, now lost, by the humanist Juan de Lucena) to the sovereigns or to the pope, and others in person. But the king was adamant and obtained royal control of the Inquisition from the pope with a strong letter of May 13, 1482, and with more money. Out of the group of the first inquisitors active in various cities, Tomás de Torquemada was appointed the first inquisitor general in 1483. His authority as a Castilian and his introduction of the new Castilian Inquisition in Aragón was strongly protested by the Aragonese conversos and by the Cortes; the ancient *fueros* (special laws) of that kingdom prohibited torture and secret witnesses and forbade foreigners from taking posts in its administration. This led to the assassination of Pedro Arbués, one of the first two Aragonese inquisitors, in the cathedral of Saragossa on September 15, 1485, a crime used by the king and by the local Inquisition to eliminate entire families of conversos, some prominent, and to obtain the popular support they needed. While the Castilian Cortes usually voiced opposition to the legal and moral abuses of the Inquisition, the Aragonese Cortes had legal grounds to attack its very existence publicly, not only politically but also theologically, because the Cortes felt that heretics could be sufficiently controlled by a revived medieval, papal, or episcopal tribunal.

The Inquisition was governed by a centralized Supreme Council (Suprema), headed by the inquisitor general, who enjoyed a status equal to—though in fact superior to—a government minister. The inquisitor general supervised the activity of a network of fifteen district tribunals that covered the whole of Spain. At the peak of inquisitorial activities, tribunals were created in 1569 in Mexico and Lima and in 1610 in Cartagena. Each of the tribunals was served by a group of "familiars," laymen or clergymen, and also of "commissaries," always members of the clergy. All were scrupulously prepared to receive and transmit information and accusations, to assist in the arrest and transportation of defendants, and to participate in the official ceremonies and *autos de fe*. Each tribunal consisted of at least three local inquisitors, specialists in canon law, some attorneys for the prosecution and the defense, several notaries who produced hundreds of thousands of documents (today preserved mostly in the Archivo Nacional in Madrid), and guards. There were also several consultors, clergymen well versed in theology, who evaluated the propositions attributed to the defendants' speech or writings, many times out of context.

Such a complex structure was meant to be financially self-supporting. According to the *Instrucciones* of Torquemada and the subsequent body of inquisitorial jurisprudence, when a person was jailed by the Inquisition, his or her possessions were confiscated, to be returned at the time of release. This was one of the reasons that many trials were lengthy and that the inquisitors sometimes felt compelled to be stringent in their verdicts, especially at the Inquisition's beginnings. As the numbers of conversos diminished, from about 1520, Pope Paul IV decreed in 1559, during the tenure of the famous inquisitor Fernando de Valdés, that the revenues from at least one of each of the cathedral canonries and collegiate churches be appropriated to the Inquisition. Even when added to revenues from confiscations and other resources, these monies were never sufficient. The Inquisition was always a bankrupt operation, and the study of the political and diplomatic intricacies of the inquisitorial finances has become its own field of study.

The exact numbers of conversos prosecuted and of those executed in the first forty years, roughly 1481 to 1520, will never be known. Most of the extant documents are too vague, and the figures supplied by historians such as Juan Antonio Llorente are suppositions. Nothing more accurate can be said than that "several thousand" conversos, but no more than between five and six thousand, were put to death, usually by burning at the stake. The figures for later periods are better documented. Although many original documents from the district tribunals are lost or were destroyed in the course of the many Spanish revolutions, the relaciones de causas, annual summaries of the current and completed cases that the local tribunals sent to the Supreme Council, can supplement the missing documents. The computerization of these data may some day yield more exact figures. A provisional conclusion is that in the period from 1540 to 1700 the tribunals in Spain and its dependencies prosecuted 5,007 conversos; 11,311 moriscos (Muslim converts to Christianity); and 3,499 Protestants; and that 49,092 cases for all kinds of offenses were examined. The total number of persons executed in this period for all kinds of crimes was 776 in person and 707 in effigy. These figures show that the activity of the Inquisition declined after the violent first period, which was directed specifically against the conversos.

The inquisitorial tribunals worked in absolute secrecy, and most of their decisions were communicated to the interested parties in private autos de fe. Public autos de fe were much less frequent. Since they were expensive, they were undertaken only when it was believed that such a spectacle would serve as a warning, but the populace soon lost interest in them. They took place either in a large church or in an open plaza, and consisted of a solemn procession followed by a mass during which the accusations and penalties were read to those convicted after a sermon of indoctrination: this was the essential "act of faith." If any execution had been decreed, lay guardsmen

took the condemned to the quemadero (place of execution) to be burnt.

The Inquisition had jurisdiction only over baptized persons, including Marranos and conversos. The few Jews that appeared before the Inquisition prior to the Expulsion acted either as witnesses against conversos or as defendants in cases of intentionally anti-Christian blasphemy or impeding the activity of the Inquisition. Modern studies have shown, ironically, that the majority of the people prosecuted were old Christians (people who were not of Jewish descent). Between 1540 and 1700, 14,319 persons were accused of advancing "scandalous propositions"; other crimes sufficient for prosecution included blasphemy, bigamy, superstitions of various kinds, and solicitation of women by priests in the confessional.

In general, the Inquisition was the main instrument of social control by the establishment in Spain and to a more limited extent in Hispanic America for four centuries. It changed the scope of its attention according to the needs of each period, from conversos to Erasmians and Lutherans, biblical scholars with progressive ideas, spiritual reformers with suspicious attitudes, satirical writers, liberal thinkers, and whatever threatened the status quo. The Inquisition has become famous because it was established to inquire into the sincerity of the judeoconversos. But it is important above all because its repression halted the progress of Spain. Especially after the discovery of the New World, it was prepared as no other country was to lead the whole world in the enterprises of the Renaissance; it soon became paralyzed by the "pedagogy of fear"—as Bartolomé Bennassar called it—that the Inquisition exercised. Temporarily suppressed by the liberal Cortes of Cádiz in 1813, the Inquisition was finally abolished by royal decree in 1834. It was a miracle of inner spiritual resources that, the Inquisition notwithstanding, Spain was able to produce its remarkable Golden Age and to create in Spanish America a world after its own image.

BIBLIOGRAPHY

Alcalá, Angel. Los orígenes de la Inquisición en Aragón. Zaragoza, 1984.

Alcalá, Angel, et al. The Spanish Inquisition and the Inquisitorial Mind. Highland Lakes, N.J., 1987.

Bennassar, Bartolomé. L'inquisition espagnole XVe–XIXe siècle. Paris, 1979.

Kamen, Henry. Inquisition and Society in Spain. Bloomington, Ind., 1985.

Lea, Henry Charles. A History of the Inquisition in Spain. 4 vols. New York, 1906. Spanish edition, 3 vols., Madrid, 1984.

Llorente, Juan Antonio. A Critical History of the Inquisition of Spain. 1823. Reprint, Williamstown, Mass., 1967. An abridgment of the following title.

Llorente, Juan Antonio. Historia crítica de la Inquisición española (1822). 4 vols. Reprint, Madrid, 1980.

Pérez Villaneuva, Joaquín, and Bartolomé Escandel, eds. *Historia de la Inquisición en España y América*. Vol. 1. Madrid, 1984.

ANGEL ALCALÁ

ISABEL (1470–1498), princess of Castile; queen of Portugal. The eldest child of Fernando and Isabel of Castile, Isabel traveled throughout Spain with her mother and was witness to the important events of her parents' reign—the war against Granada, the Inquisition, the expulsion of Jews from Spain, and the return of Columbus from his first voyage to the New World.

Born at Dueñas near Valladolid, Isabel had an abiding affection for her mother, and they remained close throughout her life. She possessed a serious disposition and was deeply religious. The Italian humanists Antonio and Alessandro Geraldino and Lucio Marineo Siculo served as her tutors, educating her well in both religion and classical literature and language.

Isabel married Afonso, son of King João II of Portugal, in Lisbon on November 22, 1490. She was widowed in July 1491 when Afonso died following a fall from his horse. She returned to Castile and spent the next six years in mourning, rejecting all offers to remarry. Finally she consented to marry King Manuel I of Portugal, but stipulated that the Jews be expelled from Portugal. Manuel complied with her wishes, and the wedding took place on September 30 in Valancia de Alcántara. That same month her brother, Prince Juan, died, making Isabel and Manuel heirs to the Castilian throne.

Isabel was in the early months of pregnancy when she and Manuel traveled to Castile for the formal declaration of their Castilian inheritance. But Isabel would never rule Castile: she died in childbirth on August 23, 1498.

BIBLIOGRAPHY

Azcona, Tarsicio de. *Isabel la Católica: Estudio crítico de su vida y su reinado*. Madrid, 1964.

Miller, Townsend. *The Castles and the Crown: Spain 1451–1555*. New York, 1963.

Prescott, William H. *History of the Reign of Ferdinand and Isabella the Catholic*. Boston, 1838.

Sanceau, Elaine. *The Reign of the Fortunate King, 1495–1521*. Hamden, Conn., 1969.

THERESA EARENFIGHT

ISABELA, LA. See *Settlements*, article on *La Isabela*.

ISABEL AND FERNANDO. Isabel of Castile (1451–1504), queen of Castile from 1474 to 1504 (as Isabel I), and Fernando of Aragón (1452–1516), king of Aragón (as Fernando II) from 1479 to 1516 and king of Castile (as Fernando V) from 1474 to 1504, ruled Spain as joint monarchs at a time of momentous change. Owing as much to the personal qualities of these monarchs as to the press of events, their rule is exemplified by four significant developments in 1492. Known later as the Catholic monarchs, Isabel and Fernando conquered the Muslim Kingdom of Granada, expelled the Jews from Spain, and sent Christopher Columbus on his mission of exploration. The year 1492 also marks the completion by Antonio de Nebrija of the first Spanish grammar, which is dedicated to Isabel. This standardization of the language facilitated the introduction of Spanish into the regions of the New World that came under Spain's influence. The king and queen are discussed together here because of the interplay of their personalities and policies, their shared genius for seizing opportunities, and the great abilities demonstrated by both in their joint rule. Many of their actions and motives are not considered praiseworthy today—in part because of changed perceptions of political morality, in part because of the hindsight of five hundred years.

Isabel was born at Madrigal de las Altas Torres, in Castile, on April 22, 1451. Fernando was born in Sos, in Aragón, on March 10, 1452. In 1453, the Christian city of Constantinople, considered Europe's bulwark at the eastern end of the Mediterranean, fell to the Muslim Turks. Throughout the lifetimes of the queen and king and for a century or more after, Christian Europe perceived Muslim Asia and Africa as a threat. The Spanish kingdoms, neighboring Muslim Granada and separated from Africa only by the Strait of Gibraltar, were viewed as a frontier outpost of Christianity. The rulers and chroniclers of the largest of the Iberian kingdoms, Castile, had, since the Muslim conquest eight centuries earlier, identified the monarchy with the effort to regain lost territory in what is known as the reconquest.

Hereditary kings (and an occasional queen) in Spain exercised authority as did others in medieval Europe—as mediators within society and dispensers of titles, wealth, and honors, the extent of their power depending on a combination of the force they could command and the loyalty they could instill, one often dependent on the other. Castile's kings, in particular, presented themselves as military leaders with a God-given mission. They claimed in the cause of reconquest nearly unlimited personal power and, in practice, owed much of their effectiveness among clergy, nobles, and commoners to their role as head of a community united against the other world power, Islam. From the royal point of view, the ruler, as head of the community, had to carry out God's wishes (and thwart Satan's stratagems). And although Muslims and Jews had long resided within Castile and the other Iberian kingdoms, theoretically they did so as royal wards, outside the dominant community and at the sufferance and service of the Crown. The Castilian monarchy was paid for principally by booty and by sales taxes on internal and foreign trade. War and commerce were thus integral to royal power.

When Isabel and Fernando married on October 19, 1469, at ages eighteen and seventeen, respectively, Isabel was heir apparent to Castile, its *princesa,* and Fernando was prince of Aragón and king of Sicily. They were cousins, both of them children of kings of the Trastamara dynasty. Isabel's grandfather, Enrique III, had been king of Castile, and his younger brother, the grandfather for whom Fernando was named, had ruled Aragón. Isabel was the daughter of Enrique's only son, Juan II of Castile, and Juan's second wife, Isabel of Portugal. A brother, Alfonso, had been born in 1453. On July 21, 1454, Isabel's father died. Her older half brother, Enrique IV, succeeded him. (Alfonso was, since male, by custom next in line for the Crown, followed by the infanta Isabel.) The modest household of the dowager queen moved to nearby Arévalo, where Isabel spent her childhood. Arévalo was a provincial center, the market town for a region devoted to farming, yet in contact with Castile's larger towns and cities and linked to a commercial network encompassing all of the Mediterranean basin as well as northern Europe.

The infanta's formal education is undocumented, though it is recorded that at Arévalo Isabel had contact with Franciscan friars known for their austerity and learning. Her informal education would have included exposure to the culturally distinct communities of Muslims and Jews in Arévalo, separate from but tolerated by the Christian majority. From Arévalo the royal chancery, which wintered there in 1454, prepared Enrique IV's expedition against the Muslim kingdom of Granada. The enterprise was meant to strengthen his authority among Castilian nobles, clergy, and commoners by taking charge of the reconquest and to pressure the Granadans into remembering their agreement to pay tribute to the king of Castile.

Isabel and Alfonso were brought to Enrique's court when she was ten or eleven, by late 1461. A first child, daughter Juana, was born to the king and queen the following February. Her birth induced a party of dissident nobles led by Alfonso Carrillo, archbishop of Toledo and head of a powerful noble family, to step up previous demands for reforms, to spread rumors that the child was not the king's, and to insist that the infante Alfonso be recognized as the royal heir. Protracted negotiations between the parties failed. At Ávila, on June 5, 1465, the

The Castilian Succession from Juan I to Carlos I

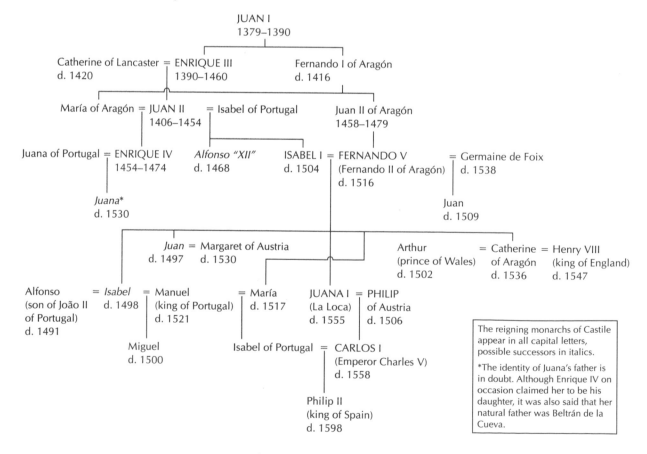

dissidents deposed Enrique in effigy and proclaimed the twelve-year-old Alfonso king. Civil war ensued, lasting three years, until, on July 5, 1468, Alfonso died suddenly, purportedly of plague. His supporters turned to seventeen-year-old Isabel, who rather than take up Alfonso's title won Enrique's agreement to end the war and to recognize her as his heir. Thereafter, the critical issue was her marriage. When the king revealed himself to be seeking a husband for her who would remove her from Castile or be unacceptable to its people, Isabel, backed by Carrillo, made her own choice. She chose Fernando of Aragón, who had expressed willingness to come to Castile. Castilians had indicated an acceptance of Fernando, in terms of his birth and reputation, as a suitable husband for an aspirant to the Crown. The engagement was arranged without consulting Enrique.

At age seventeen, Fernando already enjoyed renown as a hero of several sieges. As his father's lieutenant, he had had a taste of governing, and he had fathered two, perhaps three, children by two mothers. His father, Juan II of Aragón, had been born and raised in Castile, became through marriage king of Navarre, then succeeded to Aragón's Crown in 1459. His mother, Juan's second wife, Juana Enríquez, was also Castilian, the daughter of Castile's admiral, Fadrique Enríquez. Reputedly headstrong and ambitious, she had, though not yet its queen, made certain Fernando was born in Aragón, coming to the village of Sos just before his birth, and then put off his baptism for nearly a year, until his father had become regent of Aragón and the ceremony could be held with royal pomp in the cathedral in Zaragoza. An older half brother, the king's son Carlos of Viana, fortuitously died when Fernando was nine. That year, his father named Fernando royal lieutenant in Catalonia; his mother was to exercise authority for him. She did so with a high-handedness that led to mother and son being expelled from Barcelona and retreating to Gerona, where she directed the repulse of a Catalan siege. Four years later, at age twelve, Fernando himself led forces in defeat of the Catalans. With his valorous feat, a well-phrased appeal, and Valencia's delight in his victory over its chief rival, Barcelona, he gained from Valencia's council large annual loans for his father's hard-pressed government. When his mother died of cancer in 1468, Fernando gave her funeral eulogy. He had just finished presiding over the *corts*, Aragón's parliament, when Isabel's emissaries arrived to escort him to Castile and their wedding.

Isabel and Fernando first met in Valladolid on October 14, 1469, and they married there five days later. Both were well aware that Castile was the prize, and that they were jointly gambling for it—Enrique was only forty-four years old, and Isabel's claim and requisite aristocratic backing were shaky. Isabel's supporters had beforehand required of Fernando and his father an agreement that, while in tone suggesting that Fernando would wield a good deal of power, acknowledged that Isabel alone had the right to become proprietary ruler of Castile. Juan and Fernando thus forbore asserting a claim to the Crown of Castile based on the fact that Juan was the male next in line of succession to Enrique IV. Isabel and her advisers never lost sight of that relationship. The birth of a daughter, Isabel, on October 2, 1470, made the principle of female succession vital to both parents. Isabel and Fernando had discovered an immediate affinity in working together, indeed a mutual love and respect, and both showed themselves mindful of the advice of Juan of Aragón, that neither was powerful without the other.

From late 1469 to 1474, the fortunes of the young couple seesawed. Enrique, furious at their marriage, reinstated his purported daughter, Juana de Castilla (known as La Beltraneja), as heir apparent. Isabel and Fernando relied upon the power and purse of the archbishop, Carrillo; upon Fernando's grandfather, the admiral; and upon their position as king and queen of Sicily, which permitted them to form international alliances and to receive crucial funding from taxes on the sale of the island's abundant grain. To their advantage in Castile was the worsening economy and Enrique's wavering response to it. Showing themselves to be astute and capable, while seeking popular support, they slowly gained the backing of some key Castilian towns and nobles. Slowly Enrique was prevailed upon by his counselors, notably the Mendoza clan, to come to terms with his sister and his cousin, her husband. They reconciled at the end of 1468; Isabel was once more to be designated royal heir. When, on December 12, 1474, Enrique died, Fernando was in Aragón, fighting the French. Isabel, in Segovia, upon hearing the king had died, observed the proper rites of mourning, then, on December 13, had herself acclaimed queen of Castile. Fernando hurried back and was acclaimed king, but the arrangement that would remain in force had been proclaimed throughout the land: Isabel was the proprietary ruler of Castile.

The land, however, had first to be won. Raising the banner of Juana, who may or may not have been Enrique's daughter and who was then thirteen years old, Afonso, king of Portugal, resolved to marry her and gain back her inheritance. He invaded Castile, joined by some of its chief nobles. Again there was civil war, its end signaled by Afonso's return to Portugal after being bested by Fernando's forces outside Toro on March 1, 1476. Although Isabel and Fernando spent several more years gaining effective control, after Toro the realm was substantially theirs.

In the course of this crisis they had established the characteristics of their reign. They had taken on proven

ISABEL OF CASTILE AND FERNANDO OF ARAGÓN. Anonymous portraits, Flemish school.

advisers, most notably Pedro González de Mendoza, then archbishop of Seville and cardinal of Spain, who served them until his death in 1495 as chief minister, and Hernando de Talavera, the Hieronymite friar who became Isabel's chaplain and who was a principal architect of the monarchs' treasury arrangements and their administrative bureaucracy. They had found, too, a source of revenue and manpower in establishing under royal supervision a national hermandad, or brotherhood, a permanent league of the towns. The business of winning support during the war had reinforced their belief in the importance of public opinion and had developed their skill at molding it. They also had successfully forged what would become a lifelong practice of working in tandem.

The royal motto they shared, *tanto monta,* "as much one as the other," came to signify their cooperation. Fernando took as his emblem the double yoke, the *yugo* (its initial letter, *y* , standing for Isabel), worn by a team of oxen. Her emblem was a sheaf of arrows, *flechas* (the *f* standing for Fernando); the barbs of those arrows were held at ready, a warning to Castilians not acknowledging the reach of royal authority or that greatest of royal functions, the right to mete out justice.

In mid-April of 1476, they first convened the Cortes, or parliament, at Isabel's birthplace, Madrigal. Representatives of seventeen towns were called and nobles and high clergy were assembled to confirm the Princess Isabel in succession, to vote revenues, and to set up the Santa Hermandad, which would come to supplant the Cortes as a source of royal funding. These measures pointed to the future, as did more stringent restrictions on Muslims and Jews, who were ordered to wear distinguishing insignia and were forbidden their own communal justices. Afterward, Isabel went to reinstate royal authority in Extremadura, a seat of rebellion (and the region from which came a number of the future conquistadores of America), and

Andalusia, a center of noble autonomy crucial to Castile's relations with the Mediterranean and the Atlantic. In the great port city of Seville, so long under the sway of two dominant noble families, the Guzmán and the Ponce de León, the queen undercut their power: she had the hermandad established, royal administrators imposed, and castles and forts put under royal authority. She entered the city in state. She meted out justice severely, quickly, and publicly and reestablished respect for the monarchy. Under royal license, maritime expeditions then went out from Seville and the adjoining Andalusian coast with the purpose of challenging the Portuguese in the Atlantic Ocean, along the African coast, and in the Canary Islands.

Fernando joined Isabel in Seville in the fall of 1477. On June 30, 1478, Isabel gave birth to a son and heir, Prince Juan. That fall, at royal solicitation, a papal bull conceded to the Crown the right to appoint two or three priests as inquisitors. Isabel immediately appointed an investigatory commission in Seville, which reported widespread and adamant heresy among converts from Judaism. First in Seville, in early 1480, inquisitors appointed by the Crown began to try accused heretics, sentencing some to penance and loss of property, others to execution. Fernando, king of Aragón after his father's death in 1479, instituted a similar system there. A new Inquisition, encompassing all of Spain, was instituted with goals analogous to the royal policies made patent in the Cortes held at Toledo in 1480: to unify administration, to centralize power, to produce revenues, to instill fear and respect for the monarchy, and to create a climate of opinion supportive of a strongly national church identified with a state intent on crusade against the Muslims of Granada and even beyond. The overarching purpose was for Spain under its monarchs to regain the balance lost by the fall of Constantinople and, ultimately, to retake Jerusalem, the center of the faith and the goal of all previous crusades.

When, on December 27, 1480, Granadans took the Christian town of Zahara by surprise, Isabel and Fernando called their realms to war. The story of the next ten years is carved into the choir stalls of Toledo's cathedral. They depict over fifty of the Muslim towns taken in annual campaigns, beginning with Alhama in the heart of Granada. Its three great mosques were converted into churches. Isabel herself is said to have created ornaments for Santa María de la Encarnación, the first church consecrated in the first conquest. The monarchs counted on both a reinvigorated chivalry and a new army, on nobles and on royal appointees; as time went on, however, they relied more and more on recruits from the towns and less on the private armies of the nobility. Scaling operations gave way to heavy artillery, which battered walls, set fire to towns, and terrorized inhabitants into surrender. That Granada was rent internally by civil war was used to advantage (as similar situations among the Aztec and Inca would be used by the conquistadores in America).

To help fund the massive ongoing war, the Spanish monarchs received from the pope the right to the tithe and to the revenues from sale of bulls of crusade. The Inquisition turned over confiscated wealth—how much it took in and how much of it passed on no one knows, just as no one knows the amount of booty the Crown received from captured towns. The monarchs levied forced loans on nobles and clergy and on Jewish and Muslim communities. They sent out agents to set quotas and to collect men, money, and provisions from the towns and their hermandades. Andalusian towns, above all Seville, bore the brunt of this war effort.

Fernando commanded the armies. He and Isabel made policy decisions jointly and in council. She directed provisioning and recruiting, and at crucial junctures joined Fernando in camp before a besieged stronghold, by her presence enheartening the armies. Hers was the steady, relentless determination in fielding the annual campaigns. When in early 1484 Fernando decided that making war against the French threatening Aragón was more important than a campaign against Granada, Isabel chose to go south herself to direct that year's effort on land and to set a naval blockade of aid to Granada from Africa. Fernando, unable to fund a campaign against the French, arrived in time to attack and take Alora and Setenil. From then on the first matter of business for both monarchs was the war against Granada. In 1485 Ronda fell, and with it the western third of the kingdom. That winter they gave a brief audience to a Genoese sailor, Christopher Columbus, who made an unusual proposal, but they were occupied by the war. As for Aragón, the monarchs paid it sporadic attention, governing largely through viceroys. In 1486 Fernando, through the *sentencia de Guadalupe*, freed peasants in Aragón who were still tied to the land.

The populations of defeated towns were dealt with in various ways. The most cooperative simply came under Castilian domination; others were exiled, to be replaced by Castilian settlers. In 1487, the monarchs made an example of Granada's main port of Málaga. When it capitulated only after a grueling siege of four months, they carried through on an earlier ultimatum by enslaving and selling off most of its inhabitants. In November of 1491 the surrender of the city of Granada was formally arranged. Granadans might remain in the city and retain their property and religion. They would become subjects of the Crown of Castile. The Spanish entered the Alhambra on January 1 or 2, 1492, a momentous beginning for a momentous year. Thereafter, Talavera, as Granada's first archbishop, energetically sought to convert the populace to Christianity.

DOUBLE EXCELENTE COIN. Bearing likenesses of Isabel and Fernando, this coin was introduced in 1497 and minted until 1536. It was part of a new system of national coinage introduced after the absorption of Islamic Granada in 1492 and the arrival of quantities of gold and silver from the New World. The Latin inscription reads: (obverse) "Fernando and Isabel, by the grace of God, king and queen," (reverse) "Protect us under the shadow of Thy wings."

AMERICAN NUMISMATIC SOCIETY

Royal initiatives after Granada's fall were all of a piece: preparations for the pursuit of conquest into Africa, the expulsion of the Jews, the expedition of Christopher Columbus and another to the Canary Islands, an alliance with Egypt against the Turks, and the marriages of their five children. The overriding vision was an imperial one—to achieve hegemony over Christendom and to bring as much of the world as they could to the Roman Catholic faith.

An advance into Africa was the next step against Islam, and African gold was a powerful lure. Accordingly, Isabel and Fernando secured royal control of key ports facing Africa: Cádiz, Málaga, and, in 1500, Gibraltar. The 1479 peace treaty with Portugal had recognized Spanish economic interests in Africa east of Gibraltar (principally in the kingdom of Fès). In 1494 the Treaty of Tordesillas, which drew a line of demarcation between Spanish and Portuguese spheres of expansion, further acknowledged Spain's control. The royal couple planned to take Melilla (in present-day Morocco), a hub of the gold trade. By 1496 expeditions had occupied all the Canary Islands and from there were probing the nearby African coast. A visitor to Spain wrote in 1494, upon seeing preparations for an expedition to Africa, that no doubt Africa would soon belong to the Crown of Castile, and that then, with Africa conquered, it would be easy for the monarchs to take Jerusalem.

A decree dated March 31, 1492, signed by Isabel and Fernando in Granada, ordered all Jews to convert or leave the country by the end of July. It gave as principal reason the pernicious influence of some of them on the New Christians, recent converts from Judaism. It did not mention that Jews in Spain had decreased in number, wealth, and value to the Crown, nor that they had become ever more unpopular in the years of religious war.

Delegates at Madrigal in 1476 had stated the prevailing belief that Jews refused to acknowledge the divine will: "Well you know your highnesses, that following divine law, by the coming of the Holy of the Holies [the Messiah] the authority and jurisdictions of the Jews cease."

The decree presented the expulsion as the last step in a slow and steady progression, directed by royal policy, toward an extreme religious homogeneity. A document of 1477 signed by Isabel, forbidding certain acts against the Jews, had reflected a traditional royal stance: "The Jews are mine and they are under my protection and power." The Crown had over the centuries both stoked latent hostility to Jews and kept it tamped down: royal disdain had reinforced popular prejudice; royal power had held it in check. From 1480 the war, popular opinion, the growing strength and acceptance of the Inquisition, and ebbing royal intercession on behalf of Jews had foreshadowed the decree. Jews who proselytized were subject to the Inquisition, and Jews were in fact sentenced to burn at the stake in cases at Huesca in 1489 and at La Guardia in 1491. Against this background, it was but a step to argue that Spanish Jewry must be expelled.

Isabel and Fernando were accustomed to thinking about communities as corporate entities and to moving people en masse. Within this context, their decision can be understood as the fruit of a war-nurtured ruthlessness and a hardening of their shared conviction, their moral certainty, that the promptings of the royal hearts emanated from God. In 1492, as Spain's monarchs were accorded a place among Europe's foremost for defeating the Muslims, the presence of Jews showed Spain to Europe as old-fashionedly heterodox. To the Crown, the edict was more than anything else a mopping-up operation, subsidiary to the work of the Inquisition. That it happened so late was an embarrassment to Spain at the time; that it happened at all would subsequently become one.

In the quest for unity and orthodoxy, the rulers promoted within Spain a moral cleansing, beginning with the clergy, who expected in turn to raise the general level of morality and devotion to faith and crown. The year 1492 also marked the beginning of the rapid ascent to first minister of the brilliant and forceful Franciscan friar Francisco Jiménez de Cisneros. Cisneros succeeded in influence both Hernando de Talavera, who devoted himself to Granada as its first archbishop, and Cardinal Pedro González de Mendoza, who died in January of 1495. The king and especially the queen relied upon Cisneros for his skill in administration and his strength of belief and commitment to reform.

With Spain ascendant in 1492, the extravagant scheme of Christopher Columbus appeared worth risking. We have only hints as to what he proposed to the monarchs. They had been intrigued by Cristóbal Colón from the first

THE MADONNA OF THE CATHOLIC KINGS. Unknown artist. On the right is Isabel. On the left is Fernando and their son Juan.

MUSEO DEL PRADO

audience, in late 1485 or early 1486, when—according to the chronicler Andrés Bernáldez—he showed them a world map and "awakened in them a desire to know those lands." They most likely heard then of his plan to seek the rich and strategic eastern part of India and to find the Grand Khan by sailing around the globe. This account of Columbus's scheme accords with informed court opinion of 1493, when Peter Martyr (Pietro Martire d'Anghiera) wrote of Columbus having discovered an archipelago, new to Europeans, off the Malay peninsula of Asia.

Between the initial meeting and 1492, Fernando ordered a copy of Ptolemy's *Geography*. Isabel recalled Columbus to court, talked to him over time and at length, and held out hope of sponsorship once the war was won. With Granada conquered, the royal reputation was so high that even a failed expedition would not dim it. Within three weeks of the decree against the Jews, a concession to Columbus was signed by the king and queen, stating, "We send Cristóbal Colón with three caravels through the Ocean Sea to the Indies on some business that concerns the service of God and the expansion of the Catholic faith and our benefit and utility."

The enterprise cost the Crown little, and the funds were drawn from the two agencies that had managed wartime funding: the *cruzada*, that is, the sale of indulgences, and the hermandad. Isabel probably did offer to pawn her jewels, yet doing so was, in today's terms, only a question of cashflow, as she was offering not prized possessions but customary collateral. Columbus sailed for Castile, which had long laid claim to Atlantic places. The monarchs interpreted his initial discovery as "lands toward India" and the immediate royal interest was in clearing title with Portugal, which was accomplished at Tordesillas in 1494. The second voyage, sponsored primarily to strengthen the Spanish presence in the newfound lands, had profit as a motive as well. Thus, while Columbus wielded delegated political authority, the Crown retained an economic monopoly, and royal treasury officials sailed with the expedition. The monarchs' view on conquest overseas prevailed. They asserted lordship over native rulers and the royal right to seek material and spiritual recompense, through native labor and tribute and through missionary activity. The right to sponsor exploration was itself a royal monopoly, forbidden to nobles and all others unless by royal license.

Isabel, hoping that Columbus had found East Asian lands (a discovery that would promise both riches and a route that would allow competing with the Portuguese and outflanking the Muslims) as well as out of a natural curiosity, wrote Columbus in 1494 for more information on geography, flora, and fauna. Lacking a satisfactory answer, and with rumors circulating of mismanagement, little gold, and a wealth mostly in souls, Fernando and Isabel in 1495 sent a royal agent to investigate. The following year, they were furious to hear that Columbus had brought back three shiploads of wealth, which turned out to be Amerindians he was selling as slaves. They ordered the Indians seized until it was ascertained whether they had been justly enslaved (that is, for cannibalism or for attacking Spaniards), and, if so, they would claim the profits for themselves. They dispatched missionaries in 1497, and from then on their interest in the Indies was royal oversight of self-sustaining settlements, including plantations and sugar mills. Native peoples were to become Christian and to provide settlers and Crown with labor and tribute. Still, despite their disillusionment with him, the king and queen showed a continuing fondness for Columbus. His sons came to court as pages. Even so, step by step the Crown imposed royal governors to supersede him and his family in what would be called America.

The expansive spirit of 1492 was caught by Elio Antonio Nebrija, who dedicated the first Spanish grammar to Isabel with the explanation that "language is the companion of empire." The postwar atmosphere was one of power and grandeur. The court now traveled—there was as yet no fixed royal residence—in a retinue over one thousand strong, including grandees, young nobles at court school, musicians and chaplains, household retainers, and a burgeoning administrative staff made up chiefly of *letrados*, who were lawyers and clergy, an increasing number of them educated at the University of Salamanca. The *letrados* staffed the royal councils: those of state (from 1494), justice, finance, hermandad (until disbanded in 1498), and Inquisition (established by 1488). The chancery sat permanently at Valladolid, and a second court of justice (audiencia) was instituted in Granada. The nobility retained seats on the council of state and enjoyed a resurgence of power, especially those who had served in the war. The economy flourished, especially in the south and in Barcelona, with an upsurge in trade with the Mediterranean and northern Europe. In Barcelona, on October 25, 1492, Prince Juan received, as he had elsewhere in his parents' realms, the formal oath as crown prince of Aragón. This promised a Spain unified in his person, and, indeed, at bottom all the measures taken that year had at their root dynastic hope and dynastic aspiration.

The five royal children had their own households. The oldest, the infanta Isabel, however, was much with her parents. When her husband, Afonso, heir to João of Portugal, died within eight months of their marriage in 1490, she returned to Castile, until in 1497 she wed Manuel, Afonso's cousin and Portugal's new king. The marriages arranged for all the children reflected a policy of alignment with some of Europe's chief states, directed toward hemming in the most powerful of all, France. In 1497 Prince Juan married Margaret of Austria, whose mother had inherited the duchy of Burgundy and whose father, Maximilian of Habsburg, controlled an extensive domain in Germany and Austria. Juan's sister, the infanta Juana, married Margaret's brother, Archduke Philip. Catalina wed first Arthur, heir to Henry VII of England, in 1501, and, after he died, his brother, Henry, in 1509. Isabel and Fernando did not live to see Henry VIII divorce this last child of theirs, known to the English-speaking world as Catherine of Aragón, yet misfortune had arrived even earlier. Prince Juan, never strong, died in 1497, within six months of his wedding, his doctors concluding it was from overfondness for Margaret and their connubial bed. Margaret shortly after was delivered of a stillborn child. Within a year, young Isabel died in childbirth and her infant son, Miguel, survived less than two years. Her widower, Manuel, then married her sister, María, and the couple succeeded to Portugal's throne. From 1500, Juana and her husband, Philip, were heirs apparent to their parents' realms.

Family tragedy, appearing to doom the vision of dynastic continuity and Spanish unity, was paralleled by delay in the plans for an African expedition, because of embroilments with France in Italy. In 1494, when Charles VIII of France invaded Italy to take Naples, Fernando and Isabel leagued with Venice, Milan, Maximilian of Habsburg, and Pope Alexander VI. Spain sent an expeditionary force to Italy. Its leader, Gonzalo Fernández de Córdoba, con-

firmed the monarchs' reputation for genius in appointments. Known to history as the Great Captain, he retook Naples and showed himself a master of strategy, timing, and military discipline. The pope and the curia, in appreciation of Spanish intervention at Naples and in acknowledgment of Isabel's and Fernando's services to Christendom, bestowed upon them the honorary title of *los Reyes Católicos* (the Catholic monarchs). In 1498 a new French invasion of Italy caused a Spanish expedition poised for Africa to sail for Naples once again.

It is probably not unrelated that as the century ended four royal heirs had died, Isabel had been critically ill, and more stringent measures against social deviation had been imposed. A royal edict of 1499 declared death to any Jew entering Spain unless for the express purpose of being baptized. In 1500 and 1501 Jewish slaves were ordered deported or converted to Christianity. Legislation attacked gypsies. Homosexuality was punishable by death. Laws were enacted against luxurious dress. In 1502 all books were ordered reviewed and licensed, blasphemy was harshly punished, a campaign against priests living with concubines was launched. Further, no reconciled converso, until the fourth generation, was permitted to sit on the royal council, signaling the onset of an official policy of *limpieza de sangre*, purity of blood. In 1499, Cisneros, echoing the expulsion of the Jews, instituted a similar royal policy for Castile's Muslims: they were to be baptized or to emigrate. From 1499 through 1501, Fernando put down outbreaks of armed resistance to the policy in Granada. By 1502, through mass baptisms, most Muslims had become moriscos, and many others had left, chiefly for Africa.

Isabel died on November 26, 1504. Reportedly she had not been well since the death of her oldest daughter and had worsened with each subsequent tragedy, up to the last, which was Juana's patent lack of inclination to rule,

TOMB OF ISABEL AND FERNANDO. Royal Chapel, Granada.

her mounting mental instability, and her beloved husband's obvious dislike of Castile and affection for France. The queen was buried, as she had instructed, in Franciscan garb, in Granada.

After Isabel's death Fernando was no longer king in Castile, but, with Philip's death in 1506 and with Juana's mental instability, he ruled Castile as regent from 1508. In 1510 his armies conquered Tripoli. He proposed conquest of the eastern Mediterranean and planned to lead a crusade against the Turks, but once again troops were deflected to Italy in a campaign against the French. In 1505 he married Germaine de Foix, the niece of Louis XII of France. They had one son, in 1509, who lived less than a day. Fernando died on January 23, 1516. By the terms of his will, he was buried beside Isabel, in Granada.

Isabel and Fernando's reign was a model to their grandson and successor, Charles V, who made of Spain an empire, and to his son, Philip II, who tried mightily to carry on what they had begun. Fernando and Isabel have in the intervening five centuries been interpreted and reinterpreted in accord with the times and the writer's predilections. Today, Isabel has come to stand for religious devotion; Fernando, for Machiavellian statecraft. Both monarchs were in fact deeply devout and both excelled as rulers, though they never separated (as did Machiavelli's prince) the exigencies of statecraft from the promptings of morality. At issue, rather, is their concept of morality. Operating within it, they established one of Europe's most powerful nation-states and set Spain on the road to world empire. Most remarkable of all was their sharing of royal power, their success in lifelong cooperation.

[See also; *Columbus, Christopher,* article on *Columbus in Spain; Jews; Inquisition; Muslims in Spain; Reconquista; Spain; Treaty of Tordesillas,* and biographies of numerous figures mentioned herein.]

BIBLIOGRAPHY

Contemporary Chronicles

Anonymous. *Crónica incomplete de los Reyes Católicos (1469–1476).* Edited by Julio Puyol. Madrid, 1934.

Bernáldez, Andrés. *Memorias del reinado de los Reyes Católicos.* Edited by Manuel Gomez Moreno and Juan de la Mata Carriazo. Madrid, 1962.

Enriquez del Castillo, Diego. *Crónica del rey Don Enrique el cuarto.* Edited by Cayetano Rosell. Vol. 70 of *Biblioteca de Autores Españoles.* Madrid, 1953.

Palencia, Alfonso de. *Crónica de Enrique IV.* Edited by Alfonse Paz y Melia. 4 vols. Madrid, 1973–1975.

Pulgar, Hernando de. *Crónica de los reyes católicos.* Edited by Juan de la Mata Carriazo. 2 vols. Madrid, 1943.

Santa Cruz, Alonso de. *Crónica de los Reyes Católicos.* Edited by Juan de la Mata Carriazo. 2 vols. Seville, 1951.

Valera, Diego de. *Crónica de los reyes católicos.* Edited by Juan de la Mata Carriazo. Madrid, 1927.

Historical Studies

Azcona, Tarsicio de. *Isabel la Católica.* Madrid, 1964.

Clemencin, Diego. *Elógio de la Reina Católica Doña Isabel.* Madrid, 1821.

Fernández-Armesto, Felipe. *Ferdinand and Isabella.* New York, 1975.

Ladero Quesada, Miguel Angel. *España en 1492.* Madrid, 1978.

Liss, Peggy K. *Isabel the Queen.* Forthcoming.

Mariejol, Jean Hippolyte. *The Spain of Ferdinand and Isabella.* Translated and edited by Benjamin Keen. New Brunswick, N.J., 1961.

Suárez Fernández, Luis. *Los Reyes Católicos.* 5 vols. Madrid, 1989–1990.

Vicens Vives, Jaime. *Historia crítica de la vida y reinado de Fernando II de Aragón.* Zaragoza, 1962.

PEGGY K. LISS

ISIDORE OF SEVILLE (c. 560–636), Roman Catholic saint; Hispano-Roman theologian and encyclopedist; bishop of Seville (584–600). Isidore was a man of great learning with broad intellectual interests, especially the secular learning of the Greek and Roman civilizations. He is noted for his theological, ecclesiastical, and historical writings and his biographical essays of ecclesiastical and secular figures of his age.

Two secular works, *Etymologiae* and *De natura rerum,* were of great importance for the organization of the field of science and influenced later medieval conceptions of astronomy and geography. *Etymologiae,* an encyclopedic compilation of the remnants of secular learning up to his age, provided a wide range of information in a concise and accessible form for a time desperately in need of it. *De natura rerum* is a longer and more detailed examination of Books III, XIII, and XIV of *Etymologiae.* It is an important exposition of the physical sciences of the early Middle Ages, specifically astronomy, cosmography, and physical geography. Early medieval science relied not on systematic observation or reasoned proof but rather on the learning of the past or on divine authority. Therefore, *Etymologiae* and *De natura rerum* often contain serious contradictions, particularly concerning the sphericity of the earth and the existence of certain undiscovered, perhaps mythical, islands in the Atlantic Ocean near the coast of Africa. Isidore's works were used as the foundations for later research and as such were important sources for late medieval cartographers such as Paolo del Pozzo Toscanelli and Martin Behaim.

BIBLIOGRAPHY

Díaz y Díaz, Manuel C., ed. *Isidoriana: Colección de estudios sobre Isidoro de Sevilla, publicado con ocasión del XIV centenario de su nacimiento.* León, 1961.

Fontaine, Jacques. *Isidore de Séville et la culture classique dans l'Espagne wisigothique.* 2d ed. Paris, 1983.

Fontaine, Jacques, ed. *De natura rerum, Isidore de Séville: Traité de la nature, suivi de l'Epître en vers du roi Sisebut à Isidore.* Paris, 1960.

Perez de Urbel, Justo. *San Isidoro de Sevilla: Su vida, su obra y su tiempo.* Barcelona, 1940.

Theresa Earenfight

ISLAND CARIBS. See *Indian America*, article on *Island Caribs.*

ITALY. For discussion of Italian republics and city states, see *Florence; Genoa; Naples; Rome; Venetian Republic.*

J, K

JAMAICA. Jamaica is the third largest of the Greater Antilles, after Cuba and Hispaniola (La Española), and like them has a mountainous central area and shallow plains rimming the coast. The island is about 240 kilometers (150 miles) long and nearly 80 kilometers (50 miles) across at its broadest point; the highest mountain reaches an impressive 2,245 meters (7,400 feet). During the fifteenth century the island seems to have supported a population of about 60,000 Taínos, a subgroup of the Arawaks.

The Taínos lived in villages under chiefs, or caciques, and liked to choose sites close to the sea, for they were great fishers. For starch they had the omnipresent cassava bread; they also hunted a variety of small animals. Their canoes were sometimes very large, and they shared with the other Arawak groups the use of hammocks and tobacco. A little gold was to be found on Jamaica, and they made ornaments from it.

Christopher Columbus visited Jamaica on his second voyage, anchoring in what is now Saint Ann's Bay, which he called Santa Gloria. He was astonished by the island's beauty, calling it "the fairest that eyes have beheld." However, the Taínos in Saint Ann's Bay, and in the next port westward, Río Bueno, did not appear friendly, and Columbus chose to discourage an attack by shooting some, using his crossbowmen, and threatening others with a savage dog. These were tactics the Spaniards had already used on the native inhabitants of the Canaries.

Columbus then sailed off from Montego Bay, but after reconnoitering the south coast of Cuba returned to Jamaica. He made landfall at Montego Bay and then sailed round the island's west and south coasts; here he encountered nothing but friendliness from the inhabitants. He did not return to Jamaica until June 1503, at the end of his fourth voyage, when he was forced to beach his two water-logged caravels at Saint Ann's Bay. Here he was marooned for just over a year, until a vessel from Santo Domingo fetched him and his men away.

During this enforced stay, Columbus succeeded in remaining on friendly terms with the Taínos from a neighboring village, who supplied him with food. He had great difficulties, however, in controlling his crews, who mutinied, set up roving bands, and caused all manner of trouble. In reading about the problems within this quite small group, we can better understand the way in which the Spaniards ran riot throughout the Americas. Columbus had used his beached ships as his base, and their remains may one day be found at Saint Ann's Bay.

The Spaniards returned to Jamaica in 1510, when the first governor, Juan de Esquivel, founded the city of Sevilla la Nueva close by the place where Columbus had been marooned. Here a small town with a substantial stone fort and a church grew up, though the capital was moved in

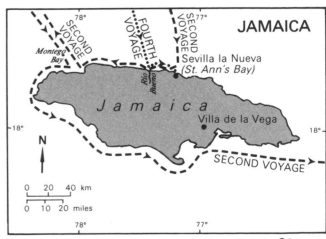

387

1534 to the south side of the island, where Villa de la Vega was built on the banks of the Río Cobre. Jamaica proved to have little gold and to be of value chiefly for its agricultural products: cassava bread, sugar, hides, and lard. The relations between the Spanish settlers and the Taínos do not seem to have been too bad, but the normal pattern of population decline through disease prevailed, until the native inhabitants were virtually extinct. Jamaica survived as a backwater of the Spanish empire until the British seized the island in 1655.

[See also *Indian America*, article on *Taínos*; *Settlements*, article on *Sevilla la Nueva*.]

BIBLIOGRAPHY

Black, Clinton V. *The History of Jamaica*. Kingston, Jamaica, 1983.
Osborne, Francis J. *History of the Catholic Church in Jamaica*. Chicago, 1988.
Padrón, Francisco Morales. *Jamaica española*. Seville, 1952.

DAVID BUISSERET

JAPAN. See *Cipangu*.

JEWS. [This entry includes four articles that focus on Jewish life and culture relative to events in the period of overseas European expansion:

Jews in Spain
Conversos
Expulsion from Spain
Jews in the New World

See also *Inquisition; Muslims in Spain; Religion*, article on *European Traditions*.]

Jews in Spain

The first Jewish settlements in Spain probably date back to the destruction of the Second Temple in A.D. 70. No historical document mentions them before the Council of Elvira (Illiberis, near present Granada) around the year 305. The laws the council adopted set the tone for later ones, outlawing marriage outside the ethnic group, providing for excommunication for sexual intercourse between Jew and Christian, as well as for clerics eating with Jews, and prohibiting the blessing of Christian agricultural products by Jews. Under the Visigothic monarchy (419–711) several kings decreed open persecution of the Jews, and even accused them of treason and conspiracy against the throne. The Muslim conquest was greeted by Iberian Jews who expected the new Semitic rulers to extend to them the limited tolerance of other religions prescribed in the Qur'an.

Not much is known about the life of the Jewish communities in the first centuries of Islamic rule. With the disintegration of the Córdoba caliphate in 1031 into twenty-three small *taifa*, or independent kingdoms, some Jews acted as prime ministers. The most famous were Samuel ha-Nagid (993–1055 or 1056) in Granada and Yekutiel ibn Hassan in Saragossa. As the Jewish physician Hasdai ibn Shaprut (c. 915–975) had done while serving as one of the ministers of Caliph 'Abd ar-Rahman III in the tenth century, these leaders encouraged the intellectual development of their coreligionists, competed for artists and writers, and attracted those Jews skillful in the techniques of agriculture and tannery to their states. Some historians rightly speak of this period, until the end of the thirteenth century, as the Jewish golden age in Spain.

It was in this milieu that writers like Solomon ibn Gabirol (c. 1022–c. 1070), Bahya ben Joseph ibn Pakuda (eleventh century), and Judah ha-Levy (c. 1075–1141) in Saragossa; Moses ibn Ezra (c. 1060–1139) and Abraham ibn Ezra (c. 1090–1164) in Toledo; and the great Moses ben Maimon (Maimonides; 1135–1204) in Córdoba produced works that influenced Western philosophy and Christian biblical scholarship and theology. These and other Spanish Jewish writers—except Judah ha-Levy—wrote in Arabic and had to be translated into Latin and Hebrew. Some of them led a wandering life because of the successive waves of Muslim invaders, the Almoravids in 1086 and the Almohads after 1174. Maimonides left Spain at age seventeen never to return; he died in Egypt. The Christians maintained a peaceful, although restricted, coexistence with Jews through the next century.

In Toledo, Murcia, and other cities, the so-called schools of translators were founded, in which teams of Christians and Jews, fluent in several languages, translated several Greek classic works from Arabic into Latin and Spanish. After the early medieval period, when most Spanish Jews lived in small towns and made their living in agriculture, the Jews slowly moved to cities under the personal protection of the kings, and though some continued rural activities, most engaged in small-scale commerce (cloth, cattle, grain, dried fish), craftsmanship (builders, silversmiths, shoemakers, tailors, tanners), and money lending. Spanish Jews were not on the whole bourgeois, and only a few reached high social echelons as financial advisers, tax contractors, doctors and *bayles*, administrators of the royal patrimony with jurisdiction over Christian subjects. *Juderías* (Jewish settlements) were organized in *aljamas*, Jewish communities juridically structured under the authority of a *nasi*, a chief justice; the *aljamas* were relatively independent microsocieties within the surrounding Christian society. In the thirteenth and fourteenth centuries, there were many instances of cooperation between Christians, Moors, and Jews under kings

בעל הבית נגש ביתנו שאומרים היהודה

READING THE TORAH IN A SPANISH SYNAGOGUE. From a fourteenth-century Hebrew Haggadah.

who enjoyed and sometimes used the title "emperor of the three religions."

The *Siete partidas* of Alfonso X, "the Wise" (1252–1284), a juridical doctrine in seven parts that was promulgated as law in 1342, manifests the ancient ambivalence of Christians about Jews: relative protection of the Jews as special subjects is juxtaposed with the hope that "those who come from the lineage of Christ's crucifiers" will soon be convinced to accept baptism. This increasingly restrictive attitude resulted from both external and internal motives. Spain felt the influence of two church councils, Lateran IV (1215) and Vienne (1311–1312), which legislated a set of statutes that weakened the peaceful coexistence of Christians and Jews. Successive regional councils, like one in Zamora (1312) and another in Salamanca (1335), aligned the church of Castile with the church at large. This official attitude was greatly enhanced by the new mendicant orders, especially the Dominican Order, which had been founded by a Spaniard. Christian enmity toward Jews in general as well as Jewish and Christian enmity toward those Jews who either individually or in groups were converting to Christianity, especially in times of persecution, became more apparent.

Among the devices used by Christians against the Jews were formal disputations that offered Christians the opportunity to convince Jewish scholars of the truth of Christian doctrine. The most famous occurred in Barcelona (1263) between Moses ben Nachman (Nachmanides) and Pau Christiá, a converso, and a century and a half later in Tortosa (1413–1414) between the converso Jerónimo de Santa Fe and almost twenty rabbis from all over Aragón. The results were disastrous for the Jews: all the rabbis who participated in the dispute of Tortosa converted except Joseph Albo (c. 1380–c. 1444), who retired to Soria and wrote his pietist *Book of the Principles*.

Popular persecutions of Jews usually occurred during the tenure of weak monarchs or at the death of those who had most protected and used them. Such was the case after the death of Jaime I of Aragón (1276) and after the deaths of Alfonso X (1284), Pedro I (1369), and Juan I (1390) of Castile. The persecutions and mob killings of Jews that took place in 1391 throughout Spain started in Seville, encouraged by an overly zealous cleric in temporary charge of that important see, and it quickly spread to other cities and towns. The great Rabbi Hasdai ben Abraham Crescas (1340–1410), author of *Or Adonai* (The light of the Lord), escaped death because he was in Zaragoza with the Aragonese court, but his son was killed in Barcelona together with many Jews, who were buried in the cemetery in Montjuïc (the mount of the Jews). Thousands were killed in hundreds of cities and towns, and many more thousands converted. That year marks the beginning of the end of Spanish Jewry. Many of the medieval *aljamas* never recovered; they either dispersed or disappeared.

By the beginning of the fifteenth century, the fate of Spanish Judaism was sealed. A new series of *taqqanot* (ordinances) agreed to in Valladolid in 1432 tried to reconstruct it, again allowing the *aljamas* to have their own schools, special jurisdiction, and penal authorities. Jews were allowed to practice usury within the legal limits, since the marginal social positions into which they had been compelled to retire forced them into the service industries. But there were many other political interests at stake: the status of the conversos was becoming more and more ambiguous and the Jewish minority was becoming negligible in numbers and in power and, therefore, politically disposable. According to lists of the *aljamas* and of the royal taxes allocated proportionally to them, in the second half of the fifteenth century there were in Castile only 224 *aljamas*, most of them in very small towns. Toledo did not have more than forty Jewish families. The kingdom of Aragón had only twenty-five *aljamas*: three in Catalonia (Lleida, Girona, Cervera), three in modest towns in Valencia (Murviedro, Castellón, Burriana), and the rest in Zaragoza and other towns in Aragón proper.

Despite the historical importance of the Jewish presence in Spain for centuries, and of the role it played in Jewish history, the Jews did not leave a permanent mark on Spanish literary culture, both for religious and linguistic reasons. The great Jewish scholars were unknown even to the best Spanish Christian scholars. The Spanish language retains no more than twenty words of Hebrew origin, almost all of biblical import. There were no Jews of note who wrote in Spanish, with the exception of Rabbi Sem Tob of Carrión, who wrote *Proverbios morales* in the mid-fourteenth century. Even connections between the Jews and Christopher Columbus—for instance, that he used maps produced by the so-called Jewish school of cartographers from Majorca; or that he was helped by Abraham Zacuto, the Jewish professor at the University of Salamanca, and by his *Almanach*—need careful scrutiny. The general Jewish influence on Spain was social and financial rather than cultural. In the second half of the fifteenth century, that influence was very much diminished although three Jewish leaders of the time—Abraham Seneor, Mair Melamed, and Isaac Abravanel—were the financial advisers to the Crown. Even so, the Jewish people as a group paid a high price in terms of a general antipathy that ultimately determined their expulsion.

BIBLIOGRAPHY

Ashtor, Eliyahu. *The Jews of Moslem Spain.* 3 vols. Philadelphia, 1973–1984.

Baer, Yitzaak. *A History of the Jews in Christian Spain.* 2 vols. Philadelphia, 1961.

Borchsenius, Paul. *The Three Rings: The History of the Spanish Jews.* London, 1963.

Neuman, Abraham Aaron. *The Jews in Spain: Their Social, Political, and Cultural Life during the Middle Ages.* 2 vols. Philadelphia, 1944.

Suárez Fernández, Luis. *Judíos españoles en la edad media.* Madrid, 1980.

ANGEL ALCALÁ

Conversos

A Spanish expression for convert or converted, *conversos* or *cristianos nuevos* (new Christians as distinguished from old Christians) or *confesos* (those who confessed the Christian faith) was the name given to those individuals who were known to have converted to Christianity from Judaism or Islam. Since the Muslim converts were also called *moriscos,* the word *conversos* was applied almost exclusively to *judeoconversos.* One would be considered a converso if one converted personally or if a conversion could be documented within the last four generations of a family. Hence there arose the popular Spanish expression "por los cuatro costados" (from four sides). Cervantes

uses this image in Sancho Panza's famous line about "men that have four inches of old Christian fat in their souls" (*Don Quixote* 2.4).

There were always notable Jewish converts in Spain. The most famous are Moses Sephardi, converted in Huesca as Petrus Alphonsi in 1106, who was the author of important scientific works and of *Disciplina clericalis,* an influential collection of Oriental tales; Rabbi Abner of Burgos, baptized in 1321 as Alfonso de Valladolid; and Rabbi Solomon ha-Levi, who converted with his brothers and children as Pablo de Santa María in 1390, and later became bishop of Burgos, chancellor of Castile, and the author of biblical commentaries and anti-Jewish polemics. But Jews started to convert in great numbers during and after the persecutions of 1391. By the mid-fifteenth century some conversos had reached high positions in Christian society through marriage into the nobility, through careers in the church, or through achievement in the professions open to them. Old Christians, infuriated at being dominated by former Jews now exacting high taxes from them for the king, revolted in Toledo in 1449, when for the first time a popular uprising tried to prevent conversos from occupying any post in the municipal administration, a precedent of what was known later as statutes of *limpieza de sangre* (purity of blood, i.e., of ancestry), strongly opposed by some converso scholars like Alfonso de Cartagena (son of Pablo), Juan de Torquemada, and others. The accusation that conversos were judaizing (observing Jewish practices) in secret was common, though it was without evidence; nonetheless, the Inquisition was founded to investigate such claims. How many conversos actually were *judaizantes* is still much discussed. Some Jewish historians (Yitzaak Baer, Isaac S. Révah, Haim Beinart) hold that the vast majority of conversos were Marranos (Jews who submitted to forced conversion but maintained Jewish practices in secret). In this case, the accusations of the Inquisition would have been accurate. Other historians (Benzion Netanyahu and others) believe that the vast majority of conversos were almost assimilated into the Christian majority by 1492 in social and religious habits, and that because of the influence and social prestige of the conversos, the *juderías* (Jewish settlements) had been dwindling long before. In fact, the Inquisition prosecuted hardly more than 5 percent of the estimated converso population of 600,000 in a country of less than six million. Of course, there were always pockets of heroic Jewish resistance, instances of which occurred well into the eighteenth century. Most of the conversos, however, assimilated so quickly and profoundly into the mainstream of the country that dozens of them wrote classics of Spanish literature of the Golden Age, while practically all the spiritual writers, reformers, and mystics of sixteenth- and seventeenth-century Spain—such as John of Ávila,

Teresa of Ávila, John of the Cross, Fray Luis de León—were descended from conversos.

Whatever the probability that Columbus might have been of distant converso descent (it would be wrong to say Jewish descent), it is true that from the very beginning of his activities in Spain he was helped by some Jews (Isaac Abravanel, Abraham Seneor) and by a group of conversos, either clerics (Diego de Deza, later archbishop of Seville and the second Grand Inquisitor, and Hernando de Talavera, later first bishop of Granada) or courtiers. When Columbus was dismissed by Isabel in Granada on January 10, 1492, after his third and last attempt to win her support, he was recalled by an emissary of Fernando, who had been convinced by four of his Aragonese courtiers—Luis de Santángel, Gabriel Sánchez, Juan Cabrero, and Juan de Coloma, all of them prominent conversos—that Columbus's venture was worthy of support. Conversos were active on every level of Spanish society, and as courtiers they participated in the enterprise of discovery.

BIBLIOGRAPHY

Benito Ruano, Eloy. *Los orígenes del problema converso.* Barcelona, 1976.

Domínguez Ortiz, Antonio. *Los judeoconversos en España y América.* Madrid, 1971.

Manzano, Juan Manzano. *Cristóbal Colón: Siete años decisivos de su vida, 1485–1492.* Madrid, 1973.

Netanyahu, Benzion. *The Marranos of Spain from the Late Fourteenth to the Early Sixteenth Century according to Contemporary Hebrew Sources.* 2d revised and enlarged ed. New York, 1973.

Serrano y Sanz, Manuel. *Orígenes de la dominación española en América: Los amigos y protectores aragoneses de Cristóbal Colón.* Madrid, 1918.

ANGEL ALCALÁ

Expulsion from Spain

On March 31, 1492, Fernando and Isabel signed a decree ordering the Jews of Spain either to be baptized or to leave the country by July 31. The decree was in fact the culmination of a series of experiments by the Crown to deal with the social and political problems concerning Jews. While it put an end to the long coexistence of Christians and Jews in Spain, the Expulsion also tried to prevent backsliding by the conversos. Ironically, this problem was to prove even more intractable. The decision was unexpected and it even astonished the prominent Jewish leaders in close contact with the court such as Isaac Abravanel, administrator of the royal tax system, and Abraham Seneor, chief rabbi of Castile, but several steps had been taken at court that should have forewarned them.

The Cortes of Castile that met in Madrigal in 1476 had reiterated laws issued in 1461 and earlier prohibiting Jews, especially women, from dressing richly in silk or displaying gold or silver and ordering them to wear "a distinctive round red cloth in the chest near the shoulders"; this was afterward changed into "a red star with six legs". The Cortes also curtailed the independent jurisdiction of the *aljamas* (Jewish communities) with regard to several issues. In 1480 the Cortes that met in Toledo confined the Spanish Jews in separate walled neighborhoods for the first time; their gates had to be shut at night. In the same year several Jews and conversos were discovered in Seville plotting to help African Moors to reinforce Granada against the Christian campaign; this discovery led to the first *auto de fe* in February 1481, and also to a first, partial expulsion of Jews from Andalusia decreed on January 1, 1483. Three years later Fernando ordered all Jews expelled from the Aragonese dioceses of Zaragoza and Albarracin, though these decrees were not fully carried out.

The text of Fernando's decree makes an explicit statement of the goal of expelling the Jews and says that the sovereigns had hoped "that by such separation the situation would be remedied." The situation they allude to is the status of the conversos.

The recovery of the *juderías* (Jewish settlements) after 1432 had raised apprehension on the part of some clerics that hundreds of thousands of converts might either return to Judaism or become an uncommitted mass of passive, agnostic, and syncretistic unbelievers, unable to be sincere Christians if the Jewish minority was allowed to stay. According to the decree of expulsion, in its first ten years of operation (1481–1491), the Inquisition had been ineffective "because of the contact, intercourse, and communication that they [conversos] have with the Jews." The text makes clear that the Expulsion, if painful, was a decision imposed on the Crown by the failure of the Inquisition to control the conversos socially, economically, or religiously, a control much more important politically for the internal peace of the country than keeping the few thousands of reluctant Jews on its soil.

The Crown decided to solve the internal social unrest caused by the divisions among old Christians, Jews, sincere new Christians, and Marranos by sacrificing a minority that had already become politically disposable. A careful study of the decree shows that the Expulsion had been decided long before and was to take place when the circumstances would allow. The end of the Granada war on January 1, 1492, and the consequent release of formerly needed funds made it possible to yield both to the long-standing demands of Columbus for his venture as well as to the pressures of the Inquisition to suppress the Jews.

The lists of tax contributions by the *aljamas* that have

been preserved for the years immediately before the Expulsion show that the majority of Jews were poor and lived mostly in rural areas. Estimates of the number of Jews in Spain in 1492 are much lower than the 800,000 proposed by the Jesuit Juan de Mariana (1536–1624) and taken for granted by Juan Antonio de Llorente (1756–1823) in his *History of the Inquisition;* they are lower than the 160,000 proposed by Yitzak Baer (1966). There were probably about 100,000 (fewer according to some scholars) Jews out of a total population of nearly six million. Given the small numbers and the poverty of the Jews, it is unlikely that greed on the part of Fernando and Isabel was a motive for the Expulsion; the rulers sometimes confessed that it would have been more advantageous to keep the Jews as taxpayers and workers.

The Decree of Expulsion was directed against Jews as adherents of a religion; there is in the text of the decree no trace of the so-called Spanish anti-Semitism that found expression in statutes of *limpieza de sangre* (purity of blood, i.e., of ancestry). At that time, few objected to accepting as full Spaniards those Jews who abandoned Jewish practices. Everything suggests that, in view of the massive and constant conversions since 1391, the monarchs and their advisers expected the majority of Jews to convert. Their expectations were partly vindicated when entire *juderías*, such as the one in Murcia, converted. In addition, many exiles returned to be baptized, and of the three leading Jews at that time, two converted— Abraham Seneor and Mair Melamed —leaving Isaac Abravanel as the sole important leader of the Sephardim (Jews of Spain). Abravanel sailed from Valencia at the head of those who chose to go to Italy.

As the July 31 deadline approached, all Jews felt pressed to dispose of their property. Since the decree of Expulsion forbade them to take gold and silver out of the country, land and houses were sold for movable property, such as mules or donkeys. About two-thirds of the Sephardim left; they underwent much suffering as they migrated to the countries where they settled: Portugal, North Africa, France, the Low Countries, the Papal States, Naples, Venice, and the Ottoman Empire.

The social importance of the Jews in 1492 and the numbers of Jews expelled have been exaggerated by some historians. The Expulsion did not cause the so-called decadence of Spain. The few important positions held by Jews and the professions in which Jews were active were filled either by new converts or by descendants of earlier converts. In any case, the Inquisition, because of its support of the statutes of purity of blood, made it impossible for the conversos and for Spain to succeed in the long run.

It was a coincidence that Columbus embarked on his first voyage across the Atlantic at dawn on August 3, just two days after the official deadline for expulsion. August 2, a Thursday, was the Ninth of Ab, a Jewish holiday, when, as a Jewish saying says, "those who work will never see a blessing therefrom." Hypothetical arguments have been constructed from this fact, suggesting the possible converso lineage of Columbus, who might have wished to keep the holiday as an ancestral family habit. But other scholars have suggested that the town of Palos, which he could not offend, celebrates on that day the festivity of its patron, the Virgin. To infer that he had a "Jewish agenda" or that he wanted to explore new lands of freedom for his fellow "Jews" sounds from a historical point of view absolutely preposterous.

BIBLIOGRAPHY

Baer, Yitzak. *A History of the Jews in Christian Spain.* 2 vols. Philadelphia, 1966.
Kriegel, Maurice. "La prise d'une décision: L'expulsion des juifs d'Espagne en 1492." *Revue Historique* 240 (1978).
Netanyahu, Benzion. *Don Isaac Abravanel.* Philadelphia, 1982.
Suárez Fernández, Luis. *Documentos acerca de la expulsión de los judíos.* Valladolid, 1964.

ANGEL ALCALÁ

Jews in the New World

Jews, Moors, and recent converts to Christianity were barred from immigrating to the Spanish Indies. This prohibition was included in the first instruction sent by Queen Isabel to Nicolás de Ovando, first royal governor of La Española (Hispaniola), Spain's first colony in the New World, in 1501. Reiterated over the years, the prohibition was expanded to include the children and grandchildren of converts. Enforced both by royal officials and by the transplanted Holy Office of the Inquisition, the policy remained in force throughout Spain's rule in the Americas. In this way, the Spanish Crown continued the dual policy it had developed with respect to Jews and persons of Jewish descent over the course of the fifteenth century: Spanish Jewry was to be converted or expelled from Spain; converts from Judaism and their descendants were not to be accorded equal status with other Spanish Christians either at home or in the New World.

The policy was put into effect through laws of *limpieza de sangre* ("clean blood") that barred conversos from engaging in any honorable public activity: to enter a university, practice a profession, hold public office, ride a horse, or sail to the Indies. Under these laws, descent from a Jewish ancestor became an indelible stain in one's blood which nothing, not even baptism, could eradicate. The old religious distinction between Jew and Catholic now became a racial distinction between New Christians of Jewish descent and Old Christians who had been converted from paganism in earlier centuries.

These legislative and social barriers led to the emergence of a new social class, the *conversos* (converts), who stood midway between Catholics and Jews and were wholly accepted by neither. The conversos were distrusted and resented by Old Christians who fought to retain their own superior status in society. Conversos were condemned by contemporary Jews as apostates. But Jewish history later enshrined the conversos as crypto-Jews or Marranos, on the supposition that, although forced to conform outwardly to Catholicism, they really remained loyal to their Jewish faith.

The Jews were expelled from Spain at the same time that Columbus set sail on his first voyage in the summer of 1492. Despite the obstacles placed in their way, unknown numbers of Jews and conversos followed in the explorer's wake. The new lands now coming into view beyond the sea gave hope to some conversos that they could disappear into a life free of harrassment by the Inquisition, which continually suspected them of backsliding into Judaism. Other conversos were motivated by the same desire for wealth and glory that drove their Old Christian countrymen to join the profitable enterprise of the Indies. Such a man, for example, was Simon Vaez Sevilla, a merchant of New Spain who was denounced to the Inquisition as a Jew but who survived several trials by torture to emerge a free man. Professing Jews found their way to America because of the pressing need for a refuge imposed upon them by the order of expulsion. At that time, Jews were prohibited from entering most countries of Europe and pirates stood off the coast of Spain to capture shiploads of refugees heading for Africa. In these desperate circumstances, some Jews came to America in the hope of finding some distant place where they could practice Judaism without being molested. Luis de Carvajal the Younger, his mother, and five sisters died at the stake for this miscalculation. Crypto-Jews like the Carvajals, or Tomás Treviño de Sobremonte and Francisco Maldonado de Silva are honored in Jewish history as martyrs to their faith.

A variety of strategems were employed by Jews, conversos, and their descendants to enter areas prohibited to them. Certificates of clean blood could be bought from complaisant priests; soldiers, sailors, and servants did not need to show these at all. And from time to time, the Spanish Crown, sunk in debt and increasingly corrupt, sold the privilege of immigration to classes of persons whom it legally excluded. There were conversos in Columbus's successive crews and among the conquistadores. In 1528 one Hernando Alonso, who had fought with Hernando Cortés, had the dubious honor of being the first person in the New World to be burned at the stake for

Judaizing (practicing Jewish customs though a baptized Catholic). Alonso was accused of having baptized a child in wine, not a Jewish custom. From the record, it is unclear whether he was a secret Jew, a converso and thus vulnerable to his personal enemies, or the victim of a political plot—the first, but certainly not the last, instance in which an accusation of Judaizing was to be used to destroy a political opponent.

Most Jews and conversos followed less dramatic occupations. The records of the Inquisition show that those brought before it on charges of Judaizing followed the whole gamut of trades of that day—from shoemaker to clergyman, from merchant to weaver to the vicar-general of the Mexican province of Michoacán. Necessary as their skills may have been, persons of Jewish descent were not permitted to take their place in society. The revelation that someone had Jewish ancestry was enough to arouse a paranoid perception that society was being infiltrated by "Jews," whom the church inveighed against unceasingly. Weekly sermons and periodic autos de fe where presumed heretics were incinerated either in person or in effigy primed the populace constantly to be on the lookout for signs of the presence of Jews. Judaic concepts such as monotheism, and the prohibition against graven images found no place in these warnings. Rather, congregations were exhorted to report persons who changed their underwear on Friday or stripped a tendon from a leg of lamb before cooking it. Such admonitions placed every household at the mercy of gossip, particularly as informers were rewarded by receiving a portion of the goods confiscated from the accused. As in the conquest of the indigenous peoples, faith mingled companionably with greed. The most spectacular case occurred in Lima in 1635, when sixty-four suspected Judaizers, most of them prosperous merchants, were arrested in one coordinated operation. The arrests led to the immediate flight of capital from the viceroyalty, the deaths and imprisonment of the accused in an auto de fe four years later, and the emergence of the Lima branch of the Inquisition as the wealthiest in the world.

Portugal, a nation of some one million people on the eve of the encounter with the New World, faced the imperial necessity of holding down Brazil as well as its global galaxy of commercial entrepôts in India, Africa, and China. Under these circumstances, the Crown could not afford to sacrifice too many of its subjects. Having forcibly converted all Portuguese and Spanish Jews within its borders in 1497 in order to evade a contractual obligation to expel them, the Crown proceeded, within limits, to permit its *novo cristãos* (New Christians) to colonize Brazil. The Inquisition was never established in Brazil itself; nevertheless, suspected Judaizers could be, and were, sent to Lisbon or even Goa to be tried by tribunals there. Inquisition records show that in Brazil also, New Christians were engaged at all levels of the economic and social structure, including the church. Economically, they were especially important as owners and managers of sugar mills. Interestingly, although *novo cristãos* were free to travel, and frequently did, to places such as Amsterdam and Hamburg where they would have been free to revert to Judaism, most chose to return to their homes under Portuguese rule, with all the risks that entailed, and even helped defend coastal cities against raids by the Dutch.

Only in the Dutch dependencies and, from time to time, in the French- and English-ruled islands, was it possible to live openly as a Jew in the New World. Those individuals who left Brazil for the safety of Curaçao, Bonaire, or Aruba took their skills with them, spreading the technology for manufacture of sugar out of cane to the various islands where it is still a staple industry. The Jewish community of Curaçao also included shipowners, sailors, slavers, and merchants who were at the core of the island's thriving oceanic trade in the seventeenth and eighteenth centuries.

Spanish America benefited from the talents of personalities of "tainted" ancestry such as Sister Juana Inés de la Cruz, dubbed the "Tenth Muse" by admirers of her poetry; Bernardino de Sahagún, the Franciscan monk who transcribed what we know today of Nahua (Aztec) culture; Antonio de León Pinelo, the polymath who laid the foundations for scholarship in Latin America. Brazilian culture was enriched by Bento Teixeira Pinto, author of the *Prosopopeia,* who died after four years in an Inquisition prison and public humiliation as a Judaizer; and the eighteenth-century Portuguese poet Antonio José da Silva, burned in Lisbon in 1739 as a pertinacious Jew.

These persons and unknown others, against great odds, lived creative lives while undergoing traumatic transformation from Jew to Catholic. Neither Jews nor Jewish culture survived the sustained attack of the Inquisition. There is thus no continuity between conversos and crypto-Jews who lived under Spanish or Portuguese colonial rule and contemporary Latin American Jewish communities.

BIBLIOGRAPHY

Böhm, Günter. *Nuevos antecedentes para una historia de los judíos en Chile colonial.* Santiago, 1963.

Cohen, Martin. *The Martyr. Luis de Carvajal: The Story of a Secret Jew and the Mexican Inquisition in the Sixteenth Century.* Philadelphia, 1973.

Emmanuel, Isaac S., and Suzanne A. Emmanuel. *History of the Jews of the Netherlands Antilles.* 2 vols. Assen, 1970.

Lewin, Boleslão. *El judío en la época colonial: Un aspecto de la historia río-platense.* Buenos Aires, 1939.

Liebman, Seymour B. *The Inquisition and the Jews in the New World: Summaries of Procesos, 1500–1810, and Bibliographic Guide.* Coral Gables, Fla., 1974.

Novinsky, Anita. *Cristãos novos na Bahia.* São Paulo, 1972.

JUDITH LAIKIN ELKIN

JIMÉNEZ DE CISNEROS, FRANCISCO (1436–1517), Spanish prelate and statesman. During his long life, Cisneros occupied the most important political and spiritual offices of the Crown of Castile: cardinal-archbishop of Toledo, inquisitor-general, and governor of the realm. No Castilian prelate has since possessed such power. Judgments about his achievements are contradictory. To some, he was an intransigent, overzealous friar; to others, a model prelate and statesman.

For the first fifty-six years of his life, Cisneros gave little indication of future greatness. A graduate of Salamanca with a bachelor's degree in law, he went to Rome to pursue an administrative career in the church. His nomination by Paul II in 1471 to a benefice in the archdiocese of Toledo angered the archbishop of Toledo, Alfonso Carrillo, who placed him in jail. But Cardinal Pedro González de Mendoza intervened on behalf of Cisneros and appointed him chaplain of the bishopric of Sigüenza in 1480. Four years later, Cisneros decided to retire from the world and took orders as an Observant Franciscan, living in the convents of La Salceda and El Castañar. But in 1492 he was persuaded by Queen Isabel to replace Hernando de Talavera, now archbishop of Granada, as her personal confessor. With this appointment, Cisneros began his rise to prominence; three years later he was appointed archbishop of Toledo.

Cisneros, like the Catholic monarchs Isabel and Fernando, wished to improve the education, discipline, and morale of the clergy, both regular and secular. His most energetic church reform was that of his own order, where he forced the lax *conventuales* to join the more rigorous and edifying Observant Franciscans in honoring their vows of poverty, chastity, and obedience. Female orders were also visited to ensure that their convents were adequately endowed and had edifying spiritual direction. Cisneros held two synods in the archdiocese of Toledo (Alcalá de Henares, 1497; Talavera de la Reina, 1498), and much of the legislation of these synods, which urged parish priests to catechize their parishioners, to teach children the Christian doctrine, and to keep records of baptisms, anticipated the Tridentine reforms. Evidence in present-day Toledo suggests that this legislation was implemented by many parish priests.

The foundation of a new university at Alcalá de Henares in 1498 formed part of the prelate's reform program. This university was to be a center for the teaching of theology, and the curriculum included not just Thomas Aquinas but also Duns Scotus and nominalism. Cisneros was enthusiastic about what was called the New Learning, and he employed at Alcalá a bevy of humanists, translators, and philologists to study the various translations of the Bible. The culmination of their efforts was the magnificent but ill-fated Complutensian Polyglot Bible that included texts in Hebrew, Latin, and Greek printed in parallel columns. Quick to recognize the utility of the printing press for his reform efforts, Cisneros encouraged the translation and printing of many religious and mystical works, thus making them accessible to a new public.

With the death of Queen Isabel in 1504, the political situation in Castile deteriorated. In 1505 Fernando retired to Italy after ceding the government of Castile to his son-in-law, Philip I of Flanders, who died a year later. Cisneros acted as regent until Fernando returned in 1507, when he presented to Cisneros a cardinal's hat, a worthy accompaniment to the title of inquisitor-general he had received earlier that year. In 1516, after Fernando's death, Cisneros again served as regent until the new heir, the future emperor Charles V, arrived in Castile. That Cisneros was able to survive and rule during these turbulent periods, when powerful nobles split into opposing factions and sought to advance their own interests, suggests that he possessed political skills of a high order.

Cardinal Cisneros has been described as the last of the crusading prelates, and this phase of his personality is best seen in the North African campaigns. In 1507 he financed the conquest of Mazalquivir (in present-day Algeria) and in 1509 personally supervised the conquest of Oran, accompanying the fleet and praying while the soldiers fought—"behaving like a new Moses," according to one observer. The New World did not escape the prelate's purview. After 1500 he was active in organizing expeditions of Franciscan missionaries and in the creation of the first episcopal sees. In response to the problems associated with the Indian labor communes (encomiendas), Cisneros sent to the Antilles three Hieronymites with instructions about the reorganization of the Indian population and the administration of the new territories.

Cisneros's attitude toward the minorities of Castile—the Jews and Muslims—seems to have been mixed. His lack of patience with the moderate, humane methods of Cardinal Talavera in the treatment and conversion of Muslims in the newly conquered Kingdom of Granada is well known. Cisneros implemented a policy of coercion and mass baptism, which eventually led to an uprising of the Granada moriscos that was barely contained. In other cases, however, the record differs. Although a strong supporter of the Holy Office and its prerogatives, Cisneros as inquisitor-general ushered in a more temperate period after the fanaticism of the inquisitor Diego Rodríguez Lucero. The prelate had Arabic books burned in Granada, but he claimed a large collection of Arabic books plundered in Oran for his new university in Alcalá. His treatment of conversos, or Jewish converts, in the city of Toledo was far from intolerant. After he became inquisitor-general, several Toledo conversos who had been arrested earlier by the Holy Office were absolved and freed, most notably the *maestrescuela* of the Toledo cathedral, Francisco Álvarez de Toledo-Zapata, who became a friend of the prelate. Cisneros encouraged a new confraternity, La Virgen y Madre de Dios, composed largely of conversos who met in the archbishop's palace. And on the roster of those employed to work on the famous Polyglot Bible were many Jewish converts whose knowledge of Hebrew was indispensable to the undertaking.

BIBLIOGRAPHY

Azcona, Tarsicio de. *La elección y reforma del episcopado español en tiempo de los reyes católicos.* Madrid, 1960.
Elliott, John H. *Imperial Spain 1469–1716.* New York, 1966.
García de Oro, José. *Cisneros y la reforma del clero español en tiempo de los reyes católicos.* Madrid, 1970.
García de Oro, José. "Francisco Jiménez de Cisneros." In vol. 2 of *Diccionario de historia eclesiástica de España.* Edited by Quentín Aldea et al. 5 vols. Madrid, 1972–1987.
Gómez de Castro, Alvar. *De las haçanas de Francisco Jiménez de Cisneros.* Edited and translated by José Oroz Reta. Madrid, 1984. Originally published as *De rebus gestis a Francisco Ximenio Cisnerio.* Alcalá, 1569.

LINDA MARTZ

JIMÉNEZ DE QUESADA, GONZALO

(1492/1506–1579), conqueror of New Granada (Colombia). Born in either Córdoba or Granada, Jiménez de Quesada was educated in law and served for a time in the Chancery of Granada. In 1535 he was named superior justice (alcalde mayor) in Pedro Fernández de Lugo's expedition to occupy Santa Marta.

Once established at Santa Marta, Fernández de Lugo commissioned Jiménez de Quesada to ascend the Magdalena River until he found its source. A force of six hundred men, one hundred horses, and six ships set out on April 5, 1536. The expedition found little of note until it reached the Magdalena's confluence with the Opón, where the native peoples had salt cones that the Spaniards guessed had come from a developed culture in the interior.

Jiménez de Quesada abandoned exploration of the Magdalena River and took the remaining men, numbering under two hundred, up the Opón and into the mountain valleys. Venerated by the Indians as children of the sun and moon, the Spanish were allowed to pass until they reached the Bogotá valley. There they began to loot the gold jewelry of the inhabitants, even robbing tombs. The Indian province of Tunja (roughly the modern department of Boyacá) was also raided. Santa Fé de Bogotá was founded on August 6, 1538, as part of Jiménez de Quesada's preparations to leave the province and go to Spain to seek a royal grant of its government. The Spanish city provided a juridical basis for his pretensions and rewards for his followers in the form of land and encomiendas.

Before Jiménez de Quesada could depart for Spain, Nicolás Federmann arrived from Venezuela, to be followed not many months later by Sebastián de Belalcázar, who had crossed the mountains from Quito. Federmann joined Jiménez de Quesada but Belalcázar attempted to overthrow his power on behalf of Francisco Pizarro, whose royal grant included part of southern Colombia, but not the Bogotá area. When that failed, he withdrew to Quito.

Jiménez de Quesada sailed from Cartagena on July 8, 1539. He was unable to secure appointment as governor of New Granada and spent a number of years in other parts of Europe before returning to Spain. Eventually granted the title of Marshal of New Granada and certain incomes, he returned to the province in 1555. A popular leader of the Spanish residents, he did not leave Bogotá until 1569, when he lead an ill-fated expedition in search of El Dorado. Jiménez de Quesada worked his way east as far as the Venezuelan Llanos before turning back. He spent the final years of his life writing an account of his conquests and a book of sermons, both now lost. In 1575 he participated in a campaign against rebellious Indians. He died of Hansen's disease in 1579 at Mariquita, New Granada.

BIBLIOGRAPHY

Arciniegas, German. *The Knight of El Dorado.* Translated by Mildred Adams. 1942. Reprint, Westport, Conn., 1968.

Cunninghame-Graham, R. B. *The Conquest of New Granada, Being the Life of Gonzalo Jiménez de Quesada.* London, 1922.

Markham, Clements R. *The Conquest of New Granada.* London, 1912.

Parry, J. H. *The Discovery of South America.* New York, 1979.

PAUL E. HOFFMAN

JOÃO II (1455–1495), king of Portugal (1481–1495). A man of exceptional intelligence and strength, João II, "the Perfect Prince," ruled Portugal after the death of his father, Afonso V, in 1481. João brought prosperity to Portugal, which enabled him to concentrate on exploration and to build a Portuguese overseas empire founded on the economic and political benefits from the voyages of discovery.

JOÃO II OF PORTUGAL.   KUNSTHISTORISCHES MUSEUM, VIENNA

During the last years of Afonso's reign, João was virtually co-ruler with his father. He managed the Crown's monopoly of the trade with Africa and was put in charge of the Junta dos Mathemáticos. The Junta, a maritime advisory committee responsible for overseas expansion, created a comprehensive plan for the discoveries, incorporating both land and sea exploration. He focused his attentions eastward, primarily on Asia and Africa. During João's reign Diogo Cão explored central Africa (1482) and Bartolomeu Dias rounded the Cape of Good Hope (1487).

Columbus brought his petitions for support of his westward voyages to João in 1484 and 1488. João rejected Columbus's theories as incorrect and mathematically improbable, so Columbus took his petitions to the court of Castile where he eventually received financing from Fernando and Isabel. When Columbus returned from his first voyage in 1493, weather conditions forced him to land in Portugal, not Castile as he had planned. Upon hearing the details of Columbus's voyage, João asserted that because the lands discovered were south of the Canary Islands, they were not within the jurisdiction of Castile but rather belonged to Portugal, according to the Treaty of

Alcáçovas (1479). Pope Alexander VI, in his bull *Inter caetera* (1493), attempted to resolve the dispute by pushing westward the Line of Demarcation. (Although there is no evidence of prior visits to Brazil by European navigators, it is likely that João suspected its existence since he knew of Paolo del Pozzo Toscanelli's map indicating possible islands in the Atlantic and suggesting a westward route to the Indies.) João disputed the papal bull, and in 1494 the disagreement was resolved by the Treaty of Tordesillas, which granted Columbus's discoveries to Castile but moved the Line of Demarcation farther west, allowing Portugal later to claim Brazil.

João married Leonor of Viseu, a member of one of the most powerful noble families in Portugal. In 1491 their only son, Afonso, married Isabel, daughter of Fernando and Isabel of Castile, but the marriage was tragically brief. After only a few months, Afonso died in a riding accident. João turned to his young cousin Manuel, the duke of Beja, and began grooming him for succession.

João strengthened royal authority by limiting the power of the nobility. Even his wife's family connections did not stop his ruthless treatment of his brothers-in-law, the powerful dukes of Bragança and Viseu; he ordered the execution of Bragança and murdered Viseu with his own hands. He harbored Spanish Jews exiled by Fernando and Isabel in 1492, including Abraham Zacuto, the famous astronomer from Salamanca. His motives were not entirely altruistic: the Jews were allowed to stay for eight months only and were taxed for the privilege of entrance to the kingdom. Just before his death in 1495 João completed plans for Vasco de Gama's voyage to India, work that was brought to fruition during the reign of Manuel I.

BIBLIOGRAPHY

Domingues, Mário. *Di João II, o homen e o monarca: Evocação histórica.* Lisbon, 1960.

Gaspar de Naia, Alexandre. *D. João II e Cristóbal Colón: Factores complementos na consecução de um mesmo objectivo.* Lisbon, 1951.

Oliveira Marquês, A. H. de. *History of Portugal.* 2 vols. New York, 1972.

Oliveira Martins, Joaquim Pedro. *O principe perfeito.* 3d ed. Lisbon, 1923.

Sanceau, Elaine. *The Perfect Prince: A Biography of the King Dom João II.* Porto, 1959.

THERESA EARENFIGHT

JOHN. For discussion of Spanish kings, see under *Juan.* For discussion of Portuguese kings, see under *João.*

JUAN (1478–1497), crown prince of Spain; the only son of Isabel and Fernando. Juan's birth in Seville was greeted with extraordinary enthusiasm, for he would inherit the united kingdoms of Castile and Aragón, to which later would be added the kingdoms of Navarre and Granada. He and his children thus would be the first monarchs in nearly eight hundred years to rule a united Spain. Juan's education was wide ranging and firmly grounded in Renaissance humanism; his tutors included Lucio Marineo Siculo and Pietro Martire d'Anghiera (Peter Martyr). Juan, who learned the art of governance as he accompanied the peripatetic court of Fernando and Isabel, later established his own court in Almazán. He was present at the fall of Granada in 1492 and the royal reception in Barcelona on April 20, 1493, which celebrated the return of Columbus from his first voyage to the New World.

Juan's marriage on April 3, 1497, in Burgos to Margaret of Austria, daughter of Emperor Maximilian I, was part of a double matrimonial alliance that joined the royal family of Castile and Aragón with the Austrian House of Habsburg. The alliance, which was designed to offset the power of France, also united Juan's sister Juana with Maximilian's son and heir, Philip the Handsome. The carefully crafted alliance lasted only a matter of months, however. Juan's health had been fragile since childhood, and he died suddenly on October 6, 1497, in Salamanca. The only child of the marriage was a stillborn daughter. Juan was buried in Ávila at the monastery of Santo Tomás.

BIBLIOGRAPHY

Camón Aznar, J. *Sobre la muerte del principe Don Juan.* Madrid, 1963.

Maura, Duque de. *El principe que murió de amor, Don Juan, primogénito de los reyes católicos.* Madrid, 1944.

Miller, Townsend. *The Castles and the Crown: Spain 1451–1555.* New York, 1963.

Suárez Fernández, Luis, and M. Fernández Álvarez. *La España de los Reyes Católicos (1474–1516).* Vol. 17 of *Historia de España.* Edited by Ramón Menéndez Pidal. 2 vols. Madrid, 1966.

THERESA EARENFIGHT

JUAN II (1397–1479), king of Aragón (1458–1479). Juan, son of Fernando I of Antequera and Leonor of Albuquerque, was already an experienced monarch when he inherited the Crown of Aragón in 1458 following the death of his brother King Alfonso V (Alfonso the Magnanimous). He had ruled Navarre since 1420 by right of his first wife, Blanca, and had served as lieutenant in Aragón during Alfonso's extended absence in Naples.

Juan's rule of the realms of the Crown of Aragón was turbulent and marked by a decade of bitter civil war (1462–1472), which devastated the economy of Barcelona. He clashed with France over possession of the counties of Roussillon and Cerdagne, an issue that would not be resolved until the reign of his son Fernando the Catholic.

His dealings with Castile were equally stormy, dating to 1420 when he and his brother, Enrique, the infantes of Aragón, interfered in Castilian affairs. As king of Navarre he attempted to manipulate the Castilian succession, hoping to unite the various Spanish kingdoms within his own family. His quarrel with his son Carlos of Viana brought Navarre close to war with Castile. When Carlos died in 1461, murder was suspected, but there was no evidence to accuse Juan of the crime.

Carlos's death cleared the way for Fernando, Juan's son by his second wife, Juana Enríquez, to inherit the Crown of Aragón. At Juan's death in 1479 the Crown of Aragón was a far-flung domain, which included the peninsular realms of Aragón, Catalonia, and Valencia as well as the Mediterranean kingdoms of Mallorca, Sardinia, Sicily, and Naples.

BIBLIOGRAPHY

Bisson, Thomas N. *The Medieval Crown of Aragon: A Short History.* Oxford, 1986.

Vicens Vives, Jaime. *Juan II de Aragón (1398–1479): Monarquía y revolución en la España del siglo XV.* Barcelona, 1953.

Vicens Vives, Jaime. *La politique méditerranéenne et italienne de Jean II d'Aragon entre 1458 et 1462.* Bern, 1950.

Vicens Vives, Jaime. *Els Trastàmares (segle XV).* Barcelona, 1956.

THERESA EARENFIGHT

JUANA DE CASTILLA (1462–1530), princess of Castile and alleged daughter of King Enrique IV of Castile, known as Juana la Beltraneja. Juana was the central figure in a prolonged crisis concerning the succession to the throne; it fractured the kingdom and led to nearly a decade of civil war in Castile. The problem of the succession centered on the uncertainty of Juana's parentage, an issue that has never been definitively resolved, although no convincing evidence exists to prove the claims of her illegitimacy. King Enrique was alleged to be impotent, and his first marriage to Blanca of Navarre was nullified on those grounds. He was wed again, to Juana of Portugal, but it was six years before a child was born on February 28, 1462. Soon after her birth, rumors began to circulate concerning the king's impotence and the queen's indiscretions. It was said that Juana was the illegitimate daughter of the king's closest adviser, Beltrán de la Cueva—hence her derogatory nickname "la Beltraneja."

Although on May 9, 1462, the Cortes of Castile judged Juana to be heir to the throne, the controversy did not subside. When a faction of nobles and clergy in the court pressured Enrique to repudiate Juana, he began to waver on the question of her legitimacy and she became a pawn in the ensuing struggle. The Sentence of Medina del Campo (1465), which repudiated Juana in favor of

Enrique's brother Alfonso, was a tacit admission by Enrique of Juana's illegitimacy, but he later revoked his repudiation. In the civil war that followed, rival factions rallied behind either Juana, supported by Beltrán de la Cueva and the Mendoza family, or Prince Alfonso, who had the formidable support of Alfonso Carrillo, the archbishop of Toledo. When Prince Alfonso died in 1468, Juan Pacheco and Carrillo pledged their support to Enrique's sister, Princess Isabel. Enrique conceded to the strength of Pacheco and Carrillo and signed the Treaty of Toros de Guisando (September 18, 1468), which designated Isabel as heir. This action temporarily pacified the situation and shifted the balance of power in favor of the Isabelline faction. But the calm was broken in 1469 when Isabel married Fernando of Aragón and a serious rift developed in relations between her and Enrique. In 1470 Isabel was repudiated once again in favor of Juana, who was declared true heir and was betrothed to the duke of Guienne, the younger brother of Louis XI of France; the duke, however, died before the marriage. Isabel and her supporters, in an alliance with the majority of the nobles and townspeople, were gaining strength.

At the time of Enrique's death in 1474 he had neither firmly settled the issue of Juana's legitimacy nor declared anyone as heir. Isabel was proclaimed queen, but Juana's partisans, especially King Afonso V of Portugal, did not give up the cause. Juana was betrothed to Afonso; they called themselves the king and queen of Castile, and the civil war continued. Fernando's defeat of Afonso's Portuguese troops at Toro in 1476 and the birth of a male heir, Juan, in 1478 to Fernando and Isabel signaled the end of Juana's attempts to gain the throne of Castile. She retired to the convent of Santa Clara in Coimbra, calling herself queen of Castile until her death in 1530.

BIBLIOGRAPHY

Ferrara, Orestes. *Un pleito sucesorio: Enrique IV, Isabel de Castilla y la Beltraneja.* Madrid, 1945.

Miller, Townsend. *The Castles and the Crown: Spain 1451–1555.* New York, 1963.

Phillips, William D., Jr. *Enrique IV and the Crisis of Fifteenth-Century Castile, 1425–1480.* Cambridge, Mass., 1978.

Sarasola, Modesto. *Isabel la Católica y el destino de doña Juana, la Beltraneja.* Valladolid, 1955.

THERESA EARENFIGHT

JUANA I (1479–1555), queen of Castile (1504–1555), known as La Loca. Juana, called the "mad queen of Castile," was the third child of Isabel I and Fernando V. She succeeded to the throne of Castile after the death of Isabel in October 1504 because of the vacancy created by the untimely deaths of her brother, Juan (1497), older sister, Isabel (1498), and Isabel's son, Infante Manuel (1500). Her incapacity to rule provoked a series of succession crises that ensued after the deaths of her husband, Philip (1506), and her father (1516).

Juana's marriage to Philip the Handsome, archduke of Austria and duke of Burgundy, in 1496 was part of a double matrimonial alliance between Castile and Emperor Maximilian I, in which her brother Crown Prince Juan was betrothed to Philip's sister Margaret. Among the six children of Philip and Juana were Charles and Ferdinand, each of whom successively bore the title of Holy Roman Emperor.

Juana had been moody and temperamental since childhood, and her marriage to Philip exacerbated her emotional instability. She was devoted to him and was particularly jealous of his numerous infidelities. The first clear signs of serious mental illness were evident as early as 1502, when because of her pregnancy she was forced to remain in Castile when Philip returned to Flanders. Her condition steadily worsened, so that when Isabel died in 1504 she named Juana as successor to Castile but stipulated that if Juana was incapable of ruling, Fernando should serve as regent for Charles, then six years old.

When Philip returned to Castile in 1506, he asserted that Juana was sane and declared that as her husband he was within his rights to rule as king. But because Philip was not especially interested in the Spanish kingdom, Fernando feared that he would be an absentee king. Juana retreated into seclusion, and the animosity between Philip and Fernando intensified. Many prominent nobles, seeking to use the easily manipulated archduke for their own political advantage, allied with Philip against Fernando, and he

bowed to their strength. On June 23, 1506, he signed the Agreement of Villafafila, which granted Philip full rights to rule Castile and denied Juana any role in government. Philip's reign was brief, however. He died in September of the same year, and Castile was faced with a succession crisis.

Fernando, who had left Castile for his kingdom in Naples, ordered the Castilians to obey Juana. But in the absence of strong royal authority, civil unrest grew as nobles asserted their independence and towns rebelled. Juana's mental state deteriorated markedly after Philip's death. She refused to let his casket be entombed and ordered that it accompany her throughout her nocturnal travels in Castile. When she abandoned all responsibilities as queen, Cardinal Francisco Jiménez de Cisneros assumed control as regent until Fernando's return in 1507. Fernando ruled Castile, with Juana as nominal queen, until his death in 1516. Castile once more was threatened with civil unrest, and a faction of the nobility tried to rule in Juana's name. The cardinal again served as regent until Charles was recognized as king in 1518. Juana, queen in name only, withdrew completely from the world and lived under guard as a recluse in the royal castle at Tordesillas until her death in 1555.

BIBLIOGRAPHY

Dennis, Amarie. *Seek the Darkness: The Story of Juana la Loca.* Madrid, 1953.

Imann, Georges. *Jeanne le Folle.* Paris, 1947.

Pfandl, Ludwig. *Juana la Loca.* 7th ed. Madrid, 1955.

THERESA EARENFIGHT

TOMB OF JUANA I AND FELIPE EL HERMOSO (PHILIP I, KNOWN AS PHILIP THE HANDSOME). Royal Chapel, Granada.

NATIONAL TOURIST OFFICE OF SPAIN, NEW YORK

KAMAL. The first European to mention the *kamal* was probably Niccolò de' Conti, around 1440. The Portuguese historian João de Barros, describing Vasco da Gama's first encounter with the Muslim navigator *(mu'allim)* from Gujarat who was to show him the way to India, reported that the navigator was not impressed by Da Gama's large wooden astrolabe and others of metal used for finding solar and stellar altitudes. The navigator told Da Gama that the mariners of "Cambaya" (Cambay, a formerly important port in Gujarat) and India used an instrument of "three tablets," one of which he had in his possession. In Book 4 of *Décadas de Asia* (1552–1615), Barros compares the use of this exotic instrument to the *balestilla* (cross-staff). The Portuguese called the *kamal: tavoletas* (or *tábuas) da Índia* and *balestilha do mouro. Tavoletas* were brought back to Portugal, and the sixteenth-century works of João de Lisboa and André Pires mention them; it has been suggested that the revival in the sixteenth century of the cross-staff as a nautical instrument was influenced by knowledge of the *kamal.*

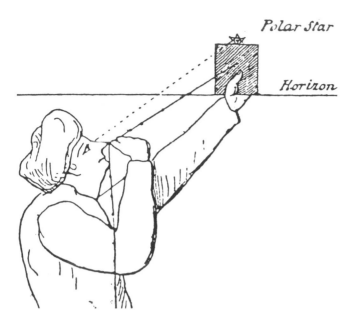

Polar Star

Horizon

USE OF THE *KAMAL*.   AFTER CONGREVE, 1850

The tablets of a *kamal* were of horn or of wood and of different sizes, and each had a central hole where a string was attached. The string was divided by appropriately placed knots, giving readings in numbers of *isba'* (finger [breadth]). In use, the bottom edge of the tablet (chosen for being of appropriate size) was aligned on the horizon, and the top edge was aligned on the celestial body, the altitude of which was to be measured (compare the use of the cross-staff). The knot that, when held between the teeth or to the nose of the observer, kept the string taut indicated the altitude. The *kamal* was used primarily to measure stellar altitudes *(qiyas)* in order to ascertain directly or by analogy the altitude of the polestar, and thus the latitude. In a variant form of *kamal*, the knots on the string indicated not *isba'*, but the altitude of the polestar at various places on the western coast of India. The few *kamal*s that have been described and illustrated in the literature can no longer be located.

It seems clear that the *kamal* was paralleled in China by the *qian xing ban* (guiding star stretch-boards), twelve ebony plates and an ivory piece, measuring *zhi*, mentioned by a sixteenth-century Chinese author, Li Zu, and in use, presumably, earlier. Some transmission from China to India seems probable. The name *kamal*, which James Prinsep learned from a navigator on a ship from the Maldives, has not been found in any other source and may not be the original term or form. Apart from the Portuguese names, the only alternative name that has been found is *khashaba* (a piece of wood), used by the Arab *mu'allim*s Ahmad ibn Majid (fl. 1460–1550) and Sulayman al-Mahri (first half of the sixteenth century); the former also uses in poetry the variant *khadaba*. The Arabic word *kamal* means "perfection, completion," but in this case might represent the assimilation of the New Persian, Arabic, Turkish, and Urdu word *kaman* (bow, arch, arc) or a derivative of the Greek word *kámilos* (rope), possibly through another Indo-European language such as Hindi or Maldivian, or even of a loan word from a South Indian Dravidian language; the Chinese might also be connected. The individual tablets were called *lawh* in Arabic.

[See also *Cross-Staff*.]

BIBLIOGRAPHY

Congreve, H. "A Brief Notice of Some Contrivances Practised by the Native Mariners of the Coromandel Coast, in Navigating, Sailing and Repairing Their Vessels." 1850. Reprinted in vol. 3 of *Instructions nautiques et routiers arabes et portugais des XVe et XVIe siècles*, edited by Gabriel Ferrand, pp. 24–30. Paris, 1928.

Maddison, Francis. *Medieval Scientific Instruments and the Development of Navigational Instruments in the XVth and XVIth Centuries*. Agrupamento de estudos de cartografia antiga, vol. 30. Coimbra, 1969.

Needham, Joseph, Wang Ling, and Lu Gwei-Djen. "Civil Engineering and Nautics." Part 3 of vol. 4 of *Science and Civilisation in China*. Cambridge, 1971.

Prinsep, James. "Note on the Nautical Instruments of the Arabs." 1836. Reprinted in vol. 3 of *Instructions nautiques et routiers arabes et portugais des XVe et XVIe siècles*, edited by Gabriel Ferrand, pp. 1–24. Paris, 1928.

Tibbetts, G. R. *The Navigational Theory of the Arabs in the Fifteenth and Sixteenth Centuries*. Agrupamento de estudos de cartografia antiga, vol 36. Coimbra, 1969.

Tibbetts, G. R. *Arab Navigation in the Indian Ocean before the Coming of the Portuguese, Being a Translation of* Kitab al-Fawa'id fi usul al-bahr wa'l-qawa'id *of Ahmad b. Majid al-Najdi*. Oriental Translation Fund, new series, vol. 42. London, 1971.

FRANCIS MADDISON

Christopher Columbus
and the
Age of Exploration

Volume 2
L–Z

L

LA COSA, JUAN DE. See *Cosa, Juan de la.*

LANDFALL CONTROVERSY. "In 1492, Columbus sailed the ocean blue." Despite the appalling geographical ignorance of schoolchildren, many would recognize these words. But just where did Columbus land? Virtually every island in the Bahamas chain, from the Berry Islands on the north to Grand Turk on the south, a distance of more than three hundred miles, has been suggested as the landfall site. This lack of knowledge of where Columbus first landed can be traced, first, to the fact that Columbus was searching for something else: densely populated lands and vast stores of wealth. These islands were mere way stations on the way to his prime objective. That objective, as he noted in his journal at the time, was the noble island of Cipangu (Japan) or, if he overshot that island, the mainland of China. Instead he found Cuba and some of the other great islands of the Caribbean. Second, the limited wealth of the islands, such as it was, consisted primarily of the bodies of their inhabitants, and this wealth was quickly exhausted by slave-raiding expeditions, at which point the islands ceased to be of any real interest to the Spaniards.

The cartography of the period following the discoveries does not help us much in solving the mystery. San Salvador, as Columbus named the landfall island, or Guanahani, as he reported the island was called by its inhabitants, was often placed by cartographers at differing and widely separated islands in the Bahamas. Charting the earth's surface was plagued by uncertainty, the result of the limited scientific methods available to establish latitude and longitude and the often conflicting and confused reports of navigators.

Nor do the early Spanish histories of the discoveries help in solving the mystery. Gonzalo Fernández de Oviedo's *Historia general y natural de las Indias* (1535) states that the first lands discovered were called the "white islands" (*islas blancas*) because these sandy isles seemed to be white, that Columbus named them "the princesses," and that Guanahani was adjacent to them and to another island called "Caicos." This passage—late though it is—gives support to proponents of the Grand Turk as the landfall island since that island is surrounded by small sandy islets (of exceptional whiteness) and is adjacent to the Caicos Islands. But other histories, such as Antonio de Herrera y Tordesillas's four-volume *Historia general de los hechos de los castellanos en las Islas, y Tierra Firme de el Mar Océano* (1601–1615), in discussing Juan Ponce de León's 1513 discovery of Florida while sailing from San Juan, Puerto Rico, through the Bahamas from south to north, locates the island of San Salvador, "the first that Admiral Don Christóval Colón discovered," in the central or northern Bahamas.

Although the islands first sighted by Columbus rapidly declined in importance, their significance at the time is evident from the names he bestowed upon them and the order in which he did so. The first island, which served to validate the lifetime of faith and reason that Columbus had invested in his great enterprise, he named San Salvador in honor of the Savior Jesus Christ; the second, Santa María de la Concepción, in honor of the Virgin Mary; the third, La Fernandina, in honor of King Fernando; and the fourth, La Isabela, in honor of Queen Isabel.

Eighteenth- and Nineteenth-Century Theories

Although the location of Columbus's landfall was not a matter of great concern in the first century after his

Columbus's Landfalls in the Bahamas in 1492

			EARLY THEORIES			
Columbus's Name (Indian Name)	M. Fernández de Navarrete	Washington Irving	A. B. Becher	J. B. Murdock	G. V. Fox	George Gibbs
1. San Salvador (Guanahani)	Grand Turk	Cat Island	San Salvador (Watlings)	San Salvador (Watlings)	Samana Cay	Grank Turk
2. Santa María	Caicos	Conception Island	Long Island	Rum Cay	Crooked Island	Caicos
3. Fernandina (Yuma)	Little Inagua	Great Exuma	Great Exuma	Long Island	Long Island	Little Inagua
4. Isabela (Saometo)	Great Inagua	Long Island	Crooked Island	Crooked Island Fortune Island	Fortune Island	Great Inagua
5. Islas Arenas or Cuban Coast		Mucarras	Ragged Islands Port Nipe	Ragged Islands Bay of Gibara	Ragged Islands Port Padre	

	TWENTIETH-CENTURY THEORIES					
Columbus's Name (Indian Name)	Northern Landfall		Central Landfall			Southern Landfall
	Arne Molander	John Hathaway Winslow	S. E. Morison M. Obregon	Pedro Grau y Triana	Joseph Judge	Robert Power
1. San Salvador (Guanahani)	Egg Island	Great Harbor Cay	San Salvador (Watlings)	San Salvador (Watlings)	Samana Cay	Grand Turk
2. Santa María	New Providence	New Providence	Rum Cay	Rum Cay	Crooked Island Acklins Island	Providenciales
3. Fernandina (Yuma)	Andros	Andros	Long Island	Long Island	Long Island	Mayaguana Acklins Island
4. Isabela (Saometo)	Long Island (Southern)	Hurricane Flats	Crooked Island	Crooked Island	Fortune Island	Great Inagua
5. Islas Arenas or Cuban Coast	Ragged Islands	Fragoso Cay	Ragged Islands	Ragged Islands	Ragged Islands	Ragged Islands

SOURCE: Joseph M. Laufer, *Discovery 500*, Spring, 1990.

voyage, in the eighteenth century scholars became interested as they began to study the history and character of the area. The first to comment on the location of the landfall was Mark Catesby, in the first volume of his *Natural History of Carolina* (1731), in which he identified Cat Island ("formerly called Salvador, or Guanahani") in the northern Bahamas as the landfall site. His choice was given added luster when Washington Irving, in his *Life and Voyages of Christopher Columbus* (1828), supported this designation. In the meantime, however, Juan Bautista Muñoz, commissioned by the Spanish king to write *Historia del Nuevo Mundo* (1793), concluded that the island Columbus named San Salvador was Watlings Island in the central portion of the Bahamas chain. And, in 1825, Martín Fernández de Navarrete, in his five-volume *Colección de los viages y descubrimientos que hicieron por mar los españoles desde fines del siglo XV con varios documentos inéditos* (1825–1837), came to the conclusion that Columbus's landfall must have been the Grand Turk, the southernmost island of the Bahamas chain, now under

separate political jurisdiction as part of the Turks and Caicos Islands.

Subsequent historians, naval officers, geographers, journalists, and amateurs with a wide variety of professional or nonprofessional skills offered other candidates for the landfall, including Mayaguana, Samana, South Caicos, Concepción (Conception Island), Eleuthera, Lignum Vitae Cay (Great Harbour Cay in the Berry Islands), Egg and Royal islands, and Plana Cays, or reiterated the choice of Cat, Watlings, or Grand Turk. On the four-hundredth anniversary of the discovery of America, the World's Columbian Exposition sent a special commissioner, Frederick A. Ober, to the Bahamas to determine the site of the first landfall. Ober published his report, *In the Wake of Columbus* (1893), noting that "no two investigators agree as to the first landfall without disagreeing as to the second; and if they happen to coincide on the first, it is only to fall out over the fourth." Ober concluded, however, that the weight of opinion favored Watlings Island.

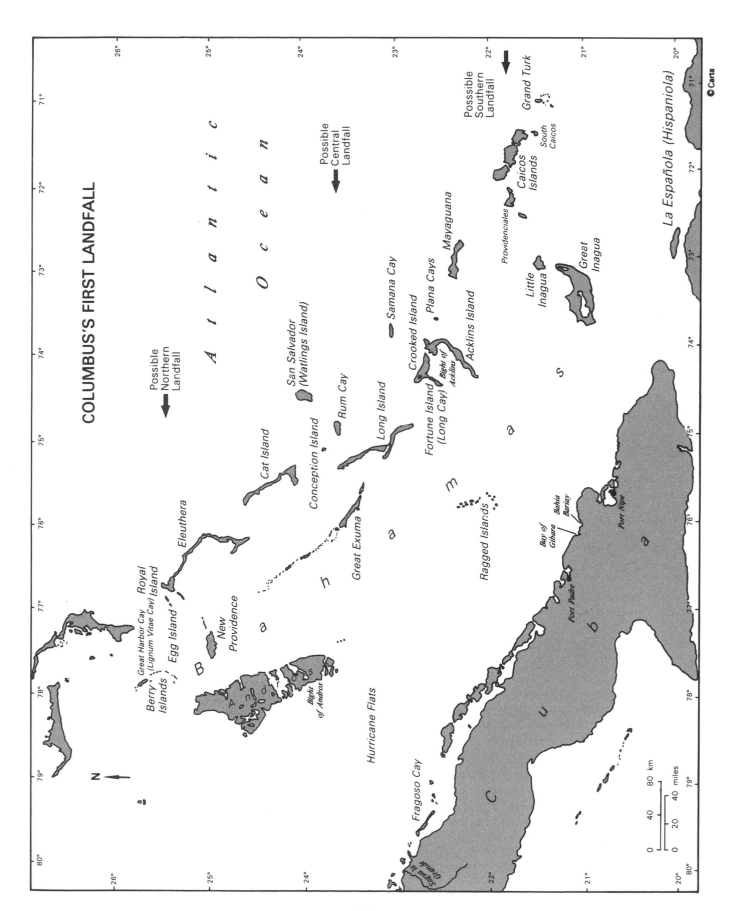

COLUMBUS'S FIRST LANDFALL

Possible Northern Landfall

Possible Central Landfall

Posssible Southern Landfall

Atlantic

O c e a n

San Salvador
(Watlings Island)

Rum Cay

Conception Island

Cat Island

Eleuthera

Royal
(Lignum Vitae Cay) Island

Great Harbor Cay

Egg Island

Berry
Islands

New
Providence

B

A n d r o s

Bight of Andros

Hurricane Flats

Great Exuma

Long Island

Samana Cay

Crooked Island

Fortune Island
(Long Cay)

Bight of
Acklins

Plana Cays

Acklins Island

Mayaguana

Caicos
Islands

South
Caicos

Providenciales

Grand Turk

Little
Inagua

Great
Inagua

Ragged Islands

Fragoso Cay

Bay of
Gibara

Bahia
Bariay

Port Padre

Port Nipe

La Española (Hispaniola)

Sagua la Grande

C   u   b   a

N

80 km

40 miles

40

20

0

© Carta

403

The Twentieth-Century Debate

The debate over the Columbus landfall intensified as the five-hundredth anniversary of the landing approached and popular interest in the question mounted. The intensity of the debate rose to a particular peak with the publication in 1986 in *National Geographic* of the results of an extensive examination of the question by Joseph Judge, the senior associate editor of the magazine. Judge's candidate for the landfall was Samana Cay, a judgment that was supported by a high-tech attempt to duplicate the voyage across the Atlantic and the subsequent route to Cuba, by an attempt to match Columbus's description of the landfall island with Samana, and by a quick archaeological investigation on the now uninhabited island itself.

Too often the protagonists in the landfall debate, who met in conferences and debates in the late 1980s and early 1990s, tended to dismiss the claims of their opponents with ill-concealed contempt, turning what might have been well-mannered scholarly debate into a series of undignified squabbles. The participants occasionally approached the question in the spirit of religion, relying on faith and inferences, rather than in the spirit of scientific caution.

Columbus's Journal. Few of the modern participants in the landfall debate have recognized the wisdom of Justin Winsor, editor of the eight-volume *Narrative and Critical History of America* (1884–1889), who wrote that "the main, or rather the only source for the decision of this question is the Journal of Columbus; and it is to be regretted that Las Casas did not leave unabridged the parts preceding the landfall, as he did those immediately following, down to October 29. Not a word outside of this Journal is helpful."

All arguments on the question of the landfall, as Winsor pointed out, ultimately depend upon the journal of Columbus, the original of which was presented to Queen Isabel, who had scribes make a copy for Columbus. Both are lost. The friar and historian Bartolomé de las Casas made an abstract of Columbus's journal from the returned copy (sometimes quoting, as Winsor noted, Columbus's exact words) for use in his *Historia de las Indias*. Fernando Colón, the Admiral's son, seems also to have had access to this copy (or possibly to another) of the original log and made use of it in preparing his book on the life of his father, which has come down to us in the form of his 1571 *Historie del S. D. Fernando Colombo*. Whether Las Casas worked from the first copy or even a copy of the copy, the possibility of transcription errors makes all estimates of Columbus's course and distances covered problematic. In the Las Casas transcription of Columbus's journal, numerous words and numbers have been crossed out and corrected; moreover, Las Casas himself noted the difficulty of determining the original meaning of some of the passages of the journal. No one can know how many words of the original log (or of the second copy) were wrongly transcribed and left uncorrected.

Las Casas has been accused not only of distortions, conscious or unconscious, in his rendition of the Columbus log but even of falsifying its contents to support his own views. Most such attacks on his honesty, however, are now discounted and his commitment to recording Columbus's journal with accuracy and goodwill conceded.

Samuel Eliot Morison. The debates of the 1980s and 1990s, starting with papers presented at the 1981 meeting of the Society for the History of Discoveries, took as the accepted wisdom (or principal target) the conclusion of the American scholar Samuel Eliot Morison. He had concluded in 1942, in his *Admiral of the Ocean Sea*, a Pulitzer Prize–winning biography of Columbus, that "there is no longer any doubt that the island called Guanahani, which Columbus renamed after Our Lord and Saviour, was the present San Salvador or Watlings." Morison went on to assert that "that alone of any island in the Bahamas, Turks or Caicos groups, fits Columbus's description. The position of San Salvador and of no other island fits the course laid down in his Journal, if we work it backward from Cuba."

The assumed landing in Cuba was, in Morison's opinion, Bahia Bariay, a wide harbor backed by several mountain peaks, one of which Columbus described as having on its summit "another little peak like a pretty little mosque," which later Spanish settlers named "La Teta de Bariay." Virtually all the theorists of the landfall island concede Bahia Bariay to be Columbus's Cuban terminus. One theorist, however, John Hathaway Winslow, has postulated a landing point in Cuba west of Bahia Bariay, at the river Sagua la Grande, which he feels is a better match than Bahia Bariay with Columbus's log and which supports his own candidate for the landfall island, Lignum Vitae (Great Harbour Cay) in the Berry Islands, the farthest north and west of the proposed landfall islands.

Despite the assurance with which Morison stated his conclusion, his argument depended (as he himself noted) on drawing a number of conclusions from frequently contradictory or at least confusing evidence. Nowhere is this more evident than in Morison's adjustment of Las Casas's report of Columbus's calculation of distances sailed between the landfall island and Cuba. Morison postulates that Columbus used a smaller "league" to describe along-shore distances in comparison with over-water distances, a hypothesis that seems to be derived more from the need to make the distances reported in the log conform to the postulated route than from any logical theory. The alternate league (a league of about 1.5 nautical miles instead of 3.18 nautical miles) is proposed first to explain why Columbus described the second island, Rum Cay, a small island with a five-mile north-south coast and a ten-mile east-west coast, as ten leagues long and five leagues wide. The choice of Rum Cay for the second island forces Morison to make another significant assumption. That is that Rum Cay could be initially perceived as a string of six islands that upon closer observation turns out to be a single island with six hillocks. The difficulty in Morison's reasoning to explain the lack of a proper fit between the Columbus log and the course reported between the first and second islands is matched by all the other proposed landfall theorists, though the major difficulty for each appears at different stages in the course between the landfall and the arrival in Cuba.

Mauricio Obregon, a participant in some of the landfall debates and an accomplished pilot and yachtsman, had flown over and sailed through the islands with Morison and others. Obregon defended Morison's judgment concerning the Watlings Island landfall, though he made some modifications in the subsequent route laid down by Morison.

The fatal weakness of all landfall theories, it is important to remember, rests on the absence of the original log. All the theories necessitate arbitrary assumptions about the direction of Columbus's movement, the distances sailed, and the length of the league or mile he used. Since the Spanish words for *east* and *west* are susceptible to mistranscription, since it is not always clear whether Columbus was referring to a mile or the much longer league, and since distances, particularly when recorded in roman numerals, can be easily confused, it is little wonder that all participants in the landfall debate require the reader's indulgence to explain some gap in the route and accept a reality on sea or land that cannot be derived from the text of Columbus's journal. None of the participants in the debate lacks ingenuity, however, in explaining why the anomalies in his route should be accepted while those of his opponents should not.

Physical Descriptions. The evidence least capable of distortion in transmission is the physical description of the island in the log. In what Las Casas recorded as the actual words (*palabras formales*) of the Admiral, Columbus described the first island as quite large (*bien grande*), level, without mountains, and with a large lake or lagoon in the middle (*una laguna en medio*) and *muchas aguas* (which might mean bodies of water or possibly sources of drinking water). Columbus also described the island as having at least one coast running north-northeast, a harbor that would hold all the ships in Christendom, reefs surrounding much of the island, and a peninsula that could be cut through to make a site for a fortress. In addition, it was green with many trees and heavily populated. This physical description, in words that are Columbus's own, is less capable of mistranscription than the directions and distances of his prior and subsequent sailing. More difficult to deduce from the journal than the physical description of the island is its exact size. The size can be estimated by calculating the time Columbus may have taken in surveying the island by longboat, though it is unclear from the account in his log exactly what route was followed, whether the longboat could have been assisted by sails, and whether it returned to the precise spot from which it departed.

Assuming that the physical description of the island in Las Casas's transcription of the log is the most reliable of all the evidence of the landfall, the two suggested islands that most closely fit the description are Watlings and Grand Turk. The absence of any archaeological evidence of native habitation on Grand Turk was, until the discovery by William Keegan in December 1989 of a Lucayan site on the southern end of the island, a near-fatal flaw in the Grand Turk candidacy. With that discovery, the island's claim was enhanced. More difficult to reconcile with the physical description of the island in Columbus's log is Samana Cay, the candidate of Capt. Gustavus Vasa Fox of the U.S. Navy in 1882 and, more than a hundred years later, of Joseph Judge of *National Geographic*. Judge has argued long and forcefully that there are "many waters" and a lake or lagoon in the middle of "his" island and has found other parallels to the description of the island and the course to and from it in the Columbus log. But, despite the prestige of the National Geographic Society sponsorship, few scholars have been converted to the Samana Cay solution. Judge bitterly attacked Mauricio Obregon for his presumed role in encouraging the 5th Ibero-American Quincentenary Conference, meeting in Puerto Rico in May 1987, to declare that San Salvador/Watlings Island would be considered the landfall of Columbus for purposes of the celebration of the Quincentenary, even though the declaration did not imply that the issue was definitely settled.

Cartographic Evidence. It might be assumed that the geographical location of the landfall island could be most easily determined from the cartographic evidence. But the maps on which the landfall island and surrounding islands are recorded form an unreliable guide. In part this was because, as the *Atlas Maritimus and Commercialis*, published in London in 1728, put it, "there is not any of these Islands worth naming, any more than they have been worth possessing: And Columbus, first Discoverer, soon found Places of more Importance to him." Guanahani, as the island was called by the inhabitants who greeted Columbus, appears on many of the maps that were drawn in the several centuries following the discovery, but as one student of the cartographic evidence has said, "this island, at least at first glance, appears to float about the central Bahamas." The earliest map on which Guanahani is found is the world map of Juan de la Cosa, of about 1500, which also records an island named Samana to the south. Unfortunately, on the Cosa map and later ones, both islands lack a precise outline and a consistent location. Alonso Cháves's *Espejo de navegantes,* the earliest set of sailing directions for the Bahamas (c. 1530), describes Samana as east-southeast of Guanahani at a distance of eight leagues, both islands being at twenty-five degrees north latitude.

Although identification must be speculative, Kim Dian Gainer believes that the Samana island on Juan de la Cosa's map represents Rum Cay, and "therefore the first cartographic evidence we have is consistent with a landfall on Watling rather than Samana Cay." "One thing is certain," Gainer adds: "this Samana is not today's Samana Cay." After an exhaustive study of all the relevant maps, Gainer concluded that the preponderance of evidence for the location and relationship of the various islands of the Bahamas on early maps "appears to favor a Watling landfall rather than one on Samana Cay. . . . The only maps that do not seem to favor a Watling landfall are those that fall outside the Spanish tradition." Nevertheless, the cartographic evidence is sufficiently uncertain that other candidates for the landfall should not be ruled out on that evidence alone.

The Latitude Question. The latitude of the landfall island has also been a persistent subject of debate. Columbus asserted in his journal entry for October 13 that he was not surprised by the color of the natives of San Salvador because their complexion resembled that of the natives of the Canary Islands and were located on an east-west line directly west of Hierro (Ferro) in the Canaries. San Salvador is at twenty-four degrees, six minutes; Ferro, twenty-seven degrees, forty-six minutes. Was Columbus navigating by latitude sailing rather than dead reckoning? The former method, by which the navigator maintains a constant elevation angle to the solar and stellar meridians, is far more accurate than sailing by dead reckoning, which relies on compass headings and estimates of the ship's speed, both subject to great errors. Samuel Eliot Morison argued that Columbus used dead reckoning as his navigational method, but this is not inconsistent with trying to "run down" a latitude that would carry him from the Canaries directly to Cipangu and which could be done by taking nightly observations of Polaris—the North Star—as well as by dead reckoning. It is clear that Columbus did not attempt to plot his course by celestial navigation, though he admired those men of learning, like the astronomer Josephus Vizinho, adviser to the Portuguese king João II, who were experts in such matters. It is also clear that he was wildly off in many of his estimates of his

latitude in the New World. But so were most navigators of his time.

In fact, the latitude of Hierro is several degrees north of the latitude of San Salvador and even farther north of Samana and Grand Turk. Arne B. Molander, one of the participants in the landfall debate, uses Columbus's attempted latitude sailing and his belief that he was at twenty-eight degrees north latitude to support his candidate for the landfall: Egg and Royal islands off the northern end of Eleuthera in the northern Bahamas. On the other hand, Robert Power and Josiah Marvel, proponents of the southern landfall at Grand Turk, cite the fact that Grand Turk and Hierro on the Juan de la Cosa map and other early maps are on the same latitude to support their conclusion, on the theory that Columbus, as will be noted below, was deceived by the magnetic variation of the compass in the Western Hemisphere into thinking he was sailing due west when in fact he was being diverted toward the south.

National Geographic sought to trace Columbus's route from the Canary Islands utilizing computers to calculate the effect of ocean currents or leeway (the sideways slip of a sailing vessel owing to the force of the wind). The expedition, under the direction of Luis Marden, sought to check the accuracy of the 1941 attempt of Lt. John W. McElroy, USNR, Morison's collaborator, to follow Columbus's log day by day. McElroy made no allowance for leeway or ocean currents on the assumption that they were negligible or canceled out, and his route ended near Watlings Island. Marden's ended near Samana Cay. Marden's work was challenged by Philip L. Richardson and Roger A. Goldsmith of the Woods Hole Oceanographic Institution, using historical wind and current data assembled as part of their ongoing investigations into the currents and circulation of the world's oceans. Applying this data to the track of *Santa María,* and correcting flaws in the Marden study, Richardson and Goldsmith brought Columbus's ships to within twenty-five kilometers of Watlings Island.

Despite the learned debate about current, leeway, the length of a league, and the magnetic variation of the compass (all continuing matters of debate over Columbus's route), the attempt to replicate the course of a voyage across three thousand miles of ocean to the exact site of a tiny landfall island is fraught with difficulties. It is little wonder that doubts about the exact course of Columbus's route across the ocean continue to puzzle students of the voyage.

Proponents of the Grand Turk landfall, several degrees of latitude farther to the south, face an even greater difficulty in explaining why Columbus landed so much farther south of the latitude he assumed he was following. The explanation given by advocates of Grand Turk is framed in terms of Columbus's misunderstanding of the effects of magnetic declination of the compass as his ships sailed across the Atlantic. Marvel and Power assert that if Columbus's compass was, as was customary, calibrated for local magnetic variation at its place of manufacture, presumably Seville, at 5⅝ degrees east, then the contrary westerly magnetic variation in the western Atlantic would cause a vessel "sailing across the Ocean by dead reckoning to veer imperceptibly to the south." They are encouraged by the fact that Richardson and Goldsmith concede that with a different assumption of the extent of westerly magnetic variation as it may have existed in 1492—a matter about which no one can speak with certainty—Grand Turk becomes "a reasonable candidate" for the landfall.

The presumption of the magnetic variation theory is that while assuming he was sailing due west, Columbus would increasingly be headed farther south than he realized. "A northward displacement of the lands of the New World near the Tropic of Cancer of at least six degrees," Marvel notes, "is consistently found on Discovery Period charts." The inference is drawn by supporters of the southern route that navigators, including Columbus, were unable to recognize the true direction they were following because of the magnetic shift in the compass as the ships moved across the Atlantic. This assumption, however, can be questioned for a number of reasons, not the least of which is that Columbus was the first to notice (on September 13, 1492) the shift from easterly to westerly variation in the compass. He observed and commented on the shift in the course of his first three voyages. Although he was not, as his son Fernando claimed, the discoverer of westerly variation, Columbus recognized the diurnal rotation of Polaris and the necessity to make the appropriate adjustments in determining one's latitude. On his third voyage, on the night of August 15–16, 1498, when sailing from Margarita Island to La Española, he noticed that the compass needles were suddenly showing a westerly variation of about seventeen degrees. As Morison noted, "If he had not discovered this variation, and altered his course accordingly, he would have missed Hispaniola [La Española]." Although Columbus often misjudged his latitude, such inaccuracies, whether caused by irregularities in Columbus's compass needle or other factors, seem unlikely to be determinative of the true landfall site.

Archaeological Evidence. Archaeological excavations undertaken in the Bahamas in recent years give us evidence that may confirm some of the observations found in Columbus's log. Charles A. Hoffman has found Spanish objects in an otherwise undisturbed pre-contact site on Watlings Island. William F. Keegan has located the densest concentration of Lucayan habitations in the Bahamas (including a settlement stretching along the shore for more than three miles) in the Acklins Island area, bordering on the shallow lagoon made up of Fortune, Crooked, and Acklins islands. In addition he unearthed a leg bone of a crocodile (hitherto unknown in the Bahamas) on a site near the northwestern cape of Crooked Island, which may represent the creature described as a "serpent" that Columbus and his men killed after it slithered into a shallow pond where Columbus was collecting fresh water for his ships. The archaeological evidence, which is sparse on Samana and Grand Turk, tends to support those who point to Watlings as the landfall island.

Northern or Southern Bahamas? A significant weakness of the southern landfall theory is the fact that Columbus records that he understood from the Indians on San Salvador that if he went to the south, or around the island to the south, he would find a king who had much gold, including "large vessels of it." Columbus, in his log, recorded his intention to go to the southwest in search of gold and precious stones, a direction he presumably followed although he did not specifically record his course when he left San Salvador. It is the horseshoe-shaped group of islands made up of Fortune, Crooked, and Acklins, surrounding a shallow lagoon, that Keegan concludes is the best match for the fourth island, named by Columbus "Isabella," an island identified by the Indians Columbus took with him from San Salvador as "Samonet, where the gold is." Columbus was unable to reach the king of the island because of the shallowness of the bay or bight that lay between his ships and the reported site of the king's village. Because he was eager to continue his voyage of exploration, and because he was somewhat doubtful about the reports he had received from the Indians "from not understanding them well and also from recognizing that they are so poor in gold that any little bit that the king may wear seems so much to them," Columbus decided to push on. If Columbus's communication with the Indians of San Salvador was free of error, in both its initial transmission and its notation in the log used by Las Casas, and if it referred to a king in the islands of the Bahamas rather than on the larger island of Cuba farther south, and if Columbus sailed in the direction he said he intended to, then the landfall island would more likely be in the northern rather than the southern portion of the Bahamas. But, like much of the evidence set forth in the landfall debate, such facts and inferences are always subject to error or misinterpretation.

Two participants in the landfall debate, Christopher C. Larimore and John Hathaway Winslow, have argued that Columbus would have been able to sail through, in the one case the Bight of Acklins, and in the other the Bight of Andros, because of changes in the sea depths in those areas since 1492. But such changes seem doubtful in the light of the work of Keegan and the geologist Neil Sealey.

The Historical Perspective. It would be futile to recount all the arguments and reasoning behind each of the candidates for the landfall. All are ingenious, but they all depend upon a fragile superstructure of evidence. From the historian's point of view, the question of which island was Columbus's landfall is of minor interest. Just as Columbus soon left the island behind in his memory, so the historian is more concerned about what followed than with the famous first sighting and landing in the New World. For the historian, these moments comprise less a series of firsts or events than a complex process of the movement of Europeans into a world inhabited by people of whom they had no knowledge.

The fact and location of the landfall is an important historical datum and a subject worthy of careful scrutiny, but it is more interesting to the public than to the historian. Part of this interest is commercial. The public is fascinated by the historical past and willing to pay much to "see" it. The island on which Columbus landed is expected to be heavily visited well beyond the quincentennial year. Hotels and resorts will be built in proximity to the presumed site of the landing. The government of the Bahamas is well aware of the attraction of San Salvador to a world of tourists to whom "The Past is a Foreign Country," to quote the title of David Lowenthal's book on the subject of our pervasive and nostalgic attempt to recapture the past. For the same reason, the government of the Turks and Caicos Islands is also aware of the advantage of having the Grand Turk designated the landfall island of Columbus. Indeed, all the islands that have a claim to be the site where Columbus first set foot in the New World stand to benefit monetarily from the public's fascination with historical firsts. From a scholarly as well as a touristic point of view the question of the landfall of Columbus might more profitably remain open rather than closed.

[See also *Compass*, article on *Declination of the Compass*; *Navigation*; *Tides and Currents*.]

BIBLIOGRAPHY

De Vorsey, Louis, Jr., and John Parker. *In the Wake of Columbus: Islands and Controversy*. Detroit, 1985.

Discovery Five Hundred (Newsletter of the International Columbian Quincentenary Alliance) 5, no. 2 (Spring 1990). Special issue: Columbus Landfall.

Gainer, Kim Dian. "The Cartographic Evidence for Columbus Landfall." *Terrae Incognitae* 20 (1988): 43–68.

Jane, Cecil, trans. *The Journal of Christopher Columbus*. With an appendix by R. A. Skelton on "The Cartography of Columbus's First Voyage." New York, 1960.

Judge, Joseph. "Our Search for the True Columbus Landfall." *National Geographic* 170, no. 5 (1986): 564–605.

Keegan, William F. "The Columbus Chronicles." *The Sciences* (New York Academy of Sciences) (January–February 1989): 46–55.

Keen, Benjamin, trans. and ed. *The Life of the Admiral Christopher Columbus by His Son Ferdinand*. New Brunswick, N.J., 1959.

Marvel, Josiah. "On the First Landfall of Christopher Columbus in the New World: Textual and Cartographic Evidence Supporting the Hypothesis That It Took Place on Grand Turk Island." Typescript. 1990.

Morison, Samuel Eliot. *Admiral of the Ocean Sea: A Life of Christopher Columbus*. Boston, 1942.

Morison, Samuel Eliot. "Columbus and Polaris." *American Neptune* 1, no. 1 (1941): 6–25; 1, no. 2 (1941): 123–137.

Morison, Samuel Eliot, and Mauricio Obregon. *The Caribbean as Columbus Saw It*. Boston, 1964.

Ober, Frederick A. *In the Wake of Columbus*. Boston, 1893.

Peck, Douglas T. "Reconstruction and Analysis of the 1492 Columbus Log from a Sailor-Navigator Viewpoint," Rev. ed. Multilith. 1988.

Richardson, Philip L., and Roger A. Goldsmith. "The Columbus Landfall: Voyage Track Corrected for Winds and Currents." *Oceanus* 30 (1987): 2–10.

Sealey, Neil E. "An Examination of the Geography of Three Major Contenders for Columbus's First Landfall in 1492." Mimeograph. 1990.

Winsor, Justin. "Columbus and His Discoveries." In vol. 2 of *Narrative and Critical History of America*. 8 vols. Boston, 1884–1889.

WILCOMB E. WASHBURN

LAS CASAS, BARTOLOMÉ DE (1484–1566), Spanish defender of the Indians, theologian, and historian. The son of a merchant, Las Casas was born and raised in Seville, then a great Spanish commercial and cultural center. He was eight when Columbus returned from his first voyage, and in his *Historia de las Indias* (History of the Indies), recalled how he and his father watched a solemn procession led by Columbus and his crew, followed by the first Indians to set foot in the Old World, as it passed through the streets of Seville on Palm Sunday, 1493. His father, Pedro de las Casas, and three uncles accompanied Columbus on his second voyage of 1493 that brought some two thousand colonists to La Española (Hispaniola). In 1502, Bartolomé, aged eighteen, himself went over to manage the land and Indians that Columbus had granted his father. Although troubled by the disastrous situation of the Taino Indians, whose numbers were rapidly dwindling as a result of the ruthless exploitation and slavehunting expeditions initiated by Columbus, the young Las Casas was concerned above all with bettering his fortunes and even appears to have taken part in a military campaign organized by Governor Nicolás de Ovando against the Indians in the eastern part of the island.

BARTOLOMÉ DE LAS CASAS. Engraving from *Retratos de los Españoles illustratres con un epitome de sus vidos*, 1791.

In 1506 Las Casas returned to Europe where he remained for several years. His close, friendly ties with the Columbus family are suggested by the fact that in 1506 he accompanied the Admiral's older brother, Bartolomé Colón, to Rome to inform Pope Julius II of the opportunities for the spread of the faith created by the discovery of the New World. In Rome, too, in 1507, Las Casas was ordained to the priesthood (he had already taken the tonsure, probably in 1501). Meanwhile Columbus had died, and in 1507 Las Casas returned to La Española with Columbus's son and heir, Diego Colón, second Admiral and Viceroy of the Indies. Las Casas undoubtedly hoped that the condition of the Indians would improve under Diego's milder rule, but the viceroy, hampered by his disputes with the Crown over the extent of his rights and with royal officials on the island, proved unable to achieve reform.

Favored, like his father, by the Columbus family, Las Casas received a good piece of land and a grant of Indians from Diego and combined the profitable activities of agriculture, stockraising, mining, and trade with the office of *doctrinero*, a parish priest who provided religious instruction to the Indians. In 1510 a group of Dominican friars arrived in the island. Horrified by the barbarous treatment of the Indians, they delegated one of their number, Antonio Montesino, to preach a sermon that would drive home to the settlers the wickedness of their deeds. The angry colonists responded by calling on the friars to retract their sentiments or pack up and sail for home. In reply, Montesino mounted the pulpit the following Sunday and let loose an even more terrific blast against mistreatment of the Indians. Although Las Casas sympathized with the Dominicans, he did not agree with their denunciation as mortal sin of the encomienda system of forced Indian labor. He was still a priest-colonist, a man of good will who treated his own Indians kindly but was interested above all in promoting his *granjerías*, or enterprises. In 1513–1514 he served as military chaplain in the conquest of Cuba—a conquest whose atrocities he vainly tried to prevent—and was again rewarded for his services with a large grant of Indians. His Cuban agricultural and stockraising enterprises prospered, and he coldly rebuffed a Dominican friar who reproached him for neglecting the religious instruction of the natives.

In 1514, however, he experienced a conversion, apparently the awakening of a dormant sensitivity as a result of the horrors he had seen about him. He renounced his own encomienda of Indians and, in 1515, accompanied by Antonio Montesino, set sail from Santo Domingo, determined to inform King Fernando and his ministers that the encomienda system was destroying the Indians and must be abolished.

Las Casas arrived in Spain at a propitious time, for in late 1516 Fernando, who had been indifferent or hostile to reform, died and was succeeded as regent by the aged Cardinal Francisco Jiménez de Cisneros. Las Casas presented the cardinal with a plan, supported by Diego Colón, for the removal of the Indians from individual encomiendas and their resettlement in self-sustaining villages with Spanish administrators. These villages would pay tribute to the Crown and contribute a limited number of workers for mining, and the encomenderos would be compensated for their loss of workers. Las Casas envisaged a parallel colonization by Spanish peasants who would live and work side by side with the Indians, teach them to live in a civilized way, and gradually bring into being an ideal Christian community. Cisneros authorized the experiment, but assigned its supervision to a group of Jeronymite friars (known for their successful management of large estates), with Las Casas to accompany them as "Protector of the Indians." The Jeronymites, lukewarm toward the project from the first and swayed by the hostile attitude of the settlers, soon gave as their opinion that the

Indians were unfit to live by themselves in a civilized way; they also complained of Las Casas's interference with the new trade in Bahaman slaves.

Fleeing La Española to escape arrest for disobeying the Jeronymites, Las Casas returned to Spain and resumed his struggle in defense of the Indians. Cisneros died in 1517, and the arrival in Spain of the young King Carlos I (the future Emperor Charles V), surrounded by Flemish courtiers who took a broader view of the royal interest in the Indies than the late King Fernando or his ministers, favored Las Casas's reformist projects. He won approval for a new scheme that combined a program of peasant colonization of Tierra Firme (Venezuela) and of Indian conversion with exploitation of the pearl and gold resources of the region by a company based in Santo Domingo. But the project ended in a complete fiasco, for the peasants recruited by Las Casas abandoned him on reaching the islands to join in the profitable slave trade, and his mission outpost of Cumaná was destroyed by Indians provoked by slavehunting raids organized by the very same Caribbean interests on whose support Las Casas had naively counted.

The disastrous failure of the Venezuelan colonization project produced what the French scholar Marcel Bataillon called Las Casas's "second conversion." Las Casas himself tells that after the fiasco of Cumaná in 1521 he felt he was dead and buried—perhaps meaning that he was buried in the Dominican convent in Santo Domingo, which he entered in 1522, and became dead to the world that he had known. The Las Casas who "died" in 1521 was the priest-reformer who proposed to reconcile Spanish private interests and Indian welfare and himself did not scruple to share in the profits of colonial enterprise; the Dominican friar who emerged from the convent in 1531 after almost ten years of immersion in juridical-theological study advanced a revolutionary creed based on solid doctrinal foundations. Henceforth Las Casas's ideology centered on the right of the Indians to their land, on the principle of self-determination, and on the subordination of all Spanish interests (including those of the Crown) to Indian interests, material and spiritual. Las Casas argued that the papal grant of America to the Crown of Castile had been made solely for the purpose of conversion and gave the Spanish Crown no temporal power or possession in the Indies. The Indians had rightful possession of their lands by natural law and the law of nations. All Spanish wars and conquests in the New World were illegal. Spain must bring Christianity to the Indians by the only method "that is proper and natural to men . . . namely, love and gentleness and kindness."

With the passage of time, Las Casas's thought became progressively more radical. His final program called for the suppression of all encomiendas, liberation of the Indians from all forms of servitude except a small voluntary tribute to the Crown in recompense for its gift of Christianity, and the restoration of the ancient Indian states and rulers, the rightful owners of those lands. Over these states the Spanish king would preside as "Emperor over many kings" in order to fulfill his sacred mission of bringing the Indians to the Catholic faith and the Christian way of life. The instruments of that mission should be friars, who would enjoy special jurisdiction over the Indians and protect them from the corrupting influence of lay Spaniards. These elements of Las Casas's final program may be called truly utopian and were never taken seriously by the Crown. But the main thrust of his program after his "second conversion"—the demand that the encomienda be abolished and the colonists be denied control over Indian tribute and labor—fully coincided with the royal interest in curbing the power of the conquistadores and preventing the rise of a powerful colonial feudalism in the New World. This coincidence explains the official support that Las Casas's reform efforts received in the reign of Carlos I (Charles V of the Holy Roman Empire), 1516–1556.

The common view of Las Casas as waging a lonely struggle to convince a reluctant Crown to accept colonial reform could not be more mistaken. The most elementary interests of the Crown demanded that the catastrophe of the West Indies, where the Indians had become an extinct race, should not be repeated in the newly conquered rich and populous empires of Mexico and Peru. But the Crown had to move cautiously, for it feared a revolt by the aggressive conquistadores. As early as 1523, when Las Casas was still secluded in his monastery, King Carlos sent Hernando Cortés an order forbidding the establishment of encomiendas in New Spain (the former Aztec Empire), because "God had created the Indians free and not subject." But in the face of Cortés's disobedience, backed by his hard-bitten followers, the Crown chose to retreat.

Far from waging a lonely struggle in defense of the Indians, then, Las Casas enjoyed the support of powerful political and social forces including the Crown, royal officials, and important members of the clergy, all of whom had an obvious interest in the preservation of the Indian population. Even the Cortes (parliament) of Castile intervened in the Indian question; summoned by Charles V in 1541, it asked that the abuses committed by the Spaniards in the Indies be ended lest the native population disappear.

Las Casas owed his leadership of this broadly based struggle in defense of the Indians to his militant, combative spirit; his mastery of scholastic philosophy and Church doctrine, which he displayed with telling effect in his famous debate in 1551–1552 with the humanist Juan Gimés de Sepúlveda over the justice of wars against the

Indians; his gifts as a propagandist, illustrated by the simple yet profoundly moving style of his *Brevíssima relación de la destruición de las Indias* (Very brief account of the destruction of the Indies); and his great political talent, his ability to negotiate, maneuver, and even compromise without sacrificing essential principles.

Las Casas and his followers won a major victory with the issuance of the New Laws of the Indies (1542). These laws appeared to doom the encomienda. They forbade the enslavement of Indians, ordered the release of slaves to whom legal title could not be proved, barred compulsory personal service by the Indians, and proclaimed that existing encomiendas were to lapse on the death of the holder. Las Casas himself, named Bishop of Chiapas, then a province of Guatemala, went out in 1545 to ensure compliance with the New Laws in a region that was a hotbed of slavehunting and other abuses against the natives. Received with hostility by the settlers who rejected his authority and even threatened him with death, and denied support by the audiencia (high court) for the region, Las Casas had to return to Spain. Meanwhile, faced with a storm of protest by the colonists throughout the Indies and a great revolt in Peru, the Crown had yielded to pressure and agreed to a compromise that recognized the right of inheritance by the heir of an encomendero; this right was gradually extended for a number of generations.

Under pressure, Charles V had made a partial retreat from his own pro-Indian policy; his son, Philip II, in effect abandoned that policy on his accession to the throne in 1556. Faced with a desperate financial crisis, Philip increased the burden on Indians paying tribute to the Crown and moved toward a rapprochement with the colonial oligarchies, allowing them greater control over the Indians on their estates and encomiendas. Simultaneously the influence of Las Casas and his Indianist movement virtually disappeared from the Spanish court. What Marcel Bataillon calls "the anti-Lascasian reaction" of Philip's reign was reflected, among other ways, in decrees forbidding colonial clergy to use the spiritual arms of the church: excommunication, interdict, and denial of absolution—weapons that Las Casas and his followers had systematically employed to secure compliance with Indian protective legislation. Despite the collapse of his Indian policy, Las Casas continued to the end of his life his struggle for justice for the Indians. One of his last actions was to send a letter to Pope Pius V asking the pontiff to order, on pain of excommunication, an end to the unjust wars against the Indians and the violent expropriation of their lands on the pretext of their conversion. The depth of Las Casas's disillusionment with Spain's Indian policy is suggested by his testament, notarized on March 5, 1564, in which he affirmed that on

account of the "great sins and injustices" committed by the Spaniards in the Indies, and "the robberies and murders and usurpations of the states and lordships of the natural kings and lords," God must vent upon Spain "His force and wrath."

An integral part of Las Casas's campaign in defense of the Indians was his authorship of a large body of works that made important contributions to anthropology, political theory, and history. In his debate with Sepúlveda, a spokesman for the encomenderos who invoked Aristotle to prove that the Indians were slaves by nature and that their conquest was a just war, Las Casas eloquently affirmed the equality of all races and the essential unity of mankind. He elaborated these arguments in his great *Apologética historia sumaria* (Apologetical history), not published until 1909, an immense accumulation of ethnographic data used to demonstrate that the Indians met all the requirements laid down by Aristotle for the good life. In this work he also developed a rudimentary theory of cultural evolution, applied to all Indian societies, that enabled him to examine the customs and beliefs of an Indian people dispassionately and within the framework of its own culture. This relativist approach even led him to develop the daring argument that Indian human sacrifice was not proof of depravity but evidence of a profound religious feeling. The theory also suggested comparison of Indian cultures with civilizations of other times and places that appeared to represent about the same state of development. Las Casas may justly be called the father of anthropology.

In his tract *De regia potestate* (Concerning the royal power), written in opposition to the encomenderos' proposal for a grant of the perpetual encomienda, which would convert their Indian tributaries into hereditary serfs, Las Casas advanced what his modern Spanish editors call three "democratic dogmas." First, all power derives from the people; second, power is delegated to rulers in order that they may serve the people; third, all important governmental acts require popular consultation and approval. These democratic ideas had medieval antecedents, but in their new context, challenging the right of the king to dispose of his Indian subjects, those old ideas acquired a subversive, revolutionary tinge.

For students of Columbus and his voyages, Las Casas's monumental *History of the Indies*, written between 1527 and 1562 but not published until 1875, has a special interest and value, for it is in considerable part a biography of Columbus and incorporates the single best source of information on the Discovery: Las Casas's abstract—part summary and part direct quotations—of Columbus's lost Diario, the journal of his first voyage to America.

Las Casas passionately admires the Admiral, chosen "among all the sons of Adam" for the providential task of opening "the doors of the Ocean Sea." He sees a divine design in the pattern of his life until his arrival in Castile, endows him with great virtues, and bitterly criticizes the injustice and ingratitude with which the Spanish monarchs treated him and his family. But when Las Casas turns to discuss Columbus's arbitrary, exploitive conduct with the Indians, his tone changes. The hero Columbus becomes flawed, and Las Casas charges him with "inexcusable ignorance" of the rights of the Indians. Viewed from this perspective, the sufferings of the Admiral—his imprisonment, the loss of part of his privileges, and other injustices—are explained by Las Casas as divine punishment for Columbus's offenses against the Indians, a punishment meant to purge him of his sins and save him from eternal damnation. Despite this alternation between praise and blame, Las Casas leaves no doubt of his overwhelmingly favorable opinion of Columbus.

In the aftermath of World War II, which led to the collapse of regimes and colonial systems based on racism and the right of the strong to dominate the weak, Las Casas's teachings concerning the unity of mankind, the principle of self-determination, and the right of all people to the satisfaction of their elementary material and cultural needs have acquired a new relevance. The influence of his ideas is particularly evident in the growing acceptance by many clergy, especially in Latin America, of the so-called theology of liberation. This doctrine teaches that the church, returning to its roots, must again become the church of the poor. In Latin America today, the poorest of the poor are precisely the Indians who were the principal objects of Las Casas's care and compassion. The theology of liberation also teaches that the church must cease to be an ally of the rich and powerful and commit itself to the struggle for social justice, to "the preferential option for the poor." Clearly, these doctrines have much in common with Las Casas's own teachings.

[See also Black Legend; Encomienda; Exploitation of Indians; Indian America; Missionary Movement.]

BIBLIOGRAPHY

Friede, Juan, and Benjamin Keen, eds. Bartolomé de las Casas in History: Toward an Understanding of the Man and His Work. De Kalb, Ill., 1971.

Hanke, Lewis. Aristotle and the American Indians. London, 1959.

Hanke, Lewis. The Spanish Struggle for Justice. Philadelphia, 1949.

Wagner, Henry R. The Life and Writings of Bartolomé de las Casas. Albuquerque, 1967.

BENJAMIN KEEN

LAST WILL AND TESTAMENT OF COLUMBUS.
See Writings, article on Last Will and Testament.

LATITUDE.
Terrestrial latitude is the angular distance from the equator measured north or south on an arc of ninety degrees extending from the equator to either one of the poles. The linear distance of a degree of latitude on the earth's surface, its length, will depend, of course, on the figure of the earth adopted. The first known measurement of the circumference of the earth was made by Eratosthenes in the second century B.C., a calculation of extraordinary accuracy if the value of the somewhat flexible Greek stade is taken as 159 meters. Two centuries before, the latitude of Marseilles had been measured by Pytheas to within fifteen minutes of arc of its true value by using the gnomon to measure the sun's noonday shadow at the equinox. The gnomon could also be used to establish the terrestrial meridian, from the bisection of shadows of equal length either side of noon. And once latitude had been established, it could also be used to find the sun's declination. A table could then be drawn for other dates that would enable latitude to be calculated on any day in any locality by measuring the height of the sun at local apparent noon. Historically, then, the measurement of latitude, at least in principle, presented no difficulty.

During the fifteenth and sixteenth centuries latitude at sea was determined by observations of the North Star according to the Regiment (rule) of the North Star, a formula given in early Portuguese and Spanish navigation manuals. The rule gave the correction to the altitude of the North Star for its position in relation to the pole of the sky using the Guard Stars to trace its counterclockwise movement round the axis of the earth's rotation. Alternatively, latitude at sea could be obtained by measuring the meridian altitude of the sun using tables of the sun's declination or by measuring the altitude of any star at its culmination, which could be judged either by the relative positions of other stars or, less satisfactorily, from its compass bearing.

Despite the enormous impact on the scholarly world of the rediscovery of Ptolemy, whose Geography defined positions on the globe by their angular distance north or south of the equator and east and west of a chosen meridian, the fifteenth-century seaman still thought of observations of sun or star altitudes simply in terms of altura (height). Although parallels and meridians were starting to appear on maps, it was not until 1502 that a scale of latitude appeared on a sea chart.

The earliest altitude observations of the sun, as of the North Star, had been made to check the linear distance traveled in a north-south direction between a first observation, at the port of departure (typically Lisbon), and subsequent observations; the difference between readings was multiplied by 16⅔ (later 17½) to give the distance in leagues, corresponding to the accepted length of a degree of the meridian. Once the Portuguese in their explorations had reached the Gulf of Guinea, however, and a major part of the voyage was in an east-west direction, such a procedure became navigationally meaningless. Also, once the equator had been crossed, and the North Star lost, it became essential to develop techniques that would enable the navigator to use the sun to define latitude. This was the task undertaken by the mathematical commission appointed by King João II of Portugal, and the commission's findings were tested by José Vizinho in Guinea in 1485 and encapsulated in the new "Regiment of the Sun." A table of the sun's declination simplified by Vizinho from the tables of the astronomer Abraham Zacuto allowed the navigator to calculate his latitude at local apparent noon anywhere in the world. The procedures laid down in the Regiment of the Sun were far from simple. The sun's maximum altitude would first be observed, generally by the mariner's astrolabe, and the sun's declination for the day extracted from the table. The rules for applying the declination differed according to whether the observer was north or south of the equator (a difficulty in itself in equatorial latitudes), whether the declination was north or south, and whether, when both latitude and declination were either north or south, the declination was greater or less than the latitude.

In integrating the new methods, standard navigational practice now came to include observing the latitude each day, recording the courses made good and the estimated distances sailed, and, from the resulting position (the dead-reckoning position) and the observed latitude, determining the distance traveled east or west. The objective was to sail to a position one hundred leagues east or west of the destination and sail down the latitude to it. When in due course a latitude scale was added to the charts, the procedures laid down in the Regiment of the North Star would be used to derive latitude directly in degrees and fractions (or minutes). Latitude navigation in substantially this form was to endure well beyond the time when longitude observations became possible with the aid of a timekeeper, for the determination of latitude from the sun's meridian altitude is relatively simple, in terms of both observation and calculation.

[See also *Altura Sailing; Circumference; Longitude; Navigation.*]

BIBLIOGRAPHY

Albuquerque, Luís de. *Astronomical Navigation.* Lisbon, 1988.

Cotter, Charles A. *A History of Nautical Astronomy.* London, 1968.

Taylor, E. G. R. *The Haven Finding Art: A History of Navigation from Odysseus to Captain Cook.* London, 1956.

M. W. RICHEY

LAWSUITS (PLEITOS COLOMBINOS).

The Pleitos Colombinos are the texts of litigation between the heirs of Christopher Columbus and the Spanish Crown. The initial litigation stretched from 1508 to 1536 and then was continued by the family to 1790. The various legal suits of the Pleitos are filed in six *legajos* (batches of collected documents) on deposit in the Archivo General de Indias (Seville), dated 1508 to 1536. They concern the interpretation of Christopher Columbus's privileges as the circumstances of discovery and conquest drastically changed a risky venture into an unprecedented enterprise. Currently being published, this litigation will fill eight printed volumes.

The conflict with the Crown arose over the definitions of privileges, governmental and judicial powers, territorial extent, and economic rights and obligations. The privileges and contractual rights of Columbus, amended by confirmations and changes, are the substance of the litigation.

The judgments and compromises of the litigation drew the map of the Spanish enterprise in the Indies. Moreover, one can trace in the Pleitos the participation of bankers, merchants, entrepreneurs, soldiers, settlers, and professionals in the economy. The Pleitos Colombinos also shed light on the way the Spanish legal system functioned.

The inheritance litigation waged over ten generations is a separate series of lawsuits initiated after the extinction of the direct line of Columbus's descendants. It is briefly mentioned at the end of this discussion.

The Substance of the Conflict: The Capitulations of Santa Fe. An original agreement, comprising "capitulations" between the Spanish monarchs, Isabel and Fernando, and Columbus, was signed in two parts at the encampment of the Spanish army before the city of Santa Fe de la Vega de Granada on April 17 and 30, 1492. The opening reads: "The things supplicated and which your Highnesses give and declare to Christopher Columbus in some satisfaction for what he will discover [*ha de descubrir*] in the ocean-seas, and for the voyage which now, with the aid of God, he is about to make therein, are as follows." In the main points of the agreement, Columbus was given the following:

1. The position of viceroy and governor "over all the islands and mainland which by his hand and industry may be discovered or acquired in the said oceans," with the right to propose to the Crown a list of three names for every governmental post from which an appointee was to be selected by the sovereigns.
2. The position of admiral of the said islands and mainland, with the salaries, prerogatives, and privileges enjoyed by the high admiral of Castile, and with the right in person or by his representative to adjudge controversies regarding merchandise and commerce.
3. One-tenth of the net profits of the Crown in all the

articles and merchandise, whether pearls, precious stones, gold, silver, spices, or others, which might be bought, exchanged, found, acquired, or obtained within the limits of his jurisdiction.

4. The right to contribute and enjoy a participation of one-eighth in every expedition.

According to a memorial by Columbus, each of the articles was notarized separately, the whole being registered and signed "I, the King, and I, the Queen."

The so-called *título*, dated April 30, in Granada, contained the formal appointment to the office of Admiral of the Ocean Sea and to the titles and privileges of viceroy and governor. This document indicated the royal intention of making all three appointments hereditary, whereas the assumption of the first document was that only the admiralty would be hereditary. The prolix text also reads: "You may have the power to punish and chastise delinquents and may exercise the powers of Admiral, Viceroy and Governor, you and your lieutenants, over all that concerns and appertains to the said office and to each of them; and that you shall have and levy the fees and salaries annexed, belonging and pertaining to the said offices."

These were provisions written in anticipation of realizations of Alexandrian proportions on the part of Columbus and simultaneously with no intention to abdicate any privileges of sovereignty on the part of the Crown, no matter what the result of Columbus's venture. Although these clauses were prolix and judged by posterity as badly drawn, with blame liberally apportioned by litigants and historians, it is unrealistic to expect that an airtight legal agreement would have been produced under the complex historical circumstances—the siege of Granada, the recent victory over the Muslim foe of centuries, and the unanticipated discovery of a hemisphere.

Anticipation and Reality. The formula suggested by Columbus for his profit was unsustainable: one-tenth of the royal profit from the enterprise; one-eighth return on one-eighth of investment by him in the trade as it would develop; and one-third of any profit due him by virtue of his title of Admiral of the Ocean Sea. This would have added up to about 55 percent of the income from the enterprise of the Indies, a sum greater than that set aside for the Crown. The issue of the one-third of royal profit that was claimed by the admiral of Castile (from seizures at sea), a clause Columbus copied when he demanded the privileges of admiral, does not appear in the capitulations as such, but it had a phantom existence through the demands that Columbus lodged with the Crown subsequently and throughout his life. It should be understood that the income of the admiral of Castile from raids at sea was utterly distinct from Columbus's license to carry on legitimate trade. It should also be noted that the admiralty of the Ocean Sea of the *título* did not include hereditary privileges in the Spanish ports.

Upon first landing on an unknown island, Columbus was rudely disappointed not to find himself in Cathay or even to be able to obtain local information about his legendary goal. But on his return to Spain, he persuaded the Crown of the vast potential of his discovery, especially as a source of gold. Columbus lost no time after his triumphant return in obtaining a confirmation of the agreements. A document of May 28, 1493, stated that the capitulations and the offices of admiral, viceroy, and governor covered lands in the same area granted to Spain in the papal bull of May 4, 1493, by Alexander VI that drew the famous Line of Demarcation between the spheres of influence of Spain and Portugal.

Reconfirmation of the capitulations was again obtained four years later, in Burgos on April 23 and 30, 1497. This document repeats the capitulations, with an added clause

Decree of Isabel and Fernando. Confirming the favors bestowed on Admiral Christopher Columbus before the Discovery. Barcelona, May 28, 1493. First page.

Archivo General de Indias, Seville

stating that it was the royal will that they "be valid and be observed in favor of him and his children and descendants, now and hereafter forever, in entirety, and if it were necessary [the king and queen] make the said grant anew."

Anticipation that Columbus might indeed discover more lands, peoples, treasure, products, and markets led to greater care in the preparations for the following voyages. The admiral's monopoly on discovery of what was beginning to appear to be a vast region was the first privilege infringed upon by the man put in charge of the Indies fleets, Juan Rodríguez de Fonseca. In April 1495, he allowed Spaniards free navigation to the recently discovered lands, with the exception of lands protected under treaty with Portugal and those actually touched by Columbus. This order was retracted, however, on June 2, 1497, when Columbus received a confirmation of his rights from the Crown.

It is at this point that Columbus began to feel threatened and began to collect the documents of his privileges, honors, rights, claims to possession, and income. Questions about the extent of his jurisdiction, his monetary rights, the appointment of judges and officials, and other colonial initiatives, such as the granting of Indian labor, were cleared up only gradually before courts of law and through successive appeals.

On February 22, 1498, Columbus received royal permission to establish a *mayorazgo*, or entailed estate, including all his titles, privileges, and possessions. This document established the line of succession to the next of kin and repeated the entitlements given in perpetuity.

Events and Claims. Christopher Columbus never instituted a lawsuit during his lifetime. Instead, his complaints about the infringement of his rights by the treasury officials were lodged directly with the *fiscal,* or government solicitor. These concerned the method of determining his share of the royal profits. He insisted that his part of the profit be calculated on the gross receipts and that costs and expenses be taken from the portion that was left. He pleaded directly for the enforcement of his rights by the Crown. But royal officials insisted that costs and expenses be deducted before any distribution could be made. An agreement to this effect, to last for three years, was signed on June 12, 1497. The officials accused Columbus of taking more than his share, an accusation supported by the growing disaffection of the unruly colonists in La Española (Hispaniola), who presented their own case against Columbus and his brother Bartolomé in Spain.

Complaints about the abuse of his judicial powers, financial claims, administrative irregularities, and violations of agreements with settlers resulted in the suspension of the Admiral's governmental prerogatives, and the sequestration of his properties. Sent by the Crown to investigate Christopher's and Bartolomé's administration of the colony of La Española, Francisco de Bobadilla, as *juez pesquisidor* (investigative judge), forced the return of the brothers to Spain in October 1500. These facts, and the alleged infringement of Columbus's privileges, became the basis for the disputes with the Crown recorded in the Pleitos.

Columbus undertook a third and a fourth voyage, and the territorial extent of his claims was built on all four voyages. Doubts about where he had been and whether he had exercised the act of possession became one focus for conflict between the Admiral and the Crown; the actual contacts he made with the new lands during his voyages were the issue. On the first voyage he touched the Bahama Islands and discovered the north coasts of Cuba and of La Española. The second voyage took him through the Lesser Antilles. He then added the south coasts of La Española and Cuba and the island of Jamaica to the map. His third voyage made a landfall at Trinidad. He discovered the Dragon's Mouth (Boca del Dragón, the Gulf of Paria between Venezuela and Trinidad) and sailed along the mainland coast of the Paria Peninsula. After sighting the island of Margarita, he returned to the town of Santo Domingo and to Spain. His last exploration was along the coast of Central America from Honduras (Isla de Piños) to Darién. Since his having been at the coasts of South and Central America was a certainty, conflict arose over the extent of his claims to this mainland in terms of the capitulations of Santa Fe.

A parallel controversy arose over the scope of his governmental powers. One reading of the capitulations and confirmatory documents—granting the posts of viceroy and governor-general of all the lands discovered, with the right to submit three names for appointments to office, and with no restrictions specified—would have created a greater and more powerful monarchy than Spain, with rights to hang Spaniards, enslave Indians, and reap enormous profits. At what point could the Spanish kings interfere when their viceroy proved incapable of orderly government and was faced with the rebellion of Spanish subjects? Was Columbus to be allowed to appoint his own men and to dominate the administration of justice?

Precedent in Spain gave the viceroy of a region (for instance Naples) the full confidence of the king. Since viceroys were chosen on the basis of their demonstrated competence, Columbus's own failure at government in Santo Domingo led to a revocation of his rights, as interpreted by the *fiscal*. The reports of a royal agent, Juan de Aguado (1495), and Bobadilla's commission precipitated the first infringements on Columbus's privileges of government. Although the titles and privileges of the admiralty were restored to him before the third voyage, no mention was made of the governorship or the viceroyalty. In 1501, Nicolás de Ovando was appointed governor of La Española explicitly because of the failure of Columbus, "who had made ill use of his grant [*merced*], and had indulged in excesses of the administration of justice." Thus Columbus was relieved of his offices of viceroy and governor.

In 1504, after the death of the queen, King Fernando tried a novel solution by offering Columbus the fiefdom of Carrión de los Condes, near Valladolid, in return for relinquishing his claim to the Indies. Columbus declined the offer and continued his complaints until his death in 1506, when his son Diego Colón, called "the second Admiral," inherited his rights and added new complaints.

Beginning of the Litigation and Its Procedures. In 1508 Diego instituted the first suit of the Pleitos Colombinos with the branch of the Council of Castile, which eventually became the Council of the Indies (Consejo de Indias). Demanding recognition of succession to his father's rights, he claimed the viceroyalty of all the lands discovered and to be discovered, including Puerto Rico and especially Veragua. This was the "Tierra Firme" stretching along the mainland Caribbean coast. Columbus discovered and reconnoitered the area in 1503 when he landed at the mouth of the Veragua River, a stream that flows into the Caribbean Sea about seventy-five miles west of the present Canal Zone. Diego insisted on his right to appoint officers and he claimed one-tenth of all royal revenues, including customs taxes.

On economic matters, the *fiscal* generally conceded the rights of Diego to profits from his father's discoveries, subject to an agreed-upon distribution. He referred to a law of 1480 (Toledo) that prohibited the grant of the administration of justice in perpetuity and thus left the door open to appeal on grounds of both economic claims and governmental powers.

A positive change in Diego's fortunes came with his marriage to María de Toledo, who was a niece of the powerful house of the duke of Alba. In a decisive turn of events, Diego, who was personally well-received at court, was appointed governor-general of the Indies without prejudice to the rights of the parties to the pending suit and "for such period as it may be the royal pleasure and will" in royal orders dated August 9 and December 9, 1508.

A conflict then arose over the extent of his grant, which rested upon the clause "all the islands and mainland which . . . he [Columbus] discovered or acquired in the said oceans." While the contract may have been intended literally to cover all the lands discovered, it eventually would have included the hemisphere from Florida to Mexico and Peru, to which he opened the way. This was the interpretation taken up by the heirs of Columbus. The government contended that only those parts actually discovered by Columbus or by someone commissioned by him were to be included under the contract.

According to the Crown, the Andalusian voyages sponsored by Fonseca established other claims to the South American coasts. There were about eleven such voyages before 1506, directed to various stretches of the coasts of South and Central America. The settlements of Puerto Rico and Cuba became bases for explorations toward the north. (Four voyages eventually entered the lawsuit.) Once the American hemisphere was revealed in a magnitude not predicted by anyone, the royal councils acted to limit the title of the Columbus family to the Caribbean area. Diego continued his suit and made a request to the king in a letter of September 7, 1509, to participate in certain royal revenues. The response, dated November 14, 1509 states: "To the claim that you are entitled, [the answer is] no, concerning participation in the tithes, fines imposed, and income from our lands—no, concerning the tithes and fines; as to the gold found, there is doubt. The matter will be considered by our Council to your satisfaction and justice will be done you."

After Diego married María de Toledo, the duke of Alba helped to expedite his son-in-law's legal proceedings by writing letters to the king, to Fonseca, and to Fernando Vega, president both of the Military Order of Santiago and of the royal council (not yet the Council of the Indies) with jurisdiction over the suit.

The Judgment of Seville. On May 5, 1511, the judges rendered the judgment of Seville, the first stock-taking of the relationship of the Columbus claims to the reality of America. Successive judgments were each to be limited to specific issues under litigation. The decision confirmed Diego's privileges as perpetual viceroy and governor-general of the islands discovered by his father, in accordance with the capitulations made with Fernando and Isabel. These privileges, however, were circumscribed so as to uphold the sovereignty of the Crown, allow supervision of the viceroy's acts, and protect the rights of colonists. The viceroy's powers were further limited by the establishment of a royal audiencia, or high court, on August 5, 1511. A royal order of November 15, 1511, confirmed the judgment, which satisfied neither side and led to new appeals.

Diego Colón announced his appeal from his palace in Santo Domingo on December 29, 1512. He accompanied it with an extended list of claims and grievances. This provoked the *fiscal*, who also challenged the judgment. The claims and counterclaims, all officially certified, were then exchanged between the lawyers of the parties and made available to the members of the Council of the Indies.

Diego Colón, his uncle Bartolomé, María de Toledo, and others were meanwhile also negotiating directly with the king and later the emperor. Attempts to circumvent restrictions, for instance, by claims to governorships of Puerto Rico, later extended to New Spain, and Peru had their roots in ill-defined clauses. The lack of geographic knowledge, the unreliability of agents, and other such uncertainties increased rather than decreased during the first decades of expansion. Extralegal issues must be kept in mind when considering the sequence of filings, appeals, and judgments, which do not follow a consistent sequence of demand and response.

The Pleito del Darién. The major issues of contention can be summarized as follows:

1. Diego's claim to the right to appoint judges and exercise judicial powers as viceroy and governor over all the lands discovered. The reply by the *fiscal* restated the illegality of hereditary granting of judicial powers because of the impossibility of knowing the qualifications of the successors to the person first designated.
2. The demand for the salaries of all three offices of admiral, viceroy, and governor, plus a grant for a guard of honor. According to Fonseca, the latter was an exclusive right of kings. The *fiscal* argued that these privileges were only granted to Christopher Columbus and did not descend to his son; also, the salary of an admiral was only paid while on duty at sea.
3. Diego claimed the right of appointment to all offices, whether of civil or criminal jurisdiction, and exemption from *residencia* (account of his administration) for himself. Again, according to the *fiscal*, these privileges were granted to Columbus only and not to his heirs.
4. The right, deriving from the office of admiral, to judicial powers in the Casa de la Contratación (House of Trade/Colonial Office) in Seville on matters relating to the Indies. This was denied by the *fiscal* as not included in the contract.
5. The right to appoint officials to the Casa de la Contratación. The *fiscal* alleged that only Christopher Columbus, by special grant, enjoyed rights of this kind and that they could not go to his heirs.
6. Diego's claim to one-tenth of all royal profits and revenues from the islands and mainland discovered and to be discovered. The *fiscal* denied this reading of the contract.
7. A claim to one-tenth of the customs duties *(almorifazgo)*. Since trade with the Indies was now open to all Spaniards who paid this tax, Diego's right to a one-eighth share in all expeditions had been rendered valueless and should be compensated by a share in the customs duties. The *fiscal* maintained that this tax was royal revenue and neither Columbus nor his son had a right to any part of it. In fact, if they had received any monies from this source, they would have to be repaid.

These issues were the substance of the second lawsuit. The arguments presented by the *fiscal* answered the claim by Diego that he should be appointed governor of the province of Darién (Panama) now being settled, as the land had been discovered by his father. It was also declared that Urabá and Veragua were on one and the same coast. Moreover, in order to exploit his properties, Diego insisted that he should receive grants of Indian labor *(repartimientos)*. The Pleito del Darién introduced the new feature of depositions from witnesses produced by both sides. This is the very heart of legal procedure, and such documents make up the volumes of *probanzas* (testimonies) collected in the Pleitos. Questions were formulated by lawyers for both sides and posed to witnesses gathered in localities where statements could be notarized. Each witness had to declare his origin, age, and profession and that he was beholden to neither party. Ranging widely in social rank and age (from twenty-three to eighty-five years), a host of seamen, pilots, companions of Columbus, rivals, experts, lawyers, supporters, and adversaries testified. Each side also produced copies of texts, royal letters, provisions, and other previous documents.

The representative for Diego Colón, the attorney Juan de la Peña, submitted his petition of appeal of the judgment of Seville on January 3, 1512. The Crown responded in 1512 with the "lawsuit between the *fiscal* of their Majesties against the Admiral of the Indies concerning the island of Darién [Panama]."

The critical issue that ensued in the flow of claims and counterclaims was the contention of the opponents of Columbus that the discovery of the South American coast had not been made by him. They alleged that Columbus had only touched at the Dragon's Mouth, near Trinidad, and Paria and had then returned, leaving the exploration of Veragua to others. Among the witnesses interrogated in Santo Domingo was Bartolomé Colón. He provided testimony on the fifth question that dealt with this issue. He supported the claim of Columbus's discovery of Veragua by testifying that, due to indisposition of the Admiral, he himself had taken possession in the name of the king and queen. He also stated that the Andalusian discoveries had only been possible because the Admiral had first brought news of the coast.

The *fiscal* likewise rounded up witnesses in Santo Domingo to prove that other pilots had discovered Darién. Information was exchanged and depositions continued to be taken in Santo Domingo (November 10, 1513) and in Puerto Rico, Cuba, Jamaica, and Spain (1514–1515). Frequent mention of certain places in Spain—Moguer, Palos, Huelva and Seville—show the Andalusian involvement in the ventures. A deposition in favor of Diego was taken in Salamanca from the oldest witness, Rodrígo Maldonado, eighty-five years old, a member of the city council and of the board of churchmen, lawyers, and seamen who examined Columbus before the discoveries.

According to Maldonado, that group agreed that "it was impossible that what the Admiral said could be true, and against the opinion of the majority the said Admiral argued." Witnesses in Palos had stated that Columbus had been mocked on account of his plan. Here was testimony to Columbus's heroic foresight and steadfastness.

In the spring of 1515 Diego Colón thought he had proved his case, only to suffer the setback of another request by the *fiscal* for more depositions and postponements. The *fiscal* gathered thirteen friends of the Pinzón brothers; three of the brothers had been on the first voyage as partners of Columbus and were later his rivals. In Palos, on October 1, 1515, a member of Martín Alonso Pinzón's crew swore that Pinzón discovered America and that if not for Captain Pinzón the voyage would have been a failure. By October 11, 1516, Diego had decided to address himself directly to King Carlos I, who was in the Low Countries, and he succeeded in obtaining an order from Brussels directing the Council to speed the decision. This was followed shortly by an order to suspend the matter (Mechelen; April 15, 1517) until the king's arrival in Spain, "because we are now informed that many of the questions touch our prerogative and sovereignty and should not be decided without consulting the King."

Diego pursued his interests at court in 1511 and again in 1513. He remained there from 1515 to 1520, with time out in 1517 to look after his government in La Española. Diego was able to befriend Carlos I, and in 1520, when the king became Holy Roman Emperor Charles V, Diego lent him 10,000 ducats, a sum greater than the cost of his father's first voyage.

The Judgment of La Coruña. A judgment considered very favorable to Diego Colón was rendered at La Coruña on May 22, 1520. The forty-two clauses of the judgment are a definition of intent and procedure by the Spanish government with respect to the Columbian privileges. A new feature is an evident concern for the Indians: "Inasmuch as God created the Indians free, the laws relating to them shall be observed. . . . Investigators of Indian affairs shall have the right only to question whether the Indians have committed misdeeds, or actions against the faith, and report their findings, but shall have no right to give orders in connection therewith." There is also an order to the treasurer to pay Diego the sum of 365,000 maravedis per annum from that time forward, which is granted "as a contribution to his costs."

Still, Diego was dissatisfied with any limitation put upon him, especially with regard to the geographical extent of his authority. He had to contend especially with the claims based on the Andalusian expeditions to the South American coasts by (1) Alonso de Ojeda, Amerigo Vespucci, and Juan de la Cosa; (2) Pedro Alonso Niño and Cristóbal Guerra; (3) Vicente Yañez Pinzón; and (4) Diego de Lepe (all dating from 1499 to 1500); and the exploration of Panama and discovery of the "South Sea" by Vasco Núñez de Balboa in 1513. Diego took up another strategy; he advocated before the Council of the Indies an extension of the privileges granted to his father, to include Panama and Mexico. All administrative offices would be appointed from lists submitted by him. Diego considered himself entitled to consideration for the governorships held by Hernando Cortés and Pedro Arias de Ávila. Diego died on February 23, 1526, worn out by his labors (according to Oviedo).

Decision at Valladolid. The appeal of the judgment of La Coruña, which led to a case of eight *capítulos*, was initiated when Diego was recalled from La Española in 1524. It was continued by María de Toledo and was closed in Valladolid on June 25, 1527. The suit was not only an appeal of the judgment of La Coruña but also contained new claims by both sides based on interpretations of the original capitulations of Santa Fe. The briefs submitted by the attorneys for the Colón interests and those of the *fiscal* moved the Council of the Indies to nullify the judgments of Seville (1511) and of La Coruña (1520) and to propose a completely new case to be heard by the Council. An interlocutory appeal by both parties led to a confirmation of that decision. The litigation with the government started afresh under the guiding hand of María de Toledo on behalf of her children, four girls and three boys. The eldest, Luis, was the successor to the *mayorazgo*.

The Judgment of Dueñas. The appeal against the decision of Valladolid resulted in a suit that was terminated by the judgment of Dueñas, containing an elaborate settlement of thirty clauses (August 27, 1534). It left both sides unsatisfied and left unanswered three questions: (1) whether the Admiral should be put in possession of the viceroyalty and governorship; (2) whether he was entitled to the one-tenth of all income from his admiralty; and (3) whether he was entitled to one-tenth of the income from the importation of brazilwood.

The Final Arbitration, 1536. In the last suit (1535–1536) of the Pleitos Colombinos proper, the twenty-eight questions of the interrogatory solicited information on the most extreme claims by the *fiscal* and the Pinzón party: that Columbus had not discovered America at all, but that Pinzón had. The Pinzóns had challenged Diego in a lawsuit of 1513, the arguments of which were incorporated by the *fiscal*. Luis Colón, in his turn, claimed that he was entitled to all the Indies from Florida to Peru. At this point a number of factors, including the rapid growth of Spain's enterprise in the Indies, the unthinkable prospect of validating the exact wording of the original capitulations, and the unworkable interim decisions, prompted a compromise decision that brought an end to the Pleitos Colombinos. Cardinal Garcia de Loayza, president of the Council of the Indies, and Gaspar de Montoya of the Council of Castile reached the decision on June 28, 1536.

This arbitration was extended somewhat by an order of July 7 and confirmed by the emperor on September 8, 1536, and March 24, 1537.

In this judgment Luis Colón renounced the following privileges granted to Columbus by Fernando and Isabel:

1. The claim to one-tenth of the revenue of the Indies.
2. The title of viceroy (the viceroyalty in this case being defined as the islands of La Española, Puerto Rico, Cuba, and Jamaica and parts of Veragua and Paria).
3. The claims to the right to appoint officials in the New World.

He was granted:

1. A perpetual annuity of ten thousand ducats payable on the revenues of La Española.
2. The island of Jamaica in fief, with full rights of government, subject only to the supreme sovereignty of the Spanish king.
3. A fief of a tract of land of twenty-five square leagues (which was larger than Jamaica) in the province of Veragua.
4. The titles of duke of Veragua and marquis of Jamaica.
5. The title of admiral of the Indies, with the privileges of office.
6. The right of appointment to the office of *alguacil mayor* (chief constable) of La Española. This was a fee-paying position that Luis Colón soon assigned to his brother Cristóbal.
7. The right to found a town on his sugar estate in La Española and to appoint municipal officers for it.

Life pensions were also granted for the daughters. Diego, the youngest child, still a minor, was made a member of the Order of Santiago, with the income therefrom. María de Toledo was awarded a sum of four thousand ducats payable over a period of four years in partial payment for the sums she had spent in the pursuit of the litigation. The sisters of Luis Colón were given noble names.

Further Litigation. But this was not the end of the litigation or of Luis Colón's attempts to sustain his claims. Two matters of continuing dissension were the designation of the ports where duties were owed the admiralty (with documents dating from 1537 to 1541) and the extent of the admiralty's jurisdiction there (1554). Next came the disastrous expedition mounted by María de Toledo and Luis Colón to settle Veragua. To this was added the effect of Spanish inflation on the sums of money settled upon in 1536. Luis's candidacy for the governorship of Peru came to nothing. María de Toledo died in 1549, but Luis Colón pursued his claims until the compromise of 1556, which was the ultimate settlement between the last direct descendant of Columbus and the Crown. The following are the terms of this compromise:

1. Luis renounced his fief in Veragua but was allowed to establish a *señorio* (hereditary estate) and received the titles of duke of Veragua and marquis of Jamaica.
2. Luis retained only the title of admiral, without income and authority.
3. Luis retained the right to appoint the chief constable in La Española. (There was no mention of a town on the sugar estate, the economy of the island having collapsed.)
4. He received the title of duke de la Vega.
5. The estate was awarded an increase in the annuity to seventeen thousand ducats, drawn on the account of La Española, except during the lifetime of Luis Colón, when it was to come from customs receipts in Seville.

During the following years, new litigation involved missing or diminished payments of Luis Colón's pension. When Luis, the last in the direct line of succession, died in 1572, his nephew Diego inherited the pension.

On balance the Pleitos are a remarkable illustration of the rise of monarchical sovereignty over private lordship. The individual judgments did not furnish broad resolutions of the issues but were rendered piecemeal as a consequence of the enormous growth of the royal enterprise of the Indies.

The Columbus Legacy. The rivalries that endured for ten generations after the extinction of the direct line reveal the wide-ranging social world of the family. They are not properly part of the Pleitos, but they tell the story of the Columbus legacy, of the connections among the family in the colonies, for instance. The Columbus clan in Europe contains names of the highest nobility. The family's quarrels with the Crown included, of course, conflicts over the order of descent as well as claims that continued to arise from reconsideration of the capitulations of Santa Fe and subsequent suits. A late eighteenth-century lawsuit brought by Mariano Colón de Larreátegui y Embrún, eleventh admiral and ninth duke of Veragua, was decided on June 16, 1790. He traced his claim to the *mayorazgo* to its descent from Luis Colón to his nephew Diego. This question of genealogy, first brought by the Larreátegui family in 1650, was thus finally brought to a successful conclusion by the famous statesman of the Spanish Enlightenment and chief justice of the king's court, Gaspar Melchor de Jovellanos. From this settlement emerged today's line of bearers of the titles of Columbus and the claimants of his income, converted to a fixed pension.

[See also *Book of Privileges; Santa Fe Capitulations.*]

BIBLIOGRAPHY

Duro, Cesareo Fernandez, ed. *Colección de documentos inéditos relativos al descubrimiento, conquista y organización de las antiguas posesiones Españolas de ultramar.* Vols. 7–8. Madrid, 1885–1932.

Garcia-Gallo, Alfonso. "El título jurídico de los reyes de España sobre las Indias en los Pleitos Colombinos." *Revista de la Faculdad de Derecho de México* 26, nos. 101–102 (1976): 129–155.

Gil, Juan. "Pleitos y clientelas colombinas." *Annali della Facolta di Scienze Politiche* (Genoa) 3 (1983–1986): 182–199.

Muro Orejón, Antonio. "Cristóbal Colón: El original de la capitulación de 1492 y sus cópias contemporaneas." *Annuario de Estudios Americanos* (Seville) 7 (1950): 505ff.

Pleitos Colombinos. 8 vols. Edited by Antonio Muro Orejón et al. Seville, 1964–1984. Vol. 1, *Proceso hasta la sentencia de Sevilla* (1967); vol. 2, *Pleito sobre el Darién* (1983); vol. 3, *Probanzas del Almirante de las Indias* (1984); vol. 8, *Rollo del proceso sobre la apelación de la sentencia de dueñas y probanzas del fiscal y del Almirante (1534–1536)* (1964).

Ramos Pérez, Demetrio. *Los Colón y sus pretensiones continentales.* Casa Museo de Colón, Seminario de la Universidad de Valladolid. Valladolid, 1977.

Schoenrich, Otto. *The Legacy of Columbus: The Historic Litigation Involving His Discoveries, His Will, His Family and His Descendants.* 2 vols. Glendale, Calif., 1949.

Vigneras, Louis André. *The Discovery of South America and the Andalusian Voyages.* Chicago, 1976.

URSULA LAMB

LEAD AND LINE. Essentially a plumb bob on the end of a long line, the lead and line (also called sounding-line) is used to determine the depth below the surface of the sea of the seabed and also to take samples of the seabed. Such a simple instrument, fulfilling an obvious need, no doubt had a long history dating back to ancient times. Possibly the earliest illustration of a lead and line is in an English manuscript of sailing directions, which dates from around 1460 to 1480. A lead and line appears on the engraved title page of Lucas Janszoon Wagenaar's *Spieghel der Zeevaerdt* (Leyden, 1584). From the similarity of the earliest illustrations and descriptions of the lead and line to those of the present time, David W. Waters has argued that the early sixteenth-century English predecessors were similar, and no doubt this is equally true of the late medieval period. An example from a seventeenth-century English seaman's manual gives a lead weight of 14 pounds (6.3 kilograms) on a thin line of 200 fathoms (370 meters) for use in deep water, and a weight of 7 pounds (3.2 kilograms) on a thicker line for use in depths of less than 20 fathoms (37 meters). The shorter line was marked at intervals by leather or cloth; for example, at 2 fathoms and 3 fathoms with black leather or at 7 fathoms with red cloth. Another contemporary manual notes that the deep-water line is marked first at 20 fathoms and then at every 10 fathoms with small knots in short strings attached to the line and says that the weight is hollow, so that hard tallow or a white woolen cloth with a little tallow can be placed inside it to bring up a sample of the seabed, for example, fine black sand or "white soft woormes." The lead and line was especially useful in those waters over a continental shelf, where depths change abruptly, but was also valuable for avoiding shoals and dangerous rocks in shallow and tidal coastal waters. An experienced mariner was able to "locate himself by the contours, colour, smell, taste, and texture of the seabed." In *The Art of Navigation in England in Elizabethan and Early Stuart Times*, Waters quotes a fifteenth-century traveler in the Baltic who said that in that sea navigators used lead and line, but not chart or compass.

BIBLIOGRAPHY

Taylor, E. G. R. *The Haven-Finding Art: A History of Navigation from Odysseus to Captain Cook.* Rev. ed. London, 1971.

Waters, David W. *The Art of Navigation in England in Elizabethan and Early Stuart Times.* London, 1958.

Waters, David W. *The Rutters of the Sea: The Sailing Directions of Pierre Garcie. A Study of the First English and French Sailing Directions.* New Haven, Conn., and London, 1967.

FRANCIS MADDISON

LEIF ERICSSON. See *Ericsson, Leif.*

LEÓN, JUAN PONCE DE. See *Ponce de León, Juan.*

LIBRARY OF COLUMBUS. Only ten extant items remain from Christopher Columbus's personal library, and there is no record of how large it might have been during the discoverer's lifetime. After the Admiral died, his library was eventually incorporated into the extensive book collection of his son, Fernando Colón, who spent much of his life browsing bookstalls all over Europe, becoming one of the greatest bibliophiles of the sixteenth century. In the back of most of his books, Fernando carefully recorded the date and place of purchase of each; he left an unfinished catalog of all the books he owned. Thus, those books owned by his father are clearly distinguished by autograph and marginal notes. When Fernando died in 1539, he willed his library (known as the Libreria Fernandina) to his nephew, Luis Colón, the son of Diego Colón and the grandson of Christopher. The will stipulated that if Luis renounced the legacy, the library would go first to the cathedral chapter at Seville, and, if rejected by the cathedral, to San Pablo Monastery in Seville. Numerous legal delays in processing the will and in Luis's renunciation of the books kept the library in storage at Fernando's residence (although Bartolomé de las Casas probably held some of the books) until 1544. In that year, it was moved to San Pablo Monastery, and in 1552 the library was transferred to the cathedral.

Estimates of the size of the Libreria Fernandina range from twelve thousand to twenty thousand books and manuscripts. Care for the library varied for the next three centuries. By royal command, some items were removed to the national archives in the 1560s. No list of the removed items exists, and they seem to have disappeared. The books were stored and abandoned in the cathedral until the period from 1684 to 1709, when a cathedral librarian was named who shelved the library, repaired some damage, and drew up a new inventory. The collection at that point had shrunk to around four thousand books. After 1709, the library was again neglected. Until 1832 children were allowed to run freely through the library and sad tales are recorded of the destruction of books by their unsupervised play.

In 1832 a new librarian was named who again preserved the books and actually added to the collection by buying contemporary volumes for the library. But, even with this renewed care, many of the volumes were stolen and resold in the bookstalls of Paris, London, and Amsterdam in the nineteenth century. The great Columbus scholar Henri Harrisse brought a halt to the thefts by writing exposés in the 1880s. Since then, the Biblioteca Colombina, as the library is now called, has been made into a professionally run library filling four rooms of the cathedral buildings. Centuries of neglect and plunder have reduced the core collection owned by Fernando and his father today to about two thousand items.

The surviving items identified as once owned by Christopher Columbus are now stored in a special bookcase. They include seven books, two notebooks, and a palimpsest:

1. Pierre d'Ailly. *Imago mundi.* Louvain, 1480–1483 (date uncertain). Columbus's copy also contained a small collection of treatises on various topics such as astronomy and geography.
2. Enea Silvio Piccolomini (Pope Pius II). *Historia rerum ubique gestarum.* Venice, 1477.
3. Marco Polo. *De consuetudanibus et conditionibus orientalium regionum.* A Latin summary by Francesco Pipino of *Il milione.* Antwerp, 1485.
4. Pliny the Elder. *Historia naturalis.* An Italian translation by Cristoforo Landino. Venice, 1489.
5. Plutarch. *Las vidas de los ilustres Varones.* A Castilian translation by Alfonso de Palencia. Seville, 1491.
6. Anonymous. *Concordantiae Bibliae Cardinalis S.P.* No publisher, no date (probably fifteenth century).
7. Saint Antoninus of Florence. *Summa confessionis.* No publisher, 1476.
8. A "notebook" of folios copied by Christopher Columbus and others now titled *Libro de las profecías* (Book of Prophecies) containing lengthy passages from scripture and the pseudepigrapha; the church fathers; ancient, medieval, and contemporary Christian theologians; and Jewish and Muslim writers.
9. A loose-leaf "notebook" copied by Christopher Columbus and others containing selections from Abraham Zacuto's *Almanach perpetuum coelestium motium.*
10. A fifteenth-century palimpsest containing Seneca's *Tragedies.*

Other books suspected to have been owned by the Admiral are a copy of John Mandeville's *Travels,* Julius Capitolinus's *De locis habitabilibus,* a copy of the *Alfonsine Tables* (astrological calculations), Albertus Magnus's *Philosophia naturalis,* and a Bible including pseudepigraphical texts. If Columbus made a living in Castile as a book dealer in the 1480s (as recorded by Andrés Bernáldez and Bartolomé de las Casas in their histories), his private library may have been very fluid as he bought and sold books.

How many books Columbus personally owned is unknown. In his own writings, Columbus cited, referenced, or quoted over sixty ancient, medieval, and contemporary writers from Christian, Jewish, and Muslim cultures. He read voraciously in his own collection, in other private book collections, and in the great monastery libraries at Santa Maria de La Rábida and Nuestra Señora Santa Maria de Las Cuevas. Although these two libraries were destroyed and no catalogs remain, it has been estimated that each contained around ten to twelve thousand books and manuscripts.

Columbus was mostly a self-taught reader. It is likely that as a boy in Genoa he attended a school established for the children of the cloth guild, where he learned some elementary Latin. As a young man, he and his brother Bartolomé learned to read and write Latin, Spanish, and Portuguese well enough to enable them to study difficult scientific and theological books, achieving a level of intellectual refinement to make mathematical calculations and analyze sophisticated scientific, historical, and theological arguments. Reflecting on his intellectual life in 1501, Columbus stated, "During this time, I have searched out and studied all kinds of texts: geographies, histories, chronologies, philosophies, and other subjects" (from the cover letter to the Book of Prophecies).

The importance of the Columbus Library, of course, is that it gives us some idea about his intellectual preparation for his "Enterprise of the Indies," and it testifies to the breadth of his interests. Explorers rarely go forth and probe; they have preconceived notions that cause them to envision the unknown environment of terrae incognitae.

They search for definite objects that they believe to exist based on both empirical and nonempirical information available to them. Further, it became evident to Columbus that he would have to debate leading intellectuals to gain support for his enterprise; thus, he read everything that he could in his effort to present his case effectively before learned councils. He intensified his studies while waiting in Spain for backing from the monarchs.

Columbus's book collecting and study enabled him to impress his contemporaries with his deportment, confidence, and knowledge before learned commissions. Before these groups, he presented maps drawn by himself and his brother, Bartolomé, and quoted frequently from ancient and contemporary texts as well as the Bible. His manner was that of a man well prepared and well versed in his subject to argue his theses with numerous citations from respected sources at his fingertips.

Although he was well read when he presented his case before commissions and monarchs, it is likely that only two of the books that survive from his personal library were read by him before the first voyage, Enea Silvio Piccolomini's *Historia rerum ubique gestarum* and Pierre d'Ailly's *Imago mundi*. These two books and the scriptures were the most powerful influence upon him and his ideas. He collected, or read, his other books at a later date.

Controversy surrounds the dates at which he began accumulating scholarly data to support his dream of crossing the Ocean Sea. The evidence suggests that he was reading his copy of Piccolomini's *Historia* as early as 1481, although this date is strongly disputed by G. Caraci and P. Taviani. Columbus had undoubtedly read d'Ailly's *Imago mundi* by 1488, for an early marginal note refers to Bartolomeu Días's return to Portugal.

The *Historia* by Piccolomini gave Columbus a solid background in fifteenth-century historical geography and its lore. It aided him immeasurably in imagining the world and its features. The book so stimulated him that he made copious marginal notes throughout the text with extensive summaries of information on the flyleaves.

D'Ailly's *Imago mundi* was undoubtedly his best-loved book other than the Bible. He annotated it with more marginal notes than any other book that survives of his library. D'Ailly was a diligent encyclopedist who opened authoritative and influential ancient and medieval authors to Columbus. The *Imago mundi* led him to understand a working interrelationship between science and theology. It was a key document for forming an image of the Ocean Sea in his mind and the relationship of land masses to that sea and to each other. The *Imago mundi* supported Columbus's calculations (actually miscalculations) about the circumference of the earth and the distance from Europe to Asia.

COPY OF THE LETTER FROM PAOLO DAL POZZO TOSCANELLI TO CANON MARTINS. Transcribed by Columbus on a blank page in his copy of Enea Silvio Piccolomini's *Historia rerum*. The letter is Toscanelli's response to an inquiry by Martins (writing for King Afonso V of Portugal) concerning the possibility of sailing west to Asia. Toscanelli replied on June 25, 1474, with a detailed letter and a map, the originals of which are lost. Columbus would have found in Toscanelli's letter support for his ideas as to the circumference of the earth.   BIBLIOTECA COLOMBINA, SEVILLE

Columbus probably did not read the other books in his personal library until after the first voyage. The most controversial issue is the date at which he read Marco Polo's book of travels to Asia. Juan Gil in his *El libro de Marco Polo* (1986) has made definitive studies of this text that suggest that it was not read or annotated until the mid-1490s. There is no evidence as to when Columbus read Pliny, and he may not have read the Plutarch book at all (the marginal notations in it are in the hand of his son Fernando). The Bible concordance has no notes in it, but it is well larded with highlighting marks commonly used by Columbus and others (hands with fingers and other symbols pointing to key texts).

Both the palimpsest, on which is copied Seneca's *Tragedies*, and the copy of Saint Antoninus's *Summa confessionis*, may or may not have belonged to Columbus. Ownership of the two items remains in doubt, and whether either was read by Columbus is also a guess, as neither contains marginal notes. He did quote a passage from Seneca in the Book of Prophecies, however.

The notebooks pose their own problems. According to the marginal notations in the books of Columbus that survive, and according to Fernando in his biography of his father, Columbus collected important information in notebooks. Most of these notebooks have disappeared. Columbus used and referred to the material collected from Zacuto's almanac over the years. The notebook of prophecies is a collection of biblical and nonbiblical sources (with marginal notations) which Columbus planned to use in writing a lengthy apocalyptic poem to the monarchs (a genre common to the fifteenth century).

There has been little reason to reproduce the books owned by Columbus. Césare de Lollis reproduced all the marginal notes with brief text to which they referred (1892–1894). In 1930, E. Buron reproduced and translated into French the *Imago mundi* by Pierre d'Ailly with Columbus's notes. A study and translation of the Book of Prophecies has been completed by Delno C. West and August Kling.

The most impressive reproduction of the Columbus Library is the Colección Tabula Americae (Madrid, 1983–). Under the general editorship of Francisco Morales Padron, several Columbian documents, including key books from Columbus's personal library, are being printed in exact facsimile from the original. Accompanying each volume is a modern translation in Spanish and a commentary on each book.

[See also *Museums and Archives; Writings*, especially the articles on *Book of Prophecies* and *Marginalia*.]

BIBLIOGRAPHY

Caraci, G. "Quando cominciò Colombo a scrivere le sue postille?" In *Scritti geografici in honore di Carmelo Colamonico*. Naples, 1963.

Harrisse, Henri. *La Colombine et Clément Marot*. Paris, 1886.

Harrisse, Henri. *Grandeur et décadence de la Colombine*. Paris, 1885. Spanish translation, *Grandeza y decadencia de la Colombina*. Seville, 1886.

Huntington, Archer. *Catalogue of the Library of Ferdinand Columbus*. New York, 1905.

Lollis, Césare de, ed. *I scritti di Cristoforo Colombo. Raccolta di documenti e studi pubblicati dalla R. Commissione Colombiana per quarto centenario dalla scoperta dell'America*, part 1. Rome, 1892–1894.

María Martínez, T. *Obras y libros de Hernando Colón*. Madrid, 1970.

Streicher, Fritz. *Die Kolumbus-originale: Eine paleographische Studie*. Spanische Forschungen der Gorresgesellschaft, vol. 1. Munich, 1928.

Taviani, Paolo E. *Christopher Columbus: The Grand Design*. London, 1985.

West, Delno C., and August Kling. *The "Libro de las profecías" of Christopher Columbus*. Gainesville, Fla., 1991.

DELNO C. WEST

LINE OF DEMARCATION. The Line of Demarcation refers to an imaginary line set in the Atlantic Ocean separating the zones of exploration and colonization reserved to Spain and Portugal, respectively. The circumstances that brought this about were the following. While the Portuguese, under the direction of Prince Henry the Navigator (d. 1460), were exploring the west coast of Africa and beginning to settle Madeira and the Azores, Portugal and Castile were disputing control over the Canary Islands. These issues were resolved when Afonso V of Portugal (r. 1438–1481) concluded the Treaty of Alcáçovas with Fernando of Aragón (r. 1479–1516) and Isabel of Castile (r. 1474–1504) on September 4, 1479. The treaty reserved to Portugal the west coast of Africa, Madeira, the Azores, and the Cape Verde Islands, while the Canaries fell to Castile.

When Columbus sailed westward across the Atlantic, he was under strict instructions from Fernando and Isabel not to intrude on any of the places reserved for Portugal. Nevertheless, in the Castilian interpretation of the Treaty of Alcáçovas, the Portuguese were limited to the waters adjacent to West Africa and the western Atlantic was open to anyone. Columbus gave Spain claim to the vast reaches of the New World, a circumstance unforeseen when the Treaty of Alcáçovas was drawn up. When he stopped in Lisbon on his return, João II (r. 1481–1495) received him warmly on March 9, 1493. Referring to the treaty, the king made the point that "according to the capitulation between the Catholic Kings and himself that conquest belonged to him." In the king's judgment, whatever lands might be discovered south of the Canaries and west of Guinea would belong to Portugal. Columbus responded that he had not seen the capitulation, but the king and queen had forbidden him to go to any part of the west coast of Africa, reserved for Portuguese exploitation. The Portuguese historian Rui de Pina reported that João II, annoyed by Columbus's tendency to exaggerate and probably regretting that he had not sponsored his voyage (Columbus had approached him before he turned to Castile), held that whatever he had discovered fell within his own lordship of Guinea or West Africa. João II's claim in effect challenged whatever rights Spain might have as a result of Columbus's voyage. The Spanish ambassador in Lisbon informed Fernando and Isabel that Portuguese preparations for a voyage of discovery might jeopardize their rights.

Unlike the Portuguese, the Spanish sovereigns had not previously sought papal authorization for the work of exploration, but now, in order to secure an undisputed title to the newly discovered lands, they appealed to Pope Alexander VI. Exercising the plenitude of papal power, the pope issued four bulls relating to this matter in 1493. In

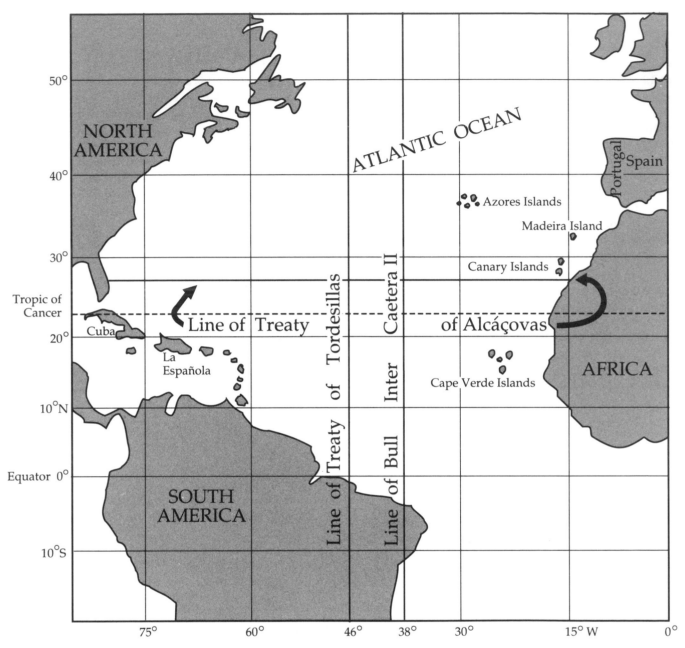

LINES OF DEMARCATION. Between Spanish and Portuguese spheres of influence, according to the Treaty of Alcáçovas, the Treaty of Tordesillas and the papal bull *Inter caetera II*.   AFTER SAMUEL ELIOT MORISON, *ADMIRAL OF THE OCEAN SEA*, LITTLE, BROWN AND CO., 1942.

the bull *Inter caetera* of May 3, after applauding the desire of the king and queen to spread the Catholic faith, he confirmed their dominion over the islands and lands already discovered and those that might be discovered, provided they were not already held by another Christian ruler.

Recognizing that the language of this document left open the possibility of conflict with Portugal, Fernando and Isabel approached the pope once again. This time he drew up two additional bulls in June, though predating them to May 3–4. *Eximiae devotionis*, dated May 3, conferred on the Spanish rulers the same rights in the lands they discovered as the Portuguese had in theirs. The third bull, also called *Inter caetera* and dated May 4, clarified the grant to Spain by drawing "a line from the Arctic or North Pole to the Antarctic or South Pole." The line was "distant one hundred leagues to the west and the south of any of the islands commonly called the Azores

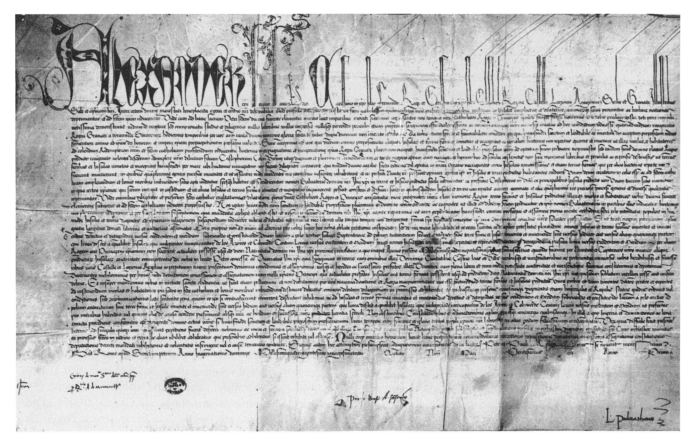

PAPAL BULL *INTER CAETERA*. Issued by Alexander VI and dated May 4, 1493.   ARCHIVO GENERAL DE INDIAS, SEVILLE

and Cape Verde." The pope, asserting his authority as the successor of Saint Peter and the vicar of Jesus Christ on earth, granted to Spain all the islands and mainlands discovered to the west and south of that line that were not subject to another Christian ruler.

Columbus may very well have suggested the idea of a line of demarcation to the king and queen. In their letter to him of September 5, 1493, they referred to "the line that you said ought to be in the papal bull." The line was probably set one hundred leagues west of the Azores because Columbus encountered milder temperatures west of that line, as he noted in the journal of his third voyage and in his letter to the king and queen concerning it. In any case, the Portuguese expressed their objections to this bull, prompting Fernando and Isabel to ask the pope for a further emendation.

In the fourth bull (*Dudum siquidem*), dated September 26, 1493, and sometimes called "the bull of extension," the pope took into account the fact that Columbus was ready to sail on his second journey to the New World (he sailed on September 25 from Cádiz). Alexander VI now amplified his previous gift by giving Spain title to all islands and mainlands to be discovered by sailing west-ward or southward toward the Orient and India. All previous grants to kings, princes, infantes, or military orders (an obvious reference to Henry the Navigator and the Order of Christ) were nullified.

The Portuguese were greatly disturbed by this latest papal bull because it gave Spain a right to the eastern route to the Indies and to lands off the West African coast. Though willing to accept the principle of demarcation, João II decided to negotiate directly with Fernando and Isabel. The ensuing negotiations between Spain and Portugal resulted in the Treaty of Tordesillas signed on June 7, 1494, settling the Line of Demarcation 370 leagues west of the Cape Verde Islands, where the king of Portugal suggested. All lands discovered (even if by Spaniards) east of this line would belong to Portugal, while those to the west would be reserved for Spain. That proved to be a great boon to Portugal because it subsequently guaranteed its rights to Brazil.

[See also *Treaty of Alcáçovas; Treaty of Tordesillas.*]

BIBLIOGRAPHY

Batllori, Miguel. "The Papal Division of the World and Its Consequences." In vol. 1 of *First Images of America: The*

Impact of the New World on the Old. Edited by Fredi Chiappelli. 2 vols. Berkeley, 1976.

Morison, Samuel Eliot. *Admiral of the Ocean Sea: A Life of Christopher Columbus.* Boston, 1942.

Pérez Embid, Florentino. *Los descubrimientos en el Atlántico y la rivalidad castellano-portuguesa hasta el tratado de Tordesillas.* Seville, 1948.

Weckmann, Luis. *Las bulas alejandrinas de 1493 y la teoría política del papado medieval: Estudio de la supremacia papal sobre islas, 1091–1493.* Mexico City, 1949.

JOSEPH F. O'CALLAGHAN

LISBON. The capital of Portugal is situated on the Tagus River. Conquered by various peoples, Lisbon was called Olissippo by the Romans (205 B.C.) and Ashbouna by the Moors (A.D. 716). In 1147 it was seized by Afonso Henriques (1111?–1185), the founder of the Portuguese monarchy, and in 1255 it was raised to the status of capital of the kingdom. Lisbon was a strategic port on the Atlantic, and the great discoveries and the expansion of maritime commerce in the fifteenth century turned it into one of the largest and richest European capitals. At the end of the century its population was about 60,000 and a century later, 120,000.

Two factors turned Lisbon into a renowned capital: nautical science and the development of the bourgeoisie. Prince Henry the Navigator surrounded himself with cosmographers, cartographers, and navigators and was responsible for greatly developing nautical science. Naval building improved, leading to the appearance of the caravel, a light type of ship. The Portuguese made numerous advances in navigation. In the fifteenth century they discovered the Madeira archipelago, the Azores, Cap Vert, and the coast of Guinea, from which came African slaves, gold, rubber, ivory, pepper, and pimenta longa. Sugar, rye, honey, dyes, and cattle were transported from the Atlantic islands through merchants from Genoa, Biscay, and Seville as well as by Arab and Jewish merchants. In its role as mediator between the Mediterranean populations and the centers of production in northern Europe, Lisbon became a formidable cosmopolitan bazaar. But in spite of Portugal's superiority in navigation and naval construction, it did not have its own capital for investment or easy access to great markets; thus, it relied on German and Italian capital and Spanish money.

Enormous privileges were granted to foreign merchants; the role of the Italians, especially the Genoese, after the fourteenth century, was essential to commerce in the metropolis. Flemish, German, and French ships also cast anchor frequently in the port, and in 1478 taxation was reduced and legal protection was extended to them. The discovery of America enlarged the economy; in Lisbon there began to arrive dyes, parrots, and, most important, after the middle of the sixteenth century, sugar from Brazil.

The society had an ambiguous character: an ecclesiastical class of nobles was based in a mercantile economy whose power was concentrated in the hands of a dynamic bourgeoisie, devoted to trade. Many were Jews who converted to Catholicism after 1497 and were called new Christians. A small bourgeoisie of tradesmen and craftsmen was also involved in commerce. In the fourteenth century the society was divided into distinct groups: clergy, nobility, and the general population, each with its own juridical differences and behavioral values. The third group was composed of farmers, merchants, craftsmen, and servants.

Economic prosperity enhanced artistic creativity, which in Lisbon was reflected by such masterpieces as the Jeronimos monastery and the Belém Tower, built in 1515 to celebrate overseas discoveries. In the 1460s Nuno Gonçalves painted Saint Vicente's altar in the cathedral of Lisbon. In the sixteenth century various masterpieces reflecting Italian influence were produced.

The Portuguese intelligentsia, concentrated in Lisbon, focused on scientific and experimental studies; two remarkable examples are those of García d'Orta in the field of botany and Pedro Nunes in cosmology. The expulsion of the Jews from Spain brought 120,000 immigrants to Portugal, including scientists, philosophers, and other professionals; some played an important role in the intellectual life of the metropolis. Among them, for example, was Abraham Zacuto, whose work was used by Christopher Columbus.

The seven or eight years that Columbus spent in Portugal are surrounded by shadows, and many facts and dates are uncertain. He apparently arrived in Lisbon after 1477. At that time Italian merchants controlled 78 percent of the sugar trade; the Genoese company Centurione, which Columbus represented, probably sent him to the Azores and Madeira. The experience acquired in Lisbon through his contacts with Portuguese navigation experts was decisive for his future life course. He married Felipa Moniz y Perestrelo, the daughter of the governor of Porto Santo; this is where he lived, according to some authors, for a number of years and where his son Diego was born. He had access to his father-in-law's documents and maps concerning navigation in the Atlantic and lived among men of the sea who stimulated his imagination with their stories. He went to Lisbon in 1481 and presented his project to King João II, who refused it when a committee of nautical scientists branded Columbus a "dreamer." After his wife's death he was in debt and burdened by his little son, and he left Lisbon.

Portuguese society offered a model of cultural and

PORT OF LISBON. Engraving from Théodor de Bry's *Americae*. Frankfurt, 1594.

NATIONAL MARITIME MUSEUM, GREENWICH

religious coexistence that had no equal beyond the Pyrenees. But after the establishment of the Inquisition and the beginning of discriminatory and exterminative policies by the state and the church, the creative bourgeoisie was debilitated or expatriated, and Lisbon went into a decline.

BIBLIOGRAPHY

Castelo Branco, Fernando. *Museus de Lisboa.* Lisbon, 1961.

Freire, Eduardo de Oliveira. *Elementos para a história do municipio de Lisboa.* 17 vols. Lisbon, 1882–1911.

Godinho, Vitorino Magalhães. *Estrutura da antiga sociedade portuguesa.* 2d ed. Lisbon, 1975.

Godinho, Vitorino Magalhães. *Os descobrimentos e a ecônomia mundial.* 2d ed. 4 vols. Lisbon, 1983.

Heers, Jacques. *L'occident au XIV et XV siècles: Aspects économiques et sociaux.* 3d ed. Paris, 1970.

Marques, A. H. Oliveira. *História de Portugal.* Vol. 1. Lisbon, 1972.

Mauro, Fréderic. *O porto de Lisboa, estudo de história econômica seguido de um catalogo bibliográfico e iconográfico.* Lisbon, 1960.

ANITA WAINGORT NOVINSKY
Translated from Portuguese by Paola Carù

LITERATURE. [This entry includes three articles that survey the appearance of Christopher Columbus as a figure in literature:

Columbus in European Literature
Columbus in Hispanic Literature
Columbus in American Literature

For discussion of Columbus's own literary output, see *Writings.* For discussion of scholarly research on Columbus and his times, see *Bibliography.*]

Columbus in European Literature

Christopher Columbus enters French literature through the interest shown his discovery by François Rabelais (c. 1483–1553) and Michel de Montaigne (1533–1592). Rabelais was inspired by Pietro Martire d'Anghiera's *De orbe novo* (1530) to write the fourth and fifth books of *Pantagruel* (1533). The protagonist's navigations are viewed ironically, but Rabelais's admiration for Columbus leads him to place the oracle sought by Panurge in Cathay, the happy land dreamed of by the discoverer. Besides having written a letter to Etienne de La Boétie in which he speaks admiringly of the discovery of the New World, Montaigne devotes several paragraphs of his *Essais* (1588) to the American Indians. Montaigne's benevolence toward the "savages" in the chapter "Des cannibales" was later shared by Rousseau and Montesquieu.

Many French poets showed respect for Columbus in their work, among them Marie Anne du Boccage who wrote a didactic epic poem, *La Colombiade, ou la foi porté au Nouveau Monde* (1756). Blaise Pascal (1623–1662) cites Columbus in the eighteenth letter of the *Provinciales* (1657), written to a Jesuit priest, declaring that the king of Spain had done well to believe Columbus rather than those who denied the existence of the antipodes. Voltaire (1694–1778) also admired Columbus and went so far as to state that all that had occurred before the discovery of America seemed of no consequence compared to this great event. The New World and its inhabitants appeared in many of Voltaire's volumes, including *Candide* (1759). His tragedy, *Alzire* (1736), is set in the city of Los Reyes. Jean-Jacques Rousseau (1712–1778) wrote *Christophe Colombe, ou la découverte du Nouveau Monde* as a piece to be put to music. The three acts in verse portray Columbus as a sort of deus ex machina, whose friendship toward the natives is distinctly modern.

Columbus is the subject of two fictionalized biographies of this period: Lamartine's (1790–1869) *Christophe Colomb* and a chapter in Jules Verne's (1828–1905) *Histoire des grands voyages et des grands voyageurs*. According to Verne, Columbus's genius lay in his perseverance and audacity: his greatness stemmed not from his arrival in the New World, but from his having left the Old. During this same period Fernand Denis's *Ismael Ben Kaizar, ou la découvert du Nouveau Monde* (1829) was published. The novel presents an almost entirely fictionalized Columbus, who is conceived as a romantic character. Commissioned by Pope Pius IX, Count Roselly de Lorgues published *Christophe Colomb* (1856), intended to encourage the beatification of the discoverer. In 1881 Gustave Flaubert's *Bouvard et Pécuchet* appeared posthumously. Bouvard reproaches Bossuet for not having spoken of America, while Vacombeil declares the necessity of exalting the discovery. Bouvard and Pécuchet feel weighed down by the world's stupidity upon learning that the inconsistent chatter they hear is repeated on the other side of the globe. Hence, Flaubert demonstrates that stupidity spares no one.

During the 1900s Columbus's almost mad audacity is conjured up in André Breton's *Manifeste du surréalisme* (1924). The most salient drama written on the navigator is Paul Claudel's (1868–1955) *Le livre de Christophe Colomb* (1928). Ferdinando Taviani in his *La parabola teatrale: Un saggio sulteatro di Paul Claudel* (1969) has pointed out that Claudel's play releases the spectator from traditional space and time, permitting a view from above, as God might view the world. Similar to the way in which Dante viewed a world that was structurally Ptolemaic and morally hierarchical, Claudel sees a tired multitude seeking to build a destiny for itself on a lost planet.

Guillaume Apollinaire (1880–1918) invokes in the poem *Toujours* (from *Calligrammes*) a Columbus who brings about the oblivion of the Old World. A clear quote from the Admiral can be found in *Le maître de Santiago* (1947) by Henri-Marie-Joseph Millon de Montherlant, in which it is said that the enterprise of the Genoese "is the most sublime thing that has ever happened to the World." The French-speaking Swiss writer Blaise Cendrars (Frédéric Sauser, 1887–1961) in his poem *Christophe Colomb* speaks of the Admiral falsifying for the crew the calculation of the miles covered. The Belgian writer Michel de Ghelderode (1898–1962) was moved to write his baroque

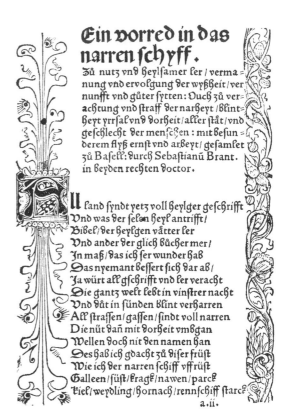

Das Narrenschiff. Basel, 1494. First page of the work containing the first literary reference in German to the islands discovered by Columbus. Library of Congress, Rare Book Division

play *Christophe Colombe* (1929), after reading Baudelaire's poem *Le voyage*. Despite its numerous historical errors, the text is interesting for its portrayal of Columbus trying to redeem himself of his own transitoriness by "doing," thus seeking self-perpetuation through action. The Belgian Charles Bertin's *Christophe Colomb* presents Columbus as burdened with a sense of absolute solitude, just as the New World and his own personal victory are within reach.

An examination of Columbus as he appears in German literature should begin with the poem *Das Narrenschiff* (1494) by Sebastian Grant, which vaguely recalls Columbus's first voyage in a cutting satire on stupidity. In the following years, Jakob Ayrer (1540–1605) wrote *Die Schöne Sidea*, whose similarity with Shakespeare's *Tempest* is remarkable. In his preface to the *Mantissa codicis jurus gentium diplomatici*, Gottfried Wilhelm Leibnitz (1646–1716) characterizes Columbus as a great Genoese of even greater fame.

Although he did not refer directly to Columbus, Friedrich Maximilian von Klinger (1752–1831) chose America as the setting for his drama *Der Wirrwarr, oder Sturm und Drang* (1776), which was staged in 1777 and whose title would later become the name of the first movement of German romanticism. In his poem *Columbus,* Friedrich von Schiller (1759–1805) enthusiastically praises Columbus's courage, in which he discerns the human ability to create reality out of nothingness.

As Johan Peter Eckermann writes in *Gespräche mit Goethe in den letzen Jahren seines Lebens* (1836–1848), Johann Wolfgang von Goethe (1749–1832) claimed that Columbus's groping was of a person who already knew what he had to find. References to America are found in both *Wilhelm Meisters Lehrjahre* and in the lyric poem *Glückliche Fahrt.* In the former, America is portrayed as a space open to the future and is praised for not having a past made of ruins.

The playwright August Friedrich Ferdinand von Kotzebue (1761–1819) also treated American themes in his work. In *La Colombona,* the Swiss author Johann Jakob Bodmer (1698–1783) perceives Columbus as a sort of prophet inspired by God. Joachim Heinrich Campe's (1746–1818) *The Discovery of America,* a didactic and moralistic dialogue addressed to the youth of the period, portrays Columbus as an intelligent man determined to reach his goal. In *Kolomb,* Friedrich Hölderlin (1770–1843) declares that had he, the poet, wished to lead a heroic life, he would have wanted to be a hero of the seas, adding that he would have enjoyed going to Genoa to visit the house in which Columbus spent his youth. In 1818, August Platen (1796–1835) wrote the ballad *Columbus Geist* in which Columbus appears as a shadow hovering over the ocean who pessimistically predicts Europe's downfall to Napoleon, who is locked in the prison of Saint Helena.

Heinrich Heine (1797–1856) devoted his long poem, *Vitlipuzli,* to the tragedy of the Aztec civilization destroyed by Hernando Cortés. He writes that Columbus was a true hero and compares his generous, luminous soul to the sun. He asserts that it would have been better for Columbus never to have been born, or at least to have retained his anonymity, than have his pure, great name linked with that of a criminal.

Although many German thinkers (including Kant, Hegel, and Marx) wrote on the discovery of the New World, it was Friedrich Wilhelm Nietzsche (1844–1900) who acutely rendered Columbus's yearning for immortality. Besides likening himself to Columbus in *Die fröhliche Wissenschaft,* Nietzsche in his poem *Colombus novus* (published as *Yorik-Colombo* in 1884) imagines Columbus as a navigator holding the helm of his ship as space and time shimmer in the distance.

Sigmund Freud's (1856–1939) antipathy toward Columbus is quite singular, especially since he believed that he shared many traits with the discoverer— whom he did not consider to be a great man. During the 1900s, Hans Joachim Haecker interpreted Columbus as a Strindberg-

esque figure; Walter Hasenclaver and Kurt Tucholsky portrayed him as an expressionist; and Hans Kyser, as a progressive. In Peter Hack's first book, *Die Eröffnung des indischen Zeiltalter,* Columbus can be compared to Brecht's Galileo. This brief overview of the treatment of Columbus in German literature concludes with Thomas Mann's (1875–1955) little-known work *Meerfahrt mit Quichote* (1934), in which Columbus is specifically mentioned and the sea is seen as a metaphor for infinity.

There are a few other texts in European literature that are worthy of note: the ambitious *Kolombus* by the Czech author Jaroslav Hilbert and the Dutch author G. Gorris's *Christoffel Columbus, laatste Kruisvaarder.* Two important dramas must also be noted: *Cristoval Colon* by the Yugoslavian Mirolsva Krleza and Nikos Kazantzàkis's *Cristoforo Colombo.* Krleza treats Columbus as a man whose future reputation has yet to be determined, a man crucified by his shipmates, who do not understand him. In Kazantzàkis's text Columbus becomes a sinner through God's will—obeying a higher plan that transcends his individual fate.

The expression *Novyk Mir* (New world)—which later became the title of an important Russian literary magazine founded in the 1920s—was first used by Maksim Grek, a Greek monk who moved to Russia in 1518 with the intention of revising liturgical texts. The first direct reference to Columbus in Russian is made by the monk Simeon Polckij (1629–1680) in a semiserious poem contained in his *Carmina Varia.* The discovery of America is given the same importance as that of vodka and hair dye. Columbus is said to have sailed around the globe, to have fought against sea monsters, and to have found the new lands for his lord, the king of Spain.

In 1761, Mikhail Vasilyevich Lomonosov called the explorers of the Bering Strait "Russian Columbuses." The Ukrainian poet and philosopher Grigory Skovorada wrote *Americus Colombus* in 1772, drawing inspiration from the episode of the dove sent by Noah, following the Flood, to search for land. In his *Scena iz Fausta* (1825), Aleksandr Pushkin (1799–1837) scolds the Spanish for having brought syphilis to Europe. Nevertheless, he was benevolent toward Columbus, whom he cites twice in his *Istorija Petra–Istorija Pugačeva* (1832–1834), stating that Karamzin discovered Russia, just as Columbus discovered America.

In 1925, on a ship bound for New York, the poet Vladimir Majakovskij (1893–1930) wrote a piece entitled *Christofor Kolomb,* in support of an article from a Madrid newspaper that claimed that Columbus was a Spanish Jew. But in previous poems Columbus is described as a sturdy noose of Genoese rope, an allusion to the insults hurled by his shipmates just as land was coming into view. Other Russian texts that should be mentioned are Ilia Ilf and Evgenij Petrov's play *Kolumb,* a satirical piece written in

1928, and Joseph Brodsky's *Less than One: Selected Essays* (1986) in which Columbus is quoted as discoverer of the West Indies.

Although Columbus is the subject of much Italian literature, its quality, ironically, is inferior to works published in other languages. The Florentine writer Giuliano Dati's poem *La historia della inventione delle diese isole Canaria indiane, extracta d'una epistola di Cristoforo Colombo* is essentially a translation from the Castilian of the letter Columbus wrote to Luis de Santángel describing his first journey.

Columbus receives better treatment in the works of Giordano Bruno (1548–1600) and Tommaso Campanella (1568–1639). In *La cena delle ceneri,* Bruno compares the Genoese navigator to the mythical Tifi, although he expresses serious reservations about the impact of the Old World on the New. In Campanella's *La città del sole,* a Genoese ship's captain describes a utopian island that is reminiscent of Thomas More's *Utopia;* other works of his also mention Columbus. Francesco Guicciardini (1483–1540) exalts the discoverer's audacity in his *Storia d'Italia.*

Fortune foretells a Ligurian's passing through the Pillars of Hercules in Torquato Tasso's (1544–1595) *Gerusalemme liberata.* Giacomo Leopardi (1798–1837) treated Columbus with a sophisticated aesthetic—albeit from a peculiar psychological angle. In *Diario di Cristoforo Colombo e Pietro Gutierrez,* Leopardi imagines Columbus on the night before his discovery of the New World; he is seen as a man whose sense of anticipation and risk seems to be the only means of battling against the tedium of existence and the gray ambitions of a mediocre life.

Few Italian dramas inspired by Columbus are worthy of note, although two nineteenth-century dramas by Paolo Giacometti—*Cristoforo Colombo alla scoperta dell'America* and *La morte di Cristoforo Colombo*—received vast public acclaim, and Antonio Gazzoletti's monologue *Le ultime ore di Cristoforo Colombo* reduced at least two generations to tears. Among the plays on Columbus published during the 1900s, two are of interest: *L'Ammiraglio degli oceani e delle anime* by Rosso di San Secondo (1887–1956), which portrays Columbus in a lyrical form as a "Bearer of Christ" (not only for the inhabitants of the New World, but also for a ship boy of his crew) and *Isabella, tre caravelle e un cacciaballe* by Dario Fo, which, while mocking the great Navigator, reluctantly recognizes his glory.

A good example of narrative works on Columbus published during the 1800s is Anton Giulio Barrili's cycle: *Le due Beatrici, Terra vergine, I figli del cielo, Fior d'oro,* and *Raggio di Dio.* The humorous tone used by Cesare Pascarella (1858–1940) in *La scoperta dell'America* is taken up in the second half of the twentieth century in works by Achille Campanile, Massimo Simili, and Umberto Eco,

who render Columbus the protagonist of quite amusing short stories.

Cristoforo Colombo nella leggenda e nella storia (1923) by Cesare de Lollis and *Il Genovese* (1951) by Paolo Revelli have a lively narrative style. Though lacking in historical fact, these stories have contributed enormously to making the Admiral a sentimental hero.

The most important Italian prose on Columbus remains Paolo Emilio Taviani's *La meravigliosa avventura di Cristoforo Colombo,* in which he summarizes his preceding fundamental books on Columbus and his achievement in a more popular style while retaining the scrupulous accuracy of his earlier books.

BIBLIOGRAPHY

Bedarida, H. "Christophe Colomb dans la littérature française." In *Genova municipale.* Vol. 10. Genoa, 1930.

Conti, S. *Un secolo di bibliografia colombiana 1880–1985.* Genoa, 1986.

Gerbi, A. *La disputa del Nuovo Mondo: Storia di una polemica.* Milan and Naples, 1975.

Marcialis, N., ed. *E i russi scoprirono l'America.* Rome, 1989.

Martini, D. G. *Cristoforo Colombo tra ragione e fantasia.* Genoa, 1986.

Martini, D. G. *Cristoforo Colombo, l'America e il teatro.* Genoa, 1988.

Pike, R. "The Image of the Genoese Age of Literature." In *Hispania.* Madrid, 1963.

Spina, Giorgio. *Cristoforo Colombo e la poesia.* Genoa, 1988.

Taviani, P. E. *La meravigliosa avventura di Cristoforo Colombo.* Novara, 1989.

Wetzel, E. *Der Kolumbus: Stoff im Deutschen Geistesleben.* Breslau, 1935.

DARIO G. MARTINI
Translated from Italian by Francesca Giusti

Columbus in Hispanic Literature

The figure of Columbus in Hispanic literature is part of Iberoamerican cultural history as well as of the world vision of its peoples and cultures. Although a figure blurred and modified by myth, legend, and folktale, Columbus has not always been blindly revered in the Hispanic world. The historical character, the legendary discoverer, the navigator par excellence, the visionary and persevering man who, against all odds, ultimately achieved his dreams, has been a rich source of creative inspiration, but he has been a problematic figure as well. Although among the Spanish of his time, Columbus may have been admired as an instrument of imperial expansion, he has, for many Hispanic Americans in the twentieth century, become the symbol of a legacy of colonialism, exploitation, and destruction. Nevertheless, in Iberian literature, his historical reputation never exceeded the proportions of his real accomplishments as recorded in his Letter of Discovery (1493) and in the chronicles and historical narratives. And in Hispanic America, the letter and his journal, published in the nineteenth century, have attained the status of foundational texts of Hispanic American letters. In Spain and in Hispanic America, then, both documents occupy privileged places, but for different reasons.

For the Spanish, Columbus's letter substantiated and legitimized the Castilian Crown's exclusive right to commercial, religious, and political enterprises in other lands. The fact that a new continent had indeed been discovered was realized and confirmed only after Columbus's death in 1508. But by then, the discoveries, explorations, conquests, and settlements had been realistically described by Spanish writers for what they were: a collective Spanish or Portuguese enterprise.

The first literary reference to Columbus by a Spanish writer is attributed to Ambrosio Montesinos, Queen Isabel's favorite poet, who during the time of the first voyage wrote a short poem (published in 1508) that captures the anxiety felt over the fate of those who had departed with Columbus. Juan Sobriano Segundo, an erudite author, wrote a poem in Latin, dedicated to King Fernando, which includes a few verses devoted to the "Discovery of New Islands" and credits the king with the propagation of Christianity. There are, on the one hand, references to mistreatment of the Indians in such plays as Micael de Carvajal's *Las cortes de la muerte* (Death's courts, 1552–1557) and, on the other, praises of the conquistadores' prowess as in Francisco de Herrera's *Elegies VII and XI* (1582). The poet Juan de Castellanos, a soldier and conquistador and later a priest who died in Colombia, was the first to devote a lengthy poem to Columbus in his biographical sketches of conquistadores, *Elegías de varones ilustres de Indias* (Elegies of illustrious men of the Indies), written between 1570 and 1592. Here Columbus is depicted as a "renowned navigator" whose mission—the fulfillment of the prophecy of completion of the world—justifies the nobility, titles, and wealth he has earned. King Fernando is portrayed as the most likely person to have supported the enterprise. Castellanos was the first one to include in a literary work the sixteenth-century popular versions of the genesis of Columbus's enterprise: that it was the outcome of practical experience rather than intellectual speculation; that his certainty about its feasibility depended on his knowledge of a prior discovery; and that he possessed Paolo dal Pozzo Toscanelli's letter and map concerning a westward route to the Indies.

Few writers of Spain's literary golden age (1500–1680) paid attention to Columbus, although Francisco de Quevedo wrote a poem, "Túmulo de Colón" (Tumulus for Columbus), in which a fragment of the sunken *Santa María* "speaks" of him as "venerable and saint." It was Lope de Vega, however, the creator of Spanish national drama, who wrote the first important European work devoted to Columbus. Written between 1595 and 1605, *El Nuevo Mundo descubierto por Cristóbal Colón* (The New World discovered by Columbus) was published in 1614. Structurally and thematically a problematic play, it nevertheless stands as the first effort to dramatize crucial scenes in the Admiral's life: from his requests for support from the monarchs of Portugal, England, and Spain to his triumphant return to Spain in 1493. Columbus is portrayed as a man divinely inspired to carry out the important mission of disseminating Christianity (although his honor is shared by King Fernando). He stands above all other humans, while his companions represent the lust for gold, a characterization that was to become paradigmatic in subsequent treatments of Columbus and the conquistadores. Using allegorical characters, Lope de Vega examines the controversial political, ethical, and moral issues related to the new lands and their inhabitants. Scenes of Indian dances, songs, and love affairs and their first reactions to the men who come from the sea, even when articulated within the dramatic conventions popular in the seventeenth century, capture the wonder and the surprise of both groups at that encounter. The play portrays the Indians' "distinctiveness" and stresses their response to accepting Christianity as their new religion.

The texts after Lope de Vega's play enunciated, reformulated, and transformed the various biographical episodes in Columbus's life to form a mythic version, beginning with the hero's birth and first wanderings along the Mediterranean and extending through his quest for support for his enterprise, the perilous voyage, his discoveries in the New World, his first triumphant return, and his ultimate ruin and death in obscurity and poverty.

During the Enlightenment, only a few authors dealt with Columbus's story, and their portrayals reflect the negative nuances of the Black Legend. In the early nineteenth century, Spanish writers subscribed to the neoclassic tradition as seen in the odes "Al Mar" (To the sea) and "Juan Padilla" by Manuel José Quintana and "El Oro" (Gold) by Catalan poet Manuel Cabanyes. *Cristóbal Colón* (1790), a play by Luciano Comella, portrays Columbus's tragic return to Spain in chains and depicts him as a man who is condemned to imprisonment by the intrigues of his enemies but is finally saved by the queen's intervention.

The figure of Columbus underwent further metamorphosis under the influence of romanticism and realism. The narrative of his life was strongly shaped by Sir Walter Scott's and Alphonse de Lamartine's works, Washington Irving's biography of Columbus, and, most important, by James Fenimore Cooper's *Mercedes of Castile; or The*

Voyage to Cathay, dealing with the first voyage. Francisco José Orellana, Cooper's most fervent Spanish follower, popularized Columbus in his best historical novel, *Cristóbal Colón* (1868). Some plays, seeking to portray an adventurous, dramatic, and sentimental Columbus, concern themselves with love affairs and duels, as in Patricio de Escosura's *La aurora de Colón* (1838). In other works he was identified with Spain's glorious past: Antonio Ribot y Fonserré's *Cristóbal Colón o las glorias de España* (1840), Tomás Rodriguez Rubí's *Isabel la Católica* (1863), Cabanyes's poem "Colombo," Duque de Rivas's "Oda a Cristóbal Colón," Ramón de Campoamor's dramatic poem *Recuerdos de un gran hombre* (1853), and Angel Lasso de la Vega's "Colón y España" (1859). In still other works Columbus was identified with the Wandering Jew, as in Eugenio Sánchez de la Fuente's *Colón y el judío errante* (1843), or was the object of romantic attraction, as in Juan de Dios de la Rada's *Cristóbal Colón* (1860) in which Beatriz out of passionate love tries everything possible to persuade him not to follow his mission.

With the coming of the four hundredth anniversary of 1492 the literary production increased. Several Columbian romances were published such as V. García-Escobar's *Romancero de Cristóbal Colón* (1866) and *Romancero General* (1873), José Velarde's *Romancero de Colón* (1887), and Narciso Campillo's five romances about Columbus at La Rábida in *Nuevas poesías* (1867). Catalan Jacinto Verdaguer portrayed Columbus as Christ-bearer in his well-known *La Atlántida* (1877), and several authors presented him on the verge of death reminiscing about his past misfortunes, as in Luis M. de Larra y Wetoret's play *La agonía* (1861), Vicente W. Querol's poem "Colón" (1890), and Victor Balaguer's play *La última hora de Colón* (1868).

In the twentieth century Columbus caught the attention of hundreds of writers. Novelist Vicente Blasco Ibáñez, in *En busca del Gran Khan* (In search of the Grand Khan, 1938), authored one of the best novels about Columbus ever written in Spain. The latest versions of the Columbus story, for example, Alberto Miralles's plays *Cataro Colón* (1969) and its revised version, *Colón* (1981), portray the nation and Columbus as more concerned with commercial and trade profits than with spiritual matters.

To Hispanic Americans Columbus's letter and journal marked the first step toward the integration of the New World into the Old, starting a transformation that is still in progress. They generated a dialogical relationship between historical and literary texts that goes back to the nineteenth century and is present in the historical reformulations of contemporary writers. For Colombian Nobel laureate Gabriel García Márquez—as for many Hispanic Americans—Columbus's letter is the first masterpiece of magical realism as literary narrative, and Columbus's journal, surrounded by "mysteries which he himself propitiated," constitutes the second work of Caribbean literature.

Washington Irving's biography (1828) influenced many early portraits of Columbus in Hispanic American literature. In "Los compañeros de Colón" (1832), a neoclassic poem by Cuban José María Heredia, Columbus is envisioned as "a prophetic inspired genius." Another Cuban poet, Gertrudis Gómez de Avellaneda, devoted a hymn to a statue of Columbus in 1863. For other writers, under the influence of Victor Hugo, Columbus represents the human race, which had conquered the New World and bestowed upon it liberty and progress—an outlook seen in Olegario V. Andrade's *La Atlántida* (1881) and José Joaquín Ortiz's *Colón y Bolívar, Colombia y España,* and *Los colonos.* A wide variety of other themes were sounded in the literature: for Rafael Pombo, in *Isaac y Colón,* Columbus was the evangelist bent on a messianic mission; for Peruvian José Santos Chocano, America, in *Alma América* (1906), was the outcome of the energy and dream of a woman (Queen Isabel) and a man (Columbus); for Nicaraguan Rubén Darío, Columbus was both the bringer of the Spanish language and the "unfortunate discoverer" who left a legacy of misery in the Americas; for Mexican Amado Nervo, he was the symbol of the ultimate voyager; for Chilean Vicente Huidobro, he was the son or god of the sea.

Later in the twentieth century Columbus became less a symbol of spiritual conquest, of Hispanism (Gabriela Mistral, Blanco Fombona), and was portrayed more critically, as in the work of Nobel Prize laureate Pablo Neruda of Chile, to whom he represents all the evils of colonialism. Possibly the most technically and ideologically innovative literary representations have been written in the last few decades. Nicaraguan poet Ernesto Cardenal in *El estrecho dudoso* (1966) re-creates the discovery of Central America, emphasizing the themes of disillusionment and the beginning of the loss of identity for American communities. Columbus's presence in García Marquéz's novel *El otoño del patriarca* (Autumn of the patriarch, 1975), a text interpolated by other fictional texts, recasts Columbus's traditional image as discoverer of the New World with that of Columbus as modern positivist. In 1976 Venezuelan playwright José I. Cabrujas staged *Acto cultural o Colón, Cristóbal, el Genovés alucinado* (Cultural act or Columbus, Christopher, the Genoese hallucinated) an iconoclastic treatment in which Columbus's voyage of discovery becomes a metaphor for the characters' psychological voyage to the discovery of their intimate frustrations and fears.

In 1979 Cuban novelist Alejo Carpentier published *El arpa y la sombra* (The harp and the shadow), a powerful novel in which the author orchestrates a chorus of voices through a mixture of genres (confession, travelogue, letter, history, drama), anachronism, and various historical perspectives to provide a complex, but human image of Columbus. He is not a saint or a genius or a victim or a scoundrel but rather a convincing schemer who at the end complains that during the last four hundred years no one has been able to portray him adequately because "having come from mystery, I returned to mystery." Argentinian writer Abel Possé in *Los perros del paraíso* (The dogs of paradise, 1983) reelaborates Columbus's voyage, emphasizing through the image of dogs the legacy of violence bequeathed by that "infamous" 1492 voyage. And in Mexican novelist Carlos Fuentes's *Cristóbal Nonato* (Christopher unborn, 1987), Columbus is an unborn fetus who discovers in the Mexico of 1992 a grotesque country with such an enormous national debt that hope and optimism are impossible to sustain.

BIBLIOGRAPHY

Bierstadt, A. O. "Columbus in Romance." *Magazine of American History* 28 (1982): 272–279.

Dille, Glen F. "El descubrimiento y la conquista de América en la comedia del Siglo de Oro." *Hispania* 71 (1983): 422–502.

Flint, Weston. "Colón en el teatro español." *Estudios Americanos* 22 (1961): 165–186.

Flint, Weston. "The Figure of Christopher Columbus in French, Italian and Spanish Drama." Ph.D. diss., University of North Carolina, 1957.

Gárate Córdoba, José María. *La poesía del Descubrimiento.* Madrid, 1977.

Lasso de la Vega, Angel. "Colón y el descubrimiento en la antigua poesía castellana." *La Ilustración Española y Americana* (Madrid) 19 (May 12, 1890): 322.

Moríñigo, Marcos A. *América en el teatro de Lope de Vega.* Buenos Aires, 1954.

Oyuela, Calixto. "Colón y la poesía." Vol. 2 of *Estudios literarios.* Buenos Aires, 1943.

Palencia-Roth, Michael. "Prisms of Consciousness: 'The Worlds' of Columbus and García Márquez." In *Critical Perspectives on Gabriel García Márquez.* Edited by Bradley A. Shaw and Nora Vera-Golwin. Lincoln, Neb., 1986.

Regazzoni, Susanna. *Cristoforo Colombo nella letteratura spagnola dell' ottocento.* Milano, 1988.

Regazzoni, Susanna. "La historia de Cristóbal Colón en el siglo decimonónico: ¿Biografías o novelas?" *Rassegna Iberistica* 29 (Sept. 1987): 15–23.

Shannon, Robert M. *Visions of the New World in the Drama of Lope de Vega.* New York, 1989.

ASELA R. LAGUNA

Columbus in American Literature

Not until after the American Revolution did writers in the United States look to Christopher Columbus as a figure of significance. Indentured to religion and (increasingly) to politics, prerevolutionary poetry and prose had little concern for matters of exploration, even less for an Italian who had sailed for the Spanish Crown. As all forms of colonial writing attest, Americans had no doubt that they had come to a New World. But only after the founding of the nation did poets and orators connect the New World to Columbus and begin to fashion images of the Admiral according to American specifications.

Among the formative expressions of praise from the early years of the Republic were the ceremonies at the first Columbus Day festivities in Boston in 1792, Philip Freneau's poem "Pictures of Columbus, the Genoese" (1788), and Joel Barlow's epic *The Columbiad* (1807), first written as *The Vision of Columbus* in 1787. Together with Washington Irving's *History of the Life and Voyages of Christopher Columbus* (1828), these works shaped images of Columbus that prevailed throughout the nineteenth century.

Boston's tricentennial celebration of Columbus's landing featured an address by Jeremy Belknap and an ode sung by a select choir. According to Belknap, Columbus discovered America and opened to European commerce "a new world." According to the choir, Columbus uncovered a land—"fair Columbia"—hidden since creation until at the appointed time she opened her arms to embrace "her adopted children." Ideas of regeneration thus joined with those of self-reliance to define a nation that looked to the past with designs on the future: while Columbia could nourish and harbor, Columbus could serve as a symbol of ongoing exploration.

Freneau's "Pictures of Columbus" and Barlow's *Columbiad* contemplate the future from radically different perspectives, one deeply personal, the other resolutely political. Freneau presents Columbus as a dreamer with practical resolve who sails on a voyage of discovery because he sees "blunders" on the existing maps. Frustrated by an arrangement of land he cannot accept, he designs his own globe, places "a new world" far to the west, and then embarks in search of what he has already envisioned. Barlow's poem begins at a tragic end with an imprisoned Columbus bemoaning "a world explored in vain" and then salutes the value of republican institutions in a series of visions offered by Hesper, the guardian genius of the "western continent."

Although Barlow's *Columbiad* celebrates an event in which Columbus played the principal role, its emphasis celebrates consequences in which he has no part. The burden of the poem is to link event and consequence, to bring Columbus and the reader to see the continuity of New World experience. And despite the patches of tedium in this curious epic, Barlow's characterization of an unnamed and largely uninhabited continent links a fifteenth-century "discovery" to a nation celebrating its uniqueness at the beginning of the nineteenth century.

COPYRIGHT, 1892, BY F. E. WRIGHT.

(51)

TITLE PAGE OF WASHINGTON IRVING'S *LIFE AND VOYAGES OF CHRISTOPHER COLUMBUS*. From a four-hundredth-anniversary issue published in New York in 1892.

Washington Irving's *History of the Life and Voyages of Christopher Columbus* (1828) comes at its subject from a different perspective. Under reproach for his lengthy stay in Europe when American literature was struggling to find a voice of its own, Irving hoped that a biography of Columbus would silence his critics. After two years he completed a study that added nothing significant to existing accounts. But his biography did validate the dual image of the Admiral that had been defined in the late years of the eighteenth century and added disquieting thoughts on the consequences of Europeans coming to the hemisphere. Repeatedly during his first voyage Irving's Columbus calms the superstitious fears of his mariners. He is not only a courageous leader but a "visionary," both "practical and poetical," concerned with knowledge rather than exploitation. Yet Columbus is implicated in a darker drama of history: Irving concludes that the arrival of Europeans in the New World was fatal to

"the indolent paradise of the Indian." His study posits a fall from Eden in a New World, with European avarice embodying the evil. As the representative of Europe and its civilization, Columbus bears a responsibility for destroying innocence; as the hero of a biography written to demonstrate Irving's commitment to an American literary agenda, Columbus is magnanimous, misjudged in his aspirations. Irving's genuine and complex ambivalence brings him to add one romantic perspective to another, to glorify Columbus and then to mourn paradise defiled.

By 1830, the figure of Columbus had been praised, split into male and female components (Columbus and Columbia), and given romantic dimensions that served a variety of expressive purposes. Irving's misgivings did not express the majority view. More indicative of popular feeling were the words of James Kirke Paulding in a letter to President James K. Polk in 1845: the moment at which Columbus first glimpsed "this Continent" yielded consequences "greater and more lasting, than ever emanated from any human being since the fall of Adam." The consequences were dependent on self-approbation: the better Americans felt about themselves, the more they praised Columbus.

Few novels were devoted to Columbus. Typically, they were flimsy attempts at narrative, unsure of their historical ground. Susanna Rowson's *Reuben and Rachel; or, Tales of Old Times* (1798) and James Fenimore Cooper's *Mercedes of Castile* (1840), for example, are labored efforts that subordinate the Admiral to formulaic concerns. But markedly different poets found Columbus and the idea of discovery useful to their purposes—among them James Russell Lowell, a Boston Brahmin; Sidney Lanier, a Confederate soldier and accomplished musician; Emma Lazarus, a spokeswoman for Jewish causes whose sonnet "The New Colossus" (1883) is carved on the Statue of Liberty; Paul Laurence Dunbar, a midwestern African American trained as a lawyer; and Joaquin Miller, a self-promoting Far Western adventurer from Liberty, Indiana. Lowell's "Columbus" (1844) portrays the explorer on his first voyage, solitary in his dreams, convinced that Europe no longer nourishes the human spirit. Lazarus's "1492" (1883) describes a year saddened by the persecution of Jews in Spain but joyful at the unveiling of a "virgin" world that will nourish the downtrodden. Dunbar's "Columbian Ode" (written in 1893, the year of the Columbian Exposition) contrasts Old World scholars blinded by superstition and Columbus whose vision fathoms the unknown. Lanier's brooding "Centennial Meditation of Columbia" (1876) and Miller's declamatory "Columbus" (1896) reveal still other ways in which Columbus served as a source for poetic expression. More profound in achievement are Walt Whitman's "Passage to India" (1871) and "Prayer of Columbus" (1874): the first yearns for a spiritual passage to truth; the second dramatizes Whitman's identification of himself with the discouraged dreamer Columbus became. Along with the more conventional work of other writers, Whitman's poems bring us to see the pervasive and sometimes eloquent romanticism that surrounded the figure of Columbus in the nineteenth century.

Although writers in the twentieth century have devoted less attention to Columbus, William Carlos Williams's study *In the American Grain* (1925) and Hart Crane's poem *The Bridge* (1930) attend to the Admiral's voyages in strikingly modern ways. The idea that the American image of Columbus reflects the American view of America is borne out again in Williams's impressionist meditations on the explorers who came early to the North American continent—Columbus, Hernando Cortés, and Hernando de Soto, among them. Williams portrays Columbus as someone who found a New World of purity and left a legacy of poison that claimed him as well as others. But Williams does not cast specific blame for what became a lethal encounter; rather, his explorers are helpless in their destructiveness, beset with an instinctive evil that haunts both conquerors and victims. Likewise an ensemble piece, though far more mystical in its vision, Crane's *The Bridge* renders a symbolic portrait of Columbus returning from his initial voyage with the supposed gift of Cathay, the first of the unifiers or "bridgers" who set the conditions for integrating past and present. Whereas Williams plunges Columbus into the plot of a fallen world, Crane presents his mistaken navigator as a prophet lifted above the mundane, ennobled by his consciousness.

Brief but salient allusions likewise suggest the diverse ways in which writers have assimilated the idea of Columbus. In her book-length study, *Woman in the Nineteenth Century* (1845), Margaret Fuller praises Isabel of Castile for giving Columbus the means of voyaging to the "New World." "This land," she continues, "must pay back its debt to Woman, without whose aid it would not have been brought into alliance with the civilized world." Henry David Thoreau enjoins in the concluding chapter of *Walden* (1853), "Be a Columbus to whole new continents and worlds within you." If Tom Sawyer landed on a wrecked riverboat, Huckleberry Finn remarks in Mark Twain's *Adventures of Huckleberry Finn* (1884), "you'd think it was Christopher C'lumbus discovering Kingdom Come." The invocation of the New World at the end of F. Scott Fitzgerald's *The Great Gatsby* (1925), the reference to Columbus standing an egg on end in the swirling conversations of William Faulkner's *Go Down, Moses* (1942), the mention of the Admiral taking native Americans back to Spain in the double-edged dialogue of Alice Walker's *The Color Purple* (1982)—such allusions testify to the continued presence of this explorer in the American literary imagination, no matter the debate over what he found or encountered, no matter the perspective on the consequences of his landing.

BIBLIOGRAPHY

Elliott, Emory. *Revolutionary Writers: Literature and Authority in the New Republic, 1725–1810.* New York, 1982.

Franklin, Wayne. *Discoverers, Explorers, Settlers: The Diligent Writers of Early America.* Chicago, 1979.

Kolodny, Annette. *The Lay of the Land: Metaphor as Experience and History in American Life and Letters.* Chapel Hill, N.C., 1975.

Mitchell, Lee Clark. *Witnesses to a Vanishing America: The Nineteenth-Century Response.* Princeton, 1981.

Pearce, Roy Harvey. *The Continuity of American Poetry.* Princeton, 1961.

Spengemann, William. *The Adventurous Muse: The Poetics of American Fiction, 1789–1900.* New Haven, 1977.

Tichi, Cecelia. *New World, New Earth: Environmental Reform in American Literature from the Puritans through Whitman.* New Haven, 1979.

TERENCE MARTIN

LODESTONE. Widely distributed in the composition of volcanic rocks, lodestone (or loadstone; the first component of the word derives from an Old English word for way or journey; French, *aimant naturel;* Italian, *calamita*), or magnetite, is a mineral consisting mainly of black oxide of iron (Fe^3O^4). The attractive properties of lodestone were known in ancient Greece and Rome and in the Muslim world. It is supposed that the earliest western compasses consisted of a lodestone placed on a piece of wood and floated on water, but the Chinese used, for divination, a spoon-shaped piece of lodestone on a polished surface *(sinan)*. Lodestones were used to magnetize, or remagnetize, floating compass needles and pivoted compass needles. Lodestones are listed in ships' inventories of the late thirteenth and fifteenth centuries: in 1294 an Italian ship had two lodestones with two charts and a pair of dividers; in 1410–1412, two English ships had, respectively, "1 sailing piece [sc. lodestone]" and "12 stones, called adamants, called sailstones . . ."; the latter were bought in Flanders. Columbus's son Fernando Colón in a passage referring to the observed "northwesting" of the compass needles in July 1496, on the third voyage, says that he believes that each piece of lodestone has points that, when applied to the needle, can make it point east, west, or south, and that this is why "he who makes the compass-needle covers the lodestone with a cloth, all but the north point of it. . . ."

In the sixteenth century the foundations were laid for the science of terrestrial magnetism, which was to have

ARMED LODESTONE. Circa 1700. A copper mounting holds the roughly shaped lodestone and its steel pole-pieces.

MUSEUM OF THE HISTORY OF SCIENCE, OXFORD

far-reaching effects on the design of the marine compass. Following the publication at London in 1600 of William Gilbert's *De magnete,* the lodestone with polished poles and mounted with pole pieces or ground to a sphere (*terella,* little earth) to simulate the earth's magnetic system became important items in the apparatus used for "philosophical" experiments.

[See also *Compass.*]

BIBLIOGRAPHY

Balmer, Heinz. *Beiträge zur Geschichte der Erkenntnis des Erdmagnetismus.* Veröffentlichungen des schweizerischen Gesellschaft für Geschichte der Medezin und der Naturwissenschaften, vol. 20. Aarau, Switzerland, 1956.

Mitchell, A. Crichton. "Chapters in the History of Terrestrial Magnetism. Chapter II—The Discovery of the Magnetic Declination." *Terrestrial Magnetism and Atmospheric Electricity* 42 (1937): 241–280.

Needham, Joseph, Wang Ling, and Kenneth Girdwood Robinson. "Physics." Part 1 of vol. 4 of *Science and Civilisation in China.* Cambridge, 1962.

Radelet de Grave, P., and D. Speiser. "Le *De Magnete* de Pierre de Maricourt. Traduction et commentaire." *Revue d'histoire des sciences et de leurs applications* 28, pt. 3 (1975): 193–234.

Waters, David W. *The Art of Navigation in England in Elizabethan and Early Stuart Times.* London, 1958.

Wiedemann, Eilhard. "Über Magnetismus." *Aufsätze zur arabischen Wissenschaftsgeschichte.* Edited by Wolfdietrich Fischer. Vol. 1, pp. 28–37. Hildesheim and New York, 1970.

FRANCIS MADDISON

LONGITUDE. The idea of defining position on the earth's surface in circular measure goes back to Ptolemy (A.D. 100–165), although Hipparchus (fl. 146–127 B.C.) before him had already proposed a geographical grid of latitude and longitude. Terrestrial longitude is the angle at the pole between a prime meridian (Ptolemy's went through the Fortunate Isles) and the meridian of the place in question (in the modern system measured through 180 degrees east and west from the prime meridian). The measurement of latitude from the altitude of the sun or a circumpolar star at meridian altitude was developed without great difficulty. But the accurate calculation of longitude, because the earth's rotation is synonymous with time, proved virtually impossible at sea until the advent of the marine chronometer in the eighteenth century. The idea that differences of longitude could be measured by timing an astronomical event, such as an eclipse or the conjunction of planets, that could be seen simultaneously by observers in different places was familiar to both the ancient Greeks and medieval astronomers, and Arab mathematicians had drawn up time differences for ephemerides compiled for Toledo so that they could be used in other places. The rate of the earth's rotation, however, is such that one degree of longitude corresponds to four minutes of time, and by the year 1500 the best mechanical clocks were subject to an error of about ten minutes a day. The Flemish astronomer Gemma Frisius proposed the use of a mechanical clock to find longitude and, had a sufficiently accurate one been available, the time of a celestial event (say an eclipse) could have been predicted for one meridian and timed at another and in this way the difference of time, and thus of longitude, established.

The lunar-distance method of determining longitude was proposed by Regiomontanus (Johann Müller) in 1474; it relies on the fact that whereas the stars appear to revolve from east to west at just over fifteen degrees every hour, the moon lags behind at a rate of about one-half degree every hour. In 1514 Johann Werner suggested measuring the lunar distance, the angle between the moon and the sun or a zodiacal star, to determine longitude at sea. However, because of its proximity to the earth, the moon will be seen at different positions in the sky by observers in different geographical locations, a parallax error that could amount to two degrees. The method was theoretically sound but only became practicable toward the end of the eighteenth century, when sufficiently precise instruments were available for the observations and the precise positions of the fixed stars, and of the moon against that background for years to come, were published in the nautical almanac. Fixing longitude by the eclipses of Jupiter's satellites had to await the invention of the telescope. For some time attempts were made to link longitude with magnetic variation, an idea finally discredited by João de Castro in 1538.

So long as it could not be determined at sea, longitude was of little consequence to the pilot, who continued to keep a careful account of the distance traveled east-west with reference to the observed latitude and the position derived from the courses made good and the estimated distances run. However, determination of longitude became a crucial issue when Pope Alexander VI decreed a meridian one hundred leagues west of the Azores as the dividing line between the Portuguese and Spanish discoveries in the Western Hemisphere. Spain would own all that lay west of the meridian, Portugal all that lay east. Adjustments were made and agreement reached with the Treaty of Tordesillas (1494), but the determination of longitude became increasingly important as transatlantic commerce grew and the question of the anti-meridian in the Eastern Hemisphere was raised concerning rival claims to the Spice Islands. Distances in leagues were sometimes converted into degrees of longitude and compared with Ptolemy's *Geography* to establish the position of newly discovered lands within that framework. In *Portuguese and Spanish Attempts to Measure Longitude in the 16th Century*, W. G. L. Randles cites the example of Giovanni da Verrazano, who in 1524, having sailed 1,200 leagues to an undiscovered land in the west, converted the distance into degrees of longitude, allowing for the convergence of the meridians in the latitude sailed, in order to see how close he had come to China, which was the objective of the voyage. Columbus probably had similar considerations when he sought to determine longitude by observation of eclipses while at anchor in the Caribbean in 1494 and 1504. He used the tables of Regiomontanus and Abraham Zacuto. He miscalculated the true longitude on the earlier occasion by 22° 30', on the later by 38'. Randles gives little credence to Amerigo Vespucci's claim to have observed lunar distances off the Venezuelan coast in 1499.

Ruy Faleiro, the Portuguese astronomer who was engaged for the preparations for Ferdinand Magellan's expedition (1519–1522) and was to have accompanied it, drew up detailed instructions for determination of longitude from observations of the latitude of the moon, lunar distances, and magnetic variation. Faleiro was unable to undertake the voyage and was replaced by Andres de San Martín who, using the tables of Regiomontanus and Zacuto, made a series of five observations along the eastern coast of South America. Of the two results that survived, one is wildly inaccurate, the other uncannily close. In the sixteenth century, the precision of both tables and instruments was wholly inadequate to the needs of navigation, let alone cartography. Randles quotes a letter from the cartographer Lopo Homem to the king of Portugal that refers to a master chart of the route to India drawn up by Pedro Nunes on which longitudes had been determined by lunar and solar eclipses. Portuguese pilots had been ordered to use the new chart, and, according to Homem, it had been the cause of shipwrecks. Portuguese pilots were thus reduced to having their charts made secretly in Spain by traditional methods.

[See also *Latitude; Line of Demarcation; Navigation; Treaty of Tordesillas.*]

BIBLIOGRAPHY

Randles, W. G. L. *Portuguese and Spanish Attempts to Measure Longitude in the 16th Century.* Coimbra, 1985.

Taylor, E. G. R. *The Haven Finding Art: A History of Navigation from Odysseus to Captain Cook.* London, 1956.

M. W. RICHEY

LOUIS XI (1423–1483), king of France. The elder son of Charles VII, Louis was on bad terms with his father from early on. He joined a revolt of the nobility in 1440 and was sent off to govern Dauphiné in 1446. Louis never again saw his father, who, angered by his independence, dispatched an army to Dauphiné in 1456. Louis sought refuge with Duke Philip of Burgundy until his father died in 1461 and he ascended the throne.

As king, Louis alienated the nobility by his tight-fisted fiscal policy and use of non-noble officials. In 1465 the nobles organized the League of the Public Weal to oppose him. With the skillful use of force and duplicity, which earned him the tag "Universal Spider," Louis defeated the nobles but was forced to concede to them a permanent exemption from the major tax, the taille.

One who refused to submit was Charles the Bold of Burgundy (r. 1467–1477). Determined to unite his separated domains of Burgundy and the Low Countries, Charles formed alliances with the kings of England and Aragón and the Holy Roman Emperor. The major issue with Aragón involved Cerdagne and Roussillon on the north slope of the Pyrenees, which Louis had invaded in 1462. Aragonese efforts to regain them failed, and France annexed them in 1475. Louis convinced the Swiss, the best soldiers of the day, that Charles's pretensions were a threat to them. In 1477 the Swiss smashed Charles's forces in the Battle of Nancy and killed him.

Louis immediately moved to take control of those of Charles's lands that were French fiefs—Burgundy, Picardy, Artois, and Flanders. Charles's daughter Mary held on to Flanders, the Low Countries, and the Franche-Comté. Ignoring Louis's demand that she wed his son, she married Maximilian of Habsburg. In 1482 Maximilian and Louis signed a treaty by which Louis's gains of 1477 were confirmed. The death of René of Anjou in 1480 passed Provence to Louis, giving France ports on the Mediterra-

Louis XI.   ELSEVIER PUBLISHING PROJECTS, AMSTERDAM

nean and making the French a factor in Mediterranean naval wars.

Louis's relentless efforts to force the nobility into submission and to raise taxes resulted in a dramatic increase in royal authority but also made him feared and despised. When the Spider King died in 1483, passing the throne to his son Charles VIII, few mourned him.

BIBLIOGRAPHY

Champion, Pierre. *Louis XI.* 2 vols. Paris, 1911.

Commynes, Philippe de. *Memoirs.* Edited by Samuel Kinser. Translated by Isabelle Cazeaux. 2 vols. Columbia, S.C., 1969.

Kendall, Paul. *Louis XI, the Universal Spider.* New York, 1971.

FREDERIC J. BAUMGARTNER

LOUIS XII (1462–1515), king of France. A second cousin to Charles VIII, Louis was a member of the Orléans branch of the Valois dynasty. As a youth Louis was forced to marry Louis XI's deformed daughter Jeanne. His resentment was a factor in his rebellion against the government of Anne of Beaujeu, who was governing France for her brother Charles. Captured in battle in 1488, Louis spent three years in prison. But in April 1498 Charles died childless, and Louis gained the throne. He quickly secured an annulment of his marriage to Jeanne and married Anne of Brittany, Charles's widow, attaching her duchy permanently to the Crown.

Louis had inherited the Visconti claim to the duchy of Milan, and in 1499 he led the second French invasion of Italy and occupied Milan. He then negotiated a treaty with Fernando of Aragón in 1500, dividing the Kingdom of Naples between them. But Fernando quickly moved to control all of Naples, and by 1503 it was securely in Spanish control.

The election of Julius II in 1503 put a strongly anti-French partisan in the papacy. After manipulating Louis into crushing Venice at Agnadello in 1509, the pope turned his Holy League into an anti-French alliance. Louis's response was to call a general council at Pisa in 1511, but its only result was Louis's excommunication as a schismatic. Julius's anti-French policy culminated in the French defeat at Novara in 1513 and eviction from Milan. More trouble for France followed when Henry VIII of England invaded Artois in 1513 and occupied Tournai. Louis was forced to conclude peace with his enemies.

In hopes of having a son, Louis agreed to marry Henry's sister Mary, Queen Anne having died in January 1514. His young bride's disruption of his life weakened his already poor health, and the "Father of the People," so called for his enlightened domestic policy, died on January 1, 1515, passing the throne to his cousin and son-in-law, Francis I.

BIBLIOGRAPHY

Bridge, John. *A History of France from the Death of Louis XI.* 5 vols. New York, 1929.

Febvre, Lucien. *Life in Renaissance France.* Translated by Marian Rothstein. Cambridge, Mass., 1977.

Quilliet, Bernard. *Louis XII, Père du peuple.* Paris, 1986.

FREDERIC J. BAUMGARTNER

LUNAR PHENOMENA. To sailors in the time of Columbus the moon was important because of its effect on tides and because lunar eclipses could be used to determine longitude. The exact influence of the moon on tides, however, was imperfectly comprehended before Isaac Newton described the law of universal gravitation, and the relation of the sun and the moon was not understood.

Observers tried to determine the recurring cycles (saros cycles) of eclipses since antiquity. The exact hour of the beginning or the end of an eclipse could not be determined correctly since a satisfactory theory of lunar movements did not exist. From the beginning of the sixteenth century, the time of a lunar eclipse was used to determine the geographic longitude of a place. It was also thought that longitude could be determined by observing the stars during occultation by the moon, by observing the opposition of the moon and Venus, and by using other equally fallible methods. Because of insufficient knowledge of the perturbations of the orbit of the moon, however, sixteenth-century methods were inherently imprecise.

Determining longitude and latitude—and therefore the exact position of a ship—was a crucial problem for

1298	1900	1901
Eclipfis Solis	Eclipfis Lune	Eclipfis Lune
29 3 2	9 12 2	2 18 29
Iulii	Nouembris	Maii
Dimidia duratio	Dimidia duratio	Dimidia duratio
0 36	1 38	1 42
Puncta tria	Puncta decem	

1902	1902	1902
Eclipfis Solis	Eclipfis Lune	Eclipfis Lune
30 19 24	14 12 20	29 13 36
Septembris	Octobris	Februarii
Dimidia duratio	Dimidia duratio	Dimidia duratio
1 8	1 1	1 26
Puncta decem	Puncta tria	

FIFTEENTH-CENTURY STUDY OF LUNAR ECLIPSES. Regiomontanus's *Ephemeria*, a page showing lunar and solar eclipses. Nürnberg, 1475. LIBRARY OF CONGRESS, RARE BOOK DIVISION

navigators. The first half of the fifteenth century saw the beginning of fairly accurate findings of latitude and longitude, that is, with insignificant errors of observation, on board caravels and other ships.

The most common way to determine longitude during navigation was based on the lunar eclipse. The process, although certain in principle, had the drawback of infrequent occurrence, since to be useful, the determination of longitude had to be done often in the progress of a voyage. Furthermore, the moment of eclipse or reappearance of the moon was always estimated imprecisely; because of this, the process almost always involved enormous errors. Columbus, whose navigational abilities are unquestioned today, determined longitudes with errors of twenty degrees.

Navigators in the seventeenth century finally understood that the solution of the problem of determining longitude lay in the construction of an accurate timepiece. This enterprise engaged various scientists, Christiaan Huyghens in particular. It was John Harrison (1693–1776) who succeeded in finding the solution in the second half of the eighteenth century by developing the marine chronometer.

BIBLIOGRAPHY

Albuquerque, Luís de. *Astronomical Navigation*. Lisbon, 1988.
Costa, A. Fontoura da. *A marinharia dos descobrimentos*. 2d ed. Lisbon, 1939.
Cotter, Charles A. *A History of Nautical Astronomy*. London, 1968.
Randles, W. G. L. *Portuguese and Spanish Attempts to Measure Longitude in the 16th Century*. Coimbra, 1985.
Taylor, E. G. R. *The Haven-Finding Art: A History of Navigation from Odysseus to Captain Cook*. Rev. ed. London, 1971.

LUÍS DE ALBUQUERQUE
Translated from Portuguese by Paola Carù

MADEIRA. The archipelago of Madeira lies in the Atlantic Ocean about 560 kilometers (350 miles) from Morocco and 800 kilometers (500 miles) from continental Portugal. Known to the Romans as the Purple Islands, they were rediscovered by João Gonçalves Zarco and Tristão Vaz Teixeira in 1418 and 1420. Under the orders of Prince Henry the Navigator the two largest islands of the group, Madeira and Porto Santo, were settled rapidly; two of the island groups, the Selvagens and the Desertas, are uninhabited. Together, the two inhabited islands, which boast one of the finest climates in the world, comprise the Funchal district of Portugal.

Some fifty years after colonization had begun, Columbus established important connections with Madeira. In the summer of 1478, Paolo di Negro, an associate of the wealthy Genoese merchant, Luigi Centurione, engaged him in Lisbon to go to Madeira to purchase Madeiran sugar for Centurione's account. Di Negro had been paid 1,290 ducats in advance to make this purchase, but he failed to provide Columbus with the required amount of cash to pay for the sugar he had sent him to buy; it appears that he intended to pay for part of the sugar with woolen goods. However, these found no takers and Columbus was unable to meet his obligations with the scanty sum of 103 ducats that di Negro had sent him and was forced to proceed to Genoa with a short consignment of sugar.

Not long after his return from the sugar-buying voyage to Madeira and Genoa, in 1479, Columbus established an even firmer connection with Madeira as a result of his marriage to a young noblewoman, Felipa Perestrelo y Moniz, the daughter of Bartolomeu Perestrelo, the first governor and *donatário* (grant holder) of the island of Porto Santo, and of Isabel Moniz, his second, or third, wife.

It was at Prince Henry's instigation that, within a few years of the settlement of Madeira, the hardy malvasia grape vine was imported from Crete and the sugarcane from Sicily. Both were in due course to play their part in making Madeira a great wine exporter. Several sugar mills had been built in the island by Genoese merchants. The Genoese also shipped out of the islands large quantities of valuable products, such as orchilla, pastel, cotton, and hides.

Porto Santo, the island that Bartolomeu Perestrelo had governed and where his son succeeded him never prospered like Madeira. It was only natural, however, that, with his brother-in-law established in Porto Santo, Columbus should settle on the island that, coupled with Madeira, was the advance headquarters of the exploration of the Atlantic. For the next two or three years, from 1480 to 1483, Columbus made his home first in Porto Santo, where his first son was born, and then at Funchal, the small but thriving capital of Madeira, where his curiosity was constantly being whetted by meeting with sailors and ship captains who had been to the edge of the unknown world and by the fact that he himself was living on the frontiers of the Atlantic.

Columbus's third and last known contact with Madeira took place in 1498, on his third voyage to America. At that time Spain was at war with France, and a French fleet was said to be lying off Cape St. Vincent, waiting to despoil Columbus's fleet. Accordingly, he made a wide sweep to the south, passing near the African coast, instead of taking the straight course to Porto Santo, which was his first objective. On June 7, the fleet arrived at Porto Santo, after a journey of at least 1,050 kilometers (650 miles). The inhabitants, believing his fleet to be French corsairs, took to the hills with their flocks and herds. That same night he set sail for Madeira. On June 10 he anchored in Funchal roads. In his *Historia de las Indias,* Bartolomé de las Casas writes that the local inhabitants outdid themselves in their welcome: "in the town [Funchal] he was given a very fine reception and much entertainment, for he was very well known there, having been a resident thereof for some time. He stayed there six days, completing his lading of water, wood, and other things necessary for his voyage."

In the opinion of many experts, the greatest part of Columbus's education in the sea belongs to Madeira, and his own son was supposed to have said that the fact that his father had lived in Madeira "was the beginning of the discovery of the New World."

BIBLIOGRAPHY

Albuquerque, Luís de, and Alberto Vieira. *The Archipelago of Madeira in the XV Century.* Translated by Martin A. Kayman and M. Filomena Mesquita. Funchal, 1988.

Cruz, Visconde do Porto da. "A Estada de Cristovam Colombo na Madeira." *Revista de Arqueologia* 2 (1936): 283–288.

Pereira, Eduardo C. N. "Cristóvão Colombo no Porto Santo e na Madeira." *Das Artes e da História da Madeira.* 22 (1956): 20–27.

Treen, Maria de Freitas. "Columbus in Madeira and Porto Santo." *Bulletin of the American Portuguese Society* (Fall 1976): 1–3.

Vieira, Alberto. "Colombo: A Ilha, os homens e a história." *Diário de Notícias* (Madeira). May 30, 1987.

REBECCA CATZ

MADRID. Madrid, a comparatively minor town in twelfth-century Castile, was growing steadily at the close of the Middle Ages and came into its own when Philip II decided to establish his court there in 1561. Situated on the Manzanares River more than two thousand feet above sea level and bounded on the north by the Sierra de Guadarrama, Madrid is surrounded by productive and fertile agricultural lands. Though evidence of settlement dates back to prehistoric times, Madrid first gained notoriety in 932 when Ramiro II of León knocked down its walls. After the fall of Toledo in 1085 it passed into Christian hands along with other towns in the Tagus valley. In the twelfth century the town received various royal privileges that were incorporated in the *fuero,* or municipal charter, granted by Fernando III in 1222. The town itself was divided into parishes (*colaciones*) and the municipal district into four *seismos,* or regions. The determination of the boundaries of the municipal district was the source of frequent conflict with neighboring Segovia.

From the thirteenth century onward municipal law was largely shaped by royal actions as the Crown intensified its efforts to control town government more effectively. In 1346 Alfonso XI replaced the open municipal council with a council composed of a limited number of regidores chosen by the king. In the fifteenth century the regidores nominated several persons for the offices of alcalde, or judge, and alguacil, or police inspector, and the king made his appointments from these nominees, who usually came from the principal families of the city. The king also named a corregidor to supervise the administration of justice and to maintain law and order. Taken together all these officials constituted the ayuntamiento, a governing body with responsibility for revenues, public works, and other matters affecting the municipality. The *Libros de acuerdos del concejo de Madrid* (Books of agreements of the council of Madrid) contain acts relating to municipal government from 1464 onward. As the town continued to grow in importance, the Cortes was convened there on several occasions in the fourteenth and fifteenth centuries. Madrid was one of the eighteen towns with representation in the Cortes in the reign of Fernando and Isabel. Sessions of the audiencia, or royal tribunal, were occasionally held there in accordance with a decree of Juan I in 1387.

At the end of the fifteenth century Madrid was still a comparatively small town. According to data from 1530, the city had a population of four thousand, in contrast to Segovia, with fifteen thousand, and Medina del Campo with twenty thousand. On the other hand, Madrid's location in the geographic center of the peninsula made it more and more attractive in the economic development of the Kingdom of Castile. When Philip II decided to make it his capital in 1561, Madrid also had the advantage of being close to the new royal palace of El Escorial. The establishment of Madrid as the capital aided the growth of population, which rose to thirty-seven thousand in 1594. Not until after 1606, however, did Madrid achieve permanent status as the political and financial capital of the realm.

BIBLIOGRAPHY

Domingo Palacio, Timoteo. *Documentos del archivo general de la villa de Madrid.* 6 vols. Edited by Agustín Millares Carló and Eulogio Varela Hervías. Madrid, 1888–1943.

Gibert, Rafael. *El Concejo de Madrid: Su organización en los siglos XII a XV.* Madrid, 1949.

MacKay, Angus. *Spain in the Middle Ages: From Frontier to Empire, 1000–1500.* New York, 1977.

O'Callaghan, Joseph F. *A History of Medieval Spain.* Ithaca, 1975.

JOSEPH F. O'CALLAGHAN

MAGELLAN, FERDINAND (1480?–1521), Portuguese navigator. Although Magellan (Fernão de Magalhães, in Portuguese; Magallanes, in Spanish) was a Portuguese, his great journey across the Pacific was purely Spanish in its impact: it reached the Orient via a westward passage and thus completed the work Columbus had undertaken but had to abandon when the American landmasses blocked his way. Magellan himself technically did not circumnavigate the globe, for he died on Mactan Island, near Cebu, in the Philippines. Rather, his officer Juan Sebastián de Elcano finished the circuit, although along a return passage already well established by the Portuguese. Much of this return distance Magellan probably had himself sailed earlier in his career while in the service of Portugal; if so, he himself had also traveled effectively around the globe, though not all upon the same voyage or in consecutive years.

Magellan was born into petty nobility, probably in the village of Sabrosa, near Vila Real in the province of Tras-os-Montes. The date, never established with certainty, was around 1480, which made him of prime age to seek social and economic advancement in the great Indies enterprise that followed the return of Vasco da Gama from Calicut in 1500. In fact, he enlisted in the service of Francisco de Almeida, the first Portuguese viceroy, and sailed for the Orient in 1505. He filled minor positions there for the next eight years—in Goa, Cochin, Quilon, and possibly Mozambique. Then he accompanied Diogo Lopes de Sequeira on his ill-fated voyage to Malacca in

FERDIN·MAGELLANVS·SVPERATI ANTARTIC° FRETI·ANGVS TIIS· CLARISS·

FERDINAND MAGELLAN.   ELSEVIER PUBLISHING PROJECTS, AMSTERDAM

1508–1509. Returning to India, he was shipwrecked on some shoals near the Maldive Islands. Here he first came to the attention of the chroniclers for bravely refusing to abandon his subordinates.

It is also known that even before the fall of Malacca to the Portuguese in 1511, he had become a close friend of Francisco Serrão, one of the first European visitors to the Moluccas, or Spice Islands, and manager of the Portuguese Crown factory at Ternate. Magellan himself may have sailed as far as Ambon, at 128 degrees east longitude, before returning to India. From Serrão it would seem he obtained detailed information about the islands' location and their products. Magellan returned to Portugal in 1513, though it is far from certain that he maintained further correspondence with Serrão, as has been claimed, or that this played a part in the subsequent maturation of his daring plans for a voyage to the islands from the Americas.

One of the principal Portuguese military operations closer to home (and one that certainly diverted men and matériel from further adventures in Asia) was devoted to empire building in Morocco. Soon after his return from India, Magellan took part in a campaign under the duke of Braganza at Azamour, where he appears to have distinguished himself in battles and skirmishes; he was appointed quartermaster of war spoils. After his return to Portugal, he petitioned King Manuel I for modest recompense of his services. At the same time, however, rumors spread that he had sold captured cattle back to the enemy, whereupon the monarch obliged him to return to Africa to clear his name—which he succeeded in doing. Nonetheless, Manuel refused to increase his yearly stipend, as Magellan requested. This soured him and seems to have been instrumental in his decision to leave Portugal.

Exactly when Magellan conceived his plan of sailing to the Moluccas via a passage around or through the American continents is not known. He may well have had the idea before returning to Portugal from India, though he seems to have worked out the final details in Lisbon with a Portuguese cartographer, Rui Faleiro—including the idea that the Moluccas actually lay on the Spanish side of the 1494 Line of Demarcation as extended around to the Eastern Hemisphere. By then he was in disfavor, and though seemingly he tried to present it to Manuel as a more efficient way of reaching the islands, after his unhappy treatment he resolved to take it to Manuel's rival, Carlos I of Spain, or actually to Bishop Juan Rodríguez de Fonseca, head of the Spanish Consejo de Indias.

Magellan's contract and the arrangements for his voyage were much like those of Columbus in that the voyage was sponsored by commercial sources such as merchants of Seville and Antwerp, and the *capitulación* he received made him and his cocaptain, Faleiro, adelantados and gave them a share of the profits. (Faleiro, however, demurred to go at the last moment.) In September 1519, five small vessels, none in good condition, *Santo Antonio, Trinidad, Concepción, Santiago,* and *Victoria* (the heaviest at 120 *toneladas*), passed the bar at Sanlúcar de Barrameda. Their crews were even more international than most of the age. Besides Spaniards and Basques, they included Genoese, Sicilians, Neapolitans, Germans, Greeks, Flemings, an Englishman, and even some Malays and Africans. The largest foreign contingent, however, was thirty-seven Portuguese. Also with the expedition were Magellan's brother-in-law, the Portuguese Duarte Barbosa, author of an early description of the East, and Antonio Pigafetta, a gentleman of Vicenza, who went as a passenger and later became the expedition's most famous chronicler.

Magellan expected rightly to find a passage to the south, though certainly not so southerly as it proved to be. From the easternmost part of Brazil, the ships coasted on the lookout for a westerly passage, exploring the bay of Rio de Janeiro and the Rio de la Plata before wintering in Patagonia from March to August 1520. During this time Magellan effectively dealt with a serious mutiny, and subsequently, *Santo Antonio* deserted the fleet. When a strait was finally found to the Pacific, Magellan skillfully navigated it at the cost of *Santiago,* which foundered on a

reef, though with the loss of only one life. Next, after coasting northward along Chile for a thousand miles or so, he effected an arduous Pacific crossing of ninety-eight days. His starting point had the effect of aligning the remaining three ships with a belt of easterly trade winds, but it also caused them to bypass all the great archipelagoes to the south, which might have provided refreshment; in the whole passage only two islands were sighted—seemingly one in the Tuamotu group and one in the Line Islands. Thereafter, Magellan steered to a still more northerly course in hopes of reaching the coast of China for surer relief than the Moluccas might have provided. This took the expedition to Guam, whose thieving natives prompted them to call the group the Ladrones. Finally, on April 7, the little fleet reached Cebu in the Philippines. Less than three weeks later, Magellan was dead, killed in a skirmish on Mactan Island after the Spaniards became involved in a brawl between indigenes.

Command was then assumed by the Portuguese captain, João Serrão, but he, too, was slain by natives within a short time, along with Duarte Barbosa. Command then devolved upon Elcano, a capable Basque who had been involved in the Patagonian rebellion earlier in the voyage. Of his three remaining vessels, *Concepción* had to be abandoned, but after calling at Brunei in Borneo and

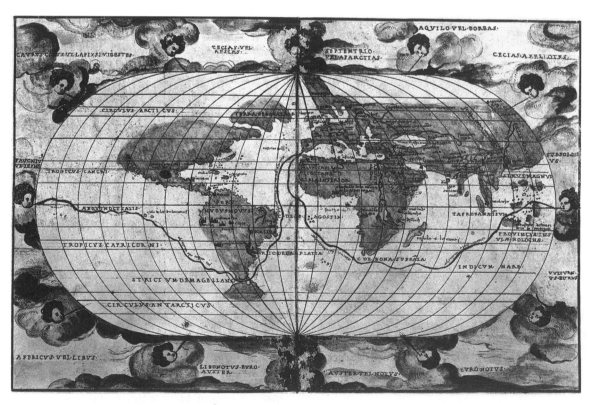

THE ROUTE OF MAGELLAN'S VOYAGE. From an atlas by Battista Agnese produced for Charles V, the Holy Roman Emperor, in Venice in 1552.

returning to the Philippines, Elcano reached the Moluccas at Tidore. Thereafter, the rotting *Trinidad*'s captain elected to try to recross the Pacific. Elcano, however, returned via India and the Cape of Good Hope, arriving home in September 1522, three years after the expedition had departed. Needless to say, Elcano was happy to assume credit for what belonged nearly in full to the expedition's fallen leader. It was only the testimonies of others, among them Pigafetta's, that eventually provided a true picture of what had ensued and restored to Magellan his place as perhaps the greatest pilot and navigator of the early discovery era.

The triumphal return of Elcano in *Victoria* might have obscured the achievement of Magellan temporarily—but hardly the implications of his journey. The Spanish had signed the Treaty of Tordesillas in 1494, but at the time, no one could ascertain longitude with any certainty—nor did either the papal bull *Inter caetera* or the treaty itself specifically say that Portuguese or Spanish influence must end exactly at the edge of the hemispheres where the Atlantic line cut around on the opposite side of the globe. Worried that Spain might try to claim bits of the Orient as on the other side of the line, Manuel in 1514 obtained the bull *Praecelsae devotionis,* limiting the demarcation line to the Atlantic and awarding all the Asian Indies to Portugal—something the Spanish Crown scorned, however.

Armed with Elcano's reports, the Emperor Charles V weighed upon the Portuguese monarch, João III, for a binational commission composed of distinguished seamen and representatives to negotiate an agreement on the issue. It met on the bridge over the tiny Caia River, which formed the border of Spain and Portugal between Elvas and Badajoz. Among those present were Elcano himself, Fernando Colón, Diogo Lopes de Sequeira, and Sebastian Cabot. The Spanish delegation at first maintained that the Moluccas were on their side of the line. Then, when the Portuguese vehemently denied this, the Spanish even called for a papal investigative commission to visit the Far East and decide the question.

Debate dragged on for years until in 1529, by the Treaty of Zaragoza, João agreed to buy from Spain for 350,000 gold dobras all rights to exclusive access and usufruct of the islands. Under a clause of the treaty, the Spanish were supposed to pay back the sum should the islands be shown by future science to lie within the Portuguese sphere. That they did indeed lie within the purview of the Portuguese was subsequently shown by modern methods of determining longitude—but not until the eighteenth century. By then the Portuguese had long since been expelled from the islands by the Dutch and the issue forgotten.

Magellan had both "discovered" and died in the Philippines (named in honor of Prince Philip, later Philip II).

The archipelago actually lay to the west of the Moluccas, but even though the Spanish had given up their rights to those Spice Islands, they had no intention of yielding what they considered rightfully theirs, no matter what the location might ultimately prove to be. Thereafter, Portuguese protests over the repeated Spanish incursions into the area went unheeded—and the issue was effectively settled only by the Union of Crowns in 1580.

In modern times, the sole aspect of the voyage that remains universal knowledge is that of Magellan's great circumnavigation. But his achievement in fact was his discovery and skillful passage of the straits named for him and his successful crossing of the unknown Pacific Ocean to Asia, thus fulfilling the great objective that had eluded Columbus.

BIBLIOGRAPHY

Albo, Francisco. "Diário o derrotero del viaje de Magellanes." In vol. 4 of *Colección de los viajes y descubrimientos.* Edited by Martin Fernández de Navarrete. 5 vols. Madrid, 1835–1837.

Denucé, Jan. *Magellan, la question des Moluques et la première navigation du globe.* Brussels, 1911.

Guillemard, F. H. H. *The Life of Ferdinand Magellan and the First Circumnavigation of the Globe.* London, 1890.

Jong, Marcus de, ed. *Um roteiro inédito . . . [de Vazquito Gomes Gallego (?)].* Coimbra, 1937.

Medina, José Toribio de. *El descubrimiento del Océano Pacifico: Vasco Nuñez de Balboa, Hernando de Magallanes y sus compañeros.* 3 vols. Santiago de Chile, 1914–1920.

Nowell, Charles E., ed. *Magellan's Voyage around the World: Three Contemporary Accounts.* Evanston, Ill., 1962.

Queiroz Velloso, José Maria de. *Fernão de Magalhães, a vida e a viagem.* Lisbon, 1941.

GEORGE D. WINIUS

MALINCHE (fl. 1519), native American princess, known also as Doña Marina; interpreter for Hernando Cortés during the Spanish conquest. Malinche was the daughter of a high-ranking lord of the region of Coatzacoalcos, on the southeastern fringe of the Aztec empire. Her father died while she was still young, and her mother, protecting the inheritance for Malinche's half-brother, later passed her on to coastal merchants. She was then sold by these traders to the ruler of Tabasco and was presented by him to the Spanish newcomers along with nineteen other women in 1519. Her native name, perhaps Malinalli (twisted grass) or some variant, was changed by the Spaniards to Marina when she was baptized. Because the reverential *-tzin* was added to her native name to yield Malintzin, so *doña* was appended to Marina in recognition of her high native status.

Marina became Cortés's most important ally in the Spanish conquest of Mexico, although he barely mentions her in his letters to the Spanish king. She served Cortés as interpreter, adviser, confidante, and mistress. As interpreter, Marina demonstrated considerable linguistic skills, being conversant in Nahuatl and a coastal Maya dialect.

Marina was not only a translator of words, but an interpreter of native customs and intentions. She was intensely loyal to Cortés and guided his path through the political maneuverings and cultural confusions that faced him on his trek to the Aztec capital. She was not only responsive to Cortés's needs and goals, but on occasion took the initiative in achieving those goals. She endured many hardships, including the frantic Noche Triste (the "sad night" of the Spaniards' retreat from the Aztec capital in early July 1520) and Cortés's arduous march to Honduras following his capture of Tenochtitlan (Spanish, Tenochtitlán).

Marina was also Cortés's mistress; she bore him a son, Don Martín Cortés, who should not be confused with Cortés's legitimate son by his second wife, also named Martín. Once Marina's usefulness had ceased, Cortés married her to one of his men, Juan de Jaramillo. She was given estates in her native province, but little is known of her later life.

Marina is a symbol of cultural contact and blending; she is also considered by Mexicans as a traitor to the native way of life. Early on, the Mexica ruler Motecuhzoma II recognized her pivotal role in the fall of his empire and transformation of his culture; the news that she was accompanying the newcomers "pierced Motecuhzoma's heart."

BIBLIOGRAPHY

Anderson, Arthur J. O., and Charles E. Dibble. *The War of Conquest: How It Was Waged Here in Mexico.* Salt Lake City, 1978.

Díaz del Castillo, Bernal. *The Conquest of New Spain.* Baltimore, 1963.

Orozco y Berra, Manuel. *Historia antigua y de la conquista de Mexico.* Vol. 4. Mexico City, 1960.

Rodríguez, Gustavo A. *Doña Marina.* Mexico City, 1935.

FRANCES F. BERDAN

MANDEVILLE, JOHN. Mandeville's *Travels,* composed most likely in French around the mid-fourteenth century, was the most widely read European book about the world during the late Middle Ages. Its unknown author represents himself as a far-traveling English knight, Sir John Mandeville of St. Albans, who has written this narrative upon returning home after thirty-four years of travels. The book was soon translated into nearly every European language as well as Latin and survives in more than 250 manuscripts (almost three times the number that Marco Polo's travel account engendered). As one of the earliest printed books, it enjoyed special popularity in the two decades from 1480 to 1500. The book presents a first-person account of supposed travels based on the eyewitness authority of a narrator who is at once pious, curious, skeptical, and tolerant.

The first part of the book (a prologue and fifteen chapters) portrays the world that European pilgrims would encounter in taking one of the several land or sea routes to the Holy Land. Mandeville describes the possible itineraries; informs readers of distances, local history, customs, marvels, relics, and foreign alphabets; and explains at some length the pilgrimage sites in and around the Holy Land. Chapter 15 is a summary of Islamic customs and beliefs and includes a lecture by the sultan about the sinfulness of Western Christians and their consequent crusading failures.

The second part of the book recounts Mandeville's exploration of the wonders of the little known, non-Christian world farther east. He discovers there fantastic animals and humans of surprising shapes, powers, and behaviors (some of which are parodies or reminders of Christian practices). He discourses on the roundness of the earth and the possibility of its circumnavigation. He describes journeys to the home of the Amazons, the Well of Youth (at which he drank), the land of the pygmies (whose laborers are giants), the dominion of the great Chan of Cathay, the region of the Tartars, the realm of the legendary Prester John, the bastion of the Muslim terrorists known as the Assassins, the Vale Perilous (which Mandeville but not all his companions survived), the Isle of Bragman (a utopia where people live in preternatural harmony), and at the easternmost edge of the world the earthly paradise, about which Mandeville says (in a Middle English manuscript version), "ne can I not speken propurly, for I was not there." Near the end of the book he states his conviction that "wee knowe not whom God loueth ne whom God hateth" and that most of these non-Christian peoples seem to know the "God of Nature" through their "naturelle wytt."

Although no copy of the *Travels* known to have been read by Columbus has yet come to light, there is direct and indirect evidence that the Admiral knew Mandeville's account. Three of his contemporaries—his son Fernando Colón, Bartolomé de las Casas, and Andrés Bernáldez—indicate he read Mandeville. It is also apparent from Columbus's writings that the book was an influential source or confirmation for several of his fundamental ideas and motivations.

First, Columbus would have been struck by the chapter in which Mandeville asserts that the earth is circumnavigable and that it is both inhabitable and inhabited worldwide. Mandeville's conviction about these matters is based on his alleged authority as a world traveler, his calculations with an astrolabe, and the experience of an unnamed northern European who, he says in a lengthy anecdote, sailed around the world twice—once in each direction.

Second, Columbus's assumptions about the Caribbean peoples he met would have been shaped by Mandeville's depiction of the world east of Jerusalem as a series of increasingly marvelous societies, each one older, more advanced, and ethically superior to the one before. At the eastern edge of Asia—where Columbus thought he had arrived—Mandeville encounters the perfect natives of the Isle of Bragman, then the near-Edenic island of Taprobane with its Bahamas-like two seasons and shallow seas, and at last Eden itself.

Finally, Columbus would have found in Mandeville's book an emphasis on the centrality of Jerusalem that matched his own abiding crusader's concern to rescue the Holy Land for Christianity. The Jerusalem pilgrimage that occupies the first half of the *Travels* balances the exotic Asian journeying of the rest of the book and emphasizes the spiritual objective that ought to motivate every Christian voyager. From the Book of Prophecies and other of his writings it is apparent that Columbus understood his worldly explorations as a form of pilgrimage and that the attainment of Jerusalem, literally or allegorically, was his ultimate goal.

BIBLIOGRAPHY

Bennett, Josephine W. *The Rediscovery of Sir John Mandeville.* New York, 1954. Reprint, New York, 1971.

Campbell, Mary B. *The Witness and the Other World: Exotic European Travel Writing, 400–1600.* Ithaca and London, 1988.

Seymour, M. C., ed. *Mandeville's Travels.* Oxford, 1967.

Zacher, Christian K. *Curiosity and Pilgrimage: The Literature of Discovery in Fourteenth-Century England.* Baltimore and London, 1976.

CHRISTIAN K. ZACHER

MANUEL I (1469–1521), king of Portugal. Manuel the Fortunate inherited the Kingdom of Portugal in 1495 when his cousin King João II died without a legitimate heir. Manuel strengthened the monarchy, enacted legal reform, and supervised the political organization of Portuguese claims in the New World.

Manuel carried out João II's plan for the exploration of India and presided over the global expansion of Portugal. During Manuel's reign, Vasco da Gama sailed around the Cape of Good Hope to India (1498), and by 1505 the Portuguese had begun the territorial organization of India. In 1500 Pedro Álvares Cabral claimed Brazil for Portugal, and in 1502 present-day Uruguay and Argentina were explored. In 1511 the first large-scale Portuguese expedi-

tions were sent to chart the Pacific via Da Gama's route. By 1521 the fleet of the Portuguese navigator Ferdinand Magellan, sailing in the service of Emperor Charles V, had circumnavigated the globe.

In 1497 Manuel married Isabel, daughter of Fernando and Isabel, and at her insistence he expelled the Jews from Portugal. When the Castilian prince Juan died in 1498, Isabel and Manuel were named heirs to Castile. But Castile slipped out of Manuel's grasp when Isabel died in childbirth (1498), followed two years later by their son, Miguel. In 1500 Manuel married Isabel's sister María who bore him eight children, among them his heir, João III, and Isabel, future wife of Emperor Charles V. In 1518, a

MANUEL I. From an illuminated manuscript, 1521.

ARQUIVO NACIONAL DA TORRE DO TOMBO

year after the death of María, he married Leonor, the sister of Emperor Charles V, who bore him two children. Manuel died in 1521 and is buried in the abbey of the Hieronymite monastery in Lisbon.

BIBLIOGRAPHY

Domingues, Mário. *D. Manuel e a epopeia dos descubrimentos: Evocação histórica*. Lisbon, 1960.

Goes, Damião de. *Crónica do felicissimo Rei D. Manuel*. 4 vols. Coimbra, 1926.

Oliveira Marquês, A. H. de. *History of Portugal*. 2 vols. New York, 1972.

Sanceau, Elaine. *The Reign of the Fortunate King, 1495–1521*. Hamden, Conn., 1969.

THERESA EARENFIGHT

MAPPAMUNDI. In the Middle Ages, *mappamundi* (from Latin *mappa,* napkin; and *mundus,* world; pl., *mappaemundi*) designated a world map whatever its form or purpose. In modern terminology, the word is restricted to images of the world determined by religious or ideological considerations executed in a more or less schematic manner. Although such images were known in Asia and the Islamic world, the expression refers to a body of documents specific to the West. Originating in the monasteries, *mappaemundi* combined in one representation a few scientific elements (derived from classical antiquity) with ideas taken from biblical and patristic texts. Usually oval or circular in form, *mappaemundi* primarily accompanied texts and had essentially didactic and moral functions, illustrating the narratives of traditional Christianity.

The commonest maps give a tripartite representation of the inhabited world *(oikoumene)* within a T-O *(orbis terrarum)* scheme. The three continents, Europe, Asia, and Africa, are encircled by the ocean and are separated by the Mediterranean (the vertical element of the T) and by the Don and the Nile (the horizontal elements of the T). Jerusalem, placed at the intersection of the two elements, is thus at the center of the world, at least on maps dating from after the Crusades. The whole is oriented toward the east, from which flow the rivers of the terrestrial paradise. A second type of *mappamundi,* which derived from the Greeks, represents the whole world in parallel zones or "climates," the habitable temperate zones of the two hemispheres being symmetrically arranged on either side of the central torrid zone which, like the two polar zones, was considered uninhabitable. Quadripartite *mappaemundi* include elements from the first two types. The tripartite *oikoumene* of the northern hemisphere is flanked in the southern hemisphere by a fourth continent, inhabited or not, called the Antipodes.

As *mappaemundi* gradually became dissociated from texts, taking on increasingly imposing dimensions, their contents and appearance evolved under the double influence of nautical cartography (from the fourteenth century) and the revival of Ptolemaic geography (from the beginning of the fifteenth century). From nautical cartography, exemplified by portolan charts, *mappaemundi* borrowed the network of rhumb lines and scale (though here not functional); a good delineation of the Mediterranean and Black sea areas, contrasting with a dramatically less accurate depiction elsewhere; and an interest in the geographical knowledge produced by recent voyages such as those of Marco Polo in Asia in the thirteenth century and the Portuguese navigators along the African coast in the fifteenth century. Ptolemy's *Geography,* translated into Latin in 1406–1407 and widely diffused in printed editions after 1475, offered on the other hand a learned cartographic model that simultaneously revived some archaic geographical concepts (such as the closed Indian Ocean and a Mediterranean Sea twenty degrees too long) and reintroduced the idea of the rigorous location of places on a grid marked in latitude and longitude produced by projection. One of the best-known *mappaemundi* of the late Middle Ages, that drawn by Fra Mauro in 1459, is a compendium of geographical sources that uses the Marco Polo narratives, the Portuguese exploration of Africa, the portolan charts, and Ptolemy's *Geography.*

From among these "transitional" *mappaemundi,* historians have sought to identify first, any that could have aided the development of Columbus's project or illustrate the presuppositions behind it, and second, any that mark the stages of the establishment of the idea of a new continent. Among the first, the most important is the map that Paolo dal Pozzo Toscanelli presented to the Portuguese court in 1474 in defense of the idea that the western route to India across the Atlantic was shorter than the eastern route around the southern tip of Africa, toward which Portuguese colonial policy was oriented. In 1483, when this project was examined by a committee of cosmographers in the service of João II, Columbus had not yet annotated the works that would eventually help him to transform his intuition into a full theory; the Toscanelli map, of which he obtained a copy, was doubtless his most important scientific support. He had moreover himself copied the letter that accompanied the map, thus demonstrating the interest that it had for him. Unfortunately, the map is lost, and the fairly precise description given by the written sources do not allow it to be identified certainly among surviving *mappaemundi* (the suggestion that it was similar to the Genoese world map of 1457 is open to many objections), nor to come to unanimity of opinion about a reconstruction. It may be

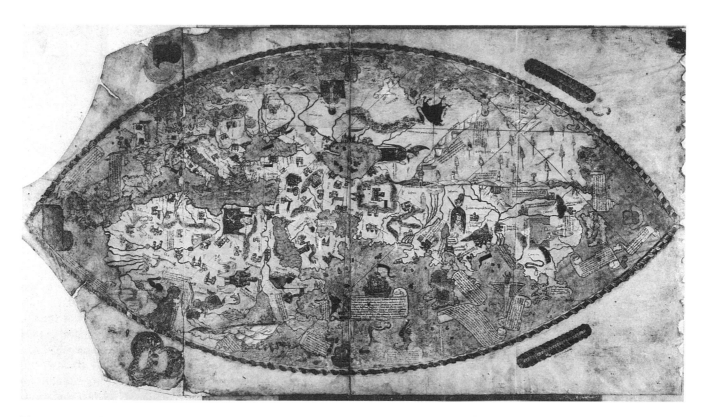

MAPPAMUNDI BY PAOLO DAL POZZO TOSCANELLI.   Manuscript on vellum, 1457. Not the map that Toscanelli presented to the Portuguese court in 1474, which is lost, it nevertheless shows his conception of the distance west from Europe to Asia. This is a typical "transitional" *mappamundi*, incorporating elements from portolan charts, Ptolemaic geography, the new knowledge of Africa derived from Portuguese exploration, and the accounts of Marco Polo's travels.   BIBLIOTECA NAZIONALE CENTRALE, FLORENCE

supposed that the map was graduated in latitude and longitude, but historians are divided about what system of projection might have been used. In the end, we know nothing of Columbus's practice in the drawing of his maps.

The classic sources of Columbus biography, particularly Andrés Bernáldez, suggest that Columbus presented to the Spanish sovereigns and their specialist advisers at Salamanca (1486–1487) and at Santa Fé (1491) a map on which he, or his brother Bartolomé, had drawn "the lands and seas to discover." This map was probably also shown by Bartolomé to Henry VII of England during his mission of 1488. But the ambivalence of the term *mappamundi* conceals whether it was actually a *mappamundi* or a nautical chart, and no document of either type can be certainly identified as drawn by the brothers. The geographical vestiges that best correspond with Columbus's vision of the world are those found on the globe of Martin Behaim, which derived from a prototype common to several late-fifteenth- and early-sixteenth-century *mappaemundi*. This prototype was developed by the German cartographer Henricus Martellus, who worked in collaboration with the Florentine engraver Francesco Rosselli,

and it underlies several surviving manuscript and printed *mappaemundi* from the 1490s.

One of these was acquired in 1961 by Yale University Library. It has a latitude scale and is also the only non-Ptolemaic *mappamundi* of the fifteenth century to be divided for longitude. There is no direct proof that this map was known to Columbus, but it illustrates several of his leading ideas. The very large east-west extent of the *oikoumene* (270 degrees) and the reduced distance to be sailed between the Canaries and Cipangu (90 degrees) are measures that correspond to those that Toscanelli had deduced from Marinus of Tyre and Marco Polo, and were known to Columbus. Converted into marine leagues on the median line of the map, the 90 degrees correspond approximatively with the 1,142 leagues that Columbus reckoned he had sailed when he arrived in the Caribbean Islands that he took to be Cipangu. The same world map, which shows Bartolomeu Dias's voyage of 1488, depicts Africa with a prolongation into the southern hemisphere and therefore even more difficult to circumnavigate than supposed because it is also extended to the east by a cape, called a *promontorium passum* in Ptolemy's *Geography*, that enclosed the Indian Ocean.

The eastern route to India pursued by the Portuguese for so many years thus seemed extremely difficult. Such a picture of the world at this date could well have influenced the Spanish authorities to give support to Columbus.

Such *mappaemundi,* in which "the beginning of the Indies" faced the West across an ocean of no great width, dominated cartographic production until about 1506. Such a presentation appears in the Contarini map engraved by Rosselli in 1506, and the texts it carries indicate clearly that the author believed that Columbus had reached the coast of Asia. In the map by Johan Ruysch that accompanied the 1508 Rome edition of Ptolemy's *Geography,* the North American lands explored by the Côrte-Reals and the Cabots are parts of Asia, but the coast visited by Columbus belongs to a continent separated from Asia by a stretch of open sea. This may indicate a direct influence from Bartolomé Colón, the presumed author of three anonymous and undated sketches, sections of a world map drawn to illustrate the voyage along the central coast of America during Columbus's fourth voyage. These sketches, found as marginal drawings in a copy of Columbus's letter from Jamaica (July 7, 1503), give the first general picture of the lands discovered by Columbus. The route across the narrow ocean is marked by the Spanish islands, with the exception of Cuba. Asia, with the *serici montes,* is next to Honduras and extends as far as Venezuela. A tiny strait separates this continent from the South American coast, where the hinterland is labeled "Mondo Novo." Columbus, if these sketches are authentic, was thus convinced that he had discovered, at least in South America, a New World. Nonetheless it is in the large world map of Martin Waldseemüller, published at Strasbourg in 1507, that the first cartographic expression of South America appears.

BIBLIOGRAPHY

Almagia, Roberto. "I mappamondi di Enrico Martello e alcuni concetti geografici di Cristoforo Colombo." *La Bibliofilia* 42 (1940): 288–311.

Destombes, Marcel, ed. *Mappemondes A.D. 1200–1500: Catalogue préparé par la commission des cartes anciennes de l'Union géographique internationale.* Amsterdam, 1964.

Liethäuser, Joachim C. *Mappaemundi: Die geistige Eroberung der Welt.* Berlin, 1958.

Randles, William G. L. "The Evaluation of Columbus' 'India' Project by Portuguese and Spanish Cosmographers in the Light of the Geographical Science of the Period." *Imago Mundi* 42 (1990).

Skelton, R. A. "The Cartography of Columbus' First Voyage." Appendix to *The Journal of Christopher Columbus.* Translated by Cecil Jane, annotated by L. A. Vigneras. London, 1960.

Woodward, David. "Medieval Mappaemundi." In vol. 1 of *The History of Cartography,* edited by J. B. Harley and David Woodward. Chicago and London, 1987.

ISABELLE RAYNAUD-NGUYEN
Translated from French by Anthony Turner

MAPS. For discussion of the history of mapmaking through the Age of Exploration, see *Cartography.*

MARGARET OF AUSTRIA (1480–1530), daughter of Maximilian I; princess of Spain (1497); regent of the Netherlands (1507–1530).

As daughter of Emperor Maximilian I and his first wife, Mary of Burgundy, Margaret played an important role in the diplomatic marriages that linked the Austrian Habsburg family with the kingdoms of Castile and Aragón. As an infant Margaret was betrothed to the French dauphin Charles VIII (1482), but Charles repudiated her to marry Anne of Brittany. To offset the power of France, a double marriage was negotiated in 1495 by Maximilian and Fernando of Aragón. Margaret was betrothed to Juan, prince of Asturias and heir to the throne of Castile and Aragón, and her brother, Philip the Handsome, to Juan's sister, Juana of Castile. Juan and Margaret were married in Burgos on April 3, 1497, but the marriage was tragically brief, ending only months later with Juan's sudden death on October 6 in Salamanca.

Margaret returned to Flanders in 1499, and in 1501 she married Duke Philip of Savoy. When Philip died in 1504, she was briefly under consideration as a possible bride for Henry VIII of England. The death of her brother, Philip, in 1506 and the madness of his wife, Juana, forced Maximilian to appoint Margaret to the regency of the Netherlands for her young nephew, Charles. Her competent governance of the Netherlands, notably her mediation of alliances between Maximilian, England, Spain, and the papacy in 1513, prompted Charles to retain her as regent after the death of Maximilian in 1519 until her death in 1530.

BIBLIOGRAPHY

Boom, Ghislaine. *Marguerite d'Autriche.* Brussels, 1946.

Bruchet, Max Pierre Marie. *Marguerite d'Autriche, duchesse de Savoie.* Lille, 1927.

Iongh, Jane de. *Margaret of Austria, Regent of the Netherlands.* Translated by M. D. Herter Norton. New York, 1953.

Winker, Elsa. *Margarete von Österreich: Grande Dame der Renaissance.* Munich, 1966.

THERESA EARENFIGHT

MARÍA (1482–1517), princess of Castile; queen of Portugal.

María, daughter of Fernando and Isabel of Castile, was

the second wife of King Manuel I of Portugal. They were married in Alcácer do Sal on October 30, 1500. By marrying María, Manuel hoped to revive his plan to unite Portugal and Castile under his personal rule, a goal that had suffered a setback with the deaths of his first wife, María's older sister Isabel, in 1498 and their two-year-old son, Miguel, in 1500. The Castilian succession, however, eventually passed not to María but to her sister Juana and Philip the Handsome of Austria. Nevertheless, by all accounts, María and Manuel had a happy marriage, overseeing the expansion of Portugal from a continental kingdom to an overseas empire.

María was born in Granada in 1482; her twin sister was stillborn. Little is known of María's childhood, but of all the children of Fernando and Isabel, she appears to have led the most peaceful life. Like her brothers and sisters, she was educated by the court tutors, the Italian humanists Antonio and Alessandro Geraldino and Lucio Marineo Siculo. She traveled frequently with her mother and the peripatetic court, taking part in the momentous events of fifteenth-century Castile—the Inquisition, the conquest of Granada, and Columbus's return from his voyages to the New World.

María had eight children who lived to adulthood: João (1502), the future king João III; Isabel (1503), future wife of Emperor Charles V; Beatriz (1504); Luis (1506); Fernando (1507); Afonso (1509); Enrique (1512); and Duarte (1515). María died in March 1517, two months after giving birth to a stillborn boy christened Antonio.

BIBLIOGRAPHY

Azcona, Tarsicio de. *Isabel la Católica: Estudi crítico de su vida y su reinado.* Madrid, 1964.

Miller, Townsend. *The Castles and the Crown: Spain 1451–1555.* New York, 1963.

Prescott, William H. *History of the Reign of Ferdinand and Isabella the Catholic.* Boston, 1838.

Sanceau, Elaine. *The Reign of the Fortunate King, 1495–1521.* Hamden, Conn., 1969.

THERESA EARENFIGHT

MARINE COMPASS. See *Compass,* article on *Marine Compass.*

MARINUS OF TYRE (fl. c. A.D. 100–135), geographer. Almost all our knowledge of Marinus is derived from Ptolemy's *Geography* (about A.D. 148), which calls him the most recent contemporary geographer. Marinus's lost work, written in Greek and referred to by Ptolemy as "the *diorthosis* [rectification] of the map," went through several editions, and as Ptolemy implies, aimed at improving the tradition of world mapping, long connected with Greek mathematical geographers.

The impetus for scientific world cartography came primarily from Eratosthenes of Cyrene (c. 275–194 B.C.), who, assuming that the earth is a sphere, determined its circumference by comparing the angle of the sun at Alexandria at midday on the summer solstice with the angle 5000 stades (about 890 kilometers) south at Syene (Aswan). From these measurements he calculated the angle of the arc of a circle between Alexandria and Syene subtended at the earth's center as one-fiftieth of 360 degrees, thus reaching a fairly close approximation to the circumference of the earth. Eratosthenes's map of the world (c. 225 B.C.) was later criticized by Hipparchus (fl. 162–126 B.C.) and others.

By the second century more detailed knowledge had resulted from the expansion of the Roman Empire. Ptolemy criticized Marinus because of the way he claimed to rectify the geographical *pinax* (world map, presumably of Eratosthenes). Marinus proposed an orthogonal system for a map of the world based on the latitude-longitude ratio of Rhodes, whose latitude was reckoned as 36° N. But his assumption that a degree of longitude equaled 400 stades and a degree of latitude equaled 500 meant that his approximations decreased in accuracy as one moved away from the latitude of Rhodes. Marinus estimated the north-south extent of the *oikumene* (known world) as 87 degrees or 43,500 stades; this placed Thule (probably Shetland) at 63° N instead of 66° N as reckoned by Pytheas of Marseilles and Eratosthenes. Marinus reckoned the longitude of the known world on the latitude of Rhodes as 225 degrees; the difference in longitude between the Canary Islands and Weihai, China, is in fact about 140 degrees. Marinus's calculation relied on exaggerated figures of travel times; he accepted seven months as the west-to-east traveling time from Kashgar (in western China) or thereabouts to Luoyang (on Hwang Ho River) and four months as the north-to-south traveling time from the territory of the Garamantes (in the Fezzan) to Agisymba (Lake Chad area). Marinus claimed to determine the extent of *klimata* (belts of latitude, literally "inclinations" to the earth's axis) and one-hour belts of longitude, though it seems that he did so by putting lists of places together, not by mapping. Although Ptolemy considered the use of *klimata* inexact, the concept of *klimata* persisted until the Renaissance. Marinus's work was rediscovered by the Arab geographer al-Mas'udi (d. A.D. 956/957), who mentions a colored map attributed to Marinus showing the seven *klimata.* No "Marinus" maps are known to have survived the Middle Ages in western Europe.

The information available on Marinus in the Renaissance was to be found in Greek, Latin, or Arabic manuscripts or in Greek or Latin editions and, later, vernacular editions, of Ptolemy's *Geography*. Columbus read about Marinus in Pierre d'Ailly's *Imago mundi* (1410), a book printed around 1483. Of particular interest in the time of Columbus was Marinus's estimate of 225 degrees longitude for the whole *oikumene* on the parallel of Rhodes; if this estimate was right, there would be only 135 degrees of unknown territory between the Canaries and the east coast of China. This assumption led Columbus to believe that a westward voyage from Europe to China was possible.

BIBLIOGRAPHY

Dilke, O. A. W. *Greek and Roman Maps.* Ithaca, N.Y., 1985.

Dilke, O. A. W., and the editors, "Updating the Map: Ptolemy's Criticism of Marinus of Tyre." In vol. 1 of *The History of Cartography,* edited by J. B. Harley and David Woodward. Chicago, 1987.

Ptolemy, Claudius. *Geography of Claudius Ptolemy.* Edited by E. L. Stevenson. New York, 1932.

Temporini, Hildegard, ed. *Aufstieg und Niedergang der römischen Welt.* Berlin, 1978.

O. A. W. Dilke

MARTELLUS, HENRICUS (fl. late fifteenth century), cartographer. Among the geographic charts of the fifteenth century that were based on Portuguese originals that have since disappeared, one stands out from the rest. It is the *mappamundi* designed by a German cartographer who worked in Italy and became known by his Latin name, Henricus Martellus Germanus. The map, four manuscript copies of which are included in the *Insularium illustratum Henrici Martelli Germani,* was later engraved and can be dated around 1490. Martellus worked in Florence in the last quarter of the fifteenth century in association with the engraver Francesco Roselli, who probably engraved not only this chart but also at the beginning of the next century, those of Contarini and others.

This map is the first to record the places reached in the voyage to the southern tip of Africa. Recorded are the results of the second voyage of the Portuguese navigator Diogo Cão, who sailed as far as Cape Padrão, and the voyage of Bartolomeu Dias, who rounded the Cape of Good Hope and reached the Indian Ocean.

The previous absence of these southern regions in Portuguese cartography can certainly be attributed to the policy of secrecy of the Portuguese king João II. Martellus must nonetheless have had access to information from Portugal. In his new toponymy, twelve of the place names derive from the voyage of Cão and twenty-one from the voyage of Dias.

Among the chart's various legends is the following:

"Hec est vera forma moderna affrice secundum descriptione Portugalensium inter mare Mediterraneum et oceanum meredionalem" (This is the true modern shape of Africa, according to the description of the Portuguese, between the Mediterranean Sea and the Southern Ocean). Another has given rise to much debate among scholars:

"Ad hunc usque montem qui vocatur niger per venit classis secûdi regis portugalie cuius classis p[er]fectus erat diegus canus qui in memoriam rei erexit colûnam marmorea cum crucis in signe et ultra processit usque ad serram pardam que distat ab môte nigro mille miliaria et. hic moritur" (The armada of the king of Portugal sailed as far as this mountain, which they call Negro. It was commanded by Diogo Cão, who erected stone pillars with crosses in memory of the king, and proceeded on his way until he got as far as the Serra Parda, which is located at a distance of one thousand miles from Mount Negro, and ends there).

Some scholars have interpreted "hic moritur" as "there he ended [his days]" or "there he died," asserting that the phrase refers to Diogo Cão, who may have died there, which would explain why he is undocumented after the return of this expedition. Others, however, think the phrase refers to the mountain, and thus means that the Serra Parda "ends there." (Evidence for the second interpretation may be a document found very recently that seems to indicate that Diogo Cão indeed survived the voyage.)

But the *mappamundi*'s real importance lies elsewhere. It is the first that shows the southern tip of Africa, which is depicted, so to speak, experimentally. Its workmanship is extremely modern in relation to its date, which we know from another legend referring to Dias's last voyage: "Hunc usq ad ilhe de fonti p[er]venit ultima navegatio portugalesium, ano dm. 1489" (The last Portuguese navigation reached as far as the Island of the Fountain in the year of the Lord 1489). The chart was certainly made a few months after Dias returned to Lisbon in December of 1488. This would mean that the Portuguese prototype on which Martellus based his map was made immediately after the return of the navigator, which was the usual practice. No known Portuguese chart represents the results of Dias's voyage, and though Martellus's map was certainly based on some chart, it is not extant.

Various references to these Portuguese charts, on which were methodically and progressively recorded the latest advances in navigation, attest to their existence. Some have been found in modern times—namely, the chart of Pedro Reinel, dated around 1485, and that of Jorge de Aguiar, dated 1492. These charts, and their very perfection, which presupposes antecedents, are proof of the development of Portuguese cartography in the fif-

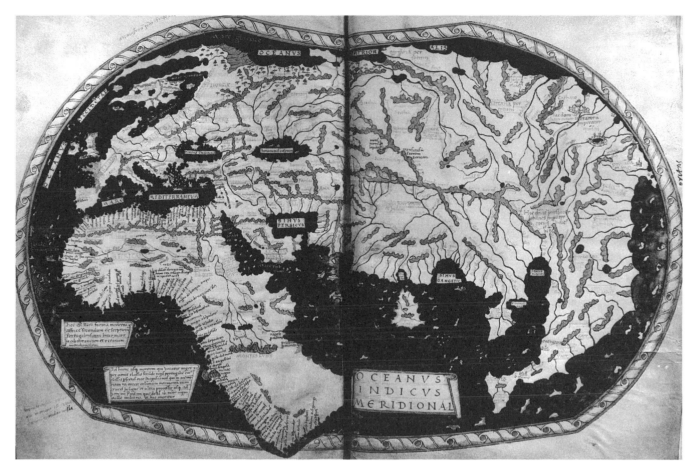

WORLD MAP OF HENRICUS MARTELLUS, 1489.

teenth century. Although Martellus must have based his map on such a chart, it contains an error that is not found in the Portuguese models that are known. His coordinates are incorrect; the African continent is unduly extended about six degrees to the south and dislocated by about twenty degrees to the east.

According to the Portuguese historian Jaime Cortesão, and as corroborated by Armando Cortesão, the errors could have been the result of misinformation circulated by King João II in an effort to make people believe that the African route was far longer than it actually is; Martellus was probably provided with this erroneous information. King João's policy of secrecy explains his showing Christopher Columbus (or his brother Bartolomé) a chart on which the voyage of Dias was represented with false latitudes. The king's objective was to discourage Portugal's rivals from following the southeastern route. It is probably not by chance that the first known Portuguese map to represent the southern tip of Africa—the so-called Cantino planisphere of 1502—was a clandestine chart secretly obtained by bribing a cartographer.

Aside from its representation of Africa, Martellus's *mappamundi* is a typical chart drawn according to Ptolemaic conceptions. It represents the Indian Ocean in a characteristically Ptolemaic form and, of course, it does not show any continent between western Europe and the extremity of Asia. It allows us to see the world as it was conceived on the eve of the first voyage of Christopher Columbus.

BIBLIOGRAPHY

Almagiá, Roberto. "I mappamondi di Enrico Martello e alcuni concetti geografici di Cristoforo Colombo." *La Bibliofilia* (Florence) 42 (1940): 288–311.

Castro, Augusto César da Silva, Jr. "Diogo Cão e a legenda de Henrique Martellus." In vol. 2 of *Actas do Congresso Internacional de história dos descobrimentos (1960)*. Lisbon, 1961.

Cortesão, Armando, and Avelino Teixeira da Mota. *Portugaliae Monumenta Cartographica*. 6 vols. Lisbon, 1960. Vols. 1, p. 10, and 5, p. 170.

Crone, G. R. *Maps and Their Makers: An Introduction to the History of Cartography*. 2d ed. London, 1962.

Nunn, George Emra. *The Geographical Conceptions of Columbus*. American Geographical Society, research series no. 14. New York.

Ravenstein, Ernest George. *Martin Behaim: His Life and His Globe.* London, 1908.
Vietor, Alexander O. "A Pre-Columbian Map of the World, Circa 1489." *Yale University Library Gazette* 37 (July 1962): 8–13.

ALFREDO PINHEIRO MARQUES
Translated from Portuguese by Rebecca Catz

MARTÍNEZ DE IRALA, DOMINGO (1509–1557),

Spanish conquistador; known as the Father of Paraguay. Born in Vergara, Guipúzcoa, in Spain, Martínez de Irala was the second son of Martín Perez and Marina de Albisúa Toledo. Following his older brother's death, he received an entailed estate from his parents, but in 1534 he transferred it to a brother-in-law and sailed for the Río de la Plata with Pedro de Mendoza, the newly appointed adelantado for the region.

Mendoza founded Buenos Aires in February 1536 but failed to find the great wealth he had hoped for. Soon under seige at Buenos Aires, he sent Juan de Ayolas to scout farther up the river in search of a way to Peru. During the second of these trips, Irala was left in charge of the ships and men posted at Candelaria (modern Corumbá?) while Ayolas marched westward. According to some accounts, Irala participated in the founding of Asunción, Paraguay, on August 15, 1537. (The city's government was created in 1541.) Following Mendoza's return to Spain and Ayolas's disappearance, Martínez de Irala emerged as a popular leader among the remaining colonists. In June 1539, he was elected governor of Paraguay. He continued to search for Ayolas until early in 1540 when news of Ayolas's death reached the governor. A year later, Irala withdrew the garrison at Buenos Aires.

The arrival on March 9, 1542, of the royally appointed replacement for Mendoza as governor and adelantado, Alvar Núñez Cabeza de Vaca, began the most controversial years of Martínez de Irala's life. Cabeza de Vaca claimed that Irala was plotting against him, but other sources indicate that Irala played the obedient subordinate until April 25, 1544, when failure of Cabeza de Vaca's efforts to reach El Dorado (or Peru) led the royal treasury officials and ordinary soldiers to overthrow him. Irala again was elected governor.

As governor between 1544 and 1556, Irala oversaw the solidification of the Spanish presence in Paraguay. He was unable to make peace with all the Indian groups antagonized during the previous decade, although most were pacified. Among the many explorations he authorized to the north and west of Asunción, his own in 1548 to the foothills of Bolivia was the most spectacular. Beginning in 1554, he sent explorers east to find routes to the Brazilian coast. His rule was challenged on a number of occasions; the Crown had even appointed a new governor, Diego de

Sanabría, in 1547, but the new governor and his son of the same name died before reaching Asunción. Martínez de Irala's own royal appointment as governor finally occurred in 1554. In 1556 he oversaw the granting of encomiendas, a measure he had previously resisted. He died on October 2, 1556, at the age of forty-seven.

BIBLIOGRAPHY

Morison, Samuel Eliot. *The European Discovery of America: The Southern Voyages, A.D. 1492–1616.* New York, 1971.
Warren, Harris G. *Paraguay: An Informal History.* Norman, Okla., 1949.

PAUL E. HOFFMAN

MARTYR, PETER. See *Anghiera, Pietro Martire d'.*

MAXIMILIAN I (1459–1519), German king from 1486

and Holy Roman Emperor-elect in 1493. Maximilian, son of Emperor Frederick III (1415–1493) and Leonor of Portugal, never formally received papal confirmation of his title of emperor. According to the terms of an agreement signed in Trent (1508), he declared that he would use the title of Holy Roman Emperor-elect until his coronation in Rome, which never took place.

Maximilian used his matrimonial alliances and military skill to bring the Austrian House of Habsburg to prominence in European affairs, especially in the west. His marriage in 1482 to Mary of Burgundy, daughter of Duke Charles the Bold, brought with it the wealth and territory of Flanders and the Franche-Comté. Maximilian increased his influence in 1495 through a double marriage alliance with Fernando of Spain. According to the terms of this diplomatic coup, Maximilian's only surviving legitimate son, Philip the Handsome, was betrothed to Juana of Castile, and his daughter Margaret was to marry Juan, prince of Asturias and heir to the thrones of Aragón, Castile, and Granada. Prince Juan died in 1497, followed by Philip in 1506, leaving Juana's son and Maximilian's grandson, the future Emperor Charles V, heir to the Castilian Crown as well as the territories in the Low Countries. Maximilian paved the way for the addition of Hungary and Bohemia to his territories by negotiating the marriages of his granddaughter Mary to King Louis II of Hungary and his grandson Ferdinand to Anne of Bohemia.

Until the death of his father in 1493, Maximilian had little German territory or political power and was preoccupied with his territories in the Low Countries. He was named co-regent of the Netherlands in 1477, and he became the ruling duke of Burgundy at the death of his wife, Mary (1482), and titular co-regent for his son, Philip, in 1488. Although Maximilian derived his political power from

MAXIMILIAN I. Engraving by Albrecht Dürer.

rial princes, who claimed to be the representatives of the popular will. In his dealings with the German princes, Maximilian was at a disadvantage because he constantly needed revenue for his campaigns against the French in Italy and northern France and the Ottoman Turks in eastern Europe. His financial difficulties were exacerbated by his desire to establish a permanent army. Maximilian was forced to bargain for his much-needed funds by promising administrative reforms of the imperial government. The reform movement was initiated by Berthold of Henneberg, the powerful archbishop of Mainz, but the reforms were stymied by the chaotic nature of German territorialism. His most lasting reforms were the creation of an imperial chamber court and imperial "circles" designed to maintain the peace. The Diet of Worms (1495) was a turning point in the constitutional history of the empire, but the reform movement ultimately failed because the princes and the emperor were unable to work together.

Maximilian had wide-ranging interests and was well read and reasonably intelligent. He furthered the humanist program of the Renaissance through his patronage of the University of Vienna and the University of Freiburg. He cultivated the fine arts, especially the work of artists such as Albrecht Dürer and the composers Heinrich Isaac and Ludwig Senfl. Maximilian did much to advance military organization and the newer technologies of warfare. His use of improved weapons such as lightweight lances and firearms made his foot soldiers, the Landsknecht, feared throughout Europe.

By the time of his death in 1519 Maximilian had established the foundations for the enduring dominance of the Habsburg family in European politics. He is buried not in his monumental tomb in Innsbruck but in the Chapel of St. George in Wiener Neustadt.

BIBLIOGRAPHY

Benecke, Gerhard. *Maximilian I (1469–1519): An Analytical Biography*. London, 1982.

Seton Watson, Robert William. *Maximilian I: Holy Roman Emperor*. Westminster, 1902.

Waas, Glenn Elwood. *The Legendary Character of Kaiser Maximilian*. New York, 1941.

Wiesflecker, Hermann. *Kaiser Maximilian I: Das Reich, Österreich und Europa an der Wende zur Neuzeit*. 4 vols. Vienna, 1971–1986.

THERESA EARENFIGHT

MAYAS. See *Indian America*, article on *Mayas*.

MEDICI FAMILY. Members of the Medici family, which originated in the Mugello region north of Florence,

Flanders, it was the source of many of his thorniest problems. The strength of the Flemish townspeople and their reluctance to be ruled by a foreign prince clashed violently with Maximilian's autocratic style. His policy of appointing officials from his Habsburg realms rather than from local territories was especially unpopular. He became embroiled in uprisings in Flanders in 1482 and 1488, and the Flemish burghers held him captive for several months during the latter rebellion. In addition, the acquisition of Flanders and the advent of Habsburg influence in western Europe inevitably led to conflict with the French kings Louis XI and Charles VIII.

Within his German realms he fared little better. Despite his personal popularity among the German people, Maximilian was considered an outsider, interested only in establishing the Habsburg family as a ruling dynasty. His territorial expansion, which began with his Burgundian marriage, raised Maximilian and the Habsburg family far above the competing German princes, thus making it nearly impossible for the imperial electors to refuse the Habsburgs the title of emperor without risking civil war. A deep rift developed between Maximilian and the territo-

migrated to that city in the early thirteenth century. They established themselves in the district around the church of San Lorenzo, investing in urban real estate and engaging in moneylending and cloth manufacture while still maintaining property in the Mugello. In the turbulent 1200s and 1300s, the family played a modest role in Florentine politics, filling some offices and participating in the factional conflicts that were so typical of the age. In 1400, the family was one of dozens of prominent Florentine lineages who controlled the city's economy and political life and constituted an urban elite. Giovanni di Bicci de' Medici (1360–1429) laid the foundation for the family's prominence in the fifteenth century by building a vast fortune from his banking operations in the Roman Curia. His son Cosimo (1389–1464) expanded his father's business operations, developing a network of branches in Rome, London, Bruges, Geneva, and Venice. In 1458, Cosimo's tax returns revealed that he was the richest citizen in Florence; he may well have been the wealthiest European of his time.

A factional conflict erupted in Florence in the late 1420s and early 1430s, which resulted in the exile of Cosimo and his cousin Averardo in 1433. But a year later, the two returned to Florence in triumph and established a regime of their partisans, which governed Florence for the next

LORENZO DE'MEDICI. Bust by Andrea del Verrocchio.

NATIONAL GALLERY OF ART, WASHINGTON, D.C.

sixty years. The foundations of this Medicean hegemony were (1) the family's vast wealth, which enabled Cosimo to build a large network of dependent clients; (2) constitutional reforms, which guaranteed that only Medici partisans filled the key offices of the state; and (3) the political astuteness of Cosimo and his successors. Cosimo projected an image of himself and his family as civic benefactors by maintaining peace and prosperity and by embellishing the city with palaces, villas, and restored churches and monasteries, most notably, San Lorenzo and San Marco. Even with these formidable assets, however, the Medici regime encountered opposition from disgruntled citizens: some who deplored the erosion of republican institutions and values, and others who wished to replace the Medici with their own faction. The most serious challenge to the regime was the Pazzi conspiracy (April 1478), in which Lorenzo de' Medici was wounded and his brother Giuliano was killed by assassins in the cathedral. The Pazzi conspirators failed to rouse the citizenry to their cause, and many were hunted down and executed.

Lorenzo (1449–1492) had succeeded to his father Piero's position as the leading citizen of Florence in 1469 when he was only seventeen. During his short life, he achieved an extraordinary reputation as statesman, patron of the arts, scholar, and poet. No other European of his time could match Lorenzo's versatility, which was a rare combination of political acumen, scholarly expertise, and poetic sensibility. He maintained close personal ties with the rulers of Italian states and was given credit for maintaining a fragile peace in the peninsula. He was particularly intimate with Pope Innocent VIII (r. 1484–1492), who bestowed a cardinal's hat on Lorenzo's son Giovanni. This was an important aspect of Lorenzo's strategy to build an Italian context for his family's power and influence.

After Lorenzo's death in 1492, Medici fortunes experienced a dramatic decline. His son Piero (1471–1503) was a less skillful politician than his father, and he alienated a number of influential citizens. He had initially opposed the efforts of King Charles VIII of France to claim the Kingdom of Naples as his inheritance. When a French army moved across the Alps in the summer of 1494 and threatened Florence, Piero abandoned the city. Opponents of the Medici established a republican regime, which was strongly influenced by the Dominican friar Girolamo Savonarola. This regime controlled Florence for fourteen years before it was overthrown and replaced by a pro-Medici party. From 1512 to 1527, the Medici dominated Florentine politics, while maintaining a republican form of government. After a brief interlude (1527–1530), when the city was governed by anti-Mediceans, the family again reasserted its control over the city. After a brief period of instability, Medici control of the Florentine state was solidified in 1537 under Cosimo (1517–1574), the first grand duke of Tuscany. His descendants ruled Florence for two hundred years before the family died out in 1737.

After Lorenzo's death, the most prominent members of the Medici family were two of its popes, Leo X (r. 1513–1521) and Clement VII (r. 1523–1534). Although they provided critical support for the family's control of Florence, they were unsuccessful in suppressing the Protestant revolt, and both failed in their attempts to limit the expansion of Spanish power in Italy. Clement VII supported the efforts of the Dominicans and Franciscans to convert the Indians in the New World, and he established a diocesan organization for the Roman Catholic church in the Caribbean and in Central and South America.

BIBLIOGRAPHY

DeRoover, Raymond. *The Rise and Decline of the Medici Bank, 1394–1494.* Cambridge, Mass., 1963.

Hale, John R. *Florence and the Medici: The Pattern of Control.* London, 1977.

Kent, Dale. *The Rise of the Medici: Faction in Florence, 1426–34.* Oxford, 1978.

Rubinstein, Nicolai. *The Government of Florence under the Medici (1434–94).* Oxford, 1966.

Stephens, John. *The Fall of the Florentine Republic, 1512–1530.* Oxford, 1983.

GENE A. BRUCKER

MEDICINE AND HEALTH. On the eve of the great voyages of the late fifteenth century, the practice of medicine in western Europe was in a transitional stage. Medieval Christianity discouraged all investigation of natural causes and this, in turn, retarded the development of medical inquiry. The scholastic dedication to rationalism, buttressed by new readings of Aristotle, did not penetrate deeply into the fabric of medieval society. For the vast majority of the population, disease was viewed as a punishment for sins or the result of some commerce with the devil. While individual illness could be cured by divine intervention encouraged simply by the ministrations of prayer, epidemic disease had to be countered by more public religious expressions such as mass processions, the building of churches, and the erection of inspiring religious statues. Medical practice was thus more a function of culture than of biology.

A powerful agent of change presented itself in a totally unanticipated form. The Black Death (most likely bubonic plague) arrived in western Europe between 1347 and 1351 with devastating results and was followed by other epidemics in 1361–1363, 1371, 1375, and 1396–1397. The bubonic plague had originated in Asia. It was carried to Europe by black rats (*Rattus rattus*) aboard sailing vessels

to Mediterranean ports. The black rats quickly infected local rodents with the deadly bacillus, *Pasteurella pestis,* and before the urban rats died the infection was carried from the rodent population to human hosts by fleas that shared the rodents' burrows. The sudden presence of thousands of dead rats in a community was an unmistakable sign of impending disaster.

The arrival of *Pasteurella pestis* in western Europe could not have come at a worse time. The famine years of 1345 to 1347 had left a weakened and highly susceptible population. Those persons living in crowded and dirty medieval cities were obvious targets since the accumulation of garbage and sewage attracted rodents and the flying vectors they harbored. Once *Pasteurella pestis* reached the human population, it was passed on not only by fleas but occasionally from person to person, generally from the mucus sprayed by the coughing or sneezing of someone already infected. High fevers, abscesses, and carbuncles brought death to about half of those infected within four or five days; in some parts of Europe, entire towns were virtually wiped out. Those who managed to survive were left in such a frail condition that they were easy prey to secondary infections. Besides bubonic plague, smallpox, tuberculosis, scabies, erysipelas, leprosy, and trachoma all reached epidemic proportions and wreaked demographic havoc in western Europe in the fourteenth and fifteenth centuries.

There is no general agreement on the average life span in western Europe on the eve of the great discoveries. It was certainly less than twenty-nine years of age, probably closer to twenty-eight. This low average figure reflects a very high infant and young-child mortality rate. It is believed that over one-third of the population died before reaching the age of five. Though the epidemics commanded most attention, poor diet, horrible hygienic practices, and the general lack of competent medical care all contributed to low life expectancy.

The heavy toll exacted by the recurring epidemics in western Europe for the first time prompted genuine public concern with medical education, the regulation of medical practice, the construction of hospitals, the need for hygiene, and the elusive search for effective therapy. There were few large advances in medical knowledge, but social pressure rather than religious discourse clearly began to affect the direction of medical inquiry. Spain affords one good example of the European response to epidemic disease, and in Spain it was the Black Death especially that encouraged the medical effort.

The rapid spread of the Black Death throughout Iberia left some cities with less than half of their original populations. The kingdoms of Aragón and Catalonia were hit as hard as any regions of Europe. The city of Barcelona, for example, had a population of about 50,000 in 1340. Ten years later the number had been reduced to 38,000 and by 1377 to 20,000. This demographic devastation alerted the Iberian medical community to the matter of contagiousness. The institution of quarantine emerged as the first response. Ships calling at Spanish ports were sometimes required to remain at anchor in the harbor for forty days (thus the word quarantine) before anyone could disembark. Concern with prophylaxis prompted the construction of elementary sewage systems, the cleaning of public latrines, and a more systematic regulation of public market places and slaughter houses.

In the century that followed the cataclysm of the plague, many uneducated Spaniards turned to religious practices in their search for solace, but an increasing number of educated Spaniards began to free themselves from the bondage of superstition, alchemy, and astrology to search for rational explanations of disease. A new emphasis was placed on medical education at the leading Spanish universities. Anatomy was at the core of the curriculum and grave robbers began to provide corpses for classroom dissection. The propriety of dissection of the human body occasioned much anxious wrangling but the process was fundamental to the new questions addressed by Spanish physicians. Without it medical science simply could not exist.

The University of Salamanca, founded by King Fernando III of Castile in 1243, had offered medical training on a regular basis since 1252; by the fifteenth century Valencia, Seville, Barcelona, Valladolid, Lerida, and Alcalá de Henares were making major contributions as well. If not yet ready to compete with Salerno and Padua in Italy and Montepellier in France, they were improving rapidly. By attending lectures and listening to the explication of texts,

BLOODLETTING. A standard treatment. From a fifteenth-century illuminated manuscript.   ELSEVIER PUBLISHING PROJECTS, AMSTERDAM

medical students sought to master Hippocrates, Galen, Ibn Sina (Avicenna), and Ibn Rushd (Averroës) during their four-year course of study; they were expected to question these venerable authorities as well. Responsibility for the systematic acquisition and transmission of medical knowledge was institutionalized rather than passed on casually from a "practitioner" to any interested party. Institutionalization made certain elements of control possible.

With the establishment of an environment for academic medicine, the quest for better teaching materials took on new meaning. In the hope of providing more appropriate tools for disciplined inference, Jewish scholars in Toledo, especially Alvaro de Castro and Diego Sobrino, began the arduous task of translating medical treatises from Greek and Arabic. By the late fifteenth century Spanish presses had begun to accelerate their diffusion of medical treatises and in the classroom, as well as the clinic, these scholarly works were taken seriously for the first time. The medical literature used in Spanish universities in the fifteenth and sixteenth centuries was heavily indebted to the Greeks, especially Galen and Hippocrates. It is not surprising that Spanish physicians embraced a modified humoral theory of medicine, according to which disease resulted from a disequilibrium of the body's four basic qualities: hot, cold, wet, and dry. Therapy, as a result, was designed to restore that equilibrium through the use of foods and medicines that harbored the appropriate hot or cold, wet or dry therapeutic properties. It was one of those theories not quickly killed by fact.

At approximately the same time that medical education was institutionalized, hospitals were established throughout the Iberian kingdoms. During the second half of the fifteenth century, general hospitals could be found in Madrid, Zaragoza, Burgos, Toledo, Salamanca, Barcelona, and Seville, and more specialized institutions for the mentally impaired in Barcelona, for women in Madrid (Hospital de la Pasión), and for lepers in Seville (Hospital de San Lázaro). A special military hospital was established in Granada to care for Christian soldiers wounded during the wars of the Reconquista. By the time that Columbus began his first voyage to America the practice of medicine to a large extent had been taken out of the monasteries and much of the Spanish medical community had rejected the deductive method in favor of the experimental.

Equally important were the early steps to regulate medical practice. During the earlier Middle Ages, the regulation of medicine seemed designed more to guard morals than to promote public health or medical competence. The *fueros* (bodies of regional laws) were concerned that male doctors might use their influential positions to corrupt their female patients and therefore prohibited all treatment of women unless parents or husbands ordered the treatment or were present during the specific procedures. But gradually regulatory control directed itself to the charlatan, the quack, and the medical incompetent. The *Siete partidas* provided that a false doctor who caused a person's death be banished for five years and provided that a pharmacist who dispensed medicine without a doctor's order could be tried for murder if the patient died. But it was not until the second half of the fifteenth century that comprehensive laws for the licensing of physicians were ordered by the Spanish monarchs.

On March 30, 1477, nine years before they met Columbus for the first time, King Fernando and Queen Isabel signed a significant *pragmática* (a royal edict) in Madrid establishing a special council known as the *protomedicato*. Designed to safeguard the public interest, the *protomedicato* was charged with examining all doctors, surgeons, curers, apothecaries, and sellers of herbs to determine their competence in their respective fields. If they were judged to be competent they were given a formal letter of approval and a license to practice. Those who continued their activities without the license were subject to stiff fines; a special prosecutor, the *promotor fiscal,* was attached to the council to bring charges against violators. In addition to licensing doctors, the *protomedicato* also heard all complaints brought by the public against the medical profession. Its decision in these cases was final as the enabling act provided that there would be no appeal to any other royal tribunal. It is significant that the decree establishing the *protomedicato* was made applicable to all existing Spanish kingdoms and possessions and all future possessions that the Crown might acquire. Following the voyages of Columbus, the *pragmática* of 1477 would be applied in the New World.

The royal decree establishing the *protomedicato* was supplemented by a series of other regulatory measures in the decades that followed its promulgation. The most important of these was a statute that provided that all practicing physicians have a medical degree from an approved university in addition to two years of internship with a certified doctor. Evidence of compliance had to be presented to the *protomedicato*. All these regulatory measures were hesitant steps in the right direction but in and of themselves they were insufficient to make a major impact on health care, much less to establish the dominion of humanity over disease.

A new round of epidemics swept through the Iberian kingdoms in the two decades prior to the voyages of Columbus. Though not as severe as the Black Death of the fourteenth century they took a heavy toll. The plague visited Barcelona in 1478, 1483, 1489, and 1490; Mallorca in 1475; Zaragoza in 1486 and 1490; and Valencia in 1489. Typhus apparently made its European debut in Spain when it struck Granada in 1489 and 1490; it reportedly caused over 17,000 deaths in the Spanish army, making it a much more effective killer than the Moors the Spanish were attempting to drive off Iberian soil. Some of the Spanish adventurers, servants, and slaves would carry these deadly pathogens, along with others, to the New World on the Atlantic voyages that began in 1492.

The first European travelers to the New World crossed the Atlantic on small, crowded ships that lacked proper sanitary facilities. These vessels were designed to carry freight, not passengers, and the travelers often shared their space with animals. They had the choice of finding a niche in the stench of the hold, surrounded by seasick passengers, or sitting on a cluttered deck exposed to the elements and the epithets of hardened sailors. Seldom would they encounter a doctor aboard. When all went well, the time between landfalls was only about a month and a half, but ocean calms often lengthened the journey. The diet for the trip (primarily salted meat, salted flour, biscuit, lard that quickly became rancid, dried grains, peas, and beans, and about a quart of water per day) was barely tolerable even when the ration was not attacked by rats or fouled by seawater. The absence of fresh fruit, vegetables, and meat left the travelers weak and vulnerable to scurvy, especially if poor dietary practices prior to the initial boarding had lowered their resistance. Scurvy seemed to attack the whole body, causing swelling of the joints, excruciating pain in the back and kidneys, hemorrhaging from the mucous membranes, general weakness, and the swelling of gums and loss of teeth. Shipboard deaths were not uncommon in the late fifteenth and early sixteenth centuries, especially when climatic conditions, improper navigation, or malfunctioning of the vessels unexpectedly lengthened the duration of the journey. Short trips in the Caribbean were less prone to the ravages of scurvy but the disease was the chief cause of mortality among Spanish seamen.

For native Americans the most dramatic impact of the European contact was the introduction of new epidemic diseases. Isolated for millennia from the gene pools of the Old World, the Indian populations of the Americas had few immunological defenses against Old World diseases. Smallpox, typhus, measles, pertusis, tuberculosis, and pneumonia, once turned loose, devastated the Indians of the New World and in time left only remnants of once vibrant preconquest societies. Some of Columbus's sailors returned to Europe with a new disease thought to be of American origin, syphilis, which spread through Europe with a vengeance during the last few years of the fifteenth century.

The early Spanish chroniclers offered Europe tantalizing descriptions of the botanical bounty of the New World at a time when medicinal plants were in great demand. Samples of jalap, sarsaparilla, sneezewort, sassafras, wormwood, creosote, chinchona bark (from which quinine is extracted), peyote, and countless other plants found their way back to Europe and worked their way into the *Materia medica*. The Spanish physician Nicolás Bautista de Monardis collected these specimens in Seville and in 1565 published his *Dos libros, el uno que trata de todas las cosas que traen de nuestras Indias Occidentales que sirven al uso de medicina*. It soon inspired an English translation under the overly optimistic title *Joyfull Newes out of the Newe Worlde* (London, 1577). Many of the plants did not live up to expectations, but the medical syncretism of the Old World and the New World had begun.

[For further discussion of disease in the New World, see *Disease and Demography*. See also *Syphilis* for further discussion of its origins and spread.]

BIBLIOGRAPHY

Crosby, Alfred W. *The Columbian Exchange: Biological and Cultural Consequences of 1492*. Westport, Conn., 1972.

Entralgo, Laín. *Historia universal de la medicina*. Barcelona, 1981.

Granjel, Luis S. *La medicina española renacentista*. Salamanca, 1980.

McNeill, William H. *Plagues and Peoples*. Garden City, N.Y., 1976.

Twigg, Graham. *The Black Death: A Biological Reappraisal*. London, 1984.

Zinsser, Hans. *Rats, Lice, and History*. Boston, 1934.

MICHAEL C. MEYER

MEDINACELI, DUKE OF.

MEDINACELI, DUKE OF. The fifth duke of Medinaceli, Luis de la Cerda (d. 1501), played a critical role in introducing Christopher Columbus into the royal court of Spain. The duke of Medinaceli was the most logical Spanish nobleman for Columbus to ask for help with his enterprise of the Indies because he was one of the great sea lords of Spain. His ancestors had been among the first conquerors of the Canary Islands, and he was lord of the strategic port of Puerto de Santa María.

When Columbus approached him in late 1485, the duke was in Puerto de Santa María, where he had married his third wife, Catalina Bique de Orejón, a local citizen. He was eager to expand his shipping business and considered outfitting three or four ships for Columbus. But he decided that Columbus's plan would more appropriately be sponsored by the monarchs. So from his village of Rota, he wrote to the queen recommending Columbus.

Columbus could not have chosen a better patron in the merchant and shipping world of Spain's southern coast. The duke was descended from Castilian kings and was closely related to the most powerful member of the royal court, Cardinal Pedro González de Mendoza. The duke

was the cardinal's nephew, and the duke's granddaughter was married to the cardinal's son. The connections worked marvelously well. By early 1486, Columbus was at the royal court presenting his plan to Fernando and Isabel. The queen placed her chief accountant, Alonso de Quintanilla, in charge of the project, and Quintanilla wrote to the duke that the proposal was risky but if it succeeded Her Highness would give him a share of it.

We can reconstruct this story from a letter that the duke wrote to Cardinal Mendoza on March 19, 1493. At the time, the duke was in his town of Cogolludo north of the city of Guadalajara, supervising the building of a palace. On the recommendation of the cardinal, he had hired the Italian-trained architect, Lorenzo Vázquez, to design a Renaissance building for him. In the midst of this building project, he received word that Columbus had returned safely from his first voyage.

The duke of Medinaceli wrote to tell his uncle about the great event and asked for two favors. Since he had supported and recommended Columbus, he wanted a share of the new shipping business. He asked that all the cargoes in this new trade should be loaded and unloaded in Puerto de Santa María.

He did not get this, but he did receive his second request, that he be permitted to send some of his own caravels every year. One of the ships that participated in Columbus's second voyage was captained by an employee of the duke, Alonso de Ojeda. And the duke may have been the principal investor in Ojeda's later voyages of exploration to the coast of South America.

Meanwhile, the duke's palace in Cogolludo lagged. By the time he died in 1501, only the facade had been built, and the structure remains in the same incomplete state today.

BIBLIOGRAPHY

Gutiérrez Coronel, Diego. *Historia genealógica de la casa de Mendoza*. Edited by Angel González Palencia. 2 vols. Cuenca, 1946.

Layna Serrano, Francisco. *Castillos de Guadalajara*. Madrid, 1962.

Medinaceli, Duke of. "Letter to the Grand Cardinal of Spain, about the Duke's early support of Columbus." In *The Conquerors and the Conquered*. Vol. 1 of *New Iberian World: A Documentary History of the Discovery and Settlement of Latin America to the Early 17th Century*. Edited by John H. Parry and Robert G. Keith. 5 vols. New York, 1984.

HELEN NADER

MEDINA SIDONIA, DUKE OF.

MEDINA SIDONIA, DUKE OF. Hereditary noble titles were a new invention in Castile during Christopher Columbus's lifetime, and one of the richest of these new titles was duke of Medina Sidonia, which King Juan II bestowed on the count of Niebla, Juan Alfonso de Guzmán, in 1445. The dukes of Medina Sidonia were exceptionally wealthy because they were lords of the important port of Sanlúcar de Barrameda and because the king gave them as a hereditary property the royal taxes on the annual tuna catch in the Straits of Gibraltar. The second duke, Enrique de Guzmán (duke from 1468 until his death in 1492), was an important commander in the war against Granada. Some historians believe that Christopher Columbus asked the duke of Medina Sidonia to finance his project to sail west to the Indies because the duke was one of the patrons of the monastery of La Rábida and owned property around Huelva, where Columbus's sister-in-law and her husband lived. If Columbus did so, it would have been sometime between 1485, when Columbus came to Castile, and 1492, when Fernando and Isabel agreed to sponsor the project. No documentary evidence exists that Columbus approached the duke of Medina Sidonia, however, and there is some reason to believe that authors have confused this nobleman with the duke of Medinaceli, whose early support for Columbus is well documented.

BIBLIOGRAPHY

Manzano Manzano, Juan. *Cristóbal Colón: Siete años decisivos de su vida, 1485–1492.* 2d ed. Madrid, 1964.
Pierson, Peter. *Commander of the Armada.* New Haven, 1989.
Rumeu de Armas, Antonio. *La Rábida y el descubrimiento de América.* Madrid, 1968.

HELEN NADER

MEMORIAL ARCHITECTURE. See *Monuments and Memorials.*

MÉNDEZ, DIEGO (c. 1472–c. 1536), captain of *La Capitana.* Méndez, by all accounts, emerges as the true hero of Columbus's disaster-plagued fourth voyage to America, for which he enlisted as *escudero,* "gentleman volunteer." Little is known of his early life except that he came from the Segura region of Spain and had served for a time as majordomo for Columbus. The recorded history of his heroic exploits begins in Veragua, a gold-rich area in the western part of present-day Panama, where Columbus was attempting to establish a settlement.

The apparent permanence of the settlement was causing a rapid deterioration in the once-friendly relations with the local Indians. Méndez, who had become a trusted aide of the Admiral, observed the increase in the numbers and hostility of the natives and undertook a bold reconnoitering expedition. He returned with the warning that the area's principal chieftain, the cacique El Quibián,

had assembled thousands of warriors and was clearly planning an attack. Méndez advised the Admiral and his brother Bartolomé Colón, who was to remain in charge of the new settlement as adelantado (military and political leader), that the only safe course was to seize El Quibián and his principal subordinates and outlined a plan to do so. The daring plan was approved and carried out with great skill by Colón, Méndez, and a force of about eighty men. The cacique was taken prisoner, together with several key subordinates and their families. Through the laxness of guards, El Quibián was able to escape, enabling him to continue his campaign against the Spaniards.

On April 6, 1503, the day the Admiral was to depart the area with three of his four ships, a force of about four hundred armed natives attacked the settlement. Seven of the Spanish force were killed and several others wounded, including the adelantado. As Méndez later recorded, "This fight lasted three full hours, and Our Lord miraculously gave us the victory, we being so few and they so numerous." When the fight was over, the captain of the Admiral's flagship, Diego Tristán, who had been sent ashore in a ship's boat to take on a final supply of water, ignored the advice of Méndez and proceeded up the river to find good sweet water. The regrouped natives attacked and killed Tristán and all his men but one, who managed to escape and report the disaster. Remembering the loss of the entire force left at La Navidad in La Española on the first voyage, Columbus realized that the situation ashore had become untenable, and he reluctantly decided it would be prudent to abandon the settlement. Méndez constructed a raft out of two dugout canoes and cross timbers and in two days transported to the ships all the garrison, together with the food and gear that had been stored ashore. The worm-eaten hulk of the caravel *Gallego* was abandoned. When Méndez came aboard with the last load, the Admiral embraced him and promoted him to captain of the flagship *La Capitana,* to replace Tristán. On Easter Sunday, April 16, 1503, the three remaining ships departed for La Española.

Of this voyage Méndez wrote, "as the ships were all pierced and worm-eaten . . . we soon had to abandon one of them . . . for not even the entire crew with pumps, kettles and pots were able to keep ahead of the water which leaked in through the worm holes." After seventy torturous days of fighting head winds and strong adverse currents, the two remaining ships, barely afloat, finally were able to reach Puerto Santa Gloria in Jamaica where the Admiral found it necessary to run them aground to keep them from sinking.

Although they were now in fact marooned, the immediate problem was food. Méndez gave out the last rations of hardtack and wine and took off into the interior of the island with three men to bargain with the caciques for food. He found the natives to be friendly and eager to trade food for beads, bits of lace, hawkbells, and other such trinkets he had to offer. One important cacique named Huareo agreed to furnish provisions regularly, to be paid for when delivered. At the eastern end of the island, Méndez established a friendship with a cacique named Ameyro from whom he purchased a "splendid canoe in exchange for a fine chamber pot, a coat and a shirt." The cacique also provided six natives to paddle. Loading the canoe with provisions, Méndez proceeded westerly along the coast until he reached Puerto Santa Gloria.

Columbus then requested that Méndez go to La Española in the canoe to arrange with Governor Nicolás de Ovando for their rescue. He was afterward to proceed to Spain at the first opportunity to deliver to the sovereigns a report of the voyage. (That letter, dated July 7, 1503, which eventually was delivered by Méndez, has become known as the "Lettera Rarissima" from an Italian transcript.) Méndez's first attempt was thwarted by hostile natives, but he escaped and returned to the stranded ships. Another attempt was made at once, with more thorough preparations. A second canoe was added to the expedition under the charge of Bartolomeo Fieschi, a Genoese who had commanded the abandoned *Vizcaína*. The second attempt, with an armed party under the adelantado following them along the shore to the eastern end of the island, was successful, but all suffered from the intense heat. Their supply of water gave out, and one of the Indians died of thirst and exhaustion. After four trying days, they arrived at Cape Tiburon, the southwestern peninsula of La Española.

After much difficulty, Méndez finally located the governor in Jaraguá. Ovando received him cordially but made excuse after excuse for not sending relief to Columbus. He detained Méndez for seven long months before granting him permission to go to Santo Domingo. There Méndez was able to purchase on the Admiral's account one of a fleet of three caravels just then arrived from Spain. Having appropriately supplied the caravel and seen it depart for Jamaica, Méndez, in the other ships of this opportune fleet, sailed directly for Spain to carry out the further instructions of the Admiral.

After proceeding with the letter to court, Méndez remained there for some time with the Admiral's son Diego to work for the restitution of promised titles and privileges that had been stripped from Columbus and his heirs. When the Admiral finally returned to Spain, Méndez continued to serve him and was present at his deathbed.

BIBLIOGRAPHY

Irving, Washington. *The Life and Voyages of Christopher Columbus and His Companions.* 3 vols. New York, 1849.

Morison, Samuel Eliot. *Journals and Other Documents on the Life and Voyages of Christopher Columbus.* New York, 1963.

WILLIAM LEMOS

MENDOZA, ANTONIO DE (1491–1552), first Spanish viceroy of New Spain (Mexico) and second viceroy of Peru. Mendoza was born in Alcalá la Real, Spain, the second son of the second count of Tendilla, Íñigo López de Mendoza, and his second wife and third cousin, Francisca Pacheco. The count was the captain general of Granada during and following its conquest by Fernando and Isabel. He was the head of a principal family among the twenty-two families that constituted the House of Mendoza, one of the three great houses of the Castilian nobility. Antonio's brothers included Diego Hurtado de Mendoza, noted for his history of Granada and the novel *Lazarillo de Lormes,* and Bernardino de Mendoza, famous for his naval exploits in the Mediterranean.

Prior to his service in Mexico, Antonio de Mendoza served as ambassador to Hungary (1526–1528) and as a royal chamberlain in Isabel of Portugal's court. While still a teenager, he saw military service in suppressing a rebellion in Granada.

Mendoza was appointed viceroy of New Spain in 1535, six years after he first had been approached about taking that office. His rule, which lasted until 1550, was notable for strengthening the royal government through legal and institutional development. He also reformed the royal treasury, regularized the assessment of tributes on native Americans, and issued laws governing mining and the mint. He so reduced Hernando Cortés's effective power that Cortés went to Spain to seek the emperor Charles V's favor, which, however, he did not obtain. Mendoza promoted education and advocated the founding of a university. He commissioned explorations of the American southwest by Francisco Vázquez de Coronado (1540–1542) and voyages that carried Spanish exploration as far as Oregon. In 1543 he established a Spanish colony in the Philippines.

Mendoza personally led the army that crushed the Mixton rebellion in 1541, a rising of native Americans in Jalisco that might have destroyed the Spanish colony had not other Indians remained loyal to the Spanish. Mendoza also steered New Spain through the crisis of the New Laws of 1542. Faced with the potential for a Spanish revolt against royal control because the New Laws decreed an end to encomiendas, Mendoza suspended execution of the laws and worked to effect a compromise that allowed a continuation of the encomienda but under tighter royal control and for a limited number of generations. His success in thus avoiding a rebellion may be contrasted with Viceroy Blasco Núñez Vela's enforcement of the New

Laws in Peru and the resulting rebellion that cost him his life.

Once order had been restored in Peru, Mendoza was sent to be its second viceroy (1551–1552). When he arrived, Peru was in political turmoil because the audiencia of Lima had issued a decree abolishing personal service by Indians, a practice outlawed in 1542 but still customary in Peru. Mendoza attempted to moderate but not abolish this custom. Ill before he made the journey to Peru, Mendoza died on July 21, 1552, after only ten months and nine days in office.

BIBLIOGRAPHY

Aiton, Arthur S. *Antonio de Mendoza, First Viceroy of New Spain.* Durham, N.C., 1927.

Rubio Mañé, Ignacio. *Introducción al estudio de los virreyes de Nueva España, 1535–1746.* 4 vols. Mexico City, 1955.

PAUL E. HOFFMAN

MENDOZA, PEDRO GONZÁLEZ DE (1428–1495),

cardinal, archbishop of Toledo, and confidant of Fernando and Isabel. Mendoza's parents, the marquises of Santillana, intended him for a church career and arranged for his appointment as archdeacon of Guadalajara. In 1445, the young cleric went to the University of Salamanca, where he lived on his comfortable income as archdeacon, studied canon law, and translated the *Aeneid* and some books of Ovid's *Metamorphoses* at the request of his father, who was one of Spain's most renowned poets. Mendoza was appointed bishop of Calahorra (1454) and began to travel with the royal court, first representing the political interests of his militarily powerful brothers in the succession wars during the reign of King Enrique IV, then persuading Cardinal Rodrigo Borja (the future Pope Alexander VI) to support the claims of Princess Isabel. This political success launched his career up the ladder of lucrative church appointments: bishop of Sigüenza, archbishop of Seville, cardinal of Santa Croce (1472), and archbishop of Toledo (1485–1495). He also received royal and papal legitimation of his two sons and noble titles for them.

As primate of Spain and a permanent resident of the royal court, Cardinal Mendoza exercised so much influence over Fernando and Isabel that he was popularly called "the third king of Spain." Many writers speculate that, in order to have gained the confidence of the monarchs, Christopher Columbus must have been supported by Cardinal Mendoza.

BIBLIOGRAPHY

Azcona, Tarsicio de. *La elección y reforma del episcopado español en tiempo de los Reyes Católicos.* Madrid, 1960.

Azcona, Tarsicio de. *Isabel la Católica: Estudio crítico de su vida y su reinado.* Madrid, 1964.

Medina y Mendoza, Francisco de. *Vida del Cardenal D. Pedro González de Mendoza.* Memorial Histórico Español, vol. 6. Madrid, 1853.

Villalba Ruiz de Toledo, F. Javier. *El Cardenal Mendoza ante la guerra civil castellana.* Madrid, 1983.

HELEN NADER

MENÉNDEZ DE AVILÉS, PEDRO (1519–1574),

adelantado of Florida. A notable Spanish, sixteenth-century naval leader, explorer, and colonizer, Pedro de Menéndez was born in Avilés. He went to sea as a youth and led his own ship against French corsairs in the Bay of Biscay. Young Menéndez's exploits brought him a royal appointment to command the Indies fleets. He also became a ship owner in the transatlantic trade; two large galleasses were built to his order, of which one, *San Pelayo,* was of almost a thousand-tons burden.

In 1565, King Philip II contracted with Menéndez to pacify and colonize Florida, which extended from Newfoundland to the Florida Keys and west to St. Joseph's Bay in the Gulf of Mexico. Under the contract, Menéndez was named adelantado (governor and captain general), but agreed to bear much of the cost of the Florida enterprise. In return, he would enjoy certain monopolies and exemptions, and was promised a large Florida land grant, with the title of marquis, should his venture succeed.

In outfitting his Florida expedition, Menéndez used *San Pelayo* and utilized a network of relatives and friends from a closely knit Asturian family group. These associates supplemented his funds and furnished him with manpower for the Florida enterprise. In turn, they hoped to share Menéndez's royal favor and expected to receive lands in Florida. Menéndez paid his own soldiers' passage to America and promised them town lots and plantation allotments. The royal troops were to be paid from the king's treasury.

In the meantime, Jean Ribault had explored Florida for France, leaving a short-lived colony at Port-Royal, near present-day Beaufort, South Carolina. In 1564, another French captain, René Goulaine de Laudonnière, built Fort Caroline on the St. Johns River. In 1565, Ribault returned to Port-Royal with reinforcements.

On September 8, 1565, Menéndez landed in Florida and founded San Agustín (St. Augustine), the oldest continuously occupied city in the United States. Menéndez dealt rapidly with the French forces, capturing Fort Caroline and killing Jean Ribault with many of his followers. He then established reliable sources of supply in Cuba and Yucatán for his Florida colony and quelled soldiers' mutinies in the Florida garrisons. After that, Menéndez proceeded with his explorations of the east coast of North America. He signed treaties with many of the native American groups, but found himself opposed by Indians who had been allied with the French. Menéndez built forts and missions in the Florida peninsula and north to Chesapeake Bay and founded the city of Santa Elena on present-day Parris Island. He dispatched expeditions to Newfoundland and overland from Santa Elena to the Appalachian Mountains. In none of his explorations did Menéndez find the passage he sought through the continent to the Pacific and the riches of Asia.

In 1567, Menéndez was appointed captain general of Spain's first royal armada for the Indies and designed its new vessels, fast galleys called *galizabras*. While commanding the armada, Menéndez was also named governor of Cuba; his lieutenants governed it in his absence, together with Florida. He also proposed to the king his own solution for determining longitude.

As the axis of Spanish Florida began to shift northward by 1569, the south Florida forts and missions were abandoned, and more than two hundred settlers, among them Menéndez and his wife and household, came to Santa Elena to develop farms and raise livestock. Although the Spanish Crown established a subsidy to sustain the Florida garrisons and granted Menéndez another royal contract to extend his jurisdiction to Pánuco in Mexico, relations with the native Americans of Florida deteriorated into mutual hostility and war.

The settlers at Santa Elena were confined to the poor coastal soils; lacking peace with the Indians, they could not penetrate to the fertile Georgia and Carolina uplands. The Jesuit missionaries on Chesapeake Bay were killed by the Indians, and the order terminated its Florida efforts. Menéndez's enterprise was showing unmistakable signs of its eventual failure.

In February 1574, after the Sea-Beggars (Dutch rebels against Spanish rule) had captured the fortress of Middelburg, on an island on the coast of the Spanish Netherlands, Philip II ordered Menéndez to clear the English Channel of enemy vessels and reinforce the Spanish garrisons in the Netherlands. As he prepared to sail, Menéndez fell ill, evidently of typhus. He died September 17, 1574, and the fleet he had gathered at Santander never sailed.

BIBLIOGRAPHY

Lyon, Eugene. *The Enterprise of Florida: Pedro Menéndez de Avilés and the Spanish Conquest of 1565–1568.* Gainesville, Fla., 1976.

Lyon, Eugene. *Santa Elena: A Brief History of the Colony, 1566–1587.* Columbia, S.C., 1982.

Manucy, Albert C. *Florida's Menéndez: Captain-General of the Ocean Sea.* St. Augustine, Fla., 1965.

Ruidíaz y Caravía, Eugenio. *La Florida: Su conquista y colonización por Pedro Menéndez de Avilés.* 2 vols. Madrid, 1893–1894.

EUGENE LYON

MERCATOR, GERARDUS (1512–1594), Flemish cartographer, cosmographer, and instrument maker. Gerardus Mercator was born Gerhard Kremer on March 5, 1512, in the small town of Rupelmonde, Spanish Netherlands (present-day Belgium), to which his parents had recently moved from the German village of Gangelt. The family was poor. Gerhard learned what Latin he could in local schools and after his father's death in 1526–1527 his uncle sent him to 's Hertogenbosch to study at a school, one of the largest and best in Europe, run by the Brethren of the Common Life. After three and a half years with the brothers, Gerhard went to Louvain, where he enrolled at the university in 1530 as one of the poor students at Castle College. By this time he had Latinized his name to Mercator. He studied philosophy and took his master's degree in 1532.

Louvain was, at this time, a great center of learning, and Mercator made the acquaintance, among others, of the greatest astronomer and mathematician of the Low Countries, Gemma Frisius, and of the Louvain goldsmith and engraver Gaspar van der Heyden (à Myrica). Through association with these men and private study, he acquired a thorough knowledge of geography, astronomy, cartography, and surveying, including triangulation. He also learned the arts of making astronomical and surveying instruments of brass, of engraving on brass and copper, and of italic handwriting. Mercator commenced his cartographic career in Louvain but moved to Duisburg, Germany, in 1552, probably because of the repressive intolerance of the Spanish Netherlands in religious matters, and spent the rest of his life there. Besides compiling and publishing maps, Mercator also wrote a highly influential manual of italic handwriting (the first to be published outside of Italy; 1540), and attempted a "harmonization," or reconciliation, of the Four Gospels (1592). He was much involved with theological issues throughout his life and even his cartographic work (witness the introduction to his *Atlas*) was firmly rooted in religious conviction. Mercator died on December 2, 1594.

During an active career of almost sixty years, Mercator produced a long series of important and influential cartographic works: a map of the Holy Land (1537), the double-cordiform world map of 1538, a map of Flanders (1540), a pair of globes, terrestrial and celestial (1541 and 1551), maps of Europe (1554) and the British Isles (1564), the great world map (1569), a scholarly edition of Ptolemy's *Geography*, with maps (1578), and his atlas (first part, 1585; first complete edition, 1595).

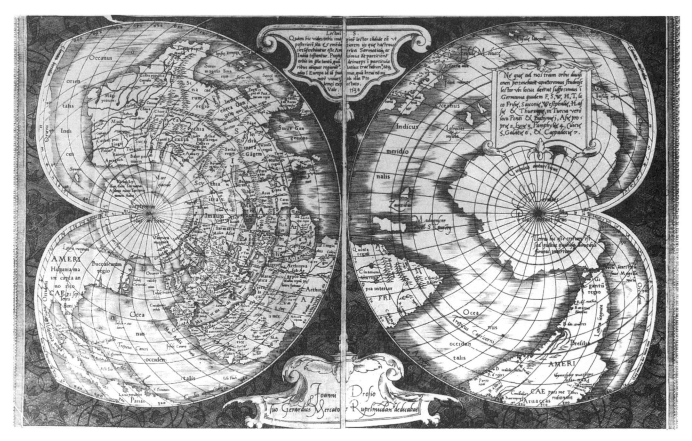

MERCATOR'S DOUBLE-CORDIFORM WORLD MAP OF 1538. This copperplate engraving is the earliest extant map to use the name *America* for both northern and southern continents. The famous Mercator projection came later, with the publication of a world map in 1569.

Mercator's research on geomagnetism anticipated Humphrey Gilbert's work by fifty years. He developed the idea that there was a magnetic pole located on the earth and not in the heavens, and suggested that its location could be determined by noting the angle of magnetic declination at two points on the earth and extending those rhumbs until they intersected.

No cartographer has been as important for the advancement of navigation as Mercator. His terrestrial globe of 1541 already showed three innovations that were developed with the navigator in mind, for it was intended that the globe actually be used at sea. First, the lines radiating from the compass roses printed on the globe are not great circles but actual loxodromes, lines of constant compass direction, and hence spiral in toward the poles. Secondly, because of the reliance that mariners placed on the compass, Mercator showed the North Magnetic Pole (in the form of *magnetum insula*), locating it in the ocean above Scandinavia. Finally, Mercator's globe was made with a hollow wooden ball, not the more usual plaster over papier-mâché, and so would stand up better to travel

and would better accept the points of the compass used to make measurements on it. The companion celestial globe, too, was viewed very much as a working tool and could be used for determining the locations of stars, the latitude of a place, zodiacal signs and degrees, the time of culmination of a star, and the duration of twilight.

Using a globe in the cabin of a pitching ship would have been an awkward operation, however, and its scale is severely limited. Flat maps, on the other hand, drawn on any of the projections then known, could not preserve the true angular relationships between places, so that navigators attempting to steer a course measured on the typical "plane chart" of the time were forced to make constant correction to be assured of a reasonably accurate landfall. Mercator set out to make a world map in sheets that would preserve the directional relationships between places and the result is the wall map of the world (1569) on the projection that bears his name. Although later mathematicians have shown how the projection can be derived using trigonometry or calculus, Mercator worked it out by trial and error, by plotting on flat paper the spiral rhumb lines from his globe of 1541. The Mercator projection has the unique attribute that any compass direction can be represented by a straight line. If a mariner wished to sail, say, between Gibraltar and Hispaniola, he simply laid a straightedge between the two points and measured the angle between this line and any meridian. If he then followed this steady compass course he would reach his destination. His course would not be the straightest possible; plotted on a globe, it would describe a spiral and not the straight line of a great circle course. But a true great circle course requires constant change in compass direction and was well beyond the abilities and instruments of sixteenth-century seamen. Mercator's chart, used in connection with a magnetic compass (and an awareness of compass deviation) gave the sailor the most reliable guide he had ever possessed.

The Mercator projection is unsurpassed for its purpose and still used on virtually all nautical charts published today, but its acceptance was slow, and apparently few navigators in the sixteenth century availed themselves of it. Several large world maps of the early seventeenth century used it as did the great sea atlas of Sir Robert Dudley, the *Arcano del mare* (1647), but so conservative was the nautical community that the use of Mercator's projection on charts for practical seamen did not become common until the end of the eighteenth century.

Mercator's *Atlas,* besides contributing the title that has come to stand for "book of maps," was tremendously influential. With its accurate and austere maps, it offered stiff competition to the later editions of the *Theatrum orbis terrarum* of Abraham Ortelius, whose florid and decorative engravings were beginning to appear dated. And whereas Ortelius had reengraved at uniform size the best available maps and published them under the names of their original authors, Mercator systematically conflated and edited all existing information to create a new work of synthesis, bearing only his name. In 1604 the copper plates of Mercator's atlas were sold to Jodocus Hondius of Amsterdam, a consummate businessman who, with his son, saw the Mercator atlas through twenty-nine editions between 1609 and 1641 and did much to launch the golden age of Dutch atlas production and to make Mercator's name a household word.

BIBLIOGRAPHY

Averdunk, Heinrich, and J. Müller-Reinhard. *Gerhard Mercator und die Geographen unter seinen Nachkommen.* Petermanns geographische Mitteilungen, supplement 182. Gotha, 1914. Reprinted Amsterdam, 1969.

Bagrow, Leo, and Robert W. Karrow, Jr. *Mapmakers of the Sixteenth Century and Their Maps: The Catalog of Cartographers of Abraham Ortelius, 1570.* Chicago, forthcoming.

Osley, A. S. *Mercator: A Monograph on the Lettering of Maps, etc., in the 16th Century Netherlands. With a Facsimile and Translation of His Treatise on the Italic Hand and a Translation of Ghim's Vita Mercatoris.* New York, 1969.

Smet, Antoine de. "Gerard Mercator." *National biografisch woordenboek* 10 (1983): 431–455.

ROBERT W. KARROW, JR.

METAL. Pre-Columbian native Americans knew how to work gold, silver, and copper. Some understood crude smelting, annealing, and soldering and used the processes to create works of art, but most of their tools were made of stone, bone, wood, and horn. When Columbus brought the first iron and steel tools to the New World, native American technology changed forever.

Copper was already commonly used by many groups in the New World. The Arctic Eskimos had copper scrapers, and Northwest Coast tribes made cold-worked copper plaques that served to indicate rank. Native Americans throughout eastern North America traded awls and pins made from northern Great Lakes raw copper. The Aztecs cast a copper-gold alloy, using the lost-wax method, and the Incas knew how to make bronze, and even how to control the tin content. Copper, however, was of little interest to the European explorers.

When Columbus arrived in the Caribbean, he found native Americans wearing ornaments of gold painstakingly extracted from placer mines. These small amounts of gold spurred expansion to the mainland, where the conquistadores found the gold and silver treasures of the Aztecs of Mexico and the Incas of Peru. Much of this treasure had been made for aesthetic purposes and for prestige, but its artistic value was lost when the silver and gold were melted down for shipment to Spain.

American Resources. Searching for the sources of the Aztec and Incan treasures, the Spaniards discovered silver west of Mexico City as early as 1531; they made large silver strikes in Zacatecas in 1546 and in Peru at Potosí in 1545. They also found some gold in Chile and New Granada. All mines were by law the property of the Crown, but colonists could exploit them upon payment of a large royalty. Although shipping costs were high and fraud through juggling books or smuggling was common, the mines brought such wealth into Europe that the resultant inflation lasted through the seventeenth century.

The conquistadores, steeped in Christian legends, believed there existed a third great treasure to match those in Mexico and Peru, and stories of Cíbola and El Dorado spurred exploration into the North American plains. This search failed, but a third source of mineral wealth did in fact exist; it was not discovered until 1848 in California, when it launched a gold rush the following year.

Until the middle of the sixteenth century, the Spanish

miners used smelting to extract silver from rich ores. Smelters used water- or hand-powered bellows and charcoal as fuel. In Mexico, the production of charcoal denuded the surrounding countryside of timber.

In 1556, German immigrants to New Spain introduced the patio amalgamation process for the extraction of silver from low-grade ores, and by the 1570s Potosí had adopted the technique. In the patio process, mules or native American labor prepared a paste from crushed ore, water, mercury, and other materials in a large open courtyard called a patio. The silver combined with the mercury as an amalgam, and the rest was washed away. Heating the amalgam drove off the mercury and left the silver behind. The mercury, reclaimed for future use, was so important to this mining process that it became a government monopoly.

The mine at Potosí was the richest of all, yielding about half the world's silver production between 1546 and 1601. But the price for this wealth could be counted in the deaths of native American miners. Although the viceroys of New Spain and Peru issued mining codes to protect them, conditions for miners grew steadily worse through the years.

European Uses of Metal in the New World. In return for the wealth of the New World, Spain introduced metal coins, arms and armor, and metal tools and equipment.

Coinage. Native Americans had no formal system of money, using instead barter and exchange systems based on such items as cacao beans and cotton textiles. Trade relationships of the Spanish colonists in the New World were crude as well. Columbus brought with him only a few coins, and the million-maravedi shipment of coins to La Española in 1505 did not stabilize the monetary system. Silver bars were debased by copper and lead, and scales and weights were unreliable. These problems were not solved until the establishment of the first New World mint in 1535.

Arms and armor. Spanish exploration of the New World coincided with the apex of the armorer's art in Europe. Sixteenth-century armor was designed for three functions: war, tournaments, and ceremony. Most Spanish soldiers in the New World wore armor designed for war, especially helmets. These ranged from a simple steel cap to more elegant curved and pointed helmets. Other armor varied from heavy Gothic suits to simple chain-mail shirts. It is an indication of their importance that weapons and coats of mail were exempt from the sales tax.

The success of cavalry depended on proper equipment. Metal parts for riding gear, such as spurs, stirrups, horseshoes, and horse armor, came from Spain. The conquistadores in Peru were so desperate for iron for horseshoes that they substituted silver and gold.

The Spanish military brought with it artillery and primitive firearms called harquebuses. These arms were important for their psychological effect, but the harquebus was unwieldy and difficult to load and fire, and the cavalry considered the weapon ungentlemanly. Although the sixteenth century saw improvements in firearms, they had limited use in the guerrilla warfare practiced by so many native Americans.

The crossbow was more common than the harquebus, but it also was of limited use, often misfiring or breaking down. Other, more useful, weapons in the Spanish arsenal were halberds, swords, rapiers, daggers, and lances. The smiths of Toledo were famous for their high standards of craftsmanship in producing swords, and a lance in the hands of a mounted man was a formidable weapon against warriors on foot.

Native Americans had little protection against Spanish weapons, although the padded armor of the Aztecs, called the *escaupil,* was adequate to repel Indian arms. Inca soldiers wore similar quilted armor, and many Spanish soldiers adopted it.

Native Americans took Spanish arms and armor as spoils of war and turned them against the Spaniards. They did not at first understand the complexities of the harquebus, but the Indians of southern Chile and the North American plains eventually adopted horses and firearms, which also changed the way they hunted. The native Americans had already developed bronze arms such as maces, heavy clubs, and hand axes, but these were simply copies of earlier stone forms and were no match for Spanish steel. Nevertheless, the Spaniards' superiority in arms and armor, and their use of cavalry, are not sufficient to explain their conquest of the New World. In the Caribbean islands the impact of European diseases and the use of native American allies also played a large role in the military strategies of the conquistadores.

Metal tools and equipment. The introduction into the New World of metal objects was of greater cultural importance than was the use of arms and armor by the conquistadores. Export of these items was tightly controlled by Spain, although the goods brought to the New World may have originated with Spanish trading partners. Knives, for instance, came from Flanders, Holland, Bohemia, and Germany, harquebuses from Holland, and clocks from Germany. Duties exacted at each point of shipment increased the cost of the import to the New World consumer as much as 75 percent; prices were the highest at the farthest outposts of the empire.

Because the monopoly on trade discouraged the independent development of many industries in the New World, all sorts of metal goods made the transatlantic passage. Sewing equipment included thimbles, scissors, pins, and wool shears. The medical kit contained copper cupping instruments, syringes, razors, lancets, and barber's scissors. A well-stocked kitchen contained tin cups, bowls, cruets, graters, and funnels, iron spoons and pans, pewter plates and bowls, bronze ollas and copper kettles, butcher knives, and spits.

Building tools and equipment included axes of various kinds, adzes, sledgehammers, crowbars, saws, chisels, augurs, planes, hinges for doors and windows, door knockers and latches, and nails of various sizes, including spikes, roofing nails, and tacks. Wagons had special metal needs such as tire nails, harping irons, cleats, washers, bolts, and linchpins. The construction of ships also demanded metal, including fastening nails, a cauldron for tar, hatchets, and iron water barrel hoops.

Religious observances, too, required special paraphernalia. Spain sent tin flasks for holy oils, copper vessels for holy water, tin and brass lanterns, silver chalices, small bells and large church bells with iron support frameworks, iron utensils for making communion wafers, and clarions, bassoons, and trumpets. And finally, the Spaniards brought with them such household and personal items as metal timepieces and jewelry, iron shoehorns, steel boxes, locks and keys, and brass picture frames and candlesticks.

Native American Adoption of Spanish Metal. Utilitarian metal items quickly replaced their native American functional equivalents in stone, bone, wood, or ceramic. New World agriculture was based on the use of the hoe and digging stick to cultivate crops, and metal garden hoes, spades, and plows were sometimes a welcome addition to native American farmers. Hunting and fishing groups added metal fishhooks and projectile points to their technology. Metal pots quickly replaced pottery and basketry vessels for cooking.

If a metal tool was more efficient than its native American analogue, it was adopted quickly. But if there was no parallel native American tool, the Spanish metal substitute might be either ignored or adapted for another use. Thus a piece of metal equipment sometimes lost its original meaning and became a personal ornament or item of prestige among native Americans.

[See also *Agriculture; Arms, Armor, and Armament.*]

BIBLIOGRAPHY

Borah, Woodrow. *Early Colonial Trade and Navigation between Mexico and Peru.* Ibero-Americana, no. 38. Berkeley, Calif., 1954.

Cespedes, Guillermo. *Latin America: The Early Years.* New York, 1974.

Haring, C. H. *The Spanish Empire in America.* New York, 1947.

Lewis, Oscar. "Plow and Hoe Culture: A Study in Contrasts." In Oscar Lewis, *Anthropological Essays.* New York, 1970.

Means, Philip Ainsworth. *Fall of the Inca Empire and the Spanish Rule in Peru, 1530–1780.* New York, 1932.

Scholes, France V. "The Supply Service of the New Mexican Missions in the Seventeenth Century." *New Mexico Historical Review* 5 (1930): 93–115; 5 (1930): 185–210; 5 (1930): 386–404.

Spencer, Robert F., and Jesse D. Jennings, et al. *The Native Americans.* New York, 1965.

Steward, Julian K. *Handbook of South American Indians.* Vol. 5. Bulletin 153, Bureau of American Ethnology. Washington, D.C., 1949.

Tarassuk, Leonid, and Claude Blair, eds. *The Complete Encyclopedia of Arms and Weapons.* New York, 1986.

Torre Revello, José. "Merchandise Brought to America by the Spaniards (1534–1586)." *Hispanic American Historical Review* 23 (1943): 773–780.

West, Robert C., and John P. Augelli. *Middle America: Its Lands and Peoples.* Englewood Cliffs, N.J., 1966.

D. K. ABBASS

MINERAL RESOURCES. The Americas are richly endowed with minerals of all kinds, but many were not discovered in the time of Columbus or in the century following his landfall. And even among some that were known, such as zinc, the technologies of the era either made little or no use of them or, as in the case of other base metals, the primitive methods of land transport and the small size of transoceanic vessels did not encourage their export. Virtually all the demand, therefore, was for precious metals and gemstones.

The Europe of the late fifteenth century had begun a long period of demographic and economic growth, which in turn involved a need for gold and silver as a necessary medium of exchange in a society where credit mechanisms were rudimentary and paper money did not yet exist. Because gold and silver were so vital, people went to even more ruthless lengths to obtain them in the years following the Columbian discoveries than they did in Brazil two centuries later or in the California gold rush of 1849. In fact the "gold lust" of the Spaniards after Columbus's first voyages of discovery became the engine of European emigration, as well as the basis for the Black Legend of Spanish cruelty.

Gold. In Columbus's lifetime or very soon after, Spaniards found gold-bearing sands and gravels in the riverbeds of La Española, Cuba, and Puerto Rico, and along the Caribbean shores of Central America. Within a generation after his death, they found more gold in southern and central Mexico and in the Andes, particularly of Colombia, but also in other locations between there and Chile.

Gold worth an estimated eight million pesos was produced in the Antilles between 1494 and around 1530, in what historians have termed the "island cycle" because the alluvial gold was exhausted in about thirty-five years. Mining methods then were almost identical to those used in the California gold rush of 1849: gravel was washed in pans or in a wooden sluice of running water nearby. Nearly all this work was carried out by Arawak labor gangs pressed into service by the early conquistadores. Their maltreatment occasioned a famous protest by Antonio de Montesinos on the Sunday before Christmas, 1509, in a thatched chapel on Santo Domingo. His sermon led to the Crown's promulgating a round of laws intended to protect the Indians and ensure their good treatment.

Prior to about 1515 most of the gold came from La Española; thereafter, most was found in Puerto Rico and to a lesser extent in Cuba (which produced only about half as much). Alluvial gold continued to be important for some time afterward, but the scene of production passed to Panama until about midcentury when gold from this source was nearly exhausted. Meanwhile, veins of gold were discovered in the highlands of Honduras and Nicaragua and, ultimately, in western Mexico, in Micho-acán and Nueva Galicia. In South America, gold was mined at sites in the province of Quito, and in Colombia, in the region called Antioquia, in various regions of Upper and Lower Peru, and in Chile.

General histories have made much of the hoards of gold extorted from the Aztec Motecuhzoma II and the Inca Atahualpa, but though these represented a large and easy acquisition, they scarcely compared with the total amount

GOLD DISK WITH FIGURES. From Chimu, Peru, fourteenth to fif-teenth century. The Spanish discovery of such objects fueled the conquest of the Andes.

THE METROPOLITAN MUSEUM OF ART, THE MICHAEL C. ROCKEFELLER MEMORIAL COLLECTION, BEQUEST OF NELSON A. ROCKEFELLER, 1979. (1979.206.766)

mined before midcentury by the Spaniards themselves. For instance, compare Atahualpa's ransom of 971,000 pesos worth of fine gold (over seven times that of Motecuhzoma's treasure) with the best estimates for gold that arrived—legally—and was registered at the Casa de la Contratación in Seville during the nineteen years between 1541 and 1560: over sixteen million pesos worth. And were the smuggled amounts known, that figure would likely double. (This article does not deal with the discovery and production of gold in Brazil because hardly any was found until the 1690s and thereafter, long after the time of the discoveries.)

Silver. Although gold has received most of the popular attention, it was silver that produced by far the greatest Spanish New World treasure. Moreover, because of its bulk and the more complicated industrial effort needed to extract it from the rather low-quality ore that prevailed in the Americas, it was considerably more difficult for its miners to escape payment of Crown duties. Little or none was found in the Antilles during the first decades of the expansion, however, and it was not until the conquest of Mexico by Hernando Cortés that an appreciable quantity came into Spanish hands. Even then, the amount of silver in possession of the indigenous peoples was far less than that of gold: it was less esteemed and less was found in superficial deposits. Ultimately, however, the amounts of silver extracted from both Americas dwarfed the quanti-ties of gold. Shortly after the conquest of Mexico, Spaniards took over mining operations already being worked by Indians near Taxco, Zumpango, and Sultepec and a few years later, in Nueva Galicia at Tamazula and Compostela. Then, in the late 1540s, nearly a decade after the conquest of Peru, Gonzalo Pizarro moved into the Inca mines at Porco in Upper Peru. Production both there and in Mexico was limited before 1556, however, because the Europeans were using Indian methods to extract ore, and the yield was low.

It was only in 1556 that improved technology permitted an increase in production, and the quantities of silver obtained soon dwarfed those produced before midcen-tury. This was because of the invention by a colonial miner, Bartolomé de Medina, of the patio process, which led to an enormous increase in efficiency. It involved a complicated and sophisticated method of applying mer-cury to the crushed ore to glean silver from sulphurous compounds and the base metals—mostly tin and cop-per—with which it was alloyed. (American silver ore, though there were great quantities of it, was much inferior to that from European mines, as in Styria.) Meanwhile, literally dozens of huge new deposits were being discov-ered, most notably at Potosí in Upper Peru (1545), and in Mexico at Zacatecas (1546) and at Guanajuato and Pachuca (1550s). Soon surface deposits were exhausted and the miners began to dig shafts; until the eighteenth century, ores had to be hauled in baskets up wooden ladders on the shoulders of laborers.

The laborers, of course, were almost entirely Indians, and they were obliged to serve under the encomienda system of the allocation of indigenes to conquistadores, supposedly in return for their (religious) education. In Peru, Spaniards did not need to innovate a forced labor system as in Mexico and the Caribbean; they simply adapted the corvée-like mita system from the peasants' former Inca overlords and obliged the same lower classes to serve for stated intervals with them instead. The mine's exploitants were Spaniards, or after a generation or so, criollos—that is, their American-born heirs and descendants. Spanish (Roman) law claimed all products of the subsoil for the Crown, but it in turn awarded exploitation rights to the proprietors who had discovered or inherited the diggings. It bestowed on them a highly privileged status in order to ensure uninterrupted production. First and foremost, they could not be foreclosed by their creditors. In return, they paid a percentage of their yield, traditionally one-fifth, to the Crown and were obliged to bring their silver to government offices, which combined the functions of assaying, remelting, and taxing; there the silver was cast into uniform ingots, which bore identifying numbers. As part of the procedure, officials claimed the government's share for the royal treasury and then returned the remainder to the producers as their legitimate property.

In the course of the sixteenth century ownership of mines became highly diffuse, and workings were seldom in the hands of one individual or even one family. This was due partly to original partnership divisions but also to financial arrangements. The refining processes needed to produce pure silver from its ore were so expensive and complex that few of the mine proprietors possessed all the necessary equipment, mercury, chemicals, and labor. Hence the industry was characterized by intertwined clusters of capital devoted to various stages of production.

But that the new technology was effective—and the prospecting for new mining sites significant—there can be little question. It will afford some idea of how much yields increased during the second half of the sixteenth century if one considers that in no five-year period after 1560 did (legal) silver export from Mexico fail to exceed the total export of the entire period prior to 1550. Moreover, during the same century, Peruvian production, mainly from Potosí, dwarfed Mexican production by about four to one.

Other Minerals. Other metals, even those that were by-products of silver production, were seldom of more than local importance. Although tin, lead, zinc, and copper existed in abundance in the Americas, they are never found in export figures, for they were cheaply available on the European market. Had cannon foundries existed in the Indies (these could have been practicable in Mexico), there might have been greater industrial use of tin and copper. But as it was, Spanish colonial policy restricted the growth of such manufactures to avoid their competing with metropolitan industry (but also, perhaps, out of fear of their being used in rebellions).

Mercury, however, was the one exception, for it was used in the patio process and was largely responsible for the increased silver production after Medina's invention. Much was imported from Almadén in Castile, but appreciable quantities were discovered at Huancavelica in Peru around 1570, making the Peruvian mines nearly independent of Europe. Mexico, however, continued to require Spanish mercury throughout the century; if ships bearing mercury did not arrive as expected, production lagged visibly.

Gemstones. Less discussed in the literature than the extraction of metals is that of precious stones, which were found mostly in Colombia, in the Muzo, Coscuez, and Salmondoco mines. These appear to have been known by the indigenes prior to the conquest by Gonzalo Jiménez de Quesada. (Semiprecious stones existed in almost all American regions in abundance, but they were never items of great commercial importance.) There are no production figures available on American emeralds, rubies, or opals in the sixteenth century, and the royal government did not attempt consistently to control their production and hence tax them successfully. (Only diamonds have attracted the attention of Latin American economic historians, but their description lies beyond the compass of this article. They were not discovered in the Americas until 1720.) What is most interesting is that both the emeralds and the rubies from Colombia were of higher quality—less flawed and of better color and greater size—than those found in Asia where these gems fetched considerably higher prices than they did in Europe. Europeans appear instead to have prized diamonds, which in the sixteenth and seventeenth centuries came chiefly from mines in south India, in Golconda.

Evidence from shipwrecks suggests that American colonial jewelers were imaginative in incorporating these stones into high-quality pieces of silver- and goldsmithery, which were then brought into Europe by Spaniards returning from colonial service. There is also reason to believe that much of the gemstone production of Colombia was bought up by professional traders, who sent it off to Asia, where diamonds were common enough, but where the larger and better colored rubies and emeralds found in South America were desired by rulers and their nobility. But because jewels could so easily be concealed, as in seams of clothing, only passing references can be gleaned from memoirs as to what their distribution might have been like; it would seem that a great proportion traveled from Seville to Lisbon, where they made their way via professional traders to Goa and hence into the courts of Asian princes.

Columbus had been searching for Asia, not for the New World he encountered. Had not the presence of precious metals been immediately detected, there would have been little incentive for European colonization of the new lands in the late fifteenth and early sixteenth centuries. As it was, the ensuing gold rush virtually guaranteed European expansion into the Western Hemisphere.

[See also *Metal*.]

BIBLIOGRAPHY

Diffie, Bailey W. *Latin American Civilization: Colonial Period.* Harrisburg, Pa., 1945.

Hamilton, Earl J. "Imports of American Gold and Silver into Spain, 1503–1660." *Quarterly Journal of Economics* 43 (1931).

Haring, Clarence H. "American Gold and Silver Production in the First Half of the Sixteenth Century." *Quarterly Journal of Economics* 29 (1915).

Haring, Clarence H. *Trade and Navigation between Spain and the Indies in the Time of the Hapsburgs.* Cambridge, Mass., 1918.

Slicher van Bath, Bernard H. "Het Latijns-Americaanse goud en zilver in de koloniale tijd." *Economisch en sociaal-historisch jaarboek* 47 (1984).

Wagner, Henry R. "Early Silver Mining in New Spain." *Revista de Historia de America* 14 (1942).

GEORGE D. WINIUS

MISSIONARY MOVEMENT.

MISSIONARY MOVEMENT. From the time Columbus first made contact with the natives of the New World, one of the prime motivations for exploration and settlement was the desire on the part of the Spaniards to spread Christianity. The discovery and conquest of the Americas came immediately on the heels of the Reconquista, which had prepared the Spaniards for the new enterprise and had linked Christianization with territorial expansion. Although the methods were not always the same, the motive was similar. An important legacy of the Spaniards in the Americas is the prevalence of the Roman Catholic faith and the art and architecture it inspired.

Although no priest seems to have accompanied Columbus on his first voyage, there was no absence of religion on board. Columbus was a devout Christian, and all commentaries on the voyage speak of the important place religious devotions had in the daily life of the expedition. On the return voyage, for example, the crew, when caught in a storm, pleaded for divine intercession and at first landfall made a religious pilgrimage in thanksgiving. These, of course, were the norms of the time. The important role of missionary activity to Columbus himself is evidenced by the signature he routinely used after the voyage, *Xpo Ferens*, "He who carries Christ."

On the second voyage, Columbus brought Bernardo Buil and other friars with him, not just to minister to the Spanish settlers but also to Christianize the Indians and ensure their good treatment. In fact, the stipulated purpose of the second voyage, other than to relieve the Spaniards left on La Española, was to convert native Americans to Christianity. Second was the establishment of a trading colony. Thus the tone of the voyages of exploration and conquest was set very early. A quarter of a century later, Bernal Díaz del Castillo, a foot soldier in the conquest of Mexico, summarized his motivation as a desire to serve God and his king as well as to get rich.

The role of the missionary on an expedition was to provide spiritual support for the conquerors and to spread the Gospel among the natives. The expeditions were more corporate operations than organized military bands. Each participant provided something for the common good. Men came with their own provisions, equipment, and animals. If the expedition was successful, each received part of the booty in proportion to his investment. Similarly, the priest contributed his service as a spiritual intermediary and could receive a share usually equivalent to that of an officer. Whether he did or not depended on his status. The Catholic priesthood consists of two quite different groups. The parish priest is most often a member of the secular clergy. He lives in the world and is largely indistinguishable from other members of society, save for his celibacy and dress. Other priests are regulars, members of formally organized religious orders, such as the mendicants (Franciscans and Dominicans, among others). They follow special rules of life, often taking vows of poverty, for instance, above and beyond the vows of celibacy and obedience. Both secular and regular clergy participated in the exploration and conquest of the New World. But the regulars could not receive a portion of the booty, at least for themselves, whereas the seculars could.

In purely missionary contexts, the regulars had a slight advantage. The internal organization of the regular clergy allowed for small groups of friars to operate with limited immediate supervision, for they were somewhat self-governing bodies. The secular priest depended upon his religious superiors for authority and supervision. Thus regulars were often missionaries, and the secular clergy took over the religious administration of communities after they had been Christianized.

The missionaries played an important role in the legitimization of the conquest. Early political thinkers concluded that Spain's claim to the New World could be legally justified only in the missionary context. Consequently missionary activity had to precede military subjugation. If native peoples openly embraced Christianity and

Spanish sovereignty, no war could be made against them. As a result of the preaching of individuals such as Bartolomé de las Casas, the Spanish monarchs ordered that the natives had to reject Christianity and sovereignty before being subjected to war. To comply with this order a document known as the Requerimiento (Requirement) was read aloud to natives before the onset of battle. It outlined European history and the basics of Christian theology: the natives then were "informed" and, of their free will, could accept Christianity and Spanish rule or reject it.

The conquests of two major regions of the Americas, Mexico and Peru, provide good examples of the activity of seculars and regulars, and their relationships to missionary activity and the conquering armies. In Mexico two principal clerics accompanied Hernando Cortés — Bartolomé de Olmedo and Juan Díaz. Olmedo, a Mercedarian friar, was Cortés's private chaplain and served the spiritual needs of the army. Díaz, a secular priest, was more a member of the expedition in his own right and also served as chaplain for the troops. Both priests played major roles in the missionary activity of the expedition. Díaz baptized the nobles of Tlaxcala, Cortés's first important Indian allies. Olmedo usually celebrated mass when Cortés wanted to provide an especially good show for the natives. Olmedo died shortly after the conquest of Mexico; Díaz continued as a parish priest until his death.

In the conquest of Peru, similarly, a regular and a secular priest accompanied the expedition. The regular, Vicente de Valverde, was present when Francisco Pizarro

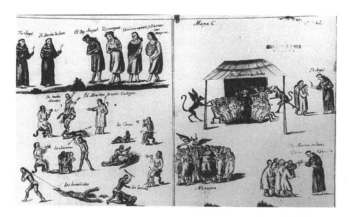

INTRODUCING CHRISTIANITY TO NEW SPAIN. A European view, from the *Crónica de Michoacán*, an eighteenth-century copy of an earlier postconquest document. The text reads: "It is demonstrated here that once it was known that the Great Caltconzin surrendered to Cortés and the king ... from Tzireo to Iguatzio ... they started to surrender and ask for baptism ... and it is shown here ... punishments given to the ones who did not follow Christian morals ... in their tribes."

ARCHIVO GENERAL DE LA NACIÓN, MEXICO CITY

captured the Inca ruler Atahualpa, but as a Dominican not permitted private wealth, he did not receive a share of the booty. Nevertheless, he played an important role in the conquest. As one of the most highly educated of the company, he was a personal adviser to Pizarro and spiritual leader of the band. He ultimately became bishop of Cuzco, which included all of the newly conquered territory. Juan de Sosa, on the other hand, was a secular priest who, though he was not present when Atahualpa was captured, collected a share of the booty. Like Díaz, he was more of a private member of the expedition who also happened to be a priest. He too came to serve as a chaplain for the troops.

Once the active phase of a conquest had ended, the role of the church was to continue the "spiritual conquest" of the land. As noted, this occupation usually fell to the regulars. Among the religious orders the most active, certainly in the early phases of the Spanish settlement of the Americas, were the Franciscans, who supplied twelve priests for the first organized missionary expedition to Mexico. This group arrived in 1524, led by Martín de Valencia. They were followed in 1526 by twelve Dominicans, led by Tomás Ortiz, and in 1533 by seven Augustinians under the guidance of Francisco de la Cruz. By 1559 the missionary corps had swelled to 802 religious in some 160 monasteries.

In Peru a similar pattern emerged. The Franciscans were among the first missionaries to arrive, along with Dominicans and Mercedarians. All three orders seem to have been established in Peru shortly following the conquest. The Franciscan mission was initially led by Marcos de Niza, who led a small expedition down from Mexico, although upon reaching what is now southern Panama, they seem to have returned home. In 1534 and 1535 the order established monasteries first in Quito and later in Los Reyes (present-day Lima). In 1540 twelve Dominicans arrived under the leadership of Francisco Toscano. The first Mercedarians appeared in Lima in 1535, and by 1540 they had established four monasteries, in Lima, San Miguel de Piura, Cuzco, and Guamanga.

Although the Augustinians were active in Mexico, they did not participate in the early missions in Peru. As late as 1551 the order had become established in South America, but in the sixteenth century they ranked noticeably behind the other three. In contrast, the Mercedarians participated in the spiritual conquest of Peru but did not arrive in Mexico until much later in the century. In 1593 they established a college and house of novices under the direction of the Guatemalan province. It was not until 1619 that an independent Mexican province was created.

The friars and priests encountered several obstacles to their evangelizing. The two major problems were those of communication and of the sheer size of the native population. Friars either had to teach the natives Spanish or learn the Indian tongues themselves. Clearly the more reasonable option was that they learn the native languages, which they did. In many ways the early missionaries functioned as linguists. They listened to the languages, learned them aurally, and then wrote them down, assigning Spanish letters to the native sounds. Unfortunately there was not always a close fit between the sounds represented in Spanish and those in the Indian languages. Most notably, Spanish has no letters for the sounds "k" or "w" in most contexts but must use constructions such as "que" or "hua." The friars did not even distinguish some sounds, such as vowel length or the glottal stop, the closing off of the vocal path by the glottis and the release of air when it reopens. The glottal stop is important in the Aztec language, Nahuatl, but the Spanish friars often missed it. The early linguistic efforts usually fell to the regulars, especially the Franciscans, but eventually the secular clergy followed suit, and soon one sure method of securing a clerical position became learning a native language. The major languages, Nahuatl in Mexico and Quechua in Peru, were taught in the universities that were later founded in the colonies.

The importance of native languages in the spiritual conquest is demonstrated by the fact that the first book printed in the New World was a catechism written in Nahuatl and published in 1539 in Mexico. Throughout the sixteenth century, works in native languages continued to be an important portion of the total number of publications. Of nearly two hundred published in Mexico in the sixteenth century, thirty-five were in Nahuatl; other languages included Tarascan, Maya, Otomi, and Timucuan (from Florida). In colonial Peru similar works appeared in Quechua, Aymara, Guarani, and many other native languages.

Another means of bridging the language gap was the sixteenth-century equivalent of comic strips. This novel idea came from Jacobo de Testera, an Italian Franciscan in Mexico. He used little stick figures to portray the important features of Christian doctrine. These little catechisms have come to be known as "Testerian catechisms" in his honor. They were used with some frequency in Mexico and to a more limited extent in Peru.

Theatrical presentations soon became a popular means for spreading Christian doctrine. In all likelihood the friars used pantomime early on to explain the gospel stories. Once they had mastered the native languages, they presented European passion plays, translated into Indian languages. These plays were wildly popular—so well received that in many communities native Americans still put them on in one form or another after nearly five hundred years.

As the priests confronted the natives, several theological problems arose. Some thought that perhaps the Indians were not human, a notion that was quickly dispelled; in 1536 a papal bull confirmed Indian humanity. But then the friars wondered about the best way to proceed with the missionary effort. Should they imitate the ancient church and have the neophytes undergo a long complicated theological indoctrination before offering them the benefits of the sacraments? Or should they baptize them straight away and work later on perfecting their understanding of dogma? Although the friars were aware of the threat from pre-Columbian religions, they considered the natives more receptive to the gospel than other groups with whom they had had experience—particularly the Muslims. Native Americans were merely "heathens," that is, they had never heard the gospel of Christ (although some Christians did argue that Saint Thomas, or others, had brought Christianity to the New World in the ancient past). In contrast, the Muslims were thought of as "infidels," people who had heard the gospel but rejected it. Among the early friars there was even a romantic notion that the Indians were particularly receptive to the gospel, that in fact once they had all been baptized the Second Coming would occur. With this prospect in mind, the friars in most areas baptized first and preached second. One Franciscan lay brother, Peter of Ghent, is said to have baptized 100,000 natives in one day!

Once the initial contact was made and the friars settled into the native villages, the missionary activity became routine. On a regular basis, often daily, the priests convened the Indians for indoctrination. Men, women, and children were trained separately, according to their needs and abilities. As soon as they could, the friars established schools for the children, recognizing that they could be a potent tool for converting the elders. In Mexico, they pursued a special approach for the sons of the Indian nobility. These boys were shipped off to a school located in Santiago Tlatelolco in a neighborhood of Mexico City, where they were trained to occupy their rightful place in the native social and political order but also taught Spanish, Latin, and church doctrine. Some scholars have looked upon this as an early, intentional effort to develop a native priesthood, although this contention cannot be proved. The important role of children in the missionary effort is reflected in a legend of three children from Tlaxcala who were martyred by their parents for having openly embraced and preached Christianity.

Although the papal bull clearly established that the Indians were human, they were not offered all the sacraments of the church. In general the Indians received baptism, were often confirmed, attended mass regularly, and took the Eucharist several times a year. Sixteenth-century norms required at least an annual confession. But the administering of unction, usually reserved for the critically ill, was relatively uncommon among the natives.

Logistically it was difficult for the priests to administer the sacrament, given the thousands of natives each man tended. Matrimony was required. The native nobles often had multiple wives, something the friars abhorred. The priests forced them to recognize their first wife as the true wife and abandon the rest. Often a noble suffered circumstantial amnesia and could not remember who had come first, allowing him to choose his favorite. The sacrament of ordination, entrance to the priesthood, was denied the natives on the ground that they were newcomers to the faith. It was not until the eighteenth century that significant numbers of native Americans entered the priesthood.

The first century following Columbus's voyage saw Christianity spread throughout the Western Hemisphere. By 1592 missionaries had penetrated far into the American Southwest, the southern reaches of modern Chile, the jungles of South America, and the plains of Argentina. Their effort rivaled the military conquest of the Americas, and more important, it left a lasting mark that remains to the present day.

[See also *Religion*.]

BIBLIOGRAPHY

Phelan, John Leddy. *The Millennial Kingdom of the Franciscans in the New World*. Berkeley, 1970.

Ricard, Robert. *The Spiritual Conquest of Mexico*. Translated by Lesley Bird Simpson. Berkeley, 1966.

Tibesar, Antonine. *Franciscan Beginnings in Colonial Peru*. Washington, D.C., 1953.

JOHN F. SCHWALLER

MONTEJO, FRANCISCO DE (c. 1479–1553), Spanish conqueror of Yucatán. Born in Salamanca, Montejo went to the Americas in 1514 with Pedro Arias de Ávila (Pedrárias). From Castilla del Oro (Panama) he left for Cuba at an unknown date prior to 1518. There he acquired a ranch and other properties. In 1518, he was a captain in the Juan de Grijalba expedition, and in 1519 he joined Hernando Cortés's expedition, also as a captain. When the expedition founded the town of Veracruz, Montejo was elected one of its judges, or alcaldes.

Montejo twice served Cortés as an emissary to Charles V (1521, 1526), on the first occasion helping to secure Cortés's appointment as captain general of New Spain over the opposition of Diego Velázquez, governor of Cuba. He obtained a royal contract for the conquest of Yucatán on December 8, 1526, and sailed from Spain in the summer of 1527 with four ships and five hundred men. He landed first at Cozumel Island but abandoned it for the mainland. He marched inland against light Indian resistance until he was defeated at Aké (in north-central Yucatán). Leaving a small force in Yucatán, Montejo went to New Spain for reinforcements. Appointed governor of Tabasco, he went there in 1529 and withdrew the men he had left in Yucatán. He resumed the conquest of Yucatán in 1530 with the founding of Campeche. By 1533, a series of campaigns seemed to establish Spanish control over western and northern Yucatán. Montejo subsequently gave the enterprise to his natural son Francisco de Montejo, who carried out the reconquest of Yucatán between 1537 and 1545, following a Maya uprising from 1533 to 1545 that had driven the Spaniards from most of the peninsula.

In 1533 the elder Montejo turned his attention to Honduras, part of which he had claimed as early as 1529. He was appointed royal governor of Honduras-Higueras in 1535, at a time when the Indians were in rebellion and Spaniards were leaving. Because he lacked financial resources, Montejo did not immediately take up his office. Instead, Pedro de Alvarado, governor of Guatemala, administered Honduras. Their rival claims to the province led to disputes in 1537 and again in 1539. In the interim, Montejo suppressed a major Indian revolt (1537–1539) and instituted modest administrative and economic reforms.

Alvarado's return to Guatemala in 1539 led to Montejo's removal as governor of Honduras and an agreement between them exchanging Chiapas, which was part of Alvarado's grant, for Montejo's claims to Honduras. Following Alvarado's death in 1541, the colonists of Honduras called Montejo to be governor (1542). However, other men were appointed governor by the audiencia of Santo Domingo and the viceroy of Mexico, and Montejo was again removed from office. The audiencia of Santo Domingo appointed him governor in 1543, but he had to give up that office when the newly created audiencia of Los Confines began its rule in the spring of 1544. Following his residencias (an inquiry at the end of his term of office) in Honduras and Chiapas, he returned to Yucatán to assume its governorship. In 1549 he was removed from that position as well. He returned to Spain where he died in 1553, having obtained few of the rewards he had sought because he had never had enough money to field large forces and because he did not cultivate patrons whose favor might have protected his claims from rivals.

BIBLIOGRAPHY

Chamberlain, Robert S. *The Conquest and Colonization of Yucatán, 1527–1550*. Washington, D.C., 1948.

Chamberlain, Robert S. *The Conquest and Colonization of Honduras, 1502–1550*. Washington, D.C., 1953.

PAUL E. HOFFMAN

MONTEZUMA. See *Motecuhzoma II*.

MONUMENTS AND MEMORIALS.

Monuments to Christopher Columbus exist throughout the United States, Mexico, Central and South American countries, and various locations in the Caribbean; Spain and Italy also boast several monuments to Columbus. Since the practice of erecting commemorative statuary to a nondivine, nonsacred, or nonaristocratic person is a modern one, originating in Europe, public monuments to Columbus did not exist much before the nineteenth century. Stylistic diversity within this large but chronologically limited group, therefore, can be attributed in part to historical developments in art; flexibility in the portrayal of Columbus—conceptually as well as physically—also accounts for the wide range of types of monuments.

The United States

The earliest notice of a Columbus monument appears in a journal of 1782 written by an officer in Comte de Rochambeau's army during the American War of Independence: "You see several notable buildings [in Philadelphia] ," wrote Jean-Baptiste-Antoine de Verger, "including the mansion where the Congress meets [Independence Hall] . . . ascending the staircase, you see the statues of Christopher Columbus and of Penn." No trace of this statue has been found, nor are there any remains of a monument created by New York's Tammany Society, also known as the Columbian Order, on the occasion of the tricentennial of Columbus's first voyage. Designed as an obelisk and of a material resembling black marble, the 1792 Columbus monument bore scenes of Columbus's life on each of its four faces. Ephemeral as these two works were, they nevertheless adumbrated the strong American interest in Columbian monuments, an interest that produced the largest number of Columbus statues in any nation. Moreover, the tradition that began in 1792 has continued unbroken to the late twentieth century.

Not all the eighteenth-century Columbian monuments were transitory. The French consul in Baltimore erected a stone obelisk on the grounds of his estate in 1792; it was moved to the Samuel Ready Institute in the 1960s. The erection of the first figural sculpture of Columbus in the United States took place in Boston, where in 1849 a Greek or Italian businessman (the sources differ) presented a marble statue of Columbus to the city. (The first figural sculpture of Columbus in the Western Hemisphere was modeled in London in 1831 and erected at Government House, Nassau, Bahamas, in 1832; it is of metal, painted white.) Although without aesthetic distinction, the Boston statue presaged many later American monuments in theme and design, being a single figure of a young man clad in fifteenth-century dress and accompanied by nautical motifs. The monument raised in Philadelphia in 1876 is similar in physical features and enlarges on the idea of Columbus as a sailor and navigator, his right hand resting

PHILADELPHIA, 1876. Statue of Christopher Columbus.

PHOTOGRAPH: E. B. HESTON

on a globe and his left holding a map; an anchor lies at his feet. Both the Boston and Philadelphia statues were produced in Italy and may have had a similar source. The Philadelphia monument, the gift of Italian Americans in celebration of the centennial of the Declaration of Independence and the world's fair, was the first statue of Columbus in the United States to be funded entirely by public subscription.

In addition to municipal funding or public subscription,

benefactors sometimes gave monuments to the community. St. Louis and Sacramento are among the cities that received Columbus statuary from private sources, the former as a gift of Henry D. Shaw in 1886 and the latter as a gift of D. O. Mills, a former resident, in 1882. The St. Louis statue, a bronze cast in Germany, was sited in Tower Grove Park, another of Shaw's bequests to the city. Mills presented Larkin Goldsmith Mead's three-figure ensemble to the state capitol in Sacramento and, though objections have been raised periodically because the legislature neither asked for the work nor was consulted about its acceptance, it has remained a featured part of the capitol interior for more than a century. Meade carved the marble in Italy and chose the unusual theme of Columbus explaining his theories to Queen Isabel; a page looking on seems added to balance the composition. The subject and its realization remain unique among Columbian monuments.

The federal government commissioned depictions of more or less the same theme—the 1492 landing—for nearly all the representations of Columbus in the U.S. Capitol. The bronze doors installed in 1863 and moved in 1871 (and again in 1961) to the east entrance to the

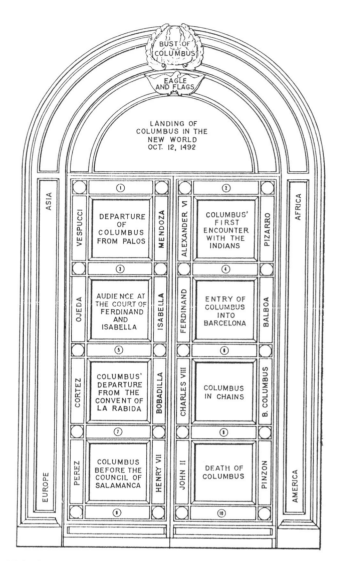

State Capitol, Sacramento, California, 1868. *Columbus's Last Appeal to Isabella*, Larkin Goldsmith Mead.

California State Capitol Museum

U.S. Capitol, 1863. The bronze doors at the eastern entrance to the Rotunda depicting events in the life of Columbus were designed and modeled by Randolph Rogers in Rome in 1858. They were cast in Munich in 1861. In November 1863 the doors were installed between Statuary Hall and the House extension. Because of their massiveness and great beauty, it was felt they were worthy of a more central location, and in 1871 they were moved to the Rotunda entrance. In 1961 the doors were moved again, thirty-two feet east, when the East Front of the Capitol was extended. The doors, also called the Rogers Doors, have two valves with four panels in each valve, surmounted by a semicircular tympanum. The tympanum depicts Columbus's first landfall in the New World. The eight panels depict various scenes from Columbus's life, as shown in the schematic representation. In niches on the sides of the doors and between the panels are sixteen small statues of contemporaries of Columbus: political figures, colleagues, and other explorers. Between the panels (numbers 1 to 10) are representations of historians who have written of Columbus. On the extreme edges of the doors are personifications of the continents of Asia, Europe, Africa, and America.

Architect of the Capitol

U.S. CAPITOL, 1844. *Discovery of America*, Luigi Persico.

ARCHITECT OF THE CAPITOL

Rotunda and the marble group (1836–1844) formerly at the east-facade stairway illustrate variations on this theme. The marble group, a sixteen-foot-high tableau by Luigi Persico that has been in storage since 1958, juxtaposed an armored Columbus holding a globe aloft with an awkwardly contorted seminude Indian female poised as though to flee. The doors, on the other hand, eschew the emblematical quality of Persico's statuary in favor of a carefully pictorial narrative of the main events in Columbus's life, in which the first landing in the New World is clearly the most important event. Modeled in Rome by Randolph Rogers and cast in Munich by F. von Müller, the doors have as their inspiration the North Doors of the Baptistry of Florence cathedral, which depict the life of Christ in a work by Lorenzo Ghiberti. The Capitol doors culminate in a lunette in which is placed the thematically crowning representation, Columbus's 1492 landing. As in Persico's rendition, the native Americans witnessing Columbus's debarkation are presented as awestruck, frightened primitives, a stereotype inspired and reinforced by the large mural, *The Landing of Columbus at the Island of Guanahani, West Indies* (also known as *The Landing of Columbus on San Salvador*), by John Vanderlyn, installed in the Rotunda in 1847.

The 1892 celebrations of the quadricentennial of Columbus's landing provided at least part of the impetus for the spur of commissions for Columbian monuments at the end of the century. In New York, the monument at Columbus Circle was dedicated on October 12, 1892, a Columbus fountain for Central Park was planned but eventually abandoned, and a replica of Jeronimo Sunol's monument in Madrid was donated to the city. In Chicago, site of the 1893 World's Columbian Exposition, a fountain ornamented by a huge statue of Columbus was given to the city and statues by Mary Lawrence, Daniel Chester French, Howard Kretchmer, and Frédéric Auguste Bartholdi were exhibited at the fair. The last two became public monuments, Kretchmer's statue moved to the lakefront and Bartholdi's (cast in silver by the Gorham Company) replicated in bronze for Providence, Rhode Island. Other quadricentennial monuments to Columbus were raised in Columbus, Ohio; Boston; Baltimore; Willimantic and New Haven, Connecticut; and Scranton, Pennsylvania.

Twentieth-century Columbian monuments are also geographically widespread, with statues or busts in Pueblo, Colorado (1905); Walla Walla, Washington (1910); Detroit

CHICAGO, 1893. Small-scale bronze cast of *Columbus Sighting Land*, Frédéric-Auguste Bartholdi. The full-size original, not extant, was cast in silver for the World's Columbian Exposition.

GRAHAM GALLERY, NEW YORK

(1912); Washington, D.C. (1912); St. Paul, Minnesota (1931); Pittsburgh (1958); Memphis (1992); and Norristown, Pennsylvania (1992).

With few exceptions the sponsoring organizations of Columbian monuments have been Italian American, often under the aegis of one of the more than one hundred and fifty Italian newspapers once published in the United States. The editor of *Il Progresso d'Italia*, Carlo Barsotti, conceived of the Columbus Circle monument in New York and brought his idea to fruition; *La Tribuna Italiana* and *L'Eco d'Italia* helped raise funds for the monuments in Detroit and Philadelphia, respectively. Whatever the agency of their collective action, Italian Americans tended to choose only Italian sculptors working in Italy to carry out their commissions and this common source meant that many American monuments share stylistic traits, not only in representing a certain type of Columbus—young, with shoulder-length hair, and wearing a short Spanish tabard—but in depicting him with the attributes of a navigator, such as a globe, map, or anchor.

The most imposing of the American monuments is that

CHICAGO, 1893. Statue of Columbus at Drake Fountain, Richard Park. This work, although inspired by the celebrations of 1893, was not exhibited at the World's Columbian Exposition.

COLUMBUS, OHIO, 1892. Statue of Christopher Columbus, after Mary Lawrence. THE OHIO HISTORICAL SOCIETY

by Gaetano Russo in New York City. The statue was carved in Rome and the whole ensemble was brought to New York on an Italian warship courtesy of the Italian government. Located at the southwest entrance to Central Park, the monument rises about 24 meters (77 feet) and thus holds its own with the surrounding tall buildings. A grim-looking Columbus stands atop a rostral column (a column decorated with the prows of boats, the vessels here being bronze). He appears to be caught in mid-action, with his hand on a ship's rudder. The pedestal on which the assemblage sits is terraced with steps and culminates in a rectangular base marked with red granite corner posts. On the front of the base, above a bronze relief of the departure from Spain, a marble genius holds a globe; at the rear, a marble eagle grasps the shields of Italy and the United States.

NEW YORK CITY, 1892. Monument to Columbus at Columbus Circle, Gaetano Russo.   *BULLETIN OF PAN AMERICAN UNION*

CHICAGO, c. 1932. Statue of Christopher Columbus, Carlo Brioschi.   PHOTOGRAPH: E. B. HESTON

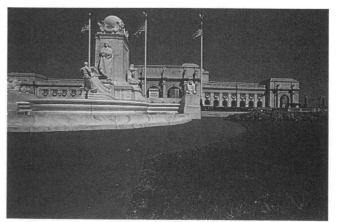

WASHINGTON, D.C., 1912. Two views of the statue of Christopher Columbus at Union Station, Laredo Taft.

NATIONAL PARK SERVICE

In contrast, the so-called national monument in Washington, D.C. (1912), sponsored by the U.S. Congress and the National Council of the Knights of Columbus, and the work of the sculptor Laredo Taft and the architect Daniel Burnham, offers a different conception: a fountain with a central shaft in front of which a cloaked and contemplative Columbus stands. To either side of Columbus, on the shaft, are personifications of the New World—a crouched Indian reaching for an arrow in the quiver on his back—and of the Old World—a meditative and mature European. Atop the shaft a globe rests on four large eagles with spread wings.

Most twentieth-century monuments tend to reflect the conceptions of earlier works. Statues of Columbus in Richmond, Virginia (1927), and in Newark (1927), Hoboken (1931), and Atlantic City, New Jersey (1958), testify to the strength of the navigator motif found in the Italian-produced works in Boston, Philadelphia, and New York; these later works were all carved by Italian sculptors. An Italian sculptor born abroad but whose career was conducted entirely in the United States, Carlo Brioschi, portrayed a slightly different and more theatrical Columbus for monuments now in Chicago (1933) and St. Paul (1931), each of which concentrates on a figure of mystical mien and dreamlike gestures.

Central and South America, the West Indies, and Mexico

The most appropriate location for monuments to Columbus would be the West Indies, locus of most of his activity in the Western Hemisphere. In 1891, the Chicago *Herald* raised a rough construction of local stone or coral on Watlings Island (Guanahani or San Salvador), the spot

SANTO DOMINGO, DOMINICAN REPUBLIC. Statue of Christopher Columbus. *BULLETIN OF PAN AMERICAN UNION*

presumed by some scholars to be the place of Columbus's first landfall. More traditional monuments were erected at other sites of Columbus's later voyages to Cuba and La Española (Hispaniola). Those in Haiti were destroyed in 1986 after the overthrow of the Duvalier regime. In Santo Domingo, the capital of the Dominican Republic, however, a monument partially funded by public subscription and erected in 1886 still dominates the city. The monument is unusual in including a nude female native American on the pedestal, her finger tracing the inscription; it is otherwise typical of the land-discovering genre of Columbian statuary found most often in North American renditions, although the bronze statue surmounting the high marble base was said to have been cast in France.

Cuba has been the home of several Columbian monuments of varying kinds, from busts to tombs. When the Cuban revolution of 1868 toppled Bourbon rule, a statue of Columbus by a French sculptor replaced a statue of Isabel II, queen of Spain until that year, that stood in the center of a park in Havana. In 1878, when Spanish rule was reinstated, the statue of Isabel returned, and the statue of Columbus was moved to the grounds of the captain general's palace. A chapel called El Templete, built to commemorate the site where the first mass was celebrated in Cuba, shelters a bust of Columbus that stands on a column. Elsewhere in Cuba, the towns of Cifuentes,

WATLINGS ISLAND, 1891. Monument to Christopher Columbus sponsored by the *Chicago Herald*.

BULLETIN OF PAN AMERICAN UNION

HAVANA, CUBA. *Christopher Columbus in Chains*, by Vallmitjana.
BULLETIN OF PAN AMERICAN UNION

Bayamo, Cárdenas, and Colón all possessed public statues of the Admiral by the turn of the century.

The Caribbean monuments to Columbus include two tombs, one in the Cathedral of Santo Domingo where Columbus's body was moved at the request of his son Diego in the sixteenth century. In 1796, however, his remains were transferred to Havana where another tomb was constructed (there is a similar tomb in Spain, where, after the Spanish-American War, Columbus's bones were transferred).

Columbus monuments in Mexico, Central America, and South America reflect the historical perspectives of the encounter between Europeans and Indians as seen by the Europeans during the nineteenth century. Thus, almost all the monuments, the gift or inspiration of Europeans or Europeans of mixed descent, include some reference to religion and almost all refer to—or in some fashion resemble—the statues of conquistadores liberally sprinkled throughout the region. Therefore, some of the Columbus monuments offer rallying points for protest demonstrations on the part of Indians. In Mexico, for instance, the huge 1877 monument by Charles-Henri-Joseph Cordier, a French sculptor who resided in Mexico, has been the target of mestizo outrage because it symbolizes a Spanish invasion that debased and then ignored a thriving and mature culture. The monument's elaborate tableau pays homage not only to the Admiral but, in life-size figures of bronze on a marble base, to two priests

who befriended Columbus in Spain and two missionaries to the New World. Columbus himself is portrayed as a conqueror, or even as a conjurer, for he plucks a veil from the globe he holds.

Most monuments in Central and South America, like those in the United States, appear to have been prompted by the quadricentennial observances. Honduras erected a bronze statue in Trujillo for the occasion, and Guatemala raised a unique monument in Guatemala City that placed a standing Columbus at the summit of two bronze globes, one atop the other. Earlier, in 1866, Empress Eugénie of

SAN JUAN, PUERTO RICO. Statue of Christopher Columbus.
COURTESY OF THE MUNICIPIO DE SAN JUAN

MEXICO CITY, 1877. Monument to Christopher Columbus by the French sculptor Charles-Henri-Joseph Cordier.

BULLETIN OF PAN AMERICAN UNION

France commissioned from Vincenzo Vela, a Swiss-Italian sculptor, a statue of Columbus to be erected at Colón (later Aspinwall) on the Isthmus of Panama. In Vela's conception, Columbus is shown wearing vaguely religious garb and standing beside a crouching Indian maiden, his right hand touching her gently as though to protect her.

The elaborate monument in Lima, Peru, by Salvatore Revelli seems to have been influenced by Vela's monumental grouping and is related to Genoa's monument to Columbus, not surprisingly since the artist Revelli was also a contributor to that multiauthored work. However, one source gives the date of the Lima monument's dedication as 1850, too early for Revelli to have known Vela's work; another identifies Revelli's ensemble as having been displayed at the 1867 Paris Exposition Universelle; in this case Revelli's sculpture apparently has been mistaken for that of Vela. In any event, Revelli's interpretation of Columbus's relation to the half-clothed Indian woman—a personification of America—merges a patriarchal attitude with a religious overtone. The Indian woman is coiled against Columbus's side, an arrow at her feet, and he in turn presses a cross into her left hand. His right arm draws his cloak around her as though to shield her from prying eyes and his face tilts heavenward. Columbus appears to

be presenting his charge to God. The base of the monument concentrates on nautical elements in relief, the work of another Italian, Guiseppe Palombini.

Elsewhere in South America, the Columbus monuments portray a single figure. The government of Chile raised a monument in Valparaíso, a heroic-sized bronze statue of Columbus clasping a crucifix. In Buenos Aires, the Italian residents of Argentina contributed a statue of Columbus to the 1910 festivities accompanying the country's centennial. Perhaps because the celebrations commemorated the country's independence from Spain, this monument least resembles the conquistador influence. Over 6½ meters (22 feet) high, the statue instead presents Columbus, a map his only attribute, in a pose suggestive of thoughtful deliberation rather than of discovery or proselytizing. The monument to Columbus in Bogotá, Colombia, has been moved from its original site on what was the Avenida de Colón to the Avenida Eldorado. The figure, with its outstretched arm, tops a tripartite base of stone and towers over the flat terrain. Maracaibo, Venezuela, in contrast, erected a smaller but unique monument that

GUATEMALA CITY, 1893. Monument to Christopher Columbus.

BULLETIN OF PAN AMERICAN UNION

BOGOTÁ, COLOMBIA. Monument to Christopher Columbus.

LIMA, PERU. Monument to Columbus by Salvatore Revelli.

joins a bust of the Admiral to the top of a large globe that outlines on its side the contours of South America.

Europe

Among European countries, Italy and Spain compete in claiming Columbus as a national hero. The award for the greatest number of memorials dedicated to Columbus must go to Spain. Commemorative monuments may be found in Barcelona, Palos, Madrid, Huelva (a city near the monastery of La Rábida), Granada, Salamanca, and Seville. Of these, the most artistically meritorious are those at Barcelona and Madrid (the one at Granada is actually dedicated to Fernando and Isabel). Funded in part by public subscription, Barcelona's memorial was designed by a Catalonian architect, who then supervised the artists employed on the gigantic project, which took six years to complete. On the day of dedication, June 1, 1888, the ships of several nations gathered in the harbor to salute the ceremonies. The queen regent of Spain, Queen Cristina, participated in the monument's unveiling. Nearly 74 meters (240 feet) high, the monument, which stands at the harbor, is the largest of the memorials to the Admiral and won many encomiums in the nineteenth century. Columbus surmounts a Corinthian column, the base of which holds four personifications of fame, their backs arched and arms upflung. Below the column is an octagonal pedestal peopled with bronze figures representing persons known to the Admiral, as well as personifications of Castile, Aragón, León, and Catalonia. The eight lions at the foot of the monument are made of iron.

The monument in Madrid, which originated as a novel form of commemorating the 1879 marriage of King Alfonso XII to María Cristina, was unveiled in 1884 to great acclaim. Much of the praise went to the marble statue of Columbus by Jeronimo Sunol that topped the ensemble (a replica of which is located in Central Park, New York City), an original conception representing the Admiral with the standard of Castile in his right hand, his left hand outstretched and his head upraised. He appears, therefore, to be offering thanks to God, a supposition reinforced by the almost epiphanic expression animating Columbus's face. The other two parts of the monument are a square base, ornamented with both reliefs and detached figures, and an octagonal pillar. The descriptive detail of the base is late Gothic, a period style that accords well with the figural accompaniments, the Spanish coats of arms, and other embellishments. Placed in a garden setting on one of the main thoroughfares of Madrid, the site has now become more urbanized and a second, modern addition to the park, inscribed with Columbian texts and a fountain, complete the newer arrangements.

The premier Italian monument, erected in Genoa in 1862, is an altogether less soaring edifice. Though its parts are elaborate, it also is less extravagantly placed within the urban milieu. Begun in 1846, the commission took several years to complete because of a series of events, including the 1848 revolution, the death of the sculptor chosen to execute the statue of Columbus itself, and the construction of Genoa's main railroad station on the site where the cornerstone of the monument was first laid. Moved to the Piazza Acquaverde in front of the station, and now on a traffic island there, the monument eventually received the contributions of nine sculptors, some of whom, like Aristedemo Costoli, Santo Varni, and Revelli went on to create other Columbian sculpture.

Franco Sborgi has argued that the Genoese monument is of national importance because of the number of artists who contributed to it, since they constituted a pantheon of Italian sculptors. But it can also be argued that so many workers produced an unevenness of style, for the monument can be said to have its high and low points aesthetically. The figures of Columbus and the native American woman beside him represent the sculpture's best parts; in comparison, the reliefs on the base depicting the debate at Salamanca, Columbus arriving in the New World, Columbus presenting the fruits of the New World to the Spanish monarchs, and Columbus in chains appear less well-designed and are poorly executed. Nonetheless, the Genoese monument remains the foremost sculptural commemoration of Columbus, primarily because, as we have seen, all Italian American monuments in the United States and many of the monuments in Central America and South America echo its main features. In addition, its location in the birthplace of Columbus draws attention to the city's Columbian art.

[For further discussion of representations of Columbus in the visual arts, see *Iconography*.]

BIBLIOGRAPHY

Bump, Charles Weathers. "Public Monuments to Columbus." Reprinted in *Selected Papers on Columbus and His Time.* Council on National Literature, 1989.

"Columbus in Statuary." *Bulletin of the Pan-American Union* 34, no. 6 (1912): 775–789.

Curtis, William Eleroy. "The Columbus Monuments." *The Chautauquan* 16, no. 2 (1892): 138–146.

Fryd, Vivien Green. "Two Sculptures for the Capitol: Horatio Greenough's *Rescue* and Luigi Persico's *Discovery of America*." *The American Art Journal* 19, no. 2 (1987): 17–39.

Ponce de Leon, Nestor. *The Columbus Gallery.* New York, 1893.

Sborgi, Franco. "Colombo, Otto Scultori e un Piedistallo." *Studi di Storia delle arti* (Genoa) 5 (1983–1985): 329–458.

BARBARA GROSECLOSE

MOTECUHZOMA II (1467–1520), Aztec ruler. Motecuhzoma (Nahuatl, Angry Lord; also spelled Moteuczoma, Moteczoma, and, in a common but corrupted English form, Montezuma) was the ninth official ruler of Mexico Tenochtitlan (Spanish adaptation of Classical Nahuatl is Tenochtitlán), the preeminent member (with Tetzcoco [Spanish, Texcoco] and Tlacopan [Spanish, Tlacopán]) of the Triple Alliance that dominated a tribute empire covering much of western Mesoamerica at the time of the Conquest. He was the son of Axayacatl, the sixth Tenochca ruler (r. 1469–1481), and a princess of Itztapallapan, a community south of Mexico Tenochtitlan ruled by a dynasty derived from that center. As the great-grandson and namesake of Motecuhzoma I (r. 1440–1469), he also bore the appellation Xocoyotl (or, in the honorific form, Xocoyotzin, "the younger"). Born probably in 1467, in his youth he distinguished himself as a warrior, attaining the highest military rank, that of *tlacatecatl*. He succeeded his uncle, Ahuitzotl (r. 1486–1502).

According to various post-Conquest accounts, before his accession Motecuhzoma had been especially noted for his humility and religiosity. However, soon after his coronation he allegedly demonstrated his pride and arrogance by replacing all commoners on the palace staff with nobles. Inheriting a flourishing empire, he surrounded himself with particularly elaborate court ceremony, requiring all his subjects, even those of high rank, to render him slavish obeisance.

He continued to expand the empire, concentrating particularly on western Oaxaca, and he was credited with the conquest of over forty major communities in this and adjoining regions. He had less success in contending with the chief Central Mexican rival of the Triple Alliance, the powerful province of Tlaxcallan and its major allies, Huexotzinco and Cholollan. A bitter dispute between Tlaxcallan and Huexotzinco that arose about 1507/1508 appeared to provide an excellent opportunity finally to crush both of these traditional enemies, especially after Huexotzinco virtually submitted to Mexico Tenochtitlan following its defeat by Tlaxcallan. However, the Tlaxcalteca successfully defended themselves against all Triple Alliance attacks, and Huexotzinco reestablished its traditional ties with its erstwhile ally just before the arrival of Hernando Cortés. The preservation of the independence of the Tlaxcalteca was to have momentous consequences, as they played a crucial role in the overthrow of Mexico Tenochtitlan as steadfast Spanish allies.

Many omens of impending doom reportedly plagued Motecuhzoma II's last years. Just before the Conquest, he ordered his likeness, adjoining those of his royal ances-

tors, to be carved in the living rock at the base of the hill of Chapultepec, west of the capital. The expected return of Topiltzin Quetzalcoatl, the semilegendary Toltec ruler, to reclaim his throne appears to have significantly influenced him in his initial dealings with Cortés. Taken captive after receiving the Spanish force peaceably in the fall of 1519, Motecuhzoma II was held hostage in his father's palace until June 1520. According to the Spanish accounts, he died from wounds received while attempting to placate his own people who, under a new ruler, his brother, Cuitlahuac, had risen in revolt. Because of his seeming vacillation and his passive acceptance of his long imprisonment by Cortés, Motecuhzoma II remains a controversial and ambiguous figure. His cousin Cuauhtemoc, however, who after Cuitlahuac's death from smallpox became the final ruler of Mexico Tenochtitlan and conducted the desperate defense of the city in 1521, has become a Mexican national hero.

BIBLIOGRAPHY

Barlow, Robert H. "El derrumbe de Huexotzinco." *Cuadernos Americanos* 39, no. 2 (1948): 147–160.

Barlow, Robert H. "Las conquistas de Moteczuma Xocoyotzin." *Memorias de la Academia Mexicana de la Historia* 8, no. 2 (1949): 159–172.

García Granados, Rafael. "Moctezuma II." In vol. 1 of *Diccionario biográfico de historia antigua de Méjico.* Mexico City, 1952.

Nicholson, H. B. "The Chapultepec Cliff Sculpture of Motecuhzoma Xocoyotzin." *El México Antiguo* 9 (1959): 379–444.

Ramírez, José Fernando. "Moteczuma." Edited by Rafael García Granados. *Memorias de la Academia Mexicana de la Historia* 5–6 (1946–1947).

Romerovargas Yturbide, Ignacio. *Motecuhzoma Xocoyotzin o Moctezuma el Magnífico y la invasión de Anahuac.* 3 vols. Mexico City, 1963.

H. B. NICHOLSON

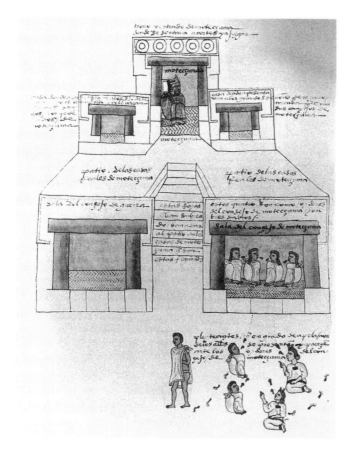

MOTECUHZOMA'S PALACE. Motecuhzoma sits at the pinnacle, chiefs just below him, and war and judiciary councils below them. From the Codex Mendoza, 1541. Original in the Bodleian Library, Oxford.
LIBRARY OF CONGRESS

MUHAMMAD XI. See *Boabdil.*

MUSEUMS AND ARCHIVES. [This entry includes two articles: *Collections of Columbus Memorabilia* and *Overview of Documentary Sources.* The first discusses the types of artifacts that illuminate modern scholarly understanding of Columbus and his times and surveys institutions that collect, preserve, and study such materials. The second focuses on the documentary sources at the foundation of Columbus scholarship. For further discussion of these sources, see *Book of Privileges; Library of Columbus; Writings,* articles on *Book of Prophecies* and *Marginalia.* Alternative sources of Columbus research are discussed in *Archaeology.*]

Collections of Columbus Memorabilia

The basic sources for the study of Columbus's life are items associated with him, his family, and his associates. These consist of objects he owned or used, correspondence and other papers he originated or received, and contemporary public records and writings relating to Columbus in his time. These materials are sometimes to be found in private collections maintained by heirs or descendants, and frequently in public repositories such as archives, libraries, and museums. Among the best known collections in the United States of artifacts and other materials related to the Age of Discovery are the numerous museums and art galleries of the Smithsonian Institution in Washington, D.C., the Metropolitan Museum of Art and the American Museum of Natural History in New York City, and the Museum of Art in Philadelphia. The largest public libraries are the Library of Congress in Washington, D.C., the New York Public Library, and Boston Public Library. In addition to the U.S. National Archives in Washington, similar resources exist as separate entities although on a much more limited scale in the state capitals and are to be found as well as part of major libraries and historical societies.

Three-dimensional objects illustrating the character or life of an adventurer like Columbus would have included personal memorabilia, the tools of his occupation, and items related to his preoccupations. These may range from his sea chest, maps, navigational instruments, the books and charts he owned and used, and arms and armor, for example, to parts of his ships and their equipment, such as anchors. Artifacts of this character, if they survived, generally are carefully maintained and featured on display for the general public in national history or naval museums.

Equally important are records documenting Columbus's achievements, such as personal journals and diaries, letters sent and received, and official documents relating to or attesting to his attainments. These may be retained by descendants or collectors or maintained in national or local archives and sometimes in libraries. Finally, there are contemporary manuscript or printed accounts of Columbus and his accomplishments in private collections and public libraries.

Regrettably, extremely few surviving artifacts can be positively documented to have been associated with Christopher Columbus and his son Diego Colón or related to their voyages. The greatest number of these materials are in Spain. They consist chiefly of books that Columbus owned and annotated, several manuscripts that he authored, and a limited amount of his correspondence. The majority of official correspondence and state papers relating to his voyages are the property of the Spanish government and maintained in the Archivo General de Indias in Seville. A few documents relating to Christopher Columbus and Diego Colón, as well as a large collection of documents and records relating to later members of the family, are retained by the family of the present duke of Veragua and the duchess of Berwick and Alba in Madrid, head of another branch of the Columbus family. It is reported that she owns a number of original documents, a few relating to Christopher Columbus and others to his son, Diego Colón, which have been the subject of a volume entitled *Autográfos de Colón*. Following are brief accounts of the chief repositories of Columbian memorabilia.

Archivo General de Indias, Seville. The largest number of personal papers of Christopher Columbus and his son Diego relating to the voyages and the establishment of settlements in the New World are assembled in this special archive of the Spanish government. Consisting of Christopher Columbus's and Diego Colón's correspondence with the Catholic sovereigns, commissions, edicts, and the like, the archives comprise a total of approximately one hundred documents ranging from 1488 to the 1540s. A great number of these had remained the property of Columbus's descendants and passed from one generation to another of the dukes of Veragua until the nineteenth century. They were then purchased by the Spanish government from the incumbent duke of Veragua.

Duke of Veragua, Madrid. Remaining in the possession of the family of the present duke are claimed to be more than five thousand papers of the Columbus family, mostly dating after the death of Diego Colón. Notable among them are three documents signed by the Catholic sovereigns: the original grant of title dated April 30, 1492, naming Columbus admiral, viceroy, and governor of all the lands and islands he was about to discover; the deed dated May 28, 1493, naming Columbus captain general of the armada sailing for the Indies; and the original document dated June 20, 1493, granting Columbus a coat-of-arms, which is illustrated therein.

Biblioteca Colombina, Cathedral of Seville. This library of some twelve thousand to twenty thousand items was founded in 1551, based upon the bequest of Fernando Colón of approximately seven thousand manuscripts in addition to the printed books he had collected in his lifetime. The library contains a collection of printed books that Christopher Columbus owned prior to his first voyage and which he carried on his voyages as well as several others he acquired later. That he read and consulted them is attested by the presence of numerous postils in his handwriting. These books are displayed within a locked, free-standing case.

Featured in Fernando Colón's collection is a manuscript

of the navigator's Book of Prophecies, which Columbus had prepared for Queen Isabel in 1501–1502 with the assistance of the monk Gaspar Gorricio. The manuscript consists of a letter addressed by Columbus to King Fernando and Queen Isabel introducing the collection of excerpts from the Bible in addition to a number of ancient and medieval works predicting or implying the discovery of the New World and proving that his plans for discovery were not antagonistic to scripture.

The cathedral of Seville also owns a cross traditionally claimed to have been made of the gold brought from America by Columbus.

Real Academia de la Historia, Madrid. The library of this learned organization, comparable to the Royal Society of London or the American Philosophical Society, owns an original letter from Columbus to the Catholic sovereigns and a fifteenth-century (c. 1475) manuscript copy of Ptolemy's *Geography* bearing Columbus's rubric on the flyleaf.

Biblioteca Nacional, Madrid. The Department of Manuscripts of Spain's national library contains a holograph letter dated January 4, 1493, from Columbus to Rodrigo de Escobedo designating him chief of the first community established in the New World; another dated 1496–1497 from Columbus to the Catholic sovereigns relating to the discovery of La Española (Hispaniola); and a painting on wood claimed to be the earliest portrait of Columbus. It was not painted from life, however, and is believed to be Italian from about 1552.

Museo Naval, Madrid. Featured in this repository of artifacts relating to Spain's naval and maritime history is the first chart of the West Indies, drawn by Juan de la Cosa in 1500 and executed on two oxhides. The Museo Naval also owns a later copy of the Toscanelli map of 1474 and a portrait of Columbus.

Museo del Ejercito, Madrid. In the extensive collections of this museum of Spanish military history is a wide range of late-fifteenth-century arms and armor such as Columbus and his men would have worn and cannon and other weapons of the type they brought with them to the New World. None of the items is known to have been associated with Columbus's voyages, however.

Palazzo Municipale, Genoa. The chief treasure relating to Columbus in Italy is his manuscript of the Book of Prophecies entitled *Cartas, privilegias, cedulas y otras escrituras de Don Christoval Colon, Almirante Mayor del Mar Oceano, Visorey y Gobernador de las Islas y Tierra Firma* (Letters, privileges, contracts and other documents of Don Christopher Columbus, Great Admiral of the Ocean Sea, Viceroy and Governor of the Islands and the Mainland). Contained in a small folio volume of parchment bound in Spanish leather, having two silver ornaments, and enclosed in a leather bag, it was originally protected by a silver lock, now lacking. The reverse of the title page bears the Columbus arms as augmented by Columbus. The volume consists of forty-two leaves with attestations of notaries and alcaldes of Seville in whose presence the copies were made.

Following a copy of the bull of Alexander VI establishing the Line of Demarcation are nine pages of arguments by Columbus describing his contract with the Catholic sovereigns and defending his rights. Ten more pages contain a letter from Columbus to the governess of Prince Don Juan (Juan de Austria); a memorandum relating to the various copies he made of his contracts with the sovereigns and their disposition; two autograph letters from Columbus to Nicolò Oderigo, the Genoese ambassador to Spain; a copy of the reply from the director of the Banco di San Giorgio of Genoa to a letter from Columbus; an original letter from King Philip II to Ottaviano Oderigo, doge of Genoa, congratulating him upon the acquisition of this collection of documents; and a memorandum relating to Lorenzo Oderigo, who gave the collection to the Republic of Genoa. At the end of the volume is a sketch, *The Triumph of Columbus*, believed to have been drawn by Columbus. These manuscripts had been sent by Columbus to his friend Nicolò Oderigo to be deposited in the Banco di San Giorgio. Apparently Oderigo kept them for himself and it was not until 1669 that a descendant, Lorenzo Oderigo, presented them to the municipality.

During Napoleon's occupation of Italy, one copy of the manuscripts was taken to Paris, where it remains in the French ministry of foreign affairs. The other copy was acquired by Count Michelangelo Cambiasi, who surrendered it to the municipality of Genoa in 1887.

Archivio Notarile di Stato, Genoa. This repository contains a number of notarial acts of the fifteenth century relating to members of Columbus's family.

Casa Museo Colón, Las Palmas, Canary Islands. In the ancient barrio of Vegueta in Las Palmas is a house that tradition has always identified with the name of Nauta Genoves and associated with Columbus. Acquired in 1951 by the Cabildo of the Grand Canaries, it has been converted into a museum, with a Columbus Hall containing some early sixteenth-century cannons, models of Spanish caravels, a replica of a mariner's astrolabe based on the drawing in the Ribeiro map, and a copy of a portrait of Columbus. Collections of archaeological artifacts of the "Cultura Esmeraldeña" from the island of Tolita, of pre-Hispanic cultures of Mexico such as the Olmecs, and of the city of Teotihuacán are exhibited. Graphic wall displays illustrate the history of the peopling of the Americas, forms of economy in indigenous America, and the principal cities and cultures of the Americas. The museum contains no original artifacts associated with Columbus or his voyages.

Chicago Historical Society. Numerous objects that remained unclaimed or unwanted after the close of the World's Columbian Exposition of 1893 were eventually deposited with the Society, some transferred from the Field Museum of Natural History. Of particular interest are three anchors, one found at Cap-Haitien alleged to have been from *Santa María,* another claimed to have been lost off the coast of Trinidad by one of Columbus's ships on the third voyage, and an anchor found in the Ozamà River, Dominican Republic, believed to have belonged to one of the ships of Columbus or his son. Although one or more of these may be authenic as claimed, their records have been misfiled and it is no longer possible to determine with certainty which is which.

Other artifacts claimed to be associated with Columbus are bricks said to have been taken from Columbus's house in Santo Domingo, an iron cross and doors from the convent of Santa Maria de La Rábida, secured at the time the building was burned; late fifteenth-century doors, three wooden shutters, and a threshold from the home in Porto Santo, Madeira, of Bartolomé Perestrelo, Columbus's father-in-law, all bearing seals of authentication by the Spanish government; and a hawkbell said to have been brought to the Americas by the first Spaniards seeking gold. Few if any of these items are satisfactorily documented.

Library of Congress, Washington, D.C. The Library's collections contain one of the four copies made under the direction of Christopher Columbus in 1501–1502 of the Book of Privileges, a collection of various grants, commissions, charters, and privileges made to Columbus by the Catholic sovereigns, in addition to copies on paper of the bulls of Pope Alexander VI of May and October 1493. This copy, consisting of forty-five folio pages on vellum, was purchased for the Library in 1901.

The Library also owns a collection of approximately three hundred mounted photographs of Columbus documents formerly owned by the duke of Veragua, the originals of which, for the most part, are now in the Archivo General de Indias, in addition to a collection of photographs of pages of the Book of Privileges in the Municipal Palace in Genoa.

Columbus Chapel, Boal Mansion Museum, Boalsburg, Pennsylvania. Founded in 1951 and installed in the Boal family estate is a collection of materials relating to later descendants of Christopher Columbus and collateral branches of the family. Featured is the interior of a sixteenth-century chapel from a Spanish castle said to have been once owned by Diego Colón, which later became the home of Columbus's descendants. It was brought from Spain in 1909 and re-erected on the Boal family estate. In the interior are a grand escutcheon of the Columbus arms, numerous religious paintings, and other items, such as a reliquary with fragments said to be from the left arm of the True Cross. A portable "admiral's desk" is claimed to have been associated with Christopher or Diego. The museum also holds a collection of more than 165,000 pages of documents spanning four and a half centuries, from 1451 to 1902. More than half of the papers relate to three Columbus descendants of the late eighteenth and early nineteenth centuries—Joseph Joaquim Colón, his son Diego Mariano, and his grandson, Diego Santiago. Many of the records concern the endless conflict between this line of the Columbus family, which ended when Diego Santiago died without an heir, and the branch holding the dukedom of Veragua. None of the documents is positively identified to have been associated with Christopher Columbus or his sons.

Upon her death, Diego Santiago's wife left the family fortune to her French nephews and nieces, one of whom became the wife of an Irish American named Theodore Boal. It was as a consequence of this marriage that the chapel interior and collection of papers were brought to the United States.

The Columbus Memorial Lighthouse, Dominican Republic. Still under construction in 1991 is a landmark known as "El Faro a Colón," a lighthouse erected as a memorial to Christopher Columbus. The installation will contain six museums dedicated to aspects of the explorer's career. Included are a library of rare and hard-to-find books; an archive concerned with the history of the planning and construction of the lighthouse project, containing architectural plans and models; and a unit devoted to the history of cartography, featuring a collection of maps of the Americas. One of the museums will be dedicated to underwater archaeology, with artifacts recovered from sites in the region; another will be devoted to ceramics produced over the past five centuries. Central in theme to the installation is a museum commemorating Columbus himself, featuring displays of collections of coins, stamps, portraits, and works in gold and silver.

BIBLIOGRAPHY

[Bedini, Silvio A., and José Ibañez-Cerda]. *Colón y su tiempo.* Madrid, 1976.

Casa Museo Colón: *Guia Didactica.* Grand Canaries, n.d.

Davenport, Frances G. "Documents. Texts of Columbus's Privileges." *American Historical Review* 14 (1909): 764–777.

Garner, Richard L., and Donald C. Henderson. *Columbus and Related Family Papers, 1451–1902. An Inventory of the Boal Collection.* University Park, Pa., 1975.

Pérez Montás, Eugenio, and Manuel Valverde Podesta. "The Columbus Memorial Lighthouse." *La Española* (Dominican Republic Commissión del Quinto Centenario) 92, no. 3 (October 1988): 66.

Putnam, Herbert. "The Columbus Codex." *The Critic,* March 1903, pp. 244–251.

Watts, Pauline Moffitt. "Columbus's Crusade." *Humanities* 6, no. 6 (1985): 15–17.

SILVIO A. BEDINI

Overview of Documentary Sources

Considering the significance of his voyages of discovery from 1492 through 1503, original documents that deal with Christopher Columbus are scarce. Ninety-three such documents are located in nine archives in Spain, one in Italy, and one in Mexico. None of the diaries of the four voyages is a holograph; the diaries consist of abstracts prepared by Bartolomé de las Casas. Careful textual analysis can reveal original portions of the diaries. The total array of information on Columbus is a composite of scattered holograph documents, printed copies and translations of documents that are now lost, and corroborative documents by contemporaries.

The most important collection of material on Columbus was the library built up by his youngest son Fernando. Known today as the Biblioteca Colombina, this library once held all Columbus's personal papers and thousands of books that were still rarities in sixteenth-century Europe. The collection, housed in the cathedral of Seville, has dwindled to some two thousand items from an estimated twelve to twenty thousand in the original bequest. Several books contain marginal notes by Columbus.

Another important collection is that of Martín Fernández de Navarrete (1765–1844), who was commissioned by the king of Spain in 1789 to copy extensively the documents of voyages and discoveries in all Spanish archives. The materials in the Navarrete Collection are held in the Museo Naval, Madrid, which is a major resource for maritime history since the time of Columbus, although caution is advised in using printed versions of the collection because of occasional errors in paleographic transcription.

In anticipation of the four hundredth anniversary of the discovery of America in 1892, the Italian government commissioned the gathering of all known information on Columbus and his voyages from libraries and archives throughout Europe. The result was the compilation of the *Raccolta di documenti e studi pubblicati dalla R. Commissione Colombiana per quarto centenario dalla scoperta dell'America* (six parts, 14 vols. and supplement). The *Raccolta* remains the single best source of documents for Columbian research.

Documents on the early life of Columbus are preserved in the archives of the city of Genoa and also in its notarial archives. Some of these documents have been published by the city in Italian, German, and English editions. The earliest manuscript biography of the Admiral, by Hernán Pérez de Oliva (1531), is in the Yale University Library.

Correspondence between Columbus and Paolo dal Pozzo Toscanelli can be found in the Biblioteca Colombina in Seville.

The diaries of the four voyages are the focus of most Columbian research. The journal of the first voyage is based on an abstract by Las Casas, *El libro de la primera navegación*, which is in the Biblioteca Nacional, Madrid. Columbus's synoptic report to the Spanish Crown has survived only as a printed document, the earliest copy being in the New York Public Library. No original or abstract exists for the second voyage, thus forcing historians and commentators to reconstruct the voyage mainly from letters by Michele da Cuneo, a Latin summation by Nicolo Syllacio, and the observations of Fernando Colón. The journal of the third voyage depends on an abstract by Las Casas; the original manuscript is in the library of the Real Academia de la Historia in Madrid. Columbus's summary report to the Crown was copied by Las Casas and is in the Biblioteca Nacional, Madrid. The fourth or "high" voyage was abstracted by Las Casas in his *Historia de las Indias* and is also recounted by Fernando Colón in *Historie del S. D. Fernando Colombo*. The Royal Instructions for the voyage were copied by Columbus in his Libro de Privilegios (Book of privileges), which is in the library of the Real Academia de la Historia. The Archivo de Simancas preserves a copy of the muster and payroll for the fourth voyage.

The Archivo General de Indias, Seville, retains the Pleitos Colombinos (in the section of the Patronato), which are a rich source of corroborative material regarding the voyages and the claims of discovery. The texts of these lawsuits brought by and against Columbus and his heirs have been published at various times, but their accuracy is frequently held in question by scholars. Holograph documents of major importance can also be found in the archives as part of the collection of the Casa de la Contratación; pertinent documents are also in the section Indiferente General.

The Archivo General de Protocolos, Seville, has two original Columbus documents and many others pertaining to relatives and crew members; it is an important depository of primary sources.

The Archivo de la Casa de Alba, Madrid, contains many significant documents, especially correspondence, on Columbus and his heirs. As is true with many other subjects, the archives of private families in Spain are rich and indispensable sources of history.

One of the best known and later works of Columbus, the Libro de las Profecías (Book of prophecies), is housed in the Biblioteca Colombina in Seville and a copy is at the Archivo Histórico Nacional, Madrid. As noted above, the Biblioteca Nacional has several essential documents in its section of reserved manuscripts.

Detailed citation of Columbian documents is an unusually complex matter because what is known about Columbus is taken from a composite of extant originals, early copies of original documents that have been lost, and printed abstracts of information once contained in the Columbus library as preserved and enriched by Fernando Colón. One is best advised to consult either the major compilation of documentary material in the *Raccolta* or the more reliable translations cited below.

After the surge of interest in Columbiana receded in the early twentieth century, attention was focused on archival lacunae and errors in publication. Alicia Bache Gould worked through much archival minutiae to develop her *Nueva lista documentada de los tripulantes de Colón* (Newly documented list of Columbus's crew). Her work has shown the need for even more careful synthesis of widely scattered data.

Most English-speaking scholars recognize the preeminent work of Samuel Eliot Morison, whose *Admiral of the Ocean Sea* remains the classic biography of Columbus. Morison's careful attention to documentary detail is seen in the first, two-volume edition (1942), and his publication of several key documents in *Journals and Other Documents* provides the English reader with a ready and reliable source of documentary information, since the paleography of sixteenth-century originals is uniformly difficult.

BIBLIOGRAPHY

Dunn, Oliver C., and James E. Kelly, Jr. *The Diario of Christopher Columbus's First Voyage to America, 1492–1493.* Norman, Okla., 1989.

Morison, Samuel Eliot. *Admiral of the Ocean Sea: A Life of Christopher Columbus.* 2 vols. Boston, 1942.

Morison, Samuel Eliot. *Journals and Other Documents on the Life and Voyages of Christopher Columbus.* New York, 1963.

Taviani, Paolo Emilio. *Christopher Columbus: The Grand Design.* London, 1985.

Varela, Consuelo. *Cristóbal Colón: Textos y documentos completos.* Madrid, 1984.

CHARLES W. POLZER

MUSLIMS IN SPAIN. The first Spaniards in the Americas were unlike other European Christians in one crucial respect: for more than seven hundred years their ancestors had lived near, with, or even as Muslims. Yet for the next century subsequent generations would gradually eliminate the physical presence of Muslims and any cultivation of their significance. Between the early seventeenth century and the end of World War II, this exclusion of the Muslim past from Spanish national identity came to dominate historical scholarship. As a result, the respective histories of Christians, Jews, and Muslims in Spain fell to three almost mutually exclusive sets of academic specialists.

However, Américo Castro's *España en su historia* (1948; English ed., *The Structure of Spanish History,* 1954) generated a debate that restructured the study of Spanish history for generations to come. In that work Castro insisted that modern Spanish identity was inconceivable without the centuries of interaction among Christians, Muslims, and Jews. Conversely, Claudio Sánchez-Albornoz, in *España: Un enigma histórico* (1956), described modern Spanish culture as essentially continuous with its pre-Islamic, that is, Roman or Visigothic, past. While late twentieth-century scholarship has mediated these extremes, it has leaned toward Castro, stressing the significance of intercommunal interaction while accounting for its changing patterns and structures with greater subtlety and precision. These changes occurred in three major phases.

During the first phase, from the eighth to the eleventh century, Muslims controlled most of the Iberian peninsula, assimilating much of the indigenous population to Islam and incorporating unconverted Jews and Christians as quasi-autonomous subject communities, while leaving Christians in control of a number of kingdoms in the far north. During this period, religious differences did not determine social relations.

Arab Muslims arrived in Egypt in the 630s and 640s, as others were expanding into Syria and Iran. By the beginning of the eighth century, this expansion had reached present-day Morocco, and most of North Africa's indigenous Berber peoples had become Muslim. In 711, a Berber-Arab army of about seven thousand, led by Tariq ibn Ziyad, landed near modern-day Gibraltar (Jebel Tariq), assisted by the flotilla of Count Julian, the Byzantine exarch of Ceuta. A few months later, a decisive defeat of the Visigothic king Roderick opened the way to rapid conquest. Within a year, Muslims controlled virtually everything south of the Duero and Ebro rivers. Although raiding across the Pyrenees continued after Charles Martel's victory at Poitiers (732), the Muslims, or Moros (Moors) as the Christians called them, made no effort to eliminate remaining Christian kingdoms south of the Pyrenees, to which a number of defeated Visigothic nobles had fled. Thus the anti-Muslim resistance that soon began in these kingdoms was led largely by Christians whose territory had never been conquered. For that reason, many scholars have accepted the concept of Reconquista as a subjective reality but not as an objective fact.

As early as 716, the Muslims were calling their territory "al-Andalus," a term that may have come from "Vandalicia," the Visigothic name for the peninsula's southernmost province. At first Berbers outnumbered Arabs; soon both groups constituted a minority of the Muslim population, which was increasingly made up of indigenous, Hispano-Roman converts (*musalima* or *muwalladun*). However, the spread of Arabic language and culture facilitated interaction and intermarriage among the various Muslim groups, unconverted Christians (Mozarabs), and Jews. The growth of bilingualism in Romance and Arabic promoted further cross-fertilization. An important symbol of this cultural fusion is the literary genre of the *muwashshah,* long Hebrew or Arabic poems that end with short passages in Romance, known as *kharja*s, the oldest poetic texts in any European vernacular.

Al-Andalus was administered by representatives of the Muslim caliph in the East until a refugee prince, Abd ar-Rahman I, established the Umayyad dynasty, which ruled until 1012. By the reign of the dynasty's most famous member, Abd ar-Rahman III an-Nasir (r. 912–961), al-Andalus was open to wider Muslim culture, to increased contact with Byzantium and Greek learning, and especially to the technological diffusion that the expansion of Islam had encouraged. Political, cultural, and economic interaction across religious frontiers was common, especially by Christians wanting to take advantage of the general superiority of Muslim culture in areas such as medicine. The last member of the Umayyad dynasty symbolized this intermixing in his nickname Sanchuelo, which derived from his maternal grandfather, the Christian king of Pamplona.

The second phase of changes occurred from the eleventh to the fifteenth century. Al-Andalus shrank substantially, yet Christians tended to treat subject Jews and Muslims (now known as Mudejares) along the lines Muslims had treated subject Jews and Christians, and bilingualism continued to promote important cross-cultural exchange.

When Umayyad rule ended, al-Andalus divided into a number of separate states, often known as Party Kingdoms. Simultaneously, the strength and quality of Christian leadership improved. In 1085, Alfonso VI of Castile occupied Toledo. The chief architect of the Reconquista, Alfonso VIII (r. 1158–1214), defeated a large Muslim army at Las Navas de Tolosa (1212) and thereby opened the way to rapid Christian advances. By 1248, Córdoba, Valencia, and Seville were also in Christian hands. The one major remaining Muslim kingdom, Granada, was ruled by the founder of the Nasrid dynasty, Muhammad I al-Ghalib (r. 1238–1273), who exchanged a tributary relationship with Castile for an independence that would last 250 years.

Despite these major changes in the balance of power, cultural boundaries remained porous and Muslims remained tolerated as a subject population, partly for practical reasons. Like Jews, Muslims performed occupa-

tional and economic functions that Christians did not, and without Muslim numbers the Christians could not populate and maintain the prosperity of their conquered territories. Some Muslims became Christians (conversos); others retained their identity, even as knowledge of Arabic declined, helped by the inspiration of Muslim Granada, where, in the last part of the fourteenth century, the Alhambra was completed, symbolizing efforts to preserve the best of Muslim culture from the threat of extinction.

Ironically, this state of affairs produced some of the most productive intercommunal exchange and some of the Muslims' greatest cultural achievements. Alfonso X, known as the King of the Three Religions, fostered collaborative learning. Raymond Lull (d. 1315), well-known Majorcan scholar and writer, knew Arabic better than Latin and was influenced by Sufism and the teachings of the Jewish philosopher Maimonides, who was in turn also influenced by Muslim thinkers. The Mudejares were responsible for a cultural synthesis, especially in architecture, that affected even areas like Aragón and Castile, which did not have direct contact with Muslims. Some craftsmen working in the Mudejar style were actually Christians.

The third phase of structural changes occurred from the fifteenth to the seventeenth century. During this period, religious affiliation began to define social relations. As religion emerged as the unifying factor among rival Christian leaders, intolerance of Muslims increased. Even when baptized and relocated, Muslims proved unassimilable. Increasingly the symbol of everything Christians were not, they were ultimately expelled.

The union of Aragón and Castile in 1469 led to the rapid conquest of remaining Muslim centers. Although the Granada capitulation treaty (1492) contained promises of continued religious tolerance for Muslims, now dubbed Moriscos (a pejorative form of Moros), pressure for their conversion grew. At first Christian leaders tried aggressive persuasion; however, when such measures as the public burning of Islamic books led to Morisco revolts, Christian leaders resorted to more forceful means. A 1501 decree gave Moriscos a choice between baptism and expulsion. At midcentury, even more extreme orders banned the use of Arabic, the wearing of Arab dress, and the covert practice of Islam, which was widespread. In the ensuing half-century, the presence of the Morisco nemesis helped harden Spanish Christian notions of religious and racial purity. In 1609, Philip III gave the final expulsion order, despite the major economic loss it entailed. During the next five years, an estimated 300,000 to 500,000 Moriscos left, some for France, some for Egypt or Constantinople, most for North Africa, where their incomplete assimilation has resulted in the partial survival of Andalusian culture.

Some, as corsairs, continued to affect Mediterranean affairs for years to come.

The Moriscos were not absorbed for many reasons. Granada's intransigence in its last decades had left Muslims suspect. As Spain committed more and more fighting men to the New World and at the same time attempted to become an imperial power, the Moriscos' identification with foreign Muslim enemies, such as the Ottomans, became increasingly threatening. In fact, the Moriscos did look to other Muslims for inspiration and support, both in their covert practice of Islam and their mounting of rebellions. For example, in their 1569 revolt, Granada Moriscos sought and received the help of the Ottoman governor of Algiers. Although knowledge of Arabic had declined sharply, the Moriscos cultivated their identity through Aljamiado literature, which they wrote in Romance using Arabic script. With Muslims viewed as racially alien as well as religiously disloyal, the intermarriage that had characterized earlier times became impossible. A higher birth-rate among Moriscos, partly the result of the increase of celibacy among Christians, may also have been threatening.

Nine hundred years of interaction had left Spain's "three histories" inextricably intertwined. Even in defeat, Muslim culture continued to exert its influence, as in Charles V's Renaissance palace in the Alhambra and the cathedral in the middle of the Great Mosque at Córdoba. Muslim culture, as absorbed by Spanish Christians, also indirectly influenced the New World in the form of family honor codes, home design, and the plateresque style of architecture. Romance and Spanish have been filled with Arabic loanwords, be they chemical, culinary, agricultural, technological, social, or scientific. Muslims introduced new crops, such as sugar cane, rice, cotton, and a number of fruits. Their wind-tower technology still heats and cools some Spanish homes, and their irrigation technologies still water some Spanish fields.

The significance of Islam for the Spaniards extended beyond Spain. When Spanish explorers happened upon the Americas, they were seeking a route to the Indian Ocean, where Muslim power was still increasing, so as to gain direct access to one of the world's most lucrative economic systems. By 1500, Muslims had rounded the Malay Peninsula and the northern coasts of Sumatra and Java and were pressing into the Moluccas and what became the Philippines. By the time Ferdinand Magellan

EXPULSION OF THE MUSLIMS FROM SPAIN. Drawing by Vincente Carducho.

MUSEO DEL PRADO

THE ALHAMBRA. Court of the Lions.   SPANISH NATIONAL TOURIST OFFICE

sailed across the Pacific from Mexico and arrived in the Philippines in 1521, conversions to Islam were increasing as far north as Manila. Muslim expansion into Southeast Asia was the result of the long-term, hemispheric political and economic changes that had brought them to al-Andalus in the first place. Likewise, the Spanish triumph in the Philippines, which reduced Muslims to a minority, was part of global political and economic changes that had begun with the Reconquista and were soon to displace the Ottomans in Europe and the Mediterranean. This connection between the geographical extremities of Islamic power is symbolized by the Spanish name for Muslims in the Philippines, Moros (Moors), the same name they had been given at home so long ago.

[See also Granada; Ottoman Empire; Reconquista; Spain.]

BIBLIOGRAPHY

Burns, Robert Ignatius. Muslims, Christians, and Jews in the Crusader Kingdom of Valencia: Societies in Symbiosis. Cambridge, 1985.

Cardaillac, Louis. Morisques et Chrétiens: Un affrontement polémique (1492–1640). Paris, 1977.

Castro, Américo. The Spaniards: An Introduction to Their History. Translated by Willard F. King and Selma Margaretten. Berkeley, Los Angeles, and London, 1971.

Chejne, Anwar G. Islam and the West: The Moriscos, A Social and Cultural History. Albany, 1983.

Glick, Thomas F. Islamic and Christian Spain in the Early Middle Ages. Princeton, 1979.

Gómez, Emilio Garcia. "Moorish Spain: The Golden Age of Cordoba and Granada." In Islam and the Arab World, edited by Bernard Lewis. New York, 1976.

Hess, Andrew C. The Forgotten Frontier: A History of the Sixteenth-Century Ibero-African Frontier. Chicago, 1978.

Jackson, Gabriel. The Making of Medieval Spain. New York, 1972.

McKendrick, Melveena. The Horizon Concise History of Spain. New York, 1972.

Watt, W. Montgomery, and Pierre Cachia. A History of Islamic Spain. Edinburgh, 1965.

MARILYN ROBINSON WALDMAN

MYTH OF COLUMBUS.

MYTH OF COLUMBUS. The myth of Columbus portrays his life and accomplishments in simplistic terms, echoing the portrayals of heroes in classical mythology. The complexity of Columbus's character and the full historical context of his life and voyages are ignored in order to illustrate moral lessons about good and evil. Such portrayals are common in textbooks, but they have also appeared in books designed for adult audiences.

The myth of Columbus stems in part from incomplete historical evidence. Even if his life were fully documented, it is likely that some distortions would have occurred over time, simply because he was a transcendent historical character. As it is, parts of his life are well-documented despite the passage of five hundred years, and other parts remain obscure. Columbus himself wrote little about his background and consciously exaggerated his accomplishments as an adult, bitterly blaming others for the misfortunes and reverses he suffered. Both his bitterness and his exalted sense of his own worth have come down to us in the biography attributed to his second son, Fernando, and in the historical works of Bartolomé de las Casas, who had access to Columbus's family papers in the first half of the sixteenth century. The uneven availability of sound evidence plus distortions promulgated by Fernando and Las Casas have both contributed to the myth.

Of the dozens of misconceptions and distortions that characterize the mythic view of Columbus, only a few will be discussed here. One persistent misconception deals with his supposedly mysterious origins. Fernando's biography and many other sources contemporary with Columbus indicated that he was Genoese, and the few times Columbus mentioned his birthplace, he named Genoa. No one seemed to doubt it before the end of the seventeenth century. Nonetheless, from then on a series of writers claimed that Columbus was English, Spanish, Portuguese, Greek, or some other nationality. In the nineteenth century the notion surfaced that he and his family were of Jewish ancestry, wherever they originated. Columbus's own reticence and the scant documentation discovered for his early life encouraged these speculations.

In the late nineteenth century, however, Italian scholars uncovered a wealth of notarial documents and other papers that proved beyond a shadow of a doubt that Columbus's family was Genoese, originating in the mountains that formed part of the city's hinterland. Columbus was born in or near the city of Genoa, probably in mid-1451. His ancestors were Christian landowners, wool-workers, minor merchants, shopkeepers, and sometime participants in Genoa's volatile partisan politics. Although Fernando's biography went to great lengths to suggest that the family was quite distinguished socially and intellectually, nothing in the documentation supports that suggestion. In fact, the family's humble position in Genoese society may explain Columbus's reticence about it. He was highly ambitious for status, wealth, and fame; revealing his true origins would not have helped him achieve his ambitions.

Because the family owned land, and because Columbus's father held a few minor official posts in Genoa, it is highly likely that the family was Christian and always had been: Jews could neither own land nor hold official posts. Columbus's own writings emphasize his strong Christian beliefs and his sense of being chosen by God to advance the spread of Christianity. He urged Fernando and Isabel, the royal sponsors of his 1492 voyage, to bar Jews and Muslims from the lands he had claimed for Castile, and he suggested that they use the profits from those lands to finance the Christian recapture of Jerusalem from the Muslims of the Ottoman Empire. Despite the findings of scholars, the myth that Columbus's origins are shrouded in mystery and that he may have been of Jewish ancestry continues to appear.

Another myth—or set of myths—deals with the formulation of Columbus's great notion that one could reach Asia in the far east of the known world by sailing west. Fernando's biography emphasizes the scholarly sources for that idea: the academic geographers whose works were newly available in the late fifteenth century after Johannes Gutenberg's invention of movable type. He also mentioned his father's experience at sea and the tales told by other mariners and merchants, but his obvious aim was to portray his father as a scholar and an intellectual, not just a mariner. From Fernando's efforts comes the myth of Columbus the scientist and intellectual. By contrast, modern scholars generally agree that Columbus's experiences of Atlantic winds and currents planted the seeds for his great notion, inspiring him to collect tales of possible lands to the west. Columbus went to sea as a teenager, eventually traveling over most of the Mediterranean and into the Atlantic on commercial voyages for various Genoese merchants. He found himself in Lisbon in 1476 and remained in Portugal and its Atlantic islands for nearly a decade, when he was not at sea. During that period, he probably continued as a seagoing merchant, battening on the contacts he retained with his Genoese homeland and with the Italian communities established in Portugal. Undoubtedly he traveled to the Atlantic islands belonging to both Portugal and Castile, West Africa, and the British Isles, and perhaps Iceland as well. In Portugal he married into an Italian-Portuguese family of some distinction; his wife's family had important mercantile, maritime, and political connections. During his Portuguese sojourn he formed the idea of sailing west to establish a shorter route to the markets of Asia, but his formulation may have had little to do with research. Scholars now think that he sought out academic sources only later, to improve the chances that his idea would find official acceptance and financial support.

At the opposite end of the spectrum from the myth of Columbus the intellectual and scientist is the anti-heroic myth that Columbus had some secret knowledge of what lay west of Europe in the Ocean Sea. Fernando's biography mentions various mariners who claimed to have seen land far to the west of Europe. From one of them, the argument goes, Columbus acquired certain knowledge that land could easily be reached by sailing westward from Europe. The success of his voyage was therefore a certainty, rather than an audacious gamble. Some modern authors have claimed that Viking voyages four centuries before Columbus produced maps of parts of North America. A few claim that Columbus had seen such a map, which provided him with proof that his notion would succeed, or even inspired the notion in the first place. In other words, they credit the Vikings not only with their own voyages in the eleventh century, but with inspiring Columbus's voyages in the fifteenth. Most scholars dismiss all supposed Viking maps as forgeries and argue that, first, even if they were authentic, the chances are very slim that Columbus could have known about them, and, second, if he had known about them, he would have sailed northwest rather than southwest to find the lands depicted. Even without maps, however, proponents of the myth of secret knowledge continue to argue that Columbus learned about the location of western lands from others, rather than formulating his notions independently.

Another set of heroic myths about Columbus deals with his search for support. The king of Portugal declined to sponsor him, presumably because the Portuguese were already pursuing an eastern sea-route to Asia toward the south around the African continent. Nonetheless, the king sent out a secret expedition to test Columbus's theory. In the heroic view of Columbus, his rejection and betrayal by the king of Portugal is usually presented as the first of a long series of trials in which he was unjustly denied and shamefully treated by nearly everyone he approached for support. Although there is some truth to such views, they still perpetuate a heroic myth about Columbus that distorts the historical record.

Seeking other royal sponsorship, Columbus moved to Spain in 1485, eventually persuading Queen Isabel of Castile and her consort, King Fernando of Aragón, to support his scheme. His long wait for royal backing and his repeated rejections by royal commissions are used in the heroic myth to show his perseverance in the face of ignorance and prejudice. In this view, Spain and its monarchs deserve almost no credit for the success of the 1492 voyage. Columbus did have to wait seven years before persuading the monarchs to support him. What the heroic myth ignores is that his geographical calculations of the size of the earth were quite wrong according to the best academic geographers of his day. It is hardly surprising that he failed to persuade them. Moreover, through the years that the Spanish monarchs kept Columbus in a state of frustrated anticipation, they provided him with several grants for his expenses, even when the royal treasury was dangerously strained by the war against Muslim Granada. When they finally agreed to sponsor his voyage, they did so despite the judgment of their expert advisers that his scheme was impractical.

Columbus embarked in 1492 in search of the famous markets of Asia and any other lands he might encounter along the way. Columbus's subsequent relations with the Spanish monarchs are distorted by a broad set of myths about his character and behavior that can fit either the heroic or the anti-heroic version of his life. Landing on an island in the Caribbean after a calm voyage of thirty-three days from the Canary Islands, he was sure he had arrived in Asia. He dubbed the local inhabitants "Indians," and the islands the "West Indies," assuming that he was somewhere in South Asia, west of the East Indies that Marco Polo had visited. Concerned with producing a profit to justify the support he had received, Columbus searched during the next several months for the rich ports of the Great Khan. Not finding them, he shifted his emphasis to a search for local trade goods and other commodities such as slaves that might be used to produce commercial profits in the immediate future. He also detained several natives against their will to take back to Spain, Christianize, and train as interpreters. The heroic myth of Columbus ignores the implications of these

actions and portrays him in one-dimensional terms as a daring explorer with only high-minded objectives.

Columbus was greeted as a hero upon returning to Spain and received substantial administrative responsibilities from the queen of Castile, in whose name he had claimed the islands. Within a few years, however, he proved incapable of carrying out those responsibilities, and the queen conferred them on others. Although the myth of Columbus blames Spanish ingratitude for his change of fortune, scholars have ample evidence to show that he brought his troubles on himself. Among other actions that turned the Crown against him, Columbus was eager to capture local inhabitants in the West Indies to sell as slaves. That was one of the easiest ways to turn a profit until the land could be developed. Despite strong sentiments by the Crown that slave-taking could only be justified in the context of a just war, Columbus continued to take slaves in other circumstances. Coupled with his obvious inability to govern the Spanish colonies established in the islands, his actions led to his ignominious arrest and to the Crown's withdrawal of his administrative duties. Personally, however, Columbus continued to enjoy honorable and friendly treatment from the monarchs, and he and his family grew rich from the offices and commercial privileges they held in the Indies. In the heroic myth of Columbus, his troubles with the Crown are blamed on the perfidy and greed of others, never on his own actions and flaws in character. Indeed, Columbus himself promulgated this interpretation in his letters to the Crown and in his subsequent legal battles to regain his titles and monopolies.

In all, Columbus made four voyages across the Atlantic, returning from the last in 1504, shortly before Queen Isabel died. By then the Crown had begun the process of colonizing the islands and bringing settlers under bureaucratic control, even as it continued to sponsor further exploration. Many individuals had been given royal approval for their expeditions, breaking the exclusive monopoly that had once been given to Columbus. Angry and disappointed, Columbus spent his last two years trying to regain all of the titles, offices, and privileges that had been withdrawn. He died in 1506, wealthy and still possessing many honorific and financial rewards, but embittered nonetheless.

The anti-heroic myth of Columbus sees only the negative sides to his character and his actions in the Western Hemisphere. In this portrait, Columbus emerges as an insensitive and brutal slaver, interested only in gold, who began the destruction of indigenous societies in the Caribbean by waging a genocidal war against the native peoples. To writers appalled by the destruction of native societies that followed in the wake of European expansion, Columbus stands as the first evil example of the European conqueror.

Not surprisingly, the interpretation favored by scholars relies on all the documentary evidence available and produces a view that avoids simplistic conclusions of every stripe. Columbus was not only a skilled mariner, master salesman, and daring explorer, but also an inept and arrogant administrator, and a merchant whose conscience was not troubled by taking and selling slaves. Columbus worked tirelessly to enhance the wealth and status of his family, but he was also a religious visionary who dreamed of recapturing Jerusalem for the glory of Christianity. In many ways he was a figure larger than life, whose reality lies somewhere between the heroic and the anti-heroic myths that have formed around him. Nonetheless, because of the far-reaching consequences of his voyages and the general human trait to seek simple explanations for complex reality, the mythic views of Columbus seem likely to continue.

[For detailed discussion of Columbus's life and works, see the various articles under *Columbus, Christopher.*]

BIBLIOGRAPHY

Books that Promote Simplistic Heroic Myths about Columbus

Columbus, Ferdinand. *The Life of the Admiral Christopher Columbus*. Translated by Benjamin Keen. New Brunswick, 1959.

Irving, Washington. *The Life and Voyages of Christopher Columbus*. 1828. Edited by John Harmon McElroy. Reprint, Boston, 1981.

Las Casas, Bartolomé de. *Historia de las Indias*. 3 vols. Edited by Agustín Millares Carló. Mexico City, 1951.

Books that Promote a Balanced Interpretation of Columbus

Ballesteros Beretta, Antonio. *Cristóbal Colón y el descubrimiento de América*. 2 vols. Barcelona, 1945.

Heers, Jacques. *Christophe Colomb*. Paris, 1981.

Taviani, Paolo Emilio. *Christopher Columbus: The Grand Design*. Translated by William Weaver. London, 1985.

Winsor, Justin. *Christopher Columbus and How He Received and Imparted the Spirit of Discovery*. Boston, 1892.

CARLA RAHN PHILLIPS

NAMING OF AMERICA. See *America, Naming of.*

NAPLES. The Kingdom of Naples grew from the early twelfth-century Norman conquests of Byzantine, Lombard, and Muslim lands in southern Italy and Sicily to become one of the great powers of Renaissance Italy. Limited to the lower third of the Italian mainland by the revolt of Sicily in the Sicilian Vespers of 1282, the Kingdom of Naples itself became the object of Angevin-Aragonese dynastic rivals in the late Middle Ages and continued to be fought over by their French and Spanish heirs after the 1494 invasion of Italy. With the Spanish victory and viceroyalty established by 1503 in neat parallel with the Spanish conquests in the New World, the Kingdom of Naples remained under Spanish rule through the sixteenth and seventeenth centuries.

The fluctuating fortunes of Neapolitan political history had already become a commonplace by the time of the Spanish conquest. In *The Prince*, Niccolò Machiavelli used Naples and Milan as examples of newly acquired principalities to be tamed; and in *The Discourses*, he argued that the Kingdom of Naples, typical of a state without equality, was incapable of establishing a republic. In his *History of Italy*, Francesco Guicciardini combined his themes of internecine quarrels and princely caprice in the Italian states with the standard portrait of an ineffectual and division-riven Kingdom of Naples. He coined an inverted aphorism to characterize the 1494 fall of Naples: "The French king—beyond the example even of Julius Caesar—first conquered, then saw." Even after three-quarters of a century of Spanish rule, the Venetian ambassador in 1580 still portrayed the Kingdom of Naples with its "frequent and turbulent revolutions" as the prime exemplar of "the various and marvelous mutations of states and governments which are diversely represented in history." Despite being "put in perpetual bondage so many times by its enemies," Naples was uniquely capable of transforming itself from conquered to conqueror, "always boasting liberty and dominion equal to the greatness of these same enemies."

Unstable political formations reflected the internal organization of a kingdom fractured by a factious feudal nobility whose agricultural interests allied them with foreign merchants and inhibited communal towns from developing native commerce and industry. The feuding local nobility maintained its regional power based largely upon the profits of raw agricultural exports shipped by Tuscan, Venetian, Catalan, and Genoese merchants to northern Italian cities. In the fifteenth century, the Adriatic ports of Manfredonia, Barletta, and Bari provided the chief products, olive oil, wheat, and wool, while the city of Naples continued to be an important port for silk exports, textile and metal imports, and products exchanged in western Mediterranean trade. Caught between foreign mercantile expansion and native baronial domination of the provincial communes, the kingdom remained compartmentalized into regional, unarticulated markets and dependent upon foreign investment and foreign demand, ripe for foreign intervention and conquest.

Population growth exacerbated the problem of the lack of economic integration. In the sixteenth century, the kingdom's population doubled from about 1.3 million inhabitants to 2.5 million. And no division better exemplifies the extremes found in the kingdom than the dichotomy between capital city and countryside. The capital city of Naples, with over 100,000 inhabitants in 1500, grew to be the largest city in western Europe, with 250,000 inhabitants at the end of the sixteenth century. At the same time, no city in the kingdom's twelve provinces numbered more than 20,000 during this period. From the late Middle Ages, then, the city of Naples was the unique cosmopolis of a rural kingdom, and the resident Angevin and Aragonese courts provided a brilliant cultural life for its teeming population.

The Angevin dynasty of Naples (1268–1435) came to the kingdom through papal invitation after the defeat of Frederick II, his son Manfred, and the Hohenstaufens. Before the 1348 plague, Angevin Naples basked in the Guelph sun of banking, financial, and commercial interests. King Robert (1309–1343) was a patron of Petrarch and of the young Boccaccio, who lived, worked, and studied in Naples from the age of fourteen to twenty-seven between 1327 and 1341. Since this cadet French dynasty owed its investiture to the pope, it attempted to solidify its claims in the kingdom by granting new titles and ever-greater privileges to the increasingly independent native nobility. Baronial antagonism erupted in civil wars that racked the kingdom during the reign of the last of the Neapolitan Angevins, the childless Queen Giovanna II (1414–1435). From her death in 1435, her Angevin heir, René of Anjou, fought over the Kingdom of Naples with Alfonso V, king of Aragón and Sicily since 1416, who was attempting to create an empire in the western Mediterranean, often at the expense of the Genoese.

Alfonso (1443–1458) successfully conquered Naples in 1443 and established himself as one of the most able rulers and generous patrons of fifteenth-century Italy. He forged diplomatic ties with Milan, repaired quarrels with the papacy, but adamantly maintained aggressive action against the rival Genoese, who were driven further into the pro-Angevin French camp. Alfonso's literary and humanist patronage, which gained him the title of "the Magnanimous," fostered a court of talented humanists including such long-term residents as Panormita, Lorenzo Valla, Bartolomeo Facio, Giannozzo Manetti, and Giovanni Pontano.

Alfonso's illegitimate son and successor in Naples, Ferrante (1458–1494), continued such patronage, but shifted his cultural largesse to vernacular works, music, and law in accordance with personal interest and contemporary exigencies. Ferrante employed all the propaganda skills of the humanist movement in order to combat the interminable opposition from René and Jean of Anjou (the Angevin claimants to Naples), from Genoese and papal resistance to Catalan-Aragonese pretensions in the Tyrrhenian Sea, from two revolts by local baronial factions aligned to the Angevin French forces, and from the Ottoman Turkish threat after the occupation of Otranto in 1480–1481. Influenced by the late fifteenth-century crisis in Naples, Neapolitan humanist literature was characterized by realistic examination of the role of fortune and virtù (ingenuity or ability) and the uncertainty of military

action and dedicated itself to princely values intent upon overcoming internal and external political threats. (Christopher Columbus, according to his son Fernando's *Life,* is reputed to have been in command of a corsair ship in the service of René of Anjou during this period, possibly in 1472–1473.)

The French invasions of Italy in 1494 marked the end of an independent Neapolitan dynasty. First conquered by Charles VIII of France and then fought over by French and Spanish troops in the last decade of the fifteenth century, Naples became the proving ground for numerous military innovations championed by the victorious Spanish general, Gonzalo Fernández de Córdoba, the Great Captain. Among the poignant stories of the French invasions, none strikes more deeply than the faithful service of the great Neapolitan poet Jacopo Sannazaro to the last Aragonese king, Federico (1496–1502), in French exile.

Naples emerged from the wars as a cornerstone in the Spanish imperial system in Italy. The Spanish conquest of Naples subordinated the independent nobles' pretensions to the Crown, erected a bulwark against Turkish and French invasions, and established a bureaucratic government that further elaborated the long tradition of Neapolitan law. The Viceroy Pedro de Toledo (1532–1553) is credited with giving Naples its definitive Spanish character as well as solidifying an alliance with Tuscany through the marriage of his daughter Eleonora to Cosimo I, duke of Florence. Finally, in an irony of history typical of the inversions of fortune in Naples, the Aragonese dynasty's most hated Italian enemies, the Genoese, eventually became bankers to the Spanish Crown in the sixteenth century and, thus, indirectly conquered the Kingdom of Naples through trade and finance.

BIBLIOGRAPHY

Abulafia, David. *The Two Italies: Economic Relations between the Norman Kingdom of Sicily and the Northern Communes.* Cambridge, 1977.

Bentley, Jerry H. *Politics and Culture in Renaissance Naples.* Princeton, 1987.

Calabria, Antonio, and John A. Marino, eds. and trans. *Good Government in Spanish Naples.* New York and Bern, 1990.

Croce, Benedetto. *History of the Kingdom of Naples.* Translated by Frances Frenaye. Chicago, 1970.

Ryder, Alan. *The Kingdom of Naples under Alfonso the Magnanimous: The Making of a Modern State.* Oxford, 1976.

JOHN A. MARINO

NARVÁEZ, PÁNFILO DE (1470?–1528), Spanish conquistador. Born either in Valladolid or Cuellar, Narváez came to the New World looking for adventure. By 1509 he commanded a company of archers in the conquest of

Jamaica. Tall, bearded, affable, and hearty, with a deep, booming voice, Narváez was invited to join his old friend Diego Velázquez de León in the conquest of Cuba in 1513. His company of battle-hardened veterans cut a bloody swath through the island, so sickening the chaplain, Bartolomé de las Casas, that he abandoned the army with a holy curse on his lips, later writing that Narváez himself had killed two thousand Indians in the gruesome slaughter. For his efforts Narváez received rich grants of land and Indians to serve his whims. His wealth grew even more when he married a rich widow, María de Valenzuela.

In 1520 Velázquez sent him to the mainland to arrest the insubordinate Hernando Cortés. On May 27, after weeks of fruitless negotiation, the outnumbered army of Cortés infiltrated the Narváez encampment at Cempoala (near present-day Vera Cruz) in a brilliant and daring night attack. Narváez himself was badly wounded and lost an eye, and his entire army was captured. Most of his men joined Cortés for a renewed march on the Aztec capital, Tenochtitlán, but Narváez was imprisoned and later returned to Spain.

His phenomenal success in Cuba, where the royal share of profit from the gold mines added immense sums to the Spanish treasury, gave Narváez easy access to the king. In 1527 he returned once more to the New World, this time with an army, a fleet, and a royal grant allowing him to explore, settle, and govern Florida. But, unnerved by the harrowing Atlantic voyage, a fourth of his army deserted when the fleet made its first stop at Santo Domingo. Other losses followed, but Narváez finally managed to land his forces near Tampa Bay on April 14, 1528, where he took possession in the name of the Spanish king.

Foolishly sending his fleet away, Narváez marched his men north and west to the supposedly rich town of Apalache. Here they found a hostile reception in a miserable little village. After several more weeks of fruitless marching through dense forests and disease-ridden swamps, Narváez ordered his men to build boats for an attempt to reach Mexico. Short of food, the men slaughtered and ate their horses, turning the hides into water containers and fashioning tools from the spurs, bits, and stirrups. One way and another, Narváez and his men constructed five bargelike vessels. With about fifty men in each boat they set off along the coast on September 22, 1528. The water bottles rotted almost immediately and food quickly ran out. In about a month they passed the mouth of the Mississippi, but two of the boats were lost. Desperate and hungry, Narváez told his men to fend for themselves as best they could, sailed off, and was lost in the waters of the Gulf of Mexico. The others landed, and four survivors, including Alvar Núñez Cabeza de Vaca, eventually made their way across the continent and back to Mexico.

BIBLIOGRAPHY

Davenport, Harbert, ed. "The Expedition of Pánfilo de Narváez, by Gonzalo Fernández de Oviedo." *Southwestern Historical Quarterly* 27 (1923).

Goodwyn, Frank. "Pánfilo de Narváez, a Character Study of the First Spanish Leader to Land an Expedition to Texas," *Hispanic American Historical Review* 29 (1949).

Hallenbeck, Cleve. *Alvar Núñez Cabeza de Vaca: The Journey and Route of the First European to Cross the Continent of North America.* Glendale, Calif., 1940.

Vigil, Ralph H. "A Reappraisal of the Expedition of Pánfilo de Narváez to Mexico in 1520." *Revista de Historia de America,* nos. 77–78 (1974).

HARRY KELSEY

NAUTICAL CHARTS. Despite the inclusion of nautical information in a few world maps and in some maps of islands, the only charts effectively used by sailors in the decades before Columbus's first voyage to the Western Hemisphere are of two types: those now known as portolan charts and the earliest plane charts produced by Portuguese hydrographers. The name portolan chart is derived from the name for written sailing directions *(portolani).* Used in the Mediterranean from the late thirteenth century, these charts are distinguished from other medieval and Renaissance maps by the remarkable accuracy with which the regions are shown. These manuscripts, drawn in ink on vellum, divide into two groups: small atlases, each with openings devoted to a particular maritime basin, and large, single charts of the Mediterranean and the Black seas.

The portolan charts were true navigational instruments and, regardless of when they were drawn, exhibit similar characteristics. Their most prominent feature is the network of rhumb lines *(marteloio)* on which they are constructed. This complex system of straight lines spreads out from the center of a circle or from several implicit circles, placed side by side. The lines represent the thirty-two directions of the wind rose, each wind distinguished by color. Black represents the eight main winds; green, the half winds; and red, the quarter winds.

A second prominent characteristic is the scale, present in all these charts. Normally, the scale's large divisions are subdivided into five parts; the value of these parts, known to the users, was indicated only in the late examples. A third characteristic is the profusion of place-names, written perpendicular to the coastlines in the interior of the land masses. These place-names—written in black or red, according to their importance—identify the ports, havens, capes, reefs, bays, and promontories that the sailor needed to know. The principal, though not exclusive, concern of these charts is the outline of the coast. Inlets,

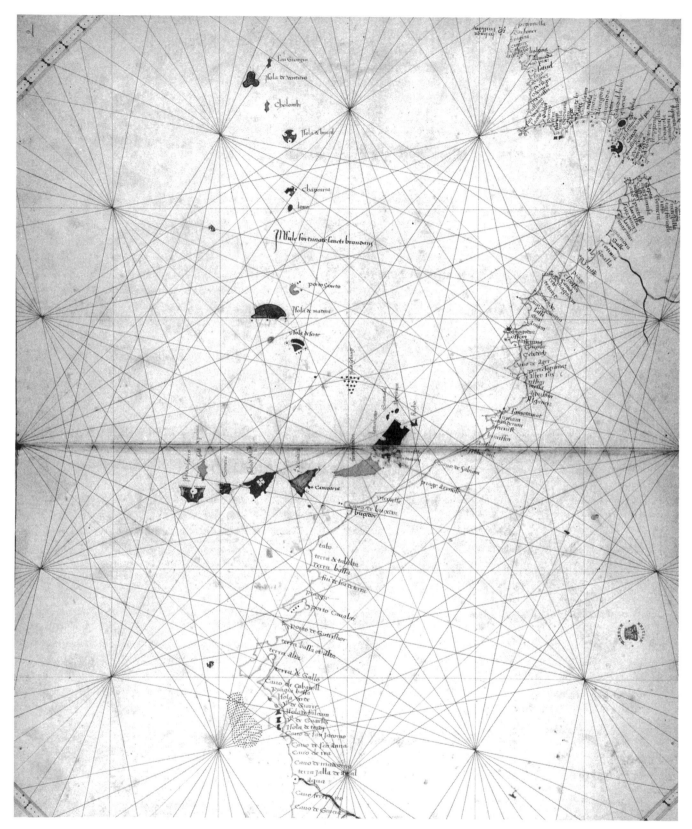

NAUTICAL CHART BY GRAZIOSO BENINCASA, 1467. Showing the Iberian and West African coasts, the Strait of Gibraltar, and Atlantic islands.

promontories, and estuaries are emphasized. Reefs are indicated by small crosses, sandbanks and shallows by dots, and islands and deltas by color.

Surviving examples indicate that these charts were owned mainly by princes and scholars, who influenced their geopolitical, theoretical, and religious content. However, these charts were originally intended for and developed by seamen. They reflect a specific navigational technique, dead reckoning, which was still in use at the time of Columbus. Essentially, this technique depends on the mariner's knowledge of the course set and the distance run, to which, respectively, the *marteloio* and the scale correspond. To effect a cross-sea route, the user would open a pair of dividers on the chart with one point on the port of departure and the other on the destination. He then looked for the closest parallel rhumb line, which showed the direction to follow. Since the chart had neither top nor bottom, the mariner could turn the chart in any direction he intended to sail and from which he would try not to deviate. If he lost his course, the mathematical tables, known as the *toleta de marteloio*, used since at least 1436, allowed the navigator to make the best use of the chart's network system in order to recover the course. Columbus's log book for the first voyage shows him trying to follow a constant course, guided by a magnetic compass, carefully measuring with a sandglass the distance run between each change of course, and scrupulously pricking off this distance on his charts, an operation that he calls *echar punto* or *cartear*.

At the end of the thirteenth century, merchants and explorers started to sail beyond the Mediterranean and to confront the unique problems of ocean navigation. Nautical charts began to take account of the nautical mile of a different value in the Atlantic and of the importance of the tides, which controlled the entry to and exit from harbors. The cartographic region was enlarged, and in the fifteenth century, charts were extended to the "Mediterranean Atlantic" between Madeira, the Azores, and the Canaries. Other Atlantic islands, both real (Cape Verde Islands) and imaginary (Antilia), were added, and, lastly, the West African coast beyond Cape Bojador, the southern limit of medieval navigation, was incorporated into the charts.

The addition of new lands, made at different times and using names that rarely agreed with other sources, has provoked endless controversies about the priority of one nation's discovery over another's and the anticipation by the charts of knowledge of a certain region before its documented discovery. For example, it has been claimed, though unconvincingly, that the island of Antilia, first identified on the 1424 Zuane Pizzigano chart, is a depiction of the most easterly part of the American continent. Such discussions obscure the more important aspects of the charts: the capacity of the rhumb-line system to be enlarged indefinitely allowed it to record, with remarkable confidence, the outline and respective position of newly attained lands. The empirical knowledge gained by seamen became known internationally, which is reflected in the charts' mixture of Latinate languages. Information concerning new discoveries consequently circulated rapidly, despite the official secrecy imposed by governments and merchant associations.

The Columbus brothers, particularly while in Lisbon, were apparently familiar with the most recent Portuguese discoveries and their incorporation into sea charts. Fernando Colón reports that Christopher Columbus had observed with interest charts belonging to his father-in-law, Bartolomeo Perestrelo, himself a navigator and erstwhile governor of Porto Santo. Most telling are the marginal annotations in books from Columbus's library, which reveal that Bartolomé Colón witnessed the return of Bartolomeu Dias to Lisbon and that he was aware of the *Carta navigationis* in which Dias recorded his voyage. Columbus himself noted the charts' inaccurate rendering of the length of the north-south journey from England to Guinea in comparison to positions established by a quadrant measuring solar altitude.

Having observed such discrepancies, Columbus showed his concern in correcting charts, for, like many sea officers in the fifteenth century, the Columbus brothers were chart makers. That they practiced this craft as a trade is, however, not certain, even during their stay in Seville. Nevertheless, both are said to have been talented draftsmen, and several documents, notably the logbooks and the accounts of the lawsuits against the Crown (the *Pleitos Colombinos*), reveal Columbus plotting the smallest of islands in a chart. His successors in the exploration of the American continent used the "charts that the Admiral had made, because he alone can make charts of all he discovered." At the end of the formal introduction to his journal of the first voyage, Columbus announces his intention "to make a new sea chart where he will place all the seas and the lands of the Ocean Sea in the places where they belong and under their winds."

Though none of the charts ascribed to the Columbus brothers carries their signatures, two of them merit special attention. The first, drawn on a relatively large scale and showing La Española (Hispaniola), is the sketch preserved in the collection of the dukes of Alba. This is a rare, if not unique, example of preparatory rough sketches for hydrographic use. By assembling several of them, the chart allows a far larger region to be drawn. The writing on this sketch is probably that of Columbus, and precise details given on the northwest coast of the island and the site of "Natividad" (La Navidad) suggest that it was drawn, at the latest, in the course of the second voyage, in December 1493.

The second is the anonymous chart preserved in the Bibliothèque Nationale, Paris. The attribution of this chart to Columbus is fraught with difficulties. However, this document is noteworthy as much for the maritime and commercial experience it illustrates as for its representation of the world. The same parchment, in effect, juxtaposes a portolan chart of the Atlantic with a tripartite *mappamundi*. The Atlantic portolan chart extends from Iceland to the mouth of the Congo River in Africa, with detailed commentaries near points on the coast that Columbus frequented after 1476. The *mappamundi*, on the other hand, is surrounded by celestial spheres (thereby displaying a geocentric universe) and shows Africa all the way to the Cape of Good Hope. Two maps in one, they share legends in Latin, the majority of them borrowed from Pierre d'Ailly's *Imago mundi*, a work central to the theoretical education of Columbus. This unusual linking of two types of maps recalls Columbus's own reference to his maps, "all of which also carry a sphere."

Except for the rough sketch drawn by the Admiral himself, the first nautical charts that incorporated hydrographic material from the voyages of Columbus are later than 1500. They are large manuscript planispheres that include first-hand documentation. One is Turkish and may owe its outline to a chart drawn in 1498. It was obtained from a companion of Columbus, who became a slave in the Ottoman fleet. Another, the oldest, is Spanish and was signed by Juan de la Cosa in 1500. Cosa was the cartographer of the second voyage, and he himself explored the Venezuelan coast in 1499. The other charts are Italian (Cantino, 1502; Caverio [Canerio], c. 1505), but they are copies of the *padrão real,* the official Portuguese chart. In light of the scale of these documents and their silence concerning specific areas, they give little information regarding Columbus's first landfall or the shape of the coast surveyed during the fourth voyage. Finally, contrary to the *mappaemundi,* they give only a slight hint of Columbus's conviction that he had reached Asia.

On the other hand, each of these documents is instructive regarding the difficulties encountered by the cartographers of this period, especially in the compilation of a new map of the entire world from discrete and disjointed individual surveys. Cartographers devised new solutions, which themselves generated other difficulties. The elements they had to contend with were magnetic variation, scale, and latitude. For example, Juan de la Cosa's map places the northern Bahamas at an excessively high latitude, and Jamaica, La Española, and Puerto Rico, which should be on the same parallel, are rotated fourteen degrees from the horizontal. There may be two explanations for this: the magnetic variation in the West Indies at this time and the use of two different scales—one for the Old World, another for the New World—which made the islands too large to fit in their correct positions. In spite of these problems, Cosa's map accurately depicts the course of Columbus's second voyage. This may be seen by placing a straightedge on the map, connecting Ferro (Hierro) in the Canary Islands to Dominica in the West Indies; the straightedge will be parallel to the west-by-south rhumb line, as indicated by Columbus himself. The Cantino map, famous for being the first to show the Line of Demarcation, is equally important in the history of nautical charts for its accurate delineation of Africa. This accuracy results from the fact that from about 1485 Portuguese hydrographers had been sent to the African coast in order to measure solar altitude, or latitude, with a quadrant and thereby more precisely establish the positions of specific places.

The Caverio chart (c. 1505) was one of the first charts to show a latitude scale. The use of latitude measurements reflects an enormous step forward in the history of surveying space, but it conflicted with essential aspects of the portolan charts. For example, dead reckoning functions with magnetic north; the quadrant uses geographic north. In addition, when using the same length for one degree in any parallel of the chart, the dead-reckoning method does not take into account the convergence of meridians. Thus, this new type of nautical chart, which was to be called a plane chart, was difficult for navigators. Sailors tried to get around the problem by using two or more scales of latitude for different areas on the same chart.

In 1516, the Caverio chart was used by Martin Waldseemüller as a model for the first printed planisphere shaped as a nautical chart, the *Carta marina navigatoria Portugallen navigationes,* and meridians showing longitude appear on charts very soon after Magellan's circumnavigation. But neither printed charts nor longitude would be of any practical use for navigation or chart making for a long time.

[See also *Cartography; Dead Reckoning; Latitude; Longitude; Mappamundi; Sailing Directions.*]

BIBLIOGRAPHY

Campbell, Tony. "Portolan Charts from the Late Thirteenth Century to 1500." In vol. 1 of *The History of Cartography,* edited by J. B. Harley and David Woodward. Chicago and London, 1987.

Harrisse, Henry. *The Discovery of North America.* Paris, 1892. Reprint, Amsterdam, 1961.

Kelley, James E., Jr. "The Map of the Bahamas Implied by Chave's Derrotero. What Is Its Relevance to the First Landfall Question?" *Imago Mundi* 42 (1990): 26–45.

Martínez, Ricardo Cezero. "Aportación al estudio de la carta de Juan de la Cosa." In *Géographie du monde au moyen âge et à la Renaissance,* edited by Monique Pelletier. Paris, 1989.

Mollat du Jourdin, Michel, and Monique de la Roncière, with Marie-Madeleine Azard, Isabelle Raynaud-Nguyen, and Marie-Antoinette Vannerau. *Sea Charts of the Early Explorers.* Translated by L. le R. Dethan. New York, 1984.

Raynaud-Nguyen, Isabelle. "Les portulans: Textes et iconographie." *Iconographie médiévale.* Paris, 1990.

Skelton, R. A. "The Cartography of Columbus' First Voyage." In *Journal of Christopher Columbus.* Translated by Cecil Jane. London, 1960.

ISABELLE RAYNAUD-NGUYEN
Translated from French by Mary Pedley

NAVIDAD, LA. See *Settlements*, article on *La Navidad*.

NAVIGATION. [This entry includes two articles that survey European technologies of navigation at the time of European overseas exploration and expansion:

Art, Practice, and Theory
Instruments of Navigation

For related general discussions of navigating at sea, see *Cartography; Shipbuilding; Tides and Currents; Weather and Wind.*]

Art, Practice, and Theory

Western nautical science based on measurement, rather than on traditional skills, originated in the Mediterranean, where by the end of the thirteenth century the navigator was in possession of the mariner's compass, systematically compiled sailing directions based on compass direction and estimated distance, and the portolan chart. Distance was estimated with the help of the timeglass, or running-glass, and a trigonometrical table or diagram, essentially solutions for a series of right-angle triangles, that told him how far he had been pushed off his intended course by headwinds and how to regain it. Mediterranean navigation, which developed rapidly during the thirteenth century in response to expansion of trade by Italian city-states with Egypt and the Levant and, to a lesser extent, the voyages of the Crusades, was essentially based on dead reckoning, the determination of position from the course and distance made good since the last known position. There was no means of fixing position offshore, but the Mediterranean seaman would seldom have been out of sight of land for more than a few days at a time, and although there are known currents the sea is virtually tideless and thus without tidal streams. Further, since both sailing directions and the chart were based on magnetic compass bearings, magnetic declination, or variation, was of no account, and, in a sea that stretches east and west over a narrow belt of latitude, neither was the convergence of the meridians toward the poles. In this special environment dead reckoning was developed to a fine art.

It was the Portuguese, during the fifteenth century, who developed and adapted Mediterranean methods of navigation to the more stringent demands of the open ocean and thus made the great European voyages of discovery possible. It was in Portugal, probably during the period 1478 to 1485, that Columbus acquired his knowledge of navigation.

On the Atlantic coasts of Europe a knowledge of the tides had been central to navigation, both to predict the depth of water within ports and harbors and to determine the direction and strength of the tidal stream that could so affect a passage. The assumption, acceptable within a narrow latitude belt, that meridians lay parallel to one another, became meaningless once latitude navigation had been introduced, for it became clear that an east-west course could carry a ship north or south of its intended latitude. Magnetic variation, too, became a problem on long voyages; positions defined by magnetic bearings on the chart often became irreconcilable with those obtained by astronomical observation.

The tides are of course caused by the attraction of the moon and, to a lesser extent, the far more distant sun on the waters of the earth. As long ago as the seventh century, Bede the Venerable had propounded his own theory of the tides and concluded, among other things, that although high water does not necessarily arrive simultaneously at all places on a meridian, it does occur at any one place when the moon is at the same position in the sky. The daily retardation of both the moon and the tides, which results from the fact that while the earth rotates on its axis once in twenty-four hours, the moon revolves counterclockwise around the earth (taking the high waters with it) in about thirty days, was accepted by Bede as forty-eight minutes. Seamen, however, were accustomed to telling the time at sea in terms of a compass bearing of the sun, so that each of the thirty-two points represented forty-five minutes, which was found to be a more convenient figure for the daily retardation of the tide. If they knew the time of high water at new moon they could thus use the compass rose to find the time of high water on any other day when the age of the moon, the time elapsed since new moon, was known. The "establishment of the port" at any place is the interval between the time the moon crosses the meridian and the time of high water. In early tide tables these values were expressed for different places in terms of compass directions, so that a phrase like "Flood tide, moon north-east, south-west" would mean that at new moon high water would occur three hours after the moon had crossed the midnight line and meridian. The lowest ebb would be six hours later and the following day the figures would be forty-five minutes later. To find the age of the moon the seaman needed to know the golden number (or prime), which he could deduce from the date, and that gave him the epact, from which he could calculate the moon's age by rote.

The earliest tidal diagram to survive is on the splendid Catalan atlas, dated 1375, attributed to Abraham Crescas and presented to the French court by the king of Aragón. It shows, in the form of a circular diagram and in terms of the eight named Mediterranean winds (directions were thus identified), the bearing of the moon at high and low water on the first day of new moon for a number of ports on the Atlantic seaboard. In the mid-sixteenth century, the Breton cartographer Guillaume Brouscon produced a handier form of tidal chartlet on which ports were linked with the appropriate bearings on the compass rose to show the establishment. Duarte Pacheco Pereira, the distinguished Portuguese pilot and contemporary of Columbus, devotes a chapter of his *Esmeraldo de situ orbis* (1505) to computing "the ebb and flow of the sea in the greater part of Spain and likewise in other regions where there are tides."

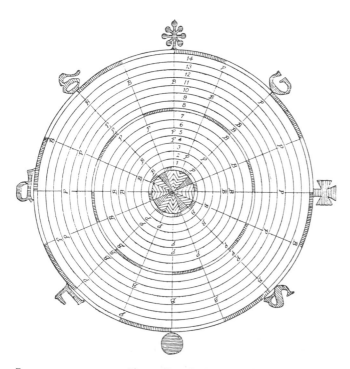

ESTABLISHMENT OF PORT. The earliest depiction of the establishment of port, from the Catalan Atlas of 1375. Bearings of the moon at high water (the *P*s) and low water (*B*s) are shown in terms of the winds for fourteen ports, identified by number. Number thirteen, for instance, is Sandwich; fourteen is the mouth of the Seine.

FROM E. G. R. TAYLOR, *THE HAVEN-FINDING ART*, LONDON, 1956

Navigators of the waters of the European continental shelf were clearly concerned with tides, the depth of water, and the nature of the sea bottom, samples of which could be brought up by a sounding lead armed with tallow. Pilot books, based on the accumulated experience of shipmasters and pilots, are of course as old as seafaring itself, and they reflect the navigational practice of their time and place. Thus the emphasis in the earliest surviving English "rutter" (from the French, *routier*), possibly dating from the fourteenth century, was all on tides and depths: "Upon Lizard there is great stones, as it were beans, and it is ragged stone. Upon Portland there is fair white sand and 24 fathoms," reads one passage; another, "A south moon maketh high water within Wight, and all the havens be full at west-south-west moon between Start and the Lizard." By contrast, Mediterranean pilot books emphasized direction and distances between coastal points. The earliest to survive, the *Compasso da navigare*, dating from between 1250 and 1260, is written in Italian and gives instructions, in terms of compass points and distance measured in Mediterranean miles (one Mediterranean mile equals five-sixths of the Roman mile), for navigating around the Mediterranean coasts eastward from Cape St. Vincent along the European shore and then along the African shore to Safi in Morocco; a bearing is then given between Safi and Cape St. Vincent. This last feature counters the idea that the early navigator was expected to cling to the coast, but such pilot books were nevertheless coastal in character as compared with later Iberian pilot books, which gave, for instance, lists of latitudes, tidal information, and sailing routes that took into account the ocean wind and current circulation. The *Compasso* distinguishes sixty-four directions, or rhumbs, arrived at by successively halving and rehalving the four quarters of the horizon, from which we can deduce that by then the magnetized needle must have been attached to the compass card. Directions in the Mediterranean were defined in terms of winds, which were named after their place of origin or character. There were eight named divisions, the four cardinal points, Tramontana (north), Mezzodi (south), Levante (east), and Ponente (west), and the four winds Greco, Scirocco, Garbino, and Maestro. Intermediate directions were named by combining the rhumbs, as, for example, "Tramonta a quarter wind Greco." The compass and wind roses on portolan charts, however, continued to show for the most part a sixteen-fold division. The division used in northern Europe, based on the four cardinal points, north, south, east, and west, proved less complicated and was adopted by the Portuguese and later the Spanish during the Age of Discovery.

The first written evidence for the existence of the mariner's compass dates from 1187, when Alexander Neckham, an English monk who lectured in the University of Paris, described how seamen, when the sun and stars were covered by clouds, used an iron needle magnetized by a piece of lodestone and floating in a bowl of water to indicate the direction of north. It is clear from the context, however, that when Neckham wrote the device had been in use for some time, and there is evidence from the changing pattern of trade in the last thirty years of the century that Genoese ships were already regularly sailing out of sight of land using the stone and needle technique. By the end of the thirteenth century, with the card attached to the needle, the compass had become a seagoing instrument indicating all directions all the time. There is no evidence that the magnetic compass was introduced to the Mediterranean by the Arabs or from China, as is sometimes held.

Whether sea charts in any recognizable form were used in antiquity is a matter of dispute; in any case, all knowledge of them seems to have been forgotten by the Middle Ages. The earliest extant reference to the chart is in the Latin account of a voyage made by King Louis IX of France from his new port of Aigues-Mortes to Tunis in 1250. The fleet was forced by heavy weather to seek shelter in Cagliari Bay, and to reassure the king he was shown the position on a sea chart (although the Latin chronicler calls it a *mappamundi*). The earliest surviving sea chart is the Carte Pisane, dated about 1290 and now in the Bibliothèque Nationale in Paris. It is clearly not the first portolan chart (a name taken from the port books or sailing directions from which, it may be assumed, the displayed information was derived, but it remains one of the most important documents in the history of navigation and deserves particular attention. Almost certainly of Genoese origin, it is drawn on an outstretched sheepskin, the neck (unusually) to the right. The coastline presents an astonishingly faithful representation of the shape of the Mediterranean. The chart carries no graticule, but a scale of miles is displayed in two places, each at a right angle to the other, presumably to take into account shrinkage. The portolan chart was indeed the first map of any kind to carry a scale, and for that reason alone is held to mark a turning point in the history of cartography. If one compares the Carte Pisane, for example, with a contemporary land map such as the Hereford world map, it is obvious that whereas the former is scientifically based, the latter is based on theology. The origins of the chart remain obscure and the problem of sources apparently intractable. But, as E. G. R. Taylor has pointed out, the nautical chart did not develop gradually but appeared suddenly, complete and excellent in all its essential features, which remained unaltered for over 250 years.

At the beginning of the thirteenth century the Hindu (Arabic) system of numerals was introduced to the West, largely through the influence of Leonardo of Pisa (Fibo-

nacci). Arithmetic was thus brought within reach of the ordinary man, including the navigator. One of the most intriguing features of the Carte Pisane is the construction diagram by means of which the network of rhumbs showing direction was laid down, for it is based on Euclid's method of making a perpendicular and shows the clear intervention of a mathematician. The coastline will have been drawn from information collected by trading ships, from local pilot books, and no doubt from the sketches of the pilots themselves, and then transferred to the chart by the method of scale squares still used by draftsmen today. The portolan chart is not based on any projection, but tests on a number of charts in the British Library suggest that the network of rhumbs was laid down before the coastline. It is tempting to relate the Carte Pisane historically with the *Compasso da navigare*, but all we can be sure of is that some central authority must have been responsible for collating the work necessary for each, and that neither document would have been possible without the magnetic compass.

To navigate with the chart the pilot or master would join, say, his point of departure with his destination using a straight-edged rule and then with dividers (compasses) find the rhumb most closely parallel. Traced back to its parent rose, this rhumb would give him the course. A color code was used for the rhumbs: black or brown for the eight winds, green for the eight half winds, and red for the sixteen quarter winds. Distance run at sea was estimated by the master or pilot from their experience of the ship in different conditions, using the timeglass as a measure of time. (The common log was not introduced until the sixteenth century.) The experienced seaman would be able to estimate the speed of the ship fairly accurately, based on his seaman's eye and notes on previous passages in differing wind and sea conditions. Leeway, the angle between the ship's fore-and-aft line and the wake, would be added or subtracted from the course steered to derive the course made good; a line with a wooden block on the end was sometimes towed astern to indicate the leeway angle. Because a sailing vessel's course is governed by the wind direction and it is seldom possible to maintain the same course throughout the voyage, it was important to keep an accurate record of the courses made good and the distances run. Estimates were normally made every hour, and at the end of each watch, or perhaps once a day, the pilot would calculate from the record the ship's progress toward its destination. The Mediterranean seaman had access to a set of what were in effect trigonometrical tables, the *toleta de marteloio*, first referred to by the Catalan mathematician Ramon Lull late in the thirteenth century. The tables, similar in concept to the modern traverse table, told the pilot how far the ship had diverged from the intended track for each of the quarter winds in a quadrant, and how far he had progressed along the intended track. A second part of the table gave him the distance along each of the quarter winds he would have to sail to regain the intended track. By the middle of the thirteenth century mathematical navigation was sufficiently advanced for the tables to be used outside the Mediterranean, but there is no hard evidence that they were. When altitude navigation was introduced by the Portuguese, the rules for "raising a degree," by means of which distance run was deduced from the course made good and the change in the sun's altitude, took the place of the *toleta*.

Although pilots had steered by the sun and stars from time immemorial, there is no evidence that astronomical navigation, in the sense of fixing position through observation of the sun and stars, was used in the Mediterranean before the seventeenth century, nor, within the confined limits of latitude of that sea, can there have been much call for it. The accuracy of dead reckoning in the Mediterranean from early on can be gauged by comparing the coastal outline of the Carte Pisane, slewed round a point to correct for the easterly variation, with a modern map of the area.

In 1317 King Dinis of Portugal appointed as hereditary admiral of his fleet the Genoese Manuel Pessagno, who brought with him a number of seamen skilled in the use of Mediterranean methods. There can be no doubt that by the time of the discoveries Portuguese pilots and masters would have been thoroughly familiar with Mediterranean dead-reckoning techniques. However, once they had passed Cape Bojador in 1435, beyond which was supposed to lie the sea of darkness, the Portuguese explorers found dead reckoning less and less adequate as they proceeded southward along the Atlantic coast of Africa. In uncharted waters, an indication of position only in relation to last known position presented problems, and the errors were of course cumulative. However, the crucial issue became the return from the Guinea coast to Portugal, since the most expeditious route, it was soon established, involved taking a long leg westward into the Atlantic to cross the northeast trades and pick up the variables more or less in the latitude of the Azores, a voyage that could take over two months out of sight of land. The route back, termed the *volta del mar*, varied according to the season, the intended landfall, and the point of departure.

That there were people in Portugal capable of adapting astronomy to the needs of navigation is shown by early tables, such as the 1339 Almanac of Coimbra. It seems more likely, however, that the initiative in this innovation came from pilots, who would undoubtedly have noticed the difference in altitude of the North Star at Lisbon and in Guinea. Latitude is of course defined by the elevation of the polestar, but the procedures introduced by Portuguese pilots in the 1450s to check distance sailed in a north-south direction between two observations of the North Star had nothing to do with establishing latitude, which indeed was not then marked on charts. The difference in angle between the two observations was to be multiplied by 16⅔ to give the linear distance in leagues (a figure later changed to 17½, still an underestimate). Observations were made with the seaman's quadrant, a simplified version of the astronomer's instrument, and in the early days of altura navigation, as it was called, it became the practice to mark on the scale the names of the various capes, islands, and landmarks whose star altitudes had been observed. At the same time, astronomers at home were compiling lists of latitudes, which by 1473 had reached the equator. It should be emphasized, however, that until latitude navigation was introduced after 1485 (when João II's mathematical commission worked out the procedures), altura navigation did not involve concepts of latitude.

The North Star does not of course lie on the axis of the earth's rotation, the pole of the sky, but describes a small circle in its counterclockwise path about it. This means that a correction has to be made to the altitudes observed to allow for the star's position in relation to the true pole, a correction that can be ascertained by the position of the Guard Stars in the Little Dipper (Ursa Minor). A mnemonic, in the form of an imaginary figure in the sky with the pole at his stomach, his head above, feet below, and outstretched arms left and right, had been used by the medieval seaman to help him remember the midnight positions of the Guards throughout the year; the mnemonic would be used to tell the time by Polaris. A similar mnemonic was now adapted to give the navigator the correction to the altitude of the North Star, originally when it was at the height of the true pole (as it would be twice every twenty-four hours) and later at any one of eight positions on its circle of declination. An observation would be made on departure, typically at Lisbon, and a further observation two or three days later when the Guards were in the same position relative to the star. Later versions of the Regiment (rule) of the North Star, as the instructions were called, gave the corrections in degrees and fractions of a degree, principally for measuring departure altitudes from points other than Lisbon.

As the equator was approached and finally crossed, in 1471, observations of the North Star became impossible, and although procedures were worked out for observing one of the circumpolar stars in the Southern Cross, the obvious body for these observations was now the sun. The sun, however, in its apparent path around the earth follows the ecliptic, not the equinoctial, and a daily correction must therefore be made to its noonday altitude to allow for its declination, the angular distance north or

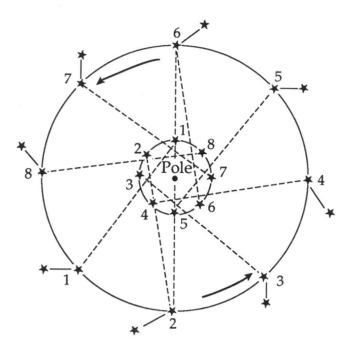

USE OF THE GUARD STARS. The relative positions of the two Guard Stars for different altitudes of the North Star.

JOURNAL OF THE INSTITUTE OF NAVIGATION, LONDON

south of the equator, or equinoctial. The practice had already developed of observing the sun to check linear distance traveled in a north-south direction, provided the observations were not more than a day or two apart—in other words, provided that the declination had not changed so as to significantly affect the result. Tables of the sun's declination had of course long been used by Iberian astronomer-astrologers, and in 1484 King João II of Portugal appointed a mathematical commission to look into the feasibility of using observations of the sun to determine latitude at sea. This was one of the most significant developments in the history of navigation and marks the foundation of positional astronomy. A leading member of the commission was José Vizinho, a Jewish scholar and former pupil of Abraham Zacuto. Vizinho, who had been a member of the commission that rejected Columbus's offer to the king of Portugal, was author, or perhaps editor, of the *Regimento do astrolabio e do quadrante*, the oldest surviving Portuguese navigation manual of which it seems likely hand-copies had been available to masters and pilots. Such copies would date from the 1480s, though the earliest known printed version is from 1509. The manual must have epitomized the conclusions of the mathematical commission and summarized the new navigational techniques. In 1485 Vizinho was sent on a voyage to Guinea (Columbus claims to have been on the same voyage) to test the practicability of the

procedures proposed for observing the sun and to check the values of declination from Zacuto's tables.

The surviving copy of the manual dating from 1509, known as the Manual of Munich, is in two parts, the second of which is a Portuguese translation of Johannes de Sacrobosco's treatise *De sphaera* (On the sphere), a thirteenth-century textbook on cosmography based on the *Almagest*. The first part contains instructions for determining latitude by the sun's meridian altitude, with seventeen examples differing according to whether the observer is north or south of the equator and whether the declination is north or south; rules for observing the North Star; rules for raising the pole (replacing the *toleta de marteloio*); a list of latitudes north of the equator; and a calendar for the year starting on March 1, with the sun's position within the signs of the zodiac and its daily declination. The next printed copy to survive, dating from circa 1519 and known as the manual of Evora, contains in addition rules for telling time by the North Star and instructions for finding the time of high water.

The rule for raising a degree became necessary when instead of sailing direct for a destination, the pilot would attempt to sail to a point one hundred leagues east or west of it and then sail along the altura (or latitude) to it. The rule, instead of dealing in terms of relative direction, as had the *toleta de marteloio*, told the pilot how far the ship must sail on each of the eight rhumbs to raise one degree and how far east or west it will have sailed in the process. The procedure at sea now became to observe the latitude daily, from sun or star, to record carefully the courses made good and estimated distances run, and to determine from the observed latitude and the mean course and distance sailed the distance made good east or west. It is possible that the introduction of latitude navigation, that is to say measurement of angular distance north or south of the equator, owed something to the publication about this time of Ptolemaic maps with a latitude scale. In any event, it quickly became apparent that, to get the full benefit of the new methods, latitude would have to be marked on the charts. This required a resurvey of the African coast based on dead reckoning and observed latitudes instead of on magnetic bearing and distance. In the 150 years following the doubling, or rounding, of Cape Bojador (1434), some three hundred miles of coastline had been surveyed each year, the results closely guarded in the Casa de India e Guinea in Lisbon, where the chief cosmographer to the king was responsible for keeping the master charts up to date and compiling sailing directions, almanacs, and manuals, as well as for training and certifying pilots.

The marine chart, to the seaman at least, was essentially a compass chart, on which the direction of the rhumbs corresponded with the rhumbs on his compass card. The compass was assumed to point true north, and, in spite of the convergence of the meridians, north-south lines on the chart were assumed to be parallel. Further, courses between points were assumed to be straight lines, not great circles. All this raised problems once a latitude scale was marked on the chart (the first was in 1502), for it became impossible to relate celestially observed latitudes with a chart based on bearing and distance. A solution attempted by the Portuguese cartographer Pedro Reinel on his 1504 chart of the North Atlantic was to provide an oblique meridian in the vicinity of Labrador to enable the seaman to reconcile his latitude with the direction of the coastline. But the seaman would have none of it; he expected the bearings on his chart to coincide with those on his compass. Columbus is credited with the first written mention of magnetic variation, but the language he uses ("northeasting" and "northwesting") is that of the Portuguese pilots, who could scarcely have failed to notice the phenomenon when they ran down the latitude to their destination. But it was little understood, was attributed to various causes, and its importance was underrated. It was not until 1538 that João de Castro would conclude that variation was not linked to longitude.

The sphericity of the earth had never been in doubt, and Sacrobosco's text printed in the navigation manuals gave a thorough description of it. But the plain chart still took no account of the fact that on a sphere north-south lines converge at the poles. In practice, however, pilots had to compensate for convergence; on the crossing from Brazil to the Cape of Good Hope, for example, it was the custom to increase the estimated distance sailed each day to compensate for chart error. Pedro Nunes, the Jewish mathematician and scholar who was cosmographer to the king of Portugal, in a tract in defense of the sea chart published in 1537, examined the problem of convergence and showed that on the sphere the direct line from one place to another is not a line of constant bearing, as it is on a plane surface. Rhumb lines, he showed, spiral toward the poles, but it was another fifty years before Gerardus Mercator published his world atlas on a projection that allowed the seaman to go on treating his rhumbs as straight lines.

There were numerous attempts in the early part of the sixteenth century to improve the instrumental accuracy of both the mariner's astrolabe, which was used largely for observations of the sun, and the seaman's quadrant; Nunes, in particular, applied his invention of the nonius (a contrivance for graduating mathematical instruments) to increase precision in reading the scale. It is difficult to assess the accuracy of either instrument at sea. The large astrolabe, such as the one Vasco da Gama used ashore at St. Helen's Bay in 1497, seems to have become at some point standard equipment for onshore observations, and

on that particular occasion it certainly proved its value. Of the instruments used at sea, smaller and generally of brass or bronze, all one can say with any certainty is that they proved accurate enough to enable the pilot to approach a destination on an east-west bearing so that he would eventually be able to identify landmarks. In 1499 Vasco da Gama brought back from the Indian Ocean the Arabic *kamal*, or *tavoletas de India*, as the Portuguese called it, a tablet of wood through which a knotted line was threaded and the tablet held, by means of the line, at a distance from the eye such that it just spans the space between the body observed and the horizon, thus giving the altitude. Pedro Álvares Cabral's pilot was charged with the mission of assessing the astrolabe, quadrant, and *kamal* on the first long voyage after Da Gama's return. His report on the *kamal* was unfavorable. However, another instrument based on the same principle, the forestaff, began to appear at sea in the early years of the sixteenth century. It was similar to but not identical with the Jacob's staff used by medieval surveyors and consisted of a wooden staff about a meter long with a movable crosspiece or transversal to measure the required angle of altitude. It seems to have been more popular with Spanish than with Portuguese seamen (except as used for measuring angular distances between the constellations), possibly because

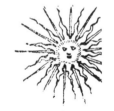

ORIZONTE

OBSERVING THE SUN. With the mariner's astrolabe. Earliest known illustration, from Pedro de Medina's *Regimento de navigacion*.

NATIONAL MARITIME MUSEUM, GREENWICH

Nunes had condemned its use, perhaps because of the ocular parallax error.

The early years of the sixteenth century witnessed the climax of Portuguese navigational achievements, and the works of Pedro Nunes, João de Castro (the chief pilot of the Portuguese Indies fleet), and Duarte Pacheco Pereira, whose *Esmeraldo de situ orbis* (1505) remains the classic guide to navigation at the time, are fitting monuments. Portuguese understanding of the wind and current systems of the ocean had enabled them to sail with confidence into the Atlantic and round the Cape to India and the Far East, and their observations of the sun and stars laid the foundation of astronomical navigation at sea. Systematic surveys of the African coast using observed latitudes increased the reliability and usefulness of the sea chart. Less than ten years after Columbus had discovered America, the Catholic monarchs, Fernando and Isabel, aware that the fate of the Indies would ultimately depend on the skill of the pilots in the Indies fleet, in 1502 established in Seville the Casa de la Contratación, the principal functions of which were the training and certification of pilots, the maintenance of the Padron Real (a master chart of all the known seas), and the inspection and certification of navigational instruments. The key figure in this enterprise was the pilot major, and over the next fifty years the position was held by a succession of distinguished navigators, including Juan de la Cosa, Amerigo Vespucci, and Sebastian Cabot. In 1519 the post of chief hydrographer was created, and four years later that of cosmographer, who was responsible for the manufacture of charts and navigating instruments. The first hydrographer was the eminent Portuguese cartographer Diogo Ribeiro, who in 1525 introduced a marked improvement in survey techniques in which positions were charted by observed latitudes and magnetic bearings corrected for variation.

The invention of printing led to a greater dissemination of navigational knowledge, both in the wider circulation of navigation manuals and in the ability to reproduce exact copies of charts in large numbers. The *Compasso da navigare*, the thirteenth-century pilot book, was first printed in Venice in 1490, and a rutter of the European coasts attributed to Cadamosto was printed in the same year. Columbus's letter to his sovereigns on his return from the first voyage was printed in Spanish that April, and four further editions were published within a year. The almost total lack of navigational works printed in Portugal during most of the sixteenth century explains why Portuguese nautical science, once so jealously guarded, was now, during the period of Spanish colonial expansion, disseminated largely by Portuguese cartographers, pilots, and shipmasters employed abroad. The first navigation manual to be printed in Spanish, Fernández de Enciso's

Suma de geographia (1518), which included sailing directions for American waters and which preserved the four-year solar declination tables prepared by Abraham Zacuto for Vasco da Gama's Indian voyage, was loosely based on a hand-copy of a work by the Portuguese Andres Pires. The second was an important work, *Tractado del esphera* (1535), by the Portuguese navigator Francisco Faleiro. With his brother Ruy, Faleiro had been closely involved with the navigational preparations for Magellan's circumnavigation. Pedro de Medina's *Arte de navegar* (1545) and Martin Cortés's *Breve compendio de la esfera e del arte de navegar* (1551) were both works of seminal importance to the development of navigation whose origins can be traced to the Portuguese manuals of Munich and Evora.

The problem of finding longitude would remain for another two hundred years, until the invention of the marine chronometer allowed time at sea to be treated as a measure of the earth's rotation. But there were attempts to solve the problem. Columbus twice, in 1494 and in 1504, observed lunar eclipses to this end using Zacuto's astronomical tables, but his objective was cosmographical rather than navigational. Vespucci claimed to have determined the longitude off the coast of Venezuela in 1499, but the claim is not generally credited. Magellan took with him instructions drawn up by Ruy Faleiro for determining longitude by lunar distances, and observations were made along the eastern seaboard of South America, but the results are not easily interpreted.

[See also *Altura Sailing; Dead Reckoning; Latitude; Longitude; Lunar Phenomena; Nautical Charts; Piloting; Solar Phenomena.*]

BIBLIOGRAPHY

Albuquerque, Luís de. *Astronomical Navigation.* Lisbon, 1988.

Albuquerque, Luís de. *Instruments of Navigation.* Lisbon, 1988.

Cortesão, Armando. *History of Portuguese Cartography.* 2 vols. Coimbra, 1969.

Da Costa, A. Fontoura. *A Marinharia dos descobrimentos.* Lisbon, 1933.

Hourani, G. F. *Arab Seafaring in the Indian Ocean in Ancient and Early Medieval Times.* Princeton, 1951.

Mota, Teixeira de. "Atlantic Winds and Ocean Currents in Portuguese Nautical Documents of the Sixteenth Century." *Proceedings of the Royal Society of Edinburgh,* section B, 23 (1972).

Pacheco Pereira, Duarte. *Esmeraldo de situ orbis.* Translated and edited by G. H. T. Kimble. London, 1937.

Randles, W. G. L. *Portuguese and Spanish Attempts to Measure Longitude in the 16th Century.* Coimbra, 1985.

Taylor, E. G. R. "The Navigating Manual of Columbus." *Journal of the Institute of Navigation* 5, no. 1 (1952): 42–54.

Taylor, E. G. R. *The Haven Finding Art: A History of Navigation from Odysseus to Captain Cook.* London, 1956.

Waters, David W. *The Rutters of the Sea.* New Haven and London, 1967.

Waters, David W. *Reflections upon Some Navigational and Hydrographic Problems of the XVth Century Related to the Voyage of Bartolomeu Dias, 1487–88.* Lisbon, 1988.

M. W. RICHEY

Instruments of Navigation

Navigation is an art and a craft as well as a science. People have regularly found their way across vast areas of sea without the benefit of any technological devices, using no other aids than their memory of traditional, codified star lore and local marine conditions, together with their own cumulative experience, as the Polynesians still did in very recent times. Even after the introduction of navigational instruments, seamanship still relied on the observation of winds and currents and other natural phenomena; as late as 1697, Martin Martin noted how the inhabitants of St. Kilda preferred to observe the direction of the flight of birds than to use a compass.

Very little is known about the practice of navigation in northern Europe and the Mediterranean region in early times. It may be inferred from Lucan's *Bellum civile* (A.D. 62 or 63) that observation of the stars in relation to the top of the mast and to the marine horizon was a navigational technique practiced in the Mediterranean. In addition to the polestar (at that time several degrees away from the celestial pole), Sirius, a bright star, may also have been important and may have been the original Stella Maris. Norse sagas refer to a *husanotra,* apparently a device used in navigation, but its nature and exact function remain unclear, as is the possible influence of the Northmen's open sea navigation in the North Atlantic upon that in more southerly latitudes. Most intentional sea voyages were coastal, only occasionally and briefly venturing out of sight of land. In northern Europe especially, the continental shelf and tidal waves encouraged the use of lead and line, probably the most ancient of navigational instruments. By the end of the thirteenth century, sailors on the Mediterranean could have used a chart, a magnetic compass, and sailing directions (written instructions for navigation in a particular area), and possibly a timeglass (sandglass). The Mediterranean is virtually tideless and there are many islands to provide stages or shelter during a voyage. To a large extent, sailing was concentrated during the summer months when the visibility was good and the sea tended to be calm. Sailing was by dead reckoning, that is, by attempting to determine the ship's position by calculation of the distance and direction traveled from the starting point. Directions were given in the sailing directions, according to the traditional wind directions, as winds, half-winds, or quarter-winds, and the distance sailed was measured by estimating the ship's speed and relating it to the time elapsed from departure.

But the determination of position at sea is pointless if there is no geographical framework to which it can be related. In the case of a sea such as the Mediterranean, almost entirely surrounded by land, the need was for accurate mapping of the coasts and the ports. Charts (it is customary to refer to land maps as "maps," and to sea maps as "charts") showing a network of lines radiating from a compass rose and parallel lines enabled a navigator to set a course from a port on one coast of the Mediterranean to a port on the opposite coast, using his magnetic compass to help him steer the ship along, or close to, one of these "rhumb" lines. The introduction to the Mediterranean seafaring community, during the latter part of the twelfth and during the thirteenth centuries, of the magnetic compass and the chart is, perhaps, the first important impact of a wider science and technology on the practical, traditional, world of the seaman, but the details of its impact remain obscure. When, in 1377, Ibn Khaldun (b. Tunis 1332; d. Cairo 1406) prepared the *Muqaddima,* the prolegomena to his universal history, he described the Mediterranean chart and its use, but added that nothing similar existed for the "Surrounding Sea" (the Atlantic Ocean) and therefore ships did not enter that sea because, if they lost sight of shore, they would be unlikely to find their way back.

As the Portuguese found when they began to explore as far as Guinea along the west coast of Africa in the fifteenth century, the winds and currents in the ocean were such as to encourage them to sail back to Portugal in a large arc toward the west, rather than to return by their outward, coastal, route; this was known as the Guinea track and later as the Elmina track. From about 1460, when sailing in the Atlantic Ocean out of sight of land, they adopted an elementary form of astronomical navigation. As they sailed northward, the sailors observed the polestar, measuring its altitude with the aid of a quadrant; when its altitude matched that observed at Lisbon, they then had merely to sail due east in order to reach Lisbon. This simple idea was beset with problems: possible invisibility of the polestar because the sky was overcast, errors in keeping to the required course because of wind or rough seas, and the fact that the polestar was not then as close to the true celestial pole as it is today. This last problem was resolved by ingenious mnemonic diagrams *(rodas)* giving the altitudes of the polestar at successive positions in its apparent rotation about the true pole. To enable a similar procedure to be used in daylight, tables of the midday position of the sun (solar declination), called *regimentos,* were produced. The astronomical techniques required for oceanic navigation, such as "running down the latitude" described above, were gradually refined and generalized.

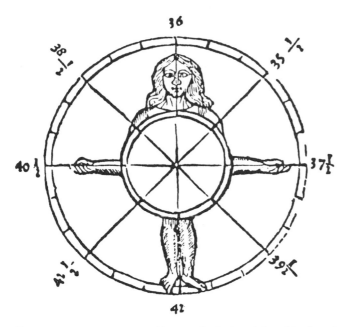

RODA DAS ALTURAS DO NORTE. Mnemonic device giving altitudes of the polestar at Lisbon. The head of the man represents north, and eight altitudes of the polestar on its circle of declination are given. From Valentim Fernandez's *Reportório dos tempos*, Lisbon, 1518.

When in 1497–1498 Vasco da Gama sailed around the Cape of Good Hope and by way of the east coast of Africa discovered, for Europeans, a sea-route to India, he took with him a number of quadrants and astrolabes, but we do not know whether the latter were traditional planispheric astrolabes or mariner's astrolabes. When he wished accurately to determine his latitude in the Bay of St. Helena, he set up his large astrolabe on land; this underlines the difficulty of using angular sighting instruments on the moving deck of a ship, a difficulty only partly overcome by averaging successive observations. At Malindi (present-day Kenya), Da Gama took on board a local, possibly Indian, navigator to guide him across the Indian Ocean; this navigator, no doubt fully cognizant of the traditional rutters in verse that were learned by heart, scorned Da Gama's instruments, saying that the only instrument used by his fellow navigators was a wooden tablet with a knotted string attached, now generally known as the *kamal,* an alternative approach to oceanic navigation despite the long tradition in Islamic lands of metal, angle-measuring instruments such as the astrolabe and the quadrant. In fact, any astronomer, Hellenistic or later, Islamic or European, from the time of Ptolemy of Alexandria (about A.D. 150) could have indicated to a mariner some form of altitude navigation, but the application of this knowledge required not only developments in cartography and its associated concepts, but also a

communication between astronomer and seaman that was rare in the early history of navigation. Other navigational problems that beset late medieval navigators venturing upon oceanic voyages were the varying magnetic declination (a magnetic needle, as in a marine compass, does not usually point to true geographical north because magnetic north lies to the east or west of true north and moves about over time) and the impossibility then of knowing longitude, the other coordinate apart from latitude required to determine a ship's position at sea. Magnetic variation was proposed by Edward Wright (1558–1615) in his preface to William Gilbert's *De magnete* (1600) as a means of determining longitude, and Galileo favored lunar distances, but it was the development of the marine chronometer that provided the practical solution. It was not until John Harrison constructed his chronometers in the mid-eighteenth century that this solution was achieved. However, the transportation of clocks for finding longitude (albeit on land) by comparing local time with standard time had been proposed as early as 1530 by Gemma Frisius in his *De principiis astronomicae et cosmographiae,* published at Louvain and Antwerp.

Accurate angular measurement, whether in the vertical plane (for solar and stellar observation) or in the horizontal (for azimuths), requires instruments. The few astronomical instruments and compasses available in the medieval period were not suited for use at sea on the deck of a moving vessel. From the end of the fifteenth century, adaptations of these instruments were devised for mariners. The *pilóto-mayor* (chief navigator) of the Casa de la Contratación (House of Commerce), founded in Seville in 1503, was charged, among other matters, with examining

THREE FIFTEENTH-CENTURY EQUINOCTIAL SUNDIALS. The middle example includes a compass needle. The instrument is oriented by use of its hour-ring and a compass.

MUSEUM OF THE HISTORY OF SCIENCE, OXFORD

and certifying instruments made by the navigators of the Casa. In 1523, it was found necessary to create the post of *cosmógrafo, maestro de hacer cartas, astrolabios y otros ingenios de navegación* (cosmographer, master of the manufacture of charts, astrolabes and other navigational devices). Practical navigators, therefore, were responsible for the supervision of the production and use of instruments, because in Spain, as in Portugal, the nature of the incentive to create an astronomical navigation and the absence of a nascent instrument-making industry resulted in the manufacture of nautical instruments remaining for some time in the hands of the practical navigators. In northern Europe, however, by the time the translation of Spanish nautical books brought astronomical navigation first to the Dutch and then to the English, specialist instrument-making workshops, which had proliferated for the manufacture of astrolabes, sundials, magnetic compasses, dividers, and other instruments for rich amateurs of science, land-travelers, surveyors, and mathematicians existed to fulfill the demand for navigational instruments and flourished from the latter part of the sixteenth century onward.

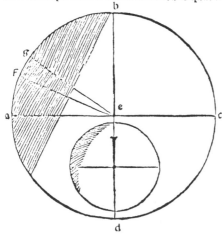

faber o que correram as sombras polla distancia que ha a hum pō to firo: τ faremos nossa obseruação per esta arte. Tomaremos a altura do sol pello estrelabio: τ na lamina das sombras.a.b.c.d. que no centro.e.tem o estilo perpendicular: notaremos o lugar da circuferencia que a sombra nos amostra: o qual seja neste exemplo. ho pōto.f.per quātes graes se apartado ponto.d. como faziamos no outro modo de tomar a altura do polo: ymaginando q̄ a agulha nos amostra ho meridiano posto que assi nā seja: τ situaremos o sol no globo como cōuē: τ dahi apouco espaço de tēpo é que a sombra faça mudança sensiuel: tornaremos a tomar o sol pello estrelabio: τ notar outra vez o lugar da sombra q̄ seja no ponto.g. τ situaremos segūda vez ho sol em seu lugar no globo: ou começādo do meridiano jmaginario como ao principio: ou

ESTORMENTO DE SOMBRAS. As illustrated and discussed in Pedro Nunes's *Tratado da sphera* (Lisbon, 1537). A horizontal plate, *a, b, c, d*, has an inset compass. In the center, at *e*, is a vertical style that casts a shadow of the sun on a scale of degrees around the circumference of the plate (the lines *ef* and *eg* show possible positions of the shadow). The compass has a south-pointing needle.

The voyages of Christopher Columbus occurred between the beginnings of the use of any reliable instrument in oceanic navigation and the serious attempts to improve upon this primitive situation, as when João de Castro tried an instrument *(estormento de sombras)* newly designed by Pedro Nunes in the course of his journey to Goa in 1538 (Armando Cortesão and Luís de Albuquerque, eds., *Obras completas de D. João de Castro,* vol. 1, Coimbra, 1968, pp. 115ff.). Columbus certainly used a quadrant, marine compasses, charts, timeglasses, log and line, lead and line, and probably portable sundials, and he had with him an "astrolabio" on the first voyage, but of what type remains unknown. All of these, with the exception of the quadrant and the astrolabe, formed part of a navigator's equipment from the beginning of the twelfth century onward. However, the mariners for whom *Le grand routier et pilotage* of Pierre Garcie (dated in May 1438; the earliest known printed edition dates only from 1521) was written had no chart, though it was assumed that they had lead and line and a compass. The quadrant, no doubt, was part of Columbus's Portuguese background, for despite his Genoese origins and his later association with the Spanish court, Columbus was a Portuguese navigator in training, experience, and exploratory aims. Evidence of this is found in the detailed analyses of his language by Consuelo Varela and by R. J. Penny.

[See also *Armillary Sphere; Astrolabe; Compass; Cross-Staff; Kamal; Lead and Line; Quadrant; Timeglass.*]

BIBLIOGRAPHY

Albuquerque, Luís de. "Astronomical Navigation" and "Instruments for Measuring Altitude and the Art of Navigation." In vol. 2 of *History of Portuguese Cartography*, edited by Armando Cortesão. Agrupamento de estudos de cartografia antiga, vol. 8. Coimbra, 1971.

Fontoura da Costa, A. *A marinharia dos descobrimentos.* 2d ed. Lisbon, 1939.

Godinho, Vitorino Magalhães. "Navegação oceánica e origens da náutica astronómica." Reprinted in vol. 1 of *Ensaios,* pp. 179–227. Lisbon, 1968.

Ife, B. W., ed. and trans. *Christopher Columbus. Journal of the First Voyage (Diario del primer viaje) 1492. Together with an Essay on Columbus's Language by R. J. Penny.* Warminster, 1990.

Maddison, Francis. *Medieval Scientific Instruments and the Development of Navigational Instruments in the XVth and XVIth Centuries.* Agrupamento de estudos de cartografia antiga, vol. 30. Coimbra, 1969.

Marcus, G. J. *The Conquest of the North Atlantic.* Woodbridge, Suffolk, 1980.

Poulle, Emmanuel. *Les conditions de la navigation astronomique au XVe siècle.* Agrupamento de estudos de cartografia antiga, vol. 27. Coimbra, 1969.

Taylor, E. G. R. *The Haven-Finding Art: A History of Navigation from Odysseus to Captain Cook.* Rev. ed. London, 1971.

Turner, Anthony. *Early Scientific Instruments: 1400–1800.* London, 1987.

Varela, Consuelo, ed. *Cristóbal Colón: Textos y documentos completos. Relaciones de viajes, cartas y memoriales.* Madrid, 1982.

FRANCIS MADDISON

NEW SEVILLE. See *Settlements,* article on *Sevilla la Nueva.*

NIÑA. Columbus's favorite ship, *Niña,* was a caravel and smallest of the three ships of his first voyage of discovery. After *Santa María,* his flagship, was wrecked on a reef just off the northern coast of La Española on Christmas morning, 1492, he transferred to *Niña* and made her his flagship for the return voyage to Spain. Despite encountering two fierce storms en route, she safely carried him home with the triumphant, world-changing news of his historic discoveries. In an entry in his log on February 12, 1493, Columbus states, "If she had not been very staunch and well found, I fear we would have been lost."

On departure from Palos, Spain, on August 3, 1492, at the start of the first voyage, *Niña* sailed with the traditional lateen rig of most caravels. With their triangular sails gracefully set on long slanting yards, these sharp-ended, light-displacement caravels were fast, maneuverable, and capable of sailing close to the wind, making them relatively independent of the variable directions of coastal winds. Having earlier participated in Portuguese voyages of discovery along the Atlantic coast of Africa, Columbus knew of the prevailing east to west trade winds at the latitude of the Canary Islands, from which he planned to take his departure on a westerly course to the Indies. With the wind coming from astern, the triangular lateen sails were less effective and far more difficult to handle than square sails. Accordingly, on arrival at the Canary Islands, he converted *Niña* to a "carabela redonda," a class of ship with rigging similar to the *Pinta*'s, with square sails on mainmast and foremast but retaining the small lateen mizzen to help in retaining much of her ability to sail to windward.

A bowsprit, an unnecessary appendage with the lateen rig but an important adjunct to the square rig, was also installed to accommodate a headstay for the new foremast and the bowlines of both the foresail and mainsail. Bowlines were attached by means of a bridle at about the midpoint of the two vertical edges of the square sails and led as far forward as possible. The purpose of the bowlines, in conjunction with the tack lines, was to haul forward the leading edges of the two sails to both flatten and steady them to improve the ship's ability to sail as close as possible into the wind.

Niña's registered name was *Santa Clara* after the patron saint of Moguer where she had been constructed. Such religious names were typical of Spanish ships of the period. Also typical was her nickname *Niña,* the feminization of the name of her popular master and owner, Juan Niño of Moguer. As with all ships built prior to the seventeenth century, no original plans or even sketches of the *Niña* exist. More is known about *Niña* than about any other ship of the period, however. This is principally because of the *Libro de armadas,* a four-hundred-page bundle of handwritten documents discovered in the Archive of the Indies in Seville by Eugene Lyon in 1986. It records the complete bill of lading of *Niña* for her 1498 resupply voyage to the colony at Santo Domingo, capital of La Española. Lyon calculated this 1498 lading to be just over fifty-two tons. It also has been documented that on a commercial voyage to Rome in 1497, she carried a cargo of fifty-one tons. Michele da Cuneo, a Genoese nobleman who accompanied Columbus aboard *Niña* in the exploration of Cuba and Jamaica during the second voyage, recorded in his excellent historical account that *Niña* was "about 60 tons," a figure that probably reflects her maximum capacity. For the 1498 voyage, *Niña* had a small fourth mast, a lateen-rigged countermizzen, stepped on her stern aft of the mizzenmast.

The Portuguese *Livro nautico* is considered to be the best source of information on the dimensional proportions and general characteristics of a typical caravel of the Columbus period. Capt. José María Martinez–Hidalgo, Spain's foremost authority on Columbus's ships and former director of the Maritime Museum in Barcelona, bases his design of *Niña* on this source and uses ratios of 1 for beam, 2.4 for length of keel, and 3.33 for length of hull. Master shipwrights of the period would know from personal and inherited experience that to carry a cargo of no more than sixty tons, a ship of the caravel type should have roughly the following dimensions: beam, twenty-one feet; length of keel, fifty feet (21 × 2.4); length of hull, seventy feet (21 × 3.33); and draft of slightly less than six feet.

Contrary to a few reports that have been ridiculed by most maritime historians, *Niña* had a full-length main deck, which extended from bow to stern. Her sheer line forward was unbroken by any raised forecastle deck such as had been constructed on *Pinta.* Since *Niña* was still lateen-rigged when she left Palos, such an elevated structure at the bow would have obstructed the free movement of the lower end of her long slanting main yard from one side of the ship to the other. From *Niña*'s remarkable success at repeatedly surviving severe storms on each of her three voyages to the New World, it seems

MODEL OF NIÑA. By José María Martinez-Hidalgo.

MUSEU MARÍTIM DE BARCELONA

BIBLIOGRAPHY

Fonseca, Quirino da. *A Carvela Portuguesa.* 2 vols. Lisbon, 1973.
Martinez-Hidalgo, José Mariá. *Columbus' Ships.* Barre, Mass., 1966.

WILLIAM LEMOS

NIÑO, JUAN (fl. late 1400s), owner and master of *Niña.* Niño was a leading member of one of the most respected seafaring families of Moguer, all of whom were strong supporters of Columbus. Their social and economic status in Moguer was comparable to that of the Pinzón family in Palos. As with the Pinzóns, the willingness of the Niños to join Columbus in his effort to find the Indies by sailing west across the Mar Tenebroso (Dark Sea) strongly influenced local seamen to overcome their reluctance to sign on for such a dubious venture.

Eldest of three brothers who participated in the first voyage, Juan Niño owned *Niña* and sailed aboard her as master. The official name of his caravel was *Santa Clara,* but, as was customary, the ship was always referred to by her nickname, *Niña.* This use of the feminine form of the owner's family name was a typical reflection of the affection and respect in which Juan Niño was held by all with whom he sailed. He is reported to have been Columbus's favorite shipmate. It is easy to understand how such a relationship might have developed aboard *Niña* during her encounter with two fierce storms while homeward bound on the first voyage. Her survival was evidence of superb seamanship, to which the veteran Juan Niño undoubtedly contributed in full measure. As a demonstration of his respect, Columbus reportedly took Niño with him on the triumphant journey from Seville across Spain to the royal court in Barcelona at the conclusion of the first voyage.

Another incident that may have contributed to their mutual respect occurred in mid-October 1492. The crewmen of all three ships, having been at sea for two months since departing Palos, had given up hope of finding land to the west and had become fearful for their lives. Because of the incessant easterly winds prevailing in the ocean, the crewmen believed that if they went any farther to the west they could never make it back to Spain against the head winds they assumed would be opposing them. Niño is reported to have joined with the masters of the other two ships to report these fears to the Admiral. It is not recorded whether the three masters themselves shared that fear, but it was appropriate for them to make known to the fleet commander the concerns of the crews. The Admiral, attempting to assuage their anxiety, replied that God had given them these favorable winds and would give them other favorable winds to return. He then suggested

that she did not suffer from the absence of a raised forecastle. Like *Pinta,* however, she had a raised half deck aft of the mainmast.

Access to the hold was provided by two center-line hatches in the main deck. The main cargo hatch in the waist, just forward of the mainmast, was of a size such that a wine tun (barrel) of 1 meter by 1.5 meters could be lowered through it. A second smaller hatch was located aft under the half deck. Both hatches were fitted with covers to prevent heavy seas sweeping over the deck from pouring into the hold. Her hold was open from stem to stern with no watertight bulkheads to control flooding.

The excavation by the Institute of Nautical Archaeology during the 1980s of the remains of two discovery-era caravels wrecked by severe storms in the Caribbean, one on Molasses Reef in the Turks and Caicos islands and the other at Highborn Cay in the Bahamas, has provided important construction details not previously available. This new information, combined with documented rules of thumb used by shipwrights of the Age of Discovery, has made it possible to construct a more authentic replica of caravels of the period than could be done in the past.

that they might set a limit of three or four days and hold to the course they were following; if they did not sight land within that time, they could turn back if they wished. With this agreement they continued their voyage, and within that time they found land.

Niña was one of the twenty ships composing the armada of the second voyage, and Niño sailed again as her master, departing the Bay of Cádiz on September 25, 1493, only six months after returning from the first voyage. After their arrival, Columbus decided that, for his planned exploration of Cuba in the spring of 1494, he needed a fast, maneuverable caravel of shallow draft as his flagship rather than the large and cumbersome *Mariagalante* in which he had sailed from Spain. He chose his old favorite, *Niña,* and purchased her from Niño, who then decided to return to Spain in one of the ships being sent back for additional provisions. Regrettably, from that time onward, the historical record of this respected seafarer is blank.

BIBLIOGRAPHY

Gould, Alicia B. *Nueva lista documentada de los tripulantes de Colón en 1492.* Madrid, 1984.

Irving, Washington. *The Life and Voyages of Christopher Columbus and His Companions.* 3 vols. New York, 1849.

WILLIAM LEMOS

NIÑO, PERALONSO (fl. late 1400s), chief pilot of *Santa María.* Member of a respected seafaring family from Moguer, Niño was well known in the seaport region of Huelva, Moguer, and Palos and very helpful to Columbus in overcoming the initial refusal by seafaring men in the three villages to be led by this unknown foreigner who proposed to reach Cipangu (Japan) and Cathay (China) by sailing west across the Mar Tenebroso (Dark Sea). Although most of the official records of the second voyage have been lost, it is believed that Niño also accompanied the Admiral on the outward-bound portion of that voyage, returning to Spain with the fleet of Antonio de Torres on March 7, 1494. He next participated in a 1496 voyage of two caravels and a nao, which he commanded, laden with provisions for the colony at La Isabela, then capital of La Española.

Niño arrived there early in July and delivered a message from the Spanish sovereigns ordering that the capital be transferred from La Isabela on the north coast to a new colony to be established on the south coast, which became present-day Santo Domingo. He also delivered a letter from the Admiral stating that the slave trade could continue provided that the Indians were genuine prisoners of war. Accordingly, three hundred Indians, all designated as "prisoners," were rounded up and sent to market

in Spain aboard Niño's ships. The proceeds of their sale were used by Bishop Juan Rodríguez de Fonseca, agent of the Crown, to help finance Columbus's third voyage.

In mid-1499, Bishop Fonseca authorized a number of adventurers to undertake privately funded expeditions to the New World. Peralonso Niño was quick to respond to this opportunity and, like Alonso de Ojeda before him, sought financial support from wealthy merchants in Seville. The only merchant who was willing to provide the necessary funds was Luis Guerra, but his offer was conditional: his brother, Cristóbal Guerra, must be in command of the expedition. Niño's financial condition was such that his only recourse was to accept a subordinate position on his own expedition.

Early in June 1499, Niño sailed from the port of Palos in a small caravel of only fifty tons burden, manned by a crew of thirty-three men. His landfall on the unnamed southern continent was only a short distance from that of Columbus, whose route he had followed. Proceeding to the northwest through the Gulf of Paria and entering the Caribbean, he headed directly for the island of Margarita, just off the northeast coast of present-day Venezuela, which Columbus had reported as being rich in pearls. Finding the natives hospitable and the pearls beautiful, large, and plentiful, the crew remained there for several weeks.

Accounts of the voyage by early historians indicate that, after amassing a substantial quantity of pearls, Guerra and Niño proceeded along the coast to the west for an unspecified but probably short distance. At their first attempt to go ashore, they were confronted by hostile Indians who had previously been stirred up by the belligerent Ojeda. Guerra, who had wisely permitted the more experienced Niño to exercise de facto command of the expedition, insisted at this point on a hasty retreat and departure with their precious cargo from this hostile coast. After an uneventful voyage home, they reached Spain early in February 1500.

On February 13, 1502, Peralonso Niño sailed once again from Cádiz as chief pilot of the flagship of a magnificent fleet of thirty ships carrying twenty-five hundred mariners, colonists, and men-at-arms to Santo Domingo, the new capital of La Española. Aboard the flagship was Nicolás de Ovando, newly appointed governor of the Indies. The outward-bound passage was uneventful, but the attempted return voyage was a disaster. Ignoring a timely warning by Columbus of an approaching hurricane, Ovando ordered the fleet to sail. The ill-fated ships had just entered the Mona Passage between La Española and Puerto Rico when the hurricane struck. Several ships capsized at sea, and most of those that survived the initial burst of fury were driven ashore and pounded to bits. Only five of the thirty ships survived. Over five hundred men were lost, among them the fleet commander, Antonio de Torres, and his chief pilot, Peralonso Niño.

BIBLIOGRAPHY

Gould, Alicia B. *Nueva lista documentada de los tripulantes de Colón en 1492*. Madrid, 1984.
Irving, Washington. *The Life and Voyages of Christopher Columbus and His Companions*. 3 vols. New York, 1849.

WILLIAM LEMOS

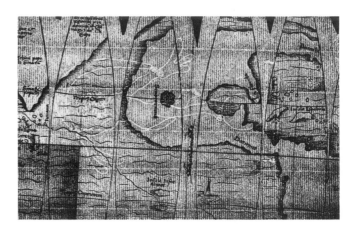

GLOBE GORES FOR THE "AMBASSADORS' GLOBE." Nürnberg, circa 1530. Detail, showing a northwest passage (as a long strait running east to west along upper right side of image).

NORTHWEST PASSAGE. As merchants and explorers came gradually to realize that America formed a separate continent between Europe and the East, they took up the search for the Northwest Passage to Asia. England, because it was excluded from sharing in the riches of eastern commerce by the prior discoveries and monopolistic claims of Spain and Portugal, based on the terms of the Treaty of Tordesillas (1494), was particularly interested in a northern route. "There is left one way to discover, which is unto the North," the merchant adventurer Robert Thorne the Younger wrote in an address to King Henry VIII in 1531.

The first voyage in search of the Northwest Passage apparently was that of Sebastian Cabot for Henry VIII in 1508–1509, but contemporary records are sparse. J. A. Williamson suggests that Cabot may have sailed through Hudson Strait into Hudson Bay, which he believed to be open ocean on the route to the East. The evidence rests partly on Cabot's later claims to have discovered the Northwest Passage and also on maps that appear to show the discovery, the earliest being a woodcut globe made in about 1530 in Nürnberg. It is depicted in a portrait of ambassadors at Hampton Court in England, painted by Hans Holbein in 1533. The Northwest Passage appears on the globe as a long strait between America and Asia, with its eastern entrance located about 50° to 55°N.

The globe appears to have been the prototype for a series of maps and globes showing a northwest "Fretum arcticum sive fretum trium fratrum" (Arctic strait or strait of the three brothers). The three have been identified as the Côrte-Real brothers, Portuguese explorers of Labrador in 1500–1501.

The most influential works were those of Gemma Frisius, the Flemish geographer, and his celebrated pupil Gerardus Mercator. Their terrestrial globes (Gemma's, 1536; Mercator's, 1541) became well known in England. Gemma Frisius's globe depicting the "Fretum trium fratum" came to be accepted as an authoritative record of Cabot's discovery of the Northwest Passage. Cabot's own world map, revised and published in London in 1549, was on display in Queen Elizabeth's gallery in Whitehall in the

1560s and was consulted by promoters of northern exploration. Upon returning to England in 1547 after forty years in Spanish service, Cabot was hailed as the leading expert on Arctic exploration.

In the 1560s plans for the discovery and exploration of the Northwest Passage were taken up with Sir Humphrey Gilbert, the leading promoter. His manuscript *Discourse of a Discoverie for a Newe Passage to Cataia* (1566) set out proof of the existence of a northwest, as opposed to a northeast, passage. Published in 1576, the *Discourse* was illustrated by a reduced version of a large world map of 1564 prepared by Ortelius (Abraham Oertel), which shows an easy route into the Pacific. The publication was intended to encourage the newly founded Company of Cathay, which dispatched Martin Frobisher's three expeditions (1576, 1577, 1578), the first to be sent to the northwest in the reign of Elizabeth I.

In 1576 the discovery of the so-called Frobisher Strait seemed to open a passage to the Pacific. The strait was in fact an inlet, now known as Frobisher Bay, on the coast of Baffin Island. The queen named the newly discovered land "Meta Incognita" (Unknown Goal). The second voyage (1577) was a more elaborate operation, in which the queen invested a thousand pounds. One of its aims was to extract ore, samples of which had been brought back from the first voyage. The enterprise had become a treasure hunt. The third voyage in 1578 carried 120 colonists in eleven ships to establish a mining settlement, but that plan was aborted by a shipwreck. Seeking to regain the Frobisher Strait, he made a new discovery by sailing two hundred leagues into Hudson Strait, which he called "The Mistaken Straightes." It seemed to be "the passage which we seeke to find to the rich countrey of Cathaya."

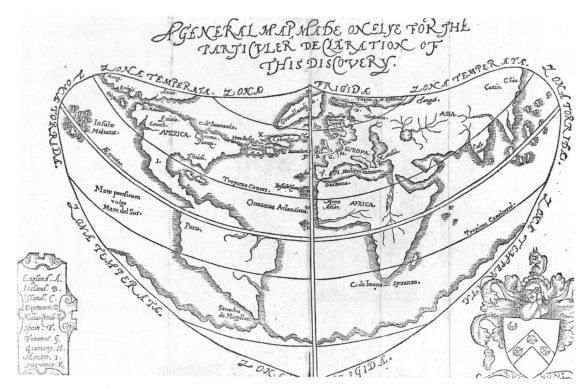

WORLD MAP FROM SIR HUMPHREY GILBERT'S *DISCOURSE*, 1576. A passage to the Pacific can be seen in the upper left corner of the map.

Frobisher returned with more supplies of ore, but the previous samples had proved to be worthless. The Company of Cathay and its financial promoter, Michael Lok, were bankrupt. Interest in the voyages, however, prompted a spate of publications in England and abroad. Dionyse Settle's account of the second voyage (1577) was issued in three foreign editions. George Best's *True Discourse,* an account of the three voyages published in London in 1587, has been described as a manual of "Arctic seamanship."

Of special interest were the reports of Eskimos (Inuits). One had been brought home from the first voyage in 1576, and three from the second in 1577. Their Asiatic appearance encouraged the belief in the Northwest Passage. Michael Lok described the Eskimo as Frobisher's "strange man of Cathay." Drawings of individuals and scenes from the second voyage made the Eskimos famous throughout Europe, and they gained ethnographical significance as the stereotype of exotic peoples. William C. Sturtevant and David B. Quinn comment that these Eskimos are rare examples of named individuals whose portraits have come to typify whole populations.

Frobisher's discoveries suggested two possible routes, which are depicted on the maps in Best's *Discourse.* The world map illustrating the first voyage shows "Frobusshers Straightes" as a wide channel between America and one of Mercator's mythical polar islands. On the map of the North Atlantic, perhaps by James Beare, illustrating the third voyage, "The Mistaken Straightes" lie immediately north of the continent, and "Frobisshers Streights" are marked farther to the north between the islands of Meta Incognita. The landmass of Greenland is depicted still farther north.

This map helps explain a major cartographic error by which Frobisher Strait and Meta Incognita came to be displaced from North America to Greenland. The maps Frobisher took with him, "Carta de navegar de Nicolo et Antonio Zeni . . . MCCCLXXX" published in 1558 and Mercator's world chart of 1569, mark to the south of the latitude of Iceland the nonexistent island of Frisland (a duplicate of Iceland) and locate the southern tip of Greenland at 65°40' instead of 59°45' N. Thus Frobisher identified his first landfall as being on Frisland, whereas it was near Cape Farewell on the southern tip of Greenland. Best's map shows "West-Ingland olim West Friseland" in mid-Atlantic and fits Greenland into the north of America.

For the next three hundred years Frobisher Strait and Meta Incognita were depicted in southern Greenland. Their true location remained unknown until the American explorer Capt. C. F. Hall, on an expedition in 1861–1862,

ESKIMO SCENE. From Dionyse Settle's account (Nürnberg, 1580) of Frobisher's second voyage. The father, mother, and child shown on the shore are the three Eskimos brought to London in 1577.

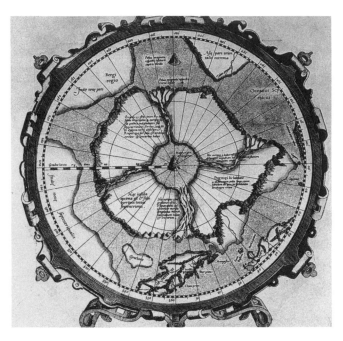

GERARDUS MERCATOR'S WORLD MAP OF 1569. Inset, showing polar regions.

identified with the help of the Eskimos the site of Meta Incognita from relics on Kodlunarn Island, which means "white man's island."

The three voyages of John Davis in 1585, 1586, and 1587 had their origin in plans of the geographer John Dee to exploit Sir Humphrey Gilbert's rights to American lands north of 50° N. Dee abandoned the project, but his associate Adrian Gilbert of Sandridge, Devon, Sir Humphrey's brother, obtained the patent for discovery. Davis, also of Sandridge, sailed as navigator, and William Sand-

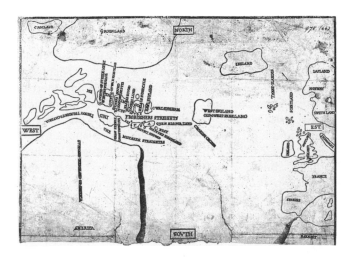

MAP OF FROBISHER'S DISCOVERIES. From George Best's *True Discourse of the Late Voyages of Discoverie*, 1578.

erson, the London merchant, provided the financing.

On the first voyage, in 1585, Davis sailed up the strait named after him to 66°40' N, which he found clear of ice. He reported to Sir Francis Walsingham, secretary of state, that "the northwest passage is a matter nothyne doubtful . . . the sea nauigable, voyd of yse, the ayre tollerable, and the waters very depe." On the second voyage the next year, he returned to the strait without gaining much new information. On the third, in 1587, he reached his farthest point north, naming it Hope Sanderson at 72°49' N. Crossing the strait, he came upon "a very great gulfe," which was Hudson Strait. Without realizing it he had rediscovered Frobisher's "Mistaken Straightes" of 1578. On his return, he reported to Sanderson that at 73° he had found the sea all open: "The passage is most certaine, the execution most easie." Davis had in fact discovered the entrance to Lancaster Sound, where the Northwest Passage begins.

Davis gave a report of his voyages in *The Worldes Hydrographical Description* (London, 1595). For a record of his discoveries he referred the reader to the terrestrial globe of Emery Molyneux, which was published in 1592 at Sanderson's expense. The globe shows the northern outlet of Davis Strait as the only route available for a northwest passage. Frobisher's discoveries are marked in southern Greenland. The globe thus makes clear why Davis never realized that he was sailing in the same region as Frobisher and had rediscovered the same strait and bays.

In the early years of the seventeenth century the search

TERRESTRIAL GLOBE OF EMERY MOLYNEUX, 1592. Detail, showing a northwest passage and the discoveries of John Davis.

for the Northwest Passage centered on Hudson Strait. In 1602 George Weymouth sailed to the northwest for the English East India Company (founded in 1600), carrying letters from Elizabeth to the emperor of China. He explored Frobisher Strait, proving it to be a bay, and noted the current from Hudson Strait.

In 1610 Henry Hudson set out to explore the inlets of Davis Strait. He passed through Hudson Strait into Hudson Bay; he saw the bay as a spacious sea and thought he had found the passage. The expedition wintered in James Bay. The men mutinied, and Hudson was set adrift and never seen again. The survivors on their return reported that they had found the passage.

Thomas Button and Robert Bylot, who had been on Hudson's voyage, returned to Hudson Bay in 1612 to look for him. After navigating the west coast of the bay, they realized they had not found a passage. Bylot sailed again in 1615 with William Baffin as chief pilot and explored Baffinland. In 1616 Baffin and Bylot searched Davis Strait and reported it to be a great bay. This phase of exploration ended with the separate expeditions of Capt. Luke Foxe of Hull and Thomas James of Bristol to Hudson Bay, where they encountered each other in 1631.

The English voyages in search of the Northwest Passage had been pursued with great determination under the harshest of conditions. Thomas Blundeville, the mathematician, commented on Arctic voyages in 1613, "I can greatly commend those valiant mindes that doe attempt such desperate voyages, and the rather when they doe it for knowledge sake, and profit their Countrey, and not altogether for private gaine and lucre."

Admiral Sir William Monson made a more practical assessment in his "Discourse Concerning the North-west Passage," revised for publication before his death in 1643: "If the passage be found, I confess there is something gained in the distance, but nothing in the navigation. . . . Little good is like to ensue of it, because of the hazard of cold, of ice, and of unknown seas." Recommending the route via the Cape of Good Hope, he wrote, "Let me now appeal to the opinion of any mariner whether it were not better for a man to sail six thousand leagues in a certain and known navigation. . .than three thousand in an uncertain sea as we shall find to the northward."

The Northwest Passage nevertheless remained a dominant feature of the world map, and the straits captured the imagination even of the poets. John Donne, referring to the western end of the passage, the Strait of Anian, wrote, probably in 1623:

CAPTAIN LUKE FOXE'S POLAR MAP. Showing path of his voyage to Hudson's Bay, where he met the expedition of Thomas James in 1631.

Is the Pacific Sea my home? Or are
The eastern riches? Is Jerusalem?
Anyan, and Magellan, and Gibraltar,
All straits, and none but straits, are ways to them,
Whether where Japhet dwelt, or Cham, or Shem.
  ("Hymn to God my God, in my Sicknesse," 1635)

[See also *Canada*.]

BIBLIOGRAPHY

Cumming, W. P., R. A. Skelton, and D. B. Quinn. *The Discovery of North America*. London, 1971.

Monson, William. "Sir William Monson's Naval Tracts." In *A Collection of Voyages and Travels,* edited by A. Churchill and J. Churchill, vol. 3. London, 1732.

Quinn, D. B., ed. *New American World: A Documentary History of North America to 1612*. New York, 1975.

Skelton, R. A. *Explorers' Maps*. London, 1958.

Sturtevant, William C., and David B. Quinn. "This New Prey: Eskimos in Europe in 1567, 1576, and 1577." In *Indians and Europe,* edited by Christian F. Feest. Aachen, 1987.

Wallis, Helen. "England's Search for the Northern Passages in the Sixteenth and Early Seventeenth Centuries." In *Unveiling the Arctic,* edited by Louis Rey. Calgary, 1984. Also in *Arctic* 37 (1984): 453–472.

Williamson, J. A. *The Cabot Voyages and British Discovery under Henry VII*. Cambridge, 1962.

HELEN WALLIS

NUEVA CÁDIZ. See *Settlements*, article on *Nueva Cádiz*.

NÚÑEZ CABEZA DE VACA, ALVAR. See *Cabeza de Vaca, Alvar Núñez*.

NÚÑEZ DE BALBOA, VASCO. See *Balboa, Vasco Núñez de*.

O

OJEDA, ALONSO DE (1466–c. 1515), ship's captain and squadron commander. Ojeda was one of the many gentlemen adventurers who eagerly accompanied Columbus on the second voyage, anticipating excitement and riches. He soon distinguished himself both afloat and ashore by his boldness and energy. He was a native of Cuenca and had been brought up as a page in the service of the Duke of Medinacelli, one of the most powerful nobles in Spain and an important ally of Fernando and Isabel in their efforts to expel the Moors from Spain. Ojeda, ever ambitious, made good and frequent use of his close connections with the nobility.

After the seventeen ships of the second voyage reached the north coast of La Española and a new settlement named La Isabela had been established, Columbus placed Ojeda in command of an expedition into the interior to find the long-sought mines of Cibao, reported by the Indians to be rich in gold. Immediately after participating in the first Mass to be celebrated in the New World on January 6, 1494, the Feast of the Epiphany, Ojeda set off. Two weeks later he returned with enough samples of gold to cause Columbus to write to the sovereigns that he hoped soon to "be able to give them as much gold as the iron mines of Biscay." Unfortunately, while leading a second expedition into the interior, the impulsive Ojeda overzealously punished a cacique (native chief) and two other Indians for a minor infraction. "This," wrote Bartolomé de las Casas, author of *Historia de las Indias*, "was the first injustice, with vain and erroneous pretension of doing justice, that was committed in these Indies against the Indians, and the beginning of the shedding of blood, which has since flowed so copiously in this island." Despite this rash act, Ojeda retained the trust of Columbus and later was instrumental in putting down a strong uprising by the Indians.

Ojeda did not accompany Columbus on his third voyage, being ambitious to gain a command of his own. As a welcome visitor to the royal court, he was able to read letters from Columbus recounting his discovery of the island of Trinidad and the mainland coast of present-day Venezuela, glowingly described as abounding in drugs and spices, gold and silver, and pearls. Excited by these tidings, Ojeda sought authorization to undertake a voyage of discovery to this new region. Bishop Juan Rodríguez de Fonseca, principal agent of the Crown in managing the affairs of the Indies and no friend of Columbus, promptly granted Ojeda a commission to trespass on the Admiral's domain. With the avid assistance of wealthy merchants in Seville, Ojeda soon equipped a squadron of four ships at Puerto de Santa María near Cádiz. He chose Juan de la Cosa, famed for his 1500 chart of the New World, as his chief pilot. Also joining him on the voyage was Amerigo Vespucci whose widely published account of this voyage, falsely dated two years early without mention of Ojeda, resulted in the New World being named America.

Departing Puerto de Santa María on May 20, 1499, Ojeda, although trying to adhere to Columbus's course, made landfall about six hundred miles southeast of the point where Columbus had first sighted South America. From this point Ojeda sailed along the coast to the northwest, stopped briefly at Trinidad, and making use of a chart of the area drawn by Columbus, passed through the Gulf of Paria into the Caribbean and proceeded along the coast to the west. Like Columbus, he neglected to avail himself of a treasure trove of large and beautiful pearls available in quantity along the shores of the island of Margarita just off the north coast of Venezuela. Instead, he chose to continue along the coast, discovering en route the islands now known as Bonaire, Curaçao, and Aruba. He finally reached as far west as the northern tip of present-day Colombia, not realizing how close he was to the Isthmus of Panama and the Pacific Ocean. Having failed to find any of the Oriental splendors he had sought, he turned to the north and took course for La Española, ignoring specific instructions to stay away from that island. Repulsed there, he stopped at several islands in the Bahamas, carrying off numerous natives to be sold as slaves when he reached Cádiz in June 1500.

Even though Ojeda had failed to find any of the riches he sought for himself and the merchants of Seville, his exploration of virtually the entire northern coast of the southern continent secured for him an authorization for a second voyage to establish a colony on that coast. He soon found associates willing to join him in fitting out another squadron of four ships and sailed from Cádiz in January 1502. This venture also came to naught when the Indians, repeatedly provoked by Ojeda, became hostile. In May, Ojeda's discontented partners rebelled, took him prisoner, and sent him to La Española, where he arrived in September 1502.

In 1508, King Fernando, sole ruler of Spain following the death of Isabel on November 26, 1504, sought an able commander to establish colonies on the coast of gold-rich Veragua (Panama). Juan de la Cosa, the chart maker, interceded in favor of Ojeda and won for him the post of governor of New Andalusia, an undefined area including what is now the Caribbean coast of Colombia. At his own expense, Juan de la Cosa fitted out three ships in which he set sail for La Española with about two hundred men. This final venture of Ojeda, like so many of his past ventures, also was doomed to failure by his belligerence toward the Indians. His recklessness resulted in the death of his staunch supporter Juan de la Cosa by a poison-tipped arrow. Ojeda managed to escape to La Española where he later died in poverty.

BIBLIOGRAPHY

Gould, Alicia B. *Nueva lista documentada de los tripulantes de Colón en 1492.* Madrid, 1984.

Irving, Washington. *The Life and Voyages of Christopher Columbus and His Companions.* 3 vols. New York, 1849.

WILLIAM LEMOS

ORELLANA, FRANCISCO DE (c. 1511–1546), Spanish explorer and soldier; first European to descend the Amazon River. Born in Trujillo, Spain, Orellana may have been related to the Pizarros. In about 1527 he went to the Indies, probably to Nicaragua. From there he went to Peru, probably after 1533. In 1535 he helped to conquer Portoviejo and became a resident of the Spanish town of that name. He took a dozen horsemen to Lima during the first Inca rebellion in 1536 and sided with the Pizarros in the battle of Las Salinas on April 26, 1538. Later that year he founded Guayaquil, Ecuador, and served as its first captain general and governor.

When Gonzalo Pizarro set out from Quito in 1540 in search of the mythic El Dorado and the land of cinnamon in the Coca River basin on the eastern slopes of the Ecuadorian Andes, Orellana joined the expedition as the leader of twenty horsemen and was given the position of second-in-command. In February 1542, he was sent to search for food with fifty men and a small boat that the Spanish had built on the banks of the Coca River. Unable to return upstream against the current, Orellana continued down the Coca and Napo rivers into the Amazon River. During a stop at Aparia, the land was claimed for Spain and a second ship was built. He later claimed to have encountered and fought with the "Amazons" of mythic fame. His boats entered the Atlantic Ocean on August 26 and sailed northwest to Nueva Cádiz, Cubagua, where they arrived on September 9 and 11, 1542. His party was the first group of Europeans to navigate the length of the Amazon River.

Returning to Spain, Orellana obtained the governorship of the south side of the Amazon Basin west of the Tordesillas Line of Demarcation. He departed Sanlúcar de Barrameda on May 11, 1545, with four ships and four hundred Spaniards. By the time he reached the mouth of the Amazon River in December, he had only two ships and less than half of the men.

The expedition worked its way one hundred leagues upstream before pausing for the first three months of 1546 to build a brigantine to replace one of the ships. Over fifty men died of hunger during this delay. Ascending another twenty leagues, the party lost the last of the original ships. Orellana broke off his efforts not long after this shipwreck and died before he could return down the Amazon. His widow and the remaining members of the expedition abandoned the enterprise and sailed to Margarita, arriving in December 1546.

BIBLIOGRAPHY

Benites Vinueza, Leopoldo. *Los descubridores del Amazonas: "La expedición de Orellana."* Madrid, 1976.

Medina, José Toribio. *The Discovery of the Amazon.* Translated by Bertram T. Lee. Edited by H. C. Heaton. New York, 1934.

PAUL E. HOFFMAN

ORTELIUS, ABRAHAM (1527–1598), Flemish cartographer and publisher. Abraham Oertel, known by the Latinized name Ortelius, was born into the family of an Antwerp antique merchant. His education evidently did not extend much beyond the curriculum of the typical

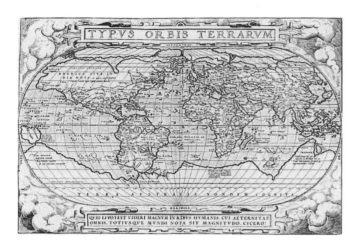

ORTELIUS'S MAP OF THE WORLD. From *Theatrum Orbis Terrarum*.
ELSEVIER PUBLISHING PROJECTS, AMSTERDAM

Latin school, where he also received some instruction in Greek and mathematics. His father died when he was twelve and his mother took over the family business. Together with his sisters, Anne and Elizabeth, Abraham took up the coloring of maps and was admitted to the painters' guild as an "illuminator of maps" in 1547. In time he took over the operation of the family shop and dealt in antiques, coins, maps, and books, with the book and map trade gradually becoming his primary occupation.

Having prospered, he began to form an extensive collection of medals, coins, and antiques (which he exhibited in his home as a kind of private museum), as well as a library of many volumes. He traveled widely on business, studied the history and geography of the places he visited, made contacts with scholars and editors, and carried on an extensive correspondence, some of which has been preserved and forms the primary source of information about his life and work.

Ortelius's career as a cartographer began in 1564 when he published a large and ambitious wall map of the world, followed in the next few years by several other separate maps. But his chief monument, and his greatest contribution to the Age of Discovery, was his atlas, the *Theatrum orbis terrarum* (Theater of the world), published in Antwerp in 1570. Earlier collections of maps had been published (most notably, those accompanying Ptolemy's *Geography*), but Ortelius's contribution was to collect the newest and best maps available for all parts of the world, have them engraved to a uniform size, and publish them together in book form. The result is usually thought of as constituting the first modern atlas. The atlas seems to have had its origins in the need to supply merchant-traders in the Low Countries with geographical information so that they could calculate freight costs and plan efficient trade routes while avoiding wars and civil disturbances. The appeal of the *Theatrum,* however, went well beyond the commercial world, and scholars all over Europe were virtually unanimous in their praise. Gerardus Mercator summed up the value of the *Theatrum* when he thanked Ortelius for having "selected the best descriptions of each region and collected them into one manual, which can be bought at small cost, kept in a small space and even carried about wherever we please."

Demand for the *Theatrum* was remarkable. Altogether some twenty-four editions appeared during Ortelius's lifetime, and another ten after his death in 1598. The original Latin text of the geographical descriptions that accompanied the maps was translated into the major vernacular languages of Europe, and by 1608, editions had been published in Dutch, German, French, Spanish, English, and Italian. The number of map sheets grew from 53 in 1570 to 167 in the last edition, in 1612. Answering the need for even lower costs and greater portability were the pocket-sized versions of the *Theatrum,* of which thirty editions were published. One of the unique contributions of the *Theatrum* was Ortelius's scrupulousness in crediting individual cartographers and his inclusion of a catalog of all the maps known to him, a document of primary importance for the history of sixteenth-century cartography.

It is difficult to overemphasize the importance of Ortelius's atlas for the spread of information about the world, including the relatively new discoveries in America. The first edition included only a single map of North and South America, but by 1590, eight new maps had been added, showing the results of Spanish and French explorations up to about mid-century. Maps of central Mexico, Sinaloa, and the West Indies appeared in editions after 1579, and five years later these were joined by maps of northwestern South America, the southeastern United States, and the San Luis Potosí region of Mexico. A new map of the Americas appeared in 1587 and one of the Pacific Ocean in 1590. These were far from being the earliest depictions of the New World on printed maps, but they were certainly the most widely available. The unique value of Ortelius's atlas as a compendium of geographical knowledge is attested by the fact that at the court of Philip II, with the resources of the great cosmographers and the Casa de la Contratación at its disposal, the *Theatrum* was consulted regularly as a tool of statecraft.

BIBLIOGRAPHY

Bagrow, Leo, and Robert W. Karrow, Jr. *Mapmakers of the Sixteenth Century and Their Maps: The Catalog of Cartographers of Abraham Ortelius, 1570.* Chicago, forthcoming.
Hessels, Jan H. *Abrahami Ortelii (geographi antverpiensis) et virorum eruditorum ad eundem et ad Jacobum Colium Orte-*

lianum . . . epistulae. Cambridge, 1887. Reprint, Osnabrück, 1969.

Koeman, Cornelis. *The History of Abraham Ortelius and His Theatrum orbis terrarum.* New York, 1964.

ROBERT W. KARROW, JR.

OTTOMAN EMPIRE. The name of this empire came from Osman, a Turkish nomad chief (d. 1324) who founded it at the turn of the fourteenth century near the northwest edge of the Anatolian plateau. Although Europeans spoke of it as an empire, the Ottomans themselves wrote of it as the *Al-i Osman,* or "House of Osman." By Columbus's time, the Ottomans had conquered the Balkans, including Constantinople (1453) as well as most of Anatolia; the Byzantine state of Trebizond fell in 1461 and the major Anatolian Muslim rival of the Ottomans, the emirate of Karaman, was conquered in 1468.

Sultan Mehmed II the Conqueror (r. 1444–1446, 1451–1481) had been responsible for these last additions to Ottoman soil, and in his lifetime the empire increased in size by about 50 percent. In fact, one of his armies briefly occupied the Italian port of Otranto in the last months of his reign. The sultanate of his son, Bayezid II (r. 1481–1512), did not add to the empire so much as consolidate it: strategic points in the Aegean and the Danube delta came under Ottoman rule, but in the main Bayezid II had to fend off, in the early years of his reign, the attempts of his brother Jem to supplant him and, in his later years, the rise of Isma'il I to power in Iran and the Safavid attempts to arouse the nomads of Anatolia against Ottoman rule. One notable addition to the population of the empire was a number of Jews, refugees from Spain who left their homes in 1492. By the end of the century they had established themselves in Thessaloníki (Salonika) and Istanbul, where they had set up a printing press.

Bayezid's successors set a faster tempo for conquest. Selim I (r. 1512–1520), known as Selim the Grim, defeated the Safavids at the Battle of Chaldiran (1514) and briefly occupied their capital, Tabriz. After this time Ottoman rule over Anatolia remained secure. In 1516 Selim marched east and south against the Mamluks of Syria and Egypt. At Marj Dabiq, near Aleppo, Selim's army defeated the Mamluks, and at the beginning of 1517 he entered Cairo. With the conquest of the Mamluk domains the Ottomans came to rule over Arabic-speaking lands and became the protectors of Mecca and Medina, the holy cities in Arabia. Further, the Ottomans now had a third sea frontier to defend, for to the Black Sea and the eastern Mediterranean was now added the Red Sea and its outlet onto the Indian Ocean, for which the Ottomans contested with the Portuguese during the sixteenth century.

Selim's son and successor was Süleyman the Magnificent (r. 1520–1566), whom the Turks called Kanuni, or the lawgiver. Süleyman caught the imagination of European authors, artists, and travelers, not least for his conquests of Rhodes, Iraq, Yemen, and parts of Hungary and his subordination of much of the North African coast and lands north of the Black Sea and the Danube. Most celebrated was his siege of Vienna in 1529. In all, Süleyman spent ten of his forty-six years of rule on campaigns.

At the death of Süleyman in 1566, the area under direct Ottoman control included about 1,190,000 square kilometers (460,000 square miles) in Asia, 570,000 (220,000) in Europe, and 490,000 (190,000) in Africa, for a total of around 2,255,000 square kilometers (870,000 square miles). An additional 905,000 square kilometers (350,000 square miles) lay under tributary rulers in central Europe and south Russia. Ottoman writ held sway along the coast of North Africa, in Egypt and the Nile basin, the coasts of Arabia, the Fertile Crescent (Syria, Iraq), Anatolia as far east as Lake Van and as far north as Kars, the Balkans, and most of Hungary; nor was it ignored in the tributary states of Walachia, Transylvania, Moldavia, and the Khanate of Crimea.

The Ottomans had originally ruled over a population that was largely Christian, especially in the Balkans, but by the sixteenth century Islam was predominant in most of Anatolia, and the conquests of Selim I and Süleyman had added large Muslim populations. In North Africa and the Levant, most people spoke Arabic; in Anatolia, while Turkish was the lingua franca, Christians spoke Greek or Armenian; and in the Balkans, Turkish at this time was more a language of administration, with the overwhelmingly Christian population speaking their traditional languages: Greek, the Slavic languages, Hungarian, and Rumanian.

The Ottomans were Muslims and ruled with a view to the protection and expansion of Muslim dominion. Nonetheless, they allowed non-Muslims to practice their religions in return for additional taxes and restrictions. The organized Christian and Jewish communities enjoyed a certain amount of autonomy and were responsible to the sultan through the community's head. Mehmed the Conqueror and his successors appointed the patriarchs of the Greek Orthodox and Armenian churches, and at some point the Jews had a grand rabbi. The sultans placed garrisons in some of the cities of the empire for the protection of the Christians and Jews.

The Ottoman Empire was the first of the "gunpowder empires" in the Near East: the Ottoman armies won at Chaldiran and Marj Dabiq thanks to their use of gunpowder weapons. What impressed European observers the most, however, was the organization of Ottoman governance, for the Ottoman enterprise rested upon the services of officials many of whom, at all levels of government, were legally slaves. The Habsburg ambassador Oghier Ghiselin de Busbecq suggested that the Ottoman government was a true meritocracy, not bound by a traditional nobility. In some years the central government sent out men to conscript Christian youths, a process known as the *devshirme*. These youths were converted to Islam and schooled for a number of years, with some graduates joining the bureaucracy, where in principle a talented man could rise to head the imperial administration as grand *vezir*, and with others, joining the Janissary Corps, the crack infantry of the sultans.

Although the empire included a number of large and historic cities (Istanbul, Damascus, Jerusalem, and Cairo), it was fundamentally an agrarian society, and during the age of Columbus there was little long-distance trade in agricultural commodities. The spice and silk trades flourished, however, and it was not until the later sixteenth century that the shift of trade routes around the horn of Africa and the influx of American silver had an impact upon the Ottoman economy. There were Ottomans who took an interest in what was occurring in other markets. For their part, Europeans, especially in the Habsburg domains and Italy, had an interest in this formidable enemy and possible trading partner. Although they did not know much of the Ottomans' early history, diplomats and merchants gathered together accounts of court life and attempted to influence Ottoman decisions through quiet diplomacy with some of the higher bureaucrats and grand *vezirs*. These accounts have not lost their interest or charm with the slow opening of the vast Ottoman archives to modern researchers.

BIBLIOGRAPHY

Inalcik, Halil. *The Ottoman Empire: The Classical Age.* London, 1973. Reprint, 1990.

Tietze, Andreas, ed. *Turkologischer Anzeiger.* An annual of current literature in all languages. Vienna, 1976–.

RUDI PAUL LINDNER

OVANDO, NICOLÁS DE (c. 1451–1511), governor of the Indies (1501–1509). Born in Brozas, Extremadura, died in Seville, May 29, 1511, Ovando was the son of Capt. Diego de Ovando, who, in the civil wars preceding the marriage of Isabel of Castile and Fernando of Aragón, opted for the winning side. In 1473 his younger son Nicolás was given the commandery of Lares in the Order of Alcántara. As a member of the military order, called frey rather than fray, he took monastic vows in addition to one that obliged him to fight the infidel.

Because of Nicolás de Ovando's performance in the civil wars and his proven loyalty to the Crown, Queen Isabel in

OVANDO ORDERS THE FIRST CONSTRUCTION OF SHIPS IN THE NEW WORLD. Engraving from Théodor de Bry's *Americae*. Frankfurt, 1594.

1501 appointed him to the post of first royal governor of the Indies, in succession to Christopher Columbus. Under the Admiral, the infant colony in Santo Domingo had fallen into disarray, and the interim attempt to cope with the difficulties by Francisco de Bobadilla had failed. Ovando arrived on April 15, 1502, with a fleet of thirty ships and about twenty-five hundred settlers. Among them were soldiers, artisans, and professionals, some of whom brought their families, and priests.

During the decade of Ovando's administration he followed his instructions from the Crown, which can be grouped under four headings: to implement the transfer of powers of government from Columbus to the Crown; to establish royal jurisdiction over planters, miners, and future towns; to encourage economic development; and to put the church on a firm foundation.

Ovando brought with him royal laws comparable, by and large, to those practiced by the military orders during the years of the reconquest. His "mission of civilization" was to convert the Indians to the Catholic faith and teach them to live as Spaniards. He thus represented the continuity of an ancient tradition.

La Española, however, was not Spain, nor were the Indians Moors. The Spanish colonists, moreover, were split in their loyalties, many supporting the Columbuses. The physical setting, the challenges to authority, and the demands on the governor to do justice by both the Indians and the settlers under Crown law demanded adjustments in almost every detail.

Ovando's powers to deal with Columbus were legally

justifiable, but his actions were shadowed by his lengthy abandonment of the marooned discoverer in Jamaica. His confrontation with the natives, whom he feared as possible agents of rebellion, led to the infamous hanging of the cacique Anacaona. The settlement of the countryside by the system of repartimiento (Indian forced labor) cost many Indian lives and was destructive of the indigenous culture. But in the more customary enterprises of stabilizing a mixed rural and mining economy, founding towns, stimulating construction of stone houses, and planning a cathedral and a hospital, which represented the "civilizing" mission of Castile, he carried out the will of the Crown. Recalled in 1509, Ovando, who had by then been elected and confirmed as *comendador mayor* of Alcántara (that is, as head of this military order of knights), left La Española. This colony had become a little Spain, with the Americas a challenge yet to be met.

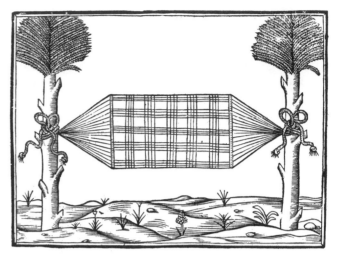

BIBLIOGRAPHY

Lamb, Ursula. "Cristóbal de Tapia v. Nicolás de Ovando: A Residencia Fragment." *Hispanic American Historical Review* 33 (1953).

Lamb, Ursula. *Frey Nicolás de Ovando, Gobernador de las Indias (1501–1509).* 2d ed. Santo Domingo, Dom. Rep., 1977.

Demorizi, Emilio Rodríguez. *El Pleito Ovando-Tapia: Comienzo de la vida urbana en America.* Santo Domingo, Dom. Rep., 1978.

URSULA LAMB

TWO WOODCUTS FROM OVIEDO'S *HISTORIA GENERAL*. *Top*: A hammock, a native American invention that soon found use in European sailing vessels. *Bottom*: Indian in a canoe. These are from the second edition of the *Historia general*, published in Salamanca in 1547 under the title *Cronica de las Indias*.

NEW YORK PUBLIC LIBRARY, RARE BOOK DIVISION

OVIEDO, GONZALO FERNÁNDEZ DE (1478–1557), royal official.

Known widely among historians and bibliographers simply as Oviedo, Gonzalo Fernández de Oviedo y Valdés spent almost fifty years in the New World and wrote two important works on the Indies and Tierra Firme (present-day Colombia and Panama). The first, *De la natural historia de las Indias*, published at Toledo in 1526, treated of the flora, fauna, and geography of the Caribbean, principally La Española, and of Tierra Firme. In one chapter he described the customs and folklore of the native inhabitants, displaying little regard for their humanity or capacity. The second work, *Historia general y natural de las Indias, islas y Tierra Firme del mar Océano,* was a larger and more significant manuscript, which, though it too included natural history and comment on Indian societies, chiefly chronicled Spain's political adventures in the same regions. The first part was published at Seville in 1535; the second at Valladolid in 1557, the year of Oviedo's death. Additional parts, suppressed probably by his ideological rival, Bartolomé de las Casas, did not appear in print until the nineteenth century.

Born at Madrid of Asturian parents, Oviedo briefly entered the service of the Infante Juan, only son of Fernando and Isabel, and came to know Columbus and the Pinzón family. During two years of military service in Italy he acquired a Renaissance taste for literature and the arts. On returning to Spain at age twenty-four, he married the Toledo beauty Margarita de Vergara, who died ten months later in childbirth. He would marry twice more.

In 1514 he made the first of his twelve Atlantic crossings, sailing (along with Bernal Díaz del Castillo and Hernando de Soto) on the expedition of Pedro Arias de Ávila (Pedrárias Dávila) to assume newly appointed duties as *veedor*, or inspector of gold smelting, on Tierra Firme. With Pedrárias, who established a tyrannical governorship at Darién, Oviedo had a continually hostile relationship. In 1532 he received the newly minted position of chronicler of the Indies, and the inspectorship of gold foundries passed to a son. In the following year he assumed the additional post of *alcalde*, or governor, of the fortress at Santo Domingo.

In his travels Oviedo became the first New World field naturalist, describing and illustrating in his own hand numerous animals, fish, and plants. To him also linguists owe their first knowledge of Indian words from which were derived such terms as *canoe, hurricane, maize,* and *hammock.* His nature writings enjoyed a wide vogue in Spain and throughout Europe.

Oviedo's attitude toward the native peoples had a strong impact in Spain, where Las Casas singled him out as "a deadly enemy of the Indians" for the way in which he denigrated their customs and capacities. In Oviedo's vision the Indians were lazy, corrupt, vicious, idolatrous, bestial, and deserving of enslavement, the last of which he himself practiced. In his famous disputation with Las Casas in 1550, Juan Ginés de Sepúlveda relied heavily on the *Historia general* in his attempt to demonstrate that the Indians were lacking in intellectual and religious capacity and thus could be justly warred upon. On the other side, Las Casas in his formal argument, the *Apologética historia,* answered the royal historian's positions point by point.

As a footnote, Oviedo deserves to be remembered as the first Spaniard to read aloud in the New World the formidable theological proclamation called the *Reque-rimiento,* which, if not heeded by its native audience, justified war and enslavement. On June 14, 1514, Oviedo dutifully declaimed before a deserted village inland from Darién, to the laughter of a military guard. He died on July 27, 1557, at Santo Domingo.

BIBLIOGRAPHY

Hanke, Lewis. *All Mankind Is One: A Study of the Disputation between Bartolomé de las Casas and Juan Ginés de Sepúlveda in 1550 on the Intellectual and Religious Capacity of the American Indians.* De Kalb, Ill., 1974.

Pérez de Tudela Bueso, Juan, et al. *Homenaje a Gonzalo Fernández de Oviedo en el IV centenario de su muerte.* Madrid, 1957.

Pérez de Tudela Bueso, Juan. "Vida y Escritos de Gonzalo Fernández de Oviedo." In Gonzalo Fernández de Oviedo, *Historia general y natural de las Indias,* vol. 1. Madrid, 1959.

Restrepo Uribe, Fernando. "Gonzalo Fernández de Oviedo, primer cronista de Indias." *Boletín de Historia y Antigüedades* 74, no. 757 (April–June 1987): 245–257.

Michael Gannon

P

PACHECO PEREIRA, DUARTE (c. 1460–c. 1533), Portuguese explorer, navigator, conquistador, cosmographer, and author of *Esmeraldo de situ orbis*. Duarte Pacheco Pereira, called the Great Pacheco and the Portuguese Achilles by the poet Luis Vaz de Camões, was born in Lisbon, the son of the seafarer and solider João Pacheco and Isabel Pereira. Little is known of his early life. Recent studies have challenged the view that young Pacheco Pereira was present in North Africa at the Portuguese conquest of Arzila and the occupation of Tangier in 1471. However, during the reign of João II (1481–1495), he made several voyages to the Guinea coast of Africa and explored the region around the Senegal River and the kingdom of Benin, whose capital he visited four times. In 1488 when Bartolomeu Dias was returning from his expedition around the Cape of Good Hope, he picked up Pacheco Pereira, who was seriously ill, from the island of Principe in the Gulf of Guinea and brought him back to Portugal. About that time, Pacheco Pereira, already a knight in the household of King João, became a member of the king's guard. He resided in Lisbon and because of his navigational experience was a technical adviser to the Portuguese delegation that was given the task of negotiating the Treaty of Tordesillas (1494) and signed the document as a witness.

In Book I, chapter 2 of Pacheco Pereira's *Esmeraldo de situ orbis,* there is an ambiguous statement regarding an expedition in 1498 "in which your Highness ordered us to explore the Western region, . . . a very large landmass with many large islands adjacent." It is not clear whether the author uses the word *us* to refer to himself or to the Portuguese in general. Some scholars assert that he, rather than Pedro Álvares Cabral, discovered Brazil. Others argue that his 1498 voyage was to the north and that it touched Florida, and therefore that the Portuguese discovered the North American mainland. Still others conjecture that the 1498 explorers sighted the Yucatán. Though it seems that there was indeed a 1498 voyage to the west, it most probably did not touch Brazil or King Manuel I would have proudly announced the news to Europe, as he did in 1501 after Cabral's landfall the previous year. Furthermore, there is no evidence that Pacheco Pereira was a member of Cabral's armada, as some writers have alleged.

In 1503 Pacheco Pereira was captain of one of the three ships in Afonso de Albuquerque's expedition to India. While there, he organized the defense of Cochin against the attacks of the ruler of Calicut. His military exploits earned him great praise from the most important Portuguese chroniclers of the sixteenth century.

He returned to Lisbon in mid-1505 as captain of one of the ships in the armada of Lopo Soares and was warmly received by King Manuel. It was about this time that he began writing *Esmeraldo de situ orbis*, which he described as "a book of cosmography and navigation." He seems to have completed all or most of it by 1508. Toward the end of 1508, King Manuel ordered him to track down the French corsair Mondragon; in a battle off Cape Finisterre on January 18, 1509, he sank one ship and captured three others as well as Mondragon himself. In 1511 he commanded a fleet sent to the aid of Tangier, which was besieged by the king of Fès. By 1512 he had married Antónia de Albuquerque, daughter of Jorge Garcês, secretary of King Manuel, and maternal granddaughter of Duarte Galvão, who had held a similar post under King João II.

In 1519 Pacheco Pereira was named governor of São Jorge da Mina for three years. In 1522 he was arrested and brought back to Portugal at the orders of King Manuel's successor, João III (r. 1521–1557). After a period of imprisonment, he was released by João and granted a pension. The exact date of his death is unknown, although there is evidence that he died in late 1532 or early in 1533.

Duarte Pacheco Pereira's *Esmeraldo de situ orbis*, first published in 1892, almost four centuries after being penned (the original manuscript is missing and only two eighteenth-century copies exist), combines a partial chronicle of Portuguese overseas discovery with a cosmography of the world. It also attempts—not always successfully—to synthesize the wisdom of the ancients with Portuguese experience. For example, the author believed that six-sevenths of the world was land enclosing a sea. At the same time, his projections regarding latitude were some of the most accurate of his day. The two extant manuscripts also give detailed sailing instructions for coasting the western part of Africa, with descriptions of that region.

BIBLIOGRAPHY

Bensaude, Joaquim. *L'astronomie nautique au Portugal à l'époque des grandes découvertes*. Bern, 1912.

Carvalho, Joaquim Barradas de. *À la recherche de la spécificité de la renaissance portugaise: L' "Esmeraldo de situ orbis" de Duarte Pacheco Pereira et la littérature portugaise de voyages à l'époque des grandes découvertes*. 2 vols. Paris, 1983.

Dias, Carlos Malheiro. *História da colonização portuguesa do Brasil*. 3 vols. Porto, 1921–1926.

Morison, Samuel Eliot. *Portuguese Voyages to America in the Fifteenth Century*. Cambridge, Mass., 1940.

Pacheco Pereira, Duarte. *Esmeraldo de situ orbis*. Translated and edited by G. H. T. Kimble. London, 1937.

Pacheco Pereira, Duarte. *Esmeraldo de situ orbis*, 3d ed. Lisbon, 1954.

Francis A. Dutra

PACIFICATION, CONQUEST, AND GENOCIDE.

The people who met Christopher Columbus at the end of his first voyage, the Taínos (from their word for "noble," or "good"), were described by Columbus as the best and most gentle people on earth. In 1492 there may have been as many as two million (estimates range from one hundred thousand to eight million) Taínos living on La Española (Hispaniola). The chroniclers described Jamaica and Puerto Rico as equally populous and the Bahamas and Cuba as supporting somewhat less dense populations. Within fifty years the Taíno peoples who occupied these islands were replaced by native peoples from other islands and the mainland and by Africans.

The destruction of the native West Indian societies occurred in two stages. The first came between 1492 and 1500 under the administration of Christopher Columbus, who undertook what he called the "pacification" of the Taínos. The second stage commenced with the arrival of

Governor Nicolás de Ovando in 1502. Ovando destroyed what remained of the Taíno political structure on La Española and encouraged the brutal conquest of neighboring islands. These stages were separated by a brief respite during the two-year administration of Francisco de Bobadilla.

It must be noted that historical accounts of this period draw heavily on the writings of Bartolomé de las Casas. Las Casas, who arrived in La Española in 1502, was the first priest ordained in the New World, in 1510; he was appointed "protector of the Indians" by Cardinal Francisco Jiménez de Cisneros, archbishop of Toledo. Because of their moral and political overtones, his writings have been used to support modern political objectives. On the one hand, his denunciation of his countrymen's treatment of native peoples was so severe that it was used to fuel the anti-Hispanic sentiments embodied in the Black Legend of the seventeenth and eighteenth centuries, which drew upon the most horrifying details in the Las Casas polemic, and was intended not to reform Spanish policy but to denigrate Spanish character. On the other hand, Las Casas's use of exaggeration to amplify his argument has led others to reject his history as inaccurate. The following discussion seeks a middle ground.

Pacification. Christopher Columbus's efforts to establish a colony on La Española were directed toward one end: he sought to extract the wealth of the Indies and to export it to Spain to enrich himself and the Crown. During the seven years that he was governor of La Española, he enumerated three sources of wealth: gold, brazilwood (a source of a red dye), and slaves. Complicated interactions between Columbus, his countrymen, and the native Taínos affected which of these sources was emphasized at any particular time. Columbus was clearly most interested in gold. He demanded that every Taíno over fourteen years of age pay one Flemish hawkbell (85 grams or 3 ounces) of gold or an arroba (11 kilograms or 25 pounds) of cotton every three months. These payments were to be collected by the Taíno caciques.

At first, relations with the Taínos were amiable. Columbus established a lifelong bond with the Taíno cacique Guacanagarí. Guacanagarí helped to salvage the contents of *Santa María*, which sank on December 24, 1492; it was in his village that the first Spanish fort, called La Navidad, was built; he also accompanied Columbus during the forced occupation of the interior in March 1495. Given Columbus's relationship with Guacanagarí, it is inferred that those who willingly submitted to his demands were treated as friends, while those who opposed him were treated as enemies.

Although native rights were not acknowledged, the issue was one of power and not race. The treatment of the Taínos was undeniably cruel, but it paralleled the treatment of Spaniards. Spaniard and Indian alike had their ears and noses cut off for stealing, and Spaniards who committed treason were hung. When Ovando burned the chiefs of Jaraguá in 1502, the Taino *cacica* (female chief) Anacaona was hanged because a person of her rank had earned that form of execution over a form—burning—suited for persons of lower rank.

Columbus began his colony with both a friend and an enemy. His friend, Guacanagarí, was not blamed for the destruction of La Navidad. Blame and retribution centered on Caonabó, who was arguably the most powerful cacique on the island. The area over which he ruled was one of the five principal *cacicazgos* on the island; it was located in the Cibao, the primary gold-producing region on La Española. Guacanagarí was a lesser cacique whose influence may not have extended much beyond his village.

One of Caonabó's names, Guacaonabo (Taíno caciques had many names that reflected their power and political alliances), was translated as "gold house." The name was interpreted as meaning that he controlled the gold deposits. Although his *cacicazgo* did include major gold deposits, the Taínos did not display the same enthusiasm for gold as did the Spanish. The capture of Caonabó became Columbus's first objective and was accomplished by subterfuge in 1494.

By 1494 the Taínos were already tired of the burdens that were placed on them. As Las Casas described the situation, even the most miserable of convicts from Spain demanded royal treatment from the natives and simply took what they desired. The situation was made worse by a famine that began in 1494. Many of the Taínos moved away from the Spaniards or went into hiding, held the Spaniards in mortal horror, refused obedience, and began to avenge themselves against individual Spaniards.

The only solution for the Taínos was to defeat the Spaniards. An army of at least fifteen thousand (but perhaps as many as one hundred thousand) was assembled in the central part of the island with Guarionex as the reluctant commander-in-chief. The Taíno forces were joined by certain Spaniards in open rebellion against Columbus. The Admiral and his brother Bartolomé Colón marched into the interior with an army of two hundred footsoldiers, twenty horsemen, twenty dogs, and Guacanagarí and his men. Vastly outnumbered, and faced with certain defeat, Bartolomé staged a midnight raid on the villages in which the Taínos were assembling. This breach of Taíno battle etiquette proved effective. Fourteen chiefs were captured, including Guarionex. Las Casas wrote that the next morning about six thousand men arrived without weapons and begged for the release of their leaders. The leaders who had instigated the uprising were burned, but Guarionex and others were released. In this way the interior of the island was "pacified."

In an effort to maintain peaceful relations, Columbus promised Guarionex and the other chiefs that, in return for tribute payments, he would keep the Spaniards from roaming free. In effect, the Taínos would have only one master, Christopher Columbus. This solution proved unsuccessful. The tribute demanded was beyond their means, even after the demands were halved. Moreover, the inability of the Taíno chiefs to meet tribute payments may have been caused by the loss of up to one-third of the native population in the central area. The gold fields were not producing a good return, and there was growing discontent among Spaniard and Taíno alike. With the conquest of the interior completed, efforts were made to bring the rest of the island into the tribute system. The *cacicazgo* of Jaraguá, in the west, was approached and began to pay tribute in the form of cotton and food, and *cacicazgos* on the east coast continued to supply Spanish ships with cassava bread.

Treatment of the Indians was strongly influenced by relations among the Spaniards. The Spaniards continued to fight among themselves, and despite promises to the Taíno chiefs, the colony was out of control. When a group of three hundred disenchanted colonists left La Española in 1498, the three hundred who remained were equally divided between Columbus, who controlled the center of the island, and Francisco Roldán whose rebels held the west. Roldán took up residence in Jaraguá, thus ending tribute payments to Columbus, and both groups plundered the *cacicazgos* on the north coast.

The peace that was negotiated between Roldán and Columbus included the allocation of native peoples to individual Spaniards. This practice of allocating Indians and their land in *repartimientos,* and later encomiendas, was to characterize the Spaniards' treatment of native peoples in their other colonies. In theory, encomenderos were responsible for the spiritual and corporal well being of their natives. In practice, the natives were often treated as slaves.

Columbus also drew royal disfavor over the issue of slavery. As early as 1493, Columbus proposed the export of natives to Spain, citing the activities of the Portuguese in Africa as an example. Columbus sent 550 slaves to Spain in 1495. In 1499 he proposed the export of slaves and dyewood as the means for resurrecting La Española's failed economy. The Crown resisted all efforts to send native West Indians to Spain as slaves. When Columbus awarded one Taíno to each of the colonists who left La Española in 1498, Queen Isabel set the natives free and returned them to La Española.

When Francisco de Bobadilla arrived at Santo Domingo in July 1500, his first sight was of two gallows, a Spaniard hanging from each. Five Spaniards had been executed in the past week and five others awaited execution. Bobadilla had been sent by the Crown to investigate turmoil in the colony and to become the new governor after he had completed his investigations. Instead, he immediately seized control of the government, arrested Christopher Columbus and Bartolomé and Diego Colón and sent them back to Spain in chains. After the removal of Columbus there was a brief respite. Bobadilla returned control of the colony to the Crown. The award of larger shares of gold placers encouraged the three hundred Spaniards who remained, and gold for the first time produced good returns.

Conditions also improved somewhat for the Taínos. A royal *cédula* (decree) declared that the Indians were free vassals of the Crown of Castile. The Spanish contingent was small, and there were no new repartimientos, uprisings, or reprisals. However, no Indians were released from previous repartimientos, and they continued to suffer under the burden of being the major suppliers of food as well as the source of labor for the gold mines. This brief peace was soon shattered.

Conquest. In April 1502, Nicolás de Ovando replaced Bobadilla as governor. Ovando arrived with about twenty-five hundred persons, and the new arrivals had an immediate and devastating impact. Las Casas reported that sickness broke out and that one thousand of the new arrivals died and more became ill. The Spaniards who headed directly for the gold fields introduced diseases into an already unhealthy environment where the death toll among the Taínos reached 25 to 30 percent of each *demora* (work gang).

The *demora* was supposed to provide a measure of protection to the Indians. Indians would work in the mines for only six to eight months, after which they would return to their fields. In theory, the natives retained their freedom in exchange for a period of labor. In practice, the system failed to instill a sense of responsibility toward the Indians. While slaveowners had to see to the needs of their slaves, if only because they represented a financial investment, the *demora* was a revolving door of free labor. Indians in a *demora* were treated as expendable because new Indians were always arriving and because the period of labor was limited. Their labor was lost when their period of service ended.

Ovando also brought a change of emphasis. The principal effort of his first two years was to gain control of the entire island. He accomplished this by breaking apart the native political structure. In the fall of 1503, Ovando marched his forces into the *cacicazgo* of Jaraguá. The leaders of Jaraguá had peacefully submitted to tribute demands of Bartolomé Colón in 1496 and had cooperated with Roldán when he took control of this area. Ovando had eighty-four caciques burned and hanged, including the paramount *cacica*, Anacaona. Attention was next

directed to the conquest of the southeastern peninsula in 1504, during which the *cacicazgo* of Higüayo was overrun and the last major Taíno cacique was deposed. All the natives were then assigned in repartimientos to the Crown or to individual Spaniards.

Throughout this period the Crown maintained that the Indians were vassals entitled to proper care and wages. These rights were largely ignored by Spaniards in La Española and were eventually abrogated. In 1503, Queen Isabel declared that the rebellious people "called Cannibals" could be captured and sold as slaves. In May 1509, in response to the dramatic decline in the Taíno population, King Fernando ordered Ovando to import all the Indians he could from neighboring islands.

The Bahamas became the immediate focus of slaving expeditions, and were depopulated by 1520. Pietro Martire d'Anghiera reported that forty thousand Lucayans were removed from the Bahamas. The Lucayans commanded a high price, 150 pesos per person, compared to the normal rate of five pesos, because they were in demand as divers on the pearl coast. The conquest soon spread to the neighboring islands. Cuba, Puerto Rico, and Jamaica were all brutally conquered. Las Casas claimed that the conquest of Cuba was so brutal it caused him to renounce his encomienda and to become an activist for native rights.

Genocide. Defined as the systematic extermination of a national or racial group, the term *genocide* is used here to characterize the extinction of the Taínos within two generations of the arrival of Columbus. Warfare, forced labor, disease, and miscegenation were the main agents of extermination. Las Casas claimed that three to four million Taínos were living in La Española in 1492, and he mourned the loss of five hundred thousand Lucayan souls. Historical demographers have increased the former number to eight million by using certain projection techniques, while at the same time discounting the latter. However, archaeologists who work with the material evidence have put the Taíno population at somewhere between four hundred thousand and two million. For the Bahamas, a population of about forty thousand is reasonable. The loss of several million native peoples in the West Indies is the most devastating result of contact with Europeans.

It is in the polemical writings of Las Casas that the mistreatment of the Indians is most completely expressed. Las Casas continuously chastises his countrymen for their disregard of native rights. He describes conditions in these words: "they thought nothing of knifing Indians by the tens and twenties and cutting slices off them to test the sharpness of their blades" and "they [the Taínos] saw themselves each day perishing by the cruel and inhuman treatment of the Spaniards, crushed to the earth by horses, cut in pieces by swords, eaten and torn by dogs, many buried alive and suffering all kinds of exquisite tortures.''

But were such random acts of violence the exception or the rule? The worst offenses occurred during the Conquest. As colonists settled onto encomiendas, their profits depended on the well-being of their subjects. There was no economic benefit to killing Taínos for sport.

During the Conquest, Spanish battle strategy seems to reflect the lessons of their war with the Moors. On a large scale, horses, dogs, and European weapons were used to devastating effect. But to the surprise of the Taínos, the Spanish would then initiate amiable relations provided the defeated submitted to their demands. This behavior reflects certain expectations of conquest and submission. Other European tactics were also employed. Caciques were taken hostage to ensure the cooperation of their subjects, individuals were made an example of to frighten others into submission, and punishments such as hanging, burning, and facial disfigurement were exacted.

The purpose of conquest warfare was not to destroy the native population, but to secure the cooperation of the people in the extraction of wealth. Although casualties in war were certainly high, these would have been greatly exceeded by deaths in the gold fields. The *demora* system, with its 25 to 30 percent mortality, has been described above. Death resulted from inadequate nutrition (workers were fed only cassava bread) and to unhealthful conditions that promoted the spread of diseases.

The greatest loss of human life came from diseases. Native Americans presented "virgin soil" conditions to infectious European parasites, conditions under which mortality can reach 30 to 100 percent. More than a dozen potentially fatal diseases were carried into the Americas by unhealthy Europeans. It is clear that Taínos were dying from European diseases as early as 1493. However, the continued operation of *cacicazgos* in La Española indicate that diseases had only local effects prior to the smallpox epidemic of 1517, by which time most of the Taínos were already dead.

In their *Essays in Population History,* the historical demographers Sherburne Cook and Woodrow Borah projected annual rates of decline from 1496 to 1504 that exceeded 30 percent per year and totaled more than three million people of an original population of seven to eight million. Yet while this massive islandwide depopulation was supposedly going on, the *cacicazgo* of Jaraguá continued to function and to pay tribute. It is impossible that this *cacicazgo* could have survived intact while undergoing such massive depopulation.

Finally, the native societies lost their identity through the intermarriage of Spaniard and Indian and by bastardization. There were few Spanish women on La Española. An accounting in 1514 listed 392 *vecinos* (inhabitants) of whom 92 had Spanish wives and 54 had native wives. The outbreak of syphilis in La Española and Europe is evidence that a number of the Spaniards and Taínos engaged in intercourse. The result was the creation of a mestizo population, today the largest segment of Hispanic Americans.

Archaeologists have examined this exchange of cultural and genetic information as a process called transculturation. The adoption of native pottery by the Spaniards is one of the most obvious types of transculturation. The replacement of native peoples by those with a European ancestry is another. Taíno culture disappeared by 1505, Taíno art by 1530, and the Taíno population by 1545.

[See also *Black Legend; Disease and Demography; Encomienda; Indian America,* especially the article on *Taínos; Slavery; Syphilis.*]

BIBLIOGRAPHY

Cook, Sherburne F., and Woodrow Borah. "The Aboriginal Population of Hispaniola." In vol. 1 of *Essays in Population History.* Berkeley, Calif., 1971.

Crosby, Alfred W. *The Columbian Exchange: Biological and Cultural Consequences of 1492.* Westport, Conn., 1972.

Keegan, William F., ed. *Hispanic/Native American Interactions in the Caribbean: A Sourcebook.* New York, 1991.

Las Casas, Bartolomé de. *Historia de las Indias.* 3 vols. Mexico City, 1951.

Sale, Kirkpatrick. *The Conquest of Paradise.* New York, 1990.

Sauer, Carl Ortwin. *The Early Spanish Main.* Berkeley, Calif., 1966.

Wilson, Samuel M. *Hispaniola: Caribbean Chiefdoms in the Age of Columbus.* Tuscaloosa, Ala., 1990.

WILLIAM F. KEEGAN

PAINTING. For discussion of Columbus as a figure in painting, see *Iconography,* articles on *Early European Portraits* and *American Painting.*

PALOS DE LA FRONTERA. In 1492, when Columbus launched his momentous voyage from Palos, the town was barely a century old. King Juan I of Castile had legally separated the squatter settlement of Palos from the town of Moguer in 1380, established it as a town, and sold it to a nobleman from Seville, Alvar Pérez de Guzmán, for 160,000 maravedis.

Pérez de Guzmán proceeded to develop the economic infrastructure of his new town in order to attract families. He received from the king an exemption from all royal taxes for the first fifty families that would settle in Palos. With almost no level land for plowing and growing wheat, Pérez de Guzmán planted olive trees on the hillsides and built a warehouse on the beach where local seamen could store their merchandise and auction their fish. He drew up municipal ordinances and founded a town government. After his death in 1394, his heirs authorized the building of a Franciscan monastery, Santa María de La Rábida, within the municipal boundaries.

The town council, which was elected annually by the local citizens upon approval by the lord, expanded the town's economy. By the mid-fifteenth century, Palos had a municipal shipyard, extensive salt pans, and a town marketplace. The town's financial obligation to its lord was to pay a 5 percent sales tax on the fish auctioned to wholesalers and to harvest the lord's olive crop during November.

Prosperity attracted new settlers, even though these latecomers did not receive the royal tax exemptions. Most Palos citizens made their living from the sea as fishermen, import-export merchants, shipbuilders, and pirates. Fish, olive oil, and salt were the town's major exports, and wheat its major import. By 1478, the town's population had grown to six hundred households.

Palos became an extremely prosperous town and its lordship a valuable possession. In 1479, a descendant of Alvar Pérez de Guzmán sold one-twelfth of the town's lordship to the duke of Medina Sidonia for the price of 2,200,000 maravedis. On June 24, 1492, another descendant sold his half of the lordship to Queen Isabel for 16,400,000 maravedis, which the royal treasury paid in annual installments during the next six years.

The town of Palos had already entered the royal service a month earlier. In a town meeting in the parish church of San Jorge on May 23, 1492, the town crier read an order from Queen Isabel commanding Palos to contribute two caravels for royal service for twelve months. The town clerk, Francisco Fernández, recorded that in addition to the usual two town judges and three town councilmen, two noncitizens were present: a Franciscan from La Rábida, Juan Pérez, and a foreign businessman, Christopher Columbus. The town council released municipal funds to lease two Palos caravels, *Niña* and *Pinta,* and local business leaders from the Pinzón family agreed to captain the ships.

BIBLIOGRAPHY

Ladero Quesada, Miguel Angel. "Palos en vísperas del descubrimiento." *Revista de Indias* 38 (1978): 471–506.
Manzano Manzano, Juan. *Cristóbal Colón, siete años decisivos de su vida (1485–1492).* Madrid, 1963.

HELEN NADER

PANÉ, RAMÓN (d. around 1498), author of early ethnological study of the Taínos. Ramón Pané arrived in La Española on Columbus's second voyage. Following orders from the Admiral, he went to live among the indigenous people of the island in order to study their "beliefs and idolatries." Pané learned their language, listened to their sacred songs and mythical tales, and submitted his findings in a report that he gave to Columbus around 1498. Known as *Relación acerca de las antigüedades de los indios* (Report on the antiquities of the Indians), this document is the first book written on American soil in a European language and marks the beginning of the ethnological study of American peoples.

The importance of this report went almost unnoticed, and its data were scarcely used because of problems understanding the text. In Spain, the manuscript was passed from Pietro Martire d'Anghiera (Peter Martyr) to Bartolomé de las Casas and Fernando Colón. The first two took note of its content, and Fernando included it in its entirety in his biography of his father, *History of the Admiral Cristopher Columbus by His Son.* Fernando Colón's work, which was left unpublished at his death in 1539, was brought to Venice, and in 1571 an Italian translation was printed by Alfonso de Ulloa. Fernando's original manuscript and Pané's original report are lost. All that have survived are d'Anghiera's notes in Latin, the summary in Spanish by Las Casas, and Ulloa's translation.

Many of the difficulties with the text could have been avoided if the original Italian translation had been better written. But Ulloa left an incomplete and hastily prepared manuscript. The translation is hence an uncertain rendering, with extensive use of indigenous terminology and several lacunae.

Following careful editing and research, the text now reveals a fascinating mythical world. It tells of the creation of the sun, the moon, the sea, and the fish; of the appearance of humans on the earth and their exploits until they arrived at the Caribbean islands; of the acquisition of fire and the cultivation and use of yucca and manioc; and of the transition from a nomadic to a sedentary life and the subsequent codification of habits and customs. It also lists the functions and attributes of the gods who inhabit the pantheon: the Supreme Being, lord of agriculture and sea activities; the Mother of God, mistress over the springs and tides and a compassionate protector of women in labor; and the Twins, the givers of the sun and the rain, among others. Finally, it narrates the moment when one of these gods announces the fateful forecast that strangers who wore clothes would come and devastate the land and people.

The reports transcribed by Pané have kept something of the original tone of the sacred hymns and epic legends, thus constituting an early record of the oral poetry and the narrative prose of the Antilles. They also serve to explain the arcane meaning of numerous handicrafts created by the Taíno potters and engravers and thus add an unexpectedly rich chapter to the history of the pre-Hispanic arts of the region, which was hitherto missing. Pané's account is no longer the forgotten evidence of an obscure friar; it has become one of the fundamental works of Hispanoamerican culture.

BIBLIOGRAPHY

Pané, Ramón. *Relación acera de las antigüedades de los Indios.* 8th ed. Mexico City, 1989.

José Juan Arrom
Translated from Spanish by Paola Carù

PAPACY. In the fifteenth and sixteenth centuries, the papacy was preoccupied with four principal concerns: the institutional unity of the Roman Catholic Church, peace among Christian princes and a crusade against Islam, church reform, and the defense and propagation of the faith.

Determined to prevent another Western Schism such as that of 1378 to 1417, during which the Roman, Avignonese, and Pisan popes each laid claim to the papacy, the popes from Martin V (r. 1417–1431) onward worked to preserve church unity by affirming the supreme authority of the Roman pontiff. Conciliarism, which asserted the ultimate authority of councils over the church and called for their frequent and regular convocation as set out by the Council of Constance (1414–1418), was stymied at the Council of Pavia-Siena (1423), sabotaged and discredited at Basel (1431–1449), refuted at Ferrara-Florence-Rome (1438–1445), deflated at Pisa-Milan-Asti-Lyon (1511–1512), and eviscerated at Lateran V (1512–1517). The attempt of the College of Cardinals to give the church an oligarchic constitution was countered by successive pontiffs' packing the college with their relatives and clients, and it ultimately failed when Sixtus V in 1587 legislated the transformation of the baronial cardinals into docile bureaucrats. The efforts of national states to set up autonomous local churches (e.g., the English Statutes of Provisors and Praemunire, 1351–1393; the French Pragmatic Sanction of Bourges, 1438; and the German Acceptance of Mainz, 1439) were in some cases checked and replaced by concordats regulating the relations between the papacy and the local church (e.g., for the Holy Roman Empire by the Concordat of Vienna, 1448; for France by that of Bologna, 1516; and for Spain by a series of papal bulls, culminating in *Eximinae devotionis affectus* of 1523). In other cases independent Protestant churches were established (e.g., Sweden in 1524 and England in 1534).

To guarantee the independence of the papacy from secular control, the popes labored to regain full sovereignty over their traditional Papal States in central Italy by subduing rebellious local lords and republican movements and by securing their territory's integrity and independence through a series of foreign alliances. Rome, the capital of the Papal States, was gradually transformed into the center of ecclesiastical and civil government with papal palaces and chapels, curial offices, cardinals' residences, and educational and cultural institutions. Christian pilgrims thronged its churches and processional thoroughfares, and visited the recently discovered (1578) catacombs. Some of the greatest artists and architects of this period such as Botticelli, Michelangelo, Raphael, Bramante, and Caravaggio contributed to making Rome a treasury of sacred art.

As head of Latin Christendom the papacy worked to end conflicts among Christians and to rally them to a defense of the Christian religion against Islam. Despite a series of papally supported campaigns to check the advance of the Turks in the Balkans and assist the embattled Byzantine Empire, Muslim forces defeated a huge Christian army at Kossovo in Serbia (1448), took Constantinople (1453), and within ten years conquered almost all the lands south of the Save and Danube rivers. The armies of Süleyman later took Belgrade in 1522, Rhodes in 1523, and most of Hungary in 1526, and unsuccessfully laid siege to Vienna in 1529.

Pope Paul III sent aid to the frontline Habsburg lands but found that his efforts to reconcile the Valois and Habsburgs, so that Emperor Charles V could confront the Turks, were hampered by King Francis I's alliance with Süleyman. As a member of the Holy League allied with Venice, Genoa, and Spain, the papacy provided money and ships for the failed efforts of 1537–1540, for the successful defense of Malta in 1565, and for the great but temporary Christian victory of Lepanto in 1571. That same year, however, Cyprus was conquered by the Turks. With offers of indulgences and patronage rights, the papacy successfully encouraged the Iberian monarchs to complete the Reconquista of Spain (Granada fell in 1492) and to take the fight against Islam to North Africa and the Arabian Sea.

As heads of the Roman Catholic Church the popes were called upon to reform the officials, procedures, and fees of the Roman Curia and to eliminate institutional abuses and moral misconduct throughout Christendom. Because many of these reforms involved a diminution in papal prerogatives and revenues at the very time the popes were struggling to strengthen their authority and to finance a restoration of Rome and the Papal States and a crusade against the Turks, the pontiffs were slow to act. They did, however, actively support the reform efforts of others: the movements to restore a pristine observance of rules by the older monastic and mendicant orders, the foundation of new religious orders (e.g., Theatines, Ursulines, Barnabites, Jesuits, and Oratorians), and local reforms by bishops, civil authorities, and special legates.

Beginning with the pontificate of Paul III (r. 1534–1549), the papacy assumed a role of leadership, enacting measures to reform the Curia, celebrating the Council of Trent (1545–1563), which issued numerous decrees reforming clerical education, preaching, appointment to church office, and religious practices, and finally seeing to the enforcement of these decrees. By the end of the sixteenth century the papacy was the driving force behind Catholic reform.

The defense and propagation of the Roman Catholic Church was the papacy's primary responsibility. Its efforts to restore communion with the Eastern Christian churches on the basis of an agreement on essential beliefs and practices resulted in the often only temporary unions negotiated at the Council of Ferrara-Florence-Rome (1438–1445) with the Greeks and Armenians (1439), Copts (1442), Syrians (1444), and Maronites on Cyprus (1445), and in the permanent union at the Fifth Lateran Council (1512–1517) with the Maronites of Lebanon. Protracted and confusing negotiations, however, ultimately failed to bring the Ethiopian church into permanent communion with Rome. In 1553 a group of the Chaldean Christians of Mesopotamia formally united with Rome, and in 1599 those of the Malabar coast of India also recognized papal authority at the Synod of Diamper. The largest group to enter permanently into union with Rome was the Ukrainians in 1595.

The efforts to suppress heresy within the Latin church were seldom successful. Despite persecution, the followers of Peter Waldo (d. 1217), known as Waldensians, survived in Savoy to be later absorbed for the most part by Protestantism. So too were the Lollard followers of John Wycliffe (d. 1384) in England and the Hussite disciples of Jan Huss (d. 1415) in Bohemia. Not appreciating at first the seriousness of the challenge coming from such Protestant theologians as Martin Luther (1483–1546) and Ulrich Zwingli (1484–1531), the papacy attempted to manage the problem by diplomacy and then resorted to public condemnations. Its effort to rally Catholic theologians, prelates, and lay leaders to a defense of the Catholic Church succeeded for the most part only in regions of southern Germany and the Rhineland. The English monarchs, with the exception of Mary I (r. 1553–1558), took that country at first into schism and then into Protestantism. Recourse to military means kept the followers of John Calvin (1509–1564) in check in France and present-day Belgium, but not in the Netherlands or Scotland.

But the most effective ways by which the papacy met the challenge of Protestantism were to clarify and explain Catholic doctrine at the Council of Trent (1545–1563), to support the preaching of the Capuchins (founded 1528) and the educational work of the Jesuits (f. 1540), and to suppress heresy through such instruments as indices of prohibited books and the Spanish (f. 1478) and Roman (f. 1542) inquisitions. The vast bulk of the cases tried by these tribunals, however, involved questions of moral conduct, and the Spanish institution at first dealt primarily with feigned conversions from Judaism.

The task of propagating Catholicism in the newly discovered lands was entrusted by the papacy to the rulers of Portugal and Spain. Because the conversion of natives was considered more easily accomplished if political control were in the hands of a Christian, the popes invoked a theocratic theory generally accepted by canonists of the high and later medieval period, and as the acknowledged vicars of Christ to whom, it was believed, belongs the earth and all that is in it, they granted particular Christian princes dominion over certain territories. The grant of islands as papal fiefs may have been based on the Donation of Constantine.

To encourage the crusading efforts of the Iberian kings, the popes over the centuries issued bulls granting them special ecclesiastical patronage rights in the conquered lands. Thus in 1095 Urban II by the bull *Tuae dilectissime* granted to Pedro I of Aragón and his successors patronage rights over all the churches (except bishoprics) established on lands taken from the Moors. Eugenius IV in 1436 by the bull *Laudibus et honore* granted these same rights to Juan II of Castile and his successors. Not until *Orthodoxae fidei* (1486) of Innocent VIII were these patronage rights extended to include bishoprics, major canonries, and dignities in cathedral and principal churches, and other well-endowed benefices in Granada, the Canary Islands, and Puerto Real, a town recently founded near Cádiz by Fernando and Isabel. By the bull *Eximiae devotionis sinceritas* (1493), Alexander VI granted to the Spanish monarchs and their successors the right of presentation to all ecclesiastical benefices in the newly discovered lands of America. That this grant also included bishoprics was clarified only in 1508 by Julius II's bull *Universalis ecclesiae regimini* addressed to Fernando of Aragón and his daughter Juana of Castile. Sovereignty over the American territory had been granted to Fernando and Isabel and their successors by Alexander VI's bulls *Inter caetera divinae* of May 3–4, 1493, and *Dudum siquidem* of September 26, 1493.

The Portuguese had received similar grants of sovereignty earlier. Although Clement IV by *Sicut exhibitae* (1344) had granted to a member of the royal house of Castile, Luis de Cerda, permission to conquer and hold as a papal fief the Canary Islands (a military feat de Cerda never accomplished), Eugenius IV by *Romanus pontifex* (1436) granted to King Duarte of Portugal the right to conquer and hold independently these islands. Exclusive Portuguese sovereignty over Saracen lands in West Africa and those of infidels and pagans farther to the south and elsewhere to be conquered and Christianized was granted by *Romanus pontifex* (1455) of Nicholas V to Afonso V of Portugal. A year later at the request of King Afonso and his uncle Henry the Navigator, who was Administrator of the Order of Christ, Calixtus III by *Inter caetera quae* confirmed the grants of his predecessors and turned over to the Order of Christ ordinary spiritual jurisdiction over the conquered region from Capes Bojador and Não (also known as Nam, Nun, and Noun) in West Africa south to India and beyond. Leo X by *Dum fidei constantiam* (1514) confirmed the order's jurisdiction and accorded to the Portuguese kings the right to propose candidates for church offices in these overseas lands. When Julius III incorporated the grand mastership of the Order of Christ into the Crown of Portugal by the bull *Praeclara charissimi* (1551), the order's jurisdictional rights also passed to the Portuguese kings.

Although having recourse to the papacy had helped sort out some of their rival claims, the Spanish and Portuguese monarchs also came to their own negotiated agreement in the Treaty of Alcáçovas (1479). In addition to settling the disputed Castilian succession, Portugal recognized Castilian sovereignty over the Canary Islands, and Fernando and Isabel acknowledged Portuguese control over the Azores, the Madeiras, the Cape Verde Islands, and the West African mainland. By his bull *Aeternae Regis clementia* (1481), Sixtus IV confirmed the concessions made by Nicholas V and Calixtus III to the Portuguese and agreed to punish with spiritual penalties anyone who violated the terms of the Treaty of Alcáçovas. Thus the later division of the new lands between Castile and Portugal by Alexander VI's *Inter caetera divinae* (1493) had both papal and secular precedents. Similarly when the Spanish and Portuguese monarchs independently agreed after ten months of negotiations to settle their differences by moving the Line of Demarcation to 370 leagues west of the Azores and Cape Verde Islands in the Treaty of Tordesillas of June 7, 1494, the papacy once again confirmed this accord by the bull *Ea quae* (1506) of Julius II. In all these agreements the Iberian monarchs agreed to work as vicars of the pope for the propagation of the Christian religion in their lands.

The delegation to the Iberian monarchs of responsibility for the church in the new lands was not complete, however. The papacy formally instituted new dioceses and gave final approval to the appointment of their bishops. Popes also acted to encourage the creation of an indigenous clergy. They supported Portuguese efforts in this regard. In 1518 Leo X, acting on the advice of King Manuel I, appointed the son of the Christian king of the Congo, Ndoadidiki Ne-Kinu a Mumemba (c. 1495–c. 1531), also known by his Christian name of Henrique, as titular bishop of Utica, vicar apostolic of the Congo, and coadjutor to the bishop of Funchal. That same year, moreover, the pope issued the brief *Exponi nobis* order-ing ordinaries to train and ordain to the priesthood native Christians. The Lisbon monastery of San Eloi had already trained native clergy for Africa and Asia for many years. In 1541 the Seminary of the Holy Faith opened in Goa to train similar indigenous clergy, and in 1571 another seminary opened on São Tomé Island to train African clergy. A seminary to train native clergy for Japan did not produce its first priests until 1601.

When Spanish efforts to create an indigenous clergy faltered, papal intervention was required. In Mexico the College of Santiago de Tlateloco was founded in 1536 to train local clergy but soon desisted owing to fierce criticism by those who held that the Indians, if not incapable of Christianity, were too new to the Christian religion, dull, incontinent, inconstant, and proud to be ordained. At the urging of the Dominicans Bishop Julián Garcés and Fray Bernardino de Minaya, Paul III issued the bull *Sublimis Deus* (1537), which affirmed that Indians were capable of becoming Christians and that even as non-Christians they should retain their liberty and possessions. The First Mexican Provincial Council (1555) and the Second Provincial Council of Lima (1567–1568) prohibited the ordination of natives, but both decrees had to be modified in subsequent councils because of a 1576 decree of Gregory XIII allowing the ordination of mestizos. Thus, at significant points the popes intervened to ensure that missionary churches under Iberian royal patronage were in substantial conformity with the practices of the Catholic Church elsewhere.

[See also *Inquisition; Line of Demarcation; Missionary Movement; Reconquista; Religion; Rome; Spirituality of Columbus; Treaty of Alcáçovas; Treaty of Tordesillas.*]

BIBLIOGRAPHY

Bontinck, François. "Ndoadidiki Ne-Kinu a Mumemba, premier évêque Kongo (c. 1495–c. 1531)." *Revue africaine de théologie* 3 (1979): 149–169.

Boxer, Charles R. *The Church Militant and Iberian Expansion, 1440–1770.* The Johns Hopkins Symposia in Comparative History, no. 10. Baltimore, 1978.

Castañeda Delgado, Paulino. *La teocracia papal y la conquista de América.* Vitoria, 1968.

Hanke, Lewis. *All Mankind Is One: A Study of the Disputation between Bartolomé de Las Casas and Juan Gines de Sepúlveda in 1550 on the Intellectual and Religious Capacity of the American Indians.* De Kalb, Ill., 1974.

Muldoon, James. *Popes, Lawyers, and Infidels.* Philadelphia, 1979.

Pastor, Ludwig von. *History of the Popes from the Close of the Middle Ages.* Vols. 1–22. Translated by Frederick Ignatius Antrobus and Ralph Francis Kerr. St. Louis, 1923–1932.

Prodi, Paolo. *Il sovrano pontifice: Un corpo e due anime: Le monarchia papale nella prima età moderna.* Annali dell' Istituto storico italo-germanico, Monografia 3. Bologna, 1983.

Ricard, Robert. *The Spiritual Conquest of Mexico: An Essay on the Apostolate and the Evangelizing Methods of the Mendicant Orders in New Spain, 1523–1572.* Translated by Lesley Byrd Simpson. Berkeley, 1966.

Setton, Kenneth M. *The Papacy and the Levant (1204–1571).* 4 vols. Memoirs of the American Philosophical Society, vols. 114, 127, 161, 162. Philadelphia, 1976–1984.

Shiels, W. Eugene. *King and Church: The Rise and Fall of the Patronato Real.* Chicago, 1961.

Thomson, John A. F. *Popes and Princes, 1417–1517: Politics and Polity in the Late Medieval Church.* London, 1980.

NELSON H. MINNICH

PEDRÁRIAS. See *Ávila, Pedro Arias de.*

PERESTRELO Y MONIZ, FELIPA (c. 1454–c. 1484), wife of Christopher Columbus. Felipa Perestrelo y Moniz was born to one of the most illustrious noble families of Portugal. She was the daughter of Bartolomeu Perestrelo, the son of Filippo Pallastrelli of Piacenza, and Isabella Moniz, Bartolomeu's second or third wife.

On August 26, 1479, Christopher Columbus left Genoa for the last time and returned to Lisbon, where he had met and would marry Felipa Perestrelo y Moniz. The date of the wedding is unknown, but it is assumed to have occurred either between Epiphany and Lent, 1479, or between September 20 and October 21, 1479. These dates are probable, for Gonzalo Fernández de Oviedo states that Columbus "made himself a naturalized subject of that land by his marriage," and on August 25, 1479, Columbus stated that he was still "civis Januae" (citizen of Genoa). Hence, either he was not yet married or he had been married only a few months and had not yet acquired his new citizenship.

According to Columbus's son Fernando Colón, Columbus met his wife in the chapel of the Convento dos Santos, where they were later married. Columbus told his son that the marriage was based on love, but this claim does not exclude the possibility that there were other, mundane considerations for Columbus's choice of a bride.

One was her noble lineage. Both her father and mother were descendants of noble families. Throughout Columbus's life there is evidence that he aspired to the state of nobility denied him by birth. Nobility, more than money, was the reward he stipulated for his voyage of discovery. His wife's family was just what he wished his own father's had been—and, indeed, as he persuaded himself that it had been, boasting of it to his son Fernando, who perpetuated the illusion in his biography of his father.

A second possible reason for considering the marriage was the fact that, according to Fernando Colón and Bartolomé de las Casas, Felipa's father, Bartolomeu Perestrelo, had been "a great seafaring man." Although historians may regard this characterization as an exaggeration, there is some justification for the claim. Felipa's father, who had been dead for twenty years when she married Columbus, may have been neither great seafarer nor explorer, but he had been governor of Porto Santo. The fact that Prince Henry the Navigator had assigned him an island of such importance to Atlantic exploration suggests that Bartolomeu Perestrelo not only had been descended from nobility but had known the sea. It is interesting to note that the husband of his wife's stepsister, Pedro Correa da Cunha, was the present governor of Porto Santo. He would now be Columbus's brother-in-law, and in light of the significance of the island, the potential importance of the relationship was undoubtedly evident to Columbus.

It is not possible to claim with certainty that Columbus's marriage influenced his great plan. But it is evident that the marriage was important to the genesis of the great discovery.

Christopher Columbus and Felipa Perestrelo y Moniz had one child, Diego Colón, who was born on Porto Santo around 1480. Little more is known of the Admiral's wife, who died before Columbus left Portugal in 1485.

BIBLIOGRAPHY

Ballesteros Beretta, Antonio. *Cristóbal Colón y el descubrimiento de América.* Vol. 1. Barcelona and Buenos Aires, 1945.

Taviani, Paolo Emilio. *Christopher Columbus: The Grand Design.* London, 1985.

Treen, Maria de Freitas. *The Admiral and His Lady: Columbus and Filipa of Portugal.* New York, 1989.

PAOLO EMILIO TAVIANI

PETER MARTYR. See *Anghiera, Pietro Martire d'.*

PHILIP II (1527–1598), king of Spain. When his father, Charles V, abdicated in 1555–1556, Philip inherited Spain and its possessions in America, Italy, and the Low Countries. From the first, this vast empire was threatened by hostile powers, the most important of which were France and the Ottoman Empire. The French were distracted by civil wars after their defeat by Philip's armies at Saint-Quentin (1557), but the Turks continued to present a threat even after the Spanish-Italian naval victory at Lepanto (Náypaktos) in 1571.

In 1566, Philip's efforts to reform both church and state in the Netherlands led to revolt. His army, though superior to others of the day, was able to secure only the ten southern provinces by 1579. The north soon proclaimed its independence as the United Provinces of the Netherlands, but the king's exalted conception of royal

PHILIP II. At age fifty-nine.

ELSEVIER PUBLISHING PROJECTS, AMSTERDAM

and strengthened continually thereafter. A French colony in Florida was destroyed in 1565, and Caribbean strongholds were fortified after the English raids of 1585–1586. After the defeat of the Armada in 1588 led Philip to rebuild and strengthen his Atlantic fleet, the American colonies remained almost inviolate for the remainder of his reign.

Internally, revolts by the descendants of the conquistadores in 1552–1554 and in 1565 convinced Philip that the colonies were threatened by anarchy. A committee under the presidency of Juan de Ovando reformed the Council of the Indies (1570–1572) and promulgated the Ordinances of 1573, which confirmed the rights of the Indians and attempted to set them on the road to self-government by locating them in fixed settlements. Disorder among the colonists and Indian raids on the frontiers were suppressed by two unusually competent viceroys, Martín Enríquez in Mexico and Francisco de Toledo in Peru. A *recopilación* of all laws pertaining to the Indies was begun, and in 1571 the Inquisition was extended to America. Philip may therefore be credited with establishing the basic system of Spanish colonial administration. He seems to have been in general agreement with the views of Bartolomé de las Casas, though unlike the Dominican, he questioned the morality of African slavery. The king's reformist impulses were constrained only by the desperate need for American bullion.

In the end, even the riches of the Indies proved insufficient to support Philip's policies, and Spain entered upon a long period of economic decline the ravages of which were evident well before his death. The reign of Philip II was nevertheless regarded as a golden age, and the king himself enjoyed a large measure of personal popularity. Hardworking, conscientious, and dignified, he was respected by his subjects for his piety and devotion to justice. His personal life, however, was tragic. His first wife, Maria of Portugal, died after two years of marriage, leaving him a son, Carlos, who died at twenty-three after being placed under arrest for his violent and unstable behavior. Philip was widely, and falsely, accused of murdering him. An unhappy marriage to Mary I of England was barren, and a third wife, Elizabeth of Valois, died young, leaving him two daughters to whom he was devoted. He had four sons by his fourth wife, Anne of Austria, but three of them died in childhood, leaving the survivor, the indolent Philip III, to inherit an exhausted empire that nevertheless spanned the entire world.

authority and his devotion to the Catholic cause made it impossible for him to abandon the struggle. Meanwhile, English support for the rebels caused Philip to launch the disastrous Armada of 1588 and a second invasion attempt in 1597; fear of an alliance between the French Huguenots and their Dutch coreligionists led to a series of campaigns in France after 1589. Within Spain, Philip was forced to suppress rebellions by the Moriscos (1568–1570) and the Aragonese (1591). In spite of these problems, Philip invaded Portugal in 1580 and asserted his claim to the Portuguese throne after King Henry died without heirs. He was now the ruler of a second vast empire, though he was careful to preserve Portuguese institutions and governed with the aid of Portuguese ministers.

Philip's vigorous defense of his prerogatives and the ongoing war with the Turks were enormously expensive. His policies would have been impossible without the treasures of the New World, which during most of his reign contributed between 20 and 25 percent of Spain's total revenues. Protection of the American colonies and of their lifeline, the annual treasure fleet, was therefore one of the king's primary strategic goals. This elaborate system of convoys was established at the beginning of his reign

BIBLIOGRAPHY

Elliott, J. H. *Imperial Spain.* New York, 1963.
Lynch, John. *Spain under the Habsburgs.* 2 vols. 2d. ed. New York, 1981.
Parker, Geoffrey. *Philip II.* Boston, 1978.
Pierson, Peter. *Philip II of Spain.* London, 1975.

WILLIAM S. MALTBY

PICCOLOMINI, ENEA SILVIO. See *Pius II.*

PILOTING. The art of piloting, or pilotage, is conveniently distinguished from open-ocean navigation by the fact that it is a skill based on experience and judgment, whereas ocean navigation relies on measurement and mathematics. The distinction, however, cannot be too rigidly drawn. Although astronomical navigation, which is the salient feature of ocean navigation, was developed by the Atlantic-coast Portuguese and Spaniards during the Age of Discovery, mathematical navigation was born in the Mediterranean, where the deep basins and steep coastal formations and the absence of tidal streams favored techniques based on accurate measurements. The mariner's compass, the nautical chart, and the pilot books based on precise bearings and distances were all Mediterranean developments.

On the Atlantic seaboard conditions were quite different. The rise and fall of the tide governed not only the depths in harbors and anchorages but also the ebb and flow of the often fierce tidal streams that dominated coastal passage making. During the Columbian period, the skill of the pilot lay in his ability to conduct his ship from cape to cape in coastal waters; he drew on his knowledge of off-lying dangers, local sets (directions in which local currents flow), landmarks and seamarks, bottom depths, bottom composition, and tides. By the beginning of the fourteenth century Genoese ships were trading directly with ports in the English Channel, across the Bay of Biscay from Cape Finisterre to within soundings, or within the one-hundred-fathom line, in the approaches to the Channel, using the nautical chart, the magnetic compass, and the sounding lead. No doubt Mediterranean methods were then adapted to the tidal waters and shallow depths on the continental shelf of northwest Europe. The Portuguese, too, were by this time trading with Galway and Flanders and would have been familiar with the Breton and English methods of pilotage, which were largely dependent on the log and line and traditional knowledge gained from centuries of experience.

In Columbus's day the speed of a ship through the water was a matter of estimate, not direct measurement, and one of the skills of the pilot was determining the course and distance made good each day on the basis of his estimate of speed over a given period of time or on each leg of a traverse. In the Mediterranean, the tideless conditions favored the use of compass, bearing-and-distance chart, timeglass (to measure intervals of time), and the *toleta de marteloio*. With these methods he could determine the course made good since the last known position—the process known as dead reckoning. On the

Atlantic seaboard, currents of unknown velocity and the ebb and flow of the tides upset this straightforward pattern, and the pilot had to rely more on his own resources and the traditional knowledge acquired, likely as not, through a long period of apprenticeship. As late as 1632, Adriaan Metius, a Dutch mathematician who wrote on astronomy and navigation, held that the determination of the number of miles run in twenty-four hours by a ship in ballast or laden with cargo could neither be described, explained, nor taught; only by long experience could the art of estimating the speed of voyages along familiar routes be mastered. Once the system of altura navigation had been introduced, there was some independent check of the distance traveled in a north-south direction, but the interpretation still depended on the pilot's judgment. The pilot took account of the conditions of lading, the strength of the wind, and the points of sailing taken on a course (running, making to windward, or reaching). He knew his ship, and though he might on occasion time the passage of a chip thrown overboard between two bolt-heads, using the repetition of some jingle to measure the interval of time, by and large he would trust his own judgment in estimating speed.

The timeglass, turned every half hour or hour, was used both to regulate the watch keeping and to help keep the reckoning. By night, the pilot would keep time by observing the constellation Little Dipper (Ursa Minor) and the star Kochab, the brighter of the two Guard Stars, using mnemonic rules based on the midnight position of the Guard Stars throughout the year. By day he would use a compass bearing of the sun, treating the compass rose as a clock face, each of the thirty-two points representing forty-five minutes, an inherently inaccurate system that nevertheless sufficed. Before the solution of the longitude problem, time of day, as opposed to measurement of the passage of time, was required principally for the prediction of tides. The "establishment of the port" at any place is the interval between the time the moon crosses the meridian and the actual time of high water, generally expressed in early tide tables and diagrams as a compass direction. From the "golden number," deduced from the date, from which he could calculate the epact, the pilot was able to determine the age of the moon (information he would later get from his almanac) and so the state of the tide for any port where the establishment was known.

During the Age of Discovery, the pilot was the ship's navigator. In the latter part of the fifteenth century, when oceanic navigation, which was necessarily mathematically based, was introduced, the manner in which the pilot exercised his responsibilities necessarily changed too.

[See also *Altura Sailing; Compass; Nautical Charts; Navigation; Timeglass; Timetelling.*]

BIBLIOGRAPHY

Crone, Ernst. *How Did the Navigator Determine the Speed of His Ship and the Distance Run?* Coimbra, 1969.

Waters, David W. "Early Time and Distance Measurements at Sea." *Journal of the Institute of Navigation* 8, no. 2 (1955): 153–173.

Waters, David W. *The Rutters of the Sea.* New Haven and London, 1967.

M. W. Richey

BIBLIOGRAPHY

Bascolo, Alberto. *Il genovese Franceso Pinelli amico a Siviglia di Christoforo Colombo.* Saggi su Christoforo Colombo. Rome, 1986.

Manzano Manzano, Antonio. *Christóbal Colón: Siete años decisivos de la vida, 1485–1492.* Madrid, 1964.

Taviani, Paolo Emilio. *Christopher Columbus: The Grand Design.* London, 1985.

Paolo Emilio Taviani
Translated from Italian by Rodica Diaconescu-Blumenfeld

PINELLI, FRANCESCO (c. 1450–1509), primary financier of Columbus's first voyage. Pinelli was born to an ancient family, which was among the wealthiest in Genoa in 1528. He lived in Valencia for a time and then moved to Seville as a civil servant to the Crown. He acted as the monarchs' guarantor for a loan of five million maravedis they had contracted with the duke of Medina Sidonia, and Pinelli himself loaned them one million maravedis for the purpose of transporting the last Saracen king of Granada to Africa.

The Spanish monarchs made no cash contributions to Columbus's first voyage. Rather, they provided two caravels (*Pinta* and *Niña*) that they had received from the inhabitants of Palos as fines for crimes they had committed. Money for the expedition was raised through loans made to the minister Luis de Santángel by Italian merchants residing in Spain. The largest of these (1,140,000 maravedis) came from Pinelli. Other loans came from Giannotto Berardi, Jacopo di Negro, Luis Doria, Gaspare Spinola, Francesco Rivarolo, and Francesco Castagno.

There are also several factors linking Pope Innocent VIII to the sponsorship of the voyage. First is the fact that the Pinellis, a Genoese family, were related to the Cibo family, to which the pope belonged. And documents, which scholars are still examining, have recently been uncovered in Genoa, Spain, and the Vatican that point to the pope's direct involvement in the project. Moreover, it is known that Martín Alonso Pinzón, before returning to Palos and joining Columbus's venture, was in Rome for the unloading of a ship's cargo. According to certain indications from the *Pleitos Colombinos*, he probably visited the papal court while in Rome. And finally, Monsignors Antonio and Alessandro Geraldini, who gave substantial support to Columbus between 1486 and 1492, undoubtedly had direct contact with the pope.

It is difficult, however, to draw a complete picture of the sponsorship of the voyage. It is only certain that those who invested in it knew they would make money if the voyage went well. If it did not, they would, in any case, have earned the favor of the Spanish monarchy and, apparently, the papacy.

PINTA. The *Pinta* was a caravel, the sort of vessel most frequently used by both the Portuguese and the Spanish in voyages of discovery during the late fifteenth and early sixteenth centuries. With their relatively light displacement, shallow draft, and sharp-ended hulls, and driven by the relatively efficient sails of their traditional lateen rig, they were fast, maneuverable, and capable of sailing to windward. These qualities minimized the frustrations of shoal waters and adverse winds likely to be encountered when exploring the unknown.

Like so much about ships of the period, the derivation of the caravel is controversial. Most maritime historians, however, credit the Arabs with development of both the lateen rig and the basic hull form. The Moors called a ship of this type a carabo or caravo from which the Spanish and Portuguese derived the diminutive forms carabela and caravela.

Pinta, by all accounts, was the fastest of the three ships of Columbus's fleet on his historic first voyage of discovery. This is readily explained by her finer lines as compared to those of *Santa María* and by her slightly greater length as compared to that of *Niña*. At some time prior to *Pinta*'s departure from Palos on the first voyage, her rig had been changed from the traditional lateen rig to "carabela redonda," square-rigged on foremast and mainmast with lateen-rigged mizzen. This was a far more practical rig for prolonged downwind open-ocean sailing, yet retained an only slightly reduced capability to sail to windward. Her conversion to a square-rigged configuration made it possible to improve her seaworthiness by the addition of a small raised forecastle deck, which, with her former lateen rig, would have been an obstruction to the lower end of her long, slanting lateen yard. A bowsprit, an unnecessary appendage with the lateen rig but an important adjunct to the square rig, had also been installed for accommodating the headstay of the foremast and the bowlines of the foresail and mainsail. Bowlines were attached by means of a bridle at about the midpoint of the two vertical edges of the square sails and led as far forward as possible. The purpose of bowlines, in conjunction with tack lines, was to haul forward the leading edges of the square sails to flatten and steady them for improved performance in sailing as close as possible into the wind.

There is consensus among maritime historians that *Pinta* had a cargo-carrying capacity of about sixty-five tons. From that value and from commonly used contemporary rules of thumb for hull proportions, it has been possible to arrive at reasonable assumptions of hull dimensions and shape. For a late-fifteenth-century caravel, the accepted hull proportions were in the approximate ratio of 1 for breadth or beam, 2.4 for length of keel, and 3.33 for overall length of hull. The master shipwright builder of *Pinta* would have known from his own long experience and from knowledge inherited from his father and forefathers that if the ship was to be of sixty-five tons burden her hull dimensions, using these ratios, should be roughly twenty-two feet for breadth or beam, fifty-three feet for length of keel, and seventy-three feet for overall length of hull.

Access to the hold was provided by two center-line hatches in the main deck. The main cargo hatch in the waist, just forward of the mainmast, was of a size such that a wine tun (barrel) of 1 meter by 1.5 meters could be lowered through it. A second smaller hatch was located aft under the half deck. Both hatches were fitted with covers to prevent heavy seas sweeping over the deck from pouring into the hold, which had no watertight bulkheads to control flooding.

In order to move beyond the mere external appearance of discovery-period ships and develop hard evidence of specific construction details, it is necessary is examine the relatively recent important findings of nautical archaeologists. The Institute of Nautical Archaeology at College Station, Texas, deserves great credit for important work in this field.

In 1982 the institute formed a group headed by Donald Keith to locate, survey, and excavate the wrecks of discovery-period ships in the Caribbean. Two shipwrecks they have surveyed and excavated are deemed to be of the discovery era. One is located on Molasses Reef near the Turks and Caicos Islands and the other just off the north shore of Highborn Cay in the northern Bahamas. The size and shape of the reasonably intact mound of stone ballast at the Molasses Reef wreck site indicates that the ship was of the approximate tonnage of *Pinta*, a common size for caravels of that period. A Florida-based treasure hunting company, Caribbean Ventures, which discovered the wreck, claimed it to be *Pinta* and one of four caravels in a fleet commanded by Vicente Yáñez Pinzón used during a voyage of exploration in 1499–1500. (Pinzón had been captain of *Niña* on Columbus's first voyage.) It is known that shortly after departing La Española on the return trip to Spain, Pinzón's ships encountered a severe storm and two of the caravels were lost. Most maritime historians,

however, believe there is insufficient evidence to support the claim that it is, in fact, *Pinta*.

Under the mounds of stone ballast at both the Molasses Reef and Highborn Cay shipwreck sites the institute's team found sections of the wooden hulls, which revealed valuable construction details. Substantial portions of hand-hewn keel, keelson, floor timbers, and other structural members were recovered and provided important information on their shape, dimensions, and methods of assembly and attachment. Among recovered artifacts were authenticated fifteenth-century wrought-iron breech-loading cannons (lombards) with separate breech blocks, breech-loading as well as muzzle-loading swivel guns with various types of shot for all, and several large anchors. Numerous wrought-iron hull fastenings and other fittings were found scattered about the sites. Iron gudgeons and pintles, hinge-like fittings used to fasten the rudder to the sternpost, provided information on the thickness of the sternpost and rudder. Several sets of iron rigging components provided indications of how the ships' standing rigging had been fastened to the hulls. With this sort of detailed information from shipwrecks, our knowledge of Columbus-era ships has been enhanced to a degree that now permits replicas of the two principal types, naos and caravels, to be constructed with high assurance of authenticity.

BIBLIOGRAPHY

Keith, Donald. *The Molasses Reef Wreck*. Institute of Nautical Archaeology. College Station, Tex., 1987.

Martinez-Hidalgo, José María. *Columbus' Ships*. Barre, Mass., 1966.

WILLIAM LEMOS

PINTO, FERNÃO MENDES (c. 1510–1583), merchant adventurer and author. Pinto's *Peregrination* is one of the most remarkable traveler's tales of the sixteenth century. It purports to be an autobiographical account of twenty-one years in the life of a man who traveled to almost every known—and unknown, at the time—part of Asia. In the year 1537, Pinto says, he sailed for India where he was shipwrecked, taken captive, and sold innumerable times. He was based in Malacca where he arrived in 1539, in the employ of the captain of the fortress whom he served as an ambassador-at-large to the neighboring kingdoms of Sumatra, Malaysia, and Martaban. Around 1540, after spending time in Burma and Siam, he shifted his activities to trading voyages in the China Seas and is known to have made four voyages to Japan.

Pinto claims to have been one of the first Europeans to have reached Japan, in 1542 or 1543, aboard a Chinese pirate junk that was blown off course and landed on the

FERNÃO MENDES PINTO. Statue dedicated in Almada, Portugal, 1983.

From its inception the work was enjoyed as an amusing traveler's tale, the first in European literature to tell of pirate battles on the high seas in the distant lands of the Orient. But this was far from the author's intention. A close reading reveals that *Peregrination* is a work of corrosive satire in which the author attacks the religious and political institutions of sixteenth-century Portugal. It is also a sweeping condemnation of the ideology of the crusade against the Moors, an extension of the crusade to liberate Iberia; this ideology was the justification for the overseas empire of the Portuguese, at least in Africa and Asia, and lay behind many of its excesses. Written in a period of religious strife, it is a rare book indeed in its plea for religious tolerance as a moral injunction from God. It is an early, if not the first, example, at the beginning of the age of European colonialism, of a literary work questioning the morality of the overseas conquests of the Portuguese.

Pinto's book is unquestionably an amalgam of everything he ever saw, heard, or read about Asia. But his genius lay in his ability to interweave it all into what has been described by Maurice Collis as "the most authentic picture of 16th-century Asia that has been written or that ever will be written."

BIBLIOGRAPHY

Collis, Maurice. *The Grand Peregrination*. 2d ed. London, 1990.

Le Gentil, Georges. *Les portugais en Extrême-Orient: Fernão Mendes Pinto, un précurseur de l'exotisme au XVIème siècle*. Paris, 1947.

Pinto, Fernão Mendes. *The Travels of Mendes Pinto*. Translated and edited by Rebecca D. Catz. Chicago, 1989.

Saraiva, António José. *Fernão Mendes Pinto ou a sátira picaresca da ideologia senhorial*. Lisbon, 1958. Reprint in *História da Cultura em Portugal* 3 (1962): 343–496.

REBECCA CATZ

island of Tanegashima—some fifty years after Columbus thought he had reached the Cipangu (Japan) he sought. If Pinto is to be believed, he was one of a group of three Portuguese who were indeed the first Europeans to set foot in Japan—thereby fulfilling Columbus's dream.

Sometime during his years in Asia, Pinto amassed a fortune. It was as a wealthy merchant on his third voyage to Japan that he met Francis Xavier, in 1551, and lent him the money to build the first Christian church in Japan. In 1554 Pinto joined the Society of Jesus (Jesuits) and took part in and paid for a diplomatic and evangelical mission to Japan. Two years later he was separated from the order at his own request, and in 1558 returned to Portugal.

Disappointed in his hopes of obtaining a royal sinecure, Pinto left the court after four years of fruitless petitioning. He married and retired to an estate in Almada, across the river from Lisbon. There he raised a family and wrote *Peregrination*, which became a classic of Portuguese literature; in the seventeenth century it rivaled in popularity Cervantes's *Don Quixote*.

PINZÓN, FRANCISCO MARTÍN (died c. 1500), master of *Pinta*. Francisco Martín Pinzón was the youngest member of the highly regarded Pinzón family of Palos. He was considered to be a competent mariner but seems to have lacked the forcefulness and ambition of his famous brothers, Martín Alonso and Vicente Yáñez, who overshadow him in the historical record. Nevertheless, when Martín Alonso Pinzón, the oldest and most reknowned of the brothers agreed to participate in the first of Columbus's voyages as captain of *Pinta*, he chose his young brother to serve as master instead of Cristóbal Quintero, *Pinta*'s owner, who normally would have been given that position.

Although the captain was in overall command of the ship, the master was in charge of the crew and responsible for their performance at sea and in port. Other responsibilities included the proper stowage of the cargo and all the ship's supplies and provisions, getting the ship under way with all appropriate sails set, managing the operation of the ship at sea, and anchoring the ship in a suitable location at the destination port. Unfortunately, no historical record exists of Francisco Martín's performance as master of *Pinta*. Whenever *Pinta* is mentioned in Columbus's log of the first voyage, as it is on a number of occasions, reference is made only to the captain.

On the return voyage to Spain in January and February 1493, *Pinta* became separated from *Niña* during a severe storm in the vicinity of the Azores. Driven to the northeast by the storm, *Pinta* finally made landfall on the northwest coast of Spain and sought refuge in the harbor of Bayona, near Vigo, to effect repairs. Not knowing whether *Niña* had survived the storm but certain that he had been first to reach Spain with news of the discoveries, Martín Alonso Pinzón sent word to the sovereigns in Barcelona announcing his arrival and requesting permission to come to court in person to make his report. To his dismay, and undoubtedly to that of Francisco Martín as well, the request for an audience was rebuffed. Crestfallen, the two Pinzóns set sail for Palos, reaching there on March 15 only a few hours after the Admiral's safe arrival. The sight of *Niña* already there, riding securely at anchor, was a shock. When they disembarked, they retired quietly to their home in Palos.

According to Alicia B. Gould, noted historian who spent many years searching for documentation of members of the crews of Columbus's ships of discovery, "Francisco Martín Pinzón has no historical importance, neither in that year [1492] nor later. Not one action nor one word about him comes down to us of his performance aboard ship in 1492, even though he held a position of importance; and of his later life very little is known." A notarial record in the Archive General of Simancas regarding the death of his mother, Mayor Vicente, in 1505 indicates that Francisco Martín Pinzón had predeceased her on an unspecified date. Apparently his death was as unheralded as his life seems to have been.

BIBLIOGRAPHY

Gould, Alicia B. *Nueva lista documentada de los tripulantes de Colón en 1492*. Madrid, 1984.

Manzano, Juan Manzano. *Los Pinzones y el descubrimiento de América*. 3 vols. Madrid, 1988.

WILLIAM LEMOS

PINZÓN, MARTÍN ALONSO (d. 1493), captain of *Pinta*. Martín Alonso Pinzón has been credited by many as the one person, apart from Columbus, most responsible for the success of the first voyage. In judicial proceedings (known as the Pleitos) between the heirs of Columbus and the Spanish Crown, convened in 1513, the Crown attempted to establish that Columbus was merely the nominal head of the voyage of discovery. It was Martín Alonso Pinzón, the Crown asserted, who had instigated, organized, and carried it out. Although controversy on this subject continues, most historians agree that the preponderance of evidence supports the view that Columbus conceived the plan to reach the Indies by sailing west, was responsible for convincing the sovereigns of its merit, and provided the leadership that resulted in discoveries of such significance to the world.

Yet there is little doubt that Martín Alonso and, to a lesser extent, his brothers Vicente Yáñez and Francisco Martín, all of the maritime village of Palos, were highly influential in overcoming the initial refusal by seafaring men in Palos, Moguer, and Huelva to participate in the dubious venture. They had no wish to be led by an unknown foreigner who foolishly, in their view, proposed to reach the distant Oriental regions of Cipangu (Japan) and Cathay (China) by a western route across the Mar Tenebroso (Dark Sea). To many of them, that sea abounded in countless terrors. In many testimonials offered during the Pleitos, Martín Alonso Pinzón was lauded as the most capable and honored ship captain in all the seaports of the Palos region. When Columbus came to him for help in recruiting seamen, he quickly volunteered to be captain of *Pinta*, one of the two ships provided for the venture by the town of Palos under orders from the Spanish sovereigns. During the Pleitos, a witness reported that Martín Alonso exhorted seamen of the region with the words, "Friends, come away with us. You are living here in misery. Come with us on this voyage, and to my certain knowledge, we shall find houses roofed with gold and all of you will return prosperous and happy." Another witness reported, "It was because of this assurance of prosperity and the general trust in him that so many agreed to go with him."

Also during the proceedings, Arias Pérez Pinzón, the older of Martín Alonso's two sons, testified that in early 1492 a friend of his father's, employed as a cosmographer in the Vatican Library, had given Martín Alonso a copy of a document indicating that Japan could be reached by sailing westward across the Atlantic. His father, impressed by this story, decided to attempt such a voyage himself. Soon thereafter, Martín Alonso discovered that Columbus was at the Franciscan friary of La Rábida, preparing to leave for France after learning that the Spanish sovereigns had rejected his plan for reaching the Indies. Martín Alonso, according to his son, showed Columbus his copy of the Vatican document and persuaded him to visit the sovereigns once more. Having done this, Columbus finally was successful in gaining royal approval for his enterprise. On returning to Palos, however, he tried for two months to procure ships and recruit men before turning for help to Martín Alonso, who succeeded where Columbus had failed.

Other testimony asserted that two interventions by Martín Alonso just prior to the first landfall in the Indies were vital to the success of the first voyage. By October 6, having lost faith in Columbus's pronouncements that they would reach the Indies at a distance of no more than 750 leagues (approximately 2,115 nautical miles) west of the Canary Islands, the seamen of the *Santa María* began to grumble and urge that the ship return to Spain before it became too late. According to testimony in the Pleitos, Martín Alonso proclaimed his support of Columbus and persuaded the men to continue on. Four days later, on October 10, against the opposition of the seamen of all three ships, Martín Alonso, with cries of "Adelante! Adelante! [Onward]," reportedly again convinced the men to continue the journey for three more days.

The Las Casas transcript of Columbus's log of the first voyage confirms an intervention by Martín Alonso on October 6, but of a different nature. The entry on that day states, "This night Martín Alonso said that it would be well to steer southwest by west for the island of Cipangu as indicated by the chart that Cristóbal Colón had shown him. It did not appear to the Admiral that they ought to change course because if the new course was incorrect they might miss the island and it would be safer to continue to the west and discover the mainland before going to the islands." The transcript for October 10 makes no mention of Martín Alonso but does confirm grumbling by the crew: "The men could now bear no more and complained of the long voyage. The Admiral cheered them on as best he could, telling them of great rewards they would soon gain and adding that they complained in vain because having set out for the Indies they must continue until, with the help of God, they found them."

Two days later, at two o'clock in the morning of October 12, 1492, Rodrigo de Triana, a seaman on *Pinta,* made the first sighting of land in the Indies, later confirmed to be an island of the Bahamas, which was called Guanahani by the natives. Martín Alonso Pinzón quickly verified the sighting and ordered the already loaded lombard to be fired as the signal of landfall and shortened sail to permit the flagship to catch up. When *Santa María* arrived, the Admiral also shortened sail and, with the fleet headed straight for an uncharted lee shore, ordered all three ships to lay-to until daylight. Finding a suitable anchorage on the leeward side of the island, the Admiral, accompanied by Martín Alonso Pinzón, Vicente Yáñez Pinzón (captain of *Niña*), Rodrigo de Escobedo (secretary of the fleet), and Rodrigo Sánchez (comptroller of the fleet), went ashore with royal banners flying. After a prayer of thanksgiving, Columbus took possession of the island for the king and queen and named it San Salvador.

The fleet departed San Salvador to the southwest on October 15, taking with them six natives as guides. They sighted and assigned names to a number of islands, finally reaching the north coast of Cuba on October 28. After exploring along this coast for three weeks without finding evidence of the anticipated splendors and riches of the Orient, Martín Alonso became impatient and decided to strike off on his own. The Las Casas transcript of the log entry for November 21 states, "This day Martín Alonso Pinzón sailed away with the *Pinta* without the permission and contrary to the wish of the Admiral but rather through greed, thinking that an Indian whom the Admiral had ordered aboard that caravel would give him much gold; and so he went away without waiting, without the excuse of bad weather, merely because he wished to do so." Testimony given in the Pleitos stated that after departing, Martín Alonso sailed east and discovered a large island that he believed to be Cipangu. He christened a river on its north coast with his name ("Río de Martín Alonso") and found evidence of gold in the mountains.

On January 6, 1493, Martín Alonso rejoined the Admiral who had also come upon the same island and named it La

MARTÍN ALONSO PINZÓN.   MUSEO NAVAL, MADRID

Española (Hispaniola). Having lost *Santa María* on a reef on Christmas night, Columbus was making preparations to return to Spain in *Niña*. The two remaining ships of the expedition headed east along the north coast of La Española, exploring as they went, and on January 16 took departure for Spain. A severe storm just west of the Azores separated them once again. *Pinta* was driven by the gale to a landfall on the northwest coast of Spain and sought refuge in the port of Bayona in Galicia.

Not knowing whether *Niña* had survived the storm but certain that he had been first to reach Spain with news of the discoveries, Martín Alonso promptly sent word to the sovereigns in Barcelona, announcing his arrival and requesting permission to come to court in person to make his report. Confident of a favorable response and eager to make the journey to Barcelona as early as possible, he remained in Bayona awaiting the expected summons. To his dismay, his request for an audience was rebuffed. Crestfallen, he set sail for Palos, reaching there on March 15 only a few hours after the Admiral's safe arrival. The shock of finding *Niña* already there, riding securely at anchor, struck a mortal blow. Older than Columbus, he was broken in health from the rigors of the voyage and mortified over the honors to be bestowed upon a man whose authority he had been unwilling to acknowledge. Martín Alonso Pinzón went directly to his country home near Palos and died in despair within the month.

BIBLIOGRAPHY

Gould, Alicia B. *Nueva lista documentada de los tripulantes de Colón en 1492*. Madrid, 1984.

Manzano, Juan Manzano. *Los Pinzones y el descubrimiento de América*. 3 vols. Madrid, 1988.

WILLIAM LEMOS

PINZÓN, VICENTE YÁÑEZ (c. 1461–c. 1513), captain of *Niña* and explorer. Vicente Yáñez Pinzón and his brothers Martín Alonso and Francisco Martín, captain and master, respectively, of *Pinta* on Columbus's first voyage, were respected members of the seafaring community of Palos and well known in the adjoining communities of Huelva and Moguer. Their commitment to Columbus and his enterprise helped overcome the initial reluctance of local seamen to sign on as crewmen in such a questionable venture. During the first voyage, Martín Alonso became disgruntled at finding no evidence of the anticipated riches of the Orient and left the formation to explore on his own without authorization from Columbus. But Vicente Yáñez loyally remained with the Admiral. On Christmas night when *Santa María* ran aground through the negligence of Juan de la Cosa, her owner and master, Vicente Yáñez again proved his loyalty by sending one of

Niña's boats to assist Columbus. He also refused to grant refuge to La Cosa, who had fled from his grounded ship, disregarding a direct order from the Admiral to set out a kedge anchor by which the ship might have been hauled off the reef.

The death of the eldest brother, Martín Alonso, soon after his return from the first voyage and the initial failure of the Spanish sovereigns to recognize the Pinzóns' vital role in the voyage instilled in the two surviving brothers a feeling of jealous hostility toward Columbus. Neither of the brothers took part in any of Columbus's subsequent voyages. When command of private expeditions became available in 1499, Vicente Yáñez was quick to respond. His perceived hostility toward Columbus worked in his favor, since Bishop Juan Rodríguez Fonseca, who was granting authorizations for expeditions, had long harbored a similar hostility.

Unlike Alonso de Ojeda and Peralonso Niño, other maritime adventurers who had obtained financial backing for their expeditions from wealthy merchants in Seville, Vicente Yáñez was obliged to fit out his four caravels on credit from mercenary ship outfitters in Palos. Among his crew were two nephews, several seamen, and a pilot who had been with Columbus when he discovered the Gulf of Paria and the continental landmass of South America. They put to sea from Palos early in December 1499, bypassing both the Canary Islands and the Cape Verde Islands and pressing on instead to the southwest for the southern mainland.

Pinzón deliberately took a more southerly course than Columbus had on his third voyage in order to make a landfall farther south on the mainland. This course took him across the equator. At that point, the North Star was no longer visible, and he was deprived of the only celestial means known to him for determining his latitude. The southern skies were completely foreign to him. But since seafarers of the period kept track of their position principally by dead-reckoning navigation—that is, by keeping a record of compass courses, estimated speeds, and leeway—Pinzón probably did not feel handicapped by the disappearance of the North Star. He continued on to the southwest until he reckoned his latitude to be eight degrees south of the equator, at which point he changed course to the west to find land. On January 28, 1500, nearly two months after leaving Palos, he finally sighted the easternmost promontory of the southern continent. As a sign of his relief, he named it Santa María de la Consolación and took formal possession for the Spanish Crown.

Finding the natives in the area decidedly inhospitable, Pinzón reportedly sailed off to the northwest, indicating that his landfall had been at what is now Cabo de São Roque at about five degrees south latitude rather than his reckoned eight degrees, a not unusual discrepancy in dead reckoning after nearly two months at sea. In a second attempted landing along the coast, he and his crew encountered more hostile Indians, resulting in the death of several Spaniards and the wounding of many more. Sailing on to the northwest, Pinzón recrossed the equator and was astounded to find that the seawater was so fresh he was able to refill his casks. Standing in toward the coast, he discovered the mouth of an immense river that was, of course, what we now know as the Amazon. Here, for the first time on this voyage, he found the Indians to be friendly. But finding no gold or other riches, he departed, emulating other early explorers by carrying off thirty-six of the natives as captives.

The North Star having reappeared above the horizon, Pinzón proceeded along the coast to the northwest with renewed confidence, passing the mouths of the Essequibo and Orinoco rivers, which had already been encountered by Ojeda, and eventually reached the Gulf of Paria, where Columbus had discovered the southern continent. Landing there and finding a magnificent stand of tall, straight trees, he ordered some to be cut down and loaded aboard as cargo. There is no record of his attempt to acquire any of the plentiful and valuable pearls along the coast just to the west of Paria. Instead, he set off for La Española, arriving there in late June 1500 and stopping only briefly to refit his ships for the long voyage home.

Departing La Española in July, Pinzón sailed north to the Bahamas, presumably profiting from the experience gained with Columbus in 1492 when they had headed north to find the favorable band of westerly winds to take them swiftly home. His four ships, apparently anchored at a location for which there is no existing record, were struck by a fierce hurricane, which sank two of his ships and severely damaged the remaining two. The survivors, Pinzón among them, returned to La Española, repaired the damages, and set off once again for Spain, anchoring at Palos at the end of September. The merchants to whom Pinzón was in debt for most of the expenses of the expedition promptly seized the two ships and their cargo. A petition to the Crown saved him from imprisonment and ruin, but the damage done by the hurricane stripped him of any financial gain from the voyage.

On September 5, 1501, Vicente Yáñez Pinzón received royal authorization to colonize and govern the lands he had discovered in the vicinity of the Amazon River, but there is no record of his ever exploiting that authorization. In 1506 and again in 1508, expeditions under the joint command of Pinzón and Juan Díaz de Solís attempted in vain to find a strait or passage to the Indian Ocean. On the 1508 expedition they sailed as far as forty degrees south latitude, but the honor of discovering the strait was to go to Ferdinand Magellan. In belated recognition of the important contributions made by the Pinzón family to the discovery of the Indies, Emperor Charles V, in 1519, granted their descendants a coat of arms emblazoned with three caravels and an island covered with Indians.

BIBLIOGRAPHY

Gould, Alicia B. *Nueva lista documentada de los tripulantes de Colón en 1492.* Madrid, 1984.

Manzano, Juan Manzano. *Los Pinzones y el descubrimiento de America.* 3 vols. Madrid, 1988.

WILLIAM LEMOS

PIUS II (1405–1464), pope, diplomat, poet laureate, bishop, and historian. Enea Silvio (Latin, Aeneas Silvius) was born at Corsignano, Piccolomini, Tuscany (later called Pienza after his papal name). The eldest of eighteen children of an impoverished aristocratic family, he was educated at Siena and Florence. As secretary to the bishop of Fermo, he attended the Council of Basel from 1431 to 1435, but fled because he was involved, as secretary to the bishop of Novara, in a plot against Pope Eugenius IV. He became secretary to Cardinal Nicolas Albergati and attended the Congress of Arras. Next he journeyed to Scotland, while suffering terribly after walking barefoot through snow to carry out a vow, to persuade James I to harass the English; the cardinal hoped that this would end the Hundred Years' War. In 1436 he returned to Basel and played a part in "deposing" Eugenius IV, who retaliated by dissolving the council. In 1440, Felix V (a layman and duke of Savoy, elected by the council the previous year but not recognized by the Vatican) made Enea Silvio papal secretary. Two years later, Emperor Frederick III appointed him poet laureate and private secretary; in 1445 he made his peace with Eugenius. He took holy orders in 1446, and promotion was rapid: he became bishop of Trieste in 1447, bishop of Siena in 1450, and a prince and cardinal in 1456.

In 1458 he was elected pope, taking the name Pius II, with the help of Rodrigo Borgia (later Pope Alexander VI). When Pius's open letter to Sultan Muhammad II suggesting that he convert to Christianity proved ineffective, he proposed a new crusade. In 1464, despite loss of German support, he set out from Venice as a crusader, but died at Ancona.

Enea Silvio produced numerous works in many spheres. Before he became a cleric, he wrote poems in Tuscan and Latin; a novel, *Historia de Eurialo et Lucretia,* in the style of Boccaccio; a Plautine play, *Chrysis;* and letters and essays on many subjects. His commentaries on the Council of Basel are exhaustive.

His geographical work, also known as *Cosmographia,* has the full title *Historia rerum ubique gestarum locorumque descriptio;* since it was never completed, its

Pius II. Engraving, from André Thevet's *Portraits et vies des hommes illustres*. Paris, 1584.

constituent parts are often quoted under their own titles. Perhaps his most important comments from this work concern long-distance voyages. In *De mundo in universo*, Pius writes

> It has been disputed whether this island [the known world] can be circumnavigated. Strabo the Cretan [actually of Amasia in Pontus] thought the Southern Sea could certainly not be navigated because of intolerable heat, or the northern because it was frozen. Solinus quotes Juba as claiming that in the whole of the South . . . all the sea encircling Africa, from India back to Spain, is navigable, adding stopping-places and distances. Pliny of Verona [actually of Comol] . . . quotes Cornelius Nepos [in fact, Strabo] as writing that one Eudoxus, a contemporary, fleeing from King Lathyrus, sailed from the Arabian Gulf as far as Cadiz.

From this extract and its context it is clear that Pius rejected Ptolemy's notion that southern Africa is connected to southern Asia. It may have been his influence that led to the alteration of the coastline in the pre-1460 Wilczek-Brown Ptolemaic map of southern Africa.

Pius's use of the word *hodie* (today) in his description of navigation in the eastern Atlantic reflects the assertion of the ancient Roman scholar Pliny the Elder: "totus hodie navigatur occidens" (today men sail over the whole of the West). He shows no sign of having seen Fra Mauro's map of 1459. His descriptions of Asiatic peoples are likewise derived from ancient geographers. It is probably thanks to Pius's work that an Arctic island inhabited by Aronphei appears in Johan Ruysch's map in the 1508 Rome edition of Ptolemy, of which a palimpsest has been deciphered. When Columbus reached Cuba, he thought it was Cipangu (Japan), evidently concluding from Solinus as quoted by Enea Silvio that the inhabitants were Seres, "mild, very quiet and preferring to show their bodies rather than dress."

Pius II's impact on Columbus and other Renaissance explorers should not be exaggerated. As a keen interpretation of classical geographers, his work was read with attention. His interest in contemporary geography, however, was linked not so much with exploration as with his attempt to limit Turkish expansion. He was a close friend of Nicholas of Cusa, corresponded regularly with him, and at the outset of his papacy promoted him. It is hence likely that Pius II furthered Nicholas's cartographic activities; however, any connection between these activities and areas of exploration is speculative.

BIBLIOGRAPHY

Aeneas Silvius (Pius II) *Opera*. Basel, 1571. Reprint, Frankfurt am Main, 1967.

Dilke, O. A. W., and Margaret S. Dilke. "The Wilczek-Brown Codex of Ptolemy Maps." *Imago Mundi* 40 (1988): 119–124.

Gasparrini Leporace, Tullia. *Il mappamondo di Fra Mauro*. Rome, 1956.

McGuirk, Donald L. "Ruysch World Map: Census and Commentary." *Imago Mundi* 41 (1989): 133–141.

Mitchell, R. J. *The Laurels and the Tiara: Pope Pius II, 1458–1464*. London, 1962.

O. A. W. Dilke

PIZARRO, FRANCISCO (1478–1541), Spanish conqueror of the Incas and governor of Peru. Francisco Pizarro was the illegitimate son of Gonzalo Pizarro, a royal captain of infantry and member of a recently established hidalgo family in Trujillo, Extremadura, Spain, and Francisca González, a servant of nuns and the daughter of a poor farmer. Pizarro spent much of his childhood in his paternal grandfather's home as well as with his mother's humbler relatives. He may have done agricultural work or practiced a manual trade in his earlier years. The sixteenth-century chronicler Francisco López de Gómara reported that the infant Pizarro was left at a church door, was suckled by a sow, and later was reluctantly recognized by his father and put to work herding swine. However, James Lockhart presents documentary evidence that this was a malicious story invented by Gómara, whose intention was to enhance the qualities and military successes of Hernando Cortés, Pizarro's rival.

Pizarro had some military experience in Italy before he arrived in the New World in 1502 in the fleet of Nicolás de Ovando, the governor of La Española. He either accompanied his uncle, Juan Pizarro, or was sent to join him in Santo Domingo. He became a leader in La Española, joined Alonso de Ojeda's expedition to the Gulf of Urabá in 1509, and shortly thereafter was left in charge of it as lieutenant general when Ojeda was recalled. He was second in command to Vasco Núñez de Balboa when he saw the Pacific for the first time. Governor Pedrárias (Pedro Arias de Ávila) sent Pizarro to arrest Balboa, and thereby conferred on him the enterprise of the discovery and conquest of Peru.

Pizarro was a tall, hollow-cheeked, thin-bearded, grim man of few words, ambitious but never flashy. He was well respected. When Panama was founded in 1519, he was a prominent citizen, council member, one of the largest encomenderos, and later an alcalde. Pizarro was formed

FRANCISCO PIZARRO. Engraving.

ELSEVIER PUBLISHING PROJECTS, AMSTERDAM

by his experience in the New World. He was pragmatic and defended the customs of the Americas over Spanish legalism, valued seniority in the colonies, and despised those with less experience. He favored his old companions and resented all royal or ecclesiastical supervision. Though proud of his hidalgo lineage and willing to appeal to his rank over his subordinates, he preferred to fight as a footman, the only way to fight in the isthmian jungles. He was illiterate, had never learned noble pastimes, and knew nothing of business or law, and so preferred the plebian amusements of gambling and sporting and liked to work. He was indifferent to everyone, never offered praise, was suspicious and implacable, but able to cut through verbiage and pretense. His ambition was to rule Peru as the governor and to leave his legacy to his descendants.

When the first Peru expedition was organized (1523–1524), Pizarro was senior to almost anyone else in Panama and had the longest experience of command. He was therefore put in charge. Pizarro and Diego de Almagro bore the heaviest burden of the financial support and Fernando de Luque contributed in lesser measure. In 1526 Pizarro led a second expedition to Peru, but it retired to Gallo Island off the coast of Ecuador. In 1527 Pedro de los Ríos, the governor of Panama, gave the men on Gallo the choice of returning to Panama or remaining on Gallo. Pizarro spoke in favor of remaining and thirteen men did so. No record exists of Pizarro's exact words, but the flowery speech attributed to him is not in keeping with his character. In 1528–1530 Pizarro returned to Spain by way of Panama, and in a document called the Capitulation, the Crown granted him the governorship of Peru and authorization to conquer the country. He was also made a knight of the Order of Santiago. Among the men he recruited for this expedition were his brothers Juan, Hernando, and Gonzalo, and many Trujillans and other Extremadurans.

In 1532 his expedition occupied Tumbes in the northern part of the Inca Empire, where he founded the first Peruvian settlement, San Miguel (Piura). When he entered Cajamarca to capture the Inca Atahualpa, he found it deserted and the Inca encamped nearby. When Atahualpa returned on November 16, 1532, he was ambushed by Pizarro's troops. Atahualpa offered a ransom of a room filled with gold and silver in return for his life, but Pizarro had him executed in July 1533. Though Pizarro at first founded Jauja as the capital of Peru and Cuzco, he later abandoned it and moved the capital to Lima in 1535. He later founded Trujillo and San Juan de la Frontera (Huamanga, now Ayacucho). Charles V made Pizarro a marquis in 1537 but Pizarro never chose a territorial title. In 1536–1537 the Indians laid a siege to Cuzco, which Almagro ended, seizing the city for himself. Pizarro's army defeated

Almagro at the battle of Salinas (Cuzco) in 1537 and executed him. In retaliation the partisans of Almagro's son, Diego de Almagro, assassinated Pizarro in Lima in 1541.

Pizarro left four mestizo children by two Indian mistresses. Francisca Pizarro, his legitimized daughter by Inés Yupanqui Huaylas, a daughter of Huayna Capac, lived the longest of all his children, received Pizarro's encomienda, and married his brother Hernando. His son Gonzalo Pizarro was also legitimized. His second mistress, Añas Yupanqui, a daughter of either Atahualpa or Huayna Capac, known as Doña Angelina, bore two (never legitimized) sons, Francisco Pizarro, a companion to Garcilaso de la Vega, and Juan Pizarro, who died in childhood.

BIBLIOGRAPHY

Cieza de León, Pedro de. *Tercera parte de la crónica del Perú.* Lima, 1946.
Hemming, John. *The Conquest of the Incas.* San Diego, 1970.
Lockhart, James. *The Men of Cajamarca.* Austin, Tex., 1972.
Pérez de Tudela, Juan, ed. *Crónicas del Perú.* Vol. I. Madrid, 1963.

JEANETTE SHERBONDY

PIZARRO, GONZALO (c. 1512–1548), youngest brother of Francisco Pizarro and his successor as governor of Peru. Gonzalo Pizarro was the illegitimate son of Gonzalo Pizarro and María Alonso and like his full brother, Juan Pizarro, was brought up in his father's household. He was quite young when the Incas were defeated at Cajamarca and is mostly known for the great rebellion he led against the Crown's authorities. He was arrogant, rash, and imprudent. While Hernando's ambition was to return to Spain with his wealth, Gonzalo Pizarro's was to stay in Peru and maintain the Pizarro family power and interests.

He became a major actor in the conquest of Peru upon the death of Juan Pizarro during the siege of Cuzco, when Hernando Pizarro made him captain of cavalry. After the battle of Salinas, Francisco groomed him as his second in command. He founded La Plata (Charcas) and had encomiendas in Cuzco, Charcas, and Arequipa. He was sent to Quito to govern the region and while there, led an expedition into the Amazon. When he returned, he learned that Francisco had been assassinated and that, even though Francisco had designated Gonzalo in his will as his successor, Vaca de Castro, the royal representative, had cheated him of his governorship. Vaca de Castro banished him to Charcas. When the first viceroy, Blasco Núñez de Vela, arrived in 1544, Pizarro organized a rebellion of the Peruvian Spaniards and was appointed governor of Peru by the audiencia. He ruled for about four years. In 1548, however, the royal forces of Pedro de la Gasca defeated Pizarro at the battle of Jaquijahuana, near Cuzco, and he was executed.

BIBLIOGRAPHY

Hemming, John. *The Conquest of the Incas.* San Diego, 1970.
Lockhart, James. *The Men of Cajamarca.* Austin, Tex., 1972.

JEANETTE SHERBONDY

PIZARRO, HERNANDO (1501–1578), brother of Francisco Pizarro, second-in-command in the conquest of Peru. Hernando Pizarro, the legitimate son of Gonzalo Pizarro and Isabel de Vargas, was his older brother, Francisco Pizarro's, right-hand man in the conquest of Peru. His upbringing in his father's household in Trujillo, Extremadura, Spain, had been very different from Francisco's. He was fully literate, had had extensive military experience in Europe as captain of infantry, had a horse, was knowledgeable in financial affairs, and was more comfortable with words than Francisco and even witty. His one outstanding personal trait, however, was self-centeredness. In appearance he was a massive, heavy man.

At Cajamarca he led a group of horsemen in the ambush of Atahualpa. His share in the ransom was the largest after Francisco's. He led the expedition that took the temple of Pachacámac. As Francisco Pizarro's major emissary to Spain, he conveyed part of the king's portion of the ransom to Spain as well as his own share. The Crown immediately sent him back to Peru, where he took over as lieutenant governor of Cuzco from his younger brother, Juan. He led the defense of Cuzco during the siege in 1536–1537, but when Cuzco was seized by Diego de Almagro, he was imprisoned. Upon his release, he defeated Almagro's army at the battle of Salinas and executed Almagro. He led an expedition into Collasuyu and in 1539 returned to Spain, where the Crown imprisoned him indefinitely for the execution of Almagro. He married his niece, Francisca Pizarro, Francisco's sole heir, in 1552, thus consolidating their vast wealth.

BIBLIOGRAPHY

Hemming, John. *The Conquest of the Incas.* San Diego, 1970.
Lockhart, James. *The Men of Cajamarca.* Austin, Tex., 1972.

JEANETTE SHERBONDY

PIZARRO, JUAN (c. 1509–1536), brother of Francisco Pizarro, Spanish conqueror of Peru. Illegitimate son of Captain Gonzalo Pizarro and María Alonso, Juan Pizarro grew up in his father's household in Trujillo, Extremadura, Spain, in the style of a hidalgo. He could sign his name but was otherwise illiterate. He was popular, magnanimous, and considerate. As a brother of Francisco, he was put in positions of responsibility even though he was young, the second youngest of the four Pizarro brothers in the conquest of Peru. At Cajamarca, Francisco put him in charge of one-half of the foot soldiers. He received the fourth largest share in the gold and silver of Atahualpa's ransom. He was a member of the council of Cuzco at its founding and represented the Pizarro family interests. He led the Pizarro faction in resisting Almagro's takeover of Cuzco. Juan was appointed captain general and then corregidor of Cuzco. He was mortally wounded in the seige of Cuzco and died two weeks later. He never married, but had at least one mestizo daughter in Peru, Isabel, to whom he left a dowry.

BIBLIOGRAPHY

Hemming, John. *The Conquest of the Incas.* San Diego, 1970.
Lockhart, James. *The Men of Cajamarca.* Austin, Tex., 1972.

JEANETTE SHERBONDY

PIZZIGANO CHART. The Pizzigano chart, dated 1424 and signed by Zuane Pizzigano, is preserved in the James Ford Bell Library of the University of Minnesota, Minneapolis. It is intricately bound up with the debate concerning a possible pre-Columbian discovery of America by the Portuguese.

In 1954, the chart was introduced in extravagant terms by the Portuguese historian Armando Cortesão, to whom we are indebted for its study and publication in a work published by the University of Coimbra. In the opinion of Cortesão, the chart represents the Antilles, Caribbean islands, which are given Portuguese names. If this were so, the discovery of America would have to be attributed to the Portuguese, and at a date far earlier than the one generally accepted today. (Note that even in Portugal, the first steps toward the discoveries promoted by Henry the Navigator were just being taken in 1424.) An acceptance of this idea would be nothing less than revolutionary and would detract considerably from the glory of the discoveries of the successive navigators who touched at the American continent, beginning with Christopher Columbus in 1492.

Needless to say, the opinions advanced by Armando Cortesão did not meet with unanimous acceptance among the international community of scholars of the history of discovery and ancient cartography. Quite the contrary, his conclusions were rejected by the great majority of them, especially the numerous defenders of the glories of Columbus. Even in Portugal, Cortesão's hypotheses were regarded as somewhat unsubstantiated. Among Portuguese specialists, Jaime Cortesão, in his latest publications, has reexamined, accepted, and developed the theses presented by his brother, regarding them as support for his own views on the policy of secrecy of the Portuguese Crown concerning western voyages and discoveries, a policy that began as far back as the time of Henry the Navigator. Few Portuguese scholars, however, share his enthusiasm.

The enigmatic document at the center of the debate is an Atlantic chart representing the European and African coasts (as far south as the Canary Islands) and a great number of islands, including the "fantastic isles" hypothetically identified with the Azores. To the West, beyond these, two large islands are represented ("Antilia" and "Satanazes") as well as two smaller islands ("Saya" and "Ymana").

The question arises as to whether these last four islands, especially, should be related to some actual discovery of land or rather added to the list of the many numerous fantastic islands with which Mediterranean cartography populated the Atlantic. According to Amando Cortesão, these islands represent the Antilles, and their names are typical Portuguese words. Moreover, he claims, the representation of the larger Antilles island would have some connection with the Portuguese myth of the "Island of the Seven Cities" (the myth that seven Portuguese bishops escaped from the invasion of the Iberian Peninsula by the Arabs and went to an island in the West, with Portuguese populations following them, and there they founded seven cities). Its appearance may also have been related to rumors within the circles of cartography, which came by way of a Portuguese model that found its way to Italy, of actual discoveries made by the Portuguese in the West in an earlier period. Cortesão also argues that the chart shows an incipient representation of the archipelago of Cape Verde, in the form of an island called "Himadoro" surrounded by islets south of the Canaries, which would suggest that the discoveries along the African coast would also have to be pushed back to an earlier time.

Without doubt, some of these hypotheses are quite acceptable, but others are less so. Even if the Portuguese origin of the place names and the general character of the chart were confirmed, it would still have to be proved that the land masses represented are not fantastic, that they correspond to an actual discovery of lands, and that those lands are American.

Even apart from these issues, the implications of this chart are by no means insignificant. As Jaime Cortesão notes, it is the earliest European map on which the main focus is no longer the Mediterranean but rather the Atlantic and the lands, real or fantastic, in and around it.

[For further discussion and an illustration of the Pizzigano chart, see *Cartography.*]

BIBLIOGRAPHY

Campbell, Tony. "Census of Pre-Sixteenth-Century Portolan Charts." *Imago Mundi* 38 (1986): 67–94.
Cortesão, Armando. *The Nautical Chart of 1492 and the Early Discovery and Cartographical Representation of America.* Coimbra, 1954.

Cortesão, Armando. "Pizzigano's Chart of 1424." *Revista da Universidade de Coimbra* 24 (1970).

Harley, J. B., and David Woodward, eds. *The History of Cartography.* Vol. 1, *Cartography in Prehistoric, Ancient and Medieval Europe and the Mediterranean.* Chicago, 1987.

Marques, Alfredo Pinheiro. "Novos elementos sobre a cartografia portuguesa vinte e sete anos depois da primeira publicacão dos portugaliae monumenta cartographica" (New materials relating to Portuguese cartography twenty-seven years after the first publication of "Portugaliae Monumenta Cartographica"). In vol. 6 of *Portugaliae Monumenta Cartographica,* edited by Armando Cortesão and Avelimo Teixeira da Mota. Lisbon, 1988.

Marques, Alfredo Pinheiro. *Origem e desenvolvimento da cartografia portuguesa na época dos descobrimentos.* Lisbon, 1988.

Marques, Alfredo Pinheiro. "Um novo mapa e a sua representação do Atlantico pre-Colombiano." *Oceanos* (Lisbon) 1 (1989): 55–57.

Taylor, E. G. R. "Imaginary Islands: A Problem Solved." *Geographical Journal* 130 (1964).

Vigneras, Louis-André. *La búsqueda del paraíso y las legendarias islas del Atlántico.* Valladolid, 1976.

ALFREDO PINHEIRO MARQUES
Translated from Portuguese by Rebecca Catz

PLANTS. See *Flora.*

PLEITOS COLOMBINOS. See *Lawsuits.*

POLITICAL INSTITUTIONS. [This article surveys the political landscape of Europe in the Age of Discovery and focuses on the structures of Spanish power and authority. For discussion of other European nations and city states, see *England; Florence; France; Genoa; Naples; Portugal; Rome; Venetian Republic.* See also *Papacy.* For discussion of the political organizations of the peoples of the New World, see *Indian America,* especially the articles on the Aztecs, Incas, and Mayas. The political institutions of Africa and Asia are discussed in *Africa; China; Cipangu; Ottoman Empire.*]

As the European Middle Ages drew to a close, the two great universal powers, the papacy and the empire, were in decline. The Renaissance popes had only recently overcome the challenge of conciliarism, that is, the idea that a general council had supreme authority in the church, even over the pope. Despite the increasingly loud cry for reform of the church in head and members, the popes were fearful of convoking a reform council, lest the specter of conciliarism should reappear. The Holy Roman Empire, ruled by the Habsburgs from their base in Austria, was in the process of disintegration into a collection of petty autonomous states. The empire's southern frontier was menaced by the presence of the Ottoman Turks in the Balkan peninsula. New nation-states were beginning to take shape in England, France, Spain, and Portugal. As the Hundred Years' War came to an end, England suffered through the dynastic Wars of the Roses and then enjoyed a resurgence under the Tudor dynasty that came to power in 1485. France, freed of the burden of the Hundred Years' War, also endured a period of civil war as the dukes of Burgundy tried to create an independent kingdom on France's eastern frontier. When King Charles VIII (r. 1483–1498) embarked on an adventuresome policy by invading Italy in 1494, he not only aroused the opposition of the papacy and the north Italian states, but initiated a long rivalry between France and Spain. Portugal, under Kings João II (r. 1481–1495) and Manuel I (r. 1495–1521) continued the work of colonization and exploration in the Atlantic begun by Henry the Navigator (d. 1461). Before the close of the century the Portuguese captain Bartolomeu Dias reached the southernmost tip of Africa and Vasco da Gama completed the roundtrip from Portugal to India.

The most momentous development in fifteenth-century Spain was the union of Castile and Aragón, the two most powerful Hispanic kingdoms. The basis for the union was laid in 1469 by the marriage of Isabel of Castile (r. 1474–1504) and Fernando of Aragón (r. 1479–1516). The fundamental equality of the sovereigns and their joint action was symbolized in various ways such as their motto, *tanto monta, monta tanto* ("one is equal to the other"), and the yoke and the arrows they adopted as their arms. In 1494 Pope Alexander VI accorded them the honorific title "los reyes católicos," or "the Catholic monarchs," in recognition of their triumph over the Moors of Granada and their establishment of religious unity in their realms.

The union of their kingdoms was a purely personal one, as each retained its identity and distinctive institutions and laws. Isabel, as queen proprietress of Castile, exercised the fullness of authority in her kingdom, but in 1475 she shared that responsibility with Fernando, so much so that public documents ordinarily were issued in the names of both. Fernando in 1481 also acknowledged her as coruler in Aragón. Although they might have simply called themselves monarchs of Spain, they maintained the traditional royal intitulation that recorded the separate identity of the eighteen kingdoms and several counties under their rule. After 1492 the Kingdom of Granada was added to the list.

The idea of the state as an entity distinct from the sovereigns, the people, and the territory of the realm was well developed in the time of Fernando and Isabel. The state was an abstraction, something intangible, but nevertheless having a real existence. Described as the *estado del reino* (state of the realm) or the *cosa publica* (republic), it was often compared to the human body. As the head of the body politic, the ruler was responsible for preserving and maintaining the state. The sum of the ruler's rights and powers was expressed by the term *corona real* (royal crown). The development of a patriotism that exalted the homeland of Castile and extolled the virtues of the Castilian nation assisted the monarchs in carrying out their responsibilities.

Fernando and Isabel's primary task was to restore the authority and prestige of the monarchy that had been seriously undermined by the ineptitude of preceding rulers. Poets and theorists, hoping that the king and queen would bring about a new age of greatness for Spain, exhorted them and applauded their efforts.

The monarchy retained a secular character that distinguished it from the monarchies in France and England where so much emphasis was placed upon the priestly or sacred character of the institution. Neither Fernando nor Isabel was anointed and crowned by an archbishop as was customary elsewhere. Rather, each was acclaimed and received an oath of allegiance and pledged to uphold the laws of the land. Although it is commonplace to describe their government as a form of royal absolutism, one should understand that in relative terms. Royal authority was always limited by circumstances and even by institutions. The Catholic monarchs made those institutions work more effectively and so greatly strengthened royal power.

As yet there was no fixed capital, although Valladolid and Toledo (and Granada after its fall in 1492) were favorite residences. The monarchs were basically itinerants, traveling their realm in the company of their household and court. In order to carry out their responsibilities, they surrounded themselves with persons distinguished by talent rather than ancestry. The magnates were drawn to the monarchy by honors and stipends, but the duties of administration most often were entrusted to members of the lesser nobility or the bourgeoisie. A major change in administration was the prominent role given to legists (*letrados*) trained in Roman law, whose principal concern was to maintain and expand the authority of the Crown. The royal council, or *consejo real*, reorganized in the Cortes of Toledo in 1480, advised the monarchs on all affairs touching the Kingdom of Castile, but it also acted on its own initiative. Prelates, nobles, and others might attend the council, but the voting members were one prelate, three knights, and eight or nine legists. The council retained a traditional function as the highest judicial tribunal, but it assumed more and more responsibility for government, administration, finance, and foreign policy. The secretaries, with custody of the royal seals, were especially influential because they had direct and continual access to the sovereigns. They intervened in all major and minor affairs and served as a link between the king and queen and the council. Aragonese affairs were handled by the Consejo de Aragón, whose members ordinarily remained with the king in Castile rather than in Aragón.

Several additional councils were created for exceptional purposes. In the late thirteenth and early fourteenth centuries the towns had organized associations, or hermandades, in times of crisis to defend their rights. In 1476 Fernando and Isabel established the Santa Hermandad and placed it under the control of the Consejo de la Santa Hermandad. As its purpose was to restore law and order in the towns and in the countryside, the hermandad maintained a militia that guaranteed public security and pursued criminals. Abuses, however, provoked the townspeople who asked that the hermandad be dissolved. Only in 1498, when the king and queen were satisfied that it had done its work, did they take that step.

As the military orders of Calatrava, Santiago, and Alcantara had participated in the factional struggles of the preceding reigns, Fernando and Isabel decided to bring the extensive resources of the orders under royal control. With papal consent, they united the administration of the orders to the Crown between 1489 and 1494. They also created the Consejo de las Ordenes in 1495 to administer the orders on their behalf. Pope Adrian VI in 1523 annexed the masterships to the Spanish Crown in perpetuity. After the papacy approved the establishment of the Inquisition in Castile, the Catholic sovereigns set up the Consejo de la suprema y general Inquisición in 1483 through which they controlled the appointment of inquisitors and directed their activities. Though this was primarily a Castilian institution, its authority also extended to Aragón. Finally, the Consejo de las Indias, established at Seville in 1511, controlled all activities relating to the exploration and colonization of the New World.

Fernando and Isabel convened the Cortes of Castile in 1476 and 1480 to promulgate their reform program but neglected to summon it again until 1498. By the more efficient collection of taxes and the development of other financial resources, the Crown was not dependent upon subsidies voted by the Cortes. The Cortes was summoned in 1498 and on several occasions thereafter principally to acknowledge the heir to the throne. The Cortes could scarcely claim to represent the estates of the realm because the prelates and magnates seldom attended, and only eighteen towns, with two representatives each, were entitled to speak for the third estate. The Castilian Cortes met only nine times in Isabel's reign of thirty years, and Fernando summoned the Catalán parliament, or *corts*, only seven times. Meetings of the parliaments of Aragón and Valencia were equally infrequent. Thus by careful manipulation, the monarchy thwarted any challenge that the Cortes might represent.

Fernando and Isabel took seriously their responsibility to administer justice to all and for that purpose promulgated many laws, or *pragmáticas*, which were printed in 1503. They also authorized Alonso Díaz de Montalvo to publish in 1484 a collection of laws entitled *Ordenanzas reales de Castilla*. New editions of the laws of Catalonia and Aragón were published by Fernando's order. The monarchs also encouraged the towns to revise and publish their *fueros* (municipal charters) and ordinances, eliminating contradictory laws or others no longer in force. The printing press disseminated the books of laws more widely than ever before.

The royal council remained the supreme tribunal, but the audiencia, a special court of justice that was developed in the fourteenth century, was now revitalized and, called the *chancilleria*, was established at Valladolid. Ordinances drawn up in 1486 regulated the activities of the president, the *oidores*, who were responsible for civil cases, and the alcaldes, who dealt with criminal matters. There were also noble judges who heard suits involving the nobility. For the most part, these judges were laymen rather than clergy as had often been the case in the past. In view of the great territorial extension of the Kingdom of Castile, a similar tribunal to handle litigation south of the Tagus River was created at Ciudad Real in 1494 and transferred to Granada in 1505.

Fernando and Isabel greatly increased their revenues by recovering estates alienated from the Crown and by the more efficient collection and administration of taxes. Royal income rose from 27 million maravedis in 1470 to 317 million in 1504. Although the royal council had general oversight of finances, a more elaborate administrative apparatus was developed. The *mayordomo mayor* (chief steward) and three subordinate *contadores mayores* (chief accountants) were entrusted with daily responsibility for managing the royal finances. The tax system was essentially the same as before, even to the point of continuing the immunities of the nobility and the clergy. The most important sources of revenue were the *alcabala*, or sales tax (about 70–80 percent of the total revenue), customs duties known as *diezmo* and *almojarifazgo*, the *servicio y montazgo* levied on transhumant sheep, ecclesiastical contributions such as the *tercias reales* (two-ninths of the tithe), and papal subsidies for the crusade against Granada. Of lesser value were the *servicios* voted by the Cortes. The Crown also benefited from its monopoly of salt and the coinage. The Crown still contracted with tax farmers who were authorized to collect various taxes, provided that the government received a specified amount. The tax farmer retained any surpluses as profit. The towns also contracted to pay fixed sums.

The office of *adelantado mayor* (provincial governor), which had had responsibility for territorial administration, was now in a state of decline. Many of its duties were taken over by corregidores, usually knights or legists dispatched permanently to most of the Castilian towns after 1480. As these officials enjoyed supreme judicial and administrative authority, the towns lost much of their traditional autonomy. By nominating the regidores who formed the municipal council, or *cabildo*, and the procurators whom the towns sent to the Cortes, the Crown exercised far more direct control over municipal affairs than ever before.

Some towns that had once depended directly on the Crown had been alienated by the preceding Trastámara kings and were now held in lordship by nobles or prelates. Fernando and Isabel established a few minor lordships and attempted to clarify seigneurial jurisdiction.

The king and queen reemphasized the principle that all able-bodied citizens had the responsibility to be prepared to defend the realm. In practice the royal army was formed by the municipal militias, by contingents brought by the military orders, and by the nobles in fulfillment of their duty as royal vassals. As a consequence of a concerted effort to develop a permanent army, the Crown had at its disposal in 1504 a force of about eight thousand, consisting of men-at-arms, light cavalry, artillery, and infantry.

By restoring the prestige and authority of the monarchy and repairing the governmental structures that had been so damaged during the previous three-quarters of a century, Fernando and Isabel prepared Spain to dominate Europe in the sixteenth century.

[See also *Isabel and Fernando; Spain.*]

BIBLIOGRAPHY

Azcona, Tarsicio de. *Isabel la Católica: Estudio critico de su vida y su reinado.* Madrid, 1964.

Ladero Quesada, Miguel Angel. *La Hacienda Real de Castilla en el siglo XV.* La Laguna de Tenerife, 1973.

Lunenfeld, Marvin. *The Council of the* Santa Hermandad: *A Study of the Pacification Forces of Ferdinand and Isabella.* Coral Gables, Fla., 1970.

Lunenfeld, Marvin. *Keepers of the City: The* Corregidores *of Isabella I of Castile (1474–1504).* Cambridge, 1987.

JOSEPH F. O'CALLAGHAN

POLO, MARCO (1254?–1324), Italian traveler and writer. Most of what is known about Polo, his travels in Asia, and the origin of his famous book is drawn from the biographical portions of that ghostwritten masterpiece. He was born of a Venetian merchant family of Dalmatian ancestry, and, as a young man, accompanied his father, Niccolò, and uncle, Maffeo, on an overland journey to Mongol China, where they resided from 1275 to 1292. This trip was preceded by a visit of the elder Polos to the court of Kublai Khan in the late 1260s. The earlier journey was the outcome of a commercial venture among the western Mongols; but when Niccolò and Maffeo returned to the West, they came as ambassadors of the Grand Khan bearing the request to the pope to dispatch one hundred learned missionaries to undertake the conversion of the Mongols to Christianity. This request was only partially fulfilled when, accompanied by the seventeen-year-old Marco, they returned to China in an embassy appointed by Pope Gregory X, who, as the former papal legate in the Holy Land, had strong interests in extending Christianity in Asia.

According to his book, Polo served the Mongol government in an official capacity, which enabled him to travel in southern China and Indochina on fact-finding missions for the Grand Khan. Whether his book derived from the notes and memoranda prepared during these official trips is

MARCO POLO. As depicted on the frontispiece of the first printed edition of Marco Polo's book of travels (Nürnberg, 1477), showing the author as a young German knight.

unknown. The chance to return home was provided by the family's appointment as members of a bridal party that escorted a Mongol princess to the court of the Persian khan. The return journey was made by the sea route from China, through the straits of Singapore and Malacca, to Ceylon, along the western coast of India, and thence to Hormuz on the Persian Gulf—an itinerary that attracted considerable interest among European explorers of a later period.

Polo's book was produced while he was imprisoned in Genoa (1298–1299) following his capture during a naval battle between Venice and Genoa. In prison he met the author of several Arthurian romances, Rustichello (or Rusticiano) of Pisa, to whom he related his experiences in Asia and who composed them in the distinctive Italianized French dialect of Rustichello's own surviving romances. It was probably Rustichello who gave Polo's book its flourishes of chivalric rhetoric and much of its legendary content. The book, known in English as *The Travels*, circulated under various titles: *The Description of the World*, *The Million*, *The Book of the Customs and Conditions of the Oriental Regions*, and simply *The Book of Marvels*. Its Italian title, *Il milione*, may reflect the skepticism of readers as to the author's truthfulness, although the word became attached to Polo's surname and may have originally been part of it. *Description of the World* was probably the more appropriate title, since it conveyed Polo's intention to compose a grand ethnographical and geographical encyclopedia of the peoples and places he had encountered in his travels (and some he had not).

During the fourteenth and fifteenth centuries, the book was translated into most of the European vernacular languages and twice into Latin. Francesco Pipino's Latin translation (1320), which was commissioned by the Dominicans, and which in its printed edition (1485?) was read by Columbus, was preceded by a prolog in which the translator argued the book's usefulness for converting pagans. The *Description* survives in some 140 manuscript copies, which vary greatly because of deletions and interpolations by generations of translators and copyists. After the invention of printing, the book appeared in almost 160 separate editions from 1477 on.

Lingering suspicion as to the author's possible exaggerations did not appear to diminish its appeal to readers who were strongly attracted to exotic travel writing and similar books of "marvels" such as Sir John Mandeville's *Travels* (1356?). Its influence on geographical knowledge and cartography only gradually became apparent as in the world maps of Abraham Crescas (1376?) and Fra Mauro (1459), which it provided with names and physical locations. The European voyages of exploration and discovery during the late fifteenth and the sixteenth centuries gave

Polo's book new influence. The efforts of Pope Eugenius IV (1431–1447) and the Council of Ferrara-Florence (1438–1442) to unite the western and eastern churches and to expand the bounds of Latin Christendom promoted interest in earlier reports of Christians in India and China such as those of Polo concerning the Church of Saint Thomas at Mylapore, India, and the Nestorian communities among the Mongols. The papal secretary and humanist, Poggio Bracciolini, published in 1492 a narrative of the travels of the Venetian Niccolò de' Conti (c. 1395–1469) in Southeast Asia, which was republished in Portuguese (1502) and Spanish (1503) translations in volumes that also included Polo's book.

Giovanni Battista Ramusio (1485–1557), Polo's first biographer, was the source of the report that Prince Pedro, Henry the Navigator's brother, acquired a copy of the *Description* from the Venetians. Columbus's interest in the book is shown by the annotations in his personal copy and by his lament to the Spanish sovereigns in the prologue to his logbook concerning the lost opportunity to convert the subjects of the "Great Khan of India." Polo's influence on Columbus and his successors was possibly more inspirational than scientifically nautical. His descriptions of the wealth of the Spice Islands and the Indies were appealing to the "insular romanticism" of Europeans who compiled gazeteers of the world's islands. Ramusio, the anthologist of sixteenth-century travel writing, compared Polo very favorably with Columbus, and by reprinting the *Description* in his collection of famous voyages (1559) made a place for Polo in the history of European exploration and discovery. By 1600 the growth of geographical knowledge had displaced Polo and his book from among the canon of authorities of European expansion.

BIBLIOGRAPHY

Moule, A. C., and Paul Pelliot. *Marco Polo: The Description of the World.* 2 vols. London, 1938.

Olschki, Leonardo. *Marco Polo's Asia: An Introduction to His "Description of the World" Called "Il Milione."* Translated by John A. Scott. Berkeley and Los Angeles, 1960.

Reichert, Folker. "Columbus und Marco Polo—Asien in Amerika," *Zeitschrift für historische Forschung* 15, no. 1 (1988): 1–63.

Yule, Sir Henry. *The Book of Ser Marco Polo the Venetian concerning the Kingdoms and Marvels of the East.* 3d ed. Revised by Henri Cordier. 2 vols. London, 1926.

W. R. JONES

PONCE DE LEÓN, JUAN (1474–1521), Spanish explorer and founder of San Juan, Puerto Rico. Ponce de León was born in San Servás de Campos, province of Palencia, in Old Castile in 1474, the year attested by him in an inquiry into the death of Cristóbal de Sotomayor during Puerto Rico's general Indian uprising in 1511. He was a veteran of the reconquest of Spain from the Moors and volunteered in 1493 for Columbus's second voyage of discovery to the New World.

He was the nephew of Rodrigo Ponce de León, Spain's outstanding hero of the Reconquista, first duke and marquis of Cádiz, and third count of Arcos. Ponce de León has been erroneously described as a "peon," or laborer. The contemporary meaning of *peon* was "foot soldier," and on that second voyage even noble caballeros had to walk, since there were no horses.

In La Española he founded the town of Salvaleón de Higüey, and on June 24, 1506, with a crew of one hundred, he sailed to the place he had landed in 1493, identified in nautical charts as *aguada*, or "watering place." There he built a fort and houses, which were destroyed during the 1511 Indian uprising but were soon rebuilt and named San Germán by Miguel Díaz d'Aux. In 1508 he also founded the town of Caparra, which was resettled in 1520 on the site of present-day San Juan as a capital city.

On February 23, 1511, he was commissioned by the king to conduct punitive expeditions against the Carib Indians. These forays took him as far as the Gulf of Darien and Yucatán in Mexico, in the course of which he discovered the "islands of Bimini," which he named Florida.

Ponce de León was an outstanding conquistador, settler, and partner in an agricultural enterprise with the king of Spain. When a court ordered him to vacate the governorship of Puerto Rico in favor of Columbus's heir, Diego Colón, King Fernando invited him to court to reward him for his deeds. As compensation for the lost governorship, the king, on September 27, 1514, appointed him adelantado of the lands he had discovered, known as Bimini and Florida, which extended from forty leagues north of Panuco in Mexico to Newfoundland.

A scientific-minded and cultured nobleman, Ponce de León served at one time or another as notary, Indian overseer, government comptroller and treasurer, public works overseer, surveyor, gold prospector, king's courier to Vasco Núñez de Balboa and Pedrárias Dávila (Pedro Arias de Ávila) in Darién, warden of Fortaleza Palace in San Juan, municipal assemblyman of San Juan, land and sea captain, navigator, and cosmographer. His ship's log for the trip from Puerto Rico to Florida and Yucatán in 1513 shows that he developed a graphical system for estimating accurate latitudes from his quadrant readings; this preceded the Nonio and Vernier instruments for measuring distances too small for visual reading.

Acting as a military engineer, he designed fortresses and towns. Their streets radiated from a central plaza containing a church, hospital, city hall, and jail nearby to which would be a tall post where punishment was meted out. The residential lots were sized according to the citizens' standing in the community.

Ponce de León discovered Mexico in 1516, landing at San Juan de Ulúa near Veracruz, as attested by Spanish records and Maya codexes. His sea chart guided Hernando Cortés who landed there in 1519. It was Ponce de León who dispatched an armed ship to Veracruz to reinforce Cortés for a counterattack on the Indians who had driven him from the capital city of Tenochtitlán.

Ponce de León's chart and log of his 1513 voyage to Florida and Yucatán provide one possible solution to the identity of the first island discovered in the New World, Guanahani; Guanahani was known in the neighboring island of Ciguateo (now Eleuthera) by the name of Guanimá (now Cat Island). During that same voyage he discovered the Gulf Stream while crossing it from the Bahamas toward Florida. He describes in his ship's log its tremendous force: on a very clear day the current near the coast was stronger than a stiff contrary wind.

Ponce de León settled at Charlotte Harbor in Florida in 1521, but that year the Calusa Indians attacked the settlement. An arrow pierced Ponce de León's armor and his left thigh, forcing him to sail to Havana for treatment, where he died. His remains now rest in a marble mausoleum in the San Juan cathedral. He has been remembered in history mostly for his putative search for the "Fountain of Youth" spoken of in Indian legends. But he was in reality a man of many achievements and the first European to land in and explore the continental United States.

BIBLIOGRAPHY

Tió, Aurelio. *Nuevas fuentes para la historia de Puerto Rico.* Barcelona, 1961.

AURELIO TIÓ

PORTOLANO. See *Cartography; Nautical Charts; Sailing Directions.*

PORTO SANTO. Porto Santo, one of the Madeira Islands, sometimes called the golden island or the windmill island, lies 64 kilometers (40 miles) northeast of Funchal, Madeira. The island is 11 by 6 kilometers (7 by 4 miles) with a circumference of 38 kilometers (24 miles). Its capital is Vila Baleira.

Porto Santo is low lying and flat except for the high peaks at each end. The population in the fifteenth century is estimated at six hundred inhabitants. The highest point is Pico do Facho (*facho* means "torch," and it was from this peak that signals warning of approaching pirates were sent). The climate is drier and warmer than Madeira. Wind blows every day and the original settlers built windmills to pump water and grind grain. Very little now grows in the chalky limestone soil, and the landscape has an ocher color except after a rain, when it becomes light green.

The island was discovered by mariners trading between Bristol, England, and Genoa in the 1340s. A legendary account claims that during 1344, Robert McKean in his cog *Le Welyfare* abducted his lover, Anna of Hereford; thirteen days later his ship met a storm and was wrecked off Madeira. Moors picked up the survivors and imprisoned them, from whence the story of the islands spread. The Medici Map of Genoese origin dated 1351 indicates this island with the name Porto Santo (Italian, Porto Seo).

The island's association with Christopher Columbus begins with the forebears of his wife. In 1419, João Gonçalves and Tristram Vaz were blown to Porto Santo by a storm. In their company was Bartolomeu Perestrelo, whose daughter, Felipa Moniz, would marry Columbus in 1479. In 1446, the island had been granted by royal charter to Bartolomeu Perestrelo, making him lord proprietor during the reign of Dom Duarte, king of Portugal. The island was controlled by him and his heirs until April 7, 1497, except for the period from 1458 to 1470 when it was owned by Pedro Correira da Cunha, governor of Graciosa. The Perestrelo family regained ownership in 1470, and in 1497, the island was incorporated under the Crown of the Portuguese kingdom to be governed by the laws and king of Portugal.

In the traditional account, Columbus, Felipa, and their infant son stayed with Bartolomeu Perestrelo II in Porto Santo for two years (1478–1480) while Columbus tried to set himself up as a sugar trader in Funchal. By this time, the island had been ruined for agriculture by infestations of rabbits and the harvesting of dragon trees; earlier documents show the island to have been a source of beef, wild pig, and wild rabbit.

Still standing is the church where Columbus was supposed to have worshiped, Nossa Señhora da Piedade, which dates from 1494. Down a narrow lane beside the church is a white-washed house dating from the time Columbus was in the islands. A museum in Vila Baleira dedicated to Columbus was opened in 1987.

[See also *Madeira.*]

BIBLIOGRAPHY

Azurara, Gomes Eanes de. *Crónica da Guiné.* Edited by Livraria Civilizacão. Oporto, 1973.

Cadamosto, Luis de. *Navegacão de Luis de Cadamosto.* Lisbon, 1944.

Carita, Rui. *Historia da Madeira, 1420–1566.* Funchal, 1989.

Frutuoso, Gaspar. *As Saudades da Terra.* Lisbon, 1590. Reprint, edited by Alvaro Azevedo. Funchal, 1873.

J. DONALD SILVA

PORTUGAL. Portugal emerged as an independent nation in the year 1140 by liberating the western corner of the Iberian Peninsula, which had been overrun by the Moors. Under Afonso III (r. 1248–1279), who finally drove the last of the Moors southward across the sea, Portugal achieved its present-day boundaries, which from 1263 remained permanently fixed. Under Dinis I (r. 1279–1325), Portugal entered upon an era of colonial and maritime expansion. A Genoese, Manuel Pessagno, was hired as hereditary admiral of the Portuguese navy, and some twenty Genoese seamen entered the service of the king of Portugal—forerunners of Columbus, a later compatriot whose exploits were to be far more significant for both Portugal and the world.

On the death of King Fernando I (r. 1367–1383), whose sole heiress was married to Juan I of Castile, a popular revolution overthrew the dynasty out of fear of Spain's claiming the throne. In 1385, João of Aviz, illegitimate son of Pedro I (r. 1357–1367), was proclaimed king after a resounding victory on the battlefield of Aljubarrota. That same year, João married Philippa of Lancaster, daughter of John of Gaunt, and the Portuguese court entered one of the most promising periods in its history. The couple's third son, Henry, who became known as the Navigator, earned a large place in the history of Portugal and the world for his contributions to nautical science.

The first stage of the overseas expansion of Europe can be regarded as beginning with the capture of Ceuta (on the Moroccan coast) by the Portuguese in 1415. Ceuta was literally the opening gun in the great adventure that did not end until a large part of the known world came within the sphere of Portuguese influence. The three oldest sons of King João I were anointed for their heroism in the capture of such a glorious prize, though no one could foresee then that Ceuta was the initial step toward the conquest of Africa. But the main impulses behind the Age of Discovery undoubtedly were a mix of religious, economic, strategic, and political factors, all of which were celebrated in the literature of the period. The lyricism of the Middle Ages, the melancholy and simple melodies that distinguished the abundant poetry of Galicia and Portugal, was to give way to a severe but exultant prose—the chronicles of the historians who found more inspiration in the exploits of warriors and crusaders, explorers and adventurers, than in the love affairs of peasant girls and shepherds. History and historical evocation were the most original forms of expression during the fifteenth century.

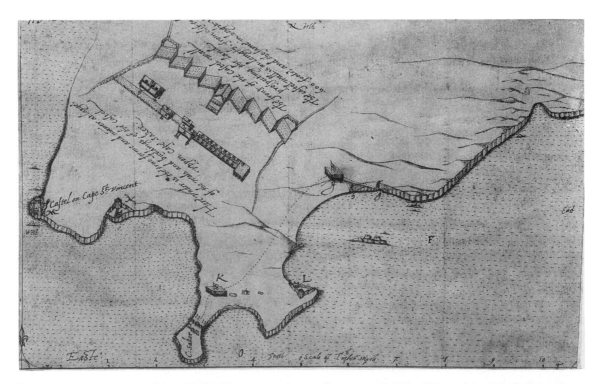

PLAN OF THE WORKS OF CAPES SAKER AND ST. VINCENT IN SOUTHERN PORTUGAL. Showing some of the installations where, according to tradition, Henry the Navigator sponsored much research and innovation in the art of navigation. The site advantageously faced Africa and the shipping routes between the Mediterranean and the Atlantic. This English drawing is from 1587.

The seizure of Ceuta in 1415 and, more important, its retention were probably inspired mainly by crusading ardor to deal a blow at the infidel and the desire of the half-English princes of Portugal to be dubbed knights on the field of battle in a spectacular manner. But there is no doubt that the occupation of Ceuta enabled the Portuguese to obtain some information about the territory of the native peoples in the Upper Niger and Senegal river regions where there was gold. Under the aegis of Prince Henry the Navigator, Portuguese ships went out along the coast of Africa, following up on the information.

The next stage in the Portuguese expansion began with the discovery, or rather the rediscovery, of the islands that lay not far from Portugal proper—the Azores and Madeiras. In all probability they were rediscovered by Portuguese vessels returning from the African coast. The Madeiras became a Portuguese outpost at a very early date after their rediscovery by João Gonçalves Zarco who sighted Porto Santo in 1418. The formal discovery of the Azores has been attributed to Gonçalo Velho Cabral who, in 1431, was instructed by Prince Henry to sail westward in search of these islands, which appeared on early maps. The colonization of both uninhabited archipelagoes followed quickly.

The next step toward conquering Africa geographically was to round Cape Bojador (present-day Boujdour, Western Sahara) and move on to Cape Verde. But for a long time terror inspired by ancient legends kept the Portuguese from sailing around the cape. In 1433 Henry sent out Gil Eanes to prove that it was possible to go beyond Bojador. Eanes failed on that trip but succeeded on a second try, demonstrating that it was possible to sail southward beyond the line that ignorance had set as the outward limit of navigability. In 1444 a voyage under the command of Nuno Tristão pushed still farther south and saw for the first time the lands where black Africans lived, far beyond the territories of the Islamized Moors. Between 1445 and 1448, caravel after caravel sailed out of Portugal bent on expanding the knowledge already acquired and pushing the known frontier farther and farther south. After a hiatus, the voyages resumed, and from 1470 to 1475, under Afonso V (r. 1438–1481), they were leased on a monopoly basis to Fernão Gomes, a wealthy Lisbon merchant. He discovered a large stretch of the Guinea coast, which was opened up to Portuguese enterprise and trade.

From 1480 on, the *mare clausum* (closed sea) policy in the Gulf of Guinea was enforced by Prince João, son and heir of Afonso V, who had placed him in charge of the African voyages. Coast guard squadrons had orders to execute on sight any intruder who was found south of the parallel of the Canaries. In 1481 the prince ascended the throne as João II (r. 1481–1495) and issued orders to Diogo de Azambuja to construct a castle at São Jorge da Mina (on what was later known as the Gold Coast), which was completed in 1482 and became the principal source of gold in the fifteenth century. It is believed that Columbus made one or two voyages to São Jorge in the company of Azambuja.

About the same time, João II ordered the first voyage of exploration undertaken by Diogo Cão (1482–1484) to sail beyond the then known limits of the African coast, south of the Gulf of Guinea, below the equator. He reached the Zaire River, sailed beyond it, and got as far as Cape Lobo on the coast of Angola, where he mistakenly believed he had reached the tip of Africa and the waters of the Indian Ocean. On this voyage he made contact with the Kingdom of the Congo where he established friendly relations that were later to bear fruit.

In the meantime, while the first voyage of Diogo Cão was underway, another explorer, João Afonso de Aveiro, was sent overland into the interior of Africa, starting from the coasts of Benin and present-day Nigeria. He announced on his return that he had heard of the presence in the area of Prester John, a legendary African potentate for whom the Europeans had been searching for years. Toward the end of 1484 or the beginning of 1485, Columbus appeared in audience before the king with a proposal for reaching the Indies by sailing west. King João submitted his proposal to a scientific council, which rejected it. It was at that time that a disappointed Columbus left Portugal for Spain. It is possible that one of the reasons for his rejection, among others, was the information brought back by Diogo Cão and João Afonso de Aveiro, information that led the king to believe that the Portuguese were already on the threshold of India.

During the years 1485–1486, Diogo Cão was sent out on a second expedition. He had passed beyond the limits of his first voyage and reached a point on the African coast called Serra Parda when he realized he had been mistaken in believing he had reached the tip of Africa on his previous voyage. There now appeared to be no end to the African coast, which continued farther south. He set up a commemorative pillar and returned to Portugal in 1486 with a plan for reaching southern Africa by cutting a wide circuit to the west, as Vasco da Gama was to do later on his momentous journey to India in 1497–1499.

The crusading impulse and the search for Guinea gold were soon reinforced by the quest for Prester John. This mythical potentate was vaguely located in the "Indies"—an elastic term often embracing Ethiopia and East Africa as well as what little was known of Asia. The passage of time, travelers' tales such as Marco Polo's, and wishful thinking combined to build up the medieval belief that Prester John was a mighty schismatical Christian priest-king. As early as the twelfth century the news had spread over Europe that

Prester John was real and had communicated with the pope. His domains were believed to lie somewhere behind those of the Islamic powers, which occupied a wide belt of territory from Morocco to the Black Sea. The opening up of the route to the Far East via the cape was undoubtedly partly motivated by the desire of the Portuguese to locate Prester John and, with his assistance, squeeze Islam from two sides. Both Prince Henry and, long after Henry's death, King João II were obsessed by the desire to establish contact with Prester John.

King João decided to investigate both by land and by sea. Two expeditions were sent out almost at the same time. The one would travel overland via Egypt and the Red Sea to take passage on an Arab dhow for Indian ports to study Indian Ocean navigation, to see the lands in which spices grow, and then to cross the sea again and seek the Christian realm of Prester John in Abyssinia. The other was to pursue the Atlantic route from the point at which Diogo Cão had turned back. João picked his men carefully. Pero da Covilhã and Afonso de Paiva, polyglot adventurers with diplomatic tact and fluent Arabic, would risk the perils of wandering disguised through Muslim lands, while the stout seaman Bartolomeu Dias would lead his caravels beyond all distances known to Europeans.

It was Dias who was destined to discover the Cape of Good Hope and prepare the way for the exploit of Vasco da Gama in reaching the Indies. In August of 1486, Dias departed from Lisbon with three ships, the purpose of which was to continue the work so promisingly begun by Diogo Cão who had reached a spot on the coast of southwestern Africa (present-day Namibia), where he set up a pillar and moved down the African coast. Dias finally rounded and pushed up the other side of Africa to halfway between the cape and Port Elizabeth before turning back. He had found Africa's southern limit and demonstrated that it was possible to navigate around it and into the Indian Ocean. Dias returned from the cape in December of 1488. It is believed that Columbus was present at court when Dias announced his discovery.

João II now began preparations for the voyage that was to be commanded by Vasco da Gama, but the king died in 1495, before they were far advanced. The fruits of the seeds sown by him and by Prince Henry the Navigator and other forgotten pilots and navigators were now reaped by King Manuel I (r. 1495–1521), starting with Da Gama's voyage in 1497–1499. On July 9, 1497, the little fleet of four vessels sailed down the Tagus. Four months later Da Gama cast anchor in St. Helena Bay, South Africa, and then quickly rounded the cape and proceeded up the east coast of Africa. After calling at various Arab-Swahili ports along the coast, Da Gama reached Malindi, where he received the help of Ahmad Ibn Madjid, the most famous Arab pilot of his age, who knew the Indian Ocean better than any other man alive. Thanks to his guidance, the Portuguese

were able to reach Calicut, the major emporium of the pepper trade on the Malabar coast, thereby ushering in a new era for India and the world—an age of maritime power and authority based on control of the seas by European nations.

On April 22, 1500, a year after Da Gama's return to Portugal, Pedro Álvares Cabral, on his way to India, sailed much farther west into the South Atlantic than Da Gama had and sighted land. A week later Cabral took possession of this unknown territory in the name of Portugal, but since his business lay elsewhere, he did not linger. He simply took on water and named the newly found land Terra da Vera Cruz. Thus, the vast country of Brazil was discovered—by chance, if we are to believe the common version, and its exploration was left largely to chance for a long time afterward.

Portuguese naval supremacy in the Indian Ocean was achieved early on with Francisco de Almeida's great victory over a combined Muslim fleet off Diu in 1509, and it was not seriously challenged until the appearance of the Dutch and English in the Indian Ocean nearly a century later. But the foundations of the Portuguese eastern empire were laid by Afonso de Albuquerque who wrested the landlocked island of Goa from the Muslim sultan of Bijapur in 1510. By capturing Malacca in 1511, Albuquerque secured the main emporium for the spice trade and the strategic key to the South China Sea and to Indonesia. With the seizure of Hormuz in the Persian Gulf in 1515, he obtained control of those waters and of one of two routes by which the spice trade was carried on with the Levant.

The three key strong points of Hormuz, Goa, and Malacca were soon supplemented by a large number of other fortified settlements and trading posts extending from Sofala to southeastern Africa to Ternate in the Moluccas. In addition, the Portuguese established a number of unfortified settlements. Elsewhere, native shipping was allowed to continue as before, provided that the owners took out Portuguese licenses. Unlicensed ships were liable to be seized or sunk, particularly if they belonged to Muslim traders. East of Malacca the situation was different. Beyond Malacca, the Portuguese were merely one more cog in the existing pattern of trade, nor was it long before they had to compete with the Spaniards who were seeking the same goal from the opposite direction. Once the Spaniards realized that Columbus had not discovered the golden lands of Cathay and Cipangu so enthusiastically described by Marco Polo, and before they found the treasures of Aztec Mexico and Inca Peru, one of their chief objectives was to get around the newfound American continent that was barring their way to East Asia. This they finally achieved with what must surely rank as the most outstanding voyage of all time—the circumnavigation of the world organized and begun by the Portuguese Ferdinand Magellan, in the service of the Crown of

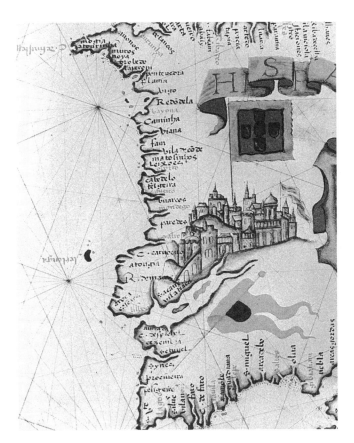

THE PORTUGUESE COAST. In the center, Lisbon and the Tagus River. From Diego Homen's atlas, 1563.

UNIVERSITY OF LIVERPOOL LIBRARY, SPECIAL COLLECTIONS

heavy annual emigration from the mother country was needed to fill the gaps in manpower caused by tropical diseases and battles with the Dutch during the first forty years of the seventeenth century.

During the early part of the reign of Sebastião (r. 1568–1578), divisions and conflicts within the Portuguese court led to neglect of the defenses of India. In 1578, Sebastião led the Portuguese to a resounding defeat on the battlefield of Morocco. His death in that battle threw the nation into a dynastic crisis, since he died without an heir. For two years, the aged Cardinal Henrique, brother of King João III (r. 1521–1557), sat on the throne of Portugal, but he died in 1580, also without an heir.

Then came forced union with Spain, after Philip II backed his claim to the Portuguese throne with well-placed money and military might. For sixty years, Spanish interests prevailed and Portugal was dragged into every conflict in which the Spaniards were involved. Spain's enemies determined those whom Portugal engaged in combat. The effects were disastrous for the immense Portuguese Empire, which was now open to depredations actually directed against Philip II and Spain. This period (known as the "Spanish captivity" to the Portuguese) also left the Portuguese vulnerable to the ambitions of the Dutch, whose incursions in the waters of the Far East ruined the Portuguese Empire there. Only Macao on the Chinese coast remained in Portuguese hands.

The opening years of the seventeenth century saw a bitter clash of rivalries and ambitions among all the European states, which now joined in the scramble for overseas possessions. In addition to the Dutch and English, the French East India Company was established in 1604, and even Denmark founded a similar enterprise in 1616, constructing a fortress and commercial depots on the Malabar coast of India.

On December 1, 1640, Portuguese insurgents assassinated the Spanish viceregal adviser, Miguel de Vasconcelos, and escorted Philip IV's representative in Portugal, Margaret of Savoy, to the frontier. John of Braganza, a descendant of King Manuel I, was proclaimed king of Portugal. The revival of independent Portugal was now complete, and another cycle in the national history was about to begin.

[See also *Africa; Colonization*, article on *Portuguese Colonization; Lisbon;* and biographies of figures mentioned herein.]

Castile, and completed by the Basque Juan Sebastián de Elcano, who sailed *Victoria* into the harbor of Sanlúcar de Barrameda on September 8, 1522, after an absence of almost three years.

The Portuguese Empire reached its peak during the sixteenth century and then went into decline. With the appearance of European rivals in the Far East and Africa, Portugal was unable to do more than maintain what it already possessed. It lost the prestige it had gained from being for so many years the sole European influence in these areas. For a long time the Portuguese expended their fortune and energy in preventing the Dutch in particular from seizing their possessions in Brazil, India, the Indonesian islands, and Africa. One of their problems was a shortage of manpower; there were never enough soldiers to man the forts. Exact figures for the Portuguese overseas population in the sixteenth and seventeenth centuries are lacking, but apparently there were never more than between six and ten thousand able-bodied men manning an empire that at its peak extended from South America to the Spice Islands. The population in Portugal at this time probably fluctuated at around a million, and a

BIBLIOGRAPHY

Boxer, Charles Ralph. *Four Centuries of Portuguese Expansion, 1415–1825.* Berkeley and Los Angeles, 1969.

Lach, Donald F. *The Century of Discovery.* Vol. 1 of *Asia in the Making of Europe.* Chicago and London, 1965.

Pattee, Richard. *Portugal and the Portuguese World.* Milwaukee, 1957.

Sanceau, Elaine. *Good Hope: The Voyage of Vasco da Gama.* Lisbon, 1967.

Sanceau, Elaine. *The Reign of the Fortunate King, 1495–1521.* Hamden, Conn., 1969.

REBECCA CATZ

POSTILS. For discussion of Columbus's marginal notations in the books he owned, see *Library of Columbus; Writings*, article on *Marginalia*.

PRESTER JOHN. Prester (the Priest) John was the legendary monarch of an imaginary Christian kingdom variously located in India, central Asia, and Africa. The first mentions of Prester John in western European letters appear in the twelfth century. In his *Chronicon*, the historian Otto of Freising relates that in 1145 he interviewed a Syrian bishop in Rome who described a kingdom far to the east ruled by a Nestorian Christian named Prester John. Nestorian Christians were usually Persians, so it is not incongruent that the bishop told Otto that Prester John was a descendant of the Magi. He had been on his way with armies to aid the crusaders in the Holy Land but was unable to cross the Tigris River. He was said to have lingered for several years in hopes that it would freeze over during the winter and allow his forces to pass.

Somewhat later in the same century, around 1165, a letter purportedly written by Prester John himself to the Byzantine emperor, Manuel I, began to circulate in western Europe. In this letter, Prester John describes his fantastic kingdom in some detail. Located but three days' journey from the Terrestrial Paradise, he says, it is replete with precious and magical stones and with plants and animals that have special powers. Its inhabitants live in perpetual peace and harmony and may drink from the waters of a "transparent spring" located at the foot of Mount Olympus, waters that endow them with eternal youth and health. The history of this letter is complex. It was probably originally written in Latin in western Europe, though some versions claim to be translations from Arabic or Greek. Many manuscripts survive; they frequently contain additions and variations reflective of shifting popular conceptions regarding the "marvels of the East."

These twelfth-century sources engendered an ongoing series of attempts to communicate with or actually visit Prester John. In 1177, Pope Alexander III wrote a letter to Prester John proposing to instruct him in Roman Christianity and to help him secure a church of his own in Jerusalem. In the thirteenth century, a new phase of European contacts with inner Asia and the Far East was inaugurated by the westward surges of the Mongols under Genghis (Chingis) Khan. European travelers, from Gio-

PRESTER JOHN. From Francisco Alvares's *Truthful Information of the Lands of Prester John*, 1540.

vanni da Pian del Carpini in the middle of the century to Odoric of Pordenone in the early decades of the fourteenth century, sought to locate the legendary kingdom somewhere within the previously unknown regions opened to them.

In his *History of the Mongols*, Carpini calls Prester John the king of Greater India and describes in some detail a bizarre battle between his forces and a "black people" called Ethiopians. Willem van Ruysbroeck, writing an account of a journey to the court of Mangku Khan in the 1250s, says that Prester John is a Nestorian Christian, the ruler of a people called the Naimans whose home appears to be somewhere in the steppes of inner Asia. In his famous *Travels (Il Milione)*, written in the final years of the thirteenth century, Marco Polo devotes several passages to Prester John. He relates that the dominions of Prester John and his descendants lay in a region called Tenduc and that he ruled a people named the Kerait (Kairites). He apparently considered Prester John to be a hereditary title rather than the name of a particular individual. In one passage he describes how the first Prester John was slain in battle by Genghis Khan; in another he mentions that the present ruler of Tenduc is of the lineage of Prester John and bears that title, though his given name is George. The letters of Giovanni da Montecorvino, written from Peking (Beijing) in the first decade of the fourteenth century, and the narrative of Odoric of Pordenone, written somewhat later, both parallel the account of Marco Polo.

Sometime around the middle of the fourteenth century, an obscure Florentine Franciscan by the name of Giovanni dei Marignolli wrote an account of a papal legation to the Far East in which he describes the kingdom of Prester John as being located in Ethiopia. The tradition of locating Prester John's kingdom in East Africa rather than on the eastern fringes of Asia seems to have prevailed among the Portuguese explorers of the fifteenth century. Portuguese navigators working their way down the west coast of Africa sought to establish contact with this legendary ruler and to establish a workable access to his kingdom. In 1499, when Vasco da Gama returned to Portugal from his famous voyage around the southern tip of Africa, he reported hearing of a king who ruled the interior somewhere near Mozambique.

Christopher Columbus's readings—of Marco Polo's *Travels*, for example—would have acquainted him with the legendary kingdom of Prester John. But he does not seem to have been as preoccupied with locating it as he was with reaching Cipangu (Japan) and the court of the Grand Khan. At least one of Columbus's prominent successors in the exploration of the Caribbean, Juan Ponce de León, seems to have believed that at one point he might be proximate to the Fountain of Youth supposedly located in Prester John's kingdom. According to the sixteenth-century *Historia general y natural de las Indias* by Gonzalo Fernández de Oviedo, in 1512 Ponce de León and his men heard tales of the existence of the Fountain of Youth in the Bimini Islands north of Cuba. Their efforts to locate it, which apparently were not casual, provide evidence of the enduring power of the imagined presence of this isolated Christian monarch and the unparalleled riches of his kingdom.

[See also *Geography, Imaginary; Grand Khan; Terrestrial Paradise.*]

BIBLIOGRAPHY

Boas, George. *Essays on Primitivism and Related Ideas in the Middle Ages.* New York, 1978.

Gumilev, L. N. *Searches for an Imaginary Kingdom: The Legend of the Kingdom of Prester John.* Cambridge, 1987.

Lach, Donald F. *Asia in the Making of Europe.* Vol. 1. Chicago, 1965.

Polo, Marco. *The Travels.* New York, 1958.

Quinn, David B., ed. *America from Concept to Discovery: Early Exploration of North America.* Vol. 1 of *New American World: A Documentary History of North America to 1612.* New York, 1979.

Yule, Henry. *Cathay and the Way Thither: Being a Collection of Medieval Notices of China.* Taipei, 1966.

PAULINE MOFFITT WATTS

PRINTING. Although printing with movable characters was invented in China in the early eleventh century A.D., it is generally accepted that the technique was reinvented in the West by Johann Gensfleisch zur Laden (c. 1394/1399–1468), better known as Johann Gutenberg, and was first used at Mainz in the 1450s, at a time when technical and commercial conditions in Germany were ripe for such a development. It is, however, probable that others in Europe were working toward the same invention at about the same time.

Mainz was a metalworking center, and Gutenberg was familiar with the goldsmith's craft. When in 1428 local patrician families like his own were deprived of their civic privileges in the Guild Rebellion, he settled in Strasbourg, where, as early as the mid-1430s, he and his partners began the slow elaboration of certain processes connected with printing. As he was secretive about his inventions, contemporary documents are not explicit about them. In 1448 he was back in Mainz. The development and application of his inventions required considerable investment, so in 1449 or 1450 he turned to a lawyer, Johann Fust, for a substantial loan. A subsequent sum was also loaned by Fust in exchange for a partnership in Gutenberg's project. In 1455, by which time Gutenberg had perfected the process of printing with movable metal types, Fust appears to have foreclosed on him, for reasons which remain unclear. Some, at least, of Gutenberg's stock and equipment passed to Fust, who thenceforth ran a printing office with Gutenberg's former associate, a calligrapher named Peter Schöffer. Together they produced, or at least completed, the famous Mainz Psalter of 1457, the first known book printed in the West to carry a date and also the name of its printers.

The magnificent forty-two-line folio Bible printed at Mainz in the period 1453–1455 is usually attributed to Gutenberg and named after him; it was either nearing completion or already finished at the time of his apparent dispute with Fust. Although Gutenberg continued to have access to printing equipment after 1455, it is not certain what he produced, because he never put his name to any printed item.

Gutenberg's invention required him to adapt various techniques, instruments, and material already employed by skilled metalworkers, printers of woodcuts, and scribes. He also developed completely new ones. Probably his most outstanding achievement was to invent an adjustable mold in which thousands of pieces of type, all of the same height but of varying widths (the letters *i* and *m,* for example, require bodies of different widths), could be cast rapidly yet with great precision. Gutenberg so perfected the processes involved in printing that they were not fundamentally altered until the nineteenth century.

Presses, often operated by peripatetic German craftsmen, spread from the Rhine Valley to much of the rest of Europe within some twenty years of the invention of printing. Printed books first appeared in Italy in 1465, Bohemia in 1468, France and Switzerland in 1470, Spain perhaps in 1472, Hungary and Poland in 1473, the Low Countries in 1473 or 1474, and England in 1475 or 1476. From the outset, printing was a business, and most printers were motivated by profit rather than any more high-minded ambitions. Commercial cities like Venice, Lyons, Basel, and Seville, situated on major trade routes

THE GUTENBERG PRESS. A reconstruction at Mainz.

ELSEVIER PUBLISHING PROJECTS, AMSTERDAM

along which printed books could be distributed like other merchandise, were generally more important printing centers than university cities such as Oxford or Heidelberg. When, for instance, the great humanist printer Aldo Manuzio (Aldus Manutius) began printing in 1494 or 1495, he chose to work in Venice, a commercial center that dominated European printing in the fifteenth and early sixteenth centuries, rather than Florence. Modern reassessments of Manuzio's career emphasize the importance of economic considerations for even the most scholarly of printers.

About 77 percent of all books printed in the fifteenth century were in the international language, Latin, allowing printers to export their products to other countries. Indeed, the rise and influence of humanism throughout Europe was closely linked to that of printing. The new craft's early opponents have too frequently been thought to reflect a universal contemporary judgment that printed books were an inferior substitute for the manuscripts that the first printed editions imitated. Italian humanists were enthusiastic patrons of the presses, however. Pico della Mirandola, for example, chose printed rather than manuscript versions of several works, presumably because he believed the former to be more accurate. In the sixteenth century, humanist scholars and certain notable printers cooperated closely. Erasmus, for instance, was associated with Josse Bade in Paris, Johann Froben in Basel, and Manuzio in Venice; he even spent considerable time revising his *Adagia* in the latter's office.

Initially, apart from the printing of indulgences, administrative forms and notices, and the ephemeral broadsheets (which have disappeared in incalculable numbers), the early presses tended to print time-honored works of the ancients and of the Middle Ages, reproducing in particular those texts that had already been most in demand before the advent of printing. Only later did contemporary authors begin to write specifically to be printed and publishers need to search for new works to satisfy demand.

By far the largest proportion of books printed at the time of Columbus were religious (over 40 percent), and it is no coincidence that the first printed book was the Bible. The scriptures became widely available in Latin and in some of the vernacular languages, leading, in the sixteenth century, to intense debate among both Catholics and Protestant Reformers about the desirability of general access to Holy Writ. While numerous works of scholastic theology for the universities and simple manuals for confessors were issued, liturgical editions and books of hours became a staple for the new presses. Likewise, devotional works proved best-sellers. The most popular were the fifteenth-century *Imitation of Christ,* attributed to Thomas à Kempis, of which some one hundred Latin and vernacular editions appeared before 1501, and the thirteenth-century *Golden Legend* by Jacobus de Voragine, of which at least 130 Latin and vernacular editions were printed before 1501. Indeed, a major effect of the advent of printing was to multiply the number of books of popular piety generally available.

The range of works printed in the fifteenth century was extremely varied, however; commercial considerations underlay the process of selection from among the thousands of works available in manuscript. Classical, medieval, and contemporary literature account for some 30 percent of the presses' known output, law for just over 10 percent, and books on scientific subjects for approximately 10 percent, while one of the most profitable categories for publishers would have been schoolbooks. It is certain that huge numbers of Latin grammars, particularly that of Donatus, were printed, but whole editions, now lost, must have been thumbed to pieces by students.

Classical works became widely available, often in scholarly editions printed in Italy, but, despite the humanists' recent rediscovery of works by the ancients, it was the classical texts popular throughout the Middle Ages that were most frequently issued. In the course of the second half of the fifteenth century many printed editions appeared of Aesop, Aristotle, Boethius, the pseudo-Cato, Cicero, Juvenal, Livy, Lucian, Ovid, Persius, Plautus, Sallust, Seneca, Terence, Vegetius, and Virgil. Works by these authors were read throughout Europe, as were vernacular translations of Latin works, printed translations from other vernacular languages, and works originally written in the vernacular in which they were printed. Boccaccio, Dante, Petrarch, and amatory romances were universally popular. The medieval chronicles and other works considered by contemporaries to be historical were frequently issued. Aristotle, Euclid, Pliny, and Ptolemy were among the scientific authors most often printed.

The eventual effects of the wide dissemination of ideas and information permitted by printing constituted a communications revolution. This has tempted some historians to view the advent of the presses as a major turning point in Western history and to attribute almost every intellectual or ideological development which took place after Gutenberg to his invention. Not only does the output of the presses in Columbus's lifetime provide much evidence of continuity with the manuscript age, however, but early printing generally did not hasten the acceptance of new ideas or knowledge. It should also be remembered that printing was a neutral medium exploited by both innovators and conservatives. However revolutionary its eventual consequences, it neither did away with the scribes—who often copied printed books—nor did it convert a largely oral culture to a written one overnight.

A major effect of the advent of printing was the rise of a new industry with its related crafts and a large wholesale import-export trade of books. France, Italy, Germany, and the Low Countries were net exporters of printed books while countries on the periphery of Europe, like Spain, Portugal, England, and Poland, were importers. The production and availability of books were dramatically increased by printing: by 1500 there were some 250 printing centers, which had issued at least 27,000 surviving editions. In two generations, more than 10 million books had been produced mechanically at a time when the population of Europe numbered fewer than 100 million inhabitants. But, rather than immediately creating a new demand, the presses supplied the burgeoning market that already existed for manuscript books, a result of increasing levels of literacy during the first half of the fifteenth century.

Although printing enormously increased the availability of books, which were generally cheaper than manuscripts, it does not seem immediately to have had a radical effect on levels of literacy or on the ownership of books. The same sorts of readers who once acquired manuscripts simply acquired a greater amount of written material. Indeed, the collapse of many printers in Italy in the 1470s and again by 1500 suggests that the market was limited and printing rapidly glutted it.

As a result of the new availability of books, scholars could now readily consult a range of works that previously would have taken them a lifetime to copy or acquire. Large collections were made, the most notable of which—although untypically extensive—was that of Columbus's illegitimate son, Fernando Colón, who had amassed more than 15,000 volumes in his Seville library by the time of his death in 1539. Liberated from the need constantly to travel to study manuscripts or to spend time copying them or having them copied for their own use, scholars enjoyed increased opportunities both for wider research and for comparing conflicting ideas, a significant development in intellectual history.

While errors always crept into manuscript text and diagrams as they were copied and recopied, some works becoming hopelessly garbled in the process, the possibility of printing numerous identical copies of a work encouraged scholarly editors to correct such errors and to publish the most accurate version they could. This had the effect of fixing texts, various forms of which had previously coexisted. Books could also be regularly revised in the light of new discoveries, as happened with successive editions of Ptolemy's *Geography*. This work had lost its maps during the Middle Ages and was provided with substitutes only after its first printed edition; the maps were subsequently updated as new information became available.

PRINTING. Woodcut by Jost Amman.

Yet all editors and printers were not scholars, and printing also allowed defective texts to be widely disseminated, and outmoded orthodoxies and traditional prejudices to be reinforced. For example, Diego de Valera's popular *Historia de España abreviada*, first printed at Seville in 1482, continued to be issued in the mid-sixteenth century without a mention of the discovery of the Americas in its section dealing with world geography. Eventually, printing led to changes in the presentation of reading matter as printed books ceased to be modeled on manuscripts. The numerous scribal abbreviations that had made reading so slow were gradually abandoned by printers who found them impractical to reproduce; cumbersome manuscript glosses were streamlined; a range of sizes of types allowed different elements of a page to be distinguished at a glance; layout was simplified; the need to economize on paper resulted in cramped typesetting; and the addition of more systematic indexes permitted easy reference. This, in turn, led to different ways of reading and consulting books.

Columbus certainly had access to printed books, some of which he possessed and annotated; several of his own copies are still conserved in the Biblioteca Colombina in Seville. It is known that he read printed versions of Ptolemy's *Geography*, Pierre d'Ailly's *Imago mundi*, Enea Silvio Piccolomini's *Historia rerum ubique gestarum* (Universal history), Pliny's *Natural History*, Plutarch's *Lives*, and the *Book of Marco Polo* (Italian title, *Il milione*). It was probably from the printed tables of Johann Müller (Regiomontanus) that Columbus attempted his calculations of longitude on his second and fourth voyages.

In their turn, Columbus's discoveries were rapidly broadcast by the presses: his *Epistola de insulis nuper inventis* (Letter on the newly discovered islands) was printed at Barcelona, Rome, Basel, and Paris in 1493, and at least nine separate editions in Spanish, German, and Latin appeared before 1500. It is questionable, however, how wide interest in the New World was outside Spain and Portugal until the mid-1550s. Throughout Europe in the fifteenth century the largely fabulous *Travels* of Sir John Mandeville had been more widely read than the more trustworthy narrative of Marco Polo's journeys to the Far East. A parallel development was seen in the following century when, even at Seville, the very hub of administration and commerce with the new Spanish colonies in the Americas, more books were printed providing semifictional descriptions of journeys to Turkey and the Holy Land than reliable accounts of the New World.

Later in the sixteenth century, well after Columbus's death, printing was to have a marked effect upon the standardization of the vernacular languages and upon literacy. It was also instrumental in the rapidity with which some new intellectual or ideological movements, notably the Reformation (embodied in writings in the vernacular languages), swept across Europe.

In 1539 the first press arrived in the lands discovered by Columbus. It was founded in Mexico City as a branch office of the Seville press owned by the Cromberger family.

[See also *Library of Columbus* for further discussion of works owned by Christopher Columbus and his son, Fernando Colón. For further discussion of works related to contemporary knowledge of exploration and discovery, see *Travel Literature* and biographies of writers mentioned herein.]

BIBLIOGRAPHY

Bühler, Curt F. *The Fifteenth-Century Book: The Scribes, the Printers, the Decorators.* Philadelphia, 1960.

Carter, John, and Percy H. Muir, eds. *Printing and the Mind of Man.* 2d ed. Munich, 1983.

Catalogue of Books Printed in the XVth Century Now in the British Museum. 12 vols. London, 1908–1971.

Eisenstein, Elizabeth L. *The Printing Press as an Agent of Change:*

Communications and Cultural Transformations in Early-Modern Europe. 2 vols. Cambridge, 1979.

Escolar, Hipólito. *Historia del libro.* 2d ed. Madrid, 1988.

Febvre, Lucien, and Henri-Jean Martin. *The Coming of the Book.* Translated by David Gerard. London, 1976.

Lowry, Martin. *The World of Aldus Manutius: Business and Scholarship in Renaissance Venice.* Oxford, 1979.

Martin, Henri-Jean. *Histoire et pouvoirs de l'écrit.* Paris, 1988.

Martin, Henri-Jean, and Roger Chartier, eds. *Histoire de l'édition française.* 4 vols. Paris, 1983–1986.

Scholderer, Victor. *Johann Gutenberg: Inventor of Printing.* 2d ed. London, 1970.

CLIVE GRIFFIN

PTOLEMY (fl. around A.D. 127–148), Greek scientist who worked in Alexandria, Egypt. The works of Ptolemy (Greek, Klaudios Ptolemaios) cover astronomy, geography, optics, astrology, music, and other fields. While his astronomical work *Almagest* outlined *klimata* (latitude belts), his *Geography* (*Geographike hyphegesis*, Manual of geography) particularly interested explorers.

Book 1 of the *Geography* outlines Ptolemy's aims: to give coordinates of numerous places and geographical features and to make recommendations for creating a world map and regional maps. He criticizes Marinus of Tyre for lack of consistency, for exaggerating the dimensions of the known world, and for using a projection suited mainly to the latitude of Rhodes. Books 2 and 3 cover Europe; Book 4, Africa; Books 5 through 8, Asia and a summary. Rejecting orthogonal (cylindrical) world mapping, Ptolemy describes three alternative projections. For regional maps he accepts orthogonal projection, but with proportions for each region based on its mean latitude. He considers Thule (Shetland to him) as the farthest point north at 63° N and Agysimba and Prasum promontory, east Africa, as the farthest south at 16°25'S. He considers the due north-south distance of the *oikumene* (known world) to be about 40,000 stades, which, with a stade equal to 184.81 meters (the commonest equivalent under the Roman Empire), gives 7,392 kilometers (4,580 miles). He estimated the east-west distance from the Canaries to Sera, the supposed capital of China, and Cattigara (possibly Hanoi) to be 180 degrees, against Marinus's estimate of 225 degrees. This gave the east-west extent of the *oikumene* on the parallel of Rhodes as 72,000 stades (13,306 kilometers, or 8,250 miles).

At several points in Books 1 and 2, Ptolemy mentions maps that accompanied the *Geography*, using phrases such as "we shall draw maps." But in Book 8 he writes, "we have had maps drawn." He mentions ten maps of Europe, four of Africa, and twelve of Asia, and a world map. Some manuscripts contain the note, "I, Agathos Daimon, a technician of Alexandria, drew a map from the *Geography* of Ptolemy," which must refer to a world map from between the second and the sixth century. The Arabic writer al-Mas'udi (d. ca. 956) mentions a colored map of the *Geography* containing, he says, 4,530 cities and over 200 mountains.

The Byzantine monk Maximus Planudes (c. 1260–1310) discovered a copy of the *Geography* in 1295. Since it had no maps, he reconstructed them from Ptolemy's textual coordinates. The Florentine Jacobus Angelus made the first Latin translation (perversely called *Cosmographia*) in 1406. Place-names were transliterated from a Greek manuscript (Vaticanus Urbinas graecus 82) to a Latin manuscript (Vaticanus latinus 5698) in 1415.

The first Latin printed editions were published in Bologna, Rome, and Ulm between 1477 and 1482, which led to an enormous expansion of readership. Regional maps made on the cartographer Donnus Nicolaus's (fl. 1460s–1470s) trapezoidal projection appeared in the Ulm editions, which were printed in black-and-white; the maps could be colored by hand. Christopher Columbus had a copy of the Vicenza first edition of 1475, without maps. Now in Madrid, his copy bears a common version of his signature, *Christo ferens,* and annotations in his hand. It is obvious that he took account of Ptolemy's as well as Marinus's distances. His brother Bartolomé also had access to printed Ptolemaic maps.

As the results of Portuguese discoveries sponsored by Prince Henry the Navigator emerged, it became apparent that Ptolemaic maps must be amended. Much earlier their depiction of north Britain had been recognized as incorrect. The shapes of Africa and much of Southern Asia—implying an enclosed Indian Ocean—were known to contradict facts. One method of coping with these errors was to include *tabulae modernae* (updated maps); thus Scandinavia, hardly known to Ptolemy, appeared in Claudius Clavus's version (1427).

Columbus's discoveries did not destroy Ptolemy's reputation or remove his name from updated atlases; instead, the *tabulae modernae* system was extended to the New World. The name "America," from Amerigo Vespucci, first appeared in 1507 in a work preparatory to an edition of Ptolemy by Martin Waldseemüller and Matthias Ringmann. In this work the name is applied to South America, but is clearly intended to apply to the whole hemisphere. Among many Ptolemaic world maps that show the American continents is that of Johan Ruysch (1508). The distinction between ancient Ptolemaic maps and contemporary atlases was foreshadowed in Waldseemüller's 1513 edition and was finally effected by Gerardus Mercator, who edited the ancient Ptolemaic maps in 1578 and modern maps at various other periods as independent volumes.

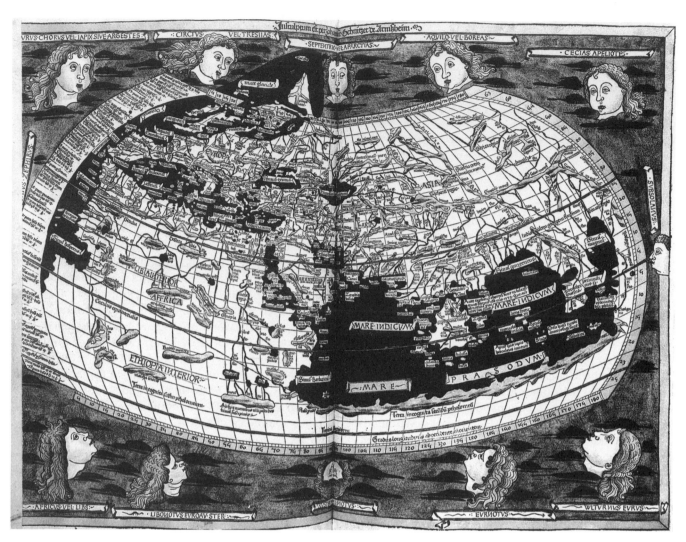

PTOLEMAIC WORLD MAP. From an early printed edition of *Geography*. Ulm, 1482.

BIBLIOGRAPHY

Campbell, Tony. *The Earliest Printed Maps: 1472–1500.* London, 1987.

Davies, Arthur. "Origins of Columbian Cosmography." *Studi Colombiani* 2 (1952): 59–67.

Dilke, O. A. W. *Greek and Roman Maps.* Ithaca, N.Y., 1985.

Harley, J. Brian, and David Woodward, eds. *The History of Cartography.* Vol. 1, *Cartography in Prehistoric, Ancient, and Medieval Europe and the Mediterranean.* Chicago, 1987.

Ptolemy. *The Geography of Ptolemy.* Translated by E. L. Stevenson. New York, 1932.

O. A. W. DILKE

PUERTO RICO. The smallest of the Greater Antilles (after Cuba, Hispaniola, and Jamaica), Puerto Rico is also the most easterly. Its topography is similar to that of the other large islands, with central mountains giving way to plains along the shore. During the fifteenth century it was the frontier of the Taíno people, for the smaller islands to the east were held by the Caribs.

The Taínos of Puerto Rico, or Boriquén as they called it, resembled their cousins to the west. They too lived in villages under caciques (chiefs) and sustained themselves with fish and cassava bread. They built swift canoes, wove hammocks, and worked the gold that was relatively abundant on their island. They seem to have been notable particularly for their addiction to a ball game somewhat resembling pelota; their courts for this game can still be seen on the island.

Columbus reached Boriquén in November 1493 and was well received by the inhabitants. Spanish occupation began in 1508, under the direction of Juan Ponce de León, and relations with the Taínos were at first amicable.

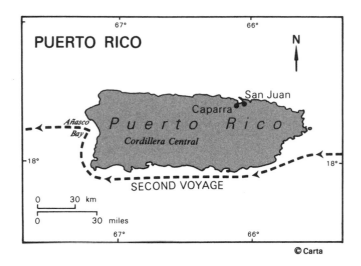

PUERTO RICO

Añasco Bay

Puerto Rico

Caparra   San Juan

Cordillera Central

SECOND VOYAGE

0   30 km

0   30 miles

© Carta

Perhaps the Spaniards were seen as a counterweight to the Caribs, whose perpetual attacks had made the Taínos abandon eastern areas of the island. However, the conquerors' usual cruelties in their quest for gold eventually incited resistance, and in 1511 the Taínos broke into formal revolt. This was soon put down, however, and then began the usual pattern of a catastrophic decline in the native population, partly through brutal treatment but more, no doubt, through the ravages of European diseases.

In 1510 a capital was founded at Caparra, but this site was soon abandoned for the adjacent one at Puerto Rico, on its magnificent bay. Eventually the island took the name of this town, and the town took the name of San Juan, which had been given the island by Columbus. Like the other islands, Puerto Rico became a backwater once Spanish attention was diverted to the gold-rich mainland. Some sugar cultivation was practiced, using slaves imported from Africa, and there were vast cattle ranches. But the island's chief value to Spain lay in its port of San Juan, which over the years was heavily fortified and which became one of the main stopovers for the yearly flota, which maintained communications between Spain and her colonies.

[See also *Indian America*, articles on *Island Caribs* and *Taínos*.]

BIBLIOGRAPHY

Alegria, Ricardo. *Descubrimiento, conquista y colonización de Puerto Rico 1493–1599*. San Juan, 1975.

DAVID BUISSERET

QUADRANT. Three types of quadrant (Latin, *quadrans;* Spanish, *cuadrante;* Portuguese, *quadrante*) have been distinguished in the literature: (1) the *quadrans vetustissimus* (the most ancient quadrant; this term is recent), (2) the *quadrans vetus* (the old quadrant), and (3) the *quadrans novus* (the new quadrant), which is the astrolabe-quadrant. Essentially, a quadrant is a flat plate of wood or metal in the form of a circle, with a plumb line and bob suspended from a hole close to the apex and with a scale of ninety degrees engraved along the circumferential arc; a pair of sight vanes attached to one of the radial edges enabled the instrument to be used for measuring angular elevations. A form of sundial, known as a horary quadrant, was engraved above the degree scale with lines for unequal (planetary) hours and a solar declination scale, and served for use in a particular latitude (the *quadrans vetustissimus*). Such quadrants, known in Islam and medieval Europe, were improved during the twelfth century by the addition of a sliding cursor, enabling the quadrant to be used in any latitude (the *quadrans vetus*). Horary quadrants had a sliding bead on the plumb line, which was held taut either against the solar declination or the date on the declination scale or against the appropriate point on the declination scale on the cursor, which had previously been adjusted for the latitude, while the bead was moved to the declination on the day of use (in the first case) or to the six-o'clock-hour line (in the second case). The plumb line was then allowed to hang freely, and the quadrant was directed toward the sun until the shadow of the foresight fell squarely on the backsight. The position of the bead in relation to the hour lines indicated the time.

When Columbus referred to a quadrant, he would have meant either an instrument of the simplest type (merely an angle-measuring device with a plumb bob and a scale of degrees) or perhaps a *quadrans vetus*. The earliest known representation of a quadrant intended for nautical use does not occur until the 1563 (posthumous) edition of Valentim Fernandes's *Reportório dos tempos* (1st ed., Lisbon, 1518) at the beginning of a chapter entitled "the Regiment [that is, rule] in order that one may be guided, with the quadrant or the astrolabe, by the Pole Star." Compared with the earliest surviving medieval quadrant (c. 1300), Fernandes's quadrant had a much smaller area devoted to the hour lines, no sliding cursor for latitude adjustment (but what were probably declination scales for two different latitudes), and the scale of ninety degrees along the arc was emphasized by lengthening the five-degree and ten-degree intervals, to make it easier to determine the altitude of a celestial body (e.g., the polestar), using the sight vanes and the plumb line. Fernandes explains how to navigate with the quadrant, but his method was already superseded by 1563. The navigator, on leaving Lisbon, is instructed to mark, on the quadrant, where the plumb line falls while observing the polestar with the Guards of the Little Dipper (Ursa Minor) lying east-west relative to that star. When, later, at sea, he wanted to know his north-south distance from Lisbon, he should determine the difference in degrees between the position of the plumb line at his original observation and that of a new observation; then he should convert to distance with one degree equal to 16⅔ leagues. Such a quadrant could have been used in this way at sea for several centuries previously, but its use in navigation is associated with the development of the technique of "running down the latitude."

In the thirteenth century, Prophatius Judaeus of Montpellier reduced the essential circles of the planispheric astrolabe to a quarter of a circle, thereby enabling them to be drawn on a quadrant (for use in a single latitude). This

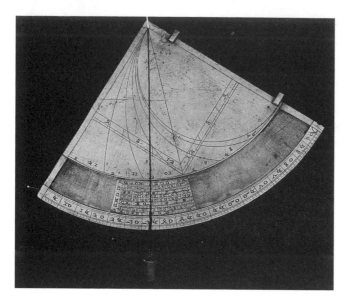

HORARY QUADRANT. This example, from about 1300, is the only surviving *quadrans vetus.*

MUSEUM OF THE HISTORY OF SCIENCE, OXFORD

astrolabe-quadrant was known as the *quadrans novus.* Medieval examples, European or Islamic, are very rare; however, many examples from the Ottoman Empire survive. From the late seventeenth century until the early years of the present century, the astrolabe-quadrant (typically with the astrolabe lines on one side, and a sine/cosine quadrant on the other) was very popular, probably because it provided the *muwaqqit* (time-keeper) in a mosque with a conveniently cheap instrument for determining prayer times.

BIBLIOGRAPHY

Maddison, Francis. *Medieval Scientific Instruments and the Development of Navigational Instruments in the XVth and XVIth Centuries.* Agrupamento de estudos de cartografia antiga, vol. 30. Coimbra, 1969.

Millás Vallicrosa, J. M. "La introducción del cuadrante con cursor en Europa." *ISIS* 18 (1932): 218–258. Reprinted in *Estudios sobre historia de la ciencia española,* by J. M. Millás Vallicrosa. Pp. 61–78. Barcelona, 1960.

Poulle, Emmanuel. *Les instruments astronomiques du moyen âge.* Astrolabica, vol. 3. Paris, 1983.

Schmalzl, Peter. *Zur Geschichte der Quadranten bei den Araben.* Munich, 1929.

Turner, Anthony. *Early Scientific Instruments: Europe 1400–1800.* London, 1987.

FRANCIS MADDISON

QUINCENTENARY. [This entry includes three articles concerning various historical perspectives on the epochal events of 1492:

Caribbean Perspectives
American Indian Perspectives
Hispanic Perspectives

For discussion of how Columbus is remembered in social and artistic media, see *Celebrations; Columbianism; Columbian Societies; Iconography; Literature; Monuments and Memorials.*]

Caribbean Perspectives

Columbus and his crew landed on an island in the Caribbean in October 1492. What was it about this event that would lead it to radically change the world? Why should that date more than any other (according to Tzvetan Todorov, 1984) have marked "the beginning of the modern era"? Why is it that, as contemporary people, it is with Columbus that our intellectual genealogy begins? Most urgently of all, how are "we"—who are inhabitants of the part of the world where Columbus landed and consequently of both European and non-European civilizational and racial origins—to look back on and interpret that event?

Spain, and Europe in general, are preparing to celebrate this event and have chosen to call it "the First Encounters." But the view from the Americas and the Caribbean, unlike that from Europe, must confront the fact that a non-European and indigenous collective historical memory also exists. This memory, in marked contrast to the triumphalist schoolbook stereotype that "in 1492, Columbus sailed the ocean blue" and "discovered America," is scarred. As Wendy Rose (1990) reminds us, for some people this epochal event "is a time of mourning."

Consider that within one generation of 1492, Columbus, the Spanish settlers, and the new diseases that they brought to the Caribbean had virtually "destroyed all the native human life" on the islands (Rose, 1990). Thus, José Marti of Cuba mourned that "a page had been torn from the Book of the Universe!" Moreover, the linkage of that event to the forcible capture and Middle Passage travail of the peoples of Africa to serve as substitute slave labor for the former native population is also historical reality.

So, how are "we"—as descendants of both the invaders and the invaded, the enslavers and the enslaved, whose process of conflictual interaction laid the foundation of the culture of the Americas—to look back on, interpret, and mark that event of 1492? Indeed, how are all later immigrants of non-European (and therefore of nonwhite) origin to do so, if to do so enforces and legitimizes the relations of a socioracial hierarchy between Euro-whites (blancos) and whiter nonwhites (morenos), on the one hand, and between morenos and the Afro-blacks, on the other? If the displacement and defeat of the indigenous people who first domesticated this hemisphere is celebrated on the day when "Columbus discovered America," then so also are the "five centuries of humiliation" (Van Sertima, 1976) undergone by the peoples of Africa and their Diaspora descendants.

Hans Koning, writing about groups who are organizing a countermovement to the official celebrations of the five-hundredth anniversary of Columbus's landing in the Americas, narrated the story of a visitor to a 1492 exhibition in the Southwest entitled "First Encounters." An American Indian was demonstrating in protest outside the exhibition, and the woman called out angrily, vehemently, to him, "You are spoiling the pleasure of our children!"

This incident of the "Protest-ant" and the "Woman Celebrant" brings out the feature that is "new" with respect to how the contemporary Americas and the Caribbean are to view, interpret, and commemorate the event that lies at our origin. It sharply separates the European view of 1492 from the view whose conflictual nature the peoples of the Americas and the Caribbean are now called upon to confront and resolve.

From the historical perspective of Europe, 1492 marks the initial step in the linkage of Europe, Africa, and the Americas, as well as of its eventual rise in the nineteenth century to become a civilization of global hegemony. So without being confronted by a descendant of America's indigenous inhabitants to challenge them, as was Koning's Woman Celebrant in the Southwest, Europeans can without contradiction rephrase the earlier "vulgate" interpretation of "Columbus discovered America" into the euphemistic terms of "First Encounters."

But for us, the immediacy of the Celebrant versus Protest-ant contradiction impels us to a new question that is specific to the "New World": that is, "What are the rules that shape and govern human perception? What are the rules that allow the Woman Celebrant to live existentially in the Americas and yet continue to accept the purely triumphalist, Europe-centered terms of the displacers rather than the dualistic and conflictual terms of the Americas and the Caribbean?"

Western Thinkers. An understanding of this problem is revealed by the historian T. M. Roberts (1985), who explains that for the Americas and all the rest of the world, all that has happened is the "echo" of Western thinkers and a reflection of the "way of life" that their modes of thought have prescribed. The thinkers and actors of Western Europe continue to "transform the world in their image"—that is, in terms of their industrial-technological way of life. Moreover, the entire world has now come to see and know reality through the mediation of the conceptual frameworks generated from the varying images of the human put in place by Western European thinkers from the Renaissance onward.

So completely has this been the case that the struggles directed against this dominance (whether the formidable one of Marxism or more recently of feminism, Afrocentrism, and multiculturalism) have been couched in theoretical terms that are themselves generated from the thought patterns invented by Western European thinkers. Because of these patterns and their underlying conceptions of the human being, as Roberts points out, all humans today live in a "world radically reshaped by the West"—and, therefore, within the "world of rules" by which this reshaping has been effected (Hubner, 1983).

Returning to the example of Koning's Woman Celebrant, it is clear that she interprets the event of 1492 in terms of the United States as a generically white and Euro-American nation-state, a notion that derives from the American history she was taught in school. That history continues to perceive the event of 1492 from the perspective of Western Europe, to whose peoples the Woman Celebrant continues to be linked by the triumphalist terms of the vulgate interpretation and its "unitary system of meanings" (Castoriadis, 1981).

This perspective of the Woman Celebrant puts her in sharp opposition to the Protest-ant American Indian. For although they are of the same nation-state, they do not share a common historical consciousness. Nevertheless, paradoxically, Western thought has also entrapped the Protest-ant, making him continue to see the event of 1492 only in terms of the triumphalism of the upper-dogs. In view of this paradox, we ask why we must remain caught in the conflict described by Gregory Bateson (1969), where "we just go round and round in terms of the old premises," unable to call those premises into question.

A "Root Expansion of Thought." In his *Zen and the Art of Motorcycle Maintenance* (1972), Robert Persig challenged the schoolbook stereotype that Columbus has been made into. Rather than accepting a territorial or technological interpretation of Columbus's achievement, Persig argues that in crossing an ocean that was believed at that time to be nonnavigable, Columbus's actual feat involved a "root expansion of thought."

The point here is that Columbus's voyage, and the chain of reasoning that led to it, challenged the belief structure sustaining both the image of the earth and the rigid noble-nonnoble caste hierarchy of the feudal Christian order of that time. In the symbolic geography of the image of the earth, then, the *orbis* (world) of Christian Redemption was a Jerusalem-centered, tripartite world of Europe, Asia, and Africa. Concomitantly, the Western Hemisphere, as antipodal lands to the *orbis* (that is, as the *orbis alter*, or Other World/Earth), should have been submerged under the infinite expanse of water of the encircling Ocean Sea (of which the Atlantic was considered a part) and, as such, uninhabitable and unreachable.

Despite this theocentric Christian version of Aristotle's physics, Columbus jotted down in the margin of a page of Pierre d'Ailly's *Imago mundi*, "Between the edge of Spain and the beginning of India, the sea is short and can be crossed in a matter of a few days." Thus, Columbus's challenge to the prevailing knowledge of his age was, in his words, "Mare totum navigabile"—"All seas are navigable."

Carrying his thought further, Persig argues that our present space exploration can be effected within the context of a mode of reason that is "adequate to handle it." Thus, it does not involve a true expansion of thought. Any "really new exploration" that would look to us today the way the world looked to Columbus, according to Persig, "would have to be in an entirely new direction," since it would have to move into "realms beyond [present-day] reason."

An analogous call for a "really new exploration" has also been made by the African scholar Theophile Obenga (1987). He argues that Europe's five centuries of triumph and dominance cannot be understood without taking note of the central role played by the new type of lay intellectual who emerged in Europe during the Renaissance. It was the synergistic interaction of "this new type of intellectual" (such as printers, editors, merchants, jurists, and writers) that would lead to the profound "intellectual mutation" that gave rise to a Europe new in "social, economic, cultural, and scientific terms."

Central to this process, Obenga continues, was the Renaissance intellectuals' reconceptualization of their past through a valorization of Europe's Greco-Roman intellectual legacy. That legacy had been reinterpreted and stigmatized in Christian terms during the feudal era; but in the Renaissance it was rediscovered and enriched by astronomers, cartographers, and geographers. Among these were "men of the sea, such as Columbus and Magellan," who not only enlarged the world but also created "a new image of the earth and another conception of the cosmos."

Obenga concludes that African intellectuals, if they are to deal with the vast dimensions of the problems plaguing their continent and their peoples worldwide, have no alternative but to effect a second such "intellectual mutation." This, too, would have to be done through a reconceptualization of the history of Africa, as one reaching back to the very emergence of the phenomenon of the human "from within the animal kingdom," to the rock paintings of the Grotto-Apollo in Namibia (dating back to 28,000 B.C.), and then to the flowering of this hominization in an ancient Egypt. Thus, ancient Egypt would serve Africa in the same way the Greco-Roman world has served Europe.

Toward a New World View of 1492. In this context, the dispute over the interpretation of 1492 opens the possibility of going beyond the limits of our present nation-state system of symbolic representations and attendant modes of cognition and perception. We need to move beyond "conventional reason" in a way that parallels Columbus's "root expansion of thought." Like Obenga's new type of intellectual, we must break out of our present culture-specific mode of thought, its related perceptual matrix, and co-related socioracial and other hierarchies. Indeed, the Janus-faced character of 1492 and its aftermath (evident in its dual effects of human emancipation and enslavement) can now be seen as the result of the partial and incomplete nature of that first intellectual mutation. It effectively led to the natural sciences but left us all in the dark regarding the rules that govern our modes of thought and the perceptions that orient our collective behavior.

A New World view of 1492 therefore has to move beyond our present system of knowledge and the rules that govern its modes of self, other, and societal perceptions. It should challenge symbolic representations, such as "Columbus discovered America," which render invisible America's indigenous peoples. It should also include a radical change from the image of the human as a natural organism that preexists culture to an image of humans emerging out of the animal kingdom and only coming into being simultaneously with culture, that is, with representations and discourse.

A New World view of the event of 1492 should seek to reconceptualize the past in terms of the reality specific to the Western hemisphere. It must recognize, as Cuban novelist Alejo Carpentier points out, that all the major and hitherto separated races of the world have been brought together in the New World to work out a common destiny. This destiny would entail the transformation of an original dominant/subordinate social structure into new ones founded on reciprocal relations.

In conclusion, we must come to terms with the tragic paradox of 1492 that is reflected in Koning's incident of the Woman Celebrant and the American Indian Protest-ant. The fundamental opposition between the two is unique to the New World situation. To resolve it, we must now replicate Columbus's creation of a "new image of the earth" by creating a new "image of the human," based on a transracial mode of inclusive altruism beyond the limits of the national subject and the nation-state.

BIBLIOGRAPHY

Bateson, Gregory. "Conscious Purpose vs. Nature." In *The Dialectics of Liberation*, edited by D. Cooper. Harmondsworth, England, 1969.

Castoriadis, C. "The Imaginary: Creation in the Socio-Historical Domain." In *Disorder and Order: Proceedings of the Stanford International Symposium*, edited by Paisley Livingston. Stanford Literature Studies 1. *Anma Libri* (September 1981): 14–18.

Gonzalez, Alicia. "The New World Will Discuss Process." *The New World* 1, no. 1 (Spring 1990): 3.

Hubner, Kurt. *Critique of Scientific Reason.* Chicago, 1983.

Koning, Hans. "Don't Celebrate 1492, Mourn." *New York Times* (August 14, 1990).

Obenga, Theophile. "Sous-thème: La pensée africaine et la philosophie dans une perspective de renouvellement." Paper presented at a symposium organized by FESPAC, Dakar, December 15–19, 1987.

Persig, Robert. *Zen and the Art of Motorcycle Maintenance.* New York, 1972.

Roberts, T. M. *The Triumph of the West.* Boston, 1985.

Rose, Wendy. "For Some It's a Time of Mourning." *The New World* 1, no. 1 (Spring 1990): 4.

Thorndike, Lynn. *A History of Magic and Experimental Science.* Vol. 4. New York, 1934.

Todorov, Tzvetan. *The Conquest of America: The Question of the Other.* New York, 1982.

Van Sertima, I. *They Came before Columbus.* New York, 1976.

Wynter, Sylvia. "1492: A New World View." *The New World* 1, no. 2 (Spring/Summer 1991): 4–5. This article in *The New World* and the foregoing encyclopedia entry are based on a paper prepared for the conference " 'Race,' Discourse and the Origins of the Americas: A New World View of 1492" (The Smithsonian Institution, October 31 to November 1, 1991).

SYLVIA WYNTER

American Indian Perspectives

Out of the dark, very early one morning, a large object appeared far out in the ocean. The coming of daylight finally allowed the people on the beach to see a ship and men unlike any they had ever seen, strange in appearance and behavior. The generally accepted version of history would record that the leader of these men was called Christopher Columbus, discoverer of the New World. But in actuality he was an arrogant intruder on Guanahani, as the people called their island. It is their version of history—history as perceived by native Americans—that is presented here.

Contemporary books fail to relate how these people viewed Columbus; thus, how American Indians in general have perceived the American experience is unknown to most people. To see history through the eyes of another person is difficult, especially if the individual is from another culture, another world. And the greater the difference between cultures, the more difficult it is to overcome prejudice and recognize another's world. To begin to understand the perspective of the American Indian, consider a coin and then turn it over. It is the same coin, but it presents one image from one side; a totally different, but equal image from the other.

From the "other side" of the events of 1492, the original inhabitants of the Western Hemisphere viewed Columbus as a stranger to their land. From out of the water as far as the eye could see, he came with his people, riding a huge vessel unknown to them. How could it be that a race of "white" people existed? Why had they come here? What did they want? Why were they different? Was he an intruder or a visitor? And where did he and his men come from? These questions may very well have run through the minds of America's inhabitants as they witnessed the arrival of Columbus that October day.

The dress and behavior of the white stranger and his crew were totally foreign. There was no existing knowledge that would enable the people to address them and learn the answers to their questions. Even the wisest elders could not say who these people were. Columbus and his men had upset the balance of reality of the known world. In such circumstances, only time provides answers to such questions, and people must be patient, for what appears at first to be an answer is not always the truth.

For the American Indians, dreams and visions had produced assumptions that there were other beings who spoke foreign languages; thus, when Columbus did not fit into the realm of existing knowledge, the people presumed him to be a foreigner. Because he did not look or dress like those of their own society, it was assumed he knew no better; therefore, he must not be as intelligent. Certainly he did not speak the language, and what was more, he did not seem to want to learn. And he was obviously lost!

Time revealed that Columbus was a trespasser, not a friend. The unusual-looking stranger had his own agenda and motives, and his plan did not include sharing or helping people. He had come with a single purpose, and it did not involve trying to make their lives better. Later, the people learned that Columbus had a culture of his own, a nation, a world of other people.

Two very different worlds with separate histories now began to form a new history of "Indian" and "white" relations. In such a case, the amount of difference exemplifies the distance between ideas, values, concerns, religions, cultures, and worldviews. On a daily basis, social contact did not lessen the distance; only time brought the two sides closer together. Unfortunately, two diametrically opposed worlds will end in conflict unless each respects the other and agrees on a course of positive relations. Their incongruence continues until one dominates the other, and the result alters the evolutionary course of both peoples.

Columbus's bold entrance into the native world was construed by some to mean that he might be a messenger or the provider of new knowledge, perhaps a prophet. The material items he possessed (his huge sailing vessel was an example) and the ones he gave to the people indicated that he had more knowledge than the wisest elders of Guanahani. The material culture of the stranger was a major difference, and it had a grave effect on the native Americans. First, the foreign goods impressed them and fed their curiosity. The people were seduced by their bright colors and charm, and naturally they wanted them. Among the native Americans, gift giving underscored generosity—a cherished value—and hospitality established a friendly rapport. As Columbus and later Europeans continued to give gifts of trinkets, beads, and whiskey, native Americans responded with their own generous hospitality.

Such gift giving brought the Europeans and native Americans of different nations together on a positive basis. Or at least, so the native Americans thought, until they realized the imperialistic nature of Europeans and learned that all Europeans were not alike. During the sixteenth and seventeenth centuries, the French followed the Spanish, and then the Dutch, English, Swedes, and Russians arrived, desiring land and its bullion of gold and silver or pelts of fur to enrich their motherlands. But wanton greed had no place in the world of native Americans where the abundance of flora and fauna provided the requirements of life.

The native Americans were not as competitive as the Europeans at the same intense, individual level at which one views oneself as the philosophical center of the universe. Rather, the native people stressed sharing, generosity, and hospitality as virtues to bond their communities together, placing solidarity above the values of a single individual. In the Americas, a person alone did not survive very long; chances for a long life increased when one had a family and community to help provide food, shelter, and protection.

Through the succeeding years, every ship brought more people with the same individualistic attitude. Their sheer numbers were beyond belief. At various times, native groups described the white race as being as numerous as the "leaves on the trees" or the "stars at night." How could such a race of people multiply so? The native Americans viewed themselves as separate nations, so they did not realize they, too, were numerous. They did not see themselves as one race called "Indians," nor did any of the tribes have such a generic word in their languages, compelling many groups to invent a phrase that translated as "red man" or "red people." All together, when Columbus arrived, approximately 15 to 20 million people lived in North America (including Mexico and Central America) and an even larger number lived in South America.

The final difference between the native Americans and the Europeans was the advanced level of technology the latter possessed, especially in the eighteenth and nineteenth centuries. As the British dominance over the French and Spanish gave way to the white Americans in the Revolution, the white Americans' superior military weaponry won the final victories over the native nations. The gunpowder, cannon, pistols, and rifles of the white Americans prevailed over the superior knowledge of the land and the ways of nature of the native Americans. The end of the 1800s marked the ultimate defeat of the native Americans and witnessed the emergence of their conquerors as a leading power in the world. This stage of events in the Americas enabled the whites to write their own ethnocentric version of history that has become the accepted perspective of the non-Indian mainstream in the United States.

A history written by conquerors dismisses the perspective of those who were suppressed and attempts to negate the history of others who are not dominant in the culture. American history has failed to include accounts of other minorities and of women, and has stressed the strength of the victorious culture. As a result, politics and economics have been seen as the driving emphases of American civilization; other important aspects of the culture, such as its social, cultural, and religious elements, have been neglected.

An "Indian" version of the American experience should present multiple versions from the many native nations. But, lacking these, a categorical "Indian" version does exist, and it needs to be widely acknowledged for a correction of the historical record. More than five hundred tribal nations existed, and their collective view would present the Indian perspective of the history of the Americas. Because of ethnocentrism on the part of scholars of history and anthropology and other experts who study the American experience, the record of Indian-white relations is incomplete. This prejudice has produced a one-sided view, that of Anglo-America; the other side, Indian America, needs to be heard.

The encounter between Columbus and the American Indians on the shores of Guanahani on that early Friday morning, October 12, 1492, should be reexamined so that the history of their meeting and the events that followed it will be balanced and accurate.

BIBLIOGRAPHY

Berkhofer, Robert F., Jr. *The White Man's Indian: Images of the American Indian from Columbus to the Present.* New York, 1978.

Horsman, Reginald. *Race and Manifest Destiny: The Origins of American Racial Anglo-Saxonism.* Cambridge, Mass., 1981.

Martin, Calvin, ed. *The American Indian and the Problem of History.* New York, 1987.

McNickle, D'Arcy. *They Came Here First: The Epic of the American Indian.* Philadelphia, 1949.

Washburn, Wilcomb E. *The Indian in America.* New York, 1975.

Donald L. Fixico

Hispanic Perspectives

When Christopher Columbus returned to Spain after his first voyage to the Western Hemisphere, he took with him news of territories previously unknown. Across ensuing centuries, these lands and the peoples inhabiting them would be incorporated into the European worldview and its economic and political activities. Inclusion of the Americas in the accumulated knowledge and understanding of the Old World was a much slower task than its incorporation into the European political system or its rapidly evolving mercantile-capitalist economic system. A variety of landscapes, plant and animal species, ethnic groups, and social and thought systems were suddenly to be included within a worldview that Europe had taken centuries to elaborate and that encompassed the familiar neighboring lands, people, and cultures. In this view, there was no ready fit for the New World.

Assimilating the Discoveries. A first intellectual undertaking was establishing the contours of the land masses and locating their place on the earth. Spanish navigators and foot soldiers relentlessly explored the islands and the mainland, mapped the shorelines, and described the physical and ecological features they encountered. The information they sent back, leaking out from Seville, allowed Europeans to piece together a reasonably accurate picture of the area within four decades. The New World was recognized as an independent landmass lying between the Western and Eastern parts of the Old World. Geographical curiosity eventually led navigators to discover the spherical shape of the planet and its rotation.

Plants and animals unknown in Europe were acknowledged; others that looked familiar were treated by analogy and given European names, in spite of being native species. Fads for exotic items led to some plants being acclimated in Spanish gardens, although their use as staples was postponed for a few centuries. These new lands and new species shattered many European assumptions about the world. They stunned people but were easy to absorb; they were simply added to the old panoply of known objects.

The New World's peoples and societies raised more philosophical issues and led to elevated debates. Were the beings with whom relations were to be established human, at the same level as Africans, Asians, and Europeans? In practical terms, there was little hesitation: Spanish sailors and soldiers met native females. But on a higher level, did the natives deserve respect as human beings, were they entitled to freedom, and could they be expected to behave morally and comprehend the Gospel, the supreme value in European culture? Natives were brought back to Spain as slaves by Columbus, but it was immediately ordered that they be returned and freed. A debate raged for decades among jurists and theologians of the court to ascertain whether the Crown could legitimately subjugate alien Americans, impose upon them the obligations of vassals, such as paying tribute, and make them participate in Christendom. Emperor Charles V even considered the idea of relinquishing control of the Indies and bringing the settlers home.

Practical reasons prevailed and the Conquest of the New World went on. Indians were thereafter regarded as fully rational people, vassals and Christians, although this did not prevent their maltreatment or exploitation. They were free and entitled to self-government under the suzerainty and guidance of the Crown. A paternalistic attitude prevailed, and Indians were treated as minors.

New World Peoples and Resources in Europe's Hands. Native Americans were thus reckoned as members of the wider world, but they still needed to be accepted on their own ground. Uncovering their self-identity and putting their creations on an equal footing with other world experiences required a longer intellectual process. Recognition of the Indian self began early, amid an attempt to suppress them. Missionaries, intending to understand Indian customs and minds in order to instill the Gospel more effectively, described pre-Columbian usages, institutions, and creeds. There is a fascinating contradiction between the denial of Indians' ways and the information about them that was rescued for future generations. Modern ethnography arose from these detailed accounts of remote cultures. Understanding these peoples often led to empathy. The notion of an open-minded and good-natured person—the "noble savage" of the eighteenth-century Enlightenment to come—began to emerge from the early contacts between Spaniards and natives. As Europeans strove to come to grips with the Americas, humankind came to be seen as not inescapably tarnished by original sin: there could still be humans living in a state of innocence; maybe it was civilization that had blemished humans; history could extend back beyond the biblical past; perhaps even paradise could be found on earth. A sense of cultural relativism, dear to our time, emerged.

Among the products of the New World that were shipped back were precious metals. Silver mined in Potosí and Mexico was the most important during the sixteenth and seventeenth centuries. By the eighteenth century, Brazilian gold production took the lead, and silver mining was later revived in Mexico. Both public and private remittances of precious metals reached Spain and Portugal and were spent on luxury goods or hoarded, but most silver and gold coins entered into circulation.

The money supply exploded, increasing the purchasing power for goods and the spread of credit. Consumption rose in Spain, encouraging production and imports. Inflation, however, soon came to harm the Spanish economy. Money drained away toward the rest of Europe, paying for imports and services or defraying the expenses incurred in Spain's expanding involvement in European affairs and wars. In the end, all the European nations, especially the most industrialized, shared in the tide of precious metals flowing from the New World. Europe also obtained the means of payment used in its import trade with the Orient. The global expansion that capitalist exchange acquired in early modern times was largely based on opportunities created by the monetary flow from the New World. Economic conditions changed, but so did economic thinking and behavior. Economic realities were hard to explain within the old moral framework. Theories such as the inflationary effect of increasing monetary supply were then formulated and policy conclusions were drawn. Modern monetarism can be traced back to the arrival of the "American treasure."

Emergence of the Hispanic New World. The union of Castile and Aragón, under Isabel and Fernando, created a powerful state led by a dominant monarchy. It was helped by a professional government bureaucracy checking both the nobility and feudal corporate rights. In the vast Americas, where the vice-kingdoms of New Spain and Peru were quickly established, the Crown had the opportunity to impose its vision of government for secondary kingdoms. The establishment of a semifeudal "nobility" was checked; as in Spain, the church was curbed through the *Patronato Real,* which gave the Crown control over all aspects of Roman Catholic practice. Control rested with Crown bureaucrats whose loyalty was to Spain. Justice was administered in local courts with the right of appeal to the audiencia or to the Council of the Indies in Spain; treasury officials collected taxes and remitted the portion not needed for American expenses back to Seville; public order was maintained. Only as American-born Spaniards with regional vested interests infiltrated the administrative structure, during the Habsburg decline, did colonial interests compete significantly with Crown aims. In Spain itself, the flow of silver from the Americas enabled the Crown to depend less on the goodwill (and contributions) of the estates, stemming the growth of their role in any kind of parliamentary system. The autocrat could afford to act independently.

By 1600 over 243,000 Spanish people had migrated, and during the next fifty years another 195,000 legal passages were noted. These migrants included government bureaucrats, priests and friars, merchants, craftsmen, soldiers of fortune, and ne'er-do-wells. The Americas served as an escape valve for ambitious men. Many came to improve their fortunes, and even when the éclat of the conquest era was over, the lure of the mines and the opportunities

to obtain land or establish themselves in the growing cities were known throughout the Iberian Peninsula and beyond. The Crown encouraged male migrants to take female members of their families to the colonies, but the migration of women was always less than that of men. In addition, by the end of the sixteenth century, the forced migration of African slaves was becoming regionally significant.

Unlike previous mercantile expansion along the coasts of Africa and Asia, where trading enclaves were established, in the Americas, conquerors became settlers in cities. The city was seen as the site of civilization; cities became centers from which novelties and modern ideas, fashions, and practices radiated. Although the Americas had been home to some highly developed urban peoples, they became a laboratory in which Spanish urban ideals were imposed. Cities were established where the Spanish wanted or needed them. They quickly took on the classic grid pattern that still characterizes them, with the church, the cabildo (council hall), the jail, and the homes of prominent citizens clustered around a central square. Within little more than a century, definitive networks of cities were established in the areas of active colonization—Mesoamerica and the Andean region. Through these networks, settlers were connected to the far-off metropolis, and rural hinterlands to the cities.

The catastrophic decline of the native American population, which was overwhelmingly due to Old World diseases, freed up space into which many Iberians moved. Contact between the two societies and tribute exigencies, paid in European plants and animals, modified indigenous production and led to some European products being integrated into indigenous life. Miscegenation led to a mestizo population that became Hispanicized in urban areas and maintained an indigenous cultural identification in rural areas. In some regions of Brazil and the Caribbean, African slaves contributed indelibly to another social and cultural hybrid. Iberian and African migration increasingly opened up the New World and was followed in later centuries by massive European migration, as well as indentured labor from areas as far away as India and China.

In those regions whose indigenous population maintained a critical mass, the encounter unleashed a centuries-long struggle between the attempt to impose Iberian structures and the determination to maintain indigenous ways. This ever-evolving dialectic produced a new society in which, in spite of differences in power and access to resources, all sides were modified.

The New World, which had evolved independently for thousands of years, abruptly entered the human, biotic, economic, and political exchanges of the Old World. Sooner or later this had been bound to occur; there was simply no place on a shrinking globe for an isolated continent to hide. For Europeans, the inclusion of this new reality was difficult intellectually; in the Americas, the process was painful and destructive for the people and the environment in which they lived. On both sides of the Atlantic, exchanges of people, species, and goods expanded consumption and contributed to the economic evolution. Indeed, the encounter forced the opening up of our collective understanding of nature, humanity, and society; it was the underpinning of the rise of modern times.

BIBLIOGRAPHY

Crosby, Alfred. *The Columbian Exchange: Biological and Cultural Consequences of 1492.* Westport, Conn., 1972.

Elliott, John H. *Imperial Spain, 1469–1716.* New York, 1964.

Hamilton, Earl J. *American Treasure and the Price Revolution in Spain, 1501–1650.* New York, 1934.

Pagden, Anthony. *The Fall of Natural Man: The American Indian and the Origins of Comparative Ethnology.* New York, 1982.

Parry, John H. *The Spanish Seaborne Empire.* New York, 1966.

NICOLÁS SÁNCHEZ-ALBORNOZ and DEBORAH L. TRUHAN

QUINTERO DE ALGRUTA, JUAN (b. 1466), boatswain. Quintero was boatswain aboard *Pinta* on Columbus's first voyage of discovery and shared with the Admiral and Pedro de Terreros the distinction of participating in all four voyages. As boatswain, he was in charge of all gear having to do with the efficient and safe operation of the ship. Prior to departure, he directed the proper stowage of all cargo and when underway checked that its lashing remained secure. At sea it was also his duty to check the condition of all spars, sails, rigging, and pumps; to lead the seamen and ship's boys in effecting necessary repairs and carrying out sail-handling and ship-maneuvering orders of the master or pilot; to keep the ship's boats fitted out and ready for use; and to ensure that the wood fire in the stove was extinguished every night.

Quintero was twenty-six years old in 1492. Like Martín Alonso Pinzón, his captain, he was from the seaport town of Palos and no doubt had been recruited by Pinzón to be boatswain of *Pinta*. Columbus had encountered strong resistance to his efforts to recruit experienced seamen to undertake his planned voyage to the west across the Mar Tenebrosa (Dark Sea) to reach Cipangu (Japan), Cathay (China), and the many islands of the Indies. He was a stranger to the seafaring men of the Huelva, Moguer, and Palos region, and they were extremely dubious of the venture's prospects of success. Only when the Pinzón and Niño families of Palos and Moguer, respectively, gave their support to Columbus did it become possible to convince any of these men to become a part of the enterprise. In later years, Quintero, a staunch supporter of the captain of *Pinta*, testified in the Pleitos as to the vital role of Martín Alonso Pinzón in convincing the reluctant seamen to join him and his brother Vicente Yáñez Pinzón, captain of *Niña*, in making the voyage. He also spoke of Martín Alonso's role in calming the seamen on October 10, 1492, when they wished to turn back toward Spain. Land would be sighted in a few days, he told them, and, of course, it was.

Although Quintero participated in all four voyages of discovery, he never sailed on the same ship as Columbus. Perhaps because of this, no mention of his name is found in any of the several accounts of the voyages. But his selection by Martín Alonso Pinzón to the important position of boatswain of *Pinta* and his eventual rise to the position of master of *Gallega* on the fourth voyage attest to his competence in seamanship.

BIBLIOGRAPHY

Gould, Alicia B. *Nueva lista documentada de los tripulantes de Colón en 1492.* Madrid, 1984.

Irving, Washington. *The Life and Voyages of Christopher Columbus and His Companions.* 3 vols. New York, 1849.

WILLIAM LEMOS

R

RÁBIDA, LA. When Columbus's ships sailed from Palos through the narrow estuary to the Atlantic on August 3, 1492, they passed the coastal promontory of La Rábida. From this headland rose a Franciscan monastery, Santa María de La Rábida, that had played an important part in financing the voyage.

The headland took its name from a Muslim fortified monastery (*rabat*) that once stood on the site. Franciscans founded the monastery of Santa María there in 1412. During the fifteenth century, the number of friars grew to twenty-six, and the monastery gained the reputation of sending missionaries to convert the natives of the Canary Islands.

A Spanish historian, Antonio Rumeu de Armas, has finally swept away centuries of exaggerated claims about when Columbus arrived at La Rábida and what kind of help he received there. Rumeu researched the Franciscan archives, the royal treasury accounts, and court records. He discovered that Christopher Columbus stayed at the monastery of Santa María de La Rábida on three occasions.

Columbus first came to La Rábida in 1491, when he arrived with his twelve-year-old son Diego. No one in the region had ever seen him before, and he spoke with a foreign accent. The head of the monastery (whose identity is unknown) provided the travelers with the hospitality of the house. One of the brothers, Juan Pérez, who had worked in the royal accounting office when he was a boy and later became confessor to Queen Isabel, engaged Columbus in conversation about the royal court.

Juan Pérez sent a letter to the queen, asking that she give Columbus's scheme another hearing, and received a favorable reply two weeks later. Riding a mule rented from a citizen of the town of Moguer (Juan Rodríguez Cabezudo), Pérez went to the court in Santa Fe, where he told the queen that Columbus and his son were ragged, without connections, and without funds. The monarchs sent generous assistance, twenty thousand maravedis in florins, to Columbus.

While Juan Pérez negotiated on his behalf at court, Columbus put his stay in the monastery to good use. He visited the towns of Palos, Moguer, and Huelva to talk with pilots and publicize his plans. When Pérez and the royal secretary Juan de Coloma reached an agreement—which came to be known as the Santa Fe Capitulations—Columbus left Diego behind at La Rábida and arrived at court in time to see the Castilian banners raised in Granada on January 2, 1492.

Columbus and Juan Pérez returned to the monastery on the night of May 22—Columbus's second stay at La Rábida. For the next two months, Columbus worked to equip and man his little fleet in Palos, all the time residing in the monastery. He sent Diego to live with Beatriz de Arana before the fleet departed on August 3, 1492.

Columbus's final stay at La Rábida occurred when he brought *Niña* back to Palos after the first voyage, on March 15. He spent the next two weeks in the port, probably visiting his Franciscan friends at the monastery. He departed for Seville on March 29 and never returned to La Rábida.

LA RÁBIDA MONASTERY.   MUSEO NAVAL, MADRID

BIBLIOGRAPHY

Rumeu de Armas, Antonio. *La Rábida y el descubrimiento de América: Colón, Marchena y fray Juan Pérez.* Madrid, 1968.
Sale, Kirkpatrick. *The Conquest of Paradise: Christopher Columbus and the Columbian Legacy.* New York, 1990.

HELEN NADER

RATIONS. See *Equipment, Clothing, and Rations.*

RECONQUISTA. The reconquest is the central theme of medieval Spanish history. Generations of the Spanish people were taught that for seven hundred years their ancestors almost singlehandedly held back the Muslims threatening to engulf Christian Europe. In spite of this romantic view, the reconquest is not an artificial concept created by modern historians to render the history of medieval Spain intelligible; rather, it is an idea that developed in the ninth-century Kingdom of Asturias.

The origins of the reconquest go back to the collapse of Visigothic Spain as Muslim forces invaded from North Africa in 711. In later history and literature this event was described as *la pérdida de España* (the loss of Spain). As the Muslims overran Spain, some hardy survivors held out in the mountains of Asturias. Their leader, Pelayo, the first king of Asturias (r. 718–737), declared that he would achieve the *salus Spanie* (salvation of Spain), and the restoration of the Gothic people. His victory over the Muslims at Covadonga in 722 traditionally is taken to mark the beginning of the reconquest. The inexorability of the struggle was stressed by a ninth-century chronicler who stated that the Christians would wage war against the enemy by day and night "until divine predestination commands that they be driven cruelly thence. Amen!" That hope proved to be illusory, but the ideal of the expulsion of the Muslims and the restoration of the Visigothic monarchy was embedded thereafter in the consciousness of Spanish Christians and recurs again and again in medieval history and literature.

For nearly three hundred years following the initial Muslim invasion, the Christians remained on the defensive, so that one could hardly speak of reconquest. Nevertheless, the breakup of the caliphate of Córdoba in the eleventh century enabled the Christian rulers to make significant progress in the reconquest. The fall of Toledo in 1085, Zaragoza in 1118, and Lisbon in 1147 moved the frontier to the Ebro and the Tagus rivers. Invasions by the Almoravids and Almohads from Morocco in the late eleventh and twelfth centuries halted expansion temporarily, but the Castilian victory at Las Navas de Tolosa in 1212 opened Andalusia to conquest. In the first half of the thirteenth century the kings of Portugal occupied the Alemtejo and the Algarve, as Jaime I of Aragón (r. 1213–1276) subjugated the Balearic Islands and Valencia.

Meanwhile Fernando III of Castile-León (r. 1217–1252) conquered Córdoba and Seville and reduced the Kingdom of Granada to tributary status. In the late thirteenth and fourteenth centuries the kings of Castile tried to gain control of the Straits of Gibraltar so as to seal off the classic invasion route from Morocco. The final Moroccan invasion by the Benimerines was halted by Alfonso XI's triumph at Salado in 1340, but for nearly a century and a half thereafter the Christians failed to press the reconquest.

The reconquest originated as a war to recover territory, but it also assumed the character of a holy war between two mutually exclusive societies. Religious beliefs regulated every aspect of life in both Christian and Muslim Spain, so much so that there was no possibility of full integration. The reconquest was a war not to propagate Christianity or to convert the Muslims but rather to expel them as intruders whose entire way of life was alien to that of the Christians. The reconquest was transformed into a crusade in the twelfth century, as the popes assured those who fought the Moors in Spain they would receive the same indulgences given to those who went off to liberate the Holy Land. From the thirteenth century onward the principal campaigns against the Spanish Muslims had the canonical status of crusades. The bull of crusade remained a characteristic feature of religious practice well into modern times both in Spain and in the Spanish colonies.

The reconquest was accompanied by repopulation or colonization. As the Muslims withdrew before the Christian advance into the Duero River valley and into Extremadura, the newly occupied lands had to be settled. Fortified urban settlements were established that were directly dependent upon the king, and royal charters ensuring personal freedom and other liberties were issued to attract settlers. The military orders founded in the twelfth century received lordships in the frontier region stretching from below the Tagus to the borders of Andalusia. When Andalusia, Valencia, Murcia, and the Algarve were taken, a substantial Muslim population was incorporated into Christian territory. The Mudéjars, as they were called, were expelled from Andalusia following an uprising in 1264, but they remained in Valencia until the seventeenth century.

Fernando of Aragón (r. 1479–1516) and Isabel of Castile (r. 1474–1504) brought the reconquest to completion. Appealing to the pope for crusading indulgences in 1485, they expressed the hope that "these infidels . . . will be ejected and expelled from Spain." In 1492 they informed the pope that "this kingdom of Granada, which was occupied for over seven hundred and eight years by the infidels . . . has been conquered." Some publicists argued that the reconquest would be complete only when Morocco, thought to have once been part of the Visigothic kingdom, was conquered, but the attraction of the New World soon diverted the Spanish monarchs from North Africa.

The territorial integrity of Christian Spain was now restored, but the problem of creating one people remained. Whereas religious minorities previously enjoyed a measure of religious tolerance and juridical autonomy in Spain, the new idea of the nation-state made that difficult to sustain. For that reason the Jews in 1492 and the Muslims of Granada in 1502 were given the option of accepting Christianity or of being expelled from the realm. Thus the ideal of political, juridical, and religious unity was achieved, at least in theory.

The reconquest helped develop among medieval Spanish Christians a pioneer psychology. A people always living on a frontier, they were ever-ready to give up the security of a settled and peaceful place to seek something better, even though the risks might be great. The long centuries of reconquest and repopulation prepared the people of Spain for the task of overseas exploration and colonization.

[See also *Muslims in Spain.*]

BIBLIOGRAPHY

Collins, Roger. *Early Medieval Spain: Unity in Diversity, 400–1000.* New York, 1983.

Lomax, Derek W. *The Reconquest of Spain.* New York, 1978.

MacKay, Angus. *Spain in the Middle Ages: From Frontier to Empire, 1000–1500.* New York, 1977.

O'Callaghan, Joseph F. *A History of Medieval Spain.* Ithaca, N.Y., 1975.

JOSEPH F. O'CALLAGHAN

RELIGION. [This entry includes two overviews of religion at the time of European overseas exploration: one on European religious traditions and one on the religious systems of indigenous American peoples first encountered by Europeans. See also *Inquisition; Jews; Missionary Movement; Muslims in Spain; Papacy; Reconquista; Spirituality of Columbus.*]

European Traditions

The religious world of Europe in the fifteenth and sixteenth centuries was marked by contention and dissidence. Communities of Jews lived in scattered urban centers throughout Europe, and in the Iberian Peninsula there was a persistent, if often fragile, tradition of *convivencia* (coexistence) among Jews, Muslims, and Christians. Historians of the period, however, habitually assume that most Europeans were at least nominally Christian and had been so for centuries. But what being a Christian—even in a nominal sense—actually meant in terms of belief and practice is another matter. The urgent resurfacing of this ancient issue, as old as Christianity itself, was prompted by external circumstances as well; western Christendom was threatened from without by the persistent incursions of the Muslim Turks into the territories of Byzantium and the Holy Land. This concatenation of religious tensions reshaped both the sacred and the secular worlds in which Europeans lived and thought in fundamental ways.

The origins and dynamics of the spectrum of reform movements that emerged in sixteenth-century Europe remain controversial, but both Protestant and Catholic reformations manifested certain common patterns. When considered within the larger scope of the later medieval and Renaissance periods, they appear to have had a number of important, interrelated historical precedents. These included earlier endemic forms of religious dissent and independent lay pieties that had established themselves in various parts of Europe. Another precedent of a different sort was the development of humanist philology and hermeneutics in Renaissance Italy. These interpretive techniques and the readings they produced would exercise considerable influence on Biblical exegesis in the sixteenth century. In the social and political arenas, the Great Schism of the late fourteenth century and the reconsolidation of papal power in the course of the fifteenth and sixteenth centuries engendered new permutations in the ongoing conflicts with secular rulers.

The best-known heresies of pre-Reformation Europe were those of the Waldensians, the Lollards, and the Hussites. The Waldensians, who traced their origins back to the twelfth century, at one time or another claimed followers in various parts of the continent. The Lollards were concentrated in England and the Hussites in Bohemia and Moravia. There were certainly essential differences among them, but they all shared a resistance to the absolute authority of the pope and ecclesiastical law. To varying degrees they developed alternative doctrines and liturgies in seeking to establish themselves as separate Christian churches. In so doing they can be said to have anticipated the Lutherans and other Protestant sects; some of Luther's early followers were drawn from the Hussite movement.

Other important spiritual traditions, though remaining peripheral to Roman Catholic orthodoxy, were never declared heresies. In the German Rhineland, a lineage of popular preachers inspired by the great Meister Eckhart promised direct union of the aspiring soul with God. Their sermons bypassed the conventional confessional structures of the church and other avenues proffered by the system of indulgences and the intercession of saints, intertwining the messages of mysticism, dissent, and salvation.

In Italy, and then in transalpine Europe, the legend and

MARTIN LUTHER. Gold medal, 1521.

AMERICAN NUMISMATIC SOCIETY

teachings of Saint Francis guided an assortment of groups both within and without the mendicant order that bore his name. Within the order, first the Spirituals and later the Observants espoused shifting blends of radical poverty and apocalyptic expectations derived from Francis's contemporary Joachim of Fiore and other influential sources. Outside the order, the Beguines, the Fraticelli, and other lesser-known sects adopted associated views.

Accompanying such heresies and heterodoxies were curious local and regional admixtures of Christian and non-Christian doctrine, and residual beliefs and practices of pre-Christian Europe. Probably the most famous infiltration of non-Christian ideas occurred among the Cathars of southern France. Its doctrines, Persian in origin, activated the Albigensian Crusade and a Dominican inquisition sponsored by the papacy that did not altogether succeed in eradicating them. Recent scholarship has demonstrated that other nameless syncretisms, often idiosyncratic and usually very restricted in their influence, prevailed well into the early modern period. They continued to attract the attention and energies of inquisitors and evangelists from the mendicant and Jesuit orders.

These vibrations in the religious life of later medieval and Renaissance Europe resonated in its intellectual world as well. In the course of the fifteenth century, the Italian humanists' recovery and study of antique texts previously unknown in western Europe led to more nuanced understandings of the religion and philosophy of the pagans, Jews, and early Christians of the Greco-Roman world. In seeking to identify and date these texts and to discover their proper cultural contexts, the humanists became versatile in historical and comparative linguistics. Scholars such as Lorenzo Valla and Desiderius Erasmus applied these philological techniques to the text of the Bible itself.

Their work demonstrated that it, like all other texts, was the complex product of accruements and emendations made over a period of time. Scripture was, then, the word of human beings as much as it was the Word of God.

The emergent awareness of the historicity of scripture stimulated important new editions of the two Biblical testaments. Among these were the versions published by Erasmus at Basel in the early decades of the sixteenth century and the great Complutensian Polyglot Bible produced by a team of Jewish and Christian scholars at the University of Alcalá de Henares and printed in 1514–1517 under the patronage of the Franciscan reformer, Cardinal Francisco Jiménez de Cisneros.

This revivification of Holy Writ through the arcana of scholarship and the medium of print both fed and was fed by the rise in literacy and the demand for more widespread dissemination of the Bible through vernacular translations. Such translations would play an important role in the promulgation of sixteenth-century reforms. Martin Luther rendered the New Testament into German in 1522 and completed his version of the entire Bible in 1534.

The traditions of religious dissent and the culture of humanism also influenced the ongoing contest among secular rulers, the papacy, and the episcopate for temporal as well as spiritual control of Christendom. A lineage of political theorists traceable back to Marsilius of Padua in the fourteenth century had argued that the church should be governed by a representative council rather than a centralized papal bureaucracy in Rome. The conciliar movements of the late fourteenth and early fifteenth centuries enjoyed the support of secular rulers since the movements were tied more to local and regional power bases and so gave the rulers more influence in ecclesiastical affairs. Further ammunition was provided in the early fifteenth century when Lorenzo Valla demonstrated that the Donation of Constantine, a key document used by popes in making their claims for temporal authority, was in fact a forgery.

In England and France, where political bases were relatively consolidated, the rulers enjoyed greater autonomy with regard to the papacy and exercised considerable control over ecclesiastical appointments and institutions. In Germany and Italy power was fragmented and conflicts between sacred and secular claims were chronic. The religious world of Spain was subject to circumstances that differed from the mixes that prevailed in other parts of Europe. These circumstances played a not insignificant role in Spain's emergence as a colonial power subsequent to Columbus's voyages of discovery.

In January of 1492, the combined forces of Fernando of Aragón and Isabel of Castile conquered the Kingdom of Granada, the only territory on the Iberian Peninsula still controlled by the Muslims. On March 31, 1492, the Spanish regents issued an edict ordering the Jews resident in their domains either to convert to Catholicism or to submit to permanent exile. These events marked the end of the previous tradition of *convivencia* among Iberian Christians, Jews, and Muslims. They also signaled a revival of the crusading ideal of the Reconquista—the divinely sanctioned conversion of the non-Christian through conquest.

The Reconquista, coming as it did in the final decade of the fifteenth century, activated a complex of apocalyptic fears and expectations as well as reform movements. It permeated the ecclesiastical structures of the Spanish Catholic church and the political ideology of the court of Fernando and Isabel as well as the more fluid forms of monastic and public religious life. To more than a few observers, Fernando and Isabel's actions augured the final conversion of all infidels that would presage the end of time. Together they appeared to be the legendary "Last World Emperor" who, ancient prophecies decreed, would appear on the eve of the end of time to take Jerusalem for the Christians. A number of Christopher Columbus's letters to his monarchs indicate that he was seeking to place his discoveries within this larger apocalyptic framework.

Columbus believed that by sailing west to reach the Far East he had discovered a route that would give his regents efficient access to the wealth of the Orient and, particularly, to the lost mines of King Solomon. This wealth would provide Fernando and Isabel with the necessary means to mount a final crusade against the Turks in the Holy Land. In his letter describing the fourth voyage, Columbus pledged his services to that final crusade, promising to conduct the Christian forces to Jerusalem, presumably by sailing west across the Atlantic. He died in 1506 convinced that the end of the world was at hand. According to several contemporary accounts he was buried in the robes of a Franciscan tertiary, that branch of the order composed of laymen.

The regular members of that order, particularly the Observant Franciscans, would play a leading part in the "spiritual conquest" of Mexico in the course of the sixteenth century. Their actions and motivations were grounded in the European contexts of reconquest and reform as well. The Observant Franciscans' missionary work began with the arrival of twelve friars at Tenochtitlán (Mexico City) in 1524, shortly after Hernando Cortés's conquest of the Aztec empire. These events in the New World were contemporaneous with a cluster of important ones in the Old. In 1519, the Spanish king, Charles I, grandson of Fernando and Isabel, was elected Holy Roman emperor. The following year, Luther published his three incendiary treatises, *To the Christian Nobility of the*

German Nation (August), *On the Babylonian Captivity of the Church* (October), and *On the Freedom of the Christian Man* (November). He was excommunicated on January 3, 1521.

As had Columbus before them, a number of the early missionary chroniclers believed that events in Europe and America were interrelated in the larger plan of providential history. Works such as Diego Valadés's *Rhetorica christiana* (1579) and Gerónimo de Mendieta's *Historia eclesiástica indiana* (1596) linked the evangelization of the indigenous peoples of the New World to Protestant and Counterreformation movements in Germany and Spain. The new souls gathered into the Christian fold by the "pious" Martin of Valencia, the leader of the twelve Franciscans at Tenochtitlán would more than offset the losses suffered to the "cursed arch-heretic" Martin Luther.

In Europe, influential Catholic reformers such as Giles of Viterbo also cast the discovery of the Americas into an apocalyptic framework. In a sermon delivered before Pope Julius II in 1507, Giles argued that the many previously unknown souls revealed by the Portuguese and Spanish voyages surely presaged the age of *unus pastor, unum ovilem* prophesied in *John* 10:16. This was the age in which all infidels would finally be converted to Christianity, the Antichrist Luther would be defeated, and Jerusalem reconquered from the Turks. The discovery of a new world was somehow inseparable from visions of the end of the world, the subsumption of history in the final triumph of Christian universalism.

BIBLIOGRAPHY

Bataillon, Marcel. *Erasmo y España: Estudios sobre la historia espiritual del siglo XVI.* Mexico City, 1950.

Delumeau, Jean. *Catholicism between Luther and Voltaire: A New View of the Counter-Reformation.* London, 1977.

Ginzburg, Carlo. *The Cheese and the Worms: The Cosmos of a Sixteenth-Century Miller.* Baltimore, 1980.

Milhou, Alain. *Colón y su mentalidad mesianica en el ambiente franciscanista español.* Valladolid, 1983.

Phelan, John Leddy. *The Millennial Kingdom of the Franciscans in the New World.* Berkeley, 1970.

Ricard, Robert. *The Spiritual Conquest of Mexico: An Essay on the Apostolate and the Evangelizing Methods of the Mendicant Orders in New Spain, 1523–1572.* Berkeley, 1966.

Spitz, Lewis W. *The Renaissance and Reformation Movements.* Chicago, 1971.

PAULINE MOFFIT WATTS

Amerindian Traditions

In 1492 Columbus came upon a New World of unknown, unexpected, and astonishing religious diversity and intensity. By way of comparison, the diversity of New World religions rivaled that of Europe prior to the introduction of Christianity. North and South America—a vast continent with societies of varying degrees of social, cultural, and political complexity—contained hundreds of languages and thousands of ethnic groups. Religions approaching full-scale state religions, like those of the Incas and the Aztecs, existed alongside simpler tribal religions; all had little in common. For example, in North America alone the hunting religions of the Naskapi Indians of Labrador contrast sharply with the horticultural religions of the Pueblo peoples of New Mexico, and the religions of California Indians bear little resemblance to the religion of sacred kinship of the Natchez people on the Lower Mississippi.

Columbus's initial statements on New World religions indicate that he did not think the natives to be religious at all. In his diary of the first voyage, he mentions native religions three times. In the first instance, he suggests that the natives of San Salvador will become Christians easily because "it would seem to me that they had no religion." Of the natives of La Española, he asserts that it should be easy to convert them to Christianity, too, since they "have no religion of their own and are not idolators."

Columbus's initial statements concerning the lack of religion among Amerindians are echoed in writings from the sixteenth and seventeenth centuries. But contemporary interpreters contend to the contrary that Amerindian peoples were among the most religious peoples in the world and that the most striking similarity underpinning all New World societies was their overwhelming devotion to religion. The Indian world made religion its fundamental business. From the simplest hunting and gathering society to the high civilizations of the Aztecs and the Incas, religion was the one great behavioral force that provided social unity.

Another measure of religious intensity is the comparatively low rate of conversion to Christianity. Spanish and and later French missionaries experienced little immediate success with the native peoples and complained that they rapidly reverted to pagan ways whenever the opportunity presented itself. Conversion was rarely complete, even down to the seventeenth century.

On the other hand, Amerindian religions appear to have had considerable appeal to Europeans. There are numerous accounts of European captives who, after having been taken against their wills, chose to remain with the Indians when repatriation became available. In the history of the transatlantic encounter there are more accounts of Europeans who "went native" than Indians who "went European." Of course, few Amerindians were offered the option of full acceptance within white society, whereas European captives were frequently accorded this opportunity among Amerindians.

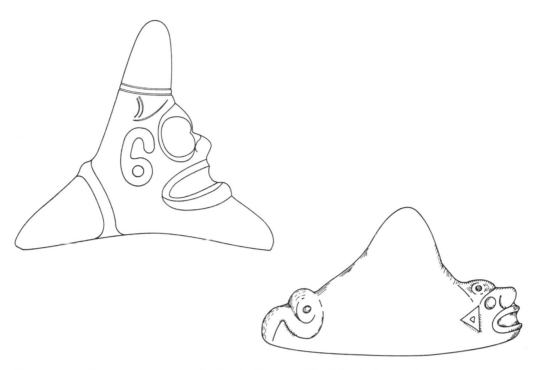

TRIANGULAR *CEMÍE* AND HUMPBACKED *CEMÍE.* Ritual objects used by Taíno Indians in the sixteenth century.

DRAWINGS BY STEPHEN D. GLAZIER

What we think of as Taíno religion is not one religion but the product of waves of migration into the Caribbean from the South American mainland. The first Amerindian group to be contacted by Columbus on San Salvador seems to have been part of a wider religious sphere that had reached an advanced level of development on La Española. The people of San Salvador traded with the Taínos, and linguistic affiliations are evidenced by the fact that Columbus successfully used Indians from San Salvador as translators. In terms of mythology, the Taínos shared much in common with the mythologies of South American peoples, especially the tribes of the Upper Orinoco and Amazon. There is also strong material evidence for connections with Mesoamerica (the Yucatán Peninsula).

From a religious standpoint, the first intense and protracted contact between Europeans and Amerindians took place on La Española. On his third voyage in 1495, Columbus commissioned a humble, poorly educated Hieronymite priest, Ramón Pané, to live with the Taínos for two years and compile a description of their religious beliefs and practices. It is unclear why Columbus chose Pané for this task. He had six priests in his command, including two better educated than Pané. It may have been that Columbus did not consider this a very important or difficult assignment or that Pané was the only priest

with experience in the native language. Columbus was motivated not only by his desire for knowledge but by his political and military needs as well. The Taínos had proved themselves earlier to be worthy adversaries in battle, and Columbus hoped to understand them better so he could more easily bring them into submission.

Little is known concerning Pané and the fate of his report to Columbus, which he completed in 1496 or 1497. The original report was lost, but it was reconstructed in 1968 by José Arrom from a 1571 Italian translation. Pané has received recognition for his accomplishments as the first ethnographer of a New World people and baptizer of the first Amerindian to become a Christian, Guaticabanú. His missionary success was short-lived, however, as Guaticabanú was killed shortly after Pané's departure from the Taíno village.

Taíno religion might be best described as animistic, emphasizing a close connection with nature. Although Columbus repeatedly professed that he found no evidence of idolatry among these peoples, Catholic priests, when they began work among the Taínos in the early sixteenth century, found that religious objects known as *cemíes* were revered. *Cemíes* were made from natural materials such as stone, wood, ceramic, seashells, and cotton. Of these, stone *cemíes* have survived in greater number. *Cemíes* were associated with fertility, funerals, divination, and healing. Much to the priests' dismay, natives treated statues of Catholic saints as if they too were *cemíes*. They buried them in the yucca fields and urinated on them to promote the fertility of their crops.

Shamans—variously known as *behiques, behutios,* and *piaïes* among the Taínos and *boyés* among the Caribs—occupied a central position in all known Amerindian societies. Their functions included healing, divining the future, and making offerings to the gods. Healing techniques varied across cultures, but a shaman from any ethnic group could easily have recognized and appreciated the practices of his counterparts elsewhere in the New World, even if separated by vast distances. Among the majority of New World peoples, the role of the shaman appears to have been distinct from that of the political leader. The distinction between political and religious authority, however, does not seem to have been as rigid in all societies. The Taínos, for example, allowed for a close relationship between religious power (the *behutio*) and political power (the cacique). Similar close relationships have been noted between religious and political leaders among the Incas and Aztecs as well as in a number of other groups in North and South America.

Early explorers saw Amerindian mythology almost exclusively in terms of Western mythology. The subtlety of Taíno religious thought was lost entirely on Europeans who took Taíno religious statements literally. For example, when the Taínos spoke of a land inhabited entirely by women, Spaniards saw in this a corroboration of the Greek myth of the Amazons. When told of a city of gold, they assumed that the Taínos were substantiating a myth concerning seven Portuguese bishops who fled with their church ornaments to an Atlantic island in order to escape from the Moors (the Seven Cities of Cíbola). Columbus himself was a man of faith who believed not only in Christian dogma but also in cyclopes, mermaids, Amazons, men with tails, and men with dogs' heads. And as is true of others, his beliefs influenced his interpretations of what he found in his new world.

Within forty years of contact, the Taínos and their religion were nearly extinct—victims of Spanish brutality and the introduction of European diseases. Of the groups encountered by Columbus himself, all have been extinct for over 350 years. The Carib Indians to the south fared better than most. They were able to maintain aspects of their religion and culture well into the eighteenth century, because they were a mobile people and Europeans had little interest in settling the smaller islands where they lived.

The religious system of the Aztecs in the valley of Mexico approached European conceptions of religion. In the strictest sense, Aztec society was not a full-scale state system, but it possessed distinguishable ritual, elaborate

NORTH AMERICAN SHAMAN. Drawing by John White, of the Virginia colony, circa 1585. Original in the British Museum.

LIBRARY OF CONGRESS

processions, a hierarchy of religious specialists, and other characteristics with which the Spaniards could identify.

By 1524, the first Franciscans had arrived to begin the work of converting the Aztecs to Christianity, and Bernardino de Sahagún left a revealing record of the debates between European and Aztec religious specialists. The Aztec priests consistently argue from tradition: "This is the religion of our fathers." When one reads these dialogues, it becomes apparent that a major difference between Christianity and the religion of the Aztecs was that the latter emphasized tolerance and pluralism. The Amerindians were looking for a way to put the Christian God alongside their own gods.

Religious tolerance and pluralism in Amerindian traditions are also noticeable in the detailed accounts of Spanish contact with the Incas of Peru, whose religious system most nearly approximated sixteenth-century European Christianity. Franciscan efforts to eliminate idolatry and syncretism revealed a great deal about New World religion. These efforts also spurred exceptionally vivid indigenous accounts such as that of Guaman Pomo, who unsuccessfully attempted to explicate and defend his native culture to the king of Spain.

Encounters between Christianity and the religions of Amerindians are excellent examples of what Cuban anthropologist Fernando Ortiz termed "transculturation." Both Christianity and native religions were inexorably changed by the process. It is easy to overestimate the effects of Christianity on native religions, and at the same time to underestimate the effects of Amerindian religions on European Christianity. This would be inaccurate. Numerically, descendants of Amerindian peoples constitute a sizable proportion of world Catholics and have enjoyed considerable influence in Rome. On the local level syncretism continues unabated, and the resiliency and intensity of Amerindian traditions is notable. Also notable is the persistence of shamans who continue to practice their trade. While much else has changed, shamanism, which has been noted frequently as a unifying factor within the diversity of Amerindian groups, is immediately identifiable and has been little altered over the past five hundred years.

BIBLIOGRAPHY

Dunn, Oliver, and James A. Kelley, Jr., trans. *The Diario of Christopher Columbus's First Voyage to America. 1492–1493.* Norman, Okla., 1988.
Hultkrantz, Åke. *The Religions of the American Indians.* Translated by Monica Setterwall. Berkeley, 1979.
Krickeberg, Walter, Herman Trimborn, Werner Muller, and Otto Zerries, eds. *Pre-Columbian American Religions.* Translated by Stanley Davis. New York, 1968.
Pané, Ramón. *Relación acerca de las antiquedades de los indios.* Translated by José Juan Arrom. Mexico City, 1974.
Stevens-Arroyo, Antonio M. *Cave of the Jagua: The Mythological World of the Tainos.* Albuquerque, 1988.
Sullivan, Lawrence E. *Icanchu's Drum: An Orientation to Meaning in South American Religions.* New York, 1988.
Todorov, Tzvetan. *The Conquest of America: The Question of the Other.* Translated by Richard Howard. New York, 1987.
Wilbert, Johannes. *Tobacco and Shamanism in South America.* New Haven, 1987.

STEPHEN D. GLAZIER

ROME. In the Renaissance period, this former capital of the ancient Roman Empire was important as the seat of the papacy, place of pilgrimage, and capital of the Papal States (one of the five major Italian states). Although the ancient Aurelian walls survived, the inhabited part of the city was restricted, because of the need for water, to the bend in the Tiber River (Campo Marzio and Regula regions) opposite the Vatican complex (the Leonine Borgo) and the Trastevere section on the right bank. Access by land to the city was along the ancient Roman highways (e.g., Aurelian, Flaminian, and Cassian from the north and Appian from the south), through the Roman Campagna where bandits flourished amid large estates given over to grain, wine, cattle, and sheep production. Larger ships docked at Civitavecchia, some thirty-eight miles from the city on the Aurelian Way, and smaller ones used Ostia at the mouth of the Tiber and ferried goods fifteen miles upstream to the city's large landing area (the Ripa Grande) in Trastevere or to the smaller facilities (the Ripetta) in Campo Marzio. Although there were various attempts from 1434 to 1511 to set up an independent Roman republic, the popes retained political control of the city but granted it significant local autonomy with its own constitution in 1469.

In the fifteenth and sixteenth centuries Rome experienced a remarkable revival. During the time of the Great Western Schism, (1378–1417), control of the city shifted among the Roman and Pisan popes, the kings of Naples, condottieri (leaders of mercenary troops) and local feudal barons (notably the rival Colonna and Orsini families). Rome was then a regional market town with a population of about seventeen thousand. What distinguished it from other such towns was the steady stream of pilgrims (about 100,000 annually) who came to pray at the tombs of the apostles Peter and Paul and the martyrs. Serving these pilgrims' needs were various religious confraternities and almost five hundred establishments providing lodgings and food. Jubilee years every quarter century could see a fourfold increase in the number of pilgrims. With the end of the Great Western Schism a unified papacy under Martin V (r. 1417–1431) took up residency in Rome in 1420. Apart from some notable periods of absence during the pontificates of Eugenius IV (1431–1447) and Pius II (1458–1464), the growing central bureaucracy of the Roman Catholic Church was permanently established in the city, attracting numerous prelates, bureaucrats, lawyers, bankers, and petitioners from throughout Christendom. Perhaps only a quarter of the city's population was native; the rest was very mobile and cosmopolitan. The Curia needed people familiar with conditions in various countries, cardinals' households often contained connationals, and relatives and countrymen frequently sought favors from the popes: for example, Venetians from Eugenius IV and Paul II (1464–1471); Spaniards from Calixtus III (1455–1458) and Alexander VI (1492–1503); Ligurians from Sixtus IV (1471–1484), Innocent VIII (1484–1492), and Julius II

(1503–1513); and Tuscans from Leo X (1513–1521), Clement VII (1523–1534), and Julius III (1550–1555). Despite repeated disasters of floods, malaria, epidemics, and famine, the city had grown to about forty thousand by the end of the fifteenth century.

Popes contributed in various ways to this growth. Martin V began the work of renovation by improving the streets, public buildings, and churches. His successor Eugenius IV restored sections of the city walls, bridges, and churches. With the help of Leon Battista Alberti, Nicholas V drew up plans to make Rome a grand monumental city and cultural center. Abandoning the Lateran palace, he moved the papacy permanently to the Vatican, restoring its palace and founding the Vatican Library. He recognized that the ancient basilica of Saint Peter's was beyond repair and envisioned a new one. Although he helped restore forty churches, his grander plans remained unrealized for a lack of time and money. Sixtus IV significantly altered the face of Rome by opening up new roads, prohibiting porches and overhangs that abutted onto existing roadways, and building the Ponte Sisto that joined Trastevere to the rest of the city. He encouraged the construction of palaces and homes by changing church law; clerics could now bequeath to others, rather than having confiscated at death, the buildings they constructed with revenues from ecclesiastical benefices. Among the many palaces built at this time, the most famous was the Cancelleria (1485–1511) of Raffaello Riario. Sixtus IV gained lasting fame for building and decorating at the Vatican the Sistine Chapel for papal ceremonies, consistories, and conclaves. Innocent VIII is remembered for having built the Belvedere villa in the papal gardens. The heart of papal Rome, known as Leonine Borgo, commanded the attention of Alexander VI who restored Castel Sant' Angelo as the papal fortress and

facilitated access to it from the Vatican. He is said to have used some of the first gold from America to decorate the ornate ceiling of Santa Maria Maggiore.

The popes of the sixteenth century further transformed Rome into a center of art and culture. Julius II concentrated on the Vatican complex, significantly enlarging the palace. Above the apartments that had been inhabited by Alexander VI he raised a new series of rooms *(stanze)* whose walls and ceiling he commissioned Raphael to decorate with a series of frescoes depicting historical events and theological themes. Michelangelo was entrusted with decorating the ceiling of the Sistine Chapel with scenes from the book of *Genesis*. In 1506 Julius laid the foundations for a new Saint Peter's basilica to be built on a Greek-cross plan designed by Bramante. Along the left bank of the Tiber he laid out the Via Giulia where he hoped in vain to locate the judicial functions of the Curia.

Under Leo X work continued on decorating the papal apartments, and when Raphael replaced Bramante as architect of Saint Peter's, a Latin-cross plan replaced the Greek. (The indulgence preached to help finance this construction occasioned Luther's Ninety-five Theses and the beginnings of the Protestant Reformation.) Leo X also welcomed to Rome many leading writers and artists and strengthened the local university, Sapienza, founded in 1303, with new faculty, a large student body, and a Greek college. The city experienced phenomenal growth (some ten thousand new homes were constructed), and Leo systematized the three streets radiating from the Piazza del Popolo and developed the Via di Ripetta that led to the smaller river harbor. The three principal commercial centers were also beautified: Piazza del Ponte (banking), Piazza Navona (general merchandise), and Campo dei Fiori (foodstuffs).

Under Clement VII a new art style developed to replace the idealized and harmonious compositions of the High Renaissance. This elongated, off-balance, strangely colored, and overly refined art is known as Clementine Mannerism. Many of its proponents left Rome at the time of the Sack (1527) and thus spread its style. Just prior to the Sack of Rome a census counted at least 53,689 inhabitants. The devastations caused by the unruly army sent by Emperor Charles V and later by a flood in 1530 reduced this number to about 32,000. But the city rapidly recovered, especially under Paul III who repaired its walls and fortifications and laid out streets to encourage development. The medieval-style center of municipal government (the Campidoglio) he transformed into a splendid Renaissance piazza according to the design of Michelangelo with the ancient bronze equestrian statue of Marcus Aurelius as its centerpiece.

Thereafter, baroque rapidly became the typical art style of the city. Pius IV (r. 1559–1565) was able to develop the

St. Peter's Square.   Elsevier Publishing Projects, Amsterdam

area atop the Quirinal along the Via Pia leading to the Porta Pia because of the restoration of the Vergine aqueduct. Tapping into this water supply, Gregory XIII (r. 1572–1585) created many fountains. He embellished the Campidoglio with the palaces of the senator and conservators and laid out connecting thoroughfares between the basilicas of Santa Maria Maggiore and San Croce and San Giovanni in Laterano. The cult of the ancient martyrs was advanced both by Saint Filippo Neri, whose Congregation of the Oratory the pope approved in 1575, and by the accidental discovery three years later of a subterranean cemetery on the Via Salaria. The discovery aroused great interest and led in 1593 to the systematic exploration by Antonio Bosio of numerous other catacombs. With the support of Cardinal Alessandro Farnese and Pope Gregory XIII, the Jesuits built their mother church, the Gesù, and the Roman College with its satellite national colleges.

Under the brief but remarkable pontificate of Sixtus V (1585–1590), Rome became definitively "the sacred city." The new aqueduct (Aqua Felice) he built to allow for the development of the hilly regions of Rome terminated in a fountain with sculpted scenes from the Old Testament. A network of straight streets centering on Santa Maria Maggiore and ending at major churches in an obelisk crowned with a cross proclaiming the victory of Christ over paganism facilitated the processions of pilgrims visiting the shrines of Christendom. The secular character and grandeur of the Belvedere garden, with its collection of ancient statuary despoiled of many of its marble items by the austere Pius V in 1566, was forever tempered by the construction of the Vatican Library wing across its inner courtyard. Work on the massive dome of Saint Peter's was completed just three months before Sixtus died in 1590. By then, Rome with a population of more than ninety thousand had a clearly religious dimension and had become a fitting capital of Catholic Christendom.

BIBLIOGRAPHY

D'Amico, John F. *Renaissance Humanism in Papal Rome: Humanists and Churchmen on the Eve of the Reformation.* Johns Hopkins University Studies in Historical and Political Science, 101st ser., no. 1. Baltimore, 1983.

Delumeau, Jean. *Vie économique et sociale de Rome dans la seconde moitié du XVIe siècle.* 2 Vols. Bibliothèque des Écoles Françaises d'Athènes et de Rome, fasc. 184. Paris, 1959.

Partner, Peter. *The Lands of St. Peter: The Papal States in the Middle Ages and the Early Renaissance.* Berkeley, 1972.

Partner, Peter. *The Papal State under Martin V: The Administration and Government of the Temporal Power in the Early Fifteenth Century.* London, 1958.

Partner, Peter. *Renaissance Rome, 1500–1559: A Portrait of a Society.* Berkeley, 1976.

Paschini, Pio. *Roma nel Rinascimento.* Storia di Roma, vol. 12. Bologna, 1940.

Pecchiai, Pio. *Roma nel cinquecento.* Storia di Roma, vol. 13. Bologna, 1948.

Stinger, Charles L. *The Renaissance in Rome.* Bloomington, Ind., 1985.

NELSON H. MINNICH

RUTTER. See *Sailing Directions.*

RUYSCH, JOHAN (d. 1533), Dutch geographer, explorer, and cartographer. Because Johan Ruysch is said to have worked first at Utrecht and then at Cologne, he is called Germanus by Beneventanus in the 1507–1508 Rome edition of Ptolemy's *Geography.* Beneventanus reports (chapter 3) that Ruysch said (*dixit*) that he had sailed from the south of England to fifty-three degrees north latitude and then stayed on that latitude until he arrived at the shores of the east *per angulum noctis* (by the angle [corner] of the night) and visited many islands. Later in the same chapter Beneventanus writes that Ruysch calls the Northern Sea (Mare Aquilonium) part of the Mare Sugenum, a huge area of sea stretching from about seventy degrees north latitude to the North Pole.

Although Beneventanus calls Ruysch a most experienced geographer and a most careful cartographer, nothing of his other work is known. Internal evidence shows clear but not perfect latinity, good draftsmanship, and depictions of coastlines ranging from near perfection to wild surmise. It has naturally been conjectured that Ruysch accompanied John Cabot on his 1497 voyage from Bristol, but he never mentions Cabot in the captions to his map; and Cape Race, Newfoundland, which on Juan de la Cosa's map is called "cauo de Ynglaterra" (Cape England), is in Ruysch's map called "C. de Portogesi."

This map, *Universalior cogniti orbis tabula,* must have been engraved shortly before the 1507–1508 Rome Ptolemy, because it records the fact that Portuguese mariners sailed to Taprobana (to him, Sumatra) in 1507. Whereas he records Portuguese discoveries around the coast of Africa accurately, he illustrates Columbus's view of the New World by combining the eastern coasts of Asia and North America to form one coast. Between Iceland and Greenland he notes that an island was completely burned in 1456. Near Greenland are remarks about magnetism upsetting compasses, with reference to a work on the fortunate discovery by Nicholas of Lynn (1355). Greenland and Terra Nova (Newfoundland) have only a shallow bay between them. Not far west of Terra Nova he places a long shore heading roughly west-northwest toward Gog Magog (cf. *Ezekiel* 38–39) and Cathaya (China). These coasts form a bay called Plisacus Sinus, near the south end of which is Zaito(n), whose caption starts (in translation): "M. Polo says that fifteen hundred miles east is a very large island called Sipa[n]g[us] [Japan]"; Ruysch says, among other things, that it has such a good climate that its inhabitants live to the age of 150.

The West Indies include a large island (Cuba?) or peninsula west of Spagnola (La Española), with a caption saying that the ships of King Fernando of Spain reached the west of it. South America is labeled "Terra sancte crucis sive Mundus novus" (Land of the Holy Cross, or New World), and Ruysch provides a long caption about its inhabitants, who are said to eat their prisoners. He credits the Spanish with naming it Mundus Novus (compare the Pesaro world map of c. 1505). On the east he records some predecessor of Ferdinand Magellan: "Portuguese sailors observed this part of this land and reached latitude fifty degrees south latitude, but did not reach the southern extremity." His fan-shaped map reaches only to thirty-eight degrees south latitude, but this enables him to include the whole of southern Africa.

It has long been known that there are notable variations in different drafts of the map. Recently a systematic catalog of these differences has been attempted, and what may be called a palimpsest has been discovered. It consists of text referring to Arctic islands and their inhabitants that has been replaced by stippling for sea.

BIBLIOGRAPHY

Dilke, Margaret S., and Antonio Brancati. "The New World in the Pesaro Map." *Imago Mundi* 31 (1979): 78–83.

Dilke, O. A. W. "Note on the Ruysch Palimpsest." *Imago Mundi* 42 (1990): 132.

Fite, Emerson D., and Archibald Freeman. *A Book of Old Maps Delineating American History.* Cambridge, Mass., 1926.

McGuirk, Donald L., Jr. "Ruysch World Map: Census and Commentary." *Imago Mundi* 41 (1989): 133–141.

Nordenskiöld, A. E. *Facsimile-Atlas to the Early History of Cartography.* Translated by J. A. Ekelöf and C. R. Markham. Reprint, New York, 1973.

Ptolemy. *Cosmographia (Geography).* Rome, 1507–1508. Facsimile with introduction by R. A. Skelton in *Theatrum orbis terrarum,* 2d ser., vol. 6. Amsterdam, 1966.

Shirley, Rodney W. *The Mapping of the World.* London, 1983.

Swan, Bradford. "The Ruysch Map of the World (1507–1508)." *Papers of the Bibliographical Society of America* 45 (1951): 219–236.

Woodward, David, ed. *Five Centuries of Map Printing.* Chicago, 1975.

O. A. W. Dilke

SAILING DIRECTIONS.

SAILING DIRECTIONS. In the time of Columbus, sailing directions were contained in portolanos (derived from the Latin *portus,* port) and rutters (from the French *route*). Portolanos are medieval Italian books containing a description of the coasts and ports of the Mediterranean and Black seas giving shipmasters all the aids they required for coasting and pilotage. The term has been used in this sense from at least 1295. The earliest surviving manuscript is *Lo compasso da navigare* (Hamilton Manuscript 396, State Library, Berlin) dated 1296, a compilation based on several earlier versions that may date back to 1232.

The contents of *Lo compasso* recall the collections of nautical directions of Greek antiquity of which, according to Strabo, there were two types: *peripli (periploi),* which gave general directions for voyages, and *limenes* (port-books), which contained details about individual ports such as how to enter and leave them and where to anchor. The anonymous *Stadiasmos of the Great Sea* (A.D. 250–300), the only ancient Greek true sea book to have survived, lists only brief pieces of information on the functions and port facilities of the towns mentioned; it gives only the distance between towns, expressed in stades. *Lo compasso,* which describes the Mediterranean and Black sea coasts, starting at Cape St. Vincent (the southwest extremity of Portugal) to the straits of Gibraltar, in a counterclockwise direction, and then from Gibraltar to Safi on the Atlantic coast of Morocco, supplies information similar to that in *Stadiasmos,* but adds two new items: the depth of anchorages expressed in *passi,* with indications of watering places, and the course to steer between the named ports. These courses are given by the names of the Mediterranean eight-rayed compass: *Tramontana* (north), *Greco* (northeast), *Levante* (east), *Sirocco* (southeast), *Ostro* (south), *Africo* or *Libeccio* (south-west), *Ponente* (west), and *Maestro* (northwest). Distances are given in Italian miles, one mile being equal to 1,230 meters. Usually distances are rounded off to the nearest 10 miles and are somewhat understated. These developments, contemporary with the production of a reliable sea compass and with the first known nautical chart constructed by geometrical methods, the *Carte Pisane* (c. 1275; Bibliothèque Nationale, Paris, Res. Ge. B. 1118), mark a turning point in the history of navigation.

Nineteenth-century writers used the word *portolano* to describe either a book of sailing directions—the generally accepted meaning—or a nautical chart constructed according to bearing and distance, which is now known as a portolan chart. There is no doubt of a close relationship between charts and sailing directions, but the exact relationship is still uncertain. R. B. Motzo, the first editor of *Lo compasso,* believed that it and the early portolan chart belonged to the same work, produced by a single author and based on the same data. A comparative analysis of place-names, however, shows that at least 30 percent of those found in the *Carte Pisane* come from another source. Further, whereas *Lo compasso* is written in Italian, the *Carte Pisane* contains a wide range of dialectical variations. Moreover, a map using data from the portolano can be constructed only by making certain adjustments to overcome the shortcomings of the text; such a map shows grossly simplified coastlines when compared to the sophisticated coastal delineation found on the earliest surviving charts. It may well be that a number of descriptions found in the portolano have their origins in an examination of contemporary charts. Thirteenth-century navigators were not content routinely to hug the shore, and several of the routes described in *Lo compasso* are quite long cross-sea passages of about 500 Italian miles (a little under 650 kilometers, or 400 miles) and even up to 700 Italian miles (roughly 900 kilometers, or 550 miles). It may well be that the drawing up of the chart made a visualization of the crossing possible—perhaps that was their intention—and that their description in the portolano is no more than a verbal translation of the chart. One thing, however, cannot be overemphasized: in the final stages of these crossings, irrespective of whether the hoped-for landfall was a headland, a small island, or a port of call, the portolan chart, because of its small scale, was no longer useful to the sailor, who now had to refer to the more detailed information in the portolano.

Only half a dozen manuscript collections of sailing directions survive from before the last quarter of the fifteenth century. Their titles differ according to the language used. In northern Europe, the oldest is called *Seebuch* (Low German), which covers coasts from Sweden to Gibraltar. Part of the text goes back to the fourteenth century and contains traces of its Italian origin. The *Leeskart* (Flemish) from the same period refers to the same shores. The French title is *routier* (literally route-book). The oldest *routier* is *Le routier de la mer,* an anonymous work, but attributed to the Vendean Pierre Garcie (end of the fifteenth century). The work covers Atlantic waters from the Scheldt to Gibraltar. It is essentially an original work, notably in including detailed descriptions of the physical features of the shore illustrated by the elevation of important points of the hinterland and coast as they would appear to an approaching sailor. Nevertheless, it too incorporated much older material, and in its turn served as a prototype for the first rutter printed in English (1528). The same word *(route)* turns up again in the sixteenth-century Portuguese term *roteiro* and the Spanish *derrotero.* All these books, following the example of the Italian portolano, focus on the information necessary for coastal navigation and landfall. All derive from the same sources and draw on each other.

If we attempt to identify sea books that Christopher Columbus might have used or to which he might have contributed, we must distinguish three different traditions. The first is the Mediterranean portolano, which Columbus, by origin Genoese, clearly used on his voyages to Chios and England. By the end of the fifteenth century, such works had been changed and enlarged when compared to the *Compasso,* since they now contained data about the Atlantic and the northern European seas taken respectively from either the *Seebuch* or Pierre Garcie's *routier,* or from sources identical to theirs. Although Mediterranean distances continued to be given in Italian miles (1,230 meters), in the ocean Portuguese leagues (5,500 meters) were used; for Atlantic ports, headlands, and channels, there are indications concerning the direction of flow of tidal streams and a definition of their

"establishment," that is, a record of the moon's position on the horizon at high water on days of new or full moons, which gives the pilot the most propitious time for entering and leaving port and place. In the first published portolano, *Questa e una opera necessaria a tutte li naviganti chi vano in diverse parte del mondo* (Bernardo Rizo, Venice, November 1490), about one-fifth of the instructions refer to non-Mediterranean seaboards. The manuscript is anonymous, but can be attributed to the Venetian Alvise Cadamosto, who in the mid fifteenth century had explored the coasts of Senegal and Gambia in the service of Prince Henry the Navigator.

The second tradition was developed in Portugal at the same time. In the final quarter of the fifteenth century the first original *roteiros*—dealing with the African coast and the Madeira, Azores, Canary, and Cape Verde archipelagoes—were being put together. Christopher Columbus followed some of these routes in the period from 1477 to 1482–1483: the route from Lisbon to Madeira regularly and the route from Lisbon to São Jorge da Mina at least once. The oldest Portuguese-produced route book, *Roteiro das ilhas e da Guiné* (available only in a codex of 1506 to 1508, known as the manuscript of Valentim Fernandes) took shape as part of the process of exploration and discloses evidence of its earlier composition. São Tiago Island, in the Cape Verde Islands, for example, is referred to under two names, the second of which, Ilha de Antonio, clearly alludes to Antonio da Noli, who accompanied Cadamosto's expedition in 1455–1456. Another clue to its real age is its layout; it is divided into geographical sections, starting with the coast of Senegal *(tytolo de çenaga)* and then São Jorge da Mina *(Ho livro das rotas do castello de Sam Jorge),* before going from the Niger delta to São Tomé Island *(A qui falla de rota do Cabo Fremoso pera ylha de Samtamtoneo);* that is, it follows the order of exploration and discovery. The route book for Flanders *(Roteiro da Flandres,* found in a much later manuscript, *Lo livro de marinharia de João de Lisboa),* very probably an original Portuguese work of the fifteenth century, covers a familiar and long-known area, and offers various categories of information, for example, distinguishing among indications of distance only *(leguas),* indications of rhumbs and distances for points along the same coast *(rotas* and *derrotas),* indications of rhumbs and distances for points on different sections of the coastline opposite each other *(travessas),* and instructions about how to enter the ports *(pousos). Roteiro das ilhas e da Guiné* indicates *travessas* between points of the Iberian and Moroccan coasts on the one hand, and archipelagoes in the Atlantic on the other hand, including the imaginary islands of contemporary nautical cartography (such as the Island of the Seven Cities and Saint Brendan's Isle), clearly showing that at least a few sections of the sea books are indebted to the descriptions in the charts. The African *roteiro* ends with information concerning the establishment of the ports of Sierra Leone and São Jorge da Mina. Therefore, in its conception and contents, it is strictly comparable to the *Portolano Rizo,* though for different shores.

The main achievements of the Portuguese in the field, which cannot be accurately dated, probably did not appear before the early sixteenth century. Two should be given special attention. First, and more important, for each of the points described by the rutter, latitude was mentioned, first in preliminary tables and then integrated in the text itself. Second, the coastal data of the region described were supplemented with information about the safest or the more direct route to sail across the ocean.

The third tradition is Spanish. Both innovations of the Portuguese sea books appear in the first methodical Spanish rutter of the sea areas discovered by Columbus in America. This *derrotero* is a later manuscript (c. 1530), never published in the sixteenth century, which is the fourth part of a general book dealing with nautical science, the *Quatri partitu en cosmografia practica, y por otro nombre espejo de navegantes.* The author, Alonso Cháves, was a well-known pilot and cosmographer to Charles V; in the opening lines of the rutter, he acknowledges his debt to the many pilots who navigated in the region. This version is a compilation of previous works by at least two copyists; despite a number of geographic discrepancies, it was a pioneering book, since it was the first general rutter of navigation to the Indies. It is divided into twenty-five chapters. The first describes the voyage from Spain to the Indies, and the last the return. Chapters 2 to 7 concern the islands, from the West Indies to the Bahamas; chapters 8 to 24 are devoted to continental shorelines. There are two successive clockwise descriptions of the coasts, one around the Caribbean and the Gulf of Mexico from Venezuela to Florida, the second around South and Central America, along the Pacific coast, from Peru to Nicaragua, and again along the Caribbean and the Atlantic Ocean south to the Straits of Magellan.

Like the Portuguese of the same period, Cháves introduced latitude data in his *derrotero.* A thorough study of these latitudes shows that they are consistent with a westerly magnetic variation of about fourteen degrees, something that Columbus observed as early as his first voyage, and that was to generate important secondary effects in contemporary nautical charts. Several indications in the text, such as false orientations of the Bahamas islands that wrench them into appropriate latitudes exactly as they appear on contemporary charts, or the dominance of cardinal bearings (52 percent of the bearings are north, south, east, or west; 27 percent are the intermediate

winds) suggest once again that a part of the *derrotero* was a verbal map. Cháves makes an interesting methodological improvement: a table of place names classified in alphabetical order referring to the corresponding chapter and paragraph, for example. "*Guanahani, isla de Lucayos,* ch. 7, 16." The text explains that this island was the first landfall reached when the Indies were discovered. There are other Columbian reminiscences, such as the description of Tierra Firme from the Gulf of Paria to the Gulf of Uraba, through the Boca del Dragon (Dragon's Mouth, the northern entrance of the Gulf of Paria), which is close to Gonzalo Fernández de Oviedo's description. The route from Spain, starting from Sanlúcar or Cádiz Bay, southwest to Tenerife and Gomera, then sailing directly from Fierro in the Canaries to the Caribbean, corresponds to Columbus's route to the Indies on his second voyage. These details are not surprising since Cháves worked in close collaboration with Fernando Colón from 1526 to 1539. They also indicate that Columbus was a link in an international tradition of sailing directions of which he was both an heir and a creator.

BIBLIOGRAPHY

Castañeda, Paulino, Cuesta Mariano, and Hernandez Pilar. *Alonzo de Chaves y el libro IV de su "Espejo de Navegantes."* Madrid, 1977.

Campbell, Tony. "Portolan Charts from the Late Thirteenth Century to 1500." In *The History of Cartography,* vol. 1, *Cartography in Prehistoric, Ancient and Medieval Europe and the Mediterranean,* edited by J. B. Harley and David Woodward. Chicago and London, 1987.

Conti, Simoneta. "Portolano e carta nautica: confronto toponomastico." *Imago et mensura mundi. Atti del IX Congresso internazionale di storia della cartografia.* Rome, 1985.

Kelley, James E., Jr. "The Map of the Bahamas Implied by Chaves's Derrotero. What Is Its Relevance to the First Landfall Question?" *Imago Mundi* 42 (1990).

Kretschmer, Konrad. *Die italienischen Portolane des Mittelalters.* Berlin, 1909. Reprint, Hildesheim, 1962.

Lamb, Ursula. "The 'Quatri Partitu en Cosmographia' by Alonso de Chaves. An Interpretation." *Agrupamento de estudos de cartografia antiga,* vol. 28. Coimbra, 1969.

Teixeira da Mota, Avelino. "Evoluço dos roteiros portugueses durante o seculo XVI." *Agrupamento de estudos de cartografia antiga,* vol. 33. Coimbra, 1969.

Waters, David W. *The Rutters of the Sea.* New Haven and London, 1967.

ISABELLE RAYNAUD-NGUYEN
Translated from French by Anthony Turner

SANTA FE CAPITULATIONS. The capitulations constitute the agreement between Christopher Columbus and the Spanish monarchs concerning the conditions under which Columbus would be permitted to lead an expedition west, into the Atlantic, over which they claimed sovereignty. The two parts of the agreement were signed in the city of Santa Fe de Granada. The first, dated April 17, 1492, spelled out Columbus's privileges and obligations, and the second, dated April 30, defined his titles. The three basic questions concerning these instruments concern their precedents, their nature, and their consequences.

The evident demand for high status, extensive powers, and financial gain by a foreign trader is what makes the agreement unique. Late-medieval precedents, such as contracts between a sovereign and a private party dealing with exploration within a given jurisdiction, are plentiful. The case of Columbus is extraordinary in the speculative, not to say chimerical, goals he presented. Columbus must have felt there was nothing to lose at this stage, when the queen was ready to support the venture on the basis of the argument that the risk was very small, practically, financially, and politically.

How the first five articles of the capitulations were spelled out in detail is revealed in the Pleitos Colombinos, the ensuing litigation. Assuming the most extensive and liberal interpretation in Columbus's favor of the financial privileges and those of office, the obstacles to full implementation can be easily imagined. The unfolding of the Pleitos reveals a larger context of medieval traditions in government (the conferring of titles) combined with the ambitions of a rising entrepreneurial class and sponsorship by a monarchy with antifeudal tendencies. The capitulations became in form, if never in substance, the basis for all subsequent agreements with explorers of the Indies. Contemporary and subsequent interpretations of the good or bad faith shown by both parties to the capitulations have tended to reflect assessments of the outcome of Columbus's venture. Such questions are yet alive today.

Columbus took the original document containing the capitulations of Santa Fe de Granada with him on his first voyage. It is known to have been on deposit with Columbus's papers in the archive of the Carthusian Monastery (La Cartuja) in Seville as late as 1520 to 1526 but has not been found in modern times. Although the original is not preserved, the text survives in the register and file kept in the archive of the Crown of Aragón in Barcelona. Columbus was quite naturally afraid of a mishap or loss of that text, so he had a copy made, witnessed, and registered on December 16, 1495, in Santo Domingo. Columbus wanted to have an authenticated copy in his possession, because of the arrival in October of that year of Juan Aguado, an investigative judge who surely needed to consult the document. This made the Admiral consider the need for an authorized duplicate,

and it was this copy he submitted in Burgos on April 23, 1497, when he requested the confirmation of his privileges. It is now in the collection of the Archive of the Indies in Seville. Of four more copies, dated 1502, referred to as the Privilegios de Veragua, two were sent to Genoa.

The variations in spelling among the copies are judged trivial by the experts. One remarkable exception is a brief clause that refers to "Christopher Columbus, in some satisfaction for *what he has discovered.*" This phrase was changed in the Navarrete Collection, the nineteenth-century edition of the document copy of Burgos (1497), to "what he shall discover."

[See also *Book of Privileges; Lawsuits.*]

BIBLIOGRAPHY

García Martínez, Bernardo. "Ojeada a las capitulaciones para la conquista de America." *Revista de Historia de America* 69 (1970): 1–41.

Schoenrich, Otto, *The Legacy of Columbus: The Historic Litigation Involving His Discoveries, His Will, His Family and His Descendants.* 2 vols. Glendale, Calif., 1949.

Thacher, John Boyd. *Christopher Columbus.* 2 vols. 1902. Reprint, New York, 1967. Spanish and English texts of the capitulations.

Ursula Lamb

SANTA MARÍA. Almost without exception, maritime historians and Columbus scholars have acclaimed *Santa María*, Columbus's flagship on his first voyage of discovery, as the most famous ship in the world. What reader of Samuel Eliot Morison's *Admiral of the Ocean Sea* could feel otherwise? Despite his extensive research, however, not even Morison was able to provide an authentic picture of *Santa María*. He reluctantly reported that "there are no data from which it honestly can be done." Ongoing research, however, has given us some details.

Columbus himself provided important information in the journal of his first voyage. He identified *Santa María* as a nao, a bulky merchant ship with substantial cargo-carrying capacity. He also provided specific information as to the number and type of her sails, listing them as "the main course with two bonnets, the fore course, spritsail, mizzen and topsail." The two bonnets, upper and lower, were horizontal strips of sail laced one above the other to the foot of the mainsail, or main course as it was then called, in light to moderate winds. As wind strengths increased, first the lower and then the upper bonnet would be removed as a substitute for reefing the mainsail. This sail plan was an early development in the transition from one mast with a single large mainsail to three masts with a variety of sails. It was a time of rapid change in rig development with the large mainsail remaining as the major driving force. The much smaller foresail, mizzen, and spritsail, while obviously providing some additional propulsive force, served more to help in directional control and maneuverability, particularly when tacking. The tiny main topsail was still an early tentative addition to the rig. This journal entry about the sails was, regrettably, the only specific reference Columbus made about his ships.

Another reason there is little specific information about ships of the period is that until the seventeenth century there were no naval architects in the modern sense of that profession. There were only shipwrights who built boats and ships the way their fathers and forefathers had built them for centuries. They drew no plans either for use in the building process or for recording their achievements.

To construct a replica or even paint an accurate picture of *Santa María*, the best one can do is to make use of as much data as possible about ships of her type from contemporary paintings and sketches, models, books, and documents of pertinent maritime history and ship construction as well as recent findings developed by nautical archaeologists from their excavations of discovery-era ships.

Most paintings and sketches of fifteenth-century merchant naos, which were commonly referred to as "round" ships, had certain features that were indeed round. The shapes of the stem and frames that governed the shape of the hull, for example, almost invariably were arcs of circles. The radii of these arcs were related to the ship's breadth or beam by simple ratios used by shipwrights of the period. Other identifying features, well illustrated by

MODEL OF *SANTA MARÍA*. The Martinez-Hidalgo model in the National Museum of American History.   THE SMITHSONIAN INSTITUTION

Vittore Carpaccio's painting *The Legend of Saint Ursula* (1495), were the forecastle overhanging the bow, the half deck with a poop deck rising above it in the stern, the graceful arch visually tying the forecastle deck to the bulwark rails port and starboard, the heavy bitt beam protruding through the bulwark planking just forward of the arch, and the distinctive round tuck stern with wales and planking sweeping gracefully upward at about a 45-degree angle to a heavy transom beam mounted atop the sternpost at the main deck level.

Several maritime museums display models of *Santa María* that show many of these features. The Naval Museum in Madrid, the Maritime Museum in Barcelona, and the National Museum of American History in Washington, D.C., have such a model based on a full-size replica designed in 1963 by Capt. José María Martinez-Hidalgo, Spain's foremost authority on Columbus's ships. His plans are reported to be the basis of the 1989 Spanish reconstruction of *Santa María*. Philips Academy in Andover, Massachusetts, has an older well-regarded model by noted English historian R. C. Anderson. Maritime museums in Newport News, Virginia; Savannah, Georgia; and Pegli, Italy, also have excellent models.

From books and documents one finds that there is consensus among maritime historians that *Santa María* was of about one hundred tons burden. In the Columbus era the burden, or cargo-carrying capacity, of a ship was measured in terms of the number of wine tuns (barrels) she could carry. Since a tun of wine weighed very close to a ton, the change from tuns to tons required no change in numerical value. From the value of one hundred tons burden and from commonly used rules of thumb for hull proportions it was possible to arrive at reasonable assumptions of hull dimensions and shape. For a late fifteenth century nao, the accepted proportions of breadth, length of keel, and length of main deck were in the simple ratios of 1:2:3. The master shipwright builder of *Santa María* would have known from his own long experience and from knowledge inherited from his forefathers that if she were to be of one hundred tons burden, her hull dimensions, using those ratios, should be roughly twenty-seven feet for breadth or beam, fifty-four feet for length of keel, and eighty-one feet for length of main deck.

Discoveries and excavations in the 1980s of three shipwrecks of the discovery period have provided particularly valuable and previously unavailable details of hull construction and shape. Two of the shipwreck sites were in the Caribbean and the third was in Red Bay, Labrador. The latter was the remarkably well-preserved 1565 wreck of a Spanish Basque galleon, the immediate successor of the nao with many similar features. Since *Santa María* is believed to have been built in the Basque region of Spain, and since hull construction methods of a particular region were very slow to change, there is good reason to believe that the hull of the Basque galleon was built using much the same methods that would have been used to build Columbus's famous flagship.

The staff of the Institute of Nautical Archaeology and the marine archaeologists of the Canadian Park Service deserve great credit for their important accomplishments in the Caribbean and Labrador, respectively. New hard evidence of hull form and construction details, when combined with documented rules of thumb used by shipwrights of the Age of Discovery, now makes it possible to construct a more authentic replica of *Santa María* than could be done in the past.

BIBLIOGRAPHY

"Marine Excavation of the Basque Whaling Vessel San Juan." Research Bulletins 123, 163, 194, 206, 240, 248, 258. Canadian Park Service. Ottawa, 1980–1987.

Martinez-Hidalgo, José María. *Columbus' Ships*. Barre, Mass., 1966.

WILLIAM LEMOS

SANTÁNGEL, LUIS DE (d. 1505), Aragonese converso and chief financial adviser to Fernando the Catholic. Santángel's personal intervention in 1492, literally at the last moment, was the decisive factor that persuaded Queen Isabel to advance the nearly five million maravedis for Columbus's first voyage.

Columbus knew of the wealthy Santángel family— merchants and lawyers who had served the Aragonese royal family for generations—through their mercantile interests in Genoa. He approached Luis de Santángel in Córdoba as early as 1486 seeking financial support for his proposal to sail westward to India. Even as he sought financial assistance from other European monarchs, particularly King João II of Portugal, Columbus maintained contact with Santángel. By 1492 the Castilians had defeated the Muslim kings of Granada and were finally able to sponsor Columbus. The Granada wars had brought the Castilian treasury close to bankruptcy, however, and to finance Columbus, Santángel had to obtain the funds from a variety of sources including the Aragonese treasury and his own personal fortune. So great was Columbus's gratitude for Santángel's support that the first news of the voyage to reach Isabel and Fernando was through the now famous letter to Santángel in which Columbus described the voyage.

Santángel's faithful service to Fernando spared his family from the persecution of Jews and conversos during the Inquisition. Fernando's personal grant of May 30, 1497, exempted Santángel and his sons from the Inquisition and guaranteed his heirs their personal and financial property.

BIBLIOGRAPHY

Columbus, Christopher. *The Authentic Letters of Columbus.* Edited and translated by William Eleroy Curtis. Chicago, 1895.

Kayserling, M. *Christopher Columbus and the Participation of the Jews in the Spanish and Portuguese Discoveries.* Translated by Charles Gross. 4th ed. New York, 1968.

Mir, Miguel. *Influencia de los Aragoneses en el descubrimiento de América.* Palma de Mallorca, 1892.

THERESA EARENFIGHT

SANTO DOMINGO. See *Settlements,* article on *Santo Domingo.*

SCIENCE. [This entry includes two articles:

Science in the Late Fifteenth Century

Science and Technology in the Age of Discovery

For further discussion of the innovations in European science and technology that supported overseas expansion, see also *Cartography; Medicine and Health; Navigation; Printing; Shipbuilding; Timetelling.*]

Science in the Late Fifteenth Century

With a few notable exceptions, science at the time of Christopher Columbus's voyage in 1492 was largely a continuation of medieval medicine, science, and natural philosophy. Scientists accepted the geocentric representation of the cosmos as firmly in the fifteenth century as in the thirteenth and fourteenth. In some fields, especially physics, logic, mathematics, and natural philosophy, actual achievements in the fifteenth century were inferior to those of the preceding two centuries. Fifteenth-century scientists stood in the tradition of late medieval science and the Greco-Arabic inheritance it received in Latin translation during the twelfth and thirteenth centuries. At the core of this large body of scientific literature, which encompassed the physical and life sciences, were the physical and philosophical works of Aristotle, which formed the basis of the curriculum of the medieval universities, and the medical works of the second-century Greek physician Galen and the early eleventh-century Persian scientist Ibn Sina (Avicenna). During the thirteenth and fourteenth centuries, scholastic natural philosophers and scientists not only absorbed Greco-Arabic science, but added their own achievements in a variety of fields. Their successors in the fifteenth century seemed content to repeat and elaborate the ideas and interpretations of their medieval predecessors.

Few scientists made important original contributions in this century. The great polymath of the period, Leonardo da Vinci (1452–1519), despite his innovations in mechanics, geology, and technology, exercised no influence on the history of science. His massive notebooks were not published until long after his death. Many scientists born in the fifteenth century, such as Nicolaus Copernicus, did not become important until after 1500.

The most notable scientists of the period were Georg von Peuerbach, Regiomontanus, Luca Pacioli, and Nicholas of Cusa. The astronomer Georg von Peuerbach (1423–1461) and his student Regiomontanus (1436–1476; born Johann Müller) produced an abridged translation from Greek into Latin of the *Almagest* of the second-century Greek astronomer Ptolemy. Peuerbach translated the first six books and Regiomontanus completed the project, although the work, entitled *Epitome of the Almagest,* was not published until 1496, twenty years after the death of Regiomontanus. Peuerbach also wrote the *New Theories of the Planets,* which Regiomontanus published around 1474 and which became the basic astronomical text up to the seventeenth century. Peuerbach's *Tables of Eclipses,* completed around 1459 but printed only in 1514, was also a standard treatise in use until the seventeenth century. Although neither made dramatic departures from traditional astronomy, Peuerbach and Regiomontanus together revised and upgraded astronomy while also defining numerous technical terms.

The famous *Summa de arithmetica, geometria, proportioni et proportionalita* (Venice, 1494) of Luca Pacioli (c. 1445–c. 1514) was an encyclopedic mathematical treatise written in Italian that included sections on arithmetic (both practical and theoretical), algebra, tables of moneys and weights, double-entry bookkeeping, and geometry. Comprehensive and useful though it was, Pacioli's work was not an original contribution to the history of mathematics.

The most original thinker among fifteenth-century scientists may have been Nicholas of Cusa (c. 1401–1464), who concluded, contrary to the generally accepted opinion of Aristotle, that the celestial motions had no center. Indeed, the entire universe had no fixed center and no circumference. Consequently, the earth could not be the center of the cosmos nor could it be an immobile body, but it was in motion in space along with the other celestial bodies. In a daring speculation, Nicholas conjectured that life may not be confined to the earth but may also exist on other celestial bodies. Bold and spectacular as they were, Nicholas's cosmological conclusions were highly idiosyncratic conclusions drawn from his own metaphysical theory, which he called the "coincidence of opposites" *(coincidentia oppositorum),* a theory that failed to win adherents and had little impact in the physical sciences.

Although theoretical medicine was largely taught and studied from the texts of Galen, Ibn-Sina, and Razi (Rhazes) as well as medieval texts based on these fundamental works, fifteenth-century surgeons—especially Heinrich von Pfolspeundt (fl. 1460) and the Sicilian surgeons of the Branca family—developed plastic surgery to the face, replacing mutilated noses and lips and providing detailed descriptions of their procedures.

Notwithstanding the century's mediocre achievements in science proper, two major activities in the second half of the fifteenth century—a wave of translations from Greek to Latin and the invention of printing around 1460—made the period important for the history of science. The new translations and the printing press marked the definite beginnings of a challenge to traditional science and natural philosophy, beginnings that would deepen in the sixteenth century and come to fruition in the seventeenth.

The New Translations. Before Greek scientific treatises could be translated, manuscripts of them had to be obtained. This was a significant preoccupation of many fifteenth-century humanists, who were aided by the fact that numerous Greek manuscripts were brought to Italy by Byzantine Greeks, many of whom fled the Turkish siege and then the capture of Constantinople. Manuscripts of works that would be neither printed nor translated during the fifteenth century were salvaged from possible destruction and preserved in European library collections, either papal, royal, or private, to become available in the sixteenth and even seventeenth centuries.

The translations were largely associated with the Italian humanist movement of the fifteenth century, which was characterized by an intense interest in classical Greek and Roman culture and literature. Unlike their medieval scholastic predecessors and contemporaries, who devoted themselves to commentaries on the works of Aristotle that had largely been translated into Latin from earlier Arabic versions, the Italian humanists were interested in the original Latin and Greek texts, not only of Aristotle, but of all Greeks and Romans. Literary style, correct grammar, and philology, which were of little concern in scholastic discourse, were of paramount interest to humanists. In their study of philosophy, Italian humanists were interested in themes of love, friendship, beauty and good citizenship, and much less concerned with natural philosophy, science, and logic than the more analytically oriented scholastic natural philosophers. Not surprisingly, humanists made few, if any, significant contributions to science.

And yet, by their translating activities, fifteenth-century humanists played a significant role in the history of science. By locating and translating Greek texts, they made available new and usually improved Latin translations of Greek authors whose works were already well known, achieving this sometimes by the discovery of better manuscripts of the Greek original. More important, however, were their translations of Greek authors whose works were previously unknown or known only in a fragmentary way during the Middle Ages.

It was in Florence that Cosimo de' Medici (1389–1464) institutionalized this interest by founding the famous Platonic Academy in 1462 or 1463. At the request of Cosimo, Marsilio Ficino (1433–1499) translated the works of Plato into Latin, thus making Plato's philosophy and cosmology available to a wide audience. His translation of Plato's works brought a weighty addition to Western philosophical and scientific literature because few of Plato's works had been available in Latin during the Middle Ages (only two-thirds of the *Timaeus,* along with the *Meno* and the *Phaedo*). At the very least, Plato's works would complement Aristotle's and to some they would offer a significant alternative. Even before his translation of Plato, however, Ficino, in April 1463, completed a translation of the *Corpus Hermeticum,* fourteen Greek works on magic that were thought to have been written by Thoth, the Egyptian god of wisdom—also known as Hermes Trismegistus—who was assumed to have lived long before Plato and Aristotle, but slightly after Moses. With their emphasis on natural magic, the Hermetic treatises, only a few of which had been known during the Middle Ages, would assume a large and significant role in shaping the world view of the late fifteenth and sixteenth centuries.

Other previously unknown works by ancient Greek authors were also translated from Greek to Latin in the fifteenth century. Among them were a two-part handbook on astronomy (*Contemplation of the Highest Orbs*) by Cleomedes (c. first century A.D.); the first book of Alexander of Aphrodisias's (fl. second to third centuries A.D.) *On the Soul* (*De anima*); Aristarchus of Samos's (c. 320–230 B.C.) *On the Sizes and Distances of the Sun and Moon; The Lives of the Eminent Philosophers* of Sextus Empiricus (third century A.D.); the *Cosmographia* (*Geography*) of Ptolemy (second century A.D.); the *Geographia* of Strabo (c. 64 B.C. – after A.D. 23); *On the History of Plants* and *On the Causes of Plants* by Theophrastus (c. 372–c. 287 B.C.), the student of Aristotle; and *The Paraphrase of Aristotle* by Themistius (around A.D. 317–c. 388).

Another category of previously unknown Greek scientific works were those that were neither translated nor printed in the fifteenth century, but which found their way into Europe, usually into Italy, from Byzantine sources and contacts. Most of these works would be translated and printed in the sixteenth or subsequent centuries. In this group, we find Proclus's (around A.D. 410–485) *Commentary on the First Book of Euclid's Elements* and his *Commentary on Plato's Timaeus;* Hero of Alexandria's (first century A.D.) *Pneumatica;* the *Arithmetica* of Nicomachus of Gerasa (fl. around A.D. 100); and the *Moralia* of Plutarch (around A.D. 46–after 119).

Humanists were also interested in traditional Greek authors whose works were well known in the Middle Ages, either from translations from Arabic, or, less often, from the Greek. During the fifteenth century, new translations were made from Greek manuscripts of the works of Aristotle, Galen, and Hippocrates.

The Impact of Printing. Although humanist interest in Greek and Latin texts was instrumental in uncovering a relatively large number of previously unknown, or little known, scientific works by ancient Greek and Roman authors and in translating many of them into Latin, often for the first time, the introduction of printing around 1450 significantly altered the way in which new and old scientific texts were presented and disseminated. In this regard, the fifteenth century marks a milestone in the history of science. Printing from fixed type largely guaranteed that an edition of, say Ptolemy's *Almagest*, would be uniform: readers in London would confront the same text and diagrams as readers in Rome. Such was never the case with manuscripts, where virtually every manuscript was a unique and idiosyncratic version of a given text.

During the second half of the fifteenth century, some 35,000 editions were printed, of which perhaps two or three thousand belonged to science broadly conceived. Most of the scientific texts that printers and publishers chose to print were drawn from the enormous array of contemporary manuscript versions of medieval treatises, with special emphasis on the works of Greek and Arabic authors such as Aristotle, Galen, Hippocrates, Ibn-Sina, and Ibn Rushd (Averröes) as well as texts of the works of Aristotle, Diogenes Laertius (third century A.D.), Theophrastus, and Philo Judaeus (c. 13 B.C. –between A.D. 45 and 50), which Aldus Manutius published between 1495 and 1498.

By their great emphasis on traditional medieval texts, fifteenth-century printers solidified and perpetuated the medieval worldview. Many of their products were commentaries on the physical works of Aristotle. In addition to the popularization of the medieval perception of the physical operation of the universe that was embodied in Aristotelian commentaries, one of the most popular and noteworthy treatises printed was the *Imago mundi* of Pierre d'Ailly (1350–1420), written in 1410 and printed in Louvain in 1483. It provided a general description of the structure of the world, both celestial and terrestrial. D'Ailly included estimates of the size of the earth and attributed to Aristotle the opinion that only a small sea intervened between western Spain and eastern India. Columbus, who owned a copy of the *Imago mundi*, annotated this passage in the margin, presumably because it favored his conviction that the distance between Spain and India was relatively small and that the ocean voyage

was feasible. Also noteworthy is a splendid version of Euclid's *Elements*, which appeared in 1482 and included clear diagrams essential for following the proofs. Numerous medical works also appeared.

But if the overwhelming number of printed scientific works were medieval in origin, significant "new" works were also printed in the fifteenth century and belong to one of two categories: ancient treatises that had been previously unknown or newly written works.

In the first category were Latin translations of Greek works, among which were Ficino's translations of the works of Plato (1484/1485) and the *Pimander*, or *Corpus Hermeticum* (1471, plus six more times in the fifteenth century); Ptolemy's *Geography* (1475); Strabo's *Geography* (1469, plus six more editions in the fifteenth century); Theophrastus's *History of Plants* and *On the Causes of Plants* (1483; the Greek text was printed in 1499); Cleomedes's *On the Contemplation of the Heavenly Orbs* (1497); and Aristarchus of Samos's *On the Magnitudes and Distances of the Sun and Moon* (1498).

Contributions by ancient Roman authors also played a role in expanding the scientific horizons of the fifteenth century. Among Latin works that were virtually unknown during the Middle Ages but were effectively rediscovered and printed in the fifteenth century were *On Medicine* (1478, plus three later printings in the fifteenth century) by A. Cornelius Celsus; *On Aqueducts* (c. 1485) by Sextus Julius Frontinus (around A.D. 35–103); *On the Nature of Things* (1473) by Lucretius (c. 100 to 90–c. 55 to 53 B.C.); *Cosmography* by Pomponius Mela (first century A.D.); and *On Architecture* (1483–1490) by Vitruvius (first century B.C.).

Of new scientific treatises composed and published after the advent of printing, the most significant were those already mentioned: *New Theory of the Planets* (around 1474) and *Epitome of the Almagest* (1496) by Regiomontanus and *Summa de arithmetica* (1494) of Luca Pacioli. Thus printing not only preserved traditional knowledge during the first forty or fifty years of its existence, but it became the vehicle for the addition of new scientific knowledge.

During the voyages of Columbus in the last decade of the fifteenth century, science was still traditionally medieval but, because of the humanist quest for original classical treatises and the introduction of printing, the groundwork had been laid for the great changes in science that would occur in the next two centuries.

BIBLIOGRAPHY

Eisenstein, Elizabeth L. *The Printing Press as an Agent of Change*. 2 vols. Cambridge, 1979.

Grant, Edward. *Physical Science in the Middle Ages*. New York, 1971. Reprint, 1977.

Hall, A. R. *The Scientific Revolution 1500–1800. The Formation of the Modern Scientific Attitude.* London, 1954.

Klebs, Arnold C. "Incunabula Scientifica et Medica: Short Title List." *Osiris* 4 (1938): 1–359.

Lindberg, David C., ed. *Science in the Middle Ages.* Chicago, 1978.

Yates, Frances A. *Giordano Bruno and the Hermetic Tradition.* New York, 1969.

EDWARD GRANT

Science and Technology in the Age of Discovery

In the middle of the fifteenth century, around the time of the birth of Columbus, Europe embarked on a tremendous period of intellectual, scientific, and technological upheaval on a scale that had not been seen before. It was arguably more fundamental and disrupting than even the Industrial Revolution or the electronics revolution of later eras.

From the time of the Crusades (1096–1291), Europe had begun to assimilate a tremendous storehouse of knowledge from the Islamic kingdoms of Spain, Africa, and the Middle East. The Muslims had not only carefully preserved the legacy of classical Greece and Rome; through the centuries, great Muslim thinkers had passed on and added to the ancient wisdom.

Mathematicians had developed the number system that we call Arabic, but that is actually from India. This was a remarkable intellectual achievement, particularly the introduction of zero, which made modern mathematics possible. By the fifteenth century, European merchants and traders had begun to adopt the new style of notation that was especially convenient for bookkeeping and accounting. The new system would later facilitate the development of higher mathematics.

The greatness of African, Asian, and Middle Eastern thinkers, and the intellectual and scientific debt Europe owed them, is not fully appreciated by most Europeans and Americans. But even the great scholars of Islam like Ibn Sina (980–1037) and Ibn Rushd (1126–1198) would have acknowledged that they could have done little on their own without the philosophers, poets, and playwrights of the ancient Mediterranean world. It was the Greeks who served as guides and models for philosophy, geometry, astronomy, and drama as we know them today. It was primarily the Greeks who secularized learning, taking it out of the hands of the temple priests and giving it to ordinary citizens. They established medicine as a branch of science, not of religion.

It is important to stress, however, that the scholars of Columbus's time and for some centuries after did not think of themselves as scientists in the way we use and understand that term. For the educated elite, natural philosophy was the study of subjects we classify as physics, biology, medicine, or chemistry. The overwhelming majority of Europeans had little access to or need for theoretical knowledge. Even the more specialized tradesmen and artisans—mechanics, miners, smiths—learned practical knowledge as apprentices or by trial and error.

Arguably the single most important classical author was Aristotle. Not only was he one of the greatest and most original thinkers of all time, but the range of his interests and the topics on which he wrote were truly encyclopedic: biology and naturalism, physics, astronomy, ethics, logic, poetics, politics, rhetoric, metaphysics, geography, and much else besides. Although initially the universities of Europe were antagonistic to Aristotle because he was a pagan, gradually a group of Christian thinkers called the Scholastics were able to synthesize the teaching of Aristotle with the teaching of the church. These schoolmen, as they were called, dominated university life at the time of Columbus.

The centers of the Scholastic influence were the great universities of Europe like Oxford and the universities of Paris, Padua, and Verona, which date from the time of the Crusades and after. It was here that Aristotle was held up as the final authority on all questions, and here that scholars, trained in the Aristotelian techniques of logic and rhetoric, refuted any challenges to Aristotle's system of the world. In addition to Aristotle himself, classical authors who followed his beliefs, like Galen in medicine or Ptolemy in astronomy, were also venerated.

In the fifteenth and early sixteenth centuries, most Europeans accepted Plato's and Aristotle's belief that everything in the world was made up of a combination of four pristine elements—earth, air, fire, and water—each of which had its own aspects and elements. Earth and water were naturally cold and dense and tended to go down; air and fire were rarified and hot and tended to go up. This system of elements explained why smoke rose and rain fell; why the ground was cold; why fire needed air to burn but was extinguished by water. There was a fifth element, ether, which was what the stars and planets were made of, an eternal, incorporeal essence that traveled in perfect circles along the nine spheres of the heavens around the central and stationary earth. Most people believed that the celestial spheres emanated rays that influenced people, elements, and events on earth, linking all creation into a vast unity. It was for this reason that astrology was an important aspect of university study, especially in medicine.

Additionally, the body contained four fluids, or humors, which were ruled by the elements and responded to the influence of certain planets. This theory explained both medicine and psychology. Each person had a humor based on the type of fluid that dominated the individual's personality; we still use the words that named the humors to describe emotional states, like *melancholy, sanguine, phlegmatic,* and *choleric.* In this period, it was not unusual for doctors to consult their patients' astrological charts before treating them or to prescribe the elimination of bodily fluids to restore the balance of humors necessary for health. Many people regularly allowed themselves to be bled by doctors to treat even simple ailments like colds.

One of the major events of the fourteenth century that recurred periodically until the eighteenth century was the bubonic plague, or Black Death, as it was known. This disease began in Asia and reached the Black Sea around 1334. Ships plying the trading ports of Europe spread it throughout the continent. Rats carried one form of the plague, but another could be transmitted by human contact. The Black Death caused fever, delirium, and swelling and was usually fatal within three or four days. In some parts of Europe, as much as three-fourths of the population died, although some towns escaped lightly or were spared. University doctors were powerless to understand or fight the plague. Some doctors ran away or hid whenever the disease appeared. Such behavior undermined confidence in the universities and indirectly in the wisdom of ancient authorities.

Another fifteenth-century event that contributed to the new critical spirit was the development of printing. Men like Johann Gutenberg and Johann Fust in Germany, William Caxton in England, and Josse Bade in France made accurate, standard versions of texts available in quantity. As a result, more people had greater access to information than ever before. The flood of books spread the spirit of the Renaissance all over Europe.

As people read books like the Bible for the first time, they began to question traditional ideas. Sometimes ancient authorities disagreed. Many lost works of Plato and his followers—especially the so-called Hermetic writings—became available after the fall of Constantinople in 1453. Neoplatonism was more mystical than Aristotelianism, and it suggested that hidden correspondences exist among the heavens, nature, and people. The only way to discover these correspondences was by study, and the Neoplatonic authors like Pico della Mirandola, Marsilio Ficino, and Johannes Reuchlin urged their followers to delve into subjects that the church and the Scholastics condemned as forbidden and heretical. At the time of Columbus the influence of Neoplatonism had not yet made the impact it would in the sixteenth and seventeenth centuries, when men like Paracelsus, Johannes Kepler, Giordano Bruno, and even Galileo Galilei made the study of nature and the rejection of Scholastic authority the basis for the rise of experimental science. For Paracelsus and Galileo, this also meant combining the knowledge of practical arts like mechanics and herbalism

with the more abstract philosophical knowledge of the university.

In another respect, the new spirit of inquiry can be seen in men like Filippo Brunelleschi, who combined studies of the ancients with innovations using improved manufacturing techniques to build such masterpieces as the cathedral of Florence. Prince Henry the Navigator of Portugal is also illustrative of this spirit. It was Henry who brought together the naval and manufacturing arts at Sagres. Henry built an observatory and a naval arsenal; his *marinheiros* (mariners) studied the wind cycle and made charts of the declination of the sun. This was a systematic combination of scholarship and investigation on a scale that had not been seen before in Europe.

Less formal but equally important experimentation was going on in fields like mining, milling, and manufacture, where skilled artisans and craftspeople devised innovative techniques and materials, often without understanding that they were violating the philosophical principles laid down by the ancient Greeks. The importation of the secret of gunpowder from China proved that combinations of substances existed that the Greeks had not considered; this reinforced the need for more practical investigations. Other important technological innovations from the East like the horsecollar and horseshoe helped the average farmer immensely; agricultural output increased as much as fivefold in this period. As the expansion of agriculture depleted the forests, the need for metals to replace items that had formerly been made of wood led to the development of new alloys; tin, for example, became the basis for the movable type used in the new printing presses.

Technological advancement in one area, like milling, for which meshed gears were perfected, was often applied to other fields, like clock making. In the time of Columbus, the clock was quickly becoming the central metaphor of town life; the precise mechanical regularity of clocks reinforced the need for accuracy and standardization.

When Columbus embarked on his voyage in 1492, he carried with him a mixture of attitudes representative of his time. Like many educated, prosperous men, he embraced both the sureties of the medieval world, which was passing away, and the uncertainties of the new era, which he would do much to create. Part of his faith that the Atlantic Ocean could be crossed and would lead to the western coast of India came from Aristotle, who believed that the world was seven parts land and one part water, exactly the relationship between the head and the body of a well-proportioned person. But Columbus had also spent time studying the Atlantic winds, a topic unknown to the ancients. His ship carried the new technology in the form of compass and cross staff; his sails combined the European square sails with the Arabian lateen sails.

Although Columbus was not a scientist in any way, he

helped bring about major economic and social changes. His inadvertent discovery of a continent wholly unknown in ancient authors created another new metaphor of sixteenth-century life: the New World. It was not only that the Americas offered seemingly endless gold and lands to be conquered. The existence of America itself forced a reevaluation of Scholastic authority. The discovery of new animals like the turkey and new plants like potatoes, tobacco, and corn, effectively demonstrated to Europeans that they now stood on the frontiers of new knowledge.

When Columbus was engaged in his voyages of discovery, the two men who embodied the revolutions to come in the next century were embarking on their careers. In 1500, Nicholas Copernicus lectured on astronomy in Rome, digesting the *Epitome of the Almagest,* one of the new texts made available by the printing revolution. Out of his studies came the heliocentric hypothesis, which would, as much as any other single event, stimulate the scientific revolution.

In 1505, near the end of Columbus's life, young Martin Luther experienced conversion during a thunderstorm. He became a monk, trained in the philosophy of William of Ockham, and chose a career as a doctor of theology at the University of Wittenberg. Luther's rejection of Catholic authority culminated in the Reformation, a movement that freed mainly northern Europe to explore questions of conscience in new ways. Although Luther himself personally condemned Copernicus, in general, northern European countries were much more tolerant of the Copernican hypothesis. This was due in part to Protestant interest in challenging traditional Catholic interpretations of the Bible and the new spirit of inquiry and debate over the meaning of scripture. The new freedom of inquiry, combined with wealth from the New World, helped shift the balance of political and intellectual power from the Mediterranean to the Atlantic in the sixteenth century.

BIBLIOGRAPHY

Barfield, Owen. *Saving the Appearances.* Hanover, N.H., 1988.
Jacob, Margaret. *The Cultural Meaning of the Scientific Revolution.* New York, 1987.
Rice, Eugene F. *The Foundations of Early Modern Europe.* Vol. 1 of *The History of Modern Europe.* New York, 1981.
Siraisi, Nancy G. *Medieval and Early Renaissance Medicine: An Introduction to Knowledge and Practice.* Chicago, 1990.

SCOTT McPARTLAND

SECOND VOYAGE. See *Voyages of Columbus.*

SETTLEMENTS. [This entry surveys six settlements dating from the early days of European presence in the Western Hemisphere. The article on Sevilla la Nueva

demonstrates in detail what can be known about such settlements through historical and archaeological research:

 La Navidad
 La Isabela
 Nueva Cádiz
 Sevilla la Nueva
 Santo Domingo
 Concepción de la Vega

For further discussion of the early phases of European settlement of the New World, see *Colonization; Exploration and Discovery,* article on exploration and discovery after 1492. See *Archaeology* for discussion of research techniques that advance understanding of this period. Other places in the New World are discussed in *Bahamas; Canada; Cuba; Cuzco; Española, La; Jamaica; Puerto Rico; West Indies.* See *Vinland* for discussion of Viking exploration and settlement of the New World prior to Columbus's voyages.]

La Navidad

La Navidad was the name given to the first settlement established by Christopher Columbus in the Americas. It is located on the north coast of present-day Haiti, near the small fishing villages of En Bas Saline and Borde de Mer Limonade.

It was near the site of La Navidad, on Christmas Eve, 1492, that Columbus's flagship, *Santa María,* ran aground and settled on a coral reef and could not be saved. On Christmas Day Columbus's men unloaded the cargo and supplies of *Santa María* with the assistance of the Taíno Indian cacique, Guacanagarí, who governed a large Taíno town. Columbus reported that the town was about one kilometer (six-tenths of a mile) from the wreck site. They placed all of the goods in two large houses belonging to the cacique, which he then gave to the Spaniards.

Because it was impossible to accommodate the crew of *Santa María* on *Niña* and *Pinta,* thirty-nine men were chosen to remain at La Navidad until Columbus could return for them. They were given food and supplies for a year, the ship's boat, and instructions to find the source of the Indians' gold in the meantime. The men of La Navidad included a physician, a gunner, a carpenter, a boat builder, a barrel maker, a caulker, and a tailor in addition to the sailors. To make fortifications, they dismantled much of *Santa María* above the water table and used the planks and timbers to fortify an area that may have incorporated the houses given by the cacique.

There are no eyewitness accounts of La Navidad's appearance. Columbus and the remaining Spaniards left La Navidad on January 4, 1493, before the fort was built. By the time they returned, it was destroyed. Columbus alleged, however, in his 1493 letter to Fernando and Isabel, that a moat, tower, and palisade were under

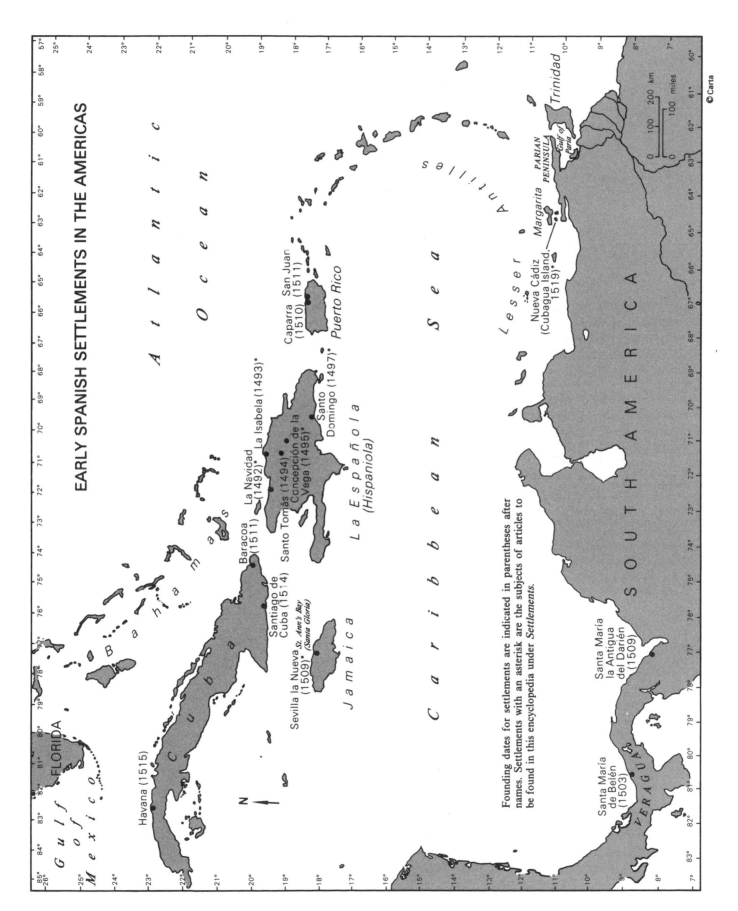

EARLY SPANISH SETTLEMENTS IN THE AMERICAS

Atlantic Ocean

Gulf of Mexico

FLORIDA

B a h a m a s

Havana (1515)

C u b a

Baracoa (1511)

Santiago de Cuba (1514)

Sevilla la Nueva (1509)* St. Ann's Bay (Santa Gloria)

Jamaica

La Navidad (1492)* La Isabela (1493)*
Santo Tomás (1494) Concepción de la Vega (1495)*
Santo Domingo (1497)*

La Española (Hispaniola)

Caparra (1510) San Juan (1511)
Puerto Rico

Caribbean Sea

Lesser Antilles

Margarita
Nueva Cádiz (Cubagua Island, 1519)*

PARIAN PENINSULA
Gulf of Paria

Trinidad

Santa María la Antigua del Darién (1509)

Santa María de Belén (1503)

VERAGUA

S O U T H   A M E R I C A

Founding dates for settlements are indicated in parentheses after names. Settlements with an asterisk are the subjects of articles to be found in this encyclopedia under *Settlements*.

0   100   200 km
0   100 miles

©Carta

607

FORT LA NAVIDAD. Engraving from Columbus's Letter to Sanchez, as published in Basel, 1493.   NEW YORK PUBLIC LIBRARY

construction. Accounts from the second voyage suggest that a well for water and a palisade may have been constructed.

Columbus returned to La Navidad eleven months later to find the settlement and surrounding Indian town burned, all the men dead, and the supplies dispersed among the Indians over a distance of several kilometers. Various accounts indicate that his men had left to trade elsewhere or had died as a result of disease or internal fighting, having antagonized their hosts by their desire for women and gold, and finally by an attack from Indians of the interior regions. Columbus investigated the circumstances of the colony's destruction and searched for the gold he believed his men had acquired, but was unsuccessful in both efforts. He soon left La Navidad and continued westward along the north coast of La Española to found La Isabela, his first intentional settlement.

The location and fate of La Navidad have captured the imaginations of many scholars over the years. Early research by Samuel Eliot Morison concluded that the site of La Navidad should be within a kilometer of the tiny Haitian fishing village of Borde de Mer Limonade. Excavations commissioned by Morison were conducted at that village in 1939 but revealed only remains from an eighteenth-century French blockhouse.

William Hodges, a medical missionary and lifelong student of Columbus, searched for La Navidad for more than twenty years. In 1975, Hodges located the site of a large Indian village at En Bas Saline, about half a kilometer (a third of a mile) inland from Borde de Mer Limonade. Aerial photographs indicate that a tributary of the region's major river, the Grande Rivière du Nord, connected the site to the shore in 1492. Excavations demonstrating that this was probably the town of Guacanagarí have been conducted there by Hodges and by the University of Florida. European artifacts, animal bone, and a series of radiocarbon dates confirmed the occupation of the town shortly after 1492.

Excavations searching for La Navidad were also conducted by Hodges from 1988 to 1990 at Borde de Mer Limonade. None of the excavations undertaken to date at any of the potential sites has unequivocally uncovered the remains of the fort itself.

BIBLIOGRAPHY

Columbus, Christopher. *The Journal of Christopher Columbus.* Translated by Cecil Jane. New York, 1989.

Deagan, Kathleen. "Columbus's Lost Colony." *National Geographic* (November 1987): 672–675.

Deagan, Kathleen. "The Search for La Navidad, Columbus's 1492 Settlement." In *First Encounters,* edited by J. T. Milanich and S. Milbrath. Gainesville, Fla., 1989.

Hodges, William H. "La Fortaleza de la Navidad: Reflections at the End of 1988." Limbé, Haiti, 1988.

Jane, Cecil. *The Four Voyages of Columbus.* New York, 1988.

Morison, Samuel Eliot. "The Route of Columbus along the North Coast of Haiti and the Site of La Navidad." *Transactions of the American Philosophical Society* 31, part 4 (1940): 239–285.

KATHLEEN DEAGAN

La Isabela

La Isabela was the first town intentionally established by Columbus in the Americas and the first place at which Europeans established a settled colony. It was founded late in 1493 about 45 kilometers (28 miles) west of present-day Puerto Plata on the north coast of the Dominican Republic. Columbus established La Isabela after he returned to La Española (Hispaniola) on his

HURRICANE ON LA ISABELA, 1485. Engraving from Théodor de Bry's *Americae*. Frankfurt, 1594.

second voyage and discovered that his earlier and inadvertent settlement of La Navidad—built the previous year in what is today Haiti—was burned to the ground.

The second voyage of Columbus was intended as a voyage of settlement. The expedition included seventeen ships, carrying 1,700 men, along with pigs, horses, cattle and other livestock, seeds and plants for crops, and the tools and equipment necessary to start a colony. The site of La Isabela was apparently chosen because of its accessibility to the Bajabonico River and proximity to a good source of stone, fertile ground for cultivation, and native trading routes into the allegedly gold-rich interior. Among the all-male settlers were craftsmen, builders, Franciscan friars, farmers, practitioners of other occupations, and representatives of social classes necessary to implement a Spanish way of life. A cabildo, or town council, was also established.

The town had a plaza at the waterfront, with several buildings constructed of limestone from a nearby quarry. These included a house occupied by Columbus, a stone church, and a fortified storehouse and barracks. Some two hundred palm-thatch huts provided housing for most of the town's inhabitants. The men at La Isabela began to suffer from disease, overwork, and food shortages almost immediately. Indian hostility also developed quickly as the native peoples of the area were pressed into service for labor at the same time that they were fast succumbing to European diseases. Mutinies developed among the men of the colony, leading at one point to Columbus's recall to Spain.

Through all these difficulties, the population of La Isabela declined steadily, dropping to 630 people in 1495, and no more than 300 people in 1496. In 1498 a new capital of La Española was established at present-day Santo Domingo. This marked the effective end of the colony at La Isabela, which was soon depopulated.

La Isabela remained in ruins after its abandonment, occupied occasionally by smugglers and fishermen. In 1526 Bartolomé de las Casas carried stones from La Isabela to be used in the Convento de San Pedro Martir in Puerto Plata. Today the site is occupied by the small Dominican fishing village of El Castillo. The government of the Dominican Republic has set aside the plaza area of La

COLUMBUS'S HOUSE. Excavated and reconstructed ruins of what is believed to have been his dwelling in the central plaza area of La Isabela.   FLORIDA STATE MUSEUM, GAINESVILLE

Isabela—fronting directly upon the bay—as a national park.

La Isabela has been the subject of numerous studies over the past century, including at least fourteen archaeological excavations. It was first tested and mapped in 1892, when the site was visited by members of the North American Commission for the four hundredth anniversary of Columbus's first voyage. The most recent and extensive excavations at the site have been carried out by José Cruxent, working through the Dirección de Parques Nacionales de la Republica Dominicana. Cruxent's extensive excavations in the central plaza area have uncovered the foundations of the barracks and storehouse, the house believed to have been that of Columbus, and other unidentified structures. He also concludes that La Isabela may have had two contemporary settlement locations about ten kilometers (six miles) apart, serving different functions. Cruxent was joined by a University of Florida team in 1989, working outside the park boundaries. That work suggested that the town was originally some 200 meters (650 feet) square.

Earlier projects by the Museo del Hombre Dominicano and others have uncovered the church foundations and excavated a number of burials from the cemetery of La Isabela. The architectural and material remains from research at La Isabela—both in the past and ongoing—have helped to reveal the details of the first and last essentially medieval community in the Americas.

BIBLIOGRAPHY

Cruxent, José. "The Origins of La Isabela." In *Columbian Consequences.* Edited by D. H. Thomas. Washington, D.C., 1990.

D'Anghiera, Peter Martyr. *De Orbo Novo.* Translated by F. A. MacNutt. 2 vols. New York, 1970.

Floyd, Troy. *The Columbus Dynasty in the Caribbean 1492–1526.* Albuquerque, N. Mex., 1973.

Cecil, Jane. *The Four Voyages of Columbus.* New York, 1988.

Major, R. H. *Letters of Christopher Columbus with Other Original Documents Relating to his Four Voyages to the New World.* 1857. Reprint, New York, 1961.

KATHLEEN DEAGAN

Nueva Cádiz

The barren, low, now uninhabited island of Cubagua is located on the eastern Venezuelan continental shelf, between Margarita Island and the Araya Peninsula. Cubagua was discovered by Columbus on his third voyage, while taking colonists to Santo Domingo, on August 15, 1498. He had divided his fleet in the Canary Islands, sending three ships to La Española and taking the remaining three south on an unscheduled exploratory voyage

that reached the island of Trinidad and the Gulf of Paria on the mainland. While exploring the area along the eastern coast of Venezuela, he encountered Indians who wore strings of fine pearls that they traded for trinkets. Columbus heard that the pearls came from the present-day Cubagua waters, but apparently did not set foot on the island because his eyes bothered him and, in any case, because he was eager to reach Santo Domingo. The news of the pearls caused a sensation in Santo Domingo as well as in Spain, and a series of official and unofficial exploratory voyages were carried out between 1499 and 1502 by Alonso de Ojeda, Peralonso Niño (Pedro Alonso Niño), Cristóbal and Luis Guerra, Rodrigo de Bastidas, and others. These voyages confirmed the presence of pearls near Cubagua and Margarita and resulted in the exploration of the coast of South America from Suriname to Panama.

The original European settlers came to Cubagua from Santo Domingo shortly after the beginning of the sixteenth century to trade for pearls. In 1519 it was decided that in order to take control of the pearl fisheries, the Indians were to be enslaved; many were brought from all over the Caribbean to toil alongside slaves from Africa on the pearl banks. Simple aboriginal huts (*bohíos*) were built. In response to the predation by Spanish ships along the Cumaná coast, the mainland Indians rebelled in 1520, killing eighty Spaniards and forcing the abandonment of the three-hundred-strong Spanish settlement on Cubagua, which totally depended on supplies from the mainland. Construction of a fortress at Cumaná by Jácome de Castellón in 1523 brought the Indians under control and led to highly profitable pearl production and spectacular masonry constructions. By 1526, the settlement on Cubagua was known as Villa Santiago and in 1528 it received the official name of Nueva Cádiz; it was the first Spanish city founded in South America. The climax of Nueva Cádiz occurred between 1530 and 1535 when its fisheries supported a total population of fifteen hundred people and shipped an average value of 800,000 pesos in pearls annually to Europe. But overexploitation caused the destruction of the pearl beds, leading to the desertion of the island. In 1541 Nueva Cádiz was destroyed by a hurricane. In 1544 French pirates burned what was left of the city and by 1545 the site had been completely abandoned, although sporadic activity in the pearl fisheries persisted throughout the sixteenth century. In recent times the highest production of 1,300 kilograms (about 2,850 pounds) was recorded for 1943.

Archaeological excavations were started by José M. Cruxent and John Goggin in 1954 and systematically continued by Cruxent between 1955 and 1961. Excavations revealed masonry structures arranged in a regular rectangular grid as well as less spectacular structures. The most

Nueva Cádiz. The archaeological site, 1958–1960.

Unidad de Fotografia Científica, I.V.I.C.

elaborate building was a Franciscan friary, with carved stone gargoyles imported either from the mainland or Spain. Some houses also had masonry stairways that led to second stories. Rouse and Cruxent reported excavations yielding large amounts of majolica, various kinds of glazed ware, olive jars, china porcelain, stamps, tiles, glass, metals, local Indian pottery as well as pottery from other parts of the Caribbean, human burial sites, remains of animal bones, and other organic refuse that reveal information on diet and pearl exploitation. By the late 1980s the ruins of Nueva Cádiz had been almost totally destroyed and looted. Plans exist to restore the site and convert it into a tourist attraction.

BIBLIOGRAPHY

Otte, E. *Las Perlas del Caribe: Nueva Cádiz de Cubagua.* Caracas, 1977.

Rouse, I. and José M. Cruxent. *Venezuelan Archaeology.* New Haven and London, 1963.

Sauer, C. O. *The Early Spanish Main.* Berkeley and Los Angeles, 1966.

Vila, P. *Visiones geohistóricas de Venezuela.* Caracas, 1969.

Willis, R. "Nueva Cádiz." In *Spanish Colonial Frontier Research,* edited by H. Dobyns. Albuquerque, N.Mex., 1982.

Erika Wagner

Sevilla la Nueva

In 1509, Diego Colón, Columbus's son and heir who had been appointed viceroy of the Indies the year before, sent Juan de Esquivel from Santo Domingo, the capital city of La Española, to found the town of Sevilla la Nueva (New Seville) on the north coast of the island of Jamaica. Esquivel took with him some sixty men in order to pacify and subdue the indigenous Arawak inhabitants as well as to settle the island.

This was one of the first moves of the Columbus heirs to enforce the terms of the contract that Columbus had drawn up with the Spanish Crown as the basis of his 1492 voyage, terms on which the Crown was now reneging. The founding of the town of Sevilla la Nueva was therefore part of a preemptive bid by Diego Colón to forestall the Crown's imposition of its own de facto absolute sovereignty over the island of Jamaica as its officials in La Española had just done in the case of Puerto Rico.

The Siting of the Town. The site of Sevilla la Nueva was selected in the context of the same imperative. Diego ordered it to be built as the capital city on the north coast of the island next to the bay of Santa Gloria where his father and his crew had been shipwrecked for a little over a year (June 25, 1503, to June 29, 1504) at the end of his fourth voyage. Diego thus was asserting the claim of the Columbus family to an island that "all the world knew" his father had "discovered."

Diego's half brother, Fernando, who had been shipwrecked with his father during that year, later wrote that it was on the site of the nearby Arawak settlement of Maima that "the Christians later founded a city named Seville." Contemporary archaeological opinion, however, is that the town was founded near to rather than on the site of Maima, which is the present-day Windsor.

Sevilla la Nueva and its environs had clearly been part of a major settlement of the Taínan-Arawak fishing and cassava complex, one that had supplied the shipwrecked Spaniards with food during Columbus and his crew's enforced stay there. With the Spaniards' arrival in 1509–1510 and their discovery that there was little gold to be had, the Crown ordered that the island be converted into a food-growing, livestock and horse-rearing complex to supply expeditions devoted to slave raiding and exploration, conquest, settlement, and evangelization of the mainland. The town of Sevilla la Nueva therefore served Spain's expansion in the Americas and the Caribbean.

History of the Town. The town's brief history as a capital consisted of three phases—the Esquivel years (1509–1512), the era of Francisco de Garay (1515–1523), and the era of Pedro de Mazuelo (1524–1534).

Esquivel, before his death in 1512, laid the foundations of the town, including erecting a Franciscan monastery staffed by a Belgian lay friar, Father Deule. The Crown had ordered Diego Colón in 1511 to see that Esquivel set in motion the evangelization and conversion of the Indians, since this was the "principal basis" on which the Crown founded its "conquest of these parts." Esquivel would later be accused of having accelerated the processes of Arawak extinction by his harsh treatment of the indigenous inhabitants.

The second phase began with the arrival in Sevilla la Nueva in May 1515 of the new governor appointed by the Crown, Francisco de Garay. This phase would see the town realize its "brilliant beginning" (Chaunu, 1959) in the context of the overall network of the state-organized mercantile system called Seville's (Spain) Atlantic I by Huguette Chaunu and Pierre Chaunu. Under Garay's leadership, the institutional bases for the town's role were established. These included the following:

1. The establishment of a Crown-Garay company and the development of hinterland estates to supply food to the mainland settlers in exchange for Indian slaves captured in slave-raiding expeditions. Skilled supervisory personnel under contract to the company were brought out to oversee and further the island's food provisioning role.

2. The establishment of Sevilla la Nueva as an Indian slave-trading entrepôt from which captured Indians from the mainland, exchanged for food provisions grown on the island by Arawak forced labor on the Crown-Garay estates, were transshipped for sale in Santo Domingo.

3. The relocation of the town from the site where it had been laid down by Esquivel to a new site, probably leading to the shift from the original name El Pueblo de Sevilla to that of Sevilla la Nueva.

4. The construction of a new fortified governor's mansion, which seems to have been of considerable Renaissance splendor. The Crown referred to it as being "as excellent as you say it is," and the Spanish art historian Angulo Iniguez described the plateresque facade, which was discovered in a well in 1937, as being "the finest decorative work to be found in the Caribbean."

5. The building of two sugar mills, which initiated a demographic shift, with the gradual replacement of encomienda and enslaved indigenous labor by that of transported African slave labor.

In 1522, Garay resigned as governor of Jamaica. He had obtained a royal patent that entitled him to conquer and settle a region on the mainland that he intended to call Garayana. He sailed from Sevilla la Nueva in 1523. Defeated in battle by the indigenous inhabitants of the mainland and foiled by Hernando Cortés, he died on the mainland without returning to Sevilla la Nueva. Given the magnitude of the expedition he had outfitted—six ships, forty-four horsemen, seven hundred foot soldiers—he had drained the town of men and resources and dealt it a blow from which it would never really recover.

The third era was presided over by the island's treasurer, Pedro de Mazuelo. He acted in conjunction with another royal official, the comptroller Juan de Torralba, to oversee the dismantling and resale of the Crown-Garay estate. In the process, they diverted much of its assets to their own purposes, as the guardian of the young Garay heir later complained to the Crown.

In 1524, the year of Garay's death on the mainland, Pietro Martire d'Anghiera (Peter Martyr), the Italian humanist-priest and first historian of the New World, was appointed mitred abbott of Jamaica with his seat in Sevilla la Nueva. D'Anghiera used the titles due him to begin the building of a stone church in the town. The church was never to be completed, however. Among the complaints made to the Crown against Mazuelo was that he diverted the Arawaks allotted to building the church to work on his own personal projects and for his private profit.

On the basis of these complaints, the Crown ordered a judicial inquiry, a *residencia*, into the tenure of Mazuelo and into those of the other royal officials of Sevilla la Nueva, including Torralba. The judge of inquiry, Gil Gonzales Dávila, initiated proceedings soon after his arrival in September 1533. But he died the following year with the *residencia* incomplete.

Through the influence of his friends at the court in Spain, Mazuelo obtained a royal letter of July 28 that formally granted him the right to shift the capital from the north coast and to a site on the south coast. The decree also gave him permission to found the new town on a site adjacent to his recently built sugar mill. This new town and capital (later to be called Santiago de la Vega, today's Spanish Town) was referred to at first also as "Sevilla," but with the qualifier, "on the bank of the River Caguaya."

Although Diego Colón had died in 1526, the revenues due him from the island had continued to be paid to his heirs. And in August 1536, the original intention that had led to Diego's founding of Sevilla la Nueva on the site where Columbus had been stranded after his shipwreck was finally validated. Judgment was passed on the lawsuit brought by the Columbus family to keep the Crown to the original terms of its agreement. As part of the settlement, sovereignty over the island of Jamaica was conceded to the Columbus family, with the Crown retaining only supreme overall jurisdiction. As Mazuelo presciently warned, this delegation of sovereignty, which took the matter of the island's fortifications out of the direct control of the Crown, made Jamaica the weak link in the Spanish chain. This led to its relatively easy capture by the English in 1655, a century and a quarter later.

Sevilla la Nueva had lapsed into oblivion when the capital was shifted to the south coast. With the capture of the island by the English, the site was allotted to a Captain Hemmings as part of his private estate. Developed as a sugar estate and worked by enslaved African labor, it would continue as such, even after slavery was abolished and slave labor replaced by wage labor.

In the early 1960s, the estate's four hundred acres were purchased by the first government of a postcolonial and independent Jamaica and turned over to the Jamaican National Trust Commission to be developed as a historical site. Since 1981, major archaeological excavations intended to map the two sites of the town have been carried out by a team of Spanish archaeologists funded by the government of Spain and led by Lorenzo Eladio Lopez y Sebastian.

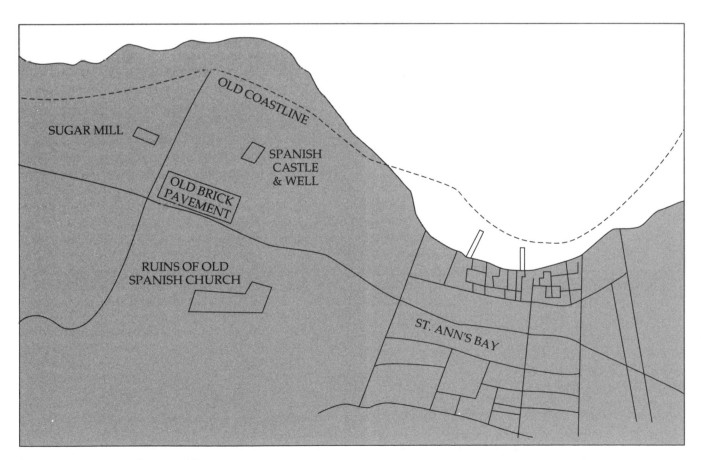

ARCHAEOLOGICAL SITES AT SEVILLA LA NUEVA.   AFTER G. A. AARONS, 1983, P. 45.

The Town's Archaeological and Historical Significance.
There are other reasons, in addition to its intimate link
with the fortress of the Columbus heirs, that make Sevilla
la Nueva significant in American-Caribbean history.

1. It is the site of Columbus's shipwrecked stay as well
as of his writing of his *Lettera rarissima* to the Spanish
sovereigns on July 7, 1503.

2. It includes the site next to the bay where two of
Columbus's caravels were abandoned. G. A. Aarons has
pointed out that although the caravel was the ship type
that opened up the New World to the Old and facilitated
the circumnavigation of Africa that proved to be a gateway
to the East, nowhere in the world does there remain a
trace of any fifteenth- or sixteenth-century caravel, nor
does any model or reproduction exist from the fifteenth or
sixteenth centuries.

The two caravels, *Santiago* and *La Capitana*, have
therefore been sought by several teams of marine archaeologists. Although begun earlier, the search was renewed
in 1981 on the basis of the collaborative efforts of the
Institute of Nautical Archaeology of Texas A&M University
and the government of Jamaica. Roger C. Smith, a
research associate, spearheaded "a site survey in order to
map the data available regarding the possible locating of
the shoreline. . . . Based on these surveys, some indication of where the coastline was located in the fifteenth and
sixteenth centuries has begun to emerge" and "possible
locations for the caravels identified" (Aarons, 1984).

3. The conversion experience of Pedro de la Renteria,
the business partner of Bartolomé de las Casas, took place
in the monastery at Sevilla in June 1514, at the very
moment that Las Casas also had a parallel conversion
experience at Sancti Spíritus, Cuba. Both men, from then
on, would dedicate their lives to the struggle for the
abolition both of the forced-labor encomienda system and
of the slave-trading system, which had been one of the
mainstays of the mercantile system of Seville's Atlantic I,
that moved Indians around the Caribbean and from the
Caribbean to the mainland.

As part of the struggle, Las Casas proposed the introduction of slaves from Africa in order to substitute for
indigenous forced and slave labor. The proposal then took
on a dynamic of its own with the first license granted in
1518, going far beyond its original limited intention.
Although Las Casas later regretted his proposal when he
discovered the unjust and coercive methods by which the
Africans had also been enslaved, his proposal would give
impetus to the process by which the transatlantic slave
trade was set in motion and the culture complex of
Africans, the indigenous peoples of the Americas, and
Europeans merged into the new civilization of the Americas and the Caribbean.

4. The town was connected, as an abbacy seat, with

d'Anghiera, whose *Decades of the New World* initiated
the narrated history of the post-Columbus New World.

5. The town is the site of architectural remains of the
facade of what seems to have been Garay's mansion
fortress. The Spanish art historian Angulo Iniguez described the plateresque complex of carvings on these
pilasters "as belonging to a quite early date going back to
the beginnings of the Renaissance style in Spain" and,
therefore, "as being of the greatest significance, not only
for the history of architecture in America, but for that of
the Iberian Peninsula itself."

As he concludes, no one "could have imagined that the
Spaniards in the first thirty years of their presence in the
island could have had built, at a time when many buildings
were still being built in the Gothic style on the [Iberian]
Peninsula, a beautiful facade according to the latest style
being diffused from Italy."

Although no map or plan of Sevilla la Nueva has been
found, the layout of the original sites has been mapped by
the Spanish archaeological team whose services were
contributed by the Spanish government. This team, which
began exploration in 1981 under the direction of Lorenzo
Eladio Lopez y Sebastian, has made some exciting discoveries, assisted by an interesting new method—the use of
subsurface interface radar to map remaining underground
structures. This method was used for the first time by the
Donohue firm of engineers and architects of Wisconsin
that specializes in techniques of remote sensing.

BIBLIOGRAPHY

Aarons, G. A. "Sevilla La Nueva: Microcosm of Spain in Jamaica."
Parts 1 and 2. *Jamaica Journal* 16, no. 4 (1983); 17, no. 7 (1984).

Accounts for the island of Santiago from the time it was settled to
the year 1536. Contaduria section, no. 1174. Archives of Seville,
Spain.

Anghiera, Pietro Martire d'. *De Orbe Novo: The Eight Decades of
Peter Martyr D'Anghiera.* Translated from the Latin with notes
and introduction by Francis A. MacNutt. New York, 1912.
Reprint, 1970.

Angulo Iniguez. *El Gótico y el Renacimiento en las Antillas.*
Seville, 1947.

Arrenz Marquez, Luis. *Don Diego Colón, Almirante, Virrey, y
Gobernador de Las Indias.* Vol. 1. Madrid, 1982.

Chaunu, Huguette, and Pierre Chaunu. *Seville et l'Atlantique,
1504–1650.* 8 vols. Paris, 1955–1959.

Columbus, Ferdinand. *The Life of the Admiral Christopher
Columbus by His Son, Ferdinand.* Translated and edited by
Benjamin Keen. New Brunswick, N.J., 1959.

Cotter, C. S. "The Discovery of the Spanish Carving at Seville."
Jamaican Historical Review 1, no. 3 (December 1948): 227–234.

Documents relating to early Spanish Jamaica in the Archivo
General de Indias. Transcribed by Irene Wright. National
Library of Jamaica.

Herskovits, M. J. *The New World Negro: Selected Papers in*

Afro-American Studies. Edited by F. S. Herskovits. Bloomington, Ind., 1966.

Jane, Cecil, ed. *Select Documents Illustrating the Four Voyages of Columbus.* 2 vols. London, 1932, 1933.

Landstrom, Bjorn. *Columbus: The Story of Don Cristobol Colon.* New York, 1967.

Las Casas, Bartolomé de. *The History of the Indies.* Translated by Andree M. Collard. New York, 1971.

Morales Padron, Francisco. *Jamaica Española.* Seville, 1952.

Pleitos de Colón (Lawsuits). *Colleción de documentos inéditos para la historia de España.* Madrid, 1875.

Wagner, H. R., with H. Parish. *The Life and Writings of Bartolomé de las Casas.* Albuquerque, N.Mex., 1967.

Wynter, Sylvia. *Major Dates: 1509–1536: With an Aftermath 1537–1655.* Kingston, Jamaica, 1984.

Wynter, Sylvia. *New Seville: Major Facts, Major Questions.* Kingston, Jamaica, 1984.

Wynter, Sylvia. "New Seville and the Conversion Experience of Bartolomé de las Casas." *Jamaica Journal* 17, no. 182 (1984).

SYLVIA WYNTER

Santo Domingo

The oldest European city in the Western Hemisphere, Santo Domingo was founded by Bartolomé Colón in 1497 on the left bank of the Ozama River. Five years later it was relocated across the river to its present site by Governor Nicolás de Ovando. According to early chronicles, this move occurred because of an ant plague, but the present location on the right bank had from the onset many advantages over the original site. Potable water was readily available, and the gold mines at Haina and Cotuí were more easily accessible.

Nicolás de Ovando designed the city "with a ruler and a compass," thereby establishing a quadrilateral pattern that was widely imitated in future urban foundations in Spanish America. The streets were laid in straight angles, calculated from the four cardinal points, and the church was constructed in front of a central square around which public buildings were located.

Though the city's wide streets and the abundance of stone and mortar buildings impressed early travelers, Santo Domingo never became a great city. It never surpassed fifty blocks, twelve of which were occupied by religious institutions.

Santo Domingo was surrounded by a mortar and stone wall reinforced with ramparts built after the mid-sixteenth century to defend it from attacks by corsairs and fugitive slaves. The city became the main exporting harbor for sugar, hides, and ginger, and its inhabitants experienced prosperity until the end of the sixteenth century. With the development of Mexico and Peru, Santo Domingo lost its importance. Portobelo, Veracruz, and Havana became the principal ports of call for the galleon fleets. The city's commercial activities gradually decreased and eventually stagnated; most of its inhabitants emigrated from the island.

In 1586, Santo Domingo fell into the hands of the English corsair Francis Drake. He burned the archives and many houses, took all the available jewels, gold, and silver as ransom, and stole the bells from the churches. For the next 150 years, the city ceased growing. Its inhabitants abandoned their houses and were replaced by professional soldiers brought from other parts of the Caribbean or Portugal. During the Thirty Years' War, Santo Domingo

PALACE OF DIEGO COLÓN, SANTO DOMINGO.

DOMINICAN REPUBLIC MINISTRY OF TOURISM

was converted into a simple military outpost on the fringes of the Spanish Empire. Its walls were rebuilt, and the fortresses and ramparts were refurbished to consolidate the network of fortified towns of San Juan, Cartagena, Portobelo, Veracruz, and La Habana (Havana), which defended the Caribbean Basin.

By becoming a military outpost, the city lost its original commercial character and its role as a communications center. The remaining population became extremely poor. Trade with Spain completely disappeared. Buildings were abandoned, and earthquakes, hurricanes, termites, rains, fungi, and vegetation eroded the sixteenth-century constructions. In the mid-seventeenth century, the development of the French colony of Saint-Domingue on the western side of the island briefly interrupted the city's decline. As the French filled their sugar plantations with African slaves, there was an increased demand for meat, which the Spaniards of Santo Domingo supplied in exchange for European merchandise. In the eighteenth century this active trade helped Santo Domingo to regain some of its lost prosperity.

BIBLIOGRAPHY

Castillo, Guillermo Céspedes del. *Latin America: The Early Years.* New York, 1974.

Floyd, Troy. *The Columbus Dynasty in the Caribbean, 1492–1526.* Albuquerque, N.Mex., 1973.

Lamb, Ursula. *Frey Nicolás de Ovando, Gobernador de las Indias (1501–1509).* Santo Domingo, 1977.

Moya Pons, Frank. *Historia colonial de Santo Domingo.* Santiago de los Caballeros, 1973.

Palm, Erwin Walter. *Los monumentos arquitectónicos de la Española.* Santo Domingo, 1984.

Ugarte, María. *Monumentos coloniales.* Santo Domingo, 1977.

FRANK MOYA PONS

Concepción de la Vega

The town of La Concepción de la Vega was founded by Christopher Columbus in 1495 during his second voyage to the New World. The discovery of gold in the Cordillera Central of La Española attracted settlers from other parts of the island, especially La Isabela, and made Concepción a center for mining. The area also produced sugar cane. The historian Bartolomé de las Casas lived and studied in Concepción.

Concepción was laid out in a checkerboard pattern, with a parade ground at the center and the city's major buildings—the cathedral, the government palace, and a fortress—around it. A Franciscan convent and a mint were also located there. An earthquake in 1562 led to the abandonment of the original site and the establishment of the town of La Vega (in the present-day Dominican Republic) nearby.

In the twentieth century, archaeological excavations of La Vega Vieja have yielded ceramic and metal household objects and numerous coins and have uncovered cemeteries, fortresses, roads, irrigation ditches, aqueducts, and the foundations of religious and secular buildings.

BIBLIOGRAPHY

Moya Pons, Frank. *Historia colonial de Santo Domingo.* Barcelona, 1974.

Pérez Montás, Eugenio. *República Dominicana monumentos históricos y arqueologicos.* Mexico, 1984.

EUGENIO PÉREZ MONTÁS
Translated from Spanish by Paola Carù

SEVILLA LA NUEVA. See *Settlements,* article on *Sevilla la Nueva.*

SEVILLE. Spanning the Guadalquivir River in southwestern Spain, Seville thrived as a commercial and industrial center during the fifteenth and sixteenth centuries. The river's broad alluvial plain surrounded Seville with fertile vineyards, fields, and orchards that provided both food and employment for inhabitants whose numbers increased to more than 100,000 in 1600. Soap manufacturing consumed quantities of oil produced from olive groves, and a ceramics industry developed, using clay from the river's banks. Artisans made casks for shipping these products as well as fish, wheat, oil, and wine to distant ports.

After Isabel directed Seville to outfit the small ships in which Columbus would attempt to discover a western route to the Indies in 1492, this protected inland seaport became the commercial capital of the Spanish Habsburg Empire. The royal government decreed in 1503 that all ships sailing between Europe and the lands claimed for Spain in the New World should pass through the port of Seville, where officials could more carefully control them. The city erected a new mint, a customs house near the river, and, at one side of the cathedral, the beautiful Lonja (the commercial exchange) designed by Juan de Herrera for the Casa de la Contratación, the royal agency supervising colonization in and commerce with the New World.

The seat of an archbishop and site of the third largest cathedral in the Christian world, Seville became the location for the first permanent tribunal of the Inquisition. Dominicans sent to this city in 1480 quickly found evidence of a network of conversos, or Christianized Jews, whom they accused of secretly practicing Jewish rites and plotting to resist attempts to purify the church. Later, in the sixteenth century, inquisitors uncovered in Seville one of the few groups of Protestants on the Iberian Peninsula.

Since 1248, Seville had been ruled as an oligarchy by

nobles loyal to the Christian monarchy that had defeated its Muslim rulers; but it also continued as the home of many moriscos, those Muslims who chose baptism over expulsion after the fall of Granada in 1492. Always suspect as false Christians, this group became identified as politically disloyal. When Philip II ordered the dispersal of moriscos throughout his kingdom following their rebellion in the mountains near Granada in 1568, more than four thousand were sent to Seville, where they were forbidden to live together, to speak Arabic, or to teach it to their children. Inquisitors prosecuted many for apostasy and blasphemy before Philip III finally ordered their expulsion in the early seventeenth century.

The dazzling wealth of some of its citizens, which often masked the city's cruel poverty, supported art, architecture, literature, and learning. Numerous printers published books in this city, where writers such as Lope de Vega, Mateo Alemán, and Miguel de Cervantes lived and worked for a time. Although Muslim influences could be seen in the buildings and fountains of an earlier period, Renaissance architecture and a developing baroque style contributed many impressive structures to the city, most notably the city hall and the Hospital de las Cinco Llagas, which was built to shelter poor women.

[See also *Casa de la Contratación; Inquisition; Jews; Muslims.*]

BIBLIOGRAPHY

Chaunu, Pierre, and Huguette Chaunu. *Seville et l'Atlantique, 1504–1650.* 8 vols. Paris, 1955–1959.

Domínguez Ortiz, Antonio. *Orto y ocaso de Sevilla: Estudio sobre la prosperidad y decadencia de la ciudad durante los siglos XVI y XVII.* Seville, 1946.

Montoto, Santiago. *Sevilla en el Imperio (siglo XVI).* Seville, 1937.

Perry, Mary Elizabeth. *Crime and Society in Early Modern Seville.* Hanover and London, 1980.

Pike, Ruth. *Aristocrats and Traders: Sevillian Society in the Sixteenth Century.* Ithaca and London, 1972.

MARY ELIZABETH PERRY

SHIPBUILDING. [*The following entry surveys the history of shipbuilding in Europe and northern Africa, focusing on technical information about discovery-era ships and how such information has been gained through underwater archaeology. For related discussions, see* Arms, Armor, and Armament; Archaeology, *article on* Underwater Archaeology. *See also* Niña; Pinta; Santa María.]

Shipbuilding in the Age of Discovery is best viewed as but one stage in an evolutionary process. As with any such process, a better understanding of any particular stage is afforded by at least a brief overview of some of the more significant preceding stages.

Archaeological discoveries of prehistoric dugout log canoes have been unearthed in many regions of the world. As crude as many of them were, they represented an advance from sitting "on" a rough log to sitting "in" a hand-hewn log canoe produced by intelligent beings using tools they had fashioned. As the need for waterborne transportation increased, the dugout canoe was made more seaworthy by fastening first one, then two or more planks to each side and bringing these planks together at each of its ends to keep water out. The log remained as a principal structural member, but its shape and function gradually changed until it evolved into what came to be known as the keel. The resulting vessel in which the shaped log had become a submerged keel was capable of carrying a number of people and a sizable cargo. It was becoming a ship.

Southern and Northern Shipbuilding Traditions

In Europe and the northern regions of Africa, this evolutionary process had two main branches, Southern and Northern. As early as 3000 B.C. waterborne transportation in Egypt had developed to a point that permitted the Egyptians to send ships as far as Crete and Phoenicia. Thus stimulated, the Cretans and Phoenicians soon had fleets of their own. As these were overtaken by Greek and Roman warships and merchantmen, a definite Mediterranean, or Southern, style developed, and the number of ships grew to include Turkish, Spanish, and Portuguese fleets. By 200 B.C. a distinct Scandinavian, or Northern, style began to evolve. Because there was little sea traffic between north and south until the time of the Crusades, these two evolutionary branches of development maintained uniquely regional characteristics.

Although there were obvious similarities between the two styles, there were also significant differences. In the older Southern methods of construction, adjacent planks were fitted together edge to edge, so that the resulting "carvel-planked" hull had a relatively smooth surface. Deck beams protruded through the planking and were supported at each deck level by thicker planks called wales. The earliest sails in both the north and the south were square or rectangular and were set on a horizontal spar or yard on a single mast mounted approximately amidships. Ships so rigged could sail only with the wind coming from abaft the beam and thus were required to wait for favorable winds when trying to sail in a particular direction. In the more populous south with its greater reliance on sea commerce, such a restriction could not be tolerated. To minimize this drawback, the lateen sail of triangular shape set on a long diagonal yard was adopted from the Arabs in about the eighth century A.D. This permitted Southern ships to make progress to windward, particularly when the two-masted rig was developed in the twelfth century A.D., freeing the ships from dependence on the direction of the wind.

LATEEN RIG. Shown on a model of a typical Southern vessel of the fifteenth to sixteenth century. Note also the carvel planking and the wales.   COMISSÃO NACIONAL PARA AS COMEMORAÇÕES DOS DESCOBRIMENTOS PORTUGUESES, LISBON

In the north, "lapstrake," or "clinker" planking methods were used. The first plank, or garboard strake, overlapped a T-shaped lip on the keel and each adjacent plank overlapped the next lower plank, as with clapboards on a wooden house, all the way up to the uppermost plank or sheer strake. Deck beams did not protrude through the planking but instead were supported by an inner shelf that extended from stem to stern. Use of the single square or rectangular sail persisted. But as population increased in the north and seagoing commerce to and from the south began to develop, Northern and Southern shipbuilding traditions melded into a common Atlantic tradition. The single square or rectangular sail had become inadequate. Additional masts and sails were added, and by the end of the fifteenth century, a true oceangoing ship rig had been developed that, in its basic configuration, persisted well into the eighteenth century.

Thus, the sail plan of a ship such as *Santa María*, Columbus's flagship on his first voyage, consisted of a foremast and mainmast carrying square or rectangular sails (referred to as "square-rigged") and a mizzenmast carrying a triangular-shaped lateen sail. In addition, a rectangular spritsail was rigged under the upswept bowsprit and a small square topsail was rigged on a slender unstayed topmast mounted as an extension of the mainmast. Beginning early in the sixteenth century, a similar small topsail was rigged on the foremast. In smaller

vessels, some regional traditions persisted. For example, many small vessels in the north continued to be built with lapstrake planking, a tradition that still survives. Larger oceangoing ships of the new Atlantic tradition, however, were all carvel-planked and square-rigged on mainmast and foremast. In addition, deck beams no longer protruded through the planking. The more watertight system of supporting the beams on an interior shelf had been adopted.

Individual sketches or paintings of ships of the discovery period by some contemporary artists cannot be relied upon to provide authentic information on many details of either the hulls or their rigging. When certain specific features are found in a number of sketches or paintings by different contemporary artists, however, one is justified in assuming that those features are reasonably authentic. Features typical of merchant ships of the period, well illustrated in Vittore Carpaccio's painting *The Legend of Saint Ursula* (1495), are the round tuck stern and general roundness of the hull, the forecastle and the aft castle, the forecastle arch, the heavy bitt beam protruding through the forward part of the bulwarks, and the lapstrake planking filling the triangular space between the bulwark rails and the forecastle deck. The profile shape of the bow almost invariably was made up of arcs of circles with radii related by a simple ratio to the maximum breadth of the ship. The cross-sectional shape of the hull was also normally made up of arcs of circles. At this transitional stage in rig development from one mast to three, the large mainsail remained as the major driving force, with the much smaller foresail, spritsail, and mizzen, although providing some propulsive force, aiding greatly in directional control and maneuverability. A tiny main topsail was still an early tentative addition to the sail plan.

Although it is possible to trace the development of ships up to the age of discovery, it is important to understand that there are no extant original plans of any fifteenth-century ship. The profession of naval architecture as we know it today did not exist at that time. The first reasonably complete construction plans were not produced until the seventeenth century, and not until late in the next century were full sets of detailed working plans generally available. Shipwrights of the period who built ships without benefit of plans had little or no formal education, as was the case with most artisans. They did, however, have a strong background of experience. They started to work as apprentices at a young age and learned to build boats and ships the way their fathers and forefathers had built them for centuries. They learned to use various simple rules of thumb formed by years of trial and error. For example, the generally accepted proportions for the principal hull dimensions of maximum breadth or beam, length of keel, and length of the main

VITTORE CARPACCIO'S *THE LEGEND OF SAINT URSULA*, 1495. Detail, showing typical merchant ships of the period in the harbor of Venice.

ALINARI/ART RESOURCE

deck for a late fifteenth-century merchant ship, called a nao in Spain and a carrack in Italy, were in the simple ratio of 1:2:3. Thus, for a ship capable of carrying a cargo of one hundred tons, such as Columbus's flagship *Santa María*, a master shipwright would know from long experience that he should choose approximate dimensions of twenty-seven feet for the beam, fifty-four feet for the keel length, and eighty-one feet for the main deck length. For caravels like *Niña* and *Pinta*, which were lighter, faster, less bulky ships, the proportions were less precise; the average ratios were 1 for beam, 2.4 for length of keel, and 3.33 for length of hull.

In addition to these ratios for principal hull dimensions, there were other rules of thumb used by master shipwrights of the fifteenth and sixteenth centuries. It should be noted that the ship's maximum beam was the key dimension to which all these rules of thumb were directly related. For example, the master frame, a major structural assemblage that determined the cross-sectional shape of the hull at its widest point, was made up of components whose size and shape were governed by the dimension of the ship's maximum beam. The master frame consisted of a flat central bottom section called a floor timber and two or three curved sections called futtocks, which extended upward to the main deck. By rule of thumb the floor timber of the master frame was usually given a length of approximately one-third the ship's maximum beam and was made flat except for slightly upturned ends where it was fastened to overlapping first futtocks, usually by means of both iron nails and wooden pegs called tree-nails. Depending on the height of the main deck above the keel, second and third futtocks were added.

These ancient rules of thumb usually were viewed as a way of doing things that was practical and simple. They were based on experience and practice rather than on scientific knowledge. Master shipwrights used them as convenient approximations, not as rigid requirements. The rules often were adjusted to accommodate the opinions of ship captains and sailing masters on the good and bad points of previous ships. Thus, without benefit of detailed drawings or even any specifications other than the anticipated use of the ship and its desired cargo-carrying capacity, shipwrights regularly built wooden ships by applying these rules of thumb to a simple yet effective method of construction known as the master frame and batten system.

That system consisted of setting up and fastening together a keel, stem, and sternpost. The master frame then was constructed and mounted on the keel at the point of desired maximum breadth, normally slightly aft of amidships. In order to control the shape of the hull both forward and aft, two intermediate frames usually were required, one between the master frame and the stem and another between the master frame and the sternpost. If the ship was to be a nao such as the Spanish *Santa María*, a transom beam would be mounted horizontally atop the sternpost at main deck level. In conformity with the simple 1:2:3 rule of thumb for hull proportions of a nao or carrack, the length of the keel would be about two times the breadth of the master frame. The combined rake or overhang of the stem and sternpost would be made such that the length of the main deck would be equal to about three times the breadth. If the ship was to be a caravel, a flat transom extending from just below the waterline to the main deck would be mounted on the sternpost. For either type hull, temporary straight flexible battens, suitably spaced, would then be bent around the master and intermediate frames from stem to stern, producing a hull form inside of which additional required frames, each consisting of a floor timber and associated futtocks, were then fashioned to fit. When all the frames were in place, the temporary battens would be replaced one at a time by permanent exterior planking, fastened to the interior frames with both treenails and iron nails.

The experience and personal practice of individual master shipwrights governed the location of the master and intermediate frames. The underbody of one English ship was designed to be similar to the shape of a fish on the theory that God had given fish an ideal shape for moving through the water. This located the master frame, and hence maximum breadth and fullness, somewhat forward of amidships. This had the advantage of providing a very fine or slender afterbody that would greatly increase the effectiveness of the rudder but would also result in a very full forebody with some undesirable characteristics. Southern shipwrights opted for a master frame location slightly aft of amidships, which (though it

FISH-SHAPED UNDERBODY. And (above) shipwrights at work. English drawings of the sixteenth century.

ELSEVIER PUBLISHING PROJECTS, AMSTERDAM

conforms with modern practice) demanded careful shaping of the afterbody to ensure adequate rudder effectiveness.

Evidence from Nautical Archaeology

The examination of contemporary paintings and the study of the use of certain rules of thumb have provided useful but severely limited information on the construction of discovery-period ships. Fortunately, recent findings of nautical archaeologists have made it possible to develop hard evidence of specific construction details used during the Columbus era. The Institute of Nautical Archaeology in College Station, Texas, deserves great credit for important work in this field. Its reports of on-site study of a number of ancient shipwrecks as well as the construction of authentic scale models by noted ship reconstructor J. Richard Steffy of the institute's staff, have contributed significantly to our knowledge of the evolution of wooden ships up through the Age of Discovery.

In 1982 a group headed by Donald Keith was formed to

locate, survey, and excavate the wrecks of discovery-period ships in the Caribbean. Two shipwrecks that have been surveyed and excavated are thought to be of the discovery era. One is located on Molasses Reef near the Turks and Caicos Islands and the other just off the north shore of Highborn Cay in the northern Bahamas. The size and shape of the reasonably intact mound of stone ballast at the Molasses Reef site indicates that the ship was of the approximate tonnage of *Pinta*, a common size for caravels of that period. A Florida-based treasure-hunting company, Caribbean Ventures, which located the wreck, claimed that it is the *Pinta,* one of Columbus's three original ships of discovery and possibly one of four caravels in a fleet commanded by Vicente Yáñez Pinzón on a voyage of exploration in 1499–1500. It is known that shortly after departing La Española on the return voyage to Spain, the fleet encountered a severe storm and two of the caravels were lost. Many maritime historians, however, believe that there is insufficient evidence to support the claim that it is, in fact, the *Pinta*.

Under the mounds of stone ballast at both the Molasses Reef and the Highborn Cay shipwreck sites the team found sections of wooden hulls, which provided valuable construction details. Substantial portions of the hand-hewn keels, keelsons, floor timbers, and attached first futtocks provided information on shape, dimensions, and methods of attachment. Among recovered artifacts were authenticated fifteenth-century wrought-iron, breech-loading lombards with breech chambers and wedges, smaller breech-loading as well as muzzle-loading swivel guns, various types of shot, and several large anchors. Numerous wrought-iron hull fastenings and other fittings were found scattered about the sites. Iron gudgeons and pintles used to fasten the rudder to the sternpost provided information on the thickness of the sternposts and rudders. Several sets of iron rigging components provided indications of how the ships' standing rigging had been fastened to the hulls. With this sort of detailed information, our knowledge of Columbus-era ships was greatly expanded.

Marine archaeologists of the Canadian Park Service, headed by Robert Grenier, discovered and excavated the wreck of a Spanish Basque whaling ship believed to be *San Juan,* documented as having sunk in Red Bay, Labrador, in 1565. Major components of her flattened hull, not revealed until after extensive excavation, had been remarkably well preserved by the icy water and mud. She was a merchant galleon, successor to the nao and thus of great interest because of her comparability to discovery-era ships. Grenier and his team of marine archaeologists recovered nearly all the major heavy structural members and most of the framing, planking, hull stringers, clamps, hanging knees, skids (or fenders), deck beams, and

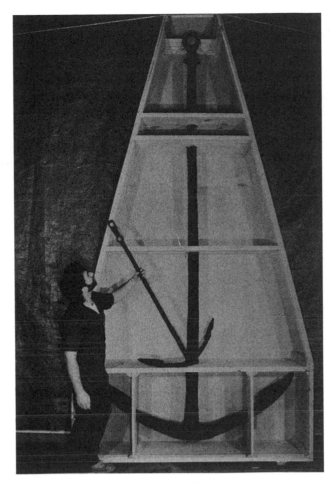

SHIP'S ANCHOR AND ANCHOR OF A SMALL BOAT FROM THE MOLASSES REEF WRECK. On display in conservation lab of the Institute of Nautical Archaeology.

INSTITUTE OF NAUTICAL ARCHAEOLOGY, COLLEGE STATION, TEXAS

supports as well as portions of the rigging. All significant pieces were measured and drawn at one-tenth scale to provide a permanent record of all components and make possible the construction of an accurate scale model.

The massive hand-hewn keel and keelson were recovered intact. At its midpoint, the keel was roughly T-shaped in cross section. Toward the bow and stern it became more Y-shaped and near its ends more U-shaped, bringing to mind its gradual evolution from the dugout canoe. The arms of the T, Y, and U cross sections seem to have been designed to take the place of the more usual garboard strakes fastened in place on each side of the keel in later ships. The maximum width and thickness of the keelson were near its expanded midpoint where it was mortised to take the foot of the mainmast, thus accurately locating the position of that major spar. Both forward and aft of this mast step, the keelson was tapered to about eight inches square at each end. The bottom face was notched to a depth of about three inches to fit tightly over the floor timbers, through which the keelson was fastened to the keel by long iron bolts.

Another key structural component, the lower portion of which was recovered virtually intact, was the master frame. This was of particular importance because it confirmed the use of ancient rules of thumb in forming the hull cross section and provided hard evidence of its shape. The floor timber was approximately one-third of the ship's maximum breadth and was flat except for a slight upward curvature at its ends where it overlapped with and was fastened to the first futtocks precisely as prescribed by one of the ancient rules of thumb. An interesting detail not found in any historical text was the manner in which the first futtocks were joined to the floor timbers using carefully fashioned mortises and tenons. The same construction technique was found in the Molasses Reef and Highborn Cay discovery-era wrecks. Here was hard evidence of shipbuilding methods in the Age of Discovery as opposed to conjecture.

Early in the recovery effort it was determined that the flattened remains of the hull could not be raised as a whole and that its individual pieces probably could not be reassembled. Recognizing the importance of providing visual evidence of sixteenth-century Spanish shipbuilding methods, the Canadian marine archaeologists wisely decided to construct a 1:10 scale model of the ship at their headquarters in Ottawa. A complete reconstruction was not attempted, but enough work was completed to permit development of hull lines, to identify important structural details visually, and to show how significant assemblages of individual pieces fit together. The result is a treasure trove of invaluable information for maritime historians.

The efforts of the Canadian Park Service marine archaeologists in excavating and analyzing the remains of this ship have been immensely valuable. The Canadian information on a post-Columbus ship, the information developed by the Institute of Nautical Archaeology on Columbus-era ships, and the evidence provided by Steffy's models of pre-Columbian ships constitute an important sequence of findings that greatly increases our understanding of ship hull form and construction during an important period of history.

BIBLIOGRAPHY

Anderson, R. C. "Italian Naval Architecture about 1445." In *Mariner's Mirror* 11. London, 1925.

Anderson, Romola, and R. C. Anderson. *The Sailing-Ship: Six Thousand Years of History*. New York, 1963.

Bradford, Ernle. *Christopher Columbus*. New York, 1973.

Culver, Henry B., and Gordon Grant. *The Book of Old Ships*. Garden City, N.Y., 1935.

Gibson, Charles E. *The Story of the Ship*. New York, 1958.

Greenhill, Basil. *Archaeology of the Boat*. Middletown, Conn., 1976.

Greenhill, Basil. *The Evolution of the Wooden Ship*. New York, 1988.

Howard, Frank. *Sailing Ships of War, 1400–1860*. New York, 1979.

Keith, Donald. *The Molasses Reef Wreck*. Institute of Nautical Archaeology. College Station, Tex., 1987.

Landstrom, Bjorn. *The Ship*. Garden City, N.Y., 1961.

Lane, Frederick Chapin. *Venetian Ships and Shipbuilders of the Renaissance*. Baltimore, 1934.

Oertling, Thomas J. *Highborn Key Wreck*. Institute of Nautical Archaeology. College Station, Tex., 1988.

WILLIAM LEMOS

SHIPS AND CREWS. [This entry gathers the names of the crew members for Columbus's four voyages to the Western Hemisphere. For further discussion of the three ships of the first voyage, see *Niña, Pinta,* and *Santa María*. For further discussion of the events of these voyages, see *Voyages of Columbus*.]

First Voyage

The following roster of the crews of the ships of the first voyage has been rigorously researched by Alicia Bache Gould and published by the Real Academia de la Historia in Madrid. Roman numerals refer to later voyages. An asterisk indicates that this crew member was left behind in La Navidad and died there.

Santa María

Christopher Columbus, captain

Juan de la Cosa, from Santona, master and owner (there is conflicting opinion about whether this Juan de la Cosa is the same as the Juan de la Cosa of the second voyage)

Peralonso Niño, from Moguer, pilot

*Diego de Arana, from Córdoba, master-at-arms of the fleet

*Rodrigo de Escobedo, from Segovia, secretary of the fleet

*Pedro Gutiérrez, baker of the royal house

Rodrigo Sánchez, from Segovia, comptroller of the fleet

*Luis de Torres, interpreter

*Maestre Juan, surgeon

*Chachu, boatswain

*Domingo de Lequeitio, boatswain's mate

*Antonio de Cuéllar, carpenter

*Domingo Vizcaíno, able seaman and cooper

*Lope, able seaman and caulker

*Juan de Medina, able seaman and tailor

*Diego Pérez, able seaman and painter

Bartolomé Bives, from Palos, able seaman

Alonso Clavijo, from Vejer, able seaman

*Gonzalo Franco, able seaman

Juan Martínez de Azoque, from Denia, able seaman

Juan de Moguer, from Palos, able seaman; also II

Juan de la Placa, from Palos, able seaman

Juan Ruiz de la Peña, from Basque Provinces, able seaman

Bartolomé de Torres, from Palos, able seaman; also II

Juan de Jerez, from Moguer, able seaman; also II

Rodrigo de Jerez, from Ayamonte, able seaman

Pero Yzquierdo, from Lepe, able seaman

Cristóbal Caro, silversmith and ship's boy; also II

Diego Bermúdez, from Palos, ship's boy; also III

Alonso Chocero, ship's boy

Rodrigo Gallego, ship's boy

Diego Leal, ship's boy; also II

*Pedro de Lepe, ship's boy

*Jácome el Rico, from Genoa, ship's boy

*Martín de Urtubia, ship's boy

Andrés de Yévenes, ship's boy

Juan, ship's boy

Pedro de Terreros, Columbus's steward; also II, III, IV

Pedro de Salcedo, Columbus's valet; also II, III

Pinta

Martín Alonso Pinzón, from Palos, captain

Francisco Martín Pinzón, from Palos, master

Cristóbal García Sarmiento, pilot; also II

Juan Reynal, master-at-arms; also II

Maestre Diego, surgeon

Juan Quintero de Algruta, from Palos, boatswain; also II, III, IV

Cristóbal Quintero, from Palos, owner and able seaman; also III

Antón Calabrés, from Calabria, Italy, able seaman; also II

Francisco García Vallejos, from Moguer, able seaman

Alvaro Pérez, able seaman

Gil Pérez, able seaman

Diego Martín Pinzón, from Palos, able seaman; also III

Sancho de Rama, able seaman

Gómez Rascón, from Palos, able seaman

Rodrigo de Triano (also known as Juan Rodríguez Bermejo), able seaman

Juan Verde de Triana, able seaman; also II

Juan Vezano, from Venice, able seaman

Pedro de Arcos, from Palos, ship's boy

Juan Arias, from Tavira, Portugal, ship's boy

Fernando Medel, from Huelva, ship's boy

Francisco Medel, from Huelva, ship's boy

Alonso de Palos, ship's boy; also II

Juan Quadrado, ship's boy

Pedro Tegero, ship's boy

Bernal, ship's boy and captain's servant

García Fernández, from Palos, steward

Niña

Vicente Yáñez Pinzón, from Palos, captain

Juan Niño, from Moguer, master and owner

Sancho Ruíz de Gama, pilot

*Maestre Alonso, surgeon

*Diego Lorenzo, master-at-arms

Bartolomé García, from Palos, boatswain; also II, IV

*Alonso de Morales, carpenter

Juan Arráez, able seaman; also II

Pedro Arráez, able seaman

Rui García, from Santona, able seaman

Rodrigo Monge, able seaman

Bartolomé Roldán, from Palos, able seaman and apprentice pilot; also III

Juan Romero, able seaman

Pedro Sánchez, from Montilla, able seaman

Pedro de Villa, from Santona, able seaman

García Alonso, from Palos, ship's boy; also II

*Andrés de Huelva, ship's boy

*Francisco de Huelva, ship's boy

Francisco Niño, from Moguer, ship's boy; also II

Pedro de Soria, ship's boy

Fernando de Triana, ship's boy

Miguel de Soria, ship's boy and captain's servant

Second Voyage

Following his triumphant appearance before the sovereigns in Barcelona upon his return from the first voyage, Columbus remained with the court making plans for the second voyage. By the end of May 1493 he had been designated captain general of the fleet and, together with Juan de Fonseca, archdeacon of Seville, was made jointly responsible for all aspects of the preparations. Fonseca, a good businessman and organizer, within five months assembled, manned, and outfitted a fleet of seventeen vessels for a six-month round-trip voyage and provided food, arms, supplies, tools, and equipment for some twelve hundred artisans and workmen who were to establish a self-sustaining colony.

Among the seventeen vessels of the fleet were three naos, ships of the same type as the original *Santa María*, which was wrecked on a reef off the north coast of La Española during the first voyage. Once again the Admiral named his flagship *Santa María*, but as usual she was normally referred to by her nickname *Mariagalante*. The other two naos were named *Colina* and *Gallega*. The remaining fourteen ships were all caravels and included gallant *Niña*, which had safely carried Columbus home to Spain on the first voyage. Twelve of these were *carabelas redondas* like *Niña*, square-rigged on foremast and mainmast, lateen on the mizzen. The two remaining ships, *San*

Juan and *Cardera,* the smallest in the fleet and chosen by Columbus specifically for exploring shoal rivers and inlets, were lateen-rigged throughout.

Columbus's log of the second voyage has never been found. Fortunately, the biography of the Admiral by his son Fernando and narrative accounts by Michele da Cuneo and Guillermo Coma, gentleman volunteers who participated in the voyage, have provided substantial information. The only official crew lists that have survived are contained in declarations by crew members of the three caravels *Niña, San Juan,* and *Cardera* stating their belief that Cuba was part of the mainland they had been seeking. These depositions, ordered by the Admiral, were taken under oath and recorded by Fernando Pérez de Luna, chief scribe and notary of the fleet. A dagger indicates participation in the first voyage also.

Niña
†Christopher Columbus, captain of the flagship and fleet commander
 Alonso Medel, from Palos, master to Cuba and remainder of voyage
 Francisco Niño, from Moguer, pilot
†Pedro de Terreros, boatswain
 Fernando Pérez de Luna, royal notary
 Diego Tristán, from Seville, gentleman volunteer
 Francisco de Morales, from Seville, gentleman volunteer
 Juan de la Cosa, chart maker (there is conflicting opinion about whether this Juan de la Cosa is the same as the Juan de la Cosa of the first voyage)
 Iñigo López de Zúñiga, the Admiral's steward
 Johan del Barco, from Palos, able seaman
 Morón, from Moguer, able seaman
 Francisco de Lepe, from Moguer, able seaman
 Diego Beltrán, from Moguer, able seaman
 Domingo, from Genoa, able seaman
 Estefano, from Venice, able seaman
 Juan de España, from Basque Provinces, able seaman
 Gómez Calafar, from Palos, able seaman
 Ramiro Pérez, from Lepe, able seaman
 Mateo de Morales, from San Juan del Puerto, able seaman
 Gonzalo, from Basque Provinces, ship's boy
 Francisco Ginovés, from Córdoba, ship's boy
 Rodrigo Molinero, from Moguer, ship's boy
 Rodrigo Calafar, from Caraya, ship's boy
 Alonso Niño, from Moguer, ship's boy
 Juan, from Basque Provinces, ship's boy
San Juan
 Alonso Pérez Roldán, from Málaga, master
 Bartolomé Pérez, from Rota, pilot
 Alfonso Rodríguez, from Cartaya, boatswain

 Johan Rodríguez, from Ciudad Rodrigo, able seaman
 Sebastián de Ayamonte, from Ciudad Rodrigo, able seaman
 Diego del Monte, from Moguer, able seaman
 Francisco Calvo, from Moguer, able seaman
 Juan Domínguez, from Palos, able seaman
 Juan Albarracín, from Puerto de Santa María, able seaman
 Nicolás Estefano, from Mallorca, cooper
 Cristóbal Vivas, from Moguer, ship's boy
 Rodrigo de Santander, from Moguer, ship's boy
 Johan Garcés, from Beas, ship's boy
 Pedro de Salas, from Lisbon, ship's boy
 Hernando López, from Huelva, ship's boy
 Fernando Pérez de Luna, royal notary
Cardera
 Cristóbal Pérez Niño, from Moguer, master
 Fenerin Ginovés, boatswain
 Gonzalo Alonso Galeote, boatswain's mate
†Juan de Jerez, from Moguer, able seaman
 Francisco Carral, from Palos, able seaman
 Gorjón, from Palos, able seaman
 Juan Griego, from Genoa, able seaman
 Alonso Pérez, from Huelva, able seaman
 Juan Vizcaíno, from Cartaya, able seaman
 Cristóbal Lorenzo, from Palos, ship's boy
 Francisco de Medina, from Moguer, ship's boy
†Diego Leal, from Moguer, ship's boy
†Francisco Niño, from Moguer, ship's boy
 Tristán, from Valduerna, ship's boy
Our only information on the following participants in the voyage comes from occasional mention of certain individuals in the various narrative accounts.
 Antonio de Torres, master and owner of flagship *Mariagalante*
†Juan Niño, from Moguer, master from Spain to La Española only
 Bartolomé Colín, captain of *India* on return voyage
 Juan Aguado, ship's captain
 Alonso Sánchez de Carvajal, judge of Baeza and ship's captain
 Pedro Fernández Coronel, ship's captain
 Ginés de Gorbalán, ship's captain
 Alonso de Ojeda, ship's captain and leader of troops ashore
†Peralonso Niño, chief pilot from Spain to La Española only
†Cristóbal García Sarmiento, pilot
†Juan Quintero de Algruta, boatswain
†Bartolomé García, boatswain
 Diego de Alvarado, later active in Peru
 Francisco de Garay, an associate of Cortés
 Juan Ponce de León, future discoverer of Florida

Juan de Luján, from Madrid, gentleman volunteer

Pedro Margarit, commander of fort in interior La Española

Melchior Maldonado, gentleman volunteer

Diego Alvarez Chanca, from Seville, fleet physician and writer of voyage narrative

Michele da Cuneo, from Genoa, writer of voyage narrative

Guillermo Coma, gentleman volunteer, writer of voyage narrative

Bernardo Buyl (or Buil), Benedictine monk

Ramón Pané, Hieronymite friar

Diego Márquez, from Seville, inspector of the colony

Francisco Morales, able seaman

†Juan de Moguer, able seaman

†Bartolomé de Torres, able seaman

†Cristóbal Caro, silversmith and ship's boy

†Juan Reynal, master-at-arms

†Antón Calabrés, able seaman

†Juan Verde de Triana, able seaman

†Alonso de Palos, ship's boy

†Juan Arráez, able seaman

†García Alonso, ship's boy

†Pedro de Salcedo, ship's boy

Diego Colón, the Admiral's youngest brother

In June 1495, a severe hurricane sank three of the four caravels at La Isabela. The hardy *Niña* once again survived. Among the ships' crews were a few shipwrights who, with the assistance of carpenters from the colony, salvaged as much as they could of the wrecked ships' timbers and equipment to build a sister ship of *Niña*. This new caravel, the first European ship to be built in the New World, was officially named *Santa Cruz* but was always called *India*. *Niña* and *India* were dangerously overloaded, carrying 255 passengers, of whom 30 were Indians, back to Spain.

Third Voyage

Columbus requested eight ships for the third voyage, two of which would depart as soon as possible with supplies for La Española. The sovereigns gave approval for this number of ships, but money for the enterprise was slow in reaching the fitting-out port of Seville. Reliable *Niña* and her sister ship *India*, sixty-ton caravels in both of which Columbus owned a half interest, were the first ships to be readied. They sailed from Sanlúcar at the mouth of the Guadalquivir River on January 23, 1498. Not until four months later, May 30, did the next six ships depart: One nao, the *Santa María de Guía*, Columbus's flagship, and five caravels, *Vaqueños, El Correo, Garza, La Gorda,* and *La Rábida*. The latter three, loaded with men and supplies for the colony on La Española, headed directly for their assigned destination from the Canary Islands while the first three ships, under the Admiral's command, took a more southerly course in hopes of discovering the rumored mainland south of the Antilles.

The following roster of the third voyage has been compiled from sources discovered at different times, some in the sixteenth century and some not until late in the twentieth. Ship assignments for most of the crewmen are not available.

Christopher Columbus, Admiral of the Ocean Sea

Pero Fernández Coronel, captain general of *Niña* and *India*

Pedro Francés, captain of *Niña*

Juan Bermúdez, captain of *India*

Pedro de Terreros, captain of *El Correo*

Hernán Pérez, captain of *Vaqueños*

Alonso Sánchez de Carvajal, captain of *Garza*

Pedro de Arana, captain of *La Gorda*

Giovanni Antonio Colombo, the Admiral's Genoese cousin, captain of *La Rábida*

Cristóbal Quintero, owner and master of *Santa María de Guía*

Andrés García Galdín, from Palos, master of *La Castilla*

Francisco García, from Palos, owner and master of *Garza*

Alfón Benítez, from Palos, master of *La Gorda*

García Alfón Cansino, from Palos, master of *La Rábida*

Juan Quintero de Algruta, from Palos, pilot

Juan Quintero Principe, from Palos, pilot

Bartolomé Roldán, able seaman

Diego Martín Pinzón, able seaman

Alfonso Pérez Mateos, from Huelva, able seaman

Alonso Pérez, able seaman

Fernando Pérez de Palos, able seaman

Domingo de Bermeo, able seaman

Juan Griego, able seaman

Diego Galindo, able seaman

Pedro de Valmaseda, able seaman

García de Vedia, able seaman

Juan de Echevarría, able seaman

Diamedes Quaralte, able seaman

Juan de Purcheta, able seaman

Luis de Area, of Palos, able seaman

Diego Ortiz, of Palos, able seaman

Ortuño, of Baracaldo, able seaman

Cristóbal Durán, from Palos, able seaman

Diego Bermúdez, ship's boy

Juan de Amezaga, from Baracalda, ship's boy

Jácome, ship's boy

Pedro de la Maza, ship's boy

Bartolomé de Sanlúcar de Barrameda, ship's boy

Juan Farfán, ship's boy

Ochoa de Etorribalzago, ship's boy

Juan Antonio, the Admiral's head steward

Pedro del Arroyal, the Admiral's steward

Pedro de Salcedo, the Admiral's servant

Andrés de Corral, the Admiral's page

The following individuals could have been either crew members or colonists:

Juan Domínguez, priest
Juan de Caizedo, priest
Juan de Castuera, priest
Maestre Diego, from Palencia, surgeon
Juan Picardo, gunner
Rodrigo Yáñez, from Lepe, cooper
Francisco Sánchez, from Lepe, cooper
Gonzalo, of Fregenal, barber
Juan Rodríguez, from Triana, tailor
Fernando Pacheco, from Seville
Pedro de Arana, from Córdoba
Juan de Amezaga, from Baracalda
Domingo de Alburquerque
Juan de Bolonia
Simón de Piamonte
Gonzalo Moreno
Juan Guillén, from Jerez de Badajoz
Juan de Vera, from Canary Islands
Andrés de Vera, from Canary Islands
Juan Portugués, from Canary Islands
Andrés del Hierro, from Canary Islands

Also without ship assignments or designated occupations were ten pardoned criminals.

The following sixteen *escuderos* (gentlemen volunteers) probably were aboard the three ships headed for La Española, but a few may have been with the explorers in the three ships commanded by Columbus:

Francisco de Alarcón
Francisco de Atienza
Francisco de Barrasa
Pero Carrillo
Luis de Castrejón
Gil Delgadillo, from Jerez de Badajoz
Diego de Escobar, from Seville
Diego de Luna
Antonio Marino
Diego Mexía, from Jerez
Lope de Ribera
Fernando de San Miguel, from Seville
Bartolomé de Torres
Gonzalo de Valdenebro
Alfonso de Vallejo
García de Villanueva, from Jerez de la Frontera
Cristóbal Sánchez de la Cida, from Jerez, in charge of
    the following labor force destined for the colony:
      Lázaro Ruíz, from Córdoba, locksmith
      Lope Alfonso, from Portugal, blacksmith
      Pedro López, blacksmith
      Cristóbal de Paz, from Seville, mason
      Bartolomé Sánchez, from Seville, mason

Antón Gutiérrez, from Seville, mason
Pedro de Requena, from Baena, mason
Alfonso Rodríguez, from Carmona, mason
Juan Gascón, mason
Juan Martínez, from Seville, tile maker
Navidad Bretón, sawyer
Benito Sánchez, sawyer
Juan Rodríguez, copper worker
Pedro Sánchez, from Baeza, gold worker
Antonio Maldonado, sword maker
Juan de Guadalajara, drummer

Twenty-eight *labradores* and *hortelanos* (farmers and vegetable gardeners) and fifty peons (unskilled laborers) were also aboard. Also destined for the colony were sixty-six *ballesteros* (crossbowmen), for a total of about 245 participants in the third voyage.

Fourth Voyage

On September 3, 1501, Nicolás de Ovando was named by the sovereigns as governor and chief justice of the Indies except for those portions of the mainland under the jurisdiction of Vicente Yáñez Pinzón and Alonso de Ojeda. On February 13, 1502, Ovando sailed from Cádiz with a magnificent fleet of thirty ships carrying twenty-five hundred crewmen, colonists, and soldiers.

At this juncture, Columbus, who had been stripped of nearly all his titles and privileges but still retained his designation as Admiral of the Ocean Sea, proposed to the sovereigns an additional voyage of discovery in the as-yet-unexplored western Caribbean in another attempt to find the long-sought strait to the Indian Ocean. The sovereigns, who particularly wanted to have such a strait discovered, were quick to approve his proposal. Four caravels were provided for this voyage, including *La Capitana,* the flagship.

La Capitana
  Christopher Columbus, Admiral of the Ocean Sea
  Diego Tristán, captain (died at Veragua and replaced by
    Diego Méndez)
  Ambrosio Sánchez, master
  Juan Sánchez, chief pilot
  Antón Donato, boatswain
  Bartolomé Colón, the Admiral's elder brother
  Fernando Colón, the Admiral's son and biographer
  Pedro Fernández Coronel, gentleman volunteer
  Francisco Ruíz, gentleman volunteer
  Alonso de Camora, gentleman volunteer
  Guillermo Ginovés, from Genoa, gentleman volunteer
  Maestre Bernal, physician and gentleman volunteer
  Martín de Arriera, cooper
  Domingo Viscaíno, caulker (died April 6, 1503)
  Diego Francés, carpenter

Juan Barba, gunner (died May 20, 1504)
Mateo, gunner (died April 6, 1503)
Juan de Cuéllar, trumpeter
Gonzalo de Salazar, trumpeter
Martín Dati, able seaman (remained in La Española)
Bartolomé García, able seaman (died May 28, 1503)
Pedro Rodríguez, able seaman (died April 6, 1503)
Juan Rodríguez, able seaman (remained in La Española)
Alonso de Almagro, able seaman (remained in La Española)
Pedro de Toledo, able seaman
Pedro de Mayo, able seaman
Juan Gómez, able seaman
Diego Roldán, able seaman
Juan Gallego, able seaman
Juan de Valencia, able seaman (died January 15, 1504)
Gonzalo Rodríguez, able seaman (died April 4, 1503)
Tristán Pérez Chinchorrero, able seaman
Rodrigo Vergayo, able seaman (remained in La Española)
Diego Portogalete, ship's boy (died January 4, 1503)
Martín Juan, ship's boy (remained in La Española)
Donís de Galve, ship's boy
Juan de Zumados, ship's boy (died April 28, 1503)
Francisco de Estrada, ship's boy
Antón Chavarín, ship's boy
Alonso, ship's boy (died April 6, 1503)
Grigorio Sollo, ship's boy (died June 27, 1504)
Diego el Negro, ship's boy
Pedro Sánchez, ship's boy
Francisco Sánchez, ship's boy
Francisco de Morón, ship's boy
Juan de Murcia, ship's boy
Grigorio Ginovés, ship's boy
Ferrando Dávila, ship's boy
Alonso de León, ship's boy
Juan de Miranda, ship's boy
Juan Garrido, ship's boy (died February 27, 1504)
Baltasar Daragón, ship's boy

Santiago de Palos
Francisco de Porras, captain and chief mutineer
Diego de Porras, chief auditor of the fleet and mutineer
Francisco Bermúdez, master
Pedro Gómez, boatswain
Francisco de Farias, gentleman volunteer
Diego Méndez, gentleman volunteer and hero of rescue mission
Pedro Gentil, gentleman volunteer
Andrea Ginovés, gentleman volunteer
Juan Jácome, gentleman volunteer
Batista Ginovés, gentleman volunteer
Bartolomé de Milán, gunner
Juan de Noya, cooper

Domingo de Arana, caulker (died April 6, 1503)
Machín, carpenter
Rodrigo Ximón, able seaman
Francisco Domingo, able seaman (died February 4, 1503)
Juan de Quijo, able seaman
Juan Rodríguez, able seaman (died April 6, 1503)
Juan de la Feria, able seaman
Juan Camacho, able seaman
Juan Grande, able seaman
Juan Reynaltes, able seaman (died April 6, 1503)
Diego Gómez, able seaman
Diego Martín, able seaman
Alonso Martín, able seaman
Gonzalo Ramírez, ship's boy
Juan Baudrojín, ship's boy (died October 23, 1503)
Diego Ximón, ship's boy
Apricio, ship's boy
Donís, ship's boy (died June 1, 1503)
Alonso Escarramán, ship's boy (died January 23, 1504)
Francisco Márquez, ship's boy
Juan de Moguer, ship's boy
Alonso de Cea, ship's boy
Pedro de Villatoro, ship's boy
Ramiro Ramírez, ship's boy
Francisco Dávila, ship's boy
Diego de Mendoza, ship's boy
Diego Cataño, ship's boy

Gallego
Pedro de Terreros, captain (died May 29, 1504)
Juan Quintero de Algruta, master
Alonso Ramón, boatswain
Gonzalo Camacho, gentleman volunteer
Rui Ferrandes, able seaman
Luis Ferrandes, able seaman
Gonzalo García, able seaman
Pedro Mateos, able seaman
Julián Martín, able seaman (died April 6, 1503)
Diego Cabezudo, able seaman
Diego Barranco, able seaman
Diego Delgado, able seaman
Rodrigo Álvares, able seaman
Pedro de Flandes, ship's boy
Bartolomé Ramírez, ship's boy (died April 6, 1503)
Antón Quintero, ship's boy
Bartolomé Dalza, ship's boy
Gonzalo Flamenco, ship's boy
Pedro Barranco, ship's boy
Juan Galdil, ship's boy (died September 9, 1504)
Alonso Penac, ship's boy
Esteban Mateos, cabin boy
Diego de Santander, ship's boy
García Polanco, ship's boy
Juan García, ship's boy

Francisco de Medina, ship's boy (jumped ship in La Española)

Juan de San Martín, ship's boy

Vizcaíno

Bartolomeo Fieschi, from Genoa, captain

Juan Pérez, master (died October 7, 1503)

Martín de Fuenterrabía, boatswain (died September 17, 1502)

Alejandre, friar, missionary

Juan Pasan, Genoese, gentleman volunteer

Francisco de Córdoba, gentleman volunteer

Marco Surjano, from Genoa, gentleman volunteer (died September 11, 1504)

Pedro de Ledesma, able seaman and mutineer

Juan Ferro, able seaman

Juan Moreno, able seaman

San Juan, able seaman

Gonzalo Díaz, able seaman

Gonzalo Gallego, able seaman (jumped ship in La Española)

Alonso de la Calle, able seaman (died May 23, 1503)

Lope de Pego, able seaman

Miguel de Lariaga, ship's boy (died September 17, 1502)

Andrés de Sevilla, ship's boy

Luis de Vargas, ship's boy

Batista Ginovés, ship's boy

Francisco de Levante, ship's boy

Pedro de Montesel, ship's boy

Rodrigo de Escobar, ship's boy

Domingo Narbasta, ship's boy (died March 26, 1504)

Pasqual de Ausurraga, ship's boy

Cheneco, cabin boy

William Lemos

SIGNATURE. The curious form Columbus adopted for signing his name after his return from his first voyage to the New World has been the subject of considerable conjecture among scholars. The earliest surviving example of Columbus's signature appears in a letter of April 1493 addressed to the Catholic monarchs, and it is found thereafter in almost all his surviving autograph documents. Between forty-five and fifty of these signatures have been preserved, each having the same pyramid of letters arranged in exactly the same way. The signature appears as follows:

.S.

.S. A .S.

X M Y

Xpo FERENS

The letters above the signature are considered to be a pious ejaculation, and it has been suggested that it can be read beginning with the uppermost letter, "I am the servant of the Most Exalted Savior Xhristus Maria Yosephus."

The final line of the signature, *Xpo Ferens,* is simply a Greek-Latin form of "Christopher." The first half of the signature, *Xpo* (for "Christo"), is derived from the Greek and the second half, *Ferens,* is Latin. Instead of the Latin "Christophorus" or the Italian "Cristoforo" for his given name, Columbus adopted the Greek-Latin form "Christoferens," assumed to signify his role as the bearer of the Christian religion to the pagan peoples in the lands he discovered. It is to be noted that in his map of the West Indies in 1500 Juan de la Cosa portrayed Columbus under the symbol of Saint Christopher bearing Christ over the waters.

This form of signature reflects to some degree the religious and social atmosphere of Roman Catholic countries during the fifteenth century and is an example of a practice not unusual in Spain. It was customary to

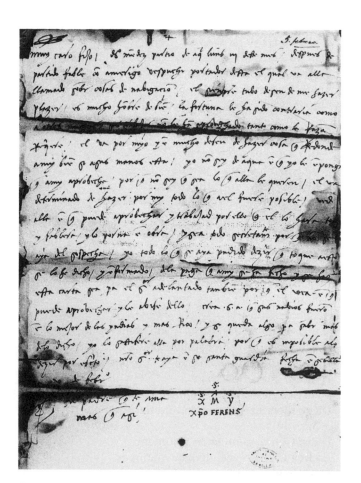

SIGNATURE OF COLUMBUS. On a letter to his son Diego in which he mentions a meeting with Amerigo Vespucci.

ARCHIVO GENERAL DE INDIAS, SEVILLE

accompany one's signature with some words of religious purport, often to identify the writer as a Christian in a country in which Jews and Muslims were proscribed and persecuted.

In his biography of his father, Fernando Colón stated that when his father "had to write anything, he would not try the pen without first writing these words, *Jesus cum Maria sit nobis in via.*" Columbus begins his Book of Prophecies with the same words.

At the time that Columbus first began using the device, he had achieved the height of his power and fame, and he undoubtedly wished to embody his seal with the importance of his newly acquired nobility. He was determined, furthermore, to extend the range of his discoveries and privileges to acquire the right to create a viceregal dynasty with virtually sovereign power over a part of the earth that promised potentially great wealth.

In the act of primogeniture Columbus prepared five years later on February 22, 1498, he established that *las armas*—his seal—should be adopted as the standard family coat of arms and that his heirs should have the right to seal documents with his arms and to sign with the monogram he himself had devised, although only after the right of primogeniture had been acquired. The monogram was to be followed by the signature "El Almirante," suggesting that he considered that the device and signature represented dignity, position, and inheritance handed down by himself as the founder of the house to his legitimate successors.

Columbus attached great importance to his signature, and in his entail he instructed his heirs to continue "to sign with my signature which I now employ which is an X with an S over it and an M with a Roman A over it and over that an S and then a Greek Y with an S over it, preserving the relation of the lines and points." These instructions were not followed by the heirs, however. Columbus never revealed their meaning, which is why they have aroused so much speculation.

The signature reveals much of Columbus's peculiar character. He considered himself mysteriously elected and set apart to achieve certain great purposes, as strongly reflected in the formality and solemnity with which he approached all his concerns. Historians attempting to solve the puzzle of the monogram have worked on the assumption that Columbus was deeply religious, accustomed to beginning his writings with *Jesus cum Maria sit nobis in via,* as his son reported, and that he intended the monogram to convey a strictly religious meaning. The puzzle becomes of particular interest in relation to the various claims that Columbus was a Jew, a Spaniard, or a Freemason.

At least eight possible meanings of the initials have been proposed. The third line is probably an invocation to Christ, Mary, and Joseph (*Christe, Maria, Yoseph*). Columbus sometimes confused the Greek *Y* with the Greek *I* that begins the names of Jesus and Joseph. The letters have therefore been variously interpreted as *Xhristus, Maria, Yosephus* or *Yesus, Maria, Yosephus.*

The four letters in the first two lines lend themselves to many combinations of which the simplest and most reasonable appears to be:

> *Servus*
> *Sum Altissimi Salvatoris*
> (Servant I am
> of the Most Exalted Savior)

It has also been suggested that Columbus may have intended the combination of letters to have a mystical meaning, in which case the significance could be established by interpreting it thus:

> *Yesu, Maria, Yoseph*
> *Sanctus, Sanctus, Sanctus*
> (Jesus, Mary, Joseph
> Holy, Holy, Holy)

Two other interpretations that have been considered are the following:

> *Sit Sibi Semper Antecedente*
> *Christus Maria Yosephus*
> (May they always go before him
> Christ, Mary, Joseph)

> *Supplex Servus Altissimi Salvatoris*
> *Iesu Maria Yosephus*
> (Suppliant servant of the Most High Savior
> Jesus, Mary, Joseph)

In the Castilian dialect in that period the letters *I, J,* and *Y* were interchangeable, and the name of the queen was often spelled "Ysabel." Some have substituted "Ysabel" for "Yosephus," thus:

> *Servidor (de) Sus Altezas Sacras*
> *Jesu Maria Jsabel*
> (Servant of Their Sacred Highnesses
> Jesus, Mary, Isabel)

Some historians claim to have detected in Columbus's signature a potential reference to his long-held plan to mount crusades against the Muslims and to achieve the liberation of the Holy Sepulcher, which can be rendered in either one of two forms as follows:

> *Sarraceno Subjuget Avertat Submovent*
> *Christus Maria Iosephus*
> (May the Saracens be subjugated,
> turned away and removed by
> Christ, Mary, and Joseph)

Salva Sanctum Altissimum Sepulcrum
Christus Maria Iosephus
(Save the most high Holy Sepulcher
Christ, Mary, and Joseph)

Still others have concluded that the signature has no mystical import at all but in an abbreviated form constitutes merely the solemn subscription of Columbus. The signature would be divided into two groups of letters, the first group of letters in the top two lines

A
X M Y

have been interpreted to signify

Christóbal Almirante Mayor [de las] Indias
Christus Maria Yosephus [or Ysabel]
(Christopher First Admiral of the Indies
Jesus, Mary, Joseph [or Isabel])

and it has been suggested that the remaining three letters

.S.
.S. .S.

may have been intended to mean

Sub. Scrip. Si.
(I have signed my name below this.)

In other of Columbus's writings, the last line of the signature sometimes varied, occasionally reading *el Almirante* ("the Admiral"), and on a few documents he used the word *Virey* ("the Viceroy"). To one *Virey* signature in the Veragua manuscripts in the Archivo General de Indias, Columbus added in lowercase letters the words *general a las yndias* above a long tail of the final letter *Y*. Another signature without this addition, which is reproduced in the duchess of Berwick y Alba's *Autógrafos de Colón*, is accompanied by a unique impression of Columbus's seal that appears to have the same monogram featured over a globe.

[See also *Coat of Arms*.]

BIBLIOGRAPHY

Colón, Fernando. *Historie di Cristoforo Colombo*. 2 vols. Milan, 1930, 2:373–378.

Streicher, F. "Die Kolumbus-Originale. Eine paläographische Studie." In vol. 1 of *Spanische Forschungen der Görresgesellschaft*. Münster, 1928.

Streicher, F. "El monogramma de las cartas de Colón." *Investigacion y progreso* (Madrid) 3, no. 6 (1929).

Thacher, J. B. *Christopher Columbus: His Life, His Work, His Remains*. 3 vols. New York, 1903, 3: 455–457.

SILVIO A. BEDINI

SLAVERY. The incidence of slavery in Europe declined after the fall of the Roman Empire and its character changed, but the institution was never threatened with extinction. In rural areas it was transformed into serfdom or at least a dependent peasantry, but in the cities slaves continued in domestic and personal service. Slavery became vital in agriculture once more only with the development of sugar plantations in the eastern Mediterranean in the aftermath of the early Crusades. Throughout the Middle Ages many parts of Europe were a ready source of slaves for the more prosperous non-Christian societies of the Mediterranean. For centuries, indeed, the Germanic peoples and Slavs were to the Middle East and North Africa what Africans would become to the Americas. Primary products and slaves were the only commodities in which Europe could interest its more sophisticated southern and eastern trading partners.

Iberia was both a battleground and a trading nexus for this north-west/south-east dichotomy. Almost all the invaders and external institutional influences that affected the Iberian Peninsula in the centuries before the Columbian expansion practiced or countenanced slavery. Romans, Visigoths, and Arabs, as well as the Christian and Muslim faiths, regarded enslavement as a normal part of any social system. Slavery thus existed continuously in Spain, and indeed in most of the rest of the world, from pre-Christian to early modern times.

Slaves always composed a minority in pre-Columbian Iberia; they made up probably less than 10 percent of the population. As elsewhere in the Mediterranean basin, slavery in both Christian and Islamic Spain was primarily an urban and domestic phenomenon, and recognition of the institution was embedded in Iberian law. The Christian advance in Iberia coincided with a burgeoning interest in and application of Roman law throughout western Europe, and Roman law provided the code for the operation of a slave system. The Castilian code from the mid-thirteenth century, known as the *Siete partidas*, is an example of this influence. The only religious constraint on the institution—not always effective before the late Middle Ages—was that Christians and Muslims not enslave people of their own faith. The political constraint was that rulers did not countenance enslavement of their own subjects.

The Muslim presence and subsequent reconquest reinforced slavery in the Iberian Peninsula. In the early Middle Ages Spain was a major point of exchange in the trade of European slaves and primary products for manufactured and luxury products from the Far East. In addition, during the long wars of reconquest, enslavement of captives reinforced the institution of slavery on both sides of the religious divide. Slaves were often captured as hostages, and organizations such as the Mercedarian Order were dedicated to the redemption of captives held by non-Christians.

The prevalence of war and raids as a source of slaves obscures the fact that the Christian kingdoms in medieval

Spain—Portugal, Castile, and Aragón —could not usually afford to buy slaves through international commercial channels. It was Islamic Iberia that was more likely to purchase slaves from outside the peninsula. Slavery was associated with prosperity and commercial exchange rather than poverty and backwardness. Indeed, as David B. Davis has pointed out, the institution has flourished most in societies recognized as being at the forefront of social, cultural, and economic advance. The shrinking of the slaving frontier within the Iberian Peninsula (with the reconquest of the Muslim south) coincided with expansion of the European economy and the victories of the Ottoman Turks in the eastern Mediterranean—the latter closing off a major source of slaves in the late Middle Ages. It also coincided with the development of the technical expertise needed to conduct long-distance overseas exploration, commerce, and military forays. Hence, just as the Iberian ability to purchase slaves increased, Africa replaced the Black Sea regions as the major source of slaves. The long Iberian historical experience of slavery, an accommodating legal system, and the preexistence of a small trans-Saharan trade ensured a smooth transition from one provenance zone to another.

In the century and a half after 1441 the Portuguese carried perhaps over fifty thousand African slaves to Europe. Several thousand more of the Guanche peoples of the Canary Islands and some aboriginal Americans in the early days of the Spanish conquest of the New World experienced a similar fate. The vast majority went to Portugal and Spain. In both countries two systems of slavery existed side by side: Muslims were the victims in one and Africans in the other, with treatment of the Muslims probably the more severe of the two. In no regions in either country did slaves form a majority, and the pattern of holdings, as before, was predominantly urban. African slaves made up 10 percent of the population of Lisbon in the mid-sixteenth century, for example. In Seville—the largest city in the peninsula—slaves composed a slightly smaller proportion overall, with about half of them of African origin. In Valencia, closer to the Mediterranean and more recently Muslim, there were fewer slaves overall and a smaller proportion of them were Africans. Muslims were enslaved from within the kingdom through judicial procedure as well as from without through raids, even after the long war of reconquest had finished.

By the early sixteenth century, not only were more slaves African, but they also worked in a wider range of occupations than had been usual in medieval times. The Portuguese, in a pattern that anticipated that of Brazil down to the mid-nineteenth century, used slaves in all activities, including some that required skills. They also used more slaves in agriculture than in earlier times, particularly south of the Tagus, but not on the type of plantation that was to become the norm in the Americas. In Spain, or at least in the cities of Seville and Valencia (for which we have the best records), domestic service continued to predominate.

It is probable that the Portuguese used some slaves in sugar production in the Algarve of southern Portugal. In the late Middle Ages, sugar cultivation spread to other parts of the peninsula from Islamic Spain, where it had long been cultivated (in Córdoba and Toledo in particular). By the early fifteenth century, a major expansion in sugar production was underway in Valencia and the Algarve just as production in the eastern Mediterranean— the major source of sugar in medieval Europe — began to decline. Spain and Portugal had thus become steps in the westward march of sugar cultivation that began in Southeast Asia in the pre-Christian era and was to reach the Pacific coastal regions of the New World some two millennia later. A rising European demand for sugar, German finance, Genoese entrepreneurship, and Iberian land (though not at this stage extensive use of African labor) composed a mix, albeit on a small scale, that was to be repeated in first the Atlantic islands and then the Americas. In the broader context it should be noted that Iberian expansion was part of a general European colonization movement to the east and northwest as well as to the Caribbean and South America, and that an element of coercion—whether indentured labor, serfdom (in eastern Europe), or slavery—was common to all.

As the two Iberian states expanded, slavery increasingly assumed much greater importance as a source of labor. Apart from the links between slavery and empire alluded to above, the regions into which the Portuguese and Spanish moved had high land-to-labor ratios, a condition historically associated with coerced labor. Given the long experience of Iberians with slavery, it is not surprising that the new settlements and conquests that were part of Iberian expansion generated genuine slave societies in that they relied on slave labor for the production of the commodities that sustained them.

Despite the continuities, however, the slavery that developed in the Iberian Atlantic settlements was fundamentally different from the institution that went under the same name in medieval Europe, Islamic states, and indigenous societies in Africa and the Americas. In these older societies the slave class lacked racial distinctiveness, and more important, slaves were usually migrants or the immediate descendants of migrants whose status might be regarded as a step toward fuller social integration over a generation or two. In the New World, slavery was no longer an institution for the minority. Eunuchs may have been much less common, but manumission or social integration of any kind was an extremely remote possibility for slaves or their descendants. In the New World the bundle of rights over others was redefined in such a way as to give much more unrestricted power to the master. Slavery may have already existed in Africa and the Americas before Europeans arrived, but the rights that the African slave owner sold to the European trader were altogether less absolute than what the latter in turn sold to the plantation owner in the Americas.

The initial Iberian movement into the Atlantic was to the offshore islands of the Canaries, Madeira, Cape Verde, the Azores, and São Tomé and Principé in the Bight of Biafra. Only the first of these was inhabited and, after a dispute with Portugal settled in the Treaty of Alcáçovas in 1479, it was taken over by Castilians. The rest were uninhabited before being settled by the Portuguese. First European contact with the islands dates from the mid-fourteenth century, but settlement of Madeira began only in the second quarter of the following century. Significantly, the clearing and irrigation of the largest and most mountainous of the Madeiran islands was carried out by slaves captured in the Canary Islands. Although the early crops were cereals rather than sugar, large initial land grants and an aggressive group of elite settlers ensured that sugar would be introduced well before the mid-fifteenth century. By the end of the century, perhaps a fifth of the population of fifteen thousand was slave. Initially the slaves were Guanches and Muslims from Iberia, but increasingly they were of African origin. For a short time the island was the largest single source of cane sugar consumed in Europe. Sugar also did well in the Canaries, the extinction of whose indigenous peoples led to further reliance on African labor. Similar efforts in the drier Azores and Cape Verde islands were less successful. The last port of call in the Old World in the westward march of sugar was São Tomé in the Bight of Biafra. Prevailing winds and currents made the island relatively easy for sailing ships to reach and, more important, leave, and the soil, precipitation, and ready access to African labor ensured an important sugar sector until Brazilian competition buried the Old World industry in the second half of the sixteenth century. The Portuguese sold perhaps twenty-five thousand African slaves to the Atlantic islands—most to Madeira and the Canaries—and almost four times as many to São Tomé.

Unlike most of the Atlantic islands, the Americas to which the Portuguese and Spanish sailed were not empty lands. The widespread adoption and modification of slavery in the New World was shaped not just by the drive to produce an exportable staple and by the cultural baggage that the Iberians brought with them. It was also influenced by the fact that slavery had long existed in the pre-Columbian Americas. A wide range of aboriginal societies, from the complex Aztec to the less developed Tupinambá in what became Brazil, held slaves. These were often war captives spared from immediate death, though

the risk of eventually being killed and eaten in the case of the Tupinambás or used for live sacrifice in the Aztec empire was very high. Female war captives became wives who rarely lost their slave status but whose children could become full members of the host society, as, for example, among the Caribs. Most slaves in the more complex societies of Central America were nevertheless generated internally through judicial process, indebtedness, or deprivation and the resulting voluntary assumption of slave status. It is likely that the slave class of the Aztec empire was growing at the time of the first Spanish contact.

Nevertheless, no Indian peoples can be said to have created a slave society in the sense of that in ancient Rome or in the Caribbean in the eighteenth century. The economic rationale for slavery among Indian groups was probably less important than motives of prestige, religion (the requirements of ritual), or sexual gratification. Most slaves were domestics, although among the Aztecs, transportation, in the absence of vehicles and horses, absorbed many of them. Slaves were also employed in the tilling of crops, including cacao in an anticipation of the post-Columbian situation, but this activity was neither labor-intensive nor dominant in the catalog of slave uses. Among the Aztecs, slave status, at least for slaves of internal origin, was likely to be temporary. Redemption by self or family, manumission on the death of the slave-owner, and the rendition of a valuable service provided routes to full integration into the community. Internal markets in slaves were not well developed. As in the medieval Mediterranean region, racial distinctiveness was not coterminous with slavery, although Europeans and Africans served as slaves to aboriginal groups in the post-Columbus era. Slaves could marry nonslaves, own property, and exercise other legal rights. In its largely noneconomic, nonracial, and temporary nature, aboriginal slavery differed sharply from the post-Columbian institution that replaced it, especially in the Dutch, English, and French colonies. Yet the Spanish in particular did take over existing aboriginal structures for the exploitation of labor. Among these were tribute labor and slavery. Indeed, the Spanish were most successful at extracting labor from native Americans where such structures were most highly developed in pre-Columbian societies.

Epidemiology was crucial to the creation of the European version of New World slavery. The Americas were a relatively isolated part of the globe compared to the Eurasian and African continents in the sense that flora, fauna, and microorganisms, as well as human societies, had evolved separately for millennia by the time the Iberians arrived. Their coming initiated a merging of two distinct epidemiological zones in the process of which the native population of the Americas was decimated and in some cases—for example, the Arawaks—exterminated. Labor shortages, owing as much to smallpox and measles as to European exploitation, developed within a few years of the initial contact. Even without the epidemiological factor Spanish and Portuguese restrictions on enslavement of native Americans in response to the advocacy of Bartolomé de las Casas, among others, slowed the enslavement and vigorous slave trade of aboriginals in the first phase of Iberian settlement. Moreover, plantation and mine owners in Spanish America and Brazil regarded Indian labor as far less productive than African and European. African slaves throughout the Iberian Americas sold for three or more times as much as their aboriginal counterparts. Systems for exploiting the forced labor of Indians, such as encomienda and repartimiento (and mita labor in Peru), were not as successful as African slavery or even wage labor in those sectors producing commodities for world markets.

If Iberians preferred Africans to Indians, the question remains, why Africans rather than Europeans, either slave or free? One explanation is that as Europeans spread they used settlement methods that had already proved useful closer to home. In northern Europe new lands typically were settled with villages and peasant labor drawn from the home society, whereas in the Mediterranean region colonizers tended to meet labor needs in new areas with alien slaves. Northern Europe had more surplus population than any of the Iberian regions in the later Middle Ages. Thus Barbados in its pre-sugar phase and the Chesapeake plantation colonies originally used white labor, albeit indentured rather than free. The Portuguese and Spanish, following the Mediterranean tradition, used slave labor from the start. A far greater proportion of the English population immigrated to the New World in the first century of English settlement than set out across the Atlantic from Spain in the sixteenth century. Epidemiology had some role in the process. Mortality in the Americas was very high for both Europeans and Africans in the early days of settlement. Whites and blacks died at similar rates on both slave ships and plantations before the nineteenth century. On the other hand, Africans had no choice, whereas Europeans, even indentured servants, could

AFRICAN SLAVES IN THE AMERICAS. Nicolás de Ovando, governor of La Española, imported Africans to work the gold mines. Engraving from Théodor de Bry's *Americae*. Frankfurt, 1594.

NATIONAL MARITIME MUSEUM, GREENWICH

usually choose not to go to a nonplantation region. The basic fact governing nearly four centuries of the slave trade to the New World was that everyone who had a choice avoided gang labor on sugar plantations and in mines.

As we might expect from the discussion so far, the early Iberian slave trade was multilateral and diffuse compared to the massive regularity of the east-west population shift of the eighteenth and nineteenth centuries. The Spanish carried American aborigines in the opposite direction, to Seville before 1500, and shortly thereafter they brought Africans from Spain to the Americas. Indeed, for a quarter of a century, all black slaves in Spanish America came from Spain, not from Africa, partly because the Treaty of Tordesillas excluded the Spanish from the African coast. The Portuguese, as we have seen, took Guanches from the Canaries to Madeira. Before initiating the transatlantic business, they shipped large numbers of Africans from Upper Guinea and what became Angola to yet another part of Africa, the Gold Coast, and exchanged them for a range of African commodities desired in Europe. On the other side of the Atlantic, over a quarter of a million aborigines from southern Brazil endured an ocean voyage up the coast as long and as miserable as any trip across the southern Atlantic before reaching the early sugar plantations in Pernambuco in northeast Brazil. The intra-Caribbean trade in Caribs also preceded the substantial shipment of slaves directly from Africa. Iberians thus organized a massive reshuffling of peoples within the New World prior to 1575 before concentrating on the traffic from Africa to the Americas.

INDIANS BEING TRANSPORTED TO SPAIN AS SLAVES.   Engraving from Théodor de Bry's *Americae*, Frankfurt, 1594.

By the last quarter of the sixteenth century, the pattern for the next three centuries was in place. By far the largest stream of peoples moving to the New World were African until the mid-nineteenth century. Down to 1625, the "New World" for this group meant Spanish America and Brazil. The major carrier—indeed, the only carrier direct from Africa at this stage—was Portugal, in whose ships over 400,000 people left the continent for the Americas. Those who reached continental Spanish America, usually Panama, Veracruz, or Cartagena in present-day Colombia, faced further long land or sea journeys before being set to work. The mainland areas of New Spain and New Granada received more Africans than did the Caribbean islands at this stage. The common impulse behind all this movement—on both sides of the Atlantic as well as across it—was the drive to obtain the labor necessary to the production of a commodity for world markets. As in pre-Columbian days, slavery continued to be associated with conventional concepts of progress, including economic prosperity, but now for the first time it was tied to the production of an export staple.

This does not mean that all slaves or even a majority in all regions were employed in sugar production and mining. The concentration of slaves in urban and domestic environments in both Portugal and Spain was repeated in the Americas. This pattern, however, was supplemented and eventually overwhelmed by the Mediterranean and Atlantic islands pattern of slaves being employed in agriculture and mining. They were rather more dominant in sugar production than in mining, where slavery was used in conjunction with various forms of commandeered aboriginal labor. Slaves were also to be found in cacao production and later the small Peruvian textile industry. Much of the output was exported. Small-scale sugar production began on La Española within twenty years of the Columbian landfall. It spread to other Caribbean islands, such as Puerto Rico, Cuba, and Jamaica, and to Mexico and Peru before the end of the sixteenth century. But the industry did not at this point make a sustained impact on the world market; rather, it concentrated on production for local consumption once the massive sugar complex of northeastern Brazil was established in the last quarter of the sixteenth century. It was this region, closest to Africa and with the lowest transportation costs for labor, that became in many ways the most thoroughgoing slave society in the New World. Although slaves dominated the export sector, there was scarcely an occupation in the economy that did not have a slave component.

Slavery as enforced by Iberians and then imitated by the French and English in the Americas was thus radically different from the institution that had existed before in Europe, Africa, or the Americas. It had become more racially exclusive, less a transitional status in the intergenerational sense, and very much oriented to a world commodity market, especially later under the French and the English. This easy transformation, however, could not have taken place without the institutional foundations in Iberia, the rest of Europe, and to a lesser extent among the aboriginal peoples of the Americas.

[See also *Encomienda; Pacification, Conquest, and Genocide.*]

BIBLIOGRAPHY

Davis, David B. *Slavery and Human Progress.* New York, 1984.

Garcia, Carlos Bosch. *La esclavitud prehispanica entre los Aztecas.* Mexico City, 1944.

Greenfield, Sidney M. "Plantations, Sugar Cane and Slavery." *Historical Reflections* 6 (1979): 85–119.

Phillips, William D. *Slavery from Roman Times to the Early Transatlantic Trade.* Minneapolis, 1985.

Russell-Wood, A. J. R. "Iberian Expansion and the Issue of Black Slavery: Changing Portuguese Attitudes, 1440–1770." *American Historical Review* 83 (1978): 1–28.

Saunders, A. C. de C. M. *A Social History of Black Slaves and Freedmen in Portugal, 1441–1555.* Cambridge, 1982.

Silva, Alfonso Franco. *La esclavitud en Sevilla y su tierra a fines de la edad media.* Seville, 1979.

Steward, Julian H., ed. *Handbook of South American Indians.* 3 vols. Washington, D.C., 1948.

Verlinden, Charles. *Péninsule ibérique–France.* Vol. 1 of *L'esclavage dans l'Europe médiévale.* Bruges, 1955.

Vogt, John L. "The Lisbon Slave House and the African Trade, 1486–1521." *Proceedings of the American Philosophical Society* 117 (1973): 1–16.

DAVID ELTIS

SOCIAL AND ECONOMIC INSTITUTIONS. The social and economic institutions of late medieval Europe grew out of the confluence of agricultural productivity, burgeoning towns, and long-distance trade. Agricultural production still consumed as much as 90 percent of human labor, and all social and economic organization depended upon control of the primary sector of food production. As medieval towns became overlords of the agrarian domain, agricultural surpluses sustained the urban division of labor that provided the catalyst for change. The increasing number of those communes newly founded after the year 1000 in Italy and northern Europe fueled their growth by exchanging goods in two long-distance economic systems. Both a southern and a northern trading circuit maintained a core of numerous and relatively large towns in Italy and Flanders through domination of distant hinterlands. Columbus's discovery of America in 1492 and Vasco da Gama's circumnavigation of Africa to establish a sea route to Asia in 1498 fit into the continuous pattern of trade, exploration, and exploitation that late medieval social and economic institutions had fostered.

The Mediterranean Sea delimited a medieval trading network first focused in the Islamic Middle East by the eighth century. In the ninth and tenth centuries, four Italian maritime communes without substantial agricultural hinterlands—Genoa, Pisa, Amalfi, and Venice—entered the system. In the course of the thirteenth century, a northern Italian commercial, banking, and industrial complex centered in Genoa, Milan, Florence, and Venice took over the system. The Italian cities reaped the profits from price differentials in the long-distance trade from the Near East home to Italy and inland to France and Germany. They also drew raw material goods from around the Mediterranean for industrial transformation and reexport. Luxury goods such as spices, silk, fine woolen cloth, leather, furs, and glass were the most important products, but ordinary bulky cargoes of salt, wine, fish, cheese, butter, oil, cotton, flax, raw wool, common dyes, nonprecious metals, and timber bolstered the carrying trade. Venice emerged as the victor in the eastern Mediterranean with an overseas empire that stretched from the Italian mainland, the Dalmatian coast, and Corfu to Crete, Cyprus, and Constantinople. Genoa pioneered westward into the Atlantic, and in 1293 a joint Castilian-Genoese fleet decisively defeated a Muslim navy to open the way to regular ties with England and Flanders. Two Genoese brothers, Ugolino and Vadino Vivaldi, even attempted an unsuccessful Atlantic voyage to the Indies in 1291.

The Germans themselves spearheaded the somewhat later development of the northern trading network, the Hanseatic League. Lübeck merchants took the lead from the mid-twelfth century, and in 1356 the Hansa became a formal association of towns rather than one only of merchants. As many as one hundred towns subscribed to the Hansa at its height as it oversaw trade in northwest Europe, the North and Baltic seas from Bruges, London, Hamburg, and Lübeck to Bergen and Novgorod. Flanders in the Low Countries, with access to the rich Rhineland, became its urbanized center of industrial production and transshipment.

A long wave of rising and declining economic activity had begun in Europe with the reestablishment of towns in the eleventh and twelfth centuries and crashed in the catastrophic outbreak of bubonic plague in 1348. Europe's internal restructuring as it came out of the century-long social and economic crisis between 1350 and 1450 set the tone for the next economic cycle that began in the third quarter of the fifteenth century. During that century of reorganization after the plague, external changes in international trade also challenged the Italian monopoly of key markets. The fourteenth-century decline of the Mongol Empire in Central Asia, which closed the land routes to Asia, adversely affected Genoese trade through her Black Sea ports. The growing power of the Ottoman Turks, who conquered Constantinople in 1453, further threatened eastern Mediterranean trade, although the Ottomans did not cut off the Venetian access to the southern route to Asia through the Red Sea until 1527. Spurred by the desire to exploit new agricultural hinterlands, to circumvent the Italian city-states' Levant trade monopoly, and to find another route to the Indies to outflank hostile Islamic middlemen, newly amalgamated European monarchical states competed among themselves to sponsor exploratory economic ventures. Fifteenth-century European expansion to Africa, Asia, and America thus capped a medieval urban and commercial revolution and stimulated the development of a single Atlantic Ocean–focused economy conflated from the two earlier trading systems.

Population Size. An important variable that affects both the structure of demand and the supply of labor, population size is a baseline indicator to begin an examination of structure and change in late medieval and early modern European social and economic institutions. Although the Black Death that devastated Europe in 1348 hit a social and economic environment already weakened from overpopulation and strained resources, the immediate three-year death toll of twenty-five million out of Europe's eighty million inhabitants was staggering. Depending on the region and whether a rural or urban setting, between one-fourth to two-thirds of the population died during the pandemic. Further, the immediate crisis was compounded by the fact that the plague bacillus, which is transmitted by infected fleas on host rats, took endemic form and ravaged various places at various times for the next three centuries. In England, plague struck in thirty of the years between 1351 and 1485; in Florence, in twenty-two years between 1348 and 1500; in Paris, in twenty-two years between 1348 and 1596; in Barcelona, in seventeen years between 1457 and 1590. By 1500 with its population ranging between sixty to seventy million, Europe had not yet recovered even one-half of its 1348 plague losses.

Population recovery depended upon a net increase of births over deaths, but this was a society in which birth and death rates closely approximated each other at thirty to forty per thousand. Because of the high mortality that especially affected children (one out of four died in the first year, and one-half never saw twenty), high fertility was necessary to maintain even stable population levels. Consequently, preindustrial Europe's population structure reflected a young age distribution with one-third or more of the population under fifteen years of age.

Ironically, because the significant measure of economic growth is product per capita, not total product, Europe's high mortality worked to long-term economic advantage. Thus, the economic effects of the devastating population losses from the plague—deserted villages and abandoned marginal land, declining agricultural prices and production, the rising price of manufactured goods, an influx of rural populations to the towns, the loosening of the power of merchant guilds, the incorporation of unskilled workers, and the weakening of the traditional landed nobility vis-à-vis the towns and the new monarchical states—led to a strengthening and rebuilding of social and economic institutions. Although rural debt and sharecropping increased, rural mobility was high as the disparity between legal contracts and enforcement weakened because of the labor shortage. Similarly, in the towns, as a result of labor scarcity and the contraction of wealth into fewer hands, salaries were high, unemployment was low, and both the demand for goods and the standard of living increased. European population decline allowed for the restarting of the economy from a stronger per capita product profile.

Late medieval economic, political, and legal constraints led Europeans to adopt unique marriage patterns and reproduction strategies to control fertility and limit family size to about 4.5 to 5 individuals per household. In northern Europe, delayed age at first marriage for both men (twenty-seven to twenty-nine years) and women (twenty-five to twenty-six years), as well as a relatively high percentage of people who never married, characterized family structure in both town and countryside. The household was the chief unit of economic production with women sharing both labor responsibilities and ownership rights. In urban Italy, in contrast, women tended to marry eight to ten years younger, could expect to bear three more children, and did not share the inheritance rights or management expectations of northern European women. Italian families, even when typically maintaining separate residence, were more closely clan-linked, and these lineages played a dominant role in political, social, and economic activity. In both models, however, patriarchal family organization largely determined women and children's work, the family/household economy, and its place in the structure of market production.

The Division of Labor and Wealth. The division of labor in society extended beyond both gender and the family. In the fifteenth century, urban workers who were engaged in activities relating to food, clothing, and shelter—that is, those activities that commanded about 98 percent of private expenditures—accounted for between 55 and 65 percent of the labor force. Specialized crafts such as metalwork, woodwork, and leatherwork comprised between 15 and 20 percent of the labor market, and miscellaneous workers as much as another 20 percent. Larger towns would boast a significant number of professionals (bankers, lawyers, doctors, notaries) who might reduce the miscellaneous total by 10 percent. All in all, the structure of demand for food, textiles, and construction determined the quantity and quality of production and the need for a diversified labor force.

Merchants, who were specialists in organizing the transport and financial arrangements concomitant with both long-distance trade and the round of innumerable internal fairs and markets, acted as middlemen between producer and consumer. An important development growing out of the merchants' capital accumulation and the immediate cash needs of craftsmen-producers encouraged merchants to advance payment to producers who often fell into indebtedness and dependence upon the merchants. Such economic leverage gradually led to a kind of employer-employee relationship. Craftsmen became wage earners while merchants made managerial decisions and enjoyed the profits. These merchant-capitalists expanded their control over production by circumventing entrenched craftsmen guilds in the towns and seeking employee-producers among seasonally underemployed peasants and agricultural laborers, especially women, in what is called the "domestic," or "putting-out" system. Overseers would provide raw materials, typically fibers for spinning and weaving in textile production, to wage earners working in their own homes. The rise of a wage-earning work force along with the division of labor in society and the emergence of the strong centralized states of the new monarchies were the key fifteenth-century developments fostering the rise of capitalism.

Wealth and income distribution followed occupation. Professionals along with members of the larger textile and merchant guilds stood at the top of the urban social and economic hierarchy. Wealth was concentrated into the hands of the few: the richest 10 percent of the population controlled one-half of the wealth, the next 30 percent about one-quarter of the wealth, and the bottom 60 percent as little as 5 to 20 percent. Typically, 10 to 20 percent of the population could be classified as poor or "beggars." The extreme concentration of the wealthy at the top and the poor at the bottom of the scale emphasizes the incipient nature of middle-class society. At the same time, the sharp distinction in this fifteenth-century urban profile from that of medieval feudal society's rigidified orders (those who prayed, those who fought, and those who worked) makes it clear that the diversification of urban occupations, the immigration from the countryside, and the raising or lowering of families and individuals by fortune or disease contributed to extraordinary social mobility and economic dynamism.

The uncertainty and antagonisms wrought in the transition to the nascent capitalist economies of the late medieval towns, especially by the post-plague social and economic dislocations, often found expression in social conflict. In the town, revolts of craftsmen and skilled workers spread throughout Italy and the Low Countries. In the countryside, social and economic discontent erupted into peasant revolts in Flanders, around Paris, and in England, Bohemia, and Catalonia. Often, as in the eleven major peasant uprisings in Germany in the century before the peasant revolt of 1525, social justice identified with Christianity in a call to traditional values and simple virtues.

Christianity also pricked individual consciences. Christianity denounced the unjust profits of usury, encouraged charitable works, and called for a renunciation of worldly goods. In his 1304–1308 Convivio, Dante allied Christianity with stoicism in articulating the belief that the vagaries of wealth undermined philosophic and spiritual imperatives: true nobility is founded on the principle that all wealth is valueless because it fills humankind inescapably with a never-satisfied lust for new treasures and at the same time with the sad fear of losing that which has been acquired. Thomas More's satiric indictment of European society's greed in his 1516 Utopia called for the abolition of private property based upon the example of native American society gleaned from Amerigo Vespucci's pirated letter describing the "natural man" of the New World. At the same time, countless contrary incantations of the positive connection between civic wealth and virtue filled the air. Leonardo Bruni, the noted early fifteenth-century humanist chancellor of Florence, proclaimed the proud belief that the possessions of the rich were a precondition for the full development of the moral life. Francesco di Marco Datini, the great merchant of Prato who was purported to be the richest man in the world at his death in 1410, linked Christianity and money in his account books, which inscribed a religious formula like "In the name of God and of profit" on the first page of each volume. The uneasy tension in mercantile consciousness between rich and poor or virtue and vice, and the capitalist spirit of worldly asceticism that Max Weber associated with the so-called Protestant ethic of Calvinist culture, long preceded the Reformation; one finds its roots in the conflict between medieval Christianity and the medieval urban revolution.

Such ambivalent mentalities came with the Europeans to the New World as explorers became exploiters seeking gold and souls or slave traders buying and selling native Africans and Americans. In practice, most good intentions of Christian moralists or the reasoned judgments of the neoscholastics of the School of Salamanca were subverted by the extractive greed and paternalistic intransigence of military commanders and missionaries. The intolerant religious zeal of anti-Muslim crusades in the Reconquista and of anti-Jewish bigotry, both exemplified in 1492 by Fernando and Isabel's conquest of Granada and expulsion of the Jews, tied Spanish secular and religious jurisdictions more closely together and carried over to confrontations with native peoples in the overseas expansion.

Despite religious scruples, capital drawn from trade and finance nevertheless continued to fuel the ever-expanding medieval urban revolution. The accumulation of fixed capital that formed the infrastructure of economic life in the city and the countryside had been on the rise from the eleventh century. All fixed capital goods—water mills, windmills, and agricultural buildings such as barns; tools such as shovels, plows, and barrels; livestock for transport, labor, textiles, and meat; and ships, carts, and bridges—remained impervious to the population losses from the plague and again illustrate the importance of per capita measurement.

Organizational and Technological Innovations. Organizational know-how, likewise, facilitated market exchange. Newly developed business techniques were employed—accounting innovations such as modern dating, the introduction of Arabic numerals and double-entry bookkeeping, the check, the endorsement, insurance, commerce manuals, partnership contracts, joint stock companies, the stock exchange, and the central bank. New forms of credit and new forms of partnerships infused money and diffused the expertise of mathematics, literacy, and business entrepreneurship into social and economic institutions.

Technological innovations also contributed to the slow maturation of the medieval economy. Agricultural improvements from the seventh-century diffusion of the heavy plow, eighth-century diffusion of the three-field system, and ninth-century diffusion of the horseshoe and harness for draft animals had contributed to the increasing surpluses to precipitate the urban revolution. Distinctions in northern and southern European agriculture—southern soils limited the range of expansion of the more effective moldboard plow and sparse southern grasslands prevented the substitution of horses for oxen—had a marked effect in creating a long-term productive disadvantage in the primary sector for Mediterranean lands. In the towns, mechanical clocks, developed at the beginning of the fourteenth century, ushered in a worldview distinguishing work hours and merchant time from the seasonal and diurnal rhythms of agricultural labor and the church's agrarian calendar.

From the thirteenth through the fifteenth centuries, technological changes in shipping, navigation, and armaments made water transport more viable, economical, and dominant. Instrumental or mathematical reckoning, facilitated by the development of the magnetic compass, water clock, astrolabe, portolan or naval charts, trigonometric tables, and the sternpost rudder, allowed for greater accuracy in determining position and speed plus the reduction of idle time in winter. Improvements in hull design and shipyard division of labor like that of the Venetian Arsenal, the greatest "factory" system in preindustrial Europe, reduced shipbuilding costs and time. After 1440, the Portuguese lateen-rigged caravel, a ship with triangular sails and a narrower hull, had the ability to utilize both following and contrary winds and to maneuver safely in the open seas and in coastal waters. Finally, the "full-rigged" ship combined the Atlantic and Mediterranean technologies: nautical instruments and the carvel-built hull with a new sail configuration of three masts with a large square sail on the mainmast, a smaller square sail on the foremast, and a lateen (triangular) sail on the mizzen (aft) mast. With the adaptation of artillery, which had been developed along with gunpowder in China and transmitted across the Eurasian steppes, the revolution in military technology that had already affected land warfare and was beginning to undermine the social hierarchy of knight-dominated armies completed the powerful naval tool necessary for long-distance trade and expansion.

A similar confluence of innovations led to the printed book. Paper came to Europe in the thirteenth century from China. Water mills provided the energy to power machines to pulp rags for paper production. Printing also made its way to Europe, again from China; and the application of movable type by the mid-fifteenth century revolutionized the dissemination of information. Between 1450 and 1500, presses in twelve countries had printed millions of books in forty thousand editions. Renaissance ideas, religious reform, and scientific knowledge all spread widely and penetrated deeply into society because of printing.

Wars, Conquests, and Colonization. Not by chance, over two-thirds of fifteenth-century book production came from Italy and Germany. Not only were these two regions cornerstones of the southern and northern trading systems, but the size of their polities, government economic policy, and the devastating wars occupying England, France, and Iberia worked to German and Italian advantage in the late fifteenth century. Since capitalist enterprise arose piecemeal, the economies of scale offered by city-states and small principalities in Italy and Germany nurtured the development of the requisite commerce and industry because mercantile elites were able to play such an important role in decision making. At the same time, war disrupted France and England during the Hundred Years' War (1337–1453) and then afterward tore them apart internally in civil wars during the English War of the Roses (1455–1485) and, especially during the Burgundian wars, in the reconstruction of a French kingdom under Louis XI (1461–1483). In Iberia, similarly, twenty years of civil wars devastated Castile and Catalonia from the 1460s through the disputed succession (1475–1479) of Enrique

IV of Castile. Like famine and disease, war and politics had an important effect upon social and economic structures.

During the Italian peace between 1454 and 1494, established as a defensive alliance after the Ottoman conquest of Constantinople, the wealth of the Italian cities increased, but Italy became a tempting prize for conquest. The 1494 Italian invasions initiated a long struggle for Italy between the new monarchies of France and Spain not settled until the Battle of Pavia in 1525. South German bankers like the Fuggers of Augsburg, who based their wealth on mercantile ties to the core of the two trading systems at Venice and Antwerp and on central European mining, exerted their greatest influence between 1490 and 1525, during the Italian wars and before the Reformation. Reformation wars in Germany, religious wars in France, and the revolt of the Netherlands not only cost lives but also consumed the finances of the new Valois and Habsburg monarchies in the sixteenth century.

The political clout of the new monarchies had been built on their own manpower and resource needs. Portugal's poverty, its small population of one million, and its Atlantic-facing position pushed it first to seek agricultural resources in North Africa, the Atlantic islands, and along the West African coast. Madeira (1420), the Azores (1425), and the Cape Verde Islands (1455) were stepping-stones of conquest and colonization on the way to an African, Brazilian, and South Asian empire. Royal monopolies on gold, slaves (some 150,000 Africans between 1450 and 1500), spices, ivory, and the rights of export and reexport bolstered the strength of the Aviz dynasty, which had come to power in opposition to the old nobility in 1385. Genoese capital helped finance sugar plantations and the slave trade and promoted the sale of African pepper to compete with Asian pepper imported by the Venetians. The Portuguese traded this sugar and pepper first at Bruges and after 1488 at Antwerp.

Spain's success resulted from the marriage between the Aragonese commercial empire plied by Catalan merchants in the western Mediterranean and Castilian population, fiscal, and agricultural resources. The Catholic monarchs, Fernando and Isabel, continued previous government policy in an impoverished kingdom with eight million inhabitants unable to provision a city large enough to sustain the royal court full time for the entire year. In Castile, agricultural production was subordinated to pastoral interests because of the profits to be made from the wool trade to Flanders and Italy and the taxes to be garnered from sheep owners. The large pastoral investors drawn from the nobility and religious institutions thus allied with the Crown to inhibit native textile industries and local town growth. Spanish social organization remained rigidly hierarchical and disproportionately stratified with 2 to 3 percent of the population owning 97

percent of the land. In Aragón, the 1462–1472 civil war revealed the weakness of a kingdom in decline from erosion of its trading empire by the Genoese, from peasant uprisings against the feudal nobility, and from town cleavage between the urban patriciate and small-scale merchants and artisans. The Union of the Crowns, nevertheless, allowed Aragonese economic institutions and bureaucratic expertise to channel Castilian dynamism. Spanish merchants operated in the Medina del Campo fair, the Burgos wool monopoly, and the iron and shipping industries of Bilbao on the north coast. In the South, the Genoese maintained their dominance in New World shipping and finance from Seville through a relationship forged long before the discoveries. Despite the booming sixteenth-century Spanish economy based on New World wealth, Spanish social and economic institutions enjoyed only a transitory success. State expenditures on military ventures, price inflation, and weakening agricultural and industrial production undermined their viability. Real economic dynamism flowed to the Spanish possessions in the Low Countries.

There, Antwerp benefited from products of the old Hansa network, from the English wool staple, from both Bavarian and Genoese financial backing, and from the decline of its neighbor, Bruges. It was able to attract the products from Portuguese and Spanish expansion and become sixteenth-century Europe's most important entrepôt, growing spectacularly from 17,000 inhabitants in 1437 to 50,000 in 1500 and 100,000 in 1555. Antwerp declined only during the revolt of the Netherlands between 1572 and 1585 and gave way to Amsterdam in the seventeenth century.

Europe in 1500, at first contact with the Americas and direct maritime contact with Asia, then, was in the midst of a significant demographic and economic recovery from the previous downturn. For about the first century of the new economic cycle, growth was self-generated and self-sustained. By 1560 when New World products had begun to exert substantial impact upon the Old World, Europe had surpassed fourteenth-century population levels and growth continued until the economic slide after 1620. The period of European expansion thus ran parallel with the two-hundred-year economic cycle of 1450 to 1650. That economic cycle owed its origins to the reorganization of social and economic institutions after the dislocations of the fourteenth-century crisis. It maintained itself through the early seventeenth century on overseas extraction and exploitation, especially African gold and American silver. It faltered in the seventeenth-century collapse of financial markets, in the stalling of commerce and industry, in the political crisis of the Spanish imperial system, and in the dissolutions of the Thirty Years' War (1619–1648) that led to Dutch and English ascendance.

The economic cycle of 1450 to 1650 witnessed the ever-increasing drive of capitalist enterprise and a reorientation of the northern and southern medieval trading networks into a single world economic system with a core in northwestern Europe. The earlier progression of agricultural productivity, urban growth, labor differentiation, and long-distance trade continued to make modern Europe. European social and economic institutions, part and parcel of the new centralized states, added newly transformed technologies unknowingly derived from China (the compass, gunpowder, and printing) to their arsenal. Europeans thus imposed their social and economic institutions, as much as their mentalities, on populations and landscapes in Africa, America, and Asia as they took over old networks, established new ones, and took off toward capitalism, industrialization, and world hegemony.

[For further discussion of innovation in European culture at the time of Columbus, see *Navigation; Political Institutions; Printing; Religion,* article on *European Traditions; Science; Shipbuilding; Timetelling; Trade.* For discussion of American cultures and societies of the period, see *Agriculture; Indian America; Religion,* article on *Amerindian Traditions.*]

BIBLIOGRAPHY

General

Abu-Lughod, Janet L. *Before European Hegemony: The World System A.D. 1250–1350.* New York and Oxford, 1989.

Braudel, Fernand. *Civilization and Capitalism 15th–18th Century.* Translated by Siân Reynolds. 3 vols. New York, 1981–1984.

Braudel, Fernand. *The Mediterranean and the Mediterranean World in the Age of Philip II.* Translated by Siân Reynolds. 2 vols. 2d ed. New York, 1972–1973.

Cipolla, Carlo M. *Before the Industrial Revolution: European Society and Economy, 1000–1700.* 2d ed. New York and London, 1980.

Cipolla, Carlo M., ed. *The Fontana Economic History of Europe.* 6 vols. Vol. 1, *The Middle Ages.* Glasgow, 1972. Vol. 2, *The Sixteenth and Seventeenth Centuries.* Glasgow, 1974.

Davis, Ralph. *The Rise of the Atlantic Economies.* Ithaca, 1973.

Goldthwaite, Richard A., ed. "Recent Trends in Renaissance Studies: Economic History." *Renaissance Quarterly* 42 (Winter 1989): 760–825.

Howell, Martha C. *Women, Production, and Patriarchy in Late Medieval Cities.* Chicago, 1986.

Jones, E. L. *The European Miracle: Environments, Economies and Geopolitics in the History of Europe and Asia.* 2d ed. Cambridge, 1987.

Miskimin, Harry A. *The Economy of Early Renaissance Europe, 1300–1460.* Cambridge, 1975.

Miskimin, Harry A. *The Economy of Later Renaissance Europe, 1460–1600.* Cambridge, 1977.

Wallerstein, Immanuel. *Capitalist Agriculture and the Origins of the European World-Economy in the Sixteenth Century.* Vol. 1 of *The Modern World-System.* New York, 1974.

Wolf, Eric R. *Europe and the People without History.* Berkeley and Los Angeles, 1982.

Spain

MacKay, Angus. "Recent Literature on Spanish Economic History." *Economic History Review* 31, no. 1 (1978): 129–145.

Phillips, Carla Rahn. "Time and Duration: A Model for the Economy of Early Modern Spain." *American Historical Review* 92, no. 3 (1987): 531–562.

JOHN A. MARINO

SOLAR PHENOMENA. The sun was still considered a planet when Christopher Columbus began his voyages in the hope of reaching India by following the apparent course of the sun. The two solar phenomena important in Columbus's lifetime were the apparent circular movement of the sun and, less important, solar eclipses.

The circular movement of the sun was essential to determining latitude. Astronomers drew up tables that gave the solar declinations for each day of one year. Observers saw the position of the sun in the ecliptic and observed its meridian height. If they knew the declination, using the information in the tables, and by means of simple arithmetical calculations, they ascertained their latitude. Quadrants and astrolabes were used for these observations; cross-staffs were introduced later.

The traditional solar tables, such as Abraham Zacuto's *Almanach perpetuum coelestium motium* (Perpetual almanac of the heavenly bodies, 1496), however, did not give declinations directly or did not give them at all. In the former case, users of Zacuto's work first consulted a table that offered the "position" of the sun—in degrees, minutes, and seconds—in a given zodiacal sign; this position corresponded to its celestial longitude. Finally, observers used a table of declinations to calculate this celestial coordinate. This procedure required more complicated arithmetical calculations (multiplication and division) that were often difficult for observers in the fifteenth century.

Tables with this structure were used by some pilots. Francisco Rodrigues mentions them in a short guide to navigation appended to the *Suma oriental* (Oriental summa) by Tomé Pires (c. 1515). We know that the cosmographer Pedro Nunes recommended that navigators use this type of table, but in practice a good arithmetician who knew how to do the necessary operations worked out simpler tables of declinations for all the days in one or four years on which navigators could read directly the solar coordinates relative to their position.

A table of the first type can be found in the *Guia náutico de munique* (Nautical guide of Munique) and was reproduced by Francisco Rodrigues. There are also fragments of quadrennial tables for the late fifteenth and the sixteenth centuries. One for the four years between 1497 and 1500 could have been used by Vasco da Gama's pilot. One of the most widespread tables was that for 1517 to 1520, the work of Gaspar Nicolas, the author of the first arithmetical book published in Portugal (1519).

Tables were worked out for four-year periods. They could be corrected at the end of the year or of the quadrennium, but this did not always happen. Thus, many quadrennial tables continued to be used well beyond the limits of their validity, requiring that observers perform further calculations to correct them. Using out-of-date tables compromised the exactness of the latitudes calculated from them.

Christopher Columbus must have known how to obtain geographical latitude by observing the sun. In one of the books that may have belonged to him, there is a handwritten note referring to the procedure, though there is doubt that the handwriting is Columbus's. Columbus was, however, familiar with Portuguese pilots and sailed in Portuguese ships to Guinea. In sailing from Europe to the Antilles, he tried to navigate at a constant latitude, using observations of the polestar to determine latitude.

Solar eclipses, like lunar eclipses, could be observed to determine geographical longitude by noting the local time of the beginning of the eclipse in the place of the observation and comparing it with the time reported in a reference table. Although Petrus Apianus (Peter Bennewitz, 1501–1552) refers to solar eclipses in his *Cosmographia* (Cosmography, 1524) as the best means to determine longitude, the method was prone to error and even Columbus made a major error when he attempted to use it.

BIBLIOGRAPHY

Albuquerque, Luís de. *Astronomical Navigation*. Lisbon, 1988.
Cotter, Charles A. *A History of Nautical Astronomy*. London, 1968.
Taylor, E. G. R. *The Haven-Finding Art: A History of Navigation from Odysseus to Captain Cook*. Rev. ed. London, 1971.
Waters, David W. *The Art of Navigation in England in Elizabethan and Early Stuart Times*. London, 1958.

LUÍS DE ALBUQUERQUE
Translated from Portuguese by Paola Carù

REPORT OF THE EXPLORATIONS OF DE SOTO. Published in Evora, Portugal, 1557. This title page reads: "A truthful report of the work that the Governor Hernando de Soto and certain Portuguese gentlemen performed in the discovery of the province of Florida."

COURTESY OF THE JOHN CARTER BROWN LIBRARY, BROWN UNIVERSITY

SOTO, HERNANDO DE

SOTO, HERNANDO DE (1497?–1542), Spanish explorer. De Soto, born in Extremadura, went with the expedition of Pedro Arias de Ávila (Pedrárias Dávila) to Costa Rica in 1513–1514. Schooled under this infamous soldier, De Soto spent his late teens mastering horsemanship, weaponry, and the art of conquering Indians. By his early twenties, he exhibited the traits for which he would be famous: he was independent, headstrong, a superb horseman, a good commander, and fearless in battle.

Following Columbus's voyages, Spain sought to penetrate the interior of the newly discovered continents. De Soto played a role in conquering and exploring more territory than any of his contemporaries. He participated as a very young man in the conquest of Costa Rica and later, in 1524, in the conquest of Nicaragua. From 1531 to 1535 he was one of the principal players in the conquest of the Incas. He is best known, however, for his exploration of the present-day southern United States in 1539 to 1542.

In 1536, after the conquest of the Incas, De Soto returned to Spain an exceedingly wealthy man and married Isabel de Bobadilla, daughter of Governor Pedrárias. But De Soto was not content to remain in Spain. He wanted a governorship of his own and the honor that would come from commanding a major expedition of exploration and conquest.

In 1537 De Soto was granted the right to conquer La Florida—an indefinite area of North America that at this time had been explored only along the Gulf and Atlantic coasts. Appointed governor of Cuba and adelantado of La Florida, De Soto landed with more than six hundred persons at Tampa Bay in May 1539. The expedition proceeded to the chiefdom of Apalachee in present-day Tallahassee, where it wintered. In the spring of 1540 the expedition proceeded northeastward through Georgia to the chiefdom of Cofitachequi in South Carolina; from there they turned northward, crossed the Appalachian Mountains, and then circled back through northwestern Georgia and central Alabama before continuing on to the chiefdom of Chicaca, west of Columbus, Mississippi, where they spent the winter of 1540–1541. In the spring they traveled northwestward, discovered and crossed the Mississippi River a few miles south of present-day Memphis, explored northern Arkansas, and then turned southwestward, skirting the Ozark Mountains. They ascended the Arkansas River before looping southward through the Ouachita Mountains and again returned to the Arkansas River, where they spent the winter of 1541–1542.

In the spring of 1542 they traveled to Guachoya, just below the junction of the Arkansas and Mississippi rivers. Here De Soto realized that there was no society comparable to that of the Aztecs or Incas in La Florida, and therefore his expedition was a hopeless failure and he was ruined. At this point he caught a fever, it is said, and died. The survivors of the expedition then attempted to reach New Spain (Mexico) by traveling overland through Texas. But midway they realized they would starve if they continued, so they returned to the Mississippi River where they spent the winter of 1542–1543 building boats. The next summer they sailed down the river and reached New Spain. Only about half of the original force had survived.

[See also *Indian America,* article on *Indians of La Florida.*]

BIBLIOGRAPHY

Albornoz, Miguel. *Hernando de Soto: Knight of the Americas.* New York, 1986.

Hudson, Charles. "A Synopsis of the Hernando de Soto Expedition, 1539–1543." In *De Soto Trail.* National Park Service, 1990.

Lockhart, James. *The Men of Cajamarca.* Austin, Texas, 1972.

Rubio, Rocio Sanchez. *Hernando de Soto.* Cuadernos Populares, no. 25. Mérida (Badajoz), 1988.

Swanton, John R. *Final Report of the United States De Soto Expedition Commission.* Washington, D.C., 1985.

CHARLES HUDSON

SOUTHERN CROSS. The constellation of the Southern Cross was generally unknown in Europe until the fifteenth century, when exploration along the African coast brought European sailors to relatively low latitudes in the Northern Hemisphere. The first navigator to mention it was the Venetian Alvise Cadamosto, who traveled to the coast of Guinea twice in the 1450s, under the sponsorship of Prince Henry the Navigator. The drawing of the constellation that appears in his report does not represent the Southern Cross accurately (though the only surviving copy dates from the late fifteenth century). He calls it the Southern Chariot because it was used in navigation in a way similar to the Northern Chariot (one of the names of Ursa Minor).

The Southern Cross was next represented more than forty years later in a letter sent to King Manuel I from Pôrto Seguro (Brazil) by Mestre José, the king's astrologist and doctor, who had sailed with Pedro Álvares Cabral. In this letter, written in an unrefined Castilian, Mestre José (perhaps a converted Castilian Jew) includes a representation of the southern stars, among them the Southern Cross. His main preoccupation was to designate a star (probably a star in either Octans or Hydrus, which are closer to the South Pole than the Southern Cross is) that could serve as a polestar for navigators in the Southern Hemisphere and to provide a *regimento* (set of rules) similar to the northern *regimento.* Later *regimentos,* such as *Guia náutico de Munique* (Nautical guide of Munique) and *Guia náutico de Evora* (Nautical guide of Evora) omit all mention of the Southern Cross.

The oldest reference to the Southern Cross is found in the *Tratado da agulha de marear* (Treatise on the nautical pointers), a short but significant text (despite its errors) summarized by the famous pilot João de Lisboa, probably before 1508. He knew the "body of rules" and represented the constellation in two engravings (one of which contains numerical errors.) He refers to how the rules can be used, not only to determine latitudes at night, but also to define the local meridian line, and therefore to know the value of the declination of the compass.

Andrea Cosali drew the Southern Cross in a letter (1515) addressed to Duke Giuliano de' Medici that was reproduced by Battista Ramusio in *Navigationi et viaggi* (Navigations and voyages; first edition, 1551). Cosali's sketch of the stars is evidence of the fascination that the Cross held for voyagers of the time. The drawing was reproduced in 1600 by Francisco da Costa in *Arte de navegar* (Art of navigation).

The text of this set of rules never filtered into cosmographers' works during the sixteenth century, but it frequently appeared in the *livros de marinharia* (books of navigation) attributed to various pilots. These works can be found as well in a large number of atlases, in which astronomical data that could be of interest to pilots were included. They are usually referred to as the "body of rules of the sun," the "body of rules of the polestar," and as the "body of rules of the Cross."

BIBLIOGRAPHY

Albuquerque, Luís de. *Astronomical Navigation*. Lisbon, 1988.

Costa, A. Fontoura da. *A marinharia dos descobrimentos*. 2d ed. Lisbon, 1939.

Cotter, Charles A. *A History of Nautical Astronomy*. London, 1968.

Randles, W. G. L. *Portuguese and Spanish Attempts to Measure Longitude in the 16th Century*. Coimbra, 1985.

Taylor, E. G. R. *The Haven-Finding Art: A History of Navigation from Odysseus to Captain Cook*. Rev. ed. London, 1971.

LUÍS DE ALBUQUERQUE
Translated from Portuguese by Paola Carù

SPAIN. In the fourteenth century, the Iberian Peninsula experienced the same catastrophes as the rest of Europe: epidemics of bubonic plague, crop failures, depopulated towns, civil wars, and business bankruptcies. The medieval society organized for war crumbled under the impact of these disasters. Out of the ruins, Spaniards during the fifteenth century created a new society organized for peace. The innovation and stability that enabled Spain to explore and settle the Americas grew out of its experience as a society that reconstructed itself during the Renaissance.

Six separate medieval monarchies coalesced during the

fifteenth century to form Spain. They were bonded together by a single ruling family, the Trastámara, an illegitimate branch of the Castilian royal family that had seized the throne of Castile during a brutal civil war between 1366 and 1369. In 1412, a brother of the Trastámara king of Castile was elected king of Aragón, Catalonia, and Valencia, and his descendants inherited the Kingdom of Navarre. When Isabel, crown princess of Castile, married Fernando, crown prince of Aragón, in 1469, they reunited the Trastámara dynasty, and went on to conquer a sixth monarchy, the Muslim Kingdom of Granada, in 1492. The individual monarchies in the union retained separate laws, customs, and languages, while their combined strengths enabled the Trastámara monarchs to pursue a single-minded policy of expansion. Aragonese commerce expanded east into the Mediterranean, and Castilian commerce turned west into the Atlantic.

The part of Spain that refashioned itself most successfully was the Kingdom of Castile, which became one of the largest, most populous, and dynamic countries of Europe. By 1530, Castile's population numbered six million, while all the other Spanish kingdoms together counted one and a half million inhabitants. The most important impetus to Castile's growth was a legal fact: Castilians were free men and women. Serfdom never developed in Castile, and King Fernando extended this freedom to the serfs of Aragón in 1485. The Spanish monarchs never allowed their subjects to be enslaved and, by royal decree in 1500, guaranteed this legal freedom to their American Indian subjects. Royal policy toward nonsubjects, however, was the opposite: non-Christians captured in war and subjects who rebelled against the royal sovereignty could be enslaved. And the monarchs permitted the purchase of African slaves from the Portuguese, who held a monopoly on slaving in sub-Saharan Africa.

Whether noble or freemen, clergy or farmers, Spaniards lived in cities, towns, and villages. Nearly all the land of Spain was incorporated in municipalities—more than 32,000 of them. The isolated farmhouse in the countryside was the rare exception. Those few people whose occupations required them to live outside of towns were regarded as outside the norms of society. Roadside innkeepers, millers, and shepherds were often depicted in popular and high literature as lecherous, venal, and violent. The fictional Don Quixote's bizarre adventures could have taken place only outside the norm of municipal life.

Spaniards were free citizens of their home cities, towns, and villages. Virtually every notarial document of the period began "I, John Doe, citizen of the town of X, and I, Jane Smith, his wife and citizen of the town of X, do hereby . . . ." These citizens governed themselves through

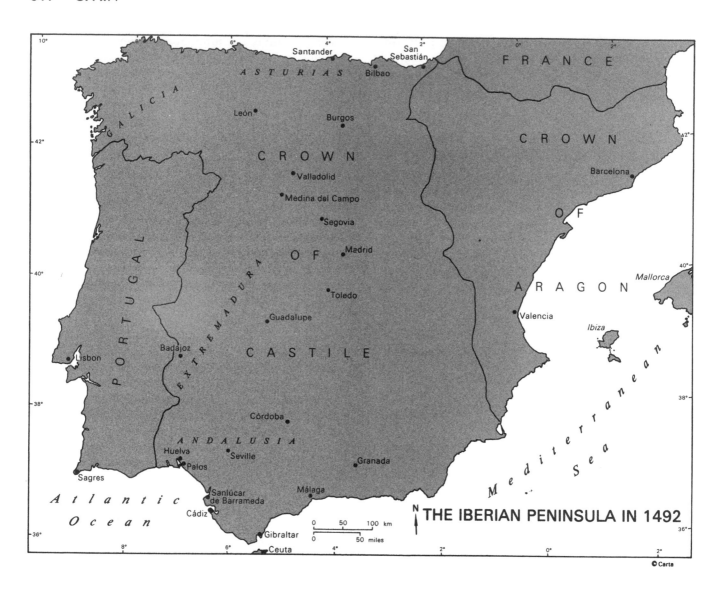

THE IBERIAN PENINSULA IN 1492

© Carta

democratic town meetings and elected town councils and judges. Each citizen's household possessed a vote, but only married men had the right to cast the vote in town meetings and to hold municipal office. Women could speak in town meetings but could not hold office or vote. Widows possessed the vote of their household but had to ask a male proxy—usually a son or the town judge—to cast their vote. Unmarried males could not vote or hold office.

The economic consequence of this free population living in self-administering municipalities was that Spanish farmers and workers were not subject to forced labor service. Farmers, who comprised over 90 percent of the population, owned their own land, lived in town, and walked out to their fields to plow, plant, and harvest. Their farming produced the staples of the Spanish diet: wheat for bread, olive oil for cooking, grapes for wine, and pork for hams and sausages. Women provided most of the

variety in the diet: they made cheese and raised the chickens and eggs that supplied most of the animal protein and cultivated gardens of legumes, green vegetables, and seasonings. During slack seasons, farmers worked as textile manufacturers, fishermen, teamsters, building contractors, livestock breeders, tanners, cabinetmakers, and soldiers, while day in and day out women spun raw wool, flax, and silk into thread.

The town council provided for the common welfare by inspecting weights and measures in the marketplace (*plaza*), hiring the town schoolteacher, and building hospitals, schools, fountains, laundries, and churches. The council managed and developed the economic infrastructure of the town's farmland by constructing dams, roads, bridges, mills, and irrigation systems. The town sheriff arrested suspects and brought them before the town judge, who heard cases, pronounced sentence, and imposed fines and punishments.

There were no regional governments (provinces were not created until the nineteenth century), so the monarchy depended on municipal governments to carry out royal policy at the local level. City and town councils wrote directly to the kings when they were carrying out their administrative duties, creating a vast treasure of testimony about everyday life witnessed by ordinary citizens. Trastámara monarchs encouraged towns and cities to form cooperative law courts (hermandades) for judging cases involving fugitives and livestock that crossed municipal boundaries. In the sixteenth century, the Habsburg kings depended on city and town councils to collect the royal taxes.

Every city and town had its own constitution (*fuero*) that defined its relationship with the king or lord and contained the municipal ordinances governing elections, commerce, contracts, and inheritance. Despite the number and diversity of law codes, an ideal of equality prevailed in the inheritance laws throughout the Spanish kingdoms. In general, all the children of a marriage, both male and female, had the right to inherit equitable portions of their parents' property. Parents could not favor one child over another nor could they exclude a child, except in extreme cases such as a child who attempted to murder a parent. Because these laws of partible inheritance were mandatory and enforced by the town judge, parents had no need to draw up wills, which were extremely rare in the fifteenth century.

These institutions and customs that were most effective in rebuilding Castile shaped Spanish settlement in America. Because town life was the norm for Spaniards, they could not conceive of a civilization without municipalities and, when they did not find towns in the Caribbean, they proceeded to build them. Spaniards founded twenty-seven towns and cities on the islands of La Española, Cuba, Puerto Rico, and Jamaica between 1496 and 1515. In between the hundreds of Indian cities and towns that already existed in central Mexico, they established another fifteen Spanish towns and cities between 1519 and 1531. Spanish America came to be, like Spain itself, a few large cities surrounded by hundreds of smaller, autonomous towns.

Enjoying legal freedom and engaging in wide-flung business enterprises, Spaniards were notorious travelers. They went as pilgrims to the Holy Land, pirates to Africa, sailors to the North Atlantic fishing banks, university students to France and Italy, churchmen to Rome and Avignon, ambassadors to Denmark, Bohemia, England, and Florence, and merchants to the trading centers of Bruges, London, and Bordeaux. At home in Spain, farmers traveled to other towns to buy and sell, to shrines for pilgrimages, to the mountains for summer pasture, to less populous regions to start new lives.

SPAIN AS THE HEAD OF EUROPE. Engraving from Sebastian Münster's *Cosmographia*, 1527. ELSEVIER PUBLISHING PROJECTS, AMSTERDAM

With travel came infections. Spain suffered the same diseases as the rest of Europe during the Renaissance, an age of unprecedented epidemics. The Black Death epidemic of bubonic plague in 1348–1350 caused up to 40 percent overall mortality in large cities, and as much as 60 percent mortality in smaller towns and villages. After that first epidemic, bubonic plague appeared in Europe at least once every generation between 1350 and 1720. Castile suffered huge population losses from plague epidemics in 1575–1577, 1596, 1601–1602, and 1630. Other infectious diseases had equally disastrous effects. An influenza pandemic in 1580 resembled the devastating influenza of 1918, in that morbidity and mortality were high among young adults, leaving a reduced number of adults of child-bearing age to replace the population lost in the bubonic plague epidemics over the next fifty years. One of the new infectious diseases was typhus, believed to have been brought to Spain and Italy in the late fifteenth century through warfare against the Turks in the Mediterranean. The chronicler Andrés Bernáldez and most of his parishioners were afflicted by this new disease in 1507, during an epidemic that swept through Castile killing about 40 percent of the population in the cities and towns it reached. The record of epidemics of smallpox in Europe and Spain is negligible before the 1560s; a milder strain of smallpox probably prevailed. Virulent smallpox entered Spain in the early seventeenth century, and held a prominent place among diseases of the seventeenth and eighteenth centuries.

No segment of the population escaped the ravages of disease. The early Trastámara monarchs were afflicted with tuberculosis, which carried them off at an average age of thirty-seven. Their successors, the Habsburg monarchs, suffered agonies with tubercular joints and respiratory crises, and more than a dozen royal children died before reaching adulthood. Whole families of aristocratic children died of smallpox during the seventeenth century, leaving a handful of lucky distant cousins to inherit multiple noble titles and vast fortunes. The flower of Castilian manhood died of influenza without ever seeing battle in the invasion of Portugal in 1580. The great city of Barcelona never recovered the population, manufacturing, and commercial losses it suffered as a result of bubonic plague deaths in the fourteenth century. In the Extremadura farm town of Cabeza de Vaca, so few citizens survived the epidemic of 1507 that they decided the place was unhealthful; they tore down the houses, salted the ground, and moved to other towns.

These demographic losses opened the way for new economic leaders. Some of Spain's most spectacular fortunes in wool, international trade, and landed estates started from modest beginnings in the early fifteenth century when Castile regained its pre–Black Death population levels and embarked on nearly a century of domestic growth. With rising fortunes came upward social mobility. Successful farmers became wealthy businessmen; they used their plow mules and oxen to transport their produce to the cities, sold it, used the profits to buy city goods, and sold these back in their home towns.

Some Spaniards did not need to be citizens of municipalities. They were the tax-exempt (hidalgo) upper classes: officers and officials who administered the royal household and court, nobles who gave military and diplomatic service to the king, and clergy. Yet like other Spaniards they resided in cities and towns. They also participated in the social mobility of the age. Soldiers rose to become knights, knights rose to become well-rewarded commanders, and victorious commanders became nobles.

Just as Spain was a monarchy of cities and towns, a

Top Grandees of Castile in 1520

Title	Date	Family	Annual Income in Ducats
Constable of Castile	1492	Velasco	50,000
Admiral of Castile	1405	Enríquez	32,000
Dukes			
Alba	1465	Toledo	30,000
Infantado	1475	Mendoza	30,000
Medina Sidonia	1445	Guzmán	50,000
Béjar	1485	Zúñiga	24,000
Medinaceli	1479	La Cerda	16,000
Alburquerque	1464	La Cueva	24,000
Arcos	1493	Ponce de León	30,000
Escalona	1472	Pacheco	24,000

noble estate was a cluster of towns. Trastámara monarchs gave away the government of royal towns as hereditary property to the military leaders who helped them gain the throne in the civil war. To ensure that these new seignorial towns would remain in loyal hands, the Trastámara monarchs required that they be placed in perpetual trusts (*mayorazgos*), of which the monarchs were the trustees and the new lords were the beneficiaries.

After 1400, the monarchs introduced another innovation, giving hereditary noble titles to lords of seignorial towns. The first hereditary title was count of Alba, granted in 1439 by King Juan II and elevated to duke of Alba in 1465 by King Enrique IV. In 1400 Castile had fewer than a dozen titled nobles; by the end of the century, the kingdom boasted more than one hundred. In 1520, Charles V ranked the titled nobles and designated the wealthiest as grandees. The dates when those hereditary noble titles were created, and the size of their annual incomes by 1520, shown in the accompanying table, indicate how quickly social status and financial fortunes were changing in fifteenth-century Castile.

The grandees of Castile were a new nobility, and thus Columbus's ambition to achieve noble status was a realistic and attainable goal. Although Fernando and Isabel refused to give hereditary lordship in the Americas to anyone, Spaniard or Indian, they did give the conquerors lifetime lordship (encomienda) over Indian towns. And their grandson, Charles V, gave two hereditary lordships in the Americas: in 1529 he gave the conqueror of Mexico, Hernando Cortés, hereditary lordship over the valley of Oaxaca, with the title "marquis of the Valley," and in 1537 he named Columbus's grandson duke of Veragua (modern Panama) and marquis of Jamaica.

The Castilian language in the fifteenth century displayed this same dynamism and, like the municipal tradition, gave cultural unity to both Spain and Spanish America. The vernacular had been the language of government and law since the thirteenth century, when the king decreed the dialect of Toledo to be the standard by which contracts and laws would be interpreted in litigation. Latin continued as the language of church, university, and foreign diplomacy, but it became a dying language, replaced by the Castilian vernacular in literature, government, and law courts.

Portugal and Aragón also abandoned Latin as an official language in the thirteenth century, but sheer numbers of population gave Castilian vernacular dominance in the peninsula. At the end of the fifteenth century, four-fifths of the inhabitants of Spain spoke Castilian. Castilian served as the most common language for intrapeninsular transactions, by its very prestige and ubiquity inspiring bilingualism even in the Portuguese authors of the period. By the beginning of the fifteenth century, Castilians developed their own Renaissance in literature, launching a ''golden century'' of poetry, chronicles, novels, and plays. In 1492, the Spanish humanist Antonio de Nebrija published a grammar of the Castilian language—the first grammar of a European vernacular—and dedicated it to Queen Isabel with the reminder that Castilian would be to Spain's empire as Latin had been to Rome's.

By virtue of its diffusion within the peninsula and its status as a literary and official language, Castilian in the fifteenth century had already developed into the modern language of nearly all Spaniards. Speakers of the modern language find little difficulty in reading Renaissance Castilian, in contrast to the vernaculars of the other countries of western Europe, which continued to use Latin in legal proceedings until well into the seventeenth century. The mobility of the Castilian people imparted a remarkable uniformity to the language despite the many political differences that separated one region from another. Even the minor dialects that persisted into the fifteenth century were mutually intelligible. Genoese and Venetians might have had difficulty finding a common comprehensible dialect of Italian; Florentine poets might have had to choose between writing in Latin, which could be read throughout Italy, or their local dialect, which was easily understood only in Tuscany. Castilian authors did not have to make such choices. And even a Genoese merchant long resident in Portugal might easily have found himself most comfortable writing in Castilian.

Along with these traditional social and cultural bonds, Spaniards shared a lively curiosity for the new and exotic. Spanish merchants traveled the markets of Europe to satisfy an almost compulsive taste for novelty among Spanish consumers. They sent back cloth and hats in the Burgundian fashion, spices and aromatics from Venetian warehouses in the eastern Mediterranean, novels of chivalry from France, and Renaissance poetry from Italy.

THE ESCORIAL. Palace and monastery intended to serve as the court of the kings of Spain. Built by Philip II between 1563 and 1584, it was one of the most ambitious architectural undertakings of the Renaissance.

ELSEVIER PUBLISHING PROJECTS, AMSTERDAM

International artists found ready markets in Spain for their skills. Musicians, painters, and architects from the Netherlands, England, and Germany were the rage in the reign of Fernando and Isabel. Moral conservatives who fought against luxurious dress found no fault with foreign styles, as long as they were not extravagant.

Spain had long been one of the great seafaring nations of Europe; by the end of the fifteenth century, it had become a leader in the new enterprise of exploring the Atlantic. Through its Renaissance transformation into a society organized for peace, Spain went beyond exploration to take the lead in colonizing the Americas.

[See also *Barcelona; Columbus, Christopher,* articles on *Columbus in Spain, The Final Years, Illness and Death; Colonization,* article on *Spanish Colonization; Córdoba; Granada; Isabel and Fernando; Jews,* article on *Expulsion from Spain; Madrid; Muslims in Spain; Reconquista; Seville; Toledo; Valencia; Valladolid.*]

BIBLIOGRAPHY

Carmichael, Ann G., and Arthur M. Silverstein. "Smallpox in Europe before the Seventeenth Century: Virulent Killer or Benign Disease?" *Journal of the History of Medicine and Allied Sciences* 42 (1987): 147–168.

Ladero Quesada, Miguel Angel. *Spain in 1492.* Bloomington, Ind., forthcoming.

McAlister, Lyle N. *Spain and Portugal in the New World, 1492–1700.* Minneapolis, 1984.

Nader, Helen. *Liberty in Absolutist Spain: The Habsburg Sale of Towns, 1516–1700.* Baltimore, 1990.

Nader, Helen. *The Mendoza Family in the Spanish Renaissance, 1350 to 1550.* New Brunswick, N. J., 1979.

Pérez Moreda, Vicente. *Las crisis de mortalidad en la España interior, siglos XVI–XIX.* Madrid, 1980.

Phillips, William D., Jr. *Slavery from Roman Times to the Early Transatlantic Trade.* Minneapolis, 1985.

Vassberg, David. *Land and Society in Golden Age Castile.* Cambridge, 1984.

HELEN NADER

SPICES. Throughout history, spices have been used as drugs, foods, preservatives, and cosmetics. From prehistory to the Age of Exploration in the sixteenth century, the demand for spices contributed to the development of intercontinental trade and even influenced the rise and fall of nations. The terms for spices in English and many other languages have a broader application than the modern meanings. A number of products were called spices that are today called aromatics, condiments, perfumes, cosmetics, preservatives, and, above all, drugs. Pharmaceutical uses were primary in accounting for their value. Because the spice products are often derived from plants that are grown only in specific locations, the trade in spices was a significant part of the international and intercontinental trade prior to the Industrial Revolution. Columbus's voyages and others that immediately followed were largely motivated by interests in shipping pharmaceuticals (spices) from the Pacific rim to Europe by the least expensive means.

Primarily, the traffic in spices came to Europe from the south in East Africa and from the east (India, China, Southeast Asia), Persia (Iran), and Arabia, with the latter often serving as a depot and controller of the Incense Road. The principal spices imported from China and Southeast Asia were aloewood (*Aquilaria malacensis*), benzoin (a resin derived from *Styrax*), camphor, cinnamon, cloves, galingale, ginger, nutmeg, sandalwood, and turmeric. From India came amomum, bdellium (which included myrrh and balm), cardamom, cinnamon (some species different from Southeast Asian cinnamon), cyperus, pepper, putchuk or costus, sandalwood, sesame, spikenard, sweet flag or calamus, sweet rush or ginger grass, and turmeric. From Persia came a number of products from saracocolla, various species of *Ferula* (giant fennel), including asafetida and panax (all-heal). Arabia produced balsam, frankincense, and myrrh. From East Africa came two different kinds of frankincense, cultivated ginger, cassia, balsam, aloes, myrrh, and ambergris (an animal product).

From classical antiquity to the sixteenth-century European explorations, there were several trade routes along which goods were transported to Europe. One route, the so-called Silk Road, went from China across Asia to the Black Sea. Another was more direct from India through Syria and Persia. Two sea routes went from India to Arabia (so-called Arabia Felix, now Yemen) and directly from the Pacific Islands of Malaysia, Indonesia, and Guinea (among others) across the Indian Ocean to the east coast of Africa and Madagascar (the so-called Spice Route). Pliny the Elder (died A.D. 79) described the trade carried in ocean-going double-outrigger canoes (which he called rafts). An important depot on the African mainland was Rhapta, located somewhere opposite Zanzibar, where African products were added to the trade. The *Periplus of the Erythraean Sea,* an anonymous sailor's and trader's guide to the trade in the Red Sea area written in Greek around the first century A.D., provides a detailed account of the spice items found in each port of call. Almost always the trade went from east and south to the north and west. One of the exceptions is saffron (crocus), which was grown in the Mediterranean area and exported to East Asia, where it was a valued drug. The Chinese developed uses for saffron as a condiment or food and learned to cultivate the plant, thereby ending their dependence on the Western export.

As demand for spices grew, new products were developed and added to the trade. Camphor was discovered in Asia, possibly Korea, and was mentioned in Arabic sources in the seventh century; by the ninth century, camphor was known by a Latin version *(camphora)* of its Asian name *(kapur)*. Cassia was first a species or kind of cinnamon produced in the Malay peninsula; at some time during the early Middle Ages, a new product was substituted for it, derived from the true *Cassia* plant, which grew in East Africa. Cassia was confused with cinnamon for many centuries thereafter, although it was an important and common laxative. In classical antiquity, a spice drug from a species of *Ferula,* called *silphium,* was so highly valued as an oral contraceptive that it was hunted out of existence. The plant grew only in a narrow band along a mountain range in Libya and resisted all attempts at cultivation. As it became extinct, an inferior substitute was employed from the *Ferula assafoetida* plant, grown in Syria and Persia, which is now used as a condiment in making Worcestershire sauce. Pepper, oranges, lemons (known as the "medical apple"), sugar, tea, coffee, tobacco, and chocolate are examples of "spice" drugs that were imported into Europe as pharmaceuticals and later were used as foods, condiments, and other categories.

As early as the New Kingdom in Egypt the importance of the spice trade was seen by the pharaohs Sahure (c. 2400 B.C.) and Hatshepsut (Hashepsowe, c. 1490–1468 B.C.), who attempted to extend their power to the land of Punt, roughly modern Somalia and Yemen, which was a central producer and trader in spices. A Roman document preserved in Justinian's *Digest* lists some fifty-four spices and a few other trade items, such as ivory and purple cloth, and the import duty on each item imposed in the port of Alexandria. The resulting unfavorable balance of trade between the Mediterranean world and spice pro-

ducers is considered a factor in the decline and fall of the Roman Empire.

During the early Middle Ages, spices were often a substitute for money. The early monks often used spices as exchange gifts when moving between monastic communities. So important were spices that approximately one-third of the drugs given in pharmaceutical prescriptions between the seventh and tenth centuries were from products produced in Asia or Africa. The Byzantine Greek term for "warehouse" or "trade depot" is *apoteca,* which came to mean "drug store" or "pharmacist" in European languages. The trade in drugs and spices increased during and after the Crusades. The disruptions in trade caused by the Crusades were a stimulant to find alternative routes, as can be seen by the voyage of Marco Polo. Because of a population increase in Europe between about 1000 and 1320, there was a sharp rise in the demand for spice drugs. Also, a general increase in prosperity enlarged the demand for spices as condiments, preservatives, perfumes, and cosmetics.

One of the best sources for information on the subject is found in *Coloquios dos simples e drogas he cousas medicinais da India* (1563), by Garcia d'Orta (c. 1500–c. 1568). For over thirty years d'Orta, a Portuguese physician in Goa, wrote an account of the spices that he saw. He corrected much of the information about the flora of South Asia because, heretofore, much of the rest of the world knew the items only by their derived products, for example, ginger only as a root, cinnamon as a bark, and pepper as a pod. D'Orta's primary interest was medicinal uses but, because of his broad curiosity, he explored regions for new plants, cultivated them in his garden, and introduced to Europe new food items, such as mangoes, mangosteens, durians, and jackfruit.

A prominent use of spice drugs, especially those with aromatic qualities, was as an ingredient in salves and unguents for flesh wounds, sores, and ulcers. A symptom of festering wounds and sore was an unpleasant smell and the fragrance was thought to be beneficial. Since most of these spice drugs were resins and resins have a mild antiseptic quality, early peoples observed a pharmaceutically active effect. One of the most prized was balsam from *Commiphora opobalsamum,* a tree that grew in a royal garden in Jerusalem and Jericho, where local kings controlled its production as a monopoly. In the first century a pint of balsam sold for one thousand denarii, a considerable sum. Spice drugs had many other uses. Indian nard was good for digestion and jaundice when taken internally, and for sores on the eyelids in ointments. Cinnamon was a menstrual regulator when drunk with myrrh, an antidote against deadly poisons, a diuretic, and, in a salve, good for sunburn. Costus stimulated the libido, expelled intestinal parasites, and, in an ointment, was good for sunburn. Sweet flag was good for the kidneys,

SUGAR PROCESSING IN THE NEW WORLD. Engraving by Théodor de Bry.

coughs, and hernias. Saffron stopped watering of the eyes, acted as an aphrodisiac, and mitigated inflammations resulting from erysipelas. Frankincense taken internally helped the arteries and bowels, but drunk in too great a quantity was thought to produce madness. Finally, the juice of the narcissus bulb was thought to be effective against cancer, a use that modern chemotherapy of cancer has confirmed.

Spice or aromatic drugs were an essential feature in making perfumes and cosmetics. In antiquity and the medieval period, until the formulation of increasingly specialized guilds, the sellers of spices were often the same as druggists, cosmeticians, and perfumers. From the early Sumerian epic legend (as early as c. 3000 B.C.), a distinguishing characteristic of a civilized person, male or female, was smell. Most spice plants have aromatic qualities. Although a few, such as iris roots, were indigenous to the West, a sizable number were trade items. The Syrians in antiquity gained a reputation as specialists in perfumes and cosmetics. A massage with aromatic oils and a wearing of perfume were a routine part of many people's lives.

Various spices' chemical actions to preserve food were known but, because of their high costs, were not often used. Pepper and, later, sugar, in particular, were seen as preventing decay of meat (the action is known to the modern world as enzyme retardation). Whereas the cost was high for sufficiently high quantities to have these results, it was possible to mask the unpleasant smells and tastes of overripe meat by adding these and other spices and condiments. Spices were added to foods for medicinal, preservative, and taste reasons. Detailed recipes using spices as condiments are prominently found in the works of Apicius (fl. early first century A.D.; *De re coquinaria*) and Platina (Bartolomeo Sacchi, 1421–1481; *De honesta voluptate et valitudine*).

Myrrh and frankincense are the spices most used in various religious rituals. Good spirits or gods were thought to enjoy pleasant, uncorrupted air, and the burning of these aromatics improved the environment for spiritual ceremony. The Christian church maintained a great demand for myrrh and frankincense in its rituals throughout the Middle Ages. Myrrh was also used to cause abortions.

BIBLIOGRAPHY

Burkill, I. H. *A Dictionary of the Economic Products of the Malay Peninsula.* 2 vols. Reprint, Kuala Lumpur, 1966.
Greene, Edward Lee. *Landmarks of Botanical History.* 2 parts. Edited by Frank N. Egerton. Stanford, Calif., 1983.
Miller, J. Innes. *The Spice Trade of the Roman Empire, 29 B.C. to A.D. 641.* Oxford, 1969.
Orta, Garcia d'. *Aromatum, et simplicium aliquot medicamentorum apud indos nascentium historia.* Antwerp, 1567. Facsimile reprint, Nieuwpook, 1963.
Riddle, John M. "The Introduction and Use of Eastern Drugs in the Early Middle Ages." *Sudhoffs Archiv* 49 (1965): 185–198.

JOHN M. RIDDLE

SPIRITUALITY OF COLUMBUS.

In popular biographies and textbooks, Columbus has frequently been depicted as the intrepid "Admiral of the Ocean Sea." In these accounts, Columbus, champion of the spirit of rational, scientific inquiry, struggled against the religious prejudices and superstitions of his day in seeking to gain acceptance for his "Enterprise of the Indies." This enterprise—Columbus's proposal that the Far East could be reached by sailing west across the Atlantic—was based upon the idea that the earth was round and that the distance separating the Atlantic coastlines of Europe from the archipelagos that lay on the outskirts of Cathay was navigable. It was the innovative nature of his beliefs regarding the size and shape of the earth that supposedly accounted for the difficulties he encountered first in Portugal and then in Spain, especially from influential ecclesiastics within the court of Fernando and Isabel.

Contemporary sources such as Bartolomé de las Casas's *History of the Indies* and Fernando Colón's biography of his father, *The Life of the Admiral Christopher Columbus*, do indeed recognize the importance of the title "Admiral of the Ocean Sea" to Columbus. In fact, both suggest that ultimately it was not the novelty of Columbus's geography and cartography (for which there were well-known ancient and medieval precedents) that impeded royal funding for his enterprise. Instead it seems that it was his persistent demand for a substantial package of titles, offices, and revenues from any lands he might discover that almost cost him the support of Fernando and Isabel.

But Columbus held dear another self-image, one that has been less frequently acknowledged in the vast literature regarding his actions and motivations. This second self-image reflects Columbus's spiritual side. It is encoded in a title, *Christoferens*, or "Christ-bearer," bestowed upon him, Columbus believed, not by any earthly ruler but by God.

The earliest known document Columbus signed with *Christoferens* is a memorandum to Fernando and Isabel dated 1493. Thereafter it appears on almost everything he signed until his death in 1506. The signature was accompanied by this curious acronym, which has not yet been definitively deciphered:

.S.

.S. A .S.

X M Y

Xpo FERENS

In his biography, Fernando Colón provides some pertinent information regarding the mystical etymology of his father's name. Columbus's given name, Fernando explains, signified that God had designated him as a second Saint Christopher. Just as the converted pagan giant had once carried the Christ Child across a treacherous river, "so the Admiral Christophorus Colonus, asking Christ's aid and protection in that perilous pass, crossed over with his company that the Indian nations might become dwellers in the triumphant Church of Heaven."

Columbus's surname, which means "dove," also held a higher meaning, according to Fernando. God had sent the "dove" Columbus to carry the message of Christianity to the New World, just as he had previously sent a dove to mark the baptism of Christ and a dove to signal the end of the Flood to Noah: "over the waters of the ocean, like the dove of Noah's ark, he [Columbus] bore the olive branch and oil of baptism, to signify that those people who had been shut up in the ark of darkness and confusion were to enjoy peace and union with the Church." And, in a letter written shortly before his death, Columbus described himself as a divinely sent messenger: "God made me the messenger of the new heaven and new earth of which He spoke in the Apocalypse of Saint John after having spoken of it through the mouth of Isaiah: and He showed me the spot where to find it."

This second self-image has proved discomfiting to Columbus scholars. It is more often than not treated as the product of his unhappy, waning years, an unfortunate but inevitable surfacing of the deposits of medieval religious sentiment in an otherwise modern prototype. But to deprive Columbus of his spiritual identity misrepresents him and his culture. There was an important religious dimension to Columbus's understanding of the genesis and historical significance of his enterprise. And his spirituality in this regard was not especially anomalous or eccentric. It was derived from and responded to a variety of contexts and environments encountered by Columbus in the books he read and in the world in which he lived.

In his *History of the Indies,* Las Casas describes Columbus as "a most observant Christian" and a man of intense personal piety. According to Las Casas, Columbus frequently confessed, took communion, and prayed at the appointed canonical hours as would members of the regular clergy. He was particularly devoted to Saint Francis and the Virgin Mary. Both his writing and speaking were laced with homilies. In addition to the signature described above, he was accustomed to insert the phrase "Jesus with Mary be with us on the journey" *(Iesus cum Maria sit nobis in via)* in his letters. He was openly angered by and intolerant of blasphemy.

Columbus seems to have had particularly close connections with the Franciscan order. When he arrived in Castile from Portugal in 1485, he first stayed at the Franciscan monastery of Santa María de La Rábida, located near the port of Palos where he had disembarked. During this five-month sojourn and a second one in 1491, he was apparently instructed and succored by several of the resident monks. His cause was supported within the royal court by Antonio de Marchena, an influential Franciscan cosmographer and by Juan Pérez, a member of the community of La Rábida, who was the confessor of Isabel. There is some reason to believe that later in life Columbus joined the Third Order of Saint Francis, which consisted of laypersons. Las Casas reported that after his second voyage to the Americas, Columbus was observed walking in the streets of Seville dressed in the sackcloth of a Franciscan penitent; Columbus's son Diego said that his father was buried in the robes of a Franciscan tertiary.

Columbus apparently developed the self-image of *Christoferens* over a period of time encompassing his stay in Spain, his four voyages to the Americas, and his unhappy last years. It can be traced through his annotations to certain books, in passages he collected for an unfinished work he named the Book of Prophecies, and in a number of letters.

Among the books Columbus read and annotated were Pliny the Elder's *Natural History,* Plutarch's *Lives,* Marco Polo's *Travels (Il milione),* a popular history written by the humanist Enea Silvio Piccolomini (Pope Pius II), and a collection of works compiled by the early-fifteenth-century philosopher and theologian Pierre d'Ailly. These works all enjoyed a relatively wide circulation in both manuscript and printed editions. They acquainted Columbus with a variety of ancient and medieval authorities and provided him with a traditional body of knowledge regarding cosmography, geography, and history. The works of d'Ailly appear to have been particularly important in the development of both the "Enterprise of the Indies" and the self-image of *Christoferens.*

Columbus's copy of d'Ailly's works was published between 1480 and 1483, but it is difficult to determine when he read it. In a note to the best-known piece in the collection, a work titled *Imago mundi,* Columbus refers to a voyage made down the west coast of Africa by Bartolomeu Dias in 1488. And in the margins to another piece, *De correctione kalendarii,* Columbus calculated the date of the vernal equinox for "this year 1491." These annotations suggest that he was actively using d'Ailly's book in the late 1480s and early 1490s—that is, prior to the first voyage of discovery.

In addition to these two titles, Columbus annotated a group of short works in which d'Ailly discussed the interrelationships among astrology, prophecy, and history. D'Ailly believed that there were divinely ordained concurrences among the unfolding of significant historical events, the fulfillments of ancient prophecies, and the appearance of certain celestial phenomena. Columbus adopted the framework of providential history and eschatology that d'Ailly set forth and sought to place his role as *Christoferens* within it.

According to one of d'Ailly's works, *Tractatus de legibus et sectis contra supersticiosos astronomos,* the world had already passed through ages marked by the ascendancy of the Hebrews, the Chaldeans, the Egyptians, and the Saracens. In each of these ages the patron planet of the dominant group had entered into conjunction with the planet Jupiter. In the present age of the Christians, Jupiter was conjoined with Mercury and the final age of Antichrist would be signed by the conjunction of Jupiter and the Moon. Columbus followed d'Ailly's theory of planetary conjunctions closely, sometimes summarizing the salient points in phrases or sentences, sometimes copying passages directly from d'Ailly's text.

D'Ailly and Columbus, though separated by several generations, shared the conviction that the world was rapidly nearing the end of the age of the Christians. They were therefore especially interested in identifying the preordained events that would mark the imminent advent of Antichrist. In seeking to do so both made use of a number of late antique prophetic texts that enjoyed considerable currency throughout the medieval period. One such prophecy, which foretold the unleashing of "a race which has been shut up within the Caspian gates," a race that would supply Antichrist with his armies, was taken by d'Ailly from Roger Bacon's influential thirteenth-century work *Opus maius.* D'Ailly and Columbus supposed that it referred to different episodes of the endemic conflicts between Christian and Muslim forces in the Holy Land and Byzantium. A second prophetic passage that attracted the attention of d'Ailly and Columbus originally derived from the seventh-century Byzantine apocalypse of Pseudo-Methodius. It outlined eight events that would augur the appearance of Antichrist. Columbus copied this passage from d'Ailly and designated it for inclusion in the Book of Prophecies.

Other prophecies guided Columbus in placing his achievements and those of Fernando and Isabel within the eschatological framework adopted from d'Ailly's works. These too were gathered by Columbus and his collaborator, the Carthusian monk Gaspar Gorricio for inclusion in the Book of Prophecies. Columbus's role as *Christoferens* is evoked in two prophecies in particular. The first is the famous passage from *John* 10:16 that predicts the penultimate conversion of all the peoples of the world to Christianity: "And I have other sheep, that are not of this fold; I must bring them also, and they will heed my voice. So there shall be one flock, one shepherd." The second

prophecy is from the Stoic Seneca's tragedy *Medea:* "The years will come, in the succession of the ages, when the Ocean will loose the bonds by which we have been confined, when an immense land shall lie revealed, and Tethys shall disclose new worlds, and Thule will no longer be the most remote of countries." In the manuscript of the Book of Prophecies Fernando Colón wrote next to this excerpt, "My father, the Admiral Christopher Columbus, fulfilled this prophecy in the year 1492." In breaking the bonds of the Ocean Sea, *Christoferens* revealed the existence of previously unknown souls; the promise of their conversion indicated that the end of postlapsarian time and space must be at hand.

Corroboration lay in another prophecy applicable to Fernando and Isabel. Attributable to a prominent medieval Iberian diplomat and apocalyptist, Arnau de Villanova (c. 1250–1312), it prophesied that "he who will restore the ark of Zion will come from Spain." That Columbus believed it was the historical destiny of his king and queen to lead the Christian forces in the final recovery of Jerusalem from the infidel is evident in the prefatory letter to the Book of Prophecies.

After reviewing his training as a navigator and mapmaker and his many years of experience at sea, Columbus declares that these skills "were of no use to me in the execution of the enterprise of the Indies." Instead, he argues, it is divine providence that guided him and that will guide Fernando and Isabel to the reconquest of Jerusalem: "Who would doubt that this light, which comforted me with its rays of marvelous clarity . . . and urged me on with great haste continuously without a moment's pause, came to you in a most deep manner, as it did to me? In this voyage to the Indies Our Lord wished to perform a very evident miracle in order to console me and the others in the matter of this other voyage to the Holy Sepulcher."

Columbus's views that Fernando and Isabel were destined to play important roles in providential history were not unique. Rather they need to be understood within the apocalyptic and prophetic contexts of medieval and early modern political imagery and ideology. In seeing his regents as emperor-messiahs, Columbus was but investing in a tradition traceable back at least to the court of Charlemagne. As his letter prefacing the first voyage suggests, he was casting his achievements not within an eccentric framework but within one that would have been familiar and operative at the royal court. If Columbus represents his regents correctly, they elected to send him on his voyage for purposes that were in significant part evangelical:

Your Highnesses, as Catholic Christians and as princes devoted to the holy Christian faith and propagators thereof, and enemies of the sect of Mahomet and of all idolatries and heresies, took thought to send me, Christopher Columbus, to the said parts of India, to see those princes and peoples and lands and the character of them and of all else, and the manner which should be used to bring about their conversion to our holy faith.

And even if (as was likely the case) the monarchs' motives were not so single-minded as Columbus suggested, there can be little doubt that he became increasingly focused upon the recovery of the Holy Land. In the letter describing the fourth voyage, Columbus offered to guide such an expedition via his new westward sea route: "Jerusalem and Mount Zion are to be rebuilt by the hands of the Christians as God has declared by the mouth of his prophet in the fourteenth Psalm. . . . Who will offer himself for this work? Should anyone do so, I pledge myself, in the name of God, to convey him safely thither, provided the Lord permits me to return to Spain."

Columbus's own readings and writings thus consistently reveal that *Christoferens* was not a peripheral part of his self-image. This spiritual self was as essential to his understanding of history and his place in it as was the Admiral of the Ocean Sea. *Christoferens* was as grounded in the religious culture of his world as was the Admiral of the Ocean Sea in the jurisdictional and seignorial cultures. The two faces of Columbus need to be understood as complementary if he and his age are not to be misrepresented in the light of contemporary bifurcations of the sacred and the secular.

[See also *Library of Columbus; La Rábida; Signature; Writings,* article on *Book of Prophecies;* and biographies of figures mentioned herein.]

BIBLIOGRAPHY

Columbus, Ferdinand. *The Life of Christopher Columbus by His Son Ferdinand.* Translated by Benjamin Keen. New Brunswick, N. J., 1959.

Milhou, Alain. *Colón y su mentalidad mesianica en el ambiente franciscanista español.* Valladolid, 1983.

Reeves, Marjorie. *The Influence of Prophecy in the Later Middle Ages: A Study in Joachimism.* Oxford, 1969.

Watts, Pauline Moffitt. "Prophecy and Discovery: On the Spiritual Origins of Christopher Columbus's 'Enterprise of the Indies.' " *American Historical Review* 90 (1985): 73–102.

PAULINE MOFFITT WATTS

STAMPS. See *Iconography,* article on *Philately.*

STRABO (64/63 B.C.–A.D. 24 or later), geographer and historian. Strabo was born in Amasia, Pontus, to a noble Greek family of partly Asiatic descent. He studied rhetoric at Nysa, Caria, and in about 44 B.C. went to Rome to study geography and philosophy, eventually becoming a Stoic. He spent several years in Alexandria, traveling south to Syene (Aswan) and the Ethiopian frontier with the Roman governor Aelius Gallus and his entourage. Although not a great traveler, he knew Asia Minor and other parts of the eastern and central Mediterranean quite well.

Strabo wrote the lost work *Historical Sketches,* in forty-seven books, and *Geography,* in seventeen books, which is extant except for parts of Book 7. The latter work describes Spain, Gaul, Britain, Italy, northern and eastern Europe, Greece, Asia Minor and the surrounding areas, the Middle East, India, and the parts of Africa known to the Romans. It is likely that Renaissance explorers made only limited use of Strabo's *Geography.* The work is discursive, and much of the text concerns areas that were relatively well known by the fifteenth century. Strabo was convinced that the inhabited world could be circumnavigated and that the North and South Atlantic were not separated by an appreciable body of land. He was obviously interested in exploring the Atlantic, writing, "We [humans] are in a way amphibious, not more landlubbers than seafarers."

In addition to recounting events such as the ancient circumnavigation of Africa commissioned by the Egyptian pharaoh Necho, Strabo stresses the importance of geometrical and astronomical contributions to geography and cartography. He discusses, though without details, Eratosthenes's measurement of the circumference of the earth and gives some details of Eratosthenes's world map. In Book 1 of *Geography* Strabo writes, "Eratosthenes says that . . . if the size of the Atlantic did not prevent it, we could even sail from Iberia to Indike [India/China] along the same parallel over more than a third of the total distance, assuming that the circle through Athens, on which we have made our calculation of the distance from India to Spain, is less than 200,000 stades in circumference." Eratosthenes reckoned the circumference of the earth at the equator to be 252,000 stades, or between 37,292 and 46,620 km (that is, between 23,120 and 28,900 miles; a stade in his day was variously reckoned at 185 meters, 148 to 158 meters, or other equivalents). By examining Strabo's text, it is clear how Ptolemy came later to make Taprobane (Sri Lanka) too large: Strabo, who orientates it wrongly, gives its length as over 5,000 stades.

The manuscript tradition of Strabo's *Geography* is tenuous. The work was evidently little read in ancient times. All extant manuscripts are derived from one source (around A.D. 850). The earliest surviving manuscript, apart from palimpsest fragments, is in the Bibliothèque Nationale, Paris (Greek manuscript no. 1397) and dates from the late tenth century. A Latin translation (Rome, 1472) by Guarinus Veronensis and Gregorius Tifernas was later revised by J. Andreas (1480) and edited by A. Mancellinus (1494). The first Greek edition did not appear until 1516. There is no evidence that Strabo included maps in the *Geography,* and none were included in the early editions; those printed in later editions were constructed from his text and from Renaissance maps.

BIBLIOGRAPHY

Aujac, Germaine. *Strabon et la science de son temps.* Paris, 1966.
Strabo. *Geography.* 8 vols. Translated by Horace Leonard Jones. 1917. Reprint, Cambridge, Mass., 1969.

O. A. W. DILKE

SYPHILIS. An infectious disease, syphilis is usually transmitted by sexual contact (venereal syphilis), but it can also be transmitted to a newborn infant by an infected mother (congenital syphilis). Its origin has long been a matter of scholarly debate. Some have maintained that it originated in the Old World and, like so many other infectious diseases, was carried to the New World by explorers in the Age of Discovery. Others, however, have argued that it existed in the New World prior to 1492 and was introduced into Europe by the returning explorers. In order to understand the terms of this debate, one must first understand how the disease affects the human body.

After an incubation period of ten to ninety days, the primary lesion, or chancre, of venereal syphilis appears in the anogenital region. Secondary lesions develop later on the skin and mucous membranes of other regions of the body. In more advanced stages (tertiary), the disease can affect bones as well as other organs.

Syphilis is one of several treponemal diseases—venereal syphilis, endemic syphilis, yaws, and pinta—that have similar symptoms. All are thought to be caused by a species of the bacterium *Treponema,* and in their more advanced stages, all but pinta affect bone in similar ways. In fact, some have argued that all these diseases are really different expressions of a single disease caused by *Treponema pallidum.* Endemic syphilis is best known from Syria and areas of Africa. Yaws primarily affects children in rural populations of the tropics. Pinta, which also occurs in the tropics, ranging from Mexico to Ecuador, primarily affects the skin and does not involve internal organs.

Venereal syphilis usually affects the skeleton in the area of the cranial vault, the bones of the nasal area, and the tibia of the lower leg. In the cranial vault, venereal syphilis typically produces a "worm-eaten" scarred pattern of lesions on the outer table of the frontal bone termed "caries sicca." This condition frequently is accompanied by extensive destruction of the bone around the nose area and the upper jaw. In the remainder of the skeleton, the disease causes inflammation of the periosteum, a tissue adjoining the bone's exterior surface that has the capability to form new bone. The inflamed periosteum produces characteristic bony lesions that range from small striated extensions to large lesions with rough surfaces. Yaws produces very similar skeletal effects. In congenital syphilis, the teeth are frequently deformed, a condition termed "mulberry molars" or "Hutchinson's teeth."

Syphilis now is controlled by the antibiotic penicillin. Prior to the discovery of its effectiveness in treating the disease in about 1910, syphilis infected as many as 5 percent of people throughout the world living in urban areas. It is estimated that between 10 and 20 percent of those infected with the disease had skeletal involvement.

Those who argue that the disease originated in the Old World cite numerous passages from the Bible, as well as early literature from Greece, Italy, Spain, India, and China, that describe conditions similar to those known for syphilis. Frequently, these accounts correlate the disease with sexual encounters, further bolstering the interpretation of venereal syphilis. These advocates also argue that, in the early literature, syphilis was confused with leprosy and that the hospitals and colonies set up to isolate lepers from the rest of society actually contained many individuals suffering from syphilis. This argument is supported by early accounts mentioning the effective use of ointments containing mercury, a substance of little use in treating leprosy but widely employed in treating syphilis.

Critics of the Old World origin of syphilis point out the uncertain diagnoses of the disease and its likely confusion with a multitude of other diseases having similar symptoms. The mercury-based ointments may have been aimed not at leprosy but at related diseases other than syphilis. Recent studies of human remains from leper cemeteries have failed to find any skeletal evidence of syphilis. And an analysis of large samples of human remains from Europe, including over ten thousand from Czechoslovakia alone, turned up no examples of the disease. On the other hand, several skeletons from Southeast Asia (Borneo, Australia, and the Mariana Islands) that predate 1492 seem to have skeletal lesions matching those expected with syphilis or a related treponemal disease.

Evidence for the other side of the debate—that syphilis existed in the New World prior to 1492—now seems overwhelming. Many skeletons have been found from a variety of pre-Columbian archaeological sites that show all the features of both venereal and congenital syphilis. Given the high frequency of affected individuals at some sites, the highly diagnostic nature of the lesions, and the geographical distribution of the disease throughout the Western Hemisphere, there seems little doubt that syphilis, or a closely related treponemal disease, was in the Americas prior to 1492.

Those who argue for a New World origin also cite an apparent epidemic of syphilis that struck Europe in about A.D. 1500. The rapid spread of the disease throughout Europe at that time indicates to them that it must have been a "new" disease among populations having no prior immunity. Alternative explanations are that epidemics of syphilis had struck before but were not recognized as such or that the epidemic was stimulated by the unprecedented population movements that occurred throughout Europe at that time.

Collectively, however, the evidence suggests that treponemal disease, including syphilis, was present in the New World long before 1492. The disease may also have been present in the Old World prior to that year, but the evidence for that is concentrated mostly in Southeast Asia. It seems very likely that, whereas many diseases crossed the Atlantic with Columbus and subsequent European voyagers and caused great mortality among the native New World populations, syphilis and related treponemal diseases may have traveled in the opposite direction.

[See also *Disease and Demography*.]

BIBLIOGRAPHY

Baker, Brenda J., and George J. Armelagos. "The Origin and Antiquity of Syphilis: Paleopathological Diagnosis and Interpretation." *Current Anthropology* 29 (1988): 703–737.

Crosby, Alfred W., Jr. "The Early History of Syphilis: A Reappraisal." *American Anthropologist* 17 (1969): 218–227.

Ortner, Donald J., and Walter G. J. Putschar. *Identification of Pathological Conditions in Human Skeletal Remains*. Washington, D.C., 1985.

Quétel, Claude. *History of Syphilis*. Translated by Judith Braddock and Brian Pike. Baltimore, 1990.

Steinbock, R. Ted. *Paleopathological Diagnosis and Interpretation*. Springfield, Ill., 1976.

DOUGLAS H. UBELAKER

T

TAÍNOS. See *Indian America*, article on *Taínos*.

TALAVERA, HERNANDO DE (1428–1507), bishop of Ávila (1485); archbishop of Granada (1492). Hernando de Talavera was one of the main characters in the making of the legend of Columbus. He has often been depicted as the stalwart foe of Columbus's plans, rejecting the enterprise of the Indies and showing his ignorance and resistance to progress. The evidence, however, shows otherwise.

A member of a hidalgo family of modest means from the area of Sigüenza, Talavera was educated at the University of Salamanca, thanks to the financial support of one of his relatives. He studied moral philosophy and theology in what was then the usual curriculum for those not interested in the law. A man of great austerity and simple piety, he joined the Hieronymite Order at age thirty-five. He rose to prominence swiftly, being named prior of the monastery of the Prado in Valladolid and, soon after, confessor to the Castilian queen, Isabel.

As an ecclesiastic in the inner circle of the Castilian court, he played a central role in the diplomatic negotiations with Portugal after the conclusion of the civil war between the followers of Juana de Castilla (La Beltraneja) and Isabel. He was also instrumental in negotiating the agreements by which the Crown recovered income and lands alienated to the nobility during the reign of Enrique IV.

His service to the queen and the realm was rewarded by his appointment as bishop of Ávila and then as archbishop of the newly established see of Granada after the conquest of the city in 1492. As archbishop he instituted a benevolent policy of gentle persuasion toward the Muslims, avoiding any attempts at forced conversion. This attitude and his opposition to the establishment of an inquisitional tribunal in Granada drew the ire of the Inquisition. Because he enjoyed the favor of the queen, he was spared, and the Inquisition limited its displeasure to charging some of his relatives with heresy. Soon after Isabel's death in 1506, however, Talavera was imprisoned and accused of befriending Moors and conversos, of hindering the work of the Inquisition, and, finally, of being of Jewish descent. The archbishop remained in prison until an appeal to Pope Julius II brought a dismissal of the charges as fictitious and slanderous. His exoneration, however, was of little solace, for Talavera died soon afterward in 1507.

As confessor to the queen, Talavera presided over the so-called Junta de Salamanca, which through most of 1486–1487, received, assessed, and rejected Columbus's proposal for a westerly voyage to the Indies. The consensus of most historians is that Talavera's opposition to the project rested on two legitimate considerations: First, that the voyage might be considered an incursion into Portugal's Atlantic possessions, and second, that Columbus's demands and expected rewards were excessive. On both counts Talavera's objections were valid. Peace with Portugal, after the defeat of efforts to secure the Castilian throne for Juana de Castilla, had been obtained at great cost, and the security of Castile's western frontier was a prerequisite before the final push against Granada. Columbus's conditions and demands were indeed exorbitant.

Thus, Talavera's decision was not based on animosity toward Columbus or on ignorance. By not rejecting Columbus's proposal outright and by granting Columbus a small pension, Talavera guaranteed that the proposal would be resubmitted after the conclusion of the Granada campaign and that the future Admiral of the Ocean Sea would remain in the service of Castile.

BIBLIOGRAPHY

Nader, Helen. *The Mendoza Family in the Spanish Renaissance, 1350–1550.* New Brunswick, N.J., 1979.
Mariéjol, J. H. *The Spain of Ferdinand and Isabella.* Translated and edited by Benjamin Keen. New Brunswick, N.J., 1961.

TEOFILO F. RUIZ

TECHNOLOGY. See *Science.*

TENOCHTITLAN. See *Indian American,* article on *Aztecs and Their Neighbors.*

TERRESTRIAL PARADISE. Within the Judeo-Christian tradition, the terrestrial paradise is a garden created by God that was the abode of Adam and Eve before the Fall. The principal description of the terrestrial paradise in scripture occurs in *Genesis.* According to *Genesis* 2:8, the garden of Eden was situated in the East. Its verdant flora were watered by a river that flowed forth from the garden in four branches: Pison, Gihon, Hiddekel, and Euphrates. From these branches the whole earth was watered. After the expulsion of Adam and Eve from the garden, God surrounded it with cherubim and a "flaming sword which turned every way" to prevent humankind from reentering (*Genesis* 3:24).

A second description of the terrestrial paradise is found in *Ezekiel* 28:13–19, which relates that the "garden of God" was located at the top of a holy mountain and was rich in precious stones of many kinds. From it God cast out the "son of man." Neither the *Genesis* nor the *Ezekiel* account indicates that God destroyed the terrestrial paradise after exiling humankind from it. Therefore, it was widely presumed still to exist and was incorporated into the geography, cartography, and travel literature of the medieval Latin West.

Medieval geographies are characterized by their fusions of Greco-Roman and Judeo-Christian sources. Works such as Aristotle's *On the Heavens* (fourth century B.C.), Pliny the Elder's *Natural History* (first century A.D.), Martianus Capella's *The Marriage of Philology and Mercury* (late fourth to early fifth century A.D.), and Macrobius's *Commentary on the Dream of Scipio* (fifth century A.D.) were among the most important antique pagan sources for medieval cosmographers and geographers.

These works conceived of the earth as round and encased in three layers of concentric spheres consisting of the elements of water, air, and fire. The inhabitable part of the world, called the *oikumene* by the Greeks, extended from the coastlines of Britain, France, Spain, and North Africa in the west to the Ganges River in the East. Its northern and southern limits were somewhat vaguer, but generally were extended to the Baltic Sea and to the mouth of the Arabian Gulf. The *oikumene* was completely surrounded by the Ocean Sea.

In a lineage of authoritative medieval texts that can be traced from Isidore of Seville's *Etymologiae* (seventh century) to Pierre d'Ailly's *Imago mundi* (fifteenth century), this ancient image of the world was embellished with peoples and places derived from scripture and popular legends. In these accounts, Jerusalem was usually located at the center of the world in accordance with *Ezekiel* 5:5 ("This is Jerusalem: I have set it in the midst of the nations and countries that are round about her"), and the terrestrial paradise was placed in the east beyond India, in accordance with *Genesis* 2:8. Some writers, notably the tenth-century Syrian Moses Bar-Cepha in his *On Paradise,* make the terrestrial paradise an island separated from the *oikumene* by the band of Ocean Sea. It is often described as being elevated in height because it remained untouched by the inundations of the Flood described in *Genesis* 6–7.

Such combinations of real and imagined geographies are manifest in medieval *mappaemundi* (world maps). A series of well-known *mappaemundi* that includes the family of maps named for the eighth-century Iberian monk Beatus of Liebana, the thirteenth-century Psalter and Ebstorf world maps, and the mid-fifteenth-century maps of Giovanni Leardo share certain elements. They are all oriented with the east at the top, where they locate the terrestrial paradise. Usually depicted in some detail, the terrestrial paradise includes the figures of Adam and Eve bracketing the tree of wisdom entwined by a snake. Sometimes the garden is surrounded by tongues of flame; sometimes it is an island in the Ocean Sea, as in the famous Fra Mauro map (1459). From the garden the four streams flow, visibly feeding all the waters delineated on the map.

The terrestrial paradise is also mentioned in a widely circulated sequence of tales of legendary journeys. The sixth-century Irish monk, Saint Brendan, purportedly found it in the North Atlantic. In the twelfth century, the mythical Christian king of the Far East, Prester John, supposedly sent a letter to the Byzantine emperor in which he remarked that his kingdom was but three days journey from paradise. During the same century there also proliferated a genre of stories concerning the travels and exploits of Alexander the Great. In one of these popular romances of Alexander, the *Iter ad paradisum*, Alexander is said to have reached the gates of paradise during his eastern campaigns.

The terrestrial paradise is also an important locus in the great cosmic journey of Dante's *Divine Comedy*. Echoing *Ezekiel*, Dante places it at the top of the mountain of Purgatory. And, as had Moses bar-Cepha and others, he also made Purgatory and its paradisal summit an island, located in the waters of the southern hemisphere, directly opposite Jerusalem, the navel of the *oikumene* of the northern hemisphere. *Purgatorio* culminates with Dante the pilgrim taking a purificatory bath in the rivers of the terrestrial paradise in preparation for his ascent to the celestial spheres.

John Mandeville's fictitious *Travels*, originally composed in French in 1366, proved to be an especially attractive example of the genre of imaginary journeys. In it, he recorded his travels to Jerusalem and thence to the kingdom of Prester John and mentioned being in the vicinity of paradise, though he never actually saw it. Mandeville's *Travels* was rapidly translated into several vernaculars and circulated widely in both manuscript and printed versions.

Christopher Columbus read and annotated a copy of Mandeville's *Travels*. It supplied him, as did a number of other works, with the geographical and literary frameworks for the terrestrial paradise. There seems little doubt that he believed that it actually existed and expected to find it in the course of his voyages of exploration. Columbus's letter to Fernando and Isabel describing the third voyage contains a lengthy passage in which he considers the question of the location of the terrestrial paradise, reviewing a variety of standard theories. He concludes that he has just passed close to it, citing as evidence the fresh water he found pouring into the sea at a point that he called the Dragon's Mouth (Boca del Dragón). He was actually in the Gulf of Paria between Trinidad and Venezuela. The fresh water Columbus took to be the four rivers of the terrestrial paradise was streaming from the mouth of the Orinoco River.

BIBLIOGRAPHY

Boas, George. *Essays on Primitivism and Related Ideas in the Middle Ages.* New York, 1978.

Graf, Arturo. *Miti, leggende e superstizioni del medio evo.* Milan, 1984.

Kimble, George H. T. *Geography in the Middle Ages.* New York, 1968.

Major, R. H., ed. and trans. *Christopher Columbus: Four Voyages to the New World.* Gloucester, Mass., 1978.

Wright, John Kirkland. *Geographical Lore of the Time of the Crusades.* New York, 1925.

PAULINE MOFFITT WATTS

THIRD VOYAGE. See *Voyages of Columbus.*

TIDES AND CURRENTS. Early explorers quickly learned from Columbus to sail westward from the Canary Islands in the northeast trade winds and north equatorial current. Returning from the Caribbean they sailed northward into the region of eastward currents and westerly winds. Both wind and current were very important in providing propulsion for the ships and affecting their course and speed. As they approached land, explorers were concerned about tides: swift tidal currents could carry them helplessly onto rocks or shoals, and large variations of sea level could play havoc with anchoring.

Tides. In mid-ocean, where it is a matter of no concern to mariners, the mean range of the tide is only a few feet and tidal currents are generally not strong. Near shore, tides and their associated currents are usually amplified, sometimes severely. Northwestern France and southwestern England have tides reaching forty feet as does the Bay of Fundy between Maine and Nova Scotia. More typical along the coasts of North America and Africa are tides of about five feet, although in two regions—the mouth of the Amazon River and off Guinea Bissau in West Africa—they reach fifteen feet and are accompanied by swift currents. Despite the Caribbean's low tides, which are usually less than two feet, tidal currents there reach several knots around islands and through passages. Although tidal height variations are well known and predictions are routinely prepared for the world's harbors, tidal currents—which can have complicated patterns around shoals, islands, and headlands—are not nearly so well known even today. Safely sailing through dangerous reefs in the presence of these swift currents requires considerable expertise and some luck. It was probably a tidal current that carried Columbus's becalmed *Santa María* onto a reef north of La Española where she was lost. Columbus was forced to switch to *Niña*, on which he successfully returned home, narrowly surviving several winter gales.

Tides are caused by the gravitational attraction of the moon and sun with the moon's influence being more than twice that of the sun. The tide at any given place consists of a number of partial tides each of which is related to the complicated motion of the earth relative to the moon and sun. Most regions have semidiurnal tides, or two high tides each day 12.4 hours apart caused by the moon. Some regions such as the Gulf of Mexico have a diurnal tide, that is, only one high tide each day. Mixed tides, consisting of two markedly unequal high tides each day, occur in the Gulf of St. Lawrence and in the Caribbean. Significant variations in sea level and associated currents can also be generated by the wind and atmospheric pressure changes.

Although these changes are not tidal, they can augment tides and tidal currents, modify their timing, and make them much more hazardous.

Currents. Since the winds are the primary driving force of surface ocean currents, their patterns are strongly linked. Large-scale ocean currents and winds generally flow clockwise around the mean mid-latitude high-pressure region in the North Atlantic. Currents, however, tend to be skewed to the west and are much narrower and swifter on the western sides of ocean basins. Thus, in the west, wind and current patterns do not necessarily match.

The most comprehensive data of surface currents are historical ship drifts measured over the past hundred years by both merchant and navy ships. Ship drift measurements of surface current are determined from the difference between shipboard navigational fixes and the estimated velocity of the ship through the water. Most current atlases and pilot charts are based on these data, which show the general currents. The Gulf Stream begins in the Straits of Florida and flowing at a speed of four to five knots follows along the coast northeastward to Cape Hatteras. Its speed must have been difficult for southward-sailing explorers to stem, especially around Cape Hatteras with its dangerous shoals and through the Florida Straits where the stream is bounded on both sides by shoals. Sailors probably hugged the shore where there is a weaker current and sometimes even a counterflow. A short time after Columbus's voyages Spanish mariners learned to sail northeastward in the stream and then eastward to Spain with favorable winds and currents.

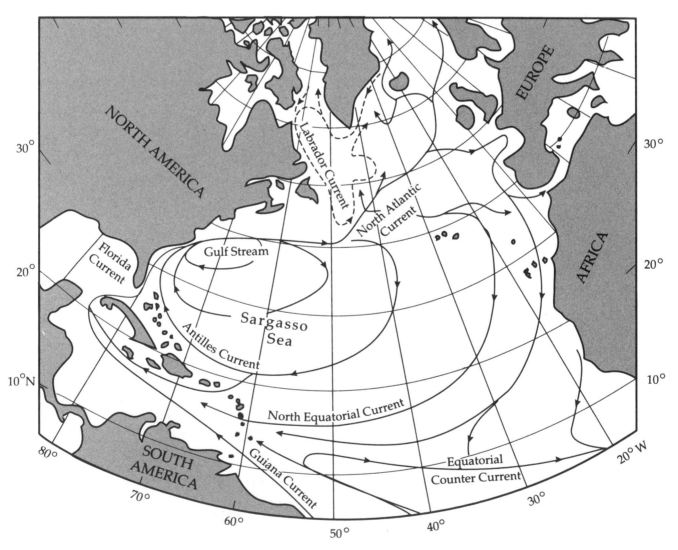

NORTH ATLANTIC CURRENTS. Chart showing main features of the upper layer circulation. Currents are simplified and schematized.

AFTER SVERDRUP, JOHNSON, AND FLEMING, 1942

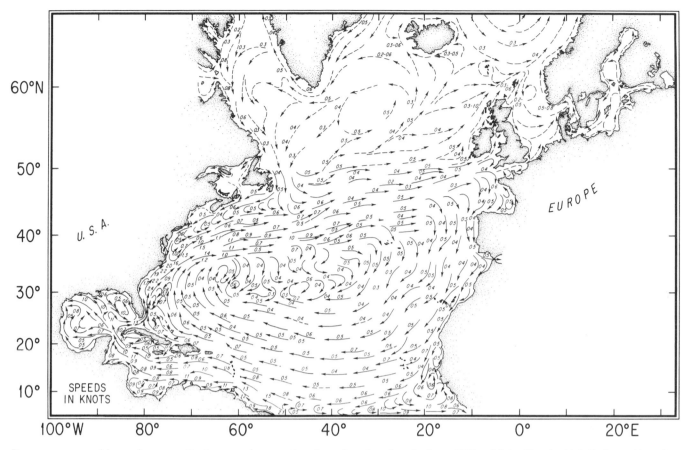

PILOT CHART OF THE NORTH ATLANTIC. Surface currents as taken from the pilot chart for June 1978 published by the U.S. Defense Mapping Agency. Along the Canary Islands–to–Caribbean route, velocity values are typically 0.5 knots, although the technique used to obtain these values tends to inflate speeds.

WOODS HOLE OCEANOGRAPHIC INSTITUTION, WOODS HOLE, MASSACHUSETTS

Downstream from Cape Hatteras the Gulf Stream leaves the coast, meanders widely, and sheds intense eddies or current rings, which populate both sides of the stream. In this region the instantaneous stream is approximately a hundred kilometers wide, but the meanders cause its time-averaged width to be much wider. Downstream of the Grand Banks of Newfoundland the stream breaks down into numerous current filaments and eddies, and the main currents become difficult to follow. The most energetic eddies are located in the stream south of New England; the strength of these eddies decreases as one moves away from the mean axis of the stream.

Roughly half of the volume of water transported by the Gulf Stream through the Straits of Florida originates in the South Atlantic and flows northward as a warm current across the equator into the Caribbean and Gulf of Mexico. A deep cold compensating current flows southward across the equator at depths of from one thousand to four thousand meters. This large-scale circulation—northward in the upper thousand meters and southward in deeper water—is responsible for the northward heat flux in the Atlantic and is an important factor in climate. The other half of the transport in the Straits of Florida is return flow from the stream that has recirculated and entered the Caribbean through numerous passages. The stream increases in transport to the north, reaching its maximum south of Nova Scotia. The major part of this flow recirculates westward on both sides of the stream as countercurrents, but some continues eastward across the Atlantic, splitting southeast of Newfoundland into northward and southward branches. Because of strong eddies and swift current filaments, the mean flow is difficult to map even today. The northward branch mixes with other waters, is cooled, and eventually turns into deeper colder water during winter, forming the beginning of the southward flow that much later crosses the equator. The southward branch flows clockwise around the Atlantic and into the Caribbean. The north equatorial current part of this branch is some of the steadiest flow of the ocean—both winds and currents flow southwestward with very little

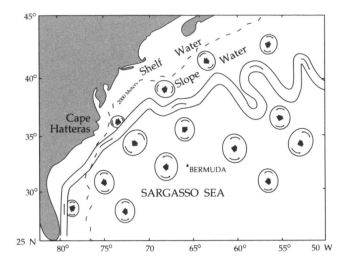

THE GULF STREAM. A schematic, synoptic representation of the path of the Gulf Stream and the distribution and movement of rings. The width of the Stream is typically around 100 km and the diameter of rings, 200 km. The rings usually move westward but can also interact with the Stream and drift downstream. The general fate of rings is coalescence with the Stream after a few months to a few years. Swirl speeds in young rings are similar to speeds in the Stream.

WOODS HOLE OCEANOGRAPHIC INSTITUTION, WOODS HOLE, MASSACHUSETTS

variation in time. There are even eddies here, however, and currents are not always southwestward despite the average pattern. Sailing to the Caribbean is usually a delight, but returning directly to Europe is not easy. The only option is to sail northward into the westerlies as Columbus discovered on his first voyage.

Farther to the south are located very swift equatorial currents, which have enormous seasonal variations. The south equatorial current flows westward in the vicinity of the equator, splitting near the eastern tip of Brazil. Most of the current flows northwestward along the coast of South America as the swift (up to three to four knots) north Brazil current, then Guiana current, and then Caribbean current. During the latter half of each year most of the near surface north Brazil current turns offshore at five to ten degrees north, forming the origin of the eastward-flowing north equatorial countercurrent, which has speeds of three knots in the west and meanders with a two hundred-mile north-south displacement and five hundred-mile wavelength, the distance between successive meander crests. During the first half of the year the countercurrent is replaced by a generally westward current. At this time the north Brazil current continues up the coast. This seasonal variation of currents modulates the northward heat flux in the Atlantic. Amazon River water

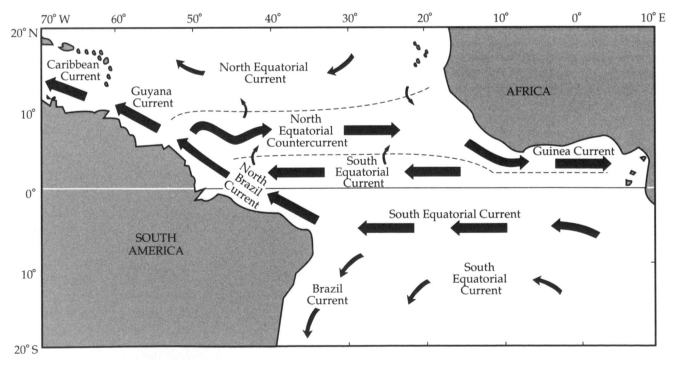

TROPICAL CURRENTS. Schematic map of major tropical currents between July and September, when the North Equatorial Countercurrent flows swiftly eastward across the Atlantic into the Guinea Current. From January through June the countercurrent disappears and westward velocities are seen in this area. Heavier arrows show swiftest currents, generally greater than 0.5 knots.

AFTER RICHARDSON AND WALSH, 1986

enters the Atlantic near the equator forming large pools and filaments of fresh water, which are carried northwestward up the coast of South America and eastward into the countercurrent. These swift equatorial currents and their strong seasonality could have been difficult for early explorers to navigate. Those heading south along the coast toward the eastern tip of Brazil would have found very strong currents against them and, during the second half of the year, the southeast trades against them, too. Sailing northwestward along the coast would have been much easier. South of the eastern tip of Brazil the currents and winds are much more favorable for sailing southward. Early mariners soon learned to pass well clear of the eastern tip of Brazil when sailing from Europe to the South Atlantic.

The strong current seasonality observed in the equatorial region from ten degrees north to ten degrees south is caused by the seasonal shifting of trade winds: the northeast and southeast trades converge toward the intertropical convergence zone, or doldrums, which lie near the equator. In the latter half of the year the wind pattern shifts northward and the doldrums generally lie between five and ten degrees north coinciding with the countercurrent and largely responsible for it; during the first half of the year the doldrums lie close to the equator. Often in spring the easterly trades along the equator are replaced by westerly winds. The result is a swift eastward current jet within a few degrees of the equator. The doldrums are known for their very light breezes, so before the days of engine power, sailing vessels often lay becalmed there for weeks drifting unknowingly large distances sometimes eastward in the countercurrent or the jet along the equator and sometimes westward in the south equatorial current. On his third voyage, Columbus sailed southwestward from the Cape Verde Islands reaching the doldrums in the middle of July 1498, where he was becalmed for eight miserable days in terrible tropical heat. At this time Columbus probably drifted eastward in the countercurrent, which is usually well developed during July. Finally, the cool trade winds reappeared, filled Columbus's sails, and drove him toward Trinidad where he made landfall nine days later.

The currents through passages into the Caribbean can be very swift and are difficult to describe in the general sense because they vary with the large-scale currents as well as with local winds, eddies, and tides. One can imagine that each passage has its own complicated and different flow pattern, depending on the direction of wind and the configuration of islands and sea floor. Eddies can be generated in the lee of islands, some stationary, some carried downstream. The numerous shoals and low islands in the Bahamas plus the time-varying currents there must have been particularly tricky for early navigators.

Numerous recent wrecks attest to the difficulty of sailing in these waters even today. More detailed information of these waters can be found in the Coast Pilots, Sailing Directions, and Tide and Tidal Current Tables.

BIBLIOGRAPHY

Richardson, P. L. "Gulf Stream Rings." *Oceanus* 19, no. 3 (1976): 65–68.

Richardson, P. L., and D. Walsh. "Mapping Climatological Seasonal Variations of Surface Currents in the Tropical Atlantic Using Ship Drifts." *Journal of Geophysical Research* 91 (1986): 537–550.

Robinson, Allan R., ed. *Eddies in Marine Science.* Berlin, 1983.

Stommel, Henry. *The Gulf Stream.* London, 1958.

Sverdrup, H. U., M. W. Johnson, and R. H. Fleming. *The Oceans.* New York, 1942.

U.S. Naval Oceanographic Office. *Oceanographic Atlas of the North Atlantic Ocean, Section 1, Tides and Currents.* Bay St. Louis, Miss., 1965.

Warren, Bruce A., and Carl Wunsch, ed. *Evolution of Physical Oceanography, Scientific Surveys in Honor of Henry Stommel.* Cambridge, Mass., 1981.

Philip L. Richardson

TIMEGLASS. A timeglass (also called sandglass, hour glass, or running glass) consists of two conical phials joined at the apexes and held in a symmetrical frame that can be placed either end up. A fine material, sometimes sand but more commonly finely ground eggshell or other material is sealed into the phials and can trickle in a known amount of time from the upper phial to the lower; the time depends upon the quantity and nature of the material and upon the diameter of the aperture at the junction of the two phials. In other languages, the timeglass was called *horologium* (Latin); *horloge de mer* or *sablier* (French); *orologio, ampoletta,* or *clessidra* (Italian); *ampulheta* (Portuguese); *ampolleta* (Spanish); and possibly also *dyoll* (English), which presents linguistic problems (perhaps a misreading of *fyoll*), but seems confirmed by the mention of "smale diale sonde" in a tract (after 1534) on the circumnavigation of England.

The construction of any timeglass clearly presupposes a certain skill in glassblowing (known in Syria from the first century b.c.), but the earliest timeglasses consisted of two independently blown phials joined by wax and binding, with a small brass plate pierced by an aperture between them. Later, in the eighteenth century, timeglasses were blown in one piece, the narrow aperture being created by drawing out the softened glass. Timeglasses could be made to run for periods from a few minutes up to several hours and measured equal intervals of time. Thus, they were used at sea with the log for determining speed and distance sailed (dead reckoning) and for dividing the day

TIMEGLASS. A fifteenth-century *ampoletta* of one-half-hour duration.   NATIONAL MARITIME MUSEUM, GREENWICH

and night into watches. However, continuous periods of time measurement achieved by reversing the timeglass as quickly as possible each time it had run (or starting another at that moment) were likely to be inaccurate, and the pitching and rolling of a ship were not conducive to constant interval measurement.

The history of the timeglass is obscure. The timeglass was apparently not known in antiquity, nor is the first definite Muslim evidence, in sixteenth-century Turkey, earlier than medieval European evidence. About the year A.D. 1000, al-Biruni, in Ghazni, Afghanistan, preferred sand to water in time measurers, but there is no reason to suppose that he was referring to a glass-phial device, rather than to an open clepsydra (water clock) in which

sand was substituted for water, as also, probably, was al-Khazini, writing in A.D. 1121/1122. In Europe, references are ambiguous until the fourteenth century, when the clerk of the English king's ship *La George* recorded in 1345/1346 the sums he paid in Flanders for twelve glass horloges and another four of the same sort. There are several subsequent references in the fourteenth century: in France in 1380, to a large *orloge de mer* comprising *deux grans fiolles plains de sablon* (two large phials full of sand); in Catalonia in 1380 as a wedding-present; in France in 1392 to 1394 in a recipe for filling domestic timeglasses; and in Switzerland, where the tolling of a town bell was to be regulated by a timeglass. A fresco by Ambrosio Lorenzetti in the Palazzo Publico in Siena uses a timeglass to symbolize temperance; it is uncertain whether the painting, as now seen, dates from 1338/1339 or nearly twenty years later. The next known illustration of a timeglass is found in a German-Hebrew Pentateuch of 1395, in which the timeglass, hanging by a becket from a hook on a wall, is timing a lesson. Only the first of these fourteenth-century references comes from a nautical context, but they show that, by the beginning of the fifteenth century, the timeglass was well known and not uncommon. No medieval timeglasses have survived intact; only a few fragments have been found.

Columbus refers to the *ampolleta* in his account of his first voyage. By extension of meaning, he uses this word to mean "the time the timeglass measures," by which he means always half an hour.

BIBLIOGRAPHY

Balmer, R. T. "The Operation of Sand Clocks and Their Medieval Development." *Technology & Culture* 19 (1978): 615–632.

Drover, C. B., P. A. Sabine, C. Tyler, and P. G. Coole. "Sand-Glass 'Sand,' Historical, Analytical, Practical." *Antiquarian Horology* 3 (1960): 62–72.

Junger, Ernest. *Das Sanduhr Buch.* Frankfurt am Main, 1957. French translation, *Le traité du sablier.* Paris, 1981.

Naish, G. P. B. "The Dyoll and the Bearing-Dial." *Journal of the Institute of Navigation* 7 (1954): 205–8.

Turner, A. J. " 'The Accomplishment of Many Years': Three Notes towards a History of the Sand-glass." *Annals of Science* 39 (1982): 161–172.

Turner, A. J. "Water-clocks, Sand-glasses, Fire-clocks." Part 3 of vol. 1 of *The Time Museum: Catalogue of the Collection.* Rockford, Ill., 1984.

Varela, Consuelo, ed. *Cristóbal Colón. Textos y documentos completos. Relaciones de viajes, cartas y memoriales.* Madrid, 1982.

Waters, David W. *The Art of Navigation in Elizabethan and Early Stuart Times.* London, 1958.

Waters, David W. "Early Time and Distance Measurement at Sea." *Journal of the Institute of Navigation* 8 (1955): 153–173.

FRANCIS MADDISON

TIMETELLING. Although the measurement of time has preoccupied humankind from the earliest periods of civilization, it was at best still only approximate during the Age of Discovery and in fact until a relatively modern period. The most common timekeeping devices prevalent in the fifteenth century in both the West and in the East were the sundial and the water clock (clepsydra), neither of which was capable of the precise measurement required for astronomical observations or navigation.

Water and Sand Clocks. Like the sundial, the water clock was commonly used in the Middle East and Far East as well as in the Western world from a very early period. Knowledge of Islamic forms of both sundials and water clocks was transmitted to the West by translations of Arabic texts. Notable among these were five books of the *Libros del saber de astronomía* (Books of knowledge of astronomy) compiled in about 1277 for King Alfonso X of Castile (Alfonso the Wise) and containing descriptions of a water clock, mercury clock, candle clock, and two sundials.

It is not known with certainty whether the water clock of the European medieval period was derived entirely from the Islamic water clock or was a continuation of the Roman anaphoric clock tradition. Basically, an anaphoric clock was a form of celestial calculator consisting of a constant-flow clepsydra and a disk on which were painted the signs of the zodiac and a number of stars behind a fixed grill, which represented the hours and the observer's local coordinates. It was already in use in European monastic houses in the twelfth century and possibly earlier. The earliest known description is found in a tenth- or eleventh-century manuscript in the Benedictine monastery of Santa María de Ripoli in the Pyrenees. The device's primary purpose was not to measure time in hours but to strike an alarm to awaken the bell ringer who would then strike the monastery bell to announce the canonical hours or offices that governed the daily life of the community. Several of the regulations of the early twelfth-century Cistercian rule confirm the widespread use of clepsydrae in monastic houses, including one rule that specified that the sacristan was to be instructed to set the "clock" and cause it to strike before lauds on winter weekends unless it was daylight. In the eleventh century similar instructions were issued by Abbot William of Hirsau to his sacristan.

In addition to its monastic functions, the water clock was used in rural areas in medieval Spain to control water distribution for irrigation. The sinking-bowl form as well as the *gadus* (a bucket of the noria or waterwheel, punctured in such a manner as to function as a makeshift outflow clepsydra) served this purpose, as did the sand clock, in which fine sand performed the same function as water. The sand clock was especially popular with astrologers and mariners. (Later, in the late fifteenth century, the mechanical clock was also adapted for regulating water rights. Such a timekeeper was installed by the local lord, Père Bon, at his castle in the village of Collosa near Alicante. Constructed by a Valencian clockmaker, Micer Rubi, it was welcomed by the villagers because for the first time "the water of irrigation is divided into hours." A clock installed at Granada in the 1490s governed water flow for irrigation by the striking of "the Irrigation Bell.")

Until the late fourteenth century, large sand clocks, constructed in some of the larger cities by Mallorcan artisans identified as "cartographers," were installed in the towers of the communities' tallest public buildings. Keepers were employed to maintain them and to strike a bell each hour as indicated by the flow of sand. Such a timekeeper was ordered for the city of Barcelona by King Juan I of Aragón, and others were recorded in use in Tortosa and Zaragoza.

Mechanical Clocks. Late in the fourteenth century sand clocks were replaced by mechanical clocks installed in cathedrals and some monasteries in the major cities of Aragón and Castile. The earliest were in Tortosa and Burgos. The records indicate that for the most part the late fourteenth-century clock makers working in Spain were Jews, in addition to a few Catalans and Mallorcans.

The origin of the mechanical clock in the Western world has never been satisfactorily explained. Horological scholars have long debated the conflicting traditions relating to its introduction. One proposes that it was brought from China by seafarers to a major Italian port—Livorno, Amalfi, or Venice—at the beginning of the fourteenth century and from there proliferated through Italy and then the rest of Europe. Another tradition suggests that it evolved from an alarm developed for timing roasting spits in monastic kitchens or for awakening the bell ringer in time to toll the bell marking the divisions of the day.

In any event, by the early fourteenth century, the mechanical clock had revolutionized time measurement in Western society. The earliest public clock of record was installed in 1309 in the bell tower of the Church of San Eustorgio in Milan, and others soon followed. The cathedral at Beauvais had "a clock with bell" before 1324, and by 1335 the Church of San Gottardo in Milan had a clock with a bell that struck the twenty-four hours, the number of each hour indicated by the number of strokes. Many of the earliest public clocks were water-powered but were subsequently replaced with mechanical movements designed to strike bells at periodic intervals, making it possible at last for the populace to regulate their day.

Evidence indicates that these pioneering clocks only struck the hours—a dial for visual timekeeping was a later addition. By the mid-fourteenth century, public clocks were equipped with bells and simple dials as well as complicated astronomical dials and automatons. And at the end of the century clocks not only struck the hours and quarters but indicated them visually along with the day of the week, the month, the lunar phases, and conjunctions of the heavenly bodies. Mechanical clocks like these had now made their appearance on church and monastery buildings in a number of the larger Spanish cities, including the cathedrals of Barcelona, Tarragona (in Aragón), Valencia, Burgos, Seville, and Lérida.

It was not until the early sixteenth century that clock making evolved as a professional craft in its own right, brought about primarily by the demand for timepieces from the European royal courts and the rising class of bourgeois and wealthy merchants. Portable clocks and watches for domestic use evolved principally as possessions of the privileged, the princes, and the prelates. Generally they were products of great artistry involving the skills of the goldsmith and engraver as well as the mechanician. The time measurement function of these "toys of the wealthy" remained during this period of secondary importance to their interest as curiosities or as symbols of affluence and status. (They were often featured in portraits of individuals of power to denote position and wealth.)

The early clocks were weight-driven, having a crown wheel and verge escapement regulated by a foliot, which was subsequently replaced by the more accurate balance wheel. In time the spring drive replaced the falling weight as a power source, making it possible for the timepiece to assume various portable forms including the neck watch, the table clock, and the traveling clock.

Timekeeping at Sea. The early mechanical timekeepers usually lost or gained a great deal during the course of twenty-four hours, and it was not until much later even that a minute hand was added. Because of their lack of accuracy, they served no purpose for the astronomer or navigator. To measure time at sea, sailors consulted the stars at night or used a time glass or sand glass *(reloj de arena* or *ampoletta)*. These glasses were produced in Venice, and because of their extreme fragility, a ship would carry as many as one or two dozen on a voyage. The flowing sand of the form used on fifteenth-century vessels measured thirty minutes. On shipboard the time glasses were maintained by a ship's boy (grummet) whose responsibility was to turn it immediately when the sand ran out. Consequently, the accuracy of time measurement depended on the degree of the grummet's diligence.

According to Columbus's journal, the ship's crew was divided into two watches, called *cuartos* or *guardias*. Each watch was of four hours' duration, and each was supervised by one of the ship's officers. Whether a standard procedure existed for changing the hours of watches on early Portuguese and Spanish ships is not known, but Columbus noted that on his ships, watches were changed

at 3:00, 7:00, and 11:00. Columbus may have selected 7:00 for his first watch because it was approximately the time of sunset, and he developed the rest of his schedule from there at four-hour intervals. (It is to be noted that in Italian timekeeping the first hour began at half an hour after sunset, a practice that continued until the seventeenth century.)

The timing of the time glasses was corrected at noon and at night. Utilizing the card of the ship's compass as a sundial, the shipmaster or seaman would insert a pin at the center of the card, which would throw its shadow upon the center of the north point at exactly noon; at this moment the glass would be turned, establishing the correct time. For timing events Columbus used, in addition to the time glasses and the changing of the watch, the canonical hours or offices of prayer, which he undoubtedly learned during his stay at the monastery at La Rábida.

Columbus and other navigators of his time were probably also equipped with an early form of an instrument called the nocturnal, possibly hand drawn on paper. Through an opening at the center of this instrument or card, the polestar could be sighted at night and a movable arm representing the Little Dipper turned until it reached Kochab, one of the Dipper's two brightest stars. In this manner the precise position and the time were indicated.

Timetelling's importance in navigation was related to the need to determine longitude at sea. But until the late sixteenth century the accuracy of the timepieces used at sea—the sort used by Columbus—was at best only approximate within a quarter of an hour. In 1530 Rainer Gemma Frisius proposed the use of mechanical clocks on shipboard for determining longitude, but this was not yet possible because mechanical clocks were not sufficiently accurate. English voyagers, too, proposed using clocks at sea in the late sixteenth century, but the problem was not to be satisfactorily resolved until the last quarter of the eighteenth century when the English clockmaker John Harrison invented the chronometer. In the interim many sought a solution by devising specialized timepieces capable of being used on shipboard, but none was successful.

It was not until the scientific revolution of the seventeenth century when the clock became an important tool in the new sciences that it achieved precision. The growing preoccupation with astronomy, navigation, microscopy, and mechanics in particular brought about a closer relationship between the scientist and the craftsman who designed and constructed the tools of science. The greatest need was for tools of measurement of increasing precision, and although it was realized that in principle the clock could serve a multitude of scientific needs, it first had to be improved, particularly in its regulation.

Following the invention of the pendulum regulator,

conceived by Galileo in 1642 and first patented by Christian Huygens in 1657, improvements in the clock followed in rapid succession, including the English inventions of the anchor escapement, the compensated pendulum, the dead-beat escapement, and the balance spring. The establishment of the Royal Astronomical Observatory at Greenwich, England, in 1675 provided even greater impetus for developing clocks and watches of increasing accuracy.

[See also *Hourglass; Navigation*, article on *Instruments of Navigation*.]

BIBLIOGRAPHY

Bedini, Silvio A. *The Pulse of Time: Galileo Galilei, the Determination of Longitude, and the Pendulum Clock.* Florence, 1990.

Drover, C. B. "A Medieval Monastic Water-Clock." *Antiquarian Horology* 1, no. 5 (December 1954): 54–58, 63.

Glick, Thomas F. *Irrigation and Society in Medieval Valencia.* Cambridge, Mass., 1970.

Glick, Thomas F. "Medieval Irrigation Clocks." *Technology and Culture* 10, no. 3 (July 1969): 424–428.

Herrero García, Miguel. *El reloj en la vida española.* Madrid, 1955.

North, John D. "Monasticism and the First Mechanical Clocks." In *The Study of Time II: Proceedings of the Second Conference of the International Society for the Study of Time.* Edited by J. T. Fraser and John Lawrence. New York, 1975.

Vielliard, Jeanne. "Horloges et horlogers Catalans à la fin du moyen âge." *Bulletin Hispanique* 63 (1961): 161–168.

Whitrow, G. J. *Time in History.* New York, 1988.

SILVIO A. BEDINI

TOBACCO. See *Flora*, article on *Tobacco*.

TOLEDO. At the time of Columbus's voyages, the city of Toledo was one of the most important of Spain. It was a center of commerce and trade, a meeting site for the itinerant Castilian Crown and Cortes, and the see of the most powerful Castilian prelate, the archbishop of Toledo.

Toledo's prominence owed much to its central location. It straddled the major trade routes with Lisbon to the west, and with the southern and northern cities of the Crown of Castile. As the largest city of New Castile, Toledo was the center of a flourishing local and regional economy.

The city's population in 1492 is unknown, but Fernando Colón, writing in the early 1500s, estimated that it was between 18,000 and 20,000 souls. In the first recorded census of 1528, the population was about 29,490 inhabitants and rose to a high point of 62,060 in 1571.

The Toledo political scene was dominated by two rival factions: the Ayalas, the counts of Fuensalida; and the Silvas, the counts of Cifuentes. When these factions were not involved in open warfare, Toledo was governed by a city council presided over by a Crown-appointed corregidor, whose business it was, among other things, to steer the city council along paths favored by the Crown. After the comunero revolt of 1520–1521, the clans' bloody street battles subsided, although rivalry continued in other spheres.

A powerful figure in the city was the archbishop of Toledo, who presided over an enormous archdiocese, an impressive income, and vast opportunities for patronage. The Toledo prelates frequently occupied other high offices, as presidents of royal councils, close royal advisers, or inquisitor-generals of Castile. Men of prodigious influence, they played an important role in local politics and society. As church revival took on more urgency under the leadership of Cardinal-Archbishop Francisco Jiménez de Cisneros, Toledo experienced a proliferation of new religious, charitable, and educational foundations, confraternities, and lay groups devoted to religion. The patrimony of Toledo owes much to the munificence of its prelates.

Below these powerful figures were the more numerous and lesser-known citizens, among them a sizable population of Jews. By 1485, when the Inquisition arrived in the city, many Jews had converted to Christianity. Known as conversos, in 1486 they accounted for about 20 percent of the population. The political, social, and financial success of many conversos engendered tensions throughout the fifteenth and sixteenth centuries.

Despite setbacks from the Inquisition, the Toledo merchant and financial community, dominated by conversos, remained dynamic. After the conquest of Granada, several Toledo conversos established themselves as collectors of the royal tax levied on Granada silk. This connection was probably instrumental in the development of Toledo's silk industry, which came to dominate the city's manufacturing activities in the sixteenth century.

Toledo citizens were active in exploring new regions of the ever-expanding empire. Some families made their fortune by participating in the conquest of the Canary Islands, and many formed commercial companies to trade with the New World. Some people dedicated themselves to evangelization in remote parts of the empire, including the Philippines and Japan, others filled posts in the imperial bureaucracy, and some emigrated in search of a better life.

From the 1580s onward the Toledo economy experienced a decline, and the city lost much of its regional monopoly to the new capital, Madrid. What had been a dynamic, varied, and intellectually curious society of merchants, clerics, artisans, professionals, and local elites slowly faded to a frail, provincial society, living in a city that retained little of its former glory except for the importance of the church.

BIBLIOGRAPHY

Benito Ruano, Eloy. *Toledo en el siglo XV: Vida política.* Madrid, 1961.

Martz, Linda. "Converso Families in Toledo: The Importance of Lineage." *Sefarad* 48 (1988): 117–196.

Martz, Linda. *Poverty and Welfare in Habsburg Spain: The Example of Toledo.* Cambridge, 1983.

Phillips, Carla Rahn. "Time and Duration: A Model for the Economy of Early Modern Spain." *American Historical Review* 92 (1987): 531–562.

LINDA MARTZ

TOLEDO Y ROJAS, MARÍA DE (d. 1549), wife of Diego Colón, second Admiral of the Indies; daughter-in-law of Christopher Columbus; vicereine of the Indies. María Toledo y Rojas was the daughter of María de Rojas and Fernando de Toledo, lord of Villorias, grand falconer, *comendador mayor* of León, and member of the order of Santiago. Her father's brother was the second duke of Alba. She was married to Diego Colón in 1508 with a promised dowry of one million maravedis (2,667 ducats) drawn from her mother's property. In addition, she stood eventually to inherit a portion of her parent's joint property. Diego Colón offered her a marriage settlement of two thousand ducats. During the decades that followed, she and her kinsmen in the house of Alba were strong advocates for Colón's claims as heir to the Santa Fe Capitulations.

Accompanying her husband to Santo Domingo in 1509, she quickly established a miniature court and just as quickly began to bear children in a succession interrupted primarily by Diego's absences in Spain in 1511, 1513, and 1515 to 1517. In preparation for the latter journey, Diego named her cogovernor of La Española, with Gerónimo de Agüero, his former tutor. She had no real power; the audiencia and various royal agents had taken command of the government. Indeed, she was unable to prevent them from taking encomiendas and offices from Diego's friends and appointees. In 1518 she (and perhaps Diego) took her children, Felipa, María, Juana, and Isabel, to Spain to join her husband in seeking satisfaction of his claims under Christopher Columbus's agreements with the Catholic monarchs.

It is not known whether she traveled with him as he followed Charles V's court during 1518 and 1519. But she did return to Santo Domingo with him in 1520. Their first son, Luís, was born in 1521. During the next three years she bore two more sons, Cristóbal and Diego. The latter had not been born when his father was again summoned to Spain in the fall of 1523. She remained at Santo Domingo until 1529, seeing to the probating of her husband's will in May 1526 (he died in February).

Confirmed as tutor for her son Luís and thus empowered to exercise his rights, she soon came into conflict with the audiencia of Santo Domingo, royal appointees, and some municipal councils. When challenged by a royal official, she is said to have made the telling reply that a particular action followed the custom in the domains of the duke of Alba; the official rejoined that they were in the domains of the king. Because no resolution of the different visions of the admiral's power was possible at Santo Domingo, in 1529 she journeyed to Spain in order to preserve her son's rights as she understood them. Historians differ as to whether Luís and the other children accompanied her at this time.

Another reason for her journey was that her late husband's appeal of the decisions of 1520 (regarding the second lawsuit in the Pleitos Colombinos) was consolidated in 1527 into an entirely new lawsuit. María's father represented the family in 1527 and 1528; her presence was necessary because the royal attorney objected that even he could not speak for Luís. The lawsuit was concluded in 1534 with a settlement that left unanswered the important questions of whether Luís should be put in possession of the viceroyalty and governorship and what revenues he was to enjoy as admiral. A new lawsuit resulted, from which came the settlement of 1536–1537. During the years these cases were being heard, María continued to appoint officials and claim revenues according to her interpretation of her son's privileges.

Under the terms of the settlement of 1536–1537, Luís received a fixed income in place of the percentage of royal revenues and certain admiralty fees he had received, Jamaica and a land grant in Veragua (Panama), and new titles, but had to give up the title of viceroy of the Indies. His unmarried sisters and youngest brother, Diego, received lifetime pensions. María was awarded four thousand ducats over a four-year period to repay her costs in pursuing the litigation since 1526 and a lifetime pension of one thousand ducats a year. She later assigned this to her daughter María, probably as part of her dowry.

Adding to María's achievements in providing for her family were the marriages of her daughters María, Juana, and Isabel, although she did not live to see all of them. María married Sancho de Cardona, admiral of Aragón. Juana married Luís de la Cueva, brother of the third duke of Albuquerque, in 1536. Isabel married Jorge de Portugal, count of Gelves, in 1531. The oldest daughter, Felipa, became a nun.

Having thus provided for the financial security of her family, María joined her son in lobbying for his appointment as captain general of La Española, a title he was given in 1540. She apparently accompanied him back to Santo Domingo that year and remained there for the rest of her life, exercising such influence as she could over Luís.

The last years of her life were marked by her success in breaking up Luís's marriage in 1542 to María de Orozco and by the disastrous effort in 1546 to colonize Luís's land grant in Veragua. She undoubtedly had a hand in Luís's marriage in 1547 to María de Mosquera. The Mosquera marriage probably brought new financial resources to the family as well as strengthened ties to an important, wealthy local family, whose founder, Juan de Mosquera, had been a poor immigrant in the earliest days of the colony. Ties to another important and wealthy family resulted from the marriage of María's second son, Cristóbal, to Leonor Zuazo, daughter of Alonso Zuazo, once Diego Colón's antagonist and then his supporter in the struggle over power in 1517 and 1518. María de Toledo died at Santo Domingo on May 11, 1549.

BIBLIOGRAPHY

Colección de documentos inéditos relativos al descubrimiento, conquista, y organización de las antiguas posesiones españolas de América y Oceanía, sacados de los archivos del reino, y muy especialmente del de Indias. Edited by Joaquín F. Pacheco et al. 42 vols. Madrid, 1864–1884. Vols. 37, pp. 436, and 40, pp. 373–397.

Floyd, Troy S. *The Columbus Dynasty in the Caribbean.* Albuquerque, N.Mex., 1973.

Thacher, John Boyd. *Christopher Columbus, His Life, His Work, His Remains.* 3 vols. 1903–1904. Reprint, New York, 1967.

PAUL E. HOFFMAN

TOMB OF COLUMBUS. See *Burial Places.*

TORDESILLAS, TREATY OF. See *Treaty of Tordesillas.*

TORQUEMADA, TOMÁS DE (1420–1498), first inquisitor general. Tomás de Torquemada was the son of Pedro Fernández de Torquemada, of Jewish lineage, and nephew of the Dominican theologian Cardinal Juan de Torquemada (1388–1468), who in 1450 defended the conversos in Rome in his famous *Treatise against Midianites and Ishmaelites.* Torquemada entered the Dominican convent of San Pablo, Valladolid, founded by his uncle, and soon became the prior of Santa Cruz in Segovia, a position that he held for twenty-two years. He knew Isabel, then living as a princess in Segovia, who made him her confessor, whereby he gained special authority over her as well as over Fernando. Contrary to the common understanding, Torquemada did not request that the Inquisition be established, although he was associated with it from its beginning in 1478. In 1482 his order asked him to oversee the foundation of the convent of Santo

Tomás in Ávila, to which he retired in 1496, and where he died. Also in 1482, the sovereigns named him as one of several inquisitors in Castile and León, kingdoms without any inquisitorial tradition. Feeling the need to organize a tribunal with unified jurisdiction and knowing Torquemada's abilities, in 1483 they asked Pope Sixtus IV to appoint him inquisitor general of Spain, including Aragón, thus superseding the medieval Aragonese (papal, or so-called French) inquisition. Helped by fellow inquisitors, Torquemada wrote in 1486 the *Instrucciones,* the basic by-laws of the Spanish Inquisition for its entire duration. He then organized its Supreme Council as an ecclesiastical branch of the government, divided Spain into districts, and supervised inquisitorial activities until Pope Alexander VI appointed four bishops both to help and restrain him. In 1492 he not only supported but actively promoted the expulsion of the Jews, although neither his title nor his name appear in the text of the decree of expulsion. Torquemada, rightly or wrongly, became the symbol of religious—and even general—intolerance. In 1808 French troops desecrated his remains. His life and activities continue to be reevaluated by contemporary scholarship.

BIBLIOGRAPHY

Huerga Criado, Pilar. *El inquisidor general Torquemada.* Madrid, 1984.

Meseguer Fernández, Juan. "Tomás de Torquemada, inquisidor general." In vol. 1 of *Historia de la Inquisición en España y América,* edited by J. Pérez Villanueva and B. Escandell. Madrid, 1984.

Wood, Clement. *Torquemada: Rack of the Inquisition.* New York, 1930.

ANGEL ALCALÁ

TORRES, ANTONIO DE (fl. late 1500s), ship's captain and fleet commander. Torres was owner and master of Columbus's flagship on his second voyage. The principal purpose of the voyage was to establish a self-sustaining colony on La Española, and to that end a grand fleet of seventeen vessels was manned and outfitted in Cádiz with food, arms, supplies, and equipment for more than twelve hundred seamen, officials, ecclesiastics, artisans, workmen, and men-at-arms. The fleet sailed from Cádiz on September 25, 1493, for an intended six-month round-trip voyage.

Twelve of the vessels, under the overall command of Torres, then sailed from La Isabela, the newly established colony on La Española, on February 2, 1494, to return to Spain for additional supplies. Following the example set by Columbus on the return to Spain from the first voyage, Torres proceeded along the north shore of the island to its eastern end and then headed to the northeast until he caught the favorable westerly winds, arriving in Cádiz on March 7, 1494, after a swift passage.

Torres returned to La Española that fall with four caravels laden with supplies requested by Columbus and with a message of approval from the sovereigns, dated August 16, 1494. Torres again set sail from La Isabela on February 24, 1495, with the four caravels laden with about five hundred male and female Indian slaves. For some reason he chose a more southerly route than he had used previously and wasted a month beating to windward along the northern coasts of La Española and Puerto Rico. Running low on food and water, he finally changed course to the north to find the westerlies. These favorable winds sped him on to the island of Madeira where he was able to reprovision before resuming his voyage to Cádiz. The suffering of the Indians, confined below decks, can only be imagined. About two hundred of them died and were cast overboard. The remainder, many of whom were sick, were disembarked in Cádiz about May 1, 1495, and put up for sale in Seville by Bishop Juan Rodríguez de Fonseca.

There followed an interval in which there is no record of Torres. He reappears in 1502 as captain of the flagship of a magnificent fleet of thirty ships carrying twenty-five hundred mariners, colonists, and soldiers. Aboard the flagship was Nicolás de Ovando, newly appointed governor of the Indies (except those portions under the jurisdiction of Vicente Yáñez Pinzón and Alonso de Ojeda). The fleet sailed from Cádiz on February 13, 1502, and arrived in Santo Domingo, the new capital of La Española, in early April.

The fleet remained anchored until July in the mouth of the Ozama River, the site of Santo Domingo, and was making preparations to return to Spain when Columbus arrived at the mouth of the river, seeking refuge for his four caravels from an approaching hurricane. The Admiral, having gained experience from two previous hurricanes in the Caribbean, urged that the fleet not leave port until the storm had passed. Ovando refused Columbus access to the harbor and scoffed at the hurricane warning. The fleet sailed and had just entered the Mona Passage between La Española and Puerto Rico when the hurricane struck. Several ships capsized at sea, and most of those that survived the first winds were driven ashore and destroyed. Only five of the thirty ships survived, and over five hundred men were lost, among them the fleet commander, Antonio de Torres.

BIBLIOGRAPHY

Gould, Alicia B. *Nueva lista documentada de los tripulantes de Colón en 1492*. Madrid, 1984.
Irving, Washington. *The Life and Voyages of Christopher Columbus and His Companions*. 3 vols. New York, 1849.

WILLIAM LEMOS

TOSCANELLI, PAOLO DAL POZZO (1397–1482),

Florentine mathematician, astronomer, astrologer, and geographer. Toscanelli (Latin, Paulus de Puteo Toscanello; also Paulus medicus, physicus, astronomus, etc.) was born and died in Florence, where he spent most of his long life. He studied medicine and other subjects at the University of Padua, gaining his doctorate in 1424. His most important extant work is a treatise on comets, *Immensi labores et graves vigilie Pauli de Puteo Toscanello super mensura comete* (Immense toils and serious lucubrations of Paolo dal Pozzo Toscanelli on the measurement of comets), which contains celestial maps showing the successive positions of each comet at its appearance. His fame as a geographer rests on his knowledge and appreciation of the voyages of Marco Polo, his interviews with travelers visiting Florence from distant lands (such as Tatars from the Don and clerics from Ethiopia), and his connection, whether direct or not, with Columbus's plans for exploration.

While in Padua he became a close friend of Nicholas of Cusa, with whom he shared an interest in geography. In 1425, he met the Florentine architect Filippo Brunelleschi, who designed the dome and lantern of the cathedral of Florence. When the city was hit by an earthquake in 1453, the Signoria consulted Toscanelli as an astrologer. In 1468 he constructed an astronomical gnomon in Brunelleschi's lantern, where an opening let the sun's rays shine on the gnomon (later replaced), so that the timing of solstices, eclipses, and other astronomical data could be established. The opening also allowed the sun to shine on a stone set in the floor of the cathedral at noon on the summer solstice. Both these astronomical devices helped establish latitude and longitude.

According to Bartolomé de las Casas's *Historia de las Indias*, Afonso V of Portugal asked Canon Fernão Martins to write to Toscanelli about the possibilities of sailing west to Asia. On June 25, 1474, Toscanelli replied with a detailed letter and a map. The originals of both are lost, but a presumed copy of the letter attached to Columbus's copy of Enea Silvio Piccolomini's geographical work was made public after Columbus's death. J. Henry Vignaud's attempts to prove that this letter was spurious are no longer accepted by most scholars.

In his letter, Toscanelli says that he is very glad that the king is seeking a shorter sea route to the spice-producing areas than by way of Guinea. He includes a map or chart, made with his own hands, "in which are drawn your shores and the islands from which you may begin to sail continuously west, and the lands which you must reach, and how far you must deviate from the pole or the equator, and for what distance, that is, for how many miles you should sail to reach most fertile lands producing all spices and gems." He claims that, as the land distance from Lisbon east to the coast of the Far East covers 230 degrees, only 130 degrees of sea separate Lisbon from the east coast of Asia (at 100 kilometers [62½ miles] to the degree, this distance would be 13,000 kilometers [8,125 miles]). Toscanelli claimed that only 116 degrees separated Cape Verde from the coast of Asia and that both the legendary island of Antilia and Cipangu (Japan) lie on the route, there being only 50 degrees between the two.

In contrast to Ptolemy's implication that the unknown world was 180 degrees across from east to west, and Marinus of Tyre's implication that it was 135 degrees across, the actual distance at the latitudes involved is nearly 250 degrees. If there had been no intervening land, this stretch of open ocean would have proved an insuperable obstacle. Toscanelli's estimate of 62½ miles to a degree was the middle of three estimates (56⅔, 62½, and 66⅔ miles) given by Fra Mauro in his 1459 world map. Columbus, following Pierre d'Ailly, who in turn was indebted to Alfraganus (al-Farghani), preferred the smallest figure, 56⅔ miles.

Toscanelli's map may have resembled the 1894 reconstruction by Hermann Wagner, with cylindrical projection similar to that of Marinus and with the west coast of Cipangu placed about 1,000 miles from the nearest point of China (Marco Polo had placed Cipangu 1,500 miles from China, and Toscanelli may have done likewise or modified the distance from his interviews). The map may have had

a directional line past Antilia, wherever that was thought to be, and from Cipangu to Quinsay (Hangchow, China). According to W. G. L. Randles, the extant map corresponding most closely to Wagner's reconstruction of Toscanelli's is the world map (c. 1490) by Henricus Martellus Germanus (Yale University Library).

Toscanelli's letter and map had no immediate effect. Columbus's plans were rejected by a Portuguese royal committee of cosmographers appointed in 1483–1484 and by similar committees in Spain in 1486–1487 and 1491. During that period, learned men in both countries were arguing for or against the plans, with both sides appealing to Aristotle and even to *Genesis*. To explain the emergence of dry land from water, the Spanish converso Paul de Burgos (c. 1350–1435) had maintained that on the third day of creation, when God said "Let the waters under the heaven be gathered together unto one place, and let the dry land appear," God moved the sphere of water so that the spheres of earth, water, air, and fire were no longer concentric. Ptolemy writes in his *Geography*, "From mathematical calculations it may be assumed that the collective surface of land and sea is in all its parts spherical"; he knew of no land in Asia beyond islands near its east coast. Arguments from such authorities were likely to be sterile, whereas Toscanelli, by combining the statistics of a mathematical geographer with an economic

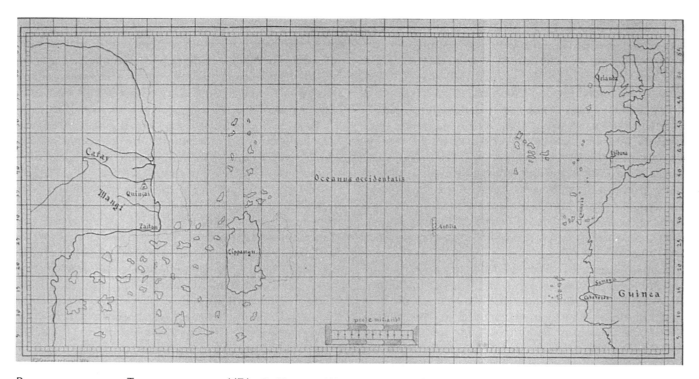

RECONSTRUCTION OF THE TOSCANELLI CHART OF 1474. By Hermann Wagner, 1894. Based on presumed copy of the Toscanelli letter to Canon Martins that is copied into Columbus's copy of Enea Silvio Piccolomini's *Historia rerum*.

FROM *NACHRICHTEN DER K. GESELLSCHAFT DER WISSENSCHAFTEN ZU GÖTTINGEN* (1894), P. 313.

factor (the search for spices and jewels), may well have helped to influence the new committee and the Royal Council of Castile in 1491, some years after his death. The *mappamundi* that Columbus exhibited at that time may have been Toscanelli's map with the distance shortened.

BIBLIOGRAPHY

Morison, Samuel Eliot. *Admiral of the Ocean Sea: A Life of Christopher Columbus.* 2 vols. Boston, 1942.

Randles, W. G. L. "The Evaluation of Columbus' 'India' Project by Cosmographers in the Light of the Geographical Science of the Period." *Imago Mundi* 42 (1990): 50–64.

Uzielli, Gustavo. *La vita e i tempi di Paolo dal Pozzo Toscanelli.* Rome, 1983.

Vignaud, J. Henry. *The Columbian Tradition on the Discovery of America and of the Part Played Therein by the Astronomer Toscanelli.* Oxford, 1920.

Vignaud, J. Henry. *Toscanelli and Columbus.* London, 1902.

O. A. W. Dilke

TRADE. [The following entry includes two articles on trade in the Age of European Exploration:

Mediterranean Trade

Caribbean Trade

For further discussion of the importance and impact of trading, see *Atlantic Rivalry.*]

Mediterranean Trade

By about 1460 the Western world had begun to recover from the demographic devastation wrought by the Black Death of the mid-fourteenth century. Although scholars argue about the nature and extent of the revitalization, it seems clear that populations were beginning to rise, labor wages remained relatively high, and demand for both domestic and imported goods increased as the century wore on. The augmented output of raw materials, such as metals, wool, and wood, and industrial products, such as cloth, glass, arms, and soap, satisfied much domestic demand and also provided valuable commodities for exchange with other Christian countries, both Mediterranean and northern, and with Muslim countries and lands farther east.

The Mediterranean economy of the second half of the fifteenth century was, however, still largely agrarian and localized. Although only about one in ten Europeans lived in cities, these urban centers needed to import large amounts of foodstuffs. Some food came from the countryside controlled by the cities, from estates often owned by rich burghers, but in times of shortfall, and often on a regular basis, more had to be imported. Civic governments were adamant about ensuring food supplies since

shortages could easily lead to social disruption—something civic officials everywhere wanted to avoid. Thus, cities usually allowed unrestricted importation of necessaries, with the only predictable tariffs being levied on wine in Spain and southern Italy. Cities like Genoa or Naples that were poor in local agricultural production had to import vast amounts of grain, salt, oil, fish, and sometimes wine. Fernand Braudel has estimated that the average European consumed annually about 440 pounds of grain, and given frequent disruptions in local supply, it could prove profitable to import grain even from enormous distances. Sicilian and Apulian grain could be found in Flanders, and German wheat in Egypt, while Crimean grain was routinely sold as Genoese bread.

As the European economy began to grow after 1460 or so, industry also picked up momentum. The development of printing in the 1450s created new markets for both expensive volumes and cheap pocketbooks, tracts, and broadsheets; it also stimulated the paper and ink industries. The Venetians started a new woolens industry in 1458, although it had stagnated by the early sixteenth century. Venice also made substantial additions to its arsenal shipyards in 1473, and the manufacture of soap and glass increased over the years. Production of cloth—including woolens, silks, linens, and cottons, and fancy velvets, damasks, and brocades—also expanded. Flemish and English cloth sold regularly in Mediterranean ports, and cheaper grades of light woolens from Florence had a ready market at Levantine fairs. Richer grades were always in demand, increasingly so in the Levantine markets where domestic production had fallen off. This high rate of production stimulated demand for raw material, usually imported into production centers like Florence; alum, needed in the cleaning and dying process of wool and extracted at only a few places in Europe; and dyestuffs, the best quality and variety of which came from Asia. Milanese arms and armor and firearms still commanded a steady market, although competition from Spain and southern Germany was growing.

Short-haul trade provided the bulk of Mediterranean traffic, but the real profits were to be made in luxury trade with Asia. Traditionally, oriental products reached the West by caravan to the Black Sea ports like Tana, or up the Persian Gulf and through Mesopotamia to Syria, or up the Red Sea to Egypt's ports, especially Alexandria. When the Turks captured Constantinople in 1453, they effectively blocked European trade with the Black Sea ports, restricting already diminishing trade with the northern caravan routes and producers in the Black Sea region. The silks, drugs, aromatics, and spices that had traveled overland from India and China now filtered through Turkish hands if they came through at all. This area had provided wheat and slaves, which were now at the mercy of the "infidel," as were the valuable alum mines of Focea, captured from the Genoese in 1455.

Farther south in Syria and Egypt, an area ruled by the Mamluks and threatened by further Turkish advances, the situation was one of social decline and general impoverishment. Although Beirut, Damascus, Tripoli, and Alexandria remained important transit ports between east and west, their native economies based on fancy cloth, glass, and even grain and cotton disintegrated, as high taxation for defense and recurring epidemics hammered the population. This forced the Mamluk authorities to raise tariffs, force the purchase by western merchants of certain surplus goods, especially pepper, and otherwise raise the revenues from the transit trade. Glass and silks, once major export items, were now imported by the Venetians.

Venice, long the most vital and powerful maritime nation in the Mediterranean, dominated Western trade with the Levant. Venetians brought to that region cheap cloth from England and northern Italy, oil, honey, nuts, and sometimes wheat, copper, and tin from northern Europe, and soap, glass, and coral from Venetian lands. The Venetian galley fleets returned with cotton, precious stones, dyes, aromatics, and spices from Malaysia, Burma, India, Ceylon, and China. As European economic production rose, less specie was needed to pay for these goods. In addition, the prices of spices, especially pepper and ginger, fell dramatically after mid-century because of economic conditions in the East, which sweetened the appeal of the spice trade for Europeans.

Venice handled much of this in large, regularly sailing fleets of galleys sponsored and controlled by the state. Upon their arrival at Alexandria or Beirut, huge fairs (*mudda*) were held, which facilitated exchange between the East and West. According to the foremost authority on the Levant trade, Eliyahu Ashtor, during the second half of the fifteenth century, "the spice trade flourished more than in any time before." Venetian merchants were responsible for about 60 percent of this trade, with a gross annual average around the end of the century of 650,000 ducats out of some 1.1 million ducats.

Until the Turkish conquest of the northeast Mediterranean, the Italian city-state of Genoa controlled trade in this region through a number of important trading colonies. The chief entrepôt was the Aegean island of Chios, which remained the key to eastern Genoese trade even after the surrender of Pera (1453) and the losses of Focea and Lesbos (1462). Genoa accounted for about 140,000 ducats per annum in trade with Egypt and Syria in the late 1400s, but whereas the Levant trade was vital for Venice, it represented only about 25 percent of Genoa's trade volume. Because of its location in the western Mediterranean, Genoa traditionally looked both east and west. Like Venice, Genoa served as a transit point for Mediterranean goods going north, especially to Milan, Switzerland, and the fairs of France, but Genoa also came to dominate trade between the eastern Mediterranean and Iberia, England, and Flanders.

The Genoese used a variety of ships, each specializing in a certain type of cargo. Some carried high-bulk goods such as alum, wheat, or lumber; smaller, faster ships would transport higher-priced, lower-bulk items. Although the Genoese used galley fleets, in general their trade was not under state control, as the Venetians' was; rather it was guided by individual initiative on the part of merchants and shipowners. This lent a good deal of flexibility to Genoese practices, although it also exposed merchants to greater risks. Indeed, as the Turks gobbled up Genoa's eastern colonies, the metropolis did practically nothing. On the other hand, Genoese ships did not have to make mandatory stops, often sailing directly from Chios to Flanders or from England to Chios. In addition, the Genoese could ship foreign goods, thus serving the interests of foreign individuals and states, as they did in transporting alum from Tolfa in the Papal States.

The stability, continuity, and experience of Genoese traders and their practices contrast favorably with those of their rivals. Although all Mediterranean countries carried out coastal trade in commodities like wine, wheat, and salt (wheat, in fact, was a very important item in Genoese trade), few could carry on sustained trade with the East like Venice or even Genoa, at least not before 1500. Catalan trade declined as political and economic conditions in the region were disrupted, especially during the war between Aragón and France in the 1460s. French overseas trade was also upset by this war, as it had been by the long war with England that had only recently ended. The French monarch Louis XI, however, had a lively interest in Levant trade, and he established regular galley voyages from Marseilles to Alexandria in the 1470s and 1480s. The Italian cloth and banking center of Florence dealt most heavily with the old Byzantine, now Turkish, centers, which tended to alienate the rival Mamluks and resulted in only a small traffic in Levantine spices. Florence's attempt at establishing a galley fleet at this time is evidence of Italian merchant vitality, despite the fact that the effort failed. Naples was a great center for the exchange of goods, but owing to a policy of free trade its own goods were frequently handled by foreign traders.

The profits from longer-distance luxury trade were substantial. European demand for oriental products increased over the second half of the century, which tended to raise their value. In general, the costs of delivering these items to European markets fell at least slightly. These two factors augmented the profit margin. Freight charges, commissions, and duties at home and abroad added about 25 percent to the price paid in the Levant, but profits still lay in the range of 20 to 25 percent for spices and 45 to 50 percent for cotton from the East. Freight charges tended to drop as ships got larger, and other dues could fluctuate according to local conditions. Duties paid in the Levant amounted to about 40 percent of transport costs, but the uncertainty created by the Turkish threat kept this an unstable figure. Since the Mamluks counted on Western support against the potential threat of the Turks, however, they tried to tread lightly (though on several occasions they sequestered Western merchants for the misdeeds of other Europeans). All the same, the profits were high, compared with the 9 to 10 percent gained from trade with central Europe (whose overland freight charges were very high). Trade with the East would continue to grow, but in what direction?

There must have been those who, like the brothers Ugolino and Vadino Vivaldi in the 1290s, dreamed of making direct commercial contact with the producers themselves in the East. Such direct contact would eliminate the costs of coastal voyages in the waters of the Indian Ocean, Red Sea, and Persian Gulf, and of caravan transport from southern ports. The often corrupt and unpredictable Mamluks and their charges could be avoided, and if the Turks were to capture the Mamluk ports, then a continued supply would be ensured. Cutting out these middlemen could more than compensate for the costs of increased sailing time.

Although the Venetians were generally contented with their Levant trade and saw its volume and profits increase over the latter half of the fifteenth century, the Genoese and Portuguese, who were already trading in the Atlantic, were far more likely to seek alternative routes to the East. The Genoese were well established in the North African coastal trade and, along with the Portuguese, probed down the Atlantic coast. Many Genoese served with or for the Portuguese and other Iberian rulers or were independent merchants trading out of Cádiz or Lisbon. The independent-mindedness of the Genoese well served the Iberian monarchs who were already attempting early forms of mercantilism, especially the Portuguese in the Madeiras and the Canaries. The colonial practices of the Genoese and to a lesser extent the Venetians, honed in the Aegean and Cyprus, proved apt models for later Iberian expansion. The tightly organized Venetian state galley fleets were as well direct precursors of the East Indian fleets of Spain and Portugal.

In many ways economic conditions in the Mediterranean during the latter half of the fifteenth century made European expansion into and beyond the Atlantic almost inevitable. Venetian domination of the trade with Mamluk ports, and the Turkish threat to those ports, made alternative routes to the East very appealing to such western powers as Genoa, Spain, and Portugal. Falling prices of spices, dyes, and aromatics in the East seemed to ensure continued high profits, as did generally improving demographic and economic conditions in the West. The Genoese had proven that long continuous voyages, such as that from Chios to Flanders, were practical and profitable. The Genoese and Venetians had also established models for both extractive and trading colonies, such as the alum mines of Focea and highly successful *fondouks*, or trading headquarters, in Alexandria, Damascus, and Beirut. The Genoese and Iberians, seeking to tap into African gold, ivory, slaves, and some spices, had long traded with North Africa, and during the fifteenth century they expanded commercial contacts well down the African Atlantic coast. By the time the westward-looking Genoese Christopher Columbus approached the Spanish monarchs and convinced them to support his venture, any economic arguments he made must have sounded self-evident.

[See also *Florence; Genoa; Spices; Venetian Republic.*]

BIBLIOGRAPHY

Ashtor, Eliyahu. *Levant Trade in the Later Middle Ages.* Princeton, 1983.

Heers, Jacques. *Gênes au XVe siècle: Activité économique et problèmes sociaux.* Paris, 1961.

Kedar, Benjamin. *Merchants in Crisis: Genoese and Venetian Men of Affairs and the Fourteenth-Century Depression.* New Haven, 1976.

Lane, Frederic C. *Venice and History: The Collected Papers of Frederic C. Lane.* Baltimore, 1966.

Lopez, Robert S. "Venice and Genoa: Two Styles, One Success." *Diogenes* 71 (1970).

Pike, Ruth. *Enterprise and Adventure: The Genoese in Seville and the Opening of the New World.* Ithaca, N.Y., 1966.

Tracy, James D. *The Rise of Merchant Empires (1350–1750).* New York, 1990.

Verlinden, Charles. *The Beginnings of Modern Colonization.* Ithaca, N.Y., 1970.

JOSEPH P. BYRNE

Caribbean Trade

Once Columbus had discovered America, the Spanish monarchy wanted to monopolize all production in the new lands as well as all the mercantile transactions between Spain and the Indies. To achieve this goal, the Crown established a system whereby the production of the colonies was regimented according to a complicated system of royal rights, licenses, and grants that regulated the cultivation or exploitation of specific products. This system of trading colonies followed the model of the *factorías* set up by the Portuguese in Africa.

A *factoría* was a commercial outpost owned by two or more partners who divided the profits derived from trading with the natives; labor was provided by white artisans and craftsmen employed under a rigid wage system. Columbus used this experience in Africa to set up the first *factoría* at La Isabela in the island of La Española. Given the harsh working conditions imposed by Columbus on the Spanish laborers, a rebellion soon broke out and the *factoría* collapsed, thus forcing the Spanish Crown to reconsider its colonization scheme in the New World.

Within the new colonial framework initiated in 1502, the Spanish monarchs set up a fiscal policy that guaranteed a steady revenue for the royal exchequer. A tax of one-fifth was placed on all gold found in the Indies; another, the *alcabala*, put a 10 percent surcharge on all operations of buying and selling carried out in the colonies; and yet another, the *almojarifazgo*, imposed a 7.5 percent duty on all merchandise imported by the colonists. Thus, what the monarchs could not obtain by directly controlling colonial commerce and production they could get by taxing all the economic activities in the New World.

These activities were supervised by the Casa de la Contratación, which started its operations in Seville in 1503. Without its permission, no voyages or commercial transactions could be undertaken between Spain and the Indies. In each port of the New World the Casa maintained officials to supervise the production of gold, silver, precious stones, and many agricultural products. Other functionaries collected taxes, kept the account books of the royal exchequer, and gave permission to navigate and trade between the different regions. These officials included factors, inspectors, accountants, and treasurers, and their counterparts in Seville.

Spain's monopolistic policies put heavy restrictions on colonial trade. According to a policy established in 1503, there could be no commerce with foreigners. Therefore, foreigners could not go to the Indies to trade without the risk of severe punishment. Ships could leave for the Indies only from the port of Seville. Colonial products could not be sent to any port other than Seville or Cádiz, thus leaving all the other ports of the Iberian Peninsula outside the great stream of trade generated by colonization.

Such control had its most noticeable effects on prices, since the Casa de la Contratación responded generally to the interests of Seville's merchants rather than to the needs of the colonists. Thus, throughout the sixteenth century, it was almost impossible for the colonists legally to obtain merchandise directly from other parts of Spain or Europe; items they needed had first to be imported into Spain from other European countries. After paying maritime insurance, freight rates, and other duties, such merchandise cost up to six times its original price when it arrived at the colonies. On the other hand, the merchants of Seville often paid the lowest possible prices for colonial products in order to maximize their profits, a practice resented by the colonists.

The Spanish monopoly on the colonial market was also resented by the European merchants who were seeking means to expand their external markets. To circumvent the trade controls, many non-Spanish merchants maintained agents in Seville and various colonial cities operating through third parties. These foreign merchants acted as shipowners, exporters, and importers or as moneylenders and financiers for the many Spanish businessmen in Seville who were always in need of money. Even Charles V became deeply indebted to foreign merchants. As the sixteenth century advanced, Seville's economic life became more dependent upon foreign investors who anxiously awaited the return of ships from the New World to receive their payments, rents, and commissions. There were entire years during which the shipments of gold coming from Mexico and other colonies were mortgaged even before embarking to Spain. Because of this foreign domination over Spanish trade and finances, almost all the gold, silver, and other products that arrived in Seville were finally handed over to the very nations Spain wanted to keep away from its colonies. By 1589, Seville had some fifteen thousand foreign residents out of a total population of only ninety thousand.

Other responses elicited by the European opposition to Spain's monopoly in the New World were piracy and contraband. As early as 1513, for example, French pirates waited around the Canaries for Spanish ships coming from the Indies. In 1522, a French pirate named Jean Fleury attacked a ship sailing from Santo Domingo to Seville with a cargo of sugar, which Fleury stole and took to France. Soon, these pirates moved into the Caribbean. Piracy had a drastic effect on prices in the Indies as freight and insurance rates rose several times, and it presented a grave problem to the Spanish monopoly. In 1543, the Crown decided to protect its trade between Seville and the New World by ordering its ships to make their trips together in well-guarded fleets. These fleets were to leave twice a year from Seville and return through the ports of Veracruz in Mexico and Nombre de Dios on the Isthmus of Panama. The system of fleets, however, did not function regularly until 1566 when the use of galleons was inaugurated.

The fleets notably altered the rhythm and flow of navigation in the Caribbean and eventually completed the isolation of Santo Domingo, Puerto Rico, Jamaica, and the eastern part of Cuba as Mexico and Peru gained in importance within the Spanish Empire. Ships bound from Seville to the Caribbean islands could sail from Spain only with the fleet. But upon arriving in the Caribbean, they would have to proceed without protection through pirate-infested waters as the fleet continued on to other ports. Thus, navigation and trade to these islands became more expensive as freight rates rose in proportion with maritime insurance. Havana became the most important port in the Caribbean, and Santo Domingo, Puerto Rico, and Jamaica were left on the sidelines. Havana was on the gulf route, and its port was a much more convenient spot for the fleets to stop and take on provisions of food and water for the return voyage.

The inhabitants of the Caribbean islands were always in great need of wheat, wine, flour, cloth, soap, perfume, cloves, shoes, medicine, paper, dried fruit, iron, steel, knives, nails, and many other articles. Since Spain could not provide them except at high prices and under monopolistic conditions, the colonists increasingly turned to smugglers. Evidence of contraband appeared as early as 1527, when an English ship appeared in the harbor of Santo Domingo and asked to be admitted to rest its crew and take on fresh water on the pretext that it had been thrown off its course to North America. Although the authorities permitted it to anchor, they soon discovered that the English were seeking to establish trade with the city's residents. Moreover, the colonial authorities realized that despite existing prohibitions, there were abundant signs that African slaves were being introduced as contraband by the Portuguese and Germans who brought these blacks from the coasts of Guinea and Senegal.

As the sixteenth century progressed, the contraband trade became the norm in the Caribbean. In the early years, the colonists in the islands had patiently awaited Spanish ships to buy their products. But as the arrival of ships became more and more infrequent, the people gradually turned to French, English, and Portuguese smugglers. Indeed, contraband offered the inhabitants of these islands distinct advantages over the official Spanish trade. The smugglers sold their goods at cheaper prices and offered higher prices for the colonists' sugar, hides, and other products, and the colonists avoided paying export taxes to the Spanish government.

At first the colonists preferred trading with the Portuguese smugglers since the latter spoke a similar language and offered the merchandise most desired by the Spaniards—African slaves. But because Portugal, like Spain, possessed little industry, most of the manufactured goods needed by the residents were produced in other countries, particularly England and France, and were cheaper when obtained directly from French, English, and Dutch intermediaries. The willingness of the colonists to trade with the smugglers was intolerable to the Consulado of Seville and the Casa de la Contratación, even though their system of fleets was placing the islands on the sidelines of the official trade routes.

Dozens of cedulas, royal orders, and laws were sent from Seville to the colonial authorities commanding an end to the contraband that reduced the fiscal revenues, and the merchants of Seville continually sent representatives to apply pressure on the islands' governments. But in only a few cases was this pressure successful. Contraband continued to flow into the islands without hindrance throughout the sixteenth century, for the lack of European manufactured goods affected all the population, and everyone, authorities and commoners alike, were equally involved in a business necessary to their subsistence.

[See also *Casa de la Contratación.*]

BIBLIOGRAPHY

Céspedes del Castillo, Guillermo. *Latin America: The Early Years.* New York, 1974.

Haring, Clarence H. *Trade and Navigation between Spain and the Indies in the Time of the Habsburgs.* Gloucester, Mass., 1964.

Moya Pons, Frank. *Historia colonial de Santo Domingo.* Santiago de los Caballeros, 1973.

Parry, John H. *The Spanish Seaborne Empire.* London, 1967.

Pike, Ruth. *Enterprise and Adventure: The Genoese in Seville and the Opening of the New World.* Ithaca, N.Y., 1966.

FRANK MOYA PONS

TRAVEL LITERATURE. Columbus's claim that he could reach the East by sailing west from Spain across the ocean was inspired as much by his reading of travel and geographical writers—most of them medieval, but some classical and contemporary—as by his varied experiences at sea. Before 1492, most likely during the time he lived in Portugal and Spain, Columbus began the eclectic perusal of such authorities; his reading is reflected in his own subsequent writings and attested by his son Fernando, Andrés Bernáldez, and other contemporaries. He continued his bookish investigations throughout the decade of his four voyages, less, it seems, to entertain new ideas than to find confirmation of his conviction that he had indeed reached Asia. Some of the works Columbus (perhaps with his brother Bartolomé) read and annotated for their information about the earth have survived, although they probably constitute only a fraction of the "books of cosmography, history, chronicle, and philosophy" that Columbus in 1501 said that he had studied for years (*Cristóbal Colón: Textos y documentos completos, relaciones de viajes, cartas y memoriales*, ed. Consuelo Varela [Madrid, 1982]). A few of these annotated volumes and certain other travel and geographical works known to Columbus made important contributions to the argument that he presented to his sponsors about the feasibility of a westward voyage of discovery.

Crucial to this argument was his belief in the greatest possible eastward extension of Asia and in a correspondingly narrow Ocean Sea. In Ptolemy's *Geography* (compiled in the second century A.D. but discovered by western Europeans only in the fifteenth century), Columbus found authority for the notion that the continuous Eurasian landmass covered half of the earth's circumference. He relied, in addition, on the learned opinion of the contemporary Florentine geographer Paolo dal Pozzo Toscanelli that Asia extended thirty degrees farther east than even Ptolemy had estimated. These views were strongly corroborated by Pierre d'Ailly's *Imago mundi* (1410), a standard handbook of geographical lore for the later Middle Ages. The annotations in Columbus's copy of this book reveal his close attention to d'Ailly's verdict that Asia stretched farther into the ocean than Ptolemy had figured and that the sea between Spain and China was narrow. D'Ailly discussed but did not take a position on the age-old question of whether a fourth continent existed and was inhabited; Columbus also encountered uncertainty and skepticism about the existence of the antipodes in Aeneas Sylvius's (Enea Silvio Piccolomini, later Pius II) *Historia rerum ubique gestarum* (1477), a copy of which survives from the Admiral's library.

While these old and new geographers strengthened Columbus's faith in the possibility of a short ocean voyage to the Indies, several medieval travel narratives shaped his expectations about the places and peoples he eventually found there. Columbus borrowed what he needed from the scholarly experts to bolster his ideas—and he occasionally disputed their authority; but the *Travels of Marco Polo* (*Il milione*, Italian title), a copy of which he owned; John Mandeville's *Travels*, which Bernáldez, Las Casas, and his son Fernando Colón affirmed he read; and a few other accounts of Atlantic exploration he may have known, impressed him because they seemed to reflect the results of actual traveling.

Polo's narrative offered the fullest description of the Orient available in the West, and his merchant-traveler's focus on its wealth resonated with Columbus's own mercantile motives. What Columbus remarked on in his copy of Polo was the prevalence of gold, the signs of the far-flung Chinese trading network, the rich centers of civilization, and the vastness of Asia. Polo also taught Columbus about Cipangu (Japan), which supposedly lay fifteen hundred miles from Cathay; indeed, Polo's estimate of that distance was what convinced Toscanelli (and Columbus in turn) that westward ocean voyage could be relieved by a stop at Japan or at any of the thousands of islands beyond the mainland that Polo reported.

Mandeville's *Travels*, the most popular European travel account of the Middle Ages, would have affected both practical and visionary dimensions of Columbus's enterprise. Mandeville argued that the earth was circumnavigable, that it was inhabited everywhere, and that an anonymous northern European had already sailed around the globe. His portrayal of Asian peoples as ethically superior to Europeans helped define Columbus's assumptions about the Caribbean natives he met. And Mandeville's emphasis on the ultimate centrality of Jerusalem coincided with Columbus's crusading desire to help rescue the Holy Land for Christianity.

An important letter written to Columbus in 1497 by an English businessman, John Day, refers to narratives or news of two late medieval English voyages into the Atlantic that Columbus either knew of or wished to know of. Columbus seems to have requested from Day a copy of *Inventio fortunata*, a now-lost Latin narrative allegedly composed by Nicholas of Lynn, following travels in the North Atlantic during the mid-fourteenth century, and generally known to various geographers and mapmakers in Europe in Columbus's time. In the same letter, Day promised the Admiral a copy of the chart drawn by John Cabot while coasting along his unidentified North American landfall.

Day's letter is a sobering reminder of how much is not known about Columbus's sources of information and access to books. In his Genoese youth he may have heard or read about the centuries-long exploits of Genoese traders in distant Asia and about voyages like those of the Vivaldi brothers in 1291 into the Atlantic. He sailed with the Portuguese to Africa and must have been familiar with the record of their exploration south into the Atlantic; the time he spent in the Atlantic islands and his apparent visits to Ireland and Iceland would have made him knowledgeable about accounts of assorted European ventures in the Atlantic toward the end of the Middle Ages. It is clear, however, that he read widely and frequently, and his own writings show that he habitually blended his reading with his maritime experience.

[See also *Library of Columbus* and biographies of figures mentioned herein.]

BIBLIOGRAPHY

Andrews, K. R., N. P. Canny, and P. E. H. Hair, eds. *The Westward Enterprise: English Activities in Ireland, the Atlantic, and America, 1480–1650.* Liverpool, 1978.

Campbell, Mary B. *The Witness and the Other World: Exotic European Travel Writing, 400–1600.* Ithaca, N.Y., and London, 1988.

Gil, Juan, ed. *El Libro de Marco Polo.* Madrid, 1986.

Keever, Edwin F., trans. *Imago Mundi by Petrus Ailliacus.* Wilmington, N.C., 1948.

Morison, Samuel Eliot. *Admiral of the Ocean Sea: A Life of Christopher Columbus.* 2 vols. Boston, 1942.

Phillips, J. R. S. *The Medieval Expansion of Europe.* New York, 1988.

Taviani, Paolo Emilio. *Christopher Columbus: The Grand Design.* London, 1985.

Vigneras, L. A. "The Cape Breton Landfall: 1494 or 1497; Note on a Letter from John Day." *Canadian Historical Review* 38 (1957): 219–228.

CHRISTIAN K. ZACHER

TREATY OF ALCÁÇOVAS.   The Treaty of Alcáçovas was concluded by Fernando and Isabel of Spain and Afonso V of Portugal on September 4, 1479. The treaty was ratified by the Spanish rulers at Toledo on March 6, 1480, and by Afonso V at Évora on September 8, 1480; Pope Sixtus IV confirmed it in his bull *Aeterni Regis* on June 21, 1481.

The treaty resolved several outstanding issues. The most pressing was the controversy over the succession to the kingdom of Castile. Afonso V abandoned his efforts to uphold the rights to the Castilian throne of Juana de Castilla (La Beltraneja), the daughter of King Enrique IV. Given the option of retiring to a convent or marrying the son and heir of Fernando and Isabel, Juana chose the former, entering the monastery of Santa Clara de Coimbra in 1480. As a guarantee of permanent peace between the two realms, Isabel, the daughter of Fernando and Isabel, was betrothed to Afonso, a grandson of Afonso V.

The eighth article of the treaty was the most important from the point of view of overseas expansion because it established spheres of influence in the Atlantic Ocean. The treaty confirmed Portugal in possession of "all the trade, lands, and traffic in Guinea, with its gold mines, and whatever other islands, coasts, and lands" that might be discovered, as well as Madeira, the Azores, the Cape Verde Islands, and any other islands that might be found and conquered below the Canaries and opposite Guinea. The Canary Islands were explicitly reserved to Castile. Fernando and Isabel also promised not to allow any of their subjects or foreigners living in their dominions to travel to or to conduct business in the islands and lands of Guinea already discovered or to be discovered, without the permission of the king of Portugal.

Portugal derived the greatest benefit from the treaty in that Castile was now effectively limited to the Canary Islands and the sea routes leading to them. The treaty said nothing about navigation westward across the Atlantic, but it did reserve to Portugal complete and sole control of navigation along the Guinea coast. While Castilians might travel to the Canaries, they were prohibited from intruding in those ocean spaces reserved to Portugal. Fernando and Isabel strictly upheld these restrictions on navigation in the Atlantic, but when Columbus presented his proposals to them, their horizons were expanded. That may explain why in the Santa Fe Capitulations, their agreement with Columbus, Fernando and Isabel entitled themselves "lords of the ocean seas." When Columbus returned from his epic voyage to the New World, João II of Portugal cited the Treaty of Alcáçovas to lay claim to whatever lands Columbus had discovered. As a consequence, Fernando and Isabel appealed to Pope Alexander VI to set down the Line of Demarcation between the Portuguese and Spanish areas of discovery. The conclusion of the Treaty of

Tordesillas between Spain and Portugal in 1494 eventually resolved these issues.

[See also *Line of Demarcation; Treaty of Tordesillas.*]

BIBLIOGRAPHY

Davenport, Florence Gardiner. *European Treaties Bearing on the History of the United States and Its Dependencies to 1648.* 4 vols. Washington, D.C., 1917–1937.

Diffie, Bailey W., and George D. Winius. *Foundations of the Portuguese Empire, 1415–1580.* Minneapolis, 1977.

Pérez Embid, Florentino. *Los descubrimientos en el Atlántico y la rivalidad castellano-portuguesa hasta el tratado de Tordesillas.* Seville, 1948.

JOSEPH F. O'CALLAGHAN

TREATY OF TORDESILLAS.   The Treaty of Tordesillas was signed on June 7, 1494, by Spain and Portugal. The purpose of the treaty was to establish the Line of Demarcation in the Atlantic Ocean, assigning the lands west of the line to Spanish exploration and colonization and those east of the line to Portugal. The treaty was the consequence of a long debate between the two kingdoms that reached a critical stage when Columbus landed in the New World in 1492. Inasmuch as João II (r. 1481–1495) of Portugal challenged Spain's rights to the newly discovered lands, Fernando of Aragón (r. 1479–1516) and Isabel of Castile (r. 1474–1504) appealed to Pope Alexander VI, who upheld Spanish pretensions. In the papal bull *Inter caetera,* the pope, on May 3, 1493, confirmed Spain's rights. Nevertheless, as the wording was vague, he issued another bull, also called *Inter caetera,* dated May 4, in which he drew the Line of Demarcation from the North to the South Poles, assigning the lands one hundred leagues west and south of the Azores and the Cape Verde Islands to Spain, provided they were not subject to any other Christian ruler. Still later, on September 26, in response to Spanish requests for further clarification, he declared in the bull *Dudum siquidem* that Spain was entitled to all lands discovered by sailing westward or southward toward the Orient and India.

João II was dissatisfied by these papal decisions and proposed negotiations with Fernando and Isabel. Their representatives concluded the Treaty of Tordesillas on June 7, 1494. The Spanish sovereigns ratified it at Arévalo on July 2 and João II did so on September 5 at Setúbal. Although both sides agreed not to submit the treaty to the papacy for approval, Pope Julius II, at the request of King Manuel I of Portugal (r. 1495–1521), confirmed it in 1506.

The treaty consisted of four clauses. As the king of Portugal suggested, the first clause drew "a stripe or straight line from pole to pole, from the Arctic pole to the Antarctic pole, that is, from north to south," 370 leagues

THE TREATY OF TORDESILLAS. The first attempt to define global spheres of influence. Signed by representatives of João II of Portugal and Isabel and Fernando of Spain, June 7, 1494; ratified July 2, 1494.   ARQUIVO NACIONAL DA TORRE DO TOMBO

west of the Cape Verde Islands. Everything east of the line, to the north and south, would belong to Portugal, and everything west would pertain to Spain. As a consequence, the Western Hemisphere fell to Spain and the Eastern to Portugal. In the second clause each party pledged not to explore in the regions reserved to the other and to yield lands that they might by chance discover in the other's region. The third clause provided for a period of ten months in which to establish the meridian marking the zones. Each party agreed to send one or two ships, with pilots, astronomers, and mariners to the Island of Grand Canary, from which they would sail directly to the Cape Verde Islands and then westward to determine the point where the line should be fixed. As this was eventually seen to be impractical, it was not carried out. In 1495 the two kingdoms agreed to abandon that idea but to inform one another of new discoveries. The fourth clause granted permission to Castilian subjects to cross the Portuguese zone on the way west, but without stopping to explore. This was important for Columbus who had already started on his second voyage and of necessity had to cross the Portuguese zone. The treaty

allowed an exception: if Columbus before June 20 should discover any lands beyond the first 250 leagues, they would belong to Castile. Any others east of that point would be reserved to Portugal.

In practical terms the most important consequence of the Treaty of Tordesillas was that it gave Portugal undisputed title to Brazil. Even so, the difficulty of determining exactly where the Line of Demarcation ought to run provided the basis for continuing disputes over the extent of Brazil and also over claims to islands in the Pacific Ocean. For example, although the Portuguese had reached the Moluccas Islands in 1512, Spain claimed them after Ferdinand Magellan's ships landed there in 1521. The Treaty of Zaragoza, signed in 1529, finally recognized the Portuguese title to the islands. A similar dispute arose concerning the Philippines, which the Spaniards had occupied, even though the Portuguese claimed that those islands also fell within their zone. The Treaty of San Ildefonso, concluded in 1777, brought these controversies to a close by establishing the western limits of Brazil and confirming Spanish rights to the Philippine Islands.

[See also *Line of Demarcation; Treaty of Alcáçovas.*]

BIBLIOGRAPHY

Davenport, Frances. *European Treaties Bearing on the History of the United States and Its Dependencies to 1648.* 4 vols. Washington, D. C., 1917–1937. Vol. 1, no. 9, pp. 84–100.

Diffie, Bailey W., and George D. Winius. *Foundations of the Portuguese Empire, 1415–1580.* Minneapolis, 1977.

El Tratado de Tordesillas y su proyección. 2 vols. Valladolid, 1973.

Morison, Samuel Eliot. *Admiral of the Ocean Sea: A Life of Christopher Columbus.* Boston, 1942.

Nowell, Charles E. "The Treaty of Tordesillas and the Diplomatic Background of American History." In *Greater America: Essays in Honor of Herbert E. Bolton.* Berkeley, 1945.

Pérez Embid, Florentino. *Los descubrimientos en el Atlántico y la rivalidad castellano-portuguesa hasta el tratado de Tordesillas.* Seville, 1948.

JOSEPH F. O'CALLAGHAN

TRISTÃO, NUNO (d. 1446), navigator and knight. Knowledge of the life of Nuno Tristão stems from narratives that are described by the chronicler Eanes Gomes de Azurara in his *Crónica dos feitos da Guiné* (Chronicle of the events in Guinea). During the reign of Prince Henry the Navigator, the navigator Tristão was also a merchant and a warrior. When he began his trips to the western coast of Africa, he often attacked practically defenseless coastal populations with the goal of capturing Africans to be sold as slaves. Besides capturing slaves, he also hunted seals, which were profitable for their oil and skins. He sometimes traded with the natives, who sought peaceful contacts with the navigators, a practice that was still common between 1440 and 1450. Further, his trips contributed to expanded exploration of the coast.

Chroniclers report that Prince Henry gave Tristão a caravel for his first expedition and explicitly recommended that he go beyond the "Pedra da Galé, over there, as far as possible" and that he should capture native Africans in any possible way. Tristão's voyage in 1422 set him in competition with another warrior-navigator, Antão Gonçalves, who was likewise engaged in sorties and slaving raids. Tristão was thus prompted to follow Gonçalves's route and to accomplish his goals with Gonçalves as an occasional companion.

Tristão reconnoitered farther to the south than he had been ordered, reaching Cape Blanc. The following year, still in a caravel, he continued his mission, but did not travel farther than the island of Adegete, some 40 kilometers (25 miles) from the point he had previously reached. The island was later called Arguim, the site of a farm-fortress built by the Portuguese. Tristão's penultimate voyage took place in 1445. He left Lagos in his caravel and traveled toward the island of Garças, not far from Arguim. After realizing that it would be impossible to take prisoners in that place, he kept sailing south and explored the coast to a place called Palmar on a fifteenth-century Italian map. Since he could not engage in trade with the local population, he landed with the intention of taking prisoners, but this venture was not very successful. In 1446 he intended to explore the coast south of Cape Vert. However, upon reaching the coast of Guinea, he arrived at the mouth of a large river (historians are still divided as to this river's identity) that he and his crew entered in search of a village. There, they were attacked by Guinean warriors, who killed twenty of the twenty-two Portuguese, Nuno Tristão among them.

BIBLIOGRAPHY

De Lery, Jean. *History of a Voyage to the Land of Brazil Otherwise Called America.* Translated by Janet Whatley. Berkeley, 1990.

Diffey, Bailey W. *Prelude to Empire: Portugal Overseas before Henry the Navigator.* Lincoln, Neb., 1960.

Diffey, Bailey W., and George D. Winius. *Foundations of the Portuguese Empire, 1414–1850.* Edited by Boyd C. Shafer. Minneapolis, 1977.

Morison, Samuel Eliot. *Portuguese Voyages to America in the Fifteenth Century.* New York, 1965.

LUÍS DE ALBUQUERQUE
Translated from Portuguese by Paola Carù

TUPINAMBÁS. See *Indian America*, article on *Tupinambás*.

VALENCIA. The capital of a former Muslim kingdom on the east coast of the Iberian peninsula that fell to the Aragonese in 1238, Valencia in the fifteenth century experienced profound tensions as the economic and social monopolies of the urban medieval craft guilds were challenged by peasants and foreigners.

The greater participation of the peasantry in the crafts throughout the century was opposed by the artisans, who tried to retain their monopoly of markets and protect themselves from rural competition. The development of shipyards in the first half of the fifteenth century brought expansion of crafts linked to the arsenals and shipyards; metalworking was revived by the manufacture of armor, weapons, and artillery for the armies of Alfonso V. The rural textile industry, which depended on contracts and raw material from native and foreign merchants based in the city, unsettled the old order and brought about modifications to the production system. New construction, including renovation and refurbishment of existing structures, sought to impose a Christian order on the old Muslim town and upgraded the building crafts—masonry and carpentry—and the profession of master builder.

Increase of foreign goods competed with local production, which was too weak to resist the products of other cities and states. Artisans and a section of the bourgeoisie who favored a protectionist trade policy were pitted against nobles who favored a liberal trade policy because they exported the majority of their agricultural production through foreign intermediaries. The Crown was pulled in both directions, wishing to protect local industry but grateful for the revenue produced by foreign trade.

Of the groups of foreigners, Italians—Florentines, Sienese, Romans, and Genoese—were the best integrated and most prosperous, especially as silk makers and papermakers. The Sienese specialized in banking. In the final quarter of the century, Valencia was one of the great printing centers of Europe, with seven German printers operating in the city. Valencia's commercial community included merchants from the Empire (Germans and Swiss), France, Portugal, and the other Spanish kingdoms.

Christians were a majority of the population by the fifteenth century, although the Muslim minority continued to play an important role in the economy and life of the city because of the links it retained with the Berbers and the Kingdom of Granada. Despite the warfare of the Reconquista, contacts between Christians and Muslims were maintained, under royal protection. The tiny Jewish community disappeared in 1492.

BIBLIOGRAPHY

Berger, Philippe. *Libro y lectura en la Valencia del renacimiento.* Valencia, 1987.

Bisson, Thomas N. *The Medieval Crown of Aragon.* New York, 1991.

Hadjiiossif, Jacqueline Guiral. *Valencia, puerto mediterraneo en el siglo XV.* Valencia, 1989.

JACQUELINE GUIRAL HADJIIOSSIF

VALLADOLID. Center of the most important demographic and urban region of Castile, Valladolid underwent a great overall development during the fourteenth and fifteenth centuries. Situated in the center of the basin of Castile and close to the River Duero, Valladolid is an easy gateway to the north and a natural link with both the eastern and western regions.

The starting point of this expansion was the increasing importance of Valladolid's political function. Even though the Castilian-Leonese monarchy did not have a fixed capital, the frequent presence of the court in Valladolid made it the de facto capital of the kingdom. It was also one of the favorite spots at which to hold the Cortes, the parliamentary assembly. The political importance of Valladolid is also attested to by the fact that it was the place where Isabel, princess of Castile, and Fernando, heir to the throne of Aragón and king of Sicily, were married on October 19, 1469.

Another factor that greatly contributed to the development of Valladolid was the establishment of the Audiencia Real, or Chancillería—highest appellate court for civil suits and criminal cases. In 1442 King Juan II of Castile designated Valladolid as the seat of the Chancillería, but his ordinance was not effective until Isabel established it as such in 1485.

Political progress in the fourteenth and fifteenth centuries was not paralleled by the development of the urban nucleus. The city's territory was still defined by the wall erected in the first decades of the fourteenth century, although the area outside expanded owing to the increasing importance of Valladolid.

The economy of the city was characterized by three elements: agriculture and cattle raising, luxurious crafts, and commerce. The chief crops of the area, wheat and barley, were enough to satisfy the more immediate necessities of the villagers. There was also a good provision of wine produced in the valleys of the Duero and the Pisuerga rivers. Livestock was abundant with a predominance of sheep, although cows, goats, and pigs were also raised.

Even though the most important industrial activity was the weaving of wool into cloth of ordinary quality, in the fourteenth and fifteenth centuries Valladolid saw an enormous growth of luxurious crafts: silversmithing, jewelry, furriery, painting, enameling, armors' craft, and tailoring. This growth was related to the presence of nobles and their retinues in the village.

From a very early date Valladolid held annual fairs, which were attended by an important number of foreign merchants, mostly Italians and Flemish. These fairs lost their importance in 1491, however, when the sovereigns made those of Medina del Campo the general fairs of the whole kingdom.

From an ecclesiastical point of view, Valladolid was dependent on the bishopric of Palencia. The highest position in the clergy was that of the collegiate chapter of Santa María la Mayor. In Valladolid there were other numerous monasteries and convents, the most important being that of San Benito. Established by King Juan I of Castile in 1390, San Benito had become the head of the majority of the Benedictine monasteries of Castile and León by the end of the fourteenth century.

The University of Valladolid, created in the thirteenth century, had four schools at the beginning of the fifteenth century: law, arts, theology, and medicine. It was world famous for its highly specialized surgical work. In addition to the university, other centers of study known as *colegios* were established in the last third of the fifteenth century by illustrious ecclesiastical patrons with the idea of providing the monarchy and the clergy with a new generation of more educated public servants and priests. The two most important *colegios* were Santa Cruz, established by Cardinal Pedro González de Mendoza, and San Gregorio, established by Alonso de Burgos.

In May of 1505, a few months after returning from his fourth journey to America, Christopher Columbus, following the court, moved to Segovia. There he presented his claims to King Fernando about his titles of admiral, viceroy, and governor, and all the rights and privileges associated with them. Without having reached a solution Columbus moved to Valladolid in April 1506 where his family had a modest house. There he spent his last days enduring the pain of gout and arthritis. He died on May 21, 1506; his body was deposited in the convent of San Francisco, and his obsequies were celebrated in the parochial church of Santa María la Antigua. A few years later his remains were transported to Seville. The house where he is supposed to have lived and died, known today as Casa de Colón, serves as a museum and houses the Department of the History of America.

BIBLIOGRAPHY

Highfield, Roger, ed. *Spain in the Fifteenth Century, 1369–1516.* New York, 1972.

Mariéjol, Jean H. *The Spain of Ferdinand and Isabella.* New Brunswick, N.J., 1961.

Ribot García, Luis A., et al. *Valladolid, corazón del mundo hispánico: Siglo XVI.* Valladolid, 1981.

Ruiz Asencio, Manuel, and Julio Valdeón Baruque. *Historia de Valladolid: Valladolid medieval.* Valladolid, 1980.

Trevor Davies, R. *The Golden Centuries of Spain, 1501–1621.* New York, 1967.

FRANCISCO GAGO JOVER

VÁZQUEZ DE AYLLÓN, LUCAS. See two entries under *Ayllón, Lucas Vázquez de.*

VENETIAN REPUBLIC. Poised in a lagoon near the northern end of the Adriatic Sea, medieval Venice turned away from the Italian mainland from which its first settlers had migrated, fleeing the poverty, disorganization, and warfare that accompanied the fall of ancient Rome. Offering nothing at first but fish and salt, its merchants traveled eastward, extending their realm from nearby ports to the cities of the Balkan coast, Greece, Crete, Cyprus, the whole of the Levant, and Egypt, until their chosen leader, called doge, could claim domination by Venice and its gold ducats of *quartum et dimidium* (one-quarter plus one-eighth) of the world that Rome had once ruled. But in the centuries that encompassed the birth and death of Columbus, who sought a route to the east that avoided the routes that Venice dominated, the city turned westward. From 1404–1406, when it seized neighboring Padua, Vicenza, and Verona, until 1571, when at the battle of Lepanto it reached the zenith of its Mediterranean career, Venice claimed one-half of northern Italy, thanks to its well-run standing army, one of the first in Europe, and the unyielding policies forged by black-robed councilors in the halls of the ducal palace— the seat of one of Europe's first republican governments.

Venetian greatness was built on trade. A prerogative of the city's elite of noblemen and citizens was the license to trade under the Venetian standard, which gave access to Mediterranean ports and participation in the state fleets, escorted by armed galleys, that sailed to the Black Sea, the Levant, Alexandria, and Flanders. Meanwhile, merchandise from Asia, Africa, and northern Europe was purveyed by foreign merchants at the Rialto, the single bridge across the city's serpentine Grand Canal, and its commercial center. Organized merchant communities kept their representatives there, housed in office blocks such as those named for the Germans—the Fondaco dei Tedeschi— and the Turks—the Fondaco dei Turchi. The numerous foreigners in Venice seemed almost to overwhelm the indigenous population, who were daily exposed to conflicting faiths and customs and a symphony of languages. Meanwhile, native craftsmen organized in guilds produced glass, lace, and ships of great renown. After 1500, Venice continued to flourish but at a slackening pace: its appetite for commercial activity was curbed by Turkish encroachment in the eastern Mediterranean and by the lure of mainland territories, which the city's noblemen sought as a haven from the risks of maritime trade. Thus the seafaring merchant princes of Venice turned landlord following the conquest of the hinterland.

The transformation of the nobility that occurred during the age of exploration was a crucial social and political series of events, since Venice's distinctive political institutions were designed to foster the interests of that class. During the fourteenth century, participation in the government of Venice was limited to a set of noble families

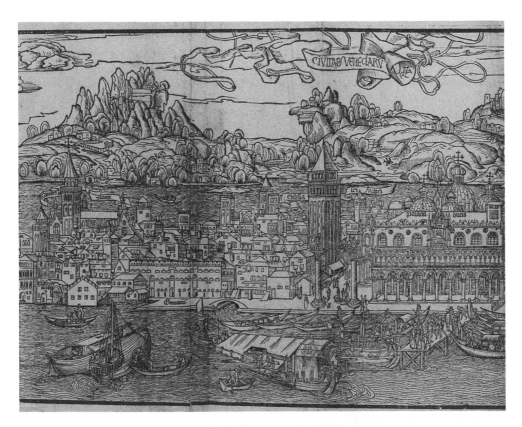

VENICE IN **1486.** Woodcut, from Breydenbach's *Journey to the Holy Land.*

and their legitimate heirs; this limitation was called the *serrata* (locking) of the Great Council, the largest of the city's deliberative bodies. Thenceforth, Venice's republican machinery expanded, always powered by birth and driven by privilege. The fifteenth century brought the rise in influence of the Senate, which stood behind the strategy of expansion, and the elevation of the Collegio, an advisory circle around the doge that included sets of counselors, "sages" expert in naval, military, and diplomatic affairs, and members of the Council of Ten, the secretive body created to guard against treachery. Coincidental with this governmental elaboration, the ancient custom by which the whole assembled people approved the election of the doge was ended. The sixteenth century saw the further extension of the influence of the distinctly undemocratic Ten and the creation of councils of censors, reformers, and inquisitors. Although the aristocratic government of Venice departed steadily from the more democratic practices of the traditional commune, its processes of discussion and decision making, as well as its handling of foreign affairs, were a legacy to later nation states. Sent as ambassadors to courts and cities on three continents, Venetian nobles pioneered modern diplomacy, and their achievement was witnessed by their famous *relazioni* (reports), minutely describing foreign customs, courts, and personalities.

Venetian government was run by nobles dedicated to their own self-interest as much as to the common welfare. An increase in the numbers of aristocrats in the fifteenth century dating from the downturn that began with the Black Death of 1348 occasioned bitter competition for positions, both among those seeking honorable office without pay and those seeking lesser positions for high salaries. As the nobles competed with one another for office, for villas in the country, and for the perpetuation of lineage and reputation, their posts in the commercial (and even the cultural) world were taken by members of the "citizen" class. Made up of *cittadini originari* (citizens by birth) and citizens by privilege, who had acquired Venetian trading rights, the citizenry was a kind of lesser patriciate, quite as restricted as the nobility. Each of the two groups comprised about 5 percent of a population that fluctuated around 100,000. Among them were merchants, state secretaries, teachers, and physicians, leaders in the *scuole* (social organizations for religious and charitable purposes), and, like the noblemen they imitated, patrons of art and ideas. Lower in the social hierarchy were artisans and common laborers, servants and prostitutes, and that uniquely Venetian shipyard proletariat, the *arsenalotti* (workers in the Arsenal).

Workers, citizens, and nobles alike joined in a distinctively Venetian piety, scrupulously correct yet wary of Rome. The whole populace engaged in ritual observances that were both religious and civic, such as the procession of doge, councilors, senators, secretaries, and citizens, and the *Scuole grandi* in tableaux vivants, in celebration of Corpus Christi. Venetian neighborhoods were tightly organized around the parish church standing in each *campo* (square), where business and culture was also centered. Armed with saints' relics from around the world, more than a hundred churches brooded over Venice, and half as many monasteries and convents hugged the periphery or sat on the encircling islands. These monasteries engendered reform movements that rose again and again in these centuries, led by charismatic nobles or citizen ascetics. From the upper ranks of the Venetian secular clergy, headed by their own patriarch after 1451, reformers of international stature emerged. Their activity was eventually halted as the Roman Inquisition (after 1542) and the Council of Trent (1545–1563) moved to suppress all heterodoxy. Thereafter, Venetians conformed, but they resisted orders from Rome about censorship, prosecution of heresy, and papal authority.

In this city that looked simultaneously outward and inward, east and west, there developed, as in Florence, a culture that was unique in the history of European civilization. Patrician and citizen intellectuals studied philosophy and law, collected libraries, wrote histories, learned Greek, and mastered the humanist curriculum, while the Venetian press became the most active in Europe. Poets and painters, architects and sculptors, mathematicians and philosophers gravitated to this cosmopolis that offered, in its patrician courtyards, its schools and printshops, and its narrow and thronged *calli* (streets), unmatched opportunity for the exchange of image and idea. From this matrix emerged some of the greatest artists of the age—Giovanni Bellini, Titian, Tintoretto, Paolo Veronese—who memorialized the special light, power, and spectacle of Venice.

BIBLIOGRAPHY

Bouwsma, William J. *Venice and the Defense of Republican Liberty: Renaissance Values in the Age of the Counter-Reformation.* Berkeley and Los Angeles, 1968.

Cozzi, Gaetano, and Michael Knapton. *La repubblica di Venezia nell' età moderna: dalla guerra di Chioggia al 1517.* Turin, 1986.

Finlay, Robert. *Politics in Renaissance Venice.* New Brunswick, N.J., 1980.

Grendler, Paul F. *The Roman Inquisition and the Venetian Press, 1540–1605.* Princeton, 1977.

Hale, John R., ed. *Renaissance Venice.* London and Totowa, N.J., 1973.

King, Margaret L. *Venetian Humanism in an Age of Patrician Dominance.* Princeton, 1986.

Lane, Frederic C. *Venice: A Maritime Republic.* Baltimore, 1973.

Logan, Oliver. *Culture and Society in Venice, 1470–1790: The Renaissance and Its Heritage.* London and New York, 1972.

Mallett, Michael E., and J. R. Hale. *The Military Organization of a Renaissance State: Venice c. 1400–1617.* Cambridge and New York, 1984.

Muir, Edward. *Civic Ritual in Renaissance Venice.* Princeton, 1981.

Queller, Donald E. *The Venetian Patriciate: Reality versus Myth.* Champaign-Urbana, Ill., 1986.

Romano, Dennis. *Patricians and Popolani: The Social Foundations of the Venetian Renaissance State.* Baltimore and London, 1987.

MARGARET L. KING

VERRAZANO, GIOVANNI DA (1485?–1528), Italian navigator and explorer for France. There have been several controversies concerning the life of Giovanni da Verrazano (also spelled Verrazzano), not the least of which is the question of his birth. Was he truly a Florentine, born in Greve in Tuscany, part of the Florentine dominion, or was he the son of Alessandro di Bartolommeo da Verrazano and his wife, Giovanna, of Lyons, France? Even if he was born in Lyons (where there were several Florentine merchants), he would have and, in fact, did, consider himself a Florentine. No documentation concerning his birth or that of his brother, Gerolamo, into the Tuscan family has survived; but neither is there any real evidence of his connection to the Lyons branch of the Verrazano family, aside from the latter's investing in Verrazano's 1524 voyage to the New World.

Almost nothing is known about Verrazano's life before the preparations for his 1524 voyage under the auspices of King Francis I of France. There is a possibility that he sailed as a member of Thomas Aubert of Dieppe's 1508 voyage to Newfoundland and the Gulf of St. Lawrence. It was this mission that brought back to France the first North American natives in 1509. Participation in that voyage would explain why Verrazano is supposed to have said to Henry VIII of England in 1525 or 1526 that he had already been three times to New World shores, although he had probably been only twice by 1525.

In the period between 1509 and 1523, when the outfitting for the 1524 voyage to America began, there are several isolated mentions of Verrazano. A responsible Portuguese official recorded that in 1517 Verrazano had been in Portugal and Spain in the company of Ferdinand Magellan. Bernardo Carli, a Florentine merchant in Lyons, later wrote to his father in Florence about Verrazano, informing him that Verrazano had been in Egypt and Syria, indeed, throughout the known world, before 1524 and was esteemed as another Amerigo Vespucci or Ferdinand Magellan. It is unclear from the surviving evidence whether Verrazano was a land-based factor in the Levant or one who traveled with goods shipped to that region.

Additional evidence of Verrazano's stature in 1523 can be found in a report to King João III of Portugal from Portuguese merchants in France who were concerned about a voyage to Brazil being planned by Verrazano and the French court. By the late spring of 1523 negotiations for the expedition were under way. Although the actual royal commission by Francis I to Verrazano has not survived, several extant letters make clear the French king's involvement in Verrazano's 1524 voyage to North America.

Like Christopher Columbus and John Cabot, Verrazano hoped to find an all-water route to the Far East. Instead his six-month voyage served the purpose of charting the eastern coastline of America from Cape Fear, South Carolina, to Cape Breton in Nova Scotia. Although the original plans of the expedition called for four ships, Verrazano set out on January 1, 1524, with only one, the royal *Dauphine.* Much of the financial support for the voyage came from the group of Florentine merchants and bankers in Lyons. The Cèllere Codex in the Pierpont Morgan Library is the record of the voyage in the form of a letter to King Francis I, and it includes a description of the land, its vegetation, its people, and the prominent geographical features seen from *Dauphine* and the ship's small boats launched to explore the new territory. Early in this letter Verrazano states,

> So we anchored off the coast and sent the small boat in to land. We had seen many people coming to the seashore, but they fled when they saw us approaching; several times they stopped and turned around to look at us in great wonderment. We reassured them with various signs, and some of them came up, showing great delight in seeing us and marveling at our clothes, appearance, and our whiteness; they showed us by various signs where we could most easily secure the boat, and offered us some of their food. We were on land, and I shall now tell Your Majesty briefly what we were able to learn of their life and customs.

Bearing in mind his royal patron, Verrazano named various discoveries after Francis I's mother and sister and the king himself as well as other members of the French court. Those areas explored by Verrazano include the coasts of present-day Virginia and Maryland; New York harbor; Narragansett Bay and the harbor of Newport, Rhode Island; Nantucket; Cape Cod; Maine; Nova Scotia; and Newfoundland.

When Verrazano returned to France on July 8, 1524, he wanted to embark on another voyage right away in order to find the elusive passage to Cathay that he and others had sought for so long. When that plan fell through, he spent some time in both England and Portugal seeking support for another voyage. Later he became involved with a project under the leadership of Philippe Chabot, which led to a voyage in 1526–1527 to look for a passage to the Spice Islands. A syndicate was formed under Chabot to compete with the 1526 voyage of Sebastian Cabot under the flag of Spain. The main purpose of Verrazano's expedition was to bring back spices to be used for food and pharmaceutical applications. This trip, Verrazano's third to the New World, was full of problems and mysteries. He appears to have sailed along the eastern coast of South America, failed to navigate the Straits of Magellan, and crossed the Atlantic to try to round the Cape of Good Hope. When most of his ships failed to make it around the Cape, he went back to South America, sailed along the coast of Brazil, loaded his ships with products there, and returned to France in September 1527.

Although several historians in the eighteenth and nineteenth centuries mistakenly identified Verrazano with Jean Florin, who was executed for piracy by the Spaniards in November 1527, we now know this is incorrect, since it is certain that Verrazano conducted another expedition to America in 1528. This final voyage was to fulfill the aims of the Chabot expedition of 1526. Three groups were involved: the officers and crew of *Flamengue;* investors in Fécamp, France, who chartered the ship; and Verrazano's friends and associates who supplied trade goods and some of the crew's wages. Once again Verrazano was seeking a passage from the Atlantic to the Indies. Although no maps of this voyage have survived, he apparently explored Florida, the Bahamas, Panama, and other islands in the Caribbean. It is commonly believed that Verrazano died during this voyage and fell victim to cannibals on an island in the Caribbean. In any event, *Flamengue* returned to France without its captain but with a cargo of dyewood from the Caribbean or South America in March of 1529.

Giovanni da Verrazano was among the great navigators and explorers of the sixteenth century whose efforts directed the attention of European merchants to the riches of the New World. It is certainly fitting that the Verrazano Narrows Bridge in New York is named for the navigator who did so much to explore the eastern coastline of the United States.

BIBLIOGRAPHY

Murphy, Henry C. *The Voyage of Verrazzano.* New York, 1875.

Thrower, Norman J. "New Light on the 1524 Voyage of Verrazzano." *Terrae Incognitae* 11 (1979): 59–65.

Wroth, Lawrence C. *The Voyages of Giovanni da Verrazzano, 1524–1528.* New Haven, 1970.

MARGERY A. GANZ

VESPUCCI, AMERIGO (1454–1512), Italian navigator and cosmographer. According to a long-held tradition, Vespucci made four voyages to America: two (1497–1498 and 1499–1500) in the service of Spain and two (1501–1502

AMERIGO VESPUCCI. Detail from a sixteeth-century painting in the Uffizi Gallery, Florence.   LIBRARY OF CONGRESS

and 1503–1504) in the service of Portugal. During the first voyage, it was said, he reached Paria, thus discovering the South American continent before Columbus. This tradition was based on the so-called Letter to Soderini, which was attributed to Vespucci. Printed for the first time in Florence in 1505–1506, it was distributed in a Latin version contained in the *Cosmographiae introductio* published at Saint-Dié in 1507. Attached to it was a large planisphere by Martin Waldseemüller, who, thinking Vespucci had discovered the southern part of the New World, inscribed it with the name *America.* This is the first appearance of the name. Another work, the *Mundus novus,* also consists of letters attributed to Vespucci. It recounts his voyage of 1501–1502 and was widely read in the first years of the sixteenth century.

But during the last half of the eighteenth century, three handwritten letters by Vespucci were found in archives in Florence. All were addressed to Lorenzo Pier Francesco de' Medici, cousin of Lorenzo de' Medici (known as Lorenzo the Magnificent). The first, from Seville, July 8, 1500, tells of the 1499–1500 voyage; the second and third, from Cape Verde in June 1501 and Lisbon in 1502, recount the 1501–1502 voyage. Because of discrepancies between these letters and the ones known earlier, scholars have concluded that the traditional ones are apocryphal and probably not truthful. Vespucci, they think, made only two of the four voyages attributed to him—the ones in 1499–1500 and 1501–1502.

Amerigo Vespucci, born the son of a noble merchant family in Florence, was the third child of Nastagio di Amerigo and Lisa di Andrea Mini. In 1483, after the death of his father, he entered into the service of Lorenzo Pier Francesco de' Medici and sometime between October 1489 and March 1492 went to Seville. There he worked with two other Florentines, Donato Nicolini and Giannotto Berardi. The latter at that time also looked after the interests of Columbus, and through him Vespucci came to know the Genoese, perhaps immediately after the discovery of the New World.

Vespucci's activities in Seville are well documented until February 1496. He worked with Berardi even after Berardi ceased his association with the Medicis in 1493. After Berardi's death on December 2, 1495, he continued preparations for an expedition of four caravels Berardi had planned. They were to have been the first of eighteen ships to be sent to Haiti at a very low price to avoid Columbus's interests being damaged by other competition. The caravels sailed on February 3, 1496, but they were destroyed in a storm. Nothing is known of Vespucci's activities after this date until May 1499. Thus, there is no proof that he made the 1497–1498 voyage attributed to him in the Letter to Soderini.

It is certain, however, that on May 18, 1499, he embarked with Alonso de Ojeda and Juan de la Cosa on the first expedition to explore the coasts of the New World after that of Columbus's (1498–1499). Sources disagree on the number of ships involved (two or four) and their itinerary. According to Vespucci's letter of July 8, 1500, he reached the South American coast in twenty-four days. The expedition headed south as far as 6°30′ S and then turning north sailed as far as Trinidad and followed the coast westward to the Venezuelan littoral. After visiting Aruba and Curaçao and following the coast for three hundred leagues (to beyond the Rio Magdalena), Vespucci decided to turn back.

But we know from other sources that Ojeda was already in Haiti on September 5, 1499, and since the itinerary Vespucci describes is too long for only three and a half months' sailing, some authors have asserted that Vespucci did not push farther south than the Suriname River (six degrees north). Others have hypothesized that he had separated from Ojeda and thus continued by himself the exploration he recounts in his letter. Both explanations are open to argument.

We do not know what tasks Vespucci carried out on this expedition, for his name is not on the list of members of the crew. Perhaps he represented the Seville merchants who had contributed to the costs of the voyage. We know he made astronomical observations and tried to measure longitude by a new method, using the conjunction of the moon with Mars on August 23, 1499, as his reference.

After his return to Spain in June 1500, he was summoned to Lisbon by King Manuel. On May 13 of the following year he sailed with a fleet of ships in the service of Portugal. Again we do not know what his tasks were. It is probable, however, that the king, having learned that Vespucci had found a new system for measuring longitude, had ordered him to fix the position of the land discovered the year before by Pedro Álvares Cabral with respect to the Line of Demarcation to see whether it was east or west of the line. If it was west, it would belong not to Portugal but to Spain.

After a stay at Cape Verde (on the western coast of Africa), Vespucci headed south-southwest, reaching the South American coast at Cape Saint Augustine (8°64′ S). The exact place and date of arrival are still debated, as is the itinerary for the rest of the voyage. Again, the sources disagree. According to the most authoritative, Vespucci reached latitude forty-six degrees south, always sailing along the coast. During this expedition Vespucci, being much interested in the Indians he encountered, made long stays in their villages. He returned to Lisbon in July 1502.

After his letter of 1502 there is another documentary gap until February 5, 1505, the date of a letter from Columbus to his son Diego Colón. It is clear from Columbus's words that there was a deep friendship between the two Italian navigators. The letter proves that no rivalry existed between them.

In the following years, Vespucci, now living in Spain, busied himself with preparations for a new expedition, which, however, never sailed. On August 6, 1506, by decree of Queen Juana, he was appointed first *piloto mayor* of Spain with the task of instructing pilots bound for the Indies. He also elaborated and updated the official nautical chart, or *padron real*. He kept this position until his death at Seville on February 22, 1512.

Among his contemporaries Amerigo Vespucci was esteemed as a cosmographer. What distinguished him from the other great navigators of his time was his interest in the scientific problems connected with the discovery of the New World, whose existence, as a continent in itself separate from Asia, he was certainly one of the first—if not the first—to explain.

[See also *America, Naming of.*]

BIBLIOGRAPHY

Arciniegas, Germán. *Amerigo and the New World: The Life and Times of Amerigo Vespucci.* Translated by Harriet de Onís. New York, 1955.

Caraci, Giuseppe. *Problemi vespucciani.* Rome, 1987.

Laguarda Trias, Rolando. *El hallazgo del Rio de la Plata por Amerigo Vespucci en 1502.* Montevideo, 1982.

Pohl, Frederick Julius. *Amerigo Vespucci, Pilot Mayor.* New York, 1944.

Magnaghi, Alberto. *Amerigo Vespucci.* 2 vols. Rome, 1926.

Ilaria Luzzana Caraci
Translated from Italian by Arthur Lomas

VINLAND. Two of the Icelandic sagas, *Eiríks saga rauða* (The saga of Eric the Red) and *Grœnlendingasaga* (The saga of the Greenlanders), tell of a land called Vinland discovered by Leif Ericsson. The texts make it clear that this must be somewhere in America, but the location of Vinland had been discussed in a large body of literature for centuries without being solved until the 1960s. Scientific assessment has shown that the Kensington Stone in Minnesota and other rune stones found in North America were not genuine Norse artifacts.

As the two sagas differ radically, it is important to ascertain which of them is the more reliable. In the past, most scholars, including Gustav Storm in 1889 and Finnur Jónsson in 1912, accepted *Eiríks saga* as being mainly historically correct. This saga relates that in about A.D. 1000 Leif Ericsson sailed from Greenland to Nidaros (Trondheim) in Norway, where the Norwegian king commissioned him to preach Christianity in Greenland. On his return to Greenland, Leif lost his way at sea and came to an unknown land, where he found vines and fields of wild wheat. He sailed to Greenland that same year.

This passage can hardly be accepted as historically accurate. For one thing, it is permeated with Christian reflections alien to the Viking age. In addition, the voyage described here—nearly 5,000 nautical miles as the crow flies—would have been nearly impossible. The distance from Trondheim to one of the northernmost areas of coastal eastern North America where grapes grow is about 3,000 nautical miles. If Leif really came to North America, his situation must have been desperate. He did not know where he was, he was sailing an open boat with square sails, and he had no instrument to determine his latitude. His only chance was to follow the coast northward for another 2,000 nautical miles or more, braving autumn storms and driftice. Presumably the provisions for his crew (probably of thirty) were intended only for the direct journey to Greenland. A voyage such as that described here would have meant starvation.

The subsequent text, about Thorfinn Karlsefni's search for Vinland, seems more than dubious. According to *Eiríks saga,* Karlsefni, who should have sailed south, sails north, following Leif's route as given in the *Grœnlendingasaga.* The author furthermore credits Karlsefni with having discovered Helluland and Markland, which, in the other saga, Leif had discovered and named. In *Eiríks saga,*

Karlsefni then makes his headquarters at a place called Straumfjord, which seems to be a substitute name for Vinland, the next land mentioned in the *Grœnlendingasaga.* Here the author is forced to stop his borrowing of names from the other saga, since the use of the name Vinland in this location would be in conflict with the story in *Eiríks saga* about Leif's discovery of Vinland during a voyage from Norway. Instead, he invented the name Straumfjord.

He then sails south and makes his camp at a place called Hop, which is accorded an effusive description of all the blessings found there, vines and self-sown wheat, game and fish, almost like a fairy tale. Again the author makes use of the *Grœnlendingasaga,* for this description is almost identical with that saga's description of Vinland. Helge Ingstad (1985) offers a detailed analysis to show that the *Grœnlendingasaga* must have been used throughout this passage, but in such a way that nothing would conflict with Leif's discovering Vinland during a voyage from Norway to a land with vines. Indeed, so many essential

Norse longship. About 1000 years old. Excavated in 1904 and now on display in the Viking Ship Museum, Oslo.

elements are unreliable that *Eiríks saga* must be judged as being largely fiction.

The Icelandic scholar Jón Jóhannesson pointed out in 1956 that the author of *Eiríks saga* must have known and made use of the *Grœnlendingasaga*, probably the earlier of the two, and he concluded, "Leif did not discover Vinland on his way from Norway to Greenland, and there remains no reason to doubt that the saga of the Greenlanders preserves the original and correct account of the discovery of the new lands in the Western Hemisphere."

According to the *Grœnlendingasaga*, Bjarni Herjulfsson makes an accidental discovery of a strange coast, and then Leif Ericsson carries out a planned expedition to find this coast. Next, Leif's brother Thorvald explores the land, finding it excellent, and finally, Thorfinn Karlsefni sails to the new land with women and livestock on board in order to settle there.

Leif followed Bjarni's route in the opposite direction, sailing first northward along the coast of Greenland, probably to Disko Island, and then crossing Davis Strait, which is only about 250 nautical miles wide. He probably came to Cape Aston in Baffin Island, a flat, barren land with glaciers, that is called Helluland (Flatstone land), and then sailed south, along the coast of Labrador, which he called Markland (Land of forests). There was forest here and extensive, impressive beaches, which can hardly be anything other than the long beaches north and south of Cape Porcupine. From there Leif sailed two days and nights and came to a third land, which must be the northern coast of Newfoundland. There he landed and built "large houses." It was at this coast that the Norse settlement was discovered.

Maps by Sigurdur Stefánsson (1590) and Hans Paulsen Resen (1605) indicate a northerly Vinland. Moreover, it is important to note that Leif would have to start late, perhaps in early August, because of the ice, and that he had to settle as soon as possible, in order to have time to make the necessary preparation for winter, building houses and securing provisions by hunting and fishing. The northern part of Newfoundland lies about nine degrees south of Leif's home in Greenland, and the route indicated by the sagas, along the coasts, from his Greenland home, Brattahlid, to the north coast of Newfoundland, covers about 1,800 nautical miles. Newfoundland offered forest for timber, fish, seal, and game; there were meadows for pasture if a permanent settlement was contemplated. It was a more favorable land than Greenland, a northern land where the Greenlanders would feel at home. There was no reason for them to continue south; on the contrary, sailing on would have been a hazardous venture.

For nearly three hundred years, it has generally been held that the sagas' information about wine and grapes is historically correct. As a consequence, it has been sug-gested that Vinland was located far to the south, in Massachusetts, Rhode Island, or Virginia. But the sagas' mention of grapes is probably because of Adam of Bremen (c. 1070), who, as a German, probably did not know that in Old Norse the syllable *vin* meant "meadows" when the *i* was short and "wine" when the *i* was long, and therefore associated the word with wine and grapes. His mistake is also made very clear by his statement that "Beyond this island [Vinland] no habitable land is found in the ocean, but all that is beyond is full of intolerable ice and immense mist"—no place for vines and grapes, but an accurate description of conditions in the ocean north of the Norse settlement at L'Anse aux Meadows at the northern coast of Newfoundland (51°35' N). Since the sagas were popular stories mainly intended for entertainment, the author or the scribe must have been delighted to borrow the detail of wine and grapes from the classic work by Adam of Bremen.

Taking most of the above arguments into consideration, Helge Ingstad (1966) came to the conclusion that Vinland must be located somewhere in Newfoundland and that it might be possible to find the remains of Leif's "large houses" by a systematic investigation of the coasts from sea and air. He carried out such an investigation in 1960, and with the assistance of George Decker, a fisherman, he found a number of indistinct overgrown elevations on an ancient marine terrace in an area called L'Anse aux Meadows.

From 1961 to 1968, Helge Ingstad and a team of international scholars, including Anne Stine Ingstad (1977) as archaeological leader, carried out seven expeditions to the area. A small river, Black Duck Brook, runs through the marine terrace and flows out into a very shallow bay. Eight houses, made of turf, were found, some of which were up to 24 meters (78 feet) long. They are of Norse type, and related to Icelandic and Greenlandic houses of the Viking period. The same also applies to the form and position of the hearths. There may have been room for almost a hundred people in these houses. The middens were fairly small, which indicates that the houses cannot have been occupied for long.

Of particular interest was the smithy, a small house dug into the terrace. In the middle of the room there was a big, flat, earthfast stone anvil. On the floor lay fragments of iron, slag, and bog-ore, the smith's raw material. Large quantities of bog-ore were found under the turf in a nearby bog. Close to the smithy there was a kiln where charcoal for work in the smithy had been produced. In other words, the old Norse method of producing iron had been transferred to America.

There were a number of other interesting finds: iron nails, a piece of copper that had been melted down, a stone lamp, a needle-hone, and fragments of what are apparently pig bone. A soapstone spindle-whorl of Norse type and a bronze ring-headed pin of Viking Age type indicate the presence of women, of which the sagas speak. Artifacts deriving from Indians and Dorset Eskimos were also found; according to the sagas, the Norse traded and fought with the natives, known to the Europeans as Skraelings.

A series of radiocarbon analyses have yielded an approximate date of A.D. 1000 for the settlement, about the time that, according to the sagas, Leif Ericsson discovered Vinland.

It is now internationally acknowledged that the settlement at L'Anse aux Meadows is Norse. The Canadian government has made the area into a national park, built a Viking museum there, and made the place into a tourist attraction. UNESCO has included the settlement in its World Heritage List as one of the most valuable historical monuments in the world.

It seems reasonable to assume that, once the route to the favorable areas in North America had been discovered, other groups of Greenlanders should have sailed to the new lands during the five hundred years their community existed. An important reason for crossing to America must have been the need for timber; Greenland had none, and timber for shipbuilding was of vital importance. A few sources may indicate such traffic. The *Icelandic Annals* for 1120 note that "Eric Upsi, bishop of Greenland, sailed in search of Vinland"; nothing more is known about him. The *Skálholt Annals* for 1342 note that the inhabitants of Greenland (probably in the Western Settlement) forsook the true faith and religion and turned to the people of America. The same annals for 1347 note that a ship with eighteen men arrived in Iceland, having sailed from Markland (Labrador).

What, if anything, did Leif Ericsson's discovery mean to Columbus? It seems likely that he did not know about it, and if he did know, it is doubtful that it would have been of any importance to him. According to a biography written by his son Fernando Colón, Columbus journeyed to an island in the north, probably Iceland, in 1477. He mentions the city of Bristol; a number of Bristol ships participated in the fishery off Iceland and it is reasonable to suppose that Columbus took part in one of these voyages. It has been claimed that the young Columbus, though he did not know the language, was informed by the Icelanders about the Vinland voyages, but this is conjecture.

[See also *Icelandic Sagas* and the biography of Leif Ericsson.]

BIBLIOGRAPHY

Adam of Bremen. *History of the Archbishops of Hamburg-Bremen*. Translated with an introduction and notes by Francis J. Tschan. New York, 1959.

Columbus, Ferdinand. *The Life of the Admiral Christopher Columbus*. Translated by Benjamin Keen. New Brunswick, N.J., 1959.

Ingstad, Anne Stine. *The Norse Discovery of America*. Vol. 1. Oslo, 1977. Reprint, Oslo, 1985.

Ingstad, Helge. *Land under the Pole Star*. London and New York, 1966. English translation of *Landet under Leidarstjernen*, Oslo, 1959.

Ingstad, Helge. *The Norse Discovery of America*. Vol. 2. Oslo, 1985.

Ingstad, Helge. *Westward to Vinland*. London and New York, 1969.

Storm, Gustav. *Studies on the Vineland Voyages*. Extraits des Mémoires de la Société royale des antiquaires du nord 1888. Copenhagen, 1889.

Wahlgren, Erik. *The Kensington Stone: A Mystery Solved*. Madison, Wis., 1958.

HELGE INGSTAD

VINLAND MAP. A world map seemingly produced in the second quarter of the fifteenth century, the Vinland Map was found bound with two medieval manuscripts, one of which included an account of European travels to the land of the Tatars at the eastern edge of Asia. The map, on its western edge, included a large island described as "Vinlanda Insula" west of Greenland and Iceland. Although no known map of this period included such a place, it was nevertheless known through the Icelandic saga narratives that recounted the voyages of Norsemen Thorfinn Karlsefni Thordarson and Leif Ericsson to a land west of Greenland at the end of the tenth century A.D. and the beginning of the eleventh. The Vinland Map continues to puzzle scholars and the lay public. Is it a forgery or authentic? That is still an open question, although partisans on both sides continue vociferously to argue their points of view.

The map (and accompanying manuscripts), which came from a still undisclosed seller and location in Europe (the seller anxious to avoid tax and customs problems that might otherwise have impeded the sale), was examined and rejected by skeptical authorities in the British Museum in the 1950s. It was later purchased by a rare-book dealer from New Haven, Connecticut, Laurence Witten, who was convinced of its authenticity and importance. Thus began the long trip toward apparent respectability, which culminated in the publication of *The Vinland Map and Tartar Relation* by Yale University Press in 1965. But the publicity associated with its publication, because it coincided with the celebration of Columbus Day, created a public outcry as those unfamiliar with the unquestioned noncartographic evidence for the Norse discovery of America assailed Yale University for insensitivity and callous disregard of Italian and Spanish pride. On a

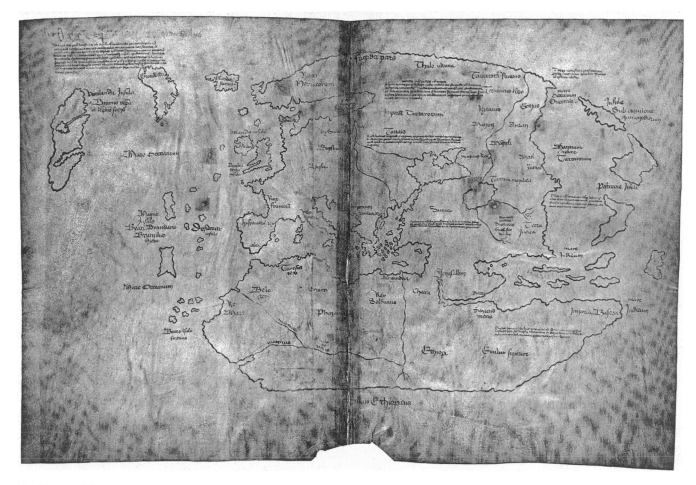

THE VINLAND MAP.

scholarly level, the fact that the work had been completed in secret by scholars associated with Yale's library (working with a library scholar from the British Museum) rather than with Yale's history department generated skepticism and hostility on the part of those excluded from the discovery. The air of secrecy with which the Vinland Map was shrouded was, in fact, simply the desire of a generous donor to Yale to avoid the irritating publicity to which he felt he would be subjected if his name were attached to the publication of the book.

In the controversy that ensued, scholarly courtesy and sometimes objectivity were often absent, and arguments concerning the motives and competence of those associated with the map were hurled by those who remained skeptical of its authenticity. A conference to bring the warring participants together was held at the Smithsonian Institution in 1966, the results of which were published in *The Proceedings of the Vinland Map Conference* in 1971. The participants, who were leading scholars in the field of the history of cartography, debated the character and

significance of the map. In considering the question of authenticity, no one was able to demonstrate through paleographic, cartographic, linguistic, or historical evidence that the map was not what it purported to be. No one, however, could dispel the serious doubts of many of the participants. It was concluded that technical analyses of the paper, ink, and binding of the document might help determine whether the map was authentic or a clever forgery. Yale University thereupon asked Walter C. Mc-Crone, director of an independent laboratory, to take samples of the ink from the map and analyze them. The results were dismaying to those who believed that no one had either the skill or the motive to forge such an exceptional document. The McCrone analysis concluded that anatase, a preparation of titanium invented only in 1920 and subsequently used in the manufacture of ink, was present on the map in significant quantities.

Yale University accepted the judgment of the McCrone laboratory, but others remained skeptical of that work, and the question of the authenticity of the map did not die. Through the agency of individuals who believed the map to be authentic, additional tests were carried on in other laboratories, most notably at the University of California, Davis, by a group led by Thomas Cahill. The Davis study asserted that the elements the McCrone laboratories had concluded derived from a substance not manufactured before 1920 was in fact present in numerous medieval manuscripts analyzed along with the Vinland Map. The Davis study thus left open the question of the map's authenticity. McCrone responded aggressively to the Davis report, reasserting the validity of his original research. As of 1990 the issue was still clouded, with further tests being undertaken by both McCrone and others in an attempt to clarify the discrepancies.

The relevance of both the Vinland Map and its accompanying documents to the Columbus story is patent. Columbus, whose careful assembling of data concerning the Ocean Sea separating Europe from Asia benefited from his own voyages north as far as Iceland and south to the Portuguese trading depots in sub-Saharan Africa, may have been aware of the reports of Norse voyages to lands beyond Iceland and Greenland in the Far North. The Vinland Map, assuming it is authentic, provides cartographic confirmation of fifteenth-century knowledge of the existence of land in what we now know to be North America. Later explorers in the sixteenth and subsequent centuries sought unsuccessfully to find the route to the riches of Asia through the northern seas, but Columbus, whether or not he knew of the existence of Vinland, chose to try to find his way to the fabled Orient through more southern seas. Nevertheless, the Vinland Map remains a tantalizing and important piece of evidence—even with its authenticity questioned—to explain European conceptions of the globe on the eve of the Age of Discovery.

[See also *Icelandic Sagas; Vinland.*]

BIBLIOGRAPHY

Cahill, Thomas A., et al. "The Vinland Map Revisited: New Compositional Evidence on Its Inks and Parchments." *Analytical Chemistry* 59 (1987): 829–833.

McCrone, Walter C. *Chemical Analytical Study of the Vinland Map; Report to Yale University.* New Haven, Conn., 1974.

McCrone, Walter C. "The Vinland Map." *Analytical Chemistry* 60 (1988): 1009–1018.

Skelton, Raleigh A., Thomas E. Marston, and George D. Painter. *The Vinland Map and the Tartar Relation.* New Haven, Conn., 1965.

Towe, Kenneth M. "The Vinland Map: Still a Forgery." *Accounts of Chemical Research* 23 (1990): 84–87.

Washburn, Wilcomb E., ed. *The Proceedings of the Vinland Map Conference.* Chicago, 1971.

Witten, Laurence C., II. "Vinland's Saga Recalled." *Yale University Library Gazette* 64 (1989): 10–37.

WILCOMB E. WASHBURN

VIVALDI, UGOLINO, AND VADINO VIVALDI

(d. 1291?), Genoese merchants and explorers. The Vivaldi brothers are often credited with the earliest European attempt to reach "the Indies" by sailing from the west coast of Africa. Sultan al-Ashraf's capture of the last crusader outposts and Pope Nicholas IV's embargo on trade with the "infidel" blocked Western access to merchandise from the Orient. The Vivaldi family had been active in tapping into the valuable overland trade from India, so the brothers now sought a way to bypass the Muslim middlemen, much as Columbus would do two hundred years later.

In the spring of 1291 the Vivaldi brothers outfitted two galleys for a long voyage. According to the Genoese annalist Iacopo Doria, whose chronicle covers the period 1280–1294, they were going "per mare Oceanum ad partes Indiae," a statement ambiguous as to both route and ultimate destination. It is known, however, that they sailed through the Straits of Gibraltar and coasted south at least as far as Cape Juby, near the Canaries. Their expedition was never heard from again. They may have intended any of three routes: circumnavigate Africa, sail up one of Africa's western rivers (believed to be branches of the Nile), or cross the Atlantic Ocean, anticipating Columbus's later voyage. No contemporary evidence is clear, and later statements about their intent are flawed by such ambiguities as Doria's.

Nevertheless, knowledge of the Vivaldis' attempt was widespread, and there are many references to the expedition in both books and maps dating from the fourteenth through sixteenth centuries. Ugolino's son Sorleone is said to have searched the east coast of Africa for his father on tips from travelers, and as late as the 1450s, Antoniotto Usodimare, a Genoese merchant, claimed to have met a descendant of a member of the ill-starred party on the west coast. The glory of the goal, the audacity of the leaders, and the mysterious conclusion of the enterprise continued to excite interest, and after Columbus's successful voyages, his fellow Genoese depicted the Vivaldis as the great discoverer's precursors with patriotic certainty. After all, the Vivaldis were not working for the Spanish. In good Genoese fashion they were working for themselves.

BIBLIOGRAPHY

Caddeo, Rinaldo. *Le navigazioni atlantiche di Alvise da Cadamosto, Antoniotto Usodimare e Niccoloso da Recco.* Milan, 1928.

Magnaghi, A. *Precursori di Colombo? Il tentativo di viaggio transoceanico dei genovese fratelli Vivaldi nel 1291.* Rome, 1935.

Moore, Gilliam. "Le spedizione dei fratelli Vivaldi e nuovi

documenti d'Archivio." *Atti della Società Ligure di Storia Patria* 82 (1972): 387–402.

Rogers, Francis M. "The Vivaldi Expedition." In *Seventy-Third Annual Report of the Dante Society.* Cambridge, Mass., 1955; 31–54.

JOSEPH P. BYRNE

VIZINHO, JOSÉ (c. 1450–c. 1520), Jewish astrologer and physician. Some scholars claim that José Vizinho was born in Portugal and some specify Viseu as his birthplace. It is thought that he was of Castilian origin since, when appointed to translate from Latin or Hebrew, he did so into Castilian, not Portuguese. In any case, he was fairly well rooted in Portugal before 1485. Because pilots on transatlantic voyages needed to know standard measurements of astronomical coordinates related to the stars or the sun, King João II of Portugal asked Vizinho to provide the necessary information.

The first and most elementary solution to the problem of maritime expeditions that lacked known coastal markers apparently began with a very simple comparison of altitudes taken at one of the meridian passages of the polestar. This was probably a widely accepted procedure. It is explained, with a slightly different purpose, in the *Tractatus de sphaera* (Treatise on the sphere) by Johannes de Sacrobosco. However, the need to proceed further and determine latitudes at sea required knowledge of books in which such problems were explained, and those who had access to these books were astrologers such as Vizinho.

Vizinho was undoubtedly familiar with the treatises on the astrolabe and the quadrant and related issues. Of special importance were works on the determination of latitudes by starting from the solar meridian altitude and its declination on the date of the observation. Many books taught how to make the determination, including the ninth-century treatise on the use of the astrolabe by Messahalla and the *Libros del saber de astronomia* (Books of astronomical knowledge) compiled by a group of scholars for Afonso X of Castile in the thirteenth century. The rules examined in these books were not complete because they did not include all possible cases.

It is very possible that Vizinho was appointed to study and complete these rules. Yet, once a *regimento* (a body of rules) was established to suit all predictable situations, it had to be verified in practice. Vizinho was assigned this task as well. Christopher Columbus notes, "In 1485 the king of Portugal sent to Guinea *magister Josepius* [José Vizinho], his physician and astrologer, to summarize the altitude of the sun in all Guinea . . . ." The experiment gave positive results and as a consequence, in 1487 and 1488, Bartolomeu Dias was able to use the *regimento* in his voyage when he rounded the southern tip of Africa.

Tables needed to calculate solar declination in using the *regimento* were included in the *Almanach perpetuum* (Perpetual almanac) by another Jewish astrologer, Abraham Zacuto. They were also published in Leiria in 1494 in parallel editions with "canons," that is, explanatory introductions, in Latin and Castilian. The Castilian version was written by Vizinho, who states that he is a disciple of Zacuto.

BIBLIOGRAPHY

De Lery, Jean. *History of a Voyage to the Land of Brazil Otherwise Called America.* Translated by Janet Whatley. Berkeley, 1990.

Diffey, Bailey W. *Prelude to Empire: Portugal Overseas before Henry the Navigator.* Lincoln, Neb., 1960.

Diffey, Bailey W., and George D. Winius. *Foundations of the Portuguese Empire, 1414–1850.* Edited by Boyd C. Shafer. Minneapolis, 1977.

Morison, Samuel Eliot. *Portuguese Voyages to America in the Fifteenth Century.* New York, 1965.

LUÍS DE ALBUQUERQUE
Translated from Portuguese by Paola Carù

VOYAGES OF COLUMBUS. [This article focuses on the details of Columbus's four voyages to America. For further discussion of Columbus's life and works, including reference to his efforts to win support for his voyages of discovery, see the various articles under *Columbus, Christopher.*]

Christopher Columbus made four voyages across the Atlantic Ocean. Clearly, the first was most important. His landfall on a tiny island in the Bahamas in 1492 changed the world dramatically and fundamentally. Although more than ten years would pass before Europe realized that Columbus had discovered, literally, a New World, not lands on the fringes of Asia, the knowledge that vast territories, new peoples, and potential riches lay within reach captured people's imaginations and stimulated efforts in every field. The age of European exploration, discovery, and colonization followed immediately; the Renaissance spread across the Old World, and people attained new heights of creativity and accomplishment. Columbus never found what he sought but the prize was far greater than he realized.

In itself, the first voyage was unremarkable: after an easy thirty-three day sail from the Canary Islands, Columbus landed on an island in the Caribbean. Given his careful but incorrect calculations, he was sure he was on the outskirts of India. Sailing southwest from San Salvador, he explored the coast of Cuba, searching for gold and spices. *Santa María* ran aground on Christmas Eve, forcing Columbus to stop exploring. He built a fortress on La Española (Hispaniola) and left a group of men there to gather the gold that the Indians said was nearby. Returning to Spain with a cargo of exotic birds, plants, gold nuggets and masks, and ten Indians, Columbus made a triumphant journey across Spain to Barcelona where King Fernando and Queen Isabel greeted him as an equal.

Columbus's second voyage followed within months. He guided seventeen ships loaded with fifteen hundred men, livestock, trees, and seeds back to La Española to establish a settlement. But this successful seaman was less adept as an administrator. His nationality and low birth reduced his authority in the eyes of many of the gentlemen adventurers who had signed on for the voyage. The hot and humid climate, difficult work, and inadequate food hampered efforts to create a viable colony. The expectations of the hidalgos for abundant, easily acquired gold were never fulfilled. Columbus spent most of the two years of this voyage trying to bring order to La Española and was able to explore only the southern coast of Cuba.

The signal event of Columbus's third voyage—his discovery of South America—was completely overshadowed at the time by strife on La Española. In fact, Columbus and his two brothers were sent home in chains by the administrator assigned by the Crown to bring order to the area. Even after this ignominious return, however, Columbus managed to regain the respect of the sovereigns and their permission for a fourth voyage of exploration. However, the powers originally promised to Columbus as Admiral of the Ocean Sea and Viceroy and Governor of the Islands were never restored, an injustice that rankled Columbus for the rest of his life.

On his fourth voyage, Columbus hoped to discover a passage to India at the western end of the Caribbean, but the strait was not there to discover. He tried to establish another tiny settlement on the Central American coast, where he found more gold than in La Española, but hostile Indians made it impossible. In his two remaining ships, so worm-eaten they looked like honeycomb, Columbus sailed as far as Jamaica where he had to beach them. He and his men were marooned for twelve months. When Columbus finally returned to Spain, Isabel was dying and Fernando had little time for the ill and aged navigator.

The First Voyage

It would be impossible to overstate the importance of Christopher Columbus's first voyage of discovery. His endeavor to reach the riches of the Orient by sailing across the Atlantic Ocean changed the face of the world as it was then known. Suddenly, the Mar Tenebrosa, the Dark Sea, was no longer dark or trackless. It could be crossed in a month, and more important, it could be recrossed back to Europe. Even though Columbus thought he had discovered the eastern extremity of Asia, the fact that people, plants, animals, and riches existed

where nothing was thought to exist before galvanized Europe. The Old World was fired with enthusiasm and the energy to learn and gain from this New World even before the size and nature of the American continents became clear.

It took Columbus twelve years to win support for his endeavor. King João of Portugal turned him down twice on the advice of court scientists and mathematicians who said his theory about a western route to the Indies was nonsense. Fernando and Isabel of Spain put him off for seven years, being more occupied with fighting the Muslim Kingdom of Granada than with sponsoring dubious sailing expeditions. But in 1492 Granada was conquered. Perhaps more important to Columbus's fortunes was the expulsion from Spain of all Jews who refused to convert to Christianity. Jewish lands, money, and other valuables were seized by the Catholic sovereigns, and this confiscated wealth helped to underwrite Columbus. So this stubborn, courageous, deeply religious Genoese mapmaker, seaman, and navigational genius was given his chance.

Christopher Columbus set out to "discover and acquire islands and mainland in the Ocean Sea" one-half hour before sunrise on August 3, 1492, just over four months after the Spanish sovereigns Fernando and Isabel had finally agreed to sponsor and help finance the venture. Efforts to obtain, outfit, and man the three ships needed for the voyage had been hampered by a number of difficulties. Columbus's notion that a western route to the Indies could be crossed before supplies ran out was ridiculed. Seamen were afraid to risk their lives in such a dangerous endeavor. Even royal commands failed to produce movement. Eager to save money, Fernando ordered the town of Palos to furnish two fully equipped and manned caravels for the voyage in penalty for earlier pirate activity against Spanish ships. Palos refused. Royal orders directed local officials to provide supplies and assistance to Columbus, but officials ignored the orders. Even the dispatch to Andalusia of Juan de Peñalosa, an officer of the royal household, could not force compliance with the sovereigns' decree. Finally, an influential Palos shipowner named Martín Alonso Pinzón announced that he and his brothers, Vicente Yáñez and Francisco Martín, would sail with Columbus. With this support, magistrates of the town were able to press a caravel, *Pinta*, into service despite the complaints of her owner, Cristóbal Quintero. Martín Alonso Pinzón agreed to sail as captain of *Pinta* with his brother Francisco Martín as her master. Vicente Yáñez Pinzón agreed to sail as captain of the caravel *Niña*, furnished by the equally influential Niño family of Moguer; her owner, Juan Niño, sailed as master of his caravel. Columbus was able to charter a third, larger vessel named *Santa María* from Juan de la Cosa and to persuade him and some of his crew to join in the venture. By the end of July, a total of eighty-seven crewmen had been recruited.

After bidding anguished farewells to family and friends, for few expected success in their venture, the crew of the tiny fleet waited for the tide and then crossed the bar of the Saltes at the mouth of the Tinto and Odiel rivers at 8:00 A.M. and sailed out into the Atlantic Ocean. Columbus set course for the Canary Islands, his point of departure for the fabled Orient. He began his log immediately. In its prologue, written for the king and queen, Columbus promised to record "very diligently" everything he saw and did each day, and to "make a new sailing chart" locating "all of the sea and the lands of the Ocean Sea in their proper places." "Above all," Columbus wrote, "it is very important that I forget sleep and pay much attention to navigation in order thus to carry out these purposes, which will be great labor." Although the original log was lost centuries ago, an excellent transcription of excerpts from it was made by Bartolomé de las Casas in his invaluable *Historia de las Indias*.

The voyage began inauspiciously: *Pinta's* rudder broke loose three days out (Columbus suspected deliberate sabotage by her owner, Cristóbal Quintero, who accompanied him but continued to oppose the voyage), and *Niña,* with her lateen rig, had difficulty keeping up with *Pinta* and *Santa María,* both square-rigged and better able to take advantage of the favorable winds from astern. Martín Alonso Pinzón was able to effect temporary repairs to the rudder, and the ship limped into Grand Canary on August 9. Columbus sailed on to Gomera to try to find a replacement for the damaged ship.

Three weeks of frustration followed, with Columbus waiting for a suitable ship to arrive (it never did) and for word from Pinzón that he had repaired the rudder (which he never sent). Columbus finally returned to Grand Canary, ordered Pinzón to make a new rudder, and directed that *Niña* be rerigged, changing her triangular lateen sails to square sails. Columbus knew the Atlantic winds blow steadily from the east or northeast in these latitudes. A square-rigged ship would have better maneuverability. He planned to return from the Indies with the westerly winds he had observed personally in the winter along the coast of Portugal and Galicia. Also, Columbus had sailed to England with the Portuguese in the past and had learned that the westerlies blew year-round in the higher latitudes. Obviously, Columbus knew how he would return to Spain. Nevertheless, the fear of being stranded somewhere at the end of the world dogged many in his crew throughout this first voyage.

When the two caravels were ready, the fleet returned to Gomera to pick up enough fresh supplies for twenty-eight days and a detachment of men left there earlier by Columbus. It then sailed west on September 6, more than a month after leaving Palos. A three-day calm kept them within sight of land, and there was some concern that a Portuguese squadron reported to be in the area might try to prevent Columbus from sailing west. Fortunately, no squadron appeared and a brisk northeast wind finally came up to move the ships on their way. Crewmen wept on September 9 when Hierro (Ferro), the westernmost of the Canaries, disappeared from view, but Columbus comforted them with promises of land and riches. He also decided to keep two accounts of distances traveled: an accurate reckoning for himself, and another for the crew that would report fewer leagues sailed "so in case the voyage were long the men would not be frightened and lose courage."

The next thirty-three days were marked by sunny skies, fair winds, and calm seas. Columbus picked up the northern fringe of the northeast trade belt, and it carried him smoothly to the outer cays of the Bahama Islands. Were the crew as convinced of ultimate success as Columbus, it would have been a peaceful voyage. Instead, according to Columbus, the days were filled with emotional highs and lows. As a number of log entries record, every imaginable sign of land was taken as real. Martín Alonso Pinzón first thought he spied land on September 18, only nine days out from Hierro. Every bird, every patch of sargasso weed, even a crab in a clump of weed ("a sure sign of land, for crabs are not found even 240 miles from shore"), was recounted in the log. Columbus knew the voyage would take some weeks, but the nervous crew wanted it to end as soon as possible. By September 24, the crew was so uneasy that, according to later testimony, some apparently planned to throw Columbus into the sea if he refused to turn back. The Admiral would calm some fears only to have new grumbling arise from another quarter. Still the fleet held together and kept on its westerly course. On October 1 Columbus's phony log showed they had sailed 1,734 miles from Hierro. His private reckoning showed 2,121 miles. On they went. Columbus had long since grown weary of the constant cries of "Land!" and had told the men that anyone making a false claim would forfeit the ten thousand maravedis reward (about eight hundred dollars) promised by the sovereigns to the first to sight the Indies. Despite this, *Niña* claimed to sight land on October 7, but by evening, it was clear the "land" was yet another cloudbank.

On October 11, birds, fresh reeds, and an apparently hand-hewn staff were sighted in the sea. Some of the crew's apprehensions were soothed, and at evening vespers, special thanks were given for the many signs of land. Columbus ordered extra lookouts and urged everyone to be especially vigilant. At about 10:00 P.M. he reported seeing a light to the west, bobbing up and down

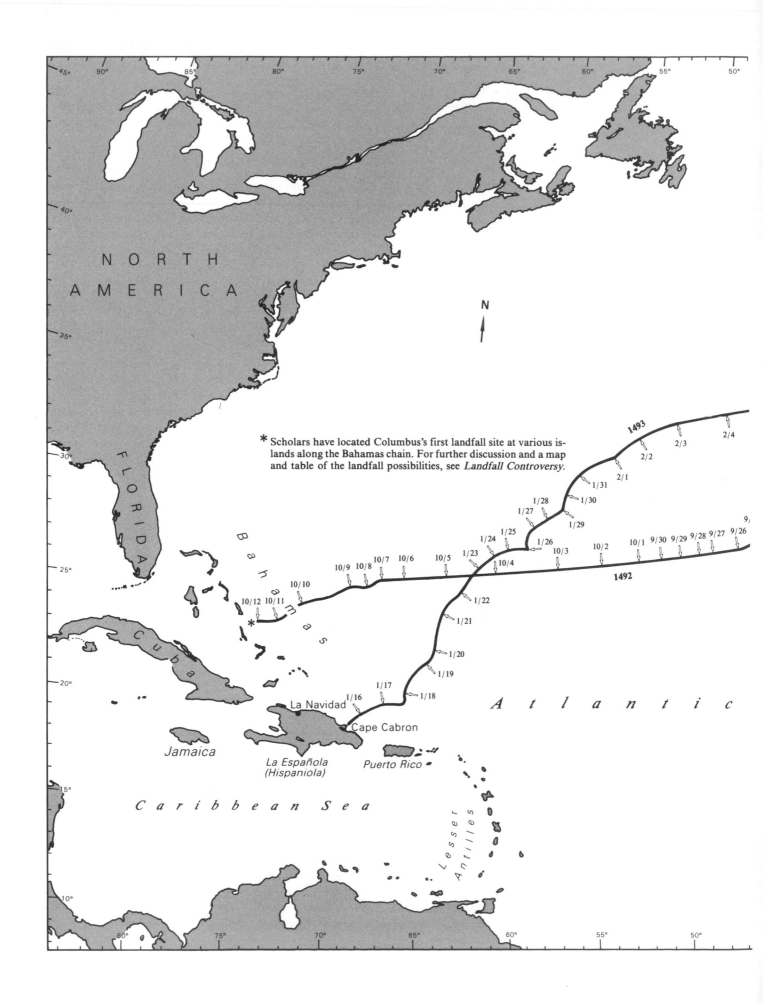

* Scholars have located Columbus's first landfall site at various islands along the Bahamas chain. For further discussion and a map and table of the landfall possibilities, see *Landfall Controversy*.

N

NORTH
AMERICA

FLORIDA

Bahamas

Cuba

Jamaica

La Navidad

Cape Cabron

La Española
(Hispaniola)

Puerto Rico

Lesser Antilles

Caribbean Sea

Atlantic

1493

1492

2/4
2/3
2/2
2/1
1/31
1/30
1/29
1/28
1/27
1/26
1/25
1/24
1/23
10/4
10/3
10/2
10/1
9/30
9/29
9/28
9/27
9/26
9/

10/5
10/6
10/7
10/8
10/9
10/10
10/11
10/12

1/22
1/21
1/20
1/19
1/18
1/17
1/16

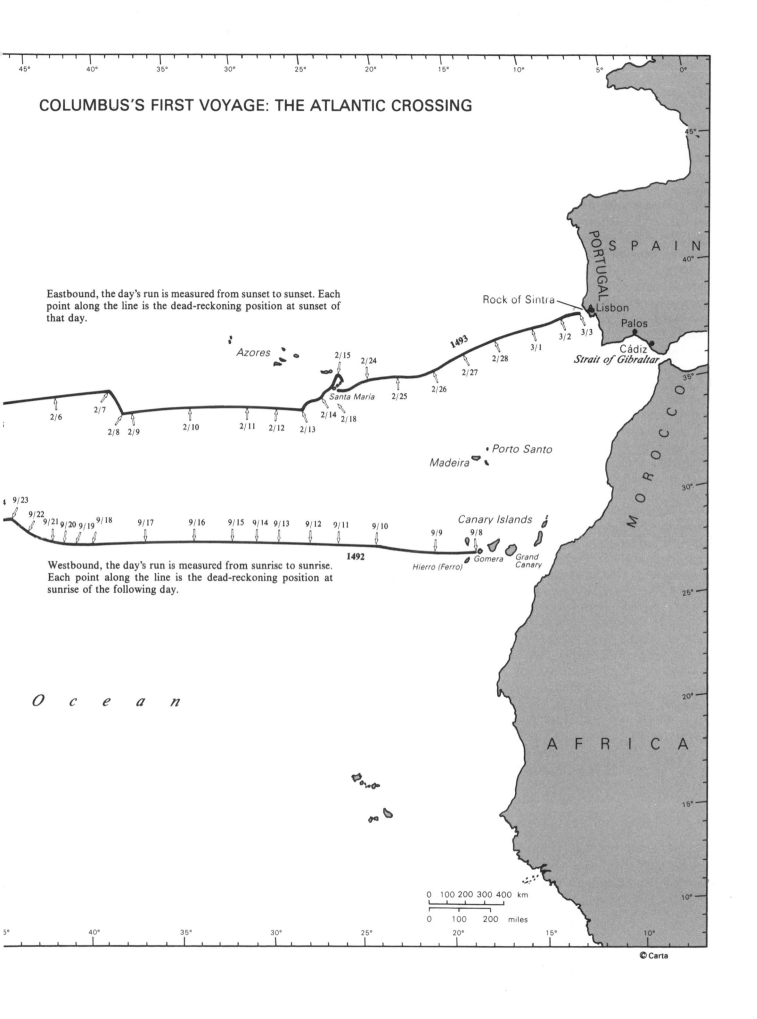

COLUMBUS'S FIRST VOYAGE: THE ATLANTIC CROSSING

Eastbound, the day's run is measured from sunset to sunset. Each point along the line is the dead-reckoning position at sunset of that day.

Westbound, the day's run is measured from sunrise to sunrise. Each point along the line is the dead-reckoning position at sunrise of the following day.

Azores

Rock of Sintra
Lisbon
Palos
Cádiz
Strait of Gibraltar

1493

2/15
2/24
2/28
2/27
2/26
2/25
2/14 2/18
Santa María
2/13
2/12
2/11
2/10
2/9
2/8
2/7
2/6

3/3
3/2
3/1

• *Porto Santo*
Madeira

9/23
9/22
9/21
9/20 9/19 9/18
9/17
9/16
9/15 9/14 9/13
9/12
9/11
9/10

Canary Islands
9/9
9/8
1492
Hierro (Ferro)
Gomera
Grand Canary

PORTUGAL
S P A I N

M O R O C C O

O c e a n

A F R I C A

0 100 200 300 400 km
0 100 200 miles

© Carta

as if being carried on a boat or by hand over rough terrain. Pedro Gutiérrez, a representative of the king's household, also saw it. A few minutes later, though, it had disappeared, and "it was something so faint that [I] did not wish to affirm that it was land," wrote Columbus.

At 2:00 A.M. on October 12, *Pinta* fired her cannon in the prearranged signal for landfall. Seaman Rodrigo de Triana had spotted a sandy beach in the moonlight. (Columbus himself was later awarded the prize for being the first to see land, based on his report of the bobbing light.) The fleet, in uncharted waters and bearing down on a lee shore before a strong following wind, was wisely ordered by Columbus to shorten sail and lay-to until dawn. At daybreak, the fleet rounded the island and found a suitable anchorage on the leeward side. Then Columbus, the Pinzón captains, secretary of the fleet Rodrigo de Escobedo, comptroller Rodrigo Sánchez, and others landed on the island called Guanahani by its natives. Making the declarations that were required, the Spanish took formal possession of the island for Fernando and Isabel. Columbus named the island San Salvador.

Columbus was sure this level, tree-covered island lay at the extremity of India. When the natives rushed to the shore, he called them *Indians,* a term subsequently applied to all aboriginals of the New World. In a scene that was to be repeated almost without change during the remainder of the first voyage, natives crowded around the richly dressed and armed strangers. The Indians were "as naked as their mothers bore them," well built with brown skin and straight, coarse, black hair. Faces and bodies were painted in black, red, white, and other colors; some carried small spears made of wood. They were curious, friendly, docile, and trusting. Eager to please the demi-gods they thought had descended from heaven, the Indians offered food, water, balls of cotton thread, parrots, and "a kind of dry leaf that they hold in great esteem." Columbus ordered his men to take nothing without offering something in exchange, and the Indians were thrilled with the beads, hawkbells, pieces of colored glass, and other baubles presented by the Spaniards.

Where did Columbus actually first set foot in the New World? The question has been debated for hundreds of years. The three favorite choices today are Watlings Island (now officially named San Salvador), Samana Cay, and Grand Turk Island. (Cat Island, East Caicos, and Concepción [Conception Island] have been vigorously promoted in the past, but their support among experts has faded.) Watlings Island was legally named San Salvador in 1926; among those who have supported it as the landfall in recent years are the respected Columbus scholars J. B. Thacher, Samuel Eliot Morison, and Mauricio Obregon. In 1985, when debate was renewed, the Society for the History of Discoveries spearheaded a new research effort, aided by the National Geographic Society. A large team of specialists (mathematicians, computer experts, archaeologists, cartographers, navigators, and translators) combined efforts and concluded that Samana Cay, first proposed as the landfall by Capt. Gustavus V. Fox in 1894, was the correct site. The debate continues.

Columbus left San Salvador on October 14. Seven Indians were taken along as guides and interpreters. Santa María de la Concepción (Crooked Island) was claimed for the Crown on October 16 and La Fernandina (Long Island) two days later. It was on Fernandina that Columbus first saw a hammock. At La Isabela (Southern Crooked Island) Columbus was told by the Indians that a great king "who wears much gold" lived in an inland village. A search party failed to find him, however, and on the twenty-fourth Columbus left in search of Cuba, described by the Indians as "very large and of great commerce . . . [with] gold and spices and great ships and merchants. And in the spheres that I saw and in world maps it [Japan] is in this region."

This reference to "spheres" may refer to the terrestrial globe produced in 1492 by Martin Behaim of Germany, which displayed the accepted view of the world at this time. While scholars debated the size of the globe, no one imagined any land mass lying between Europe and Asia. (For example, Viking discoveries were mapped as part of Asia.) Not until 1510 did some Europeans suggest a new continent had been found and many maps made in the late sixteenth century still appended the Americas to Asia. Balboa did not discover the Pacific Ocean until 1513. Additionally, Columbus based his calculations on a glaring mistake: he underestimated the length of degrees of longitude. And so did everyone else until 1670. Columbus believed a degree equaled 56.666 miles. In fact, as was learned much later, a degree of longitude at the equator measures 69 miles. Using the shorter estimate, Columbus believed Asia lay 1,100 leagues west of Europe. He sailed 1,111 leagues from the Canary Islands and found land. Where else could he be but Asia? As he wrote in the log on October 21, he planned to go to "another very large island that I believe must be Cipango [Marco Polo's name for Japan] according to the indications that these Indians that I have give me, and which they call Colba [Cuba]. In it they say there are many and very large ships and many traders. And from this island (I intend to go to) another that they call Bohío . . . I have already decided to go to the mainland and to the city of Quinsay [Hangzhou, China] and to give Your Highnesses' letters to the Grand Khan and to ask for, and to come with, a reply."

On October 28 Columbus made landfall on the north coast of Cuba and named it Juana, after Prince Juan. He coasted the northern shore for several days and then anchored in the Río de Mares (Bahía de Gibara) to make needed repairs on the ships. On November 2, believing that land of such a size must be the continent, Columbus sent Rodrigo de Jerez and Luis de Torres, who spoke Hebrew, Chaldean, and Arabic, plus two Indians, to find the Grand Khan, giving them strings of beads to trade and instructions from the sovereigns asking the khan's help in learning about his land. The delegation returned two days later, reporting they had found a large native village and had been warmly received by the inhabitants. They had seen cultivated fields of sweet potatoes, maize, and beans. The men reported "in one house alone, 12,000 pounds" of cotton and "dogs that do not bark," but they did not find the Grand Khan.

On November 12, Columbus decided to retrace his path to the east southeast in search of another island, called Bohío by the Indians, said to contain great riches. Actually, there are two islands to the southeast of Cuba, Babeque (Great Inagua) and Bohío (La Isla Española, also known as Hispaniola). The Indians told Columbus both were sources of gold, spices, and pearls. Heading east by south, two days later Columbus saw "so many islands [he] could not count them all, of good size and very high lands full of trees of a thousand kinds." Columbus believed these islands "are those innumerable ones that in maps of the world are put at the eastern end." He believed there were great riches and precious stones and spices there. He was in Tanamo Bay and decided to explore among the islands in the ship's boat, planting a cross wherever he stopped.

Departing from the bay on November 19, Columbus tried to reach Babeque, but adverse winds drove him north, not east. On November 21, while Columbus was heading back toward Cuba, Martín Alonso Pinzón "because of greed and without the permission and will of the Admiral, departed with the caravel *Pinta*, thinking that an Indian whom the Admiral had ordered put on that caravel was going to give him much gold. And so he went away without waiting and not by reason of bad weather, but because he wanted to. . . . he has done and said to me many other things." *Pinta* carried on to the east and Babeque; *Niña* and *Santa María* returned to Cuba and continued along the coast. The loyalty to Columbus of Martín Alonso's brother, Vicente Yáñez Pinzón, captain of *Niña*, is notable.

On December 5 *Santa María* and *Niña* reached the eastern end of Cuba. Believing it to be the eastern extremity of the Eurasian continent, Columbus named it Alpha and Omega (present-day Cape Maisí). From this vantage point he could see a high, mountainous land to the southeast, which the Indians called Bohío, a name Columbus believed meant "abounding in gold." Sailing there, over the objections of the Indians who said the natives living there were cannibals, Columbus named it La Isla Española, or the Spanish Island, because it reminded

him of the beauties of Castile. The Latin form, "Hispaniola," was first used by the historian Pietro Martire d'Anghiera (Peter Martyr) in a letter of October 20, 1494, and became the familiar name for the island.

Kept in place by adverse northerly winds for several days, Columbus and his men explored close to the harbor of Port Conception (today the Bay of Moustique) and on December 12, with marked solemnity, erected a great cross at the entrance to the harbor, formally claiming the island for Fernando and Isabel. By the fourteenth, Columbus was able to visit a small island opposite the harbor, which he named Tortuga. On December 16 he returned to La Española, and on December 20 the two ships anchored in what is now Acul Bay, a place that is "extremely beautiful and would hold all the ships in Christendom." As before, natives crowded the shore or rowed out to *Santa María* and *Niña* in canoes, offered food, water, small golden ornaments, in short, anything they had. Neighboring caciques (chiefs) invited the Spaniards to their villages and cried when they departed. The grand cacique Guacanagarí who ruled over the region invited Columbus to anchor closer to his village, and early in the morning of December 24, Columbus left Acul Bay and headed east with light winds.

At 11:00 P.M., the change of the watch, Columbus decided to retire to his cabin. Seas were calm and the ship almost motionless. His men had visited the coast the previous day and reported no rocks or shoals, and the Admiral had had no sleep for the past forty-eight hours because of the hundreds of Indians visiting his ships. When Columbus retired, however, so too did the rest of the crew, including the officer of the watch, Juan de la Cosa, disobeying a cardinal rule aboard ship. The helm was left to one of the ship's boys. Silently, gently, *Santa María* lodged on a coral reef. The ship's boy didn't notice anything wrong until the rudder stuck fast. Columbus jumped up instantly when the boy cried out; he woke Juan de la Cosa and ordered him to rouse the rest of the crew, launch the small boat, and cast an anchor astern to haul the ship off the reef. De la Cosa and several others leapt into the boat, but instead of doing as they were ordered, they fled to *Niña*. Her captain properly refused to let them board and sent *Niña*'s own boat to try to pull *Santa María* clear; Columbus tried to float her by cutting away the heavy mainmast. Nothing helped. The currents pushed *Santa María* farther onto the reef, and then the seams opened.

Columbus transferred his crew to *Niña* for safety reasons and at daybreak sent Diego de Arana, master-at-arms of the fleet, with a party of men to ask Cacique Guacanagarí for help. The cacique reportedly wept when he heard of the disaster and promptly sent people and large canoes to help unload the ship. Everything was

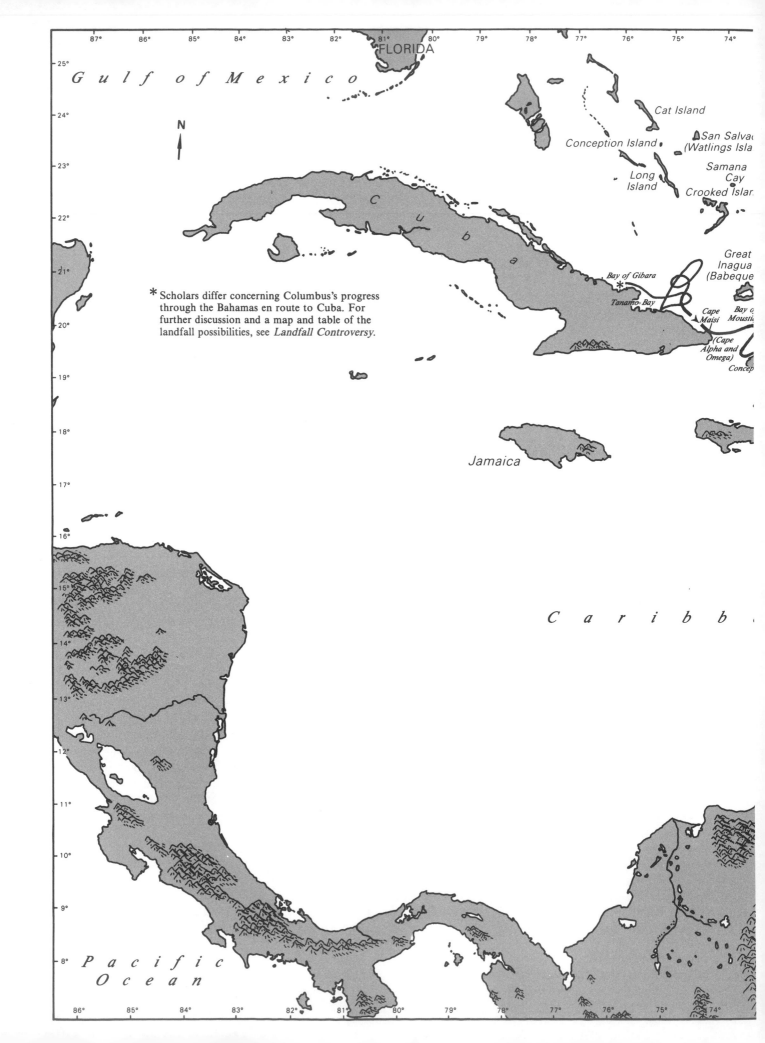

FLORIDA

Gulf of Mexico

N

Cat Island

Conception Island

San Salvac (Watlings Isla

Long Island

Samana Cay

Crooked Islan

C u b a

Great Inagua (Babeque

Bay of Gibara

*

Tanamo Bay

Cape Maisi

Bay of Moustic

(Cape Alpha and Omega)

Concep

* Scholars differ concerning Columbus's progress through the Bahamas en route to Cuba. For further discussion and a map and table of the landfall possibilities, see *Landfall Controversy.*

Jamaica

C a r i b b

Pacific Ocean

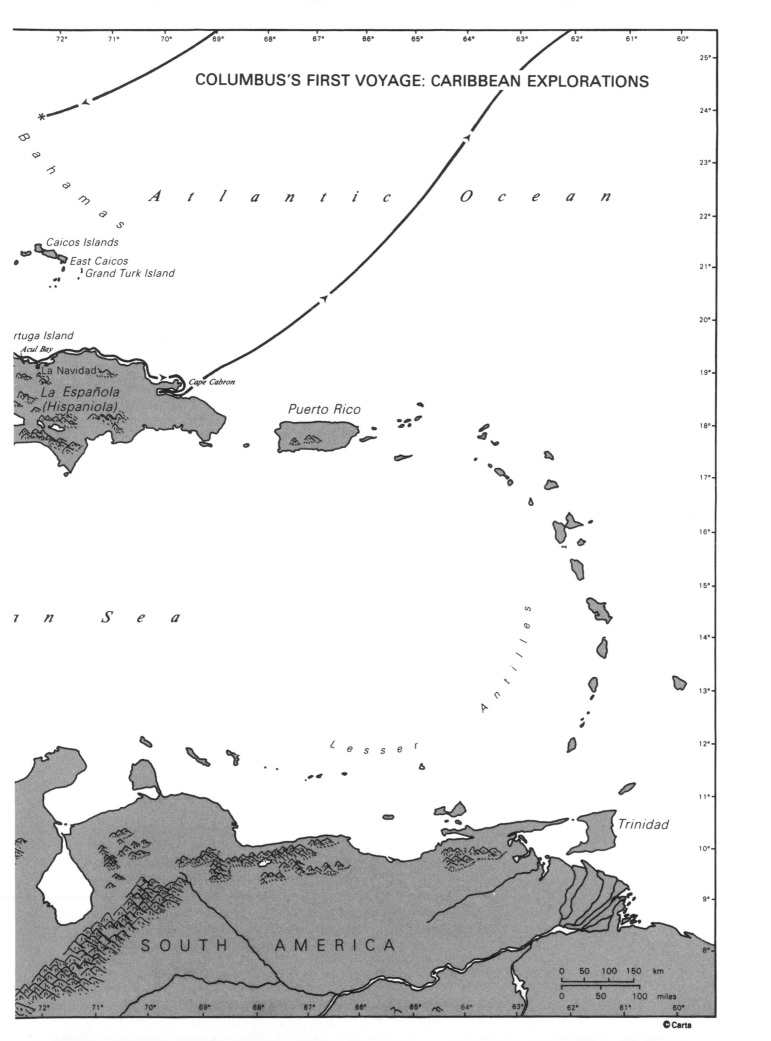

COLUMBUS'S FIRST VOYAGE: CARIBBEAN EXPLORATIONS

rescued, stored ashore, and carefully guarded by the Indians. "Not even a shoe string was lost," according to Columbus, who added, "I assure Your Highnesses that I believe that in all the world there are no better people or a better land." Columbus believed the loss of *Santa María* was an omen: "Our Lord had caused the ship to run aground there so that he would found a settlement there." Columbus had not intended to remain long in this area, largely because the cumbersome *Santa María* was "not suited to the work of discovery" close to shore.

During the ensuing days Columbus came to know the Indians, particularly Cacique Guacanagarí, and believed them when they spoke of great riches. Guacanagarí, Columbus wrote, knew where there was much gold nearby and told him that there was gold in Cipango, which they call Cybao." In Columbus's day, Japan was Cipangu (or Cipango), Marco Polo's name for it. Columbus thought Cybao (Cibao) was the Indian version of Cipangu. In fact it referred to the interior region of today's Dominican Republic.

Columbus decided to build a settlement on the coast adjacent to the grounded *Santa María* and named it La Navidad in commemoration of the day of the disaster. He ordered a tower and fortress to be constructed, and chose forty-two men to stay and find the gold mine described by Guacanagarí. As he wrote in the log, he had come to believe that everything that had happened—the gentle grounding of *Santa María* ("so softly that it was not felt, nor was there wave nor wind,") and the "treachery" of the ship's master in refusing to follow orders to cast the anchor astern and thus enable Columbus to save the ship—were signs from God that he was meant to found a settlement on La Española. When forced by these events to move ashore, Columbus saw the lush beauty of the land and, more important, learned of great riches nearby. He said, also, that he hoped "in God that on the return that he would undertake from Castile he would find a barrel of gold that those who were left would have acquired by exchange; and that they would have found the gold mine and the spicery, and those things in such quantity that the sovereigns, before three years [are over] will undertake and prepare to conquer the Holy Sepulcher."

Columbus left La Española on January 4, 1493. The reduction of the fleet to one ship precluded his staying to explore farther, and he was eager to return to Spain and report his findings to Fernando and Isabel. Before he left, he took great care to prepare the small garrison he was leaving behind at La Navidad. His orders were clear: the men were to obey Diego de Arana, Pedro Gutiérrez, and Rodrigo de Escobedo, the officers in charge; they were to show respect, honesty, and friendship toward the natives and under no circumstances injure any of them, particularly the women; they were to stay together within the

territory controlled by Guacanagarí, explore for gold, and locate a good place to build a more permanent village.

Two days later, not far from La Navidad, *Pinta* sailed into view. The two ships backtracked thirty miles to Monte Cristi where they could anchor and Pinzón could board *Niña* to explain himself. He apologized for going off on his own, claiming the weather forced him on to that course. He said when he failed to find gold on Babeque, he headed for Bohío (La Española) because other Indians claimed it was the site of riches. He had come within forty-five miles of La Navidad some twenty days earlier. Columbus privately rejected Pinzón's explanations, believing he had deliberately gone out of greed and arrogance, but decided to ignore his actions for the good of the voyage.

The two ships followed the coast of La Española to the east for six days and then anchored in a broad bay just beyond Cabo del Enamorado (Cape Cabrón) on January 13, 1493. When a contingent went ashore for *ajes*, "sweet potatoes," they encountered natives quite different from the gentle people they had previously met. Columbus suspected these ferocious, heavily painted and armed Indians to be Caribs, spoken of with fear by the Tainos and Arawaks of earlier landfalls. Caribs were cannibals and warriors who raided the settlements of their more peaceful neighbors. In fact, these were Ciguayos, different in name but not in behavior from the Caribs. They seemed friendly during initial trading, but when men were sent ashore to continue the exchange the Ciguayos attacked. The Spanish were able to drive them off and return to their ship.

The homeward leg of the first voyage began on January 16, 1493. The ships were leaking badly, little gold had been found, and the men were uneasy. At one point that morning, Columbus altered course to the southeast to explore an island said to be the home of the Caribs and another said to be inhabited only by women. But when the wind blew favorably for the return trip and Columbus recognized the dismay of his crew at his temporary change of direction, he abandoned plans for further discoveries and set course for Spain. They enjoyed pleasant weather for most of January, but the winds were easterly and hindered fast progress. Also, *Pinta's* mizzenmast was weak (Columbus was annoyed that Pinzón hadn't relaced it in the Indies), and she couldn't sail close to the wind. Columbus generally followed a course northeastward to the approximate latitude of Bermuda, where he was able to get out of the adverse easterly trade winds and steer more directly toward Spain with favorable westerly winds.

Niña and *Pinta* were separated again on February 12 not by deceit but by a severe storm that forced both captains to shorten sail and run before the wind. *Pinta* was carried northward and out of sight. The two small caravels were caught up in one of the worst storms seen in the Atlantic for years. For a week *Niña* was tossed furiously by huge waves breaking over her. Columbus ordered lots drawn for three pilgrimages to be performed in thanksgiving when and if they were delivered from the storm. Columbus himself twice drew the chick-pea marked with a cross and promised to pay the expenses of the seaman who drew the third. Short of ballast, Columbus ordered empty water and wine casks to be filled with seawater to help stabilize *Niña*. Despite these efforts, both spiritual and temporal, "all were resigned to being lost due to the terrible storm." Columbus was particularly worried that no one would know of his achievement if *Niña* perished. He wrote an account of the voyage on parchment, sealed it in waxed cloth, and placed it in a barrel, which was tossed into the sea. It was never found.

Finally, after sunrise on February 15, they sighted land. Three days later they were able to draw near enough to anchor and send a boat ashore. *Niña* had reached the island of Santa Maria in the Azores. Here, political problems added to Columbus's difficulties. The king of Portugal had sent orders to his officials in distant islands and ports to seize Columbus if he should appear. King João feared Columbus's expedition would interfere with the Portuguese rights to the eastern route to the Indies. When half the crew was sent ashore on Santa María to make a pilgrimage to a shrine in fulfillment of the pledge made at sea, they were captured and jailed by a local official. While Columbus waited anxiously for their return, the official came out to *Niña* with a boatload of armed men to take him prisoner, but the Admiral refused to yield and the Portuguese official feared coming too close. A standoff ensued during which the local contingent eventually withdrew and the remaining crew of *Niña* was able to repair some of the storm damage to their ship and fill more casks with seawater for ballast.

The harbor in which they were anchored was completely unprotected from winds out of the north, and when yet another gale blew up from that direction *Niña*'s anchor cable parted and Columbus was forced to put to sea again to save the ship. He had only half his crew at this point and only three were sailors. For two days, *Niña* "was in constant danger and difficulty." But he was able to return to the harbor on the evening of February 21, when a notary and two priests, in *Niña*'s boat with five of the captured seamen, requested permission to come aboard and see his orders from Fernando and Isabel. Columbus showed them his royal commission and the emissaries went ashore satisfied, releasing *Niña*'s boat and all the captured Spanish seamen.

On the twenty-second, Columbus weighed anchor and sailed around the island until he found a good anchorage at a place on the south coast where he might take on wood

and some stone ballast. That night, however, the wind shifted to the southwest, which was favorable for setting a course for Spain and unfavorable for sending boats to the beach for wood and stone. The decision to leave Santa Maria on a course for Spain was not difficult to make. For the next few days, Columbus and his storm-weary crew enjoyed favorable weather, but it was only a brief respite. On March 3 a violent squall split all of *Niña*'s sails and the ensuing storm drove her under bare poles throughout the day and into the night. Fortunately, at the start of the first night watch, about 7:00 P.M., the winds subsided somewhat and a full moon broke through the clouds, making it possible for a lookout to sight land ahead. Columbus set a spare mainsail and kept *Niña* offshore during the remainder of the night. At daylight on the fourth, he recognized the Rock of Sintra, a prominent landmark just north of the mouth of the Tagus River. Within a few hours, *Niña* entered the river and anchored at Rastello, later named Belém, the outer port of Lisbon.

Columbus wrote immediately to King João, requesting permission to sail to Lisbon and assuring him he had come from the Indies, not from Guinea or any other Portuguese colony. He also wrote to Fernando and Isabel of his safe return. Word spread of his achievement, and for the next several days the Tagus was thronged with boats and people eager to see the plants, animals, and, above all, the Indians brought back by the Spanish. Columbus traveled overland to Valparaiso to meet King João, who treated him with honor and respect. He also called on the queen and then returned to *Niña* and set sail for Palos on March 13, 1493. Two days later he crossed the bar of the Saltes and anchored in the harbor he had left more than seven months previously. Bells rang, shops closed, and people jammed the streets of Palos when *Niña* dropped anchor. A joyful carnival atmosphere prevailed, as it did in Seville when Columbus arrived there to await orders from the king and queen.

Pinta entered the river only a few hours after *Niña*. Martín Alonso Pinzón waited until Columbus had departed for Seville before he quietly slipped ashore. His ship blown to the north by the Atlantic storm, Pinzón had sought refuge at Bayona in Galicia. From there he wrote to Fernando and Isabel announcing his discoveries and successful return. He had waited in Bayona for their response, expecting praise and congratulations. Instead, the sovereigns replied in reproachful terms and forbade him an appearance at court. His health impaired by the rigors of the journey, Pinzón was further weakened by this rejection. He died within a few days of his return.

The sovereigns replied immediately to Columbus, addressing him as "Don Cristóbal Colón, our Admiral of the Ocean Sea and Viceroy and Governor of the Isles discovered in the Indies." They praised his achievement, invited him to court in Barcelona, and ordered him to begin immediate preparations for a return voyage to the Indies. Columbus responded with a list of ships, men, and munitions he would require, and then set out for Barcelona with six Indians, live parrots, stuffed birds, and the fruits, plants, and other materials he had collected.

In his triumphant trip across Spain, crowds gathered to see their hero and his wondrous companions. The royal reception at Barcelona was an elaborate and joyful occasion. A gold brocade canopy covered an open court, and hundreds of cavaliers and officials crowded in. Fernando and Isabel welcomed Columbus warmly and then broke protocol by inviting him to sit in their presence—something not often done by these proud rulers.

Word of the discovery spread throughout Spain and on to France, Italy, and England; spirits soared at the expansion of the world's horizons and the prospect of wealth and adventure across a sea thought to be trackless. No one fully realized yet the extent of Columbus's discovery, however; all agreed that Cuba was part of the Asian mainland and that the surrounding islands lay in the Indian Sea. The islands were called the West Indies and the New World referred to the unexplored regions of the vast Asian continent described by Marco Polo two hundred years before.

Political maneuvering for control of these lands had begun even before Columbus arrived in Palos. Upon receipt of his letter from Lisbon, Fernando and Isabel moved quickly to secure his discovery for their Crown. They had no doubt of their right to possession of this territory: during the Crusades, the Christian rulers in Europe had developed a doctrine highly favorable to themselves—it permitted their invasion and seizure of infidel territory to save it for Christianity. The pope was accorded the supreme right to dispose of captured heathen lands. Thus, Pope Nicholas V, in 1455, had awarded to Portugal all lands discovered on the African coast, and Pope Sixtus IV had confirmed, in 1481, Portuguese sovereignty as agreed with Spain in the Treaty of Alcáçovas (1479). With the Venetians controlling the overland routes to the east and Portugal jealously guarding the sea route down the western coast of Africa and eventually around the Cape of Good Hope to India, Fernando and Isabel were determined to control this new western route to fabled wealth.

On May 2, 1493, Pope Alexander VI, under pressure from Fernando, issued a papal bull granting Spain the same rights and privileges in the new territories as had been accorded Portugal in 1479. On May 3, the famous Line of Demarcation was promulgated; it ran north and south 100 leagues west of the Azores and the Cape Verde Islands, later adjusted by the Treaty of Tordesillas (June 7, 1494) to 370 leagues west of the Cape Verde Islands. Spain

was granted control of everything to the west of this line; Portugal everything to the east. But no papal bull could deter England, France, and Holland from joining in the race for territory in the New World discovered by Columbus.

The Second Voyage

Christopher Columbus's second voyage to the New World, unlike the other three, is not remembered for new discoveries made by the Admiral of the Ocean Sea. Rather, this was the voyage during which he tried and failed to establish a viable colony in what he believed to be the Indies. As viceroy, he was held personally responsible for the failure, but the blame belonged to many.

Preparations for the second voyage began while Columbus was still at the court in Barcelona reporting on the first. Fernando and Isabel were anxious to protect his discoveries for Spain, particularly against any possible Portuguese incursions. The Spanish sovereigns wanted men and arms in place as soon as possible. Formal instructions issued on May 23, 1493, directed Columbus to convert the natives to Christianity and establish a Crown trading colony on La Española. Columbus was granted full powers and control of this expedition, but because the sovereigns wanted a detailed accounting of every expenditure, the archdeacon of Seville (later patriarch of the Indies) Juan de Fonseca was named to watch over royal interests.

On September 25, 1493, crowds lined the streets and quays of Cádiz to cheer the departure of the seventeen-ship fleet. Columbus sailed on *Mariagalante*, one of three medium-sized ships, known as naos, of up to two hundred tons burden; the others were *Colina* and *La Gallega*. Antonio de Torres, owner of *Mariagalante*, was also her master. Fourteen smaller caravels, including hardy *Niña* of the first voyage, were more suitable for coastal exploration. Juan Niño sailed again as owner and master of *Niña*, this time with his brother Francisco as pilot. Cristóbal Perez Niño was master of *Cardera*. Other captains included Juan Aguado, Pedro Fernández Coronel, Alonso Sánchez de Carvajal, Ginés de Gorbalán, and Alonso de Ojeda. Most of the seamen came from Palos, Moguer, Huelva, and Lepe, as on the first voyage, although there were some Genoese and Basques among the crew. Juan de la Cosa signed on as able seaman aboard *Niña*, but he is better remembered for his 1500 chart of the New World.

Despite the gaiety and confident optimism that abounded at the fleet's departure, several facts augured ill for the voyage and, more particularly, for Columbus. His authority rankled Fonseca and his assistants; they tried in subtle ways to undercut his position. Graft and corruption characterized the provisioning of the expedition. The twenty good horses gathered by Columbus, for example, were exchanged at the last minute for inferior steeds. Some three hundred men stowed away, most of whom had been denied passage earlier; thus fifteen hundred men crowded space and drew on food and water planned for twelve hundred. Provisions themselves were substandard. Casks leaked (much of the supply of wine ran into the bilges during the first month), and biscuits and meat were of poor quality. Columbus had been given responsibility for choosing the passengers and had called for humble, hardy workers to till the soil, work mines, and build homes. However, he had been forced to take many recommended by the royal court, men who owed him no allegiance and were ill suited to the purpose of the voyage—to colonize the New World. There were soldiers, bored now that the wars against the Moors were over, adventurers, speculators, cavaliers of noble heritage, most of whom had joined the expedition for quick wealth and glory, not for the hard, mundane work envisioned by Columbus.

Among the presumed settlers on the second voyage were Ponce de León, future discoverer of Florida; Melchior Maldonado, a gentleman adventurer; Diego de Alvarado, who later fought with Pizarro; and Francisco de Garay, an associate of Cortés. Columbus's younger brother Diego accompanied him, as did Diego Alvarez Chanca, a physician from Seville who later wrote about the experience. Friar Buyl, a monk sent with twelve other ecclesiastics to convert the Indians to Christianity, brought complete equipment for the first church in the New World, a gift of Isabel.

The fleet cost some 24 million maravedis, four times the initial estimate. Part of the money to finance it came from royal church tithes and from wealth taken from the Jews expelled from Spain in 1492. Assembling such massive quantities of men, animals, food, and equipment in only five months was a prodigious feat, the first of this scale ever undertaken.

The fleet headed directly for the Canary Islands, steered well clear of Portugal, made landfall at Grand Canary on October 2, went on to Gomera for more supplies (fresh water, fruit and vegetable seeds, fowl, pigs, sheep, hogs, goats, and calves), and set sail again on October 7. They passed Hierro, farthest west of the Canaries, on the thirteenth and headed west by south (about 259 degrees). Columbus gave sealed instructions to his captains, explaining the route to take if the fleet were to become separated, but moderate winds and seas permitted them to remain together. On November 3, 1493, they sighted land.

Columbus's more southerly track on this voyage, which took the fleet to the southern Antilles, or Windward Islands, was deliberate. He wanted to explore the Carib islands he had been unable to visit at the end of his first voyage. As Chanca wrote, "Columbus rectified his course to discover [the Caribee islands] . . . because they were nearer to Spain and the route thence to La Española was direct. [And] to these islands by the goodness of God and the 'buen saber' [good knowledge] of the Admiral, we came as straight as if we had been following a well-known and customary course."

The first island was sighted on a Sunday and named Dominica. Not immediately finding a suitable harbor there, the fleet anchored off a nearby smaller island to the north. Columbus named it Mariagalante (now Marie Galante) and took formal possession for the Crown. On the fourth, he made an exploratory landing on a larger island a short distance to the west and named it Santa María de Guadalupe (now Guadeloupe). The natives fled, and when the Spanish explored their empty huts, they found human bones and skulls in addition to huge parrots, tame geese, and pineapples. Landing at a second harbor, they captured several women and boys who had been taken from their homes by marauding Caribs; the boys had been castrated and the Spanish thought they were being fattened like cattle for later slaughter. The fleet was forced to delay at Guadalupe until November 10 because a boatload of men, sent inland to explore, failed to return. Diego Márquez of Seville had taken a party of ten for purposes of plunder, and because dense foliage had made it impossible to sight the sun or stars to check direction, they became lost. Four search parties failed to find the missing men and came close to getting lost themselves. The original group managed to reach the shore just as Columbus was about to leave without them. Michele da Cuneo, an Italian gentleman on the voyage, wrote, "We thought they had been eaten by the . . . Caribs who are accustomed to do it."

The ships sailed northwest, and as they passed islands en route, Columbus named them Santa María de Monserrate (now Monserrat), Santa María la Redonda (Redonda), Santa María la Antigua (Antigua), San Martin (Nevis), San Jorge (St. Kitts), Santa Anastasia (St. Eustatius), San Cristóbal (Saba), Santa Cruz (St. Croix), Santa Ursula y las Once Mil Vírgines (Virgin Islands), and San Juan Bautista (Puerto Rico). On November 14 they landed on Santa Cruz and looted some of the native huts. A band of Carib men and women armed with poison arrows came toward them in canoes and wounded two of the Spaniards. One later died from the poison and was buried on La Española. The Caribs were captured to send back to Spain, and the fleet continued on to Puerto Rico, where the natives hid while the Spaniards took on fresh provisions.

On November 22 the ships reached the eastern end of La Española and three days later anchored at Monte Cristi. The first sign of disaster was the discovery of four corpses

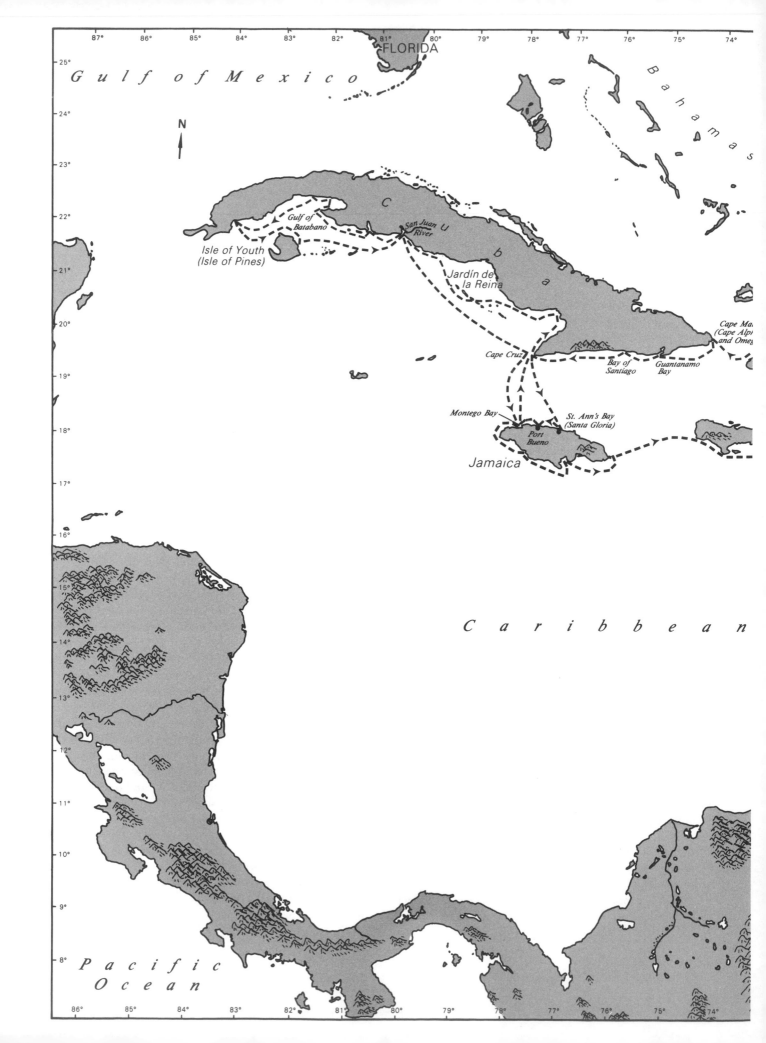

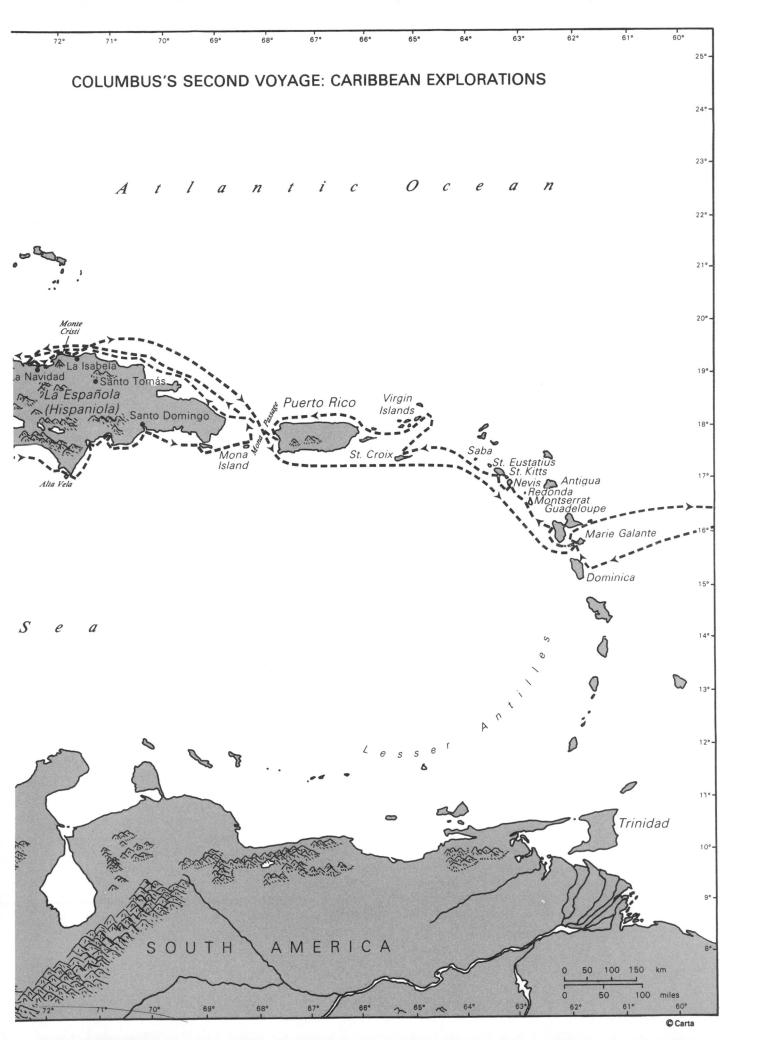

COLUMBUS'S SECOND VOYAGE: CARIBBEAN EXPLORATIONS

Atlantic Ocean

Monte Cristi

La Navidad • La Isabela
• Santo Tomás

La Española (Hispaniola)

• Santo Domingo

Mona Passage

Alta Vela

Mona Island

Puerto Rico

Virgin Islands

St. Croix

Saba

St. Eustatius
St. Kitts
Nevis • Antigua
Redonda
Montserrat
Guadeloupe

Marie Galante

Dominica

Lesser Antilles

S e a

SOUTH AMERICA

Trinidad

| 0 | 50 | 100 | 150 | km |

| 0 | 50 | 100 | miles |

© Carta

on the shore; one was bearded, a clear sign of European ancestry. On the twenty-seventh, the fleet arrived opposite the harbor of La Navidad, site of the first Spanish colony in the Indies. It was night and Columbus dared not enter, but when a few lombard shots drew no response—no shouts, no lights—his fears mounted. At midnight, a canoe of Indians approached his ship, led by a cousin of the chief, Guacanagarí, who had been friendly to Columbus on the first voyage. He explained that the Spaniards had quarreled among themselves, split up, and taken Indian wives in different parts of the island. The Carib chief Caonabó had attacked and wounded Guacanagarí when he had tried to defend the fortress. The following morning, the Spanish landed at the ruin of La Navidad. There was no treasure to be found, only several corpses lying in the open to be buried. Columbus visited Guacanagarí a few days later, and the cacique repeated the story of attack by Caonabó. He spoke of his effort to defend La Navidad and his sadness at the deaths of the Spaniards as well as several of his own people. Guacanagarí showed his own wound from the battle, but Chanca examined it and believed the cacique was feigning the injury. Columbus trusted his old friend, however. Gifts were exchanged, the Spanish receiving gold for worthless trifles.

On December 8 Columbus ordered the fleet out of La Navidad. The low, marshy area was unsuitable for any permanent settlement. They explored along the northern coast to the east and by January 2, 1494, had chosen a site for the first permanent European settlement in the New World. It was not perfect, but livestock were dying on the ship and had to be unloaded. Named La Isabela after the queen, the site lay between two rivers and was not far from the mines of Cibao. A church was constructed and the first mass held on January 6, celebrating Epiphany. Most of the Spaniards fell sick almost immediately; the climate was hot and humid, the work hard and provisions scanty. Columbus had planned to send half his fleet back to Castile laden with gold gathered by the La Navidad garrison. This was impossible now, and he was under pressure to prove to the sovereigns the richness of his discovery. Consequently, early in January, he sent two expeditions of forty men each to find the mines of Cibao that the Indians promised would yield great wealth. Alonso de Ojeda and Ginés de Gorbalán commanded the two contingents and soon returned full of optimism, reporting that large nuggets of gold lay openly in river-beds.

On February 2, twelve ships left for Castile commanded by Antonio de Torres and carrying specimens of gold, fruits and other plants (cinnamon, pepper, sandalwood), sixty parrots, and twenty-six Indians, three of them Caribs. Columbus wrote to the sovereigns asking for fresh supplies as soon as possible and saying he would be unable to make new discoveries immediately because his first duties were to find gold and secure a settlement. Five ships were left at La Española: the naos *Gallega* and *Mariagalante* and the caravels *Niña, San Juan,* and *Cordera.*

By April, a settlement of sorts existed at La Isabela. Crops had been planted and were seen to grow far more rapidly than in Spain. Two hundred small cabins roofed with thatch had been constructed, but provisions were dangerously low, native food unpalatable, and sickness prevalent. The majority of the settlers were loath to take orders from Columbus, who was viewed by them as an upstart foreigner unworthy of his newly acquired rank. They had come expecting quick, easy wealth, not debilitating heat and illness, unpalatable and insufficient food, and hard work tilling fields or mining gold. Factions had formed even before this disparate group reached La Española, and factional strife continued to plague the colony. The royal comptroller, Bernal Díaz de Pisa, and the assayer, Fermín Cedo, plotted to seize the remaining ships and return to Castile. Columbus learned of the plot and confined Díaz de Pisa on the *Mariagalante* until he could be sent back for trial.

With banners flying and trumpets sounding, the first overland march of Spanish conquistadores set forth from La Isabela on March 12, 1494. Columbus led four hundred armed men in search of the fabled mines of Cibao. Mounted cavalry and foot soldiers with swords, arquebuses, or crossbows protected the expedition, which included carpenters, masons, ditch diggers, and miners with equipment for mining gold and building fortresses. Many well-born gentlemen had refused to work at the settlement, but they carved out of the rugged mountain terrain the first road built by Europeans in the New World. Columbus named it El Puerto de los Hidalgos (Pass of the Gentlemen) in their honor, and the name endured for generations.

After making their way through this narrow pass, the Spanish got their first views of the vast fertile valley described by Las Casas as "one of the most admirable things in the world . . . so fresh, so green, so open, of such color and altogether so full of beauty that as soon as they saw it they felt they had arrived in Paradise . . . and the Admiral, who was profoundly moved by all these things, gave great thanks to God and named it Vega Real, the Royal Plain." With the help of Indians, they found a place to ford the Río Yaque del Norte and, after continuing across the valley, stopped at the Río Jánico. Here Columbus decided to establish a fort, Santo Tomás, to be a center of mining in Cibao.

Columbus stayed five days to see that work began properly, during which time Indians from miles around brought food and gold nuggets to trade with the Spaniards. Some two thousand castellanos worth of gold was officially collected, and as Cuneo recorded, "there was also exchanged in secret, against the rules and our agreement, to a value of 1000 castellanos. As you know, the devil makes you do wrong and then lets your wrong be discovered; moreover, as long as Spain is Spain, traitors will never be wanting. One betrayed the other so that almost all of them were exposed, and whoever got caught was well whipped; some had their ears slit and some the nose, which was very pitiful to see." Leaving a fifty-six-man garrison under Pedro Margarit to continue exploration and find more gold, Columbus returned to La Isabela with the bulk of the force.

The Indians had been friendly and helpful to the Spanish during Columbus's expedition inland. When he returned to La Isabela, however, word was sent by Margarit that Caonabó was rumored to be planning an attack. In fact, the Spanish had begun taking gold without trading for it and had abducted native women. Columbus sent only a small force to Santo Tomás. He was less worried about Margarit than about the situation at La Isabela. The heat and humidity, so wonderful for sugar and certain other crops, were harmful to people. Most were ill, and the well-born among them suffered also from wounded pride, being ordered by Columbus to perform hard, menial tasks. They refused, for example, to help build a flour mill, even though they needed bread as much as everyone else. Columbus resorted to strong measures to compel their obedience, thereby creating long-lasting resentment.

Although Columbus was eager to get on with further exploration of Cuba, he could not leave so large a group of discontented people at La Isabela. He decided, therefore, as a means of keeping them occupied, to send everyone able to walk on another expedition to explore the interior. On April 9, Ojeda led a force of 20 officers, 16 horsemen, 250 crossbowmen, and 110 arquebusiers to Santo Tomás to relieve Margarit. En route, Ojeda learned that three Spaniards had been robbed of their clothing by a small group of Indians. He caught one of the thieves and publicly cut off his ears and then captured the local cacique and his son and sent them to La Isabela in chains. Columbus threatened to behead them but rescinded the order when another chieftain pleaded for their lives. Las Casas records that "this was the first injustice, with vain pretension of justice, that was committed in the Indies against the Indians and the beginning of the shedding of blood which has since flowed so copiously in this island."

Columbus believed things were calm enough now to allow him to leave. He appointed a junta to manage affairs in La Isabela, presided over by his brother Diego and including Friar Buyl, Pedro Fernández Coronel, Alonso Sánchez de Carvajal, and Juan de Luján. On April 24 he set out in the three caravels: *Niña,* his flagship, with Alonso Medel as master, Francisco Niño as pilot, and chartmaker Juan de la Cosa as a seaman; *San Juan,* with Alonso Pérez Roldán as master; and *Cordera* with Cristóbal Pérez as master. Convinced as he was that Cuba was part of the Asian mainland, Columbus planned to follow its coast to reach Cathay. When he reached Cape Alpha and Omega (now Cape Maisi) at Cuba's eastern tip, he went ashore, set up a column topped by a cross, and took formal possession again of Juana, as Columbus still called Cuba. He called a council of pilots, officers, and gentlemen adventurers to discuss their route. The unanimous vote was to explore the south coast, the then popular geographical theory being that anything good is more likely to be to the south than to the north.

Landing at Guantánamo Bay on April 30, Columbus found great quantities of fish and two large iguanas roasting on open fires. No Indians were in sight. The Spaniards helped themselves to the fish and then went looking for the cooks. Their interpreter, the Taino Indian captured on the first voyage and baptized Diego Colón, managed to convince the natives that the Spaniards were friendly and offered gifts in exchange for the fish. The natives had been preparing this food for an important feast, but they were grateful the iguanas had been spared: capturing them was hard work and their meat delicious. Forty miles west of Guantánamo, the fleet entered the great Bay of Santiago lined by many Indian villages. These Indians and others who canoed out to the ships as the fleet continued westward along the coast said a great island to the south was the source of their gold. On May 3, having reached Cabo de Cruz and finding that the coastline there doubled back to the northeast, Columbus decided to head south for the promised gold of Jamaica.

On May 6, the Admiral anchored for only one night at Santa Gloria (St. Ann's Bay) and then sailed fifteen miles to the west and put in at Puerto Bueno, a better harbor, to make needed repairs on the ships. The Indians of Jamaica were more warlike than those on Cuba and hurled wooden spears and stones at the Spanish when they first tried to land. Columbus sent a boatload of crossbowmen ahead who "pricked them well and killed a number"; then they set loose a big dog "who bit them and did them great hurt, for a dog is worth ten men against Indians," wrote Cuneo. After this the Indians brought cassava, fruit, and fish to the Spaniards throughout their stay.

Columbus put back to sea and continued west along the Jamaican coast to Montego Bay. Having found no gold, he set sail for Cuba on May 13, returned to Cape Cruz, and headed northwest into a shallow archipelago, which he called El Jardín de la Reina, or Queen's Garden. Largely uninhabited, the area abounded in aromatic, lush vegetation and flamingos and other tropical birds. Some twenty days were spent sailing in and out of the intricate collection of canals and keys before heading for deeper water. After sailing farther west, they returned to the shore to take on provisions and water, encountering large numbers of peaceable Indians, most of whom said there was no end to their country. They said this part of their land was called Ornofay and that Magon lay beyond, where people had tails like beasts. Columbus believed Magon to be Mangi, a southeastern Chinese province mentioned by Marco Polo.

Continuing on, they reached the Gulf of Batabano, the westernmost point of the voyage. Similar to the Queen's Garden, these shallow waters went from milky white to green to black because of the chalk and fine sand churned up from the bottom. Ships were damaged repeatedly from running aground and being hauled off. By early June, the men wanted to go no farther. Columbus pressed on for three or four more days, though he was convinced that any land this large had to be the mainland. Because he wished to forestall accusations that he had returned prematurely (and his word had sometimes been doubted in the past), he asked the men to sign a statement that they believed Cuba to be the mainland of Asia. Punishment for retraction would be severe. Everyone willingly signed the statement. Two or three more days of sailing west would have established Cuba as an island.

Columbus began his return trip to La Española on June 13 and took on water at the Isle of Pines (now the Isle of Youth). Unable to make progress against the strong adverse winds and currents in the deeper water, he was forced to tack against the lighter winds and currents in the shoal waters around the coastal islands. Progress was exceedingly slow. On June 30, *Niña*, largest of the three ships, ran aground and was damaged when she was pulled off. Daily downpours added to the sailors' misery. After twenty-five dispiriting days, they had sailed only two hundred miles to windward. Finally, the three ships anchored in the Río San Juan, which Columbus renamed Río de las Misas because Sunday Mass was celebrated there. Staying outside of the Queen's Garden, the fleet beat to windward for ten days (July 9 to 18) in terrible weather. Las Casas wrote:

> All the winds and waters concerted to fatigue [Columbus] and heap anxiety on anxiety, difficulty on difficulty, and surprise on surprise, for he had neither the time nor the opportunity to take breath; among things that he suffered was a thundersquall so sudden, horrible and perilous that it threw the flagship on her beam ends, and with great difficulty, and it seems only with the help of God, did they strike the sails, and at the same time anchor with the heaviest anchors. Much water worked down below the floor timbers, which increased their danger, and the mariners could hardly pump it out because all were exhausted by continual labor. Provisions went so short that they had

nothing to eat but a pound of putrid biscuit and a pint of wine or its dregs except when they happened to catch some fish. . . . With these dangers and unceasing afflictions he arrived on July 18 at the cape which he had already named Cabo de Cruz, where the Indians received him well and brought him cassava bread, fish, fruits of the earth and everything they had, with great good will and pleasure. There they stayed and rested two or three days.

Because the winds were still wrong for sailing to La Española, Columbus headed for Jamaica again and sailed around the southern coast of the island. Crossing the Windward Passage to the southwestern cape of La Española, Columbus decided to explore the southern coast of that island. The ships became separated; *Niña* reached Alta Vela, an isolated rock marking the southernmost point of La Española, and waited six days for the others to catch up. Although, or perhaps because, Columbus was in bad health, he decided to raid the Carib islands and destroy their canoes so they could not attack the gentle Tainos. The ships headed toward Puerto Rico and Mona Island. Here Columbus became seriously ill with a high fever and alternate periods of coma and delirium. His officers turned around immediately and headed back for La Isabela, arriving there on September 29, 1494.

Columbus awoke to find his older brother, Bartolomé, at his bedside. Named to command three provision ships sent from Castile, Bartolomé had arrived in La Isabela just after Columbus sailed for Cuba. Their reunion was joyous—but this was the only happy note in La Isabela. During Columbus's absence, conditions in the colony had deteriorated drastically. In April, when Ojeda had been sent to Santo Tomás, Margarit had been ordered to tour the island, awing the natives with a display of power but conciliating them and treating them fairly. Columbus was convinced that just treatment of these basically friendly and helpful people would contribute to the success of the Spanish endeavor. But when Margarit marched into the Vega Real, he was anything but conciliatory: he and his men stole food and gold from the Indians, used their women, and pillaged randomly. Diego Colón's warning to change his tactics outraged Margarit, who marched to La Isabela in a fury. He was joined by a group of malcontents including Friar Buyl who, from all accounts, converted not one Indian during his months on La Española. Margarit and Buyl commandeered the ships in which Bartolomé Colón had sailed to La Española and left for Spain.

With their commander gone, bands of soldiers began roving at will and indulging in outrageous excesses against the Indians. It was only a short time before the Indians lost their timidity and retaliated. First, they attacked small groups of Spaniards. Then Caonabó led ten thousand warriors against Santo Tomás, manned by Ojeda and about fifty men. Despite a thirty-day siege by the Indians,

Ojeda held the fort and the threat receded temporarily.

In November 1494, Antonio de Torres arrived in La Isabela with four more supply ships. Along with food, the ships brought the millers, mechanics, fishermen, gardeners, and farmers the colony desperately needed. Torres also returned to Columbus the letter he had written to Fernando and Isabel and dispatched the previous year. On it were written the sovereigns' comments, dated August 16, 1494. They agreed with his plan to search for gold and establish a settlement and asked him to return to help draw the new Line of Demarcation agreed to in June. Columbus was too ill to return and sent his brother Diego in his place.

The sovereigns postponed a decision on Columbus's plan to establish a slave trade to help pay for the colony until the gold mines came into full production. Initially, he planned to send only Caribs who were the enemies of the Taínos. Fernando and Isabel did not look kindly on this proposal. But Columbus had nothing else of value to send back with Torres, apart from some gold specimens and more fruits and vegetables. When this fleet returned to Castile on February 24, 1495, it was loaded with five hundred male and female Indians to be sold at the slave market in Seville. Many of these were Taínos captured during the recent punitive expedition to the Vega Real. He has been roundly criticized for this, but Columbus was practicing a custom of his time, one sanctioned by the church and employed by Fernando in the wars against the Moors. It proved unsuccessful; two hundred died during the long voyage and the rest soon after their arrival in Spain.

After Torres left, the caciques Guatiguana, Mayrionex, and others assembled an impressive force in the Vega Real (Guacanagarí refused to join). Columbus took to the field with two hundred soldiers, twenty horses, and twenty bloodhounds, one of the most savage weapons used against the Indians by the Spaniards. Close to 100,000 natives poured into the central plain. The Spanish split up and attacked from different directions, galloping their horses, firing rifles, and charging with the dogs. The terrified Indians fled.

This left Caonabó to be dealt with, and Ojeda devised a devious plan. Going to Caonabó's headquarters, Ojeda offered him the bell from the steeple of the church in La Isabela as a gift. Caonabó believed the bell was magical, since every time it rang, all the Spanish hurried to the church. He agreed to accompany Ojeda to La Isabela to receive it but insisted a band of warriors attend him. As the story goes, Ojeda showed Caonabó a highly polished set of manacles and told him they were royal ornaments sent from heaven, that the Spanish sovereigns always wore them. He suggested that Caonabó bathe, be decorated with the manacles, and ride a horse into La Isabela

like the Spanish king. Caonabó agreed, mounted behind Ojeda, and was "decorated," at which point Ojeda galloped off at full speed. Caonabó was kept in chains in La Isabela until he could be sent to Castile.

Columbus followed his rout of the Indians with a tour of the island designed to reduce them to total submission. He reinforced existing fortresses scattered around the island and built six new ones. Desperate to raise money, he imposed a heavy tribute of gold in Vega, in Cibao, and around the mines, and demanded an equally stiff tribute in cotton from those Indians not living near the mines. Las Casas called the system irrational, burdensome, impossible, intolerable, and abominable. It soon destroyed the Indians. Docile and imprudent largely because there had been no need to be otherwise, they were unable to meet the harsh tributes imposed by the Spaniards. The unrelenting labor killed many. Others fled to the mountains and hid from the pursuing Spaniards in wretched caves or hollow tree trunks; thousands died of famine because they were too terrified of recapture to leave their hiding places to fish or gather fruit. Those forced to return to work in the fields or to search for gold died of exhaustion. Guacanagarí, Columbus's friend among the Indians, was overwhelmed by the tributes. His people reviled him for befriending the Spaniards, who had become such cruel oppressors. Las Casas says Guacanagarí hid in the mountains and died alone in misery. By 1496, the island was pacified. But by 1550, the Indians had disappeared almost completely.

During this time, Columbus's fortunes in Spain began to fall. Margarit and Friar Buyl had presented a long list of grievances to Fernando and Isabel when they returned to Spain in November 1494. The sovereigns' confidence in Columbus was shaken by the allegations; they were also concerned that some harm might have befallen him on his voyage to Cuba. They decided to send someone to investigate the charges lodged by Margarit and Buyl and to report back on conditions in general. Juan de Aguado was chosen for the task. The sovereigns said Aguado "was to be under the Admiral's authority in all things." At the same time he was to take charge in Columbus's absence and "remedy" any wrongs if he were present. Aguado had not yet left Castile when Torres returned there on April 10, 1495, with Diego Colón and the shipload of slaves. Upon hearing Diego's side of the story, the sovereigns were somewhat reassured but did not alter Aguado's conflicting orders.

With a fleet of four caravels loaded with supplies, Aguado departed Cádiz at the end of August and arrived at La Isabela in October 1495. He assumed the functions of viceroy immediately, countermanded Bartolomé's orders (Columbus had named his brother adelantado, or judge), and took depositions from the disaffected colonists.

When Columbus returned to La Isabela from the interior, he treated Aguado with deferential courtesy, assuring him he would follow his sovereigns' directions. Aguado was slightly deflated by Columbus's moderation but continued to act as overlord.

Meanwhile, in June 1495, before Aguado's arrival, the first hurricane experienced by the colonists had struck. The force of the wind and tidal surges sank three ships in the harbor. Only *Niña* survived, and she in a battered state. Columbus organized repairs to *Niña* and directed that a new ship, *Santa Cruz*, be constructed out of the wreckage of the others. While this work was going on, plans were laid to move the settlement to another site. The anchorage at La Isabela offered no protection from north winds, the climate was unhealthy, and the small amounts of gold discovered were beyond easy reach. An exploring party, sent out to find a more suitable site, chose the mouth of the Ozama River because of its fertile land, good harbor, and gold-bearing rivers. Before he sailed for Castile, Columbus directed Bartolomé to abandon La Isabela and build a new settlement, Santo Domingo, at the chosen site.

On March 10, 1496, Columbus and Aguado set out for Spain. Only five hundred men remained at La Isabela. Columbus sailed once again on *Niña*, and Aguado on *Santa Cruz*, appropriately nicknamed *India*, the first European ship built in the New World. Some 225 colonists were crowded aboard, along with thirty Indians, including Caonabó who was being taken back to exhibit to Fernando and Isabel. (The fierce Carib chieftain died of a broken spirit on the voyage.) The return trip was difficult because Columbus failed to sail beyond the reach of the adverse easterly trade winds. His route was ill chosen, in contrast to the more northerly track he had followed home after his first voyage. The ships reached only as far as Guadalupe by April 9; provisions were so low they landed there to take on a supply of native food and water. At the first anchorage, a horde of native women attacked the landing party and then calmed enough to tell the Spaniards they had no bread—their husbands, at the northern end of the island, would furnish what they needed. The two caravels proceeded to this point where the landing party was met with a fusillade of arrows. The Caribs fled when the Spaniards fired on them, but three boys and ten women were captured. Holding them as hostages, the Spaniards persuaded the Indians to teach them how to make bread from cassava roots. The crews remained for nine days, baking a three-week supply of bread and taking on firewood and water. They released all but two of the hostages and left for Spain on April 20.

By May 20, they had made little progress and provisions were so low everyone was put on rations of six ounces of bread and one and one-half pints of water a day. By June, conditions were so bad that someone suggested eating the Indians, an idea Columbus rejected. On the night of June 7–8, he ordered sails taken in, for he was sure they were off Cape St. Vincent. The pilots laughed at him, but once again his remarkable dead-reckoning ability proved accurate. On June 8 they spotted the Portuguese coast, about thirty-five miles north of São Vicente. The ships reached Cádiz on June 11, 1496.

The Third Voyage

Christopher Columbus had discovered the New World on his first voyage across the western sea, but neither he nor anyone else in Europe realized it. He discovered the South American continent on his third voyage, but again failed to comprehend the magnitude of his accomplishment. His discovery of Trinidad and the Gulf of Paria and his ceremonial taking possession on the Venezuelan coast of a continental landmass previously unknown to Europeans were overshadowed by a greed-inspired rebellion on La Española, which culminated in the Admiral's being sent home in disgrace, manacled hand and foot.

When Columbus returned from La Española in June 1496 after his second voyage, he stayed with Andrés Bernáldez, curate of Los Palacios and chaplain to the archbishop of Seville. Deeply religious, even mystical, Columbus was more comfortable in the company of ecclesiastics than in that of grandees or cavaliers. He gave Bernáldez his journals of the second voyage and other documents, which the priest used in compiling his *Historia de los Reyes Catolicos* (History of the Catholic Kings). Columbus adopted monastic garb at this time; the coarse brown habit of a Franciscan monk became his usual costume when in Spain. Fernando and Isabel wrote on July 12, 1496, expressing pleasure in his safe return and inviting him to court. Columbus set out with two Indians—Caonabó's young nephew and a brother who had been christened "Don Diego" by Bernáldez—caged parrots, jewelry, masks, winged crowns, woven cotton articles, and other Taíno artifacts. Don Diego wore a golden collar and chain that weighed six hundred castellanos. At the court, Columbus was reunited with his sons, Diego and Fernando, pages to Prince Juan. The sovereigns received him gracefully and were presented with a substantial quantity of gold, including some large nuggets. Columbus reported on his voyage to Cuba and the discovery of gold mines at Haina, which he believed might be the mines of Ophir mentioned in the Bible. Then he proposed a third voyage for which he requested eight ships. Two would sail immediately with provisions for the colony; he would lead the other six on another voyage of discovery. Fernando and Isabel were interested in everything he told them and, being satisfied with his report, readily agreed to a third voyage. But it was nearly two years before Columbus set sail.

King Fernando's political machinations were the principal cause of delay. He was preoccupied with the French invasion of Italy and its aftereffects, and he was determined to solidify and expand Spain's power through advantageous marriage alliances. The latter demanded huge sums of money and great numbers of ships and men. For example, a fleet of 130 ships was assembled to escort Fernando and Isabel's daughter Juana to Flanders for her marriage to Archduke Philip of Hapsburg and to return Philip's sister, Princess Margaret of Austria, to Spain for her marriage to Prince Juan, the heir apparent to the Spanish throne. Moreover, popular opinion held that there was little wealth in La Española, and in fact, relative to expectations, little had been returned to Castile. The benefit to royal coffers of another voyage to the Indies seemed dubious.

But finally, on April 23, 1497, orders were issued for the third voyage. Columbus was to take three hundred settlers at royal expense, including farmers, artisans, gold miners, and laborers, plus thirty women who were to pay their own way. Columbus was relieved of having to pay an eighth of the cost, as he had before, and the sovereigns appropriated a sum of 2,824,336 maravedis for the voyage. Fernando and Isabel reaffirmed Columbus's original titles, rights, and privileges and confirmed Bartolomé's appointment as adelantado. Also, the orders included a provision offering pardon to criminals (except those convicted of major crimes such as murder, treason, heresy, or sodomy) who would accompany Columbus and stay in La Española for one or two years, depending on the nature of their crime. Earlier enthusiasm for the Enterprise of the Indies had long passed; recruitment of settlers had become increasingly difficult.

Unfortunately, the promise of financial support was one thing, but actually prying money from the treasury, controlled by Juan de Fonseca, bishop of Badajoz, was something else altogether. Of the 2,824,336 maravedis appropriated in April 1497, Columbus had received only 350,094 by February 1498. Fonseca and one of his accountants, Jimeno Breviesca, threw up countless obstacles to delay the outfitting of the fleet. Before he finally was able to sail, Columbus in exasperation came to blows with Breviesca.

First to set sail, taking provisions to the colony on January 23, 1498, were sturdy *Niña* and *India*, the popular name for *Santa Cruz*, the ship built in La Isabela after the hurricane of 1495. Juan Bermúdez was captain of *India*, Pedro Francés of *Niña*. Pedro Fernández Coronel was captain general of the expedition. Four months later, the other six ships requested by Columbus were ready at last. Three caravels, *Garza*, *La Gorda*, and *La Rábida* captained by Alonso Sánchez de Carbajal, Pedro de Arana, and Giovanni Colombo, a Genoese cousin of the Admiral, were to take provisions to La Española. The other three ships, two caravels and a nao, Columbus's flagship, would

undertake the voyage of discovery. Pedro de Terreros and Hernán Pérez commanded the caravels *El Correo* and *Vaqueños*, Columbus the nao *Santa María de Guía*.

Columbus knew his chances of continuing in royal favor and holding on to the honors and titles already bestowed upon him depended on his finding major sources of gold. As Las Casas wrote, "He saw that his signal services were held of slight value, and that suddenly the reputation that these Indies at first had enjoyed was sinking and declining, by reason of those who had the ear of the Sovereigns." Fearing that Fernando and Isabel would abandon the project altogether and he himself would end in poverty, Columbus designed his route to take him to the most likely source of wealth.

His plan reflected Aristotle's doctrine that similar products existed in the same latitudes. The Portuguese had discovered gold in Guinea. If land could be found across the ocean at the same latitude, then it should be far richer than La Española. The route reflected also the prevalent belief that valuable things such as gold, spices, gems, and drugs came from hot regions, where dark-skinned people lived. Columbus planned to sail southwest until he reached the latitude of Sierra Leone and Cape St. Ann in Guinea, and then he would sail west to the meridian of La Española. If at that meridian he had not yet sighted land, he would sail south again.

Columbus's goal also was to ascertain the truth of King João of Portugal's contention that a great landmass existed west of La Española. Wishing to ensure Portugal's claim to that landmass, João had insisted that the Line of Demarcation established by papal bull be moved to 370 leagues west of the Cape Verde Islands. If land were found east of the line, it would belong to Portugal; if west, Spain would reap the benefits. Fernando, obviously preferring the second eventuality, had covered the first by arranging for his daughter, Princess Isabel, to marry João's son and heir, Manuel.

The six ships sailed from Sanlúcar de Barrameda, at the mouth of the Guadalquivir River, on May 30, 1498 and headed for Madeira, where Columbus had lived as a young man and where he was given a warm welcome. He stayed there six days replenishing water and wood and then proceeded to Gomera in the Canary Islands. On June 21 the fleet sailed from Gomera for Hierro and then split up. Columbus gave exact instructions to the captains of the three provisioning ships for the course to Dominica and thence to Santo Domingo, the new settlement on La Española. The three ships whose mission was discovery set a course for the Cape Verde Islands. Columbus had not been there before and found the name misleading: there was nothing green there; everything was dry and sterile. They stocked up on salted goat meat and water and, on July 4, headed southwest.

Columbus wrote in his journal on July 13 that "the wind

stopped so suddenly and unexpectedly and the supervening heat was so excessive and immoderate that there was no one who dared go below to look after the casks of wine and water, which burst, snapping the hoops of the pipes [wine casks]; the wheat burned like fire, the bacon and salt meat roasted and putrefied. This heat lasted eight days." Had it not been cloudy, he wrote, "many people must have perished." (One hopes the Spanish sailors removed their heavy woolen clothing, but as Morison notes, there is no evidence of these early explorers ever getting a suntan.) On July 20 the wind picked up, and they had ten days of good sailing. Water was running dangerously low, however, and Columbus had decided to head north toward Dominica to resupply when the lookout in the crow's nest, Alonso Perez, saw three rocks or mountains to the west. Columbus had planned to give the name Trinidad to the first landfall as a thankful tribute to the Trinity of his religion. That the landfall turned out to be a trinity of mountains seemed to him to be a miracle, a sign that he had been destined to discover this land. The three ships headed toward the island "and all the people glorified the divine bounty . . . singing the Salve Regina according to the custom of . . . our mariners of Spain."

On August 1 the Spaniards landed on Trinidad behind Punta de la Playa (Erin Point) to take on water. They saw signs of people, farms, and villages, but the natives kept in hiding. Columbus saw "toward the south, another island more than 20 leagues long," which was in fact Bombeador Point, part of Venezuela, his first sight of the South American continent, although he failed to recognize it as such. Keeping to the southern coast of Trinidad, the three ships sailed on to Point Arenal and on August 2 passed through the Boca de Sierpe (Serpent's Mouth), a dangerous spot where the fresh waters of the Orinoco River pour swiftly into the ocean through four channels separated by reefs. The fleet passed safely, however, and anchored on the southwest cape of Trinidad.

Soon after weighing anchor to sail north on August 4, Columbus and his men had a great fright, which he described in a letter to the sovereigns: "Standing on the ship's deck, I heard a terrible roaring which came from the southward toward the ship. And I stood by to watch, and I saw the sea lifting from west to east in the shape of a swell as high as the ship, and yet it came toward me little by little, and it was topped by a crest of white water which came roaring along with a very great noise . . . and sounded to me like the rote of surf on rocky ledges, so that even today I feel that fear in my body lest the ship be swamped when she came beneath it." Happily, no damage was done, for the great wave passed under the flagship, raising her to an immense height and then dropping her to what seemed the bottom of the ocean. Las Casas and others believed this was a tidal bore, but later experts have suggested the massive wave was probably caused by volcanic eruption.

Columbus left the Boca de Sierpe (still known as the Serpent's Mouth), headed north through the Gulf of Paria and anchored near the eastern extremity of the Parian Peninsula of the Venezuelan mainland, probably at Bahía Celeste. On August 5 he sailed south and west along the succession of mountains and headlands that constitute the peninsula. He sent boats ashore on this date, probably at Ensenada Yacera, the first positive landing of Europeans on the American mainland. They found "fish and fire and signs of people and a great house," and fruit "some like apples and others like oranges with the inside like figs"; the mountains "were covered with monkeys." The Indians fled, however, so Columbus delayed taking formal possession until the next day when the natives were on hand to witness the event.

Columbus himself may not have gone ashore for the ceremony because he was suffering from an eye infection. He was in poor health throughout this voyage, from arthritis and other maladies. Evidence is contradictory. Capt. Hernán Pérez testified later concerning the lawsuits known as the Pleitos that he was the first ashore but that Columbus, with fifty men, followed with banners and swords to perform the ceremony. On the other hand, the Admiral's page, Andrés de Corral, testified that Columbus remained on board because of his inflamed eyes and sent Capt. Pedro de Terreros to take possession. Unfortunately, Captain Terreros died on the fourth voyage and was not available to testify at the trials. In any case, although Columbus's personal presence ashore is uncertain, there is no question that men under his command landed on the South American continent in 1498. (Amerigo Vespucci sailed to Paria in 1499 with Ojeda, but changed the date to 1497 when he wrote about the voyage, unfairly claiming to have discovered the continent that bears his name.)

Over the next five days, the ships continued along the northern shore of the gulf, trading with the natives who offered food and a fermented drink made from maize and embroidered cotton kerchiefs similar to those worn by natives in Guinea. On August 6 a great cross was raised at the Rio Guiria, where "many people came out and told me that they called this land Paria." These Indians were taller than those in the Indies, with long brown hair. They wore polished gold disks like mirrors suspended around their necks. They traded these and a copper and gold alloy called "guanin," which was common to this area and was later found in Central America. The natives valued copper more than gold and sniffed all the articles offered by the Spanish to detect it. The women wore beautiful pearls, which they said they gathered in the gulf and on the Caribbean side of Paria. These Indians seemed to have a somewhat more advanced culture than that found in the Caribbean islands discovered on the first two voyages. They were more proficient in metallurgy and in weaving cotton. Some of their canoes, used to carry quantities of freight, were very large and often had a cabin built amidships.

Columbus was eager to explore this rich area, but provisions were spoiling and he had to get them to La Española. Seeking an outlet from the gulf at its western extremity, he sent *El Corréo*, the smallest of the three ships, to explore in waters too shallow for the others and discovered another vast basin fed by four large rivers. These were the four mouths of the Río Grande, the northern branch of the Orinoco. Columbus named this the Gulf of Pearls but, because of the need to deliver the provisions, decided he could not spare the time to explore it himself.

Writing to Fernando and Isabel, Columbus praised them for their sponsorship of his voyages and reminded them it took five years for Portugal to reap any benefits from Guinea. He added, "no prince of Castile is to be found . . . who has ever gained more land outside of Spain, and Your Highnesses have won these vast lands, which are an Other World where Christianity will have so much enjoyment and our faith so great an increase."

On August 13 the fleet took a dangerous departure from the Gulf of Paria through the Boca del Dragón (Dragon's Mouth) at its northeastern end where fresh water pours out and the sea rushes in. When the wind died in midcrossing, Columbus feared disaster, but fresh water overcame the salt and swept them out of the Mouth of the Dragon into the Caribbean. He sailed west along the northern coast of Paria (which he believed to be an island) seeking a back entrance to the Gulf of Pearls. He meant to keep close to the shore, but when he was forced to retire because his eyes troubled him, his pilots edged off shore. On August 15 he decided to head for La Española, "leaving the Cabo de Conches to the south and Margarita [Island] to the west." Had he explored for a day or so he would have found the rich pearl fisheries behind Margarita, but as he wrote to the sovereigns, "I omitted to prove this because of the provisions and the soreness of my eyes and because a great ship that I had was not suitable."

He did change his mind about the nature of his discovery, however, realizing that South America was a continent, not an island. He wrote in his journal, "I have come to believe that this is a mighty continent which was hitherto unknown . . . and if this is a continent, it is a matter for great wonderment and that it is such will be considered among all learned men since from it issues a river so immense that it fills a fresh sea 48 leagues long." In a letter to the sovereigns, Columbus propounded his belief that the world is not a sphere but pear-shaped with a bulge below the equator something like a woman's breast. The land he had discovered, he wrote, was the Garden of Eden, the Terrestrial Paradise, "because all men say that it is at the end of the Orient, and that is where we are." Did not Paria have a temperate climate and delicious fruit such as were found in the Garden of Eden? And what about *Genesis* 2:10? "A river flowed out of Eden to water the garden, and there it divided and became four rivers." Had not his men in Correo discovered four rivers at the western end of the Gulf of Paria? He described in some detail the many wonders he had seen—copper, lapis, amber, cotton, pepper, cinnamon, aromatic gum, ginger, gold, pearls—and drew a detailed map of the location of the gulf, including star sights, currents, and tides. But because he was ill, his men tired, and the provisions spoiling, he would return to La Española and send his brother Bartolomé back to continue the exploration of the mainland.

Columbus's amazing dead reckoning took the fleet to La Española on August 20. In *Admiral of the Ocean Sea*, historian Samuel Eliot Morison wrote of this accomplishment: "Columbus was approaching Hispaniola by a new angle, from a newly discovered continent. He had left Isabella in March 1496 and had never visited the site of Santo Domingo." At sea since May 30, Columbus had not been able to check his position against known land since July 4. He had taken a new route across the Atlantic and ended up far to the south and west of his previous Caribbean landfalls. "Yet all this time he had kept such accurate dead-reckoning that he knew the correct course for Hispaniola." Columbus was annoyed that his landfall was to leeward of Santo Domingo rather than seventy-five miles to windward as he had planned, but correctly decided that strong currents had been the cause. By any account, this was a remarkable feat of navigation.

Columbus must have been surprised when his brother Bartolomé sailed to Beata Island to meet him. Someone in Santo Domingo had spotted three caravels sailing to leeward and Bartolomé, assuming they carried Columbus, had set out to meet him. In fact, those ships has been the three provision ships Columbus had last seen in the Canary Islands. They had sailed off course and become hopelessly lost, finally fetching up at Jaraguá at the far western end of La Española. This was a clear indication that the Atlantic crossing and navigating among the Caribbean islands demanded a level of navigational expertise not all pilots possessed.

When Columbus reached Santo Domingo on August 31, 1498, he found the colony in a disastrous state. Illness— both fever and syphilis—plagued the colonists (some 160 of them, or 20 to 30 percent, probably had syphilis). The Indians had stopped paying the harsh tribute demanded by the Spaniards, mines were not being worked, farms

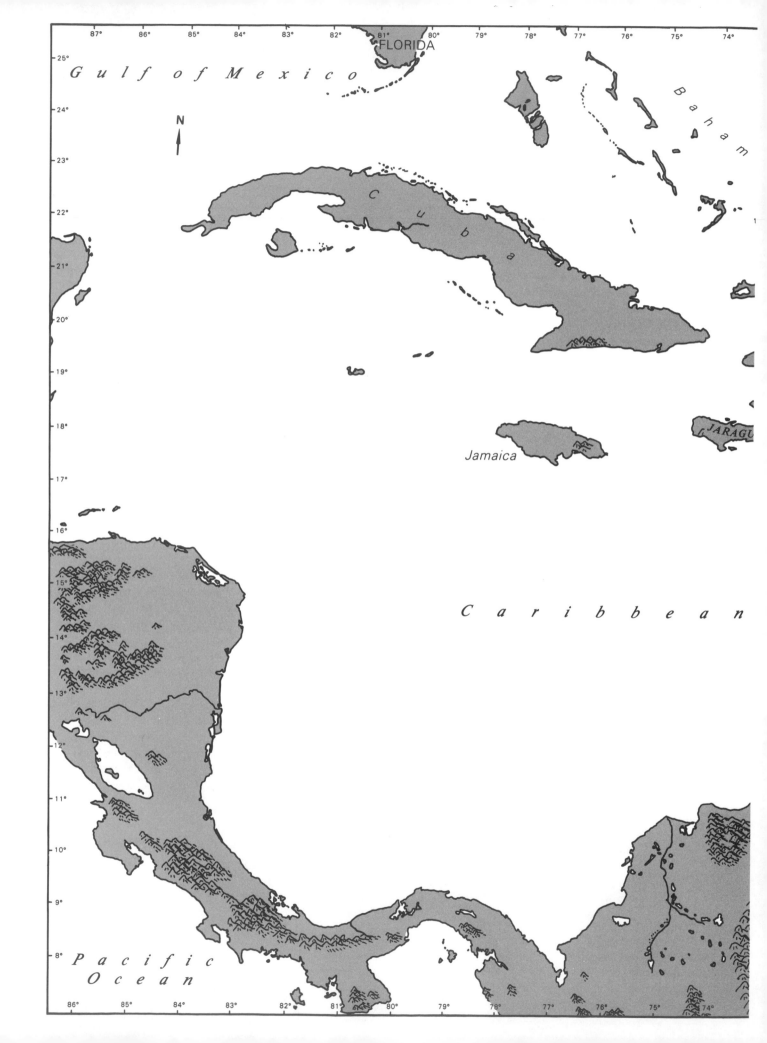

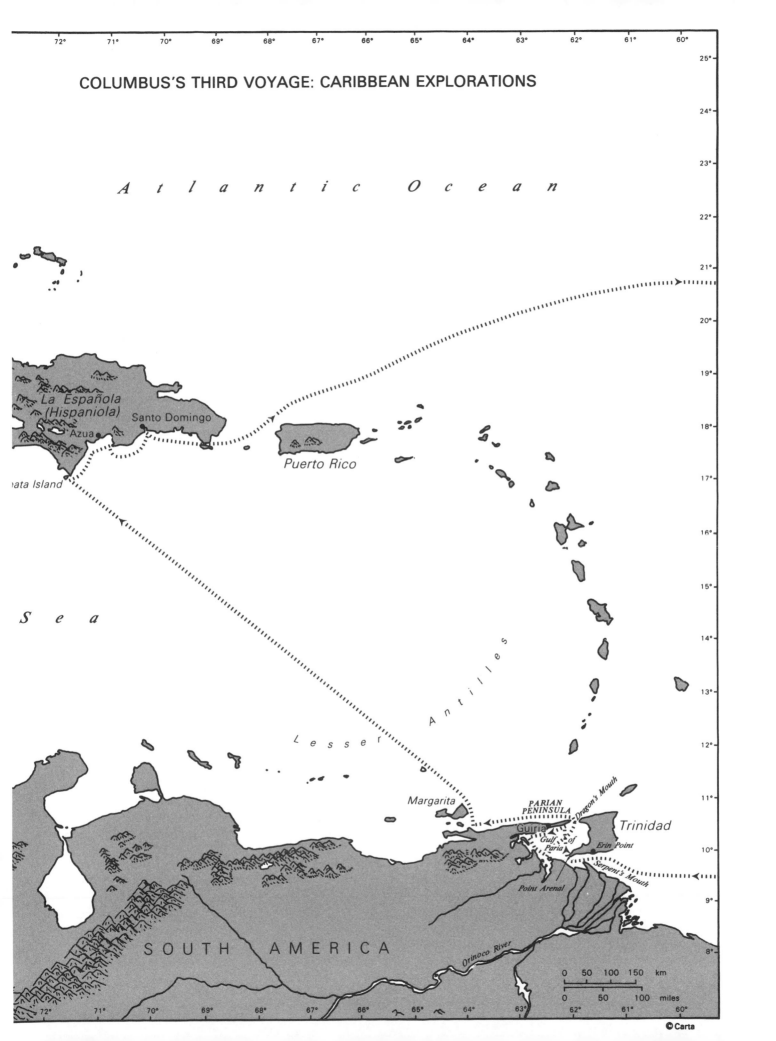

COLUMBUS'S THIRD VOYAGE: CARIBBEAN EXPLORATIONS

Atlantic Ocean

La Española
(Hispaniola)

Santo Domingo

Azua

eata Island

Puerto Rico

Sea

Lesser

Antilles

Margarita

PARIAN
PENINSULA

Dragon's Mouth

Guiria

Gulf
of
Paria

Trinidad

Erin Point

Point Arenal

Serpent's Mouth

SOUTH AMERICA

Orinoco River

| 0 | 50 | 100 | 150 | km |

| 0 | 50 | 100 | miles |

© Carta

were neglected. Most serious was a rebellion that had split the colony apart. The Spaniards hated the stern rule of that "foreigner" Bartolomé and were discontented with the climate and the chronically inadequate supply of food; above all, they were greedy for gold.

While Bartolomé had been away from La Isabela on his expedition to found the new settlement of Santo Domingo, the chief justice appointed by Columbus, Francisco Roldán, joined by a large group of malcontents, raided the armory and fanned out into the countryside, seeking gold and exploiting the Indians. Roldán abducted the wife of the then friendly cacique Guarionex, and his men were responsible for many other outrages against the natives. Bartolomé, although preoccupied with moving the colony from La Isabela to Santo Domingo on the banks of the Ozama River on the southern coast and building the new city and ships suitable for coastal trading, was nevertheless able to hold Roldán at bay at Fort Concepción, on the mule track between the two cities. When *Niña* and *India*, the advance ships of the Third Voyage, arrived with much needed provisions, the flotilla commander, Pedro Fernández Coronel, also brought royal confirmation of Bartolomé's appointment as adelantado and of Columbus's rank and privileges. Roldán had hoped the anti-Columbus faction in Spain had been able to secure the removal of the two brothers. When he learned this had not happened, he and about seventy followers moved to Jaraguá, at the western tip of the island, where Cacique Behechio permitted them to stay. Bartolomé then marched against the caciques Guarionex and Mayobanex who had joined with Roldán, captured them, burned their villages, and subdued that part of La Española temporarily. Meanwhile, however, Roldán was still at large in Jaraguá.

When the three provision ships got lost, overshot Santo Domingo, and landed at Jaraguá, many of the sailors who had signed on to mitigate criminal punishment in Spain were suborned by Roldán. Carvajal, one of the three captains, tried to reason with the rebel and then returned overland to Santo Domingo to report that he might give up his rebellion if granted amnesty. The other two captains, Arana and Giovanni Colombo, sailed back to Santo Domingo with all three ships. Roldán, joined by Pedro Requelme and Adrián de Moxica, two of the leading malcontents, moved into the Bonao Valley and planned to attack Fort Concepción. The commander, Miguel Ballester, offered Roldán pardon as directed by Columbus, but Roldán rejected it. He refused to deal with Ballester and insisted that Carbajal be sent to mediate.

On October 18, 1498, Columbus sent five ships back to Spain, loaded with brazilwood and other produce, many discontented colonists who wished to return home, and a large contingent of Indians for the slave market. He also sent two letters to Fernando and Isabel. In one he described how Roldán and others had rebelled against his

and their authority, pillaged the island, prevented the Indians from paying tribute, and stolen gold and women, including the daughters of several caciques. He requested that Roldán be summoned to Spain for judgment and complained that Fonseca's neglect of the colony, particularly the failure to provide adequate supplies of food and medicine, had been the principal cause of the settlers' discontent. He reported that he was sending home as many worthless, lazy settlers as possible and urged that industrious men be sent in their place so the natural wealth of La Española might be returned to Castile. He asked for a number of priests to help reform the dissolute Spaniards and convert the natives, and requested a man learned in the law to act as judge. He also asked that the colonists be permitted to keep Indians as slaves for two more years, using only those captured in wars or insurrections.

The second letter, written earlier, discussed his views on the shape of the earth and his discovery of Paria and the Garden of Eden; he enclosed the chart he had drawn detailing its location. He reiterated his promise to send his brother Bartolomé to continue explorations of Paria and added his intention to establish a colony there as soon as he could leave La Española. Obviously, this was not the time.

After dispatching the ships, Columbus sent Carvajal as his emissary to Roldán and his principal assistants, Adrián de Moxica, Pedro de Gámez, and Diego de Escobar. His letter to the rebels was conciliatory; he expressed concern for their feud with Bartolomé and promised them safe conduct. Terms were proposed back and forth until November, when the rebels agreed to leave for Spain in two ships provided by Columbus within fifty days. Columbus granted a number of concessions here—safe conduct, pay, slaves for their personal use or permission to take native wives in place of slaves. Two ships left Santo Domingo for Jaraguá in February 1499 but ran into violent weather and were delayed until March; one was so damaged it had to return to Santo Domingo. When Carvajal, in the replacement vessel, finally got to Jaraguá, the rebels refused to leave, claiming the ships had been deliberately delayed and were unseaworthy and ill supplied.

In another attempt to straighten things out, Columbus sailed to Azua, west of Santo Domingo, and met aboard ship with Roldán, Moxica, and others. In September Columbus agreed to the rebels' outrageous demands that all charges against them be dropped, that Roldán be reinstated as alcalde (chief judge) that fifteen rebels be allowed to return to Spain, and that the rest be given land grants, including natives living on the land, in lieu of pay. The land grant scheme, or repartimiento, was to become a cornerstone of Spanish colonial policy in the New World.

Columbus wanted to return to Spain in two caravels dispatched in October to make a personal explanation of these sorry events, but he dared not leave La Española in such an unsettled state. Instead, he wrote another letter to the sovereigns explaining that the perilous state of affairs on the island had compelled him to go along with the rebels' demands and urging them not to ratify the agreement. He repeated his request that a learned judge be sent to administer the laws of the island.

Another reason Columbus delayed his departure was the clandestine arrival of Alonso de Ojeda, whose four ships anchored off the western end of La Española. Ojeda was a favorite of Bishop Fonseca. When Columbus's letter describing Paria arrived in Castile, complete with detailed charts, Fonseca had shown them to Ojeda and then issued to him a private license to explore the area. Similar licenses were issued to Peralonso Niño and Vicente Yáñez Pinzón, undermining the authority of Columbus. Ojeda left immediately for the Gulf of Paria, accompanied by Amerigo Vespucci, a Florentine merchant, and Juan de la Cosa, the mapmaker who had sailed as a seaman on *Niña*. Ojeda departed in May 1499. Although trying to adhere to Columbus's course, he made his landfall on the southern continent some six hundred miles southeast of Trinidad but eventually passed through the Gulf of Paria into the Caribbean and proceeded along the coast to the west. He too neglected to avail himself of a treasure in beautiful pearls along the shores of the island of Margarita just off the north coast of Venezuela. Instead, he sailed on to the west finally reaching the northern tip of what is now Colombia. Having failed to find any of the Oriental splendors he had sought, he headed toward La Española for provisions. Arriving at Jaraguá, he met with Roldán's former cohorts. These men believed Roldán had deserted them by his agreement with Columbus; they wanted back pay and urged Ojeda to lead them to Santo Domingo to confront Columbus. Learning of Ojeda's arrival at Jaraguá, Columbus sent Roldán to establish order. The two crafty adventurers maneuvered for control, with Roldán finally emerging victorious. Ojeda sailed for Castile, stopping first in the Bahamas to take aboard captives for the slave market in Seville.

The turmoil in La Española continued. Roldán was now determined to enforce the laws he had so recently opposed. He imprisoned a young cavalier named Guevara, a cousin of his former lieutenant Adrián de Moxica. Moxica recruited many of his old friends to help free Guevara and kill both Roldán and Columbus. Learning of the plot, Columbus surprised and captured the ringleaders, hung Moxica, and imprisoned his accomplices. The rebels fled to Jaraguá, but Roldán followed and captured them.

La Española now began to settle down; fields were cultivated and the Indians were peaceful. Unfortunately for Columbus, events in Spain were about to culminate in his downfall. Columbus had few supporters at the court and many enemies, including Roldán's followers who spread tales of the Admiral's misrule. More important to King Fernando, gold—needed to support both his political ambitions in Europe and the colony itself—was not arriving in Castile. When more followers of Roldán returned to Spain with more tales of Columbus's tyranny and when more slaves arrived, further offending Isabel's sensibilities, the sovereigns decided to appoint someone to investigate affairs in La Española.

They appointed Francisco de Bobadilla as interim judge with powers to arrest rebels, seize their effects, and take over all royal property from Columbus, who was commanded to obey his orders. Bobadilla arrived in Santo Domingo on August 23, 1500, just at the time that Columbus had put down the rebellion led by Adrián de Moxica. As Bobadilla landed he saw seven corpses swinging from a gallows, proof to him of Columbus's cruelty. High-handedly, he seized the fortress where five other prisoners were held, released them, and took over Columbus's private quarters and possessions. (Columbus himself was at Fort Concepción at the time.) Diego was in charge in Santo Domingo, and Bobadilla jailed him. He interrogated several unhappy settlers and then issued a general license to search for gold and pay only a tenth of that found to the Crown instead of the third previously levied. When Columbus returned to Santo Domingo to meet with Bobadilla, he too was imprisoned and chained hand and foot. Later, Bartolomé joined his brothers in captivity.

The three Columbus brothers were sent home to Spain in chains. They left La Española in October 1500 aboard *La Gorda* and arrived in Cádiz at the end of the month. Alonso de Villejo, appointed to take charge of the prisoners, and Andreas Martín, master of *La Gorda*, offered to remove the manacles but Columbus refused, preferring that the sovereigns order them removed. On the sad voyage home, Columbus wrote a letter to Juana, sister of his friend Antonio de Torres and nurse to the Infante Juan, reviewing these events. Dignity intact, he made clear his outrage:

> It is now seventeen years since I came to serve these princes with the Enterprise of the Indies; they made me pass eight of them in discussion, and at the end rejected it as a thing of jest. Nonetheless, I persisted therein ... and have placed under their sovereignty more land than there is in Africa and Europe, more than one thousand seven hundred islands, without counting Hispaniola.... In seven years I, by the divine will, made that conquest. At a time when I was entitled to expect rewards and retirement, I was incontinently arrested and sent home loaded with chains, to my great dishonor and with slight service to their Highnesses.

The accusation was brought out of malice on the basis of

charges made by civilians who had revolted and wished to take possession of the land.... In this endeavor I have lost my youth, my proper share in things, and my honor.... I was judged as a governor who had been sent to take charge of a well-regulated city or town under the dominion of well-established laws, where there was no danger of everything turning to disorder and ruin; but I ought to be judged as a captain sent to the Indies to conquer a numerous and warlike people of manners and religion very different from ours, living not in regular towns but in forests and mountains. It ought to be considered that, by divine will I have brought all of these under the sovereignty of their Majesties, giving them dominion over another world, whereby Spain, heretofore poor, has become the richest of countries.

When this letter was read by Isabela, she became indignant and together with Fernando ordered that Columbus be set free. With gratitude and affection, they invited him to the court.

The Fourth Voyage

The fourth voyage of Christopher Columbus was referred to by him as El Alto Viaje, "High Voyage." He thought it would be his most significant, most profitable expedition, a fitting cap to his illustrious career. Columbus sought to discover a strait to the Indian Ocean, a shorter and more direct route to the opulent East than the route around Africa discovered in 1497 by Vasco da Gama. In fact, El Alto Viaje was the least profitable and most dangerous of all his voyages. He discovered Central America and more gold than in La Española, but he found no passage to India, returned no quantities of gold to Castile, lost many men and all four of his ships, and was marooned on a Jamaican beach for twelve months.

Six weeks after Columbus's ignominious return from La Española in chains in October 1500, the sovereigns ordered his release and invited him to the court. They sent him two thousand ducats to enable him to travel from Seville to Alhambra where they warmly received him on December 17. His brothers, Bartolomé and Diego, accompanied him, and Columbus was reunited with his sons, Diego and Fernando, who were serving as pages at the court. Isabel appears to have been genuinely upset over the harsh treatment of the Admiral by Bobadilla who in less than a year was dismissed from his position in La Española. The sovereigns agreed to restore Columbus's income and rights but turned a deaf ear to his plea that his position as viceroy be restored or that he be given a new position. In 1492, when Fernando conferred power and authority on Columbus, the scope of his discoveries could not have been anticipated. Now, merely six years later, voyages by Ojeda, Niño, Pinzón, Bastides, Lepe, Cabral, and Vespucci pointed to the vast size and richness of the South American continent. Could Fernando permit Co-

lumbus and his heirs to be governors and viceroys forever of this huge new world, with the right to tithe all trade and nominate officials? Furthermore, Columbus had failed in Fernando's eyes as colonial administrator. The job was more important now, for both England and Portugal were by this time encroaching on Spain's territories in the New World. The king planned to secure his possessions there by establishing local governmental commands at strategic places, under central control from Santo Domingo. Columbus was not the man for this vital position.

The sovereigns told Columbus that time was needed to settle things in La Española, that bad feelings still existed toward him and his brothers and it would be dangerous for them personally if they returned too soon. Bobadilla would be dismissed, but someone else would be sent to investigate events and remedy the wrongs that existed. Columbus was permitted to send a representative to ensure that his wealth and belongings were returned to him. Carvajal was chosen for this task. The new administrator would hold office for two years, after which time Columbus might return to La Española. Isabel apparently believed Columbus would be restored to his previous status after this period of time, but Fernando's conduct indicates he had no such intention.

On September 3, 1501, Nicolás de Ovando was named governor and supreme justice of the islands and mainland of the Indies. He sailed for the New World on February 13, 1502, with the largest fleet ever assembled. Thirty ships carried twenty-five hundred seamen, colonists (including seventy-three families), artisans, doctors, and soldiers, along with provisions, livestock, and munitions. Ovando had an impressive personal retinue and was allowed to take sumptuous silks and jewels to display the importance of his office. It must have been difficult at best for Columbus to view this demonstration of power and luxury which, by earlier royal decree, belonged to him.

On February 26, 1502, hardly two weeks after Ovando's triumphant departure, Columbus requested a fourth voyage to find a strait in the western Caribbean through which he could sail on to India. He knew from his own voyage to Paria and from others who had sailed there that the South American continent stretched far to the west. He also believed that the south coast of Cuba, which he still thought to be part of the Asian mainland, continued on to the west. And he had observed the strength of the current that ran westward through the Caribbean. Columbus concluded that this current must have an outlet to the west and that a strait through to the Indian Ocean must exist along the unexplored lands in the western Caribbean. In fact, the current south of Cuba does flow west; it then is deflected to the north by the Central American landmass and curves around the Gulf of Mexico to exit the Caribbean basin around the Florida cape.

Isabel may have felt that a few ships were little enough

to give to the discoverer of the New World, particularly in view of the great fleet sent with Ovando. Fernando's greed must have been aroused by the thought of a direct route to the riches of India. Portugal was growing richer with the bounty being returned around Africa along the route discovered by Vasco da Gama. If Columbus could discover a strait—and he certainly had the navigational skills to do it—da Gama's achievement would pale and Spain would gain its share of India's gold, spices, and pearls.

Formal authorization from Fernando and Isabel came on March 14, 1502. It was the last letter Columbus would receive from them. Addressing him as "Don Cristóbal Colón, Admiral of the Islands and Mainlands of the Ocean Sea in the direction of the Indies," the sovereigns said Columbus would receive ten thousand gold pesos for fitting out a fleet and all the arms and munitions he needed. He was to search for islands and continents "in the Indies in the part that belongs to us" (west of the Line of Demarcation). The gold, silver, pearls, precious stones, and spices he found were to be placed under the control of Francisco de Porras, who would sail as official comptroller. Columbus was to take no slaves. An accompanying letter of introduction to Vasco da Gama, then about to undertake a second voyage to India around the southern tip of Africa, said "it may be that you will meet on your course," indicating the sovereigns hoped that Columbus would discover a strait to the Indies and sail home around the world. They promised that his privileges would be preserved intact and confirmed anew if necessary.

Four caravels made this last voyage. Diego Tristán, a loyal servant to the Admiral, was captain of the flagship, La Capitana. Columbus, now fifty-one years old and in poor health, chose not to command the vessel himself. Bartolomé Colón sailed on Santiago de Palos, whose owner and master was Francisco Bermúdez. Francisco de Porras was titular captain, but Bartolomé, by far the better seaman, was de facto captain. Porras's brother, Diego, was auditor and Crown representative. The sister of the Porras brothers was the mistress of the treasurer of Castile, Alonso de Morales, and Morales forced Columbus to take the brothers along. El Gallego was captained by Pedro de Terreros, and Vizcaíno by Bartolomeo Fieschi, a Genoese and old family friend of the Columbuses. One hundred and forty men and boys sailed with Columbus, according to his twelve-year-old son, Fernando, who accompanied them.

The four ships set sail on May 9, 1502, heading first to Arzila, a Portuguese fortress on the Moroccan coast, to help repel an invasion of Moors. Apparently King Fernando asked that they make this detour to help maintain good relations with Manuel, king of Portugal and Fernando's son-in-law. Hostilities had ended before their arrival, so the fleet sailed on to the Canary Islands. After

reprovisioning, Columbus left Hierro behind on May 26 and set a course west by south. He reached Martinique in only twenty-one days, the fastest crossing of any of his voyages.

They rested, bathed, and repaired the ships and then sailed along the Leeward chain; by the end of June they were off the Ozama River just out from Santo Domingo. Fernando and Isabel's instructions forbade Columbus to land at La Española on this outward leg, but he had pressing reasons to request permission to enter the port. He wanted to trade Santiago for a ship more suitable for exploration and to send letters home with a large fleet about to depart for Castile. But his principal reason was to seek shelter from a tropical storm he saw brewing. Columbus knew well the subtle signs of an approaching hurricane—the oily swell from the southeast, an oppressive feeling in the air, cirrus clouds racing across the sky, perhaps twinges in his arthritic joints.

So he sent a note ashore to Ovando, requesting permission to enter and urging him to keep the fleet in port because of the impending storm. Ovando refused the request and ignored the warning. The thirty-ship armada left port and had just entered the Mona Passage when it was shattered by a massive hurricane. Only one of the ships made it to Spain—ironically, the least seaworthy of them all, aboard which Ovando had placed the four thousand pieces of gold belonging to Columbus. All the other ships were lost, either sunk with all hands or battered so heavily as to be useless. The flagship of the armada sank, killing one of Columbus's old friends, Antonio de Torres, as well as Bobadilla, Roldán, and the conquered Cacique Guarionex, and taking with it to the bottom 200,000 castellanos worth of gold. In all, more than five hundred lives were lost at sea and Santo Domingo was flattened.

Columbus and his four ships survived the storm. He had anchored close to land, possibly off the Jaina River, and was protected from winds coming from the north and west. Although the fierce winds tore three ships loose from their moorings (only Capitana's anchor held), all were able to ride out the hurricane safely. Columbus wrote (probably cursing Ovando as he did so), "What man ever born, not excepting Job, who would not have died of despair when in such weather, seeking safety for my son, brother, shipmates and myself, we were forbidden the land and the harbors that I, by God's will and sweating blood, had won for Spain?" His battered ships rendezvoused in Ocoa Bay on July 3, and the rested crews and repaired vessels left La Española on July 15.

Columbus had planned to return to Margarita Island off Venezuela and then sail downwind along the continental coast until he found the strait he sought. His decision to put in at Santo Domingo ruled out that course because he was too far north and west to beat back against both wind

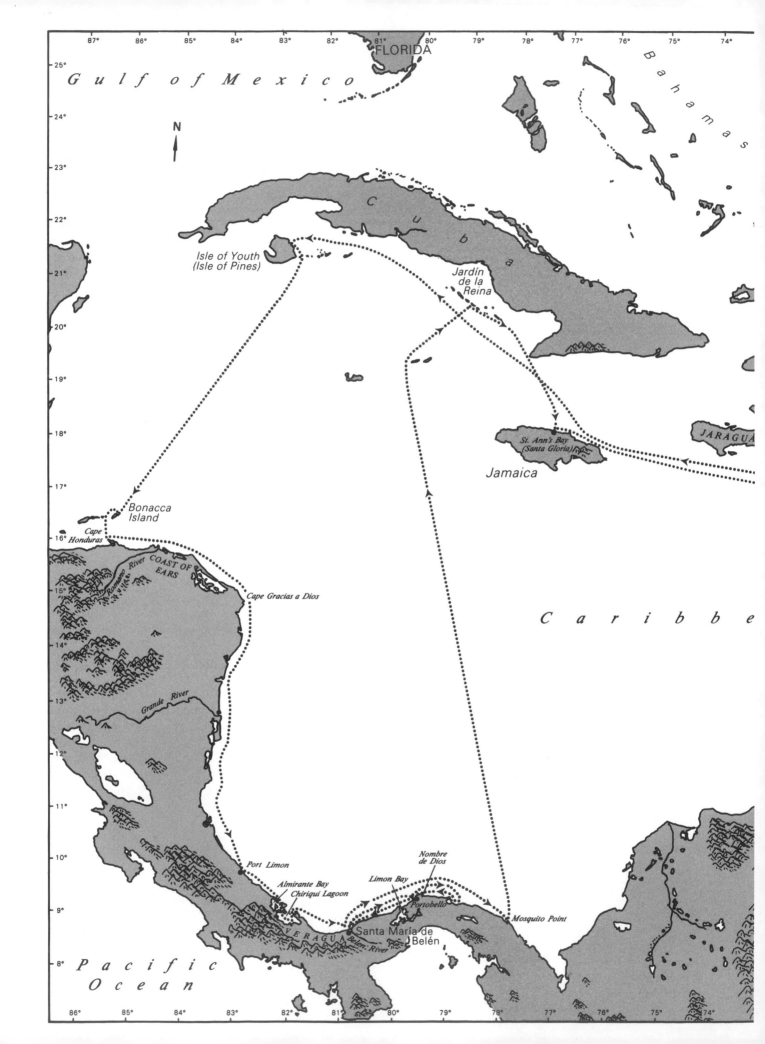

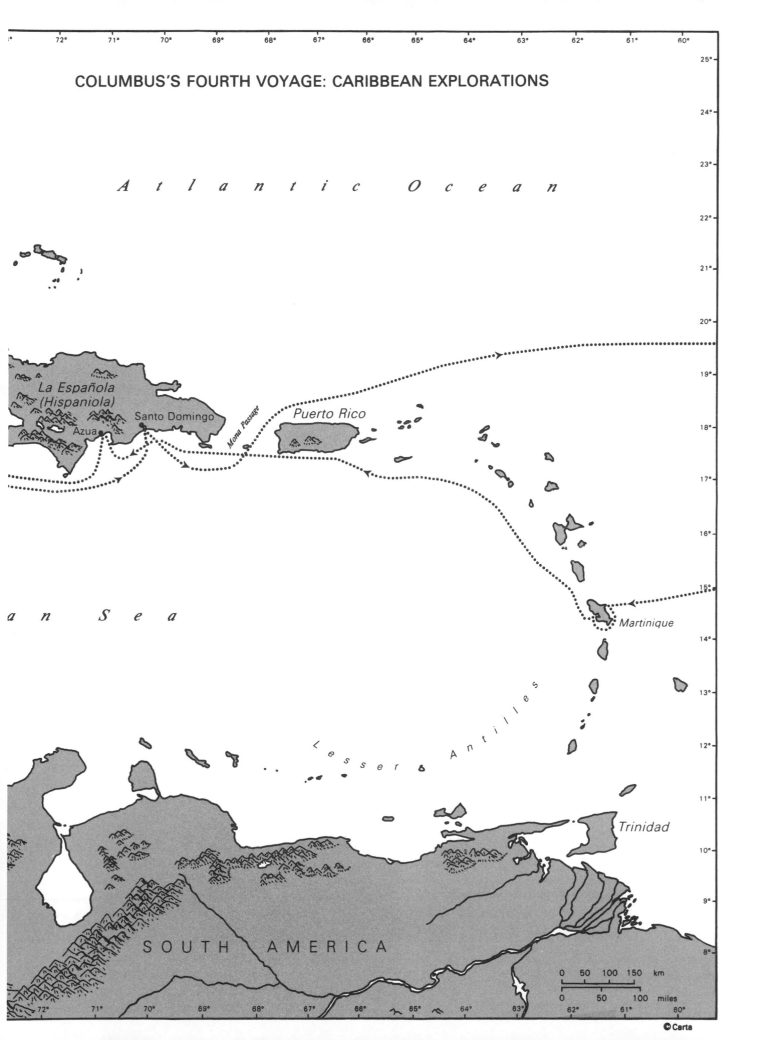

COLUMBUS'S FOURTH VOYAGE: CARIBBEAN EXPLORATIONS

A t l a n t i c   O c e a n

La Española (Hispaniola)

Santo Domingo

Azua

Mona Passage

Puerto Rico

an   S e a

L e s s e r   A n t i l l e s

Martinique

Trinidad

SOUTH AMERICA

| 0 | 50 | 100 | 150 | km |

| 0 | 50 | 100 | miles |

© Carta

and current, so he set off downwind into the western Caribbean. Light winds and strong currents carried them past Jamaica and then northwest toward Cuba. After anchoring off the Isle of Pines for three days, they picked up a stiff northeast wind and sailed 360 miles to the southwest. On the thirtieth, a seaman sighted Bonacca Island, off the Honduran coast.

Bartolomé went ashore, but the Indians had no gold or pearls to trade. A dugout canoe as long as a galley and eight feet broad, with a twenty-five-man crew, approached the ships. Women and children were sheltered by a hutlike structure of palm leaves amidships. The Spaniards captured it and exchanged the usual baubles for clay vessels, sheets of dyed cotton, flint-edged swords, and copper hatchets, all of a quality superior to what they had seen before. Like the Moors, the women covered their faces. The Indians, who were probably trading between Bonacca and the Honduran mainland, may have been part of a high culture akin to the Mayan. The Spanish captured the elderly skipper of the canoe to use him as interpreter, and he proved to be intelligent and helpful. The ships continued on toward the mainland and anchored in the lee of Cape Honduras, where they made the first landing on the mainland of North America.

After a long beat to windward they anchored off Río de la Posesión (now the Romano River), so named because Columbus took formal possession there on August 17. Father Alexander celebrated mass, and hundreds of Indians came to watch the ceremonies. They traded fowl, fish, red and white beans, and other commodities for the hawkbells, beads, and trinkets offered by the Spanish. They were darker than the Indians on La Española and tattooed or painted with designs of animals; they painted their faces "black and red . . . to appear beautiful, but they really look like devils," wrote young Fernando. Columbus called the region the Coast of the Ears because these natives had earlobes with holes as large as eggs.

The explorers then endured twenty-eight days of foul weather along the "Miskito Coast" of Honduras. Headwinds were strong, it rained fiercely, thunder and lightning tore the skies. The men were soaking wet continually, provisions were ruined, and the hard toil of pumping never ended. Still, Columbus was determined to find the strait, so they pressed on, beating off shore each day and anchoring close to shore each night: in strange waters, Columbus dared not sail after dark. Finally, on September 14, the fleet rounded the cape so aptly named Gracias a Dios (Thanks be to God) by Columbus and found favorable winds and currents. Sailing south along the Nicaraguan coast, they anchored on the sixteenth near the mouth of a large river, probably the Río Grande, where the surf was so strong one boat sent ashore for wood and water was swamped and two men drowned. Continuing

south for 130 miles, they reached Costa Rica eight days later.

On September 25 the ships anchored off what is now called Puerto Limón. Here they encountered Talamanca Indians, who were curious but superstitious. They refused to accept any gifts from the Spaniards, and when they saw a man writing, they threw powdered herbs into the air to blow the magic away. Columbus sent a boat ashore on October 2, and the men reported seeing "a great palace of wood covered with canes and within some tombs, in one of which was a corpse dried and embalmed . . . with no bad odor, wrapped in cotton cloth; and over each tomb was a tablet carved with figures of beasts, and on some the effigy of the dead person, adorned with beads and guanin, and other things that they most value." (Guanin was a copper and gold alloy.)

Taking two of the Indians as interpreters, Columbus headed southeast. When he found a channel the evening of October 5, he may have thought he had discovered the strait, but it led into Almirante Bay, not the Indian Ocean. Here Columbus "found the first sign of fine gold, which an Indian wore like a large medal on his breast and traded it." The Indians directed Columbus to another narrow strait, which again he may have thought to be the one he sought. But it led only to the landlocked Chiriqui Lagoon, thirty miles long and fifteen miles across. The fleet spent ten days in the lagoon, resting, fishing, and trading. Indians here had pure gold ornaments, not guanin. The two Indian interpreters had learned Castilian quickly. They told Columbus he was on an isthmus between two seas and that the people on the other side, a nine-day march away, had vast quantities of gold and of coral ornaments, wore rich garments, and carried swords. Columbus believed that area, called Ciguare by the natives, was actually Ciamba, Marco Polo's name for Cochin China. From this point on, Columbus concentrated on finding gold and gave up his search for the strait. He may by now have become convinced that no strait existed.

On October 17 the ships left the Chiriqui Lagoon and sailed southeast along the shore but found no harbors. They passed by five villages, one of which was called Veragua, where the Indians said gold was collected. Columbus sailed farther east but found he had passed the gold-trading part of the coast and decided to return to Veragua. Unfortunately, the rainy season began with rough seas and high adverse winds. A storm blew the fleet to Puerto Bello (now Porto Bello), a harbor just past the present Panama Canal entrance. Here they found tilled fields, good-sized villages, and amicable natives who traded spun cotton and food—but no gold. The riches of Central America lay to the west. The ships set out again but were driven back to where Nombre de Dios now is.

There they worked on their ships whose bottoms had been eaten through by *toredos* (shipworms).

Between December 6 and January 6, 1503, winds and currents battered the fleet back and forth between Puerto Bello and the Chagres River. Columbus wrote:

> The tempest arose and wearied me so that I knew not where to turn; my old wound opened up, and for nine days I was as lost without hope of life; eyes never beheld the sea so high, angry and covered with foam. The wind not only prevented our progress but offered no opportunity to run behind any headland for shelter; hence we were forced to keep out in this bloody ocean, seething like a pot on a hot fire. Never did the sky look more terrible; for one whole day and night it blazed like a furnace, and the lightning broke forth with such violence that each time I wondered if it had carried off my spars and sails; the flashes came with such fury and frightfulness that we all thought the ships would be blasted. All this time the water never ceased to fall from the sky; I don't say it rained, because it was like another deluge. The people were so worn out that they longed for death to end their dreadful sufferings.

And Fernando wrote of an occurrence, "one no less dangerous and wonderful, a waterspout which on Tuesday, December 13, passed by the ships . . . it raises the water up to the clouds in a column thicker than a water butt, twisting it about like a whirlwind." Columbus helped to exorcise the waterspout, clasping his Bible in one hand and his sword in the other as his sailors recited John's gospel.

The fleet put in twice at Puerto Gordo (Limón Bay, within sight of today's Panama Canal entrance at Cristóbal), once on December 17 and again from December 26 to January 3, after being blown back by storms. Everyone was exhausted, hungry, and sick, but finally on January 3 favorable winds let them put to sea again and on the sixth, they dropped anchor off the Belen (Bethlehem) River in Veragua. After taking soundings at the sandbar across the entrance, they entered a calm basin. Columbus decided to stay and explore inland. Bartolomé took a small group up the Veragua River and encountered the resident cacique, El Quibián, who paid a return visit to Columbus and exchanged gifts with the Admiral. On a second expedition, Bartolomé found more gold in just a few days than in four years in La Española. Columbus decided to build a settlement here and leave Bartolomé in charge while he returned to Spain for reinforcements. During the month of February 1503, the Spanish put up ten or twelve houses on the west bank of the river, the beginning of Santa María de Belén.

Many gifts were given to El Quibián to secure his friendship and keep the Spanish safe from attack. Although most of the European provisions had been exhausted, fish, maize, bananas, coconuts, and pineapples were easily found, so food seemed to be adequate. But just as Columbus was about to leave for Spain, the rains stopped and the water level of the river dropped, trapping the ships inside the sandbar. The Indians' attitude also changed. They had been willing to countenance a temporary visit from these foreigners, but when they saw houses being built they grew uneasy.

Diego Méndez, a trusted aide of the Admiral, was the first to notice suspicious Indian activity. Rowing along the coast, he found a thousand warriors gathered on the riverbank just up from the settlement. He stayed close off shore all night, holding the Indians in place. Columbus wanted more definite information before giving up his plan to establish a colony in this rich area. Méndez offered to get it, and there followed a bizarre incident. Méndez, apparently having mastered the local dialect, talked with some warriors who frankly told him they planned to attack the Spanish in two days. Méndez asked to be taken to El Quibián's village where the warriors were gathering. He claimed he wished to cure an arrow wound incurred by the chief. Although shoved about by one of the chief's sons, Méndez remained calm and staged a scene planned earlier, counting on the Indians' curiosity to make it work. Méndez sat on the ground and his companion, Rodrigo de Escobar, combed and trimmed his hair. The chief watched and then asked for the same treatment. When Escobar had cut his hair, he gave the barber's set to El Quibián. Méndez then asked for food and the two Spaniards ate a friendly dinner with the chief. The hostility of the surrounding Indians was ominous, however, and Méndez returned to warn Columbus that an attack was definitely coming. He suggested a daring plan, which was carried out with great skill by him, Bartolomé, and eighty men. El Quibián, several members of his family, and his principal subordinates were captured, as well as a good deal of gold. Unfortunately, through the laxness of his guards, the clever cacique was able to escape, but the other captives were imprisoned in the hold of one of the ships.

While this was going on, the rains resumed and raised the level of water over the bar, so that three ships could be towed out into the ocean. Bartolomé, Méndez, and seventy men were to stay at the settlement with the worm-eaten *Gallega*. While the two parties were saying good-bye, four hundred Indians armed with bows and arrows, slingshots, and spears attacked, wounding several Spaniards, including Bartolomé, and killing one. Just before the Spaniards drove off the Indians, Diego Tristán of *La Capitana* had rowed ashore in the ship's boat to take on water. Indians attacked his party, smashed the boat, and killed Tristán and all but one of his men who managed to escape and report the disaster. For eight days the situation remained tenuous. El Quibián did not attack again, but the hostages being held on *Santiago*, many of them members of El Quibián's family and thus a restraining influence on him, forced the hatch and some were able to escape. (The rest hanged themselves rather than submit to the Spaniards.)

Remembering the tragic loss of the force left at La Navidad in La Española on the first voyage, Columbus realized that the situation ashore had become untenable, and he reluctantly decided that it was prudent to abandon the settlement. Diego Méndez constructed a raft out of two dugout canoes and cross timbers. In two days he transported to the ships all of the garrison, together with the food and gear that had been stored ashore. When Méndez came aboard with the last load, the Admiral embraced him and promoted him to captain of the flagship *La Capitana* to succeed Diego Tristán. The worm-eaten *Gallega* was abandoned.

On Easter Sunday, April 16, 1503, the three remaining ships, all infested with shipworms, set sail for La Española. Within a week, *Vizcaíno* had to be abandoned at Puerto Bello because her condition was beyond repair. Her crew crowded aboard the two remaining vessels, both of which leaked badly. Columbus planned to call at Santo Domingo to repair the ships and take on provisions, and then continue on to Spain. He worked his way to the east so as to be able to make Santo Domingo on one tack. When he reached a headland, probably Punta de Mosquito, his pilots and captains prevailed on him to strike out for La Española. They thought they were east of the Caribee Islands when actually they were nine hundred miles to the west. With the ships leaking badly, they headed north on May 1. On the twelfth they reached the Jardín de la Reina, Cuba. Fernando wrote: "As we lay here at anchor ten leagues from Cuba, suffering greatly from hunger because we had nothing to eat but hard-tack and a little oil and vinegar, and exhausted by working three pumps day and night to keep the ships afloat, for they were ready to sink from the multitude of holes made by shipworms, there came on at night a great blow." *Santiago's* anchor broke loose and she crashed into *La Capitana*, severely damaging both ships. In the morning after the storm, the Spanish found only one strand of *La Capitana's* anchor cable intact.

On the twentieth of May they headed east, "the ships pierced by borers worse than a honeycomb, the people spiritless and desperate," wrote Fernando. Given the strong adverse wind and currents, they could not reach La Española. Columbus took the most sensible course available: he headed for Jamaica. From there, if the ships were still afloat, they could jump off for La Española. On the night of June 22–23, with the depth of water in the bilge increasing despite continuous pumping, they reached Jamaica. On June 25 they struggled into the reef-enclosed harbor of Santa Gloria (St. Ann's Bay). There was no way to keep the two ships afloat, so Columbus ordered they be

run ashore as far as possible and beached close together. The Spanish shored up both sides so the ships could not move and built cabins on the decks and at the fore and stern castles where they could be safe from the weather and any hostile Indians. Here they were marooned from June 25, 1503, until June 29, 1504.

One hundred sixteen men were left: six had died or deserted before Veragua, twelve had been killed at Belen, and six had since died. They had no food and Columbus could not let his men go freely ashore, knowing from past experience what they would do. Even the mild Taino Indians of Jamaica would be upset by their probable actions. Méndez and three others were sent to explore. Méndez struck a deal with a number of caciques: the Indians would provide food in exchange for beads, hawk-bells, red caps, mirrors, and so on. In exchange for a chamber pot, a cloak, and a shirt, a cacique at the eastern end of the island provided Méndez with a large dugout canoe loaded with provisions and six natives to return him by sea to the beached ships.

How could the Spanish get home? They had no tools with which to build new ships. Their only chance was to send a messenger by canoe to La Española. This involved a 180-mile trip against the wind and currents to the western cape of La Española and another 250 miles to Santo Domingo. In July, Méndez volunteered to make the crossing. With one other Spaniard and six Indians, he reached the eastern end of Jamaica but barely escaped from a hostile attack and returned alone. Columbus sent Bartolomé with a force of men to accompany Méndez to the eastern end on a second attempt. This time, Méndez and Bartolomeo Fieschi, the Genoese captain of *Vizcaíno*, each took a dugout canoe, six Spaniards, and ten Indians to paddle. If both canoes made the crossing, Méndez was to go on to Santo Domingo and Fieschi would return to Jamaica with news of their success. After seventy-two hours, during which water ran out and one Indian died of thirst, they reached the island of Navassa, a crossing of seventy-eight miles. Several of the Indians died on the island after drinking too much water too quickly; others were very ill. That night, however, they were able to make the crossing to La Española. No one would accompany Fieschi on the return trip to Jamaica, so the marooned Spaniards had no knowledge of the successful crossing.

Méndez recruited new Indian paddlers and set out for Santo Domingo. At Azua, he learned that Ovando was in Jaraguá on an expedition against the natives and went there on foot. Ovando kept Méndez at his headquarters for seven months while he brutally put down an Indian uprising. He hanged or burned alive eighty caciques including a beautiful *cacica*, Anacoana. It was not until March 1504 that Méndez finally reached Santo Domingo, again on foot. Ovando refused to let him use the small caravel in the harbor to return to Jamaica, so he was forced to wait another two months for ships from Spain.

On Jamaica, the Spanish were fearful, unhappy, and increasingly restive in their close quarters. Sure that they had been abandoned, they blamed Columbus for their troubles. With the onset of winter and bad weather, discontent reached a peak. Francisco and Diego de Porras led a conspiracy against Columbus. They may have felt themselves safe from any subsequent charges of mutiny because of their connection with Alonso de Morales, the treasurer of Castile. On January 2, 1504, Francisco entered Columbus's cabin and accused him of not trying to get back to Spain. Columbus said he wanted to return as much as anyone, but until a ship was sent, he saw no way to do so. Porras then cried, "I'm for Castile with those who will follow me." At this signal, "Castile!" the conspirators (forty-eight men, or about half the company) seized the ships. Columbus might have been murdered if a few of his loyal servants had not kept him safe in his cabin.

The rebels then seized ten dugout canoes tied up to the beached ships and fled ashore, ravaging Indian villages and stealing food and abusing women. Reaching the eastern end of the island, they set out for La Española, but heavy winds forced them to turn back. Frightened as the waves washed over the sides of the canoes, they tried to lighten them by throwing everything but their weapons overboard. Then they forced their Indian paddlers into the sea and when they clung to the sides of the canoes hacked off their hands or stabbed them. Eighteen died, but the mutineers returned safely to shore. They tried the crossing again a month later and again failed. After that, Porras and his band abandoned the canoes and started back to Santa Gloria on foot, living off the Indians and abusing them as they went.

After the rebels deserted the beached ships, the quantity of food provided by the Indians began to decrease. The actions of the Porras mutineers surely contributed to the Indians' unwillingness to help these intruders. Since most of those left with the beached ships were sick, including Columbus, it was difficult for them to gather their own food. By February, as famine loomed, Columbus had a brilliant idea. He remembered noting in his astronomical almanac that an eclipse of the moon was due and summoned all the neighboring caciques to Santa Gloria on February 29, 1504. When they had assembled, he told them his God would punish them for refusing to help him and his men and would send a sign of disapproval by making the moon disappear. The Indians were terrified when the eclipse occurred and begged Columbus to intercede with his God and save them from calamity. Columbus waited in his cabin until the eclipse was about to end and then emerged and said the moon would reappear only if the Indians continued to bring food. From then on, food was plentiful.

At the end of March, Ovando sent a small caravel to spy on Columbus and his increasingly restive men. The ship stayed out of the harbor while a small boat bearing Diego de Escobar, a former ally of Roldán, came to the shore with some wine and a slab of salt pork for the marooned men. He brought a message from Méndez saying he would come to their rescue as soon as a ship was available. Columbus sent a return message to Ovando describing his plight and begging him to send help. Publicly, Columbus reassured his men that help was coming. Privately, he believed Ovando had deliberately neglected him, fearing Columbus would be reinstated as governor of La Española. Columbus then tried to effect a compromise with the Porrases. He sent part of the pork brought by Escobar and offered them pardon if they would return to Santa Gloria and obey his command. They refused the offer. A fight between loyal and rebellious Spaniards ended in victory for the loyalists. Francisco Porras was captured, and the remaining rebels begged for pardon, which Columbus granted.

Méndez finally was able to charter a caravel commanded by Diego de Salcedo to send to Jamaica. Méndez himself sailed to Spain with Columbus's letters to the sovereigns. The survivors sailed for La Española on June 29. The voyage was long and difficult because of adverse winds and current and because the ship leaked so badly they had trouble keeping her afloat. They arrived in Santo Domingo on August 13. Ovando pretended joy at seeing the Admiral but set the Porras brothers free, a better indication of his feelings. Neither was ever punished for the mutiny. On September 12, Columbus, his son, his brother, and twenty-two others began another long and arduous journey, this time home to Spain. The mainmast broke on October 19, but Columbus and Bartolomé were able to fashion another out of one of the yards. The crossing took fifty-six days but ended safely at Sanlúcar de Barrameda on November 7, 1504.

The ailing Columbus retired to Seville, waiting to be called to the court. He waited in vain. Queen Isabel died on November 26, 1504, and Columbus was not granted permission to see her before her death. Finally, in May 1505, Columbus traveled by mule to the court, but he received nothing from King Fernando. Christopher Columbus, one of the world's greatest navigators and discoverer of the New World, died in Valladolid on May 20, 1506.

[See also *Columbus the Navigator; Equipment, Clothing, and Rations; Dead Reckoning; Grand Khan; Landfall Controversy; Lawsuits; Line of Demarcation; Navigation; Niña; Pinta; Santa María; Settlements; Ships and Crews;* and biographies of numerous figures mentioned herein.]

BIBLIOGRAPHY

Columbus, Ferdinand. *The Life of the Admiral Christopher Columbus*. Translated and annotated by Benjamin Keen. New Brunswick, N.J., 1959.

Dunn, Oliver C. and James E. Kelley, Jr. *The* Diario *of Christopher Columbus' First Voyage to America, 1492–1493*. Norman, Okla., 1987.

Fuson, Robert H. *The Log of Christopher Columbus*. Camden, Maine, 1987.

Irving, Washington. *The Life and Voyages of Christopher Columbus and his Companions*. 3 vols. New York, 1849.

Jane, Cecil. *The Voyages of Christopher Columbus*. London, 1930.

MacKie, Charles Paul. *The Last Voyages of the Admiral of the Ocean Sea*. Chicago, 1892.

Morison, Samuel Eliot. *Admiral of the Ocean Sea: A Life of Christopher Columbus*. 2 vols. Boston, 1942.

Nunn, George E. *The Geographical Conceptions of Columbus*. New York, 1924.

Parry, J. H. *The Age of Reconnaissance*. 1963. Berkeley, 1981.

Winsor, Justin. *Christopher Columbus*. Boston, 1892.

WILLIAM LEMOS

W, Z

WALDSEEMÜLLER, MARTIN (c. 1470 –1519), humanist, scholar, Roman Catholic priest, cartographer, and surveyor. The son of a butcher, Waldseemüller was probably born near Freiburg, Germany. On December 7, 1490, Waldseemüller matriculated at the University of Freiburg but soon interrupted his studies to travel to Basel, probably to work in the print shop of his uncle, Jakob Waldseemüller. At Basel it is believed he became associated with members of the printing community. He subsequently returned to the university and pursued his studies in theology; in time he was ordained a priest of the Diocese of Constance.

Nothing more is known of his career until 1506, when he arrived at Saint-Dié in the Vosges Mountains of northeastern France. Waldseemüller was soon asked to join a small intellectual circle called the Gymnase Vosgien organized by Canon Gauthier Lud, chaplain and secretary to Duke René II of Lorraine. Lud had set the Gymnase to work upon the project of producing a new translation and modern version of the *Geography*, the world atlas of Claudius Ptolemy. At the time of Waldseemüller's arrival, the philosophical circle, in addition to Lud, consisted of: Lud's nephew, Nicolas Lud; Jean Basin de Sandaucourt, a colleague and vicar of the church of Notre-Dame; and Canon Mathias Ringmann, a skilled translator of Latin and Greek. Waldseemüller, with his extensive knowledge of geography and ability to design and print maps, provided the additional skills needed for the project.

How Waldseemüller became acquainted with Lud is not known; perhaps Lud learned about him in Strasbourg in the print shop of Johann Grüninger, or it may have been there that Waldseemüller learned of Lud's project for an atlas and obtained an introduction. In any event, Lud presented the young canon to the duke of Lorraine as "a

man most knowledgeable about these matters," who was willing to work as a printer in Lud's home on the projected atlas. Following the practice of humanists of the time, Waldseemüller adopted a Greek form of his name, Hylacomylus or Ilacomilus, meaning "the miller of the lake in the forest," which was a literal translation of his name in German.

The scholars had already begun work on the atlas when the duke received from Lorenzo Pier Francesco de' Medici several marine charts depicting the newly discovered lands of the New World in addition to a French translation of the *Mundus novus,* Amerigo Vespucci's letter describing his four voyages. Lud promptly decided not only to incorporate information about the newly discovered lands into the atlas but also to make the discoveries known by other means. Work on the atlas was put aside temporarily, and the Gymnase set to work to produce a world map featuring the new lands. At the same time Basin de Sandaucourt was asked by the duke to translate the Vespucci letter into Latin for publication.

For an introduction to the world map and the atlas, Waldseemüller and Ringmann wrote a small tract on cosmography relating to the geography illustrated by the maps. This work, *Cosmographiae introductio cum quibus dam geometriae ac astronomiae principiis ad eam rem necessariis. Insuper quattuor Amerigo Vespuccii navigationes* (An introduction to cosmography with several elements of geometry and astronomy required for this science, and the four voyages of Amerigo Vespucci), was first published at Saint-Dié in April 1507, and four editions appeared before the end of the year. In his text Waldseemüller suggested that the new lands, which formed the fourth part of the world, should be named "Amerigo" or "America" to honor Amerigo Vespucci, whom he believed had discovered them. The little volume was widely distributed, and as a consequence the name "America" for the New World became generally accepted.

Next Waldseemüller produced a set of twelve gores, or triangular sections, for a terrestrial globe in which the name "America" was also incorporated, and he then designed a sea chart in which the name was again included. Entitled *Orbis typis juxta hydrographorum traditionem* (An image of the world [drawn] after those of sea charts), the chart apparently was not distributed, although it was later included in the atlas produced at Saint-Dié, but with the name "America" deleted.

Waldseemüller then turned to the design for a world map, the *Universalis cosmographia secunda Ptholemei traditionem et Americi Vespuccii aliorum que lustrationes* (A drawing of the whole earth following the tradition of Ptolemy and the travels of Amerigo Vespucci and others). Once more it featured the name "America" in the section that later was identified as South America. The map was produced in twelve large sheets reportedly in an edition of a thousand copies.

Between 1507 and 1516 Waldseemüller designed a great number of maps. In 1511 he tried unsuccessfully to interest Duke Antoine in his cartographical projects and dedicated to him the first printed wall map of central Europe, *Carta itineraria Europae*, for which Ringmann

compiled a descriptive text. A particularly interesting feature of this map is the presence on the lower border of a drawing of a compass showing magnetic declination, attesting to Waldseemüller's familiarity with a scientific phenomenon that until then had been little noted.

When the Saint-Dié edition of the *Geography* was finally published in 1513 it was not with the patronage of the duke, but at the expense of two private citizens of Strasbourg. That Waldseemüller was informed about surveying and the scientific instrumentation of his time is reflected in the detailed maps of Lorraine and the Upper Rhine he produced for the *Geography* and in a surveying instrument it is believed he invented and that was illustrated in a woodcut accompanying his treatise *Architecture et perspective rudimenta*. The significance of this instrument, which Waldseemüller named the polimetrum, lies in the fact that it was the earliest application of the principle of the theodolite to a surveying instrument and that it was the first European prototype of the theodolite, commonly used in surveying for traversing and for the simultaneous measurement of vertical and horizontal angles. It is probable that Leonard Digges learned of this instrument and from it derived his own invention of the theodolitus, which he described in his *First Book of Pantometria* (c. 1550).

In 1514 Waldseemüller was appointed cleric of the

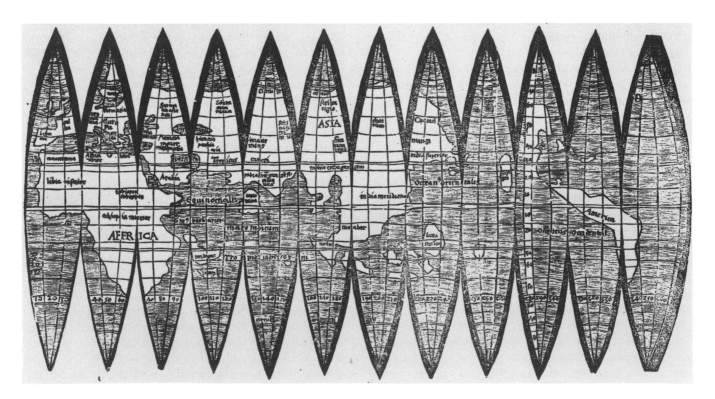

WALDSEEMÜLLER GLOBE GORES. Woodcut, Saint-Dié, 1507. The name *America* appears at right.

Diocese of Constance for the canonry at Saint-Dié, but continued his cartographical work. He produced a map of the world published in Gregor Reisch's *Margarita Philosophica nova* (1515) and in 1516 designed a large marine wall map, *Carta marina navigatoria,* which included important changes from the world map of 1507. Waldseemüller was asked by the Strasbourg printer Johann Grüninger to prepare German inscriptions for the map and to supply it with a full illustrated text in German. But before he was able to complete this task, or a new smaller version of Ptolemy's atlas he had planned, Waldseemüller died in his canon house at Saint-Dié on March 16, 1519.

BIBLIOGRAPHY

Avezac de Castera-Macaya, M. Armand P. d'. *Martin Hylacomylus Waldsemüller: Ses ouvrages et ses collaborateurs voyage d'exploration et de découvertes à travers quelques épitres dédicatoires préfaces et opuscules en prose et en vers du commencement du XVIe siècle. Notes, causeries et digressions bibliographiques et autres par un géographe bibliophile.* Paris, 1867. Reprint, Amsterdam, 1980.

Bagrow, Leo. "Carta itineraria Europae Martini Ilacomili, 1511." *Imago Mundi* 11 (1954): 149–150 and plate.

Fischer, Josef, and Franz von Wieser. *The Oldest Map with the Name America of the Year 1507 and the Carta Marina of the Year 1516 by M. Waldseemüller (Ilacomilus).* Innsbruck and London, 1903.

Kish, George. "Waldseemüller, Martin." In vol. 14 of *The Dictionary of Scientific Biography.* Edited by Charles C. Gillispie. New York, 1976.

Stevenson, E. L. "Martin Waldseemüller and the Early Lusitano Germanic Cartography of the New World." *Bulletin of the American Geographical Society* 36 (1904): 193–215.

Taylor, E. G. R. "A Regional Map of the Early Sixteenth Century." *The Geographical Journal* 71 (1928): 475–478.

SILVIO A. BEDINI

WEATHER AND WIND. Wind was the fuel that powered Columbus's voyages of discovery. His ability to take advantage of favorable winds and avoid the worst effects of unfavorable winds and weather contributed to his success as an explorer.

The Trade Winds. In planning his westward route, Columbus made perhaps his most important meteorological decision: to cross the Atlantic Ocean far enough to the south to take advantage of the northeasterly trade winds, with their typical speeds of four to sixteen knots. The northern limit of the trade-wind belt shifts with the season, ranging from about 30° N in January to 35° N in July. The southern limit of the trades shifts from near the equator in January to about 10° N in July. The trades are the world's steadiest wind system. Between 50 and 80 percent of the time the wind direction is within forty-five degrees of the most frequent wind direction. The trade

winds originate over the subtropical region of high surface pressure centered over the North Atlantic at 33° N 25° W in January and 36° N 37° W in July. The exact position of the high-pressure center can vary, and it can even develop two separate centers. When displaced to the east, it is known as the Azores high; when displaced to the west, it is known as the Bermuda high. Surface air flows outward from the center of high pressure toward the doldrums, the region of lower pressure closer to the equator. This equatorward flow in the trade-wind region is deflected to the right as a result of the rotation of the earth; this deflection, called the Coriolis effect, gives the trades their northeasterly direction over the North Atlantic Ocean.

The region occupied by the trade winds, while occasionally traversed by storms, is dominantly an area of fair weather. Skies can be exceptionally clear, though on occasion dust from the Sahara Desert travels across the Atlantic Ocean as a visible haze aloft. Average temperatures range from 68 to 80 degrees Fahrenheit (20 to 27 degrees Celsius), a few degrees lower than the ocean surface. Gentle sinking motions through the depth of the atmosphere in the trade-wind region inhibit the upward air motions needed for the development of storm systems. This sinking extends downward to within 6,000 feet of the surface, providing a lid that caps the growth of cumulus clouds in the trades; this cap is called the trade wind inversion. Overall, the relatively high pressure and sinking air motions make the trade-wind region over the North Atlantic an oceanic desert.

Even though the cumulus clouds that form beneath the trade-wind inversion are comparatively shallow (bases near 2,000 feet and tops usually less than 10,000 feet) the taller clouds poke through the inversion and can produce occasional showers. Trade-wind cumuli have many large cloud droplets that grow by colliding with and collecting smaller droplets until they eventually fall out of the clouds as raindrops. This warm-rain process differs from the typical mid-latitude or cold-rain process, which involves the systematic growth of small ice particles at lower temperatures and greater heights.

Local Wind Systems. Once Columbus reached the New World, his skills as a mariner were tested regularly as he sailed among islands that set up their own local-wind systems. These local winds include the land-sea breeze and, where local topography includes hills and mountains, the mountain-valley wind. Both types of local winds are caused by the daily cycle of heating and cooling over land.

Air temperature changes more during the course of the day over land than over water, as water maintains a more constant temperature than land. By late morning the land has warmed enough to set up a circulation in which air rises over the land, flows seaward aloft, and is replaced at low levels by the cool sea breeze, which blows landward

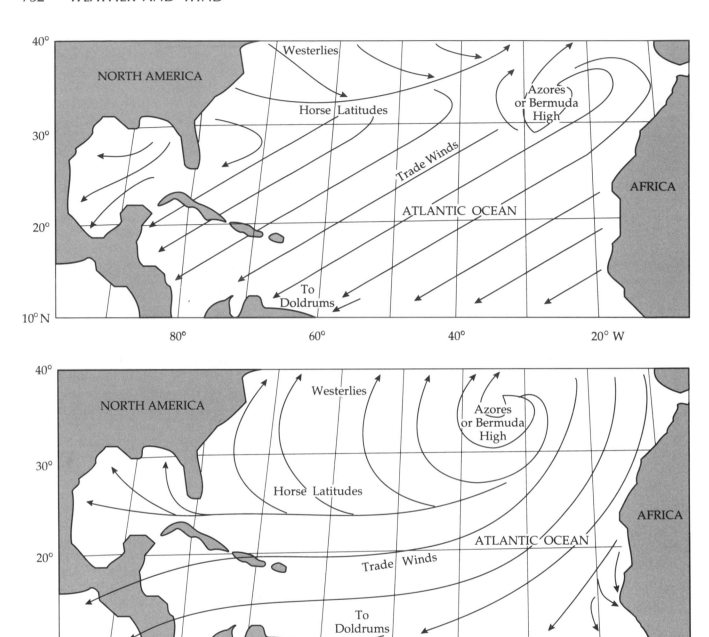

PREVAILING WINDS OVER THE WATERS COLUMBUS SAILED. Arrows show the prevailing wind directions for January *(above)* and July *(below)*. By traveling westward south of latitude 30° N, Columbus was able to take advantage of the northeasterly trade winds and the westward currents they generate. The trade winds originate near latitude 35° N in the clockwise wind flow from a high-pressure center located near longitude 25° W in January and near 35° W in July. On his eastward voyages, sailing north of latitude 30° N, Columbus was able to take advantage of prevailing westerly winds.

from the sea. At night, when the sea is warmer than the land, the direction of the circulation is reversed, and at the surface the land breeze blows seaward. The land breeze assisted Columbus's early-morning departures from islands in the Caribbean Sea. Likewise, he avoided a

dangerous lee shore by not making landings during those daytime hours when the sea breeze was strongest.

The mountain-valley wind system also shifts from day to night. During the daytime, air flows up the slope of the terrain where the mountains and hills are elevated sources

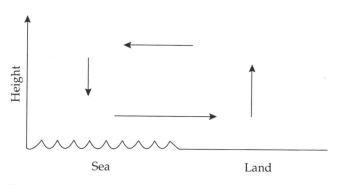
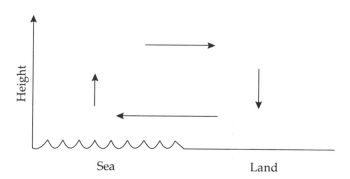

THE LAND AND SEA BREEZES. The daily circulation of air in coastal areas. By late morning the sea breeze (left) blows from the water onto the land. The sea breeze is part of a circulation that also includes rising air motion over the land, sinking air motion over the water, and, at higher altitudes, a return flow from land toward the water. At night and in the early morning hours, the circulation is reversed (right), and the land breeze blows from the land toward the water. Columbus avoided the sea breeze and took advantage of the land breeze when he landed at and departed from islands.

of heat. At night, cooling reverses this airflow to downward drainage. The mountain-valley wind system and the land-sea breeze can reinforce each other. When large-scale winds like the trades are weak, local winds predominate. In the presence of the trade winds, local winds can either reinforce or oppose the trades, depending on the orientation of sea and land. Whenever the combination of wind flows sets up convergence of winds from different directions near the surface, showers are more likely.

Records show that Columbus saw a waterspout. This meteorological phenomenon is not especially rare over the Gulf of Mexico and the Caribbean Sea, particularly when water temperatures are relatively warm. Waterspouts occur beneath cumulus clouds, usually those large enough to produce rain. Part of a rotating wind flow within the cloud that extends below cloud base, sucking up sea spray in a visible funnel, a waterspout can overturn small boats and cause damage on the decks of larger vessels. Winds at the center of a waterspout can be as strong as one hundred knots.

Tropical Storms and Hurricanes. Tropical storms (maximum sustained winds of thirty-four to sixty-three knots) and hurricanes (winds of sixty-four knots or more) occur each year in the waters Columbus sailed, and he encountered three during his voyages of discovery. Over the tropical North Atlantic and the Caribbean Sea, tropical storms usually form over warm ocean waters between 7° N and 30° N during the months from June until November. South of 25° N, the average hurricane moves northwestward at a speed of eight to twelve knots, steered by easterly winds aloft. North of 25° N, storms tend to curve back to the east under the influence of westerlies aloft.

These violent storms present special hazards for ships at sea and in port because of the high winds and seas they generate. Although the strongest winds and heaviest rains occur in the wall of the eye just outside the calm central eye of the hurricane, gale force winds may extend hundreds of kilometers outward in spiral bands of thunderstorms. Some portions of the storm are more dangerous than others. In the Northern Hemisphere, the right

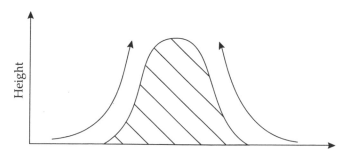
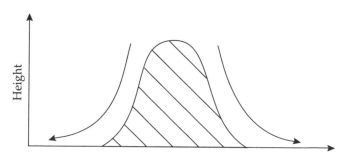

THE MOUNTAIN AND VALLEY BREEZES. The daily circulation of air in mountainous areas. During daytime hours the mountain breeze blows up the slope as the land heats (left). At night, when the land on the slope cools, the valley breeze blows down the slope (right). The mountain and valley breezes can augment the land and sea breezes. Columbus encountered such winds when he sailed into harbors of the Canary Islands, the Cape Verde Islands, and various Caribbean islands.

forward and rear quadrants contain the strongest winds because of the forward speed of the storm and the counterclockwise rotation of the winds around the storm center. The storm surge, a high sea driven shoreward by strong winds, is a particular danger on and just off shore. High tides and strong local currents can augment the storm surge.

Weather and Wind North of the Trades. While the trade winds greatly favored Columbus's journeys, his voyages were not immune to the influences of winds and weather north of the trades. During the winter season, strong cold fronts occasionally move southeastward off the North American continent. Although the arctic air behind these fronts has been considerably warmed by the time it reaches the Caribbean Sea, these northers are sometimes accompanied by showers, sudden wind shifts, and gusty winds from the northeast through northwest, as well as cooler temperatures and clear skies.

Over the open ocean, Columbus skirted the northern edge of the trades on his westward voyages. There he occasionally encountered the horse latitudes, just north of the trades, where winds are light and variable. This region was so named on account of the animals that died there during voyages of discovery and settlement when ships were becalmed in the light winds.

On his return voyages to Europe, Columbus traveled a more northerly route than on the westward voyages. In so doing, he avoided beating to windward against the trade winds and the prevailing ocean currents for part of the journey. At the more northerly latitudes, he encountered the prevailing westerlies. These are not as steady as the trades, but can be disturbed by extratropical weather systems with high winds and seas. Without a barometer, Columbus had only the signs of the clouds and the swell traveling ahead of storms approaching from the west to warn of difficult weather conditions to come.

An extratropical cyclone has a counterclockwise circulation that can be observed over a thousand miles from the center of low pressure. The fronts that extend outward from the low pressure center usually have marked wind shifts and stormy weather, particularly along and just ahead of the cold front. Such fronts stretch far southward and westward from the storm center, to latitudes south of 35°N in winter, and travel from west to east at speeds up to twenty-five knots or more. The rainbands along cold fronts can contain lines of showers with intense rainfall, gale-force winds, and high seas. Columbus encountered one such storm near the end of his first return voyage.

It speaks highly of the skill of Columbus as a mariner that, without modern meteorological and navigational instruments, he accomplished four transatlantic voyages, while encountering nearly the complete range of weather and wind conditions.

BIBLIOGRAPHY

Brooks, Charles F. "Two Winter Storms Encountered by Columbus in 1493 Near the Azores." *Bulletin of the American Meteorological Society* 22, no. 8 (1941): 303–309.

Crutcher, H. L., and R. G. Quayle. *Mariners Worldwide Climatic Guide to Tropical Storms at Sea.* Washington, D.C., 1974.

Fuson, Robert H., ed. and trans. *The Log of Christopher Columbus.* Camden, Me., 1987.

Hastenrath, Stefan, and Peter J. Lamb. *Climatic Atlas of the Tropical Atlantic and Eastern Pacific Oceans.* Madison, Wis., 1977.

Morison, Samuel Eliot. *Admiral of the Ocean Sea: A Life of Christopher Columbus.* 2 vols. Boston, 1942.

Morison, Samuel Eliot, ed. *Journals and Other Documents on the Life and Voyages of Christopher Columbus.* New York, 1963.

Palmén, Erik, and Chester W. Newton. *Atmospheric Circulation Systems: Their Structure and Physical Interpretation.* New York, 1969.

Peterson, Richard E. "Waterspout Statistics for Nassau, Bahamas." *Journal of Applied Meteorology* 17, no. 4 (1978): 444–448.

Riehl, Herbert. *Tropical Meteorology.* New York, 1954.

COLLEEN A. LEARY

WEST INDIES. The name "West Indies" was given by the Europeans in the early sixteenth century to the chain of islands that stretches in a great arc about 3,200 kilometers (2,000 miles) long from Florida to the South American coast. They saw the islands as the counterpart to the "East Indies," which they reached by sailing east from Europe, and did not at first realize that they formed part of a distinct continent; they also made the mistake of calling the inhabitants "Indians," a misnomer that has survived.

The West Indies consist of the four Greater Antilles (Cuba, Jamaica, Hispaniola, and Puerto Rico) in the west and the innumerable Lesser Antilles along the eastern rim. All these islands lie on the line of an ancient range of mountains, and they are still subject to earthquakes. In the Lesser Antilles, there is a sort of double line of islands, the ones on the Atlantic side, like Anguilla and Barbados, being relatively flat, and the ones on the Caribbean side, like Grenada and Dominica, being very mountainous. All the Lesser Antilles are small, with short rivers; some are edged with fertile plains.

The West Indian islands enjoy a moderate climate, for although they lie within the tropics, the surrounding ocean moderates temperatures. However, they are subject to hurricanes, storms of devastating force that generally sweep in from the southeast and can cause very heavy damage. On the rainy sides of the islands great forests once grew, but on Hispaniola and to a lesser extent Jamaica and Cuba, these forests have been largely de-

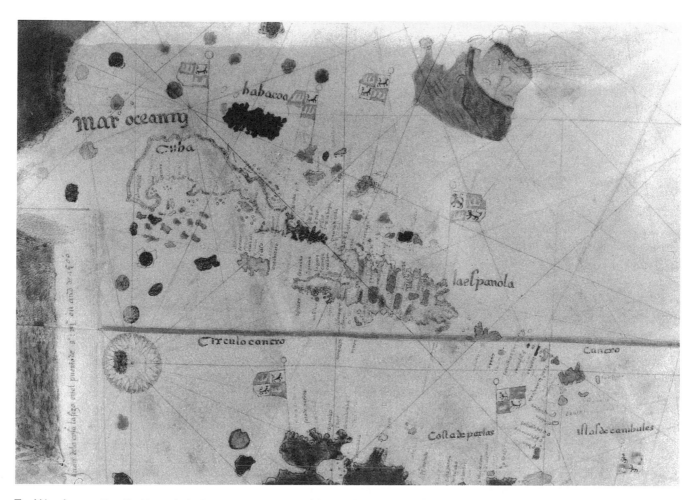

THE WEST INDIES. Detail of Juan de la Cosa's manuscript world map of 1500. The earliest surviving world map to show both the Old and New Worlds.

MUSEO NAVAL, MADRID

stroyed, which has produced a heavily eroded and dry landscape.

The West Indies were populated in a process that proceeded from the southeast to the northwest, along the line of the strongly prevailing winds and currents. Out of Venezuela came successive waves of immigrants, descendants of those peoples who originated in Asia and had long before entered the American continent in the northwest. The oldest groups still identifiable in the fifteenth century were the Ciboney and Guanahatabey, by then confined to the western end of Cuba. Throughout the rest of the Greater Antilles were the Taínos, a branch of the Arawak family. The Lesser Antilles were the home of the fierce Caribs, who when Columbus arrived were in the process of harrying the Taínos from their homes in Puerto Rico and slowly driving them westward.

It is extremely difficult to come to any firm conclusions about the populations of these native groups. The ac-

counts written by the Spaniards relied on a fairly superficial acquaintance with island societies, which in any case were rapidly reduced by the European intrusion. Archaeological investigations have given us some idea of the geographical distribution of the indigenous villages, but no very accurate notions as to their populations, since the structures have all perished and numbers have to be assessed largely from the size of kitchen middens, which may have grown in size over many years.

Here and there in the islands and on the mainland there survive groups of people closely related to the indigenous inhabitants; from these, and from the early European accounts, it is possible to have quite a good idea about how they lived. If we remain ignorant about their total numbers—which some authorities have put as high as six million—one thing is certain: the arrival of the Europeans was a demographic disaster that quite soon claimed the lives of virtually all the original inhabitants.

[See also *Cuba; Española, La; Jamaica; Puerto Rico; Indian America*, articles on *Arawaks and Caribs, Island Caribs*, and *Taínos*.]

BIBLIOGRAPHY

Milanich, Jerald T., and Susan Milbrath, eds. *First Encounters: Spanish Explorations in the Caribbean and the United States, 1492–1570*. Gainesville, 1989.

Morison, Samuel Eliot. *The European Discovery of America: The Southern Voyages A.D. 1492–1616*. New York, 1974.

Sauer, Carl Ortwin. *The Early Spanish Main*. Berkeley, 1966.

DAVID BUISSERET

WILL OF COLUMBUS. See *Writings*, article on *Last Will and Testament*.

WIND. See *Weather and Wind*.

WOMEN IN THE AMERICAS. The discovery of America was a process that began in different places at different times. In four transatlantic voyages Columbus made a brave beginning, but finding and laying claim to all that the New World had to offer required that many discoverers embark on voyages or mount up for *entradas*. Promising discoveries were followed by wars of conquest and settlements supported by Indian tribute and labor; disappointing discoveries were redeemed by taking slaves. Like Noah filling the ark, Columbus collected natives to display as curiosities, kidnapping equal numbers of males and females.

Encountering the nakedness of Arawak and Tupinambá women, discoverers in the Caribbean and Brazil thought of marvels, subhuman species such as mermaids, and Eves in new Edens. From a distance, theologians debated the rights of barbarians, but they did not question the self-evident propositions that in the natural order of things an inferior was meant to serve and a woman to be governed.

The first Spaniards to see the wonders of Mesoamerica and the Andes reported approvingly that the women of these advanced cultures were veiled and silent and did not look men in the face. Spanish etiquette, part Moorish, called for women of quality *(de calidad)* to live in near seclusion. They sat on pillows, not chairs. In the street, they donned the black mantle of the *tapada*, covering everything but one eye.

An earlier, Visigothic influence, was apparent in Spanish law. Partible inheritance was the norm. Males and females inherited equally, and unless the estate was entailed no one heir could be favored with more than "a third and a fifth." Marital gains were community property. The wife's dowry and *arras* (bridegift from the husband) remained her own. With the husband's consent, often guaranteed in the marriage contract, the wife could manage property and conduct business as freely as a widow. When her relatives failed to provide her with financial security, a woman of quality turned to her peers. To protect gentlewomen against loss of status, wealthy patrons made bequests for dowries and founded nunneries, and many a resourceful widow, citing the services of her husband and kinsmen, appealed to the king.

Paternalism, however, had its limits. As conquests in the Americas gained momentum, the actions of the conquerors regressed to those of a warrior society, treating women as the prizes of war. From the imperial halls of Mexico and Peru to the council houses of La Florida, women were deemed commodities. It was an insult to call a warrior a woman. Exchanged as pledges, tribute, or slaves, women had little to lose by casting their lot with the conquerors. One who did so was Cortés's translator and mistress, Doña Marina, known as Malinche and now maligned as the epitome of racial treachery.

The vanquishing of native Americans was first military, then sexual; the men defeated in battle were humiliated a second time when the women were ravished. In some cases the sexual conquest was legitimized. A conqueror of common origins could marry an emperor's daughter in Mexico or Peru and lay hands on her estate; in Paraguay, he could practice polygamy and make labor demands on his wives' relatives. More commonly, however, conquerors acquired one or more concubines—the common form of union with a woman of lesser rank in Spain—and sired a generation of mistrusted mestizos.

Consolidation followed discovery and conquest. Once a taxable region was securely held, Crown and Church initiated steps to curb the random violence of men of war and sanction a system of structured inequality. During the first colonial century, 440,000 Spaniards emigrated to the New World, primarily to the silver-producing colonies. Three out of ten of these emigrants were women, in contrast to the one in ten Portuguese who went to Brazil. Only New England would attract a higher proportion of female colonists than did Mexico and Peru.

Transplanted to the American viceroyalties, Iberian societies, accepting deference as natural, acquired a new dimension, namely caste. A white elite presided over tribute-paying Indian peasants and traded in African slaves; it outlawed interracial marriage, for if an *esclavo* married an *india* his children were free. Extending the meaning of *limpieza de sangre* (purity of blood) from its original sense of religious orthodoxy and *hidalgo* status to apply to racial distinctions, the elite further hardened the social boundaries with caste restrictions on the avenues to power: the bureaucracies, the professions, and the religious orders. Consequently, mestizos and mulattoes, male and female, sought the greater freedom of the frontiers.

Marriage had long been regulated under canon law as a sworn contract. In the mid-sixteenth century the Council of Trent reaffirmed matrimony to be a sacrament, and sexual acts outside of marriage to be sins. Confessors made valiant efforts to eradicate polygamy, adultery, fornication, concubinage, onanism, and sexual daydreams, while counseling the married to pay one another the "matrimonial debt." Nonetheless, commoners continued to regard marriage as a privilege of the elite; more than half of the children brought in for baptism were born of consensual unions.

The elite combined a strict sense of public honor with private flexibility. A promise of marriage often initiated sexual relations; a "protected pregnancy" did not affect the bride's reputation. There were also degrees of illegitimacy. For example, an *hijo natural,* born of unmarried parents, could be legitimized postnatally, unlike an *hijo adulterino,* a foundling, or the child of a priest.

Nunneries offered respectable seclusion for abused or erring wives, motherless girls, elderly women, and spinsters. While *Indias, mestizas,* or *mulatas* could be lay sisters, only a member of the white elite could profess as a nun. A convent often housed several women of the same family. Many nuns were socially and economically active, owning slaves, conducting their business out of convent parlors, and entertaining visitors with confections and evenings of music. For a few, such as the poet Juana Inés de la Cruz (the nun Sor Juana), the convent offered an opportunity to pursue an intellectual life.

The easy life of the elite was supported by Indian tribute and labor. The burden of tribute fell with inordinate heaviness on the women, who were the ones who wove the cotton *mantas* and picked the tiny cochineal insects off nopal cacti, and village quotas were seldom adjusted to reflect the decline in native population. The various labor drafts disrupted families: the repartimiento took the men to work in the mines and on public projects, and the semilegal *servicio personal* took the women to cities for domestic service. In order to escape both tribute and compulsory labor, men hired themselves out for wages at the mines, and the women stayed on in the cities, where they opened small stores and taverns, took in laundry and boarders, and acted as healers and midwives.

On the frontiers, the discovery of America continued. Some native societies were matrilineal, with the children belonging to their mother's clan. Some were uxorilocal, with the husband living in the wife's hometown. In some, a gender-based division of labor between hunting and farming led to nomadic husbands and sedentary wives,

with women owning the houses and fields. Other than the people themselves, these frontier areas had few resources, and as Crown and Church were united in opposition to the practice of making war to take slaves, the conquest came to a standstill. Spanish settlements on the edges of empire attempted to establish elites, but they had little revenue to support them. Nonwhite women predominated, and as always, did what they had to to survive.

[See also *Pacification, Conquest, and Genocide.*]

BIBLIOGRAPHY

Altman, Ida. *Emigrants and Society: Extremadura and Spanish America in the Sixteenth Century.* Berkeley, 1989.

Gutiérrez, Ramón A. *When Jesus Came, the Corn Mothers Went Away: Marriage, Sexuality, and Power in New Mexico 1500–1846.* Stanford, 1991.

Lavrin, Asunción, ed. *Latin American Women: Historical Perspectives.* Westport, Conn., 1978.

Lavrin, Asunción, ed. *Sexuality and Marriage in Colonial Latin America.* Lincoln, Neb., 1989.

AMY TURNER BUSHNELL

WRITINGS. [This entry includes five articles on Columbus's literary remains:

An Overview
Journal
Letters
Marginalia
Book of Prophecies
Last Will and Testament

For further discussion of documentary sources concerning Columbus, see *Bibliography; Book of Privileges; Library of Columbus; Museums and Archives.*]

An Overview

Christopher Columbus was a prolific and often eloquent reporter of his voyages and business affairs. About one hundred pieces of Columbus's writings have survived in various forms. When these are published in modern format, they comprise about 320 pages of material. Columbus wrote everything in the Castilian language, with the exception of some Latin notes in the margins of his Latin books. Even when he wrote to Italians, such as his brother Bartolomé and the city councilmen of Genoa, he wrote in Castilian. His Castilian, however, was heavily mixed with other languages: Portuguese, Latin, Italian, and the Mediterranean sailors' pidgin, "Levantisca." The earliest of his writings are some marginal notes (postils) he wrote in books that he owned and that his son Fernando preserved in his own much larger library, known as the

Biblioteca Colombina. None of these books owned by Columbus was published before 1484, although we do not know when Columbus bought the books nor when he wrote the postils. His last writings were dictated to clerks in Valladolid on May 19, 1506, the day before his death.

Forty-two of Columbus's short writings have survived in the original; they are letters and notes in his own handwriting or official documents written by a clerk and signed by Columbus. Despite the fact that Columbus never wrote Castilian or any other language correctly, his holographs are forceful, pungent, and sometimes even eloquent. These short, original writings reveal a great deal about Columbus the loving father of two sons and Columbus the hardheaded businessman. The official documents are written in correct Castilian, because Columbus was dictating to Castilian clerks who were trained to write in language that would be unambiguous and binding in a court of law. These official documents reveal Columbus the administrator of America's first European colonies.

The longest and most important of Columbus's writings are his reports on three of his voyages to America. These are Columbus's diary (Diario) of the first voyage (1492–1493) and a long letter (Primera carta de América) to King Fernando and Queen Isabel written during the return passage. He left no report on his second voyage (1493–1496), so for that voyage we depend on several reports written by passengers. Columbus also wrote a report on his third voyage (1498–1500), and a letter to the monarchs reporting on his fourth voyage (1502–1504).

None of Columbus's writings about his voyages and explorations survives in his own handwriting or in notarized copies. Bartolomé de las Casas included large parts of them in his invaluable history of America. Scholars now believe that Las Casas was a meticulous copyist of what he included, although we do not know how much he left out. Most of Columbus's other writings have come down to us in copies that were not made by clerks and, therefore, raise questions of authenticity, completeness, and accuracy.

The tone of Columbus's writings changed dramatically during his career. Until 1497, he wrote to the monarchs as he would to business partners, expressing optimism in their joint enterprise and gratitude for the confidence the monarchs had in him. During the third voyage, however, his writing fills with complaints about other explorers, the Spanish settlers, the monarchs' loss of confidence in him, and his own poor health. Ironically, these changes occur as his writing becomes more purely Castilian, with fewer and fewer words and spellings from other languages.

BIBLIOGRAPHY

Varela, Consuelo. "Prólogo, edición, y notas." In *Christopher Columbus, Textos y documentos completos: Relaciones de viajes, cartas, y memoriales.* Edited by Consuelo Varela. Madrid, 1984.

HELEN NADER

Journal

Until early in the nineteenth century, students of Columbus's first voyage had few details of the journey at their disposal. Other than the biography of Columbus attributed to his son Fernando Colón, which was published posthumously in Italian in 1571, there were only a few sources. Foremost among these was Columbus's letter to the Spanish court written on the return voyage, which, although rich in rodomontade, was meager on precise details. In addition, there were the brief accounts that opened the relations of Pietro Martire d'Anghiera (Peter Martyr), Gonzalo Fernández de Oviedo, and others.

This state of affairs ended in 1825 when Martín Fernández de Navarrete published a text he had discovered in the archives of the Duke of Infantado around 1790. The new source was sixty-seven folios in length and consisted of a detailed day-by-day account of the first voyage from the time the three ships left Palos in August 1492 until their return more than seven months later.

The new source, however, was not a shipboard log, even though it had that appearance. Rather it was a paraphrase, perhaps abridged, in the handwriting of Bartolomé de las Casas, whose own *Historia de las Indias* (completed by 1560 but not published until 1875) in turn paraphrased this source, which has come to be referred to as the journal, or Diario. About 20 percent of the Diario is not a paraphrase of some original, at least not by Las Casas, who presented it as "the very words" of Columbus. This portion of the text is characterized by being in the first person and the present tense. The degree to which the remaining four-fifths of the Diario departs from any original source is unknown. Nor do we know whether it was Las Casas, an earlier copyist, or both who changed the text.

Navarrete's edition, which introduced the Diario to the scholarly world and continued to be the basis for all transcriptions until 1892 and even later, was not an exact transcription of the holograph manuscript. Instead, Navarrete modernized and normalized the text by adding punctuation, changing the spelling, inserting paragraphing, and "correcting" words and phrases that he thought must be in error. He also attempted to fill in the various brief lacunae that exist in the Diario.

All further editions and translations of the Diario that were based on Navarrete's edition, of course, repeated his departures from the text, and added to them either deliberately or through carelessness. It was not until 1892 that, in honor of the quatercentenary of the discovery, a new and much more exact transcription was prepared under the direction of Cesare de Lollis. This edition, known as the *Raccolta* edition after the series of Columbian texts in which it appeared, came far closer to reproducing the manuscript text and, in addition, provided numerous textual notes as well as passages from the works of Fernando and Las Casas that dealt with the first voyage. This last attribute of the *Raccolta* edition has never been repeated, and so the edition retains value to the present.

Further editions and translations well into the twentieth century relied on Navarrete or on the *Raccolta,* but until 1976 none of them improved on the status quo. In that year Manuel Alvar published a two-volume edition of the Diario. In the first volume he provided a retranscription of the exact text, and in the second, a modernized version along the lines of, but superior to, those of Navarrete and others. To the first volume Alvar added extensive linguistic notes, and to the second, similarly extensive historical and geographical annotations. In the process he created the best ensemble edition then available.

Several further editions of the Diario were published in Spain and Italy during the 1980s, most of them better than any of the pre-1976 editions. Although these were not all equally satisfactory, they demonstrated that at long last the critical textual editing of the Diario according to modern standards had come to be regarded as a necessary prelude to studying the first voyage.

A marked advance in this progression was the diplomatic transcription and English translation prepared by Oliver Dunn and James E. Kelley, Jr. (1989). Although Alvar had for the first time scrupulously indicated all the changes, additions, crossovers, and marginalia in the Diario (about twelve hundred in all), he did so in his notes rather than graphically within the text itself. Dunn and Kelley, on the other hand, displayed the placement of these materials in a way that replicated the manuscript as closely as possible by means of modern typography. This innovation had the advantage of allowing users to see easily how Las Casas wrote out the text he had before him.

In addition, Dunn and Kelley's translation is the most literal yet, in any language, as they abandoned the fluid prose of most translations in favor of fidelity to the original text. These advantages combined with a thorough discussion of the paleographical issues, informative, often provocative, notes, and a detailed subject index together with a concordance (neither provided in any previous edition) to provide a valuable supplement to Alvar's edition.

These two editions rendered obsolete all editions and translations published before 1976 and 1989 respectively. Those preparing interpretations of the first voyage must rely on these editions (as well as on the facsimiles published by Carlos Sanz in 1960 and Alvar and Francisco Morales Padrón in 1984) and consult other editions only in the course of historiographical investigations.

The absence of rigorous editions of the Diario is in part responsible for the lack of authoritative studies of the activities of the first voyage, particularly the quest for Columbus's first landfall, an issue that has dominated study of the Diario from the beginning.

Form and Content. The Diario consists of approximately fifty-five thousand words, and many of these have been the object of scrutiny and controversy. In both format and content the Diario lives up to its name. It begins with an extensive prologue in which Columbus promises to investigate and conquer new lands (in Asia, he thought) for the Spanish Crown. Then follows a daily account of the voyage from Spain to the Canaries, from August 3 to August 9, 1492. Columbus remained in the Canaries until September 6, 1492, but the Diario contains no information on this sojourn, although there is some information in Fernando's biography. There is an entry in the Diario for every day from September 6, 1492, until March 15, 1493, except between November 7 and 11, when Columbus was apparently becalmed in a Cuban harbor. There are a few exceptions to the pattern; for instance, the events of October 11 and 12 are included in a single entry dated October 11.

From the perspective of the Diario Columbus's first voyage divides into five parts: September 6 to October 11, or the outward voyage; October 12 to October 27, the landfall and the cruise through the Bahamas to Cuba; October 28 to December 5, when Columbus sailed, first west and then east, along the northern coast of Cuba; December 6 to January 15, as Columbus sailed slowly along the coast of La Española, making frequent stops to inquire of the Indians after precious metals; and January 16 to March 15, the homeward voyage, which included two unscheduled stops, one of three days at Santa María in the Azores and the other for a period of over a week, when Columbus was the reluctant guest of the Portuguese court near Lisbon.

The level of detail the Diario provides varies greatly and is most dense during Columbus's six-week sojourn in La Española. In general, the detail is greatest whenever the Indians are mentioned, which many take to reflect the input of Las Casas into the extant version, although it is likely that Columbus too was interested in this new race, which he found unable to assimilate to his experience and expectations. There are also many passages in the Diario on the physiography of the New World in which Columbus found himself. Much of this is characterized by a degree of exaggeration and bewilderment that makes it difficult to evaluate in terms of matching it to modern conditions.

Of navigational details there is much, although perhaps not as much as might be expected in a shipboard log.

Some believe that this means that either Las Casas or another copyist, or even Columbus himself, omitted much of this material because it was uninteresting or unnecessary, or because of a desire on Columbus's part to keep to himself the details of the route to the New World. That which remains, however, has proved to be of great interest to most modern students of the voyage.

In addition to an apparent lack of navigational details, the Diario appears to be reticent on the matter of the disaffection of the crews, perhaps amounting to mutiny, that all other early accounts of the voyage mention. In contrast, the Diario tells of only a single incident, a few days before landfall, and even then treats it as a minor episode that Columbus had no difficulty in controlling.

On the morning of October 12, Columbus anchored at an island that the Indians seem to have called Guanahani, and which he christened San Salvador. It is all but certain that Guanahani was one of the Bahamas, but there agreement ends: no fewer than nine Bahamian islands (as well as Grand Turk and Caicos) have been advanced as the site of the landfall. This lack of unanimity is due to the fact that Columbus was uncharacteristically reticent in describing Guanahani's attributes in the Diario. He fails, for instance, even to estimate its size—it is referred to as both an "islet" and "a fairly large" island. Moreover, it is described as low-lying and green, with a lagoon "in the middle" as well as a large harbor, all criteria that many islands in the Bahamas can meet.

The remainder of the Diario's account of Columbus's journey through the Bahamas (which is described throughout as being in the words of Columbus and is by far the longest verbatim section) is similarly vague, contradictory, and intermittent. Sometimes intentions are stated but without any indication that they were carried out. Sometimes the ships seem to be in one place at the end of a daily entry and somewhere else at the beginning of the next. Some natural features are specified, only to be contradicted, and very few distances are included at all. In sum this portion of the Diario is marked by a wealth of apparent information, but only a fraction of it turns out to be testable, consistent, or plausible.

Once Columbus reached Cuba, the Diario becomes more integrated but not always more intelligible. Identifying the point at which he first reached Cuba depends entirely on matching his physical description of that place with various modern-day possibilities. Columbus's firm belief that he was on the periphery of the Far East influenced both his perceptions and the way he expressed them; superlatives became more than ever his normal rhetorical fare. Mountains were higher, rivers deeper, and harbors larger than life, as Columbus (or someone else) effectively turned the Diario into a literary rather than a nautical document.

Columbus cruised along the northern coast of Cuba, constantly inquiring of the Indians as to the whereabouts of "the Grand Khan" and associated riches until he reached the eastern end of the island and then crossed to La Española. Of the various cultures Columbus encountered on the first voyage, none impressed him as much as those on La Española. It seemed to him (if the Diario is correct) that he had at last reached an outpost of civilization. The wealth seemed greater, the political authorities more imposing, the population larger. When *Santa María* was beached and wrecked on Christmas Day, Columbus quickly had a fort erected on the site to shelter the men who would have to be left behind. He was certain both that sources of gold were close at hand and that the local ruler was well-disposed toward the opportunities Columbus believed he was offering him. Columbus continued to sail east along La Española until he reached its end, whereupon, although he was told of other interesting locales to the east, he chose to attempt the return voyage.

This, the last leg of the trip, was more eventful than its outbound counterpart. Columbus was forced to experiment with courses in order to catch the westerly winds, and the reduced fleet was subjected to several storms, one of which separated the ships and caused Columbus to fear for his survival. This storm drove *Niña*, under Columbus's command, into Portuguese territory in the Azores. After some conflict with the authorities there, Columbus renewed his voyage, only to be driven into Lisbon harbor and the clutches of his former patron turned enemy João II.

Eventually Columbus convinced João that he had not trespassed on Portuguese rights granted by the Treaty of Alcáçovas in 1479 and was permitted to sail home. Arriving in Palos on March 15, 1493, he dispatched a message to the Spanish court, then at Barcelona, and awaited their summons, which came about a month later. From Columbus's view, the voyage ended only when he received an audience with Fernando and Isabel and claimed his promised rewards.

Textual Questions. The account of the voyage in the Diario, however, ends abruptly with Columbus debarking at Palos. The most crucial question about the Diario is whether work on the shipboard log ceased at the same time. It has generally been the view of modern scholarship that, though the Diario indisputably contains both obvious and suspected errors, as well as its share of unintended distortion, it also reflects to a very great degree the shipboard log. The belief in this case is that Columbus left each entry as it stood and declined to revise earlier entries when later information came to hand, thereby accounting for most of the discrepancies that exist in the Diario. By this interpretation, the principal task of those studying the first voyage is to strip away later incrustations by Las Casas, and possibly by others, and it is widely accepted that these can be recognized in one way or another.

It is the case, for instance, that Las Casas discloses that certain data in the Diario are not Columbus's. This is most obvious when such data are anachronisms, as when Las Casas mentions the Lucayos, the name given to the Bahamas well after 1492, or when he mentions Florida by name, though it had not yet been discovered. Moreover, many of the numerous statements in the Diario about the Indians are of a nature more akin to Las Casas's frequently expressed beliefs than to any views ever expressed by Columbus. Moreover, Las Casas clearly intended that most of the some two hundred marginal notes serve as his own commentary on the text, and he occasionally interjected his own observations directly into the text. But even when these instances are identified and studied, there remains a host of anomalies that ultimately need to be explained as more than slips of the pen.

Opportunities and motives for tinkering with any documents relating to the first voyage arose long before Las Casas came into contact with the text he copied and edited. By the late summer of 1493, any records Columbus had turned over to the Spanish authorities had become political documents. By then Columbus and the Spanish authorities, on the one hand, and the Spanish and Portuguese monarchs, on the other, were already jockeying for position in the geopolitical situation that had unexpectedly arisen. The question is: how early might the log have come to be regarded as having ends other than faithfully representing things done and places seen during the first voyage? If this occurred during the voyage itself, as Columbus began to speculate on his own future role in the discoveries, then he might already have been overhauling the log even before he returned to Spain, perhaps even before he reached Guanahani.

Moreover, we cannot be certain that Columbus surrendered to the Spanish Crown the very log, whether or not revised, that he maintained during the voyage. His relations with Fernando and Isabel had always been brittle and strained; it had been only with great difficulty that he had prised any funds and concessions from them. As early as February 18, the Diario speaks of Columbus's desire to remain "master of the route of the Indies," and it would have been a guileless Columbus indeed who would have turned in the only copy of the log or, for that matter, an exact copy that could be used to circumvent him.

The trail then leads to the copy of the log that was transcribed by royal scribes and returned to Columbus just before he embarked on his second voyage several months after his return. At the time, the Portuguese emissaries were hovering around the Spanish court preparing to make a case that "the Indies" belonged to the

Portuguese Crown by right of treaty. It is reasonable to suspect that the Spanish authorities protected themselves to the extent of preparing a special recension of the log (still not yet the Diario) should they have to share it with the Portuguese.

Finally, it is necessary to consider just which one of all these possible copies (and there may have been others) eventually fell into the hands of Las Casas. Unfortunately, there is no way to know this, nor to know whether that copy had not in turn undergone further changes in the sixty years (1552 is the most widely accepted date for the creation of the Diario) after Columbus returned to Spain.

The only copy of any shipboard log, then, that is known to modern scholarship is at least two transcriptions removed from any original. Moreover, the information in any shipboard log was so valuable to several interested parties that it probably underwent changes on behalf of these parties, each of which had ample opportunity. For the moment it is necessary to defer hopes of reconstructing and interpreting Columbus's voyage in precise detail and search for evidences of revision.

One of the many aspects of the Diario's account that has aroused particular interest is the incomplete set of double numbers that are embedded in most of the daily entries for the outward voyage. There an official reckoning of distance traveled each day is accompanied by a lower figure. The latter resulted, says the Diario, from Columbus's desire to allay the fears of the crews as day after day passed with no land in sight. These so-called double distances have been interpreted in various ways; some have suggested that they show that Columbus was temperamentally inclined to dishonesty, whereas others see them as an indication of his sensitivity to the feelings of the crew or as emphasizing his navigational skills.

Whatever the interpretation, few have doubted that these numbers were part of the original shipboard log that were carried forward accurately through several transmissions until Las Casas entered them into the Diario. But there are several problems with this view. The alleged stratagem was deployed too soon to warrant such an explanation. The first false number appears in the entry for September 9, when the ships were only a few days west of the Canaries and before Columbus could have been aware of any need to minimize the distances traveled. The arithmetic of the lower distances does not match up, either proportionately or cumulatively, with other figures recorded in the Diario. Many of these figures are written in Roman numerals, which are otherwise sparingly used. These constitute serious grounds to suspect that one or another of these sets of numbers was added at some point after the outward trip.

According to the Diario, a crew member on *Pinta* sighted land early in the morning of October 12 (other sources, including Oviedo, date the sighting a day earlier). The Diario then adds that, several hours before this, Columbus had seen a mysterious light that was a sign of land or of its imminence. On the basis of this, Columbus claimed and received the reward promised to the individual who first sighted land. The story as it is told in the Diario is implausible in content and strangely placed as well. It may be that it was a later interpolation, although it is common to use this sighting as an argument for or against particular landfalls.

The description of the banners used as part of the possession-taking ceremony on Guanahani is so detailed that it suggests that it too was added for the benefit of readers other than those for whom Columbus was writing, for officials at court would not have required such information. Under the date October 13 we find another entry peculiar in itself and strangely placed. There it is reported that Guanahani was on a line due west from Hierro, the most southwesterly of the Canaries. By consulting his log, Columbus would have noticed that he had spent the equivalent of several days sailing southwest at various points in the journey. Either he had no log to consult then, he misinterpreted its testimony, or this information was added at a later point, perhaps to allay the fears of João II into whose hands Columbus (and the log?) had fallen. Whatever the case, it is evident that this datum is incomprehensible if it is treated as an integral and original part of any log.

In the combined entry for October 11 and 12, Las Casas writes (claiming to quote Columbus) that Columbus observed wounds on the Guanahani Indians, which he "believed and believe" came from Indians raiding from somewhere to the west. This emphatic juxtaposing of past and present tenses is not without counterparts in the Spanish of the time, but does not occur elsewhere in the Diario. It may be that Columbus interpolated the additional "believe" at a later point in order to emphasize that the Guanahani Indians needed protection—Spanish protection—against existing enemies. The word makes the best sense when thought of in this way, but at the same time its presence underscores that Columbus and others had no particular reasons to treat the text of the log and its successors as sacred, but simply as one of several means to desired ends.

Four times during the return trip, storms so imperiled *Niña* that Columbus ordered that lots be drawn for the purpose of determining who would make pilgrimages of thanksgiving should they survive. One chick-pea for each crew member (a total of twenty to twenty-five) was placed into a hat. One of these was marked with a cross and whoever drew the marked pea was obligated to make the required pilgrimage. In three of the four cases Columbus drew the marked pea. The odds against this happening exactly as depicted in the Diario vary according to the

circumstances of the drawing, about which we know nothing, but are at best only 1 in about 1,250. This indicates that some aspects of the stories must have been added later, probably with the purpose of showing that Columbus was marked by divine providence for special distinction, a view held by Fernando in his biography.

These and other instances suggest that it is not inappropriate to suspect that the Diario written by Las Casas in about 1552 differed in many respects from any shipboard log that Columbus kept. By this view, the Diario was the end product of a dynamic text that both influenced and was influenced by the events that surrounded its genesis, a process that took as many as sixty years to complete. This notion is supported by the fact that many diaries in history—including most famously those of Samuel Pepys and Anne Frank—were routinely and extensively revised by their authors and transmitters before being committed to posterity, yet were eventually published in a quotidian format that served to mask that fact.

In addition to this historical perspective, literary and textual critics have begun to turn their attention to the Diario in hopes of understanding more about the nature of the first documented encounter between Europe and America. In this endeavor they devote greater attention to how the Diario expresses itself than to what it says, or to whether there is a demonstrable relationship between its testimony and independently determined reality. This study is beginning to show that, in recounting his experiences on the first voyage to America, Columbus reflected closely the rhetoric of the travel accounts of the Middle Ages, which were often contrived at the metaphorical rather than the empirical level. This is particularly the case with regard to Columbus's attention to the natural world—the people, the flora, the landforms—as he came into contact with it in the West Indies.

In sum, the Diario is an extraordinarily complex text in its discursive fits and starts, its linguistic eclecticism, its panoply of beguiling, yet often elusive, detail, and its Manichean authorial posture. These elements combine to form a text that resists easy and sure analysis more than most historical documents. The application of literary and textual criticism in combination with traditional historical analysis is likely to yield results that advance the knowledge of the character of this, the primary source for knowledge of Columbus's first voyage.

BIBLIOGRAPHY

Campbell, Mary B. *The Witness and the Other World: Exotic European Travel Writing, 400–1600.* Ithaca, N.Y., 1988.

Cioranescu, Alejandro. *Primera biografía de C. Colón: Fernando Colón y Bartolomé de las Casas.* Tenerife, 1960.

Columbus, Christopher. *Diario del descubrimiento.* Edited by Manuel Alvar. 2 vols. Gran Canaria, 1976.

Columbus, Christopher. *The Diario of Christopher Columbus's*

First Voyage to America, 1492–1493. Edited and translated by Oliver Dunn and James E. Kelley, Jr. Norman, Okla., 1989.

Columbus, Christopher. *Scritti di Cristoforo Colombo.* Edited by Cesare de Lollis. 2 vols. Rome, 1892–1894.

Fuson, Robert H. "The *diario de Colón:* A Legacy of Poor Transcription, Translation, and Interpretation." *Terrae Incognitae* 15 (1983): 51–75.

Henige, David. "Edited . . . and not Precipitated; Three Recent Editions of Columbus' *diario.*" *Terrae Incognitae.* Forthcoming.

Henige, David. "Samuel Eliot Morison as Translator and Interpreter of Columbus' *diario de a bordo.*" *Terrae Incognitae* 20 (1988): 69–88.

Henige, David, and Margarita Zamora. "Text, Context, Intertext: Columbus's *diario* as Palimpsest." *Americas* 46 (1989): 17–40.

Morison, Samuel Eliot. "Texts and Translations of the Journal of Columbus's First Voyage." *Hispanic American Historical Review* 19 (1939): 235–261.

Parker, John. "The Columbus Landfall Problem: A Historical Perspective." *Terrae Incognitae* 15 (1983): 1–28.

Ramos Pérez, Demetrio. *La primera noticia de América.* Valladolid, 1986.

Tanselle, G. Thomas. "The Editing of Historical Documents." *Studies in Bibliography* 31 (1978): 1–56.

Zamora, Margarita. " 'Todas son palabras formales del Almirante': Las Casas y el *diario* de Colón." *Hispanic Review* 57 (1989): 25–41.

DAVID HENIGE

Letters

Leaving aside his marginalia, his Book of Prophecies, and his Book of Privileges, we have today about one hundred documents attributed to Columbus. Forty or forty-two of them are autographs, and the remainder consists of various copies drawn in different periods, receipts in the Archives of Protocol, two printed sheets published during the Admiral's lifetime, and twenty-five handwritten transcriptions by Bartolomé de las Casas. The documents may be classified as follows:

1. *Juridical-administrative documents.* Autograph writings include three orders of payment written in the Indies upon returning from his fourth voyage. Among the copies are: (a) the Capitulations, (b) appointment of Bartolomé Colón as lieutenant governor, (c) institution of rights of primogeniture, (d) two contracts, in part with Fonseca and in part with Antonio Mariño and Pedro Salcedo, to sell soap, (e) empowerments to the tutor of his sons, Ximeno de Briviesca, and to his Florentine brother-in-law Francesco de Bardi, and a safe-conduct to Francisco Roldán, and (f) a land distribution letter to Miguel Ballester.

2. *Reports, memorandum books, and records.* In these Columbus writes about a variety of subjects: from memorandums on the way the Indies became populated to a report on how the navigation from Laredo to Flanders should take place on the occasion of the meeting between Princess Juana and Philip, who were to be married. This report was requested by Queen Isabel, who apparently held the Admiral's nautical knowledge in high esteem. The following documents, or their signatures, are autographic: (a) muster roll of the first voyage, (b) memorandum of Antonio Torres, (c) various memorandums on the populations of the Indies, (d) memorandums of offenses, and (e) a memorandum preceding the fourth voyage. Copies by Las Casas are the records of the first and third voyages.

3. *Official correspondence.* Autograph material includes various letters to the Catholic monarchs and one to the queen, two letters to the ambassador Nicoló Oderico, one letter to the San Giorgio Bank in Genoa, letters to Fernando the Catholic and to Philip I and Juana, and two letters to Nicolás de Ovando, governor of La Española. Columbus's letter to Pope Alexander VI is a copy written perhaps by his son Fernando Colón.

4. *Private correspondence.* Eleven letters to Gaspar Gorricio and twelve letters to Columbus's son Diego are autographs. Copies by Las Casas include a letter to Juana de la Torre and the fragment of a letter to his brother Bartolomé.

These documents are preserved in various archives. The archive of the dukes of Veragua, which today is entrusted to the General Archive of the Indies in Seville (Archivo General de Indias), contains sixteen documents; twenty are stored in the ducal Archive of the Casa de Alba in Madrid; one is in the Library of the Academy of History of Madrid; one is in the General Archive of Simancas; and one is in the National Library of Madrid. The Columbus Library of Seville holds the books that Columbus glossed personally as well as a letter to the monarchs, which he copied at the beginning of his Book of Prophecies. Only three autograph letters are kept in Italy; they are deposited in the City Hall of Genoa.

The majority of Columbus's autographs are, for obvious reasons, in the first two archives mentioned above, since both ducal houses included direct descendants of Columbus and remained united for over a century. When a lawsuit separated the two families, the Albas gave the Veraguas the family archive of Columbus with the exception of one file that was permanently misplaced in their library. The Albas kept and even expanded their bequest through purchases, but the Veraguas sold their documents to the Spanish state in 1929, when they were deposited in the archive at Seville. The documents that are in Genoa are the letters that Columbus sent to Nicoló Oderico, the ambassador of the Republic of Genoa to the Catholic monarchs, which a descendant of the diplomat donated to the city. The letter to the San Giorgio Bank remained stored in the Town Hall until it was discovered in the archives of the defunct bank. Of the remaining autographs, one document is in the Royal Academy of the

History of Madrid, and three autographs, which had once been misplaced from the Royal Chancellery of the Kings of Spain, turned up in their rightful place in the Seville archive (these had not been delivered in time for the original transfer of the materials concerning America to the General Archive of the Indies in Seville in 1786).

Copies of Columbus's writings are also located in the General Archive of the Indies. Among them are Columbus's will, his recently discovered letter book, and the letter to the pope. The City Hall of Genoa as well as the Bibliothèque Nationale, Paris, and the Library of Congress in Washington, D.C., have copies of the Book of Privileges among their manuscripts.

As for the chronology of Columbus's autographs, they cover the period from 1492, date of the Diario (journal) owned by the ducal house of Alba, to December 1505, date of the last known letter by Columbus to his son Diego. We do not know of any other writings by Columbus written before 1492, since today it is certain that all the annotations to his books are later than this date. It is possible to group his autographs into various series. The first consists of the Diario of 1492. The second, a cycle of the year 1498, includes documents written during the preparation for the third voyage: the memorandum to the monarchs on the population of the Indies, various letters to Diego and Gorricio, and the muster roll of the first voyage. The third series, covering the period between the years 1500 and 1502, corresponds to the time Columbus spent in Spain between the third and fourth voyages: reports and memorandums of offenses, a letter to the queen, and some letters to Gorricio. The fourth series relates to the return from the last voyage to the New World: three receipts (the only documents written in the Indies) and letters to Diego, Gorricio, and various Italian friends.

Conveyance and Editing of the Texts. In 1493, upon returning from his first voyage and while still on board his ship, Columbus wrote a letter to Luis de Santángel, clerk of the Catholic monarchs, announcing his discoveries. In that year the letter was published nine times in a translation into Latin addressed to Gabriel Sánchez, treasurer of Aragón. Basically a letter that could be used to correspond with various addressees, it was copied three times in Italian, once in German, and twice in Castilian. It was in effect a best-seller that appeared in various editions in the following years. In this way the news of the discovery spread rapidly throughout Europe.

On March 7, 1505, an Italian version of the fourth voyage report was published in Venice. The rapidity of the copying process is demonstrated by the fact that Columbus had returned to the Iberian Peninsula only four months before. The letter apparently was published in Spanish, but we do not have a copy of it, so that the Italian version is known under the name of *lettera rarissima* (extremely rare letter), as its new editor, Bartolomeo Morelli, called it in 1810. No other publications are known to have been issued during the Admiral's life.

In 1554 the original Diario of the first voyage was about to be published. Luis Colón, a grandson of the discoverer, obtained the license and the exclusive rights to it for a period of ten years. He was an unscrupulous man and thought he could make more money out of another arrangement he had in mind: as a result the Diario, which was in his archives, was lost forever. To enhance Columbus's prestige during the Pleitos Colombinos (Columbus's lawsuits) the existence of a manuscript on the history of the Admiral was boasted by the circle of family members near to María de Toledo, Diego Colón's widow. In this book an ancestry and honorable past are claimed, and the exclusive rights of the discovery used as evidence. Various hands edited a book in which lies and truth were combined and in which a considerable amount of authentic copies of letters and notes by Columbus's hand were included. Luis decided to negotiate the sale of the manuscript in Genoa, so in 1571 the so-called *Historia del Almirante escrita por su hijo Hernando Colón* (The Admiral's history written by his son Hernando Colón) appeared on the Genoese market translated into Italian by Alfonso de Ulloa.

No previously unknown text by Columbus appeared during the seventeenth and the eighteenth centuries, for Columbus had fallen out of fashion. More appealing to the public during these years were the stories of great conquerors whose actions were more spectacular. Thus only a few texts by Columbus are known before the nineteenth century, and of these no original is known.

In 1823, G. B. Spotorno's *Codice diplomatico Colombo-Americano ossia Raccolta di documenti originali e inediti* was published in Genoa. It is a collection of documents that Columbus had gathered and is also known as *Libro de los privilegios* (The Book of Privileges). Two years later, in 1825, Martín Fernández Navarrete published for the first time the *Diarios del primero y el tercer viaje* (Logbooks of the first and the third voyages), which were copies by Las Casas that had been previously unknown as well as the autograph letters that were the property of the dukes of Veragua. For the first time autograph writings by Columbus appeared in an edition that was accessible to a wide audience. The *Carta a la Banca de San Giorgio* (Letter to the San Giorgio Bank) was printed in 1857, and the *Historia general de las Indias* (General history of the Indies) by Las Casas, which contains copies of many of Columbus's letters, was published in 1879. In 1892 the duchess of Alba published part of the letters from her archive. In that same year the Italian government published the magnificent *Raccolta Colombiana* (Columbus Collection) on the occa-

The letter to Luis de Santángel. *Left:* A folio from the Barcelona edition of 1493. *Right:* A woodcut illustration, "Trading with the Indians," from the Basel edition of 1493.

New York Public Library, Rare Book and Manuscripts Division

sion of the celebration of the fourth centennial anniversary; in this splendid edition were collected all the writings by Columbus known to that date.

Columbus became fashionable in the nineteenth century, the period of literary romanticism that glorified picturesque voyages and the sort of hero exemplified by Columbus. Perhaps the enormous amount of previously unknown documentation had an influence on Columbus's popularity. Its impact was such that the government of the United States sent Washington Irving to Madrid with the task of translating the books on the discovery that Navarrete was about to publish. Irving saw that they contained many official documents, and realizing that they might be boring for the American reader, he decided to write the Admiral's biography. He was helped in this work by Navarrete, who gave him access to the new documentation. Irving also had access to important libraries and was therefore able to publish in English for the first time a series of autographs by Columbus that were not known even in Spanish. The generosity of his friend Navarrete was so great that Irving was allowed to translate Navarrete's documents even before Navarrete published them in Spanish.

New documents continued to appear in the twentieth century. In 1902 the duchess of Alba published the famous map that represents the northern coast of La Española and a series of previously unpublished letters from her archives. Finally, in 1942 Columbus's only letter addressed to Isabel was discovered in the Archive of Simancas.

Description of the Autographs. All autographs are written on paper, the material the Admiral used to write his letters, the Book of Prophecies, and the copy of the Book of Privileges he kept in his archive. The only copies made of parchment were those sent to Nicoló Oderico and to Gaspar Gorricio.

State of preservation. The documents are well preserved. All are neat, without erasures and underlinings; marginal words appear rarely. This allows us to suppose that Columbus wrote rough drafts of his letters, a habit possibly not followed only in the incomplete autographs. The handwriting is good; the lines are straight; the left margin is altered only by the initial letters, which extend out of the block.

Heading. Both Las Casas in his *Historia general de las Indias* and Fernando Colón in his *Historie* state that Columbus would not take pen in hand without writing these words first: *Jesus cum Marie sit nobis in via* (Let Jesus and Mary be with us on our path). Nonetheless, this heading appears in only three of the autographs owned by the house of Alba, in the copy of the letter to Miguel Ballester, and in the letter to the monarchs copied at the beginning of the Book of Prophecies. It does not appear in any other autograph or in the numerous copies of the Admiral's letters made by Las Casas. As a consequence, it may be that the heading was used by Columbus on only a few occasions and that Las Casas was exaggerating in order to emphasize the piety of his hero. What Columbus's biographers, on the other hand, do not point out is that in all his writings the text is preceded by a cross, and that in the letter to the queen the heading is the abbreviation *JHS*. If this had been his habit, the Admiral would readily have included the quoted invocation under this cross, which he did not forget to write even in his promissory notes.

Signature. With the exception of the reports that are rough drafts, Columbus signed all his letters. For these he used a curious anagram—never satisfactorily explained—which he himself described when he established the rights of primogeniture in 1498. Columbus used three different types of signatures in his writings. From the beginning of 1502 he always signed with an anagram followed by the words *The Admiral,* with the exception of those authorizations for monopoly in the Indies in which he printed the word *Virrey* (Viceroy) after the anagram. The second form changed and substituted *The Admiral* with the famous and well-known Greek-Latin phrase *XPO FERENS* (Christ bearer) in capital letters. A third signature is used in three payments and in his last letter to his son Diego (wherein he wrote *xpo ferens* in small letters). These four documents were prepared by an amanuensis, and Columbus only signed them. A heading usually appears to the left of the signature, and all documents carry numbering in some of the upper corners. Doubtless, these numbers correspond to the pagination given by Columbus himself when he organized them in his archive.

Orthography and paleography. The accents are finely written and placed high and usually to the right of the letter they stress. The period serves only to indicate certain abbreviations such as *S.M.* or *V.M.* In order to mark a full stop or a semicolon, Columbus inserts vertical lines (single or double), suggesting that to a higher degree of solemnity corresponds the higher number of vertical lines. Among other details are a series of orthographical norms that Columbus never altered, such as the use of the cedilla for the groups *çe* and *çi*, the links between the letters *st, to,* and *tu,* and following *f* and *h*. He always abbreviated *que* as *q* and the toneme *ser* as γ.

[See also *Lawsuits; Library of Columbus; Signature.*]

BIBLIOGRAPHY

Columbus, Ferdinand. *The Life of Admiral Christopher Columbus by His Son Ferdinand.* Translated by Benjamin Keen. New Brunswick, N.J., 1959.

Las Casas, Bartolomé de. *Historia de las Indias.* Mexico City, 1951.

Varela, Consuelo, ed. *Cristóbal Colón: Textos y documentos completos.* 3d ed. Madrid, 1987.

CONSUELO VARELA
Translated from Spanish by Paola Carù

Marginalia

Christopher Columbus was an enthusiastic reader who read for both knowledge and pleasure. It was his habit to keep notebooks (now lost) of data and references and to lard the margins and flyleaves of the books he owned with marginal notes, known as postils. He wrote the postils mostly in Latin or Spanish, with occasional Portuguese and Italian usages. These marginal notes run in length from one abbreviated word to several pages. The postils have been edited and published in full by Césare de Lollis in volume 2 of his *Raccolta di documenti e studi pubblicati dalla R. Commissione Colombiana per quarto centenario dalla scoperta dell'America.*

In the extant books owned by the Admiral, there are between 2,700 and 2,750 postils. The figure varies according to how one counts them (some scholars would merge selected marginal notes, whereas others would count them as two). The following are estimates for each of the books Columbus owned:

1. Pierre d'Ailly, *Imago mundi,* Louvain, 1480–1483; 898 postils.
2. Enea Silvio Piccolomini (Pope Pius II), *Historia rerum ubique gestarum,* Venice, 1477; 861 postils.
3. Marco Polo, *De consuetudanibus et conditionibus orientalium regionum (Il milione),* Antwerp, 1485; 366 postils.
4. Pliny, *Historia naturalis,* Venice, 1489; 24 postils.
5. Plutarch, *Las vidas de los ilustres Varones,* Seville, 1491; 437 postils.
6. Libro de las profecías (Book of Prophecies, a notebook of prophecies collected by Columbus and others at Seville, 1501–1504); 147 postils.

Not all the marginal notations in these texts are in the

hand of Columbus. Some surely are in the hand of his brother Bartolomé, but it is difficult (sometimes impossible) to tell the difference in their handwriting. Other notes are in the hand of Columbus's youngest son, Fernando Colón. All the notes in Plutarch's *Lives*, for example, are in the son's hand. Scholars have made two attempts at a general paleographic analysis of the postils, but they vary greatly in their conclusions about who wrote which notations.

The marginalia remain basically unstudied as a source material. It is through these marginal notations, however, that one can begin to enter the mind of the explorer, develop an idea of his learning, and see the formation and progress of his objectives. The notes vary according to his purposes. Many are simply a marginal index of subjects, composed of one or two words. Others are supplemental to the text with the reader adding his own information. Still others cross-reference to other passages in the same book or to passages in other texts. Occasionally, a marginal note indicates disagreement with the text, in which case the reader almost always offers differing opinions from other authorities. Perhaps the most exciting postils are lengthy summaries of information gleaned from many sources. Usually, this type is located on the flyleaves to the book. For example, in a note to Piccolomini's *Historia rerum ubique gestarum,* where the author discusses the earth's habitable zones, Columbus states in the margin:

> Parmenides held the earth to be divided into five zones, just like the sky. He considered to be uninhabitable the two zones closest the poles because of the cold, a third directly under the course of the sun [uninhabitable] because of the heat. The contrary has been proved in the south by the Portuguese, and in the north by the English and the Swedes, who navigate in those parts.

Columbus made copious notations in the margins of the books he read for the same reason we all make notes. According to the old Chinese proverb, "The palest ink is better than the best memory." Reading is an adaptive process between the demands of the writer and the background of varied experiences occupying the mind of each reader. Through the postils one can see a selective mechanism at work where information is being extracted by a reader with certain intentions. For example, Columbus desired impeccable scholarly support for his conclusion that the world was much smaller than contemporary thinking indicated so he searched the texts for such evidences and noted it in the margins. He frequently cross-referenced such information to other authorities.

Any time a reader interacts with a text, that reader's knowledge about the contents of that text affects the nature of the information stored and retrieved by the

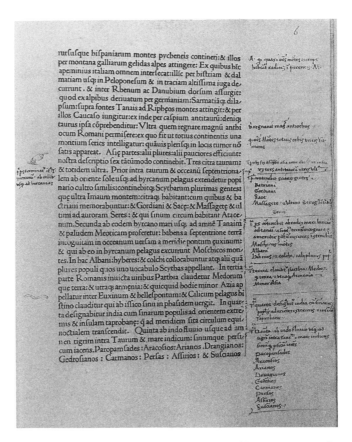

MARGINALIA. A page from *Historia rerum ubique gestarum*, by Enea Silvio Piccolomini (later Pius II). The handwriting here is almost certainly that of Columbus.   BIBLIOTECA COLOMBINA, SEVILLE

mind. In the process of understanding a text, information it contains is integrated or rejected according to the reader's existing knowledge about the topic. The reader must select, repress, relate, and organize the data being gathered according to an already set cognitive structure within his or her mind. Thus, through the postils, we can see the Admiral's mind at work. We can judge his education, learning, and style of thinking through his ability to process information on a new occasion and in a new context.

Studying the postils also helps us understand how education and information filtered from elite scientific thinkers of the fifteenth century through the schoolmasters to the public. Columbus represented a growing class of self-taught, middle-class merchants who were inspired by the ideas of cosmology, astronomy, geography, theology, and other sciences being developed in Renaissance centers of learning. He was a complex personality whose expectations were grounded in contemporary scientific theory, in his own experiences, and in legendary, visionary, and allegoric geography. His postils demonstrate the filters through which he imagined the unknown environment of terrae incognitae. In the postils written in the margins of the books he owned, we can see the well-formed, well-thought-out image of the physical world present in the mind of the explorer before he sailed.

BIBLIOGRAPHY

Lollis, Césare de. "Introduction, Ilustrazione alle postille." In *Raccolta di documenti e studi pubblicati dalla R. Commissione Colombiana per quarto centenario dalla scoperta dell'America.* Vol. 2. Rome, 1892–1894.

Raffo, Giuliano. "Sulle postille di Colombo relativo alla storia romana." In *Studi Colombiani.* Genoa, 1952.

Streicher, Fritz. "Las notas marginales de Colón en los libros de Pedro Aliaco, Eneas Silvio, y Marco Polo, estudiadas a la luz de las investigaciones paleográficas." In vol. 3 of *Investigación y progreso.* Madrid, 1929.

Taviani, Paolo E. *Christopher Columbus: The Grand Design.* London, 1985.

DELNO C. WEST

Book of Prophecies

The Book of Prophecies (Libro de las profecías) was the name given by Columbus to a work he never completed. A manuscript of materials apparently gathered in preparation for the book by Columbus and a collaborator, a Carthusian monk named Gaspar Gorricio, survives in the Biblioteca Colombina in Seville, Spain. It consists of passages excerpted from the Bible, the Apocrypha, and various patristic and medieval exegetical works. These are accompanied by a prefatory letter written by Columbus to Fernando and Isabel, some fragments of verse in Spanish, and notes in the hands of Columbus, Gorricio, Columbus's son Fernando, and Columbus's brother Bartolomé.

The dating of the manuscript of the Book of Prophecies is problematic. A note in Columbus's hand at the beginning indicates that he and Gorricio began to gather the excerpts after his third voyage to the Americas, which he completed in 1500. He appears to have composed the prefatory letter to Fernando and Isabel between September of 1501 and March of 1502—that is, between the third and fourth voyages.

It is difficult to determine precisely what Columbus had in mind for the Book of Prophecies, given the fragmentary nature of the materials that remain. Nevertheless, the excerpts do consistently manifest certain configurations and themes, and taken together with the prefatory letter, they reveal the pattern of Columbus's intention. It appears that he wanted the Book of Prophecies to place his achievements and those of his monarchs within the framework of a providential history. He believed that the end of time was near at hand and that a number of contemporary events including his own discovery of a "new world" were penultimate fulfillments of ancient prophecies.

In preparing the larger framework of providential history, Columbus made use of a number of well-known Biblical commentaries and glosses on Augustine, Isidore of Seville, and Nicholas of Lyra. But his principal source was a collection of short works on the interrelationships among history, astrology, and prophecy written between 1410 and 1414 by the late medieval thinker Pierre d'Ailly (1350–1420). Columbus used an edition of these works printed by John of Westphalia between 1480 and 1483. D'Ailly's works were not original but rather gatherings or cullings of materials drawn from a variety of late antique and medieval sources. Principal among these were Augustine, Pseudo-Methodius, and Roger Bacon. D'Ailly's works thus provided Columbus with a repertoire of established authorities upon which to base his Book of Prophecies.

Columbus's reliance upon d'Ailly's works is evident in the consistent correlations between the passages he annotated and the excerpts he selected from the works for his manuscript. These notes and excerpts are all concerned with modes of periodizing history and in particular with forecasting the advent of Antichrist. This event is presumed by d'Ailly and Columbus to be imminent. It will presage the end of postlapsarian time and space, of the cosmos and of history.

In constructing this framework, Columbus appears to have paid particular attention to d'Ailly's *Tractatus de legibus et sectis contra supersticiosos astronomos,* a treatise involving an ongoing debate among medieval philosophers and scientists regarding the use of astrology to forecast the fulfillment of prophecies and other determinant forces in historical process. In the first four chapters, d'Ailly outlines a theory in which history consists of six ages. In each age a different religion has dominated; its ascendancy was signed in the heavens by the conjunction of its particular planet with Jupiter. Thus, according to d'Ailly, the past conjunctions of Jupiter with Saturn marked the age of the Jews; with Mars, the age of the Chaldeans; with the Sun, the Egyptians; and with Venus, the Saracens. The present age of the Christians coincides with the conjunction of Saturn and Mercury, and the final age, the age of Antichrist, will see the conjoining of Jupiter and the Moon.

This linking of chronology and astronomy was derived from the ninth-century Muslim astronomer Albumazar (Abu Ma'shar) and was known to d'Ailly through Roger Bacon's *Opus maius.* According to d'Ailly's interpretation of these earlier medieval sources, the conjunction of Jupiter with the Moon, which would signal the unleashing of the forces of Antichrist, was not far off. A key passage from the fourth chapter describing the events that would

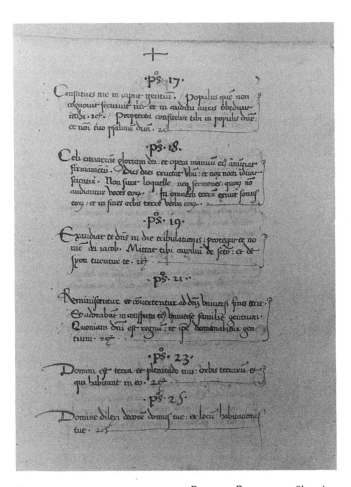

A FOLIO FROM THE MANUSCRIPT OF THE BOOK OF PROPHECIES. Showing excerpts of Biblical psalms. BIBLIOTECA COLOMBINA, SEVILLE

occur in the age of Antichrist was among the excerpts Columbus gathered for the Book of Prophecies. Further evidence was drawn from a second work by d'Ailly on the concordances between celestial phenomena and historical process (*Tractatus de concordia astronomie veritatis et narrationis hystorice*). In this treatise, d'Ailly provides a set of eight events that will augur the advent of Antichrist. They were copied verbatim from a seventh-century Byzantine Apocalypse by a figure known as Pseudo-Methodius, which enjoyed a considerable currency throughout the medieval period. Columbus's annotations indicate that he followed these passages from the works of d'Ailly carefully; both were excerpted for the Book of Prophecies.

When set within the historical context provided by d'Ailly and the other glossarists mentioned above, the selections from the Bible that form the bulk of the Book of Prophecies appear consistently to address two interrelated themes. The first is the anticipated final recovery of Mount Zion, symbol of the Holy Land, from the infidel.

The second is the penultimate conversion of all the peoples of the world to Christianity as prophesied in *John* 10:16: "And I have other sheep, that are not of this fold; I must bring them also, and they will heed my voice. So there shall be one flock, one shepherd."

Other nonscriptural materials contained in the Book of Prophecies appear to have been designed to establish the specific roles of Columbus and his monarchs within this general apocalyptic vision of history. A passage taken from Seneca's tragedy *Medea*—which predicts that "the years will come, in the succession of ages, when the Ocean will loose the bonds by which we have been confined, when an immense land shall lie revealed" —is accompanied by a note in Fernando's hand stating that "my father, the Admiral Christopher Columbus, fulfilled this prophecy in the year 1492." And a diplomatic letter to Fernando and Isabel, applying a thirteenth-century prophecy that claimed that "he who will restore the Ark of Zion will come from Spain," appears as well.

These latent patterns become more explicit in the incomplete and somewhat rambling prefatory letter addressed by Columbus to the Spanish monarchs. He begins by recalling his training and decades of experience in navigating and mapmaking. He goes on to assert, however, that it was not technical expertise but divine providence that determined the success of the Enterprise of the Indies: "In this voyage to the Indies Our Lord wished to perform a very evident miracle in order to console me and the others in the matter of this other voyage to the Holy Sepulcher." Columbus believes that he has been chosen by God to carry Christianity to the infidels of the New World in fulfillment of *John* 10:16 and that Fernando and Isabel have been designated to lead the final conquest of Jerusalem.

According to the prefatory letter, these events will unfold rapidly. Columbus points out to his regents that the calculations of d'Ailly demonstrated that but 155 years remained before the end of the world. Thus, although the Book of Prophecies is difficult to decipher, it is essential to the understanding of Columbus's conception of history and his place in it.

[See also *Antichrist; Spirituality of Columbus;* and biographies of d'Ailly and Bacon.]

BIBLIOGRAPHY

Lollis, Césare de. *Scritti di Colombo.* Vol. 2 of *Raccolta de documenti et studi pubblicata della R. Commissione Colombiana.* Rome, 1894. [Contains the text of the Book of Prophecies.]

Milhou, Alain. *Colón y su mentalidad mesianica en el ambiente franciscanista español.* Vol. 11 of Cuadernos Colombinos. Valladolid, 1983.

Watts, Pauline Moffitt. "Prophecy and Discovery: On the Spiritual Origins of Christopher Columbus's 'Enterprise of the

Indies.' " *American Historical Review* 90 (February 1985): 73–102.

West, Delno, and August Kling. *Vision and Discovery: A Study and Translation of Columbus's Libro de las profecias.* Gainesville, Fla., 1991.

PAULINE MOFFITT WATTS

Last Will and Testament

The last will and testament of Christopher Columbus were as complicated as most of his business affairs in Spain. First, he placed his assets in a perpetual trust for his son Diego. In four later acts he confirmed this trust and gave Diego instructions for the final disposition of his business affairs and charitable and pious donations.

Establishment of a Perpetual Trust *(Mayorazgo).* Christopher Columbus used an extralegal maneuver, a perpetual trust, to provide for his heirs. In Burgos after the second voyage, he petitioned Fernando and Isabel for royal permission to establish a trust, and on April 23, 1497, the monarchs issued a letter patent that gave Columbus "license and authority to make one or more trusts in favor of Sir Diego Colón, your legitimate eldest son, or any of your heirs and children." The patent allowed him to include in this trust any property, goods, and heritable offices that he had received from the monarchy.

Columbus was attempting with this trust to exempt his property from the Spanish laws of inheritance. The laws were very strict, requiring that all legitimate children receive equitable shares of their parent's estate and that the testator set aside no more than 10 percent of the estate for charitable and religious bequests. Parents had so little discretion in the partition of the estate that they rarely made wills, and when they did, it was to specify how they wanted the pious and charitable donations to be distributed.

Wealthy and noble families who wanted to prevent partition of the family fortune generation after generation found a way around the law, by establishing trusts. The Trastámara monarchs allowed parents to remove assets from the partible estate and use them as the principal of a perpetual trust *(mayorazgo).* The parents designated one of the children, usually the eldest son or daughter, as the beneficiary of the trust. After the parents' deaths, their remaining assets and liabilities were partitioned equitably among all the legitimate children of the marriage.

In Seville the next year, Columbus wrote a draft of the perpetual trust, making his son Diego the beneficiary. He finished the draft on February 22, 1498, in the midst of his preparations for the third voyage. First, he listed the offices and revenues he had received as heritable property from the monarchs: the offices of admiral of the Ocean Sea and viceroy and governor of the islands and mainland he had discovered, with their salaries and revenues; 10 percent of all the resources found there, and the right to invest one-eighth of the Indies commerce and receive one-eighth of the profits from it. He stated his desire to place "these offices, tenth, eighth, and salaries and revenues" in a perpetual trust. He placed the usual restrictions on this trust: the beneficiary could not touch the principal but had full use and possession of the income. At no time did Columbus mention how much the principal of the trust might be worth in cash, and that, too, was typical of the founding documents of perpetual trusts; the capital assets were listed, but the income was expected to grow from year to year.

Next, Columbus established the method of selecting the beneficiary of the trust. He named his son Diego as the beneficiary. If Diego should die without a male heir, Columbus's second son, Fernando, should succeed to the trust, then Columbus's brother Bartolomé, and then the youngest Columbus brother, Diego, if the latter should leave holy orders and marry. Throughout the generations, the heir should always be the eldest son of an eldest son, or the male heir most closely related to Christopher Columbus and bearing the surname Colón. He excluded females from inheriting the trust unless no male heir with the name Colón could be located anywhere in the world.

Columbus stated that he was establishing the trust this way in order to perpetuate his family name and the memory of his own attainments. He ordered Diego to display the admiral's coat of arms and to sign all documents with the same rubric that he had used—the as yet undeciphered letters arranged in a triangle—and with the title "The Admiral" no matter what other offices and titles the king might later give him.

Columbus was giving absolutely everything he possessed to Diego, yet he wanted to provide for his other son and for his brothers. So he instructed Diego to use the income from one-quarter of the trust to give an allowance to Bartolomé of up to one million maravedis per annum. Another quarter of the trust's income was to be set aside to provide Diego's half-brother, Fernando, with an annual allowance of one million maravedis. If Fernando's quarter of the principal should grow, Diego could give him up to two million maravedis per year. Columbus's youngest brother, Diego, was to receive an annual allowance sufficient to his station as a clergyman, until he received a church position.

Next, Columbus required the beneficiary of the trust to give one-tenth of the annual income in charitable donations to the poorest relatives of the Columbus family. The tenth was to be calculated by extrapolating from the income produced by the one-quarter of the revenue assigned to Bartolomé. Diego must diligently send people all over the world to seek out these poor relatives and give the money to them, especially to pay the dowries of the poorest young females—a standard type of charitable donation during the Renaissance. Christopher Columbus's two closest male relatives must audit the accounts and make sure that Diego gave 10 percent of the income in charity. Diego must also provide an allowance to a Columbus relative living with his wife and family in Genoa, making sure that they had enough to live with dignity and with enough stature to demand the benefits of Genoese citizenship.

To ensure that the family income would be secure, Columbus ordered Diego to deposit his money in the San Giorgio Bank in Genoa. The profits should be spent on financing a conquest of Jerusalem by Fernando and Isabel, or a similar crusade in Oran. In gratitude for the support that Fernando and Isabel had given him, Columbus ordered Diego and his heirs to always serve the Castilian monarchs. And in recognition of the city where he was born, he instructed Diego to work for the honor, welfare, and growth of Genoa.

Finally, Columbus provided for the disposition of his soul. He instructed Diego to build a church, to be named Santa María de la Concepción, and a hospital on the island of La Española, with a chapel in which masses would be sung for the salvation of his soul and the souls of his ancestors. Diego must also support four professors of theology on the island of La Española to teach and convert the Indians to Christianity. This endowment must be commemorated in the church by a stone plaque engraved with the information.

All of the trust was typical of Castilian trusts of the period, and Columbus appeared satisfied with it. He deposited this and his other valuable documents in the monastery of Las Cuevas in Seville, and he later affirmed the trust on three occasions.

Memorandum of Instruction for Diego. In May 1502, before leaving on his fourth voyage, he wrote a memorandum of instruction for Diego, leaving him in charge of the family's business and legal affairs and instructing him on how to manage these in the event of Columbus's death. He told Diego where the valuable papers were deposited and reminded him to tithe every year, to treat people of all stations in life with dignity, and to continue serving the king and queen. Then he ordered Diego to make specific payments to his closest female relatives. To Beatriz Enríquez de Arana, mother of Columbus's illegitimate son, Fernando, he must give ten thousand maravedis per annum payable from butcher shop leases in the city of Córdoba, and he was to treat her as lovingly as he would his own mother. To Diego's aunt, the sister of Felipa Perestrelo y Moniz, he was to give the same amount, payable quarterly.

The Admiral seems always to have treated his brother Diego with that special care and tenderness that an oldest brother displays toward a youngest. In this memo he instructed his son to provide and care for his uncle, who was living in Cádiz, "because he is my brother and has always been very obedient." He also instructed his son to persuade the king to give his brother Diego a canonry or some other church position, because he was a clergyman—an instruction that was never carried out.

Columbus gave his son good advice on the conduct of his personal affairs; he commanded him to make a monthly balance of his assets and liabilities, to seek the advice of the priest Gaspar de Gorricio, to postpone the royal arrangements for his marriage until Columbus returned, and to depend on the influence of Luis de Soria in political matters. The Admiral had appointed Alonso Sánchez de Carvajal as his business agent to collect his revenues from the Indies, and he instructed Diego to receive the money from Carvajal and pay him a per diem of five hundred maravedis for his time in La Española, as well as fifty thousand maravedis if he took care of Columbus's business in Spain.

With the money that Carvajal would bring, Diego must pay Italian investors who had advanced Columbus the capital to buy merchandise to sell in the Americas—the one-eighth of the total value of cargoes agreed on in the April 17, 1492, partnership agreement—and to pay off the Admiral's other creditors.

While these orders seem clear enough, they were in fact not clear at all. This ambiguity became apparent after Columbus returned from his disastrous fourth voyage and became embroiled in a dispute with the monarchy about just what his offices and revenues included. Until the law courts defined these, there was no way of knowing what capital assets Columbus could include as principal in the trust. The differences dividing the two parties were enormous and would take years of litigation to settle.

Amendments. Meanwhile, Columbus claimed as much as possible and even more. After returning from his fourth voyage, he stopped over in Segovia on his way to Valladolid, headquarters of the royal appeals court (*chancillería*), and wrote another memorandum to Diego on August 25, 1505. Columbus confirmed the trust and memorandum and added details that changed the proportion of donations and allowances. In this memorandum, he wrote as a hardheaded businessman who thought he was being cheated of his fair return on investment. He declared that he was entitled to one-third of all that was found in the Indies, in addition to the tenth and eighth that he claimed earlier. Although no profits had yet been realized from the Indies, he trusted that "through the benevolence of Our Lord the revenue will become very large."

In anticipation of this future revenue and apparently

more appreciative of his younger son's character and affections after their year of being shipwrecked together on Jamaica, Columbus changed his instructions to Diego about partitioning the income from the trust. Instead of dividing it into quarters and giving one of these to Bartolomé, he now ordered Diego to divide the trust's annual income into ten shares. After giving one share to charity, he would keep six shares and divide the remaining shares into thirty-five shares, which he must partition in the following way: to the Admiral's son Fernando Colón, twenty-seven shares; to the Admiral's brother Bartolomé, five shares; and to the Admiral's youngest brother, Diego, three.

As usual in Columbus's writing, this distribution seems straightforward but turns out to be a wish. In the Admiral's next words, he reveals the problem:

> My wish would be for my son Sir Fernando to receive annually 1.5 million maravedis, Sir Bartolomé 150,000, and Sir Diego 100,000. But I do not know how this can be possible, because up to now neither the source nor the amount of the income from the trust is known. I say that the procedure I have outlined above should be followed until the two-ninths grow and are sufficiently increased to provide the stated sums to Fernando, Bartolomé, and Diego. When this level of revenue has been achieved, which will be when the two-ninths are producing annual revenues of 1.75 million maravedis, then everything above that amount shall be inherited by my son Sir Diego or his heir. If this revenue should increase a great deal more, I would be pleased if the portions for Sir Fernando and my brothers were also increased.

Columbus then showed the new affection and concern he felt for his son Fernando. "The part that I order given to my son Sir Fernando I am placing in a trust for him, and this will be hereditary in his male descendants forever-more. This trust cannot be sold, traded, given away, or removed from the descendants in any way and must be treated in the same way as the trust I established for my son Sir Diego."

Columbus ordered Diego, when he had enough income from the trust and inheritance, to establish a chapel endowed with three chaplaincies to say three masses every day: one in honor of the Holy Trinity, one dedicated to the Conception of the Virgin Mary, and the other for the souls of all the faithful and for the souls of Columbus's father, mother, and wife. If this chapel could be on the island of La Española, "which God miraculously gave me, I would be very pleased if it could be on the spot where I invoked the Holy Trinity, which is in the part of the Vega that is called La Concepción."

Finally, Columbus gave Diego an intriguing instruction that reveals much about his own conscience. "I order him to be responsible for Beatriz Enríquez, mother of my son Sir Fernando, to provide for her so that she can live decently, because she is a person to whom I owe a great deal. And this must be done to clear my conscience, because this weighs heavily against my soul. It would not be proper to explain here the reason for this."

Columbus's Final Confirmation of the Trust and Instructions to Diego. Within a year, on May 19, 1506, Columbus lay on his deathbed in Valladolid. A royal judge and notary, Pedro de Hinojedo, and legal witnesses were summoned. Hinojedo testified that in his presence Christopher Columbus, who claimed to be admiral, viceroy, and governor-general of the islands and mainland discovered and to be discovered in the Indies, being ill of body, rectified and approved as valid his earlier trust and memos. Columbus named as executors of his estate his son Diego Colón, his brother Bartolomé Colón, and the treasurer of Vizcaya, Juan de Porras, and gave them his power of attorney.

Finally, Columbus appended instructions in his own handwriting ordering Diego to pay sums anonymously to a number of old friends and creditors, all of them foreigners.

> "First, to the heirs of Girolamo del Porto, father of Benito del Porto, chancellor of Genoa: 20 ducats or its equivalent.
> "To Antonio Vazo, Genoese merchant who used to live in Lisbon: 2,500 Portuguese reales, which are a little more than 7 ducats at the rate of 375 reales to the ducat.
> "To a Jew who lived at the entrance to the Jewish quarter in Lisbon, or to whomever a priest shall designate, the equivalent of one-half mark of silver.
> "To the heirs of Luigi Centurione, Genoese merchant: 30,000 Portuguese reales; at the rate of 375 reales to the ducat this is approximately 75 ducats.
> "To these same heirs and to the heirs of Paolo di Negro, Genoese, 100 ducats or its equivalent; half to one group of heirs and half to the other.
> "To Baptista Spinola or his heirs if he is dead, 20 ducats. This Baptista Spinola is the son-in-law of Luigi Centurione. He was the son of messer Nicolò Spinola de Locoli de Ronco, and, for an address, he was resident in Lisbon in the year 1482."

With this final act, Columbus reconfirmed the earlier dispositions and repaid old debts. By making these legal dispositions, he provided handsomely for his sons, his former mistress, his relatives and creditors in Genoa, Spain, and Portugal, and for the souls of his parents and wife.

[See also *Lawsuits; Signature.*]

BIBLIOGRAPHY

Columbus, Christopher. *Testamento de Cristóbal Colón.* Transcription and introduction by Demetrio Ramos. Valladolid, 1980.

Columbus, Christopher. *Textos y documentos completos: Relaciones de viajes, cartas, y memoriales.* Edited by Consuelo Varela. Madrid, 1984.

HELEN NADER

ZACUTO, ABRAHAM (c. 1450–c. 1515), navigational astronomer. Abraham Zacuto had a great influence on the development of astronomical navigation, which bloomed in the second half of the fifteenth century. His contribution was due mainly to his *Almanach perpetuum coelestium motium* (Perpetual almanac of the heavenly bodies), which was probably known in Portugal in its original version before 1493, when Zacuto took refuge there because of a Castilian law that exiled all Jews who did not convert to Catholicism.

Diogo Ortiz (known in Portugal as Diogo Calzadilha), who had taught astrology at the University of Salamanca, had taken refuge in the Portuguese kingdom after supporting Afonso V of Portugal in the disastrous war that the king had waged in support of his claim to the Crown of Castile. It is probable that he knew Abraham Zacuto before 1475, when Ortiz was forced to leave Salamanca. Knowing Zacuto's value, he apparently recommended him to the Portuguese king, thereby facilitating Zacuto's entrance into the court of Lisbon, where he received the title of royal astronomer. Zacuto offered assistance in the fields in which he was a specialist, particularly navigation. Despite his position, he fled to the Near East in 1496 because of a law of Manuel I expelling Jews.

Zacuto's *Almanach perpetuum,* probably written while he was at Salamanca, has an introduction in Hebrew, written under the name Hajibul Hagadol. This proved to be a highly influential work on navigation. Other works written by Zacuto have been forgotten, with the exception of his *Tratado breve de las influencias del cielo* (Short treatise on the influences in the heavens), an astrological book with some paragraphs on meterological information.

So-called astronomical navigation undoubtedly began much earlier than Zacuto's arrival in Portugal. Shortly after 1460 the navigator Diogo Gomes made references to the navigational use of the quadrant. Moreover, Christopher Columbus notes that in 1485 the astrologer José Vizinho systematically examined the sun in Guinea in order to test a body of rules that enabled one to determine the geographical latitude of a place by starting from the observation of the meridian height of a star. In 1487 and 1488, Bartolomeu Dias used the astrolabe to determine latitudes in his voyage around the south of Africa and into the Indian Ocean. Dias's determinations were witnessed by Columbus, who was with King João II when the king received Dias after his return.

Zacuto's importance lies in the fact that the solar declination tables, essential for the calculation of geo-

ASTRONOMICAL TABLES. From Abraham Zacuto's *Almanach perpetuum coelestium motium.* Facsimile, 1915.

graphical coordinates, were based on his tables. His *Almanach perpetuum* allowed a competent skipper to do the necessary calculations and to prepare the solar declination tables, using both single tables and, later, quadrennial tables. The tables in the *Livro de marinharia de André Pirese* (André Pirese's book of navigation) were copied for various quadrenniums, all of them based on the *Almanach perpetuum:* for 1493–1496, 1497–1500 (which might have been used by Vasco da Gama), 1501–1504, 1517–1520, 1521–1524, 1529–1532, and 1549–1552. The tables for 1517–1520 appeared in a pamphlet possibly printed in 1516 and known today as the *Guia náutico de Evora* (Nautical guide of Evora).

Four editions of the *Almanach perpetuum* exist: a well-known edition, published in Venice in 1502; a badly defined edition said to have "variations in its tables," one copy of which is reported to be in the library of the Escorial; an edition with comments by Alfonso de Córdoba and reportedly also in the library of the Escorial; and an edition printed in Venice in 1525 by Johannes Michael that follows almost literally the original edition but which is sometimes erroneously dated 1500.

This fundamental book by Abraham Zacuto was both appreciated and useful. His knowledge and his merits, though, were not rightly used to the best advantage in Portugal.

BIBLIOGRAPHY

De Lery, Jean. *History of a Voyage to the Land of Brazil Otherwise Called America.* Translated by Janet Whatley. Berkeley, 1990.

Diffey, Bailey W. *Prelude to Empire: Portugal Overseas before Henry the Navigator.* Lincoln, Neb., 1960.

Diffey, Bailey W., and George D. Winius. *Foundations of the Portuguese Empire, 1414–1850.* Edited by Boyd C. Shafer. Minneapolis, 1977.

Morison, Samuel Eliot. *Portuguese Voyages to America in the Fifteenth Century.* New York, 1965.

Waters, David W. *Reflections upon Some Navigational and Hydrographic Problems of the XVth Century Related to the Voyage of Bartolomeu Dias, 1487–88.* Lisbon, 1988.

LUÍS DE ALBUQUERQUE
Translated from Portuguese by Paola Carù

Index

A

Aarons, G.A., 614
Abbass, D.K., *as contributor*, 234–237, 466–468
Abbey, Edward Austin, 324
Abrams, Ann Uhry, *as contributor*, 321–325
Abravanel, Isaac, 391, 392
Abu Bakari II, 2
Abu Ma'shar. *See* Albumazar
Acadie, 150–151
Acamapichtli, 364
Acklins, Bight of, 407
Acklins Island, 407
Acto cultural o Colón, Cristóbal, el Genovés alucinado, 432
Adam of Bremen, 248, 313, 689
Adams, Will, 122
Ad-Din, Khayr. *See* Barbarossa
Admiral of the Ocean Sea, 404, 491, 598, 715
Adoration of the Magi, 340
Adorno, Barnaba, 165
Adrian VI, 116, 555
Aeneas Silvius. *See* Pius II
Aeterni Regis, 678
Afonso (prince of Portugal), 190, 191, 377, 678
Afonso III, 560
Afonso V, 1, 15, 119, 120, 127, 180, 182, 286, 308, 379, 396, 398, 423, 539, 561, 670, 678
Afonso de Aveiro, João, 96, 561
Afonso do Estreito, João, 181
Africa, 2–4, 253–255, 277, 531
  and Atlantic Rivalry, 52
  interior of, 251
  Portuguese knowledge of, 191
  slaves from, 142, 631, 632, 633, 634, 679
  see also specific countries
Agatharchides of Cnidus, 259
Agnadello, battle of, 438
Agreement of Villafafila, 399
Agricultural tools, 4, 6, 7,
Agriculture, 4–8, 237, 352, 682
  Aztec, 366
  changes after 1492, 6–8
  of Chibchas, 357
  diversity in, 7
  European crops in Americas, 274–276
  Mayan, 361, 363
  New World, 5, 226, 273, 356, 468, 708
  Old World, 4–5, 273–274
  slave labor, 632, 634
  and social and economic institutions, 635
  in Spain, 644
  of Taínos, 346
  technological innovations, 638
Agrippa, Henricus Cornelis, 299
Aguado, Juan, 704
Aguado, Juan de, 261, 415, 598, 711–712
Agüero, Gerónimo de, 668
Agueybaná, 346
Aguiar, Jorge de, 452
Ahern, Maureen, *as contributor*, 83–84, 210–211
Ahuitzotl, 485
Ailly, Pierre d', 8–9, 14, 23, 59, 123, 125, 250, 373, 422, 452, 504, 603, 651, 652, 658, 671, 677, 748–749
Ais, 370
Alaminos, Antonio, 262, 304
Al-Andalus, 492
Alarcón, Hernando de, 210
Al-Ashraf, Sultan, 692

Albergati, Nicolas, 549
Albigensian Crusade, 586
Al-Biruni, 664
Albisúa Toledo, Marina de, 454
Albo, Joseph, 289
Albumazar, 748
Albuquerque, Afonso de, 15, 87, 218, 219, 373, 531, 562
Albuquerque, Antónia de, 531
Albuquerque, Luís de, *as contributor*, 223, 372–374, 438–439, 640–641, 642–643, 679–680, 693, 753–754
Alcabala (tax), 675
Alcáçovas, Treaty of. *See* Treaty of Alcáçovas
Alcalá, Angel, *as contributor*, 288–290, 375–377, 390–391, 391–392, 669
Aldrovandi, Ulisse, 341, 345
Alegría, Ricardo E., *as contributor*, 345–349
Alessandrini, Angelo, 297
Alexander III, 564
Alexander VI, 9–12, 43, 53, 54, 187, 196, 384, 397, 414, 423–424, 437, 463, 538, 549, 554, 592, 669, 678, 704, 743
  death of, 12
  foreign policy, 10
  propagation of Catholicism, 11
Alexander the Great, 232, 257, 294, 295, 658–659
Alexandria (Egypt), 3
Alfonsine Tables, 13
Alfonso V, 12, 165, 397, 500, 681
Alfonso VI, 492
Alfonso VIII, 492
Alfonso X, 12–14, 36, 49, 389, 492, 665
Alfonso XI, 442, 585
Alfonso of Castile, 398

VOLUME 1: pp. 1–400; VOLUME 2: pp. 401–754.
*Numbers in boldface refer to the main entry on the
subject. Numbers in italic refer to illustrations.*

VOLUME 1: pp. 1–400; VOLUME 2: pp. 401–754.
*Numbers in boldface refer to the main entry on the
subject. Numbers in italic refer to illustrations.*

VOLUME 1: pp. 1–400; VOLUME 2: pp. 401–754.
Numbers in boldface refer to the main entry on the
subject. Numbers in italic refer to illustrations.

VOLUME 1: pp. 1–400; VOLUME 2: pp. 401–754.
*Numbers in boldface refer to the main entry on the
subject. Numbers in italic refer to illustrations.*

D

VOLUME 1: pp. 1–400; VOLUME 2: pp. 401–754.
*Numbers in boldface refer to the main entry on the
subject. Numbers in italic refer to illustrations.*

VOLUME 1: pp. 1–400; VOLUME 2: pp. 401–754.
Numbers in boldface refer to the main entry on the subject. Numbers in italic refer to illustrations.

VOLUME 1: pp. 1–400; VOLUME 2: pp. 401–754.
Numbers in boldface refer to the main entry on the
subject. Numbers in italic refer to illustrations.

VOLUME 1: pp. 1–400; VOLUME 2: pp. 401–754.
Numbers in boldface refer to the main entry on the subject. Numbers in italic refer to illustrations.

VOLUME 1: pp. 1–400; VOLUME 2: pp. 401–754.
*Numbers in boldface refer to the main entry on the
subject. Numbers in italic refer to illustrations.*

VOLUME 1: pp. 1–400; VOLUME 2: pp. 401–754.
*Numbers in boldface refer to the main entry on the
subject. Numbers in italic refer to illustrations.*

VOLUME 1: pp. 1–400; VOLUME 2: pp. 401–754.
Numbers in boldface refer to the main entry on the
subject. Numbers in italic refer to illustrations.

Maritime archaeology, **30–36**, 620–622
Markland. *See* Labrador
Márques, Diego, 201, 705
Marranos, 375, 390, 393
Marriage, 24, 474, 636, 736, 737
  Aztec, 366
  Island Carib, 350
  Maya, 361
  Taíno, 346
  Tupinambá, 354
Martel, Charles, 491
Martellus, Henricus, 62, 97, 127, 223,
  298, 449, **452–454**, 671
Martin, Andreas, 719
Martín, Benito, 304
Martin, Martin, 512
Martin, Terence, *as contributor*, 433–
  435
Martin V, 591, 592
Martínez, Fernán, 203
Martínez de Irala, Domingo, 83, **454**
Martínez-Hidalgo, José María, 515, *599*,
  600
Martini, Dario G., *as contributor*, 427–
  430
Martinique, 351
Martins, Fernão, 180, 182, 670
Martyr, Peter. *See* Anghiera, Pietro
  Martire d'
Martz, Linda, *as contributor*, 394–395,
  667–668
Marvel, Josiah, 406, 407
Marx, Chico, 335
Marx, Robert, 33
Mary I, 541
Mary of Burgundy, 284, 437, 450, 454
Mary of Spain, 454
Mary Tudor, 242, 438
Masaccio, 43
Masonry, 681
Master frame, 619, 620
Mas'udi, al-, 569
Materia medica, 460
Mathematics, 16, 51, 62, 164, 601, 604
Mato Grosso, 149
Mauro, Fra, 223, 448, 557, 658, 671
Maximilian I, 284, 384, 397, 399, 437,
  450, **454–455**
Mayas, 5, 255, **360–364**
  art and architecture, 360, 361–362
  classic, 360
  conquest of, 363
  culture at contact, 360–362
  economic system, 361

establishment of Spanish authority,
  363–364
post contact culture, 362–364
religion, 362
sociopolitical system, 361
Mayflower Compact, 157
Mayobanex, 718
Mayrionex, 711
Mazariegos, Diego de, 362–363
Mazuelo, Pedro de, 612–613
McCrone, Walter C., 691
McElroy, John W., 406
McGivney, Michael J., 160
McKean, Robert, 559
McPartland, Scott, *as contributor*, 604–
  606
Mead, Larkin Goldsmith, 476
Measles, 312, 459
Measurements
  itinerary units of, 231–234
  relationship between Greek and
    Roman, *232*
Mechanical clocks, 665–666
Medea, 652, 749
Medel, Alonso, 709
Medici, Averado de', 456
Medici, Cosimo de' (1389–1464), 456,
  602
Medici, Cosimo de' (1517–1574), 317,
  456
Medici, Giovanni, 456
Medici, Giovanni di Bicci de', 456
Medici, Giuliano de', 456
Medici, Lorenzo de', 281, 456, 686
Medici, Lorenzo Pier Francesco de', 18,
  686, 687, 729
Medici, Piero de', 456
Medici family, **455–457**
Medici Map, 559
Medicine and health, **457–460**, 602,
  604–605
  Chanca (royal physician), **115**
  humoral theory of, 458
  law, 459
  plants, 459–460
  see also Disease and demography;
    Hospitals; specific illnesses
Medieval exploration, 259–260
Medina, Bartolomé de, 469
Medina, Pedro de, 511
Medinaceli, Duke of, 53, 188, 195, **460**
Medina del Campo, 682
Medina Sidonia, Duke of, 83, **460–461**,
  536

Mediterranean Sea, 173, 174, 595, 596,
  635, 672
Meerfahrt mit Quichote, 429
Megasthenes, 294
Mehmed II, 526
Melamed, Mair, 392
Mélida, Arturo, 80
Memorial architecture. *See* Monuments
  and memorials
Méndez, Diego, 273, **461–462**, 725–727
Mendicants, 144
Mendieta, Gerónimo de, 588
Mendoza (Chile), 142
Mendoza, Antonio de, 17, 64, 210, **462–
  463**
Mendoza, Bernardino de, 462
Mendoza, Diego Hurtado de, 462
Mendoza, Iñigo López de, 462
Mendoza, Pedro de, 83, 264, 454
Mendoza, Pedro González de, 188, 375,
  380, 382, 394, 460, **463**, 682
Menéndez de Avilés, Pedro, 263, **463–
  464**
Menéndez Pidal, Ramón, 69
Mercantilism, 292
Mercator, Gerardus, 291, 300, **464–466**,
  510, 518, 525, 569
  world map of, *520*
Mercator projection, 466
Mercedarian Order, 472, 630
*Mercedes of Castile; or The Voyage to
  Cathay*, 431–432
Mercury, 467, 470
Mérida, 362
Meridians, 436, 504, 505, 510
Messahalla, 50–51, 693
Mesta, 236
Mestizos, 142, 148, 349, 535, 539, 580,
  736–737
Meta Incognita, 519
Metal, **466–468**
  American resources, 466–467, 579
  European uses of, 467–468
  native American adoption of
    Spanish, 468
  tools and equipment, 467–468
  see also Mining; specific metals
Metallurgy, 357
Metalworking, 681
Metius, Adriaan, 542
Mexico, 141, 142, 211, 212, 368, 410,
  462, 466
  agriculture, 5
  conquest of, 224, 472

VOLUME 1: pp. 1–400; VOLUME 2: pp. 401–754.
*Numbers in boldface refer to the main entry on the
subject. Numbers in italic refer to illustrations.*

O

VOLUME 1: pp. 1–400; VOLUME 2: pp. 401–754.
*Numbers in boldface refer to the main entry on the
subject. Numbers in italic refer to illustrations.*

VOLUME 1: pp. 1–400; VOLUME 2: pp. 401–754.
*Numbers in boldface refer to the main entry on the
subject. Numbers in italic refer to illustrations.*

VOLUME 1: pp. 1–400; VOLUME 2: pp. 401–754.
Numbers in boldface refer to the main entry on the subject. Numbers in italic refer to illustrations.

VOLUME 1: pp. 1–400; VOLUME 2: pp. 401–754.
Numbers in boldface refer to the main entry on the subject. Numbers in italic refer to illustrations.

W

VOLUME 1: pp. 1–400; VOLUME 2: pp. 401–754.
*Numbers in boldface refer to the main entry on the
subject. Numbers in italic refer to illustrations.*

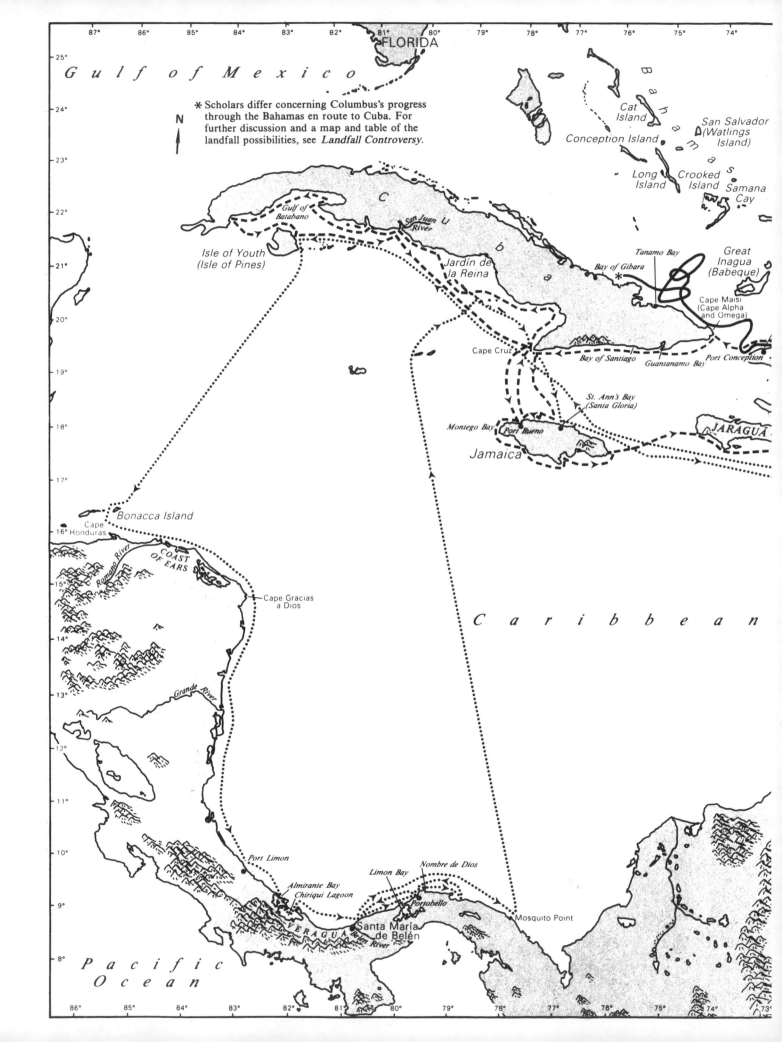

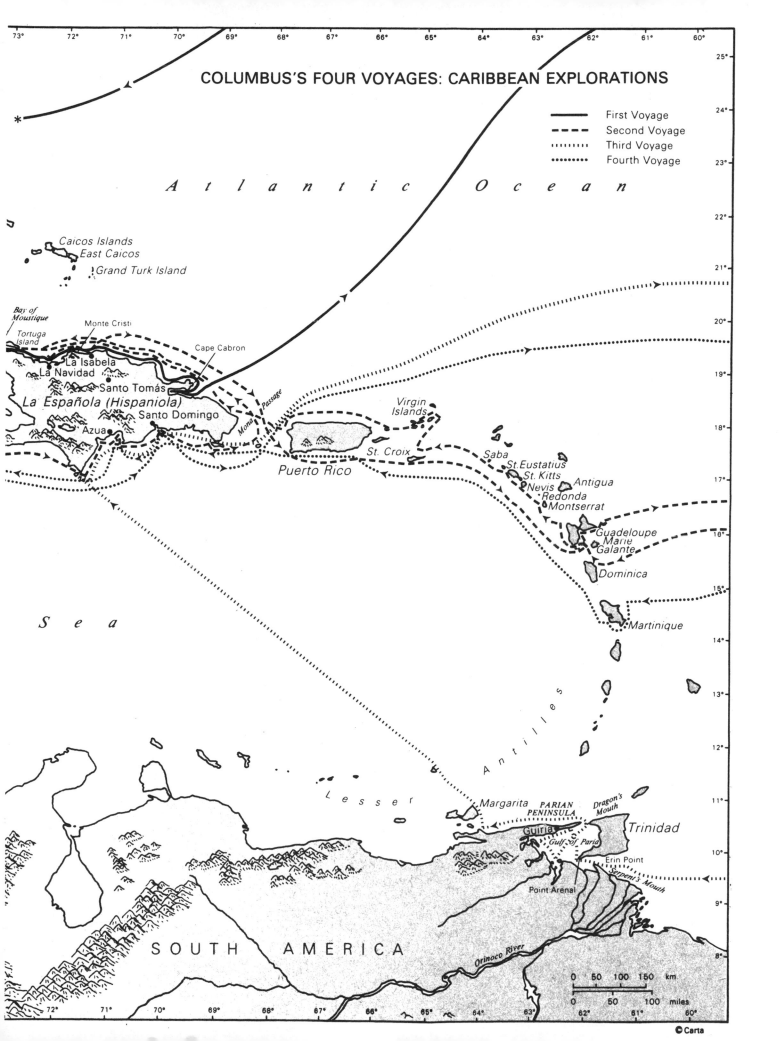

COLUMBUS'S FOUR VOYAGES: CARIBBEAN EXPLORATIONS

First Voyage
Second Voyage
Third Voyage
Fourth Voyage

Atlantic Ocean

Caicos Islands
East Caicos
Grand Turk Island

Bay of Moustique
Tortuga Island
Monte Cristi
La Isabela
La Navidad
Santo Tomás
Cape Cabron
La Española (Hispaniola)
Santo Domingo
Azua

Mona Passage

Virgin Islands

St. Croix

Puerto Rico

Saba
St. Eustatius
St. Kitts
Nevis
Redonda
Montserrat
Antigua

Guadeloupe
Marie Galante

Dominica

Sea

Martinique

Antilles

Lesser

Margarita
PARIAN PENINSULA
Dragon's Mouth
Guiria
Gulf of Paria
Trinidad
Erin Point
Serpent's Mouth
Point Arenal

SOUTH AMERICA

Orinoco River

0 50 100 150 km.
0   50   100 miles

© Carta

Other titles of interest

**WORLD EXPLORERS
AND DISCOVERERS**
Edited by Richard E. Bohlander
544 pp., 170 illus., 50 maps
80824-2 $25.95

**THE ENCYCLOPEDIA
OF NATIVE AMERICAN
BIOGRAPHY**
**Six Hundred Life Stories of
Important People, from
Powhatan to Wilma Mankiller**
Bruce E. Johansen and
Donald A. Grinde, Jr.
480 pp., 136 photos and drawings
80870-6 $22.50

**THE ENCYCLOPEDIA
OF WOMEN'S
HISTORY IN AMERICA**
Kathryn Cullen-DuPont
368 pp., 8 1/2 x 11, 44 illus.
80868-4 $22.50

**THE FRANCIS
PARKMAN READER**
Edited with an introduction
and notes by
Samuel Eliot Morison
544 pp., 1 illus., 5 maps
80823-4 $17.95

**ENCYCLOPEDIA OF
BLACK AMERICA**
Edited by W. Augustus Low
and Virgil A. Clift
941 pp., 400 illus.
80221-X $37.50

**THE MAKING OF AN
AFRO-AMERICAN**
Martin Robison Delany
Dorothy Sterling
368 pp., 3 illus.
80721-1 $14.95

**THE ENCYCLOPEDIA OF
COLONIAL AND
REVOLUTIONARY AMERICA**
Edited by John Mack Faragher
494 pp., 126 illus. & maps
80687-8 $24.50

**THE DISCOVERY AND
CONQUEST OF MEXICO**
Bernal Díaz del Castillo
Translated by A. P. Maudslay
New introduction by
Hugh Thomas
512 pp., 33 illus., 2 maps
80697-5 $16.95

**ENCYCLOPEDIA OF WESTERN
LAWMEN & OUTLAWS**
Jay Robert Nash
581 pp., 530 illus.
80591-X $27.50

**THE ENCYCLOPEDIA OF THE
THIRD REICH**
Edited by Christian Zentner and
Friedemann Bedürftig
1,162 pp., 8½ × 11, over 1200 illus.
80793-9 $50.00

ALEXANDER
Theodore Ayrault Dodge
723 pp., 234 illus., maps, and
charts
80690-8 $19.95

**CUBA or The Pursuit
of Freedom**
Updated Edition
Hugh Thomas
1,826 pp., 71 illus., 19 maps
80827-7 $39.95